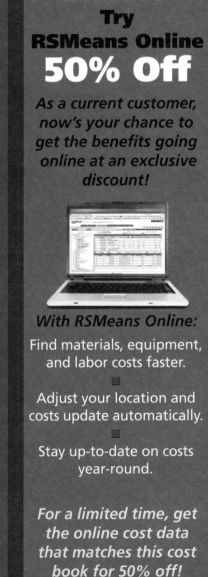

RSMeans
Quarterly Updates
700 Longwater Drive
Norwell, MA 02061
USA

Tips for Customizing Your RSMeans Cost Data By Location

The cost data found throughout the book reflects national averages.

Customize your cost data for over 930 locations throughout the U.S. and Canada.

☑ To adjust costs to your region, use the *Location Factors* found in the back of the book.

☑ To compare costs from region-to-region, use the *City Cost Indexes* found in the back of the book.

☑ For additional guidance, refer to the *How RSMeans Data Works* section towards the front of the book.

RSMeans
Reed Construction Data

Metric Conversion Formulas

Length

cm = 0.3937 in.
meter = 3.2808 ft.
meter = 1.0936 yd.
km = 0.6214 mile

in. = 2.5400 cm
ft. = 0.3048 m
yd. = 0.9144 m
mile = 1.6093 km

Weight

gram = 15.4324 grains
gram = 0.0353 oz.
kg = 2.2046 lbs.

grain = 0.0648 g
oz. = 28.3495 g
lb. = 0.4536 kg

Area

sq. cm = 0.1550 sq. in.
sq. m = 10.7639 sq. ft.
sq. m = 1.1960 sq. yd.
hectare = 2.4710 acres
sq. km = 0.3861 sq. mile

sq.in. = 6.4516 sq. cm
sq. ft. = 0.0929 sq. m
sq. yd. = 0.8361 sq. m
acre = 0.4047 hectare
sq. mile = 2.5900 sq. km

Weight, cont.

kg = 0.0011 ton (short)
ton (met.) = 1.1023 ton (short)
ton (met.) = 0.9842 ton (large)

ton (short) = 907.1848 kg
ton (short) = 0.9072 ton (met.)
ton (long) = 1.0160 ton (met.)

Common Units of Measure

Abbreviation	Measurement	Formula
SF	Square feet	Length (in feet) x Width (in feet)
SY	Square yards	Square feet / 9
CF	Cubic feet	Length (in feet) x Width (in feet) x Depth (in feet)
CY	Cubic yards	Cubic feet / 27
BF	Board foot	Length (in inches) x width (in inches) x thickness (in inches)/144
MBF	Thousand board foot	Board foot / 1,000
LF	Linear feet	12 inches of the item
SFCA	Square foot of contact area	A square foot of concrete formwork
SQ	Square	100 square feet
Ton	Ton	2,000 pounds

$399.95 per copy (in United States)
Price is subject to change without prior notice.

0302

RSMeans Facilities Maintenance & Repair

19TH ANNUAL EDITION

The *2012 Facilities Maintenance & Repair Cost Data*, 19th Annual Edition, and all of the RSMeans annual cost data books are dedicated to the memory of our respected friend and colleague, Hsiao-Cheng (John) Chiang, PE.

2012

RSMeans
A division of Reed Construction Data
Construction Publishers & Consultants
700 Longwater Drive
Norwell, MA 02061
USA

1-800-334-3509
www.rsmeans.com

Copyright 2011 by RSMeans
A division of Reed Construction Data
All rights reserved.

Printed in the United States of America
ISSN 1074-0953
ISBN 978-1-936335-35-0

Senior Editor
Stephen C. Plotner

Contributing Editors
Christopher Babbitt
Ted Baker
Barbara Balboni
Adrian C. Charest, PE
Gary W. Christensen
David G. Drain, PE
Cheryl Elsmore
Robert J. Kuchta
Robert C. McNichols
Melville J. Mossman, PE
Jeannene D. Murphy
Marilyn Phelan, AIA
Eugene R. Spencer
Phillip R. Waier, PE

Cover Design
Wendy McBay
Paul Robertson
Wayne Engebretson

President & CEO
Iain Melville

Vice President, Product & Development
Richard Remington

Vice President, Finance & Operations
David C. Walsh

Vice President, Data Aquisition & Fulfillment
Marco Piovesan

Chief Customer Officer
Lisa Fiondella

Senior Director, Product Management
Daimon Bridge

Vice President, Marketing & Business
Steven Ritchie

Engineering Director
Bob Mewis, CCC

Product Manager
Andrea Sillah

Product Marketing Manager
Ryan Cummings

Manager, Product Management
Jennifer Johnson

Production Manager
Michael Kokernak

Production Coordinator
Jill Goodman

Production Supervisor
Paula Reale-Camelio

Production
Jonathan Forgit
Mary Lou Geary
Debbie Panarelli
Sheryl A. Rose
Caroline Sullivan

Technical Support
Christopher Anderson
Tom Dion
Gary L. Hoitt
Genevieve Medeiros
Sharon Proulx
Kathryn S. Rodriguez

This book is printed using soy-based printing ink.
This book is recyclable.

Related RSMeans Products and Services

The engineers at RSMeans suggest the following products and services as companion information resources to *RSMeans Facilities Maintenance & Repair Cost Data:*

Construction Cost Data Books
Facilities Construction Cost Data 2012
Electrical Cost Data 2012
Mechanical Cost Data 2012
Plumbing Cost Data 2012

Reference Books
Facilities Planning and Relocation
Life Cycle Costing for Facilities
Cost Planning & Estimating for Facilities Maintenance
Job Order Contracting
Estimating Building Costs
RSMeans Estimating Handbook
Building Security: Strategies & Costs

Seminars and In-House Training
Facilities Maintenance & Repair Estimating
Unit Price Estimating
Means CostWorks® Training
Means Data for Job Order Contracting (JOC)
Mechanical & Electrical Estimating
Scheduling with MSProject for Construction Professionals

RSMeans on the Internet
Visit RSMeans at **www.rsmeans.com** for a one-stop portal for the most reliable and current resources available on the market. Here you can learn about our more than 20 annual cost data books, also available on CD and online versions, as well as about RSMeans seminars.

RSMeans Electronic Data
Get the information found in RSMeans cost books electronically on CD or on the Web at **MeansCostWorks.com**.

RSMeans Business Solutions
Cost engineers and analysts conduct facility life cycle and benchmark research studies and predictive cost modeling, as well as offer consultation services for conceptual estimating, real property management, and job order contracting. Research studies are designed with the application of proprietary cost and project data from Reed Construction Data and RSMeans' extensive North American databases. Analysts offer building product manufacturers qualitative and quantitative market research, as well as time/motion studies for new products, and Web-based dashboards for market opportunity analysis. Clients are from both the public and private sectors, including federal, state, and municipal agencies; corporations; institutions; construction management firms; hospitals; and associations.

RSMeans for Job Order Contracting (JOC)
Best practice job order contracting (JOC) services support the owner in the development of their program. RSMeans develops all required contracting documents, works with stakeholders, and develops qualified and experienced contractor lists. RSMeans JOCWorks™ software is the best of class in the functional tools that meet JOC specific requirements. RSMeans data is organized to meet JOC cost estimating requirements.

Construction Costs for Software Applications
Over 25 unit price and assemblies cost databases are available through a number of leading estimating and facilities management software providers (listed below). For more information see the "Other RSMeans Products" pages at the back of this publication.
RSMeansData™ is also available to federal, state, and local government agencies as multi-year, multi-seat licenses.

- 4Clicks-Solutions, LLC
- ArenaSoft Estimating
- Assetworks
- Beck Technology
- BSD – Building Systems Design, Inc.
- CMS – Construction Management Software
- Corecon Technologies, Inc.
- CorVet Systems
- Hard Dollar Corporation
- Maxwell Systems
- MC^2
- Parsons Corporation
- ProEst
- Sage Timberline Office
- UDA Technologies, Inc.
- US Cost, Inc.
- VFA – Vanderweil Facility Advisers
- WinEstimator, Inc.
- R & K Solutions
- Tririga

Table of Contents

Foreword

Our Mission

Since 1942, RSMeans has been actively engaged in construction cost publishing and consulting throughout North America.

Today, more than 65 years after RSMeans began, our primary objective remains the same: to provide you, the construction and facilities professional, with the most current and comprehensive construction cost data possible.

Whether you are a contractor, owner, architect, engineer, facilities manager, or anyone else who needs a reliable construction cost estimate, you'll find this publication to be a highly useful and necessary tool.

With the constant flow of new construction methods and materials today, it's difficult to find the time to look at and evaluate all the different construction cost possibilities. In addition, because labor and material costs keep changing, last year's cost information is not a reliable basis for today's estimate or budget.

That's why so many construction professionals turn to RSMeans. We keep track of the costs for you, along with a wide range of other key information, from city cost indexes . . . to productivity rates . . . to crew composition . . . to contractor's overhead and profit rates.

RSMeans performs these functions by collecting data from all facets of the industry and organizing it in a format that is instantly accessible to you. From the preliminary budget to the detailed unit price estimate, you'll find the data in this book useful for all phases of construction cost determination.

The Staff, the Organization, and Our Services

When you purchase one of RSMeans' publications, you are, in effect, hiring the services of a full-time staff of construction and engineering professionals.

Our thoroughly experienced and highly qualified staff works daily at collecting, analyzing, and disseminating comprehensive cost information for your needs. These staff members have years of practical construction experience and engineering training prior to joining the firm. As a result, you can count on them not only for accurate cost figures, but also for additional background reference information that will help you create a realistic estimate.

The RSMeans organization is always prepared to help you solve construction problems through its variety of data solutions, including online, CD, and print book formats, as well as cost estimating expertise available via our business solutions, training, and seminars.

Besides a full array of construction cost estimating books, RSMeans also publishes a number of other reference works for the construction industry. Subjects include construction estimating and project and business management, special topics such as green building and job order contracting, and a library of facility management references.

In addition, you can access all of our construction cost data electronically in convenient CD format or on the Web. Visit **MeansCostWorks.com** for more information on our 24/7 online cost data.

What's more, you can increase your knowledge and improve your construction estimating and management performance with an RSMeans construction seminar or in-house training program. These two-day seminar programs offer unparalleled opportunities for everyone in your organization to become updated on a wide variety of construction-related issues.

RSMeans is also a worldwide provider of construction cost management and analysis services for commercial and government owners.

In short, RSMeans can provide you with the tools and expertise for constructing accurate and dependable construction estimates and budgets in a variety of ways.

Robert Snow Means Established a Tradition of Quality That Continues Today

Robert Snow Means spent years building RSMeans, making certain he always delivered a quality product.

Today, at RSMeans, we do more than talk about the quality of our data and the usefulness of our books. We stand behind all of our data, from historical cost indexes to construction materials and techniques to current costs.

If you have any questions about our products or services, please call us toll-free at 1-800-334-3509. Our customer service representatives will be happy to assist you. You can also visit our Web site at **www.rsmeans.com**

How the Book Is Built: An Overview

A Complete Reference for the Facility Manager

This book was designed as a complete reference and cost data source for facility managers, owners, engineers, and contractors, or anyone who manages real estate. A complete facilities management program starts with a building audit. The audit describes the structures, their characteristics and major equipment, and apparent deficiencies. An audit is not a prerequisite to using any data contained in this book, but it does provide an organizational framework. A list of equipment and deficiencies forms the basis for a repair budget and preventive maintenance program. An audit also provides facility size and usage criteria on which the general maintenance (cleaning) program will be based. Together, the five sections of this book provide a framework and definitive data for developing a complete program for all facets of facilities maintenance.

Even if you have a regular building audit and preventive maintenance program in place, the information in this book will be useful.

For the occasional user, the book provides:

- a reference for time and material requirements for Maintenance & Repair tasks to fill in where your organization lacks its own historical data;
- Preventive Maintenance (PM) checklists with labor-hour standards that can be used to benchmark your program;
- a quick reference for General Maintenance (cleaning) productivity rates to analyze proposals from outside contractors;
- an explanation of Life Cycle Cost Analysis as a tool to assist in making the correct budget decisions; and
- data to validate line items in budgets.

For the frequent user, the book supplies all of the above, plus:

- guidance for getting the audit under way;
- a foundation for zero-based budgeting of maintenance & repair, preventive maintenance, and general maintenance;
- cost data that can be used to estimate preventive maintenance, deferred maintenance (repairs), and general maintenance (cleaning) programs; and
- detailed task descriptions for establishing a complete PM program.

How to Use the Book: The Details

This section contains an in-depth explanation of how the book is arranged—and how you can use it to assemble a reliable facilities maintenance estimate. It includes information about how RSMeans develops cost figures and how to completely prepare your estimate.

Section 1: Maintenance & Repair (M&R)

The Maintenance & Repair section is a listing of common maintenance tasks performed at facilities. The tasks include removal and replacement, repair, and refinishing. This section is organized according to the UNIFORMAT II system. (UNIFORMAT was originally developed for the General Services Administration as a systems approach to organizing building construction and has since become widely used in the building industry. It is now maintained and published by CSI, the Construction Specifications Institute.)

The purpose of Section 1 is to provide cost data and an approximate frequency of occurrence for each maintenance and repair task. This data is used by facility managers, owners, plant engineers, and contractors to prepare estimates for deferred maintenance projects. The data is also used to estimate labor-hours and material costs for in-house staff. The frequency listing facilitates preparation of a zero-based budget.

Under the System Description column, each task, including its components, is described. In some cases additional information (such as "2% of total roof area") appears in parentheses. The next column, Frequency, refers to how often one should expect, and therefore estimate, that this task will have to be performed. Labor hours have been enhanced, where appropriate, by 30% to include setup and delay time. In some cases, the list of steps comprising the task includes most of the potential repairs that could be made on a system. For those tasks, individual items, as appropriate, can be selected from the all-encompassing list.

Section 2: Preventive Maintenance (PM)

The Preventive Maintenance section provides the framework for a complete PM program. The establishment of a program is frequently hindered by the lack of a comprehensive

Maintenance & Repair

B30 ROOFING			B3013		Roof Covering							
B3013 105			Built-Up Roofing									
System Description			Freq. (Years)	Crew	Unit	Labor Hours	2012 Bare Costs				Total In-House	Total w/O&P
							Material	Labor	Equipment	Total		
0600	Place new BUR membrane over existing		20	G-5	Sq.							
	Set up, secure and take down ladder					.020		.75		.75	1.10	1.33
	Sweep / spud ballast clean					.500		18.70		18.70	27.50	33
	Vent existing membrane					.130		4.85		4.85	7.10	8.65
	Cut out buckled flashing					.024		.90		.90	1.32	1.60
	Install 2 ply membrane flashing					.027	.39			1.39	1.88	2.26
	Install 4 ply bituminous roofing					3.733	122	131	30	283	355	420
	Reinstall ballast					.381		14.25		14.25	21	25.50
	Clean up					.390		14.60		14.60	21.50	26
		Total				5.205	122.39	186.05	30	338.44	436.40	518.34
0700	Total BUR roof replacement		28	G-1	Sq.							
	Set up, secure and take down ladder					.020		.75		.75	1.10	1.33
	Sweep / spud ballast clean					.500		18.70		18.70	27.50	33
	Remove built-up roofing					2.500		89		89	118	146
	Remove insulation board					1.026		36		36	48	60
	Remove flashing					.024		.90		.90	1.32	1.60
	Install 2" perlite insulation					1.143	80	43		123	151	176
	Install 2 ply membrane flashing					.027	.39	1		1.39	1.88	2.26
	Install 4 ply bituminous membrane					2.800	122	98	22.50	242.50	300	350
	Clean up					1.000		37.50		37.50	55	66.50
		Total				9.040	202.39	324.85	22.50	549.74	703.80	836.69
B3013 120			Modified Bituminous / Thermoplastic									
System Description			Freq. (Years)	Crew	Unit	Labor Hours	2012 Bare Costs				Total In-House	Total w/O&P
							Material	Labor	Equipment	Total		
0100	Debris removal by hand & visual inspection		1	2 ROFC	M.S.F.							

list of equipment, actual PM steps, and budget documentation. This section fulfills all these needs. The facility manager, plant engineer, or owner can use these schedules to establish labor-hours and a budget. The maintenance contractor can use these PM checklists as the basis for a comprehensive maintenance proposal or as an estimating aid when bidding PM contracts. Selected pages, with preventive maintenance steps, can be photocopied and assembled into a customized PM program. Copies of individual sheets can also be distributed to maintenance personnel to identify the procedures required. The hours listed are predicated on work being performed by experienced technicians familiar with the PM tasks and equipped with the proper tools and materials.

The PM section lists the tasks and their frequency, whether weekly, monthly, quarterly, semi-annually, or annually. The frequency of those procedures is based on non-critical usage (e.g., in "normal use" situations, versus in facilities such as surgical suites or computer rooms that demand absolute adherence to a limited range of environmental conditions). The labor-hours to perform each item on the checklist are listed in the next column. Beneath the table is cost data for the PM schedule. The data is shown both annually and annualized, to provide the facility manager with an estimating range. If all tasks on the schedule are performed once a year, the *annually* line should be used in the PM estimate. The *annualized* data is used when all items on the schedule are performed at the frequency shown.

Section 3: General Maintenance (GM)

This section provides labor-hour estimates and costs to perform day-to-day cleaning. The data is used to estimate cleaning times, compare and assess estimates submitted by cleaning companies, or to budget in-house staff. The information is divided into *Interior* and *Exterior* maintenance. A common maintenance laborer *(Clam)* is used to perform these tasks.

Section 4: Facilities Audits

The Facilities Audit is generally the basis from which the Maintenance & Repair, Preventive Maintenance, and General Maintenance estimates are prepared. The audit provides the following:

1. A list of deficiencies for the Maintenance & Repair estimate
2. A list of equipment and other items from which to prepare a Preventive Maintenance estimate
3. A list of facilities' usage and size requirements to prepare a General Maintenance estimate

The Introduction to Facilities Audits in this section explains the rationale for the audit and the steps required to complete it successfully.

This section also provides forms for listing all of the organization's facilities, and a separate detailed form for the specifics of each facility. Checklists are provided for major building components. Each checklist should be accompanied by a blank audit form. This form is used to record the audit findings, prioritize the deficiencies, and estimate the cost to remedy these deficiencies.

Preventive Maintenance

D30 HVAC		D3025 130	Boiler, Hot Water, Oil/Gas/Comb.					
PM Components			Labor-hrs.	W	M	Q	S	A
PM System D3025 130 4950								
Boiler, hot water; oil, gas or combination fired, over 1000 MBH								
1 Check combustion chamber for air or gas leaks.			.117					√
2 Inspect and clean oil burner gun and ignition assembly where applicable.			.987					√
3 Inspect fuel system for leaks and change fuel filter element, where applicable.			.147					√
4 Check fuel lines and connections for damage.			.035	√	√	√	√	√
5 Check for proper operational response of burner to thermostat controls.			.199		√	√	√	√
6 Check and lubricate burner and blower motors.			.120					√
7 Check main flame failure protection and main flame detection scanner on boiler equipped with spark ignition (oil burner).			.186		√	√	√	√
8 Check electrical wiring to burner controls and blower.			.120					√
9 Clean firebox (sweep and vacuum).			.819					√
10 Check operation of mercury control switches (i.e. steam pressure, hot water temperature limit, atomizing or combustion air proving, etc.).			.215		√	√	√	√
11 Check operation and condition of safety pressure relief valve.			.046		√	√	√	√
12 Check operation of boiler low water cut off devices.			.085		√	√	√	√
13 Check hot water pressure gauges.			.109		√	√	√	√
14 Inspect and clean water column sight glass (or replace).			.191		√	√	√	√
15 Clean fire side of water jacket.			.433					√
16 Check condition of flue pipe, damper and exhaust stack.			.221			√	√	√
17 Check boiler operation through complete cycle, up to 30 minutes.			.887					√
18 Check fuel level with gauge pole, add as required.			.098		√	√	√	√
19 Clean area around boiler.			.182			√	√	√
20 Fill out maintenance checklist and report deficiencies.			.022		√	√	√	√
	Total labor-hours/period				1.169	1.709	1.709	5.219
	Total labor-hours/year				9.352	3.418	1.709	5.219

			Cost Each					
				2012 Bare Costs			Total	Total
Description	Labor-hrs.	Material	Labor	Equip.	Total	In-House	w/O&P
4900 Boiler, hot water, O/G/C, over 1000 MBH, annually	5.219	113	291		404	485	595

General Maintenance

01 93 Facility Maintenance

01 93 04 – Landscaping Maintenance

01 93 04.15 Edging	Crew	Daily Output	Labor-Hours	Unit	Material	2012 Bare Costs Labor	Equipment	Total	Total In-House	Total Incl O&P
0010 EDGING										
0020 Hand edging, at walks	1 Clam	16	.500	C.L.F.		13.20		13.20	16.40	20.50
0030 At planting, mulch or stone beds		7	1.143			30		30	37.50	46.50
0040 Power edging, at walks		88	.091			2.40		2.40	2.98	3.72
0050 At planting, mulch or stone beds		24	.333			8.80		8.80	10.90	13.65
01 93 04.20 Flower, Shrub and Tree Care										
0010 FLOWER, SHRUB & TREE CARE										
0020 Flower or shrub beds, bark mulch, 3" deep hand spreader	1 Clam	100	.080	S.Y.	2.92	2.11		5.03	5.85	6.92
0030 Peat moss, 1" deep hand spreader		900	.009		2.80	.23		3.03	3.37	3.86
0040 Wood chips, 2" deep hand spreader		220	.036		1.75	.96		2.71	3.12	3.68
0050 Cleaning		1	8	M.S.F.		211		211	262.00	325
0060 Fertilizing, dry granular, 3 #/C.S.F.		85	.094		6	2.48		8.48	9.70	11.35
0070 Weeding, mulched bed		20	.400			10.55		10.55	13.10	16.35
0080 Unmulched bed		8	1			26.50		26.50	33.00	41
0090 Trees, pruning from ground, 1-1/2" caliper		84	.095	Ea.		2.51		2.51	3.12	3.90
0100 2" caliper		70	.114			3.01		3.01	3.74	4.67
0110 2-1/2" caliper		50	.160			4.22		4.22	5.25	6.55
0120 3" caliper		30	.267			7.05		7.05	8.75	10.90
0130 4" caliper	2 Clam	21	.762			20		20	25.00	31
0140 6" caliper		12	1.333			35		35	43.50	54.50
0150 9" caliper		7.50	2.133			56		56	70.00	87.50
0160 12" caliper		6.50	2.462			65		65	80.50	101

Reference Section

This section contains information on Equipment Rental Costs, Crew Listings, Travel Costs, Reference Tables, Life Cycle Costing, and a listing of Abbreviations.

Equipment Rental Costs: This section contains the average costs to rent and operate hundreds of pieces of construction equipment.

Crew Listings: This section lists all the crews referenced in this book. For the purposes of this book, a crew is composed of more than one trade classification and/or the addition of power equipment to any trade classification. Power equipment is included in the cost of the crew. Costs are shown with bare labor rates and with both the in-house mark-ups and the installing contractor's overhead and profit added. For each, the total crew cost per eight-hour day and the composite cost per labor-hour are listed.

Travel Costs: This chart provides labor-hour costs for round-trip travel between a base of operation and the project site.

Reference Tables: In this section, you'll find reference tables, explanations, estimating information that support how we develop the unit price data, technical data, and estimating procedures.

Life Cycle Costing: This section provides definitions and basic equations for performing life cycle analysis. A sample problem is solved to demonstrate the methodology.

Abbreviations: A listing of the abbreviations used throughout this book, along with the terms they represent, is included in this section.

The Design Assumptions of this Book

This book is designed to be as easy to use as possible. To that end, we have made certain assumptions and limited its scope.

1. Unlike any other RSMeans publication, *Facilities Maintenance & Repair Cost Data* was designed for estimating a wide range of maintenance tasks in diverse environments. Due to this diversity, the level of accuracy of the data is +/- 20%.
2. We have established material prices based on a national average.
3. We have computed labor costs based on a 30-city national average of union wage rates.
4. Except where major equipment or component replacement is described, the projects in this book are small; therefore, material prices and labor-hours have been enhanced to reflect the increased costs of small-scale work.
5. The PM frequencies are based on non-critical applications. Increased frequencies are required for critical environments.

How to Use the Book: The Details

What's Behind the Numbers? The Development of Cost Data

The staff at RSMeans continually monitors developments in the construction industry in order to ensure reliable, thorough, and up-to-date cost information. While overall construction costs may vary relative to general economic conditions, price fluctuations within the industry are dependent upon many factors. Individual price variations may, in fact, be opposite to overall economic trends. Therefore, costs are constantly tracked and complete updates are published yearly. Also, new items are frequently added in response to changes in materials and methods.

Costs—$ (U.S.)

All costs represent U.S. national averages and are given in U.S. dollars. The RSMeans City Cost Indexes can be used to adjust costs to a particular location. The City Cost Indexes for Canada can be used to adjust U.S. national averages to local costs in Canadian dollars. No exchange rate conversion is necessary.

G The processes or products identified by the green symbol in our publications have been determined to be environmentally responsible and/or resource-efficient solely by the RSMeans engineering staff. The inclusion of the green symbol does not represent compliance with any specific industry association or standard.

Material Costs

The RSMeans staff contacts manufacturers, dealers, distributors, and contractors all across the U.S. and Canada to determine national average material costs. If you have access to current material costs for your specific location, you may wish to make adjustments to reflect differences from the national average. Included within material costs are fasteners for a normal installation. RSMeans engineers use manufacturers' recommendations, written

specifications, and/or standard construction practice for size and spacing of fasteners. Adjustments to material costs may be required for your specific application or location. Material costs do not include sales tax.

Labor Costs

Labor costs are based on the average of wage rates from 30 major U.S. cities. Rates are determined from labor union agreements or prevailing wages for construction trades for the current year. Rates, along with overhead and profit markups, are listed on the inside back cover of this book.

- If wage rates in your area vary from those used in this book, or if rate increases are expected within a given year, labor costs should be adjusted accordingly.

Labor costs reflect productivity based on actual working conditions. In addition to actual installation, these figures include time spent during a normal weekday on tasks such as, material receiving and handling, mobilization at site, site movement, breaks, and cleanup. Productivity data is developed over an extended period so as not to be influenced by abnormal variations and reflects a typical average.

Equipment Costs

Equipment costs include not only rental, but also operating costs for equipment under normal use. The operating costs include parts and labor for routine servicing such as repair and replacement of pumps, filters, and worn lines. Normal operating expendables, such as fuel, lubricants, tires, and electricity (where applicable), are also included. Extraordinary operating expendables with highly variable wear patterns, such as diamond bits and blades, are excluded. These costs are included under materials. Equipment rental rates are obtained from industry sources throughout North America—contractors, suppliers, dealers, manufacturers, and distributors.

Rental rates can also be treated as reimbursement costs for contractor-owned equipment. Owned equipment costs include depreciation, loan payments, interest, taxes, insurance, storage and major repairs.

Equipment costs do not include operators' wages; nor do they include the cost to move equipment to a job site (mobilization) or from a job site (demobilization).

Equipment Cost/Day——The cost of power equipment required for each crew is included in the Crew Listings in the Reference Section (small tools that are considered as essential everyday tools are not listed out separately). The Crew Listings itemize specialized tools and heavy equipment along with labor trades. The daily cost of itemized equipment included in a crew is based on dividing the weekly bare rental rate by 5 (number of working days per week) and then adding the hourly operating cost times 8 (the number of hours per day). This Equipment Cost/Day is shown in the last column of the Equipment Rental Cost pages in the Reference Section.

Mobilization/Demobilization——The cost to move construction equipment from an equipment yard or rental company to the job site and back again is not included in equipment costs. Mobilization (to the site) and demobilization (from the site) costs can be found in the Unit Price Section. If a piece of equipment is already at the job site, it is not appropriate to utilize mob./demob. costs again in an estimate.

Overhead and Profit

Total Cost including O&P for the *Installing Contractor* is shown in the last column on the Unit Price and/or the Assemblies pages of this book. This figure is the sum of the bare material cost plus 10% for profit, the bare labor cost plus total overhead and profit, and the bare equipment cost plus 10% for profit. Details for the calculation of Overhead and Profit on labor are shown on the inside back cover and in the Reference Section of this book. (See the "How to Use the Unit Price Pages" for an example of this calculation.)

General Conditions

Cost data in this book is presented in two ways: Bare Costs and Total Cost including O&P (Overhead and Profit). General Conditions, or General Requirements, of the contract should also be added to the Total Cost including O&P when applicable. Costs for General Conditions are listed in Division 1 of the Unit Price Section and the Reference

Section of this book. General Conditions for the *Installing Contractor* may range from 0% to 10% of the Total Cost including O&P. For the *General* or *Prime Contractor*, costs for General Conditions may range from 5% to 15% of the Total Cost including O&P, with a figure of 10% as the most typical allowance. If applicable, the Assemblies and Models sections of this book use costs that include the installing contractor's overhead and profit (O&P).

Factors Affecting Costs

Costs can vary depending upon a number of variables. Here's how we have handled the main factors affecting costs.

Quality——The prices for materials and the workmanship upon which productivity is based represent sound construction work. They are also in line with U.S. government specifications.

Overtime——We have made no allowance for overtime. If you anticipate premium time or work beyond normal working hours, be sure to make an appropriate adjustment to your labor costs.

Productivity——The productivity, daily output, and labor-hour figures for each line item are based on working an eight-hour day in daylight hours in moderate temperatures. For work that extends beyond normal work hours or is performed under adverse conditions, productivity may decrease. (See the section in "How To Use the Unit Price Pages" for more on productivity.)

Size of Project——The size, scope of work, and type of construction project will have a significant impact on cost. Economies of scale can reduce costs for large projects. Unit costs can often run higher for small projects.

Location——Material prices in this book are for metropolitan areas. However, in dense urban areas, traffic and site storage limitations may increase costs. Beyond a 20-mile radius of large cities, extra trucking or transportation charges may also increase the material costs slightly. On the other hand, lower wage rates may be in effect. Be sure to consider both of these factors when preparing an estimate, particularly if the job site is located in a central city or remote rural location. In addition, highly specialized subcontract items may require travel and per-diem expenses for mechanics.

Other Factors—
- season of year
- contractor management
- weather conditions
- local union restrictions
- building code requirements
- availability of:
  - adequate energy
  - skilled labor
  - building materials
- owner's special requirements/restrictions
- safety requirements
- environmental considerations

Unpredictable Factors——General business conditions influence "in-place" costs of all items. Substitute materials and construction methods may have to be employed. These may affect the installed cost and/or life cycle costs. Such factors may be difficult to evaluate and cannot necessarily be predicted on the basis of the job's location in a particular section of the country. Thus, where these factors apply, you may find significant but unavoidable cost variations for which you will have to apply a measure of judgment to your estimate.

Rounding of Costs

In general, all unit prices in excess of $5.00 have been rounded to make them easier to use and still maintain adequate precision of the results. The rounding rules we have chosen are in the following table.

Prices from . . .	Rounded to the nearest . . .
$.01 to $5.00	$.01
$5.01 to $20.00	$.05
$20.01 to $100.00	$.50
$100.01 to $300.00	$1.00
$300.01 to $1,000.00	$5.00
$1,000.01 to $10,000.00	$25.00
$10,000.01 to $50,000.00	$100.00
$50,000.01 and above	$500.00

How Subcontracted Items Affect Costs

A considerable portion of all large construction jobs is usually subcontracted. In fact, the percentage done by subcontractors is constantly increasing and may run over 90%. Since the workers employed by these companies do nothing else but install their particular product, they soon become expert in that line. The result is, installation by these firms is accomplished so efficiently that the total in-place cost, even adding the general contractor's overhead and profit, is no more, and often less, than if the principal contractor had handled the installation himself/herself. Companies that deal with construction specialties are anxious to have their product perform well and, consequently, the installation will be the best possible.

Contingencies

The allowance for contingencies generally provides for unforeseen construction difficulties. On alterations or repair jobs, 20% is not too much. If drawings are final and only field contingencies are being considered, 2% or 3% is probably sufficient, and often nothing need be added. Contractually, changes in plans will be covered by extras. The contractor should consider inflationary price trends and possible material shortages during the course of the job. These escalation factors are dependent upon both economic conditions and the anticipated time between the estimate and actual construction. If drawings are not complete or approved, or a budget cost is wanted, it is wise to add 5% to 10%. Contingencies, then, are a matter of judgment. Additional allowances for contingencies are shown in Division 1.

Important Estimating Considerations

The "productivity," or daily output, of each craftsman includes mobilization and cleanup time, break time and plan layout time, as well as an allowance to carry stock from the storage trailer or location on the job site up to 200' into the building and to the first or second floor. If material has to be transported over greater distances or to higher floors, an additional allowance should be considered by the estimator. An allowance has also been included in the piping and fittings installation time for leak checking and minor tightening. Equipment installation time includes the following applicable items: positioning, leveling and securing the unit in place, connecting all associated piping, ducts, vents, etc., which shall have been estimated separately, connecting to an adjacent power source, filling/bleeding, startup, adjusting the controls up and down to ensure proper response, setting the integral controls/valves/regulators/thermostats for proper operation (does not include external building type control systems, DDC systems, etc.), explaining/training owner's operator, and

warranty. A reasonable breakdown of the labor costs is as follows:

1. Movement into building, installation/setting of equipment	35%
2. Connection to piping/duct/power, etc.	25%
3. Filling/flushing/cleaning/touchup, etc.	15%
4. Startup/running adjustments	5%
5. Training owner's representative	5%
6. Warranty/call back/service	15%

Note that cranes or other lifting equipment are not included on any lines in the Mechanical divisions. For example, if a crane is required to lift a heavy piece of pipe into place high above a gym floor, or to put a rooftop unit on the roof of a four-story building, etc., it must be added. Due to the potential for extreme variation—from nothing additional required to a major crane or helicopter—we feel that including a nominal amount for "lifting contingency" would be useless and detract from the accuracy of the estimate. When using equipment rental from RSMeans, remember to include the cost of the operator(s).

Estimating Labor-Hours

The labor-hours expressed in this publication are based on Average Installation time, using an efficiency level of approximately 60%–65% (see item 7), which has been found reasonable and acceptable by many contractors. The book uses this national efficiency average to establish a consistent benchmark. For bid situations, adjustments to this efficiency level should be the responsibility of the contractor bidding the project. The unit labor-hour is divided in the following manner. A typical day for a journeyman might be:

1.	Study Plans	3%	14.4 min.
2.	Material Procurement	3%	14.4 min.
3.	Receiving and Storing	3%	14.4 min
4.	Mobilization	5%	24.0 min.
5.	Site Movement	5%	24.0 min.
6.	Layout and Marking	8%	38.4 min.
7.	Actual Installation	64%	307.2 min.
8.	Cleanup	3%	14.4 min.
9.	Breaks, Nonproductive	6%	28.8 min.
		100%	480.0 min.

If any of the percentages expressed in this breakdown do not apply to the particular work or project situation, then that percentage or a portion of it may be deducted from or added to labor-hours.

Final Checklist

Estimating can be a straightforward process provided you remember the basics. Here's a checklist of some of the steps you should remember to complete before finalizing your estimate. Did you remember to . . .

- factor in the City Cost Index for your locale?
- take into consideration which items have been marked up and by how much?
- mark up the entire estimate sufficiently for your purposes?
- read the background information on techniques and technical matters that could impact your project time span and cost?
- include all components of your project in the final estimate?
- double check your figures for accuracy?
- call RSMeans if you have any questions about your estimate or the data you've found in our publications? Remember, RSMeans stands behind its publications. If you have any questions about your estimate . . . about the costs you've used from our books . . . or even about the technical aspects of the job that may affect your estimate, feel free to call the RSMeans editors at 1-800-334-3509.

Maintenance & Repair

Table of Contents

Table of Contents (cont.)

Table of Contents (cont.)

How to Use the Maintenance & Repair Assemblies Cost Tables

The following is a detailed explanation of a sample Maintenance & Repair Assemblies Cost Table. Next to each bold number that follows is the described item with the appropriate component of the sample entry following in parentheses.

Total system costs, as well as the individual component costs, are shown. In most cases, the intent is for the user to apply the total system costs. However, changes and adjustments to the components or partial use of selected components is also appropriate. In particular, selected equipment system tables in the mechanical section include complete listings of operations that are meant to be chosen from rather than used in total.

1 System/Line Numbers (B3013 105 0700)

Each Maintenance & Repair Assembly has been assigned a unique identification number based on the UNIFORMAT II classification system.

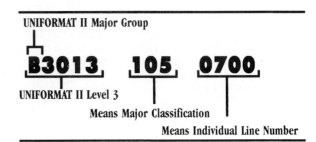

UNIFORMAT II Major Group

B3013 **105** **0700**

UNIFORMAT II Level 3

Means Major Classification

Means Individual Line Number

| B30 ROOFING | | | B3013 | | Roof Covering | | | | | | | |

B3013 105 — Built-Up Roofing

System Description	Freq. (Years)	Crew	Unit	Labor Hours	Material	Labor	Equipment	Total	Total In-House	Total w/O&P
0600 Place new BUR membrane over existing	20	G-5	Sq.							
Set up, secure and take down ladder						.75		.75	1.10	1.33
Sweep / spud ballast clean						18.70		18.70	27.50	33
Vent existing membrane				.130		4.85		4.85	7.10	8.65
Cut out buckled flashing				.024		.90		.90	1.32	1.60
Install 2 ply membrane flashing				.027	.39	1		1.39	1.88	2.26
Install 4 ply bituminous roofing				3.733	122	131	30	283	355	420
Reinstall ballast				.381		14.25		14.25	21	25.50
Clean up				.390		14.60		14.60	21.50	26
Total				5.205	122.39	186.05	30	338.44	**436.40**	518.34
0700 Total BUR roof replacement	28	G-1	Sq.							
Set up, secure and take down ladder				.020		.75		.75	1.10	1.33
Sweep / spud ballast clean				.500		18.70		18.70	27.50	33
Remove built-up roofing				2.500		89		89	118	146
Remove insulation board				1.026		36		36	48	60
Remove flashing				.024		.90		.90	1.32	1.60
Install 2" perlite insulation				1.143	80	43		123	151	176
Install 2 ply membrane flashing				.027	.39	1		1.39	1.88	2.26
Install 4 ply bituminous membrane				2.800	122	98	22.50	242.50	300	350
Clean up				1.000		37.50		37.50	55	66.50
Total				9.040	202.39	324.85	22.50	549.74	**703.80**	836.69

B3013 120 — Modified Bituminous / Thermoplastic

System Description	Freq. (Years)	Crew	Unit	Labor Hours	Material	Labor	Equipment	Total	Total In-House	Total w/O&P
0100 Debris removal by hand & visual inspection	1	2 ROFC	M.S.F.							
Set up, secure and take down ladder				.052		1.94		1.94	2.85	3.45
Pick up trash / debris & clean up				.327		12.20		12.20	17.90	21.50
Visual inspection				.327		12.20		12.20	17.90	21.50
Total				.705		26.34		26.34	**38.65**	46.45
0200 Non - destructive moisture inspection	5	2 ROFC	M.S.F.							
Set up, secure and take down ladder				.052		1.94		1.94	2.85	3.45
Infrared inspection of roof membrane				2.133		80		80	117	142
Total				2.185		81.94		81.94	**119.85**	145.45

System Description

A one-line description of each system is given, followed by a description of each component that makes up the system. In selected items, a percentage factor for planning annual costs is also given.

Frequency (28)

The projected frequency of occurrence in years for each system is listed. For example, **28** indicates that this operation should be budgeted for once every 28 years. If the frequency is less than 1, then the operation should be planned for more than once a year. For example, a value of **.5** indicates a planned occurrence of 2 times in a given year.

Crew (G-1)

The "Crew" column designates the typical trade or crew used for the task, although other trades may be used for minor portions of the work. If the task can be accomplished by one trade and requires no power equipment, that trade and the number of workers are listed (for example, "4 Rofc"). If the task requires a composite crew, a crew code designation is listed (for example, "G-1"). You'll find full details on all composite crews in the Crew Listings.

- For a complete list of all trades utilized in this book and their abbreviations, see the inside back cover of the book.

Crews

Crew No.	Bare Costs		In-House Costs		Incl. Subs O&P		Cost Per Labor-Hour		
Crew G-1	Hr.	Daily	Hr.	Daily	Hr.	Daily	Bare Costs	In House	Incl. O&P
1 Roofer Foreman (outside)	539.40	$ 315.20	$57.80	$ 462.40	$70.00	$ 560.00	$34.96	$55.27	$62.11
4 Roofers, Composition	37.40	1196.80	54.85	1755.20	66.45	2126.40			
2 Roofer Helpers	27.85	445.60	40.85	653.60	49.50	792.00			
1 Application Equipment		179.20		179.20		197.12			
1 Tar Kettle/Pot		91.00		91.00		100.10			
1 Crew Truck		182.40		182.40		200.64	8.08	8.08	8.89
56 L.H., Daily Totals		$2410.20		$3323.80		$3976.26	$43.04	$55.35	$71.00

Unit of Measure for Each System (Sq.)

The abbreviated designation indicates the unit of measure, as defined by industry standards, upon which the price of the component is based. In this example, "Cost per Square" is the unit of measure for this system or "assembly."

Labor-Hours (9.040)

The "Labor-Hours" figure represents the number of labor-hours required to perform one unit of work. To calculate the number of labor-hours required for a particular task, multiply the quantity of the item times the number of labor-hours shown. For example:

Quantity	x	Productivity Rate	=	Duration
30 Sq.	x	9.040 Labor-Hours/ Sq.	=	271 Labor-Hours

Bare Costs:
Material (202.39)

This figure for the unit material cost for the line item is the "bare" material cost with no overhead and profit allowances included. *Costs shown reflect national average material prices for the current year and generally include delivery to the facility. Small purchases may require an additional delivery charge. No sales taxes are included.*

Labor (324.85)

The unit labor cost is derived by multiplying bare labor-hour costs for Crew G-1 and other trades by labor-hour units. In this case, the bare labor-hour cost for the G-1 crew is found in the Crew Section. (If a trade is listed or used for minor portions of the work, the hourly labor cost—the wage rate—is found on the inside back cover of the book).

Equip. (Equipment) (22.50)

Equipment costs for each crew are listed in the description of each crew. The unit equipment cost is derived by multiplying the bare equipment hourly cost by the labor-hour units.

Total (549.74)

The total of the bare costs is the arithmetic total of the three previous columns: mat., labor, and equip.

Material	+	Labor	+	Equip.	=	Total
$202.39	+	$324.85	+	$22.50	=	$549.74

8 *Total In-House Costs (703.80)*

"Total In-House Costs" include suggested markups to bare costs for the direct overhead requirements of in-house maintenance staff. The figure in this column is the sum of three components: the bare material cost plus 10% (for purchasing and handling small quantities); the bare labor cost plus workers' compensation and average fixed overhead (per the labor rate table on the inside back cover of the book or, if a crew is listed, from the Crew Listings); and the bare equipment cost.

9 *Total Costs Including O&P (836.69)*

"Total Costs Including O&P" include suggested markups to bare costs for an outside subcontractor's overhead and profit requirements. The figure in this column is the sum of three components: the bare material cost plus 25% for profit; the bare labor cost plus total overhead and profit (per the labor rate table on the inside back cover of the book or, if a crew is listed, from the Crew Listings); and the bare equipment cost plus 10% for profit.

6

A10 FOUNDATIONS | A1033 | Slab on Grade

A1033 110 | Concrete, Unfinished

	System Description	Freq. (Years)	Crew	Unit	Labor Hours	2012 Bare Costs				Total In-House	Total w/O&P
						Material	Labor	Equipment	Total		
0010	**Minor repairs to concrete floor**	15	1 CEFI	S.F.							
	Repair spall				.612		21.50	3.20	24.70	32	39
	Repair concrete flooring				.061	2.46	2.59		5.05	6	7.15
	Total				.673	2.46	24.09	3.20	29.75	**38**	**46.15**
0020	**Replace unfinished concrete floor**	75	2 CEFI	C.S.F.							
	Break up concrete slab				1.664		63.60	23.20	86.80	106	129
	Load into truck				1.950		69.75	36	105.75	128	152
	Rebar #3 to #7				.139	9.80	6.80		16.60	20	23.50
	Edge form				.693	2.90	29		31.90	42	51
	Slab on grade 4" in place with finish				1.577	99	63	.75	162.75	191	225
	Expansion joint				.003	.06	.11		.17	.21	.26
	Cure concrete				.109	3.73	3.85		7.58	9.20	10.95
	Total				6.135	115.49	236.11	59.95	411.55	**496.41**	**591.71**

B1013 510 Concrete Stairs

	System Description	Freq. (Years)	Crew	Unit	Labor Hours	2012 Bare Costs				Total In-House	Total w/O&P
						Material	Labor	Equipment	Total		
1010	**Repair concrete steps**	30	1 CEFI	S.F.							
	Repair spalls in steps				.104	10.90	4.40		15.30	17.55	20.50
	Total				**.104**	**10.90**	**4.40**		**15.30**	**17.55**	**20.50**
1020	**Replace concrete steps**	75	1 CEFI	S.F.							
	Remove concrete				.520		18.45	2.72	21.17	27.50	33.50
	Install forms				.328	1.12	14.10		15.22	19.95	24.50
	Pour concrete				.567	2.49	21	.65	24.14	30.50	38
	Total				**1.416**	**3.61**	**53.55**	**3.37**	**60.53**	**77.95**	**96**
1030	**Refinish concrete steps**	3	1 PORD	S.F.							
	Prepare surface				.016		.61		.61	.79	.98
	Refinish surface, brushwork, 1 coat				.013	.07	.48		.55	.70	.85
	Total				**.029**	**.07**	**1.09**		**1.16**	**1.49**	**1.83**
2030	**Refinish concrete landing**	3	1 PORD	S.F.							
	Prepare surface				.016		.61		.61	.79	.98
	Refinish surface, brushwork, 1 coat				.013	.07	.48		.55	.70	.85
	Total				**.029**	**.07**	**1.09**		**1.16**	**1.49**	**1.83**

B1013 520 Masonry Steps

	System Description	Freq. (Years)	Crew	Unit	Labor Hours	2012 Bare Costs				Total In-House	Total w/O&P
						Material	Labor	Equipment	Total		
1010	**Repair masonry steps**	4	1 BRIC	S.F.							
	Remove damaged masonry				.074		2.61		2.61	3.47	4.28
	Clean area				.019	.04	.82		.86	1.10	1.37
	Replace with new masonry				.236	3.58	9.60		13.18	16.45	20
	Total				**.329**	**3.62**	**13.03**		**16.65**	**21.02**	**25.65**

B1013 530 Wood Stairs

	System Description	Freq. (Years)	Crew	Unit	Labor Hours	2012 Bare Costs				Total In-House	Total w/O&P
						Material	Labor	Equipment	Total		
1030	**Refinish wood steps**	3	1 PORD	S.F.							
	Prepare surface				.016		.61		.61	.79	.98
	Wash / dry surface				.001		.04		.04	.06	.07
	Refinish surface, brushwork, 1 coat				.013	.07	.48		.55	.70	.85
	Total				.030	.07	1.13		1.20	1.55	1.90
1040	**Replace wood steps**	30	2 CARP	S.F.							
	Remove stairs (to 6' wide)				.100		3.51		3.51	4.66	5.75
	New stringers (to 5 risers)				.074	.94	3.27		4.21	5.35	6.50
	Risers				.083	.63	3.67		4.30	5.55	6.80
	Treads				.123	1.56	5.45		7.01	8.95	10.85
	Total				.380	3.13	15.90		19.03	24.51	29.90
2030	**Refinish wood landing**	3	1 PORD	S.F.							
	Prepare surface				.016		.61		.61	.79	.98
	Wash / dry surface				.001		.04		.04	.06	.07
	Refinish surface, brushwork, 1 coat				.013	.07	.48		.55	.70	.85
	Total				.030	.07	1.13		1.20	1.55	1.90

B1013 540 Railing, Wood

	System Description	Freq. (Years)	Crew	Unit	Labor Hours	2012 Bare Costs				Total In-House	Total w/O&P
						Material	Labor	Equipment	Total		
1010	**Replace wood balustrade**	20	1 CARP	L.F.							
	Remove damaged balusters and handrail				.087		3.04		3.04	4.04	4.99
	Install new balusters and handrail				.473	25.50	21		46.50	56	66
	Total				.559	25.50	24.04		49.54	60.04	70.99
1030	**Refinish wood balustrade**	7	1 PORD	L.F.							
	Prepare balusters and handrails for painting				.052		1.99		1.99	2.56	3.17
	Wash / dry surface				.001		.04		.04	.06	.07
	Paint balusters and handrails, brushwork, primer + 1 coat				.089	.73	3.40		4.13	5.15	6.35
	Total				.142	.73	5.43		6.16	7.77	9.59

B10 SUPERSTRUCTURE | B1013 | Floor Construction

B1013 550 Metal Stairs

	System Description	Freq. (Years)	Crew	Unit	Labor Hours	Material	Labor	Equipment	Total	Total In-House	Total w/O&P
							2012 Bare Costs				
1010	**Repair metal steps**	15	1 SSWK	S.F.							
	Remove damaged stair tread				.099		4.89		4.89	7.60	9.15
	New stair tread				.198	39.47	9.72		49.19	58.50	67.50
	Total				.297	39.47	14.61		54.08	66.10	76.65
1040	**Replace metal steps**	40	2 SSWK	S.F.							
	Remove stairs				.168		8.30		8.30	12.85	15.45
	New stairs				.239	147.29	11.58	6.44	165.31	186	212
	Total				.408	147.29	19.88	6.44	173.61	198.85	227.45
1050	**Refinish metal steps**	3	1 PORD	S.F.							
	Prepare metal railing for painting				.019		.73		.73	.94	1.17
	Wash / dry surface				.001		.04		.04	.06	.07
	Paint metal steps, brushwork, primer + 1 coat				.015	.11	.59		.70	.88	1.08
	Total				.036	.11	1.36		1.47	1.88	2.32
2030	**Refinish metal landing**	3	1 PORD	S.F.							
	Prepare metal railing for painting				.019		.73		.73	.94	1.17
	Wash / dry surface				.001		.04		.04	.06	.07
	Paint metal landing, brushwork, primer + 1 coat				.015	.11	.59		.70	.88	1.08
	Total				.036	.11	1.36		1.47	1.88	2.32

B1013 560 Railing, Metal

	System Description	Freq. (Years)	Crew	Unit	Labor Hours	Material	Labor	Equipment	Total	Total In-House	Total w/O&P
							2012 Bare Costs				
1010	**Replace metal hand rail**	30	1 SSWK	L.F.							
	Remove damaged railings				.087		3.04		3.04	4.04	4.99
	Install new metal railings				.163	23.50	8.15	.62	32.27	39	45
	Total				.250	23.50	11.19	.62	35.31	43.04	49.99
1030	**Refinish metal hand rail**	7	1 PORD	L.F.							
	Prepare metal railing for painting				.019		.73		.73	.94	1.17
	Wash / dry surface				.001		.04		.04	.06	.07
	Paint metal railing, brushwork, primer + 1 coat				.015	.11	.59		.70	.88	1.08
	Total				.036	.11	1.36		1.47	1.88	2.32

B1013 570 — Wrought Iron Exterior Balustrade

System Description	Freq. (Years)	Crew	Unit	Labor Hours	2012 Bare Costs — Material	Labor	Equipment	Total	Total In-House	Total w/O&P
1010 Repair wrought iron balustrade	20	1 SSWK	L.F.							
Cut / remove damaged section				.325		11.40		11.40	15.15	18.70
Reset new section				.867	67.50	43		110.50	140	164
Total				1.192	67.50	54.40		121.90	155.15	182.70
1030 Refinish wrought iron balustrade	7	1 PORD	L.F.							
Prepare metal balustrade for painting				.019		.73		.73	.94	1.17
Wash / dry surface				.001		.04		.04	.06	.07
Paint metal balustrade, brushwork, primer + 1 coat				.015	.11	.59		.70	.88	1.08
Total				.036	.11	1.36		1.47	1.88	2.32

B1013 580 — Metal Fire Escapes

System Description	Freq. (Years)	Crew	Unit	Labor Hours	2012 Bare Costs — Material	Labor	Equipment	Total	Total In-House	Total w/O&P
1010 Refinish fire escape balcony, 2' wide	7	1 PORD	L.F.							
Prepare metal fire escape balcony for painting				.100		3.83		3.83	4.92	6.10
Brush on primer coat				.100	2.48	3.83		6.31	7.65	9.15
Brush on finish coat				.100	2.18	3.83		6.01	7.35	8.80
Total				.300	4.66	11.49		16.15	19.92	24.05
1020 Replace fire escape balcony, 2' wide	25	2 SSWK	L.F.							
Remove metal fire escape balcony				.500		24.50		24.50	38	46
Install new metal fire escape balcony				2.000	55	98.50		153.50	213	252
Total				2.500	55	123		178	251	298
2010 Refinish fire escape stair and platform	7	1 PORD	Flight							
Prepare fire escape stair and platform for painting				2.400		92		92	118	147
Brush on primer coat				2.400	59.40	91.80		151.20	184	220
Brush on finish coat				2.400	52.20	91.80		144	176	211
Total				7.200	111.60	275.60		387.20	478	578
2020 Replace fire escape stair and platform	25	2 SSWK	Flight							
Remove metal fire escape stair and platform				14.995		740		740	1,150	1,375
Install new metal fire escape stair and platform				59.925	1,000	2,950		3,950	5,675	6,750
Total				74.920	1,000	3,690		4,690	6,825	8,125

B1013 580 Metal Fire Escapes

System Description	Freq. (Years)	Crew	Unit	Labor Hours	2012 Bare Costs Material	2012 Bare Costs Labor	2012 Bare Costs Equipment	2012 Bare Costs Total	Total In-House	Total w/O&P
3010	**Refinish fire escape ladder**	7	1 PORD	V.L.F.						
	Prepare metal fire escape ladder for painting				.020		.77		.77	.98	1.22
	Brush on primer coat				.020	.33	.77		1.10	1.35	1.63
	Brush on finish coat				.020	.29	.77		1.06	1.30	1.58
	Total				.060	.62	2.31		2.93	3.63	4.43
3020	**Replace fire escape ladder**	25	2 SSWK	V.L.F.						
	Remove metal fire escape ladder				.250		12.35		12.35	19.10	23
	Install new metal fire escape ladder				.500	36	24.50		60.50	78	91
	Total				.750	36	36.85		72.85	97.10	114

B1013 910 Steel Decking

System Description	Freq. (Years)	Crew	Unit	Labor Hours	2012 Bare Costs Material	2012 Bare Costs Labor	2012 Bare Costs Equipment	2012 Bare Costs Total	Total In-House	Total w/O&P
0020	**Replace steel decking**	30	2 SSWK	S.F.						
	Remove decking				.011	2.23	.59	.17	2.99	3.53	4.07
	Assemble and weld decking				.011	2.23	.59	.17	2.99	3.53	4.07
	Total				.023	4.46	1.18	.34	5.98	7.06	8.14

B1013 920 Metal Grating

System Description	Freq. (Years)	Crew	Unit	Labor Hours	2012 Bare Costs Material	2012 Bare Costs Labor	2012 Bare Costs Equipment	2012 Bare Costs Total	Total In-House	Total w/O&P
0010	**Metal floor grating repairs - (2% of grating)**	10	1 SSWK	S.F.						
	Misc. welding of floor grating				.348	1.05	17.85	5.30	24.20	34	40
	Total				.348	1.05	17.85	5.30	24.20	34	40
0020	**Replace metal floor grating**	30	2 SSWK	S.F.						
	Remove grating				.011	2.23	.59	.17	2.99	3.53	4.07
	Assemble and weld grating				.059	17.70	2.96	.23	20.89	24.50	28
	Total				.071	19.93	3.55	.40	23.88	28.03	32.07

B2013 104 Copings

System Description	Freq. (Years)	Crew	Unit	Labor Hours	2012 Bare Costs				Total In-House	Total w/O&P
					Material	Labor	Equipment	Total		
2010										
Replace precast concrete coping, 12" wide	50	2 BRIC	L.F.							
Set up and secure scaffold, 3 floors to roof				.429		18.88		18.88	25	31
Remove coping				.050		1.76		1.76	2.33	2.88
Install new precast concrete coping				.229	19.60	9.10		28.70	33.50	39
Remove scaffold				.429		18.88		18.88	25	31
Total				1.137	19.60	48.62		68.22	85.83	103.88
2020										
Replace limestone coping, 12" wide	50	2 BRIC	L.F.							
Set up and secure scaffold, 3 floors to roof				.429		18.88		18.88	25	31
Remove coping				.050		1.76		1.76	2.33	2.88
Install new limestone coping				.178	15.35	7.10		22.45	26	30.50
Remove scaffold				.429		18.88		18.88	25	31
Total				1.086	15.35	46.62		61.97	78.33	95.38
2030										
Replace marble coping, 12" wide	50	2 BRIC	L.F.							
Set up and secure scaffold, 3 floors to roof				.429		18.88		18.88	25	31
Remove coping				.050		1.76		1.76	2.33	2.88
Install new marble coping				.200	35	7.95		42.95	49	56.50
Remove scaffold				.429		18.88		18.88	25	31
Total				1.108	35	47.47		82.47	101.33	121.38
2040										
Replace terra cotta coping, 12" wide	50	2 BRIC	L.F.							
Set up and secure scaffold, 3 floors to roof				.429		18.88		18.88	25	31
Remove coping				.050		1.76		1.76	2.33	2.88
Install new terra cotta coping				.200	9.20	7.95		17.15	20.50	24.50
Remove scaffold				.429		18.88		18.88	25	31
Total				1.108	9.20	47.47		56.67	72.83	89.38

System Description	Freq. (Years)	Crew	Unit	Labor Hours	2012 Bare Costs				Total In-House	Total w/O&P
					Material	Labor	Equipment	Total		
1010 Repair 8" concrete block wall - 1st floor	25	1 BRIC	S.F.							
Set up, secure and take down ladder				.130		5.75		5.75	7.45	9.25
Remove damaged block				.183		6.40		6.40	8.50	10.50
Wire truss reinforcing				.005	.23	.23		.46	.55	.65
Install block				.111	2.32	4.52		6.84	8.45	10.20
Total				.429	2.55	16.90		19.45	24.95	30.60
1020 Replace 8" concrete block wall - 1st floor	60	2 BRIC	C.S.F.							
Set up and secure scaffold				.750		33		33	44	54
Remove damaged block				4.571		160		160	213	263
Wire truss reinforcing				.260	11.25	11.50		22.75	27.50	32.50
Install block				11.111	232	452		684	845	1,025
Remove scaffold				.750		33		33	44	54
Total				17.442	243.25	689.50		932.75	1,173.50	1,428.50
1030 Waterproof concrete block wall - 1st floor	10	1 ROFC	C.S.F.							
Steam clean				2.971		105	16	121	156	190
Spray surface, silicone				.260	33	10		43	50	58.50
Total				3.231	33	115	16	164	206	248.50
2020 Replace 8" concrete block wall - 2nd floor	60	2 BRIC	C.S.F.							
Set up and secure scaffold				1.500		66		66	88	108
Remove block				4.571		160		160	213	263
Wire truss reinforcing				.260	11.25	11.50		22.75	27.50	32.50
Install block				11.111	232	452		684	845	1,025
Remove scaffold				1.500		66		66	88	108
Total				18.942	243.25	755.50		998.75	1,261.50	1,536.50
2030 Waterproof concrete block wall - 2nd floor	10	G-8	C.S.F.							
Position aerial lift truck, raise & lower platform				.250		9.35	19.95	29.30	33.50	38.50
Steam clean				11.765		413	98	511	645	785
Spray surface, silicone				.260	33	10	21	64	71	81.50
Total				12.275	33	432.35	138.95	604.30	749.50	905

14

B2013 109   Concrete Block

	System Description	Freq. (Years)	Crew	Unit	Labor Hours	2012 Bare Costs				Total In-House	Total w/O&P
						Material	Labor	Equipment	Total		
3020	**Replace 8" concrete block wall - 3rd floor**	60	2 BRIC	C.S.F.							
	Set up and secure scaffold				1.500		66		66	88	109
	Remove damaged block				4.571		160		160	213	263
	Wire truss reinforcing				.260	11.25	11.50		22.75	27.50	32.50
	Install block				11.111	232	452		684	845	1,025
	Remove scaffold				1.500		66		66	88	109
	Total				18.942	243.25	755.50		998.75	1,261.50	1,538.50
3030	**Waterproof concrete block wall - 3rd floor**	10	G-8	C.S.F.							
	Position aerial lift truck, raise & lower platform				.300		11.20	24	35.20	40.50	46.50
	Steam clean				11.765		413	98	511	645	785
	Spray surface, silicone				.260	33	10	21	64	71	81.50
	Total				12.325	33	434.20	143	610.20	756.50	913

B2013 114   Concrete Block Wall, Painted

	System Description	Freq. (Years)	Crew	Unit	Labor Hours	2012 Bare Costs				Total In-House	Total w/O&P
						Material	Labor	Equipment	Total		
1030	**Point & refinish block wall - 1st floor**	25	1 BRIC	C.S.F.							
	Set up and secure scaffold				.750		33		33	44	54
	Steam clean				2.600		91		91	121	150
	Clean & point block				3.924		173		173	225	279
	Paint surface, brushwork, 1 coat				1.040	13	40.30		53.30	65	80
	Remove scaffold				.750		33		33	44	54
	Total				9.064	13	370.30		383.30	499	617
2030	**Point & refinish block wall - 2nd floor**	25	1 BRIC	C.S.F.							
	Set up and secure scaffold				1.500		66		66	88	108
	Steam clean				2.600		91		91	121	150
	Clean & point block				3.924		173		173	225	279
	Paint surface, brushwork, 1 coat				1.040	13	40.30		53.30	65	80
	Remove scaffold				1.500		66		66	88	108
	Total				10.564	13	436.30		449.30	587	725

B2013 114 Concrete Block Wall, Painted

System Description	Freq. (Years)	Crew	Unit	Labor Hours	2012 Bare Costs				Total In-House	Total w/O&P
					Material	Labor	Equipment	Total		
3020 Point & refinish block wall – 3rd floor	25	1 BRIC	C.S.F.							
Set up and secure scaffold				2.250		99		99	132	162
Steam clean				2.600		91		91	121	150
Clean & point block				3.924		173		173	225	279
Paint surface, brushwork, 1 coat				1.040	13	40.30		53.30	65	80
Remove scaffold				2.250		99		99	132	162
Total				12.064	13	502.30		515.30	675	833

B2013 118 Terra Cotta

System Description	Freq. (Years)	Crew	Unit	Labor Hours	2012 Bare Costs				Total In-House	Total w/O&P
					Material	Labor	Equipment	Total		
1020 Replace terra cotta wall – 1st floor	50	2 BRIC	C.S.F.							
Set up and secure scaffold				.750		33		33	44	54
Remove terra cotta				1.040		37	5.45	42.45	54.50	66.50
Replace terra cotta				10.400	760	423		1,183	1,375	1,625
Remove scaffold				.750		33		33	44	54
Total				12.940	760	526	5.45	1,291.45	1,517.50	1,799.50
2010 Replace terra cotta wall – 2nd floor	50	2 BRIC	C.S.F.							
Set up and secure scaffold				1.500		66		66	88	108
Remove terra cotta				1.040		37	5.45	42.45	54.50	66.50
Replace terra cotta				10.400	760	423		1,183	1,375	1,625
Remove scaffold				1.500		66		66	88	108
Total				14.440	760	592	5.45	1,357.45	1,605.50	1,907.50
2020 Replace terra cotta wall – 3rd floor	50	2 BRIC	C.S.F.							
Set up and secure scaffold				2.250		99		99	132	162
Remove terra cotta				1.040		37	5.45	42.45	54.50	66.50
Replace terra cotta				10.400	760	423		1,183	1,375	1,625
Remove scaffold				2.250		99		99	132	162
Total				15.940	760	658	5.45	1,423.45	1,693.50	2,015.50

System Description	Freq. (Years)	Crew	Unit	Labor Hours	2012 Bare Costs				Total In-House	Total w/O&P
					Material	Labor	Equipment	Total		
1010 Repair brick wall - 1st floor										
Set up, secure and take down ladder	25	1 BRIC	S.F.	.130		5.75		5.75	7.45	9.25
Remove damage				.451		15.86		15.86	21	26
Install brick				.236	3.58	9.60		13.18	16.45	20
Total				.817	3.58	31.21		34.79	44.90	55.25
1020 Point brick wall - 1st floor										
Set up and secure scaffold	25	2 BRIC	C.S.F.	1.333		51		51	65.50	81.50
Steam clean				2.971		105	16	121	156	190
Clean & point brick				10.000	4	441		445	580	715
Remove scaffold				1.333		51		51	65.50	81.50
Total				15.638	4	648	16	668	867	1,068
1030 Waterproof brick wall - 1st floor										
Steam clean	10	1 ROFC	C.S.F.	2.971		105	16	121	156	190
Spray surface, silicone				.260	33	10		43	50	58.50
Total				3.231	33	115	16	164	206	248.50
2010 Replace brick wall - 2nd floor										
Set up and secure scaffold	75	2 BRIC	C.S.F.	1.500		66		66	88	108
Remove damage				10.401		366		366	485	600
Install brick				23.636	358	960		1,318	1,650	2,000
Remove scaffold				1.500		66		66	88	108
Total				37.037	358	1,458		1,816	2,311	2,816
2020 Point brick wall - 2nd floor										
Set up and secure scaffold	25	2 BRIC	C.S.F.	1.500		66		66	88	108
Steam clean				2.971		105	16	121	156	190
Clean & point brick				10.000	4	441		445	580	715
Remove scaffold				1.500		66		66	88	108
Total				15.971	4	678	16	698	912	1,121
2030 Waterproof brick wall - 2nd floor										
Position aerial lift truck, raise & lower platform	10	G-8	C.S.F.	.250		9.35	19.95	29.30	33.50	38.50
Steam clean				11.765		413	98	511	645	785
Spray surface, silicone				.260	33	10	21	64	71	81.50
Total				12.275	33	432.35	138.95	604.30	749.50	905

17

B20 EXTERIOR CLOSURE B2013 Exterior Walls

B2013 119 Clay Brick

	System Description	Freq. (Years)	Crew	Unit	Labor Hours	2012 Bare Costs				Total In-House	Total w/O&P
						Material	Labor	Equipment	Total		
3010	**Replace brick wall - 3rd floor**	75	2 BRIC	C.S.F.							
	Set up and secure scaffold				1.500		66		66	88	109
	Remove damage				10.401		366		366	485	600
	Install brick				23.636	358	960		1,318	1,650	2,000
	Remove scaffold				1.500		66		66	88	109
	Total				37.037	358	1,458		1,816	2,311	2,818
3020	**Point brick wall - 3rd floor**	25	2 BRIC	C.S.F.							
	Set up and secure scaffold				1.500		66		66	88	109
	Steam clean				2.971		105	16	121	156	190
	Clean & point brick				10.000	4	441		445	580	715
	Remove scaffold				1.500		66		66	88	109
	Total				15.971	4	678	16	698	912	1,123
3030	**Waterproof brick wall - 3rd floor**	10	G-8	C.S.F.							
	Position aerial lift truck, raise & lower platform				.300		11.20	24	35.20	40.50	46.50
	Steam clean				11.765		413	98	511	645	785
	Spray surface, silicone				.260	33	10	21	64	71	81.50
	Total				12.325	33	434.20	143	610.20	756.50	913

B2013 121 Clay Brick, Painted

	System Description	Freq. (Years)	Crew	Unit	Labor Hours	2012 Bare Costs				Total In-House	Total w/O&P
						Material	Labor	Equipment	Total		
1010	**Repair painted brick wall - 1st floor**	25	1 BRIC	S.F.							
	Set up, secure and take down ladder				.130		5.75		5.75	7.45	9.25
	Remove damage				.451		15.86		15.86	21	26
	Install brick				.236	3.58	9.60		13.18	16.45	20
	Paint surface, brushwork, 1 coat				.010	.13	.40		.53	.65	.80
	Total				.827	3.71	31.61		35.32	45.55	56.05

B2013 121 **Clay Brick, Painted**

	System Description	Freq. (Years)	Crew	Unit	Labor Hours	2012 Bare Costs				Total In-House	Total w/O&P
						Material	Labor	Equipment	Total		
1030	**Point brick wall - 1st floor**	25	1 BRIC	C.S.F.							
	Set up and secure scaffold				.500		22		22	29.50	36.50
	Steam clean				2.971		105	16	121	156	190
	Clean & point brick				10.000	4	441		445	580	715
	Paint surface, brushwork, 1 coat				1.040	13	40.30		53.30	65	80
	Remove scaffold				.500		22		22	29.50	36.50
	Total				15.011	17	630.30	16	663.30	860	1,058
2010	**Replace brick wall - 2nd floor**	75	1 BRIC	C.S.F.							
	Set up and secure scaffold				1.500		66		66	88	108
	Remove damage				10.401		366		366	485	600
	Install brick				23.636	358	960		1,318	1,650	2,000
	Paint surface, brushwork, 1 coat				1.040	13	40.30		53.30	65	80
	Remove scaffold				1.500		66		66	88	108
	Total				38.077	371	1,498.30		1,869.30	2,376	2,896
2020	**Point and refinish brick wall - 2nd floor**	25	1 BRIC	C.S.F.							
	Set up and secure scaffold				1.500		66		66	88	108
	Steam clean				2.971		105	16	121	156	190
	Clean & point brick				10.000	4	441		445	580	715
	Paint surface, brushwork, 1 coat				1.040	13	40.30		53.30	65	80
	Remove scaffold				1.500		66		66	88	108
	Total				17.011	17	718.30	16	751.30	977	1,201
3010	**Replace brick wall - 3rd floor**	75	1 BRIC	C.S.F.							
	Set up and secure scaffold				1.500		66		66	88	109
	Remove damage				10.401		366		366	485	600
	Install brick				23.636	358	960		1,318	1,650	2,000
	Paint surface, brushwork, 1 coat				.010	.13	.40		.53	.65	.80
	Remove scaffold				1.500		66		66	88	109
	Total				37.047	358.13	1,458.40		1,816.53	2,311.65	2,818.80

19

B2013 121 Clay Brick, Painted

	System Description	Freq. (Years)	Crew	Unit	Labor Hours	Material	Labor	Equipment	Total	Total In-House	Total w/O&P
							2012 Bare Costs				
3020	**Point and refinish brick wall - 3rd floor**	25	1 BRIC	C.S.F.							
	Set up and secure scaffold				1.500		66		66	88	109
	Steam clean				2.971		105	16	121	156	190
	Clean & point brick				10.000	4	441		445	580	715
	Paint surface, brushwork, 1 coat				1.040	13	40.30		53.30	65	80
	Remove scaffold				1.500		66		66	88	109
	Total				17.011	17	718.30	16	751.30	977	1,203

B2013 123 Field Stone

	System Description	Freq. (Years)	Crew	Unit	Labor Hours	Material	Labor	Equipment	Total	Total In-House	Total w/O&P
							2012 Bare Costs				
1010	**Repair field stone wall - 1st floor**	25	1 BRIC	S.F.							
	Set up, secure and take down ladder				.390		13.95		13.95	18.55	23
	Remove damaged stones				.173		6.15	.91	7.06	9.10	11.10
	Reset stones				.416	21	18.05	5.85	44.90	52.50	61.50
	Total				.979	21	38.15	6.76	65.91	80.15	95.60
1020	**Point stone wall, 8″ x 8″ stones - 1st floor**	25	2 BRIC	C.S.F.							
	Set up and secure scaffold				1.333		51		51	65.50	81.50
	Steam clean				2.971		105	16	121	156	190
	Clean & point stonework joints				5.714	70	252		322	405	495
	Remove scaffold				1.333		51		51	65.50	81.50
	Total				11.352	70	459	16	545	692	848
2020	**Point stone wall, 8″ x 8″ stones - 2nd floor**	25	2 BRIC	C.S.F.							
	Set up and secure scaffold				1.500		66		66	88	108
	Steam clean				2.971		105	16	121	156	190
	Clean & point stonework joints				5.714	70	252		322	405	495
	Remove scaffold				1.500		66		66	88	108
	Total				11.685	70	489	16	575	737	901

B2013 123 Field Stone

System Description	Freq. (Years)	Crew	Unit	Labor Hours	2012 Bare Costs				Total In-House	Total w/O&P
					Material	Labor	Equipment	Total		
3020 Point stone wall, 8" x 8" stones - 3rd floor	25	2 BRIC	C.S.F.							
Set up and secure scaffold				1.500		66		66	88	109
Steam clean				2.971		105		121	156	190
Clean & point stonework joints				5.714	70	252	16	322	405	495
Remove scaffold				1.500		66		66	88	109
Total				11.685	70	489	16	575	737	903

B2013 140 Glass Block

System Description	Freq. (Years)	Crew	Unit	Labor Hours	2012 Bare Costs				Total In-House	Total w/O&P
					Material	Labor	Equipment	Total		
1020 Replace glass block wall - 1st floor	75	2 BRIC	C.S.F.							
Set up and secure scaffold				.750		33		33	44	54
Remove blocks				5.200		185	27	212	272	335
Replace blocks				45.217	2,850	1,840		4,690	5,550	6,525
Remove scaffold				.750		33		33	44	54
Total				51.917	2,850	2,091	27	4,968	5,910	6,968
2020 Replace glass block wall - 2nd floor	75	2 BRIC	C.S.F.							
Set up and secure scaffold				1.500		66		66	88	108
Remove blocks				5.200		185	27	212	272	335
Replace blocks				45.217	2,850	1,840		4,690	5,550	6,525
Remove scaffold				1.500		66		66	88	108
Total				53.417	2,850	2,157	27	5,034	5,998	7,076
3020 Replace glass block wall - 3rd floor	75	2 BRIC	C.S.F.							
Set up and secure scaffold				2.250		99		99	132	162
Remove blocks				5.200		185	27	212	272	335
Replace blocks				45.217	2,850	1,840		4,690	5,550	6,525
Remove scaffold				2.250		99		99	132	162
Total				54.917	2,850	2,223	27	5,100	6,086	7,184

B2013 141 Aluminum Siding

System Description	Freq. (Years)	Crew	Unit	Labor Hours	2012 Bare Costs				Total In-House	Total w/O&P
					Material	Labor	Equipment	Total		
1010 Replace aluminum siding - 1st floor	35	1 CARP	C.S.F.							
Set up, secure and take down ladder				.520		23		23	30.50	37.50
Remove damaged siding				1.434		50		50	67	83
Install siding				5.368	161	234		395	480	575
Total				7.322	161	307		468	577.50	695.50
1020 Refinish aluminum siding - 1st floor	20	1 PORD	C.S.F.							
Set up, secure and take down ladder				1.300		49.70		49.70	64	79.50
Prepare surface				1.159		44		44	57	71
Refinish surface, brushwork, primer + 1 coat				1.231	12	47		59	74	90
Total				3.690	12	140.70		152.70	195	240.50
2010 Replace aluminum siding - 2nd floor	35	1 CARP	C.S.F.							
Set up and secure scaffold				1.500		66		66	88	108
Remove damaged siding				1.434		50		50	67	83
Install siding				5.368	161	234		395	480	575
Remove scaffold				1.500		66		66	88	108
Total				9.802	161	416		577	723	874
2020 Refinish aluminum siding - 2nd floor	20	1 PORD	C.S.F.							
Set up and secure scaffold				1.500		66		66	88	108
Prepare surface				1.159		44		44	57	71
Refinish surface, brushwork, primer + 1 coat				1.231	12	47		59	74	90
Remove scaffold				1.500		66		66	88	108
Total				5.390	12	223		235	307	377
3010 Replace aluminum siding - 3rd floor	35	1 CARP	C.S.F.							
Set up and secure scaffold				2.250		99		99	132	162
Remove damaged siding				1.434		50		50	67	83
Install siding				5.368	161	234		395	480	575
Remove scaffold				2.250		99		99	132	162
Total				11.302	161	482		643	811	982

B2013 141   Aluminum Siding

	System Description	Freq. (Years)	Crew	Unit	Labor Hours	2012 Bare Costs				Total In-House	Total w/O&P
						Material	Labor	Equipment	Total		
3020	**Refinish aluminum siding - 3rd floor**	20	1 PORD	C.S.F.							
	Set up and secure scaffold				2.250		99		99	132	162
	Prepare surface				1.159		44		44	57	71
	Refinish surface, brushwork, primer + 1 coat				1.231	12	47		59	74	90
	Remove scaffold				2.250		99		99	132	162
	Total				6.890	12	289		301	395	485
4120	**Spray refinish aluminum siding - 1st floor**	20	1 PORD	C.S.F.							
	Set up, secure and take down ladder				1.300		49.70		49.70	64	79.50
	Prepare surface				1.159		44		44	57	71
	Protect/mask unpainted surfaces				.031	.30	1.20		1.50	1.80	2.28
	Spray full primer coat				.444	7	17		24	36	42
	Spray finish coat				.500	8	20		28	40	48
	Total				3.434	15.30	131.90		147.20	198.80	242.78
4220	**Spray refinish aluminum siding - 2nd floor**	20	2 PORD	C.S.F.							
	Set up and secure scaffold				1.500		66		66	88	108
	Prepare surface				1.159		44		44	57	71
	Ptotect/mask unpainted surfaces				.031	.30	1.20		1.50	1.80	2.28
	Spray full primer coat				.444	7	17		24	36	42
	Spray finish coat				.500	8	20		28	40	48
	Remove scaffold				1.500		66		66	88	108
	Total				5.134	15.30	214.20		229.50	310.80	379.28
4320	**Spray refinish aluminum siding - 3rd floor**	20	2 PORD	C.S.F.							
	Set up and secure scaffold				2.250		99		99	132	162
	Prepare surface				1.159		44		44	57	71
	Protect/mask unpainted surfaces				.031	.30	1.20		1.50	1.80	2.28
	Spray full primer coat				.444	7	17		24	36	42
	Spray finish coat				.500	8	20		28	40	48
	Remove scaffold				2.250		99		99	132	162
	Total				6.634	15.30	280.20		295.50	398.80	487.28

B20 EXTERIOR CLOSURE — B2013 — Exterior Walls

B2013 142 — Steel Siding

System Description	Freq. (Years)	Crew	Unit	Labor Hours	2012 Bare Costs — Material	Labor	Equipment	Total	Total In-House	Total w/O&P
1010 Replace steel siding - 1st floor	35	1 CARP	C.S.F.							
Set up, secure and take down ladder				.520		23		23	30.50	37.50
Remove damaged siding				1.434		50		50	67	83
Install siding				5.266	202	230		432	520	620
Total				7.220	202	303		505	617.50	740.50
1020 Refinish steel siding - 1st floor	20	1 PORD	C.S.F.							
Set up, secure and take down ladder				1.300		49.70		49.70	64	79.50
Prepare surface				1.159		44		44	57	71
Refinish surface, brushwork, primer + 1 coat				1.231	12	47		59	74	90
Total				3.690	12	140.70		152.70	195	240.50
2010 Replace steel siding - 2nd floor	35	1 CARP	C.S.F.							
Set up and secure scaffold				1.500		66		66	88	108
Remove damaged siding				1.434		50		50	67	83
Install siding				5.266	202	230		432	520	620
Remove scaffold				1.500		66		66	88	108
Total				9.700	202	412		614	763	919
2020 Refinish steel siding - 2nd floor	20	1 PORD	C.S.F.							
Set up and secure scaffold				1.500		66		66	88	108
Prepare surface				1.159		44		44	57	71
Refinish surface, brushwork, primer + 1 coat				1.231	12	47		59	74	90
Remove scaffold				1.500		66		66	88	108
Total				5.390	12	223		235	307	377
3010 Replace steel siding - 3rd floor	35	1 CARP	C.S.F.							
Set up and secure scaffold				2.250		99		99	132	162
Remove damaged siding				1.434		50		50	67	83
Install siding				5.266	202	230		432	520	620
Remove scaffold				2.250		99		99	132	162
Total				11.200	202	478		680	851	1,027

B2013 142 **Steel Siding**

	System Description	Freq. (Years)	Crew	Unit	Labor Hours	2012 Bare Costs				Total In-House	Total w/O&P
						Material	Labor	Equipment	Total		
3020	**Refinish steel siding - 3rd floor**	20	1 PORD	C.S.F.							
	Set up and secure scaffold				2.250		99		99	132	162
	Prepare surface				1.159		44		44	57	71
	Refinish surface, brushwork, primer + 1 coat				1.231	12	47		59	74	90
	Remove scaffold				2.250		99		99	132	162
	Total				6.890	12	289		301	395	485
4120	**Spray refinish steel siding - 1st floor**	20	1 PORD	C.S.F.							
	Set up, secure and take down ladder				1.300		49.70		49.70	64	79.50
	Prepare surface				1.159		44		44	57	71
	Protect/mask unpainted surfaces				.031	.30	1.20		1.50	1.80	2.28
	Spray full primer coat				.444	7	17		24	36	42
	Spray finish coat				.500	8	20		28	40	48
	Total				3.434	15.30	131.90		147.20	198.80	242.78
4220	**Spray refinish steel siding - 2nd floor**	20	2 PORD	C.S.F.							
	Set up and secure scaffold				1.500		66		66	88	108
	Prepare surface				1.159		44		44	57	71
	Ptotect/mask unpainted surfaces				.031	.30	1.20		1.50	1.80	2.28
	Spray full primer coat				.444	7	17		24	36	42
	Spray finish coat				.500	8	20		28	40	48
	Remove scaffold				1.500		66		66	88	108
	Total				5.134	15.30	214.20		229.50	310.80	379.28
4320	**Spray refinish steel siding - 3rd floor**	20	2 PORD	C.S.F.							
	Set up and secure scaffold				2.250		99		99	132	162
	Prepare surface				1.159		44		44	57	71
	Protect/mask unpainted surfaces				.031	.30	1.20		1.50	1.80	2.28
	Spray full primer coat				.444	7	17		24	36	42
	Spray finish coat				.500	8	20		28	40	48
	Remove scaffold				2.250		99		99	132	162
	Total				6.634	15.30	280.20		295.50	398.80	487.28

B2013 143 Masonite Panel, Sealed

	System Description	Freq. (Years)	Crew	Unit	Labor Hours	2012 Bare Costs				Total In-House	Total w/O&P
						Material	Labor	Equipment	Total		
1010	**Replace hardboard panels - 1st floor**	12	1 CARP	C.S.F.							
	Set up, secure and take down ladder				.520		23		23	30.50	37.50
	Remove damaged panel				1.434		50		50	67	83
	Cut new hardboard panel to fit				2.773	120	122		242	294	350
	Total				4.727	120	195		315	391.50	470.50
2010	**Replace hardboard panels - 2nd floor**	12	1 CARP	C.S.F.							
	Set up and secure scaffold				1.500		66		66	88	108
	Remove damaged panel				1.434		50		50	67	83
	Cut new hardboard panel to fit				2.773	120	122		242	294	350
	Remove scaffold				1.500		66		66	88	108
	Total				7.207	120	304		424	537	649
3010	**Replace hardboard panels - 3rd floor**	12	1 CARP	C.S.F.							
	Set up and secure scaffold				2.250		99		99	132	162
	Remove damaged panel				1.434		50		50	67	83
	Cut new hardboard panel to fit				2.773	120	122		242	294	350
	Remove scaffold				2.250		99		99	132	162
	Total				8.707	120	370		490	625	757

B2013 145 Wood, Clapboard Finished, 1 Coat

	System Description	Freq. (Years)	Crew	Unit	Labor Hours	2012 Bare Costs				Total In-House	Total w/O&P
						Material	Labor	Equipment	Total		
1010	**Replace & finish wood clapboards - 1st floor**	25	1 CARP	C.S.F.							
	Set up, secure and take down ladder				.520		23		23	30.50	37.50
	Remove damage				2.600		115		115	152	188
	Replace wood clapboards				2.711	334.62	119.23		453.85	525	615
	Refinish surface, brushwork, primer + 1 coat				2.000	18	77		95	118	145
	Total				7.831	352.62	334.23		686.85	825.50	985.50

B2013 145 | Wood, Clapboard Finished, 1 Coat

	System Description	Freq. (Years)	Crew	Unit	Labor Hours	2012 Bare Costs				Total In-House	Total w/O&P
						Material	Labor	Equipment	Total		
2010	**Replace & finish wood clapboards - 2nd floor**	25	1 CARP	C.S.F.							
	Set up and secure scaffold				1.500		66		66	88	108
	Remove damage				2.600		115		115	152	188
	Replace wood clapboards				3.524	435	155		590	685	800
	Refinish surface, brushwork, primer + 1 coat				2.000	18	77		95	118	145
	Remove scaffold				1.500		66		66	88	108
	Total				11.124	453	479		932	**1,131**	**1,349**
3010	**Replace & finish wood clapboards - 3rd floor**	25	1 CARP	C.S.F.							
	Set up and secure scaffold				2.250		99		99	132	162
	Remove damage				2.600		115		115	152	188
	Replace wood clapboards				3.489	430.69	153.47		584.16	680	790
	Refinish surface, brushwork, primer + 1 coat				2.000	18	77		95	118	145
	Remove scaffold				2.250		99		99	132	162
	Total				12.589	448.69	543.47		992.16	**1,214**	**1,447**

B2013 147 | Wood Shingles, Unfinished

	System Description	Freq. (Years)	Crew	Unit	Labor Hours	2012 Bare Costs				Total In-House	Total w/O&P
						Material	Labor	Equipment	Total		
1010	**Repair wood shingles - 1st floor**	12	1 CARP	S.F.							
	Set up, secure and take down ladder				.052		2.30		2.30	3.04	3.76
	Remove damaged shingles				.039		1.37		1.37	1.82	2.25
	Replace shingles				.056	2	2.48		4.48	5.50	6.60
	Total				.147	2	6.15		8.15	**10.36**	**12.61**
1020	**Replace wood shingles - 1st floor**	40	2 CARP	C.S.F.							
	Set up and secure scaffold				.750		33		33	44	54
	Remove damaged shingles				2.600		91		91	121	150
	Replace shingles				4.324	154	191		345	425	510
	Remove scaffold				.750		33		33	44	54
	Total				8.424	154	348		502	**634**	**768**

B2013 147 Wood Shingles, Unfinished

System Description	Freq. (Years)	Crew	Unit	Labor Hours	2012 Bare Costs				Total In-House	Total w/O&P
					Material	Labor	Equipment	Total		
2010	**Replace wood shingles - 2nd floor**	40	1 CARP	C.S.F.							
Set up and secure scaffold				1.000		44		44	58.50	72.50
Remove damaged shingles				2.600		91		91	121	150
Replace shingles				4.324	154	191		345	425	510
Remove scaffold				1.000		44		44	58.50	72.50
Total				8.924	154	370		524	663	805
3010	**Replace wood shingles - 3rd floor**	40	1 CARP	C.S.F.							
Set up and secure scaffold				1.500		66		66	88	109
Remove damaged shingles				2.600		91		91	121	150
Replace shingles				4.324	154	191		345	425	510
Remove scaffold				1.500		66		66	88	109
Total				9.924	154	414		568	722	878

(Note: System Description headers in the table above appear in the leftmost column; Freq./Crew/Unit values 40 / 1 CARP / C.S.F. apply to each system group.)

B2013 148 Wood Shingles, Finished

System Description	Freq. (Years)	Crew	Unit	Labor Hours	2012 Bare Costs				Total In-House	Total w/O&P
					Material	Labor	Equipment	Total		
1020	**Replace & finish wood shingles - 1st floor**	45	1 CARP	C.S.F.							
Set up, secure and take down ladder				1.500		66		66	88	108
Remove damage				2.600		91		91	121	150
Replace shingles				4.324	154	191		345	425	510
Refinish surface, brushwork, primer + 1 coat				2.000	18	77		95	118	145
Total				10.424	172	425		597	752	913
1030	**Refinish wood shingles - 1st floor**	5	1 PORD	C.S.F.							
Set up and secure scaffold				.750		33		33	44	54
Prepare surface				1.667		64		64	82	102
Refinish surface, brushwork, primer + 1 coat				2.000	18	77		95	118	145
Remove scaffold				.750		33		33	44	54
Total				5.167	18	207		225	288	355

B2013 148 Wood Shingles, Finished

	System Description	Freq. (Years)	Crew	Unit	Labor Hours	2012 Bare Costs Material	Labor	Equipment	Total	Total In-House	Total w/O&P
2020	**Refinish wood shingles - 2nd floor**	5	1 PORD	C.S.F.							
	Set up and secure scaffold				1.500		66		66	88	108
	Prepare surface				1.667		64		64	82	102
	Refinish surface, brushwork, primer + 1 coat				2.000	18	77		95	118	145
	Remove scaffold				1.500		66		66	88	108
	Total				6.667	18	273		291	376	463
3020	**Refinish wood shingles - 3rd floor**	5	1 PORD	C.S.F.							
	Set up and secure scaffold				2.250		99		99	132	162
	Prepare surface				1.667		64		64	82	102
	Refinish surface, brushwork, primer + 1 coat				2.000	18	77		95	118	145
	Remove scaffold				2.250		99		99	132	162
	Total				8.167	18	339		357	464	571
4120	**Spray refinish wood siding - 1st floor**	5	1 PORD	C.S.F.							
	Set up, secure and take down ladder				1.300		49.70		49.70	64	79.50
	Prepare surface				1.159		44		44	57	71
	Protect/mask unpainted surfaces				.031	.30	1.20		1.50	1.80	2.28
	Spray full primer coat				.410	10	16		26	31	37.50
	Spray finish coat				.410	19	16		35	41	49
	Total				3.310	29.30	126.90		156.20	194.80	239.28
4220	**Spray refinish wood siding - 2nd floor**	5	2 PORD	C.S.F.							
	Set up and secure scaffold				1.500		66		66	88	108
	Prepare surface				1.159		44		44	57	71
	Ptotect/mask unpainted surfaces				.031	.30	1.20		1.50	1.80	2.28
	Spray full primer coat				.410	10	16		26	31	37.50
	Spray finish coat				.410	19	16		35	41	49
	Remove scaffold				1.500		66		66	88	108
	Total				5.010	29.30	209.20		238.50	306.80	375.78

29

B2013 148 Wood Shingles, Finished

System Description	Freq. (Years)	Crew	Unit	Labor Hours	2012 Bare Costs				Total In-House	Total w/O&P
					Material	Labor	Equipment	Total		
4320 Spray refinish wood siding - 3rd floor	5	2 PORD	C.S.F.							
Set up and secure scaffold				2.250		99		99	132	162
Prepare surface				1.159		44		44	57	71
Protect/mask unpainted surfaces				.031	.30	1.20		1.50	1.80	2.28
Spray full primer coat				.410	10	16		26	31	37.50
Spray finish coat				.410	19	16		35	41	49
Remove scaffold				2.250		99		99	132	162
Total				6.510	29.30	275.20		304.50	394.80	483.78

B2013 150 Fiberglass Panel, Rigid

System Description	Freq. (Years)	Crew	Unit	Labor Hours	2012 Bare Costs				Total In-House	Total w/O&P
					Material	Labor	Equipment	Total		
1010 Replace fiberglass panels - 1st floor	9	1 CARP	C.S.F.							
Set up, secure and take down ladder				.520		23		23	30.50	37.50
Remove damaged fiberglass panel				1.434		50		50	67	83
Install new fiberglass panel				4.727	341	206		547	640	755
Total				6.681	341	279		620	737.50	875.50
2010 Replace fiberglass panels - 2nd floor	9	1 CARP	C.S.F.							
Set up and secure scaffold				1.500		66		66	88	108
Remove damaged fiberglass panel				1.434		50		50	67	83
Install new fiberglass panel				4.727	341	206		547	640	755
Remove scaffold				1.500		66		66	88	108
Total				9.161	341	388		729	883	1,054
3010 Replace fiberglass panels - 3rd floor	9	1 CARP	C.S.F.							
Set up and secure scaffold				2.250		99		99	132	162
Remove damaged fiberglass panel				1.434		50		50	67	83
Install new fiberglass panel				4.727	341	206		547	640	755
Remove scaffold				2.250		99		99	132	162
Total				10.661	341	454		795	971	1,162

B20 EXTERIOR CLOSURE — B2013 — Exterior Walls

B2013 152 — Synthetic Veneer Plaster

	System Description	Freq. (Years)	Crew	Unit	Labor Hours	2012 Bare Costs				Total In-House	Total w/O&P
						Material	Labor	Equipment	Total		
1030	**Refinish veneer plaster - 1st floor**	10	1 BRIC	C.S.F.							
	Set up and secure scaffold				.750		33		33	44	54
	Pressure wash surface				.260		9	2	11	14	17
	Refinish surface				1.270	166	49		215	245	286
	Remove scaffold				.750		33		33	44	54
	Total				3.030	166	124	2	292	347	411
2020	**Refinish veneer plaster - 2nd floor**	10	1 BRIC	C.S.F.							
	Set up and secure scaffold				1.500		66		66	88	108
	Pressure wash surface				.260		9	2	11	14	17
	Refinish surface				1.270	166	49		215	245	286
	Remove scaffold				1.500		66		66	88	108
	Total				4.530	166	190	2	358	435	519
3020	**Refinish veneer plaster - 3rd floor**	10	1 BRIC	C.S.F.							
	Set up and secure scaffold				2.250		99		99	132	162
	Pressure wash surface				.260		9	2	11	14	17
	Refinish surface				1.270	166	49		215	245	286
	Remove scaffold				2.250		99		99	132	162
	Total				6.030	166	256	2	424	523	627

B2013 156 — Exterior Soffit Gypsum Board, Painted

	System Description	Freq. (Years)	Crew	Unit	Labor Hours	2012 Bare Costs				Total In-House	Total w/O&P
						Material	Labor	Equipment	Total		
1030	**Refinish exterior painted gypsum board - 1st floor soffit**	5	1 PORD	C.S.F.							
	Set up and secure scaffold				.750		33		33	44	54
	Prepare surface				1.159		44		44	57	71
	Paint surface, roller, primer + 1 coat				1.231	13	47		60	75	91.50
	Remove scaffold				.750		33		33	44	54
	Total				3.890	13	157		170	220	270.50

B2013 156 Exterior Soffit Gypsum Board, Painted

System Description	Freq. (Years)	Crew	Unit	Labor Hours	2012 Bare Costs				Total In-House	Total w/O&P
					Material	Labor	Equipment	Total		
1040 Replace exterior painted gypsum board - 1st floor soffit	25	2 CARP	C.S.F.							
Set up and secure scaffold				.750		33		33	44	54
Remove old exterior gypsum board				2.737		96		96	128	158
Install new exterior gypsum board				3.467	174	153		327	395	470
Paint surface, roller, primer + 1 coat				1.231	13	47		60	75	91.50
Remove scaffold				.750		33		33	44	54
Total				8.935	187	362		549	686	827.50
2010 Replace exterior painted gypsum board - 2nd floor soffit	25	1 CARP	C.S.F.							
Set up and secure scaffold				1.500		66		66	88	108
Remove old exterior gypsum board				2.737		96		96	128	158
Install new exterior gypsum board				3.467	174	153		327	395	470
Paint surface, roller, primer + 1 coat				2.462	26	94		120	150	183
Remove scaffold				1.500		66		66	88	108
Total				11.666	200	475		675	849	1,027
2020 Refinish exterior painted gypsum board - 2nd floor soffit	5	1 PORD	C.S.F.							
Set up and secure scaffold				1.500		66		66	88	108
Prepare surface				1.159		44		44	57	71
Paint surface, roller, primer + 1 coat				1.231	13	47		60	75	91.50
Remove scaffold				1.500		66		66	88	108
Total				5.390	13	223		236	308	378.50
3010 Replace exterior painted gypsum board - 3rd floor soffit	25	1 CARP	C.S.F.							
Set up and secure scaffold				2.250		99		99	132	162
Remove old exterior gypsum board				2.737		96		96	128	158
Install new exterior gypsum board				3.467	174	153		327	395	470
Paint surface, roller, primer + 1 coat				3.693	39	141		180	225	274
Remove scaffold				2.250		99		99	132	162
Total				14.397	213	588		801	1,012	1,226
3020 Refinish exterior painted gypsum board - 3rd floor soffit	5	1 PORD	C.S.F.							
Set up and secure scaffold				2.250		99		99	132	162
Prepare surface				1.159		44		44	57	71
Paint surface, roller, primer + 1 coat				1.231	13	47		60	75	91.50
Remove scaffold				2.250		99		99	132	162
Total				6.890	13	289		302	396	486.50

B2013 157 Overhang, Exterior Entry

	System Description	Freq. (Years)	Crew	Unit	Labor Hours	2012 Bare Costs Material	Labor	Equipment	Total	Total In-House	Total w/O&P
1030	**Refinish wood overhang**	5	1 PORD	S.F.							
	Prepare surface				.016		.61		.61	.79	.98
	Wash / dry surface				.001		.04		.04	.06	.07
	Refinish surface, brushwork, primer + 1 coat				.020	.18	.77		.95	1.18	1.45
	Total				.037	.18	1.42		1.60	2.03	2.50

B2013 158 Recaulking

	System Description	Freq. (Years)	Crew	Unit	Labor Hours	2012 Bare Costs Material	Labor	Equipment	Total	Total In-House	Total w/O&P
1010	**Recaulk expansion & control joints**	20	1 BRIC	L.F.							
	Set up, secure and take down ladder				.130		5.75		5.75	7.45	9.25
	Cut out and recaulk, silicone				.067	3.42	2.94		6.36	7.60	9
	Total				.197	3.42	8.69		12.11	15.05	18.25
2010	**Recaulk door**	20	1 BRIC	L.F.							
	Set up, secure and take down ladder				.130		5.75		5.75	7.45	9.25
	Cut out and recaulk, silicone				.067	3.42	2.94		6.36	7.60	9
	Total				.197	3.42	8.69		12.11	15.05	18.25
3010	**Recaulk window, 4' x 6' - 1st floor**	20	2 BRIC	Ea.							
	Set up and secure scaffold				1.333		59		59	76.50	94.50
	Cut out and recaulk, silicone				1.600	82.08	70.56		152.64	182	216
	Remove scaffold				1.333		59		59	76.50	94.50
	Total				4.267	82.08	188.56		270.64	335	405
3020	**Recaulk window, 4' x 6' - 2nd floor**	20	2 BRIC	Ea.							
	Set up and secure scaffold				1.500		66		66	88	108
	Cut out and recaulk, silicone				1.600	82.08	70.56		152.64	182	216
	Remove scaffold				1.500		66		66	88	108
	Total				4.600	82.08	202.56		284.64	358	432
3030	**Recaulk window, 4' x 6' - 3rd floor**	20	2 BRIC	Ea.							
	Set up and secure scaffold				1.500		66		66	88	109
	Cut out and recaulk, silicone				1.600	82.08	70.56		152.64	182	216
	Remove scaffold				1.500		66		66	88	109
	Total				4.600	82.08	202.56		284.64	358	434

B2013 310 Wood Louvers and Shutters

	System Description	Freq. (Years)	Crew	Unit	Labor Hours	2012 Bare Costs				Total In-House	Total w/O&P
						Material	Labor	Equipment	Total		
1010	**Repair wood louver in frame 1st floor**	6	1 CARP	Ea.							
	Set up, secure and take down ladder				.001		.05		.05	.07	.08
	Remove louver				.473		16.60		16.60	22	27
	Remove damaged stile				.078		3.45		3.45	4.59	5.65
	Remove damaged slat				.039		1.70		1.70	2.26	2.80
	Install new slat				.077	1.02	3.40		4.42	5.65	6.85
	Install new stile				.157	2.40	6.93		9.33	11.80	14.35
	Reinstall louver				.075		3.30		3.30	4.38	5.40
	Total				.900	3.42	35.43		38.85	**50.75**	**62.13**
1030	**Refinish wood louver - 1st floor**	5	1 PORD	Ea.							
	Set up and secure scaffold				.444		17		17	22	27
	Prepare louver for painting				.434		16.64		16.64	21.50	26.50
	Paint louvered surface (to 16 S.F.), brushwork, primer + 1 coat				.800	2.04	30.50		32.54	41.50	51.50
	Remove scaffold				.444		17		17	22	27
	Total				2.123	2.04	81.14		83.18	**107**	**132**
1040	**Replace wood louver - 1st floor**	45	1 CARP	Ea.							
	Set up and secure scaffold				.444		19.60		19.60	26	32
	Remove louver				.473		16.60		16.60	22	27
	Install new wood louver				.520	72.50	23		95.50	110	128
	Remove scaffold				.444		19.60		19.60	26	32
	Total				1.882	72.50	78.80		151.30	**184**	**219**
2010	**Repair wood louver - 2nd floor**	6	1 CARP	Ea.							
	Set up and secure scaffold				.889		39		39	52	64.50
	Remove louver				.473		16.60		16.60	22	27
	Remove damaged stile				.078		3.45		3.45	4.59	5.65
	Remove damaged slat				.039		1.70		1.70	2.26	2.80
	Install new slat				.077	1.02	3.40		4.42	5.65	6.85
	Install new stile				.157	2.40	6.93		9.33	11.80	14.35
	Reinstall louver				.075		3.30		3.30	4.38	5.40
	Remove scaffold				.889		39		39	52	64.50
	Total				2.677	3.42	113.38		116.80	**154.68**	**191.05**

B2013 310 Wood Louvers and Shutters

System Description	Freq. (Years)	Crew	Unit	Labor Hours	2012 Bare Costs				Total In-House	Total w/O&P
					Material	Labor	Equipment	Total		
2030 Refinish wood louver - 2nd floor	4	1 PORD	Ea.							
Set up and secure scaffold				.889		34		34	43.50	54.50
Prepare louver for painting				.434		16.64		16.64	21.50	26.50
Paint louvered surface (to 16 S.F.), brushwork, primer + 1 coat				.800	2.04	30.50		32.54	41.50	51.50
Remove scaffold				.889		34		34	43.50	54.50
Total				3.012	2.04	115.14		117.18	150	187
2040 Replace wood louver - 2nd floor	45	1 CARP	Ea.							
Set up and secure scaffold				.889		39		39	52	64.50
Remove louver				.473		16.60		16.60	22	27
Install new wood louver				.520	72.50	23		95.50	110	128
Remove scaffold				.889		39		39	52	64.50
Total				2.771	72.50	117.60		190.10	236	284
3010 Repair wood louver - 3rd floor	6	1 CARP	Ea.							
Set up and secure scaffold				1.333		59		59	78	96.50
Remove louver				.473		16.60		16.60	22	27
Remove damaged stile				.078		3.45		3.45	4.59	5.65
Remove damaged slat				.039		1.70		1.70	2.26	2.80
Install new slat				.077	1.02	3.40		4.42	5.65	6.85
Install new stile				.157	2.40	6.93		9.33	11.80	14.35
Reinstall louver				.075		3.30		3.30	4.38	5.40
Remove scaffold				1.333		59		59	78	96.50
Total				3.565	3.42	153.38		156.80	206.68	255.05
3030 Refinish wood louver - 3rd floor	4	1 PORD	Ea.							
Set up and secure scaffold				1.333		51		51	65.50	81.50
Prepare louver for painting				.434		16.64		16.64	21.50	26.50
Paint louvered surface (to 16 S.F.), brushwork, primer + 1 coat				.800	2.04	30.50		32.54	41.50	51.50
Remove scaffold				1.333		51		51	65.50	81.50
Total				3.901	2.04	149.14		151.18	194	241
3040 Replace wood louver - 3rd floor	45	1 CARP	Ea.							
Set up and secure scaffold				1.333		59		59	78	96.50
Remove louver				.473		16.60		16.60	22	27
Install new wood louver				.520	72.50	23		95.50	110	128
Remove scaffold				1.333		59		59	78	96.50
Total				3.660	72.50	157.60		230.10	288	348

	System Description	Freq. (Years)	Crew	Unit	Labor Hours	2012 Bare Costs				Total In-House	Total w/O&P
						Material	Labor	Equipment	Total		
1030	**Refinish aluminum louver - 1st floor**	5	1 PORD	Ea.							
	Set up and secure scaffold				.444		17		17	22	27
	Prepare louver for painting				.434		16.64		16.64	21.50	26.50
	Paint louvered surface (to 16 S.F.), brushwork, primer + 1 coat				.800	2.04	30.50		32.54	41.50	51.50
	Remove scaffold				.444		17		17	22	27
	Total				2.123	2.04	81.14		83.18	107	132
1040	**Replace aluminum louver - 1st floor**	60	1 CARP	Ea.							
	Set up and secure scaffold				.444		19.60		19.60	26	32
	Remove louver				.473		16.60		16.60	22	27
	Install new louver				1.783	246	93		339	385	455
	Remove scaffold				.444		19.60		19.60	26	32
	Total				3.145	246	148.80		394.80	459	546
2020	**Refinish aluminum louver - 2nd floor**	12	1 PORD	Ea.							
	Set up and secure scaffold				.889		39		39	52	64.50
	Prepare louver for painting				.434		16.64		16.64	21.50	26.50
	Paint louvered surface (to 16 S.F.), brushwork, primer + 1 coat				.800	2.04	30.50		32.54	41.50	51.50
	Remove scaffold				.889		39		39	52	64.50
	Total				3.012	2.04	125.14		127.18	167	207
2040	**Replace aluminum louver - 2nd floor**	60	1 CARP	Ea.							
	Set up and secure scaffold				.889		39		39	52	64.50
	Remove louver				.473		16.60		16.60	22	27
	Install new louver				1.783	246	93		339	385	455
	Remove scaffold				.889		39		39	52	64.50
	Total				4.034	246	187.60		433.60	511	611
3030	**Refinish aluminum louver - 3rd floor**	5	1 PORD	Ea.							
	Set up and secure scaffold				1.333		51		51	65.50	81.50
	Prepare louver for painting				.434		16.64		16.64	21.50	26.50
	Paint louvered surface (to 16 S.F.), brushwork, primer + 1 coat				.800	2.04	30.50		32.54	41.50	51.50
	Remove scaffold				1.333		51		51	65.50	81.50
	Total				3.901	2.04	149.14		151.18	194	241

B20 EXTERIOR CLOSURE — B2013 — Exterior Walls

B2013 320 Aluminum Louver

	System Description	Freq. (Years)	Crew	Unit	Labor Hours	2012 Bare Costs				Total In-House	Total w/O&P
						Material	Labor	Equipment	Total		
3040	**Replace aluminum louver - 3rd floor**	60	1 CARP	Ea.							
	Set up and secure scaffold				1.333		59		59	78	96.50
	Remove louver				.473		16.60		16.60	22	27
	Install new louver				1.783	246	93		339	385	455
	Remove scaffold				1.333		59		59	78	96.50
	Total				4.922	246	227.60		473.60	563	675

B2013 330 Steel Louver

	System Description	Freq. (Years)	Crew	Unit	Labor Hours	2012 Bare Costs				Total In-House	Total w/O&P
						Material	Labor	Equipment	Total		
1030	**Refinish steel louver - 1st floor**	5	1 PORD	Ea.							
	Set up and secure scaffold				.444		17		17	22	27
	Prepare louver for painting				.434		16.64		16.64	21.50	26.50
	Paint louvered surface (to 16 S.F.), brushwork, primer + 1 coat				.800	2.04	30.50		32.54	41.50	51.50
	Remove scaffold				.444		17		17	22	27
	Total				2.123	2.04	81.14		83.18	107	132
1040	**Replace steel louver - 1st floor**	40	1 CARP	Ea.							
	Set up and secure scaffold				.444		19.60		19.60	26	32
	Remove louver				.473		16.60		16.60	22	27
	Install new louver				1.783	246	93		339	385	455
	Remove scaffold				.444		19.60		19.60	26	32
	Total				3.145	246	148.80		394.80	459	546
2030	**Refinish steel louver - 2nd floor**	5	1 PORD	Ea.							
	Set up and secure scaffold				.889		34		34	43.50	54.50
	Prepare louver for painting				.434		16.64		16.64	21.50	26.50
	Paint louvered surface (to 16 S.F.), brushwork, primer + 1 coat				.800	2.04	30.50		32.54	41.50	51.50
	Remove scaffold				.889		34		34	43.50	54.50
	Total				3.012	2.04	115.14		117.18	150	187

B2013 330 Steel Louver

System Description	Freq. (Years)	Crew	Unit	Labor Hours	2012 Bare Costs				Total In-House	Total w/O&P
					Material	Labor	Equipment	Total		
2040	**Replace steel louver - 2nd floor**	40	1 CARP	Ea.							
Set up and secure scaffold				.889		39		39	52	64.50
Remove louver				.473		16.60		16.60	22	27
Install new louver				1.783	246	93		339	385	455
Remove scaffold				.889		39		39	52	64.50
Total				4.034	246	187.60		433.60	511	611
3030	**Refinish steel louver - 3rd floor**	5	1 PORD	Ea.							
Set up and secure scaffold				1.333		51		51	65.50	81.50
Prepare louver for painting				.434		16.64		16.64	21.50	26.50
Paint louvered surface (to 16 S.F.), brushwork, primer + 1 coat				.800	2.04	30.50		32.54	41.50	51.50
Remove scaffold				1.333		51		51	65.50	81.50
Total				3.901	2.04	149.14		151.18	194	241
3040	**Replace steel louver - 3rd floor**	40	1 CARP	Ea.							
Set up and secure scaffold				1.333		59		59	78	96.50
Remove louver				.473		16.60		16.60	22	27
Install new louver				1.783	246	93		339	385	455
Remove scaffold				1.333		59		59	78	96.50
Total				4.922	246	227.60		473.60	563	675

B2023 102 · Steel Frame, Operating

System Description	Freq. (Years)	Crew	Unit	Labor Hours	2012 Bare Costs				Total In-House	Total w/O&P
					Material	Labor	Equipment	Total		
1010 Replace glass - 1st floor (1% of glass)	1	1 CARP	S.F.							
Remove damaged glass				.052		1.82		1.82	2.42	2.99
Install new glass				.043	5.50	1.85		7.35	8.45	9.85
Total				.095	5.50	3.67		9.17	10.87	12.84
1020 Repair 3'-9" x 5'-5" steel frame window - 1st flr.	20	1 CARP	Ea.							
Set up and secure scaffold				.444		19.60		19.60	26	32
Remove window gaskets				.250		11.05		11.05	14.65	18.10
Install new gaskets				.564	102.70	24.94		127.64	146	169
Misc. hardware replacement				.333	78	14.70		92.70	105	122
Remove scaffold				.444		19.60		19.60	26	32
Total				2.037	180.70	89.89		270.59	317.65	373.10
1030 Refinish 3'-9" x 5'-5" st. frame window - 1st flr.	5	1 PORD	Ea.							
Set up, secure and take down ladder				.267		10.20		10.20	13.20	16.20
Prepare window for painting				.473		18.10		18.10	23.50	29
Paint window, brushwork, primer + 1 coat				1.000	1.85	38.50		40.35	51	63.50
Total				1.739	1.85	66.80		68.65	87.70	108.70
1040 Replace 3'-9" x 5'-5" st. frame window - 1st flr.	45	1 CARP	Ea.							
Set up and secure scaffold				.444		19.60		19.60	26	32
Remove window				.650		23		23	30.50	37.50
Install new window with frame & glazing (to 21 S.F.)				2.078	1,200	103		1,303	1,475	1,700
Install sealant				.764	6.60	33.75		40.35	51	62.50
Remove scaffold				.444		19.60		19.60	26	32
Total				4.381	1,206.60	198.95		1,405.55	1,608.50	1,864
1050 Finish new 3'-9" x 5'-5" st. fr. window - 1st flr.	45	1 PORD	Ea.							
Set up, secure and take down ladder				.267		10.20		10.20	13.20	16.20
Prepare window for painting				.236		9.05		9.05	11.75	14.50
Paint window, brushwork, primer + 1 coat				1.000	1.85	38.50		40.35	51	63.50
Total				1.503	1.85	57.75		59.60	75.95	94.20

B2023 102 | Steel Frame, Operating

	System Description	Freq. (Years)	Crew	Unit	Labor Hours	2012 Bare Costs				Total In-House	Total w/O&P
						Material	Labor	Equipment	Total		
2010	**Replace glass - 2nd floor (1% of glass)**	1	1 CARP	S.F.							
	Set up and secure scaffold				.889		39		39	52	64.50
	Remove damaged glass				.052		1.82		1.82	2.42	2.99
	Install new glass				.043	5.50	1.85		7.35	8.45	9.85
	Remove scaffold				.889		39		39	52	64.50
	Total				1.873	5.50	81.67		87.17	114.87	141.84
2020	**Repair 3'-9" x 5'-5" steel frame window - 2nd flr.**	20	1 CARP	Ea.							
	Set up and secure scaffold				.889		39		39	52	64.50
	Remove window gaskets				.250		11.05		11.05	14.65	18.10
	Install new gaskets				.564	102.70	24.94		127.64	146	169
	Misc. hardware replacement				.333	78	14.70		92.70	105	122
	Remove scaffold				.889		39		39	52	64.50
	Total				2.925	180.70	128.69		309.39	369.65	438.10
2030	**Refinish 3'-9" x 5'-5" steel frame window - 2nd flr.**	5	1 PORD	Ea.							
	Set up and secure scaffold				.889		34		34	43.50	54.50
	Prepare window for painting				.473		18.10		18.10	23.50	29
	Paint window, brushwork, primer + 1 coat				1.000	1.85	38.50		40.35	51	63.50
	Remove scaffold				.889		34		34	43.50	54.50
	Total				3.251	1.85	124.60		126.45	161.50	201.50
2040	**Replace 3'-9" x 5'-5" steel frame window - 2nd flr.**	45	1 CARP	Ea.							
	Set up and secure scaffold				.889		39		39	52	64.50
	Remove window				.650		23		23	30.50	37.50
	Install new window with frame & glazing (to 21 S.F.)				2.078	1,200	103		1,303	1,475	1,700
	Install sealant				.764	6.60	33.75		40.35	51	62.50
	Remove scaffold				.889		39		39	52	64.50
	Total				5.270	1,206.60	237.75		1,444.35	1,660.50	1,929
2050	**Finish new 3'-9" x 5'-5" st. fr. window - 2nd flr.**	45	1 PORD	Ea.							
	Set up and secure scaffold				.889		34		34	43.50	54.50
	Prepare window for painting				.236		9.05		9.05	11.75	14.50
	Paint window, brushwork, primer + 1 coat				1.000	1.85	38.50		40.35	51	63.50
	Remove scaffold				.889		34		34	43.50	54.50
	Total				3.014	1.85	115.55		117.40	149.75	187

B2023 102   **Steel Frame, Operating**

	System Description	Freq. (Years)	Crew	Unit	Labor Hours	2012 Bare Costs				Total In-House	Total w/O&P
						Material	Labor	Equipment	Total		
3010	**Replace glass - 3rd floor (1% of glass)**	1	1 CARP	S.F.							
	Set up and secure scaffold				.123		5.45		5.45	7.20	8.90
	Remove damaged glass				.052		1.82		1.82	2.42	2.99
	Install new glass				.043	5.50	1.85		7.35	8.45	9.85
	Remove scaffold				.123		5.45		5.45	7.20	8.90
	Total				.341	5.50	14.57		20.07	25.27	30.64
3020	**Repair 3'-9" x 5'-5" steel frame window - 3rd flr.**	20	1 CARP	Ea.							
	Set up and secure scaffold				1.333		59		59	78	96.50
	Remove window gaskets				.250		11.05		11.05	14.65	18.10
	Install new gaskets				.564	102.70	24.94		127.64	146	169
	Misc. hardware replacement				.333	78	14.70		92.70	105	122
	Remove scaffold				1.333		59		59	78	96.50
	Total				3.814	180.70	168.69		349.39	421.65	502.10
3030	**Refinish 3'-9" x 5'-5" steel frame window - 3rd flr.**	5	1 PORD	Ea.							
	Set up and secure scaffold				1.333		51		51	65.50	81.50
	Prepare window for painting				.473		18.10		18.10	23.50	29
	Paint window, brushwork, primer + 1 coat				1.000	1.85	38.50		40.35	51	63.50
	Remove scaffold				1.333		51		51	65.50	81.50
	Total				4.139	1.85	158.60		160.45	205.50	255.50
3040	**Replace 3'-9" x 5'-5" steel frame window - 3rd flr.**	45	1 CARP	Ea.							
	Set up and secure scaffold				1.333		59		59	78	96.50
	Remove window				.650		23		23	30.50	37.50
	Install new window with frame & glazing (to 21 S.F.)				2.078	1,200	103		1,303	1,475	1,700
	Install sealant				.764	6.60	33.75		40.35	51	62.50
	Remove scaffold				1.333		59		59	78	96.50
	Total				6.159	1,206.60	277.75		1,484.35	1,712.50	1,993
3050	**Finish new 3'-9" x 5'-5" st. fr. window - 3rd flr.**	45	1 PORD	Ea.							
	Set up and secure scaffold				1.333		51		51	65.50	81.50
	Prepare window for painting				.236		9.05		9.05	11.75	14.50
	Paint window, brushwork, primer + 1 coat				1.000	1.85	38.50		40.35	51	63.50
	Remove scaffold				1.333		51		51	65.50	81.50
	Total				3.903	1.85	149.55		151.40	193.75	241

B20 EXTERIOR CLOSURE   B2023   Exterior Windows

B2023 103   Steel Frame, Fixed

	System Description	Freq. (Years)	Crew	Unit	Labor Hours	2012 Bare Costs				Total In-House	Total w/O&P
						Material	Labor	Equipment	Total		
1010	**Replace glass - 1st floor (1% of glass)**	1	1 CARP	S.F.							
	Remove damaged glass				.052		1.82		1.82	2.42	2.99
	Install new glass				.043	5.50	1.85		7.35	8.45	9.85
	Total				.095	5.50	3.67		9.17	10.87	12.84
1020	**Repair 2'-0" x 3'-0" steel frame window - 1st flr.**	20	1 CARP	Ea.							
	Set up and secure scaffold				.444		19.60		19.60	26	32
	Remove window gaskets				.250		11.05		11.05	14.65	18.10
	Install new gaskets				.308	56	13.60		69.60	79.50	92
	Remove scaffold				.444		19.60		19.60	26	32
	Total				1.447	56	63.85		119.85	146.15	174.10
1030	**Refinish 2'-0" x 3'-0" st. frame window - 1st flr.**	5	1 PORD	Ea.							
	Set up, secure and take down ladder				.267		10.20		10.20	13.20	16.20
	Prepare window for painting				.473		18.10		18.10	23.50	29
	Paint window, brushwork, primer + 1 coat				1.000	1.85	38.50		40.35	51	63.50
	Total				1.739	1.85	66.80		68.65	87.70	108.70
1040	**Replace 2'-0" x 3'-0" steel frame window - 1st flr.**	45	1 CARP	Ea.							
	Set up and secure scaffold				.444		19.60		19.60	26	32
	Remove window				.650		23		23	30.50	37.50
	Install new window with frame & glazing (2'-0" x 3'-0")				2.078	203	103		306	380	445
	Install sealant				.764	6.60	33.75		40.35	51	62.50
	Remove scaffold				.444		19.60		19.60	26	32
	Total				4.381	209.60	198.95		408.55	513.50	609
2010	**Replace glass - 2nd floor (1% of glass)**	1	1 CARP	S.F.							
	Set up and secure scaffold				.044		1.95		1.95	2.60	3.23
	Remove damaged glass				.052		1.82		1.82	2.42	2.99
	Install new glass				.043	5.50	1.85		7.35	8.45	9.85
	Remove scaffold				.044		1.95		1.95	2.60	3.23
	Total				.184	5.50	7.57		13.07	16.07	19.30

System Description	Freq. (Years)	Crew	Unit	Labor Hours	2012 Bare Costs Material	Labor	Equipment	Total	Total In-House	Total w/O&P
2020 Repair 2'-0" x 3'-0" steel frame window - 2nd flr.	20	1 CARP	Ea.							
Set up and secure scaffold				.889		39		39	52	64.50
Remove window gaskets				.250		11.05		11.05	14.65	18.10
Install new gaskets				.308	56	13.60		69.60	79.50	92
Remove scaffold				.889		39		39	52	64.50
Total				2.335	56	102.65		158.65	198.15	239.10
2030 Refinish 2'-0" x 3'-0" steel frame window - 2nd flr.	5	1 PORD	Ea.							
Set up and secure scaffold				.889		34		34	43.50	54.50
Prepare window for painting				.473		18.10		18.10	23.50	29
Paint window, brushwork, primer + 1 coat				1.000	1.85	38.50		40.35	51	63.50
Remove scaffold				.889		34		34	43.50	54.50
Total				3.251	1.85	124.60		126.45	161.50	201.50
2040 Replace 2'-0" x 3'-0" steel frame window - 2nd flr.	45	1 CARP	Ea.							
Set up and secure scaffold				.889		39		39	52	64.50
Remove window				.650		23		23	30.50	37.50
Install new window with frame & glazing (2'-0" x 3'-0")				2.078	203	103		306	380	445
Install sealant				.764	6.60	33.75		40.35	51	62.50
Remove scaffold				.889		39		39	52	64.50
Total				5.270	209.60	237.75		447.35	565.50	674
3010 Replace glass - 3rd floor (1% of glass)	1	1 CARP	S.F.							
Set up and secure scaffold				.123		5.45		5.45	7.20	8.90
Remove damaged glass				.052		1.82		1.82	2.42	2.99
Install new glass				.043	5.50	1.85		7.35	8.45	9.85
Remove scaffold				.123		5.45		5.45	7.20	8.90
Total				.341	5.50	14.57		20.07	25.27	30.64
3020 Repair 2'-0" x 3'-0" steel frame window - 3rd flr.	20	1 CARP	Ea.							
Set up and secure scaffold				1.333		59		59	78	96.50
Remove window gaskets				.250		11.05		11.05	14.65	18.10
Install new gaskets				.308	56	13.60		69.60	79.50	92
Remove scaffold				1.333		59		59	78	96.50
Total				3.224	56	142.65		198.65	250.15	303.10

B2023 103 Steel Frame, Fixed

	System Description	Freq. (Years)	Crew	Unit	Labor Hours	2012 Bare Costs				Total In-House	Total w/O&P
						Material	Labor	Equipment	Total		
3030	**Refinish 2'-0" x 3'-0" steel frame window - 3rd floor**	5	1 PORD	Ea.							
	Set up and secure scaffold				1.333		51		51	65.50	81.50
	Prepare window for painting				.473		18.10		18.10	23.50	29
	Paint window, brushwork, primer + 1 coat				1.000	1.85	38.50		40.35	51	63.50
	Remove scaffold				1.333		51		51	65.50	81.50
	Total				4.139	1.85	158.60		160.45	205.50	255.50
3040	**Replace 2'-0" x 3'-0" steel frame window - 3rd floor**	45	1 CARP	Ea.							
	Set up and secure scaffold				1.333		59		59	78	96.50
	Remove window				.650		23		23	30.50	37.50
	Install new window with frame & glazing (2'-0" x 3'-0")				2.078	203	103		306	380	445
	Install sealant				.764	6.60	33.75		40.35	51	62.50
	Remove scaffold				1.333		59		59	78	96.50
	Total				6.159	209.60	277.75		487.35	617.50	738

B2023 110 Aluminum Window, Operating

	System Description	Freq. (Years)	Crew	Unit	Labor Hours	2012 Bare Costs				Total In-House	Total w/O&P
						Material	Labor	Equipment	Total		
1010	**Replace glass - 1st flr. (1% of glass)**	1	1 CARP	S.F.							
	Remove damaged glass				.052		1.82		1.82	2.42	2.99
	Install new glass				.043	5.50	1.85		7.35	8.45	9.85
	Total				.095	5.50	3.67		9.17	10.87	12.84
1020	**Repair 3' x 4' aluminum window - 1st floor**	20	1 CARP	Ea.							
	Set up and secure scaffold				.444		19.60		19.60	26	32
	Remove window gaskets				.250		11.05		11.05	14.65	18.10
	Install new gaskets				.431	78.40	19.04		97.44	111	129
	Misc. hardware replacement				.333	78	14.70		92.70	105	122
	Remove scaffold				.444		19.60		19.60	26	32
	Total				1.903	156.40	83.99		240.39	282.65	333.10

B2023 110 | **Aluminum Window, Operating**

	System Description	Freq. (Years)	Crew	Unit	Labor Hours	2012 Bare Costs				Total In-House	Total w/O&P
						Material	Labor	Equipment	Total		
1030	**Replace 3' x 4' aluminum window - 1st floor**	50	1 CARP	Ea.							
	Set up and secure scaffold				.444		19.60		19.60	26	32
	Remove window				.650		23		23	30.50	37.50
	Install new window with frame & glazing (to 12 S.F.)				2.078	485	103		588	690	795
	Install sealant				.555	4.80	24.53		29.33	37	45.50
	Remove scaffold				.444		19.60		19.60	26	32
	Total				4.173	489.80	189.73		679.53	809.50	942
2010	**Replace glass - 2nd flr. (1% of glass)**	1	1 CARP	S.F.							
	Set up and secure scaffold				.044		1.95		1.95	2.60	3.23
	Remove damaged glass				.052		1.82		1.82	2.42	2.99
	Install new glass				.043	5.50	1.85		7.35	8.45	9.85
	Remove scaffold				.044		1.95		1.95	2.60	3.23
	Total				.184	5.50	7.57		13.07	16.07	19.30
2020	**Repair 3' x 4' aluminum window - 2nd floor**	20	1 CARP	Ea.							
	Set up and secure scaffold				.889		39		39	52	64.50
	Remove window gaskets				.250		11.05		11.05	14.65	18.10
	Install new gaskets				.431	78.40	19.04		97.44	111	129
	Misc. hardware replacement				.333	78	14.70		92.70	105	122
	Remove scaffold				.889		39		39	52	64.50
	Total				2.792	156.40	122.79		279.19	334.65	398.10
2030	**Replace 3' x 4' aluminum window - 2nd floor**	50	1 CARP	Ea.							
	Set up and secure scaffold				.889		39		39	52	64.50
	Remove window				.650		23		23	30.50	37.50
	Install new window with frame & glazing (to 12 S.F.)				2.078	485	103		588	690	795
	Install sealant				.555	4.80	24.53		29.33	37	45.50
	Remove scaffold				.889		39		39	52	64.50
	Total				5.062	489.80	228.53		718.33	861.50	1,007
3010	**Replace glass - 3rd floor (1% of glass)**	1	1 CARP	S.F.							
	Set up and secure scaffold				.123		5.45		5.45	7.20	8.90
	Remove damaged glass				.052		1.82		1.82	2.42	2.99
	Install new glass				.043	5.50	1.85		7.35	8.45	9.85
	Remove scaffold				.123		5.45		5.45	7.20	8.90
	Total				.341	5.50	14.57		20.07	25.27	30.64

B2023 110 Aluminum Window, Operating

System Description	Freq. (Years)	Crew	Unit	Labor Hours	2012 Bare Costs				Total In-House	Total w/O&P
					Material	Labor	Equipment	Total		
3020	**Repair 3' x 4' aluminum window - 3rd floor**	20	1 CARP	Ea.							
Set up and secure scaffold				1.333		59		59	78	96.50
Remove window gaskets				.250		11.05		11.05	14.65	18.10
Install new gaskets				.431	78.40	19.04		97.44	111	129
Misc. hardware replacement				.333	78	14.70		92.70	105	122
Remove scaffold				1.333		59		59	78	96.50
Total				3.681	156.40	162.79		319.19	386.65	462.10
3030	**Replace 3' x 4' aluminum window - 3rd floor**	50	1 CARP	Ea.							
Set up and secure scaffold				1.333		59		59	78	96.50
Remove window				.650		23		23	30.50	37.50
Install new window with frame & glazing (to 12 S.F.)				2.078	485	103		588	690	795
Install sealant				.555	4.80	24.53		29.33	37	45.50
Remove scaffold				1.333		59		59	78	96.50
Total				5.950	489.80	268.53		758.33	913.50	1,071

B2023 111 Aluminum Window, Fixed

System Description	Freq. (Years)	Crew	Unit	Labor Hours	2012 Bare Costs				Total In-House	Total w/O&P
					Material	Labor	Equipment	Total		
1010	**Replace glass - 1st floor (1% of glass)**	1	1 CARP	S.F.							
Remove damaged glass				.052		1.82		1.82	2.42	2.99
Install new glass				.043	5.50	1.85		7.35	8.45	9.85
Total				.095	5.50	3.67		9.17	10.87	12.84
1015	**Replace glass - 1st floor, 1" insulating panel with heat reflective glass**	30	2 GLAZ	S.F.							
Remove damaged glass				.052		1.82		1.82	2.42	2.99
Tinted insulated glass				.213	22.50	9.10		31.60	36.50	43
Total				.265	22.50	10.92		33.42	38.92	45.99
1020	**Repair 2'-0" x 3'-0" aluminum window - 1st floor**	20	1 CARP	Ea.							
Set up and secure scaffold				.444		19.60		19.60	26	32
Remove window gaskets				.250		11.05		11.05	14.65	18.10
Install new gaskets				.308	56	13.60		69.60	79.50	92
Remove scaffold				.444		19.60		19.60	26	32
Total				1.447	56	63.85		119.85	146.15	174.10

B2023 111 Aluminum Window, Fixed

System Description	Freq. (Years)	Crew	Unit	Labor Hours	2012 Bare Costs				Total In-House	Total w/O&P
					Material	Labor	Equipment	Total		
1030 Replace 2'-0" x 3'-0" aluminum window - 1st floor	50	1 CARP	Ea.							
Set up and secure scaffold				.444		19.60		19.60	26	32
Remove window				.650		23		23	30.50	37.50
Install new window with frame & glazing (2'-0" x 3'-0")				2.078	203	103		306	380	445
Install sealant				.555	4.80	24.53		29.33	37	45.50
Remove scaffold				.444		19.60		19.60	26	32
Total				4.173	207.80	189.73		397.53	499.50	592
2010 Replace glass - 2nd floor (1% of glass)	1	1 CARP	S.F.							
Set up and secure scaffold				.889		39		39	52	64.50
Remove damaged glass				.052		1.82		1.82	2.42	2.99
Install new glass				.043	5.50	1.85		7.35	8.45	9.85
Remove scaffold				.889		39		39	52	64.50
Total				1.873	5.50	81.67		87.17	114.87	141.84
2020 Repair 2'-0" x 3'-0" aluminum window - 2nd floor	20	1 CARP	Ea.							
Set up and secure scaffold				.889		39		39	52	64.50
Remove window gaskets				.250		11.05		11.05	14.65	18.10
Install new gaskets				.308	56	13.60		69.60	79.50	92
Remove scaffold				.889		39		39	52	64.50
Total				2.335	56	102.65		158.65	198.15	239.10
2030 Replace 2'-0" x 3'-0" aluminum window - 2nd floor	50	1 CARP	Ea.							
Set up and secure scaffold				.889		39		39	52	64.50
Remove window				.650		23		23	30.50	37.50
Install new window with frame & glazing (2'-0" x 3'-0")				2.078	203	103		306	380	445
Install sealant				.555	4.80	24.53		29.33	37	45.50
Remove scaffold				.889		39		39	52	64.50
Total				5.062	207.80	228.53		436.33	551.50	657
3010 Replace glass - 3rd floor (1% of glass)	1	1 CARP	S.F.							
Set up and secure scaffold				.123		5.45		5.45	7.20	8.90
Remove damaged glass				.052		1.82		1.82	2.42	2.99
Install new glass				.043	5.50	1.85		7.35	8.45	9.85
Remove scaffold				.123		5.45		5.45	7.20	8.90
Total				.341	5.50	14.57		20.07	25.27	30.64

47

B2023 111 — Aluminum Window, Fixed

System Description	Freq. (Years)	Crew	Unit	Labor Hours	2012 Bare Costs				Total In-House	Total w/O&P
					Material	Labor	Equipment	Total		
3020 Repair 2'-0" x 3'-0" aluminum window - 3rd floor	20	1 CARP	Ea.							
Set up and secure scaffold				1.333		59		59	78	96.50
Remove window gaskets				.250		11.05		11.05	14.65	18.10
Install new gaskets				.308	56	13.60		69.60	79.50	92
Remove scaffold				1.333		59		59	78	96.50
Total				3.224	56	142.65		198.65	250.15	303.10
3030 Replace 2'-0" x 3'-0" aluminum window - 3rd floor	50	1 CARP	Ea.							
Set up and secure scaffold				1.333		59		59	78	96.50
Remove window				.650		23		23	30.50	37.50
Install new window with frame & glazing (2'-0" x 3'-0")				2.078	203	103		306	380	445
Install sealant				.555	4.80	24.53		29.33	37	45.50
Remove scaffold				1.333		59		59	78	96.50
Total				5.950	207.80	268.53		476.33	603.50	721

B2023 112 — Wood Frame, Operating

System Description	Freq. (Years)	Crew	Unit	Labor Hours	2012 Bare Costs				Total In-House	Total w/O&P
					Material	Labor	Equipment	Total		
1010 Replace glass - 1st floor (1% of glass)	1	1 CARP	S.F.							
Remove damaged glass				.052		1.82		1.82	2.42	2.99
Install new glass				.043	5.50	1.85		7.35	8.45	9.85
Total				.095	5.50	3.67		9.17	10.87	12.84
1020 Repair 2'-3" x 6'-0" wood frame window - 1st flr.	15	1 CARP	Ea.							
Set up and secure scaffold				.444		19.60		19.60	26	32
Remove putty				.667		29.50		29.50	39	48
Install new putty				.333	4.50	14.70		19.20	24.50	29.50
Misc. hardware replacement				.333	78	14.70		92.70	105	122
Remove scaffold				.444		19.60		19.60	26	32
Total				2.222	82.50	98.10		180.60	220.50	263.50
1030 Refinish 2'-3" x 6'-0" wood frame window - 1st flr.	4	1 PORD	Ea.							
Set up, secure and take down ladder				.267		10.20		10.20	13.10	16.30
Prepare window for painting				.473		18.10		18.10	23.50	29
Paint window, brushwork, primer + 1 coat				1.000	1.85	38.50		40.35	51	63.50
Total				1.739	1.85	66.80		68.65	87.60	108.80

B2023 112 | Wood Frame, Operating

	System Description	Freq. (Years)	Crew	Unit	Labor Hours	2012 Bare Costs				Total In-House	Total w/O&P
						Material	Labor	Equipment	Total		
1040	**Replace 2'-3" x 6'-0" wood frame window - 1st flr.**	40	1 CARP	Ea.							
	Set up and secure scaffold				.444		19.60		19.60	26	32
	Remove window				.473		16.60		16.60	22	27
	Install new window with frame & glazing (to 14 S.F.)				1.143	295	50.50		345.50	390	450
	Install sealant				.625	5.40	27.60		33	42	51
	Remove scaffold				.444		19.60		19.60	26	32
	Total				3.130	300.40	133.90		434.30	506	592
2010	**Replace glass - 2nd floor (1% of glass)**	1	1 CARP	S.F.							
	Set up and secure scaffold				.044		1.95		1.95	2.60	3.23
	Remove damaged glass				.052		1.82		1.82	2.42	2.99
	Install new glass				.043	5.50	1.85		7.35	8.45	9.85
	Remove scaffold				.044		1.95		1.95	2.60	3.23
	Total				.184	5.50	7.57		13.07	16.07	19.30
2020	**Repair 2'-3" x 6'-0" wood frame window - 2nd flr.**	15	1 CARP	Ea.							
	Set up and secure scaffold				.889		39		39	52	64.50
	Remove putty				.667		29.50		29.50	39	48
	New putty				.333	4.50	14.70		19.20	24.50	29.50
	Misc. hardware replacement				.333	78	14.70		92.70	105	122
	Remove scaffold				.889		39		39	52	64.50
	Total				3.111	82.50	136.90		219.40	272.50	328.50
2030	**Refinish 2'-3" x 6'-0" wood frame window - 2nd flr.**	5	1 PORD	Ea.							
	Set up and secure scaffold				.889		34		34	43.50	54.50
	Prepare window for painting				.473		18.10		18.10	23.50	29
	Paint window, brushwork, primer + 1 coat				1.000	1.85	38.50		40.35	51	63.50
	Remove scaffold				.889		34		34	43.50	54.50
	Total				3.251	1.85	124.60		126.45	161.50	201.50
2040	**Replace 2'-3" x 6'-0" wood frame window - 2nd flr.**	40	1 CARP	Ea.							
	Set up and secure scaffold				.889		39		39	52	64.50
	Remove window				.473		16.60		16.60	22	27
	Install new window with frame & glazing (to 14 S.F.)				1.143	295	50.50		345.50	390	450
	Install sealant				.625	5.40	27.60		33	42	51
	Remove scaffold				.889		39		39	52	64.50
	Total				4.018	300.40	172.70		473.10	558	657

B2023 112 Wood Frame, Operating

	System Description	Freq. (Years)	Crew	Unit	Labor Hours	2012 Bare Costs				Total In-House	Total w/O&P
						Material	Labor	Equipment	Total		
3010	**Replace glass - 3rd floor (1% of glass)**	1	1 CARP	Ea.							
	Set up and secure scaffold				.123		5.45		5.45	7.20	8.90
	Remove damaged glass				.052		1.82		1.82	2.42	2.99
	Install new glass				.043	5.50	1.85		7.35	8.45	9.85
	Remove scaffold				.123		5.45		5.45	7.20	8.90
	Total				.341	5.50	14.57		20.07	**25.27**	**30.64**
3020	**Repair 2'-3" x 6'-0" wood frame window - 3rd flr.**	15	1 CARP	Ea.							
	Set up and secure scaffold				1.333		59		59	78	96.50
	Remove putty				.667		29.50		29.50	39	48
	Install new putty				.333	4.50	14.70		19.20	24.50	29.50
	Misc. hardware replacement				.333	78	14.70		92.70	105	122
	Remove scaffold				1.333		59		59	78	96.50
	Total				4.000	82.50	176.90		259.40	**324.50**	**392.50**
3030	**Refinish 2'-3" x 6'-0" wood frame window - 3rd flr.**	5	1 PORD	Ea.							
	Set up and secure scaffold				1.333		51		51	65.50	81.50
	Prepare window for painting				.473		18.10		18.10	23.50	29
	Paint window, brushwork, primer + 1 coat				1.000	1.85	38.50		40.35	51	63.50
	Remove scaffold				1.333		51		51	65.50	81.50
	Total				4.139	1.85	158.60		160.45	**205.50**	**255.50**
3040	**Replace 2'-3" x 6'-0" wood frame window - 3rd flr.**	40	1 CARP	Ea.							
	Set up and secure scaffold				1.333		59		59	78	96.50
	Remove window				.473		16.60		16.60	22	27
	Install new window with frame & glazing (to 14 S.F.)				1.143	295	50.50		345.50	390	450
	Install sealant				.625	5.40	27.60		33	42	51
	Remove scaffold				1.333		59		59	78	96.50
	Total				4.907	300.40	212.70		513.10	**610**	**721**

B2023 113   Wood Frame, Fixed

	System Description	Freq. (Years)	Crew	Unit	Labor Hours	2012 Bare Costs				Total In-House	Total w/O&P
						Material	Labor	Equipment	Total		
1010	**Replace glass - 1st floor**	1	1 CARP	S.F.							
	Remove damaged glass				.052		1.82		1.82	2.42	2.99
	Install new glass				.043	5.50	1.85		7.35	8.45	9.85
	Total				.095	5.50	3.67		9.17	10.87	12.84
1020	**Repair 3'-6" x 4'-0" wood frame window - 1st flr.**	20	1 CARP	Ea.							
	Set up and secure scaffold				.444		19.60		19.60	26	32
	Remove putty				.667		29.50		29.50	39	48
	New putty				.333	4.50	14.70		19.20	24.50	29.50
	Remove scaffold				.444		19.60		19.60	26	32
	Total				1.889	4.50	83.40		87.90	115.50	141.50
1030	**Refinish 3'-6" x 4'-0" wood frame window - 1st flr.**	5	1 PORD	Ea.							
	Set up, secure and take down ladder				.444		17		17	22	27
	Prepare window for painting				.473		18.10		18.10	23.50	29
	Paint window, brushwork, primer + 1 coat				1.000	1.85	38.50		40.35	51	63.50
	Total				1.917	1.85	73.60		75.45	96.50	119.50
1040	**Replace 3'-6" x 4'-0" wood frame window - 1st flr.**	40	1 CARP	Ea.							
	Set up and secure scaffold				.444		19.60		19.60	26	32
	Remove window				.473		16.60		16.60	22	27
	Install new window with frame & glazing (to 14 S.F.)				1.733	400	76.50		476.50	540	625
	Install sealant				.625	5.40	27.60		33	42	51
	Remove scaffold				.444		19.60		19.60	26	32
	Total				3.720	405.40	159.90		565.30	656	767
2010	**Replace glass - 2nd floor (1% of glass)**	1	1 CARP	S.F.							
	Set up and secure scaffold				.044		1.95		1.95	2.60	3.23
	Remove damaged glass				.052		1.82		1.82	2.42	2.99
	Install new glass				.043	5.50	1.85		7.35	8.45	9.85
	Remove scaffold				.044		1.95		1.95	2.60	3.23
	Total				.184	5.50	7.57		13.07	16.07	19.30

B2023 113 | **Wood Frame, Fixed**

System Description	Freq. (Years)	Crew	Unit	Labor Hours	2012 Bare Costs				Total In-House	Total w/O&P
					Material	Labor	Equipment	Total		
2020 **Repair 3'-6" x 4'-0" wood frame window - 2nd flr.**	20	1 CARP	Ea.							
Set up and secure scaffold				.889		39		39	52	64.50
Remove putty				.667		29.50		29.50	39	48
Install new putty				.333	4.50	14.70		19.20	24.50	29.50
Remove scaffold				.889		39		39	52	64.50
Total				2.778	4.50	122.20		126.70	167.50	206.50
2030 **Refinish 3'-6" x 4'-0" wood frame window - 2nd flr.**	5	1 PORD	Ea.							
Set up and secure scaffold				.889		34		34	43.50	54.50
Prepare window for painting				.473		18.10		18.10	23.50	29
Paint window, brushwork, primer + 1 coat				1.000	1.85	38.50		40.35	51	63.50
Remove scaffold				.889		34		34	43.50	54.50
Total				3.251	1.85	124.60		126.45	161.50	201.50
2040 **Replace 3'-6" x 4'-0" wood frame window - 2nd flr.**	40	1 CARP	Ea.							
Set up and secure scaffold				.889		39		39	52	64.50
Remove window				.473		16.60		16.60	22	27
Install new window with frame & glazing (to 14 S.F.)				1.733	400	76.50		476.50	540	625
Install sealant				.625	5.40	27.60		33	42	51
Remove scaffold				.889		39		39	52	64.50
Total				4.609	405.40	198.70		604.10	708	832
3010 **Replace glass - 3rd floor (1% of glass)**	1	1 CARP	S.F.							
Set up and secure scaffold				.123		5.45		5.45	7.20	8.90
Remove damaged glass				.052		1.82		1.82	2.42	2.99
Install new glass				.043	5.50	1.85		7.35	8.45	9.85
Remove scaffold				.123		5.45		5.45	7.20	8.90
Total				.341	5.50	14.57		20.07	25.27	30.64
3020 **Repair 3'-6" x 4'-0" wood frame window - 3rd flr.**	20	1 CARP	Ea.							
Set up and secure scaffold				1.333		59		59	78	96.50
Remove putty				.667		29.50		29.50	39	48
Install new putty				.333	4.50	14.70		19.20	24.50	29.50
Remove scaffold				1.333		59		59	78	96.50
Total				3.667	4.50	162.20		166.70	219.50	270.50

B2023 113 Wood Frame, Fixed

System Description	Freq. (Years)	Crew	Unit	Labor Hours	2012 Bare Costs				Total In-House	Total w/O&P
					Material	Labor	Equipment	Total		
3030 Refinish 3'-6" x 4'-0" wood frame window - 3rd flr.	5	1 PORD	Ea.							
Set up and secure scaffold				1.333		51		51	65.50	81.50
Prepare window for painting				.473		18.10		18.10	23.50	29
Paint window, brushwork, primer + 1 coat				1.000	1.85	38.50		40.35	51	63.50
Remove scaffold				1.333		51		51	65.50	81.50
Total				4.139	1.85	158.60		160.45	205.50	255.50
3040 Replace 3'-6" x 4'-0" wood frame window - 3rd flr.	40	1 CARP	Ea.							
Set up and secure scaffold				1.333		59		59	78	96.50
Remove window				.473		16.60		16.60	22	27
Install new window with frame & glazing (to 14 S.F.)				1.733	400	76.50		476.50	540	625
Install sealant				.625	5.40	27.60		33	42	51
Remove scaffold				1.333		59		59	78	96.50
Total				5.498	405.40	238.70		644.10	760	896

B2023 116 Aluminum Frame Storm Window

System Description	Freq. (Years)	Crew	Unit	Labor Hours	2012 Bare Costs				Total In-House	Total w/O&P
					Material	Labor	Equipment	Total		
1010 Replace glass - (1% of glass)	1	1 CARP	S.F.							
Remove glass				.052		1.82		1.82	2.42	2.99
Install glass / storm window				.173	5.50	7.40		12.90	15.70	18.85
Total				.225	5.50	9.22		14.72	18.12	21.84
1030 Refinish 3'-0" x 4'-0" alum. fr. storm wdo. - 1st flr.	10	1 PORD	Ea.							
Set up and secure scaffold				.444		17		17	22	27
Prepare window frame surface				.473		18.10		18.10	23.50	29
Refinish window frame surface, brushwork, primer + 1 coat				.615	1	23.50		24.50	31.50	39
Remove scaffold				.444		17		17	22	27
Total				1.977	1	75.60		76.60	99	122
1040 Replace 3'-0" x 4'-0" alum. frame storm wdo. - 1st flr.	50	1 CARP	Ea.							
Set up and secure scaffold				.444		19.60		19.60	26	32
Remove old window				.385		13.50		13.50	17.95	22
Install new window (to 12 S.F.)				.743	113	33		146	168	195
Remove scaffold				.444		19.60		19.60	26	32
Total				2.017	113	85.70		198.70	237.95	281

B2023 116 Aluminum Frame Storm Window

System Description	Freq. (Years)	Crew	Unit	Labor Hours	2012 Bare Costs				Total In-House	Total w/O&P
					Material	Labor	Equipment	Total		
2030 Refinish 3'-0" x 4'-0" alum. fr. storm wdo. - 2nd flr.	10	1 PORD	Ea.							
Set up and secure scaffold				.889		34		34	43.50	54.50
Prepare window frame surface				.473		18.10		18.10	23.50	29
Refinish window frame surface, brushwork, primer + 1 coat				.615	1	23.50		24.50	31.50	39
Remove scaffold				.889		34		34	43.50	54.50
Total				2.866	1	109.60		110.60	142	177
2040 Replace 3'-0" x 4'-0" alum. fr. storm wdo. - 2nd flr.	50	1 CARP	Ea.							
Set up and secure scaffold				.889		39		39	52	64.50
Remove old window				.385		13.50		13.50	17.95	22
Install new window (to 12 S.F.)				.743	113	33		146	168	195
Remove scaffold				.889		39		39	52	64.50
Total				2.906	113	124.50		237.50	289.95	346
3030 Refinish 3'-0" x 4'-0" alum. fr. storm wdo. - 3rd flr.	10	1 PORD	Ea.							
Set up and secure scaffold				1.333		51		51	65.50	81.50
Prepare window frame surface				.473		18.10		18.10	23.50	29
Refinish window frame surface, brushwork, primer + 1 coat				.615	1	23.50		24.50	31.50	39
Remove scaffold				1.333		51		51	65.50	81.50
Total				3.755	1	143.60		144.60	186	231
3040 Replace 3'-0" x 4'-0" alum. fr. storm wdo. - 3rd flr.	50	1 CARP	Ea.							
Set up and secure scaffold				1.333		59		59	78	96.50
Remove old window				.385		13.50		13.50	17.95	22
Install new window (to 12 S.F.)				.743	113	33		146	168	195
Remove scaffold				1.333		59		59	78	96.50
Total				3.795	113	164.50		277.50	341.95	410

B2023 117 Steel Frame Storm Window

System Description	Freq. (Years)	Crew	Unit	Labor Hours	2012 Bare Costs				Total In-House	Total w/O&P
					Material	Labor	Equipment	Total		
1010 Replace glass - (1% of glass)	1	1 CARP	S.F.							
Remove glass				.052		1.82		1.82	2.42	2.99
Install glass / storm window				.173	5.50	7.40		12.90	15.70	18.85
Total				.225	5.50	9.22		14.72	18.12	21.84

	System Description	Freq. (Years)	Crew	Unit	Labor Hours	2012 Bare Costs				Total In-House	Total w/O&P
						Material	Labor	Equipment	Total		
1030	**Refinish 3'-0" x 4'-0" st. fr. storm wdo. - 1st floor**	5	1 PORD	Ea.							
	Set up and secure scaffold				.444		17		17	22	27
	Prepare window frame surface				.473		18.10		18.10	23.50	29
	Refinish window frame surface, brushwork, primer + 1 coat				.615	1	23.50		24.50	31.50	39
	Remove scaffold				.444		17		17	22	27
	Total				1.977	1	75.60		76.60	**99**	**122**
1040	**Replace 3'-0" x 4'-0" st. fr. storm wdo. - 1st floor**	25	1 CARP	Ea.							
	Set up and secure scaffold				.444		19.60		19.60	26	32
	Remove old window				.385		13.50		13.50	17.95	22
	Install new window (to 12 S.F.)				.743	113	33		146	168	195
	Remove scaffold				.444		19.60		19.60	26	32
	Total				2.017	113	85.70		198.70	**237.95**	**281**
2030	**Refinish 3'-0" x 4'-0" st. fr. storm wdo. - 2nd floor**	5	1 PORD	Ea.							
	Set up and secure scaffold				.889		34		34	43.50	54.50
	Prepare window frame surface				.473		18.10		18.10	23.50	29
	Refinish window frame surface, brushwork, primer + 1 coat				.615	1	23.50		24.50	31.50	39
	Remove scaffold				.889		34		34	43.50	54.50
	Total				2.866	1	109.60		110.60	**142**	**177**
2040	**Replace 3'-0" x 4'-0" st. fr. storm wdo. - 2nd floor**	25	1 CARP	Ea.							
	Set up and secure scaffold				.889		39		39	52	64.50
	Remove old window				.385		13.50		13.50	17.95	22
	Install new window (to 12 S.F.)				.743	113	33		146	168	195
	Remove scaffold				.889		39		39	52	64.50
	Total				2.906	113	124.50		237.50	**289.95**	**346**
3030	**Refinish 3'-0" x 4'-0" st. fr. storm wdo. - 3rd floor**	5	1 PORD	Ea.							
	Set up and secure scaffold				1.333		51		51	65.50	81.50
	Prepare window frame surface				.473		18.10		18.10	23.50	29
	Refinish window frame surface, brushwork, primer + 1 coat				.615	1	23.50		24.50	31.50	39
	Remove scaffold				1.333		51		51	65.50	81.50
	Total				3.755	1	143.60		144.60	**186**	**231**

B2023 117 Steel Frame Storm Window

	System Description	Freq. (Years)	Crew	Unit	Labor Hours	2012 Bare Costs				Total In-House	Total w/O&P
						Material	Labor	Equipment	Total		
3040	**Replace 3'-0" x 4'-0" st. fr. storm wdo. - 3rd floor**	25	1 CARP	Ea.							
	Set up and secure scaffold				1.333		59		59	78	96.50
	Remove old window				.385		13.50		13.50	17.95	22
	Install new window (to 12 S.F.)				.743	113	33		146	168	195
	Remove scaffold				1.333		59		59	78	96.50
	Total				3.795	113	164.50		277.50	341.95	410

B2023 119 Wood Frame Storm Window

	System Description	Freq. (Years)	Crew	Unit	Labor Hours	2012 Bare Costs				Total In-House	Total w/O&P
						Material	Labor	Equipment	Total		
1010	**Replace glass - (1% of glass)**	1	1 CARP	S.F.							
	Remove glass				.052		1.82		1.82	2.42	2.99
	Install new float glass				.043	5.50	1.85		7.35	8.45	9.85
	Total				.095	5.50	3.67		9.17	10.87	12.84
1020	**Repair 3'-0" x 5'-0" wood frame storm window**	10	1 CARP	Ea.							
	Remove putty				.667		29.50		29.50	39	48
	Install new putty				.333	4.50	14.70		19.20	24.50	29.50
	Total				1.000	4.50	44.20		48.70	63.50	77.50
1030	**Refinish 3'-0" x 5'-0" wood frame storm window**	5	1 PORD	Ea.							
	Prepare window frame surface				.473		18.10		18.10	23.50	29
	Refinish window frame surface, brushwork, primer + 1 coat				.615	1	23.50		24.50	31.50	39
	Total				1.088	1	41.60		42.60	55	68
1040	**Replace 3'-0" x 5'-0" wd. fr. storm wdo. - 1st floor**	40	1 CARP	Ea.							
	Set up and secure scaffold				.444		19.60		19.60	26	32
	Remove old window				.473		16.60		16.60	22	27
	Install new window (to 15 S.F.)				.693	160	30.60		190.60	216	250
	Remove scaffold				.444		19.60		19.60	26	32
	Total				2.055	160	86.40		246.40	290	341

B2023 119   Wood Frame Storm Window

	System Description	Freq. (Years)	Crew	Unit	Labor Hours	2012 Bare Costs Material	2012 Bare Costs Labor	2012 Bare Costs Equipment	2012 Bare Costs Total	Total In-House	Total w/O&P
2040	**Replace 3'-0" x 5'-0" wd. fr. storm wdo. - 2nd floor**	40	1 CARP	Ea.							
	Set up and secure scaffold				.889		39		39	52	64.50
	Remove old window				.473		16.60		16.60	22	27
	Install new window (to 15 S.F.)				.693	160	30.60		190.60	216	250
	Remove scaffold				.889		39		39	52	64.50
	Total				2.944	160	125.20		285.20	342	406
3040	**Replace 3'-0" x 5'-0" wd. fr. storm wdo. - 3rd floor**	40	1 CARP	Ea.							
	Set up and secure scaffold				1.333		59		59	78	96.50
	Remove old window				.473		16.60		16.60	22	27
	Install new window (to 15 S.F.)				.693	160	30.60		190.60	216	250
	Remove scaffold				1.333		59		59	78	96.50
	Total				3.833	160	165.20		325.20	394	470

B2023 122   Vinyl Clad Wood Window, Operating

	System Description	Freq. (Years)	Crew	Unit	Labor Hours	2012 Bare Costs Material	2012 Bare Costs Labor	2012 Bare Costs Equipment	2012 Bare Costs Total	Total In-House	Total w/O&P
1030	**Repl. 3'-0" x 4'-0" vinyl clad window - 1st flr.**	60	1 CARP	Ea.							
	Set up and secure scaffold				.444		19.60		19.60	26	32
	Remove window				.473		16.60		16.60	22	27
	Install new window (3'-0" x 4'-0")				1.156	390	51		441	495	570
	Remove scaffold				.444		19.60		19.60	26	32
	Total				2.518	390	106.80		496.80	569	661
2030	**Repl. 3'-0" x 4'-0" vinyl clad window - 2nd flr.**	60	1 CARP	Ea.							
	Set up and secure scaffold				.889		39		39	52	64.50
	Remove window				.473		16.60		16.60	22	27
	Install new window (3'-0" x 4'-0")				1.156	390	51		441	495	570
	Remove scaffold				.889		39		39	52	64.50
	Total				3.407	390	145.60		535.60	621	726

B2023 122 — Vinyl Clad Wood Window, Operating

System Description	Freq. (Years)	Crew	Unit	Labor Hours	2012 Bare Costs Material	Labor	Equipment	Total	Total In-House	Total w/O&P
3030 Repl. 3'-0" x 4'-0" vinyl clad window - 3rd flr.	60	1 CARP	Ea.							
Set up and secure scaffold				1.333		59		59	78	96.50
Remove window				.473		16.60		16.60	22	27
Install new window (3'0" x 4'0")				1.156	390	51		441	495	570
Remove scaffold				1.333		59		59	78	96.50
Total				4.295	390	185.60		575.60	673	790

B2023 123 — Vinyl Clad Wood Window, Fixed

System Description	Freq. (Years)	Crew	Unit	Labor Hours	2012 Bare Costs Material	Labor	Equipment	Total	Total In-House	Total w/O&P
1030 Repl. 4'-0" x 4'-0" vinyl clad window - 1st flr.	60	1 CARP	Ea.							
Set up and secure scaffold				.444		19.60		19.60	26	32
Remove window				.473		16.60		16.60	22	27
Install new window (4'-0" x 4'-0")				1.733	495	76.50		571.50	645	745
Remove scaffold				.444		19.60		19.60	26	32
Total				3.095	495	132.30		627.30	719	836
2030 Repl. 4'-0" x 4'-0" vinyl clad window - 2nd flr.	60	1 CARP	Ea.							
Set up and secure scaffold				.889		39		39	52	64.50
Remove window				.473		16.60		16.60	22	27
Install new window (4'-0" x 4'-0")				1.733	495	76.50		571.50	645	745
Remove scaffold				.889		39		39	52	64.50
Total				3.984	495	171.10		666.10	771	901
3030 Repl. 4'-0" x 4'-0" vinyl clad window - 3rd flr.	60	1 CARP	Ea.							
Set up and secure scaffold				1.333		59		59	78	96.50
Remove window				.473		16.60		16.60	22	27
Install new window (4'-0" x 4'-0")				1.733	495	76.50		571.50	645	745
Remove scaffold				1.333		59		59	78	96.50
Total				4.873	495	211.10		706.10	823	965

B2023 150 | Glass Block, Fixed

System Description	Freq. (Years)	Crew	Unit	Labor Hours	2012 Bare Costs				Total In-House	Total w/O&P
					Material	Labor	Equipment	Total		
1020 Repair window - 1st floor (2% of glass)	8	1 BRIC	S.F.							
Cut out damaged block				.433		15.38	2.26	17.64	23	27.50
Replace glass block				.452	28.50	18.40		46.90	55.50	65
Total				.886	28.50	33.78	2.26	64.54	**78.50**	**92.50**
1030 Replace glass block window - 1st floor	75	1 BRIC	S.F.							
Set up, secure and take down ladder				.267		11.75		11.75	15.30	18.95
Demolish glass block				.074		2.61		2.61	3.47	4.28
Replace glass block				.452	28.50	18.40		46.90	55.50	65
Total				.793	28.50	32.76		61.26	**74.27**	**88.23**
2020 Repair window - 2nd floor (2% of glass)	8	1 BRIC	S.F.							
Set up and secure scaffold				.889		39		39	51	63
Cut out damaged block				.433		15.38	2.26	17.64	23	27.50
Replace glass block				.452	28.50	18.40		46.90	55.50	65
Remove scaffold				.889		39		39	51	63
Total				2.663	28.50	111.78	2.26	142.54	**180.50**	**218.50**
2030 Replace glass block window - 2nd floor	75	1 BRIC	S.F.							
Set up and secure scaffold				.889		39		39	51	63
Demolish glass block				.074		2.61		2.61	3.47	4.28
Replace glass block				.452	28.50	18.40		46.90	55.50	65
Remove scaffold				.889		39		39	51	63
Total				2.304	28.50	99.01	2.26	127.51	**160.97**	**195.28**
3020 Repair window - 3rd floor (2% of glass)	8	1 BRIC	S.F.							
Set up and secure scaffold				1.333		59		59	76.50	94.50
Cut out damaged block				.433		15.38	2.26	17.64	23	27.50
Replace glass block				.452	28.50	18.40		46.90	55.50	65
Remove scaffold				1.333		59		59	76.50	94.50
Total				3.552	28.50	151.78	2.26	182.54	**231.50**	**281.50**
3030 Replace glass block window - 3rd floor	75	1 BRIC	S.F.							
Set up and secure scaffold				1.333		59		59	76.50	94.50
Demolish glass block				.074		2.61		2.61	3.47	4.28
Replace glass block				.452	28.50	18.40		46.90	55.50	65
Remove scaffold				1.333		59		59	76.50	94.50
Total				3.193	28.50	139.01		167.51	**211.97**	**258.28**

B2023 160 Aluminum Shutter

	System Description	Freq. (Years)	Crew	Unit	Labor Hours	2012 Bare Costs				Total In-House	Total w/O&P
						Material	Labor	Equipment	Total		
1030	**Refinish aluminum shutter - 1st floor**	5	1 PORD	Ea.							
	Set up and secure scaffold				.444		17		17	22	27
	Prepare shutter for painting				.434		16.64		16.64	21.50	26.50
	Paint shutter surface (to 16 S.F.), brushwork, primer + 1 coat				.800	2.04	30.50		32.54	41.50	51.50
	Remove scaffold				.444		17		17	22	27
	Total				2.123	2.04	81.14		83.18	107	132
1040	**Replace aluminum shutter - 1st floor**	60	1 CARP	Ea.							
	Set up and secure scaffold				.444		19.60		19.60	26	32
	Remove shutter				.260		11.50		11.50	15.25	18.75
	Install new shutter				.520	31	23		54	64.50	76.50
	Remove scaffold				.444		19.60		19.60	26	32
	Total				1.669	31	73.70		104.70	131.75	159.25
2030	**Refinish aluminum shutter - 2nd floor**	5	1 PORD	Ea.							
	Set up and secure scaffold				.889		34		34	43.50	54.50
	Prepare shutter for painting				.434		16.64		16.64	21.50	26.50
	Paint shutter surface (to 16 S.F.), brushwork, primer + 1 coat				.800	2.04	30.50		32.54	41.50	51.50
	Remove scaffold				.889		34		34	43.50	54.50
	Total				3.012	2.04	115.14		117.18	150	187
2040	**Replace aluminum shutter - 2nd floor**	60	1 CARP	Ea.							
	Set up and secure scaffold				.889		39		39	52	64.50
	Remove shutter				.260		11.50		11.50	15.25	18.75
	Install new shutter				.520	31	23		54	64.50	76.50
	Remove scaffold				.889		39		39	52	64.50
	Total				2.558	31	112.50		143.50	183.75	224.25
3030	**Refinish aluminum shutter - 3rd floor**	5	1 PORD	Ea.							
	Set up and secure scaffold				1.333		51		51	65.50	81.50
	Prepare shutter for painting				.434		16.64		16.64	21.50	26.50
	Paint shutter surface (to 16 S.F.), brushwork, primer + 1 coat				.800	2.04	30.50		32.54	41.50	51.50
	Remove scaffold				1.333		51		51	65.50	81.50
	Total				3.901	2.04	149.14		151.18	194	241

B20 EXTERIOR CLOSURE — B2023 — Exterior Windows

B2023 160 | Aluminum Shutter

	System Description	Freq. (Years)	Crew	Unit	Labor Hours	2012 Bare Costs Material	Labor	Equipment	Total	Total In-House	Total w/O&P
3040	**Replace aluminum shutter - 3rd floor**	60	1 CARP	Ea.							
	Set up and secure scaffold				1.333		59		59	78	96.50
	Remove shutter				.260		11.50		11.50	15.25	18.75
	Install new shutter				.520	31	23		54	64.50	76.50
	Remove scaffold				1.333		59		59	78	96.50
	Total				3.447	31	152.50		183.50	235.75	288.25

B2023 162 | Steel Shutter

	System Description	Freq. (Years)	Crew	Unit	Labor Hours	2012 Bare Costs Material	Labor	Equipment	Total	Total In-House	Total w/O&P
1030	**Refinish steel shutter - 1st floor**	5	1 PORD	Ea.							
	Set up and secure scaffold				.444		17		17	22	27
	Prepare shutter for painting				.434		16.64		16.64	21.50	26.50
	Paint shutter surface (to 16 S.F.), brushwork, primer + 1 coat				.800	2.04	30.50		32.54	41.50	51.50
	Remove scaffold				.444		17		17	22	27
	Total				2.123	2.04	81.14		83.18	107	132
1040	**Replace steel shutter - 1st floor**	40	1 CARP	Ea.							
	Set up and secure scaffold				.444		19.60		19.60	26	32
	Remove old shutter				.308		15.36	1.20	16.56	25	30
	Install new steel shutter				.617	35.40	30.90	2.34	68.64	89	104
	Remove scaffold				.444		19.60		19.60	26	32
	Total				1.814	35.40	85.46	3.54	124.40	166	198
2030	**Refinish steel shutter - 2nd floor**	5	1 PORD	Ea.							
	Set up and secure scaffold				.889		34		34	43.50	54.50
	Prepare shutter for painting				.434		16.64		16.64	21.50	26.50
	Paint shutter surface (to 16 S.F.), brushwork, primer + 1 coat				.800	2.04	30.50		32.54	41.50	51.50
	Remove scaffold				.889		34		34	43.50	54.50
	Total				3.012	2.04	115.14		117.18	150	187

B2023 162 Steel Shutter

System Description	Freq. (Years)	Crew	Unit	Labor Hours	2012 Bare Costs				Total In-House	Total w/O&P
					Material	Labor	Equipment	Total		
2040 Replace steel shutter - 2nd floor	40	1 CARP	Ea.							
Set up and secure scaffold				.889		39		39	52	64.50
Remove old shutter				.308		15.36	1.20	16.56	25	30
Install new shutter				.617	35.40	30.90	2.34	68.64	89	104
Remove scaffold				.889		39		39	52	64.50
Total				2.703	35.40	124.26	3.54	163.20	**218**	**263**
3030 Refinish steel shutter - 3rd floor	5	1 PORD	Ea.							
Set up and secure scaffold				1.333		51		51	65.50	81.50
Prepare shutter for painting				.434		16.64		16.64	21.50	26.50
Paint shutter surface (to 16 S.F.), brushwork, primer + 1 coat				.800	2.04	30.50		32.54	41.50	51.50
Remove scaffold				1.333		51		51	65.50	81.50
Total				3.901	2.04	149.14		151.18	**194**	**241**
3040 Replace steel shutter - 3rd floor	40	1 CARP	Ea.							
Set up and secure scaffold				1.333		59		59	78	96.50
Remove old shutter				.308		15.36	1.20	16.56	25	30
Install new shutter				.617	35.40	30.90	2.34	68.64	89	104
Remove scaffold				1.333		59		59	78	96.50
Total				3.592	35.40	164.26	3.54	203.20	**270**	**327**

B2023 164 Wood Shutter

System Description	Freq. (Years)	Crew	Unit	Labor Hours	2012 Bare Costs				Total In-House	Total w/O&P
					Material	Labor	Equipment	Total		
1010 Repair wood shutter - 1st floor	6	1 CARP	Ea.							
Remove shutter				.260		11.50		11.50	15.25	18.75
Remove damaged panel				.157		6.90		6.90	9.20	11.35
Install new panel				.314	4.80	13.86		18.66	23.50	28.50
Install shutter				.520		23		23	30.50	37.50
Total				1.251	4.80	55.26		60.06	**78.45**	**96.10**

B2023 164 — Wood Shutter

System Description	Freq. (Years)	Crew	Unit	Labor Hours	2012 Bare Costs				Total In-House	Total w/O&P
					Material	Labor	Equipment	Total		
1030 Refinish wood shutter - 1st floor	5	1 PORD	Ea.							
Set up and secure scaffold				.444		17		17	22	27
Prepare shutter for painting				.434		16.64		16.64	21.50	26.50
Paint shutter surface (to 16 S.F.), brushwork, primer + 1 coat				.800	2.04	30.50		32.54	41.50	51.50
Remove scaffold				.444		17		17	22	27
Total				2.123	2.04	81.14		83.18	107	132
1040 Replace wood shutter - 1st floor	40	1 CARP	Ea.							
Set up and secure scaffold				.444		19.60		19.60	26	32
Remove shutter				.260		11.50		11.50	15.25	18.75
Install new wood shutter				.520	72.50	23		95.50	110	128
Remove scaffold				.444		19.60		19.60	26	32
Total				1.669	72.50	73.70		146.20	177.25	210.75
2010 Repair wood shutter - 2nd floor	6	1 CARP	Ea.							
Set up and secure scaffold				.889		39		39	52	64.50
Remove shutter				.260		11.50		11.50	15.25	18.75
Remove damaged panel				.157		6.90		6.90	9.20	11.35
Install new panel				.314	4.80	13.86		18.66	23.50	28.50
Install shutter				.520		23		23	30.50	37.50
Remove scaffold				.889		39		39	52	64.50
Total				3.029	4.80	133.26		138.06	182.45	225.10
2030 Refinish wood shutter - 2nd floor	5	1 PORD	Ea.							
Set up and secure scaffold				.889		34		34	43.50	54.50
Prepare shutter for painting				.434		16.64		16.64	21.50	26.50
Paint shutter surface (to 16 S.F.), brushwork, primer + 1 coat				.800	2.04	30.50		32.54	41.50	51.50
Remove scaffold				.889		34		34	43.50	54.50
Total				3.012	2.04	115.14		117.18	150	187
2040 Replace wood shutter - 2nd floor	40	1 CARP	Ea.							
Set up and secure scaffold				.889		39		39	52	64.50
Remove shutter				.260		11.50		11.50	15.25	18.75
Install new wood shutter				.520	72.50	23		95.50	110	128
Remove scaffold				.889		39		39	52	64.50
Total				2.558	72.50	112.50		185	229.25	275.75

B2023 164 Wood Shutter

System Description	Freq. (Years)	Crew	Unit	Labor Hours	2012 Bare Costs				Total In-House	Total w/O&P
					Material	Labor	Equipment	Total		
3010 Repair wood shutter - 3rd floor	6	1 CARP	Ea.							
Set up and secure scaffold				1.333		59		59	78	96.50
Remove shutter				.260		11.50		11.50	15.25	18.75
Remove damaged panel				.157		6.90		6.90	9.20	11.35
Install new panel				.314	4.80	13.86		18.66	23.50	28.50
Install shutter				.520		23		23	30.50	37.50
Remove scaffold				1.333		59		59	78	96.50
Total				3.917	4.80	173.26		178.06	234.45	289.10
3030 Refinish wood shutter - 3rd floor	5	1 PORD	Ea.							
Set up and secure scaffold				1.333		51		51	65.50	81.50
Prepare shutter for painting				.434		16.64		16.64	21.50	26.50
Paint shutter surface (to 16 S.F.), brushwork, primer + 1 coat				.800	2.04	30.50		32.54	41.50	51.50
Remove scaffold				1.333		51		51	65.50	81.50
Total				3.901	2.04	149.14		151.18	194	241
3040 Replace wood shutter - 3rd floor	40	1 CARP	Ea.							
Set up and secure scaffold				1.333		59		59	78	96.50
Remove shutter				.260		11.50		11.50	15.25	18.75
Install new wood shutter				.520	72.50	23		95.50	110	128
Remove scaffold				1.333		59		59	78	96.50
Total				3.447	72.50	152.50		225	281.25	339.75

B2023 166 Metal Window Grating

System Description	Freq. (Years)	Crew	Unit	Labor Hours	2012 Bare Costs				Total In-House	Total w/O&P
					Material	Labor	Equipment	Total		
1020 Refinish 3'-0" x 4'-0" metal window grating	5	1 PORD	Ea.							
Prepare window grating surface				.308		11.75		11.75	15.15	18.80
Paint grated surface, brushwork, primer + 1 coat				.167	1.20	6.48		7.68	9.60	11.60
Total				.474	1.20	18.23		19.43	24.75	30.40
1030 Replace 3'-0" x 4'-0" metal wdo. grating - 1st floor	30	1 SSWK	Ea.							
Remove old grating				.800		28		28	37.50	46
Fabricate and install new window grating				6.275	314	310		624	820	975
Total				7.075	314	338		652	857.50	1,021

B2023 166 Metal Window Grating

	System Description	Freq. (Years)	Crew	Unit	Labor Hours	2012 Bare Costs				Total In-House	Total w/O&P
						Material	Labor	Equipment	Total		
2030	**Replace 3'-0" x 4'-0" metal wdo. grating - 2nd floor**	30	1 SSWK	Ea.							
	Set up and secure scaffold				.889		44		44	68	81.50
	Remove old grating				.800		28		28	37.50	46
	Fabricate and install new window grating				6.275	314	310		624	820	975
	Remove scaffold				.889		44		44	68	81.50
	Total				8.852	314	426		740	993.50	1,184
3030	**Replace 3'-0" x 4'-0" metal wdo. grating - 3rd floor**	30	1 SSWK	Ea.							
	Set up and secure scaffold				1.333		66		66	102	122
	Remove old window grating				.800		28		28	37.50	46
	Fabricate and install new window grating				6.275	314	310		624	820	975
	Remove scaffold				1.333		66		66	102	122
	Total				9.741	314	470		784	1,061.50	1,265

B2023 168 Metal Wire Mesh Cover

	System Description	Freq. (Years)	Crew	Unit	Labor Hours	2012 Bare Costs				Total In-House	Total w/O&P
						Material	Labor	Equipment	Total		
1020	**Refinish 3'-0" x 4'-0" mtl. wire mesh wdo. cover**	5	1 PORD	Ea.							
	Prepare metal mesh surface				.103		3.92		3.92	5.05	6.25
	Paint metal mesh surface, brushwork, primer + 1 coat				.167	1.20	6.48		7.68	9.60	11.60
	Total				.269	1.20	10.40		11.60	14.65	17.85
1030	**Repl. 3'-0" x 4'-0" mtl. wire mesh wdo. cover - 1st flr.**	30	1 SSWK	Ea.							
	Set up and secure scaffold				.444		22		22	34	41
	Remove old mesh				.800		28		28	37.50	46
	Install new wire mesh & frame (to 12 S.F.)				.452	59	20		79	91.50	107
	Remove scaffold				.444		22		22	34	41
	Total				2.141	59	92		151	197	235
2030	**Repl. 3'-0" x 4'-0" mtl. wire mesh wdo. cover - 2nd flr.**	30	1 SSWK	Ea.							
	Set up and secure scaffold				.889		44		44	68	81.50
	Remove old mesh				.800		28		28	37.50	46
	Install new wire mesh & frame (to 12 S.F.)				.452	59	20		79	91.50	107
	Remove scaffold				.889		44		44	68	81.50
	Total				3.030	59	136		195	265	316

B2023 168 Metal Wire Mesh Cover

	System Description	Freq. (Years)	Crew	Unit	Labor Hours	2012 Bare Costs				Total In-House	Total w/O&P
						Material	Labor	Equipment	Total		
3030	**Repl. 3'-0" x 4'-0" mtl. wire mesh wdo. cover - 3rd flr.**	30	1 SSWK	Ea.							
	Set up and secure scaffold				1.333		66		66	102	122
	Remove old mesh				.800		28		28	37.50	46
	Install new wire mesh & frame (to 12 S.F.)				.452	59	20		79	91.50	107
	Remove scaffold				1.333		66		66	102	122
	Total				3.919	59	180		239	333	397

B2023 170 Aluminum Window Screen

	System Description	Freq. (Years)	Crew	Unit	Labor Hours	2012 Bare Costs				Total In-House	Total w/O&P
						Material	Labor	Equipment	Total		
1010	**Repair alum. window screen**	20	1 CARP	S.F.							
	Remove screen from mountings				.052		2.57		2.57	3.97	4.77
	Repair damaged screen				.017	2.90	.86		3.76	4.51	5.20
	Remount screen				.104		5.15		5.15	7.95	9.55
	Total				.173	2.90	8.58		11.48	16.43	19.52
1020	**Refinish 3'-0" x 4'-0" alum. window screen**	5	1 PORD	Ea.							
	Prepare screen frame surface				.473		18.10		18.10	23.50	29
	Refinish screen frame surface, brushwork, primer + 1 coat				.615	1	23.50		24.50	31.50	39
	Total				1.088	1	41.60		42.60	55	68
1030	**Replace 3'-0" x 4'-0" alum. wdo. screen - 1st flr.**	50	1 CARP	Ea.							
	Set up and secure scaffold				.444		19.60		19.60	26	32
	Remove screen from mountings				.624		30.84		30.84	47.50	57
	Install new screen				1.248	252	61.80		313.80	370	430
	Remove scaffold				.444		19.60		19.60	26	32
	Total				2.761	252	131.84		383.84	469.50	551
2030	**Replace 3'-0" x 4'-0" alum. wdo. screen - 2nd flr.**	50	1 CARP	Ea.							
	Set up and secure scaffold				.889		39		39	52	64.50
	Remove screen from mountings				.624		30.84		30.84	47.50	57
	Install new screen				1.248	252	61.80		313.80	370	430
	Remove scaffold				.889		39		39	52	64.50
	Total				3.650	252	170.64		422.64	521.50	616

B2023 170 | Aluminum Window Screen

	System Description	Freq. (Years)	Crew	Unit	Labor Hours	2012 Bare Costs				Total In-House	Total w/O&P
						Material	Labor	Equipment	Total		
3030	**Replace 3'-0" x 4'-0" alum. wdo. screen - 3rd flr.**	50	1 CARP	Ea.							
	Set up and secure scaffold				1.333		59		59	78	96.50
	Remove screen from mountings				.624		30.84		30.84	47.50	57
	Install new screen				1.248	252	61.80		313.80	370	430
	Remove scaffold				1.333		59		59	78	96.50
	Total				4.539	252	210.64		462.64	573.50	680

B2023 172 | Steel Frame Screen Window

	System Description	Freq. (Years)	Crew	Unit	Labor Hours	2012 Bare Costs				Total In-House	Total w/O&P
						Material	Labor	Equipment	Total		
1010	**Repair steel frame screen window**	10	1 CARP	S.F.							
	Remove screen from mountings				.052		2.57		2.57	3.97	4.77
	Repair damaged screen				.017	2.90	.86		3.76	4.51	5.20
	Remount screen				.104		5.15		5.15	7.95	9.55
	Total				.173	2.90	8.58		11.48	16.43	19.52
1020	**Refinish 3'-0" x 4'-0" steel frame screen window**	5	1 PORD	Ea.							
	Prepare screen frame surface				.473		18.10		18.10	23.50	29
	Refinish screen frame surface, brushwork, primer + 1 coat				.615	1	23.50		24.50	31.50	39
	Total				1.088	1	41.60		42.60	55	68
1030	**Replace 3'-0" x 4'-0" st. fr. screen wdo. - 1st flr.**	40	1 CARP	Ea.							
	Set up and secure scaffold				.444		19.60		19.60	26	32
	Remove screen from mountings				.624		30.84		30.84	47.50	57
	Install new screen				1.248	50.40	61.80		112.20	151	178
	Remove scaffold				.444		19.60		19.60	26	32
	Total				2.761	50.40	131.84		182.24	250.50	299
2030	**Replace 3'-0" x 4'-0" st. fr. screen wdo. - 2nd flr.**	40	1 CARP	Ea.							
	Set up and secure scaffold				.889		39		39	52	64.50
	Remove screen from mountings				.624		30.84		30.84	47.50	57
	Install new screen				1.248	50.40	61.80		112.20	151	178
	Remove scaffold				.889		39		39	52	64.50
	Total				3.650	50.40	170.64		221.04	302.50	364

B20 EXTERIOR CLOSURE   B2023   Exterior Windows

B2023 172   Steel Frame Screen Window

	System Description	Freq. (Years)	Crew	Unit	Labor Hours	2012 Bare Costs				Total In-House	Total w/O&P
						Material	Labor	Equipment	Total		
3030	**Replace 3'-0" x 4'-0" st. fr. screen wdo. - 3rd flr.**	40	1 CARP	Ea.							
	Set up and secure scaffold				1.333		59		59	78	96.50
	Remove screen from mountings				.624		30.84		30.84	47.50	57
	Install new screen				1.248	50.40	61.80		112.20	151	178
	Remove scaffold				1.333		59		59	78	96.50
	Total				4.539	50.40	210.64		261.04	354.50	428

B2023 174   Wood Frame Screen Window

	System Description	Freq. (Years)	Crew	Unit	Labor Hours	2012 Bare Costs				Total In-House	Total w/O&P
						Material	Labor	Equipment	Total		
1010	**Repair wood frame screen window**	10	1 CARP	S.F.							
	Remove screen from mountings				.052		2.57		2.57	3.97	4.77
	Repair damaged screen				.017	2.90	.86		3.76	4.51	5.20
	Remount screen				.104		5.15		5.15	7.95	9.55
	Total				.173	2.90	8.58		11.48	16.43	19.52
1020	**Refinish 3'-0" x 4'-0" wood frame screen window**	5	1 PORD	Ea.							
	Prepare screen frame surface				.473		18.10		18.10	23.50	29
	Refinish screen frame surface, brushwork, primer + 1 coat				.615	1	23.50		24.50	31.50	39
	Total				1.088	1	41.60		42.60	55	68
1030	**Replace 3'-0" x 4'-0" wd. fr. screen wdo. - 1st flr.**	40	1 CARP	Ea.							
	Set up and secure scaffold				.444		19.60		19.60	26	32
	Remove screen from mountings				.624		30.84		30.84	47.50	57
	Install new screen				.666	97.20	29.40		126.60	146	170
	Remove scaffold				.444		19.60		19.60	26	32
	Total				2.179	97.20	99.44		196.64	245.50	291
2030	**Replace 3'-0" x 4'-0" wd. fr. screen wdo. - 2nd flr.**	40	1 CARP	Ea.							
	Set up and secure scaffold				.889		39		39	52	64.50
	Remove screen from mountings				.624		30.84		30.84	47.50	57
	Install new screen				.666	97.20	29.40		126.60	146	170
	Remove scaffold				.889		39		39	52	64.50
	Total				3.067	97.20	138.24		235.44	297.50	356

B20 EXTERIOR CLOSURE — B2023 — Exterior Windows

B2023 174 — Wood Frame Screen Window

	System Description	Freq. (Years)	Crew	Unit	Labor Hours	2012 Bare Costs				Total In-House	Total w/O&P
						Material	Labor	Equipment	Total		
3030	Replace 3'-0" x 4'-0" wd. fr. screen wdo. - 3rd flr.	40	1 CARP	Ea.							
	Set up and secure scaffold				1.333		59		59	78	96.50
	Remove screen from mountings				.624		30.84		30.84	47.50	57
	Install new screen				.666	97.20	29.40		126.60	146	170
	Remove scaffold				1.333		59		59	78	96.50
	Total				3.956	97.20	178.24		275.44	349.50	420

B2023 324 — Plate Glass

	System Description	Freq. (Years)	Crew	Unit	Labor Hours	2012 Bare Costs				Total In-House	Total w/O&P
						Material	Labor	Equipment	Total		
1020	Replace plate glass storefront - 1st floor	50	2 CARP	C.S.F.							
	Remove plate glass and frame				3.467		153		153	203	251
	Replace plate glass and frame				16.000	2,550	685		3,235	3,700	4,300
	Total				19.467	2,550	838		3,388	3,903	4,551
2020	Replace plate glass storefront - 2nd floor	50	2 CARP	C.S.F.							
	Set up and secure scaffold				1.500		66		66	88	108
	Remove plate glass and frame				3.467		153		153	203	251
	Replace plate glass and frame				16.000	2,550	685		3,235	3,700	4,300
	Remove scaffold				1.500		66		66	88	108
	Total				22.467	2,550	970		3,520	4,079	4,767
3020	Replace plate glass storefront - 3rd floor	50	2 CARP	C.S.F.							
	Set up and secure scaffold				2.250		99		99	132	162
	Remove plate glass and frame				3.467		153		153	203	251
	Replace plate glass and frame				16.000	2,550	685		3,235	3,700	4,300
	Remove scaffold				2.250		99		99	132	162
	Total				23.967	2,550	1,036		3,586	4,167	4,875

B2033 111   Glazed Aluminum

System Description	Freq. (Years)	Crew	Unit	Labor Hours	2012 Bare Costs Material	Labor	Equipment	Total	Total In-House	Total w/O&P
1020 Repair aluminum storefront door	12	1 CARP	Ea.							
Remove weatherstripping				.015		.65		.65	.86	1.06
Remove door closer				.167		7.35		7.35	9.75	12.05
Remove door hinge				.167		7.35		7.35	9.75	12.05
Install new weatherstrip				3.478	38.50	153		191.50	246	299
Install new door closer				.868	92	38.25		130.25	153	178
Install new hinge (50% of total hinges / 12 years)				.167		7.35		7.35	9.75	12.05
Hinge, 5 x 5, brass base					62.50			62.50	69	78
Oil / lubricate door closer				.065		2.85		2.85	3.78	4.66
Oil / lubricate hinges				.065		2.85		2.85	3.78	4.66
Total				4.990	193	219.65		412.65	**505.67**	**601.53**
1030 Replace 3'-0" x 7'-0" aluminum storefront doors	50	1 CARP	Ea.							
Remove door				.650		23		23	30.50	37.50
Remove door frame				1.300		57.50		57.50	76	94
Install new door, frame, and hardware				10.458	750	515		1,265	1,625	1,900
Install new glass				3.640	173.25	155.40		328.65	395	470
Total				16.048	923.25	750.90		1,674.15	**2,126.50**	**2,501.50**
2010 Replace insulating glass - (3% of glass)	1	1 CARP	S.F.							
Remove damaged glass				.052		1.82		1.82	2.42	2.99
Install new insulating glass				.277	18.90	11.85		30.75	36.50	43
Total				.329	18.90	13.67		32.57	**38.92**	**45.99**
2020 Repair aluminum storefront sliding door	12	1 CARP	Ea.							
Remove weatherstripping				.015		.65		.65	.86	1.06
Oil / lubricate door closer				.065		2.85		2.85	3.78	4.66
Oil / inspect wheel & track				.065		2.85		2.85	3.78	4.66
Install new door track / glide wheels (25% of total / 12 years)				.440	13	19.38		32.38	40	48
Install new weatherstrip				4.167	49	184		233	298	360
Total				4.750	62	209.73		271.73	**346.42**	**418.38**

B2033 130   Glazed Wood

System Description	Freq. (Years)	Crew	Unit	Labor Hours	2012 Bare Costs				Total In-House	Total w/O&P
					Material	Labor	Equipment	Total		
1020										
Repair glazed wood doors	12	1 CARP	Ea.							
Remove weatherstripping				.015		.65		.65	.86	1.06
Remove door closer				.167		7.35		7.35	9.75	12.05
Remove door hinge				.167		7.35		7.35	9.75	12.05
Install new weatherstrip				3.478	38.50	153		191.50	246	299
Install new door closer				.868	92	38.25		130.25	153	178
Install new hinge (50% of total hinges / 12 years)				.167		7.35		7.35	9.75	12.05
Hinge, 5 x 5, brass base					62.50			62.50	69	78
Oil / lubricate door closer				.065		2.85		2.85	3.78	4.66
Oil / lubricate hinges				.065		2.85		2.85	3.78	4.66
Total				4.990	193	219.65		412.65	505.67	601.53
1040										
Replace 3'-0" x 7'-0" glazed wood door	40	1 CARP	Ea.							
Remove door				.650		23		23	30.50	37.50
Remove door frame				.743		33		33	43.50	54
Install new door frame				.943	150.45	41.65		192.10	221	256
Install new oak door sill				.832	68.40	36.60		105	124	146
Install exterior door				2.105	825	93		918	1,025	1,175
Total				5.274	1,043.85	227.25		1,271.10	1,444	1,668.50
1050										
Refinish glazed wood doors	4	1 PORD	Ea.							
Paint door, door frame & trim, brushwork, primer + 2 coats				1.760	14.45	67.50		81.95	103	125
Total				1.760	14.45	67.50		81.95	103	125
2010										
Replace insulating glass - (8% of glass)	1	1 CARP	S.F.							
Remove damaged glass				.052		1.82		1.82	2.42	2.99
Install new insulated glass				.277	18.90	11.85		30.75	36.50	43
Total				.329	18.90	13.67		32.57	38.92	45.99
2020										
Repair glazed wood sliding door	14	1 CARP	Ea.							
Remove weatherstripping				.015		.65		.65	.86	1.06
Oil / lubricate door closer				.065		2.85		2.85	3.78	4.66
Oil / inspect wheel & track				.065		2.85		2.85	3.78	4.66
Install new door track / glide wheels (25% of total / 14 years)				.440	13	19.38		32.38	40	48
Install new weatherstrip				4.167	49	184		233	298	360
Total				4.750	62	209.73		271.73	346.42	418.38

B2033 130 Glazed Wood

	System Description	Freq. (Years)	Crew	Unit	Labor Hours	2012 Bare Costs				Total In-House	Total w/O&P
						Material	Labor	Equipment	Total		
2030	**Prepare and refinish glazed wood sliding door**	4	1 PORD	Ea.							
	Prepare surface				.310		11.85		11.85	15.25	18.95
	Paint door surface, brushwork, primer + 2 coats				.310	6.76	11.96		18.72	23	27.50
	Total				.621	6.76	23.81		30.57	38.25	46.45
2040	**Replace 6'-0" x 7'-0" glazed wood sliding door**	40	2 CARP	Ea.							
	Remove sliding door				1.733		76.50		76.50	102	125
	Install new sliding door				5.200	1,425	229		1,654	1,875	2,150
	Total				6.933	1,425	305.50		1,730.50	1,977	2,275
2050	**Refinish glazed wood sliding door & frame**	4	1 PORD	Ea.							
	Prepare surface				.465		17.78		17.78	23	28.50
	Paint door, door frame & trim				1.760	14.45	67.50		81.95	103	125
	Total				2.225	14.45	85.28		99.73	126	153.50

B2033 206 Solid Core, Painted

	System Description	Freq. (Years)	Crew	Unit	Labor Hours	2012 Bare Costs				Total In-House	Total w/O&P
						Material	Labor	Equipment	Total		
1010	**Repair solid core, painted, door**	12	1 CARP	Ea.							
	Remove weatherstripping				.015		.65		.65	.86	1.06
	Remove door hinge				.250		11.03		11.03	14.65	18.10
	Install new weatherstrip				3.478	38.50	153		191.50	246	299
	Install new hinge (50% of total hinges / 12 years)				.250		11.03		11.03	14.65	18.10
	Hinge, 5 x 5, brass base					93.75			93.75	104	117
	Oil / lubricate hinges				.065		2.85		2.85	3.78	4.66
	Total				4.058	132.25	178.56		310.81	383.94	457.92
1020	**Prepare and refinish solid core, painted, door**	4	1 PORD	Ea.							
	Prepare door surface				.333		12.75		12.75	16.40	20.50
	Paint door surface, brushwork, primer + 2 coats				.549	11.96	21.16		33.12	40.50	48.50
	Total				.883	11.96	33.91		45.87	56.90	69

B2033 206 | **Solid Core, Painted**

System Description	Freq. (Years)	Crew	Unit	Labor Hours	2012 Bare Costs				Total In-House	Total w/O&P
					Material	Labor	Equipment	Total		
1030										
Replace 3'-0" x 7'-0" solid core, painted, door	40	1 CARP	Ea.							
Remove door				.650		23		23	30.50	37.50
Remove door frame				.743		33		33	43.50	54
Install new door frame				.943	150.45	41.65		192.10	221	256
Install new oak door sill				.832	68.40	36.60		105	124	146
Install new solid core door				1.143	197	50.50		247.50	284	330
Install new weatherstrip				4.167	49	184		233	298	360
Install new lockset				.867	57.50	38		95.50	114	134
Total				9.345	522.35	406.75		929.10	**1,115**	**1,317.50**
2010										
Repair solid core sliding wood door	14	1 CARP	Ea.							
Remove weatherstripping				.015		.65		.65	.86	1.06
Oil / lubricate door closer				.065		2.85		2.85	3.78	4.66
Oil / inspect wheel & track				.065		2.85		2.85	3.78	4.66
Install new door track / glide wheels (25% of total / 14 years)				.440	13	19.38		32.38	40	48
Install new weatherstrip				4.167	49	184		233	298	360
Total				4.750	62	209.73		271.73	**346.42**	**418.38**
2030										
Replace 3'-0" x 7'-0" solid core sliding wood door	40	1 CARP	Ea.							
Remove sliding door				1.733		76.50		76.50	102	125
Install new sliding door frame				.998	99.90	44.10		144	168	197
Install new door track / glide wheels				1.760	52	77.50		129.50	160	192
Install new solid core door				1.143	197	50.50		247.50	284	330
Install new weatherstrip				3.478	38.50	153		191.50	246	299
Install new lockset				.867	57.50	38		95.50	114	134
Total				9.980	444.90	439.60		884.50	**1,074**	**1,277**
3010										
Replace sliding door glass - (3% of glass)	1	1 CARP	S.F.							
Remove damaged glass				.052		1.82		1.82	2.42	2.99
Install new glass				.173	8.25	7.40		15.65	18.75	22.50
Total				.225	8.25	9.22		17.47	**21.17**	**25.49**

B2033 206 Solid Core, Painted

	System Description	Freq. (Years)	Crew	Unit	Labor Hours	2012 Bare Costs				Total In-House	Total w/O&P
						Material	Labor	Equipment	Total		
3040	Repl. 3'-0" x 7'-0" solid core, w/ safety glass, ptd. dr.	40	1 CARP	Ea.							
	Remove door				.650		23		23	30.50	37.50
	Remove door frame				.743		33		33	43.50	54
	Install new door frame				.943	150.45	41.65		192.10	221	256
	Install new oak door sill				.832	68.40	36.60		105	124	146
	Install new solid core door				1.143	197	50.50		247.50	284	330
	Install new glass (3% of total glass/year)				.201	9.57	8.58		18.15	22	26
	Install new weatherstrip				4.167	49	184		233	298	360
	Install new lockset				.867	57.50	38		95.50	114	134
	Total				9.546	531.92	415.33		947.25	1,137	1,343.50

B2033 210 Aluminum Doors

	System Description	Freq. (Years)	Crew	Unit	Labor Hours	2012 Bare Costs				Total In-House	Total w/O&P
						Material	Labor	Equipment	Total		
1010	Repair aluminum door	12	1 CARP	Ea.							
	Remove door closer				.167		7.35		7.35	9.75	12.05
	Remove door hinge				.250		11.03		11.03	14.65	18.10
	Install new door closer				1.735	184	76.50		260.50	305	355
	Install new hinge (50% of total hinges / 12 years)				.250		11.03		11.03	14.65	18.10
	Hinge, 5 x 5, brass base					93.75			93.75	104	117
	Oil / lubricate door closer				.065		2.85		2.85	3.78	4.66
	Oil / lubricate hinges				.065		2.85		2.85	3.78	4.66
	Total				2.531	277.75	111.61		389.36	455.61	529.57
1020	Replace 3'-0" x 7'-0" flush aluminum door	50	1 CARP	Ea.							
	Remove door				.650		23		23	30.50	37.50
	Remove cylinder lock				.400		17.65		17.65	23.50	29
	Reinstall cylinder lock				1.156		51		51	68	83.50
	Install new door				1.224	1,325	54		1,379	1,525	1,750
	Total				3.431	1,325	145.65		1,470.65	1,647	1,900
2010	Replace wire glass - (3% of glass)	1	1 CARP	S.F.							
	Remove damaged glass				.052		1.82		1.82	2.42	2.99
	Install new wire glass				.179	24.36	7.66		32.02	36.50	43
	Total				.231	24.36	9.48		33.84	38.92	45.99

B2033 210 | **Aluminum Doors**

System Description	Freq. (Years)	Crew	Unit	Labor Hours	2012 Bare Costs				Total In-House	Total w/O&P
					Material	Labor	Equipment	Total		
2020 Repair aluminum frame and door	12	1 CARP	Ea.							
Remove weatherstripping				.015		.65		.65	.86	1.06
Remove door closer				.167		7.35		7.35	9.75	12.05
Remove door hinge				.250		11.03		11.03	14.65	18.10
Install new weatherstrip				3.478	38.50	153		191.50	246	299
Install new door closer				1.735	184	76.50		260.50	305	355
Install new hinge (50% of total hinges / 12 years)				.250		11.03		11.03	14.65	18.10
Hinge, 5 x 5, brass base					93.75			93.75	104	117
Oil / lubricate door closer				.065		2.85		2.85	3.78	4.66
Oil / lubricate hinges				.065		2.85		2.85	3.78	4.66
Total				6.024	316.25	265.26		581.51	702.47	829.63
2030 Replace 3'-0" x 7'-0" aluminum door, incl. vision lite	50	1 CARP	Ea.							
Remove door closer				.167		7.35		7.35	9.75	12.05
Remove door				.650		23		23	30.50	37.50
Install new door				1.224	1,325	54		1,379	1,525	1,750
Reinstall door closer				1.735		76.50		76.50	102	125
Install new glass				.217	10.31	9.25		19.56	23.50	28
Total				3.993	1,335.31	170.10		1,505.41	1,690.75	1,952.55
3010 Replace float glass - (3% of glass)	1	1 CARP	S.F.							
Remove damaged glass				.052		1.82		1.82	2.42	2.99
Install new glass				.201	9.57	8.58		18.15	22	26
Total				.253	9.57	10.40		19.97	24.42	28.99
3020 Repair aluminum sliding door	12	1 CARP	Ea.							
Remove weatherstripping				.015		.65		.65	.86	1.06
Oil / lubricate door closer				.065		2.85		2.85	3.78	4.66
Install new door closer (25% of total / 12 years)				.434	46	19.13		65.13	76.50	89
Oil / inspect wheel & track				.065		2.85		2.85	3.78	4.66
Install new door track / glide wheels (25% of total / 12 years)				.440	13	19.38		32.38	40	48
Install new weatherstrip				4.167	49	184		233	298	360
Total				5.184	108	228.86		336.86	422.92	507.38

System Description	Freq. (Years)	Crew	Unit	Labor Hours	2012 Bare Costs				Total In-House	Total w/O&P
					Material	Labor	Equipment	Total		
3030 **Replace 3'-0" x 7'-0" aluminum sliding door**	50	1 CARP	Ea.							
Remove door				.650		23		23	30.50	37.50
Install new door track / glide wheels				1.760	52	77.50		129.50	160	192
Install new aluminum door				1.224	1,325	54		1,379	1,525	1,750
Total				3.634	1,377	154.50		1,531.50	**1,715.50**	**1,979.50**
4020 **Repair flush aluminum, wood core, door**	12	1 CARP	Ea.							
Remove weatherstripping				.015		.65		.65	.86	1.06
Remove door closer				.167		7.35		7.35	9.75	12.05
Remove door hinge				.250		11.03		11.03	14.65	18.10
Install new weatherstrip				3.478	38.50	153		191.50	246	299
Install new door closer				1.735	184	76.50		260.50	305	355
Install new hinge (50% of total hinges / 12 years)				.250		11.03		11.03	14.65	18.10
Hinge, 5 x 5, brass base					93.75			93.75	104	117
Oil / lubricate door closer				.065		2.85		2.85	3.78	4.66
Oil / lubricate hinges				.065		2.85		2.85	3.78	4.66
Total				6.024	316.25	265.26		581.51	**702.47**	**829.63**
4030 **Replace 3'-0" x 7'-0" aluminum, wood core, door**	50	1 CARP	Ea.							
Remove door				.650		23		23	30.50	37.50
Remove door closer				.167		7.35		7.35	9.75	12.05
Install new aluminum door				1.224	1,325	54		1,379	1,525	1,750
Install door closer				1.735		76.50		76.50	102	125
Total				3.777	1,325	160.85		1,485.85	**1,667.25**	**1,924.55**
5010 **Replace tempered glass - (3% of glass)**	1	1 CARP	S.F.							
Remove damaged glass				.052		1.82		1.82	2.42	2.99
Install new glass				.201	9.57	8.58		18.15	22	26
Total				.253	9.57	10.40		19.97	**24.42**	**28.99**

B2033 210 — Aluminum Doors

	System Description	Freq. (Years)	Crew	Unit	Labor Hours	2012 Bare Costs Material	Labor	Equipment	Total	Total In-House	Total w/O&P
5020	**Repair aluminum, insulated, door**	12	1 CARP	Ea.							
	Remove weatherstripping				.015		.65		.65	.86	1.06
	Remove door closer				.167		7.35		7.35	9.75	12.05
	Remove door hinge				.250		11.03		11.03	14.65	18.10
	Install new weatherstrip				3.478	38.50	153		191.50	246	299
	Install new door closer				1.735	184	76.50		260.50	305	355
	Install new hinge (50% of total hinges / 12 years)				.250		11.03		11.03	14.65	18.10
	Hinge, 5 x 5, brass base					93.75			93.75	104	117
	Oil / lubricate door closer				.065		2.85		2.85	3.78	4.66
	Oil / lubricate hinges				.065		2.85		2.85	3.78	4.66
	Total				6.024	316.25	265.26		581.51	702.47	829.63
5030	**Replace 3'-0" x 7'-0" aluminum, insulated, door**	50	1 CARP	Ea.							
	Remove door				.650		23		23	30.50	37.50
	Remove door closer				.167		7.35		7.35	9.75	12.05
	Install new aluminum door				1.224	1,325	54		1,379	1,525	1,750
	Install door closer				1.735		76.50		76.50	102	125
	Total				3.777	1,325	160.85		1,485.85	1,667.25	1,924.55

B2033 220 — Steel, Painted

	System Description	Freq. (Years)	Crew	Unit	Labor Hours	2012 Bare Costs Material	Labor	Equipment	Total	Total In-House	Total w/O&P
1010	**Repair steel, painted, door**	14	1 CARP	Ea.							
	Remove weatherstripping				.015		.65		.65	.86	1.06
	Remove door closer				.167		7.35		7.35	9.75	12.05
	Remove door hinge				.250		11.03		11.03	14.65	18.10
	Install new weatherstrip				3.478	38.50	153		191.50	246	299
	Install new door closer				1.735	184	76.50		260.50	305	355
	Install new hinge (50% of total hinges / 14 years)				.250		11.03		11.03	14.65	18.10
	Hinge, 5 x 5, brass base					93.75			93.75	104	117
	Oil / lubricate door closer				.065		2.85		2.85	3.78	4.66
	Oil / lubricate hinges				.065		2.85		2.85	3.78	4.66
	Total				6.024	316.25	265.26		581.51	702.47	829.63

B20 EXTERIOR CLOSURE | B2033 | Exterior Doors

B2033 220 | Steel, Painted

	System Description	Freq. (Years)	Crew	Unit	Labor Hours	2012 Bare Costs				Total In-House	Total w/O&P
						Material	Labor	Equipment	Total		
1020	**Refinish 3'-0" x 7'-0" steel, painted, door**	4	1 PORD	Ea.							
	Paint on finished metal surface, brushwork, primer + 1 coat				.800	4.37	30.50		34.87	44	54.50
	Total				**.800**	**4.37**	**30.50**		**34.87**	**44**	**54.50**
1030	**Replace 3'-0" x 7'-0" steel, painted, door**	45	1 CARP	Ea.							
	Remove door				.650		23		23	30.50	37.50
	Remove cylinder lock				.400		17.65		17.65	23.50	29
	Install new door				1.224	435	54		489	550	630
	Reinstall cylinder lock				1.156		51		51	68	83.50
	Total				**3.431**	**435**	**145.65**		**580.65**	**672**	**780**
2010	**Replace tempered glass - (3% of glass)**	1	1 CARP	S.F.							
	Remove damaged glass				.052		1.82		1.82	2.42	2.99
	Install new glass				.201	9.57	8.58		18.15	22	26
	Total				**.253**	**9.57**	**10.40**		**19.97**	**24.42**	**28.99**
2030	**Prepare and refinish 3'-0" x 7'-0" steel ptd. door**	4	1 PORD	Ea.							
	Prepare surface				.333		12.75		12.75	16.40	20.50
	Refinish door surface, brushwork, primer + 1 coat				1.333	4.11	51		55.11	70	86.50
	Total				**1.667**	**4.11**	**63.75**		**67.86**	**86.40**	**107**
2040	**Replace 3'-0" x 7'-0" steel, w/ wire glass, ptd. door**	45	1 CARP	Ea.							
	Remove door				.650		23		23	30.50	37.50
	Remove door closer				.167		7.35		7.35	9.75	12.05
	Remove door frame & trim				1.300		57.50		57.50	76	94
	Install new steel door				1.224	615	54		669	750	855
	Install new steel frame				1.301	148	57.50		205.50	239	279
	Install new wire glass				.179	28.42	7.66		36.08	41	48
	Reinstall door closer				1.735		76.50		76.50	102	125
	Total				**6.556**	**791.42**	**283.51**		**1,074.93**	**1,248.25**	**1,450.55**

B20 EXTERIOR CLOSURE — B2033 — Exterior Doors

B2033 220 — Steel, Painted

	System Description	Freq. (Years)	Crew	Unit	Labor Hours	2012 Bare Costs Material	2012 Bare Costs Labor	2012 Bare Costs Equipment	2012 Bare Costs Total	Total In-House	Total w/O&P
3010	**Repair steel sliding painted door**	14	1 CARP	Ea.							
	Remove weatherstripping				.015		.65		.65	.86	1.06
	Oil / lubricate door closer				.065		2.85		2.85	3.78	4.66
	Install new door closer (25% of total / 14 years)				.434	46	19.13		65.13	76.50	89
	Oil / inspect wheel & track				.065		2.85		2.85	3.78	4.66
	Install new door track / glide wheels (25% of total / 14 years)				.440	13	19.38		32.38	40	48
	Install new weatherstrip				4.167	49	184		233	298	360
	Total				5.184	108	228.86		336.86	422.92	507.38
3020	**Refinish 3'-0" x 7'-0" steel sliding painted door**	4	1 PORD	Ea.							
	Prepare surface				.333		12.75		12.75	16.40	20.50
	Refinish door surface, brushwork, primer + 1 coat				1.333	4.11	51		55.11	70	86.50
	Total				1.667	4.11	63.75		67.86	86.40	107
3030	**Replace 3'-0" x 7'-0" steel sliding painted door**	45	1 CARP	Ea.							
	Remove door				.650		23		23	30.50	37.50
	Remove door closer				.167		7.35		7.35	9.75	12.05
	Install new steel door				1.224	615	54		669	750	855
	Install door closer				1.735		76.50		76.50	102	125
	Total				3.777	615	160.85		775.85	892.25	1,029.55
4010	**Replace steel sliding door glass - (3% of glass)**	1	1 CARP	S.F.							
	Remove damaged glass				.052		1.82		1.82	2.42	2.99
	Install new glass				.201	9.57	8.58		18.15	22	26
	Total				.253	9.57	10.40		19.97	24.42	28.99
4020	**Repair steel, insulated core, painted door**	14	1 CARP	Ea.							
	Remove weatherstripping				.015		.65		.65	.86	1.06
	Remove door closer				.167		7.35		7.35	9.75	12.05
	Remove door hinge				.167		7.35		7.35	9.75	12.05
	Install new weatherstrip				3.478	38.50	153		191.50	246	299
	Install new door closer				1.735	184	76.50		260.50	305	355
	Install new hinge (50% of total hinges / 14 years)				.167		7.35		7.35	9.75	12.05
	Hinge, 5 x 5, brass base					62.50			62.50	69	78
	Oil / lubricate door closer				.065		2.85		2.85	3.78	4.66
	Oil / lubricate hinges				.065		2.85		2.85	3.78	4.66
	Total				5.857	285	257.90		542.90	657.67	778.53

B2033 220 Steel, Painted

	System Description	Freq. (Years)	Crew	Unit	Labor Hours	2012 Bare Costs				Total In-House	Total w/O&P
						Material	Labor	Equipment	Total		
4030	Refinish 3'-0" x 7'-0" steel, insul. core, ptd. door	4	1 PORD	Ea.							
	Prepare surface				.333		12.75		12.75	16.40	20.50
	Refinish door surface, brushwork, primer + 1 coat				1.333	4.11	51		55.11	70	86.50
	Total				1.667	4.11	63.75		67.86	86.40	107
4040	Replace 3'-0" x 7'-0" steel, insul. core, ptd. door	45	1 CARP	Ea.							
	Remove door				.650		23		23	30.50	37.50
	Remove door closer				.167		7.35		7.35	9.75	12.05
	Remove door frame & trim				1.300		57.50		57.50	76	94
	Install new steel door				1.224	615	54		669	750	855
	Install new steel frame				1.301	148	57.50		205.50	239	279
	Install new insulated glass				.322	21.92	13.75		35.67	42.50	49.50
	Install door closer				1.735		76.50		76.50	102	125
	Total				6.699	784.92	289.60		1,074.52	1,249.75	1,452.05

B2033 221 Steel, Unpainted

	System Description	Freq. (Years)	Crew	Unit	Labor Hours	2012 Bare Costs				Total In-House	Total w/O&P
						Material	Labor	Equipment	Total		
1010	Repair steel, unpainted, doors	14	1 CARP	Ea.							
	Remove weatherstripping				.015		.65		.65	.86	1.06
	Remove door closer				.167		7.35		7.35	9.75	12.05
	Remove door hinge				.167		7.35		7.35	9.75	12.05
	Install new weatherstrip				3.478	38.50	153		191.50	246	299
	Install new door closer				1.735	184	76.50		260.50	305	355
	Install new door hinge (50% of total hinges / 14 years)				.167		7.35		7.35	9.75	12.05
	Hinge, 5 x 5, brass base					62.50			62.50	69	78
	Oil / lubricate door closer				.065		2.85		2.85	3.78	4.66
	Oil / lubricate hinges				.065		2.85		2.85	3.78	4.66
	Total				5.857	285	257.90		542.90	657.67	778.53
1020	Replace 3'-0" x 7'-0" steel, unpainted, doors	45	1 CARP	Ea.							
	Remove door				.650		23		23	30.50	37.50
	Remove door frame & trim				1.300		57.50		57.50	76	94
	Install new steel door				1.224	635	54		689	770	880
	Install new steel frame				1.301	148	57.50		205.50	239	279
	Total				4.475	783	192		975	1,115.50	1,290.50

B2033 221   Steel, Unpainted

	System Description	Freq. (Years)	Crew	Unit	Labor Hours	2012 Bare Costs				Total In-House	Total w/O&P
						Material	Labor	Equipment	Total		
2010	**Replace wire glass - (3% of glass)**	1	1 CARP	S.F.							
	Remove damaged glass				.052		1.82		1.82	2.42	2.99
	Install new wire glass				.179	24.36	7.66		32.02	36.50	43
	Total				.231	24.36	9.48		33.84	38.92	45.99
2020	**Repair steel, with safety glass, unptd. door**	14	1 CARP	Ea.							
	Remove weatherstripping				.015		.65		.65	.86	1.06
	Remove door closer				.167		7.35		7.35	9.75	12.05
	Remove door hinge				.167		7.35		7.35	9.75	12.05
	Install new weatherstrip				3.478	38.50	153		191.50	246	299
	Install new door closer				1.735	184	76.50		260.50	305	355
	Install new hinge (50% of total hinges / 14 years)				.167		7.35		7.35	9.75	12.05
	Hinge, 5 x 5, brass base					62.50			62.50	69	78
	Oil / lubricate door closer				.065		2.85		2.85	3.78	4.66
	Oil / lubricate hinges				.065		2.85		2.85	3.78	4.66
	Total				5.857	285	257.90		542.90	657.67	778.53
2030	**Repl. 3'-0" x 7'-0" steel, w/ safety glass, unptd. dr.**	45	1 CARP	Ea.							
	Remove door				.650		23		23	30.50	37.50
	Remove door closer				.167		7.35		7.35	9.75	12.05
	Remove door frame & trim				1.300		57.50		57.50	76	94
	Install new steel door				1.301	510	57.50		567.50	635	730
	Install new steel frame				1.301	148	57.50		205.50	239	279
	Install new wire glass				.308	49	13.20		62.20	71	82.50
	Install door closer				1.735		76.50		76.50	102	125
	Total				6.762	707	292.55		999.55	1,163.25	1,360.05
3010	**Repair steel sliding unpainted door**	14	1 CARP	Ea.							
	Remove weatherstripping				.015		.65		.65	.86	1.06
	Oil / lubricate door closer				.065		2.85		2.85	3.78	4.66
	Install new door closer (25% of total / 14 years)				.434	46	19.13		65.13	76.50	89
	Oil / inspect wheel & track				.065		2.85		2.85	3.78	4.66
	New door track / glide wheels (25% of total / 14 years)				.440	13	19.38		32.38	40	48
	Total				1.018	59	44.86		103.86	124.92	147.38

B2033 221   Steel, Unpainted

	System Description	Freq. (Years)	Crew	Unit	Labor Hours	2012 Bare Costs				Total In-House	Total w/O&P
						Material	Labor	Equipment	Total		
3020	**Replace 3'-0" x 7'-0" steel sliding unpainted door**	45	1 CARP	Ea.							
	Remove door				.650		23		23	30.50	37.50
	Remove door closer				.167		7.35		7.35	9.75	12.05
	Install new steel door				1.224	635	54		689	770	880
	Reinstall door closer				1.735		76.50		76.50	102	125
	Total				3.776	635	160.85		795.85	912.25	1,054.55
4010	**Replace tempered glass - (3% of glass)**	1	1 CARP	S.F.							
	Remove damaged glass				.052		1.82		1.82	2.42	2.99
	Install new glass				.201	9.57	8.58		18.15	22	26
	Total				.253	9.57	10.40		19.97	24.42	28.99
4020	**Repair steel, insulated core, unpainted door**	14	1 CARP	Ea.							
	Remove weatherstripping				.015		.65		.65	.86	1.06
	Remove door closer				.167		7.35		7.35	9.75	12.05
	Remove door hinge				.167		7.35		7.35	9.75	12.05
	Install new weatherstrip				3.478	38.50	153		191.50	246	299
	Install new door closer (50% of total / 14 years)				.868	92	38.25		130.25	153	178
	Install new hinge (50% of total hinges / 14 years)				.167		7.35		7.35	9.75	12.05
	Hinge, 5 x 5, brass base					62.50			62.50	69	78
	Oil / lubricate door closer				.065		2.85		2.85	3.78	4.66
	Oil / lubricate hinges				.065		2.85		2.85	3.78	4.66
	Total				4.990	193	219.65		412.65	505.67	601.53
4030	**Repl. 3'-0" x 7'-0" steel, insul. core, unptd. dr.**	45	1 CARP	Ea.							
	Remove door				.650		23		23	30.50	37.50
	Remove door closer				.167		7.35		7.35	9.75	12.05
	Remove door frame & trim				1.300		57.50		57.50	76	94
	Install new insulated steel door				1.301	685	57.50		742.50	830	950
	Install new steel frame				1.301	148	57.50		205.50	239	279
	Install new insulated glass				.322	21.92	13.75		35.67	42.50	49.50
	Reinstall door closer				1.735		76.50		76.50	102	125
	Total				6.776	854.92	293.10		1,148.02	1,329.75	1,547.05

B2033 410 Steel Single, Roll-Up

	System Description	Freq. (Years)	Crew	Unit	Labor Hours	2012 Bare Costs				Total In-House	Total w/O&P
						Material	Labor	Equipment	Total		
1010	**Repair 12' x 12' steel roll-up door**	10	1 CARP	Ea.							
	Remove overhead type door section				1.303		57.50		57.50	76.50	94
	Install new roll-up door section				4.348	462.50	215		677.50	845	980
	Total				5.651	462.50	272.50		735	921.50	1,074
1020	**Refinish 12' x 12' steel roll-up door**	5	1 PORD	Ea.							
	Set up, secure and take down ladder				.258		9.85		9.85	12.70	15.75
	Prepare door surface				2.000		76.50		76.50	98.50	123
	Paint overhead door, brushwork, primer + 1 coat, 1 side				1.493	26.46	56.70		83.16	102	124
	Total				3.751	26.46	143.05		169.51	213.20	262.75
1030	**Replace 12' x 12' steel roll-up door**	35	2 CARP	Ea.							
	Remove overhead type door				5.212		230		230	305	375
	Install new roll-up door				17.391	1,850	860		2,710	3,375	3,925
	Total				22.603	1,850	1,090		2,940	3,680	4,300

B2033 412 Steel Double, Roll-Up

	System Description	Freq. (Years)	Crew	Unit	Labor Hours	2012 Bare Costs				Total In-House	Total w/O&P
						Material	Labor	Equipment	Total		
1020	**Refinish 12' x 24' steel double roll-up door**	5	1 PORD	Ea.							
	Set up, secure and take down ladder				.533		20.50		20.50	26	32.50
	Prepare door surface				4.000		153		153	197	246
	Paint overhead door, brushwork, primer + 1 coat, 1 side				2.986	52.92	113.40		166.32	204	248
	Total				7.519	52.92	286.90		339.82	427	526.50
1040	**Replace 12' x 24' steel double roll-up door**	35	2 CARP	Ea.							
	Remove overhead type door				10.423		460		460	610	750
	Install new door				34.783	3,700	1,720		5,420	6,750	7,825
	Total				45.206	3,700	2,180		5,880	7,360	8,575

B2033 413 Steel, Single Leaf, Spring Garage Door

	System Description	Freq. (Years)	Crew	Unit	Labor Hours	2012 Bare Costs				Total In-House	Total w/O&P
						Material	Labor	Equipment	Total		
1010	**Repair 9' x 7' steel, single leaf, garage door**	10	1 CARP	Ea.							
	Repair damaged track				.068		3.02		3.02	4.01	4.94
	Remove cremone lockset				.400		17.65		17.65	23.50	29
	Install new cremone lockset				1.040	92.50	46		138.50	163	191
	Retension door coil spring				1.143		50.50		50.50	67	82.50
	Total				2.651	92.50	117.17		209.67	**257.51**	**307.44**
1020	**Refinish 9' x 7' steel, single leaf, garage door**	5	1 PORD	Ea.							
	Set up, secure and take down ladder				.258		9.85		9.85	12.70	15.75
	Prepare surface				2.000		76.50		76.50	98.50	123
	Paint garage door, brushwork, primer + 1 coat, 1 side				1.493	26.46	56.70		83.16	102	124
	Total				3.751	26.46	143.05		169.51	**213.20**	**262.75**
1030	**Replace 9' x 7' steel, single leaf, garage door**	35	2 CARP	Ea.							
	Remove door				2.602		115		115	152	188
	Install new door				2.602	950	115		1,065	1,200	1,375
	Total				5.203	950	230		1,180	**1,352**	**1,563**

B2033 420 Aluminum Single, Roll-Up

	System Description	Freq. (Years)	Crew	Unit	Labor Hours	2012 Bare Costs				Total In-House	Total w/O&P
						Material	Labor	Equipment	Total		
1010	**Repair 12' x 12' aluminum single roll-up door**	10	1 CARP	Ea.							
	Remove door section				1.303		57.50		57.50	76.50	94
	Install new door section				3.478	668.75	153.75		822.50	940	1,075
	Total				4.781	668.75	211.25		880	**1,016.50**	**1,169**
1020	**Refinish 12' x 12' aluminum single roll-up door**	5	1 PORD	Ea.							
	Set up, secure and take down ladder				.258		9.85		9.85	12.70	15.75
	Prepare surface				2.000		76.50		76.50	98.50	123
	Paint overhead type door				1.493	26.46	56.70		83.16	102	124
	Total				3.751	26.46	143.05		169.51	**213.20**	**262.75**
1030	**Replace 12' x 12' aluminum single roll-up door**	35	2 CARP	Ea.							
	Paint overhead door, brushwork, primer + 1 coat, 1 side				5.212		230		230	305	375
	Install new door				13.913	2,675	615		3,290	3,750	4,350
	Total				19.125	2,675	845		3,520	**4,055**	**4,725**

B2033 422 Aluminum Double, Roll-Up

	System Description	Freq. (Years)	Crew	Unit	Labor Hours	2012 Bare Costs				Total In-House	Total w/O&P
						Material	Labor	Equipment	Total		
1010	**Repair 12' x 24' aluminum double roll-up door**	10	1 CARP	Ea.							
	Remove door section				2.606		115		115	153	188
	Install new door section				6.957	1,337.50	307.50		1,645	1,875	2,175
	Total				9.562	1,337.50	422.50		1,760	2,028	**2,363**
1020	**Refinish 12' x 24' aluminum double roll-up door**	5	1 PORD	Ea.							
	Set up, secure and take down ladder				.533		20.50		20.50	26	32.50
	Prepare surface				4.000		153		153	197	246
	Paint overhead door, brushwork, primer + 1 coat, 1 side				2.986	52.92	113.40		166.32	204	248
	Total				7.519	52.92	286.90		339.82	427	**526.50**
1030	**Replace 12' x 24' aluminum double roll-up door**	35	2 CARP	Ea.							
	Remove overhead type door				10.423		460		460	610	750
	Install new door				27.826	5,350	1,230		6,580	7,500	8,700
	Total				38.250	5,350	1,690		7,040	8,110	**9,450**

B2033 423 Aluminum, Single Leaf, Spring Garage Door

	System Description	Freq. (Years)	Crew	Unit	Labor Hours	2012 Bare Costs				Total In-House	Total w/O&P
						Material	Labor	Equipment	Total		
1010	**Repair 9' x 7' alum., single leaf, garage door**	10	1 CARP	Ea.							
	Repair damaged track				.684		30.20		30.20	40	49.50
	Remove cremone lockset				.400		17.65		17.65	23.50	29
	Install new cremone lockset				1.040	92.50	46		138.50	163	191
	Retension door coil spring				1.143		50.50		50.50	67	82.50
	Total				3.267	92.50	144.35		236.85	293.50	**352**
1020	**Refinish 9' x 7' alum., single leaf, garage dr.**	5	1 PORD	Ea.							
	Set up, secure and take down ladder				.258		9.85		9.85	12.70	15.75
	Prepare surface				2.000		76.50		76.50	98.50	123
	Paint garage door, brushwork, primer + 1 coat, 1 side				.747	13.23	28.35		41.58	51	62
	Total				3.005	13.23	114.70		127.93	162.20	**200.75**
1030	**Replace 9' x 7' alum., single leaf, garage dr.**	35	2 CARP	Ea.							
	Remove door				2.602		115		115	152	188
	Install new door				2.602	950	115		1,065	1,200	1,375
	Total				5.203	950	230		1,180	1,352	**1,563**

B2033 430 Wood Single, Roll-Up

System Description	Freq. (Years)	Crew	Unit	Labor Hours	2012 Bare Costs				Total In-House	Total w/O&P
					Material	Labor	Equipment	Total		
1010 Repair 12' x 12' wood single roll-up door	8	1 CARP	Ea.							
Remove door section				1.303		57.50		57.50	76.50	94
Install new door section				3.478	437.50	153.75		591.25	690	795
Total				4.781	437.50	211.25		648.75	766.50	889
1020 Refinish 12' x 12' wood single roll-up door	5	1 PORD	Ea.							
Set up, secure and take down ladder				.258		9.85		9.85	12.70	15.75
Prepare door surface				2.000		76.50		76.50	98.50	123
Paint overhead door, brushwork, primer + 1 coat, 1 side				3.150	13.86	120.96		134.82	170	210
Total				5.408	13.86	207.31		221.17	281.20	348.75
1030 Replace 12' x 12' wood single roll-up door	16	2 CARP	Ea.							
Remove overhead type door				5.212		230		230	305	375
Install new door				13.913	1,750	615		2,365	2,750	3,200
Total				19.125	1,750	845		2,595	3,055	3,575

B2033 432 Wood Double, Roll-Up

System Description	Freq. (Years)	Crew	Unit	Labor Hours	2012 Bare Costs				Total In-House	Total w/O&P
					Material	Labor	Equipment	Total		
1010 Repair 12' x 24' wood double roll-up door	8	1 CARP	Ea.							
Remove door section				2.606		115		115	153	188
Install new door section				6.957	875	307.50		1,182.50	1,375	1,600
Total				9.562	875	422.50		1,297.50	1,528	1,788
1020 Refinish 12' x 24' wood double roll-up door	5	1 PORD	Ea.							
Set up, secure and take down ladder				.533		20.50		20.50	26	32.50
Prepare surface				4.000		153		153	197	246
Paint overhead door, brushwork, primer + 1 coat, 1 side				6.300	27.72	241.92		269.64	340	420
Total				10.833	27.72	415.42		443.14	563	698.50
1030 Replace 12' x 24' wood double roll-up door	16	2 CARP	Ea.							
Remove overhead type door				10.423		460		460	610	750
Install new door				27.826	3,500	1,230		4,730	5,500	6,375
Total				38.250	3,500	1,690		5,190	6,110	7,125

B20 EXTERIOR CLOSURE | B2033 | Exterior Doors

B2033 433 Wood, Single Leaf, Spring Garage Door

	System Description	Freq. (Years)	Crew	Unit	Labor Hours	Material	Labor	Equipment	Total	Total In-House	Total w/O&P
							2012 Bare Costs				
1010	**Repair 9' x 7' wood, single leaf, garage door**	8	1 CARP	Ea.							
	Repair damaged track				.068		3.02		3.02	4.01	4.94
	Remove cremone lockset				.400		17.65		17.65	23.50	29
	Install new cremone lockset				1.040	92.50	46		138.50	163	191
	Retension door coil spring				1.143		50.50		50.50	67	82.50
	Total				2.651	92.50	117.17		209.67	257.51	307.44
1020	**Refinish 9' x 7' wood, single leaf, garage dr.**	5	1 PORD	Ea.							
	Set up, secure and take down ladder				.258		9.85		9.85	12.70	15.75
	Prepare surface				2.000		76.50		76.50	98.50	123
	Paint garage door, brushwork, primer + 1 coat, 1 side				3.150	13.86	120.96		134.82	170	210
	Total				5.408	13.86	207.31		221.17	281.20	348.75
1030	**Replace 9' x 7' wood, single leaf, garage door**	16	2 CARP	Ea.							
	Remove door				2.602		115		115	152	188
	Install new door				2.602	600	115		715	810	940
	Total				5.203	600	230		830	962	1,128

B2033 513 Electric Bifolding Hangar Door

	System Description	Freq. (Years)	Crew	Unit	Labor Hours	Material	Labor	Equipment	Total	Total In-House	Total w/O&P
							2012 Bare Costs				
0120	**Remove and replace electric bi-folding hangar door motor**	15	2 SKWK	Ea.							
	Hangar door,electric bi-folding door, replace motor				3.200	435	145		580	670	780
	Total				3.200	435	145		580	670	780
0140	**Remove and replace electric bi-folding hangar door cables**	15	2 SKWK	Ea.							
	Hangar door, elec bi-folding door, replace cables				8.000	86	365		451	575	700
	Total				8.000	86	365		451	575	700
0160	**Remove and replace electric bi-folding hangar door**	20	2 SKWK	Ea.							
	Hangar door demo				77.568		3,824		3,824	5,925	7,125
	Hangar door, bi-fldg dr, remove and replace 20' x 80'				116.368	33,600	5,744		39,344	45,600	52,500
	Total				193.936	33,600	9,568		43,168	51,525	59,625

87

B2033 810 Hinges, Brass

System Description	Freq. (Years)	Crew	Unit	Labor Hours	2012 Bare Costs				Total In-House	Total w/O&P
					Material	Labor	Equipment	Total		
1010										
Replace brass door hinge	60	1 CARP	Ea.							
Remove door				.650		23		23	30.50	37.50
Remove door hinge				.167		7.35		7.35	9.75	12.05
Install new hinge				.167		7.35		7.35	9.75	12.05
Full mortise hinge, 5 x 5, brass base					62.50			62.50	69	78
Reinstall exterior door				1.388		61		61	81.50	100
Total				2.371	62.50	98.70		161.20	200.50	239.60

B2033 820 Lockset, Brass

System Description	Freq. (Years)	Crew	Unit	Labor Hours	2012 Bare Costs				Total In-House	Total w/O&P
					Material	Labor	Equipment	Total		
1010										
Replace brass door lockset	30	1 CARP	Ea.							
Remove mortise lock set				.421		18.55		18.55	24.50	30.50
Mortise lock				1.301	330	57.50		387.50	440	505
Total				1.722	330	76.05		406.05	464.50	535.50

B2033 830 Door Closer, Brass

System Description	Freq. (Years)	Crew	Unit	Labor Hours	2012 Bare Costs				Total In-House	Total w/O&P
					Material	Labor	Equipment	Total		
1010										
Replace brass door closer	15	1 CARP	Ea.							
Remove door closer				.167		7.35		7.35	9.75	12.05
Install new door closer				1.735	184	76.50		260.50	305	355
Total				1.902	184	83.85		267.85	314.75	367.05

B20 EXTERIOR CLOSURE   B2033   Exterior Doors

B2033 840   Door Opener

System Description	Freq. (Years)	Crew	Unit	Labor Hours	2012 Bare Costs				Total In-House	Total w/O&P
					Material	Labor	Equipment	Total		
1010 Automatic door opener on existing door	7	1 ELEC	Ea.							
Cutout demolition of exterior wall for actuator button				1.739		61.50	9.10	70.60	91	111
Install 1/2" E.M.T. conduit				2.462	28	126.80		154.80	188	231
Install conductor, type THWN copper, #14				1.040	12.16	53.30		65.46	79.50	97.50
Install junction box				.533	19.65	27.50		47.15	55.50	67
Install outlet				.381	10.95	19.65		30.60	36.50	44
Install plate				.100	2.65	5.15		7.80	9.30	11.25
Automatic opener, button operation				20.000	3,550	910		4,460	5,100	5,925
Total				26.255	3,623.41	1,203.90	9.10	4,836.41	**5,559.80**	**6,486.75**

B2033 850   Deadbolt, Brass

System Description	Freq. (Years)	Crew	Unit	Labor Hours	2012 Bare Costs				Total In-House	Total w/O&P
					Material	Labor	Equipment	Total		
1010 Replace brass deadbolt	20	1 CARP	Ea.							
Remove deadbolt				.154		6.80		6.80	9	11.10
Install new deadbolt				1.156	275	51		326	370	425
Total				1.309	275	57.80		332.80	**379**	**436.10**

B2033 860   Weatherstripping, Brass

System Description	Freq. (Years)	Crew	Unit	Labor Hours	2012 Bare Costs				Total In-House	Total w/O&P
					Material	Labor	Equipment	Total		
1010 Replace brass door weatherstripping	20	1 CARP	Ea.							
Remove weatherstripping				.015		.65		.65	.86	1.06
Install new weatherstrip				3.478	38.50	153		191.50	246	299
Total				3.493	38.50	153.65		192.15	**246.86**	**300.06**

B2033 870 Panic Device

				2012 Bare Costs					Total In-House	Total w/O&P
System Description	Freq. (Years)	Crew	Unit	Labor Hours	Material	Labor	Equipment	Total		
1010 **Replace door panic device**	25	1 CARP	Ea.							
Remove panic bar				.421		18.55		18.55	24.50	30.50
Install new panic bar				2.080	735	91.50		826.50	930	1,075
Total				2.501	735	110.05		845.05	**954.50**	**1,105.50**

B2033 905 Hollow Core, Painted

				2012 Bare Costs					Total In-House	Total w/O&P
System Description	Freq. (Years)	Crew	Unit	Labor Hours	Material	Labor	Equipment	Total		
1010 **Repair hollow core door**	12	1 CARP	Ea.							
Remove weatherstripping				.015		.65		.65	.86	1.06
Remove door hinge				.167		7.35		7.35	9.75	12.05
Install new weatherstrip				3.478	38.50	153		191.50	246	299
Install new hinge (50% of total hinges / 12 years)				.167		7.35		7.35	9.75	12.05
Hinge, 5 x 5, brass base					62.50			62.50	69	78
Oil / lubricate hinges				.065		2.85		2.85	3.78	4.66
Total				3.891	101	171.20		272.20	**339.14**	**406.82**
1020 **Refinish 3'-0" x 7'-0" hollow core door**	4	1 PORD	Ea.							
Prepare door surface				.333		12.75		12.75	16.40	20.50
Paint door surface, brushwork, primer + 1 coat				.549	11.96	21.16		33.12	40.50	48.50
Total				.883	11.96	33.91		45.87	**56.90**	**69**
1030 **Replace 3'-0" x 7'-0" hollow core door**	30	1 CARP	Ea.							
Remove door				.650		23		23	30.50	37.50
Remove door frame				.743		33		33	43.50	54
Install new door frame				.943	150.45	41.65		192.10	221	256
Install new oak door sill				.832	68.40	36.60		105	124	146
Install new hollow core door				1.000	108	44		152	177	208
Install new weatherstrip				3.478	38.50	153		191.50	246	299
Install new lockset				.867	57.50	38		95.50	114	134
Total				8.514	422.85	369.25		792.10	**956**	**1,134.50**

B20 EXTERIOR CLOSURE | **B2033** | **Exterior Doors**

B2033 905 — Hollow Core, Painted

	System Description	Freq. (Years)	Crew	Unit	Labor Hours	Material	Labor	Equipment	Total	Total In-House	Total w/O&P
							2012 Bare Costs				
2010	**Repair hollow core sliding wood door**	14	1 CARP	Ea.							
	Remove weatherstripping				.015		.65		.65	.86	1.06
	Oil / lubricate door closer				.065		2.85		2.85	3.78	4.66
	Oil / inspect wheel & track				.065		2.85		2.85	3.78	4.66
	Install new door track / glide wheels (25% of total / 14 years)				.440	13	19.38		32.38	40	48
	Install new weatherstrip				4.167	49	184		233	298	360
	Total				4.750	62	209.73		271.73	346.42	418.38
2030	**Replace 3'-0" x 7'-0" hollow core sliding wood door**	30	1 CARP	Ea.							
	Remove sliding door				1.733		76.50		76.50	102	125
	Install new sliding door frame				4.622	415	230	17.55	662.55	830	970
	Install new hollow core door				1.000	108	44		152	177	208
	Install new weatherstrip				3.478	38.50	153		191.50	246	299
	Lockset				.867	57.50	38		95.50	114	134
	Total				11.701	619	541.50	17.55	1,178.05	1,469	1,736

B2033 925 — Metal Grated

	System Description	Freq. (Years)	Crew	Unit	Labor Hours	Material	Labor	Equipment	Total	Total In-House	Total w/O&P
							2012 Bare Costs				
1010	**Repair metal grated door**	15	1 SSWK	Ea.							
	Remove damaged metal bar				.836		41.40		41.40	64	76.50
	Oil / lubricate door closer				.065		3.18		3.18	4.93	5.90
	Oil / lubricate hinges				.065		2.85		2.85	3.78	4.66
	Metal grating repair (3% of door area / 15 years)				.320	1.26	16.40	4.86	22.52	31.50	37.50
	Replace damaged metal bar				1.600	12.50	80.50	12.20	105.20	151	179
	Total				2.885	13.76	144.33	17.06	175.15	255.21	303.56
1020	**Prepare and refinish metal grated painted door**	4	1 PORD	Ea.							
	Prepare grated door surface				.308		11.75		11.75	15.15	18.80
	Paint grated door surface, brushwork, 1 coat				.319	2.30	12.42		14.72	18.40	22
	Total				.627	2.30	24.17		26.47	33.55	40.80

B2033 925 Metal Grated

System Description	Freq. (Years)	Crew	Unit	Labor Hours	2012 Bare Costs Material	Labor	Equipment	Total	Total In-House	Total w/O&P
1030 Replace 3'-0" x 7'-0" metal grated painted door	30	2 SSWK	Ea.							
Remove door				.650		23		23	30.50	37.50
Remove door closer				.167		7.35		7.35	9.75	12.05
Remove door hinge				.500		22.05		22.05	29.50	36
Install new grated door				15.686	785	775		1,560	2,050	2,425
Install new hinge (25% of total hinges / 30 years)				.500		22.05		22.05	29.50	36
Hinge, 5 x 5					93.75			93.75	104	117
Total				17.503	878.75	849.45		1,728.20	2,253.25	2,663.55

B2033 926 Metal Wire Mesh Door

System Description	Freq. (Years)	Crew	Unit	Labor Hours	2012 Bare Costs Material	Labor	Equipment	Total	Total In-House	Total w/O&P
1010 Repair metal wire mesh door	15	1 SSWK	Ea.							
Remove wire mesh				1.750		86.63		86.63	134	161
Wire mesh					14.07			14.07	15.45	17.60
Install wire mesh				7.000		345.45		345.45	535	640
Oil / lubricate door closer				.065		3.18		3.18	4.93	5.90
Oil / lubricate hinges				.065		2.85		2.85	3.78	4.66
Total				8.879	14.07	438.11		452.18	693.16	829.16
1020 Prepare and refinish metal wire mesh door	4	1 PORD	Ea.							
Prepare metal mesh surface				.312		11.95		11.95	15.35	19.05
Paint metal mesh door surface, brushwork, 1 coat				.319	2.30	12.42		14.72	18.40	22
Total				.631	2.30	24.37		26.67	33.75	41.05
1030 Replace metal wire mesh door	30	2 SSWK	Ea.							
Remove wire mesh door				.640		31.50		31.50	49	58.50
Remove wire mesh door frame				2.602		128		128	199	239
Install new woven wire swinging door				3.471	273	153		426	505	590
Install new metal door frame				3.200	225	160	12.15	397.15	505	590
Install new hinge (25% of total hinges / 30 years)				.500		22.05		22.05	29.50	36
Hinge, 5 x 5					93.75			93.75	104	117
Install new deadlock night latch				1.039	83	46		129	152	179
Total				11.451	674.75	540.55	12.15	1,227.45	1,543.50	1,809.50

B2033 927 | **Louvered Door**

	System Description	Freq. (Years)	Crew	Unit	Labor Hours	Material	Labor	Equipment	Total	Total In-House	Total w/O&P
						2012 Bare Costs					
1010	**Repair aluminum louvered door**	12	1 CARP	Ea.							
	Remove door				.650		23		23	30.50	37.50
	Remove weatherstripping				.015		.65		.65	.86	1.06
	Remove damaged louver				.137		6.05		6.05	8	9.90
	Install new louver				.274	15	12.10		27.10	32.50	38.50
	Oil / lubricate door closer				.065		2.85		2.85	3.78	4.66
	Install new weatherstrip				3.478	38.50	153		191.50	246	299
	Reinstall exterior door				1.388		61		61	81.50	100
	Total				6.006	53.50	258.65		312.15	403.14	490.62
1020	**Prepare and refinish aluminum louvered door**	4	1 PORD	Ea.							
	Prepare door surface				.333		12.75		12.75	16.40	20.50
	Paint door surface, brushwork, primer + 1 coat				.549	11.96	21.16		33.12	40.50	48.50
	Total				.883	11.96	33.91		45.87	56.90	69
1040	**Replace 3'-0" x 7'-0" aluminum louvered door**	50	1 CARP	Ea.							
	Remove door				.650		23		23	30.50	37.50
	Remove door closer				.167		7.35		7.35	9.75	12.05
	Install new aluminum door				1.224	1,325	54		1,379	1,525	1,750
	Install new door closer				1.735	184	76.50		260.50	305	355
	Total				3.777	1,509	160.85		1,669.85	1,870.25	2,154.55
2010	**Repair steel louvered door**	14	1 CARP	Ea.							
	Remove door				.650		23		23	30.50	37.50
	Remove weatherstripping				.015		.65		.65	.86	1.06
	Remove damaged louver				.137		6.05		6.05	8	9.90
	Install new louver				.274	15	12.10		27.10	32.50	38.50
	Oil / lubricate door closer				.065		2.85		2.85	3.78	4.66
	Install new weatherstrip				3.478	38.50	153		191.50	246	299
	Reinstall exterior door				1.388		61		61	81.50	100
	Total				6.006	53.50	258.65		312.15	403.14	490.62
2020	**Prepare and refinish steel louvered door**	4	1 PORD	Ea.							
	Prepare door surfaces				.333		12.75		12.75	16.40	20.50
	Paint door surface, brushwork, primer + 1 coat				.549	11.96	21.16		33.12	40.50	48.50
	Total				.883	11.96	33.91		45.87	56.90	69

B2033 927   Louvered Door

	System Description	Freq. (Years)	Crew	Unit	Labor Hours	2012 Bare Costs				Total In-House	Total w/O&P
						Material	Labor	Equipment	Total		
2040	**Replace 3'-0" x 7'-0" steel louvered door**	45	1 CARP	Ea.							
	Remove door				.650		23		23	30.50	37.50
	Remove door closer				.167		7.35		7.35	9.75	12.05
	Install new steel door, incl. louver				1.224	635	54		689	770	880
	Install new door closer				1.735	184	76.50		260.50	305	355
	Total				3.776	819	160.85		979.85	1,115.25	1,284.55
3010	**Repair wood louvered door**	7	1 CARP	Ea.							
	Remove door				.650		23		23	30.50	37.50
	Remove weatherstripping				.015		.65		.65	.86	1.06
	Remove damaged louver				.137		6.05		6.05	8	9.90
	Install new louver				.274	15	12.10		27.10	32.50	38.50
	Oil / lubricate door closer				.065		2.85		2.85	3.78	4.66
	Install new weatherstrip				3.478	38.50	153		191.50	246	299
	Reinstall exterior door				1.388		61		61	81.50	100
	Total				6.006	53.50	258.65		312.15	403.14	490.62
3020	**Prepare and refinish wood louvered door**	4	1 PORD	Ea.							
	Prepare door surfaces				.333		12.75		12.75	16.40	20.50
	Paint door surface, brushwork, primer + 1 coat				.549	11.96	21.16		33.12	40.50	48.50
	Total				.883	11.96	33.91		45.87	56.90	69
3040	**Replace 3'-0" x 7'-0" wood louvered door**	40	1 CARP	Ea.							
	Remove door				.650		23		23	30.50	37.50
	Remove door closer				.167		7.35		7.35	9.75	12.05
	Install new solid core door				1.143	197	50.50		247.50	284	330
	Add for installed wood louver					274			274	300	345
	Install new door closer				1.735	184	76.50		260.50	305	355
	Total				3.695	655	157.35		812.35	929.25	1,079.55

B2033 935 Aluminum Storm/Screen Door

	System Description	Freq. (Years)	Crew	Unit	Labor Hours	2012 Bare Costs				Total In-House	Total w/O&P
						Material	Labor	Equipment	Total		
1010	**Repair aluminum storm/screen door**	5	1 CARP	Ea.							
	Remove weatherstripping				.015		.65		.65	.86	1.06
	Remove screen / storm door threshold				.519		23		23	30.50	37.50
	Remove door closer				.167		7.35		7.35	9.75	12.05
	Install new screen / storm door closer				1.301	27.50	57.50		85	106	128
	Install new weatherstrip				.870	9.63	38.25		47.88	61.50	75
	Install new plain aluminum threshold				.520	5.60	23		28.60	36.50	44.50
	Total				3.391	42.73	149.75		192.48	245.11	298.11
1020	**Replace aluminum storm/screen door**	20	1 CARP	Ea.							
	Remove door				.650		23		23	30.50	37.50
	Install new anodized aluminum screen / storm door				1.487	161	65.50		226.50	264	310
	Total				2.137	161	88.50		249.50	294.50	347.50

B2033 960 Aluminized Steel Pedestrian Gate

	System Description	Freq. (Years)	Crew	Unit	Labor Hours	2012 Bare Costs				Total In-House	Total w/O&P
						Material	Labor	Equipment	Total		
1010	**Repair aluminized steel pedestrian gate**	10	1 CARP	Ea.							
	Remove gate from hinges				.286		12.60		12.60	16.75	20.50
	Oil / lubricate hinges				.065		2.85		2.85	3.78	4.66
	Install new 6' aluminized steel fencing				.360	67.50	12.54	3.27	83.31	94.50	109
	Reinstall gate				.615		27		27	36	44.50
	Total				1.326	67.50	54.99	3.27	125.76	151.03	178.66
1030	**Prepare and refinish pedestrian gate**	5	1 PORD	Ea.							
	Lay drop cloth				.090		3.45		3.45	4.40	5.50
	Prepare / brush surface				.042		1.62		1.62	2.04	2.52
	Paint gate, brushwork, 1 coat				.150	1.26	5.76		7.02	8.80	10.75
	Remove drop cloth				.090		3.45		3.45	4.40	5.50
	Total				.371	1.26	14.28		15.54	19.64	24.27
1040	**Replace pedestrian gate**	40	1 CARP	Ea.							
	Remove old gate from hinges				.286		12.60		12.60	16.75	20.50
	Install new 6' x 3' aluminized steel gate				3.117	187	109	28.50	324.50	380	440
	Total				3.403	187	121.60	28.50	337.10	396.75	460.50

B2033 961 Steel Pedestrian Gate

System Description	Freq. (Years)	Crew	Unit	Labor Hours	2012 Bare Costs				Total In-House	Total w/O&P
					Material	Labor	Equipment	Total		
1010 Repair steel gate	10	1 CARP	Ea.							
Remove gate from hinges				.286		12.60		12.60	16.75	20.50
Oil / lubricate hinges				.065		2.85		2.85	3.78	4.66
Install new 6' galvanized steel fencing				.360	55.65	12.54	3.27	71.46	81	93.50
Reinstall gate				.615		27		27	36	44.50
Total				1.326	55.65	54.99	3.27	113.91	137.53	163.16
1030 Prepare and refinish steel gate	5	1 PORD	Ea.							
Lay drop cloth				.090		3.45		3.45	4.40	5.50
Prepare / brush surface				.042		1.62		1.62	2.04	2.52
Paint gate, brushwork, 1 coat				.150	1.26	5.76		7.02	8.80	10.75
Remove drop cloth				.090		3.45		3.45	4.40	5.50
Total				.371	1.26	14.28		15.54	19.64	24.27
1040 Replace steel gate	40	1 CARP	Ea.							
Remove old gate from hinges				.286		12.60		12.60	16.75	20.50
Install new 6' x 3' galvanized steel gate				3.117	187	109	28.50	324.50	380	440
Total				3.403	187	121.60	28.50	337.10	396.75	460.50

B2033 962 Wood Pedestrian Gate

System Description	Freq. (Years)	Crew	Unit	Labor Hours	2012 Bare Costs				Total In-House	Total w/O&P
					Material	Labor	Equipment	Total		
1010 Repair wood gate	7	1 CARP	Ea.							
Remove gate from hinges				.286		12.60		12.60	16.75	20.50
Oil / lubricate hinges				.065		2.85		2.85	3.78	4.66
Replace damaged fencing				1.171	118.20	40.80	10.68	169.68	195	226
Reinstall gate				.615		27		27	36	44.50
Total				2.136	118.20	83.25	10.68	212.13	251.53	295.66
1030 Prepare and refinish wood gate	4	1 PORD	Ea.							
Lay drop cloth				.090		3.45		3.45	4.40	5.50
Prepare / brush surface				.042		1.62		1.62	2.04	2.52
Paint gate, brushwork, primer + 1 coat				.138	1.26	5.22		6.48	8.30	10.05
Remove drop cloth				.090		3.45		3.45	4.40	5.50
Total				.359	1.26	13.74		15	19.14	23.57

B2033 962 Wood Pedestrian Gate

	System Description	Freq. (Years)	Crew	Unit	Labor Hours	2012 Bare Costs				Total In-House	Total w/O&P
						Material	Labor	Equipment	Total		
1040	**Replace wood gate**	25	1 CARP	Ea.							
	Remove old gate from hinges				.286		12.60		12.60	16.75	20.50
	New 6'-0" x 3'-0" wood gate				3.468	174	121	31.50	326.50	385	450
	Total				3.754	174	133.60	31.50	339.10	401.75	470.50

B2033 963 Wrought Iron Gate

	System Description	Freq. (Years)	Crew	Unit	Labor Hours	2012 Bare Costs				Total In-House	Total w/O&P
						Material	Labor	Equipment	Total		
1010	**Repair wrought iron gate**	11	1 CARP	Ea.							
	Remove gate from hinges				.286		12.60		12.60	16.75	20.50
	Oil / lubricate hinges				.065		2.85		2.85	3.78	4.66
	Repair hand forged wrought iron				2.600	202.50	129		331.50	420	490
	Reinstall gate				.615		27		27	36	44.50
	Total				3.566	202.50	171.45		373.95	476.53	559.66
1030	**Prepare and refinish wrought iron gate**	5	1 PORD	Ea.							
	Lay drop cloth				.090		3.45		3.45	4.40	5.50
	Prepare / brush surface				.125		4.86		4.86	6.10	7.55
	Paint gate, brushwork, primer + 1 coat				.167	1.26	6.30		7.56	9.70	11.65
	Remove drop cloth				.090		3.45		3.45	4.40	5.50
	Total				.471	1.26	18.06		19.32	24.60	30.20
1040	**Replace wrought iron gate**	45	1 CARP	Ea.							
	Remove old gate from hinges				.286		12.60		12.60	16.75	20.50
	Install new hand forged wrought iron gate				3.467	270	172		442	560	655
	Total				3.753	270	184.60		454.60	576.75	675.50

B3013 105   Built-Up Roofing

System Description	Freq. (Years)	Crew	Unit	Labor Hours	2012 Bare Costs				Total In-House	Total w/O&P
					Material	Labor	Equipment	Total		
0100 Debris removal and visual inspection	0.50	2 ROFC	M.S.F.							
Set up, secure and take down ladder				.052		1.94		1.94	2.85	3.45
Pick up trash / debris & clean-up				.327		12.20		12.20	17.90	21.50
Visual inspection				.327		12.20		12.20	17.90	21.50
Total				.705		26.34		26.34	38.65	46.45
0200 Non-destructive moisture inspection	5	2 ROFC	M.S.F.							
Set up, secure and take down ladder				.052		1.94		1.94	2.85	3.45
Infrared inspection of roof membrane				2.133		80		80	117	142
Total				2.185		81.94		81.94	119.85	145.45
0300 Minor BUR membrane repairs - (2% of roof area)	1	G-5	Sq.							
Set up, secure and take down ladder				1.000		37		37	55	66
Sweep / spud ballast clean				.640		24		24	35	42.50
Cross cut incision through bitumen				.258		9.65		9.65	14.15	17.15
Install base sheet and 2 plies of glass mopped				3.294	90.50	115	26.50	232	295	350
Reinstall ballast in bitumen				.390		14.60		14.60	21.50	26
Clean up				.390		14.60		14.60	21.50	26
Total				5.973	90.50	214.85	26.50	331.85	442.15	527.65
0400 BUR flashing repairs - (2 S.F. per sq. repaired)	1	2 ROFC	S.F.							
Set up, secure and take down ladder				.010		.37		.37	.55	.66
Sweep / spud ballast clean				.009		.34		.34	.49	.60
Cut out buckled flashing				.020		.75		.75	1.10	1.33
Install 2 ply membrane flashing				.013	.19	.50		.69	.94	1.13
Reinstall ballast in bitumen				.005		.19		.19	.29	.35
Clean up				.004		.15		.15	.22	.27
Total				.062	.19	2.30		2.49	3.59	4.34
0500 Minor BUR membrane replacement - (25% of roof area)	15	G-5	Sq.							
Set up, secure and take down ladder				.078		2.92		2.92	4.28	5.20
Remove 5 ply built-up roof				3.252		115		115	153	189
Remove roof insulation board				1.333		47		47	63	78
Install 2" polystyrene insulation				.833	56	31		87	108	125
Install 4 ply bituminous roofing				3.733	122	131	30	283	355	420
Clean up				1.000		37.50		37.50	55	66.50
Total				10.229	178	364.42	30	572.42	738.28	883.70

B3013 105 Built-Up Roofing

	System Description	Freq. (Years)	Crew	Unit	Labor Hours	2012 Bare Costs				Total In-House	Total w/O&P
						Material	Labor	Equipment	Total		
0600	**Place new BUR membrane over existing**	20	G-5	Sq.							
	Set up, secure and take down ladder				.020		.75		.75	1.10	1.33
	Sweep / spud ballast clean				.500		18.70		18.70	27.50	33
	Vent existing membrane				.130		4.85		4.85	7.10	8.65
	Cut out buckled flashing				.024		.90		.90	1.32	1.60
	Install 2 ply membrane flashing				.027	.39	1		1.39	1.88	2.26
	Install 4 ply bituminous roofing				3.733	122	131		283	355	420
	Reinstall ballast				.381		14.25		14.25	21	25.50
	Clean up				.390		14.60		14.60	21.50	26
	Total				5.205	122.39	186.05	30	338.44	436.40	518.34
0700	**Total BUR roof replacement**	28	G-1	Sq.							
	Set up, secure and take down ladder				.020		.75		.75	1.10	1.33
	Sweep / spud ballast clean				.500		18.70		18.70	27.50	33
	Remove built-up roofing				2.500		89		89	118	146
	Remove insulation board				1.026		36		36	48	60
	Remove flashing				.024		.90		.90	1.32	1.60
	Install 2" perlite insulation				1.143	80	43		123	151	176
	Install 2 ply membrane flashing				.027	.39	1		1.39	1.88	2.26
	Install 4 ply bituminous membrane				2.800	122	98	22.50	242.50	300	350
	Clean up				1.000		37.50		37.50	55	66.50
	Total				9.040	202.39	324.85	22.50	549.74	703.80	836.69

B3013 120 Modified Bituminous / Thermoplastic

	System Description	Freq. (Years)	Crew	Unit	Labor Hours	2012 Bare Costs				Total In-House	Total w/O&P
						Material	Labor	Equipment	Total		
0100	**Debris removal by hand & visual inspection**	1	2 ROFC	M.S.F.							
	Set up, secure and take down ladder				.052		1.94		1.94	2.85	3.45
	Pick up trash / debris & clean up				.327		12.20		12.20	17.90	21.50
	Visual inspection				.327		12.20		12.20	17.90	21.50
	Total				.705		26.34		26.34	38.65	46.45
0200	**Non - destructive moisture inspection**	5	2 ROFC	M.S.F.							
	Set up, secure and take down ladder				.052		1.94		1.94	2.85	3.45
	Infrared inspection of roof membrane				2.133		80		80	117	142
	Total				2.185		81.94		81.94	119.85	145.45

B3013 120 Modified Bituminous / Thermoplastic

System Description	Freq. (Years)	Crew	Unit	Labor Hours	2012 Bare Costs				Total In-House	Total w/O&P
					Material	Labor	Equipment	Total		
0300 Minor thermoplastic membrane repairs - (2% of roof area)	1	G-5	Sq.							
Set up, secure and take down ladder				1.000		37		37	55	66
Clean away loose surfacing				.258		9.65		9.65	14.15	17.15
Install 150 mil mod. bit., fully adhered				2.597	80	88	12	180	229	270
Clean up				.390		14.60		14.60	21.50	26
Total				4.245	80	149.25	12	241.25	319.65	379.15
0500 Thermoplastic flashing repairs - (2 S.F. per sq. repaired)	1	2 ROFC	S.F.							
Set up, secure and take down ladder				.010		.37		.37	.55	.66
Clean away loose surfacing				.003		.10		.10	.14	.17
Remove flashing				.020		.75		.75	1.10	1.33
Install 120 mil mod. bit. flashing				.019	.83	.63	.08	1.54	1.92	2.25
Clean up				.004		.15		.15	.22	.27
Total				.055	.83	2	.08	2.91	3.93	4.68
0600 Minor thermoplastic membrane replacement - (25% of roof area)	20	G-5	Sq.							
Set up, secure and take down ladder				.078		2.92		2.92	4.28	5.20
Remove existing membrane / insulation				4.571		171		171	251	305
Install 2" perlite insulation				1.481	80	55		135	169	198
Clean adjacent membrane / patch				1.143		42.50		42.50	62.50	76
Install fully adhered 150 mil membrane				2.597	80	88	12	180	229	270
Clean up				1.000		37.50		37.50	55	66.50
Total				10.870	160	396.92	12	568.92	770.78	920.70
0700 Total thermoplastic roof replacement	25	G-1	Sq.							
Set up, secure and take down ladder				.020		.75		.75	1.10	1.33
Remove existing membrane / insulation				3.501		131		131	192	233
Remove flashing				.026		.98		.98	1.42	1.72
Install 2" perlite insulation				1.143	80	43		123	151	176
Install flashing				.037	1.66	1.26	.16	3.08	3.84	4.50
Install fully adhered 180 mil membrane				2.000	62	68	9	139	177	209
Clean up				1.000		37.50		37.50	55	66.50
Total				7.727	143.66	282.49	9.16	435.31	581.36	692.05

B30 ROOFING — B3013 — Roof Covering

B3013 125 — Thermosetting

System Description	Freq. (Years)	Crew	Unit	Labor Hours	2012 Bare Costs				Total In-House	Total w/O&P
					Material	Labor	Equipment	Total		
0100 Debris removal by hand & visual inspection	1	2 ROFC	M.S.F.							
Set up, secure and take down ladder				.052		1.94		1.94	2.85	3.45
Pick up trash / debris & clean up				.327		12.20		12.20	17.90	21.50
Visual inspection				.327		12.20		12.20	17.90	21.50
Total				.705		26.34		26.34	38.65	46.45
0200 Non - destructive moisture inspection	5	2 ROFC	M.S.F.							
Set up, secure and take down ladder				.052		1.94		1.94	2.85	3.45
Infrared inspection of roof membrane				2.133		80		80	117	142
Total				2.185		81.94		81.94	119.85	145.45
0300 Minor thermoset membrane repairs - (2% of roof area)	1	G-5	Sq.							
Set up, secure and take down ladder				1.000		37		37	55	66
Broom roof surface clean				.258		9.65		9.65	14.15	17.15
Remove / vent damaged membrane				.258		9.65		9.65	14.15	17.15
Install thermosetting patch				2.597	52	88	12	152	198	235
Clean up				.390		14.60		14.60	21.50	26
Total				4.503	52	158.90	12	222.90	302.80	361.30
0400 Thermoset flashing repairs - (2 S.F. per sq. repaired)	1	2 ROFC	S.F.							
Set up, secure and take down ladder				.010		.37		.37	.55	.66
Remove flashing				.020		.75		.75	1.10	1.33
Prime surfaces				.003		.11		.11	.16	.20
Install 2 ply membrane flashing				.007	.10	.25		.35	.47	.57
Clean up				.004		.15		.15	.22	.27
Total				.044	.10	1.63		1.73	2.50	3.03
0500 Minor thermoset membrane replacement - (25% of roof area)	10	G-5	Sq.							
Set up, secure and take down ladder				.078		2.92		2.92	4.28	5.20
Broom roof surface clean				.258		9.65		9.65	14.15	17.15
Remove, strip-in & seal joint				.593		22		22	32.50	39.50
Install base sheet and 2 plies of glass mopped				3.294	90.50	115	26.50	232	295	350
Clean up				.390		14.60		14.60	21.50	26
Total				4.613	90.50	164.17	26.50	281.17	367.43	437.85

101

B3013 125 Thermosetting

System Description	Freq. (Years)	Crew	Unit	Labor Hours	2012 Bare Costs				Total In-House	Total w/O&P
					Material	Labor	Equipment	Total		
0600 Total thermoset roof replacement	20	G-1	Sq.							
Set up, secure and take down ladder				.020		.75		.75	1.10	1.33
Remove existing membrane / insulation				3.501		131		131	192	233
Remove flashing				.026		.98		.98	1.42	1.72
Install 2" perlite insulation				1.143	80	43		123	151	176
Install new flashing				.020	.39	.75		1.14	1.52	1.80
Install thermosetting membrane				2.800	77	98	23	198	252	295
Clean up				1.000		37.50		37.50	55	66.50
Total				8.510	157.39	311.98	23	492.37	654.04	775.35

B3013 127 EPDM (Ethylene Propylene Diene Monomer)

System Description	Freq. (Years)	Crew	Unit	Labor Hours	2012 Bare Costs				Total In-House	Total w/O&P
					Material	Labor	Equipment	Total		
0600 Total EPDM roof replacement	25	G-5	Sq.							
Set up, secure and take down ladder				.020		.75		.75	1.10	1.33
Remove existing membrane / insulation				3.501		131		131	192	233
Remove flashing				.026		.98		.98	1.42	1.72
Install 2" perlite insulation				1.143	80	43		123	151	176
Install new flashing				.020	.39	.75		1.14	1.52	1.80
Fully adhered with adhesive				1.538	99.50	52.50	6.90	158.90	193	225
Clean up				1.000		37.50		37.50	55	66.50
Total				7.249	179.89	266.48	6.90	453.27	595.04	705.35

B3013 130 Metal Panel Roofing

System Description	Freq. (Years)	Crew	Unit	Labor Hours	2012 Bare Costs				Total In-House	Total w/O&P
					Material	Labor	Equipment	Total		
0100 Debris removal by hand & visual inspection	1	2 ROFC	M.S.F.							
Set up, secure and take down ladder				.100		3.74		3.74	5.50	6.65
Visual inspection				.327		12.20		12.20	17.90	21.50
Total				.427		15.94		15.94	23.40	28.15

B3013 130   Metal Panel Roofing

System Description	Freq. (Years)	Crew	Unit	Labor Hours	2012 Bare Costs Material	Labor	Equipment	Total	Total In-House	Total w/O&P
0300 Minor metal roof finish repairs - (2% of roof area)	5	2 ROFC	S.F.							
Set up, secure and take down ladder				.010		.37		.37	.55	.66
Wire brush surface to remove oxide				.020		.75		.75	1.10	1.33
Prime and paint prepared surface				.016	.62	.60		1.22	1.56	1.84
Clean up				.004		.15		.15	.22	.27
Total				.050	.62	1.87		2.49	3.43	4.10
0400 Metal roof flashing replacement - (2 S.F. per sq. repaired)	1	2 ROFC	S.F.							
Set up, secure and take down ladder				.010		.37		.37	.55	.66
Dismantle seam				.016		.60		.60	.88	1.06
Remove metal roof panels				.060		2.25		2.25	3.30	3.99
Remove damaged metal flashing				.019		.71		.71	1.04	1.26
Install new aluminum flashing				.072	1.25	2.70		3.95	5.35	6.35
Replace metal panels				.129		4.83		4.83	7.10	8.60
Clean up				.004		.15		.15	.22	.27
Total				.310	1.25	11.61		12.86	18.44	22.19
0500 Minor metal roof panel replacement - (2.5% of roof area)	20	2 ROFC	S.F.							
Set up, secure and take down ladder				.010		.37		.37	.55	.66
Dismantle seam				.016		.60		.60	.88	1.06
Remove metal roof panels				.020		.75		.75	1.10	1.33
Install new metal panel				.044	3.03	1.91		4.94	5.80	6.85
Re-assemble seam				.016		.60		.60	.88	1.06
Prime and paint surface				.016	.62	.60		1.22	1.56	1.84
Clean up				.004		.15		.15	.22	.27
Total				.126	3.65	4.98		8.63	10.99	13.07
0600 Total metal roof panel replacement	30	2 ROFC	Sq.							
Set up, secure and take down ladder				.020		.75		.75	1.10	1.33
Remove existing roofing panel				3.600		135		135	197	239
Remove flashing metal				.038		1.42		1.42	2.08	2.52
Install new aluminum flashing				.072	1.25	2.70		3.95	5.35	6.35
Install new metal panel				4.384	303	191		494	580	685
Clean up				.390		14.60		14.60	21.50	26
Total				8.504	304.25	345.47		649.72	807.03	960.20

B3013 140   Slate Tile Roofing

System Description	Freq. (Years)	Crew	Unit	Labor Hours	2012 Bare Costs Material	Labor	Equipment	Total	Total In-House	Total w/O&P
0100										
Visual inspection	3	2 ROFC	M.S.F.							
Set up, secure and take down ladder				.100		3.74		3.74	5.50	6.65
Visual inspection				.327		12.20		12.20	17.90	21.50
Total				.427		15.94		15.94	23.40	28.15
0200										
Minor slate tile replacement - (2.5% of roof area)	20	2 ROTS	S.F.							
Set up, secure and take down ladder				.010		.37		.37	.55	.66
Remove and replace damaged slates				.800	5.90	30		35.90	50.50	61
Clean up				.013		.49		.49	.71	.86
Total				.823	5.90	30.86		36.76	51.76	62.52
0300										
Slate tile flashing repairs - (2 S.F. per sq. repaired)	20	2 ROTS	S.F.							
Set up, secure and take down ladder				.010		.37		.37	.55	.66
Removal of adjacent slate tiles				.100		3.74		3.74	5.50	6.65
Remove damaged metal flashing				.052		1.94		1.94	2.85	3.45
Install 16 oz. copper flashing				.089	7.85	3.32		11.17	13.50	15.70
Reinstall tiles in position				.134		5		5	7.35	8.90
Clean up				.013		.49		.49	.71	.86
Total				.398	7.85	14.86		22.71	30.46	36.22
0400										
Total slate tile roof replacement	70	2 ROTS	Sq.							
Set up, secure and take down ladder				.020		.75		.75	1.10	1.33
Remove slate shingles				1.600		57		57	75	93
Install 16 oz. copper flashing				.178	15.70	6.64		22.34	27	31.50
Install 15# felt				.138	6.90	5.15		12.05	15.15	17.80
Install slate roofing				4.571	480	172		652	780	905
Clean up				1.333		50		50	73	88.50
Total				7.840	502.60	291.54		794.14	971.25	1,137.13

B3013 142   Mineral Fiber Steep Roofing

System Description	Freq. (Years)	Crew	Unit	Labor Hours	2012 Bare Costs Material	Labor	Equipment	Total	Total In-House	Total w/O&P
0300										
Visual inspection	3	2 ROFC	M.S.F.							
Set up, secure and take down ladder				.100		3.74		3.74	5.50	6.65
Visual inspection				.327		12.20		12.20	17.90	21.50
Total				.427		15.94		15.94	23.40	28.15

B3013 144 Clay Tile Roofing

	System Description	Freq. (Years)	Crew	Unit	Labor Hours	2012 Bare Costs				Total In-House	Total w/O&P
						Material	Labor	Equipment	Total		
0300	**Visual inspection**	3	2 ROFC	M.S.F.							
	Set up, secure and take down ladder				.100		3.74		3.74	5.50	6.65
	Visual inspection				.327		12.20		12.20	17.90	21.50
	Total				.427		15.94		15.94	**23.40**	**28.15**
0400	**Minor clay tile repairs - (2% of roof area)**	20	2 ROFC	S.F.							
	Set up, secure and take down ladder				.010		.37		.37	.55	.66
	Remove damaged tiles				.020		.75		.75	1.10	1.33
	Install new clay tiles				.073	4.40	2.73		7.13	8.85	10.35
	Clean up				.013		.49		.49	.71	.86
	Total				.116	4.40	4.34		8.74	**11.21**	**13.20**
0500	**Clay tile flashing repairs - (2 S.F. per sq. repaired)**	1	2 ROFC	S.F.							
	Set up, secure and take down ladder				.010		.37		.37	.55	.66
	Remove adjacent tiles				.208		7.76		7.76	11.40	13.80
	Remove damaged metal flashing				.052		1.94		1.94	2.85	3.45
	Install 16 oz copper flashing				.178	15.70	6.64		22.34	27	31.50
	Reinstall clay tiles				.073		2.73		2.73	4	4.85
	Clean up				.013		.49		.49	.71	.86
	Total				.533	15.70	19.93		35.63	**46.51**	**55.12**
0600	**Total clay tile roof replacement**	70	2 ROFC	Sq.							
	Set up, secure and take down ladder				.020		.75		.75	1.10	1.33
	Remove clay tile roofing				3.200		120		120	176	213
	Remove damaged metal flashing				.040		1.50		1.50	2.19	2.66
	Install 16 oz copper flashing				.178	15.70	6.64		22.34	27	31.50
	Install felt				.138	6.90	5.15		12.05	15.15	17.80
	Install new clay tiles				7.273	440	273		713	885	1,025
	Clean up				1.333		50		50	73	88.50
	Total				12.182	462.60	457.04		919.64	**1,179.44**	**1,379.79**

105

	System Description	Freq. (Years)	Crew	Unit	Labor Hours	2012 Bare Costs				Total In-House	Total w/O&P
						Material	Labor	Equipment	Total		
0100	**Debris removal by hand & visual inspection**	1	2 ROFC	M.S.F.							
	Set up, secure and take down ladder				.100		3.74		3.74	5.50	6.65
	Visual inspection				.327		12.20		12.20	17.90	21.50
	Total				.427		15.94		15.94	23.40	28.15
0300	**Minor asphalt shingle repair - (2% of roof area)**	1	2 ROFC	S.F.							
	Set up, secure and take down ladder				.010		.37		.37	.55	.66
	Remove damaged shingles				.024		.84		.84	1.11	1.37
	Install asphalt shingles				.036	.93	1.33		2.26	2.97	3.52
	Clean up				.003		.10		.10	.14	.17
	Total				.072	.93	2.64		3.57	4.77	5.72
0500	**Asphalt shingle flashing repairs - (2 S.F. per sq. repaired)**	1	2 ROFC	S.F.							
	Set up, secure and take down ladder				.010		.37		.37	.55	.66
	Remove adjoining shingles				.046		1.62		1.62	2.16	2.66
	Remove damaged metal flashing				.019		.71		.71	1.04	1.26
	Install new aluminum flashing				.072	1.25	2.70		3.95	5.35	6.35
	Install asphalt shingles				.071	1.85	2.66		4.51	5.95	7.05
	Clean up				.003		.10		.10	.14	.17
	Total				.221	3.10	8.16		11.26	15.19	18.15
0600	**Install new asphalt shingles over existing**	20	2 ROFC	Sq.							
	Set up, secure and take down ladder				.020		.75		.75	1.10	1.33
	Remove shingles at eaves and ridge				.460		17.20		17.20	25	30.50
	Install new aluminum flashing				.144	2.50	5.40		7.90	10.70	12.70
	Install asphalt shingles				1.778	92.50	66.50		159	199	234
	Clean up				.258		9.65		9.65	14.15	17.15
	Total				2.660	95	99.50		194.50	249.95	295.68
0700	**Total asphalt shingle roof replacement**	40	2 ROFC	Sq.							
	Set up, secure and take down ladder				.020		.75		.75	1.10	1.33
	Remove existing shingles				2.353		84		84	111	137
	Remove damaged metal flashing				.038		1.42		1.42	2.08	2.52
	Install 15# felt				.138	6.90	5.15		12.05	15.15	17.80
	Install new aluminum flashing				.144	2.50	5.40		7.90	10.70	12.70
	Install asphalt shingles				1.778	92.50	66.50		159	199	234
	Clean up				.258		9.65		9.65	14.15	17.15
	Total				4.729	101.90	172.87		274.77	353.18	422.50

B3013 160 — Roll Roofing

System Description	Freq. (Years)	Crew	Unit	Labor Hours	2012 Bare Costs				Total In-House	Total w/O&P
					Material	Labor	Equipment	Total		
0100 Debris removal by hand & visual inspection	1	2 ROFC	M.S.F.							
Set up, secure and take down ladder				.100		3.74		3.74	5.50	6.65
Pick up trash / debris & clean up				.327		12.20		12.20	17.90	21.50
Visual inspection				.327		12.20		12.20	17.90	21.50
Total				.753		28.14		28.14	41.30	49.65
0300 Minor roofing repairs - (2% of roof area)	1	2 ROFC	S.F.							
Set up, secure and take down ladder				.010		.37		.37	.55	.66
Cut out damaged area				.015		.56		.56	.82	1
Install roll roofing with mastic				.027	.68	.95	.22	1.85	2.35	2.77
Clean up				.003		.10		.10	.14	.17
Total				.055	.68	1.98	.22	2.88	3.86	4.60
0400 Flashing repairs - (2 S.F. per sq. repaired)	1	2 ROFC	L.F.							
Set up, secure and take down ladder				.010		.37		.37	.55	.66
Remove adjacent roofing				.015		.56		.56	.82	1
Remove damaged metal flashing				.019		.71		.71	1.04	1.26
Install aluminum flashing				.072	1.25	2.70		3.95	5.35	6.35
Install roll roofing with mastic				.054	1.36	1.89	.44	3.69	4.71	5.55
Clean up				.003		.10		.10	.14	.17
Total				.173	2.61	6.33	.44	9.38	12.61	14.99
0500 Minor replacement - (25% of roof area)	15	2 ROFC	Sq.							
Set up, secure and take down ladder				.078		2.92		2.92	4.28	5.20
Remove strip-in				1.067		40		40	58.50	71
Renew striping with 2 ply felts				2.917	102	102	23.50	227.50	285	335
Clean up				.258		9.65		9.65	14.15	17.15
Total				4.319	102	154.57	23.50	280.07	361.93	428.35
0600 Total roof replacement	20	2 ROFC	Sq.							
Set up, secure and take down ladder				.020		.75		.75	1.10	1.33
Remove existing shingles				1.333		50		50	73	88.50
Remove flashing				.019		.71		.71	1.04	1.26
Install aluminum flashing				.144	2.50	5.40		7.90	10.70	12.70
Install 4 ply roll roofing				2.917	102	102	23.50	227.50	285	335
Clean up				.258		9.65		9.65	14.15	17.15
Total				4.691	104.50	168.51	23.50	296.51	384.99	455.94

B3013 165 Corrugated Fiberglass Panel Roofing

System Description	Freq. (Years)	Crew	Unit	Labor Hours	2012 Bare Costs				Total In-House	Total w/O&P
					Material	Labor	Equipment	Total		
0100 Debris removal & visual inspection										
Set up, secure and take down ladder	5	2 ROFC	M.S.F.	.100		3.74		3.74	5.50	6.65
Visual inspection				.327		12.20		12.20	17.90	21.50
Total				.427		15.94		15.94	**23.40**	**28.15**
0200 Fiberglass roof flashing repairs - (2 S.F. per sq. repaired)										
Set up, secure and take down ladder	15	2 ROFC	S.F.	.010		.37		.37	.55	.66
Cut flashing				.010		.37		.37	.55	.66
Install new flashing				.036	.39	1.36		1.75	2.42	2.91
Clean up				.004		.15		.15	.22	.27
Total				.060	.39	2.25		2.64	**3.74**	**4.50**
0400 Minor fiberglass roof panel replacement - (25% of roof area)										
Set up, secure and take down ladder	15	2 ROFC	S.F.	.010		.37		.37	.55	.66
Remove damaged panel				.030		1.12		1.12	1.65	1.99
Install new fiberglass panel				.064	1.90	2.79		4.69	5.70	6.85
Install strip-in with joint seal				.029	.01	1.27		1.28	1.66	2.05
Clean up				.004		.15		.15	.22	.27
Total				.137	1.91	5.70		7.61	**9.78**	**11.82**
0600 Total fiberglass roof replacement										
Set up, secure and take down ladder	20	2 ROFC	Sq.	.020		.75		.75	1.10	1.33
Remove existing fiberglass panels				2.500		93.50		93.50	137	166
Install new flashing				.073	.78	2.72		3.50	4.84	5.80
Install new fiberglass panel				6.400	190	279		469	570	685
Apply joint sealer to seams				.029	.01	1.27		1.28	1.66	2.05
Clean up				.390		14.60		14.60	21.50	26
Total				9.412	190.79	391.84		582.63	**736.10**	**886.18**

B3013 170 | Roof Edges

System Description	Freq. (Years)	Crew	Unit	Labor Hours	2012 Bare Costs				Total In-House	Total w/O&P
					Material	Labor	Equipment	Total		
1010 Replace Roof edges, aluminum, duranodic, .050″ thick, 6″ face	25	2 ROFC	L.F.							
Set up, secure, and take down ladder				.010		.37		.37	.55	.66
Remove adjacent roofing				.015		.56		.56	.82	1
Remove roof edges				.080		2.81		2.81	3.73	4.60
2″ x 8″ Edge blocking				.025	.88	1.08		1.96	2.40	2.87
Cants, 4″ x 4″, treated timber, cut diagonally				.025	2.02	.92		2.94	3.57	4.17
Aluminum gravel stop with Duranodic finish				.089	10.43	4.64		15.07	17.35	20.50
Roof covering, splice sheet				.008	1.97	.27	.04	2.28	2.60	2.98
Total				.251	15.30	10.65	.04	25.99	31.02	36.78
1020 Replace Roof edges, copper, 20 oz,, 8″ face	35	2 ROFC	L.F.							
Set up, secure, and take down ladder				.010		.37		.37	.55	.66
Remove adjacent roofing				.015		.56		.56	.82	1
Remove roof edge				.080		2.81		2.81	3.73	4.60
2″ x 8″ Edge blocking				.025	.88	1.08		1.96	2.40	2.87
Cants, 4″ x 4″, treated timber, cut diagonally				.025	2.02	.92		2.94	3.57	4.17
Copper gravel stop				.139	15.70	5.20		20.90	25	29
Roof covering, splice sheet				.008	1.97	.27	.04	2.28	2.60	2.98
Total				.301	20.57	11.21	.04	31.82	38.67	45.28
1030 Replace Roof edges, galvanized, 20 ga., 6″ face	25	2 ROFC	L.F.							
Set up, secure, and take down ladder				.010		.37		.37	.55	.66
Remove adjacent roofing				.015		.56		.56	.82	1
Remove roof edge				.080		2.81		2.81	3.73	4.60
2″ x 8″ edge blocking				.025	.88	1.08		1.96	2.40	2.87
Cants, 4″ x 4″, treated timber, cut diagonally				.025	2.02	.92		2.94	3.57	4.17
Galvanized steel gravel stop				.092	2.15	3.45		5.60	7.45	8.80
Roof covering, splice sheet				.008	1.97	.27	.04	2.28	2.60	2.98
Total				.254	7.02	9.46	.04	16.52	21.12	25.08

B3013 620   Gutters and Downspouts

	System Description	Freq. (Years)	Crew	Unit	Labor Hours	2012 Bare Costs				Total In-House	Total w/O&P
						Material	Labor	Equipment	Total		
1010	**Replace aluminum gutter, enameled, 5" K type, .027" thick**	40	2 SHEE	L.F.							
	Set up, secure and take down ladder				.010		.37		.37	.55	.66
	Remove gutter				.033		1.17		1.17	1.55	1.92
	Install new gutter				.067	2.58	3.48		6.06	7.25	8.70
	Clean up				.003		.10		.10	.14	.17
	Total				.113	2.58	5.12		7.70	9.49	**11.45**
1020	**Replace aluminum gutter, enameled, 5" K type, .032" thick**	40	2 SHEE	L.F.							
	Set up, secure and take down ladder				.010		.37		.37	.55	.66
	Remove gutter				.033		1.17		1.17	1.55	1.92
	Install new gutter				.067	2.89	3.48		6.37	7.55	9.05
	Clean up				.003		.10		.10	.14	.17
	Total				.113	2.89	5.12		8.01	9.79	**11.80**
1060	**Replace aluminum downspout, 2" x 3", .024" thick**	25	2 SHEE	L.F.							
	Set up, secure and take down ladder				.010		.37		.37	.55	.66
	Remove downspout				.023		.80		.80	1.07	1.32
	Install new downspout				.044	2.05	2.32		4.37	5.20	6.20
	Clean up				.003		.10		.10	.14	.17
	Total				.080	2.05	3.59		5.64	6.96	**8.35**
1070	**Replace aluminum downspout, 3" x 4", .024" thick**	25	2 SHEE	L.F.							
	Set up, secure and take down ladder				.010		.37		.37	.55	.66
	Remove downspout				.023		.80		.80	1.07	1.32
	Install new downspout				.057	2.75	2.98		5.73	6.80	8.15
	Clean up				.003		.10		.10	.14	.17
	Total				.093	2.75	4.25		7	8.56	**10.30**
2010	**Replace galvanized steel gutter, 5" box type, 28 ga.**	40	2 SHEE	L.F.							
	Set up, secure and take down ladder				.010		.37		.37	.55	.66
	Remove gutter				.033		1.17		1.17	1.55	1.92
	Install new gutter				.067	3.89	3.48		7.37	8.65	10.30
	Clean up				.003		.10		.10	.14	.17
	Total				.113	3.89	5.12		9.01	10.89	**13.05**

B3013 620 | **Gutters and Downspouts**

	System Description	Freq. (Years)	Crew	Unit	Labor Hours	Material	Labor	Equipment	Total	Total In-House	Total w/O&P
								2012 Bare Costs			
2020	**Replace galvanized steel gutter, 6" box type, 26 ga.**	40	2 SHEE	L.F.							
	Set up, secure and take down ladder				.010		.37		.37	.55	.66
	Remove gutter				.033		1.17		1.17	1.55	1.92
	Install new gutter				.067	2.88	3.48		6.36	7.55	9.05
	Clean up				.003		.10		.10	.14	.17
	Total				**.113**	**2.88**	**5.12**		**8**	**9.79**	**11.80**
2060	**Replace round corrugated galvanized downspout, 3" diameter**	25	2 SHEE	L.F.							
	Set up, secure and take down ladder				.010		.37		.37	.55	.66
	Remove downspout				.023		.80		.80	1.07	1.32
	Install new downspout				.042	1.84	2.20		4.04	4.80	5.75
	Clean up				.003		.10		.10	.14	.17
	Total				**.078**	**1.84**	**3.47**		**5.31**	**6.56**	**7.90**
2070	**Replace round corrugated galvanized downspout, 4" diameter**	25	2 SHEE	L.F.							
	Set up, secure and take down ladder				.010		.37		.37	.55	.66
	Remove downspout				.023		.80		.80	1.07	1.32
	Install new downspout				.055	2.54	2.88		5.42	6.45	7.70
	Clean up				.003		.10		.10	.14	.17
	Total				**.091**	**2.54**	**4.15**		**6.69**	**8.21**	**9.85**
3020	**Replace vinyl box gutter, 5" wide**	20	1 CARP	L.F.							
	Set up, secure and take down ladder				.010		.37		.37	.55	.66
	Remove gutter				.033		1.17		1.17	1.55	1.92
	Install new gutter				.073	1.38	3.21		4.59	5.80	7
	Clean up				.003		.10		.10	.14	.17
	Total				**.119**	**1.38**	**4.85**		**6.23**	**8.04**	**9.75**
3060	**Replace vinyl downspout, 2" x 3"**	15	1 CARP	L.F.							
	Set up, secure and take down ladder				.010		.37		.37	.55	.66
	Remove downspout				.023		.80		.80	1.07	1.32
	Install new downspout				.038	2.08	1.99		4.07	4.80	5.75
	Clean up				.003		.10		.10	.14	.17
	Total				**.074**	**2.08**	**3.26**		**5.34**	**6.56**	**7.90**

B3013 620   Gutters and Downspouts

System Description	Freq. (Years)	Crew	Unit	Labor Hours	2012 Bare Costs				Total In-House	Total w/O&P
					Material	Labor	Equipment	Total		
4020 Replace 5" copper box gutters, 16 oz.	50	1 SHEE	L.F.							
Set up, secure and take down ladder				.010		.37		.37	.55	.66
Remove gutter				.033		1.17		1.17	1.55	1.92
Install new gutter				.067	11.70	3.48		15.18	17.25	20
Clean up				.003		.10		.10	.14	.17
Total				.113	11.70	5.12		16.82	19.49	22.75
4060 Replace copper downspouts, 2" x 3", 16 oz.	40	1 SHEE	L.F.							
Set up, secure and take down ladder				.010		.37		.37	.55	.66
Remove gutter				.023		.80		.80	1.07	1.32
Install new gutter				.042	8.45	2.20		10.65	12.10	14
Clean up				.003		.10		.10	.14	.17
Total				.078	8.45	3.47		11.92	13.86	16.15

B3023 110 Single Unit Glass Skylight

	System Description	Freq. (Years)	Crew	Unit	Labor Hours	2012 Bare Costs				Total In-House	Total w/O&P
						Material	Labor	Equipment	Total		
1010	**Repair glass skylight glazing**	6	1 CARP	S.F.							
	Set up, secure and take down ladder				.130		5.75		5.75	7.60	9.40
	Remove glazing				.069		2.43		2.43	3.23	3.99
	Install new glazing				.252	18.50	11		29.50	34.50	40.50
	Total				.451	18.50	19.18		37.68	45.33	53.89
1020	**Replace continuous skylight and structure**	40	2 CARP	C.S.F.							
	Set up and secure scaffold				.750		33		33	44	54
	Remove unit skylight				5.202		229		229	305	375
	Inspect / remove flashing				3.152	193	118		311	385	450
	Replace flashing				3.152	193	118		311	385	450
	Install new unit				12.960	2,050	565		2,615	3,000	3,475
	Remove scaffold				.750		33		33	44	54
	Total				25.966	2,436	1,096		3,532	4,163	4,858
1040	**Replace skylight and structure, double glazed, 10 to 20 S.F.**	40	G-3	S.F.							
	Set up, secure and take down ladder				.010		.37		.37	.55	.66
	Remove skylight, plstc domes,flush/curb mtd				.081		3.53		3.53	4.56	5.65
	10 S.F. to 20 S.F., double				.102	25	4.43		29.43	33	38.50
	Total				.193	25	8.33		33.33	38.11	44.81
1080	**Replace skylight and structure, double glazed, 30 to 65 S.F.**	40	G-3	S.F.							
	Set up, secure and take down ladder				.010		.37		.37	.55	.66
	Remove skylight, plstc domes,flush/curb mtd				.081		3.53		3.53	4.56	5.65
	30 S.F. to 65 S.F., double				.069	24	3		27	30.50	35
	Total				.160	24	6.90		30.90	35.61	41.31

B3023 120 Hatches

	System Description	Freq. (Years)	Crew	Unit	Labor Hours	2012 Bare Costs				Total In-House	Total w/O&P
						Material	Labor	Equipment	Total		
1020	**Replace aluminum roof hatch & structure**	40	2 CARP	Ea.							
	Set up, secure and take down ladder				.130		5.75		5.75	7.60	9.40
	Remove roof hatch				1.000		35		35	46.50	57.50
	Install 2'-6" x 3'-0" aluminum hatch				3.200	1,050	140		1,190	1,325	1,525
	Total				4.330	1,050	180.75		1,230.75	1,379.10	1,591.90

B3023 120 Hatches

System Description	Freq. (Years)	Crew	Unit	Labor Hours	2012 Bare Costs				Total In-House	Total w/O&P
					Material	Labor	Equipment	Total		
1120 **Replace galvanized roof hatch & structure**	40	2 CARP	Ea.							
Set up, secure and take down ladder				.130		5.75		5.75	7.60	9.40
Selective demo, therm & moist protect, roof acc, roof hatch, to 10 S.F.				1.000		35		35	46.50	57.50
Install 2'-6" x 3'-0" galvanized roof hatch				3.200	640	140		780	885	1,025
Total				4.330	640	180.75		820.75	939.10	1,091.90

B3023 130 Smoke Hatches

System Description	Freq. (Years)	Crew	Unit	Labor Hours	2012 Bare Costs				Total In-House	Total w/O&P
					Material	Labor	Equipment	Total		
1010 **Replace galvanized smoke hatch single unit 4' x 4'**	40	2 CARP	Ea.							
Set up and secure scaffold				.750		33		33	44	54
Inspect / remove flashing				.032	1.93	1.18		3.11	3.85	4.50
Replace flashing				.032	1.93	1.18		3.11	3.85	4.50
Galvanized steel cover and frame				2.462	1,800	107		1,907	2,125	2,425
Remove scaffold				.750		33		33	44	54
Total				4.025	1,803.86	175.36		1,979.22	2,220.70	2,542
1020 **Replace aluminum smoke hatch single unit, 4' x 8'**	40	2 CARP	Ea.							
Set up and secure scaffold				.750		33		33	44	54
Smoke vent 4' x 8'				4.000		140		140	187	230
Inspect / remove flashing				.756	46.32	28.32		74.64	92.50	108
Replace flashing				.756	46.32	28.32		74.64	92.50	108
4' x 8' aluminum cover and frame				5.246	2,800	229		3,029	3,375	3,875
Remove scaffold				.750		33		33	44	54
Total				12.259	2,892.64	491.64		3,384.28	3,835	4,429

C1013 110 — Concrete Block, Painted

System Description	Freq. (Years)	Crew	Unit	Labor Hours	2012 Bare Costs				Total In-House	Total w/O&P
					Material	Labor	Equipment	Total		
0010 Repair 8" concrete block wall - (2% of walls)	25	1 BRIC	C.S.F.							
Remove block				6.420		228	34	262	335	410
Replace block				11.111	232	452		684	845	1,025
Total				17.531	232	680	34	946	**1,180**	**1,435**
0020 Refinish concrete block wall	4	1 PORD	C.S.F.							
Prepare surface				.250		10		10	12	15
Fill & paint block, brushwork				1.376	21	53		74	91	110
Place and remove mask and drops				.370		14		14	18	23
Total				1.996	21	77		98	**121**	**148**
0040 Replace 8" concrete block wall	75	2 BRIC	C.S.F.							
Set up and secure scaffold				.750		33		33	44	54
Remove block				6.420		228	34	262	335	410
Replace block				11.111	232	452		684	845	1,025
Remove scaffold				.750		33		33	44	54
Total				19.031	232	746	34	1,012	**1,268**	**1,543**

C1013 115 — Glazed CMU Interior Wall Finish

System Description	Freq. (Years)	Crew	Unit	Labor Hours	2012 Bare Costs				Total In-House	Total w/O&P
					Material	Labor	Equipment	Total		
0010 Repair 4" glazed C.M.U. wall - (2% of walls)	25	1 BRIC	C.S.F.							
Remove damaged blocks				5.200		185	27	212	272	335
Install new blocks				15.072	815	615		1,430	1,700	2,000
Total				20.272	815	800	27	1,642	**1,972**	**2,335**
0020 Replace 4" glazed C.M.U. wall	75	2 BRIC	C.S.F.							
Set up and secure scaffold				.750		33		33	44	54
Remove blocks				5.200		185	27	212	272	335
Install new blocks				15.072	815	615		1,430	1,700	2,000
Remove scaffold				.750		33		33	44	54
Total				21.772	815	866	27	1,708	**2,060**	**2,443**

C1013 120 Glass Block

System Description	Freq. (Years)	Crew	Unit	Labor Hours	2012 Bare Costs				Total In-House	Total w/O&P
					Material	Labor	Equipment	Total		
0010										
Repair glass block wall - (2% of walls)	25	1 BRIC	C.S.F.							
Remove damaged glass block				17.829		640		640	845	1,050
Repair / replace blocks				45.217	2,850	1,840		4,690	5,550	6,525
Total				63.046	2,850	2,480		5,330	6,395	**7,575**
0020										
Replace glass block wall	75	2 BRIC	C.S.F.							
Set up and secure scaffold				.750		33		33	44	54
Remove damaged glass block				17.829		640		640	845	1,050
Repair / replace blocks				45.217	2,850	1,840		4,690	5,550	6,525
Remove scaffold				.750		33		33	44	54
Total				64.546	2,850	2,546		5,396	6,483	**7,683**

C1013 125 Stone Veneer

System Description	Freq. (Years)	Crew	Unit	Labor Hours	2012 Bare Costs				Total In-House	Total w/O&P
					Material	Labor	Equipment	Total		
0010										
Repair 4" stone veneer wall - (2% of walls)	25	1 BRIC	C.S.F.							
Remove damaged stone				7.429	53	328		381	485	590
Replace stone				41.600	755	1,695		2,450	3,050	3,700
Total				49.029	808	2,023		2,831	3,535	**4,290**
0020										
Replace 4" stone veneer wall	75	2 BRIC	C.S.F.							
Set up and secure scaffold				.750		33		33	44	54
Remove damaged stone				7.429	53	328		381	485	590
Replace stone				41.600	755	1,695		2,450	3,050	3,700
Remove scaffold				.750		33		33	44	54
Total				50.529	808	2,089		2,897	3,623	**4,398**

C1013 230 Demountable Partitions

	System Description	Freq. (Years)	Crew	Unit	Labor Hours	2012 Bare Costs Material	2012 Bare Costs Labor	2012 Bare Costs Equipment	2012 Bare Costs Total	Total In-House	Total w/O&P
1010	**Remove and reinstall demountable partitions**	5	2 CARP	C.L.F.							
	Remove demountable partitions for reuse				16.000		705		705	940	1,150
	Vinly clad gypsum wall system, material only to replace damaged					1,160			1,160	1,275	1,450
	Install new and reused vinyl clad gypsum in new configuration				34.286		1,510		1,510	2,000	2,500
	18 ga. prefinished 3'-0" x 6'-8" to 4-7/8" deep frame				3.000	483	132		615	710	820
	Reinstall doors				3.200		141		141	188	231
	Cleanup				1.000		44		44	59	72
	Total				57.486	1,643	2,532		4,175	5,172	6,223

C1013 544 Channel Frame Wire Mesh Wall

	System Description	Freq. (Years)	Crew	Unit	Labor Hours	2012 Bare Costs Material	2012 Bare Costs Labor	2012 Bare Costs Equipment	2012 Bare Costs Total	Total In-House	Total w/O&P
0010	**Repair channel frame wire mesh wall - (2% of walls)**	20	1 SSWK	C.S.F.							
	Remove damaged 1-1/2" diamond mesh panel				12.000		429		429	570	705
	Replace with new 1-1/2" diamond mesh panel				2.857	447.50	126.25		573.75	660	765
	Total				14.857	447.50	555.25		1,002.75	1,230	1,470
0020	**Refinish channel frame wire mesh wall**	5	1 PORD	C.S.F.							
	Prepare surface				.370		14		14	18	23
	Scrape surface				1.250		48		48	62	76
	Refinish surface, brushwork, primer + 1 coat				1.538	43	59		102	123	148
	Total				3.158	43	121		164	203	247

C1013 730 Plate Glass Wall - Interior

	System Description	Freq. (Years)	Crew	Unit	Labor Hours	2012 Bare Costs Material	2012 Bare Costs Labor	2012 Bare Costs Equipment	2012 Bare Costs Total	Total In-House	Total w/O&P
0010	**Repair plate glass interior wall - (2% of total)**	25	1 CARP	C.S.F.							
	Remove plate glass & frame				6.933		243		243	325	400
	Repair damaged glass				23.111	6,400	1,065		7,465	8,550	9,850
	Total				30.044	6,400	1,308		7,708	8,875	10,250

C1013 730 Plate Glass Wall - Interior

| | System Description | Freq. (Years) | Crew | Unit | Labor Hours | 2012 Bare Costs | | | | Total In-House | Total w/O&P |
						Material	Labor	Equipment	Total		
0020	**Replace plate glass interior wall**	50	2 CARP	C.S.F.							
	Set up and secure scaffold				.750		33		33	44	54
	Remove plate glass & frame				6.933		243		243	325	400
	Repair damaged glass				23.111	6,400	1,065		7,465	8,550	9,850
	Remove scaffold				.750		33		33	44	54
	Total				31.544	6,400	1,374		7,774	8,963	10,358

C1023 108 Fully Glazed Wooden Doors

	System Description	Freq. (Years)	Crew	Unit	Labor Hours	2012 Bare Costs				Total In-House	Total w/O&P
						Material	Labor	Equipment	Total		
1010	**Replace insulating glass (3% of glass)**	1	1 CARP	S.F.							
	Remove damaged glass				.052		1.82		1.82	2.42	2.99
	Install new insulating glass				.277	28	11.85		39.85	46.50	54
	Total				.329	28	13.67		41.67	48.92	**56.99**
1020	**Repair fully glazed wood door**	10	1 CARP	Ea.							
	Remove lockset				.520		23		23	30.50	37.50
	Replace lockset				1.040	92.50	46		138.50	163	191
	Oil hinges				.065		2.85		2.85	3.78	4.66
	Oil door closer				.065		2.85		2.85	3.78	4.66
	Total				1.689	92.50	74.70		167.20	201.06	**237.82**
1030	**Refinish 3'-0" x 7'-0" fully glazed wood door**	4	1 PORD	Ea.							
	Prepare interior door for painting				.433		16.55		16.55	21.50	26.50
	Paint door, roller + brush, 1 coat				1.333	1.98	51		52.98	68	84
	Total				1.767	1.98	67.55		69.53	89.50	**110.50**
1040	**Replace 3'-0" x 7'-0" fully glazed wood door**	40	1 CARP	Ea.							
	Remove interior door				.520		18.25		18.25	24.50	30
	Remove interior door frame				1.300		57.50		57.50	76	94
	Remove door closer				.167		7.35		7.35	9.75	12.05
	Install new wood door and frame				2.600	712.50	114.50		827	940	1,075
	Reinstall door closer				1.735		76.50		76.50	102	125
	Total				6.322	712.50	274.10		986.60	1,152.25	**1,336.05**

C1023 110 Steel Painted Interior Doors

	System Description	Freq. (Years)	Crew	Unit	Labor Hours	2012 Bare Costs				Total In-House	Total w/O&P
						Material	Labor	Equipment	Total		
1010	**Repair steel painted door**	14	1 CARP	Ea.							
	Remove lockset				.520		23		23	30.50	37.50
	Replace lockset				1.040	92.50	46		138.50	163	191
	Oil hinges				.065		2.85		2.85	3.78	4.66
	Oil door closer				.065		2.85		2.85	3.78	4.66
	Total				1.689	92.50	74.70		167.20	201.06	**237.82**

C1023 110 | **Steel Painted Interior Doors**

System Description	Freq. (Years)	Crew	Unit	Labor Hours	2012 Bare Costs				Total In-House	Total w/O&P
					Material	Labor	Equipment	Total		
1020 Refinish 3'-0" x 7'-0" steel painted door	4	1 PORD	Ea.							
Prepare interior door for painting				.433		16.55		16.55	21.50	26.50
Paint door, roller + brush, 1 coat				.800	4.37	30.50		34.87	44	54.50
Total				1.233	4.37	47.05		51.42	**65.50**	**81**
1030 Replace 3'-0" x 7'-0" steel painted door	60	1 CARP	Ea.							
Remove interior door				.520		18.25		18.25	24.50	30
Remove interior door frame				1.300		57.50		57.50	76	94
Remove door closer				.167		7.35		7.35	9.75	12.05
Install new steel door				1.224	635	54		689	770	880
Install new steel door frame				1.000	148	44		192	221	258
Reinstall door closer				1.735		76.50		76.50	102	125
Total				5.946	783	257.60		1,040.60	**1,203.25**	**1,399.05**
2010 Safety glass repl., (3% of glass)	1	1 CARP	S.F.							
Remove damaged glass				.052		1.82		1.82	2.42	2.99
Install new safety glass				.173	8.25	7.40		15.65	18.75	22.50
Total				.225	8.25	9.22		17.47	**21.17**	**25.49**
2030 Refinish, 3'-0" x 7'-0" steel w/ safety glass door	4	1 PORD	Ea.							
Prepare interior door for painting				.433		16.55		16.55	21.50	26.50
Paint door, roller + brush, 1 coat				.800	4.37	30.50		34.87	44	54.50
Total				1.233	4.37	47.05		51.42	**65.50**	**81**
2040 Replace 3'-0" x 7'-0" steel door w/ vision lite, & frame	60	1 CARP	Ea.							
Remove interior door				.520		18.25		18.25	24.50	30
Remove interior door frame				1.300		57.50		57.50	76	94
Remove door closer				.167		7.35		7.35	9.75	12.05
Install new steel door				1.224	635	54		689	770	880
Install new steel door frame				1.301	148	57.50		205.50	239	279
Reinstall door closer				1.735		76.50		76.50	102	125
Vision lite					93			93	102	116
Total				6.246	876	271.10		1,147.10	**1,323.25**	**1,536.05**

C1023 110 | **Steel Painted Interior Doors**

System Description	Freq. (Years)	Crew	Unit	Labor Hours	2012 Bare Costs				Total In-House	Total w/O&P
					Material	Labor	Equipment	Total		
3010 Repair 3'-0" x 7'-0" steel sliding door	14	1 CARP	Ea.							
Oil door closer				.065		2.85		2.85	3.78	4.66
Oil / inspect track / glide wheels				.065		2.85		2.85	3.78	4.66
Remove door track / glide wheels (25% of total / 14 years)				.220		9.75		9.75	12.90	15.90
Install new door track / glide wheels (25% of total / 14 years)				.440	13	19.38		32.38	40	48
Total				.789	13	34.83		47.83	60.46	73.22
3020 Refinish 3'-0" x 7'-0" steel sliding door	4	1 PORD	Ea.							
Prepare interior door for painting				.433		16.55		16.55	21.50	26.50
Paint door, roller + brush, 1 coat				.800	4.37	30.50		34.87	44	54.50
Total				1.233	4.37	47.05		51.42	65.50	81
3030 Replace 3'-0" x 7'-0" steel sliding door & frame	60	1 CARP	Ea.							
Remove interior door				.520		18.25		18.25	24.50	30
Remove interior door frame				1.300		57.50		57.50	76	94
Remove door closer				.167		7.35		7.35	9.75	12.05
Install new steel door				1.224	635	54		689	770	880
Install new steel sliding door frame				3.200	225	160	12.15	397.15	505	590
Install new door track / glide wheels				1.760	52	77.50		129.50	160	192
Install door closer				1.735		76.50		76.50	102	125
Total				9.905	912	451.10	12.15	1,375.25	1,647.25	1,923.05
4010 Replace wire glass (3% of glass)	1	1 CARP	S.F.							
Remove damaged glass				.052		1.82		1.82	2.42	2.99
Install new wire glass				.179	24.36	7.66		32.02	36.50	43
Total				.231	24.36	9.48		33.84	38.92	45.99
4030 Refinish 3'-0" x 7'-0" steel half glass door	4	1 PORD	Ea.							
Prepare interior door for painting				.433		16.55		16.55	21.50	26.50
Paint door, roller + brush, 1 coat				.800	4.37	30.50		34.87	44	54.50
Total				1.233	4.37	47.05		51.42	65.50	81

C1023 110 Steel Painted Interior Doors

System Description	Freq. (Years)	Crew	Unit	Labor Hours	2012 Bare Costs				Total In-House	Total w/O&P
					Material	Labor	Equipment	Total		
4040										
Replace 3'-0" x 7'-0" steel half glass door & frame	60	1 CARP	Ea.							
Remove interior door				.520		18.25		18.25	24.50	30
Remove door closer				.167		7.35		7.35	9.75	12.05
Remove interior door frame				1.300		57.50		57.50	76	94
Install new steel door frame				1.301	148	57.50		205.50	239	279
Install new half glass interior door				1.224	615	54		669	750	855
Install new safety glass				1.040	49.50	44.40		93.90	113	134
Reinstall door closer				1.735		76.50		76.50	102	125
Total				7.287	812.50	315.50		1,128	1,314.25	1,529.05

C1023 111 Steel Unpainted Interior Doors

System Description	Freq. (Years)	Crew	Unit	Labor Hours	2012 Bare Costs				Total In-House	Total w/O&P
					Material	Labor	Equipment	Total		
1010										
Repair steel unpainted door	14	1 CARP	Ea.							
Remove lockset				.520		23		23	30.50	37.50
Replace lockset				1.040	92.50	46		138.50	163	191
Oil hinges				.065		2.85		2.85	3.78	4.66
Oil door closer				.065		2.85		2.85	3.78	4.66
Total				1.689	92.50	74.70		167.20	201.06	237.82
1020										
Replace 3'-0" x 7'-0" steel unpainted door & frame	60	1 CARP	Ea.							
Remove interior door				.520		18.25		18.25	24.50	30
Remove interior door frame				1.300		57.50		57.50	76	94
Remove door closer				.167		7.35		7.35	9.75	12.05
Install new steel door				1.224	635	54		689	770	880
Install new steel door frame				1.000	148	44		192	221	258
Reinstall door closer				1.735		76.50		76.50	102	125
Total				5.946	783	257.60		1,040.60	1,203.25	1,399.05
2010										
Replace safety glass (3% of glass)	1	1 CARP	S.F.							
Remove damaged glass				.052		1.82		1.82	2.42	2.99
Install new safety glass				.173	8.25	7.40		15.65	18.75	22.50
Total				.225	8.25	9.22		17.47	21.17	25.49

C1023 111 | Steel Unpainted Interior Doors

	System Description	Freq. (Years)	Crew	Unit	Labor Hours	2012 Bare Costs				Total In-House	Total w/O&P
						Material	Labor	Equipment	Total		
2030	**Repl. 3'-0" x 7'-0" st. half glass unpainted dr. & fr.**	60	1 CARP	Ea.							
	Remove interior door				.520		18.25		18.25	24.50	30
	Remove interior door frame				1.300		57.50		57.50	76	94
	Remove door closer				.167		7.35		7.35	9.75	12.05
	Install new half glass interior door				1.224	615	54		669	750	855
	Install new safety glass				1.560	74.25	66.60		140.85	169	200
	Install new steel door frame				1.301	148	57.50		205.50	239	279
	Reinstall door closer				1.735		76.50		76.50	102	125
	Total				7.807	837.25	337.70		1,174.95	1,370.25	1,595.05
3010	**Repair 3'-0" x 7'-0" steel sliding unpainted door**	14	1 CARP	Ea.							
	Oil door closer				.065		2.85		2.85	3.78	4.66
	Oil / inspect track / glide wheels				.065		2.85		2.85	3.78	4.66
	Remove door track / glide wheels (25% of total / 14 years)				.220		9.75		9.75	12.90	15.90
	Install new door track / glide wheels (25% of total / 14 years)				.440	13	19.38		32.38	40	48
	Total				.789	13	34.83		47.83	60.46	73.22
3020	**Replace 3'-0" x 7'-0" steel sliding unpainted interior door**	60	1 CARP	Ea.							
	Remove interior door				.520		18.25		18.25	24.50	30
	Remove interior door frame				1.300		57.50		57.50	76	94
	Remove door closer				.167		7.35		7.35	9.75	12.05
	Install new steel door				1.224	635	54		689	770	880
	Install new steel sliding door frame				3.200	225	160	12.15	397.15	505	590
	Install new door track / glide wheels				1.760	52	77.50		129.50	160	192
	Reinstall door closer				1.735		76.50		76.50	102	125
	Total				9.905	912	451.10	12.15	1,375.25	1,647.25	1,923.05
4010	**Replace wire glass (3% of glass)**	1	1 CARP	S.F.							
	Remove damaged glass				.052		1.82		1.82	2.42	2.99
	Install new wire glass				.179	24.36	7.66		32.02	36.50	43
	Total				.231	24.36	9.48		33.84	38.92	45.99

123

C1023 112 Bi-Fold Interior Doors

System Description	Freq. (Years)	Crew	Unit	Labor Hours	2012 Bare Costs				Total In-House	Total w/O&P
					Material	Labor	Equipment	Total		
2010 Repair 2'-6" x 6'-8" bi-fold louvered door	15	1 CARP	Ea.							
Remove interior door				.520		18.25		18.25	24.50	30
Remove damaged stile				.078		3.45		3.45	4.59	5.65
Remove damaged slat				.039		1.70		1.70	2.26	2.80
Install new slat				.077	1.02	3.40		4.42	5.65	6.85
Install new stile				.157	2.40	6.93		9.33	11.80	14.35
Reinstall door				.667		29.50		29.50	39	48
Oil / lubricate door				.065		2.85		2.85	3.78	4.66
Total				1.602	3.42	66.08		69.50	**91.58**	**112.31**
2020 Refinish 2'-6" x 6'-8" louvered door	8	1 PORD	Ea.							
Prepare door for finish				.967		37		37	47.50	59
Paint door, roller + brush, 1 coat				1.143	4.43	43.50		47.93	61	75.50
Total				2.110	4.43	80.50		84.93	**108.50**	**134.50**
2040 Replace 2'-6" x 6'-8" wd. louver bi-fold dr. and fr.	24	1 CARP	Ea.							
Remove doors				.520		18.25		18.25	24.50	30
Install new door				1.600	278	70.50		348.50	400	465
Install new interior door frame				.998	107.10	44.10		151.20	176	206
Total				3.118	385.10	132.85		517.95	**600.50**	**701**

C1023 114 Aluminum Interior Doors

System Description	Freq. (Years)	Crew	Unit	Labor Hours	2012 Bare Costs				Total In-House	Total w/O&P
					Material	Labor	Equipment	Total		
1010 Repair aluminum door	12	1 CARP	Ea.							
Remove lockset				.520		23		23	30.50	37.50
Replace lockset				1.040	92.50	46		138.50	163	191
Oil hinges				.065		2.85		2.85	3.78	4.66
Oil door closer				.065		2.85		2.85	3.78	4.66
Total				1.689	92.50	74.70		167.20	**201.06**	**237.82**

C1023 114 | Aluminum Interior Doors

	System Description	Freq. (Years)	Crew	Unit	Labor Hours	Material	Labor	Equipment	Total	Total In-House	Total w/O&P
							2012 Bare Costs				
1020	**Replace 3'-0" x 7'-0" aluminum door & frame**	50	1 CARP	Ea.							
	Remove interior door				.520		18.25		18.25	24.50	30
	Remove interior door frame				1.300		57.50		57.50	76	94
	Remove door closer				.167		7.35		7.35	9.75	12.05
	Install new aluminum door				1.224	1,325	54		1,379	1,525	1,750
	Install new aluminum door frame				2.971	425	147		572	695	805
	Reinstall door closer				1.735		76.50		76.50	102	125
	Total				7.917	1,750	360.60		2,110.60	2,432.25	2,816.05
2010	**Replace safety glass (3% of glass)**	1	1 CARP	S.F.							
	Remove damaged glass				.052		1.82		1.82	2.42	2.99
	Install new safety glass				.173	8.25	7.40		15.65	18.75	22.50
	Total				.225	8.25	9.22		17.47	21.17	25.49
2030	**Replace 3'-0" x 7'-0" alum. dr., fr. & vision lite**	50	1 CARP	Ea.							
	Remove interior door				.520		18.25		18.25	24.50	30
	Remove interior door frame				1.300		57.50		57.50	76	94
	Remove door closer				.167		7.35		7.35	9.75	12.05
	Install new aluminum door				1.224	1,325	54		1,379	1,525	1,750
	Install new aluminum door frame				2.971	425	147		572	695	805
	Reinstall door closer				1.735		76.50		76.50	102	125
	Vision lite					93			93	102	116
	Total				7.917	1,843	360.60		2,203.60	2,534.25	2,932.05
3010	**Replace insulating glass (3% of glass)**	1	1 CARP	S.F.							
	Remove damaged glass				.052		1.82		1.82	2.42	2.99
	Install new insulating glass				.277	28	11.85		39.85	46.50	54
	Total				.329	28	13.67		41.67	48.92	56.99
3020	**Repair 3'-0" x 7'-0" aluminum sliding door**	14	1 CARP	Ea.							
	Oil door closer				.065		2.85		2.85	3.78	4.66
	Oil / inspect track / glide wheels				.065		2.85		2.85	3.78	4.66
	Remove door track / glide wheels (25% of total / 14 years)				.220		9.75		9.75	12.90	15.90
	Install new door track / glide wheels (25% of total / 14 years)				.440	13	19.38		32.38	40	48
	Total				.789	13	34.83		47.83	60.46	73.22

C1023 114 Aluminum Interior Doors

	System Description	Freq. (Years)	Crew	Unit	Labor Hours	2012 Bare Costs				Total In-House	Total w/O&P
						Material	Labor	Equipment	Total		
3030	**Replace 3'-0" x 7'-0" aluminum sliding door**	50	1 CARP	Ea.							
	Remove interior door				.520		18.25		18.25	24.50	30
	Remove interior door frame				1.300		57.50		57.50	76	94
	Remove door closer				.167		7.35		7.35	9.75	12.05
	Install new aluminum door				1.224	1,325	54		1,379	1,525	1,750
	Install new aluminum door frame				2.971	425	147		572	695	805
	Install new door track / glide wheels				1.760	52	77.50		129.50	160	192
	Install door closer				1.735		76.50		76.50	102	125
	Total				9.677	1,802	438.10		2,240.10	2,592.25	3,008.05

C1023 116 Fully Glazed Aluminum Doors

	System Description	Freq. (Years)	Crew	Unit	Labor Hours	2012 Bare Costs				Total In-House	Total w/O&P
						Material	Labor	Equipment	Total		
1010	**Replace insulating glass (3% of glass)**	1	1 CARP	S.F.							
	Remove damaged glass				.052		1.82		1.82	2.42	2.99
	Install new insulating glass				.277	28	11.85		39.85	46.50	54
	Total				.329	28	13.67		41.67	48.92	56.99
1020	**Repair 3'-0" x 7'-0" fully glazed aluminum door**	12	1 CARP	Ea.							
	Remove lockset				.520		23		23	30.50	37.50
	Replace lockset				1.040	92.50	46		138.50	163	191
	Oil hinges				.065		2.85		2.85	3.78	4.66
	Oil door closer				.065		2.85		2.85	3.78	4.66
	Total				1.689	92.50	74.70		167.20	201.06	237.82
1030	**Replace 3'-0" x 7'-0" fully glazed aluminum door**	50	1 CARP	Ea.							
	Remove interior door				.520		18.25		18.25	24.50	30
	Remove interior door frame				1.300		57.50		57.50	76	94
	Remove door closer				.167		7.35		7.35	9.75	12.05
	Install new aluminum door and frame				10.458	750	515		1,265	1,625	1,900
	Install new safety glass				3.640	173.25	155.40		328.65	395	470
	Reinstall door closer				1.735		76.50		76.50	102	125
	Total				17.819	923.25	830		1,753.25	2,232.25	2,631.05

C1023 120   Hollow Core Interior Doors

System Description	Freq. (Years)	Crew	Unit	Labor Hours	2012 Bare Costs				Total In-House	Total w/O&P
					Material	Labor	Equipment	Total		
1010 Repair hollow core wood door	7	1 CARP	Ea.							
Remove lockset				.520		23		23	30.50	37.50
Replace lockset				1.040	92.50	46		138.50	163	191
Oil hinges				.065		2.85		2.85	3.78	4.66
Oil door closer				.065		2.85		2.85	3.78	4.66
Total				1.689	92.50	74.70		167.20	**201.06**	**237.82**
1020 Refinish 3'-0" x 7'-0" hollow core wood door	4	1 PORD	Ea.							
Prepare interior door for painting				.433		16.55		16.55	21.50	26.50
Paint door, roller + brush, 1 coat				.533	4.43	20.50		24.93	31	38
Total				.967	4.43	37.05		41.48	**52.50**	**64.50**
1030 Replace 3'-0" x 7'-0" hollow core wood door	30	1 CARP	Ea.							
Remove interior door				.520		18.25		18.25	24.50	30
Remove interior door frame				1.300		57.50		57.50	76	94
Install new interior wood door and frame				.941	155	41.50		196.50	226	262
Total				2.761	155	117.25		272.25	**326.50**	**386**

C1023 121   Solid Core Interior Doors

System Description	Freq. (Years)	Crew	Unit	Labor Hours	2012 Bare Costs				Total In-House	Total w/O&P
					Material	Labor	Equipment	Total		
1010 Repair solid core wood door	11	1 CARP	Ea.							
Remove lockset				.520		23		23	30.50	37.50
Replace lockset				1.040	92.50	46		138.50	163	191
Oil hinges				.065		2.85		2.85	3.78	4.66
Oil door closer				.065		2.85		2.85	3.78	4.66
Total				1.689	92.50	74.70		167.20	**201.06**	**237.82**
1020 Refinish 3'-0" x 7'-0" solid core wood door	4	1 PORD	Ea.							
Prepare interior door for painting				.433		16.55		16.55	21.50	26.50
Paint door, roller + brush, 1 coat				.533	4.43	20.50		24.93	31	38
Total				.967	4.43	37.05		41.48	**52.50**	**64.50**

C1023 121 | Solid Core Interior Doors

System Description	Freq. (Years)	Crew	Unit	Labor Hours	2012 Bare Costs				Total In-House	Total w/O&P
					Material	Labor	Equipment	Total		
1030 Replace 3'-0" x 7'-0" solid core wood door	40	1 CARP	Ea.							
Remove interior door				.520		18.25		18.25	24.50	30
Remove interior door frame				.650		28.60		28.60	38.50	47
Install new interior wood door & frame				.941	305	41.50		346.50	390	450
Total				2.111	305	88.35		393.35	453	527
2010 Repair solid core sliding wood door	14	1 CARP	Ea.							
Oil door closer				.065		2.85		2.85	3.78	4.66
Oil / inspect track / glide wheels				.065		2.85		2.85	3.78	4.66
Remove door track / glide wheels (25% of total / 14 years)				.220		9.75		9.75	12.90	15.90
Install new door track / glide wheels (25% of total / 14 years)				.440	13	19.38		32.38	40	48
Total				.789	13	34.83		47.83	60.46	73.22
2030 Replace 3'-0" x 7'-0" solid core sliding wood door	40	1 CARP	Ea.							
Remove interior door				.520		18.25		18.25	24.50	30
Remove interior door frame				.650		28.60		28.60	38.50	47
Remove door closer				.167		7.35		7.35	9.75	12.05
Install new interior wood door and frame				.941	305	41.50		346.50	390	450
Install new door track / glide wheels				1.760	52	77.50		129.50	160	192
Reinstall door closer				1.735		76.50		76.50	102	125
Total				5.773	357	249.70		606.70	724.75	856.05
3040 Replace 3'-0" x 7'-0" solid core, w/ safety glass dr.	40	1 CARP	Ea.							
Remove interior door				.520		18.25		18.25	24.50	30
Remove interior door frame				.650		28.60		28.60	38.50	47
Install new interior wood door and frame				.941	305	41.50		346.50	390	450
Install new safety glass lite					76.50			76.50	84	95.50
Total				2.111	381.50	88.35		469.85	537	622.50

C1023 129 Interior Gates

	Freq. (Years)	Crew	Unit	Labor Hours	2012 Bare Costs				Total In-House	Total w/O&P
System Description					Material	Labor	Equipment	Total		
1030 Prepare and refinish interior metal gate	5	1 PORD	Ea.							
Lay drop cloth				.090		3.45		3.45	4.40	5.50
Prepare / brush surface				.125		4.86		4.86	6.10	7.55
Paint gate, brushwork, primer + 1 coat				.167	1.26	6.30		7.56	9.70	11.65
Remove drop cloth				.090		3.45		3.45	4.40	5.50
Total				.471	1.26	18.06		19.32	24.60	30.20

C1023 324 Hinges, Brass

	Freq. (Years)	Crew	Unit	Labor Hours	2012 Bare Costs				Total In-House	Total w/O&P
System Description					Material	Labor	Equipment	Total		
0010 Replace 1 1/2 pair brass hinges	60	1 CARP	Ea.							
Remove door				.650		23		23	30.50	37.50
Remove hinges				.500		22.05		22.05	29.50	36
Replace hinges				.500		22.05		22.05	29.50	36
Hinges, 1 1/2 pair					187.50			187.50	207	234
Install door				1.224		54		54	71.50	88.50
Total				2.875	187.50	121.10		308.60	368	432

C1023 325 Lockset, Brass

	Freq. (Years)	Crew	Unit	Labor Hours	2012 Bare Costs				Total In-House	Total w/O&P
System Description					Material	Labor	Equipment	Total		
0010 Replace brass lockset	30	1 CARP	Ea.							
Remove lockset				.400		17.65		17.65	23.50	29
Install lockset				1.156	220	51		271	310	360
Total				1.556	220	68.65		288.65	333.50	389

C1023 326 | Door Closer, Brass

System Description	Freq. (Years)	Crew	Unit	Labor Hours	2012 Bare Costs				Total In-House	Total w/O&P
					Material	Labor	Equipment	Total		
0010 Replace brass closer	15	1 CARP	Ea.							
Remove door closer				.167		7.35		7.35	9.75	12.05
Install new door closer				1.735	184	76.50		260.50	305	355
Total				1.902	184	83.85		267.85	314.75	367.05

C1023 327 | Deadbolt, Brass

System Description	Freq. (Years)	Crew	Unit	Labor Hours	2012 Bare Costs				Total In-House	Total w/O&P
					Material	Labor	Equipment	Total		
0010 Replace brass deadbolt	20	1 CARP	Ea.							
Remove deadbolt				.578		25.50		25.50	34	42
Replace deadbolt				1.156	275	51		326	370	425
Total				1.733	275	76.50		351.50	404	467

C1023 328 | Weatherstripping, Brass

System Description	Freq. (Years)	Crew	Unit	Labor Hours	2012 Bare Costs				Total In-House	Total w/O&P
					Material	Labor	Equipment	Total		
0010 Replace brass weatherstripping	20	1 CARP	Ea.							
Remove weatherstripping				.015		.65		.65	.86	1.06
Install new weatherstripping				3.478	38.50	153		191.50	246	299
Total				3.493	38.50	153.65		192.15	246.86	300.06

C1023 329 | Panic Bar

System Description	Freq. (Years)	Crew	Unit	Labor Hours	2012 Bare Costs				Total In-House	Total w/O&P
					Material	Labor	Equipment	Total		
0010 Replace panic bar	25	1 CARP	Ea.							
Remove panic bar				1.040		46		46	61	75
Install panic bar				2.080	735	91.50		826.50	930	1,075
Total				3.120	735	137.50		872.50	991	1,150

C1033 110 — Toilet Partitions

System Description	Freq. (Years)	Crew	Unit	Labor Hours	Material	Labor	Equipment	Total	Total In-House	Total w/O&P
1010 Replace toilet partitions, laminate clad-overhead braced, per stall	20	2 CARP	Ea.							
Remove overhead braced laminate clad partitions				1.333		59		59	78	96.50
Install overhead braced laminate clad partitions				3.478	750	153		903	1,025	1,200
Cleanup				.500		22		22	29.50	36
Total				5.312	750	234		984	1,132.50	1,332.50
1020 Replace toilet partitions, painted metal-overhead braced, per stall	20	2 CARP	Ea.							
Remove overhead braced painted metal partitions				1.333		59		59	78	96.50
Install overhead braced painted metal partitions				3.478	385	153		538	625	730
Cleanup				.500		22		22	29.50	36
Total				5.312	385	234		619	732.50	862.50
1030 Replace toilet partitions, porcelain enamel-overhead braced, per stall	20	2 CARP	Ea.							
Remove overhead braced porcelain enamel partitions				1.333		59		59	78	96.50
Install overhead braced porcelain enamel partitions				3.478	515	153		668	770	895
Cleanup				.500		22		22	29.50	36
Total				5.312	515	234		749	877.50	1,027.50
1040 Replace toilet partitions, phenolic-overhead braced, per stall	20	2 CARP	Ea.							
Remove overhead braced porcelain enamel partitions				1.333		59		59	78	96.50
Install plastic overhead braced partition				3.478	750	153		903	1,025	1,200
Cleanup				.500		22		22	29.50	36
Total				5.312	750	234		984	1,132.50	1,332.50
1050 Replace toilet partitions, stainless steel-overhead braced, per stall	30	2 CARP	Ea.							
Remove overhead braced porcelain enamel partitions				1.333		59		59	78	96.50
Stainless steel				3.478	1,025	153		1,178	1,325	1,525
Cleanup				.500		22		22	29.50	36
Total				5.312	1,025	234		1,259	1,432.50	1,657.50
1060 Replace toilet partitions, stainless steel, ceiling hung, per stall	30	2 CARP	Ea.							
Remove overhead braced porcelain enamel partitions				1.333		59		59	78	96.50
Stainless steel				4.000	945	176		1,121	1,275	1,475
Cleanup				.500		22		22	29.50	36
Total				5.833	945	257		1,202	1,382.50	1,607.50

C10 INTERIOR CONSTRUCTION | C1033 | Fittings

C1033 110 Toilet Partitions

	System Description	Freq. (Years)	Crew	Unit	Labor Hours	2012 Bare Costs				Total In-House	Total w/O&P
						Material	Labor	Equipment	Total		
2020	Replace urinal screen, stainless steel										
	Urinal Screen, remove	30	2 CARP	Ea.	1.000		35		35	46.50	57.50
	Stainless steel				2.000	580	88		668	755	870
	Cleanup				.500		22		22	29.50	36
	Total				3.500	580	145		725	831	963.50
3010	Replace shower stall, porcelain enamel, per stall										
	Shower partitons, cabinet or stall, incl. base and door	30	2 SHEE	Ea.	2.000		70		70	93.50	115
	With door, fiberglass				3.556	745	185		930	1,050	1,225
	Cleanup				.500		22		22	29.50	36
	Total				6.056	745	277		1,022	1,173	1,376

C1033 210 Metal Lockers

	System Description	Freq. (Years)	Crew	Unit	Labor Hours	2012 Bare Costs				Total In-House	Total w/O&P
						Material	Labor	Equipment	Total		
1010	Replace metal lockers, single tier										
	Remove lockers	20	1 SHEE	Ea.	.533		18.70		18.70	25	30.50
	Install 12" x 18" x 72" single enameled locker				.400	255	21		276	305	350
	Cleanup				.500		22		22	29.50	36
	Total				1.433	255	61.70		316.70	359.50	416.50

C20 STAIRS | C2013 | Stair Construction

C2013 110 Concrete Steps

	System Description	Freq. (Years)	Crew	Unit	Labor Hours	2012 Bare Costs				Total In-House	Total w/O&P
						Material	Labor	Equipment	Total		
0010	**Repair concrete steps**	15	1 CEFI	S.F.							
	Repair spalls in steps				.104	10.90	4.40		15.30	17.55	20.50
	Total				.104	10.90	4.40		15.30	**17.55**	**20.50**
0020	**Replace concrete steps**	100	2 CEFI	S.F.							
	Remove concrete				.520		18.45	2.72	21.17	27.50	33.50
	Install new concrete steps				.520	4.35	22.50	.30	27.15	35	43
	Total				1.040	4.35	40.95	3.02	48.32	**62.50**	**76.50**

C2013 115 Masonry Steps, Painted

	System Description	Freq. (Years)	Crew	Unit	Labor Hours	2012 Bare Costs				Total In-House	Total w/O&P
						Material	Labor	Equipment	Total		
0010	**Repair masonry steps, painted**	20	1 BRIC	S.F.							
	Remove damaged masonry				.083		2.92		2.92	3.88	4.79
	Replace with new masonry				.232	3.45	9.25		12.70	15.80	19.20
	Refinish surface				.014	.21	.53		.74	.91	1.10
	Total				.329	3.66	12.70		16.36	**20.59**	**25.09**
0040	**Replace masonry steps, painted**	50	2 BRIC	S.F.							
	Remove masonry steps				4.000		140		140	187	230
	Clean work area				.015		.54	.13	.67	.85	1.02
	Install new masonry steps				.891	81.50	36		117.50	137	160
	Total				4.907	81.50	176.54	.13	258.17	**324.85**	**391.02**

C2013 130 Metal Steps

	System Description	Freq. (Years)	Crew	Unit	Labor Hours	2012 Bare Costs				Total In-House	Total w/O&P
						Material	Labor	Equipment	Total		
0010	**Repair metal steps**	15	1 SSWK	S.F.							
	Remove damaged tread				.347		17.10		17.10	26.50	32
	Replace with cast iron tread, 1/2" thick				.229	46.20	11.22		57.42	68.50	78.50
	Total				.575	46.20	28.32		74.52	**95**	**110.50**

C2013 130 Metal Steps

System Description	Freq. (Years)	Crew	Unit	Labor Hours	2012 Bare Costs Material	Labor	Equipment	Total	Total In-House	Total w/O&P
0030										
Refinish metal steps	9	1 PORD	S.F.							
Prepare steps for painting				.026		.99		.99	1.28	1.59
Wipe surface				.001		.04		.04	.06	.07
Refinish surface, roller + brush, 1 coat				.025	.36	.96		1.32	1.63	1.98
Total				.052	.36	1.99		2.35	**2.97**	**3.64**
0040										
Replace metal steps	50	2 SSWK	S.F.							
Remove steps				.264		9.24		9.24	12.40	15.20
Install pre-erected steel steps				.163	110	8.15	.62	118.77	134	153
Prepare steps for painting				.026		.99		.99	1.28	1.59
Wipe surface				.001		.04		.04	.06	.07
Refinish surface				.025	.36	.96		1.32	1.63	1.98
Total				.479	110.36	19.38	.62	130.36	**149.37**	**171.84**

C2013 435 Metal Interior Stair Railing

System Description	Freq. (Years)	Crew	Unit	Labor Hours	2012 Bare Costs Material	Labor	Equipment	Total	Total In-House	Total w/O&P
0030										
Refinish metal stair railing	7	1 PORD	S.F.							
Prepare surface				.019		.73		.73	.94	1.17
Refinish surface, roller + brush, 1 coat				.015	.11	.59		.70	.88	1.08
Total				.035	.11	1.32		1.43	**1.82**	**2.25**
0040										
Replace metal stair railing	45	2 SSWK	L.F.							
Remove railing				.098		4.87	.37	5.24	7.90	9.45
Install new railing				.195	19.75	9.75	.74	30.24	37.50	43.50
Total				.293	19.75	14.62	1.11	35.48	**45.40**	**52.95**

C2013 437 Iron Interior Stair Railing

System Description	Freq. (Years)	Crew	Unit	Labor Hours	2012 Bare Costs Material	Labor	Equipment	Total	Total In-House	Total w/O&P
0030										
Refinish wrought iron stair railing	7	1 PORD	L.F.							
Prepare surface				.019		.73		.73	.94	1.17
Refinish surface, roller + brush, 1 coat				.015	.11	.59		.70	.88	1.08
Total				.035	.11	1.32		1.43	**1.82**	**2.25**

C2013 437 | Iron Interior Stair Railing

System Description	Freq. (Years)	Crew	Unit	Labor Hours	2012 Bare Costs				Total In-House	Total w/O&P
					Material	Labor	Equipment	Total		
0040 **Replace wrought iron stair railing**										
Remove railing	45	2 SSWK	L.F.	.087		3.04		3.04	4.04	4.99
Install new railing				1.300	25	64		89	127	150
Total				1.387	25	67.04		92.04	**131.04**	**154.99**

C2013 440 | Wood Steps

System Description	Freq. (Years)	Crew	Unit	Labor Hours	2012 Bare Costs				Total In-House	Total w/O&P
					Material	Labor	Equipment	Total		
0030 **Refinish wood steps**										
Prepare surface	3	1 PORD	S.F.	.026		.99		.99	1.28	1.59
Refinish surface, roller + brush, 1 coat				.026	.07	.99		1.06	1.36	1.68
Total				.052	.07	1.98		2.05	**2.64**	**3.27**
0040 **Replace wood steps**										
Remove steps	40	1 CARP	S.F.	.172		6.02		6.02	8.10	9.90
Replace steps				.325	75	14.35		89.35	102	117
Total				.497	75	20.37		95.37	**110.10**	**126.90**

C2013 445 | Wood Interior Stair Railing

System Description	Freq. (Years)	Crew	Unit	Labor Hours	2012 Bare Costs				Total In-House	Total w/O&P
					Material	Labor	Equipment	Total		
0030 **Refinish wood stair railing**										
Prepare railings for refinishing	7	1 PORD	L.F.	.026		.99		.99	1.28	1.59
Refinish surface, roller + brush, 1 coat				.026	.07	.99		1.06	1.36	1.68
Total				.052	.07	1.98		2.05	**2.64**	**3.27**
0040 **Replace wood stair railing**										
Remove railing	40	1 CARP	L.F.	.087		3.04		3.04	4.04	4.99
Replace railing				.130	2.50	5.75		8.25	10.35	12.55
Total				.217	2.50	8.79		11.29	**14.39**	**17.54**

C2023 110   Carpeted Steps

System Description	Freq. (Years)	Crew	Unit	Labor Hours	2012 Bare Costs				Total In-House	Total w/O&P
					Material	Labor	Equipment	Total		
0020										
Replace carpeted steps	8	2 TILF	S.F.							
Remove old carpet				.010		.37		.37	.49	.60
Install new carpet				.069	14.03	2.81		16.84	19	22
Additional labor				.229	28.05	9.34		37.39	42.50	49.50
Total				.308	42.08	12.52		54.60	61.99	72.10

C2023 120   Rubber Steps

System Description	Freq. (Years)	Crew	Unit	Labor Hours	2012 Bare Costs				Total In-House	Total w/O&P
					Material	Labor	Equipment	Total		
0020										
Replace rubber steps	18	2 TILF	L.F.							
Remove rubber covering				.015		.52		.52	.69	.86
Prepare floor for installation				.063		2.59		2.59	3.26	4.06
Install new rubber tread				.090	13.50	3.69		17.19	19.50	22.50
Install new rubber riser				.042	6	1.70		7.70	8.75	10.15
Total				.210	19.50	8.50		28	32.20	37.57

C2023 130   Terrazzo Steps

System Description	Freq. (Years)	Crew	Unit	Labor Hours	2012 Bare Costs				Total In-House	Total w/O&P
					Material	Labor	Equipment	Total		
0020										
Replace terrazzo steps	50	2 MSTZ	S.F.							
Remove old terrazzo tile				.052		1.83		1.83	2.43	2.99
Clean area				.020		.88		.88	1.17	1.44
Replace with new tread				.743	2.83	27.50	12.25	42.58	50	60
Total				.815	2.83	30.21	12.25	45.29	53.60	64.43

C3013 106 Vinyl Wall Covering

System Description	Freq. (Years)	Crew	Unit	Labor Hours	2012 Bare Costs Material	Labor	Equipment	Total	Total In-House	Total w/O&P
0010 Repair med. wt. vinyl wall covering - (2% of walls)	1	1 PORD	C.S.F.							
Remove damaged vinyl wall covering				1.156		45		45	57	71
Install vinyl wall covering				2.391	90	92		182	217	260
Total				3.547	90	137		227	**274**	**331**
0020 Replace medium weight vinyl wall covering	15	1 PORD	C.S.F.							
Set up and secure scaffold				.750		33		33	44	54
Remove vinyl wall covering				1.156		45		45	57	71
Install vinyl wall covering				2.391	90	92		182	217	260
Remove scaffold				.750		33		33	44	54
Total				5.047	90	203		293	**362**	**439**

C3013 202 Wallpaper

System Description	Freq. (Years)	Crew	Unit	Labor Hours	2012 Bare Costs Material	Labor	Equipment	Total	Total In-House	Total w/O&P
0010 Repair wallpaper - (2% of walls)	8	1 PORD	S.Y.							
Remove damaged wallpaper				.104		4.05		4.05	5.15	6.40
Repair / replace wallpaper				.175	8.73	6.75		15.48	18.25	21.50
Total				.279	8.73	10.80		19.53	**23.40**	**27.90**
0020 Replace wallpaper	20	1 PORD	S.Y.							
Set up and secure scaffold				.130		5.75		5.75	7.60	9.40
Remove damaged wallpaper				.104		4.05		4.05	5.15	6.40
Replace wallpaper				.175	8.73	6.75		15.48	18.25	21.50
Remove scaffold				.130		5.75		5.75	7.60	9.40
Total				.539	8.73	22.30		31.03	**38.60**	**46.70**

C3013 206 Fabric Interior Wall Finish

System Description	Freq. (Years)	Crew	Unit	Labor Hours	2012 Bare Costs				Total In-House	Total w/O&P
					Material	Labor	Equipment	Total		
0010 Repair fabric wall finish	9	1 PORD	S.Y.							
Set up, secure and take down ladder				.130		5		5	6.45	8
Remove fabric wall covering				.104		4.05		4.05	5.15	6.40
Repair / replace fabric				.234	7.02	9		16.02	19.35	23
Total				.468	7.02	18.05		25.07	30.95	37.40
0020 Replace fabric wall finish	50	1 PORD	S.Y.							
Set up and secure scaffold				1.350		59.40		59.40	79	97
Remove fabric wall covering				.104		4.05		4.05	5.15	6.40
Replace fabric				.234	7.02	9		16.02	19.35	23
Remove scaffold				1.350		59.40		59.40	79	97
Total				3.038	7.02	131.85		138.87	182.50	223.40

C3013 208 Cork Tile

System Description	Freq. (Years)	Crew	Unit	Labor Hours	2012 Bare Costs				Total In-House	Total w/O&P
					Material	Labor	Equipment	Total		
0010 Repair 12" x 12" x 3/16" cork tile wall - (2% of walls)	8	1 CARP	C.S.F.							
Remove old tiles				.620		22		22	29	36
Replace with new tile				4.426	447	170		617	710	830
Total				5.046	447	192		639	739	866
0020 Replace 12" x 12" x 3/16" cork tile wall	16	2 CARP	C.S.F.							
Set up and secure scaffold				.750		33		33	44	54
Remove old tiles				.620		22		22	29	36
Replace with new tile				4.426	447	170		617	710	830
Remove scaffold				.750		33		33	44	54
Total				6.546	447	258		705	827	974

C3013 210 Acoustical Tile

System Description	Freq. (Years)	Crew	Unit	Labor Hours	2012 Bare Costs				Total In-House	Total w/O&P
					Material	Labor	Equipment	Total		
0010 Repair acoustical tile - (2% of walls)	25	1 CARP	C.S.F.							
Remove damaged tile				1.067		37		37	50	61
Install new tile				2.737	225	121		346	410	480
Total				3.804	225	158		383	**460**	**541**
0030 Refinish acoustical tile	10	1 PORD	C.S.F.							
Wipe surface				.894	6	34		40	51	62.50
Prepare surface				.894	6	34		40	51	62.50
Refinish surface				1.529	25	58		83	103	124
Total				3.317	37	126		163	**205**	**249**
0040 Replace acoustical tile	60	2 CARP	C.S.F.							
Set up and secure scaffold				.750		33		33	44	54
Remove old tiles				1.067		37		37	50	61
Install new tile				2.737	225	121		346	410	480
Remove scaffold				.750		33		33	44	54
Total				5.304	225	224		449	**548**	**649**

C3013 212 Stucco

System Description	Freq. (Years)	Crew	Unit	Labor Hours	2012 Bare Costs				Total In-House	Total w/O&P
					Material	Labor	Equipment	Total		
0010 Repair stucco wall - (2% of walls)	20	1 BRIC	S.Y.							
Prepare surface				.023		.90		.90	1.08	1.35
Repair stucco				.532	3.51	20.52	1.71	25.74	32	39
Place and remove mask and drops				.067		2.52		2.52	3.24	4.14
Total				.621	3.51	23.94	1.71	29.16	**36.32**	**44.49**
0030 Refinish stucco wall	4	1 PORD	S.Y.							
Wash surface				.023		.90		.90	1.08	1.35
Prepare surface				.033		1.26		1.26	1.62	2.07
Refinish surface, brushwork, 2 coats				.138	2.25	5.22		7.47	9.25	11.20
Place and remove mask and drops				.033		1.26		1.26	1.62	2.07
Total				.227	2.25	8.64		10.89	**13.57**	**16.69**

C3013 212 | Stucco

	System Description	Freq. (Years)	Crew	Unit	Labor Hours	2012 Bare Costs Material	Labor	Equipment	Total	Total In-House	Total w/O&P
0040	**Replace stucco wall**	75	2 BRIC	S.Y.							
	Set up and secure scaffold				.130		5.75		5.75	7.60	9.40
	Remove stucco				.279		12.33		12.33	16.40	20
	Replace stucco				1.200	5.80	46.50	3.28	55.58	69	85
	Remove scaffold				.130		5.75		5.75	7.60	9.40
	Total				1.739	5.80	70.33	3.28	79.41	100.60	123.80
4120	**Spray refinish stucco wall**	5	1 PORD	S.Y.							
	Wash surface				.023		.90		.90	1.08	1.35
	Prepare surface				.033		1.26		1.26	1.62	2.07
	Refinish surface, spray, 2 coats				.049	2.52	1.89		4.41	5.20	6.10
	Place and remove mask and drops				.033		1.26		1.26	1.62	2.07
	Total				.138	2.52	5.31		7.83	9.52	11.59

C3013 213 | Plaster

	System Description	Freq. (Years)	Crew	Unit	Labor Hours	2012 Bare Costs Material	Labor	Equipment	Total	Total In-House	Total w/O&P
0010	**Repair plaster wall - (2% of walls)**	13	1 PLAS	S.Y.							
	Remove damage				.468		16.43		16.43	22	27
	Replace two coat plaster finish, incl. lath				.752	7.45	29	2.05	38.50	47.50	57.50
	Total				1.220	7.45	45.43	2.05	54.93	69.50	84.50
0030	**Refinish plaster wall**	4	1 PORD	S.Y.							
	Prepare surface				.033		1.26		1.26	1.62	2.07
	Paint / seal surface, brushwork, 1 coat				.063	.54	2.43		2.97	3.69	4.46
	Place and remove mask and drops				.033		1.26		1.26	1.62	2.07
	Total				.129	.54	4.95		5.49	6.93	8.60
0040	**Replace plaster wall**	75	2 PLAS	S.Y.							
	Set up, secure and take down ladder				.130		5.75		5.75	7.60	9.40
	Remove material				.468		16.43		16.43	22	27
	Replace two coat plaster wall, incl. lath				.752	7.45	29	2.05	38.50	47.50	57.50
	Total				1.350	7.45	51.18	2.05	60.68	77.10	93.90

C3013 214 — Drywall

	System Description	Freq. (Years)	Crew	Unit	Labor Hours	2012 Bare Costs				Total In-House	Total w/O&P
						Material	Labor	Equipment	Total		
0010	**Repair 5/8" drywall - (2% of walls)**	20	1 CARP	S.F.							
	Remove damage				.008		.28		.28	.37	.46
	Replace 5/8" drywall, taped and finished				.022	.25	.95		1.20	1.54	1.87
	Total				.030	.25	1.23		1.48	1.91	2.33
0030	**Refinish drywall**	4	1 PORD	S.F.							
	Place and remove mask and drops				.004		.14		.14	.18	.23
	Prepare surface				.004		.14		.14	.18	.23
	Paint surface, brushwork, 1 coat				.007	.06	.27		.33	.41	.50
	Total				.014	.06	.55		.61	.77	.96
0040	**Replace 5/8" drywall**	75	2 CARP	S.F.							
	Set up, secure and take down ladder				.014		.64		.64	.84	1.04
	Remove drywall				.008		.28		.28	.37	.46
	Replace 5/8" drywall, taped and finished				.022	.25	.95		1.20	1.54	1.87
	Total				.044	.25	1.87		2.12	2.75	3.37
0050	**Office painting, 10' x 12', 10' high walls**	5	1 PORD	Ea.							
	Spread drop cloths				.004		.14		.14	.18	.23
	Prepare drywall partitions				1.628		61.60		61.60	79	101
	Clean drywall partitions				.220	2.40	7.72		10.12	13	15.75
	Paint drywall partitions, roller + brush, 1 coat				3.062	26.40	118.80		145.20	180	218
	Remove drop cloths				.004		.14		.14	.18	.23
	Total				4.918	28.80	188.40		217.20	272.36	335.21
0060	**Office painting, 10' x 15', 10' high walls**	5	1 PORD	Ea.							
	Spread drop cloths				.005		.18		.18	.23	.29
	Prepare drywall partitions				1.850		70		70	90	115
	Clean drywall partitions				.250	2.73	8.78		11.51	14.75	17.90
	Paint drywall partitions, roller + brush, 1 coat				3.480	30	135		165	205	248
	Remove drop cloths				.005		.18		.18	.23	.29
	Total				5.589	32.73	214.14		246.87	310.21	381.48

C3013 214 Drywall

System Description	Freq. (Years)	Crew	Unit	Labor Hours	2012 Bare Costs				Total In-House	Total w/O&P
					Material	Labor	Equipment	Total		
2030 Refinish drywall, 12' to 24' high	5	2 PORD	S.F.							
Set up and secure scaffold				.015		.66		.66	.88	1.08
Place and remove mask and drops				.004		.14		.14	.18	.23
Prepare surface				.004		.14		.14	.18	.23
Paint surface, roller + brushwork, 1 coat				.007	.06	.27		.33	.41	.50
Remove scaffold				.015		.66		.66	.88	1.08
Total				.044	.06	1.87		1.93	2.53	3.12
3030 Refinish drywall, over 24' high	5	2 PORD	S.F.							
Set up and secure scaffold				.023		.99		.99	1.32	1.62
Place and remove mask and drops				.004		.14		.14	.18	.23
Prepare surface				.004		.14		.14	.18	.23
Paint surface, roller + brushwork, 1 coat				.007	.06	.27		.33	.41	.50
Remove scaffold				.023		.99		.99	1.32	1.62
Total				.059	.06	2.53		2.59	3.41	4.20

C3013 215 Fiberglass Panels, Rigid

System Description	Freq. (Years)	Crew	Unit	Labor Hours	2012 Bare Costs				Total In-House	Total w/O&P
					Material	Labor	Equipment	Total		
0010 Repair glass cloth fiberglass panels - (2% of walls)	9	1 CARP	C.S.F.							
Remove damaged fiberglass panels				2.600		91		91	121	150
Install new fiberglass panel				6.710	790	296		1,086	1,250	1,475
Total				9.310	790	387		1,177	1,371	1,625
0040 Replace glass cloth fiberglass panels	35	2 CARP	C.S.F.							
Set up and secure scaffold				.750		33		33	44	54
Remove old panels				2.600		91		91	121	150
Remove old furring				.516		18		18	24	30
Install new furring				2.101	34	93		127	160	195
Install new glass cloth fiberglass panels				6.710	790	296		1,086	1,250	1,475
Remove scaffold				.750		33		33	44	54
Total				13.427	824	564		1,388	1,643	1,958

C3013 220 Tile

	System Description	Freq. (Years)	Crew	Unit	Labor Hours	Material	Labor	Equipment	Total	Total In-House	Total w/O&P
						2012 Bare Costs					
0010	**Repair 4" x 4" thin set ceramic tile - (2% of walls)**	10	1 TILF	C.S.F.							
	Remove damaged tiles				2.600		91		91	121	150
	Replace tile / grout				10.947	206	399		605	730	885
	Total				13.547	206	490		696	851	1,035
0020	**Replace 4" x 4" thin set ceramic tile**	75	1 TILF	C.S.F.							
	Set up and secure scaffold				.750		33		33	44	54
	Remove tiles				2.600		91		91	121	150
	Replace tile / grout				10.947	206	399		605	730	885
	Remove scaffold				.750		33		33	44	54
	Total				15.047	206	556		762	939	1,143

C3013 230 Plywood Paneling

	System Description	Freq. (Years)	Crew	Unit	Labor Hours	Material	Labor	Equipment	Total	Total In-House	Total w/O&P
						2012 Bare Costs					
0010	**Repair plywood paneling - (2% of walls)**	10	1 CARP	C.S.F.							
	Remove damaged paneling				1.156		41		41	54	67
	Replace paneling				4.952	136	218		354	440	530
	Total				6.108	136	259		395	494	597
0020	**Refinish plywood paneling**	10	1 PORD	C.S.F.							
	Place mask and drops				.500		19		19	25	31
	Sand & paint, brushwork, 1 coat				.990	12	38		50	62	75
	Remove mask and drops				.500		19		19	25	31
	Total				1.990	12	76		88	112	137
0040	**Replace plywood paneling**	30	2 CARP	C.S.F.							
	Set up and secure scaffold				.750		33		33	44	54
	Remove damaged paneling				1.156		41		41	54	67
	Replace paneling				4.952	136	218		354	440	530
	Remove scaffold				.750		33		33	44	54
	Total				7.608	136	325		461	582	705

C3013 234 Wainscot

	System Description	Freq. (Years)	Crew	Unit	Labor Hours	2012 Bare Costs				Total In-House	Total w/O&P
						Material	Labor	Equipment	Total		
0010	**Repair wainscot - (2% of walls)**	10	1 CARP	C.S.F.							
	Remove damaged wainscot				1.733		61		61	81	100
	Replace wainscot				16.000	2,050	705		2,755	3,200	3,725
	Total				17.733	2,050	766		2,816	3,281	3,825
0020	**Refinish wainscot**	4	1 PORD	C.S.F.							
	Place mask and drops				.500		19		19	25	31
	Sand & paint, brushwork, 1 coat				.990	12	38		50	62	75
	Remove mask and drops				.500		19		19	25	31
	Total				1.990	12	76		88	112	137
0040	**Replace wainscot**	40	2 CARP	C.S.F.							
	Remove wainscot				1.733		61		61	81	100
	Replace wainscot				16.000	2,050	705		2,755	3,200	3,725
	Total				17.733	2,050	766		2,816	3,281	3,825

C3013 240 Stainless Steel Interior Finish

	System Description	Freq. (Years)	Crew	Unit	Labor Hours	2012 Bare Costs				Total In-House	Total w/O&P
						Material	Labor	Equipment	Total		
0020	**Replace stainless steel wall**	75	2 SSWK	C.S.F.							
	Set up, secure and take down ladder				1.500		66		66	88	108
	Remove existing stainless steel				2.342		82		82	109	135
	Replace stainless steel				13.419	725	500		1,225	1,525	1,800
	Total				17.261	725	648		1,373	1,722	2,043

C3013 410 Fireplace Mantles, Wood

	System Description	Freq. (Years)	Crew	Unit	Labor Hours	2012 Bare Costs				Total In-House	Total w/O&P
						Material	Labor	Equipment	Total		
0030	**Refinish wood surface - fireplaces**	7	1 PORD	S.F.							
	Prepare surface				.003		.13		.13	.17	.21
	Varnish, 3 coats, brushwork, sanding included				.025	.29	.94		1.23	1.53	1.86
	Total				.028	.29	1.07		1.36	1.70	2.07

C30 INTERIOR FINISHES   C3023   Floor Finishes

C3023 112   Concrete, Finished

	System Description	Freq. (Years)	Crew	Unit	Labor Hours	2012 Bare Costs				Total In-House	Total w/O&P
						Material	Labor	Equipment	Total		
0020	Refinish concrete floor										
	Add topping to existing floor 1 "	25	2 CEFI	C.S.F.	6.933	59	263	43	365	450	545
	Total				6.933	59	263	43	365	450	545

C3023 405   Epoxy Flooring

	System Description	Freq. (Years)	Crew	Unit	Labor Hours	2012 Bare Costs				Total In-House	Total w/O&P
						Material	Labor	Equipment	Total		
0020	Replace epoxy flooring										
	Strip existing flooring	15	2 CEFI	C.S.F.	3.200		141		141	188	231
	Repair and seal floor				12.735	385	467	15	867	1,050	1,250
	Total				15.935	385	608	15	1,008	1,238	1,481

C3023 410   Vinyl Tile

	System Description	Freq. (Years)	Crew	Unit	Labor Hours	2012 Bare Costs				Total In-House	Total w/O&P
						Material	Labor	Equipment	Total		
0020	Replace vinyl tile flooring										
	Remove damaged floor tile	18	1 TILF	S.Y.	.234		8.19		8.19	10.90	13.50
	Prepare surface				.645		23.49		23.49	29.50	37
	Install new tiles				.187	8.46	7.65		16.11	18.90	22.50
	Total				1.067	8.46	39.33		47.79	59.30	73

C3023 412   Vinyl Sheet

	System Description	Freq. (Years)	Crew	Unit	Labor Hours	2012 Bare Costs				Total In-House	Total w/O&P
						Material	Labor	Equipment	Total		
0020	Replace vinyl sheet flooring										
	Remove damaged floor tile	18	1 TILF	S.Y.	.234		8.19		8.19	10.90	13.50
	Prepare surface				.645		23.49		23.49	29.50	37
	Install new vinyl sheet				.407	35.55	16.56		52.11	60	70.50
	Total				1.286	35.55	48.24		83.79	100.40	121

C3023 414 | Rubber Tile

System Description	Freq. (Years)	Crew	Unit	Labor Hours	2012 Bare Costs				Total In-House	Total w/O&P
					Material	Labor	Equipment	Total		
0020 Replace rubber tile floor	18	1 TILF	S.Y.							
Remove damaged floor tile				.234		8.19		8.19	10.90	13.50
Prepare surface				.645		23.49		23.49	29.50	37
Install new tiles				1.040	105.30	42.39		147.69	169	198
Total				1.920	105.30	74.07		179.37	209.40	248.50

C3023 418 | Rubber / Vinyl Trim

System Description	Freq. (Years)	Crew	Unit	Labor Hours	2012 Bare Costs				Total In-House	Total w/O&P
					Material	Labor	Equipment	Total		
0010 Replace rubber cove base	9	1 TILF	L.F.							
Remove damaged base				.017		.61		.61	.81	1
Clean up debris				.001		.01		.01	.01	.01
Install new base				.033	1.01	1.35		2.36	2.80	3.37
Total				.051	1.01	1.97		2.98	3.62	4.38

C3023 420 | Ceramic Tile

System Description	Freq. (Years)	Crew	Unit	Labor Hours	2012 Bare Costs				Total In-House	Total w/O&P
					Material	Labor	Equipment	Total		
0010 Ceramic tile floor repairs - (2% of floors)	15	1 TILF	C.S.F.							
Regrout ceramic tile floors				16.640	15	605		620	780	970
Total				16.640	15	605		620	780	970
0020 Replace 2" x 2" thin set ceramic tile floor	50	1 TILF	C.S.F.							
Remove damaged floor tile				2.600		91		91	121	150
Prepare surface				7.172		261		261	330	410
Install new tiles				10.947	419	399		818	965	1,150
Total				20.719	419	751		1,170	1,416	1,710

C3023 428 Ceramic Trim

System Description	Freq. (Years)	Crew	Unit	Labor Hours	2012 Bare Costs				Total In-House	Total w/O&P
					Material	Labor	Equipment	Total		
0020 Replace ceramic trim	50	2 TILF	L.F.							
Remove ceramic tile trim				.015		.52		.52	.70	.86
Clean up debris				.010		.44		.44	.57	.71
Install new ceramic tile trim				.229	3.48	8.35		11.83	14.30	17.40
Total				.253	3.48	9.31		12.79	15.57	**18.97**

C3023 430 Terrazzo

System Description	Freq. (Years)	Crew	Unit	Labor Hours	2012 Bare Costs				Total In-House	Total w/O&P
					Material	Labor	Equipment	Total		
0100 Terrazzo floor repairs - (2% of floors)	15	1 MSTZ	S.F.							
Chip existing terrazzo				.089		3.14		3.14	4.16	5.15
Place terrazzo				.166	3	6.15	2.72	11.87	13.80	16.45
Remove debris				.004		.15		.15	.20	.25
Total				.260	3	9.44	2.72	15.16	18.16	**21.85**
0200 Replace terrazzo floor	75	2 MSTZ	C.S.F.							
Break-up existing terrazzo				5.943		209		209	277	340
Remove debris				.433		15.25		15.25	20.50	25
Load into truck				.650		23.25	12	35.25	42.50	51
Place terrazzo				16.640	300	615	272	1,187	1,375	1,650
Total				23.666	300	862.50	284	1,446.50	1,715	**2,066**

C3023 438 Terrazzo Trim

System Description	Freq. (Years)	Crew	Unit	Labor Hours	2012 Bare Costs				Total In-House	Total w/O&P
					Material	Labor	Equipment	Total		
0020 Replace precast terrazzo trim	75	2 MSTZ	L.F.							
Remove old terrazzo trim				.023		.81		.81	1.08	1.33
Clean area				.010		.44		.44	.57	.71
Install new precast terrazzo trim				.416	16.45	16.80		33.25	39.50	47
Total				.449	16.45	18.05		34.50	41.15	**49.04**

C3023 440 Quarry Tile

System Description	Freq. (Years)	Crew	Unit	Labor Hours	2012 Bare Costs				Total In-House	Total w/O&P
					Material	Labor	Equipment	Total		
0010 Quarry tile floor repairs - (2% of floors)										
Regrout quarry tile floor	15	1 TILF	S.F.	.166	.15	6.05		6.20	7.80	9.70
Total				.166	.15	6.05		6.20	**7.80**	**9.70**
0020 Replace quarry tile floor	50	2 TILF	S.F.							
Remove damaged floor tile				.026		.91		.91	1.21	1.50
Prepare surface				.072		2.61		2.61	3.29	4.10
Install new tiles				.109	4.19	3.99		8.18	9.65	11.50
Total				.207	4.19	7.51		11.70	**14.15**	**17.10**

C3023 450 Brick

System Description	Freq. (Years)	Crew	Unit	Labor Hours	2012 Bare Costs				Total In-House	Total w/O&P
					Material	Labor	Equipment	Total		
0020 Replace thickset brick floor	60	2 BRIC	S.F.							
Remove brick				.035		1.22		1.22	1.62	2
Prepare 2" thick mortar bed				.260	.83	10.35		11.18	14.40	17.75
Install new brick				.219	8.25	8		16.25	19.10	23
Total				.514	9.08	19.57		28.65	**35.12**	**42.75**

C3023 460 Marble

System Description	Freq. (Years)	Crew	Unit	Labor Hours	2012 Bare Costs				Total In-House	Total w/O&P
					Material	Labor	Equipment	Total		
0020 Replace thinset marble floor	50	2 TILF	S.F.							
Remove marble				.035		1.22		1.22	1.62	2
Prepare floor				.260	.83	10.35		11.18	14.40	17.75
Replace marble flooring				.347	6.25	12.65		18.90	23	27.50
Total				.641	7.08	24.22		31.30	**39.02**	**47.25**

C30 INTERIOR FINISHES | C3023 | Floor Finishes

C3023 470 | Plywood

	System Description	Freq. (Years)	Crew	Unit	Labor Hours	2012 Bare Costs				Total In-House	Total w/O&P
						Material	Labor	Equipment	Total		
0020	**Replace plywood floor**	40	2 CARP	C.S.F.							
	Remove existing flooring				1.733		76		76	102	125
	Install new plywood flooring 3/4"				1.600	117	71		188	223	262
	Total				3.333	117	147		264	325	387

C3023 472 | Wood Parquet

	System Description	Freq. (Years)	Crew	Unit	Labor Hours	2012 Bare Costs				Total In-House	Total w/O&P
						Material	Labor	Equipment	Total		
0020	**Sand and refinish parquet floor**	10	1 CARP	S.F.							
	Sand floor				.035	.86	1.24		2.10	2.59	3.11
	Refinish existing floor, brushwork, 2 coats				.026	1.28	.91		2.19	2.62	3.10
	Total				.061	2.14	2.15		4.29	5.21	6.21
0030	**Replace 5/16" oak parquet floor**	40	2 CARP	S.F.							
	Remove flooring				.023		1.02		1.02	1.35	1.67
	Repair underlayment				.014	.95	.61		1.56	1.86	2.19
	Install new parquet flooring				.065	4.56	2.87		7.43	8.85	10.40
	Total				.102	5.51	4.50		10.01	12.06	14.26

C3023 474 | Maple Strip

	System Description	Freq. (Years)	Crew	Unit	Labor Hours	2012 Bare Costs				Total In-House	Total w/O&P
						Material	Labor	Equipment	Total		
0020	**Sand and refinish maple strip floor**	10	1 CARP	S.F.							
	Sand floor				.026	1.28	.91		2.19	2.62	3.10
	Refinish maple strip floor, brushwork, 2 coats				.035	.86	1.24		2.10	2.59	3.11
	Total				.061	2.14	2.15		4.29	5.21	6.21
0030	**Replace maple floor**	40	2 CARP	S.F.							
	Remove flooring				.023		1.02		1.02	1.35	1.67
	Repair underlayment				.014	.95	.61		1.56	1.86	2.19
	Install new maple flooring				.061	5.20	2.70		7.90	9.30	10.90
	Total				.098	6.15	4.33		10.48	12.51	14.76

C3023 478 Wood Trim

System Description	Freq. (Years)	Crew	Unit	Labor Hours	2012 Bare Costs				Total In-House	Total w/O&P
					Material	Labor	Equipment	Total		
0010 Repair 1″ x 3″ wood trim	13	1 CARP	L.F.							
Remove wood				.021		.73		.73	.97	1.20
Install new trim				.173	4.52	7.64		12.16	15.10	18.15
Total				.194	4.52	8.37		12.89	16.07	**19.35**
0030 Refinish 1″ x 3″ wood trim	7	1 PORD	L.F.							
Prepare surface				.003		.13		.13	.17	.21
Varnish, 3 coats, brushwork, sanding included				.025	.29	.94		1.23	1.53	1.86
Total				.028	.29	1.07		1.36	1.70	**2.07**
0040 Replace 1″ x 3″ wood trim	75	2 CARP	L.F.							
Remove wood				.021		.73		.73	.97	1.20
Install new trim				.173	4.52	7.64		12.16	15.10	18.15
Prepare surface				.003		.13		.13	.17	.21
Varnish, 3 coats, brushwork, sanding included				.025	.29	.94		1.23	1.53	1.86
Total				.222	4.81	9.44		14.25	17.77	**21.42**

C3023 510 Carpet

System Description	Freq. (Years)	Crew	Unit	Labor Hours	2012 Bare Costs				Total In-House	Total w/O&P
					Material	Labor	Equipment	Total		
0020 Replace carpet	8	2 TILF	S.Y.							
Remove damaged carpet				.094		3.33		3.33	4.41	5.40
Install new carpet				.138	36.50	5.60		42.10	47	54.50
Total				.232	36.50	8.93		45.43	51.41	**59.90**

150

C3033 105 Plaster

	System Description	Freq. (Years)	Crew	Unit	Labor Hours	2012 Bare Costs				Total In-House	Total w/O&P
						Material	Labor	Equipment	Total		
0010	**Repair plaster ceiling - (2% of ceilings)**	12	1 PLAS	S.Y.							
	Set up, secure and take down ladder				.130		5.75		5.75	7.60	9.40
	Remove damaged ceiling				.267		9.36		9.36	12.50	15.40
	Replace plaster, 2 coats on lath				.752	6.95	29	2.05	38	47	57
	Total				1.149	6.95	44.11	2.05	53.11	67.10	81.80
0030	**Refinish plaster ceiling**	10	1 PORD	S.Y.							
	Set up, secure and take down ladder				.130		5.75		5.75	7.60	9.40
	Place mask and drops				.033		1.26		1.26	1.62	2.07
	Sand & paint				.089	1.08	3.42		4.50	5.60	6.75
	Total				.252	1.08	10.43		11.51	14.82	18.22
0040	**Replace plaster ceiling**	75	2 PLAS	S.Y.							
	Set up and secure scaffold				.130		5.75		5.75	7.60	9.40
	Remove ceiling				.267		9.36		9.36	12.50	15.40
	Replace plaster, 2 coats on lath				.752	6.95	29	2.05	38	47	57
	Remove scaffold				.130		5.75		5.75	7.60	9.40
	Total				1.279	6.95	49.86	2.05	58.86	74.70	91.20

C3033 107 Gypsum Wall Board

	System Description	Freq. (Years)	Crew	Unit	Labor Hours	2012 Bare Costs				Total In-House	Total w/O&P
						Material	Labor	Equipment	Total		
0010	**Repair gypsum board ceiling - (2% of ceilings)**	20	1 CARP	C.S.F.							
	Set up, secure and take down ladder				1.300		57.50		57.50	76	94
	Remove damaged gypsum board				2.737		96		96	128	158
	Replace 5/8" gypsum board, taped and finished				3.382	49	149		198	252	305
	Total				7.419	49	302.50		351.50	456	557
0020	**Refinish gypsum board ceiling, up to 12' high**	20	1 PORD	C.S.F.							
	Set up, secure and take down ladder				1.300		57.50		57.50	76	94
	Wash surface				.250		10		10	12	15
	Sand & paint				.990	12	38		50	62	75
	Place and remove mask and drops				.370		14		14	18	23
	Total				2.910	12	119.50		131.50	168	207

C30 INTERIOR FINISHES — C3033 — Ceiling Finishes

C3033 107 — Gypsum Wall Board

	System Description	Freq. (Years)	Crew	Unit	Labor Hours	2012 Bare Costs				Total In-House	Total w/O&P
						Material	Labor	Equipment	Total		
0040	**Replace gypsum board ceiling, up to 12' high**	40	2 CARP	C.S.F.							
	Set up and secure scaffold				.750		33		33	44	54
	Remove damaged gypsum board				2.737		96		96	128	158
	Replace 5/8" gypsum board ceiling, taped and finished				3.382	49	149		198	252	305
	Remove scaffold				.750		33		33	44	54
	Total				7.619	49	311		360	468	571
2020	**Refinish gypsum board ceiling, 12' to 24' high**	5	2 PORD	C.S.F.							
	Set up and secure scaffold				1.500		66		66	88	108
	Place and remove mask and drops				.370		14		14	18	23
	Prepare surface				.370		14		14	18	23
	Paint surface, roller + brushwork, 1 coat				.696	6	27		33	41	49.50
	Remove scaffold				1.500		66		66	88	108
	Total				4.436	6	187		193	253	311.50
3020	**Refinish gypsum board ceiling, over 24' high**	5	2 PORD	C.S.F.							
	Set up and secure scaffold				2.250		99		99	132	162
	Place and remove mask and drops				.370		14		14	18	23
	Prepare surface				.370		14		14	18	23
	Paint surface, roller + brushwork, 1 coat				.696	6	27		33	41	49.50
	Remove scaffold				2.250		99		99	132	162
	Total				5.936	6	253		259	341	419.50

C3033 108 — Acoustic Tile

	System Description	Freq. (Years)	Crew	Unit	Labor Hours	2012 Bare Costs				Total In-House	Total w/O&P
						Material	Labor	Equipment	Total		
0010	**Acoustic tile repairs - (2% of ceilings)**	9	1 CARP	C.S.F.							
	Set up, secure and take down ladder				1.300		57.50		57.50	76	94
	Remove damaged tile				1.067		37		37	50	61
	Install new tile				2.737	225	121		346	410	480
	Total				5.104	225	215.50		440.50	536	635

C3033 108 Acoustic Tile

	System Description	Freq. (Years)	Crew	Unit	Labor Hours	2012 Bare Costs				Total In-House	Total w/O&P
						Material	Labor	Equipment	Total		
0020	**Replace acoustic tile ceiling, non fire-rated**	20	1 CARP	C.S.F.							
	Set up, secure and take down scaffold				.750		33		33	44	54
	Remove old ceiling tiles				.500		18		18	23	29
	Remove old ceiling grid				.625		22		22	29	36
	Install new ceiling grid				1.000	70	44		114	136	160
	Install new ceiling tiles				1.280	75	56		131	158	187
	Sweep and clean debris				.520		25.50		25.50	33	41
	Total				4.675	145	198.50		343.50	423	507
0030	**Refinish acoustic tile ceiling/grid (unoccupied area)**	5	2 PORD	C.S.F.							
	Protect exposed surfaces and mask light fixtures				.800		30.50		30.50	39.50	49
	Refinish acoustic tiles, roller + brush, 1 coat				.267	2.50	10.20		12.70	15.90	19.45
	Total				1.067	2.50	40.70		43.20	55.40	68.45
0040	**Refinish acoustic tile ceiling/grid (occupied area)**	5	2 PORD	C.S.F.							
	Protect exposed surfaces and mask light fixtures				3.200		122		122	157	195
	Refinish acoustic tiles, roller + brush, 1 coat				.320	2.50	12.20		14.70	18.50	22.50
	Total				3.520	2.50	134.20		136.70	175.50	217.50
2030	**Refinish acoustic tile ceiling, 12' to 24' high**	5	2 PORD	C.S.F.							
	Set up and secure scaffold				1.500		66		66	88	108
	Place and remove mask and drops				.100		2		2	2.40	3
	Paint surface, roller + brushwork, 1 coat				.267	2.50	10.20		12.70	15.90	19.45
	Remove scaffold				1.500		66		66	88	108
	Total				3.367	2.50	144.20		146.70	194.30	238.45
3030	**Refinish acoustic tile ceiling, over 24' high**	5	2 PORD	C.S.F.							
	Set up and secure scaffold				2.250		99		99	132	162
	Place and remove mask and drops				.100		2		2	2.40	3
	Paint surface, roller + brushwork, 1 coat				.267	2.50	10.20		12.70	15.90	19.45
	Remove scaffold				2.250		99		99	132	162
	Total				4.867	2.50	210.20		212.70	282.30	346.45

C3033 109 Acoustic Tile, Fire-Rated

	System Description	Freq. (Years)	Crew	Unit	Labor Hours	2012 Bare Costs				Total In-House	Total w/O&P
						Material	Labor	Equipment	Total		
0010	**Replace acoustic tile ceiling, fire-rated**	20	1 CARP	C.S.F.							
	Set up, secure and take down scaffold				.750		33		33	44	54
	Remove old ceiling tiles				.500		18		18	23	29
	Remove old grid system				.625		22		22	29	36
	Install new grid system				1.200	84	52.80		136.80	163	191
	Install new ceiling tiles				1.185	117	52		169	198	232
	Sweep & clean debris				.520		25.50		25.50	33	41
	Total				4.780	201	203.30		404.30	490	583

C3033 120 Wood

	System Description	Freq. (Years)	Crew	Unit	Labor Hours	2012 Bare Costs				Total In-House	Total w/O&P
						Material	Labor	Equipment	Total		
0010	**Repair wood ceiling - (2% of ceilings)**	10	1 CARP	C.S.F.							
	Set up, secure and take down ladder				1.300		57.50		57.50	76	94
	Remove damaged ceiling				1.455		51		51	68	84
	Replace wood				5.200	149	229		378	470	560
	Total				7.955	149	337.50		486.50	614	738
0030	**Refinish wood ceiling**	6	1 PORD	C.S.F.							
	Set up and secure scaffold				.375		16.50		16.50	22	27
	Wash surface				.286		11		11	14	17
	Sand & paint, brushwork, 1 coat				.990	12	38		50	62	75
	Place and remove mask and drops				.370		14		14	18	23
	Remove scaffold				.375		16.50		16.50	22	27
	Total				2.396	12	96		108	138	169
0040	**Replace wood ceiling**	50	2 CARP	C.S.F.							
	Set up and secure scaffold				.750		33		33	44	54
	Remove damaged ceiling				1.455		51		51	68	84
	Replace wood				5.200	149	229		378	470	560
	Remove scaffold				.750		33		33	44	54
	Total				8.155	149	346		495	626	752

System Description	Freq. (Years)	Crew	Unit	Labor Hours	2012 Bare Costs				Total In-House	Total w/O&P
					Material	Labor	Equipment	Total		
0010 Replace flush valve diaphragm	10	1 PLUM	Ea.							
Turn valve off and on				.010		.57		.57	.71	.88
Remove / replace diaphragm				.300	3.10	16.40		19.50	24	29.50
Check for leaks				.013		.71		.71	.89	1.11
Total				.323	3.10	17.68		20.78	25.60	31.49
0015 Rebuild flush valve	20	1 PLUM	Ea.							
Turn valve off and on				.010		.57		.57	.71	.88
Remove flush valve				.100		5.45		5.45	6.80	8.50
Rebuild valve				.350	54	19.10		73.10	83.50	97.50
Reinstall valve				1.000		54.50		54.50	68	85
Check operation				.024		1.31		1.31	1.64	2.04
Total				1.484	54	80.93		134.93	160.65	193.92
0020 Unplug clogged line	5	1 PLUM	Ea.							
Turn valve off and on				.010		.57		.57	.71	.88
Remove water closet				2.078		113		113	142	177
Unplug line				.200		10.90		10.90	13.65	17
Reinstall water closet				.510		28		28	35	43.50
Check operation				.167		9.10		9.10	11.40	14.20
Total				2.965		161.57		161.57	202.76	252.58
0030 Replace tankless water closet	35	2 PLUM	Ea.							
Turn valve off and on				.010		.57		.57	.71	.88
Remove flush valve				.100		5.45		5.45	6.80	8.50
Remove water closet				.460		25		25	31.50	39
Install wall-hung water closet				2.759	455	136		591	670	780
Check operation				.150		8.20		8.20	10.20	12.75
Total				3.479	455	175.22		630.22	719.21	841.13
0040 Replace tankless flush valve	25	1 PLUM	Ea.							
Turn valve off and on				.010		.57		.57	.71	.88
Remove flush valve				.100		5.45		5.45	6.80	8.50
Install water closet flush valve				1.000	137	54.50		191.50	219	256
Check operation				.024		1.31		1.31	1.64	2.04
Total				1.134	137	61.83		198.83	228.15	267.42

D2013 110 Tankless Water Closet

System Description	Freq. (Years)	Crew	Unit	Labor Hours	2012 Bare Costs				Total In-House	Total w/O&P
					Material	Labor	Equipment	Total		
0050 Replace wax ring gasket	5	1 PLUM	Ea.							
Turn valve off and on				.010		.57		.57	.71	.88
Remove floor mounted tankless bowl				.667		36.50		36.50	45.50	56.50
Install new wax gasket				.083	1.83	4.55		6.38	7.70	9.40
Install floor mounted tankless bowl				1.000		54.50		54.50	68	85
Check operation				.150		8.20		8.20	10.20	12.75
Total				1.910	1.83	104.32		106.15	132.11	164.53
0080 Replace stainless steel detention water closet flush valve actuator	20	1 SKWK	Ea.							
Turn valve off and on				.010		.57		.57	.71	.88
Remove flush valve actuator				.100		5.45		5.45	6.80	8.50
Remove flush valve				.100		5.45		5.45	6.80	8.50
Detention equipment, replace toilet actuator				1.000	295	45.50		340.50	385	445
Check operation				.024		1.31		1.31	1.64	2.04
Total				1.234	295	58.28		353.28	400.95	464.92
0090 Replace stainless steel detention water closet flush valve	20	1 SKWK	Ea.							
Turn valve off and on				.010		.57		.57	.71	.88
Remove flush valve				.100		5.45		5.45	6.80	8.50
Detention equipment, replace water closet valve				1.000	320	45.50		365.50	410	475
Check operation				.024		1.31		1.31	1.64	2.04
Total				1.134	320	52.83		372.83	419.15	486.42

D2013 130 Flush-Tank Water Closet

System Description	Freq. (Years)	Crew	Unit	Labor Hours	2012 Bare Costs				Total In-House	Total w/O&P
					Material	Labor	Equipment	Total		
0010 Unplug clogged line	5	1 PLUM	Ea.							
Turn valve off and on				.010		.57		.57	.71	.88
Remove water closet				2.078		113		113	142	177
Unplug line				.200		10.90		10.90	13.65	17
Reinstall water closet				.510		28		28	35	43.50
Check operation				.167		9.10		9.10	11.40	14.20
Total				2.965		161.57		161.57	202.76	252.58

D2013 130 Flush-Tank Water Closet

	System Description	Freq. (Years)	Crew	Unit	Labor Hours	2012 Bare Costs				Total In-House	Total w/O&P
						Material	Labor	Equipment	Total		
0020	**Replace washer / diaphragm in ball cock**	5	1 PLUM	Ea.							
	Turn valve on and off				.010		.57		.57	.71	.88
	Remove and replace washer / diaphragm				.180	1.74	9.85		11.59	14.20	17.50
	Check operation				.024		1.31		1.31	1.64	2.04
	Total				.214	1.74	11.73		13.47	**16.55**	**20.42**
0030	**Replace valve and ball cock assembly**	15	1 PLUM	Ea.							
	Turn valve off and on				.010		.57		.57	.71	.88
	Remove flush valve and ball cock assembly				.300		16.40		16.40	20.50	25.50
	Install flush valve and ball cock assembly				.610	12.60	33.50		46.10	55.50	68
	Check operation				.167		9.10		9.10	11.40	14.20
	Total				1.087	12.60	59.57		72.17	**88.11**	**108.58**
0040	**Install gasket between tank and bowl**	20	1 PLUM	Ea.							
	Turn valve off and on				.010		.57		.57	.71	.88
	Remove tank and gasket				.200		10.90		10.90	13.65	17
	Install new gasket and reinstall tank				.300	2.38	16.40		18.78	23	28.50
	Inspect connection				.009		.50		.50	.62	.77
	Total				.520	2.38	28.37		30.75	**37.98**	**47.15**
0050	**Replace two piece water closet**	35	2 PLUM	Ea.							
	Turn water off and on				.010		.57		.57	.71	.88
	Remove floor-mounted water closet				1.000		54.50		54.50	68	85
	Install new bowl, tank and seat				3.019	247	148		395	455	540
	Check for leaks				.013		.71		.71	.89	1.11
	Total				4.042	247	203.78		450.78	**524.60**	**626.99**
0060	**Replace one piece water closet**	35	2 PLUM	Ea.							
	Turn water off and on				.010		.57		.57	.71	.88
	Remove floor-mounted water closet				1.000		54.50		54.50	68	85
	Install floor-mounted water closet with seat				3.019	355	148		503	575	675
	Check for leaks				.013		.71		.71	.89	1.11
	Total				4.042	355	203.78		558.78	**644.60**	**761.99**

D20 PLUMBING   D2013   Plumbing Fixtures

D2013 210   Urinal

System Description	Freq. (Years)	Crew	Unit	Labor Hours	2012 Bare Costs				Total In-House	Total w/O&P
					Material	Labor	Equipment	Total		
0010 Replace flush valve diaphragm	7	1 PLUM	Ea.							
Turn valve off and on				.010		.57		.57	.71	.88
Remove / replace diaphragm				.300	3.10	16.40		19.50	24	29.50
Check for leaks				.013		.71		.71	.89	1.11
Total				.323	3.10	17.68		20.78	25.60	31.49
0015 Rebuild flush valve	20	1 PLUM	Ea.							
Turn valve off and on				.010		.57		.57	.71	.88
Remove flush valve				.100		5.45		5.45	6.80	8.50
Rebuild valve				.350	54	19.10		73.10	83.50	97.50
Reinstall valve				1.000		54.50		54.50	68	85
Check operation				.024		1.31		1.31	1.64	2.04
Total				1.484	54	80.93		134.93	160.65	193.92
0020 Unplug line	5	1 PLUM	Ea.							
Turn valve off and on				.010		.57		.57	.71	.88
Remove and reinstall bowl				1.600		87.50		87.50	109	136
Unplug line				.200		10.90		10.90	13.65	17
Check operation				.167		9.10		9.10	11.40	14.20
Total				1.977		108.07		108.07	134.76	168.08
0030 Replace wall-hung urinal	35	2 PLUM	Ea.							
Turn valve off and on				.010		.57		.57	.71	.88
Remove urinal				2.667		146		146	182	227
Fit up urinal to wall				.196		10.70		10.70	13.35	16.65
Install flushometer pipe				.096		5.25		5.25	6.55	8.15
Install urinal				5.333	293	262		555	650	775
Check operation				.334		18.25		18.25	23	28.50
Total				8.636	293	442.77		735.77	875.61	1,056.18

D2013 310   **Lavatory, Iron, Enamel**

System Description	Freq. (Years)	Crew	Unit	Labor Hours	Material	Labor	Equipment	Total	Total In-House	Total w/O&P
0010										
Replace washer in spud connection	7	1 PLUM	Ea.							
Turn valve off and on				.022		1.21		1.21	1.51	1.88
Remove gasket or washer				.017		.92		.92	1.15	1.44
Install new gasket / washer set				.026	3.48	1.42		4.90	5.60	6.55
Install spud connection				.026		1.42		1.42	1.77	2.21
Inspect connection				.009		.50		.50	.62	.77
Total				.100	3.48	5.47		8.95	10.65	12.85
0020										
Replace washer in faucet	2	1 PLUM	Ea.							
Turn valves on and off				.022		1.21		1.21	1.51	1.88
Remove valve stem and washer				.091		4.96		4.96	6.20	7.75
Install washer				.026	.38	1.42		1.80	2.20	2.70
Install stem				.017		.92		.92	1.15	1.44
Test faucet				.010		.57		.57	.71	.88
Total				.166	.38	9.08		9.46	11.77	14.65
0040										
Replace faucets	10	1 PLUM	Ea.							
Turn valves on and off				.022		1.21		1.21	1.51	1.88
Remove faucets and tubing				.381		21		21	26	32.50
Install detention sink faucets and tubing				1.040	44.50	57		101.50	120	144
Test faucets				.010		.57		.57	.71	.88
Total				1.453	44.50	79.78		124.28	148.22	179.26
0050										
Clean out strainer and P trap	2	1 PLUM	Ea.							
Remove strainer and P trap				.157		8.55		8.55	10.70	13.35
Clean and reinstall strainer and trap				.320		17.45		17.45	22	27
Total				.477		26		26	32.70	40.35
0060										
Replace lavatory	40	2 PLUM	Ea.							
Shut off water (hot and cold)				.022		1.21		1.21	1.51	1.88
Disconnect and remove wall-hung lavatory				.800		43.50		43.50	54.50	68
Install new wall-hung lavatory with trim, (18" x 15")				2.807	375	153		528	605	710
Total				3.629	375	197.71		572.71	661.01	779.88

2012 Bare Costs (column group header over Material, Labor, Equipment, Total)

D2013 330　Lavatory, Vitreous China

System Description	Freq. (Years)	Crew	Unit	Labor Hours	2012 Bare Costs Material	Labor	Equipment	Total	Total In-House	Total w/O&P
0010　Replace washer in spud connection	7	1 PLUM	Ea.							
Turn valve off and on				.022		1.21		1.21	1.51	1.88
Loosen locknuts				.011		.60		.60	.75	.94
Remove spud connection				.017		.92		.92	1.15	1.44
Remove gasket or washer				.017		.92		.92	1.15	1.44
Clean spud seat				.021		1.13		1.13	1.42	1.77
Install new gasket / washer set				.026	3.48	1.42		4.90	5.60	6.55
Install spud connection				.026		1.42		1.42	1.77	2.21
Tighten locknut				.014		.78		.78	.98	1.22
Inspect connection				.009		.50		.50	.62	.77
Total				.163	3.48	8.90		12.38	**14.95**	**18.22**
0020　Replace washer in faucet	2	1 PLUM	Ea.							
Turn valves on and off				.022		1.21		1.21	1.51	1.88
Remove packing nut and install				.023		1.28		1.28	1.59	1.99
Remove valve stem and cap				.017		.92		.92	1.15	1.44
Remove seat washer and install				.023		1.28		1.28	1.59	1.99
Pry out washer				.017		.92		.92	1.15	1.44
Install washer				.026	.38	1.42		1.80	2.20	2.70
Install stem				.017		.92		.92	1.15	1.44
Tighten main gland valves				.012		.64		.64	.80	1
Test faucet				.010		.57		.57	.71	.88
Total				.168	.38	9.16		9.54	**11.85**	**14.76**
0040　Replace faucets	10	1 PLUM	Ea.							
Turn valves on and off				.022		1.21		1.21	1.51	1.88
Remove faucets and tubing				.381		21		21	26	32.50
Install faucets and tubing				1.040	44.50	57		101.50	120	144
Test faucets				.010		.57		.57	.71	.88
Total				1.453	44.50	79.78		124.28	**148.22**	**179.26**
0050　Clean out strainer and P trap	2	1 PLUM	Ea.							
Remove strainer and P trap				.157		8.55		8.55	10.70	13.35
Clean and reinstall strainer and trap				.320		17.45		17.45	22	27
Total				.477		26		26	**32.70**	**40.35**

D2013 330 | Lavatory, Vitreous China

	System Description	Freq. (Years)	Crew	Unit	Labor Hours	2012 Bare Costs – Material	2012 Bare Costs – Labor	2012 Bare Costs – Equipment	2012 Bare Costs – Total	Total In-House	Total w/O&P
0060	**Replace lavatory**	35	2 PLUM	Ea.							
	Shut off water (hot and cold)				.022		1.21		1.21	1.51	1.88
	Disconnect and remove wall-hung lavatory				1.485		81		81	101	126
	Install new lavatory (to 20" x 17")				2.971	187	146		333	390	460
	Install faucets and tubing				1.040	44.50	57		101.50	120	144
	Total				5.518	231.50	285.21		516.71	612.51	731.88

D2013 350 | Lavatory, Enameled Steel

	System Description	Freq. (Years)	Crew	Unit	Labor Hours	2012 Bare Costs – Material	2012 Bare Costs – Labor	2012 Bare Costs – Equipment	2012 Bare Costs – Total	Total In-House	Total w/O&P
0010	**Replace washer in spud connection**	7	1 PLUM	Ea.							
	Turn valve off and on				.022		1.21		1.21	1.51	1.88
	Loosen locknut				.014		.78		.78	.98	1.22
	Remove spud connection				.017		.92		.92	1.15	1.44
	Remove gasket or washer				.017		.92		.92	1.15	1.44
	Clean spud seat				.021		1.13		1.13	1.42	1.77
	Install new gasket / washer set				.026	3.48	1.42		4.90	5.60	6.55
	Install spud connection				.026		1.42		1.42	1.77	2.21
	Tighten locknut				.014		.78		.78	.98	1.22
	Inspect connection				.009		.50		.50	.62	.77
	Total				.166	3.48	9.08		12.56	15.18	18.50
0020	**Replace washer in faucet**	2	1 PLUM	Ea.							
	Turn valves on and off				.022		1.21		1.21	1.51	1.88
	Remove valve stem and washer				.091		4.96		4.96	6.20	7.75
	Install washer				.026	.38	1.42		1.80	2.20	2.70
	Install stem				.017		.92		.92	1.15	1.44
	Test faucet				.010		.57		.57	.71	.88
	Total				.166	.38	9.08		9.46	11.77	14.65
0040	**Replace faucets**	10	1 PLUM	Ea.							
	Turn valves on and off				.022		1.21		1.21	1.51	1.88
	Remove faucets and tubing				.381		21		21	26	32.50
	Install faucets and tubing				1.040	44.50	57		101.50	120	144
	Test faucets				.010		.57		.57	.71	.88
	Total				1.453	44.50	79.78		124.28	148.22	179.26

D2013 350 Lavatory, Enameled Steel

System Description	Freq. (Years)	Crew	Unit	Labor Hours	2012 Bare Costs				Total In-House	Total w/O&P
					Material	Labor	Equipment	Total		
0050	**Clean out strainer and P trap**	2	1 PLUM	Ea.							
Remove strainer and P trap				.157		8.55		8.55	10.70	13.35
Clean and reinstall strainer and trap				.320		17.45		17.45	22	27
Total				.477		26		26	**32.70**	**40.35**
0060	**Replace lavatory**	35	2 PLUM	Ea.							
Shut off water (hot and cold)				.022		1.21		1.21	1.51	1.88
Disconnect and remove wall-hung lavatory				1.793		98		98	122	152
Install new lavatory (to 20" x 17")				3.586	143	176		319	375	455
Install faucets and tubing				1.040	44.50	57		101.50	120	144
Total				6.441	187.50	332.21		519.71	**618.51**	**752.88**

D2013 410 Sink, Iron Enamel

System Description	Freq. (Years)	Crew	Unit	Labor Hours	2012 Bare Costs				Total In-House	Total w/O&P
					Material	Labor	Equipment	Total		
0010	**Replace faucet washer**	2	1 PLUM	Ea.							
Turn valves on and off				.022		1.21		1.21	1.51	1.88
Remove valve stem and washer				.091		4.96		4.96	6.20	7.75
Install washer				.026	.38	1.42		1.80	2.20	2.70
Install stem				.017		.92		.92	1.15	1.44
Test faucet				.010		.57		.57	.71	.88
Total				.166	.38	9.08		9.46	**11.77**	**14.65**
0020	**Clean trap**	3	1 PLUM	Ea.							
Drain trap				.021		1.15		1.15	1.43	1.79
Remove / install trap				.043		2.36		2.36	2.95	3.68
Inspect trap				.031		1.71		1.71	2.13	2.66
Clean trap				.021		1.13		1.13	1.42	1.77
Total				.116		6.35		6.35	**7.93**	**9.90**
0030	**Replace faucets**	10	1 PLUM	Ea.							
Turn valves on and off				.022		1.21		1.21	1.51	1.88
Remove faucets and tubing				.381		21		21	26	32.50
Install faucets and tubing				1.040	44.50	57		101.50	120	144
Test faucets				.010		.57		.57	.71	.88
Total				1.453	44.50	79.78		124.28	**148.22**	**179.26**

D2013 410 Sink, Iron Enamel

	System Description	Freq. (Years)	Crew	Unit	Labor Hours	2012 Bare Costs				Total In-House	Total w/O&P
						Material	Labor	Equipment	Total		
0040	**Unstop sink**	2	1 PLUM	Ea.							
	Unstop plugged drain				.571		31		31	39	48.50
	Total				.571		31		31	39	48.50
0060	**Replace kitchen sink, P.E.C.I.**	35	2 PLUM	Ea.							
	Remove PE sink				1.625		80		80	99.50	124
	Install countertop porcelain enameled kitchen sink, 24" x 21"				2.857	257	140		397	460	540
	Total				4.482	257	220		477	559.50	664
0070	**Replace laundry sink, P.E.C.I.**	35	2 PLUM	Ea.							
	Remove PE sink				1.625		80		80	99.50	124
	Install free-standing porcelain enameled laundry sink, 24" x 21"				2.667	465	131		596	675	785
	Total				4.292	465	211		676	774.50	909

D2013 420 Sink, Enameled Steel

	System Description	Freq. (Years)	Crew	Unit	Labor Hours	2012 Bare Costs				Total In-House	Total w/O&P
						Material	Labor	Equipment	Total		
0010	**Replace faucet washer**	2	1 PLUM	Ea.							
	Turn valves on and off				.022		1.21		1.21	1.51	1.88
	Remove valve stem and washer				.091		4.96		4.96	6.20	7.75
	Install washer				.026	.38	1.42		1.80	2.20	2.70
	Install stem				.017		.92		.92	1.15	1.44
	Test faucet				.010		.57		.57	.71	.88
	Total				.166	.38	9.08		9.46	11.77	14.65
0020	**Clean trap**	3	1 PLUM	Ea.							
	Drain trap				.021		1.15		1.15	1.43	1.79
	Remove / install trap				.043		2.36		2.36	2.95	3.68
	Inspect trap				.031		1.71		1.71	2.13	2.66
	Clean trap				.021		1.13		1.13	1.42	1.77
	Total				.116		6.35		6.35	7.93	9.90

D2013 420 Sink, Enameled Steel

	System Description	Freq. (Years)	Crew	Unit	Labor Hours	2012 Bare Costs				Total In-House	Total w/O&P
						Material	Labor	Equipment	Total		
0030	**Replace faucets**	10	1 PLUM	Ea.							
	Turn valves on and off				.022		1.21		1.21	1.51	1.88
	Remove faucets and tubing				.381		21		21	26	32.50
	Install faucets and tubing				1.040	44.50	57		101.50	120	144
	Test faucets				.010		.57		.57	.71	.88
	Total				1.453	44.50	79.78		124.28	**148.22**	**179.26**
0040	**Unstop sink**	2	1 PLUM	Ea.							
	Unstop plugged drain				.571		31		31	39	48.50
	Total				.571		31		31	**39**	**48.50**
0060	**Replace sink, enameled steel**	35	2 PLUM	Ea.							
	Remove sink				1.793		88		88	110	137
	Install countertop enameled steel sink, 24" x 21"				3.714	440	183		623	710	835
	Total				5.507	440	271		711	820	972

D2013 430 Sink, Stainless Steel

	System Description	Freq. (Years)	Crew	Unit	Labor Hours	2012 Bare Costs				Total In-House	Total w/O&P
						Material	Labor	Equipment	Total		
0010	**Replace faucet washer**	2	1 PLUM	Ea.							
	Turn valves on and off				.022		1.21		1.21	1.51	1.88
	Remove valve stem and washer				.091		4.96		4.96	6.20	7.75
	Install washer				.026	.38	1.42		1.80	2.20	2.70
	Install stem				.017		.92		.92	1.15	1.44
	Test faucet				.010		.57		.57	.71	.88
	Total				.166	.38	9.08		9.46	**11.77**	**14.65**
0020	**Clean trap**	3	1 PLUM	Ea.							
	Drain trap				.021		1.15		1.15	1.43	1.79
	Remove / install trap				.043		2.36		2.36	2.95	3.68
	Inspect trap				.031		1.71		1.71	2.13	2.66
	Clean trap				.021		1.13		1.13	1.42	1.77
	Total				.116		6.35		6.35	**7.93**	**9.90**

D2013 430 Sink, Stainless Steel

	System Description	Freq. (Years)	Crew	Unit	Labor Hours	Material	Labor	Equipment	Total	Total In-House	Total w/O&P
								2012 Bare Costs			
0030	**Replace faucets**	10	1 PLUM	Ea.							
	Turn valves on and off				.022		1.21		1.21	1.51	1.88
	Remove faucets and tubing				.381		21		21	26	32.50
	Install faucets and tubing				1.040	44.50	57		101.50	120	144
	Test faucets				.010		.57		.57	.71	.88
	Total				1.453	44.50	79.78		124.28	148.22	179.26
0040	**Unstop sink**	2	1 PLUM	Ea.							
	Unstop plugged drain				.571		31		31	39	48.50
	Total				.571		31		31	39	48.50
0060	**Replace sink, stainless steel**	40	2 PLUM	Ea.							
	Remove sink				1.625		80		80	99.50	124
	Install countertop stainless steel sink, 25" x 22"				3.714	645	183		828	935	1,100
	Total				5.339	645	263		908	1,034.50	1,224
0070	**Replace stainless steel detention sink faucets**	15	1 SKWK	Ea.							
	Turn valves on and off				.022		1.21		1.21	1.51	1.88
	Remove faucets and tubing				.381		21		21	26	32.50
	Detention equipment, replace fuacet valve and tubing				1.000	620	45.50		665.50	740	850
	Test faucets				.010		.57		.57	.71	.88
	Total				1.413	620	68.28		688.28	768.22	885.26

D2013 440 Sink, Plastic

	System Description	Freq. (Years)	Crew	Unit	Labor Hours	Material	Labor	Equipment	Total	Total In-House	Total w/O&P
								2012 Bare Costs			
0010	**Replace faucet washer**	2	1 PLUM	Ea.							
	Turn valves on and off				.022		1.21		1.21	1.51	1.88
	Remove valve stem and washer				.091		4.96		4.96	6.20	7.75
	Install washer				.026	.38	1.42		1.80	2.20	2.70
	Install stem				.017		.92		.92	1.15	1.44
	Test faucet				.010		.57		.57	.71	.88
	Total				.166	.38	9.08		9.46	11.77	14.65

	System Description	Freq. (Years)	Crew	Unit	Labor Hours	2012 Bare Costs				Total In-House	Total w/O&P
						Material	Labor	Equipment	Total		
0020	**Clean trap**	3	1 PLUM	Ea.							
	Drain trap				.021		1.15		1.15	1.43	1.79
	Remove / install trap				.043		2.36		2.36	2.95	3.68
	Inspect trap				.031		1.71		1.71	2.13	2.66
	Clean trap				.021		1.13		1.13	1.42	1.77
	Total				.116		6.35		6.35	**7.93**	**9.90**
0030	**Replace faucets**	10	1 PLUM	Ea.							
	Turn valves on and off				.022		1.21		1.21	1.51	1.88
	Remove faucets and tubing				.381		21		21	26	32.50
	Install faucets and tubing				1.040	44.50	57		101.50	120	144
	Test faucets				.010		.57		.57	.71	.88
	Total				1.453	44.50	79.78		124.28	**148.22**	**179.26**
0040	**Unstop, sink**	2	1 PLUM	Ea.							
	Unstop plugged drain				.571		31		31	39	48.50
	Total				.571		31		31	**39**	**48.50**
0060	**Replace sink and fittings, polyethylene**	15	2 PLUM	Ea.							
	Remove sink				3.467		170		170	213	266
	Install bench mounted polyethylene sink, 47" x 24"				6.932	1,375	340		1,715	1,950	2,250
	Total				10.399	1,375	510		1,885	**2,163**	**2,516**
0080	**Replace lab sink and fittings, polyethylene**	15	2 PLUM	Ea.							
	Remove sink				3.467		170		170	213	266
	Install bench mounted PE lab sink, 70" x 24"				5.333	1,225	262		1,487	1,675	1,950
	Total				8.800	1,225	432		1,657	**1,888**	**2,216**

D2013 444 | Laboratory Sink

System Description	Freq. (Years)	Crew	Unit	Labor Hours	2012 Bare Costs				Total In-House	Total w/O&P
					Material	Labor	Equipment	Total		
0010 **Replace faucet washer**	2	1 PLUM	Ea.							
Turn valves on and off				.022		1.21		1.21	1.51	1.88
Remove valve stem and washer				.091		4.96		4.96	6.20	7.75
Install washer				.026	.38	1.42		1.80	2.20	2.70
Install stem				.017		.92		.92	1.15	1.44
Test faucet				.010		.57		.57	.71	.88
Total				.166	.38	9.08		9.46	11.77	14.65
0030 **Replace faucets**	10	1 PLUM	Ea.							
Turn valves on and off				.022		1.21		1.21	1.51	1.88
Remove faucets and tubing				.381		21		21	26	32.50
Install faucets and tubing				1.040	44.50	57		101.50	120	144
Test faucets				.010		.57		.57	.71	.88
Total				1.453	44.50	79.78		124.28	148.22	179.26
0060 **Replace sink and fittings, polyethylene, lab.**	15	2 PLUM	Ea.							
Remove lab. sink				3.467		170		170	213	266
Install bench mounted polyethylene lab. sink, 47" x 24"				5.333	1,225	262		1,487	1,675	1,950
Total				8.800	1,225	432		1,657	1,888	2,216

D2013 450 | Laundry Sink, Plastic

System Description	Freq. (Years)	Crew	Unit	Labor Hours	2012 Bare Costs				Total In-House	Total w/O&P
					Material	Labor	Equipment	Total		
0020 **Replace washer in faucet**	2	1 PLUM	Ea.							
Turn valves on and off				.022		1.21		1.21	1.51	1.88
Remove valve stem and washer				.091		4.96		4.96	6.20	7.75
Install washer				.026	.38	1.42		1.80	2.20	2.70
Install stem				.017		.92		.92	1.15	1.44
Test faucet				.010		.57		.57	.71	.88
Total				.166	.38	9.08		9.46	11.77	14.65

D2013 450 — Laundry Sink, Plastic

System Description	Freq. (Years)	Crew	Unit	Labor Hours	2012 Bare Costs				Total In-House	Total w/O&P
					Material	Labor	Equipment	Total		
0040 Replace faucets	10	1 PLUM	Ea.							
Turn valves on and off				.022		1.21		1.21	1.51	1.88
Remove faucets and tubing				.381		21		21	26	32.50
Install faucets and tubing				1.040	44.50	57		101.50	120	144
Test faucets				.010		.57		.57	.71	.88
Total				1.453	44.50	79.78		124.28	148.22	179.26
0050 Clean out strainer and P trap	2	1 PLUM	Ea.							
Remove strainer and P trap				.157		8.55		8.55	10.70	13.35
Clean and reinstall strainer and trap				.320		17.45		17.45	22	27
Total				.477		26		26	32.70	40.35
0060 Replace laundry sink	20	2 PLUM	Ea.							
Shut off water (hot and cold)				.022		1.21		1.21	1.51	1.88
Disconnect and remove laundry sink				1.600		78.50		78.50	98	123
Install sink (23" x 18", single)				3.200	149	157		306	360	430
Install faucets and tubing				1.040	44.50	57		101.50	120	144
Total				5.862	193.50	293.71		487.21	579.51	698.88

D2013 455 — Laundry Sink, Stone

System Description	Freq. (Years)	Crew	Unit	Labor Hours	2012 Bare Costs				Total In-House	Total w/O&P
					Material	Labor	Equipment	Total		
0060 Replace laundry sink, molded stone	40	2 PLUM	Ea.							
Remove molded stone sink				1.625		80		80	99.50	124
Install laundry sink, w/trim, molded stone, 22"x23", sgl. compt.				2.667	138	131		269	315	375
Total				4.292	138	211		349	414.50	499

D2013 460 | Service/Utility Sink

System Description	Freq. (Years)	Crew	Unit	Labor Hours	2012 Bare Costs				Total In-House	Total w/O&P
					Material	Labor	Equipment	Total		
0010	**Replace faucet washer**									
Turn valves on and off	2	1 PLUM	Ea.	.022		1.21		1.21	1.51	1.88
Remove valve stem and washer				.091		4.96		4.96	6.20	7.75
Install washer				.026	.38	1.42		1.80	2.20	2.70
Install stem				.017		.92		.92	1.15	1.44
Test faucet				.010		.57		.57	.71	.88
Total				.166	.38	9.08		9.46	11.77	14.65
0020	**Clean trap**									
Drain trap	3	1 PLUM	Ea.	.021		1.15		1.15	1.43	1.79
Remove / install trap				.043		2.36		2.36	2.95	3.68
Inspect trap				.031		1.71		1.71	2.13	2.66
Clean trap				.021		1.13		1.13	1.42	1.77
Total				.116		6.35		6.35	7.93	9.90
0030	**Replace faucets**									
Turn valves on and off	10	1 PLUM	Ea.	.022		1.21		1.21	1.51	1.88
Remove faucets and tubing				.381		21		21	26	32.50
Install faucets and tubing				1.040	44.50	57		101.50	120	144
Test faucets				.010		.57		.57	.71	.88
Total				1.453	44.50	79.78		124.28	148.22	179.26
0040	**Unstop sink**									
Unstop plugged drain	2	1 PLUM	Ea.	.571		31		31	39	48.50
Total				.571		31		31	39	48.50
0060	**Replace service sink, P.E.C.I.**									
Remove sink	35	1 PLUM	Ea.	1.625		80		80	99.50	124
Install service/utility sink, 22" x 18"				5.212	675	256		931	1,050	1,250
Total				6.837	675	336		1,011	1,149.50	1,374

D2013 470 Group Washfountain

	System Description	Freq. (Years)	Crew	Unit	Labor Hours	2012 Bare Costs				Total In-House	Total w/O&P
						Material	Labor	Equipment	Total		
0060	**Replace group wash fountain, 54" diameter**	20	Q-2	Ea.							
	Shut off water (hot and cold)				.022		1.21		1.21	1.51	1.88
	Disconnect and remove group wash fountain, 54" dia.				4.800		245		245	305	380
	Install group wash fountain, terrazzo, 54" diameter				9.600	6,800	490		7,290	8,100	9,250
	Install faucets and tubing				1.040	44.50	57		101.50	120	144
	Total				15.462	6,844.50	793.21		7,637.71	8,526.51	**9,775.88**

D2013 510 Bathtub, Cast Iron Enamel

	System Description	Freq. (Years)	Crew	Unit	Labor Hours	2012 Bare Costs				Total In-House	Total w/O&P
						Material	Labor	Equipment	Total		
0010	**Inspect / clean shower head**	3	1 PLUM	Ea.							
	Turn water off and on				.010		.57		.57	.71	.88
	Remove shower head				.217		11.85		11.85	14.75	18.45
	Check shower head				.009		.50		.50	.62	.77
	Install shower head				.433		23.50		23.50	29.50	37
	Total				.669		36.42		36.42	45.58	**57.10**
0020	**Replace mixing valve barrel**	2	1 PLUM	Ea.							
	Turn valves on and off				.022		1.21		1.21	1.51	1.88
	Remove mixing valve cover / barrel				.650		35.50		35.50	44.50	55.50
	Install new mixing valve barrel / replace cover				.650	75	35.50		110.50	127	149
	Test valve				.010		.57		.57	.71	.88
	Total				1.332	75	72.78		147.78	173.72	**207.26**
0030	**Replace mixing valve**	10	1 PLUM	Ea.							
	Turn valves off and on				.022		1.21		1.21	1.51	1.88
	Remove mixing valve				.867		47.50		47.50	59	73.50
	Install new mixing valve				1.733	149	94.50		243.50	282	335
	Test valve				.010		.57		.57	.71	.88
	Total				2.633	149	143.78		292.78	343.22	**411.26**
0070	**Replace tub**	40	2 PLUM	Ea.							
	Remove cast iron tub				1.891		93		93	116	145
	Install cast iron enameled bathtub				3.782	1,025	186		1,211	1,350	1,575
	Total				5.673	1,025	279		1,304	1,466	**1,720**

D2013 530 Bathtub, Enameled Steel

System Description	Freq. (Years)	Crew	Unit	Labor Hours	2012 Bare Costs				Total In-House	Total w/O&P
					Material	Labor	Equipment	Total		
0010 Inspect / clean shower head	3	1 PLUM	Ea.							
Turn water off and on				.010		.57		.57	.71	.88
Remove shower head				.217		11.85		11.85	14.75	18.45
Check shower head				.009		.50		.50	.62	.77
Install shower head				.433		23.50		23.50	29.50	37
Total				.669		36.42		36.42	**45.58**	**57.10**
0020 Replace mixing valve barrel	2	1 PLUM	Ea.							
Turn valves on and off				.022		1.21		1.21	1.51	1.88
Remove mixing valve cover / barrel				.650		35.50		35.50	44.50	55.50
Install new mixing valve barrel / replace cover				.650	75	35.50		110.50	127	149
Test valve				.010		.57		.57	.71	.88
Total				1.332	75	72.78		147.78	**173.72**	**207.26**
0030 Replace mixing valve	10	1 PLUM	Ea.							
Turn valves off and on				.022		1.21		1.21	1.51	1.88
Remove mixing valve				.867		47.50		47.50	59	73.50
Install new mixing valve				1.733	149	94.50		243.50	282	335
Test valve				.010		.57		.57	.71	.88
Total				2.633	149	143.78		292.78	**343.22**	**411.26**
0070 Replace tub	35	2 PLUM	Ea.							
Remove tub				1.891		93		93	116	145
Install enameled steel bathtub				3.782	490	186		676	770	905
Total				5.673	490	279		769	**886**	**1,050**

D2013 550 Bathtub, Fiberglass

System Description	Freq. (Years)	Crew	Unit	Labor Hours	2012 Bare Costs				Total In-House	Total w/O&P
					Material	Labor	Equipment	Total		
0010 Inspect / clean shower head	3	1 PLUM	Ea.							
Turn water off and on				.010		.57		.57	.71	.88
Remove shower head				.217		11.85		11.85	14.75	18.45
Check shower head				.009		.50		.50	.62	.77
Install shower head				.433		23.50		23.50	29.50	37
Total				.669		36.42		36.42	**45.58**	**57.10**

D2013 550   Bathtub, Fiberglass

System Description	Freq. (Years)	Crew	Unit	Labor Hours	2012 Bare Costs				Total In-House	Total w/O&P
					Material	Labor	Equipment	Total		
0020										
Replace mixing valve barrel	2	1 PLUM	Ea.							
Turn valves on and off				.022		1.21		1.21	1.51	1.88
Remove mixing valve cover / barrel				.650		35.50		35.50	44.50	55.50
Install new mixing valve barrel / replace cover				.650	75	35.50		110.50	127	149
Test valve				.010		.57		.57	.71	.88
Total				1.332	75	72.78		147.78	173.72	207.26
0030										
Replace mixing valve	10	1 PLUM	Ea.							
Turn valves off and on				.022		1.21		1.21	1.51	1.88
Remove mixing valve				.867		47.50		47.50	59	73.50
Install new mixing valve				1.733	149	94.50		243.50	282	335
Test valve				.010		.57		.57	.71	.88
Total				2.633	149	143.78		292.78	343.22	411.26
0070										
Replace tub	20	2 PLUM	Ea.							
Remove bathtub				2.600		128		128	160	199
Install fiberglass bathtub with shower wall surround				5.200	790	256		1,046	1,200	1,400
Total				7.800	790	384		1,174	1,360	1,599

D2013 710   Shower, Terrazzo

System Description	Freq. (Years)	Crew	Unit	Labor Hours	2012 Bare Costs				Total In-House	Total w/O&P
					Material	Labor	Equipment	Total		
0010										
Inspect / clean shower head	3	1 PLUM	Ea.							
Turn water off and on				.010		.57		.57	.71	.88
Remove shower head				.217		11.85		11.85	14.75	18.45
Check shower head				.009		.50		.50	.62	.77
Install shower head				.433		23.50		23.50	29.50	37
Total				.669		36.42		36.42	45.58	57.10
0020										
Replace mixing valve barrel	2	1 PLUM	Ea.							
Turn valves on and off				.022		1.21		1.21	1.51	1.88
Remove mixing valve cover / barrel				.650		35.50		35.50	44.50	55.50
Install new mixing valve barrel / replace cover				.650	75	35.50		110.50	127	149
Test valve				.010		.57		.57	.71	.88
Total				1.332	75	72.78		147.78	173.72	207.26

D2013 710 — Shower, Terrazzo

	System Description	Freq. (Years)	Crew	Unit	Labor Hours	2012 Bare Costs — Material	Labor	Equipment	Total	Total In-House	Total w/O&P
0030	**Replace mixing valve**	10	1 PLUM	Ea.							
	Turn valves off and on				.022		1.21		1.21	1.51	1.88
	Remove mixing valve				.867		47.50		47.50	59	73.50
	Install new mixing valve				1.733	149	94.50		243.50	282	335
	Test valve				.010		.57		.57	.71	.88
	Total				2.633	149	143.78		292.78	343.22	411.26
0060	**Replace terrazzo shower surface**	30	2 PLUM	Ea.							
	Remove old terrazzo surface				3.004		105.30		105.30	140	173
	Install precast terrazzo tiles				9.014	293.15	367.25		660.40	785	940
	Install curb				2.080	108	84		192	225	267
	Total				14.098	401.15	556.55		957.70	1,150	1,380

D2013 730 — Shower, Enameled Steel

	System Description	Freq. (Years)	Crew	Unit	Labor Hours	2012 Bare Costs — Material	Labor	Equipment	Total	Total In-House	Total w/O&P
0010	**Inspect / clean shower head**	3	1 PLUM	Ea.							
	Turn water off and on				.010		.57		.57	.71	.88
	Remove shower head				.217		11.85		11.85	14.75	18.45
	Check shower head				.009		.50		.50	.62	.77
	Install shower head				.433		23.50		23.50	29.50	37
	Total				.669		36.42		36.42	45.58	57.10
0020	**Replace mixing valve barrel**	2	1 PLUM	Ea.							
	Turn valves on and off				.022		1.21		1.21	1.51	1.88
	Remove mixing valve cover / barrel				.650		35.50		35.50	44.50	55.50
	Install new mixing valve barrel / replace cover				.650	75	35.50		110.50	127	149
	Test valve				.010		.57		.57	.71	.88
	Total				1.332	75	72.78		147.78	173.72	207.26
0030	**Replace mixing valve**	10	1 PLUM	Ea.							
	Turn valves off and on				.022		1.21		1.21	1.51	1.88
	Remove mixing valve				.867		47.50		47.50	59	73.50
	Install new mixing valve				1.733	149	94.50		243.50	282	335
	Test valve				.010		.57		.57	.71	.88
	Total				2.633	149	143.78		292.78	343.22	411.26

D2013 730 Shower, Enameled Steel

System Description	Freq. (Years)	Crew	Unit	Labor Hours	2012 Bare Costs				Total In-House	Total w/O&P
					Material	Labor	Equipment	Total		
0060 Replace shower	35	2 PLUM	Ea.							
Remove shower				5.200		256		256	320	400
Install shower				4.522	730	222		952	1,075	1,250
Total				**9.722**	**730**	**478**		**1,208**	**1,395**	**1,650**

D2013 750 Shower, Fiberglass

System Description	Freq. (Years)	Crew	Unit	Labor Hours	2012 Bare Costs				Total In-House	Total w/O&P
					Material	Labor	Equipment	Total		
0010 Inspect / clean shower head	3	1 PLUM	Ea.							
Turn water off and on				.010		.57		.57	.71	.88
Remove shower head				.217		11.85		11.85	14.75	18.45
Check shower head				.009		.50		.50	.62	.77
Install shower head				.433		23.50		23.50	29.50	37
Total				**.669**		**36.42**		**36.42**	**45.58**	**57.10**
0020 Replace mixing valve barrel	2	1 PLUM	Ea.							
Turn valves on and off				.022		1.21		1.21	1.51	1.88
Remove mixing valve cover / barrel				.650		35.50		35.50	44.50	55.50
Install new mixing valve barrel / replace cover				.650	75	35.50		110.50	127	149
Test valve				.010		.57		.57	.71	.88
Total				**1.332**	**75**	**72.78**		**147.78**	**173.72**	**207.26**
0030 Replace mixing valve	10	1 PLUM	Ea.							
Turn valves off and on				.022		1.21		1.21	1.51	1.88
Remove mixing valve				.867		47.50		47.50	59	73.50
Install new mixing valve				1.733	149	94.50		243.50	282	335
Test valve				.010		.57		.57	.71	.88
Total				**2.633**	**149**	**143.78**		**292.78**	**343.22**	**411.26**
0060 Replace shower and fittings	20	2 PLUM	Ea.							
Remove shower				4.334		213		213	266	330
Install shower, fiberglass				3.302	555	162		717	815	945
Total				**7.635**	**555**	**375**		**930**	**1,081**	**1,275**

D2013 770 | Shower, Misc.

System Description	Freq. (Years)	Crew	Unit	Labor Hours	2012 Bare Costs				Total In-House	Total w/O&P
					Material	Labor	Equipment	Total		
0010 Inspect / clean shower head	3	1 PLUM	Ea.							
Turn water off and on				.010		.57		.57	.71	.88
Remove shower head				.217		11.85		11.85	14.75	18.45
Check shower head				.009		.50		.50	.62	.77
Install shower head				.433		23.50		23.50	29.50	37
Total				.669		36.42		36.42	45.58	57.10
0020 Replace mixing valve barrel	2	1 PLUM	Ea.							
Turn valves on and off				.022		1.21		1.21	1.51	1.88
Remove mixing valve cover / barrel				.650		35.50		35.50	44.50	55.50
Install new mixing valve barrel / replace cover				.650	75	35.50		110.50	127	149
Test valve				.010		.57		.57	.71	.88
Total				1.332	75	72.78		147.78	173.72	207.26
0030 Replace mixing valve	10	1 PLUM	Ea.							
Turn valves off and on				.022		1.21		1.21	1.51	1.88
Remove mixing valve				.867		47.50		47.50	59	73.50
Install new mixing valve				1.733	149	94.50		243.50	282	335
Test valve				.010		.57		.57	.71	.88
Total				2.633	149	143.78		292.78	343.22	411.26
0060 Replace shower and fittings, aluminum	25	2 PLUM	Ea.							
Remove shower				4.334		213		213	266	330
Install shower				3.302	555	162		717	815	945
Total				7.635	555	375		930	1,081	1,275
0070 Replace shower head with water conserving head	10	1 PLUM	Ea.							
Remove shower head				.217		11.85		11.85	14.75	18.45
Install new water conserving head				.400	82.50	22		104.50	118	137
Turn water on and off				.010		.57		.57	.71	.88
Total				.627	82.50	34.42		116.92	133.46	156.33
0120 Replace shower, C.M.U.	20	D-8	Ea.							
Remove C.M.U. shower enclosure				3.595		127.68	19.04	146.72	189	230
Install C.M.U. shower enclosure				6.772	129.36	275.52		404.88	500	605
Install built-in head, arm and valve				2.000	80	109		189	224	270
Total				12.367	209.36	512.20	19.04	740.60	913	1,105

D2013 770   Shower, Misc.

System Description	Freq. (Years)	Crew	Unit	Labor Hours	2012 Bare Costs Material	2012 Bare Costs Labor	2012 Bare Costs Equipment	2012 Bare Costs Total	Total In-House	Total w/O&P
0200										
Replace shower, glazed C.M.U.	25	D-8	Ea.							
Remove C.M.U. shower enclosure				4.697		167		191.50	246	300
Install glazed C.M.U. shower enclosure				9.393	467.60	383.60	24.50	851.20	1,000	1,200
Install built-in head, arm and valve				2.000	80	109		189	224	270
Total				16.090	547.60	659.60	24.50	1,231.70	1,470	1,770
0280										
Replace shower surface, ceramic tile	30	D-7	Ea.							
Remove ceramic tile shower enclosure surface				3.066		108		108	143	176
Install ceramic tile in shower enclosure				6.130	115.36	223.44		338.80	410	495
Install built-in head, arm and valve				2.000	80	109		189	224	270
Total				11.197	195.36	440.44		635.80	777	941

D2013 810   Drinking Fountain

System Description	Freq. (Years)	Crew	Unit	Labor Hours	2012 Bare Costs Material	2012 Bare Costs Labor	2012 Bare Costs Equipment	2012 Bare Costs Total	Total In-House	Total w/O&P
0010										
Check / minor repairs	1	1 PLUM	Ea.							
Check unit, make minor adjustments				.667		36.50		36.50	45.50	56.50
Total				.667		36.50		36.50	45.50	56.50
0020										
Repair internal leaks	4	1 PLUM	Ea.							
Open unit, repair leaks, close				.615		33.50		33.50	42	52.50
Total				.615		33.50		33.50	42	52.50
0030										
Correct water pressure	2	1 PLUM	Ea.							
Adjust water pressure, close				.571		31		31	39	48.50
Total				.571		31		31	39	48.50
0040										
Replace refrigerant	2	1 PLUM	Ea.							
Add freon to unit				.133	12.20	7.45		19.65	22.50	27
Total				.133	12.20	7.45		19.65	22.50	27
0050										
Repair drain leak	4	1 PLUM	Ea.							
Remove old pipe				.052		2.84		2.84	3.54	4.42
Install new pipe				.186	15.35	10.15		25.50	29.50	35
Total				.238	15.35	12.99		28.34	33.04	39.42

D2013 810 Drinking Fountain

	System Description	Freq. (Years)	Crew	Unit	Labor Hours	2012 Bare Costs				Total In-House	Total w/O&P
						Material	Labor	Equipment	Total		
0070	**Replace fountain**	10	2 PLUM	Ea.							
	Remove old water cooler				2.600		128		128	160	199
	Install new wall mounted water cooler				5.200	680	256		936	1,075	1,250
	Total				7.800	680	384		1,064	1,235	1,449

D2013 910 Emergency Shower Station

	System Description	Freq. (Years)	Crew	Unit	Labor Hours	2012 Bare Costs				Total In-House	Total w/O&P
						Material	Labor	Equipment	Total		
0020	**Inspect and clean shower head**	3	1 PLUM	Ea.							
	Turn water off and on				.010		.57		.57	.71	.88
	Remove shower head				.217		11.85		11.85	14.75	18.45
	Check shower head				.009		.50		.50	.62	.77
	Install shower head				.433		23.50		23.50	29.50	37
	Total				.669		36.42		36.42	45.58	57.10
0030	**Replace shower**	25	2 PLUM	Ea.							
	Remove emergency shower				2.600		128		128	160	199
	Install emergency shower				5.200	350	256		606	705	840
	Total				7.800	350	384		734	865	1,039

D2013 920 Emergency Eye Wash

	System Description	Freq. (Years)	Crew	Unit	Labor Hours	2012 Bare Costs				Total In-House	Total w/O&P
						Material	Labor	Equipment	Total		
0020	**Inspect and clean spray heads**	3	1 PLUM	Ea.							
	Turn water off and on				.010		.57		.57	.71	.88
	Remove spray head				.217		11.85		11.85	14.75	18.45
	Check shower head				.009		.50		.50	.62	.77
	Install spray head				.433		23.50		23.50	29.50	37
	Total				.669		36.42		36.42	45.58	57.10
0030	**Replace eye wash station**	25	2 PLUM	Ea.							
	Remove old eye wash station				2.600		128		128	160	199
	Install eye wash station				5.200	420	256		676	780	925
	Total				7.800	420	384		804	940	1,124

D2023 110 | **Pipe & Fittings, Copper**

System Description	Freq. (Years)	Crew	Unit	Labor Hours	2012 Bare Costs				Total In-House	Total w/O&P
					Material	Labor	Equipment	Total		
0010 Resolder joint	10	1 PLUM	Ea.							
Measure, cut & ream both ends				.053		2.91		2.91	3.63	4.54
Solder fitting (3/4" coupling)				.495	4.33	27		31.33	38.50	47.50
Total				.549	4.33	29.91		34.24	**42.13**	**52.04**
0020 Replace 3/4" copper pipe and fittings	20	2 PLUM	L.F.							
Remove old pipe				.071		3.88		3.88	4.84	6.05
Install 3/4" copper tube with couplings and hangers				.141	9.55	7.65		17.20	20	24
Total				.212	9.55	11.53		21.08	**24.84**	**30.05**
0030 Replace 1" copper pipe and fittings	25	2 PLUM	L.F.							
Remove old pipe				.073		3.96		3.96	4.94	6.15
Install 1" copper tube with couplings and hangers				.158	12.85	8.60		21.45	25	29.50
Total				.230	12.85	12.56		25.41	**29.94**	**35.65**
0050 Replace 1-1/2" copper pipe and fittings	25	2 PLUM	L.F.							
Remove old pipe				.104		5.70		5.70	7.10	8.85
Install 1 1/2" copper tubing, couplings, hangers				.208	21	11.35		32.35	37.50	44
Total				.312	21	17.05		38.05	**44.60**	**52.85**
0060 Replace 2" copper pipe and fittings	25	2 PLUM	L.F.							
Remove old pipe				.130		7.10		7.10	8.85	11.05
Install 2" copper tube with couplings and hangers				.260	32	14.20		46.20	53	62
Total				.390	32	21.30		53.30	**61.85**	**73.05**
0070 Replace 4" copper pipe and fittings	25	2 PLUM	L.F.							
Remove old pipe				.274		13.45		13.45	16.80	21
Install 4" copper tube with couplings and hangers				.547	118	27		145	163	190
Total				.821	118	40.45		158.45	**179.80**	**211**
0080 Replace 8" copper pipe and fittings	25	2 PLUM	L.F.							
Remove old pipe				.694		35.50		35.50	44	55
Install 8" copper tube with couplings and hangers				.918	850	47		897	995	1,125
Total				1.612	850	82.50		932.50	**1,039**	**1,180**

D2023 120 Pipe & Fittings, Steel/Iron, Threaded

	System Description	Freq. (Years)	Crew	Unit	Labor Hours	Material	Labor	Equipment	Total	Total In-House	Total w/O&P
							2012 Bare Costs				
0030	**Replace 3/4" threaded steel pipe and fittings**	75	2 PLUM	L.F.							
	Remove old pipe				.086		4.70		4.70	5.85	7.30
	Install 3/4" diameter steel pipe, couplings, hangers				.131	5.15	7.15		12.30	14.60	17.60
	Total				.217	5.15	11.85		17	20.45	24.90
0040	**Replace 1-1/2" threaded steel pipe and fittings**	75	2 PLUM	L.F.							
	Remove old pipe				.130		6.40		6.40	8	9.95
	Install 1-1/2" diameter steel pipe, couplings, hangers				.260	11.15	12.80		23.95	28	34
	Total				.390	11.15	19.20		30.35	36	43.95
0050	**Replace 2" threaded steel pipe and fittings**	75	2 PLUM	L.F.							
	Remove old pipe				.163		8		8	10	12.50
	Install 2" diameter steel pipe, couplings, hangers				.325	14.90	15.95		30.85	36.50	43.50
	Total				.488	14.90	23.95		38.85	46.50	56
0060	**Replace 4" threaded steel pipe and fittings**	75	2 PLUM	L.F.							
	Remove old pipe				.289		14.20		14.20	17.75	22
	Install 4" diameter steel pipe, couplings, hangers				.578	43.50	28.50		72	83.50	99
	Total				.867	43.50	42.70		86.20	101.25	121

D2023 130 Solar Piping: Pipe & Fittings, PVC

	System Description	Freq. (Years)	Crew	Unit	Labor Hours	Material	Labor	Equipment	Total	Total In-House	Total w/O&P
							2012 Bare Costs				
0010	**Reglue joint, install 1" tee**	10	1 PLUM	Ea.							
	Cut exist pipe, install tee, 1"				.867	1.22	47.50		48.72	60.50	75
	Inspect joints				.126		6.90		6.90	8.60	10.70
	Total				.993	1.22	54.40		55.62	69.10	85.70
0110	**Reglue joint, install 1-1/4" tee**	10	1 PLUM	Ea.							
	Cut exist pipe, install tee, 1-1/4"				.945	1.91	51.50		53.41	66.50	83
	Inspect joints				.126		6.90		6.90	8.60	10.70
	Total				1.071	1.91	58.40		60.31	75.10	93.70

D2023 Domestic Water Distribution

D2023 130 Solar Piping: Pipe & Fittings, PVC

System Description	Freq. (Years)	Crew	Unit	Labor Hours	2012 Bare Costs				Total In-House	Total w/O&P
					Material	Labor	Equipment	Total		
0210 **Reglue joint, install 1-1/2" tee**										
Cut exist pipe, install tee, 1-1/2"	10	1 PLUM	Ea.	1.040	2.33	57		59.33	73.50	91.50
Inspect joints				.126		6.90		6.90	8.60	10.70
Total				1.166	2.33	63.90		66.23	82.10	102.20
0310 **Reglue joint, install 2" tee**										
Cut exist pipe, install tee, 2"	10	Q-1	Ea.	1.224	3.38	60		63.38	79	97.50
Inspect joints				.126		6.90		6.90	8.60	10.70
Total				1.350	3.38	66.90		70.28	87.60	108.20
1020 **Install 10' section PVC 1" diameter**										
Remove broken pipe	20	1 PLUM	Ea.	1.131		61.50		61.50	77	96
Install 10' new PVC pipe 1" diameter				2.939	46.67	160.55		207.22	252	310
Inspect joints				.084		4.59		4.59	5.70	7.15
Total				4.154	46.67	226.64		273.31	334.70	413.15
1120 **Install 10' PVC 1-1/4" diameter**										
Remove broken pipe	20	1 PLUM	Ea.	1.239		67.50		67.50	84.50	106
Install 10' new PVC pipe 1-1/4" diameter				3.219	56.29	175.50		231.79	280	345
Inspect joints				.084		4.59		4.59	5.70	7.15
Total				4.542	56.29	247.59		303.88	370.20	458.15
1220 **Install 10' PVC 1-1/2" diameter**										
Remove broken pipe	20	1 PLUM	Ea.	1.445		79		79	98.50	123
Install 10' new PVC pipe 1-1/2" diameter				3.756	59.67	204.75		264.42	320	395
Inspect joints				.084		4.59		4.59	5.70	7.15
Total				5.284	59.67	288.34		348.01	424.20	525.15
1320 **Install 10' section PVC 2" diameter**										
Remove broken pipe	20	Q-1	Ea.	1.763		86.50		86.50	108	135
Install 10' new PVC pipe 2" diameter				4.583	74.75	225.55		300.30	365	445
Inspect joints				.084		4.59		4.59	5.70	7.15
Total				6.430	74.75	316.64		391.39	478.70	587.15

D2023 130 Solar Piping: Pipe & Fittings, PVC

	System Description	Freq. (Years)	Crew	Unit	Labor Hours	2012 Bare Costs				Total In-House	Total w/O&P
						Material	Labor	Equipment	Total		
2030	**Replace 1000' PVC pipe 1" diameter**	30	1 PLUM	M.L.F.							
	Remove broken pipe				113.080		6,150		6,150	7,700	9,600
	Install 1000' new PVC pipe 1" diameter				226.080	3,590	12,350		15,940	19,400	23,700
	Inspect joints				8.399		460		460	570	715
	Total				347.559	3,590	18,960		22,550	27,670	34,015
2130	**Replace 1000' PVC pipe 1-1/4" diameter**	30	1 PLUM	M.L.F.							
	Remove broken pipe				123.850		6,750		6,750	8,450	10,600
	Install 1000' new PVC pipe 1-1/4" diameter				247.620	4,330	13,500		17,830	21,500	26,400
	Inspect joints				8.399		460		460	570	715
	Total				379.869	4,330	20,710		25,040	30,520	37,715
2230	**Replace 1000' PVC pipe 1-1/2" diameter**	30	1 PLUM	M.L.F.							
	Remove broken pipe				144.490		7,900		7,900	9,850	12,300
	Install 1000' new PVC pipe 1-1/2" diameter				288.890	4,590	15,750		20,340	24,500	30,200
	Inspect joints				8.399		460		460	570	715
	Total				441.779	4,590	24,110		28,700	34,920	43,215
2330	**Replace 1000' PVC pipe 2" diameter**	30	Q-1	M.L.F.							
	Remove broken pipe				176.320		8,650		8,650	10,800	13,500
	Install 1000' new PVC pipe 2" diameter				352.540	5,750	17,350		23,100	28,000	34,200
	Inspect joints				8.399		460		460	570	715
	Total				537.259	5,750	26,460		32,210	39,370	48,415

D2023 150 Valve, Non-Drain, Less Than 1-1/2"

	System Description	Freq. (Years)	Crew	Unit	Labor Hours	2012 Bare Costs				Total In-House	Total w/O&P
						Material	Labor	Equipment	Total		
0020	**Replace old valve**	10	1 PLUM	Ea.							
	Remove old valve				.400		22		22	27.50	34
	Install new valve				.800	222	43.50		265.50	299	345
	Total				1.200	222	65.50		287.50	326.50	379

D2023 152 Valve, Non-Drain, 2"

System Description	Freq. (Years)	Crew	Unit	Labor Hours	Material	Labor	Equipment	Total	Total In-House	Total w/O&P
0020 Replace old valve	10	1 PLUM	Ea.							
Remove old valve (2")				.800		39.50		39.50	49	61.50
Install new valve (to 2")				1.600	1,150	78.50		1,228.50	1,375	1,550
Total				2.400	1,150	118		1,268	1,424	1,611.50

D2023 154 Valve, Non-Drain, 3"

System Description	Freq. (Years)	Crew	Unit	Labor Hours	Material	Labor	Equipment	Total	Total In-House	Total w/O&P
0020 Replace old valve	10	1 PLUM	Ea.							
Remove old valve				.800		39.50		39.50	49	61.50
Install new valve				1.600	1,150	78.50		1,228.50	1,375	1,550
Total				2.400	1,150	118		1,268	1,424	1,611.50

D2023 156 Valve, Non-Drain, 4" and Larger

System Description	Freq. (Years)	Crew	Unit	Labor Hours	Material	Labor	Equipment	Total	Total In-House	Total w/O&P
0020 Replace old valve, 4"	10	2 PLUM	Ea.							
Remove old flanged gate valve, 4"				5.200		265		265	330	415
Install new flanged gate valve, 4"				7.038	1,000	360		1,360	1,550	1,800
Total				12.239	1,000	625		1,625	1,880	2,215
0030 Replace old valve, 6"	10	2 PLUM	Ea.							
Remove old flanged gate valve, 6"				4.615		235		235	294	365
Install new flanged gate valve, 6"				10.399	1,700	530		2,230	2,525	2,950
Total				15.014	1,700	765		2,465	2,819	3,315
0040 Replace old valve, 8"	10	2 PLUM	Ea.							
Remove old flanged gate valve, 8"				3.871		197		197	246	305
Install new flanged gate valve, 8"				12.371	2,925	630		3,555	4,000	4,625
Total				16.242	2,925	827		3,752	4,246	4,930

D20 PLUMBING D2023 Domestic Water Distribution

D2023 156 Valve, Non-Drain, 4" and Larger

System Description	Freq. (Years)	Crew	Unit	Labor Hours	2012 Bare Costs Material	2012 Bare Costs Labor	2012 Bare Costs Equipment	2012 Bare Costs Total	Total In-House	Total w/O&P
0050										
Replace old valve, 10"	10	3 PLUM	Ea.							
Remove old flanged gate valve, 10"				3.380		172		172	215	268
Install new flanged gate valve, 10"				14.201	5,150	725		5,875	6,575	7,575
Total				17.581	5,150	897		6,047	**6,790**	**7,843**

D2023 160 Insulation, Pipe

System Description	Freq. (Years)	Crew	Unit	Labor Hours	2012 Bare Costs Material	2012 Bare Costs Labor	2012 Bare Costs Equipment	2012 Bare Costs Total	Total In-House	Total w/O&P
0020										
Remove old insulation & replace with new (1/2" pipe size, 1" wall)	15	1 PLUM	L.F.							
Remove pipe insulation				.025		1.35		1.35	1.69	2.11
Install fiberglass pipe insulation (1" wall, 1/2" pipe size)				.087	.89	3.81		4.70	5.95	7.25
Total				.111	.89	5.16		6.05	**7.64**	**9.36**
0030										
Remove old insulation & replace with new (3/4" pipe size, 1" wall)	15	1 PLUM	L.F.							
Remove pipe insulation				.025		1.35		1.35	1.69	2.11
Install fiberglass pipe insulation (1" wall, 3/4" pipe size)				.090	.97	3.98		4.95	6.25	7.60
Total				.115	.97	5.33		6.30	**7.94**	**9.71**
0040										
Remove old insulation & replace with new (1-1/2" pipe size, 1" wall)	15	1 PLUM	L.F.							
Remove pipe insulation				.025		1.35		1.35	1.69	2.11
Install fiberglass pipe insulation (1" wall, 1-1/2" pipe size)				.099	1.22	4.36		5.58	7	8.55
Total				.124	1.22	5.71		6.93	**8.69**	**10.66**
0050										
Remove old insulation & replace with new (1/2" pipe size, 3/4" wall)	15	1 PLUM	L.F.							
Remove pipe insulation				.025		1.35		1.35	1.69	2.11
Install flexible rubber tubing (3/4" wall, 1/2" pipe size)				.117	1.17	5.70		6.87	8.70	10.65
Total				.142	1.17	7.05		8.22	**10.39**	**12.76**
0060										
Remove old insulation & replace with new (3/4" pipe size, 3/4" wall)	15	1 PLUM	L.F.							
Remove pipe insulation				.025		1.35		1.35	1.69	2.11
Install flexible rubber tubing (3/4" wall, 3/4" pipe size)				.117	1.43	5.70		7.13	9	11
Total				.142	1.43	7.05		8.48	**10.69**	**13.11**

D20 PLUMBING | D2023 | Domestic Water Distribution

D2023 160 | Insulation, Pipe

	System Description	Freq. (Years)	Crew	Unit	Labor Hours	2012 Bare Costs				Total In-House	Total w/O&P
						Material	Labor	Equipment	Total		
0070	**Remove old insulation & replace w/new (1-1/2" pipe size, 3/4" wall)**	15	1 PLUM	L.F.							
	Remove pipe insulation				.025		1.35		1.35	1.69	2.11
	Install flexible rubber tubing (3/4" wall, 1-1/2" pipe size)				.120	2.46	5.85		8.31	10.30	12.50
	Total				.144	2.46	7.20		9.66	11.99	14.61

D2023 210 | Water Heater, Gas / Oil, 30 Gallon

	System Description	Freq. (Years)	Crew	Unit	Labor Hours	2012 Bare Costs				Total In-House	Total w/O&P
						Material	Labor	Equipment	Total		
0010	**Overhaul heater**	5	1 PLUM	Ea.							
	Turn valves off and on				.022		1.21		1.21	1.51	1.88
	Remove thermostat, check, and insulate				.182		9.95		9.95	12.40	15.45
	Remove burner, clean and install				.229		12.50		12.50	15.60	19.45
	Clean pilot and thermocouple				.296		16.20		16.20	20	25
	Remove burner door and install				.033		1.78		1.78	2.22	2.77
	Check after maintenance				.216		11.80		11.80	14.75	18.40
	Drain and fill tank				.615		33.50		33.50	42	52.50
	Total				1.593		86.94		86.94	108.48	135.45
0020	**Clean and service**	1	1 PLUM	Ea.							
	Check / adjust fuel burner				2.667		146		146	182	227
	Total				2.667		146		146	182	227
0030	**Replace water heater**	10	2 PLUM	Ea.							
	Remove old heater				2.600		142		142	177	221
	Install 30 gallon gas water heater				5.202	895	284		1,179	1,350	1,550
	Check after installation				.216		11.80		11.80	14.75	18.40
	Total				8.018	895	437.80		1,332.80	1,541.75	1,789.40

D20 PLUMBING

D2023 Domestic Water Distribution

D2023 212 Water Heater, Gas / Oil, 70 Gallon

	System Description	Freq. (Years)	Crew	Unit	Labor Hours	2012 Bare Costs				Total In-House	Total w/O&P
						Material	Labor	Equipment	Total		
0010	**Overhaul heater**	5	1 PLUM	Ea.							
	Remove hot water heater and insulate				.667		36.50		36.50	45.50	56.50
	Remove thermostat, check and install				.182		9.95		9.95	12.40	15.45
	Remove burner, clean and install				.229		12.50		12.50	15.60	19.45
	Clean pilot and thermocouple				.296		16.20		16.20	20	25
	Remove burner door and install				.033		1.78		1.78	2.22	2.77
	Drain and refill tank				.615		33.50		33.50	42	52.50
	Turn valve off and on				.211		11.50		11.50	14.35	17.90
	Total				2.232		121.93		121.93	152.07	189.57
0020	**Clean & service**	1	1 PLUM	Ea.							
	Check / adjust fuel burner				2.667		146		146	182	227
	Total				2.667		146		146	182	227
0030	**Replace hot water heater**	12	2 PLUM	Ea.							
	Remove old heater				2.600		142		142	177	221
	Install water heater, oil fired, 70 gallon				6.932	1,275	380		1,655	1,875	2,175
	Total				9.532	1,275	522		1,797	2,052	2,396

D2023 214 Water Heater, Gas / Oil, 1150 GPH

	System Description	Freq. (Years)	Crew	Unit	Labor Hours	2012 Bare Costs				Total In-House	Total w/O&P
						Material	Labor	Equipment	Total		
0010	**Minor repairs, adjustments**	2	2 PLUM	Ea.							
	Reset, adjust controls				1.333		73		73	91	113
	Total				1.333		73		73	91	113
0020	**Clean & service**	2	2 PLUM	Ea.							
	Drain tank, clean, and service				8.000		435		435	545	680
	Total				8.000		435		435	545	680
0030	**Replace hot water heater**	20	2 PLUM	Ea.							
	Remove water heater				26.016		1,275		1,275	1,600	2,000
	Install water heater, gas fired, 1150 GPH				51.948	24,800	2,550		27,350	30,500	35,000
	Total				77.964	24,800	3,825		28,625	32,100	37,000

D2023 220   Water Heater, Electric, 120 Gallon

System Description	Freq. (Years)	Crew	Unit	Labor Hours	2012 Bare Costs				Total In-House	Total w/O&P
					Material	Labor	Equipment	Total		
0010 **Drain and flush**										
Drain, clean and readjust	7	1 PLUM	Ea.	4.000		218		218	273	340
Total				4.000		218		218	273	340
0020 **Check operation**	3	1 PLUM	Ea.							
Check for relief valve				.010		.57		.57	.71	.88
Check for proper water temperature				.003		.14		.14	.18	.22
Fill out maintenance report				.022		1.21		1.21	1.51	1.88
Total				.035		1.92		1.92	**2.40**	**2.98**
0030 **Replace water heater**	15	2 PLUM	Ea.							
Remove old heater				4.334		237		237	295	370
Install water heater				8.667	7,375	475		7,850	8,700	9,950
Total				13.001	7,375	712		8,087	**8,995**	**10,320**

D2023 222   Water Heater, Electric, 300 Gallon

System Description	Freq. (Years)	Crew	Unit	Labor Hours	2012 Bare Costs				Total In-House	Total w/O&P
					Material	Labor	Equipment	Total		
0010 **Drain and flush**										
Drain, clean and adjust	7	1 PLUM	Ea.	4.000		218		218	273	340
Total				4.000		218		218	273	340
0020 **Check operation**	3	1 PLUM	Ea.							
Check relief valve				.010		.57		.57	.71	.88
Check for proper water temperature				.003		.14		.14	.18	.22
Fill out maintenance report				.022		1.21		1.21	1.51	1.88
Total				.035		1.92		1.92	**2.40**	**2.98**
0030 **Replace water heater**	15	2 PLUM	Ea.							
Remove old heater				8.000		395		395	490	615
Install water heater				16.000	34,900	785		35,685	39,400	44,900
Total				24.000	34,900	1,180		36,080	**39,890**	**45,515**

D2023 224 Water Heater, Electric, 1000 Gallon

	System Description	Freq. (Years)	Crew	Unit	Labor Hours	2012 Bare Costs				Total In-House	Total w/O&P
						Material	Labor	Equipment	Total		
0010	**Drain and flush**	7	1 PLUM	Ea.							
	Drain, clean and adjust				4.000		218		218	273	340
	Total				4.000		218		218	**273**	**340**
0020	**Check operation**	3	1 PLUM	Ea.							
	Check relief valve				.010		.57		.57	.71	.88
	Check for proper water temperature				.003		.14		.14	.18	.22
	Fill out maintenance report				.022		1.21		1.21	1.51	1.88
	Total				.035		1.92		1.92	**2.40**	**2.98**
0030	**Replace water heater**	15	2 PLUM	Ea.							
	Remove heater				22.284		1,125		1,125	1,425	1,775
	Install water heater				44.610	46,800	2,275		49,075	54,500	62,000
	Total				66.894	46,800	3,400		50,200	**55,925**	**63,775**

D2023 226 Water Heater, Electric, 2000 Gallon

	System Description	Freq. (Years)	Crew	Unit	Labor Hours	2012 Bare Costs				Total In-House	Total w/O&P
						Material	Labor	Equipment	Total		
0010	**Drain and flush**	7	1 PLUM	Ea.							
	Drain, clean and adjust				4.000		218		218	273	340
	Total				4.000		218		218	**273**	**340**
0020	**Check operation**	3	1 PLUM	Ea.							
	Check relief valve				.010		.57		.57	.71	.88
	Check for proper water temperature				.003		.14		.14	.18	.22
	Fill out maintenance report				.022		1.21		1.21	1.51	1.88
	Total				.035		1.92		1.92	**2.40**	**2.98**
0030	**Replace water heater**	15	2 PLUM	Ea.							
	Remove heater				31.209		1,600		1,600	1,975	2,475
	Install water heater				62.338	87,500	3,175		90,675	100,000	114,500
	Total				93.547	87,500	4,775		92,275	**101,975**	**116,975**

D2023 230 Steam Converter, Domestic Hot Water

System Description	Freq. (Years)	Crew	Unit	Labor Hours	2012 Bare Costs				Total In-House	Total w/O&P
					Material	Labor	Equipment	Total		
0020 Inspect for leaks	1	1 PLUM	Ea.							
Check relief valve operation				.038		2.06		2.06	2.57	3.21
Check for proper water temperature				.054		2.97		2.97	3.71	4.63
Total				.092		5.03		5.03	6.28	7.84
0030 Replace steam converter	20	2 PLUM	Ea.							
Remove heat exchanger				1.733		94.50		94.50	118	147
Install new heat exchanger				3.467	1,925	174		2,099	2,325	2,675
Total				5.200	1,925	268.50		2,193.50	2,443	2,822

D2023 240 Storage Tank, Domestic Hot Water

System Description	Freq. (Years)	Crew	Unit	Labor Hours	2012 Bare Costs				Total In-House	Total w/O&P
					Material	Labor	Equipment	Total		
0020 Replace storage tank, glass lined, P.E., 80 gal.	50	2 PLUM	Ea.							
Remove hot water storage tank				.578		31.50		31.50	39.50	49
Install new glass lined, P.E., 80 Gal. hot water storage tank				1.156	2,475	63		2,538	2,800	3,200
Total				1.733	2,475	94.50		2,569.50	2,839.50	3,249

D2023 245 Solar Storage Tank, 1000 Gallon

System Description	Freq. (Years)	Crew	Unit	Labor Hours	2012 Bare Costs				Total In-House	Total w/O&P
					Material	Labor	Equipment	Total		
0010 Replace 1000 gallon solar storage tank	20	Q-9	Ea.							
Remove tank				8.000		375		375	475	590
Install 1000 gallon solar storage tank				16.000	5,300	750		6,050	6,775	7,800
Total				24.000	5,300	1,125		6,425	7,250	8,390

D2023 250 | Expansion Chamber

	System Description	Freq. (Years)	Crew	Unit	Labor Hours	2012 Bare Costs				Total In-House	Total w/O&P
						Material	Labor	Equipment	Total		
0010	**Refill**	5	1 PLUM	Ea.							
	Refill air chamber				.039		2.13		2.13	2.66	3.32
	Total				.039		2.13		2.13	**2.66**	**3.32**
0020	**Remove old chamber, install new**	10	1 PLUM	Ea.							
	Remove / install expansion device, 15 gal.				.941	595	47		642	715	815
	Total				.941	595	47		642	**715**	**815**

D2023 260 | Circulation Pump, 1/12 HP

	System Description	Freq. (Years)	Crew	Unit	Labor Hours	2012 Bare Costs				Total In-House	Total w/O&P
						Material	Labor	Equipment	Total		
0020	**Pump maintenance, 1/12 H.P.**	0.50	1 PLUM	Ea.							
	Check for leaks				.010		.57		.57	.71	.88
	Check pump operation				.012		.64		.64	.80	1
	Lubricate pump and motor				.047		2.55		2.55	3.19	3.98
	Check suction or discharge pressure				.004		.21		.21	.27	.33
	Check packing glands, tighten				.014		.78		.78	.98	1.22
	Fill out inspection report				.022		1.21		1.21	1.51	1.88
	Total				.109		5.96		5.96	**7.46**	**9.29**
0030	**Replace pump / motor assembly**	10	2 PLUM	Ea.							
	Remove flanged connection pump				1.733		85		85	106	133
	Install new flanged connection pump (1/12 H.P.)				3.467	530	170		700	795	930
	Total				5.200	530	255		785	**901**	**1,063**

D2023 261 Circulation Pump, 1/8 HP

System Description	Freq. (Years)	Crew	Unit	Labor Hours	2012 Bare Costs				Total In-House	Total w/O&P
					Material	Labor	Equipment	Total		
0020 **Pump maintenance, 1/8 H.P.**	1	1 PLUM	Ea.							
Check for leaks				.010		.57		.57	.71	.88
Check pump operation				.012		.64		.64	.80	1
Lubricate pump and motor				.047		2.55		2.55	3.19	3.98
Check suction or discharge pressure				.004		.21		.21	.27	.33
Check packing glands, tighten				.014		.78		.78	.98	1.22
Fill out inspection report				.022		1.21		1.21	1.51	1.88
Total				.109		5.96		5.96	7.46	9.29
0030 **Replace pump / motor assembly**	20	2 PLUM	Ea.							
Remove flanged connection pump				1.733		85		85	106	133
Install new flanged connection pump (1/8 H.P.)				3.467	915	170		1,085	1,225	1,400
Total				5.200	915	255		1,170	1,331	1,533

D2023 262 Circulation Pump, 1/6 HP

System Description	Freq. (Years)	Crew	Unit	Labor Hours	2012 Bare Costs				Total In-House	Total w/O&P
					Material	Labor	Equipment	Total		
0020 **Pump maintenance, 1/6 H.P.**	1	1 PLUM	Ea.							
Check for leaks				.010		.57		.57	.71	.88
Check pump operation				.012		.64		.64	.80	1
Lubricate pump and motor				.047		2.55		2.55	3.19	3.98
Check suction or discharge pressure				.004		.21		.21	.27	.33
Check packing glands, tighten				.014		.78		.78	.98	1.22
Fill out inspection report				.022		1.21		1.21	1.51	1.88
Total				.109		5.96		5.96	7.46	9.29
0030 **Replace pump / motor assembly**	20	2 PLUM	Ea.							
Remove flanged connection pump				2.080		114		114	142	177
Install new flanged connection pump (1/6 H.P.)				4.160	1,325	204		1,529	1,725	1,975
Total				6.240	1,325	318		1,643	1,867	2,152

D2023 264 Circulation Pump, 1/2 HP

	System Description	Freq. (Years)	Crew	Unit	Labor Hours	2012 Bare Costs Material	2012 Bare Costs Labor	2012 Bare Costs Equipment	2012 Bare Costs Total	Total In-House	Total w/O&P
0020	**Pump maintenance, 1/2 H.P.**	1	1 PLUM	Ea.							
	Check for leaks				.010		.57		.57	.71	.88
	Check pump operation				.012		.64		.64	.80	1
	Check alignment				.053		2.91		2.91	3.63	4.54
	Lubricate pump and motor				.047		2.55		2.55	3.19	3.98
	Check suction or discharge pressure				.004		.21		.21	.27	.33
	Check packing glands, tighten				.014		.78		.78	.98	1.22
	Fill out inspection report				.022		1.21		1.21	1.51	1.88
	Total				.163		8.87		8.87	**11.09**	**13.83**
0030	**Replace pump / motor assembly, partial**	20	2 PLUM	Ea.							
	Remove flanged connection pump				2.600		128		128	160	199
	Install new flanged connection pump (1/2 H.P.)				5.200	2,200	256		2,456	2,750	3,150
	Total				7.800	2,200	384		2,584	**2,910**	**3,349**

D2023 266 Circulation Pump, Bronze 1 HP

	System Description	Freq. (Years)	Crew	Unit	Labor Hours	2012 Bare Costs Material	2012 Bare Costs Labor	2012 Bare Costs Equipment	2012 Bare Costs Total	Total In-House	Total w/O&P
0020	**Pump maintenance, 1 H.P.**	0.50	1 PLUM	Ea.							
	Check for leaks				.010		.57		.57	.71	.88
	Check pump operation				.012		.64		.64	.80	1
	Lubricate pump and motor				.047		2.55		2.55	3.19	3.98
	Check suction or discharge pressure				.004		.21		.21	.27	.33
	Check packing glands, tighten				.014		.78		.78	.98	1.22
	Fill out inspection report				.022		1.21		1.21	1.51	1.88
	Total				.109		5.96		5.96	**7.46**	**9.29**
0040	**Replace pump / motor assembly**	20	2 PLUM	Ea.							
	Remove pump / motor				2.600		128		128	160	199
	Install new flanged connection pump, bronze (1 H.P.)				5.200	3,875	256		4,131	4,575	5,250
	Total				7.800	3,875	384		4,259	**4,735**	**5,449**

D2023 267 Circulation Pump, C.I. 1-1/2 HP

	System Description	Freq. (Years)	Crew	Unit	Labor Hours	2012 Bare Costs				Total In-House	Total w/O&P
						Material	Labor	Equipment	Total		
0020	**Pump maintenance, 1-1/2 H.P.**	0.50	1 PLUM	Ea.							
	Check for leaks				.010		.57		.57	.71	.88
	Check pump operation				.012		.64		.64	.80	1
	Check alignment				.053		2.91		2.91	3.63	4.54
	Lubricate pump and motor				.047		2.55		2.55	3.19	3.98
	Check suction / discharge pressure				.004		.21		.21	.27	.33
	Check packing glands, tighten				.014		.78		.78	.98	1.22
	Fill out inspection report				.022		1.21		1.21	1.51	1.88
	Total				.163		8.87		8.87	11.09	13.83
0040	**Replace pump / motor assembly**	20	2 PLUM	Ea.							
	Remove flanged connection pump				2.600		128		128	160	199
	Install new flanged connection pump, C.I. (1-1/2 H.P.)				5.200	1,775	256		2,031	2,275	2,625
	Total				7.800	1,775	384		2,159	2,435	2,824

D2023 268 Circulation Pump, 3 HP

	System Description	Freq. (Years)	Crew	Unit	Labor Hours	2012 Bare Costs				Total In-House	Total w/O&P
						Material	Labor	Equipment	Total		
0020	**Pump maintenance, 3 H.P.**	0.50	Q-1	Ea.							
	Check for leaks				.012		.63		.63	.79	.98
	Check pump operation				.012		.64		.64	.80	1
	Check alignment				.059		3.23		3.23	4.03	5.05
	Lubricate pump and motor				.052		2.83		2.83	3.54	4.42
	Check suction / discharge pressure				.004		.21		.21	.27	.33
	Check packing glands, tighten				.016		.87		.87	1.09	1.36
	Fill out inspection report				.022		1.21		1.21	1.51	1.88
	Total				.176		9.62		9.62	12.03	15.02
0040	**Replace pump / motor assembly**	20	Q-1	Ea.							
	Remove flanged connection pump				4.400		216.70		216.70	270	335
	Install new flanged connection pump, 3 HP				8.889	7,150	435		7,585	8,400	9,625
	Total				13.289	7,150	651.70		7,801.70	8,670	9,960

D2023 310 Hose Bibb

	System Description	Freq. (Years)	Crew	Unit	Labor Hours	2012 Bare Costs				Total In-House	Total w/O&P
						Material	Labor	Equipment	Total		
0020	**Replace old valve with new**	10	1 PLUM	Ea.							
	Remove hose bibb				.217		11.85		11.85	14.75	18.45
	Install new hose bibb				.433	13.30	23.50		36.80	44	53.50
	Total				.650	13.30	35.35		48.65	**58.75**	**71.95**

D2023 320 Water Meter

	System Description	Freq. (Years)	Crew	Unit	Labor Hours	2012 Bare Costs				Total In-House	Total w/O&P
						Material	Labor	Equipment	Total		
0010	**Overhaul**	13	1 PLUM	Ea.							
	Open meter, replace worn parts				.300	3.10	16.40		19.50	24	29.50
	Total				.300	3.10	16.40		19.50	**24**	**29.50**
0020	**Remove old 5/8" meter, install new**	25	1 PLUM	Ea.							
	Remove 5/8" water meter				.325		17.75		17.75	22	27.50
	Install 5/8" threaded water meter				.650	46	35.50		81.50	95	113
	Total				.975	46	53.25		99.25	**117**	**140.50**
0025	**Remove old 3/4" meter, install new**	25	1 PLUM	Ea.							
	Remove 3/4" water meter				.371		20.50		20.50	25.50	31.50
	Install 3/4" threaded water meter				.743	83.50	40.50		124	142	167
	Total				1.114	83.50	61		144.50	**167.50**	**198.50**
0030	**Remove old 1" meter, install new**	25	1 PLUM	Ea.							
	Remove 1" water meter				.433		23.50		23.50	29.50	37
	Install 1" threaded water meter				.867	127	47.50		174.50	199	232
	Total				1.300	127	71		198	**228.50**	**269**
0035	**Remove old 1-1/2" meter, install new**	25	1 PLUM	Ea.							
	Remove 1-1/2" water meter				.650		35.50		35.50	44.50	55.50
	Install 1-1/2" threaded water meter				1.300	310	71		381	430	500
	Total				1.950	310	106.50		416.50	**474.50**	**555.50**
0040	**Remove old 2" meter, install new**	25	1 PLUM	Ea.							
	Remove 2" water meter				.867		47.50		47.50	59	73.50
	Install 2" threaded water meter				1.733	420	94.50		514.50	580	670
	Total				2.600	420	142		562	**639**	**743.50**

D2023 320 Water Meter

	System Description	Freq. (Years)	Crew	Unit	Labor Hours	2012 Bare Costs				Total In-House	Total w/O&P
						Material	Labor	Equipment	Total		
0045	**Remove old 3" meter, install new**	25	Q-1	Ea.							
	Remove 3" water meter				3.467		170		170	213	266
	Install 3" flanged water meter				6.932	2,850	340		3,190	3,550	4,100
	Total				10.399	2,850	510		3,360	3,763	4,366
0050	**Remove old 4" meter, install new**	25	Q-1	Ea.							
	Remove 4" water meter				6.932		340		340	425	530
	Install 4" flanged water meter				13.865	4,575	680		5,255	5,875	6,775
	Total				20.797	4,575	1,020		5,595	6,300	7,305
0055	**Remove old 6" meter, install new**	25	Q-1	Ea.							
	Remove 6" water meter				10.403		510		510	640	795
	Install 6" flanged water meter				20.806	7,300	1,025		8,325	9,300	10,700
	Total				31.209	7,300	1,535		8,835	9,940	11,495
0060	**Remove old 8" meter, install new**	25	Q-1	Ea.							
	Remove 8" water meter				12.998		640		640	795	995
	Install 8" flanged water meter				26.016	11,500	1,275		12,775	14,200	16,400
	Total				39.014	11,500	1,915		13,415	14,995	17,395

D2023 370 Water Softener

	System Description	Freq. (Years)	Crew	Unit	Labor Hours	2012 Bare Costs				Total In-House	Total w/O&P
						Material	Labor	Equipment	Total		
0030	**Replace softener**	15	2 PLUM	Ea.							
	Remove old unit				2.600		142		142	177	221
	Install new water softener				5.200	680	284		964	1,100	1,300
	Total				7.800	680	426		1,106	1,277	1,521

D2033 110   Pipe & Fittings, Cast Iron

System Description	Freq. (Years)	Crew	Unit	Labor Hours	2012 Bare Costs Material	Labor	Equipment	Total	Total In-House	Total w/O&P
0020 Unclog main drain										
Unclog main drain using auger	10	1 PLUM	Ea.	.630		34.50		34.50	43	53.50
Total				.630		34.50		34.50	**43**	**53.50**
0030 Replace cast iron pipe & fittings, 4″										
Remove old pipe	40	2 PLUM	L.F.	.189		9.30		9.30	11.60	14.45
Install new 4″ cast iron pipe				.378	15.45	18.60		34.05	40	48.50
Total				.567	15.45	27.90		43.35	**51.60**	**62.95**

D2033 130   Pipe & Fittings, PVC

System Description	Freq. (Years)	Crew	Unit	Labor Hours	2012 Bare Costs Material	Labor	Equipment	Total	Total In-House	Total w/O&P
0010 Unclog floor drain										
Unclog plugged floor drain	20	1 PLUM	Ea.	.650		35.50		35.50	44.50	55.50
Total				.650		35.50		35.50	**44.50**	**55.50**
0020 Unclog 4″ - 12″ diameter PVC main drain per L.F.										
Unclog main drain using auger	10	1 PLUM	L.F.	.052		2.82		2.82	3.52	4.39
Total				.052		2.82		2.82	**3.52**	**4.39**
0040 Repair joint										
Remove plastic fitting (2 connections)	10	1 PLUM	Ea.	.650		32		32	40	50
Connect fitting (2 connections)				1.300	8.20	64		72.20	89	110
Inspect joints				.163		8.90		8.90	11.15	13.90
Total				2.113	8.20	104.90		113.10	**140.15**	**173.90**
0060 Replace pipe, 1-1/2″										
Remove broken pipe	30	2 PLUM	L.F.	.145		7.40		7.40	9.25	11.50
Install new pipe, couplings, hangers				.289	4.59	15.75		20.34	24.50	30
Inspect joints				.327		17.80		17.80	22.50	28
Total				.760	4.59	40.95		45.54	**56.25**	**69.50**

D2033 130 Pipe & Fittings, PVC

System Description	Freq. (Years)	Crew	Unit	Labor Hours	2012 Bare Costs				Total In-House	Total w/O&P
					Material	Labor	Equipment	Total		
0080 Replace pipe, 2"	30	2 PLUM	L.F.							
Remove broken pipe				.176		8.65		8.65	10.80	13.50
Install new pipe, couplings, hangers				.353	5.75	17.35		23.10	28	34
Inspect joints				.327		17.80		17.80	22.50	28
Total				.855	5.75	43.80		49.55	**61.30**	**75.50**
0100 Replace pipe, 4"	30	2 PLUM	L.F.							
Remove broken pipe				.217		10.65		10.65	13.30	16.60
Install new pipe, couplings, hangers				.433	14.35	21.50		35.85	42.50	51
Inspect joints				.327		17.80		17.80	22.50	28
Total				.977	14.35	49.95		64.30	**78.30**	**95.60**
0120 Replace pipe, 6"	30	2 PLUM	L.F.							
Remove broken pipe				.267		13.10		13.10	16.35	20.50
New pipe, couplings, hangers				.533	25	29		54	64	77
Inspect joints				.327		17.80		17.80	22.50	28
Total				1.126	25	59.90		84.90	**102.85**	**125.50**
0140 Replace pipe, 8"	30	2 PLUM	L.F.							
Remove broken pipe				.325		16.55		16.55	20.50	26
Install new pipe, couplings, hangers				.650	38.50	33		71.50	83.50	99.50
Inspect joints				.327		17.80		17.80	22.50	28
Total				1.302	38.50	67.35		105.85	**126.50**	**153.50**

D2033 305 Pipe & Fittings

System Description	Freq. (Years)	Crew	Unit	Labor Hours	2012 Bare Costs				Total In-House	Total w/O&P
					Material	Labor	Equipment	Total		
3010 Unclog floor drain	10	1 PLUM	Ea.							
Unclog plugged floor drain				4.000		223		223	278	345
Solvent					26			26	28.50	32.50
Total				4.000	26	223		249	**306.50**	**377.50**
3020 Unclog 4" - 12" diameter main drain per L.F.	10	2 PLUM	L.F.							
Unclog main drain using auger				.052		2.82		2.82	3.52	4.39
Total				.052		2.82		2.82	**3.52**	**4.39**

D2033 310 Floor Drain W/O Bucket

	System Description	Freq. (Years)	Crew	Unit	Labor Hours	2012 Bare Costs				Total In-House	Total w/O&P
						Material	Labor	Equipment	Total		
0010	**Clean drain**	4	1 PLUM	Ea.							
	Remove debris from drain				1.590		87		87	108	135
	Total				1.590		87		87	**108**	**135**
0030	**Replace floor drain**	40	1 PLUM	Ea.							
	Remove floor drain				1.040		57		57	71	88.50
	Install floor drain				2.080	825	102		927	1,025	1,200
	Total				3.120	825	159		984	**1,096**	**1,288.50**

D2033 330 Floor Drain With Bucket

	System Description	Freq. (Years)	Crew	Unit	Labor Hours	2012 Bare Costs				Total In-House	Total w/O&P
						Material	Labor	Equipment	Total		
0010	**Clean out bucket**	5	1 PLUM	Ea.							
	Remove debris from bucket				4.000		218		218	273	340
	Total				4.000		218		218	**273**	**340**
0030	**Replace floor drain**	40	1 PLUM	Ea.							
	Remove floor drain				1.040		57		57	71	88.50
	Install floor drain				2.080	825	102		927	1,025	1,200
	Total				3.120	825	159		984	**1,096**	**1,288.50**

197

D2043 110 Distribution: Gutters, Pipe

System Description	Freq. (Years)	Crew	Unit	Labor Hours	2012 Bare Costs				Total In-House	Total w/O&P
					Material	Labor	Equipment	Total		
1010 General maintenance & repair	1	1 PLUM	M.L.F.							
Inspect rainwater pipes				.104		5.65		5.65	7.10	8.85
Clean out pipes				4.000		218		218	273	340
Total				4.104		223.65		223.65	280.10	348.85
1020 Replace pipe or gutter	20	1 PLUM	L.F.							
Remove 4" PVC roof drain system				.650		10.65		10.65	13.30	16.60
Install 4" roof drain system				.433	15.60	21.50		37.10	43.50	52.50
Total				.650	15.60	32.15		47.75	56.80	69.10

D2043 210 Drain: Roof, Scupper, Area

System Description	Freq. (Years)	Crew	Unit	Labor Hours	2012 Bare Costs				Total In-House	Total w/O&P
					Material	Labor	Equipment	Total		
1010 General maintenance & repair	1	1 PLUM	Ea.							
Inspect drain				.104		5.65		5.65	7.10	8.85
Clean drain				.400		22		22	27.50	34
Total				.504		27.65		27.65	34.60	42.85
1020 Replace drain	40	1 PLUM	Ea.							
Remove drain				.800		39.50		39.50	49	61.50
Install roof drain				1.600	330	78.50		408.50	460	535
Total				2.400	330	118		448	509	596.50

D2043 310 | **Rainwater Sump Pump**

	System Description	Freq. (Years)	Crew	Unit	Labor Hours	2012 Bare Costs				Total In-House	Total w/O&P
						Material	Labor	Equipment	Total		
1020	**Pump maintenance, 87 GPM**	1	1 PLUM	Ea.							
	Check for leaks				.010		.57		.57	.71	.88
	Check pump operation				.012		.64		.64	.80	1
	Check alignment				.053		2.91		2.91	3.63	4.54
	Lubricate pump and motor				.047		2.55		2.55	3.19	3.98
	Check suction or discharge pressure				.004		.21		.21	.27	.33
	Check packing glands, tighten				.014		.78		.78	.98	1.22
	Fill out inspection report				.022		1.21		1.21	1.51	1.88
	Total				.163		8.87		8.87	11.09	13.83
1030	**Replace sump pump / motor assembly**	20	2 PLUM	Ea.							
	Remove sump pump assembly				1.300		71		71	88.50	111
	Install new cast iron sump pump (87 GPM)				2.078	252	113		365	420	490
	Total				3.378	252	184		436	508.50	601

D2093 910 Pipe & Fittings, Industrial Gas

System Description	Freq. (Years)	Crew	Unit	Labor Hours	2012 Bare Costs				Total In-House	Total w/O&P
					Material	Labor	Equipment	Total		
1010 General maintenance										
General maintenance	2	1 PLUM	M.L.F.	.500		27.50		27.50	34	42.50
Total				.500		27.50		27.50	**34**	**42.50**
1030 Replace pipe and fittings	75	2 PLUM	L.F.							
Shut off valve				1.067		58		58	72.50	90.50
Remove old pipe				.162		7.95		7.95	9.95	12.40
Install 2" black steel pipe, couplings, and hangers				.325	14.90	15.95		30.85	36.50	43.50
Check for leaks				.889		48.50		48.50	60.50	75.50
Total				2.443	14.90	130.40		145.30	**179.45**	**221.90**

D2093 920 Pipe & Fittings, Anesthesia

System Description	Freq. (Years)	Crew	Unit	Labor Hours	2012 Bare Costs				Total In-House	Total w/O&P
					Material	Labor	Equipment	Total		
1010 Resolder joint	12	1 PLUM	Ea.							
Measure, cut & clean both ends				.053		2.91		2.91	3.63	4.54
Attach fitting				.578	8.65	31.50		40.15	49	60
Total				.631	8.65	34.41		43.06	**52.63**	**64.54**
1030 Replace pipe and fittings	25	2 PLUM	L.F.							
Remove old pipe				.069		3.79		3.79	4.72	5.90
Install new 3/4" copper tubing, couplings, hangers				.141	9.55	7.65		17.20	20	24
Total				.210	9.55	11.44		20.99	**24.72**	**29.90**

D2093 930 Pipe & Fittings, Oxygen

System Description	Freq. (Years)	Crew	Unit	Labor Hours	2012 Bare Costs				Total In-House	Total w/O&P
					Material	Labor	Equipment	Total		
1010 Resolder joint	12	1 PLUM	Ea.							
Measure, cut & clean both ends				.289		15.80		15.80	19.70	24.50
Attach fitting				.578	8.65	31.50		40.15	49	60
Total				.867	8.65	47.30		55.95	**68.70**	**84.50**

D2093 930 Pipe & Fittings, Oxygen

	System Description	Freq. (Years)	Crew	Unit	Labor Hours	2012 Bare Costs				Total In-House	Total w/O&P
						Material	Labor	Equipment	Total		
1030	**Replace pipe and fittings**	25	2 PLUM	L.F.							
	Remove old pipe				.069		3.79		3.79	4.72	5.90
	Install new 3/4" copper tubing, couplings, hangers				.141	9.55	7.65		17.20	20	24
	Total				.210	9.55	11.44		20.99	24.72	29.90

D2093 940 Pipe & Fittings, Compressed Air

	System Description	Freq. (Years)	Crew	Unit	Labor Hours	2012 Bare Costs				Total In-House	Total w/O&P
						Material	Labor	Equipment	Total		
1010	**General maintenance**	2	1 PLUM	M.L.F.							
	General maintenance				.500		27.50		27.50	34	42.50
	Total				.500		27.50		27.50	34	42.50
1030	**Replace pipe and fittings**	75	2 PLUM	L.F.							
	Shut off valve				1.067		58		58	72.50	90.50
	Remove old pipe				.052		2.84		2.84	3.54	4.42
	Install 2" black steel pipe, couplings, and hangers				.325	14.90	15.95		30.85	36.50	43.50
	Check for leaks				.889		48.50		48.50	60.50	75.50
	Total				2.333	14.90	125.29		140.19	173.04	213.92

System Description	Freq. (Years)	Crew	Unit	Labor Hours	2012 Bare Costs Material	2012 Bare Costs Labor	2012 Bare Costs Equipment	2012 Bare Costs Total	Total In-House	Total w/O&P
1004										
Check and adjust 3/4 H.P. compressor	1	1 SPRI	Ea.							
Check compressor oil level				.022		1.21		1.21	1.51	1.88
Check V-belt tension				.038		2.06		2.06	2.57	3.21
Drain moisture from air tank				.033		1.78		1.78	2.22	2.77
Clean air intake filter on compressor				.178		9.70		9.70	12.10	15.10
Clean reusable oil filter				.182		9.95		9.95	12.40	15.45
Check pressure relief valve				.108		5.90		5.90	7.35	9.20
Clean cooling fins				.105		5.75		5.75	7.15	8.95
Check motor				.060		3.26		3.26	4.07	5.10
Check control circuits				.182		9.95		9.95	12.40	15.45
Operation checks				.222		12.15		12.15	15.15	18.90
Fill out maintenance report				.022		1.21		1.21	1.51	1.88
Total				1.151		62.92		62.92	78.43	97.89
1006										
Replace 3/4 H.P. compressor	25	1 SPRI	Ea.							
Remove air compressor				4.457		232		232	289	360
Install new 3/4 H.P. compressor				6.250	685	340		1,025	1,175	1,375
Total				10.707	685	572		1,257	1,464	1,735
1010										
Check and adjust 2 H.P. compressor	1	1 PLUM	Ea.							
Check compressor oil level				.022		1.21		1.21	1.51	1.88
Check V-belt tension				.038		2.06		2.06	2.57	3.21
Drain moisture from air tank				.033		1.78		1.78	2.22	2.77
Clean air intake filter on compressor				.178		9.70		9.70	12.10	15.10
Clean reusable oil filter				.182		9.95		9.95	12.40	15.45
Check pressure relief valve				.108		5.90		5.90	7.35	9.20
Clean cooling fins				.105		5.75		5.75	7.15	8.95
Check motor				.060		3.26		3.26	4.07	5.10
Check control circuits				.182		9.95		9.95	12.40	15.45
Operation checks				.222		12.15		12.15	15.15	18.90
Fill out maintenance report				.022		1.21		1.21	1.51	1.88
Total				1.151		62.92		62.92	78.43	97.89
1030										
Replace 2 H.P. compressor	25	2 PLUM	Ea.							
Remove air compressor				4.457		232		232	289	360
Install new 2 H.P. compressor				8.915	3,575	465		4,040	4,500	5,200
Total				13.372	3,575	697		4,272	4,789	5,560

System Description	Freq. (Years)	Crew	Unit	Labor Hours	2012 Bare Costs				Total In-House	Total w/O&P
					Material	Labor	Equipment	Total		
3010										
Check and adjust 10 H.P. compressor	1	1 PLUM	Ea.							
Check compressor oil level				.022		1.21		1.21	1.51	1.88
Check tension on V-belt				.038		2.06		2.06	2.57	3.21
Drain moisture from air tank				.033		1.78		1.78	2.22	2.77
Clean air intake filter on compressor				.178		9.70		9.70	12.10	15.10
Clean reusable oil filter				.182		9.95		9.95	12.40	15.45
Check operation of pressure valve				.108		5.90		5.90	7.35	9.20
Clean cooling fins				.105		5.75		5.75	7.15	8.95
Check motor				.060		3.26		3.26	4.07	5.10
Check compressor circuits				.182		9.95		9.95	12.40	15.45
Perform operation				.222		12.15		12.15	15.15	18.90
Fill out maintenance report				.022		1.21		1.21	1.51	1.88
Total				1.151		62.92		62.92	78.43	97.89
3030										
Replace 10 H.P. compressor	25	2 PLUM	Ea.							
Remove compressor				17.335		870		870	1,075	1,350
Install 2-stage compressor 10 H.P.				34.632	6,500	1,725		8,225	9,325	10,800
Total				51.967	6,500	2,595		9,095	10,400	12,150
4010										
Check and adjust 25 H.P. compressor	1	1 PLUM	Ea.							
Check compressor oil level				.022		1.21		1.21	1.51	1.88
Check tension on V-belt				.038		2.06		2.06	2.57	3.21
Drain moisture from air tank				.033		1.78		1.78	2.22	2.77
Clean air intake filter on compressor				.178		9.70		9.70	12.10	15.10
Clean reusable oil filter				.182		9.95		9.95	12.40	15.45
Check operation of pressure valve				.108		5.90		5.90	7.35	9.20
Clean cooling fins				.105		5.75		5.75	7.15	8.95
Check motor				.060		3.26		3.26	4.07	5.10
Check compressor circuits				.182		9.95		9.95	12.40	15.45
Perform operation				.222		12.15		12.15	15.15	18.90
Fill out maintenance report				.022		1.21		1.21	1.51	1.88
Total				1.151		62.92		62.92	78.43	97.89
4030										
Replace 25 H.P. compressor	25	2 PLUM	Ea.							
Remove compressor				26.002		1,350		1,350	1,675	2,100
Install 2-stage compressor 25 H.P.				51.948	14,700	2,700		17,400	19,500	22,600
Total				77.950	14,700	4,050		18,750	21,175	24,700

D2093 Other Plumbing Systems

D2093 946 Compressed Air Systems, Compressors

| | System Description | Freq. (Years) | Crew | Unit | Labor Hours | 2012 Bare Costs | | | | Total In-House | Total w/O&P |
						Material	Labor	Equipment	Total		
5030	**Check operation**										
	Check operation of unit	1	1 STPI	Ea.	.320		17.80		17.80	22	28
	Total				.320		17.80		17.80	**22**	**28**

D3013 110 Fuel Oil Storage Tank, 275 Gallon

System Description	Freq. (Years)	Crew	Unit	Labor Hours	2012 Bare Costs Material	2012 Bare Costs Labor	2012 Bare Costs Equipment	2012 Bare Costs Total	Total In-House	Total w/O&P
0010 Replace 275 gallon fuel storage tank	30	Q-5	Ea.							
Remove 275 gallon tank				2.081		104		104	130	163
Install 275 gallon tank				4.156	445	208		653	750	880
Total				6.236	445	312		757	**880**	**1,043**

D3013 150 Fuel Level Meter

System Description	Freq. (Years)	Crew	Unit	Labor Hours	2012 Bare Costs Material	2012 Bare Costs Labor	2012 Bare Costs Equipment	2012 Bare Costs Total	Total In-House	Total w/O&P
0010 Preventive maintenance	5	1 STPI	Ea.							
Check fuel level meter calibration				.500		28		28	35	43.50
Total				.500		28		28	**35**	**43.50**
0020 Replace remote tank fuel gauge	20	1 STPI	Ea.							
Remove remote read gauge				2.081		116		116	145	181
Replace remote read gauge 5" pointer travel				4.167	3,875	232		4,107	4,550	5,200
Total				6.247	3,875	348		4,223	**4,695**	**5,381**

D3013 160 Oil Filter

System Description	Freq. (Years)	Crew	Unit	Labor Hours	2012 Bare Costs Material	2012 Bare Costs Labor	2012 Bare Costs Equipment	2012 Bare Costs Total	Total In-House	Total w/O&P
0010 Preventive maintenance	1	1 STPI	Ea.							
Replace filter element				.052	1.93	2.90		4.83	5.75	6.90
Total				.052	1.93	2.90		4.83	**5.75**	**6.90**
0020 Replace filter housing	30	1 STPI	Ea.							
Replace filter housing				.520	19.25	29		48.25	57.50	69
Total				.520	19.25	29		48.25	**57.50**	**69**

D3013 170 — Fuel Oil Storage: Pipe & Fittings, Copper

System Description	Freq. (Years)	Crew	Unit	Labor Hours	2012 Bare Costs Material	Labor	Equipment	Total	Total In-House	Total w/O&P
0010 Remake flare type joint										
Remake flare type joint	10	1 STPI	M.L.F.	.286		15.90		15.90	19.85	25
Total				.286		15.90		15.90	**19.85**	**25**
0020 Install 10' sect. 3/8" type L copper per M.L.F.										
Remove section 3/8" diameter copper	20	1 PLUM	Ea.	.619		33.80		33.80	42	52.50
Install 10' section new 3/8" diameter type L				1.238	37.30	67.50		104.80	126	152
Total				1.857	37.30	101.30		138.60	**168**	**204.50**
0030 Install 10' sect. 1/2" type L copper per M.L.F.										
Remove section 1/2" diameter copper	20	1 PLUM	Ea.	.642		35.10		35.10	44	54.50
Install 10' section new 1/2" diameter type L				1.284	43	70		113	135	163
Total				1.926	43	105.10		148.10	**179**	**217.50**
0040 Install 10' sect. 5/8" type L copper per M.L.F.										
Remove section 5/8" diameter copper	20	1 PLUM	Ea.	.658		35.90		35.90	45	56
Install 10' section new 5/8" diameter type L				1.316	62.50	72		134.50	159	190
Total				1.975	62.50	107.90		170.40	**204**	**246**
0050 Install 10' sect. 3/4" type L copper per M.L.F.										
Remove section 3/4" diameter copper	20	1 PLUM	Ea.	.684		37.40		37.40	46.50	58
Install 10' section new 3/4" diameter type L				1.369	66	74.50		140.50	166	199
Total				2.053	66	111.90		177.90	**212.50**	**257**
0060 Install 10' section 1" type L copper per M.L.F.										
Remove section 1" diameter copper	20	1 PLUM	Ea.	.765		41.80		41.80	52	65
Install 10' section new 1" diameter type L				1.529	98.50	83.50		182	215	253
Total				2.294	98.50	125.30		223.80	**267**	**318**
0130 Replace 1000' type L 3/8" copper										
Remove section 3/8" diameter copper	25	1 PLUM	M.L.F.	61.920		3,380		3,380	4,225	5,250
Install 1000' section new 3/8" diameter type L				123.800	3,730	6,750		10,480	12,600	15,200
Total				185.720	3,730	10,130		13,860	**16,825**	**20,450**
0140 Replace 1000' type L 1/2" copper										
Remove section 1/2" diameter copper	25	1 PLUM	M.L.F.	64.220		3,510		3,510	4,375	5,450
Install 1000' section new 1/2" diameter type L				128.390	4,300	7,000		11,300	13,500	16,300
Total				192.610	4,300	10,510		14,810	**17,875**	**21,750**

D30 HVAC | D3013 | Energy Supply

D3013 170 | Fuel Oil Storage: Pipe & Fittings, Copper

System Description	Freq. (Years)	Crew	Unit	Labor Hours	2012 Bare Costs Material	Labor	Equipment	Total	Total In-House	Total w/O&P
0150 Replace 1000' type L 5/8" copper										
Remove section 5/8" diameter copper	25	1 PLUM	M.L.F.	65.840		3,590		3,590	4,500	5,600
Install 1000' section new 5/8" diameter type L				131.640	6,250	7,200		13,450	15,900	19,000
Total				197.480	6,250	10,790		17,040	20,400	24,600
0160 Replace 1000' type L 3/4" copper										
Remove section 3/4" diameter copper	25	1 PLUM	M.L.F.	68.440		3,740		3,740	4,650	5,800
Install 1000' section new 3/4" diameter type L				136.850	6,600	7,450		14,050	16,600	19,900
Total				205.290	6,600	11,190		17,790	21,250	25,700
0170 Replace 1000' type L 1" copper										
Remove section 1" diameter copper	25	1 PLUM	M.L.F.	76.480		4,180		4,180	5,200	6,500
Install 1000' section new 1" diameter type L				152.930	9,850	8,350		18,200	21,500	25,300
Total				229.410	9,850	12,530		22,380	26,700	31,800

D3013 210 | Natural Gas: Pipe & Fittings, Steel/Iron

System Description	Freq. (Years)	Crew	Unit	Labor Hours	2012 Bare Costs Material	Labor	Equipment	Total	Total In-House	Total w/O&P
0010 Install new 2" gasket, 1 per M.L.F.										
Disconnect joint, remove gasket & clean faces	30	1 STPI	Ea.	.803		44.63		44.63	55.50	69.50
Install gasket and make up bolts				.800	4.85	44.50		49.35	61	75.50
Total				1.603	4.85	89.13		93.98	116.50	145
0020 Install new 3" gasket, 1 per M.L.F.										
Disconnect joint, remove gasket & clean faces	30	1 STPI	Ea.	.945		52.50		52.50	65.50	82
Install gasket and make up bolts				.945	5.80	52.50		58.30	72	89.50
Total				1.890	5.80	105		110.80	137.50	171.50
0030 Install new 4" gasket, 1 per M.L.F.										
Disconnect joint, remove gasket & clean faces	30	1 STPI	Ea.	1.300		72.50		72.50	90.50	113
Install gasket and make up bolts				1.300	10.40	71		81.40	100	124
Total				2.600	10.40	143.50		153.90	190.50	237

D3013 210 | Natural Gas: Pipe & Fittings, Steel/Iron

	System Description	Freq. (Years)	Crew	Unit	Labor Hours	2012 Bare Costs				Total In-House	Total w/O&P
						Material	Labor	Equipment	Total		
0040	**Install new 6" gasket, 1 per M.L.F.**	30	1 STPI	Ea.							
	Disconnect joint, remove gasket & clean faces				1.733		96.50		96.50	120	150
	Install gasket and make up bolts				1.733	18.10	96.50		114.60	140	173
	Total				3.466	18.10	193		211.10	**260**	**323**
0110	**Replace 10' of buried 2" diam. st. pipe/M.L.F.**	12	Q-4	Ea.							
	Check break or leak				.016		.89		.89	1.11	1.39
	Turn valve on and off				.010		.56		.56	.70	.87
	Excavate by hand				5.771		202.20		202.20	269	330
	Remove broken 2" diameter section				.743		38.60	.90	39.50	49	61
	Install 10' of pipe coated & wrapped				1.143	88	59.50	1.30	148.80	173	204
	Check for leaks, additional section				.900		50		50	63	78
	Backfill by hand				2.101		73.33		73.33	98	121
	Total				10.684	88	425.08	2.20	515.28	**653.81**	**796.26**
0120	**Replace 10' of buried 3" diam. st. pipe/M.L.F.**	12	Q-4	Ea.							
	Check break or leak				.016		.89		.89	1.11	1.39
	Turn valve on and off				.010		.56		.56	.70	.87
	Excavate by hand				5.771		202.20		202.20	269	330
	Remove broken 3" diameter section				.800		41.60	.90	42.50	53	66
	Install 10' of pipe coated & wrapped				1.231	145.50	64	1.40	210.90	240	283
	Check for leaks, additional section				.900		50		50	63	78
	Backfill by hand				2.101		73.33		73.33	98	121
	Total				10.829	145.50	432.58	2.30	580.38	**724.81**	**880.26**
0130	**Replace 10' of buried 4" diam. st. pipe/M.L.F.**	12	B-35	Ea.							
	Check break or leak				.016		.89		.89	1.11	1.39
	Turn valve on and off				.010		.56		.56	.70	.87
	Excavate by hand				5.771		202.20		202.20	269	330
	Remove broken 4" diameter section				1.224		53.50	17.40	70.90	86	104
	Install 10' of pipe coated & wrapped				1.882	189.50	82	26.80	298.30	340	395
	Check for leaks, additional section				.900		50		50	63	78
	Backfill by hand				2.101		73.33		73.33	98	121
	Total				11.905	189.50	462.48	44.20	696.18	**857.81**	**1,030.26**

D3013 210 Natural Gas: Pipe & Fittings, Steel/Iron

	System Description	Freq. (Years)	Crew	Unit	Labor Hours	2012 Bare Costs				Total In-House	Total w/O&P
						Material	Labor	Equipment	Total		
0140	**Replace 10' of buried 6" diam. st. pipe/M.L.F.**	12	B-35	Ea.							
	Check break or leak				.016		.89		.89	1.11	1.39
	Turn valve on and off				.010		.56		.56	.70	.87
	Excavate by hand				5.771		202.20		202.20	269	330
	Remove broken 6" diameter section				1.734		75.50	24.70	100.20	122	148
	Install 10' of pipe coated & wrapped				2.667	335	116	38	489	555	645
	Check for leaks, additional section				.900		50		50	63	78
	Backfill by hand				2.101		73.33		73.33	98	121
	Total				13.199	335	518.48	62.70	916.18	1,108.81	1,324.26
0210	**Replace 1000 L.F. of buried 2" diam. st. pipe**	75	Q-4	M.L.F.							
	Check break or leak				1.600		89		89	111	139
	Turn valve on and off				1.000		55.50		55.50	69.50	87
	Excavate with 1/2 C.Y. backhoe				23.111		944.44	526.67	1,471.11	1,750	2,100
	Remove broken 2" diameter section				74.250		3,860	90	3,950	4,900	6,100
	Install 1000' of pipe coated & wrapped				114.290	8,800	5,950	130	14,880	17,300	20,400
	Check for leaks, additional section				9.000		500		500	630	780
	Backfill with 1 C.Y. bucket				8.667		371.11	193.33	564.44	670	805
	Total				231.918	8,800	11,770.05	940	21,510.05	25,430.50	30,411
0220	**Replace 1000 L.F. of buried 3" diam. st. pipe**	75	Q-4	M.L.F.							
	Check break or leak				1.600		89		89	111	139
	Turn valve on and off				1.000		55.50		55.50	69.50	87
	Excavate with 1/2 C.Y. backhoe				23.111		944.44	526.67	1,471.11	1,750	2,100
	Remove broken 3" diameter section				80.000		4,160	90	4,250	5,300	6,600
	Install 1000' of pipe coated & wrapped				123.080	14,550	6,400	140	21,090	24,000	28,300
	Check for leaks, additional section				9.000		500		500	630	780
	Backfill with 1 C.Y. bucket				8.667		371.11	193.33	564.44	670	805
	Total				246.458	14,550	12,520.05	950	28,020.05	32,530.50	38,811
0230	**Replace 1000 L.F. of buried 4" diam. st. pipe**	75	B-35	M.L.F.							
	Check break or leak				1.600		89		89	111	139
	Turn valve on and off				1.000		55.50		55.50	69.50	87
	Excavate with 1/2 C.Y. backhoe				23.111		944.44	526.67	1,471.11	1,750	2,100
	Remove broken 4" diameter section				122.390		5,350	1,740	7,090	8,600	10,400
	Install 1000' of pipe coated & wrapped				188.240	18,950	8,200	2,680	29,830	34,000	39,700
	Check for leaks, additional section				9.000		500		500	630	780
	Backfill with 1 C.Y. bucket				8.667		371.11	193.33	564.44	670	805
	Total				354.008	18,950	15,510.05	5,140	39,600.05	45,830.50	54,011

D3013 210 | Natural Gas: Pipe & Fittings, Steel/Iron

	System Description	Freq. (Years)	Crew	Unit	Labor Hours	Material	Labor	Equipment	Total	Total In-House	Total w/O&P
							2012 Bare Costs				
0240	**Replace 1000 L.F. of buried 6″ diam. st. pipe**	75	B-35	M.L.F.							
	Check break or leak				1.600		89		89	111	139
	Turn valve on and off				1.000		55.50		55.50	69.50	87
	Excavate with 1/2 C.Y. backhoe				23.111		944.44	526.67	1,471.11	1,750	2,100
	Remove broken 6″ diameter section				173.390		7,550	2,470	10,020	12,200	14,800
	Install 1000′ of pipe coated & wrapped				266.670	33,500	11,600	3,800	48,900	55,500	64,500
	Check for leaks, additional section				9.000		500		500	630	780
	Backfill with 1 C.Y. bucket				8.667		371.11	193.33	564.44	670	805
	Total				483.438	33,500	21,110.05	6,990	61,600.05	70,930.50	83,211
0410	**Replace 10′ of hung 2″ diam. st. pipe/M.L.F.**	12	Q-1	Ea.							
	Check break or leak				.016		.89		.89	1.11	1.39
	Turn valve on and off				1.000		56		56	70	87
	Remove broken 2″ diameter section				1.626		80		80	99.50	125
	Install 10′ of black 2″ diameter steel pipe				3.250	149	159.50		308.50	365	435
	Check for leaks, additional section				.900		50		50	63	78
	Total				6.792	149	346.39		495.39	598.61	726.39
0420	**Replace 10′ of hung 3″ diam. st. pipe/M.L.F.**	12	Q-15	Ea.							
	Check break or leak				.016		.89		.89	1.11	1.39
	Turn valve on and off				.010		.56		.56	.70	.87
	Remove broken 3″ diameter section				2.420		119	5.60	124.60	154	192
	Install 10′ of black 3″ diameter steel pipe				4.837	255	240	11.20	506.20	590	700
	Check for leaks, additional section				.900		50		50	63	78
	Total				8.182	255	410.45	16.80	682.25	808.81	972.26
0430	**Replace 10′ of hung 4″ diam. st. pipe/M.L.F.**	12	Q-15	Ea.							
	Check break or leak				.016		.89		.89	1.11	1.39
	Turn valve on and off				.010		.56		.56	.70	.87
	Remove broken 4″ diameter section				2.812		138	6.50	144.50	179	222
	Install 10′ of black 4″ diameter steel pipe				5.622	350	275	13	638	745	880
	Check for leaks, additional section				.900		50		50	63	78
	Total				9.359	350	464.45	19.50	833.95	988.81	1,182.26

D3013 210   Natural Gas: Pipe & Fittings, Steel/Iron

System Description	Freq. (Years)	Crew	Unit	Labor Hours	2012 Bare Costs				Total In-House	Total w/O&P
					Material	Labor	Equipment	Total		
0440 Replace 10' of hung 6" diam. st. pipe/M.L.F.	12	Q-16	Ea.							
Check break or leak				.016		.89		.89	1.11	1.39
Turn valve on and off				.010		.56		.56	.70	.87
Remove broken 6" diameter section				4.335		220	6.70	226.70	285	350
Install 10' of black 6" diameter steel pipe				8.667	520	440	13.30	973.30	1,150	1,350
Check for leaks, additional section				.900		50		50	63	78
Total				13.928	520	711.45	20	1,251.45	1,499.81	1,780.26
0510 Replace 1000 L.F. of hung 2" diam. steel pipe	75	Q-1	M.L.F.							
Check break or leak				1.600		89		89	111	139
Turn valve on and off				100.000		5,550		5,550	6,950	8,700
Remove broken 2" diameter section				162.550		8,000		8,000	9,950	12,500
Install 1000' of black 2" diameter steel pipe				325.000	14,900	15,950		30,850	36,500	43,600
Check for leaks, additional section				9.000		500		500	630	780
Total				598.150	14,900	30,089		44,989	54,141	65,719
0520 Replace 1000 L.F. of hung 3" diam. steel pipe	75	Q-15	M.L.F.							
Check break or leak				1.600		89		89	111	139
Turn valve on and off				1.000		55.50		55.50	69.50	87
Remove broken 3" diameter section				241.950		11,900	560	12,460	15,400	19,200
Install 1000' of black 3" diameter steel pipe				483.680	25,500	24,000	1,120	50,620	59,000	70,000
Check for leaks, additional section				9.000		500		500	630	780
Total				737.230	25,500	36,544.50	1,680	63,724.50	75,210.50	90,206
0530 Replace 1000 L.F. of hung 4" diam. steel pipe	75	Q-15	M.L.F.							
Check break or leak				1.600		89		89	111	139
Turn valve on and off				1.000		55.50		55.50	69.50	87
Remove broken 4" diameter section				281.150		13,800	650	14,450	17,900	22,200
Install 1000' of black 4" diameter steel pipe				562.190	35,000	27,500	1,300	63,800	74,500	88,000
Check for leaks, additional section				9.000		500		500	630	780
Total				854.940	35,000	41,944.50	1,950	78,894.50	93,210.50	111,206

D3013 210 | Natural Gas: Pipe & Fittings, Steel/Iron

	System Description	Freq. (Years)	Crew	Unit	Labor Hours	2012 Bare Costs				Total In-House	Total w/O&P
						Material	Labor	Equipment	Total		
0540	**Replace 1000 L.F. of hung 6" diam. steel pipe**	75	Q-16	M.L.F.							
	Check break or leak				1.600		89		89	111	139
	Turn valve on and off				1.000		55.50		55.50	69.50	87
	Remove broken 6" diameter section				433.450		22,000	670	22,670	28,500	35,200
	Install 1000' of black 6" diameter steel pipe				866.740	52,000	44,000	1,330	97,330	114,000	135,500
	Check for leaks, additional section				9.000		500		500	630	780
	Total				**1311.790**	**52,000**	**66,644.50**	**2,000**	**120,644.50**	**143,310.50**	**171,706**

D3013 240 | Natural Gas: Pressure Reducing Valve

	System Description	Freq. (Years)	Crew	Unit	Labor Hours	2012 Bare Costs				Total In-House	Total w/O&P
						Material	Labor	Equipment	Total		
0010	**Check gas pressure**	5	1 STPI	Ea.							
	Check pressure				.130		7.25		7.25	9.05	11.30
	Total				**.130**		**7.25**		**7.25**	**9.05**	**11.30**
0110	**Replace pressure regulator 1/2" diam. pipe**	14	1 STPI	Ea.							
	Turn valve on and off				.010		.56		.56	.70	.87
	Remove 1/2" diameter regulator				.217		12.05		12.05	15.05	18.80
	Replace 1/2" diameter pipe size regulator				.433	46	24		70	80.50	95
	Total				**.660**	**46**	**36.61**		**82.61**	**96.25**	**114.67**
0120	**Replace pressure regulator 1" diam. pipe**	14	1 STPI	Ea.							
	Turn valve on and off				.010		.56		.56	.70	.87
	Remove 1" diameter regulator				.274		15.25		15.25	19.05	24
	Replace 1" diameter pipe size regulator				.547	96	30.50		126.50	144	168
	Total				**.831**	**96**	**46.31**		**142.31**	**163.75**	**192.87**
0130	**Replace pressure regulator 1-1/2" diam. pipe**	14	1 STPI	Ea.							
	Turn valve on and off				.010		.56		.56	.70	.87
	Remove 1-1/2" diameter regulator				.400		22.50		22.50	28	34.50
	Replace 1-1/2" diameter pipe size regulator				.800	600	44.50		644.50	715	820
	Total				**1.210**	**600**	**67.56**		**667.56**	**743.70**	**855.37**

D30 HVAC

D3013 | Energy Supply

D3013 240 | Natural Gas: Pressure Reducing Valve

	System Description	Freq. (Years)	Crew	Unit	Labor Hours	2012 Bare Costs				Total In-House	Total w/O&P
						Material	Labor	Equipment	Total		
0140	**Replace pressure regulator 2" diam. pipe**	14	1 STPI	Ea.							
	Turn valve on and off				.010		.56		.56	.70	.87
	Remove 2" diameter regulator				.473		26.50		26.50	33	41
	Replace 2" diameter pipe size regulator				.946	600	52.50		652.50	725	830
	Total				1.428	600	79.56		679.56	758.70	871.87

D3013 260 | LPG Distribution: Pipe & Fittings, Steel/Iron

	System Description	Freq. (Years)	Crew	Unit	Labor Hours	2012 Bare Costs				Total In-House	Total w/O&P
						Material	Labor	Equipment	Total		
0120	**Replace 10' st. pipe 1/2" diam. per M.L.F.**	12	1 PLUM	Ea.							
	Check break or leak				.016		.89		.89	1.11	1.39
	Turn valve on and off				.010		.56		.56	.70	.87
	Remove broken 1/2" diameter section				.826		45.10		45.10	56.50	70
	Install section of pipe 1/2" diameter				1.651	43.80	90		133.80	161	195
	Check for leaks, additional section				.900		50		50	63	78
	Total				3.402	43.80	186.55		230.35	282.31	345.26
0220	**Replace 10' st. pipe 3/4" diam. per M.L.F.**	12	1 PLUM	Ea.							
	Check break or leak				.016		.89		.89	1.11	1.39
	Turn valve on and off				.010		.56		.56	.70	.87
	Remove broken 3/4" diameter section				.853		46.60		46.60	58	72.50
	Install section of pipe 3/4" diameter				1.312	51.50	71.50		123	146	176
	Check for leaks, additional section				.900		50		50	63	78
	Total				3.090	51.50	169.55		221.05	268.81	328.76
0320	**Replace 10' st. pipe 1" diam. per M.L.F.**	12	1 PLUM	Ea.							
	Check break or leak				.016		.89		.89	1.11	1.39
	Turn valve on and off				.010		.56		.56	.70	.87
	Remove broken 1" diameter section				.982		53.50		53.50	67	83.50
	Install section of pipe 1" diameter				1.962	75.50	107		182.50	215	261
	Check for leaks, additional section				.900		50		50	63	78
	Total				3.870	75.50	211.95		287.45	346.81	424.76

D3013 260 LPG Distribution: Pipe & Fittings, Steel/Iron

System Description	Freq. (Years)	Crew	Unit	Labor Hours	2012 Bare Costs				Total In-House	Total w/O&P
					Material	Labor	Equipment	Total		
0420 Replace 10' st. pipe 1-1/4" diam. M.L.F.	12	Q-1	Ea.							
Check break or leak				.016		.89		.89	1.11	1.39
Turn valve on and off				.010		.56		.56	.70	.87
Remove broken 1-1/4" diameter section				1.169		57.50		57.50	71.50	89.50
Install section of pipe 1-1/4" diameter				2.337	95	115		210	250	298
Check for leaks, additional section				.900		50		50	63	78
Total				4.432	95	223.95		318.95	386.31	467.76
0520 Replace 10' st. pipe 1-1/2" diam. M.L.F.	12	Q-1	Ea.							
Check break or leak				.016		.89		.89	1.11	1.39
Turn valve on and off				.010		.56		.56	.70	.87
Remove broken 1-1/2" diameter section				1.300		64		64	80	99.50
Install section of pipe 1-1/2" diameter				2.600	111.50	128		239.50	280	340
Check for leaks, additional section				.900		50		50	63	78
Total				4.826	111.50	243.45		354.95	424.81	519.76
0620 Replace 10' section st. pipe 2" diam. M.L.F.	12	Q-1	Ea.							
Check break or leak				.016		.89		.89	1.11	1.39
Turn valve on and off				.010		.56		.56	.70	.87
Remove broken 2" diameter section				1.626		80		80	99.50	125
Install section of pipe 2" diameter				3.250	149	159.50		308.50	365	435
Check for leaks, additional section				.900		50		50	63	78
Total				5.802	149	290.95		439.95	529.31	640.26
1130 Replace 1000' of 1/2" diameter steel pipe	75	Q-1	M.L.F.							
Check break or leak				1.600		89		89	111	139
Turn valve on and off				1.000		55.50		55.50	69.50	87
Remove broken 1/2" diameter section				82.560		4,510		4,510	5,650	7,000
Install section of pipe 1/2" diameter				165.080	4,380	9,000		13,380	16,100	19,500
Check for leaks, additional section				9.000		500		500	630	780
Total				259.240	4,380	14,154.50		18,534.50	22,560.50	27,506

D3013 260 LPG Distribution: Pipe & Fittings, Steel/Iron

	System Description	Freq. (Years)	Crew	Unit	Labor Hours	2012 Bare Costs				Total In-House	Total w/O&P
						Material	Labor	Equipment	Total		
1230	**Replace 1000' of 3/4" diameter steel pipe**	75	Q-1	M.L.F.							
	Check break or leak				1.600		89		89	111	139
	Turn valve on and off				1.000		55.50		55.50	69.50	87
	Remove broken 3/4" diameter section				85.270		4,660		4,660	5,800	7,250
	Install section of pipe 3/4" diameter				131.150	5,150	7,150		12,300	14,600	17,600
	Check for leaks, additional section				9.000		500		500	630	780
	Total				228.020	5,150	12,454.50		17,604.50	**21,210.50**	**25,856**
1330	**Replace 1000' of 1" diameter steel pipe**	75	Q-1	M.L.F.							
	Check break or leak				1.600		89		89	111	139
	Turn valve on and off				1.000		55.50		55.50	69.50	87
	Remove broken 1" diameter section				98.150		5,350		5,350	6,700	8,350
	Install section of pipe 1" diameter				196.220	7,550	10,700		18,250	21,500	26,100
	Check for leaks, additional section				9.000		500		500	630	780
	Total				305.970	7,550	16,694.50		24,244.50	**29,010.50**	**35,456**
1430	**Replace 1000' of 1-1/4" diameter steel pipe**	75	Q-1	M.L.F.							
	Check break or leak				1.600		89		89	111	139
	Turn valve on and off				1.000		55.50		55.50	69.50	87
	Remove broken 1-1/4" diameter section				116.890		5,750		5,750	7,150	8,950
	Install section of pipe 1-1/4" diameter				233.710	9,500	11,500		21,000	25,000	29,800
	Check for leaks, additional section				9.000		500		500	630	780
	Total				362.200	9,500	17,894.50		27,394.50	**32,960.50**	**39,756**
1530	**Replace 1000' of 1-1/2" diameter steel pipe**	75	Q-1	M.L.F.							
	Check break or leak				1.600		89		89	111	139
	Turn valve on and off				1.000		55.50		55.50	69.50	87
	Remove broken 1-1/2" diameter section				130.040		6,400		6,400	8,000	9,950
	Install section of pipe 1-1/2" diameter				260.000	11,150	12,800		23,950	28,000	33,800
	Check for leaks, additional section				9.000		500		500	630	780
	Total				401.640	11,150	19,844.50		30,994.50	**36,810.50**	**44,756**

D3013 260 LPG Distribution: Pipe & Fittings, Steel/Iron

	System Description	Freq. (Years)	Crew	Unit	Labor Hours	2012 Bare Costs				Total In-House	Total w/O&P
						Material	Labor	Equipment	Total		
1630	**Replace 1000' of 2" diameter steel pipe**	75	Q-1	M.L.F.							
	Check break or leak				1.600		89		89	111	139
	Turn valve on and off				1.000		55.50		55.50	69.50	87
	Remove broken 2" diameter section				162.550		8,000		8,000	9,950	12,500
	Install section of pipe 2" diameter				325.000	14,900	15,950		30,850	36,500	43,600
	Check for leaks, additional section				9.000		500		500	630	780
	Total				499.150	14,900	24,594.50		39,494.50	47,260.50	57,106

D3013 601 Solar Panel, 3' x 8'

	System Description	Freq. (Years)	Crew	Unit	Labor Hours	2012 Bare Costs				Total In-House	Total w/O&P
						Material	Labor	Equipment	Total		
0010	**Replace solar panel 3' x 8'**	15	Q-1	Ea.							
	Remove panel				1.891		93		93	116	145
	Install 3' x 8' solar panel aluminum frame				3.783	865	186		1,051	1,175	1,375
	Total				5.674	865	279		1,144	1,291	1,520

D3023 180   Boiler, Gas

	System Description	Freq. (Years)	Crew	Unit	Labor Hours	2012 Bare Costs				Total In-House	Total w/O&P
						Material	Labor	Equipment	Total		
1010	**Repair boiler, gas, 250 MBH**	7	1 STPI	Ea.							
	Remove / replace burner blower				.600		33.50		33.50	41.50	52
	Remove burner blower bearing				1.000		55.50		55.50	69.50	87
	Replace burner blower bearing				2.000	54.50	111		165.50	199	242
	Remove burner blower motor				.976		54.50		54.50	68	84.50
	Replace burner blower motor				1.951	188	109		297	340	405
	Remove burner fireye				.195		10.85		10.85	13.55	16.95
	Replace burner fireye				.300	208	16.70		224.70	250	286
	Remove burner gas regulator				.274		15.25		15.25	19.05	24
	Replace burner gas regulator				.547	96	30.50		126.50	144	168
	Remove burner auto gas valve				.274		15.25		15.25	19	24
	Replace burner auto gas valve				.421	172	23.50		195.50	218	252
	Remove burner solenoid valve				.279		14.90		14.90	18.55	23
	Replace burner solenoid valve				.557	550	30		580	640	735
	Repair controls				.500		28		28	35	43.50
	Total				9.874	1,268.50	548.45		1,816.95	2,075.15	2,442.95
1060	**Replace boiler, gas, 250 MBH**	30	Q-7	Ea.							
	Remove boiler				21.888		1,150		1,150	1,450	1,800
	Replace boiler, 250 MBH				43.776	3,100	2,325		5,425	6,300	7,500
	Total				65.663	3,100	3,475		6,575	7,750	9,300
2010	**Repair boiler, gas, 2000 MBH**	7	Q-5	Ea.							
	Remove / replace burner blower				.600		33.50		33.50	41.50	52
	Remove burner blower bearing				1.000		55.50		55.50	69.50	87
	Replace burner blower bearing				2.000	54.50	111		165.50	199	242
	Remove burner blower motor				.976		54.50		54.50	68	84.50
	Replace burner blower motor				1.951	193	101		294	335	395
	Remove burner fireye				.195		10.85		10.85	13.55	16.95
	Replace burner fireye				.300	208	16.70		224.70	250	286
	Remove burner gas regulator				.727		36.50		36.50	45.50	57
	Replace burner gas regulator				1.455	1,150	73		1,223	1,350	1,550
	Remove burner auto gas valve				.800		39.50		39.50	49	61.50
	Replace burner auto gas valve				1.231	370	60.50		430.50	485	555
	Remove burner solenoid valve				2.600		139		139	173	216
	Replace burner solenoid valve				5.199	1,175	279		1,454	1,650	1,900
	Repair controls				.500		28		28	35	43.50
	Total				19.534	3,150.50	1,038.55		4,189.05	4,764.05	5,546.45

D3023 180 Boiler, Gas

System Description	Freq. (Years)	Crew	Unit	Labor Hours	2012 Bare Costs Material	Labor	Equipment	Total	Total In-House	Total w/O&P
2070 Replace boiler, gas, 2000 MBH	30	Q-7	Ea.							
Remove boiler				57.762		3,075		3,075	3,825	4,775
Replace boiler, 2000 MBH				109.000	18,100	5,825		23,925	27,100	31,700
Total				166.762	18,100	8,900		27,000	30,925	36,475
3010 Repair boiler, gas, 10,000 MBH	7	Q-5	Ea.							
Remove / replace burner blower				1.000		55.50		55.50	69.50	87
Remove burner blower bearing				1.000		55.50		55.50	69.50	87
Replace burner blower bearing				2.000	54.50	111		165.50	199	242
Remove burner motor				1.000		55.50		55.50	69.50	87
Replace burner motor				1.951	288	101		389	440	515
Remove burner fireye				.195		10.85		10.85	13.55	16.95
Replace burner fireye				.300	208	16.70		224.70	250	286
Remove burner gas regulator				1.300		65		65	81.50	102
Replace burner gas regulator				2.600	2,075	130		2,205	2,450	2,800
Remove burner auto gas valve				5.195		265		265	330	410
Replace burner auto gas valve				8.000	5,875	410		6,285	6,975	7,975
Remove burner solenoid valve				2.600		139		139	173	216
Replace burner solenoid valve				10.399	2,950	555		3,505	3,950	4,550
Repair controls				.500		28		28	35	43.50
Total				38.040	11,450.50	1,998.05		13,448.55	15,105.55	17,417.45
3070 Replace boiler, gas, 10,000 MBH	30	Q-7	Ea.							
Remove boiler				364.000		19,320		19,320	24,100	30,100
Replace boiler, gas, 10,000 MBH				722.400	123,900	38,360		162,260	184,000	214,500
Total				1086.400	123,900	57,680		181,580	208,100	244,600

D3023 182 — Boiler, Coal

	System Description	Freq. (Years)	Crew	Unit	Labor Hours	2012 Bare Costs				Total In-House	Total w/O&P
						Material	Labor	Equipment	Total		
1010	**Repair boiler, coal, 4600 MBH**	20	4 STPI	Ea.							
	Remove coal feeder				2.703		150.80		150.80	187	234
	Replace coal feeder				4.054	1,476.80	226.20		1,703	1,900	2,200
	Remove vibrating grates				33.592		1,872		1,872	2,325	2,925
	Replace vibrating grates				62.712	18,772	3,494.40		22,266.40	25,000	28,900
	Remove motor				.832		46.28		46.28	57.50	72.50
	Replace motor				.450	174.20	23.19		197.39	221	254
	Repair controls				5.200		288.60		288.60	360	450
	Total				109.543	20,423	6,101.47		26,524.47	30,050.50	35,035.50
1050	**Replace boiler, coal, 4600 MBH**	30	5 STPI	Ea.							
	Remove boiler				122.304		6,812		6,812	8,475	10,600
	Replace boiler, coal, 4600 MBH				244.608	92,664	13,624		106,288	119,000	137,000
	Total				366.912	92,664	20,436		113,100	127,475	147,600

D3023 184 — Boiler, Oil

	System Description	Freq. (Years)	Crew	Unit	Labor Hours	2012 Bare Costs				Total In-House	Total w/O&P
						Material	Labor	Equipment	Total		
1010	**Repair boiler, oil, 250 MBH**	7	Q-5	Ea.							
	Remove / replace burner blower				.600		33.50		33.50	41.50	52
	Remove burner blower bearing				1.000		55.50		55.50	69.50	87
	Replace burner blower bearing				2.000	54.50	111		165.50	199	242
	Remove burner blower motor				.976		54.50		54.50	68	84.50
	Replace burner blower motor				1.951	188	109		297	340	405
	Remove burner fireye				.195		10.85		10.85	13.55	16.95
	Replace burner fireye				.300	208	16.70		224.70	250	286
	Remove burner ignition transformer				.250		13.95		13.95	17.40	21.50
	Replace burner ignition transformer				.500	80.50	28		108.50	123	144
	Remove burner ignition electrode				.200		11.15		11.15	13.90	17.35
	Replace burner ignition electrode				.400	12	22.50		34.50	41	49.50
	Remove burner oil pump				.350		19.50		19.50	24.50	30.50
	Replace burner oil pump				.700	74.50	39		113.50	131	154
	Remove burner nozzle				.167		9.30		9.30	11.60	14.45
	Replace burner nozzle				.300	13.50	16.70		30.20	35.50	43
	Repair controls				.600		33.50		33.50	41.50	52
	Total				10.489	631	584.65		1,215.65	1,420.95	1,699.75

D3023 184 Boiler, Oil

System Description	Freq. (Years)	Crew	Unit	Labor Hours	2012 Bare Costs				Total In-House	Total w/O&P
					Material	Labor	Equipment	Total		
1060 Replace boiler, oil, 250 MBH	30	Q-7	Ea.							
Remove boiler				24.465		1,300		1,300	1,625	2,025
Replace boiler, oil, 250 MBH				48.930	3,250	2,600		5,850	6,825	8,125
Total				73.394	3,250	3,900		7,150	8,450	10,150
1066 Replace boiler, oil, 300 MBH	30	Q-7	Ea.							
Remove boiler				29.091		1,550		1,550	1,925	2,400
Replace boiler, oil, 300 MBH				59.480	3,825	3,150		6,975	8,150	9,700
Total				88.570	3,825	4,700		8,525	10,075	12,100
1070 Replace boiler, oil, 420 MBH	30	Q-7	Ea.							
Remove boiler				35.955		1,900		1,900	2,375	2,975
Replace boiler, oil, 420 MBH				71.749	4,275	3,800		8,075	9,450	11,300
Total				107.704	4,275	5,700		9,975	11,825	14,275
1080 Replace boiler, oil, 530 MBH	30	Q-7	Ea.							
Remove boiler				42.440		2,250		2,250	2,800	3,500
Replace boiler, oil, 530 MBH				84.881	5,400	4,500		9,900	11,600	13,800
Total				127.321	5,400	6,750		12,150	14,400	17,300
2010 Repair boiler, oil, 2000 MBH	7	1 STPI	Ea.							
Remove / replace burner blower				.600		33.50		33.50	41.50	52
Remove burner blower bearing				1.000		55.50		55.50	69.50	87
Replace burner blower bearing				2.000	54.50	111		165.50	199	242
Remove burner blower motor				.976		50.50		50.50	62	77.50
Replace burner blower motor				1.951	193	101		294	335	395
Remove burner fireye				.195		10.85		10.85	13.55	16.95
Replace burner fireye				.300	208	16.70		224.70	250	286
Remove burner ignition transformer				.286		15.90		15.90	19.85	25
Replace burner ignition transformer				.571	80.50	32		112.50	128	150
Remove burner ignition electrode				.200		11.15		11.15	13.90	17.35
Replace burner ignition electrode				.400	12	22.50		34.50	41	49.50
Remove burner oil pump				.400		22.50		22.50	28	34.50
Replace burner oil pump				.800	77.50	44.50		122	141	166
Remove burner nozzle				.167		9.30		9.30	11.60	14.45
Replace burner nozzle				.333	13.50	18.55		32.05	38	46
Repair controls				.600		33.50		33.50	41.50	52
Total				10.779	639	588.95		1,227.95	1,433.40	1,711.25

D30 HVAC | D3023 | Heat Generating Systems

D3023 184 Boiler, Oil

	System Description	Freq. (Years)	Crew	Unit	Labor Hours	2012 Bare Costs				Total In-House	Total w/O&P
						Material	Labor	Equipment	Total		
2060	**Replace boiler, oil, 2000 MBH**	30	Q-7	Ea.							
	Remove boiler				57.762		3,075		3,075	3,825	4,775
	Replace boiler, oil, 2000 MBH				148.000	17,300	7,900		25,200	28,800	33,900
	Total				205.762	17,300	10,975		28,275	32,625	**38,675**
2070	**Replace boiler, oil, 3000 MBH**	30	Q-7	Ea.							
	Remove boiler				110.000		5,850		5,850	7,275	9,125
	Replace boiler, oil, 3000 MBH				220.000	21,600	11,700		33,300	38,300	45,200
	Total				330.000	21,600	17,550		39,150	45,575	**54,325**
3010	**Repair boiler, oil, 10,000 MBH**	7	1 STPI	Ea.							
	Remove / replace burner blower				.600		33.50		33.50	41.50	52
	Remove burner blower bearing				1.000		55.50		55.50	69.50	87
	Replace burner blower bearing				2.000	54.50	111		165.50	199	242
	Remove burner blower motor				.800		44.50		44.50	55.50	69.50
	Replace burner blower motor				1.951	288	101		389	440	515
	Remove burner fireye				.195		10.85		10.85	13.55	16.95
	Replace burner fireye				.300	208	16.70		224.70	250	286
	Remove burner ignition transformer				.333		18.55		18.55	23	29
	Replace burner ignition transformer				.667	80.50	37		117.50	135	159
	Remove burner ignition electrode				.200		11.15		11.15	13.90	17.35
	Replace burner ignition electrode				.444	12	25		37	44	53.50
	Remove burner oil pump				.500		28		28	35	43.50
	Replace burner oil pump				1.000	102	55.50		157.50	182	215
	Remove burner nozzle				.167		9.30		9.30	11.60	14.45
	Replace burner nozzle				.400	13.50	22.50		36	42.50	51.50
	Repair controls				.600		33.50		33.50	41.50	52
	Total				11.158	758.50	613.55		1,372.05	1,597.55	**1,903.75**
3060	**Replace boiler, oil, 10,000 MBH**	30	Q-7	Ea.							
	Remove boiler				373.100		19,803		19,803	24,700	30,900
	Replace boiler, oil, 10,000 MBH				520.905	126,280	27,695.50		153,975.50	173,500	201,000
	Total				894.005	126,280	47,498.50		173,778.50	198,200	**231,900**

D3023 186 Boiler, Gas/Oil

System Description	Freq. (Years)	Crew	Unit	Labor Hours	2012 Bare Costs				Total In-House	Total w/O&P
					Material	Labor	Equipment	Total		
1010 Repair boiler, gas/oil, 2000 MBH	7	Q-5	Ea.							
Remove/replace burner blower				.600		33.50		33.50	41.50	52
Remove burner blower bearing				1.000		55.50		55.50	69.50	87
Replace burner blower bearing				2.000	54.50	111		165.50	199	242
Remove burner blower motor				.976		54.50		54.50	68	84.50
Replace burner blower motor				1.951	193	101		294	335	395
Remove burner fireye				.195		10.85		10.85	13.55	16.95
Replace burner fireye				.300	208	16.70		224.70	250	286
Remove burner ignition transformer				.333		18.55		18.55	23	29
Replace burner ignition transformer				.571	80.50	32		112.50	128	150
Remove burner ignition electrode				.200		11.15		11.15	13.90	17.35
Replace burner ignition electrode				.400	12	22.50		34.50	41	49.50
Remove burner oil pump				.500		28		28	35	43.50
Replace burner oil pump				.800	77.50	44.50		122	141	166
Remove burner nozzle				.167		9.30		9.30	11.60	14.45
Replace burner nozzle				.333	13.50	18.55		32.05	38	46
Remove burner gas regulator				.727		36.50		36.50	45.50	57
Replace burner gas regulator				1.455	1,150	73		1,223	1,350	1,550
Remove burner auto gas valve				.800		39.50		39.50	49	61.50
Replace burner auto gas valve				1.231	370	60.50		430.50	485	555
Remove burner solenoid valve				2.600		139		139	173	216
Replace burner solenoid valve				5.199	1,175	279		1,454	1,650	1,900
Repair controls				.600		33.50		33.50	41.50	52
Total				22.939	3,334	1,228.60		4,562.60	5,202.05	6,070.75
1050 Replace boiler, gas/oil, 2000 MBH	30	Q-7	Ea.							
Remove boiler				57.762		3,075		3,075	3,825	4,775
Replace boiler, gas/oil, 2000 MBH				115.000	27,400	6,125		33,525	37,800	43,800
Total				172.762	27,400	9,200		36,600	41,625	48,575

	System Description	Freq. (Years)	Crew	Unit	Labor Hours	2012 Bare Costs				Total In-House	Total w/O&P
						Material	Labor	Equipment	Total		
2010	**Repair boiler, gas/oil, 20,000 MBH**	7	Q-5	Ea.							
	Remove/replace burner blower				.600		33.50		33.50	41.50	52
	Remove burner blower bearing				1.000		55.50		55.50	69.50	87
	Replace burner blower bearing				2.000	54.50	111		165.50	199	242
	Remove burner blower motor				.976		50.50		50.50	62	77.50
	Replace burner blower motor				1.951	320	101		421	475	555
	Remove burner fireye				.195		10.85		10.85	13.55	16.95
	Replace burner fireye				.300	208	16.70		224.70	250	286
	Remove burner ignition transformer				.333		18.55		18.55	23	29
	Replace burner ignition transformer				.667	80.50	37		117.50	135	159
	Remove burner ignition electrode				.267		14.85		14.85	18.55	23
	Replace burner ignition electrode				.444	12	25		37	44	53.50
	Remove burner oil pump				.500		28		28	35	43.50
	Replace burner oil pump				2.602	162	130		292	340	405
	Remove burner nozzle				.167		9.30		9.30	11.60	14.45
	Replace burner nozzle				.571	13.50	32		45.50	54.50	66.50
	Remove burner gas regulator				1.300		65		65	81.50	102
	Replace burner gas regulator				2.600	2,075	130		2,205	2,450	2,800
	Remove burner auto gas valve				5.195		265		265	330	410
	Replace burner auto gas valve				8.000	5,875	410		6,285	6,975	7,975
	Remove burner solenoid valve				2.600		139		139	173	216
	Replace burner solenoid valve				10.399	2,950	555		3,505	3,950	4,550
	Repair controls				.600		33.50		33.50	41.50	52
	Total				43.266	11,750.50	2,271.25		14,021.75	15,773.20	18,215.40
2050	**Replace boiler, gas/oil, 20,000 MBH**	30	Q-7	Ea.							
	Remove boiler				1527.360		81,400		81,400	101,500	126,500
	Replace boiler, gas/oil, 20,000 MBH				3156.840	239,020	167,240		406,260	472,000	560,000
	Total				4684.200	239,020	248,640		487,660	573,500	686,500

D3023 198 | **Blowoff System**

	System Description	Freq. (Years)	Crew	Unit	Labor Hours	2012 Bare Costs				Total In-House	Total w/O&P
						Material	Labor	Equipment	Total		
1010	**Repair boiler blowoff system**	10	1 STPI	Ea.							
	Repair leak				1.000		55.50		55.50	69.50	87
	Total				1.000		55.50		55.50	69.50	87

D3023 198 Blowoff System

System Description	Freq. (Years)	Crew	Unit	Labor Hours	2012 Bare Costs				Total In-House	Total w/O&P
					Material	Labor	Equipment	Total		
1020 Replace boiler blowoff system	15	Q-5	Ea.							
Remove boiler blowoff				2.773		139		139	173	217
Replace boiler blowoff				5.556	3,550	279		3,829	4,250	4,875
Total				**8.329**	3,550	418		3,968	**4,423**	**5,092**

D3023 292 Chemical Feed System

System Description	Freq. (Years)	Crew	Unit	Labor Hours	2012 Bare Costs				Total In-House	Total w/O&P
					Material	Labor	Equipment	Total		
1010 Repair chemical feed	15	1 STPI	Ea.							
Repair controls				.040		2.23		2.23	2.78	3.47
Remove / replace agitator motor				1.951	188	109		297	340	405
Remove / replace pump seals / bearings				2.078	30	113		143	175	215
Remove / replace pump motor				1.951	193	101		294	335	395
Total				**6.020**	411	325.23		736.23	**852.78**	**1,018.47**
1030 Replace chemical feed	15	2 STPI	Ea.							
Remove / replace feeder				2.500	655	137		792	890	1,025
Total				**2.500**	655	137		792	**890**	**1,025**

D3023 294 Feed Water Supply

System Description	Freq. (Years)	Crew	Unit	Labor Hours	2012 Bare Costs				Total In-House	Total w/O&P
					Material	Labor	Equipment	Total		
1010 Repair feed water supply pump	15	1 STPI	Ea.							
Repair controls				.600		33.50		33.50	41.50	52
Remove / replace pump seals / bearings				1.600		89		89	111	139
Remove pump motor				2.078		116		116	144	180
Replace pump motor				4.167	1,950	232		2,182	2,425	2,800
Remove / replace pump coupling				1.000		55.50		55.50	69.50	87
Total				**9.445**	1,950	526		2,476	**2,791**	**3,258**
1030 Replace feed water pump	15	Q-2	Ea.							
Remove pump				11.111		565		565	705	880
Replace pump				22.222	13,400	1,125		14,525	16,200	18,500
Total				**33.333**	13,400	1,690		15,090	**16,905**	**19,380**

D30 HVAC | D3023 | Heat Generating Systems

D3023 296 | Deaerator

	System Description	Freq. (Years)	Crew	Unit	Labor Hours	2012 Bare Costs				Total In-House	Total w/O&P
						Material	Labor	Equipment	Total		
1010	**Repair deaerator**	10	1 STPI	Ea.							
	Repair controls				1.000		55.50		55.50	69.50	87
	Total				1.000		55.50		55.50	**69.50**	**87**
1030	**Replace deaerator**	20	4 STPI	Ea.							
	Remove unit				7.500		390		390	485	610
	Replace unit				179.000	28,300	10,000		38,300	43,600	51,000
	Total				186.500	28,300	10,390		38,690	**44,085**	**51,610**

D3023 298 | Separators for 9000 Ton Chilled Water System

	System Description	Freq. (Years)	Crew	Unit	Labor Hours	2012 Bare Costs				Total In-House	Total w/O&P
						Material	Labor	Equipment	Total		
1010	**Clean separator strainer**	10	Q-6	Ea.							
	Clean separator strainer				10.000		555		555	695	870
	Total				10.000		555		555	**695**	**870**
1030	**Replace separator**	20	Q-6	Ea.							
	Remove unit				22.500		1,170		1,170	1,450	1,825
	Replace separator				42.857	40,200	2,235		42,435	47,100	53,500
	Total				65.357	40,200	3,405		43,605	**48,550**	**55,325**

D3023 310 | Metal Flue / Chimney

	System Description	Freq. (Years)	Crew	Unit	Labor Hours	2012 Bare Costs				Total In-House	Total w/O&P
						Material	Labor	Equipment	Total		
0010	**Replace metal flue, all fuel SS, 6" diameter**	15	Q-9	L.F.							
	Replace flue, all fuel stainless steel, 6" diameter				.387	77.58	18.13		95.71	108	126
	Total				.387	77.58	18.13		95.71	**108**	**126**
0020	**Replace metal flue, all fuel SS, 10" diameter**	15	Q-9	L.F.							
	Replace flue, all fuel stainless steel, 10" diameter				.483	95.70	22.69		118.39	134	155
	Total				.483	95.70	22.69		118.39	**134**	**155**

D3023 310 — Metal Flue / Chimney

	System Description	Freq. (Years)	Crew	Unit	Labor Hours	2012 Bare Costs				Total In-House	Total w/O&P
						Material	Labor	Equipment	Total		
0030	**Replace metal flue, all fuel SS, 20" diameter**										
	Replace flue, all fuel stainless steel, 20" diameter	15	Q-10	L.F.	.967	178.35	47.13		225.48	255	297
	Total				.967	178.35	47.13		225.48	**255**	**297**
0040	**Replace metal flue, all fuel SS, 32" diameter**										
	Replace flue, all fuel stainless steel, 32" diameter	15	Q-10	L.F.	1.289	297.25	63.08		360.33	405	470
	Total				1.289	297.25	63.08		360.33	**405**	**470**
0050	**Replace metal flue, all fuel SS, 48" diameter**										
	Replace flue, all fuel stainless steel, 48" diameter	15	Q-10	L.F.	1.832	442.25	89.18		531.43	600	695
	Total				1.832	442.25	89.18		531.43	**600**	**695**
2010	**Replace metal flue, gas vent, galvanized, 48" diameter**										
	Replace flue, gas vent, galvanized, 48" diameter	10	Q-10	L.F.	1.895	1,230	92.25		1,322.25	1,475	1,675
	Total				1.895	1,230	92.25		1,322.25	**1,475**	**1,675**

D3023 388 — Pneumatic Coal Spreader

	System Description	Freq. (Years)	Crew	Unit	Labor Hours	2012 Bare Costs				Total In-House	Total w/O&P
						Material	Labor	Equipment	Total		
1010	**Repair spreader, pneumatic coal**	10	2 STPI	Ea.							
	Repair controls				1.000		55.50		55.50	69.50	87
	Remove conveyor bearing				1.111		62		62	77	96.50
	Replace conveyor bearing				2.222	61	124		185	222	269
	Remove conveyor motor				2.597		145		145	181	225
	Replace conveyor motor				5.195	2,250	268		2,518	2,800	3,225
	Remove / replace blower				1.200		67		67	83.50	104
	Remove blower bearings				1.000		55.50		55.50	69.50	87
	Replace blower bearings				2.000	54.50	111		165.50	199	242
	Remove blower motor				2.000		111		111	139	174
	Replace blower motor				4.000	1,150	206		1,356	1,525	1,750
	Total				22.326	3,515.50	1,205		4,720.50	**5,365.50**	**6,259.50**
1060	**Replace coal spreader**	12	4 STPI	Ea.							
	Remove spreader				65.041		3,625		3,625	4,525	5,650
	Replace spreader				130.000	6,900	7,250		14,150	16,600	19,900
	Total				195.041	6,900	10,875		17,775	**21,125**	**25,550**

D3023 390 Fuel Oil Equipment

	System Description	Freq. (Years)	Crew	Unit	Labor Hours	2012 Bare Costs				Total In-House	Total w/O&P
						Material	Labor	Equipment	Total		
1010	**Repair fuel oil equipment, pump**	10	1 STPI	Ea.							
	Remove pump seals / bearings				.600		33.50		33.50	41.50	52
	Replace pump seals / bearings				1.500	28.50	83.50		112	136	166
	Remove / replace pump coupling				.900		50		50	62.50	78
	Remove / replace impeller / shaft				.900		50		50	62.50	78
	Remove / replace motor				.650		36		36	45	56.50
	Remove strainers				.289		16.10		16.10	20	25
	Replace strainers				.578	12.50	32		44.50	54	65.50
	Total				5.417	41	301.10		342.10	421.50	521
1030	**Replace fuel oil 25 GPH pump / motor set**	15	Q-5	Ea.							
	Remove equipment				1.733		87		87	108	135
	Replace equipment				3.468	1,025	174		1,199	1,350	1,550
	Total				5.201	1,025	261		1,286	1,458	1,685
1040	**Replace fuel oil 45 GPH pump / motor set**	15	Q-5	Ea.							
	Remove equipment				1.733		87		87	108	135
	Replace equipment				3.468	1,025	174		1,199	1,350	1,550
	Total				5.201	1,025	261		1,286	1,458	1,685
1050	**Replace fuel oil 90 GPH pump / motor set**	15	Q-5	Ea.							
	Remove equipment				2.081		104		104	130	163
	Replace equipment				4.161	1,025	209		1,234	1,400	1,600
	Total				6.242	1,025	313		1,338	1,530	1,763
1060	**Replace fuel oil 160 GPH pump / motor set**	15	Q-5	Ea.							
	Remove equipment				2.597		130		130	162	203
	Replace equipment				5.195	1,075	260		1,335	1,500	1,750
	Total				7.792	1,075	390		1,465	1,662	1,953

System Description	Freq. (Years)	Crew	Unit	Labor Hours	2012 Bare Costs				Total In-House	Total w/O&P
					Material	Labor	Equipment	Total		
1010 Repair cooling tower, 50 ton	10	2 STPI	Ea.							
Repair controls				1.000		55.50		55.50	69.50	87
Remove bearings				1.200		67		67	83.50	104
Replace bearings				2.000	54.50	111		165.50	199	242
Remove fan motor				1.155		64.50		64.50	80.50	100
Replace fan motor				2.312	380	119		499	565	660
Remove / replace float valve				.500	19.85	25		44.85	53	64
Total				8.167	454.35	442		896.35	1,050.50	1,257
1030 Replace cooling tower, 50 ton	15	Q-6	Ea.							
Remove cooling tower				10.397		540		540	675	845
Replace cooling tower, 50 ton				20.779	11,820	1,080		12,900	14,300	16,500
Total				31.177	11,820	1,620		13,440	14,975	17,345
2010 Repair cooling tower, 100 ton	10	2 STPI	Ea.							
Repair controls				1.000		55.50		55.50	69.50	87
Remove bearings				4.800		268		268	335	415
Replace bearings				8.000	218	444		662	795	970
Remove fan motors				4.621		258		258	320	400
Replace fan motors				9.249	1,520	476		1,996	2,250	2,625
Remove / replace float valve				.575	22.83	28.75		51.58	61	73.50
Total				28.245	1,760.83	1,530.25		3,291.08	3,830.50	4,570.50
2030 Replace cooling tower, 100 ton	15	Q-6	Ea.							
Remove cooling tower				14.286		745		745	925	1,150
Replace cooling tower, 100 ton				28.571	16,500	1,485		17,985	20,000	22,900
Total				42.857	16,500	2,230		18,730	20,925	24,050
3010 Repair cooling tower, 300 ton	10	2 STPI	Ea.							
Repair controls				1.000		55.50		55.50	69.50	87
Remove bearings				7.200		402		402	500	625
Replace bearings				13.333	366	744		1,110	1,325	1,625
Remove fan motors				6.931		387		387	485	600
Replace fan motors				13.865	2,730	714		3,444	3,900	4,525
Remove / replace float valve				1.250	49.63	62.50		112.13	133	160
Total				43.580	3,145.63	2,365		5,510.63	6,412.50	7,622

D3033 115 Cooling Tower

System Description	Freq. (Years)	Crew	Unit	Labor Hours	2012 Bare Costs				Total In-House	Total w/O&P
					Material	Labor	Equipment	Total		
3030 Replace cooling tower, 300 ton	15	Q-6	Ea.							
Remove cooling tower				36.273		1,890		1,890	2,350	2,950
Replace cooling tower, 300 ton				72.582	28,800	3,780		32,580	36,300	41,900
Total				108.855	28,800	5,670		34,470	38,650	**44,850**
4010 Repair cooling tower, 1000 ton	10	2 STPI	Ea.							
Repair controls				1.000		55.50		55.50	69.50	87
Remove bearings				12.000		670		670	835	1,050
Replace bearings				23.529	1,720	1,310		3,030	3,550	4,200
Remove fan motors				11.552		645		645	805	1,000
Replace fan motors				25.974	7,200	1,340		8,540	9,550	11,100
Remove / replace float valve				2.350	93.30	117.50		210.80	249	300
Total				76.406	9,013.30	4,138		13,151.30	15,058.50	**17,737**
4030 Replace cooling tower, 1000 ton	15	Q-6	Ea.							
Remove cooling tower				104.350		5,400		5,400	6,750	8,450
Replace cooling tower, 1000 ton				208.700	72,500	10,850		83,350	93,500	107,500
Total				313.050	72,500	16,250		88,750	100,250	**115,950**

D3033 130 Chiller, Water Cooled, Reciprocating

System Description	Freq. (Years)	Crew	Unit	Labor Hours	2012 Bare Costs				Total In-House	Total w/O&P
					Material	Labor	Equipment	Total		
1010 Repair water cooled chiller, 20 ton	10	Q-6	Ea.							
Repair controls				1.000		55.50		55.50	69.50	87
Remove compressor				24.390		1,275		1,275	1,575	1,975
Replace compressor				48.780	15,100	2,525		17,625	19,800	22,800
Remove / replace evaporator tube				1.200	162	62.50		224.50	256	300
Remove / replace condenser tube				1.200	162	62.50		224.50	256	300
Replace refrigerant				2.667	244	149		393	450	535
Total				79.237	15,668	4,129.50		19,797.50	22,406.50	**25,997**
1030 Replace chiller, water cooled, 20 ton	20	Q-7	Ea.							
Remove chiller				50.633		2,675		2,675	3,350	4,175
Replace chiller, water cooled, 20 ton				101.000	18,900	5,375		24,275	27,500	32,000
Total				151.633	18,900	8,050		26,950	30,850	**36,175**

D3033 130 Chiller, Water Cooled, Reciprocating

	System Description	Freq. (Years)	Crew	Unit	Labor Hours	2012 Bare Costs				Total In-House	Total w/O&P
						Material	Labor	Equipment	Total		
2010	**Repair water cooled chiller, 50 ton**	10	Q-6	Ea.							
	Repair controls				1.000		55.50		55.50	69.50	87
	Remove compressor				60.976		3,156.25		3,156.25	3,975	4,950
	Replace compressor				121.951	37,750	6,312.50		44,062.50	49,500	57,000
	Remove / replace evaporator tube				1.200	162	62.50		224.50	256	300
	Remove / replace condenser tube				1.200	162	62.50		224.50	256	300
	Replace refrigerant				4.000	366	223.50		589.50	675	805
	Total				190.327	38,440	9,872.75		48,312.75	54,731.50	63,442
2030	**Replace chiller, water cooled 50 ton**	20	Q-7	Ea.							
	Remove chiller				74.074		3,925		3,925	4,900	6,125
	Replace chiller, water cooled, 50 ton				148.000	32,300	7,850		40,150	45,300	52,500
	Total				222.074	32,300	11,775		44,075	50,200	58,625
3010	**Repair water cooled chiller, 100 ton**	10	Q-6	Ea.							
	Repair controls				1.000		55.50		55.50	69.50	87
	Remove compressor				155.844		8,100		8,100	10,100	12,600
	Replace compressor				310.000	35,000	16,200		51,200	58,500	69,000
	Remove / replace evaporator tube				4.798	615	254		869	995	1,175
	Remove / replace condenser tube				4.798	615	254		869	995	1,175
	Replace refrigerant				8.000	732	447		1,179	1,350	1,600
	Total				484.439	36,962	25,310.50		62,272.50	72,009.50	85,637
3030	**Replace chiller, water cooled, 100 ton**	20	Q-7	Ea.							
	Remove chiller				116.000		6,200		6,200	7,675	9,650
	Replace chiller, water cooled, 100 ton				233.000	58,500	12,400		70,900	80,000	92,500
	Total				349.000	58,500	18,600		77,100	87,675	102,150
5010	**Repair water cooled chiller, 200 ton**	10	Q-7	Ea.							
	Repair controls				1.000		55.50		55.50	69.50	87
	Remove compressor				152.099		8,085		8,085	10,000	12,600
	Replace compressor				303.380	34,034	16,170		50,204	57,500	67,500
	Remove / replace evaporator tube				9.610	1,225	510		1,735	1,975	2,325
	Remove / replace condenser tube				9.610	1,225	510		1,735	1,975	2,325
	Replace refrigerant				13.333	1,220	745		1,965	2,250	2,675
	Total				489.031	37,704	26,075.50		63,779.50	73,769.50	87,512

D3033 130 Chiller, Water Cooled, Reciprocating

System Description	Freq. (Years)	Crew	Unit	Labor Hours	2012 Bare Costs Material	Labor	Equipment	Total	Total In-House	Total w/O&P
5030										
Replace chiller, water cooled, 200 ton	20	Q-7	Ea.							
Remove chiller				163.000		8,650		8,650	10,800	13,500
Replace chiller, water cooled, 200 ton				326.000	92,000	17,300		109,300	123,000	142,000
Total				489.000	92,000	25,950		117,950	133,800	155,500

D3033 135 Chiller, Air Cooled, Reciprocating

System Description	Freq. (Years)	Crew	Unit	Labor Hours	2012 Bare Costs Material	Labor	Equipment	Total	Total In-House	Total w/O&P
1010										
Repair recip. chiller, air cooled, 20 ton	10	2 STPI	Ea.							
Repair controls				.800		44.50		44.50	55.50	69.50
Remove fan bearing				3.600		201		201	251	310
Replace fan bearing				6.000	163.50	333		496.50	595	725
Remove fan motor				2.927		163.50		163.50	204	254
Replace fan motor				5.854	960	303		1,263	1,425	1,675
Remove compressor				24.490		1,275		1,275	1,600	1,975
Replace compressor				48.780	15,100	2,525		17,625	19,800	22,800
Replace refrigerant				2.667	244	149		393	450	535
Total				95.117	16,467.50	4,994		21,461.50	24,380.50	28,343.50
1030										
Replace chiller, 20 ton	20	Q-7	Ea.							
Remove chiller				42.857		2,225		2,225	2,775	3,475
Replace chiller, air cooled, reciprocating, 20 ton				118.000	26,400	6,300		32,700	36,900	42,800
Total				160.857	26,400	8,525		34,925	39,675	46,275
2010										
Repair recip. chiller, air cooled, 50 ton	10	Q-6	Ea.							
Repair controls				1.000		55.50		55.50	69.50	87
Remove fan bearing				3.600		201		201	251	310
Replace fan bearing				6.667	183	372		555	665	810
Remove fan motor				3.096		159		159	197	246
Replace fan motor				6.936	1,140	357		1,497	1,700	1,975
Remove compressor				60.976		3,187.50		3,187.50	3,950	4,950
Replace compressor				121.951	37,750	6,312.50		44,062.50	49,500	57,000
Remove / replace compressor motor				7.201		372		372	460	575
Replace refrigerant				4.000	366	223.50		589.50	675	805
Total				215.427	39,439	11,240		50,679	57,467.50	66,758

D3033 135 Chiller, Air Cooled, Reciprocating

	System Description	Freq. (Years)	Crew	Unit	Labor Hours	2012 Bare Costs				Total In-House	Total w/O&P
						Material	Labor	Equipment	Total		
2030	**Replace chiller, 50 ton**	20	Q-7	Ea.							
	Remove chiller				73.395		3,900		3,900	4,850	6,075
	Replace chiller, air cooled, reciprocating, 50 ton				146.000	39,000	7,775		46,775	52,500	61,000
	Total				219.395	39,000	11,675		50,675	57,350	67,075
3010	**Repair chiller, air cooled, 100 ton**	10	Q-6	Ea.							
	Repair controls				1.000		55.50		55.50	69.50	87
	Remove fan bearing				4.200		234		234	293	365
	Replace fan bearing				6.667	183	372		555	665	810
	Remove fan motor				3.900		201		201	248	310
	Replace fan motor				7.792	2,160	402		2,562	2,875	3,325
	Remove compressor				194.805		10,125		10,125	12,600	15,800
	Replace compressor				191.250	24,125	10,187.50		34,312.50	39,300	46,000
	Remove / replace compressor motor				9.359		482		482	595	750
	Replace refrigerant				6.667	610	372.50		982.50	1,125	1,350
	Total				425.640	27,078	22,431.50		49,509.50	57,770.50	68,797
3030	**Replace chiller, 100 ton**	20	Q-7	Ea.							
	Remove chiller				84.211		4,475		4,475	5,575	6,950
	Replace chiller, air cooled, reciprocating, 100 ton				168.000	71,500	8,925		80,425	90,000	103,500
	Total				252.211	71,500	13,400		84,900	95,575	110,450

D3033 137 Chiller, Water Cooled, Scroll

	System Description	Freq. (Years)	Crew	Unit	Labor Hours	2012 Bare Costs				Total In-House	Total w/O&P
						Material	Labor	Equipment	Total		
4010	**Repair water cooled chiller, 5 ton**	10	1 STPI	Ea.							
	Repair controls				.500		28		28	35	43.50
	Remove fan bearing				1.200		67		67	83.50	104
	Replace fan bearing				2.000	54.50	111		165.50	199	242
	Remove compressor				2.477		138		138	172	215
	Replace compressor				4.954	455	276		731	845	1,000
	Replace refrigerant				.667	61	37.25		98.25	113	134
	Total				11.797	570.50	657.25		1,227.75	1,447.50	1,738.50

D3033 137 Chiller, Water Cooled, Scroll

System Description	Freq. (Years)	Crew	Unit	Labor Hours	2012 Bare Costs Material	Labor	Equipment	Total	Total In-House	Total w/O&P
4030 Replace chiller, water cooled, 5 ton	20	Q-5	Ea.							
Remove chiller				18.182		910		910	1,125	1,425
Replace chiller, water cooled, 5 ton				36.364	3,400	1,825		5,225	6,025	7,100
Total				54.545	3,400	2,735		6,135	7,150	8,525
5010 Repair water cooled chiller, 10 ton	10	2 STPI	Ea.							
Repair controls				1.000		55.50		55.50	69.50	87
Remove fan bearing				3.600		201		201	251	310
Replace fan bearing				6.000	163.50	333		496.50	595	725
Remove compressor				4.954		276		276	345	430
Replace compressor				9.907	910	552		1,462	1,700	2,000
Replace refrigerant				1.333	122	74.50		196.50	225	268
Total				26.794	1,195.50	1,492		2,687.50	3,185.50	3,820
5030 Replace chiller, water cooled, 10 ton	20	Q-6	Ea.							
Remove chiller				43.478		2,250		2,250	2,825	3,525
Replace chiller, water cooled, 10 ton				86.957	6,425	4,525		10,950	12,700	15,100
Total				130.435	6,425	6,775		13,200	15,525	18,625
6010 Repair water cooled chiller, 15 ton	10	Q-5	Ea.							
Repair controls				1.000		55.50		55.50	69.50	87
Remove fan bearing				24.000		1,095		1,095	1,450	1,775
Replace fan bearing				6.000	163.50	333		496.50	595	725
Remove compressor				6.932		348		348	435	540
Replace compressor				13.865	2,050	700		2,750	3,100	3,650
Replace refrigerant				2.000	183	111.75		294.75	340	400
Total				53.797	2,396.50	2,643.25		5,039.75	5,989.50	7,177
6030 Replace chiller, water cooled, 15 ton	20	Q-6	Ea.							
Remove chiller				42.857		2,225		2,225	2,775	3,475
Replace chiller, water cooled, 15 ton				85.714	17,500	4,450		21,950	24,800	28,800
Total				128.571	17,500	6,675		24,175	27,575	32,275

D3033 140 **Chiller, Hermetic Centrifugal**

System Description	Freq. (Years)	Crew	Unit	Labor Hours	2012 Bare Costs				Total In-House	Total w/O&P
					Material	Labor	Equipment	Total		
1010 Repair centrifugal chiller, 100 ton	10	Q-7	Ea.							
Repair controls				1.000		55.50		55.50	69.50	87
Remove compressor				24.390		1,275		1,275	1,575	1,975
Replace compressor				197.000	22,100	10,500		32,600	37,300	43,900
Remove / replace condenser tube				4.800	648	250		898	1,025	1,200
Remove / replace evaporator tube				4.800	648	250		898	1,025	1,200
Remove / replace refrigerant filter				1.600	336	85		421	475	550
Remove refrigerant				.440		24.50		24.50	30.50	38
Replace refrigerant				8.000	732	447		1,179	1,350	1,600
Total				242.030	24,464	12,887		37,351	42,850	50,550
1030 Replace centrifugal chiller, 100 ton	20	Q-7	Ea.							
Remove chiller				163.000		8,650		8,650	10,800	13,500
Replace chiller, centrifugal, 100 ton				326.000	82,000	17,300		99,300	112,000	129,500
Total				489.000	82,000	25,950		107,950	122,800	143,000
2010 Repair centrifugal chiller, 300 ton	10	Q-7	Ea.							
Repair controls				1.000		55.50		55.50	69.50	87
Remove compressor				56.341		2,945.25		2,945.25	3,650	4,550
Replace compressor				455.070	51,051	24,255		75,306	86,000	101,500
Remove / replace condenser tube				12.000	1,620	625		2,245	2,550	3,000
Remove / replace evaporator tube				12.000	1,620	625		2,245	2,550	3,000
Remove / replace refrigerant filter				1.200	360	63.50	1.38	424.88	475	550
Remove refrigerant				1.319		73.50		73.50	91.50	114
Replace refrigerant				21.333	1,952	1,192		3,144	3,600	4,300
Total				560.263	56,603	29,834.75	1.38	86,439.13	98,986	117,101
2030 Replace centrifugal chiller, 300 ton	20	Q-7	Ea.							
Remove chiller				173.000		9,225		9,225	11,500	14,400
Replace chiller, 300 ton				347.000	129,500	18,400		147,900	165,500	190,500
Total				520.000	129,500	27,625		157,125	177,000	204,900

D30 HVAC — D3033 Cooling Generating Systems

D3033 140 Chiller, Hermetic Centrifugal

	System Description	Freq. (Years)	Crew	Unit	Labor Hours	2012 Bare Costs				Total In-House	Total w/O&P
						Material	Labor	Equipment	Total		
3010	**Repair centrifugal chiller, 1000 ton**	10	Q-7	Ea.							
	Repair controls				1.000		55.50		55.50	69.50	87
	Remove compressor				187.561		9,804.75		9,804.75	12,100	15,200
	Replace compressor				1514.930	169,949	80,745		250,694	287,000	338,000
	Remove / replace condenser tube				16.800	2,268	938		3,206	3,675	4,300
	Remove / replace evaporator tube				12.600	2,268	700		2,968	3,375	3,925
	Remove / replace refrigerant filter				1.600	360	89		449	505	590
	Remove refrigerant				3.516		196		196	244	305
	Replace refrigerant				29.333	2,684	1,639		4,323	4,950	5,900
	Total				1767.340	177,529	94,167.25		271,696.25	311,918.50	368,307
3030	**Replace centrifugal chiller, 1000 ton**	20	Q-7	Ea.							
	Remove chiller				242.000		12,900		12,900	16,000	20,000
	Replace chiller, 1000 ton				484.000	433,000	25,700		458,700	508,500	581,500
	Total				726.000	433,000	38,600		471,600	524,500	601,500
6010	**Repair centrifugal chiller, 9000 ton**	10	Q-7	Ea.							
	Repair controls				1.000		55.50		55.50	69.50	87
	Remove compressor				2025.974		105,300		105,300	131,500	164,000
	Replace compressor				5122.000	574,600	273,000		847,600	970,000	1,142,000
	Remove / replace condenser tube				151.204	20,412	8,442		28,854	33,000	38,600
	Remove / replace evaporator tube				113.399	20,412	6,300		26,712	30,400	35,300
	Remove / replace refrigerant filter				14.400	3,240	801		4,041	4,550	5,300
	Remove refrigerant				31.648		1,764		1,764	2,200	2,725
	Replace refrigerant				263.993	24,156	14,751		38,907	44,600	53,000
	Total				7723.618	642,820	410,413.50		1,053,233.50	1,216,319.50	1,441,012
6030	**Replace centrifugal chiller, 9000 ton**	20	Q-7	Ea.							
	Remove chiller				1452.000		77,400		77,400	96,000	120,000
	Replace chiller, 9000 ton				3306.000	3,789,000	175,800		3,964,800	4,386,000	5,010,000
	Total				4758.000	3,789,000	253,200		4,042,200	4,482,000	5,130,000

D3033 142 Chiller, Open Centrifugal

System Description	Freq. (Years)	Crew	Unit	Labor Hours	2012 Bare Costs				Total In-House	Total w/O&P
					Material	Labor	Equipment	Total		
1010 Repair open centrifugal chiller, 300 ton	10	Q-7	Ea.							
Repair controls				1.000		55.50		55.50	69.50	87
Remove compressor				56.341		2,945.25		2,945.25	3,650	4,550
Replace compressor				455.070	51,051	24,255		75,306	86,000	101,500
Remove / replace condenser tube				12.000	1,620	625		2,245	2,550	3,000
Remove / replace evaporator tube				12.000	1,620	625		2,245	2,550	3,000
Remove / replace refrigerant filter				1.200	360	63.50	1.38	424.88	475	550
Remove refrigerant				20.000		912.50		912.50	1,200	1,475
Replace refrigerant				21.333	1,952	1,192		3,144	3,600	4,300
Total				578.944	56,603	30,673.75	1.38	87,278.13	100,094.50	118,462
1030 Replace open centrifugal chiller, 300 ton	20	Q-7	Ea.							
Remove chiller				91.429		4,850		4,850	6,050	7,550
Replace chiller, 300 ton				907.440	164,445	48,165	1,045	213,655	242,000	281,500
Total				998.869	164,445	53,015	1,045	218,505	248,050	289,050
2010 Repair open centrifugal chiller, 1000 ton	10	Q-7	Ea.							
Repair controls				1.000		55.50		55.50	69.50	87
Remove compressor				187.561		9,804.75		9,804.75	12,100	15,200
Replace compressor				1514.930	169,949	80,745		250,694	287,000	338,000
Remove / replace condenser tube				16.800	2,268	875		3,143	3,575	4,200
Remove / replace evaporator tube				16.800	2,268	875		3,143	3,575	4,200
Remove / replace refrigerant filter				1.600	375	85	1.84	461.84	520	605
Remove refrigerant				35.204		1,960		1,960	2,450	3,050
Replace refrigerant				34.666	3,172	1,937		5,109	5,850	6,975
Total				1808.560	178,032	96,337.25	1.84	274,371.09	315,139.50	372,317
2030 Replace open centrifugal chiller, 1000 ton	20	Q-7	Ea.							
Remove chiller				313.000		16,600		16,600	20,700	25,900
Replace chiller, 1000 ton				3104.400	562,575	164,775	3,575	730,925	828,000	963,500
Total				3417.400	562,575	181,375	3,575	747,525	848,700	989,400

D3033 145 Chiller, Absorption

	System Description	Freq. (Years)	Crew	Unit	Labor Hours	2012 Bare Costs				Total In-House	Total w/O&P
						Material	Labor	Equipment	Total		
1010	**Repair chiller, absorption, 100 ton**	10	2 STPI	Ea.							
	Repair controls				1.000		55.50		55.50	69.50	87
	Remove / replace concentrator tube				.900	162	45		207	234	273
	Remove / replace condenser tube				6.000	810	312.50		1,122.50	1,275	1,500
	Remove / replace evaporator tube				6.000	810	312.50		1,122.50	1,275	1,500
	Remove / replace absorber tube				.900	169	45		214	242	282
	Remove / replace gang pump				1.600	6,750	80		6,830	7,525	8,575
	Remove gang pump motor				3.704		191		191	236	295
	Replace gang pump motor				7.407	4,525	380		4,905	5,450	6,250
	Add refrigerant				8.000	249	446		695	830	1,000
	Total				35.511	13,475	1,867.50		15,342.50	17,136.50	19,762
1030	**Replace chiller, absorption, 100 ton**	20	Q-7	Ea.							
	Remove chiller				155.000		8,250		8,250	10,300	12,800
	Replace chiller				310.000	125,000	16,500		141,500	158,000	182,000
	Total				465.000	125,000	24,750		149,750	168,300	194,800
2010	**Repair chiller, absorption, 350 ton**	10	2 STPI	Ea.							
	Repair controls				1.000		55.50		55.50	69.50	87
	Remove / replace concentrator tube				1.800	324	90		414	470	545
	Remove / replace condenser tube				7.200	972	375		1,347	1,525	1,800
	Remove / replace evaporator tube				7.200	972	375		1,347	1,525	1,800
	Remove / replace absorber tube				1.800	338	90		428	485	565
	Remove / replace gang pump				1.600	6,750	80		6,830	7,525	8,575
	Remove gang pump motor				3.704		191		191	236	295
	Replace gang pump motor				7.407	4,525	380		4,905	5,450	6,250
	Add refrigerant				8.000	249	446		695	830	1,000
	Total				39.711	14,130	2,082.50		16,212.50	18,115.50	20,917
2030	**Replace chiller, absorption, 350 ton**	20	Q-7	Ea.							
	Remove chiller				200.000		10,600		10,600	13,200	16,500
	Replace chiller				400.000	317,500	21,200		338,700	375,500	430,000
	Total				600.000	317,500	31,800		349,300	388,700	446,500

D3033 145 | Chiller, Absorption

	System Description	Freq. (Years)	Crew	Unit	Labor Hours	2012 Bare Costs				Total In-House	Total w/O&P
						Material	Labor	Equipment	Total		
3010	**Repair chiller, absorption, 950 ton**	10	4 STPI	Ea.							
	Repair controls				1.000		55.50		55.50	69.50	87
	Remove / replace concentrator tube				3.600	648	180		828	935	1,100
	Remove / replace condenser tube				12.000	1,620	625		2,245	2,550	3,000
	Remove / replace evaporator tube				12.000	1,620	625		2,245	2,550	3,000
	Remove / replace absorber tube				3.600	676	180		856	970	1,125
	Remove / replace gang pump				1.600	6,750	80		6,830	7,525	8,575
	Remove gang pump motor				3.704		191		191	236	295
	Replace gang pump motor				8.696	5,550	450		6,000	6,650	7,625
	Add refrigerant				8.000	249	446		695	830	1,000
	Total				54.198	17,113	2,832.50		19,945.50	22,315.50	25,807
3030	**Replace chiller, absorption, 950 ton**	20	Q-7	Ea.							
	Remove chiller				266.000		14,100		14,100	17,600	22,000
	Replace chiller				533.000	649,500	28,300		677,800	749,500	856,000
	Total				799.000	649,500	42,400		691,900	767,100	878,000

D3033 210 | Air Cooled Condenser

	System Description	Freq. (Years)	Crew	Unit	Labor Hours	2012 Bare Costs				Total In-House	Total w/O&P
						Material	Labor	Equipment	Total		
1010	**Repair condenser, air cooled, 5 ton**	10	1 STPI	Ea.							
	Repair controls				.500		28		28	35	43.50
	Remove fan motor				1.800		100		100	125	156
	Replace fan motor				2.311	330	119		449	510	595
	Total				4.611	330	247		577	670	794.50
1030	**Replace condenser, air cooled, 5 ton**	15	Q-5	Ea.							
	Remove condenser				5.195		260		260	325	405
	Replace condenser, air cooled, 5 ton				10.390	1,825	520		2,345	2,650	3,100
	Total				15.584	1,825	780		2,605	2,975	3,505
2010	**Repair condenser, air cooled, 20 ton**	10	2 STPI	Ea.							
	Repair controls				1.000		55.50		55.50	69.50	87
	Remove fan motor				2.310		129		129	161	200
	Replace fan motor				4.622	760	238		998	1,125	1,325
	Total				7.932	760	422.50		1,182.50	1,355.50	1,612

D3033 210 | **Air Cooled Condenser**

System Description	Freq. (Years)	Crew	Unit	Labor Hours	Material	Labor	Equipment	Total	Total In-House	Total w/O&P
						2012 Bare Costs				
2030 Replace condenser, air cooled, 20 ton	15	Q-5	Ea.							
Remove condenser				10.390		520		520	650	810
Replace condenser, air cooled, 20 ton				20.779	4,575	1,050		5,625	6,325	7,350
Total				31.169	4,575	1,570		6,145	**6,975**	**8,160**
3010 Repair condenser, air cooled, 50 ton	10	2 STPI	Ea.							
Repair controls				1.000		55.50		55.50	69.50	87
Remove fan motor				3.466		193.50		193.50	242	300
Replace fan motor				6.936	1,140	357		1,497	1,700	1,975
Total				11.402	1,140	606		1,746	**2,011.50**	**2,362**
3030 Replace condenser, air cooled, 50 ton	15	Q-6	Ea.							
Remove condenser				38.961		2,025		2,025	2,525	3,150
Replace condenser, air cooled, 50 ton				77.922	13,800	4,050		17,850	20,200	23,600
Total				116.883	13,800	6,075		19,875	**22,725**	**26,750**
4010 Repair condenser, air cooled, 100 ton	10	2 STPI	Ea.							
Repair controls				1.000		55.50		55.50	69.50	87
Remove fan motor				6.931		387		387	485	600
Replace fan motor				13.873	2,280	714		2,994	3,400	3,950
Total				21.804	2,280	1,156.50		3,436.50	**3,954.50**	**4,637**
4030 Replace condenser, air cooled, 100 ton	15	Q-7	Ea.							
Remove condenser				69.264		3,675		3,675	4,575	5,725
Replace condenser, air cooled, 100 ton				138.000	28,100	7,350		35,450	40,000	46,500
Total				207.264	28,100	11,025		39,125	**44,575**	**52,225**

D3033 260   Evaporative Condenser

	System Description	Freq. (Years)	Crew	Unit	Labor Hours	2012 Bare Costs Material	Labor	Equipment	Total	Total In-House	Total w/O&P
1010	**Repair evaporative condenser, 20 ton**	10	2 STPI	Ea.							
	Repair controls				1.000		55.50		55.50	69.50	87
	Remove fan motors				2.310		129		129	161	200
	Replace fan motors				4.622	760	238		998	1,125	1,325
	Remove pump and motor				20.779		1,025		1,025	1,275	1,600
	Replace pump and motor				41.558	3,650	2,050		5,700	6,575	7,750
	Remove / replace pump nozzles				5.000	47.50	250		297.50	365	450
	Remove / replace float valve				.500	19.85	25		44.85	53	64
	Total				75.770	4,477.35	3,772.50		8,249.85	9,623.50	11,476
1030	**Replace evaporative condenser, 20 ton**	15	Q-5	Ea.							
	Remove condenser				22.130		1,100		1,100	1,375	1,725
	Replace evaporative condenser, 20 ton				44.199	9,200	2,225		11,425	12,900	15,000
	Total				66.329	9,200	3,325		12,525	14,275	16,725
2010	**Repair evaporative condenser, 100 ton**	10	2 STPI	Ea.							
	Repair controls				1.000		55.50		55.50	69.50	87
	Remove fan motors				6.931		387		387	485	600
	Replace fan motors				13.873	2,280	714		2,994	3,400	3,950
	Remove pump and motor				20.779		1,025		1,025	1,275	1,600
	Replace pump and motor				41.558	3,650	2,050		5,700	6,575	7,750
	Remove / replace nozzles				25.000	237.50	1,250		1,487.50	1,825	2,250
	Remove / replace float valve				.500	19.85	25		44.85	53	64
	Total				109.642	6,187.35	5,506.50		11,693.85	13,682.50	16,301
2030	**Replace evaporative condenser, 100 ton**	15	Q-7	Ea.							
	Remove condenser				57.762		3,075		3,075	3,825	4,775
	Replace evaporative condenser, 100 ton				115.000	17,400	6,125		23,525	26,800	31,300
	Total				172.762	17,400	9,200		26,600	30,625	36,075

D3033 260 | **Evaporative Condenser**

System Description	Freq. (Years)	Crew	Unit	Labor Hours	2012 Bare Costs				Total In-House	Total w/O&P
					Material	Labor	Equipment	Total		
3010 **Repair evaporative condenser, 300 ton**	10	2 STPI	Ea.							
Repair controls				1.000		55.50		55.50	69.50	87
Remove fan motors				11.552		645		645	805	1,000
Replace fan motors				23.121	3,800	1,190		4,990	5,650	6,600
Remove pump and motor				20.779		1,025		1,025	1,275	1,600
Replace pump and motor				24.000	4,400	1,225		5,625	6,375	7,400
Remove / replace nozzles				35.000	332.50	1,750		2,082.50	2,550	3,150
Remove / replace float valve				1.000	39.70	50		89.70	106	128
Total				116.453	8,572.20	5,940.50		14,512.70	16,830.50	19,965
3030 **Replace evaporative condenser, 300 ton**	15	Q-7	Ea.							
Remove condenser				152.471		8,100		8,100	10,100	12,600
Replace evaporative condenser, 300 ton				304.560	43,740	16,159.50		59,899.50	68,000	80,000
Total				457.031	43,740	24,259.50		67,999.50	78,100	92,600

D3043 120 | **Fan Coil**

System Description	Freq. (Years)	Crew	Unit	Labor Hours	Material	Labor	Equipment	Total	Total In-House	Total w/O&P
						2012 Bare Costs				
1010 Repair fan coil unit, 1 ton	10	1 STPI	Ea.							
Remove fan motor				1.200		67		67	83.50	104
Replace fan motor				1.951	193	101		294	335	395
Total				3.151	193	168		361	418.50	499
1030 Replace fan coil unit, 1 ton	15	Q-5	Ea.							
Remove fan coil unit				1.733		87		87	108	135
Replace fan coil unit, 1 ton				3.467	815	174		989	1,125	1,300
Total				5.200	815	261		1,076	1,233	1,435
2010 Repair fan coil unit, 3 ton	10	1 STPI	Ea.							
Remove fan motor				1.200		67		67	83.50	104
Replace fan motor				1.951	320	101		421	475	555
Total				3.151	320	168		488	558.50	659
2030 Replace fan coil unit, 3 ton	15	Q-5	Ea.							
Remove fan coil unit				2.597		130		130	162	203
Replace fan coil unit, 3 ton				5.195	1,725	260		1,985	2,225	2,550
Total				7.792	1,725	390		2,115	2,387	2,753
3010 Repair fan coil unit, 5 ton	10	1 STPI	Ea.							
Remove fan motor				1.200		67		67	83.50	104
Replace fan motor				2.311	330	119		449	510	595
Total				3.511	330	186		516	593.50	699
3030 Replace fan coil unit, 5 ton	15	Q-5	Ea.							
Remove fan coil unit				2.680		134		134	168	209
Replace fan coil unit, 5 ton				5.371	2,491	268.84		2,759.84	3,075	3,525
Total				8.052	2,491	402.84		2,893.84	3,243	3,734
4010 Repair fan coil unit, 10 ton	10	1 STPI	Ea.							
Remove fan motor				1.400		78		78	97.50	122
Replace fan motor				2.312	380	119		499	565	660
Total				3.712	380	197		577	662.50	782

D3043 120 | **Fan Coil**

System Description	Freq. (Years)	Crew	Unit	Labor Hours	2012 Bare Costs				Total In-House	Total w/O&P
					Material	Labor	Equipment	Total		
4030										
Replace fan coil unit, 10 ton	15	Q-6	Ea.							
Remove fan coil unit				11.538		600		600	750	935
Replace fan coil unit, 10 ton				23.077	3,400	1,200		4,600	5,225	6,125
Total				34.615	3,400	1,800		5,200	**5,975**	**7,060**
5010										
Repair fan coil unit, 20 ton	10	1 STPI	Ea.							
Remove fan motor				1.600		89		89	111	139
Replace fan motor				2.311	455	119		574	650	755
Total				3.911	455	208		663	**761**	**894**
5030										
Replace fan coil unit, 20 ton	15	Q-6	Ea.							
Remove fan coil unit				19.512		1,025		1,025	1,275	1,575
Replace fan coil unit, 20 ton				39.024	5,250	2,025		7,275	8,300	9,725
Total				58.537	5,250	3,050		8,300	**9,575**	**11,300**
6010										
Repair fan coil unit, 30 ton	10	1 STPI	Ea.							
Remove fan motor				1.800		100		100	125	156
Replace fan motor				2.597	720	134		854	955	1,100
Total				4.398	720	234		954	**1,080**	**1,256**
6030										
Replace fan coil unit, 30 ton	15	Q-6	Ea.							
Remove fan coil unit				25.974		1,350		1,350	1,675	2,100
Replace fan coil unit, 30 ton				51.948	8,450	2,700		11,150	12,700	14,800
Total				77.922	8,450	4,050		12,500	**14,375**	**16,900**

D3043 122 Fan Coil, DX Air Conditioner, Cooling Only

System Description	Freq. (Years)	Crew	Unit	Labor Hours	2012 Bare Costs				Total In-House	Total w/O&P
					Material	Labor	Equipment	Total		
1010 Repair fan coil, DX 1-1/2 ton, cooling only	10	1 STPI	Ea.							
Repair controls				.300		16.70		16.70	21	26
Remove / replace supply fan				.650		36		36	45	56.50
Remove supply fan bearing				1.000		55.50		55.50	69.50	87
Replace supply fan bearing				2.000	54.50	111		165.50	199	242
Remove supply fan motor				1.156		59.50		59.50	73.50	92
Replace supply fan motor				1.951	188	109		297	340	405
Remove compressor				2.477		138		138	172	215
Replace compressor				3.714	243	207		450	525	625
Replace refrigerant				.267	24.40	14.90		39.30	45	53.50
Total				13.515	509.90	747.60		1,257.50	1,490	1,802
1040 Replace fan coil, DX 1-1/2 ton, no heat	15	Q-5	Ea.							
Remove fan coil unit				2.080		104		104	130	162
Replace fan coil unit, 1-1/2 ton, no heat				4.160	690	209		899	1,025	1,200
Total				6.240	690	313		1,003	1,155	1,362
2010 Repair fan coil, DX 2 ton, cooling only	10	1 STPI	Ea.							
Repair controls				.300		16.70		16.70	21	26
Remove / replace supply fan				.650		36		36	45	56.50
Remove supply fan bearing				1.000		55.50		55.50	69.50	87
Replace supply fan bearing				2.000	54.50	111		165.50	199	242
Remove supply fan motor				1.156		59.50		59.50	73.50	92
Replace supply fan motor				1.951	193	101		294	335	395
Remove compressor				2.477		138		138	172	215
Replace compressor				4.000	250	223		473	555	660
Replace refrigerant				.400	36.60	22.35		58.95	67.50	80.50
Total				13.934	534.10	763.05		1,297.15	1,537.50	1,854
2040 Replace fan coil, DX 2 ton, no heat	15	Q-5	Ea.							
Remove fan coil unit				2.167		109		109	136	169
Replace fan coil unit, DX 2 ton, no heat				4.334	750	217		967	1,100	1,275
Total				6.500	750	326		1,076	1,236	1,444

D3043 122 Fan Coil, DX Air Conditioner, Cooling Only

	System Description	Freq. (Years)	Crew	Unit	Labor Hours	2012 Bare Costs				Total In-House	Total w/O&P
						Material	Labor	Equipment	Total		
3010	**Repair fan coil, DX 2-1/2 ton**	10	1 STPI	Ea.							
	Repair controls				.300		16.70		16.70	21	26
	Remove / replace supply fan				.650		36		36	45	56.50
	Remove supply fan bearing				1.000		55.50		55.50	69.50	87
	Replace supply fan bearing				2.000	54.50	111		165.50	199	242
	Remove supply fan motor				1.156		59.50		59.50	73.50	92
	Replace supply fan motor				1.951	288	101		389	440	515
	Remove compressor				2.477		138		138	172	215
	Replace compressor				4.334	296	241		537	625	745
	Replace refrigerant				.533	48.80	29.80		78.60	90	107
	Total				14.401	687.30	788.50		1,475.80	**1,735**	**2,085.50**
3040	**Replace fan coil, DX 2-1/2 ton, no heat**	15	Q-5	Ea.							
	Remove fan coil unit				2.363		118		118	148	185
	Replace fan coil, DX 2-1/2 ton, no heat				4.727	790	237		1,027	1,175	1,350
	Total				7.090	790	355		1,145	**1,323**	**1,535**
4010	**Repair fan coil, DX 3 ton, cooling only**	10	1 STPI	Ea.							
	Repair controls				.300		16.70		16.70	21	26
	Remove / replace supply fan				.650		36		36	45	56.50
	Remove supply fan bearing				1.000		55.50		55.50	69.50	87
	Replace supply fan bearing				2.000	54.50	111		165.50	199	242
	Remove supply fan motor				1.156		59.50		59.50	73.50	92
	Replace supply fan motor				1.951	288	101		389	440	515
	Remove compressor				2.477		138		138	172	215
	Replace compressor				3.844	276.25	214.20		490.45	570	680
	Replace refrigerant				.533	48.80	29.80		78.60	90	107
	Total				13.911	667.55	761.70		1,429.25	**1,680**	**2,020.50**
4040	**Replace fan coil, DX 3 ton, no heat**	15	Q-5	Ea.							
	Remove fan coil unit				2.737		137		137	171	214
	Replace fan coil, DX 3 ton, no heat				5.474	985	274		1,259	1,425	1,650
	Total				8.211	985	411		1,396	**1,596**	**1,864**

D3043 | 122 | Fan Coil, DX Air Conditioner, Cooling Only

System Description	Freq. (Years)	Crew	Unit	Labor Hours	2012 Bare Costs				Total In-House	Total w/O&P
					Material	Labor	Equipment	Total		
5050 Repair fan coil, DX 5 ton, cooling only	10	1 STPI	Ea.							
Repair controls				.300		16.70		16.70	21	26
Remove / replace supply fan				.650		36		36	45	56.50
Remove supply fan bearing				1.000		55.50		55.50	69.50	87
Replace supply fan bearing				2.000	54.50	111		165.50	199	242
Remove supply fan motor				1.156		59.50		59.50	73.50	92
Replace supply fan motor				1.951	288	101		389	440	515
Remove compressor				2.477		138		138	172	215
Replace compressor				4.954	455	276		731	845	1,000
Replace refrigerant				.533	48.80	29.80		78.60	90	107
Total				15.021	846.30	823.50		1,669.80	1,955	2,340.50
6060 Replace fan coil, DX 5 ton, no heat	15	Q-5	Ea.							
Remove fan coil unit				3.466		174		174	217	271
Replace fan coil, DX 5 ton, no heat				6.932	1,325	350		1,675	1,900	2,200
Total				10.399	1,325	524		1,849	2,117	2,471
7070 Repair fan coil, DX 10 ton, cooling only	10	Q-6	Ea.							
Repair controls				.300		16.70		16.70	21	26
Remove / replace supply fan				.650		36		36	45	56.50
Remove supply fan bearing				1.000		55.50		55.50	69.50	87
Replace supply fan bearing				2.000	54.50	111		165.50	199	242
Remove supply fan motor				1.156		59.50		59.50	73.50	92
Replace supply fan motor				2.311	380	119		499	565	660
Remove compressor				14.513		753.75		753.75	940	1,175
Replace compressor				28.714	8,978	1,490.75		10,468.75	11,700	13,600
Replace refrigerant				.800	73.20	44.70		117.90	135	161
Total				51.444	9,485.70	2,686.90		12,172.60	13,748	16,099.50
8080 Replace fan coil, DX 10 ton, no heat	15	Q-6	Ea.							
Remove fan coil unit				6.000		310		310	390	485
Replace fan coil, DX 10 ton, no heat				12.000	2,975	625		3,600	4,050	4,700
Total				18.000	2,975	935		3,910	4,440	5,185

D3043 122 Fan Coil, DX Air Conditioner, Cooling Only

	System Description	Freq. (Years)	Crew	Unit	Labor Hours	2012 Bare Costs				Total In-House	Total w/O&P
						Material	Labor	Equipment	Total		
9090	**Repair fan coil, DX 20 ton, cooling only**	10	Q-6	Ea.							
	Repair controls				.300		16.70		16.70	21	26
	Remove / replace supply fan				.650		36		36	45	56.50
	Remove supply fan bearing				1.000		55.50		55.50	69.50	87
	Replace supply fan bearing				2.000	54.50	111		165.50	199	242
	Remove supply fan motor				1.156		59.50		59.50	73.50	92
	Replace supply fan motor				2.476	590	128		718	805	935
	Remove compressor				21.929		1,147.50		1,147.50	1,425	1,775
	Replace compressor				43.902	13,590	2,272.50		15,862.50	17,800	20,500
	Replace refrigerant				1.333	122	74.50		196.50	225	268
	Total				74.747	14,356.50	3,901.20		18,257.70	20,663	23,981.50
9590	**Replace fan coil, DX 20 ton, no heat**	15	Q-6	Ea.							
	Remove fan coil unit				22.284		1,150		1,150	1,450	1,800
	Replace fan coil, DX 20 ton, no heat				44.610	5,575	2,325		7,900	9,025	10,600
	Total				66.894	5,575	3,475		9,050	10,475	12,400
9600	**Repair fan coil, DX 30 ton, cooling only**	10	Q-6	Ea.							
	Repair controls				.300		16.70		16.70	21	26
	Remove / replace supply fan				.650		36		36	45	56.50
	Remove supply fan bearing				1.000		55.50		55.50	69.50	87
	Replace supply fan bearing				2.000	54.50	111		165.50	199	242
	Remove supply fan motor				1.156		59.50		59.50	73.50	92
	Replace supply fan motor				2.476	590	128		718	805	935
	Remove compressor				24.490		1,275		1,275	1,600	1,975
	Replace compressor				48.780	15,100	2,525		17,625	19,800	22,800
	Replace refrigerant				1.733	158.60	96.85		255.45	293	350
	Total				82.586	15,903.10	4,303.55		20,206.65	22,906	26,563.50
9610	**Replace fan coil, DX 30 ton, no heat**	15	Q-6	Ea.							
	Remove fan coil unit				25.974		1,350		1,350	1,675	2,100
	Replace fan coil, DX 20 ton, no heat				48.000	7,350	2,500		9,850	11,200	13,100
	Total				73.974	7,350	3,850		11,200	12,875	15,200

247

D3043 124 | **Fan Coil, DX Air Conditioner W/ Heat**

System Description	Freq. (Years)	Crew	Unit	Labor Hours	2012 Bare Costs				Total In-House	Total w/O&P
					Material	Labor	Equipment	Total		
1010										
Replace fan coil, DX 1-1/2 ton, with heat										
Remove fan coil unit	15	Q-5	Ea.	2.312		116		116	145	181
Replace fan coil unit, 1-1/2 ton, with heat				6.474	966	324.80		1,290.80	1,475	1,700
Total				8.786	966	440.80		1,406.80	**1,620**	**1,881**
2010										
Replace fan coil, DX 2 ton, with heat										
Remove fan coil unit	15	Q-5	Ea.	2.407		121		121	151	188
Replace fan coil unit, DX 2 ton, with heat				6.741	1,050	337.40		1,387.40	1,575	1,850
Total				9.148	1,050	458.40		1,508.40	**1,726**	**2,038**
3010										
Replace fan coil, DX 2-1/2 ton, with heat										
Remove fan coil unit	15	Q-5	Ea.	2.626		132		132	164	205
Replace fan coil, DX 2-1/2 ton, with heat				7.354	1,106	368.20		1,474.20	1,675	1,950
Total				9.979	1,106	500.20		1,606.20	**1,839**	**2,155**
4010										
Replace fan coil, DX 3 ton, with heat										
Remove fan coil unit	15	Q-5	Ea.	3.042		152		152	190	238
Replace fan coil, DX 3 ton, with heat				8.514	1,379	427		1,806	2,075	2,400
Total				11.556	1,379	579		1,958	**2,265**	**2,638**
5010										
Replace fan coil, DX 5 ton, with heat										
Remove fan coil unit	10	Q-5	Ea.	3.852		193		193	241	300
Replace fan coil, DX 5 ton, with heat				10.785	1,855	539		2,394	2,725	3,150
Total				14.637	1,855	732		2,587	**2,966**	**3,450**
6010										
Replace fan coil, DX 10 ton, with heat										
Remove fan coil unit	10	Q-6	Ea.	6.667		345		345	430	540
Replace fan coil, DX 10 ton, with heat				18.667	4,165	973		5,138	5,775	6,700
Total				25.333	4,165	1,318		5,483	**6,205**	**7,240**
7010										
Replace fan coil, DX 20 ton, with heat										
Remove fan coil unit	10	Q-6	Ea.	24.793		1,300		1,300	1,600	2,000
Replace fan coil, DX 20 ton, with heat				69.421	7,805	3,605		11,410	13,100	15,400
Total				94.215	7,805	4,905		12,710	**14,700**	**17,400**

D3043 128   Unit Ventilator

	System Description	Freq. (Years)	Crew	Unit	Labor Hours	2012 Bare Costs Material	2012 Bare Costs Labor	2012 Bare Costs Equipment	2012 Bare Costs Total	Total In-House	Total w/O&P
1010	**Repair unit ventilator, 750 CFM, 2 ton**	10	1 STPI	Ea.							
	Repair controls				.200		11.15		11.15	13.90	17.35
	Remove / replace fan				.650		36		36	45	56.50
	Remove fan motor				1.156		59.50		59.50	73.50	92
	Replace fan motor				1.951	193	101		294	335	395
	Total				3.957	193	207.65		400.65	467.40	560.85
1030	**Replace unit vent., 750 CFM, heat/cool coils**	15	Q-6	Ea.							
	Remove unit ventilator				7.792		405		405	505	630
	Replace unit, 750 CFM, with heat / cool coils				15.605	3,900	810		4,710	5,300	6,150
	Total				23.397	3,900	1,215		5,115	5,805	6,780
2010	**Repair unit ventilator, 1250 CFM, 3 ton**	10	1 STPI	Ea.							
	Repair controls				.200		11.15		11.15	13.90	17.35
	Remove / replace fan				.650		36		36	45	56.50
	Remove fan motor				1.156		59.50		59.50	73.50	92
	Replace fan motor				1.951	320	101		421	475	555
	Total				3.957	320	207.65		527.65	607.40	720.85
2030	**Replace unit vent., 1250 CFM, heat/cool coils**	15	Q-6	Ea.							
	Remove unit ventilator				11.142		580		580	725	905
	Replace unit , 1250 CFM, with heat / cool coils				22.284	4,750	1,150		5,900	6,675	7,750
	Total				33.426	4,750	1,730		6,480	7,400	8,655
2040	**Repair unit ventilator, 2000 CFM, 5 ton**	10	1 STPI	Ea.							
	Repair controls				.300		16.70		16.70	21	26
	Remove / replace fan				.650		36		36	45	56.50
	Remove fan motor				1.156		59.50		59.50	73.50	92
	Replace fan motor				2.311	330	119		449	510	595
	Total				4.417	330	231.20		561.20	649.50	769.50
2050	**Replace unit vent., 2000 CFM, heat/cool coils**	15	Q-6	Ea.							
	Remove unit ventilator				31.209		1,625		1,625	2,025	2,525
	Replace unit, 2000 CFM, with heat / cool coils				62.338	5,975	3,250		9,225	10,600	12,500
	Total				93.547	5,975	4,875		10,850	12,625	15,025

D30 HVAC | D3043 | Distribution Systems

D3043 140 | Duct Heater

System Description	Freq. (Years)	Crew	Unit	Labor Hours	2012 Bare Costs				Total In-House	Total w/O&P
					Material	Labor	Equipment	Total		
0020 Maintenance and inspection	0.50	1 ELEC	Ea.							
Inspect and clean duct heater				1.143		59		59	72.50	87
Total				1.143		59		59	**72.50**	**91**
0030 Replace duct heater	15	1 ELEC	Ea.							
Remove duct heater				.667		34.50		34.50	42.50	53
Duct heater 12 KW				2.000	1,725	103		1,828	2,025	2,325
Total				2.667	1,725	137.50		1,862.50	**2,067.50**	**2,378**

D3043 210 | Draft Fan

System Description	Freq. (Years)	Crew	Unit	Labor Hours	2012 Bare Costs				Total In-House	Total w/O&P
					Material	Labor	Equipment	Total		
1010 Repair fan, induced draft, 2000 CFM	10	1 STPI	Ea.							
Remove bearings				1.000		55.50		55.50	69.50	87
Replace bearings				2.000	54.50	111		165.50	199	242
Total				3.000	54.50	166.50		221	**268.50**	**329**
1030 Replace fan, induced draft, 2000 CFM	20	Q-9	Ea.							
Remove fan				3.151		148		148	187	233
Replace fan, induced draft, 2000 CFM				6.304	3,300	296		3,596	4,000	4,600
Total				9.456	3,300	444		3,744	**4,187**	**4,833**
2010 Repair fan, induced draft, 6700 CFM	10	1 STPI	Ea.							
Remove bearings				1.000		55.50		55.50	69.50	87
Replace bearings				2.000	54.50	111		165.50	199	242
Total				3.000	54.50	166.50		221	**268.50**	**329**
2030 Replace fan, induced draft, 6700 CFM	20	Q-9	Ea.							
Remove fan				4.522		212		212	268	335
Replace fan, induced draft, 6700 CFM				9.045	4,075	425		4,500	5,025	5,775
Total				13.567	4,075	637		4,712	**5,293**	**6,110**
3010 Repair fan, induced draft, 17,700 CFM	10	1 STPI	Ea.							
Remove bearings				1.000		55.50		55.50	69.50	87
Replace bearings				2.222	61	124		185	222	269
Total				3.222	61	179.50		240.50	**291.50**	**356**

D30 HVAC | D3043 | Distribution Systems

D3043 210 | Draft Fan

System Description	Freq. (Years)	Crew	Unit	Labor Hours	2012 Bare Costs				Total In-House	Total w/O&P
					Material	Labor	Equipment	Total		
3030										
Replace fan, induced draft, 17,700 CFM	20	Q-9	Ea.							
Remove fan				12.998		610		610	770	960
Replace fan, induced draft, 17,700 CFM				26.016	10,500	1,225		11,725	13,100	15,100
Total				39.014	10,500	1,835		12,335	13,870	**16,060**

D3043 220 | Exhaust Fan

System Description	Freq. (Years)	Crew	Unit	Labor Hours	2012 Bare Costs				Total In-House	Total w/O&P
					Material	Labor	Equipment	Total		
1010										
Replace fan & motor, propeller exh., 375 CFM	15	Q-20	Ea.							
Remove fan and motor				1.300		62		62	78	97.50
Replace fan & motor, propeller exhaust, 375 CFM				2.600	450	124		574	650	760
Total				3.900	450	186		636	728	**857.50**
1030										
Replace fan & motor, propeller exh., 1000 CFM	15	Q-20	Ea.							
Remove fan and motor				1.625		78		78	98	122
Replace fan & motor, propeller exhaust, 1000 CFM				3.250	700	156		856	965	1,125
Total				4.875	700	234		934	1,063	**1,247**
1040										
Replace fan & motor, propeller exh., 4700 CFM	15	Q-20	Ea.							
Remove fan and motor				2.600		124		124	156	195
Replace fan & motor, propeller exhaust, 4700 CFM				5.200	1,125	249		1,374	1,550	1,800
Total				7.800	1,125	373		1,498	1,706	**1,995**
2030										
Replace roof mounted exhaust fan, 800 CFM	20	Q-20	Ea.							
Remove fan & motor				2.600		124		124	156	195
Replace fan & motor, roof mounted exhaust, 800 CFM				5.200	785	249		1,034	1,175	1,375
Total				7.800	785	373		1,158	1,331	**1,570**
2040										
Replace roof mounted exhaust fan, 2000 CFM	20	Q-20	Ea.							
Remove fan & motor				3.250		156		156	196	244
Replace fan & motor, roof mounted exhaust, 2000 CFM				6.500	1,525	310		1,835	2,075	2,400
Total				9.750	1,525	466		1,991	2,271	**2,644**

D3043 220 | **Exhaust Fan**

	System Description	Freq. (Years)	Crew	Unit	Labor Hours	2012 Bare Costs				Total In-House	Total w/O&P
						Material	Labor	Equipment	Total		
2050	**Replace roof mounted exhaust fan, 8500 CFM**	20	Q-20	Ea.							
	Remove fan & motor				4.333		207		207	261	325
	Replace fan & motor, roof mounted exhaust, 8500 CFM				8.666	2,475	415		2,890	3,250	3,750
	Total				12.998	2,475	622		3,097	3,511	4,075
2060	**Replace roof mounted exhaust fan, 20,300 CFM**	20	Q-20	Ea.							
	Remove fan & motor				13.004		620		620	780	975
	Replace fan & motor, roof mounted exhaust, 20,300 CFM				26.008	6,925	1,250		8,175	9,175	10,600
	Total				39.012	6,925	1,870		8,795	9,955	11,575
3010	**Replace utility set, belt drive, 800 CFM**	10	Q-20	Ea.							
	Remove fan and motor				2.167		104		104	130	163
	Replace utility set, belt drive, 800 CFM				4.334	900	207		1,107	1,250	1,450
	Total				6.500	900	311		1,211	1,380	1,613
3020	**Replace utility set, belt drive, 3600 CFM**	10	Q-20	Ea.							
	Remove fan and motor				3.250		156		156	196	244
	Replace utility set, belt drive, 3600 CFM				6.500	1,850	310		2,160	2,425	2,800
	Total				9.750	1,850	466		2,316	2,621	3,044
3030	**Replace utility set, belt drive, 11,000 CFM**	10	Q-20	Ea.							
	Remove fan and motor				6.500		310		310	390	490
	Replace utility set, belt drive, 11,000 CFM				13.004	4,900	620		5,520	6,175	7,100
	Total				19.504	4,900	930		5,830	6,565	7,590
3040	**Replace utility set, belt drive, 20,000 CFM**	10	Q-20	Ea.							
	Remove fan and motor				16.247		775		775	980	1,225
	Replace utility set, belt drive, 20,000 CFM				32.520	6,550	1,550		8,100	9,150	10,600
	Total				48.767	6,550	2,325		8,875	10,130	11,825
4010	**Replace axial flow fan, 3800 CFM**	10	Q-20	Ea.							
	Remove fan and motor				3.823		183		183	230	287
	Replace axial flow fan, 3800 CFM				7.648	4,800	365		5,165	5,750	6,575
	Total				11.472	4,800	548		5,348	5,980	6,862

D3043 220 Exhaust Fan

System Description	Freq. (Years)	Crew	Unit	Labor Hours	2012 Bare Costs				Total In-House	Total w/O&P
					Material	Labor	Equipment	Total		
4020 Replace axial flow fan, 6400 CFM	10	Q-20	Ea.							
Remove fan and motor				4.643		222		222	279	350
Replace axial flow fan, 6400 CFM				9.285	5,350	445		5,795	6,450	7,375
Total				13.928	5,350	667		6,017	**6,729**	**7,725**
4030 Replace axial flow fan, 15,600 CFM	10	Q-20	Ea.							
Remove fan and motor				8.123		390		390	490	610
Replace axial flow fan, 15,600 CFM				16.247	8,400	775		9,175	10,200	11,700
Total				24.370	8,400	1,165		9,565	**10,690**	**12,310**
4040 Replace axial flow fan, 28,000 CFM	10	Q-20	Ea.							
Remove fan and motor				32.520		1,550		1,550	1,950	2,450
Replace axial flow fan, 28,000 CFM				64.935	14,400	3,100		17,500	19,700	22,900
Total				97.455	14,400	4,650		19,050	**21,650**	**25,350**

D3043 250 Fireplaces, Clay Flue

System Description	Freq. (Years)	Crew	Unit	Labor Hours	2012 Bare Costs				Total In-House	Total w/O&P
					Material	Labor	Equipment	Total		
0010 Replace baked clay flue, architectural	75	2 BRIC	L.F.							
Set up and secure scaffold				.022		.97		.97	1.27	1.57
Masonry demolition				.083		2.92		2.92	3.88	4.79
Remove damaged flue				.002		.10		.10	.13	.16
Install new flue lining				.224	9.75	8.90		18.65	22.50	26.50
Install new chimney				1.518	38.50	60.50		99	121	146
Remove scaffold				.022		.97		.97	1.27	1.57
Total				1.872	48.25	74.36		122.61	**150.05**	**180.59**

D3043 252 Fireplaces, Metal Flue

System Description	Freq. (Years)	Crew	Unit	Labor Hours	2012 Bare Costs				Total In-House	Total w/O&P
					Material	Labor	Equipment	Total		
0020 Replace metal pipe flue, architectural	50	2 SSWK	L.F.							
Remove damaged pipe				.008		.41		.41	.64	.77
Install new vent chimney, prefabricated metal				.306	6.35	14.35		20.70	25	30.50
Total				.314	6.35	14.76		21.11	**25.64**	**31.27**

D3043 310 Steam Converter, Commercial

System Description	Freq. (Years)	Crew	Unit	Labor Hours	2012 Bare Costs				Total In-House	Total w/O&P
					Material	Labor	Equipment	Total		
0010 Repair steam converter										
Repair heat exchanger	5	1 STPI	Ea.	5.944		330		330	415	515
Total				5.944		330		330	**415**	**515**
0020 Inspect for leaks										
Check relief valve operation	2	1 STPI	Ea.	.038		2.10		2.10	2.62	3.28
Check for proper water temperature				.055		3.04		3.04	3.79	4.74
Total				.092		5.14		5.14	**6.41**	**8.02**
0030 Replace steam converter										
Remove exchanger	30	Q-5	Ea.	2.081		104		104	130	163
Install new exchanger 10 GPM of 40F to 180F				4.160	2,900	209		3,109	3,450	3,950
Total				6.241	2,900	313		3,213	**3,580**	**4,113**

D3043 320 Flash Tank, 24 Gallon

System Description	Freq. (Years)	Crew	Unit	Labor Hours	2012 Bare Costs				Total In-House	Total w/O&P
					Material	Labor	Equipment	Total		
0010 Repair flash tank										
Repair flash tank	5	1 STPI	Ea.	5.944		330		330	415	515
Total				5.944		330		330	**415**	**515**
0030 Replace flash tank 24 gal										
Remove old tank	15	Q-5	Ea.	.743		37.50		37.50	46.50	58
Install new tank 24 gallon				1.486	635	74.50		709.50	790	910
Total				2.229	635	112		747	**836.50**	**968**

D3043 330 Steam Regulator Valve

System Description	Freq. (Years)	Crew	Unit	Labor Hours	2012 Bare Costs				Total In-House	Total w/O&P
					Material	Labor	Equipment	Total		
0010 Replace steam regulator valve 1-1/2" diameter										
Remove steam valve	6	1 STPI	Ea	.400		22.50		22.50	28	34.50
Install steam regulator valve 1-1/2" diameter				.800	2,200	44.50		2,244.50	2,475	2,825
Total				1.200	2,200	67		2,267	**2,503**	**2,859.50**

D3043 330   Steam Regulator Valve

System Description	Freq. (Years)	Crew	Unit	Labor Hours	2012 Bare Costs				Total In-House	Total w/O&P
					Material	Labor	Equipment	Total		
0110 Replace steam regulator valve 2" diameter	6	1 STPI	Ea.							
Remove steam valve				.473		26.50		26.50	33	41
Install steam regulator valve 2" diameter				.945	2,700	52.50		2,752.50	3,025	3,450
Total				1.418	2,700	79		2,779	**3,058**	**3,491**
0210 Replace steam regulator valve 2-1/2" diameter	6	Q-5	Ea.							
Remove steam valve				.867		43.50		43.50	54	67.50
Install steam regulator valve 2-1/2" diameter				1.733	3,375	87		3,462	3,825	4,350
Total				2.600	3,375	130.50		3,505.50	**3,879**	**4,417.50**
0310 Replace steam regulator valve 3" diameter	6	Q-5	Ea.							
Remove steam valve				.946		47.50		47.50	59	74
Install steam regulator valve 3" diameter flanged				1.891	4,225	95		4,320	4,775	5,425
Total				2.836	4,225	142.50		4,367.50	**4,834**	**5,499**

D3043 340   Condensate Meter

System Description	Freq. (Years)	Crew	Unit	Labor Hours	2012 Bare Costs				Total In-House	Total w/O&P
					Material	Labor	Equipment	Total		
0010 Repair meter	15	1 STPI	Ea.							
Replace drum				1.538	740	84		824	920	1,050
Replace bearings				2.597	121	142		263	310	370
Total				4.136	861	226		1,087	**1,230**	**1,420**
0030 Replace condensate meter 500 lb./hr.	30	1 STPI	Ea.							
Remove meter				.372		20.50		20.50	26	32.50
Replace meter 500#/hr				.743	2,350	41.50		2,391.50	2,625	3,000
Total				1.114	2,350	62		2,412	**2,651**	**3,032.50**
0130 Replace condensate meter 1500 lb./hr.	30	1 STPI	Ea.							
Remove meter				.743		41.50		41.50	51.50	64.50
Replace meter 1500#/hr				1.486	2,550	83		2,633	2,900	3,325
Total				2.229	2,550	124.50		2,674.50	**2,951.50**	**3,389.50**

D3043 350 Steam Traps

System Description	Freq. (Years)	Crew	Unit	Labor Hours	2012 Bare Costs				Total In-House	Total w/O&P
					Material	Labor	Equipment	Total		
1030 Replace steam trap, 15 PSIG, 3/4" threaded	7	1 STPI	Ea.							
Remove old CI body float & thermostatic trap				.325		18.10		18.10	22.50	28
Install new CI body float & thermostatic trap				.650	109	36		145	165	193
Total				.975	109	54.10		163.10	**187.50**	**221**
1040 Replace steam trap, 15 PSIG, 1" threaded	7	1 STPI	Ea.							
Remove old CI body float & thermostatic trap				.347		19.30		19.30	24	30
Install new CI body float & thermostatic trap				.693	131	38.50		169.50	192	224
Total				1.040	131	57.80		188.80	**216**	**254**
1050 Replace steam trap, 15 PSIG, 1-1/4" threaded	7	1 STPI	Ea.							
Remove old CI body float & thermostatic trap				.400		22.50		22.50	28	34.50
Install new CI body float & thermostatic trap				.800	159	44.50		203.50	231	268
Total				1.200	159	67		226	**259**	**302.50**
1060 Replace steam trap, 15 PSIG, 1-1/2" threaded	7	1 STPI	Ea.							
Remove old CI body float & thermostatic trap				.578		32		32	40	50
Install new CI body float & thermostatic trap				1.156	231	64.50		295.50	335	390
Total				1.733	231	96.50		327.50	**375**	**440**
1070 Replace steam trap, 15 PSIG, 2" threaded	7	1 STPI	Ea.							
Remove old CI body float & thermostatic trap				.867		48.50		48.50	60	75
Install new CI body float & thermostatic trap				1.733	425	96.50		521.50	590	680
Total				2.600	425	145		570	**650**	**755**

D3043 410 Radiator Valve

System Description	Freq. (Years)	Crew	Unit	Labor Hours	2012 Bare Costs				Total In-House	Total w/O&P
					Material	Labor	Equipment	Total		
0010 Replace radiator valve 1/2" angle union	50	1 STPI	Ea.							
Remove radiator valve				.217		12.05		12.05	15.05	18.80
Install radiator valve 1/2" angle union				.433	43.50	24		67.50	78	92
Total				.650	43.50	36.05		79.55	**93.05**	**110.80**

D3043 410 | Radiator Valve

	System Description	Freq. (Years)	Crew	Unit	Labor Hours	2012 Bare Costs Material	Labor	Equipment	Total	Total In-House	Total w/O&P
0020	**Replace radiator valve 3/4" angle union**	50	1 STPI	Ea.							
	Remove radiator valve				.260		14.50		14.50	18.10	22.50
	Install radiator valve 3/4" angle union				.520	47.50	29		76.50	88.50	104
	Total				.780	47.50	43.50		91	106.60	126.50
0030	**Replace radiator valve 1" angle union**	50	1 STPI	Ea.							
	Remove radiator valve				.274		15.25		15.25	19.05	24
	Install radiator valve 1" angle union				.547	54.50	30.50		85	98	116
	Total				.821	54.50	45.75		100.25	117.05	140
0040	**Replace radiator valve 1-1/4" angle union**	50	1 STPI	Ea.							
	Remove radiator valve				.347		19.30		19.30	24	30
	Install radiator valve 1-1/4" angle union				.693	70	38.50		108.50	125	148
	Total				1.040	70	57.80		127.80	149	178

D3043 420 | Cast Iron Radiator, 10' Section

	System Description	Freq. (Years)	Crew	Unit	Labor Hours	2012 Bare Costs Material	Labor	Equipment	Total	Total In-House	Total w/O&P
0010	**Replace C.I. radiator 4 tube 25"H 10' section**	50	Q-5	Section							
	Remove radiator				1.084		54.50		54.50	68	84.50
	Install C.I. radiator 4 tube 25" high 10' section				2.167	280	108.50		388.50	445	520
	Total				3.250	280	163		443	513	604.50

D3043 430 | Baseboard Radiation, 10' Section

	System Description	Freq. (Years)	Crew	Unit	Labor Hours	2012 Bare Costs Material	Labor	Equipment	Total	Total In-House	Total w/O&P
0010	**Replace radiator, baseboard 10'**	20	Q-5	Ea.							
	Remove radiator				2.262		113.50		113.50	142	177
	Install 10' baseboard radiator				4.522	355	225		580	675	800
	Total				6.783	355	338.50		693.50	817	977

257

D3043 440 Finned Radiator, Wall, 10' Section

System Description	Freq. (Years)	Crew	Unit	Labor Hours	2012 Bare Costs				Total In-House	Total w/O&P
					Material	Labor	Equipment	Total		
0010 Replace finned radiator	20	Q-5	Ea.							
Replace radiator				3.468		174		174	215	270
Install 10' finned tube, 2 tier, 1-1/4" cop tube				6.933	500	350		850	985	1,175
Total				10.401	500	524		1,024	1,200	**1,445**

D3043 450 Duct Coil, 1-Row, Hot Water

System Description	Freq. (Years)	Crew	Unit	Labor Hours	2012 Bare Costs				Total In-House	Total w/O&P
					Material	Labor	Equipment	Total		
1020 Replace coil, hot water boost, 12" x 24"	25	Q-5	Ea.							
Remove coil				.858		43		43	53.50	67
Replace coil, hot water duct, 12" x 24"				1.111	380	55.50		435.50	490	560
Total				1.969	380	98.50		478.50	**543.50**	**627**
1030 Replace coil, hot water boost, 24" x 24"	25	Q-5	Ea.							
Remove coil				1.717		86		86	107	134
Replace coil, hot water duct, 24" x 24"				3.433	470	172		642	730	855
Total				5.150	470	258		728	**837**	**989**
1040 Replace coil, hot water boost, 24" x 36"	25	Q-5	Ea.							
Remove coil				2.581		129		129	161	202
Replace coil, hot water duct, 24" x 36"				5.161	665	259		924	1,050	1,225
Total				7.742	665	388		1,053	**1,211**	**1,427**
1050 Replace coil, hot water boost, 36" x 36"	25	Q-5	Ea.							
Remove coil				3.867		194		194	242	300
Replace coil, hot water duct, 36" x 36"				7.729	825	385		1,210	1,400	1,625
Total				11.596	825	579		1,404	**1,642**	**1,925**

D3043 510 — Pipe & Fittings, Steel/Iron, Flanged

	System Description	Freq. (Years)	Crew	Unit	Labor Hours	2012 Bare Costs				Total In-House	Total w/O&P
						Material	Labor	Equipment	Total		
0010	**Install new gasket, 4" pipe size**	25	1 PLUM	Ea.							
	Disconnect joint / remove flange gasket				1.301		71		71	88.50	111
	Install new gasket				1.300	10.40	71		81.40	100	124
	Total				2.601	10.40	142		152.40	188.50	235
0030	**Replace 2" flanged steel pipe and fittings**	75	2 PLUM	L.F.							
	Remove old pipe				.231		11.35		11.35	14.15	17.70
	Install flanged 2" steel pipe with hangers				.356	18.35	17.50	.82	36.67	43	51
	Total				.587	18.35	28.85	.82	48.02	57.15	68.70
0040	**Replace 4" flanged steel pipe and fittings**	75	2 PLUM	L.F.							
	Remove old pipe				.400		19.65		19.65	24.50	30.50
	Install flanged 4" steel pipe with hangers				.800	44	39.50	1.85	85.35	99.50	119
	Total				1.200	44	59.15	1.85	105	124	149.50
0050	**Replace 6" flanged steel pipe and fittings**	75	2 PLUM	L.F.							
	Remove old pipe				.624		30.50		30.50	38.50	48
	Install flanged 6" steel pipe with hangers				1.248	66.50	63.50	1.92	131.92	154	184
	Total				1.872	66.50	94	1.92	162.42	192.50	232
0060	**Replace 8" flanged steel pipe and fittings**	75	2 PLUM	L.F.							
	Remove old pipe				.821		42		42	52	65
	Install flanged 8" steel pipe with hangers				1.642	82	83.50	2.53	168.03	197	235
	Total				2.463	82	125.50	2.53	210.03	249	300

D3043 520 — Valves

	System Description	Freq. (Years)	Crew	Unit	Labor Hours	2012 Bare Costs				Total In-House	Total w/O&P
						Material	Labor	Equipment	Total		
1010	**Repack gate valve gland, 3/8" - 1-1/2"**	10	1 STPI	Ea.							
	Remove / replace gate valve packing				.219	10.05	10.95		21	24.50	29.50
	Total				.219	10.05	10.95		21	24.50	29.50

D3043 520   Valves

System Description	Freq. (Years)	Crew	Unit	Labor Hours	2012 Bare Costs				Total In-House	Total w/O&P
					Material	Labor	Equipment	Total		
1020	**Replace gate valve, partial, 3/8" - 1-1/2"**	20	1 STPI	Ea.							
Turn valve off and on				.017		.95		.95	1.18	1.48
Remove old				.530		29.50		29.50	37	46
Install new, 3/8" - 1-1/2" size				.800	167	44.50		211.50	239	278
Total				1.347	167	74.95		241.95	**277.18**	**325.48**
2010	**Repack gate valve gland, 2" - 3"**	10	1 STPI	Ea.							
Remove / replace gate valve packing				.291	13.37	14.56		27.93	32.50	39.50
Total				.291	13.37	14.56		27.93	**32.50**	**39.50**
2020	**Replace gate valve, partial, 2" - 3"**	20	Q-1	Ea.							
Turn valve off and on				.017		.95		.95	1.18	1.48
Remove valve parts				.440		24.50		24.50	30.50	38
Replace valve parts, 2" - 3"				1.600	660	78.50		738.50	825	950
Total				2.057	660	103.95		763.95	**856.68**	**989.48**
2060	**Repack gate valve gland, 8" - 12"**	5	1 PLUM	Ea.							
Replace valve packing, 8" to 12" diameter				1.600	40	87.50		127.50	153	186
Total				1.600	40	87.50		127.50	**153**	**186**
3010	**Repack drain valve gland, 3/4"**	3	1 STPI	Ea.							
Remove / replace drain valve packing				.219	10.05	10.95		21	24.50	29.50
Total				.219	10.05	10.95		21	**24.50**	**29.50**
3020	**Replace drain valve stem assembly, 3/4"**	8	1 STPI	Ea.							
Turn valve off and on				.017		.95		.95	1.18	1.48
Remove valve stem assembly				.267		14.85		14.85	18.55	23
Replace valve stem assembly				.267	12.15	14.85		27	32	38
Total				.550	12.15	30.65		42.80	**51.73**	**62.48**
3030	**Replace drain valve, 3/4"**	20	1 STPI	Ea.							
Turn valve off and on				.017		.95		.95	1.18	1.48
Remove old valve				.308		17.15		17.15	21.50	26.50
Install new valve, 3/4"				.308	12.15	17.15		29.30	35	41.50
Total				.632	12.15	35.25		47.40	**57.68**	**69.48**

D3043 530 — Circulator Pump

System Description	Freq. (Years)	Crew	Unit	Labor Hours	2012 Bare Costs				Total In-House	Total w/O&P
					Material	Labor	Equipment	Total		
1010 **Repair circulator pump, 1/12 - 3/4 H.P.**	5	1 STPI	Ea.							
Loosen coupling from pump shaft				.009		.50		.50	.63	.78
Remove 4 stud bolts in motor				.035		1.95		1.95	2.43	3.04
Remove motor				.052		2.90		2.90	3.61	4.51
Remove impeller nut from shaft				.033		1.84		1.84	2.29	2.86
Remove seal assembly				.019		1.06		1.06	1.32	1.65
Inspect bearing brackets face				.005		.28		.28	.35	.43
Clean bearing				.016		.89		.89	1.11	1.39
Inspect shaft				.040	37.50	2.01		39.51	44	50
Clean shaft				.017		.95		.95	1.18	1.48
Install new seal and rubber				.013		.72		.72	.90	1.13
Install seal spring and washers				.006		.33		.33	.42	.52
Install impeller nut on shaft				.040	9.35	2.01		11.36	12.80	14.80
Clean pump body gasket area				.037		2.06		2.06	2.57	3.21
Install new gasket (ready made)				.010		.56		.56	.70	.87
Install impeller				.009		.50		.50	.63	.78
Install 4 stud bolts				.035		1.95		1.95	2.43	3.04
Assemble motor to bearing				.024		1.34		1.34	1.67	2.08
Install 4 stud bolts				.027		1.50		1.50	1.88	2.34
Tighten coupling				.009		.50		.50	.63	.78
Final tightening of bolts				.027		1.50		1.50	1.88	2.34
Test run				.042		2.34		2.34	2.92	3.65
Total				.505	46.85	27.69		74.54	86.35	101.68
1030 **Replace circulator pump, 1/12 - 3/4 H.P.**	15	Q-1	Ea.							
Remove pump and motor				2.597		128		128	159	199
Install new pump and motor, 1/12-3/4 H.P.				5.195	2,400	255		2,655	2,950	3,400
Total				7.792	2,400	383		2,783	3,109	3,599

D3043 530 Circulator Pump

System Description	Freq. (Years)	Crew	Unit	Labor Hours	2012 Bare Costs				Total In-House	Total w/O&P
					Material	Labor	Equipment	Total		
2010 Repair circulator pump, 1 H.P.	5	1 STPI	Ea.							
Loosen coupling from pump shaft				.009		.50		.50	.63	.78
Remove 4 stud bolts in motor				.035		1.95		1.95	2.43	3.04
Remove motor				.052		2.90		2.90	3.61	4.51
Remove impeller nut from shaft				.033		1.84		1.84	2.29	2.86
Remove seal assembly				.019		1.06		1.06	1.32	1.65
Inspect bearing brackets face				.005		.28		.28	.35	.43
Clean bearing				.016		.89		.89	1.11	1.39
Inspect shaft				.040	37.50	2.01		39.51	44	50
Clean shaft				.017		.95		.95	1.18	1.48
Install new seal and rubber				.013		.72		.72	.90	1.13
Install seal spring and washers				.006		.33		.33	.42	.52
Install impeller nut on shaft				.040	9.35	2.01		11.36	12.80	14.80
Clean pump body gasket area				.037		2.06		2.06	2.57	3.21
Install new gasket (ready made)				.013		.72		.72	.90	1.13
Install impeller				.009		.50		.50	.63	.78
Install 4 stud bolts				.035		1.95		1.95	2.43	3.04
Assemble motor to bearing				.024		1.34		1.34	1.67	2.08
Install 4 stud bolts				.027		1.50		1.50	1.88	2.34
Tighten coupling				.009		.50		.50	.63	.78
Final tightening of bolts				.027		1.50		1.50	1.88	2.34
Test run				.042		2.34		2.34	2.92	3.65
Total				.508	46.85	27.85		74.70	86.55	101.94
2030 Replace circulator. pump, 1 H.P.	15	Q-1	Ea.							
Remove pump				2.597		128		128	159	199
Install new pump, 1 H.P.				5.200	3,875	256		4,131	4,575	5,250
Total				7.797	3,875	384		4,259	4,734	5,449

D3043 540 Expansion Tank

System Description	Freq. (Years)	Crew	Unit	Labor Hours	2012 Bare Costs				Total In-House	Total w/O&P
					Material	Labor	Equipment	Total		
0010 Refill expansion tank	5	1 STPI	Ea.							
Refill air chamber				.200		11.15		11.15	13.90	17.35
Total				.200		11.15		11.15	13.90	17.35

D3043 540 | Expansion Tank

	System Description	Freq. (Years)	Crew	Unit	Labor Hours	2012 Bare Costs				Total In-House	Total w/O&P
						Material	Labor	Equipment	Total		
0020	**Replace expansion tank, 24 gal capacity**	50	Q-5	Ea.							
	Remove expansion tank				.743		37		37	46.50	58
	Install expansion tank, 24 gallon capacity				1.486	1,075	74.50		1,149.50	1,275	1,450
	Total				2.228	1,075	111.50		1,186.50	**1,321.50**	**1,508**
0120	**Replace expansion tank, 60 gal capacity**	50	Q-5	Ea.							
	Remove expansion tank				1.300		65		65	81.50	102
	Install expansion tank, 60 gallon capacity				2.602	1,700	130		1,830	2,025	2,325
	Total				3.901	1,700	195		1,895	**2,106.50**	**2,427**
0220	**Replace expansion tank, 175 gal capacity**	50	Q-5	Ea.							
	Remove expansion tank				2.597		130		130	162	203
	Install expansion tank, 175 gallon capacity				5.195	4,650	260		4,910	5,450	6,225
	Total				7.792	4,650	390		5,040	**5,612**	**6,428**
0320	**Replace expansion tank, 400 gal capacity**	50	Q-5	Ea.							
	Remove expansion tank				3.721		187		187	233	291
	Install expansion tank, 400 gallon capacity				7.442	9,900	375		10,275	11,400	13,000
	Total				11.163	9,900	562		10,462	**11,633**	**13,291**

D3043 550 | Pipe Insulation

	System Description	Freq. (Years)	Crew	Unit	Labor Hours	2012 Bare Costs				Total In-House	Total w/O&P
						Material	Labor	Equipment	Total		
1010	**Repair damaged pipe insulation, fiberglass 1/2"**	5	Q-14	Ea.							
	Remove 2' length old insulation				.086		3.80		3.80	4.94	6.10
	Install insulation, fiberglass, 1" wall - 1/2" diam.				.173	1.78	7.62		9.40	11.90	14.55
	Total				.260	1.78	11.42		13.20	**16.84**	**20.65**
1110	**Repair damaged pipe insulation, fiberglass 3/4"**	5	Q-14	Ea.							
	Remove 2' length old insulation				.090		3.98		3.98	5.15	6.40
	Install insulation, fiberglass, 1" wall - 3/4" diam.				.181	1.94	7.96		9.90	12.50	15.25
	Total				.271	1.94	11.94		13.88	**17.65**	**21.65**

D3043 550 Pipe Insulation

System Description	Freq. (Years)	Crew	Unit	Labor Hours	2012 Bare Costs				Total In-House	Total w/O&P
					Material	Labor	Equipment	Total		
1120 Repair damaged pipe insulation, fiberglass 1"	5	Q-14	Ea.							
Remove 2' length old insulation				.095		4.16		4.16	5.40	6.70
Install insulation, fiberglass, 1" wall - 1" diam.				.189	2.08	8.32		10.40	13.10	16
Total				.284	2.08	12.48		14.56	**18.50**	**22.70**
1130 Repair damaged pipe insulation, fbgs 1-1/4"	5	Q-14	Ea.							
Remove 2' length old insulation				.099		4.34		4.34	5.65	7
Install insulation, fiberglass, 1" wall - 1-1/4" diam.				.198	2.26	8.68		10.94	13.80	16.85
Total				.296	2.26	13.02		15.28	**19.45**	**23.85**
1140 Repair damaged pipe insulation, fbgs 1-1/2"	5	Q-14	Ea.							
Remove 2' length old insulation				.099		4.34		4.34	5.65	7
Install insulation, fiberglass, 1" wall - 1-1/2" diam.				.198	2.44	8.72		11.16	14	17.05
Total				.297	2.44	13.06		15.50	**19.65**	**24.05**
1150 Repair damaged pipe insulation, fiberglass 2"	5	Q-14	Ea.							
Remove 2' length old insulation				.104		4.56		4.56	5.95	7.35
Install insulation, fiberglass, 1" wall - 2" diam.				.208	2.64	9.14		11.78	14.80	18
Total				.312	2.64	13.70		16.34	**20.75**	**25.35**
1160 Repair damaged pipe insulation, fiberglass 3"	5	Q-14	Ea.							
Remove 2' length old insulation				.116		5.10		5.10	6.60	8.20
Install insulation, fiberglass, 1" wall - 3" diam.				.232	3.20	10.20		13.40	16.80	20.50
Total				.348	3.20	15.30		18.50	**23.40**	**28.70**
1170 Repair damaged pipe insulation, fiberglass 4"	5	Q-14	Ea.							
Remove 2' length old insulation				.139		6.12		6.12	7.95	9.85
Install insulation, fiberglass, 1" wall - 4" diam.				.278	4.24	12.20		16.44	20.50	25
Total				.417	4.24	18.32		22.56	**28.45**	**34.85**
1180 Repair damaged pipe insulation, fiberglass 6"	5	Q-14	Ea.							
Remove 2' length old insulation				.173		7.60		7.60	9.90	12.20
Install insulation, fiberglass, 1" wall - 6" diam.				.347	5.08	15.20		20.28	25.50	31
Total				.520	5.08	22.80		27.88	**35.40**	**43.20**

D3043 550 Pipe Insulation

	System Description	Freq. (Years)	Crew	Unit	Labor Hours	2012 Bare Costs				Total In-House	Total w/O&P
						Material	Labor	Equipment	Total		
1220	**Replace pipe insulation, fiberglass 1/2"**	5	Q-14	M.L.F.							
	Remove 1000' length old insulation				33.330		1,470		1,470	1,900	2,350
	Install insulation, fiberglass, 1" wall - 1/2" diam.				66.670	890	2,930		3,820	4,800	5,825
	Total				100.000	890	4,400		5,290	6,700	8,175
1230	**Replace pipe insulation, fiberglass 3/4"**	5	Q-14	M.L.F.							
	Remove 1000' length old insulation				34.780		1,530		1,530	2,000	2,450
	Install insulation, fiberglass, 1" wall - 3/4" diam.				69.570	970	3,060		4,030	5,050	6,125
	Total				104.350	970	4,590		5,560	7,050	8,575
1240	**Replace pipe insulation, fiberglass 1"**	5	Q-14	M.L.F.							
	Remove 1000' length old insulation				36.360		1,600		1,600	2,075	2,575
	Install insulation, fiberglass, 1" wall - 1" diam.				72.730	1,040	3,200		4,240	5,300	6,450
	Total				109.090	1,040	4,800		5,840	7,375	9,025
1250	**Replace pipe insulation, fiberglass 1-1/4"**	5	Q-14	M.L.F.							
	Remove 1000' length old insulation				38.100		1,680		1,680	2,175	2,700
	Install insulation, fiberglass, 1" wall - 1-1/4" diam.				76.190	1,130	3,350		4,480	5,600	6,825
	Total				114.290	1,130	5,030		6,160	7,775	9,525
1260	**Replace pipe insulation, fiberglass 1-1/2"**	5	Q-14	M.L.F.							
	Remove 1000' length old insulation				38.100		1,680		1,680	2,175	2,700
	Install insulation, fiberglass, 1" wall - 1-1/2" diam.				76.190	1,220	3,350		4,570	5,700	6,925
	Total				114.290	1,220	5,030		6,250	7,875	9,625
1270	**Replace pipe insulation, fiberglass 2"**	5	Q-14	M.L.F.							
	Remove 1000' length old insulation				40.000		1,760		1,760	2,275	2,825
	Install insulation, fiberglass, 1" wall - 2" diam.				80.000	1,320	3,520		4,840	6,000	7,300
	Total				120.000	1,320	5,280		6,600	8,275	10,125
1280	**Replace pipe insulation, fiberglass 3"**	5	Q-14	M.L.F.							
	Remove 1000' length old insulation				44.440		1,950		1,950	2,550	3,150
	Install insulation, fiberglass, 1" wall - 3" diam.				88.890	1,600	3,910		5,510	6,850	8,300
	Total				133.330	1,600	5,860		7,460	9,400	11,450

	System Description	Freq. (Years)	Crew	Unit	Labor Hours	2012 Bare Costs				Total In-House	Total w/O&P
						Material	Labor	Equipment	Total		
1290	**Replace pipe insulation, fiberglass 4″**	5	Q-14	M.L.F.							
	Remove 1000′ length old insulation				53.330		2,350		2,350	3,050	3,775
	Install insulation, fiberglass, 1″ wall - 4″ diam.				106.670	2,120	4,690		6,810	8,400	10,200
	Total				160.000	2,120	7,040		9,160	**11,450**	**13,975**
1300	**Replace pipe insulation, fiberglass 6″**	5	Q-14	M.L.F.							
	Remove 1000′ length old insulation				66.670		2,930		2,930	3,800	4,700
	Install insulation, fiberglass, 1″ wall - 6″ diam.				133.330	2,540	5,850		8,390	10,400	12,600
	Total				200.000	2,540	8,780		11,320	**14,200**	**17,300**
1410	**Repair damaged pipe insulation rubber 1/2″**	5	1 ASBE	Ea.							
	Remove 2′ length old insulation				.117		5.70		5.70	7.40	9.20
	Install insulation, foam rubber, 3/4″ wall - 1/2″ diam.				.234	2.34	11.40		13.74	17.40	21.50
	Total				.350	2.34	17.10		19.44	**24.80**	**30.70**
1420	**Repair damaged pipe insulation rubber 3/4″**	5	1 ASBE	Ea.							
	Remove 2′ length old insulation				.117		5.70		5.70	7.40	9.20
	Install insulation, foam rubber, 3/4″ wall - 3/4″ diam.				.234	2.86	11.40		14.26	18	22
	Total				.350	2.86	17.10		19.96	**25.40**	**31.20**
1430	**Repair damaged pipe insulation rubber 1″**	5	1 ASBE	Ea.							
	Remove 2′ length old insulation				.118		5.78		5.78	7.50	9.30
	Install insulation, foam rubber, 3/4″ wall - 1″ diam.				.236	3.26	11.50		14.76	18.60	22.50
	Total				.355	3.26	17.28		20.54	**26.10**	**31.80**
1440	**Repair damaged pipe insulation rubber 1-1/4″**	5	1 ASBE	Ea.							
	Remove 2′ length old insulation				.120		5.84		5.84	7.60	9.40
	Install insulation, foam rubber, 3/4″ wall - 1-1/4″ diam.				.239	4.34	11.70		16.04	19.90	24
	Total				.359	4.34	17.54		21.88	**27.50**	**33.40**
1450	**Repair damaged pipe insulation rubber 1-1/2″**	5	1 ASBE	Ea.							
	Remove 2′ length old insulation				.120		5.84		5.84	7.60	9.40
	Install insulation, foam rubber, 3/4″ wall - 1-1/2″ diam.				.239	4.92	11.70		16.62	20.50	25
	Total				.359	4.92	17.54		22.46	**28.10**	**34.40**

D3043 550 Pipe Insulation

	System Description	Freq. (Years)	Crew	Unit	Labor Hours	2012 Bare Costs				Total In-House	Total w/O&P
						Material	Labor	Equipment	Total		
1460	**Repair damaged pipe insulation rubber 2"**	5	1 ASBE	Ea.							
	Remove 2' length old insulation				.121		5.92		5.92	7.70	9.50
	Install insulation, foam rubber, 3/4" wall - 2" diam.				.242	5.68	11.80		17.48	21.50	26
	Total				.364	5.68	17.72		23.40	29.20	35.50
1470	**Repair damaged pipe insulation rubber 3"**	5	1 ASBE	Ea.							
	Remove 2' length old insulation				.122		5.98		5.98	7.75	9.60
	Install insulation, foam rubber, 3/4" wall - 3" diam.				.245	8.64	12		20.64	25	30
	Total				.367	8.64	17.98		26.62	32.75	39.60
1480	**Repair damaged pipe insulation rubber 4"**	5	1 ASBE	Ea.							
	Remove 2' length old insulation				.130		6.36		6.36	8.25	10.20
	Install insulation, foam rubber, 3/4" wall - 4" diam.				.260	10.90	12.70		23.60	28.50	34
	Total				.390	10.90	19.06		29.96	36.75	44.20
1490	**Repair damaged pipe insulation rubber 6"**	5	1 ASBE	Ea.							
	Remove 2' length old insulation				.130		6.36		6.36	8.25	10.20
	Install insulation, foam rubber, 3/4" wall - 6" diam.				.260	15.80	12.70		28.50	34	40
	Total				.390	15.80	19.06		34.86	42.25	50.20
1510	**Replace pipe insulation foam rubber 1/2"**	5	1 ASBE	L.F.							
	Remove 1000' length old insulation				.090		4.40		4.40	5.70	7.05
	Install insulation, foam rubber, 3/4" wall - 1/2" diam.				.180	2.34	8.78		11.12	14	17.05
	Total				.270	2.34	13.18		15.52	19.70	24.10
1520	**Replace pipe insulation foam rubber 3/4"**	5	1 ASBE	L.F.							
	Remove 1000' length old insulation				.090		4.40		4.40	5.70	7.05
	Install insulation, foam rubber, 3/4" wall - 3/4" diam.				.180	2.86	8.78		11.64	14.50	17.70
	Total				.270	2.86	13.18		16.04	20.20	24.75
1530	**Replace pipe insulation foam rubber 1"**	5	1 ASBE	L.F.							
	Remove 1000' length old insulation				.091		4.44		4.44	5.75	7.15
	Install insulation, foam rubber, 3/4" wall - 1" diam.				.182	3.26	8.88		12.14	15.10	18.40
	Total				.273	3.26	13.32		16.58	20.85	25.55

D3043 550 Pipe Insulation

	Freq. (Years)	Crew	Unit	Labor Hours	2012 Bare Costs				Total In-House	Total w/O&P
System Description					Material	Labor	Equipment	Total		
1540										
Replace pipe insulation foam rubber 1-1/4"	5	1 ASBE	L.F.							
Remove 1000' length old insulation				.092		4.50		4.50	5.85	7.20
Install insulation, foam rubber, 3/4" wall - 1-1/4" diam.				.184	4.34	8.98		13.32	16.40	19.85
Total				.276	4.34	13.48		17.82	22.25	27.05
1550										
Replace pipe insulation foam rubber 1-1/2"	5	1 ASBE	L.F.							
Remove 1000' length old insulation				.092		4.50		4.50	5.85	7.20
Install insulation, foam rubber, 3/4" wall - 1-1/2" diam.				.184	4.92	8.98		13.90	17.10	20.50
Total				.276	4.92	13.48		18.40	22.95	27.70
1560										
Replace pipe insulation foam rubber 2"	5	1 ASBE	L.F.							
Remove 1000' length old insulation				.093		4.54		4.54	5.90	7.30
Install insulation, foam rubber, 3/4" wall - 2" diam.				.186	5.68	9.08		14.76	18	21.50
Total				.279	5.68	13.62		19.30	23.90	28.80
1570										
Replace pipe insulation foam rubber 3"	5	1 ASBE	L.F.							
Remove 1000' length old insulation				.094		4.60		4.60	5.95	7.40
Install insulation, foam rubber, 3/4" wall - 3" diam.				.188	8.64	9.20		17.84	21.50	25.50
Total				.282	8.64	13.80		22.44	27.45	32.90
1580										
Replace pipe insulation foam rubber 4"	5	1 ASBE	L.F.							
Remove 1000' length old insulation				.100		4.88		4.88	6.35	7.85
Install insulation, foam rubber, 3/4" wall - 4" diam.				.200	10.90	9.78		20.68	24.50	29.50
Total				.300	10.90	14.66		25.56	30.85	37.35
1590										
Replace pipe insulation foam rubber 6"	5	1 ASBE	L.F.							
Remove 1000' length old insulation				.100		4.88		4.88	6.35	7.85
Install insulation, foam rubber, 3/4" wall - 6" diam.				.200	15.80	9.78		25.58	30	35.50
Total				.300	15.80	14.66		30.46	36.35	43.35

	System Description	Freq. (Years)	Crew	Unit	Labor Hours	2012 Bare Costs				Total In-House	Total w/O&P
						Material	Labor	Equipment	Total		
1010	**Repair unit heater, 12 MBH, 2 PSI steam**	10	1 STPI	Ea.							
	Repair controls				.200		11.15		11.15	13.90	17.35
	Remove fan motor				.976		54.50		54.50	68	84.50
	Replace fan motor				1.951	193	101		294	335	395
	Total				3.127	193	166.65		359.65	**416.90**	**496.85**
1030	**Replace unit heater, 12 MBH, 2 PSI steam**	15	Q-5	Ea.							
	Remove unit heater				.867		43.50		43.50	54	67.50
	Replace unit heater, 12 MBH, 2 PSI steam				1.733	345	87		432	490	565
	Total				2.600	345	130.50		475.50	**544**	**632.50**
2010	**Repair unit heater, 36 MBH, 2 PSI steam**	10	1 STPI	Ea.							
	Repair controls				.200		11.15		11.15	13.90	17.35
	Remove fan motor				.976		54.50		54.50	68	84.50
	Replace fan motor				1.951	288	101		389	440	515
	Total				3.127	288	166.65		454.65	**521.90**	**616.85**
2030	**Replace unit heater, 36 MBH, 2 PSI steam**	15	Q-5	Ea.							
	Remove unit heater				1.300		65		65	81.50	102
	Replace unit heater, 36 MBH, 2 PSI steam				2.600	520	130		650	735	855
	Total				3.900	520	195		715	**816.50**	**957**
3010	**Repair unit heater, 85 MBH, 2 PSI steam**	10	1 STPI	Ea.							
	Repair controls				.200		11.15		11.15	13.90	17.35
	Remove fan motor				.976		54.50		54.50	68	84.50
	Replace fan motor				1.951	320	101		421	475	555
	Total				3.127	320	166.65		486.65	**556.90**	**656.85**
3030	**Replace unit heater, 85 MBH, 2 PSI steam**	15	Q-5	Ea.							
	Remove unit heater				1.600		80		80	100	125
	Replace unit heater, 85 MBH, 2 PSI steam				3.200	620	160		780	880	1,025
	Total				4.800	620	240		860	**980**	**1,150**
4010	**Repair unit heater, 250 MBH, 2 PSI steam**	10	1 STPI	Ea.							
	Repair controls				.200		11.15		11.15	13.90	17.35
	Remove fan motor				1.156		59.50		59.50	73.50	92
	Replace fan motor				2.311	330	119		449	510	595
	Total				3.667	330	189.65		519.65	**597.40**	**704.35**

D3053 110 | Unit Heater

System Description	Freq. (Years)	Crew	Unit	Labor Hours	2012 Bare Costs				Total In-House	Total w/O&P
					Material	Labor	Equipment	Total		
4030 **Replace unit heater, 250 MBH, 2 PSI steam**	15	Q-5	Ea.							
Remove unit heater				4.160		209		209	260	325
Replace unit heater, 250 MBH, 2 PSI steam				8.320	1,425	415		1,840	2,100	2,425
Total				12.481	1,425	624		2,049	**2,360**	**2,750**
5010 **Repair unit heater, 400 MBH, 2 PSI steam**	10	1 STPI	Ea.							
Repair controls				.200		11.15		11.15	13.90	17.35
Remove fan motor				1.156		59.50		59.50	73.50	92
Replace fan motor				2.311	380	119		499	565	660
Total				3.667	380	189.65		569.65	**652.40**	**769.35**
5020 **Replace unit heater, 400 MBH, 2 PSI steam**	15	Q-5	Ea.							
Remove unit heater				6.499		325		325	405	510
Replace unit heater, 400 MBH, 2 PSI steam				13.008	2,500	650		3,150	3,575	4,150
Total				19.507	2,500	975		3,475	**3,980**	**4,660**

D3053 112 | Infrared Heater Suspended, Commercial

System Description	Freq. (Years)	Crew	Unit	Labor Hours	2012 Bare Costs				Total In-House	Total w/O&P
					Material	Labor	Equipment	Total		
0010 **Maintenance and repair**	1	1 ELEC	Ea.							
Repair wiring connections				.615		31.50		31.50	39	49
Total				.615		31.50		31.50	**39**	**49**
0020 **Maintenance and inspection**	0.50	1 ELEC	Ea.							
Inspect and clean infrared heater				1.143		59		59	72.50	91
Total				1.143		59		59	**72.50**	**91**
0030 **Replace infrared heater**	15	1 ELEC	Ea.							
Remove infrared heater				.667		34.50		34.50	42.50	53
Infrared heater 240 V, 1500 W				2.105	255	109		364	415	485
Total				2.772	255	143.50		398.50	**457.50**	**538**

D3053 114 Standard Suspended Heater

System Description	Freq. (Years)	Crew	Unit	Labor Hours	2012 Bare Costs				Total In-House	Total w/O&P
					Material	Labor	Equipment	Total		
0010 **Maintenance and repair**	2	1 ELEC	Ea.							
Remove unit heater component				.151		7.80		7.80	9.60	12
Unit heater component				.444	60	23		83	94.50	111
Total				.595	60	30.80		90.80	**104.10**	**123**
0020 **Maintenance and inspection**	0.50	1 ELEC	Ea.							
Inspect and clean unit heater				1.143		59		59	72.50	91
Total				1.143		59		59	**72.50**	**91**
0030 **Replace heater**	15	1 ELEC	Ea.							
Remove unit heater				.667		34.50		34.50	42.50	53
Unit heater, heavy duty, 480 V, 3 KW				3.200	455	165		620	705	825
Total				3.867	455	199.50		654.50	**747.50**	**878**

D3053 116 Explosionproof Industrial Heater

System Description	Freq. (Years)	Crew	Unit	Labor Hours	2012 Bare Costs				Total In-House	Total w/O&P
					Material	Labor	Equipment	Total		
0010 **Maintenance and repair**	2	1 ELEC	Ea.							
Remove explosionproof heater part				.200		10.30		10.30	12.75	15.95
Explosionproof heater part				.615	75.50	31.50		107	122	143
Total				.815	75.50	41.80		117.30	**134.75**	**158.95**
0020 **Maintenance and inspection**	0.50	1 ELEC	Ea.							
Inspect / clean explosionproof heater				1.143		59		59	72.50	91
Total				1.143		59		59	**72.50**	**91**
0030 **Replace heater**	15	1 ELEC	Ea.							
Remove explosionproof heater				.800		41		41	51	63.50
Explosionproof heater, 3 KW				3.810	7,375	196		7,571	8,350	9,525
Total				4.610	7,375	237		7,612	**8,401**	**9,588.50**

271

D3053 150   Wall Mounted/Recessed Heater, With Fan

	System Description	Freq. (Years)	Crew	Unit	Labor Hours	2012 Bare Costs Material	Labor	Equipment	Total	Total In-House	Total w/O&P
0010	**Maintenance and repair**										
	Remove heater fan	5	1 ELEC	Ea.	.250		12.90		12.90	15.90	19.90
	Heater fan				.727	86	37.50		123.50	141	166
	Total				.977	86	50.40		136.40	156.90	185.90
0020	**Maintenance and inspection**										
	Inspect and clean heater with fan	1	1 ELEC	Ea.	1.143		59		59	72.50	91
	Total				1.143		59		59	72.50	91
0030	**Replace heater**										
	Remove heater with fan	20	1 ELEC	Ea.	.667		34.50		34.50	42.50	53
	Heater with fan, commercial 2000 W				2.667	181	137		318	370	440
	Total				3.333	181	171.50		352.50	412.50	493

D3053 160   Convector Suspended, Commercial

	System Description	Freq. (Years)	Crew	Unit	Labor Hours	2012 Bare Costs Material	Labor	Equipment	Total	Total In-House	Total w/O&P
0010	**Maintenance and repair**										
	Repair wiring connections	2	1 ELEC	Ea.	.615		31.50		31.50	39	49
	Total				.615		31.50		31.50	39	49
0020	**Maintenance and inspection**										
	Inspect and clean convector heater	0.50	1 ELEC	Ea.	1.143		59		59	72.50	91
	Total				1.143		59		59	72.50	91
0030	**Replace heater**										
	Remove cabinet convector heater	15	1 ELEC	Ea.	.667		34.50		34.50	42.50	53
	Cabinet convector heater, 2' long				2.000	1,900	103		2,003	2,225	2,525
	Total				2.667	1,900	137.50		2,037.50	2,267.50	2,578

D3053 170 Terminal Reheat

	System Description	Freq. (Years)	Crew	Unit	Labor Hours	2012 Bare Costs				Total In-House	Total w/O&P
						Material	Labor	Equipment	Total		
1010	**Repair terminal reheat, 12" x 24" coil**	10	1 STPI	Ea.							
	Fix leak				1.200		67		67	83.50	104
	Total				1.200		67		67	**83.50**	**104**
1040	**Replace terminal reheat, 12" x 24" coil**	15	Q-5	Ea.							
	Remove terminal reheat unit				.858		43		43	53.50	67
	Replace terminal reheat unit, 12" x 24" coil				1.716	810	86		896	1,000	1,150
	Total				2.574	810	129		939	**1,053.50**	**1,217**
2010	**Repair terminal reheat, 18" x 24" coil**	10	1 STPI	Ea.							
	Fix leak				1.400		78		78	97.50	122
	Total				1.400		78		78	**97.50**	**122**
2040	**Replace terminal reheat, 18" x 24" coil**	15	Q-5	Ea.							
	Remove terminal reheat unit				1.284		64.50		64.50	80.50	100
	Replace terminal reheat unit, 18" x 24" coil				2.568	950	129		1,079	1,200	1,400
	Total				3.852	950	193.50		1,143.50	**1,280.50**	**1,500**
3010	**Repair terminal reheat, 36" x 36" coil**	10	1 STPI	Ea.							
	Fix leak				2.200		123		123	153	191
	Total				2.200		123		123	**153**	**191**
3040	**Replace terminal reheat, 36" x 36" coil**	15	Q-5	Ea.							
	Remove terminal reheat unit				3.852		193		193	241	300
	Replace terminal reheat unit, 36" x 36" coil				7.703	1,600	385		1,985	2,250	2,600
	Total				11.555	1,600	578		2,178	**2,491**	**2,900**
4010	**Repair terminal reheat, 48" x 126" coil**	10	1 STPI	Ea.							
	Fix leak				4.000		223		223	278	345
	Total				4.000		223		223	**278**	**345**
4040	**Replace terminal reheat, 48" x 126" coil**	15	Q-5	Ea.							
	Remove terminal reheat unit				17.937		900		900	1,125	1,400
	Replace terminal reheat unit, 48" x 126" coil				35.874	4,950	1,800		6,750	7,700	9,000
	Total				53.812	4,950	2,700		7,650	**8,825**	**10,400**

System Description	Freq. (Years)	Crew	Unit	Labor Hours	2012 Bare Costs				Total In-House	Total w/O&P
					Material	Labor	Equipment	Total		
1010 Repair heat pump, 1.5 ton, air to air split	10	1 STPI	Ea.							
Repair controls				.600		33.50		33.50	41.50	52
Remove / replace supply fan				.650		36		36	45	56.50
Remove supply fan motor				.700		39		39	48.50	61
Replace supply fan motor				1.951	188	109		297	340	405
Remove compressor				1.860		104		104	129	161
Replace compressor				3.714	243	207		450	525	625
Remove / replace condenser fan				1.800		100		100	125	156
Remove condenser fan motor				1.800		100		100	125	156
Replace condenser fan motor				1.951	193	101		294	335	395
Replace refrigerant				.133	12.20	7.45		19.65	22.50	27
Remove / replace heater				.500		28		28	35	43.50
Total				15.661	636.20	864.95		1,501.15	1,771.50	2,138
1030 Replace heat pump, 1.5 ton, air to air split	20	Q-5	Ea.							
Remove heat pump				4.336		217		217	271	340
Replace heat pump, 1.5 ton, air to air split				8.649	2,075	435		2,510	2,825	3,275
Total				12.985	2,075	652		2,727	3,096	3,615
2010 Repair heat pump, 5 ton, air to air split	10	1 STPI	Ea							
Repair controls				.600		33.50		33.50	41.50	52
Remove / replace supply fan				.650		36		36	45	56.50
Remove supply fan motor				1.156		59.50		59.50	73.50	92
Replace supply fan motor				1.951	193	101		294	335	395
Remove compressor				2.477		138		138	172	215
Replace compressor				4.954	455	276		731	845	1,000
Remove / replace condenser fan				1.800		100		100	125	156
Remove condenser fan motor				.976		54.50		54.50	68	84.50
Replace condenser fan motor				1.951	288	101		389	440	515
Replace refrigerant				.667	61	37.25		98.25	113	134
Remove / replace heater				.500		28		28	35	43.50
Total				17.681	997	964.75		1,961.75	2,293	2,743.50
2030 Replace heat pump, 5 ton, air to air split	20	Q-5	Ea.							
Remove heat pump				20.806		1,050		1,050	1,300	1,625
Replace heat pump, 5 ton, air to air split				41.558	3,425	2,075		5,500	6,375	7,525
Total				62.365	3,425	3,125		6,550	7,675	9,150

D3053 245 | **Heat Pump**

System Description	Freq. (Years)	Crew	Unit	Labor Hours	2012 Bare Costs				Total In-House	Total w/O&P
					Material	Labor	Equipment	Total		
3010 **Repair heat pump, 10 ton, air to air split**	10	Q-5	Ea.							
Repair controls				.600		33.50		33.50	41.50	52
Remove / replace supply fan				.650		36		36	45	56.50
Remove supply fan motor				.700		39		39	48.50	61
Replace supply fan motor				2.311	380	119		499	565	660
Remove compressor				4.000		201		201	250	310
Replace compressor				8.000	1,200	400		1,600	1,825	2,125
Remove / replace condenser fan				1.800		100		100	125	156
Remove condenser fan motor				1.800		100		100	125	156
Replace condenser fan motor				2.311	330	119		449	510	595
Replace refrigerant				1.067	97.60	59.60		157.20	180	214
Remove / replace heater				.500		28		28	35	43.50
Total				23.739	2,007.60	1,235.10		3,242.70	3,750	4,429
3030 **Replace heat pump, 10 ton, air to air split**	20	Q-6	Ea.							
Remove heat pump				24.490		1,275		1,275	1,600	1,975
Replace heat pump, 10 ton, air to air split				48.980	8,250	2,550		10,800	12,300	14,300
Total				73.469	8,250	3,825		12,075	13,900	16,275
4010 **Repair heat pump, 25 ton, air to air split**	10	Q-5	Ea.							
Repair controls				.600		33.50		33.50	41.50	52
Remove / replace supply fan				1.000		55.50		55.50	69.50	87
Remove supply fan motor				1.156		59.50		59.50	73.50	92
Replace supply fan motor				2.311	455	119		574	650	755
Remove compressor				10.000		500		500	625	780
Replace compressor				20.000	3,000	1,000		4,000	4,575	5,325
Remove / replace condenser fan				1.800		100		100	125	156
Remove condenser fan motor				1.800		100		100	125	156
Replace condenser fan motor				2.312	380	119		499	565	660
Replace refrigerant				2.000	183	111.75		294.75	340	400
Remove / replace heater				.500		28		28	35	43.50
Total				43.479	4,018	2,226.25		6,244.25	7,224.50	8,506.50
4030 **Replace heat pump, 25 ton, air to air split**	20	Q-7	Ea.							
Remove heat pump				61.538		3,275		3,275	4,075	5,075
Replace heat pump, 25 ton, air to air split				123.000	19,300	6,525		25,825	29,400	34,300
Total				184.538	19,300	9,800		29,100	33,475	39,375

D30 HVAC — D3053 Terminal and Package Units

D3053 245 Heat Pump

	System Description	Freq. (Years)	Crew	Unit	Labor Hours	2012 Bare Costs — Material	Labor	Equipment	Total	Total In-House	Total w/O&P
5010	**Repair heat pump, 50 ton, air to air split**	10	Q-6	Ea.							
	Repair controls				.600		33.50		33.50	41.50	52
	Remove / replace supply fan				1.000		55.50		55.50	69.50	87
	Remove supply fan motor				1.156		59.50		59.50	73.50	92
	Replace supply fan motor				4.167	1,450	215		1,665	1,850	2,150
	Remove compressor				77.922		4,050		4,050	5,050	6,300
	Replace compressor				155.000	17,500	8,100		25,600	29,300	34,500
	Remove / replace condenser fan				2.400		134		134	167	208
	Remove condenser fan motor				1.800		100		100	125	156
	Replace condenser fan motor				4.000	1,150	206		1,356	1,525	1,750
	Replace refrigerant				4.667	427	260.75		687.75	790	940
	Remove / replace heater				1.200		67		67	83.50	104
	Total				253.912	20,527	13,281.25		33,808.25	39,075	46,339
5030	**Replace heat pump, 50 ton, air to air split**	20	Q-7	Ea.							
	Remove heat pump				96.970		5,150		5,150	6,425	8,025
	Replace heat pump, 50 ton, air to air split				207.000	48,000	11,000		59,000	66,500	77,000
	Total				303.970	48,000	16,150		64,150	72,925	85,025
6010	**Repair heat pump, thru-wall unit, 1.5 ton**	10	1 STPI	Ea.							
	Repair controls				.600		33.50		33.50	41.50	52
	Remove / replace supply fan				.650		36		36	45	56.50
	Remove supply fan motor				.700		39		39	48.50	61
	Replace supply fan motor				1.951	188	109		297	340	405
	Remove compressor				1.860		104		104	129	161
	Replace compressor				3.714	243	207		450	525	625
	Remove / replace condenser fan				1.800		100		100	125	156
	Remove condenser fan motor				1.800		100		100	125	156
	Replace condenser fan motor				1.951	193	101		294	335	395
	Replace refrigerant				.133	12.20	7.45		19.65	22.50	27
	Remove / replace heater				.500		28		28	35	43.50
	Total				15.661	636.20	864.95		1,501.15	1,771.50	2,138
6030	**Replace heat pump, thru-wall unit, 1.5 ton**	20	Q-5	Ea.							
	Remove heat pump				6.709		335		335	420	525
	Replace heat pump, thru-wall, 1.5 ton				13.423	2,550	675		3,225	3,650	4,250
	Total				20.131	2,550	1,010		3,560	4,070	4,775

D3053 245 — Heat Pump

	System Description	Freq. (Years)	Crew	Unit	Labor Hours	2012 Bare Costs				Total In-House	Total w/O&P
						Material	Labor	Equipment	Total		
7010	**Repair heat pump, thru-wall unit, 5 ton**	10	1 STPI	Ea.							
	Repair controls				.600		33.50		33.50	41.50	52
	Remove / replace supply fan				.650		36		36	45	56.50
	Remove supply fan motor				1.156		59.50		59.50	73.50	92
	Replace supply fan motor				1.951	193	101		294	335	395
	Remove compressor				2.477		138		138	172	215
	Replace compressor				4.954	455	276		731	845	1,000
	Remove / replace condenser fan				1.800		100		100	125	156
	Remove condenser fan motor				.976		54.50		54.50	68	84.50
	Replace condenser fan motor				1.951	288	101		389	440	515
	Replace refrigerant				.667	61	37.25		98.25	113	134
	Remove / replace heater				.500		28		28	35	43.50
	Total				17.681	997	964.75		1,961.75	2,293	2,743.50
7030	**Replace heat pump, thru-wall unit, 5 ton**	20	Q-5	Ea.							
	Remove heat pump				16.000		800		800	1,000	1,250
	Replace heat pump, trhu-wall, 5 ton				32.000	4,150	1,600		5,750	6,575	7,700
	Total				48.000	4,150	2,400		6,550	7,575	8,950

D3053 265 — Air Conditioner, Window, 1 Ton

	System Description	Freq. (Years)	Crew	Unit	Labor Hours	2012 Bare Costs				Total In-House	Total w/O&P
						Material	Labor	Equipment	Total		
1010	**Repair air conditioner, window, 1 ton**	8	1 STPI	Ea.							
	Find / fix leak				1.000		55.50		55.50	69.50	87
	Replace refrigerant				.067	6.10	3.73		9.83	11.25	13.40
	Total				1.067	6.10	59.23		65.33	80.75	100.40
1030	**Replace air conditioner, window, 1 ton**	10	L-2	Ea.							
	Remove air conditioner				1.300		50.50		50.50	67	82.50
	Replace air conditioner, 1 ton				2.000	645	77.50		722.50	810	935
	Total				3.300	645	128		773	877	1,017.50

D3053 | **Terminal and Package Units**

D3053 266 | Air Conditioner, Thru-The-Wall

System Description	Freq. (Years)	Crew	Unit	Labor Hours	2012 Bare Costs				Total In-House	Total w/O&P
					Material	Labor	Equipment	Total		
2010										
Repair air conditioner, thru-the-wall, 2 ton	8	1 STPI	Ea.							
Find / fix leak				1.000		55.50		55.50	69.50	87
Replace refrigerant				.133	12.20	7.45		19.65	22.50	27
Total				1.133	12.20	62.95		75.15	**92**	**114**
2030										
Replace air conditioner, thru-the-wall, 2 ton	10	L-2	Ea.							
Remove air conditioner				2.600		101		101	134	165
Replace air conditioner, 2 ton				5.200	1,100	201		1,301	1,475	1,700
Total				7.800	1,100	302		1,402	**1,609**	**1,865**

D3053 272 | Air Conditioner, DX Package

System Description	Freq. (Years)	Crew	Unit	Labor Hours	2012 Bare Costs				Total In-House	Total w/O&P
					Material	Labor	Equipment	Total		
1010										
Repair air conditioner, DX, 5 ton	10	1 STPI	Ea.							
Repair controls				.600		33.50		33.50	41.50	52
Remove / replace supply fan				.650		36		36	45	56.50
Remove supply fan bearing				1.000		55.50		55.50	69.50	87
Replace supply fan bearing				2.000	54.50	111		165.50	199	242
Remove supply fan motor				1.156		59.50		59.50	73.50	92
Replace supply fan motor				2.311	330	119		449	510	595
Remove compressor				2.477		138		138	172	215
Replace compressor				4.954	455	276		731	845	1,000
Remove / replace condenser fan				1.800		100		100	125	156
Remove condenser fan bearing				1.200		67		67	83.50	104
Replace condenser fan bearing				2.000	54.50	111		165.50	199	242
Remove condenser fan motor				.976		54.50		54.50	68	84.50
Replace condenser fan motor				1.951	320	101		421	475	555
Replace refrigerant				.667	61	37.25		98.25	113	134
Remove / replace heating coils				3.900	622.50	202.50		825	940	1,100
Total				27.641	1,897.50	1,501.75		3,399.25	**3,959**	**4,715**
1030										
Replace air conditioner, DX, 5 ton	20	Q-6	Ea.							
Remove air conditioner				13.001		675		675	845	1,050
Replace air conditioner, 5 ton				26.002	4,150	1,350		5,500	6,250	7,300
Total				39.003	4,150	2,025		6,175	**7,095**	**8,350**

D3053 272 Air Conditioner, DX Package

	System Description	Freq. (Years)	Crew	Unit	Labor Hours	2012 Bare Costs				Total In-House	Total w/O&P
						Material	Labor	Equipment	Total		
2010	**Repair air conditioner, DX, 20 ton**	10	Q-6	Ea.							
	Repair controls				.800		44.50		44.50	55.50	69.50
	Remove / replace supply fan				.650		36		36	45	56.50
	Remove supply fan bearing				1.000		55.50		55.50	69.50	87
	Replace supply fan bearing				2.000	54.50	111		165.50	199	242
	Remove supply fan motor				1.156		59.50		59.50	73.50	92
	Replace supply fan motor				2.312	380	119		499	565	660
	Remove compressor				24.390		1,275		1,275	1,575	1,975
	Replace compressor				48.780	15,100	2,525		17,625	19,800	22,800
	Remove / replace condenser fan				1.800		100		100	125	156
	Remove condenser fan bearing				1.200		67		67	83.50	104
	Replace condenser fan bearing				2.000	54.50	111		165.50	199	242
	Remove condenser fan motor				.976		54.50		54.50	68	84.50
	Replace condenser fan motor				2.311	330	119		449	510	595
	Replace refrigerant				1.333	122	74.50		196.50	225	268
	Remove / replace heating coils				6.936	2,340	367.50		2,707.50	3,025	3,500
	Total				97.645	18,381	5,119		23,500	26,618	30,931.50
2030	**Replace air conditioner, DX, 20 ton**	20	Q-7	Ea.							
	Remove air conditioner				23.105		1,225		1,225	1,525	1,900
	Replace air conditioner, 20 ton				46.243	15,600	2,450		18,050	20,200	23,300
	Total				69.347	15,600	3,675		19,275	21,725	25,200

System Description	Freq. (Years)	Crew	Unit	Labor Hours	2012 Bare Costs				Total In-House	Total w/O&P
					Material	Labor	Equipment	Total		
3010										
Repair air conditioner, DX, 50 ton	10	Q-6	Ea.							
Repair controls				.800		44.50		44.50	55.50	69.50
Remove / replace supply fan				.650		36		36	45	56.50
Remove supply fan bearing				1.200		67		67	83.50	104
Replace supply fan bearing				2.222	61	124		185	222	269
Remove supply fan motor				1.156		59.50		59.50	73.50	92
Replace supply fan motor				2.597	720	134		854	955	1,100
Remove compressor				77.922		4,050		4,050	5,050	6,300
Replace compressor				155.000	17,500	8,100		25,600	29,300	34,500
Remove / replace condenser fan				1.800		100		100	125	156
Remove condenser fan bearing				1.200		67		67	83.50	104
Replace condenser fan bearing				2.222	61	124		185	222	269
Remove condenser fan motor				.976		54.50		54.50	68	84.50
Replace condenser fan motor				2.311	330	119		449	510	595
Replace refrigerant				3.333	305	186.25		491.25	565	670
Remove / replace heating coil				12.468	6,675	660		7,335	8,175	9,375
Total				265.857	25,652	13,925.75		39,577.75	45,533	53,744.50
3030										
Replace air conditioner, DX, 50 ton	20	Q-7	Ea.							
Remove air conditioner				41.558		2,200		2,200	2,750	3,425
Replace air conditioner, 50 ton				83.117	44,500	4,400		48,900	54,500	62,500
Total				124.675	44,500	6,600		51,100	57,250	65,925

D3053 274 Computer Room A/C Units, Air Cooled

	System Description	Freq. (Years)	Crew	Unit	Labor Hours	2012 Bare Costs				Total In-House	Total w/O&P
						Material	Labor	Equipment	Total		
1010	**Repair computer room A/C, air cooled, 5 ton**	10	1 STPI	Ea.							
	Repair controls				.600		33.50		33.50	41.50	52
	Remove / replace supply fan				.650		36		36	45	56.50
	Remove supply fan bearing				1.000		55.50		55.50	69.50	87
	Replace supply fan bearing				2.000	54.50	111		165.50	199	242
	Remove supply fan motor				1.156		59.50		59.50	73.50	92
	Replace supply fan motor				2.311	330	119		449	510	595
	Replace fan belt for supply fan				.400	32.50	22.50		55	63.50	75
	Remove compressor				2.477		138		138	172	215
	Replace compressor				4.954	455	276		731	845	1,000
	Remove / replace condenser fan				1.800		100		100	125	156
	Remove condenser fan bearing				1.200		67		67	83.50	104
	Replace condenser fan bearing				2.000	54.50	111		165.50	199	242
	Remove condenser fan motor				.976		54.50		54.50	68	84.50
	Replace condenser fan motor				1.951	320	101		421	475	555
	Replace fan belt for condenser fan				.400	32.50	22.50		55	63.50	75
	Replace refrigerant				.667	61	37.25		98.25	113	134
	Remove / replace heating coils				3.900	622.50	202.50		825	940	1,100
	Total				28.441	1,962.50	1,546.75		3,509.25	4,086	4,865
1015	**Replace computer room A/C, air cooled, 5 ton**	20	Q-6	Ea.							
	Remove air conditioner and condenser				13.001		675		675	845	1,050
	Replace air conditioner and remote condenser, 5 ton				35.556	19,100	1,775		20,875	23,200	26,700
	Total				48.557	19,100	2,450		21,550	24,045	27,750

D3053 274 Computer Room A/C Units, Air Cooled

	System Description	Freq. (Years)	Crew	Unit	Labor Hours	2012 Bare Costs				Total In-House	Total w/O&P
						Material	Labor	Equipment	Total		
1020	**Repair computer room A/C, air cooled, 10 ton**	10	1 STPI	Ea.							
	Repair controls				.400		22.50		22.50	28	34.50
	Remove / replace supply fan				.650		36		36	45	56.50
	Remove supply fan bearing				1.200		67		67	83.50	104
	Replace supply fan bearing				2.000	54.50	111		165.50	199	242
	Remove supply fan motor				1.156		59.50		59.50	73.50	92
	Replace supply fan motor				2.311	380	119		499	565	660
	Replace fan belt for supply fan				.400	32.50	22.50		55	63.50	75
	Remove compressor				14.513		753.75		753.75	940	1,175
	Replace compressor				28.714	8,978	1,490.75		10,468.75	11,700	13,600
	Remove / replace condenser fan				1.800		100		100	125	156
	Remove condenser fan bearing				1.200		67		67	83.50	104
	Replace condenser fan bearing				2.000	54.50	111		165.50	199	242
	Remove condenser fan motor				.976		54.50		54.50	68	84.50
	Replace condenser fan motor				1.951	320	101		421	475	555
	Replace fan belt for condenser fan				.400	32.50	22.50		55	63.50	75
	Replace refrigerant				1.333	122	74.50		196.50	225	268
	Remove / replace heating coils				5.200	830	270		1,100	1,250	1,450
	Total				66.204	10,804	3,482.50		14,286.50	16,186.50	18,973.50
1025	**Replace computer room A/C, air cooled, 10 ton**	20	Q-6	Ea.							
	Remove air conditioner and condenser				33.898		1,750		1,750	2,200	2,750
	Replace air conditioner and remote condenser, 10 ton				64.000	37,200	3,200		40,400	44,900	51,500
	Total				97.898	37,200	4,950		42,150	47,100	54,250

D3053 274 Computer Room A/C Units, Air Cooled

System Description	Freq. (Years)	Crew	Unit	Labor Hours	2012 Bare Costs				Total In-House	Total w/O&P
					Material	Labor	Equipment	Total		
1030 **Repair computer room A/C, air cooled, 15 ton**	10	1 STPI	Ea.							
Repair controls				.500		28		28	35	43.50
Remove / replace supply fan				.650		36		36	45	56.50
Remove supply fan bearing				1.200		67		67	83.50	104
Replace supply fan bearing				2.000	54.50	111		165.50	199	242
Remove supply fan motor				1.156		59.50		59.50	73.50	92
Replace supply fan motor				2.312	380	119		499	565	660
Replace fan belt for supply fan				.400	32.50	22.50		55	63.50	75
Remove compressor				21.661		1,125		1,125	1,400	1,750
Replace compressor				42.857	13,400	2,225		15,625	17,500	20,200
Remove / replace condenser fan				1.800		100		100	125	156
Remove condenser fan bearing				1.200		67		67	83.50	104
Replace condenser fan bearing				2.000	54.50	111		165.50	199	242
Remove condenser fan motor				.976		54.50		54.50	68	84.50
Replace condenser fan motor				1.951	320	101		421	475	555
Replace fan belt for condenser fan				.400	32.50	22.50		55	63.50	75
Replace refrigerant				2.000	183	111.75		294.75	340	400
Remove / replace heating coils				6.501	1,037.50	337.50		1,375	1,575	1,825
Total				89.563	15,494.50	4,698.25		20,192.75	22,893.50	26,664.50
1035 **Replace computer room A/C, air cooled, 15 ton**	20	Q-6	Ea.							
Remove air conditioner and condenser				50.314		2,625		2,625	3,275	4,075
Replace air conditioner and remote condenser, 15 ton				72.727	40,900	3,650		44,550	49,500	57,000
Total				123.042	40,900	6,275		47,175	52,775	61,075

D3053 274 — Computer Room A/C Units, Air Cooled

	System Description	Freq. (Years)	Crew	Unit	Labor Hours	2012 Bare Costs				Total In-House	Total w/O&P
						Material	Labor	Equipment	Total		
1040	**Repair computer room A/C, air cooled, 20 ton**	10	1 STPI	Ea.							
	Repair controls				.800		44.50		44.50	55.50	69.50
	Remove / replace supply fan				.650		36		36	45	56.50
	Remove supply fan bearing				1.000		55.50		55.50	69.50	87
	Replace supply fan bearing				2.000	54.50	111		165.50	199	242
	Remove supply fan motor				1.156		59.50		59.50	73.50	92
	Replace supply fan motor				2.312	380	119		499	565	660
	Replace fan belt for supply fan				.400	32.50	22.50		55	63.50	75
	Remove compressor				24.390		1,275		1,275	1,575	1,975
	Replace compressor				48.780	15,100	2,525		17,625	19,800	22,800
	Remove / replace condenser fan				1.800		100		100	125	156
	Remove condenser fan bearing				1.200		67		67	83.50	104
	Replace condenser fan bearing				2.000	54.50	111		165.50	199	242
	Remove condenser fan motor				.976		54.50		54.50	68	84.50
	Replace condenser fan motor				2.311	330	119		449	510	595
	Replace fan belt for condenser fan				.400	32.50	22.50		55	63.50	75
	Replace refrigerant				2.667	244	149		393	450	535
	Remove / replace heating coils				6.936	2,340	367.50		2,707.50	3,025	3,500
	Total				99.778	18,568	5,238.50		23,806.50	26,970	31,348.50
1045	**Replace computer room A/C, air cooled, 20 ton**	20	Q-6	Ea							
	Remove air conditioner and condenser				23.105		1,225		1,225	1,525	1,900
	Replace air conditioner and remote condenser, 20 ton				100.000	49,700	5,200		54,900	61,000	70,000
	Total				123.105	49,700	6,425		56,125	62,525	71,900

D3053 276 | Computer Room A/C Units, Chilled Water

System Description	Freq. (Years)	Crew	Unit	Labor Hours	2012 Bare Costs Material	2012 Bare Costs Labor	2012 Bare Costs Equipment	2012 Bare Costs Total	Total In-House	Total w/O&P
1010 Repair computer room A/C, chilled water, 5 ton	10	1 STPI	Ea.							
Repair controls				.600		33.50		33.50	41.50	52
Remove / replace supply fan				.650		36		36	45	56.50
Remove supply fan bearing				1.000		55.50		55.50	69.50	87
Replace supply fan bearing				2.000	54.50	111		165.50	199	242
Remove supply fan motor				1.156		59.50		59.50	73.50	92
Replace supply fan motor				2.311	330	119		449	510	595
Replace fan belt for supply fan				.400	32.50	22.50		55	63.50	75
Remove / replace heating coils				26.002	4,150	1,350		5,500	6,250	7,300
Total				34.119	4,567	1,787		6,354	7,252	8,499.50
1015 Replace computer room A/C, chilled water, 5 ton	20	Q-6	Ea.							
Remove air conditioner				13.001		675		675	845	1,050
Replace air conditioner, 5 ton				28.070	13,600	1,400		15,000	16,700	19,200
Total				41.071	13,600	2,075		15,675	17,545	20,250
1020 Repair computer room A/C, chilled water, 10 ton	10	1 STPI	Ea.							
Repair controls				.400		22.50		22.50	28	34.50
Remove / replace supply fan				.650		36		36	45	56.50
Remove supply fan bearing				1.200		67		67	83.50	104
Replace supply fan bearing				2.000	54.50	111		165.50	199	242
Remove supply fan motor				1.156		59.50		59.50	73.50	92
Replace supply fan motor				2.311	380	119		499	565	660
Replace fan belt for supply fan				.400	32.50	22.50		55	63.50	75
Remove / replace heating coils				26.002	4,150	1,350		5,500	6,250	7,300
Total				34.119	4,617	1,787.50		6,404.50	7,307.50	8,564
1025 Replace computer room A/C, chilled water, 10 ton	20	Q-6	Ea.							
Remove air conditioner				33.898		1,750		1,750	2,200	2,750
Replace air conditioner, 10 ton				42.105	13,900	2,100		16,000	17,900	20,700
Total				76.004	13,900	3,850		17,750	20,100	23,450

D3053 276 | Computer Room A/C Units, Chilled Water

	System Description	Freq. (Years)	Crew	Unit	Labor Hours	2012 Bare Costs				Total In-House	Total w/O&P
						Material	Labor	Equipment	Total		
1030	**Repair computer room A/C, chilled water, 15 ton**	10	1 STPI	Ea.							
	Repair controls				.500		28		28	35	43.50
	Remove / replace supply fan				.650		36		36	45	56.50
	Remove supply fan bearing				1.200		67		67	83.50	104
	Replace supply fan bearing				2.000	54.50	111		165.50	199	242
	Remove supply fan motor				1.156		59.50		59.50	73.50	92
	Replace supply fan motor				2.312	380	119		499	565	660
	Replace fan belt for supply fan				.400	32.50	22.50		55	63.50	75
	Remove / replace heating coils				26.002	4,150	1,350		5,500	6,250	7,300
	Total				34.220	4,617	1,793		6,410	7,314.50	8,573
1035	**Replace computer room A/C, chilled water, 15 ton**	20	Q-6	Ea.							
	Remove air conditioner				50.314		2,625		2,625	3,275	4,075
	Replace air conditioner, 15 ton				44.444	14,600	2,225		16,825	18,800	21,700
	Total				94.759	14,600	4,850		19,450	22,075	25,775
1040	**Repair computer room A/C, chilled water, 20 ton**	10	1 STPI	Ea.							
	Repair controls				.500		28		28	35	43.50
	Remove / replace supply fan				.650		36		36	45	56.50
	Remove supply fan bearing				1.200		67		67	83.50	104
	Replace supply fan bearing				2.000	54.50	111		165.50	199	242
	Remove supply fan motor				1.156		59.50		59.50	73.50	92
	Replace supply fan motor				2.312	380	119		499	565	660
	Replace fan belt for supply fan				.400	32.50	22.50		55	63.50	75
	Remove / replace heating coils				46.243	15,600	2,450		18,050	20,200	23,300
	Total				54.461	16,067	2,893		18,960	21,264.50	24,573
1045	**Replace computer room A/C, chilled water, 20 ton**	20	Q-6	Ea.							
	Remove air conditioner				23.105		1,225		1,225	1,525	1,900
	Replace air conditioner, 20 ton				47.059	15,500	2,350		17,850	20,000	23,100
	Total				70.164	15,500	3,575		19,075	21,525	25,000

D3053 278 | Multi-Zone Air Conditioner

System Description	Freq. (Years)	Crew	Unit	Labor Hours	2012 Bare Costs Material	Labor	Equipment	Total	Total In-House	Total w/O&P
1010 Repair multi-zone rooftop unit, 15 ton	10	Q-6	Ea.							
Repair controls				1.000		55.50		55.50	69.50	87
Remove fan bearings				2.400		134		134	167	208
Replace fan bearings				4.000	109	222		331	400	485
Remove fan motor				1.156		59.50		59.50	73.50	92
Replace fan motor				2.312	380	119		499	565	660
Remove compressor				17.778		890		890	1,100	1,400
Replace compressor				42.857	13,400	2,225		15,625	17,500	20,200
Replace refrigerant				1.333	122	74.50		196.50	225	268
Remove / replace heater igniter				.500	26.50	28		54.50	64	76.50
Total				73.336	14,037.50	3,807.50		17,845	20,164	23,476.50
1040 Replace multi-zone rooftop unit, 15 ton	15	Q-7	Ea.							
Remove multi-zone rooftop unit				94.675		5,025		5,025	6,275	7,825
Replace multi-zone rooftop, 15 ton				70.022	59,500	3,725		63,225	70,000	80,000
Total				164.696	59,500	8,750		68,250	76,275	87,825
2010 Repair multi - zone rooftop unit, 25 ton	10	Q-6	Ea.							
Repair controls				1.000		55.50		55.50	69.50	87
Remove fan bearings				2.400		134		134	167	208
Replace fan bearings				4.000	109	222		331	400	485
Remove fan motor				1.156		59.50		59.50	73.50	92
Replace fan motor				2.311	455	119		574	650	755
Remove compressor				22.222		1,112.50		1,112.50	1,375	1,750
Replace compressor				60.976	18,875	3,156.25		22,031.25	24,800	28,500
Replace refrigerant				2.000	183	111.75		294.75	340	400
Remove / replace heater igniter				1.000	53	56		109	128	153
Total				97.065	19,675	5,026.50		24,701.50	28,003	32,430
2040 Replace multi-zone rooftop unit, 25 ton	15	Q-7	Ea.							
Remove multi-zone rooftop unit				115.000		6,125		6,125	7,600	9,550
Replace multi-zone rooftop, 25 ton				95.808	77,000	5,075		82,075	91,000	104,000
Total				210.808	77,000	11,200		88,200	98,600	113,550

	System Description	Freq. (Years)	Crew	Unit	Labor Hours	2012 Bare Costs				Total In-House	Total w/O&P
						Material	Labor	Equipment	Total		
3010	**Repair multi-zone rooftop unit, 40 ton**	10	Q-6	Ea.							
	Repair controls				1.000		55.50		55.50	69.50	87
	Remove fan bearings				2.400		134		134	167	208
	Replace fan bearings				4.444	122	248		370	445	540
	Remove fan motor				2.000		103		103	127	159
	Replace fan motor				4.000	1,150	206		1,356	1,525	1,750
	Remove compressor				35.451		1,850		1,850	2,300	2,875
	Replace compressor				71.006	16,600	3,700		20,300	22,900	26,500
	Replace refrigerant				2.667	244	149		393	450	535
	Remove / replace heater igniter				1.000	53	56		109	128	153
	Total				123.967	18,169	6,501.50		24,670.50	28,111.50	32,807
3040	**Replace multi-zone rooftop unit, 40 ton**	15	Q-7	Ea.							
	Remove multi-zone				172.000		9,175		9,175	11,400	14,300
	Replace multi-zone rooftop, 40 ton				151.000	112,500	8,050		120,550	133,500	153,000
	Total				323.000	112,500	17,225		129,725	144,900	167,300
4010	**Repair multi-zone rooftop unit, 70 ton**	10	Q-7	Ea.							
	Repair controls				1.000		55.50		55.50	69.50	87
	Remove fan bearings				2.400		134		134	167	208
	Replace fan bearings				4.444	122	248		370	445	540
	Remove fan motor				2.601		134		134	166	207
	Replace fan motor				5.195	2,250	268		2,518	2,800	3,225
	Remove compressor				76.923		4,075		4,075	5,100	6,350
	Replace compressor				153.000	19,300	8,150		27,450	31,400	36,800
	Replace refrigerant				4.667	427	260.75		687.75	790	940
	Remove / replace heater igniter				1.000	53	56		109	128	153
	Total				251.230	22,152	13,381.25		35,533.25	41,065.50	48,510
4040	**Replace multi-zone rooftop unit, 70 ton**	15	Q-7	Ea.							
	Remove multi-zone rooftop unit				231.000		12,300		12,300	15,300	19,200
	Replace multi-zone rooftop, 70 ton				264.000	151,500	14,000		165,500	184,000	211,500
	Total				495.000	151,500	26,300		177,800	199,300	230,700

288

D3053 278 Multi-Zone Air Conditioner

System Description	Freq. (Years)	Crew	Unit	Labor Hours	2012 Bare Costs				Total In-House	Total w/O&P
					Material	Labor	Equipment	Total		
5010 **Repair multi-zone rooftop unit, 105 ton**	10	Q-7	Ea.							
Repair controls				1.000		55.50		55.50	69.50	87
Remove fan bearings				4.800		268		268	335	415
Replace fan bearings				9.412	688	524		1,212	1,425	1,675
Remove fan motor				4.334		223		223	276	345
Replace fan motor				8.696	3,150	450		3,600	4,025	4,625
Remove compressor				79.012		4,200		4,200	5,225	6,525
Replace compressor				157.600	17,680	8,400		26,080	29,800	35,100
Replace refrigerant				6.667	610	372.50		982.50	1,125	1,350
Remove / replace heater igniter				1.500	79.50	84		163.50	192	230
Total				273.020	22,207.50	14,577		36,784.50	42,472.50	**50,352**
5040 **Replace multi-zone rooftop unit, 105 ton**	15	Q-7	Ea.							
Remove multi-zone rooftop unit				347.000		18,400		18,400	23,000	28,700
Replace multi-zone rooftop, 105 ton				390.000	200,000	20,700		220,700	246,000	282,000
Total				737.000	200,000	39,100		239,100	**269,000**	**310,700**

D3053 280 Single Zone Air Conditioner

System Description	Freq. (Years)	Crew	Unit	Labor Hours	2012 Bare Costs				Total In-House	Total w/O&P
					Material	Labor	Equipment	Total		
1001 **Repair single zone rooftop unit, 3 ton**	10	2 STPI	Ea.							
Repair controls				.300		16.70		16.70	21	26
Remove fan bearings				2.400		134		134	167	208
Replace fan bearings				4.000	109	222		331	400	485
Remove fan motor				1.156		59.50		59.50	73.50	92
Replace fan motor				1.951	288	101		389	440	515
Remove compressor				2.477		138		138	172	215
Replace compressor				4.522	325	252		577	670	800
Replace refrigerant				.533	48.80	29.80		78.60	90	107
Remove/replace heater igniter				.500	26.50	28		54.50	64	76.50
Total				17.840	797.30	981		1,778.30	2,097.50	**2,524.50**
1002 **Replace single zone rooftop unit, 3 ton**	15	Q-5	Ea.							
Remove single zone				8.000		400		400	500	625
Replace single zone rooftop, 3 ton				30.476	3,600	1,525		5,125	5,875	6,875
Total				38.476	3,600	1,925		5,525	**6,375**	**7,500**

D30 HVAC | **D3053** | **Terminal and Package Units**

D3053 280 | **Single Zone Air Conditioner**

	System Description	Freq. (Years)	Crew	Unit	Labor Hours	2012 Bare Costs				Total In-House	Total w/O&P
						Material	Labor	Equipment	Total		
1003	**Repair single zone rooftop unit, 5 ton**	10	2 STPI	Ea.							
	Repair controls				.300		16.70		16.70	21	26
	Remove fan bearings				2.400		134		134	167	208
	Replace fan bearings				4.000	109	222		331	400	485
	Remove fan motor				1.156		59.50		59.50	73.50	92
	Replace fan motor				1.951	288	101		389	440	515
	Remove compressor				2.477		138		138	172	215
	Replace compressor				4.954	455	276		731	845	1,000
	Replace refrigerant				.533	48.80	29.80		78.60	90	107
	Remove/replace heater igniter				.500	26.50	28		54.50	64	76.50
	Total				18.271	927.30	1,005		1,932.30	2,272.50	2,724.50
1004	**Replace single zone rooftop unit, 5 ton**	15	Q-5	Ea.							
	Remove single zone				18.561		930		930	1,150	1,450
	Replace single zone rooftop, 5 ton				38.005	4,975	1,900		6,875	7,850	9,200
	Total				56.566	4,975	2,830		7,805	9,000	10,650
1005	**Repair single zone rooftop unit, 7.5 ton**	10	2 STPI	Ea.							
	Repair controls				.400		22.50		22.50	28	34.50
	Remove fan bearings				2.400		134		134	167	208
	Replace fan bearings				4.000	109	222		331	400	485
	Remove fan motor				1.156		59.50		59.50	73.50	92
	Replace fan motor				2.311	330	119		449	510	595
	Remove compressor				3.467		174		174	217	271
	Replace compressor				6.932	1,025	350		1,375	1,550	1,825
	Replace refrigerant				.667	61	37.25		98.25	113	134
	Remove/replace heater igniter				.500	26.50	28		54.50	64	76.50
	Total				21.833	1,551.50	1,146.25		2,697.75	3,122.50	3,721
1006	**Replace single zone rooftop unit, 7.5 ton**	15	Q-5	Ea.							
	Remove single zone				26.016		1,300		1,300	1,625	2,025
	Replace single zone rooftop, 7.5 ton				43.011	7,650	2,150		9,800	11,100	12,900
	Total				69.027	7,650	3,450		11,100	12,725	14,925

D3053 280   **Single Zone Air Conditioner**

	System Description	Freq. (Years)	Crew	Unit	Labor Hours	Material	Labor	Equipment	Total	Total In-House	Total w/O&P
						2012 Bare Costs					
1007	**Repair single zone rooftop unit, 10 ton**	10	2 STPI	Ea.							
	Repair controls				.400		22.50		22.50	28	34.50
	Remove fan bearings				2.400		134		134	167	208
	Replace fan bearings				4.000	109	222		331	400	485
	Remove fan motor				1.156		59.50		59.50	73.50	92
	Replace fan motor				2.311	380	119		499	565	660
	Remove compressor				14.513		753.75		753.75	940	1,175
	Replace compressor				28.714	8,978	1,490.75		10,468.75	11,700	13,600
	Replace refrigerant				.800	73.20	44.70		117.90	135	161
	Remove/replace heater igniter				.500	26.50	28		54.50	64	76.50
	Total				54.794	9,566.70	2,874.20		12,440.90	14,072.50	16,492
1008	**Replace single zone rooftop unit, 10 ton**	15	Q-6	Ea.							
	Remove single zone				33.898		1,750		1,750	2,200	2,750
	Replace single zone rooftop, 10 ton				48.000	10,600	2,500		13,100	14,800	17,200
	Total				81.898	10,600	4,250		14,850	17,000	19,950
1010	**Repair single zone rooftop unit, 15 ton**	10	2 STPI	Ea.							
	Repair controls				.500		28		28	35	43.50
	Remove fan bearings				2.400		134		134	167	208
	Replace fan bearings				4.000	109	222		331	400	485
	Remove fan motor				1.156		59.50		59.50	73.50	92
	Replace fan motor				2.312	380	119		499	565	660
	Remove compressor				21.661		1,125		1,125	1,400	1,750
	Replace compressor				42.857	13,400	2,225		15,625	17,500	20,200
	Replace refrigerant				1.333	122	74.50		196.50	225	268
	Remove / replace heater igniter				.500	26.50	28		54.50	64	76.50
	Total				76.719	14,037.50	4,015		18,052.50	20,429.50	23,783
1040	**Replace single zone rooftop unit, 15 ton**	15	Q-6	Ea.							
	Remove single zone rooftop unit				50.314		2,625		2,625	3,275	4,075
	Replace single zone rooftop, 15 ton				56.075	15,900	2,925		18,825	21,100	24,400
	Total				106.389	15,900	5,550		21,450	24,375	28,475

	System Description	Freq. (Years)	Crew	Unit	Labor Hours	2012 Bare Costs Material	Labor	Equipment	Total	Total In-House	Total w/O&P
2010	**Repair single zone rooftop unit, 25 ton**	10	Q-6	Ea.							
	Repair controls				.500		28		28	35	43.50
	Remove fan bearings				2.400		134		134	167	208
	Replace fan bearings				4.000	109	222		331	400	485
	Remove fan motor				1.156		59.50		59.50	73.50	92
	Replace fan motor				2.311	455	119		574	650	755
	Remove compressor				22.222		1,112.50		1,112.50	1,375	1,750
	Replace compressor				60.976	18,875	3,156.25		22,031.25	24,800	28,500
	Replace refrigerant				2.000	183	111.75		294.75	340	400
	Remove / replace heater igniter				1.000	53	56		109	128	153
	Total				96.565	19,675	4,999		24,674	27,968.50	32,386.50
2040	**Replace single zone rooftop unit, 25 ton**	15	Q-7	Ea.							
	Remove single zone rooftop unit				76.923		4,075		4,075	5,100	6,350
	Replace single zone rooftop, 25 ton				76.739	25,000	4,075		29,075	32,600	37,600
	Total				153.662	25,000	8,150		33,150	37,700	43,950
3010	**Repair single zone rooftop unit, 60 ton**	10	Q-6	Ea.							
	Repair controls				.500		28		28	35	43.50
	Remove fan bearings				2.400		134		134	167	208
	Replace fan bearings				4.444	122	248		370	445	540
	Remove fan motor				2.000		103		103	127	159
	Replace fan motor				4.167	1,450	215		1,665	1,850	2,150
	Remove compressor				93.507		4,860		4,860	6,050	7,550
	Replace compressor				186.000	21,000	9,720		30,720	35,200	41,400
	Replace refrigerant				4.667	427	260.75		687.75	790	940
	Remove / replace heater igniter				1.000	53	56		109	128	153
	Total				298.684	23,052	15,624.75		38,676.75	44,792	53,143.50
3040	**Replace single zone rooftop unit, 60 ton**	15	Q-7	Ea.							
	Remove single zone rooftop unit				188.000		9,975		9,975	12,400	15,600
	Replace single zone rooftop, 60 ton				181.000	47,800	9,650		57,450	64,500	75,000
	Total				369.000	47,800	19,625		67,425	76,900	90,600

D3053 280   Single Zone Air Conditioner

	System Description	Freq. (Years)	Crew	Unit	Labor Hours	Material	Labor	Equipment	Total	Total In-House	Total w/O&P
							2012 Bare Costs				
4010	**Repair single zone rooftop unit, 100 ton**	10	Q-7	Ea.							
	Repair controls				.500		28		28	35	43.50
	Remove fan bearings				4.800		268		268	335	415
	Replace fan bearings				9.412	688	524		1,212	1,425	1,675
	Remove fan motor				4.334		223		223	276	345
	Replace fan motor				7.407	3,150	380		3,530	3,925	4,525
	Remove compressor				98.765		5,250		5,250	6,525	8,150
	Replace compressor				197.000	22,100	10,500		32,600	37,300	43,900
	Replace refrigerant				6.667	610	372.50		982.50	1,125	1,350
	Remove / replace heater igniter				1.500	79.50	84		163.50	192	230
	Total				330.385	26,627.50	17,629.50		44,257	51,138	60,633.50
4040	**Replace single zone rooftop unit, 100 ton**	15	Q-7	Ea.							
	Remove single zone rooftop unit				296.000		15,700		15,700	19,600	24,500
	Replace single zone rooftop, 100 ton				304.000	100,000	16,200		116,200	130,000	150,000
	Total				600.000	100,000	31,900		131,900	149,600	174,500

D3053 282   Multi-Zone Variable Volume

	System Description	Freq. (Years)	Crew	Unit	Labor Hours	Material	Labor	Equipment	Total	Total In-House	Total w/O&P
							2012 Bare Costs				
1010	**Repair multi-zone variable volume, 50 ton**	10	Q-6	Ea.							
	Repair controls				1.300		72.50		72.50	90.50	113
	Remove fan bearings				2.400		134		134	167	208
	Replace fan bearings				4.444	122	248		370	445	540
	Remove fan motor				2.000		103		103	127	159
	Replace fan motor				4.000	1,150	206		1,356	1,525	1,750
	Remove compressor				77.922		4,050		4,050	5,050	6,300
	Replace compressor				155.000	17,500	8,100		25,600	29,300	34,500
	Replace refrigerant				3.333	305	186.25		491.25	565	670
	Remove / replace heater igniter				1.000	53	56		109	128	153
	Total				251.400	19,130	13,155.75		32,285.75	37,397.50	44,393
1040	**Replace multi-zone variable volume, 50 ton**	15	Q-7	Ea.							
	Remove multi-zone variable volume unit				160.000		8,475		8,475	10,600	13,200
	Replace multi-zone variable volume unit, 50 ton				219.000	104,000	11,600		115,600	129,000	148,000
	Total				379.000	104,000	20,075		124,075	139,600	161,200

D3053 282   Multi-Zone Variable Volume

	System Description	Freq. (Years)	Crew	Unit	Labor Hours	2012 Bare Costs				Total In-House	Total w/O&P
						Material	Labor	Equipment	Total		
2010	**Repair multi-zone variable volume, 70 ton**	10	Q-7	Ea.							
	Repair controls				1.300		72.50		72.50	90.50	113
	Remove fan bearings				2.400		134		134	167	208
	Replace fan bearings				4.444	122	248		370	445	540
	Remove fan motor				2.601		134		134	166	207
	Replace fan motor				5.195	2,250	268		2,518	2,800	3,225
	Remove compressor				76.923		4,075		4,075	5,100	6,350
	Replace compressor				153.000	19,300	8,150		27,450	31,400	36,800
	Replace refrigerant				4.667	427	260.75		687.75	790	940
	Remove / replace heater igniter				1.000	53	56		109	128	153
	Total				251.530	22,152	13,398.25		35,550.25	41,086.50	48,536
2040	**Replace multi-zone variable volume, 70 ton**	15	Q-7	Ea.							
	Remove multi-zone variable volume unit				231.000		12,300		12,300	15,300	19,200
	Replace multi-zone variable volume unit, 70 ton				304.000	145,500	16,200		161,700	180,000	207,000
	Total				535.000	145,500	28,500		174,000	195,300	226,200
3010	**Repair multi-zone variable volume, 90 ton**	10	Q-7	Ea.							
	Repair controls				1.300		72.50		72.50	90.50	113
	Remove fan bearings				2.400		134		134	167	208
	Replace fan bearings				4.444	122	248		370	445	540
	Remove fan motor				2.601		134		134	166	207
	Replace fan motor				6.504	2,100	335		2,435	2,725	3,150
	Remove compressor				92.308		4,890		4,890	6,125	7,625
	Replace compressor				183.600	23,160	9,780		32,940	37,700	44,200
	Replace refrigerant				6.667	610	372.50		982.50	1,125	1,350
	Remove / replace heater igniter				1.500	79.50	84		163.50	192	230
	Total				301.323	26,071.50	16,050		42,121.50	48,735.50	57,623
3040	**Replace multi-zone variable volume, 90 ton**	15	Q-7	Ea.							
	Remove multi-zone variable volume unit				296.000		15,700		15,700	19,600	24,500
	Replace multi-zone variable volume unit, 90 ton				395.000	167,000	21,000		188,000	210,000	241,500
	Total				691.000	167,000	36,700		203,700	229,600	266,000

D3053 282 Multi-Zone Variable Volume

System Description	Freq. (Years)	Crew	Unit	Labor Hours	2012 Bare Costs Material	Labor	Equipment	Total	Total In-House	Total w/O&P
4010 Repair multi-zone variable volume, 105 ton	10	Q-7	Ea.							
Repair controls				1.300		72.50		72.50	90.50	113
Remove fan bearings				4.800		268		268	335	415
Replace fan bearings				9.412	688	524		1,212	1,425	1,675
Remove fan motor				4.334		223		223	276	345
Replace fan motor				8.696	3,150	450		3,600	4,025	4,625
Remove compressor				79.012		4,200		4,200	5,225	6,525
Replace compressor				157.600	17,680	8,400		26,080	29,800	35,100
Replace refrigerant				7.333	671	409.75		1,080.75	1,250	1,475
Remove / replace heater igniter				1.500	79.50	84		163.50	192	230
Total				273.987	22,268.50	14,631.25		36,899.75	42,618.50	50,503
4040 Replace multi-zone variable volume, 105 ton	15	Q-7	Ea.							
Remove multi-zone variable volume unit				347.000		18,400		18,400	23,000	28,700
Replace multi-zone variable volume unit, 105 ton				444.000	187,000	23,600		210,600	235,000	270,500
Total				791.000	187,000	42,000		229,000	258,000	299,200
5010 Repair multi-zone variable volume, 140 ton	10	Q-7	Ea.							
Repair controls				1.300		72.50		72.50	90.50	113
Remove fan bearings				7.200		402		402	500	625
Replace fan bearings				14.118	1,032	786		1,818	2,125	2,525
Remove fan motor				4.334		223		223	276	345
Replace fan motor				11.594	4,050	600		4,650	5,200	6,000
Remove compressor				106.370		5,654.25		5,654.25	7,025	8,775
Replace compressor				212.169	23,801.70	11,308.50		35,110.20	40,200	47,300
Replace refrigerant				8.666	793	484.25		1,277.25	1,475	1,750
Remove / replace heater igniter				2.000	106	112		218	256	305
Total				367.751	29,782.70	19,642.50		49,425.20	57,147.50	67,738
5040 Replace multi-zone variable volume, 140 ton	15	Q-7	Ea.							
Remove multi-zone variable volume unit				516.000		27,400		27,400	34,200	42,700
Replace multi-zone variable volume unit, 140 ton				592.000	229,000	31,400		260,400	291,000	335,500
Total				1108.000	229,000	58,800		287,800	325,200	378,200

D3053 284   Single Zone Variable Volume

System Description	Freq. (Years)	Crew	Unit	Labor Hours	2012 Bare Costs				Total In-House	Total w/O&P
					Material	Labor	Equipment	Total		
1010 Repair single zone variable volume, 20 ton	10	Q-6	Ea.							
Repair controls				1.000		55.50		55.50	69.50	87
Remove fan bearings				2.400		134		134	167	208
Replace fan bearings				4.000	109	222		331	400	485
Remove fan motor				1.156		59.50		59.50	73.50	92
Replace fan motor				2.312	380	119		499	565	660
Remove compressor				17.778		890		890	1,100	1,400
Replace compressor				48.780	15,100	2,525		17,625	19,800	22,800
Replace refrigerant				1.333	122	74.50		196.50	225	268
Remove / replace heater igniter				1.000	53	56		109	128	153
Total				79.760	15,764	4,135.50		19,899.50	22,528	26,153
1040 Replace single zone variable volume, 20 ton	10	Q-7	Ea.							
Remove single zone variable volume unit				71.545		3,795		3,795	4,725	5,925
Replace single zone variable volume unit, 20 ton				64.945	27,060	3,437.50		30,497.50	34,100	39,200
Total				136.489	27,060	7,232.50		34,292.50	38,825	45,125
2010 Repair single zone variable volume, 30 ton	10	Q-6	Ea.							
Repair controls				1.000		55.50		55.50	69.50	87
Remove fan bearings				2.400		134		134	167	208
Replace fan bearings				4.000	109	222		331	400	485
Remove fan motor				1.156		59.50		59.50	73.50	92
Replace fan motor				2.476	590	128		718	805	935
Remove compressor				26.667		1,335		1,335	1,650	2,100
Replace compressor				73.171	22,650	3,787.50		26,437.50	29,700	34,200
Replace refrigerant				2.667	244	149		393	450	535
Remove / replace heater igniter				1.000	53	56		109	128	153
Total				114.536	23,646	5,926.50		29,572.50	33,443	38,795
2040 Replace single zone variable volume, 30 ton	10	Q-7	Ea.							
Remove single zone variable volume unit				104.142		5,527.50		5,527.50	6,900	8,600
Replace single zone variable volume unit, 30 ton				92.147	32,670	4,895		37,565	42,000	48,500
Total				196.289	32,670	10,422.50		43,092.50	48,900	57,100

D3053 | 284 | Single Zone Variable Volume

	System Description	Freq. (Years)	Crew	Unit	Labor Hours	2012 Bare Costs				Total In-House	Total w/O&P
						Material	Labor	Equipment	Total		
3010	**Repair single zone variable volume, 40 ton**	10	Q-6	Ea.							
	Repair controls				1.000		55.50		55.50	69.50	87
	Remove fan bearings				2.400		134		134	167	208
	Replace fan bearings				4.000	109	222		331	400	485
	Remove fan motor				1.156		59.50		59.50	73.50	92
	Replace fan motor				4.000	1,150	206		1,356	1,525	1,750
	Remove compressor				35.451		1,850		1,850	2,300	2,875
	Replace compressor				71.006	16,600	3,700		20,300	22,900	26,500
	Replace refrigerant				3.333	305	186.25		491.25	565	670
	Remove / replace heater igniter				1.000	53	56		109	128	153
	Total				123.346	18,217	6,469.25		24,686.25	28,128	32,820
3040	**Replace single zone variable volume, 40 ton**	10	Q-7	Ea.							
	Remove single zone variable volume unit				143.000		7,590		7,590	9,450	11,800
	Replace single zone variable volume unit, 40 ton				122.100	43,890	6,517.50		50,407.50	56,000	65,000
	Total				265.100	43,890	14,107.50		57,997.50	65,450	76,800
4010	**Repair single zone variable volume, 60 ton**	10	Q-6	Ea.							
	Repair controls				.500		28		28	35	43.50
	Remove fan bearings				2.400		134		134	167	208
	Replace fan bearings				4.444	122	248		370	445	540
	Remove fan motor				2.000		103		103	127	159
	Replace fan motor				4.167	1,450	215		1,665	1,850	2,150
	Remove compressor				93.507		4,860		4,860	6,050	7,550
	Replace compressor				186.000	21,000	9,720		30,720	35,200	41,400
	Replace refrigerant				4.000	366	223.50		589.50	675	805
	Remove / replace heater igniter				1.000	53	56		109	128	153
	Total				298.018	22,991	15,587.50		38,578.50	44,677	53,008.50
4040	**Replace single zone variable volume, 60 ton**	10	Q-7	Ea.							
	Remove single zone variable volume unit				189.200		10,092.50		10,092.50	12,500	15,700
	Replace single zone variable volume unit, 60 ton				184.800	57,200	9,817.50		67,017.50	75,500	87,000
	Total				374.000	57,200	19,910		77,110	88,000	102,700

D3053 286 | Central Station Air Conditioning Air Handling Unit

System Description	Freq. (Years)	Crew	Unit	Labor Hours	2012 Bare Costs				Total In-House	Total w/O&P
					Material	Labor	Equipment	Total		
1010										
Repair central station A.H.U., 1300 CFM	10	1 STPI	Ea.							
Repair controls				.300		16.70		16.70	21	26
Remove blower motor				1.200		67		67	83.50	104
Replace blower motor				1.951	320	101		421	475	555
Total				3.451	320	184.70		504.70	579.50	685
1040										
Replace central station A.H.U., 1300 CFM	15	Q-5	Ea.							
Remove central station A.H.U.				8.667		435		435	540	675
Replace central station A.H.U., 1300 CFM				17.335	6,475	870		7,345	8,200	9,450
Total				26.002	6,475	1,305		7,780	8,740	10,125
2010										
Repair central station A.H.U., 1900 CFM	10	1 STPI	Ea.							
Repair controls				.300		16.70		16.70	21	26
Remove blower motor				1.200		67		67	83.50	104
Replace blower motor				2.311	330	119		449	510	595
Total				3.811	330	202.70		532.70	614.50	725
2040										
Replace central station A.H.U., 1900 CFM	15	Q-5	Ea.							
Remove central station A.H.U.				9.456		475		475	590	740
Replace central station A.H.U., 1900 CFM				18.913	9,950	950		10,900	12,100	13,900
Total				28.369	9,950	1,425		11,375	12,690	14,640
3010										
Repair central station A.H.U., 5400 CFM	10	1 STPI	Ea.							
Repair controls				.300		16.70		16.70	21	26
Remove blower motor				1.400		78		78	97.50	122
Replace blower motor				2.312	380	119		499	565	660
Total				4.012	380	213.70		593.70	683.50	808
3040										
Replace central station A.H.U., 5400 CFM	15	Q-6	Ea.							
Remove central station A.H.U.				19.496		1,025		1,025	1,275	1,575
Replace central station A.H.U., 5400 CFM				39.024	14,600	2,025		16,625	18,600	21,400
Total				58.521	14,600	3,050		17,650	19,875	22,975
4010										
Repair central station A.H.U., 8000 CFM	10	1 STPI	Ea.							
Repair controls				.300		16.70		16.70	21	26
Remove blower motor				1.600		89		89	111	139
Replace blower motor				2.311	455	119		574	650	755
Total				4.211	455	224.70		679.70	782	920

D3053 286 | **Central Station Air Conditioning Air Handling Unit**

	System Description	Freq. (Years)	Crew	Unit	Labor Hours	2012 Bare Costs Material	Labor	Equipment	Total	Total In-House	Total w/O&P
4040	**Replace central station A.H.U., 8000 CFM**	15	Q-6	Ea.							
	Remove central station A.H.U.				25.974		1,350		1,350	1,675	2,100
	Replace central station A.H.U., 8000 CFM				51.948	23,300	2,700		26,000	29,000	33,300
	Total				77.922	23,300	4,050		27,350	30,675	35,400
5010	**Repair central station A.H.U., 16,000 CFM**	10	1 STPI	Ea.							
	Repair controls				.300		16.70		16.70	21	26
	Remove blower motor				1.800		100		100	125	156
	Replace blower motor				2.597	720	134		854	955	1,100
	Total				4.698	720	250.70		970.70	1,101	1,282
5040	**Replace central station A.H.U., 16,000 CFM**	15	Q-6	Ea.							
	Remove central station A.H.U.				41.026		2,125		2,125	2,650	3,325
	Replace central station A.H.U., 16,000 CFM				82.192	46,700	4,275		50,975	56,500	65,000
	Total				123.217	46,700	6,400		53,100	59,150	68,325
6010	**Repair central station A.H.U., 33,500 CFM**	10	1 STPI	Ea.							
	Repair controls				.300		16.70		16.70	21	26
	Remove blower motor				2.601		134		134	166	207
	Replace blower motor				5.195	2,250	268		2,518	2,800	3,225
	Total				8.096	2,250	418.70		2,668.70	2,987	3,458
6040	**Replace central station A.H.U., 33,500 CFM**	15	Q-6	Ea.							
	Remove central station A.H.U.				82.192		4,275		4,275	5,325	6,650
	Replace central station A.H.U., 33,500 CFM				164.000	97,500	8,550		106,050	118,000	135,000
	Total				246.192	97,500	12,825		110,325	123,325	141,650
7010	**Repair central station A.H.U., 63,000 CFM**	10	1 STPI	Ea.							
	Repair controls				.300		16.70		16.70	21	26
	Remove blower motor				4.334		223		223	276	345
	Replace blower motor				8.696	3,150	450		3,600	4,025	4,625
	Total				13.329	3,150	689.70		3,839.70	4,322	4,996
7040	**Replace central station A.H.U., 63,000 CFM**	15	Q-7	Ea.							
	Remove central station A.H.U.				160.000		8,475		8,475	10,600	13,200
	Replace central station A.H.U., 63,000 CFM				320.000	184,000	17,000		201,000	223,500	256,500
	Total				480.000	184,000	25,475		209,475	234,100	269,700

D3053 310   Residential Furnace, Gas

System Description	Freq. (Years)	Crew	Unit	Labor Hours	2012 Bare Costs Material	Labor	Equipment	Total	Total In-House	Total w/O&P
1010 Repair furnace, gas, 25 MBH	10	Q-1	Ea.							
Repair controls				.500		28		28	35	43.50
Remove fan motor				.976		54.50		54.50	68	84.50
Replace fan motor				1.951	193	101		294	335	395
Remove auto vent damper				.274		14.25		14.25	18.05	22.50
Replace auto vent damper				.547	67.50	28.50		96	110	129
Remove burner				1.000		49		49	61.50	76.50
Replace burner				2.000	239	98.50		337.50	385	450
Total				7.248	499.50	373.75		873.25	1,012.55	1,201
1030 Replace furnace, gas, 25 MBH	15	Q-9	Ea.							
Remove furnace				2.000		94		94	119	148
Replace furnace				4.000	620	188		808	920	1,075
Total				6.000	620	282		902	1,039	1,223
2010 Repair furnace, gas, 100 MBH	10	Q-1	Ea.							
Repair controls				.500		28		28	35	43.50
Remove fan motor				.976		54.50		54.50	68	84.50
Replace fan motor				1.951	288	101		389	440	515
Remove auto vent damper				.289		15.05		15.05	19.05	23.50
Replace auto vent damper				.578	87	30		117	134	156
Remove burner				1.200		59		59	73.50	92
Replace burner				2.400	540	118		658	740	860
Total				7.894	915	405.55		1,320.55	1,509.55	1,774.50
2030 Replace furnace, gas, 100 MBH	15	Q-9	Ea.							
Remove furnace				3.250		153		153	193	240
Replace furnace				6.499	720	305		1,025	1,175	1,375
Total				9.749	720	458		1,178	1,368	1,615

D3053 310 Residential Furnace, Gas

	System Description	Freq. (Years)	Crew	Unit	Labor Hours	2012 Bare Costs				Total In-House	Total w/O&P
						Material	Labor	Equipment	Total		
3010	**Repair furnace, gas, 200 MBH**	10	Q-1	Ea.							
	Repair controls				.500		28		28	35	43.50
	Remove fan motor				.976		54.50		54.50	68	84.50
	Replace fan motor				1.951	320	101		421	475	555
	Remove auto vent damper				.325		16.95		16.95	21.50	26.50
	Replace auto vent damper				.650	98	34		132	151	176
	Remove burner				3.077		151		151	189	236
	Replace burner				10.403	1,200	510		1,710	1,950	2,300
	Total				17.882	1,618	895.45		2,513.45	**2,889.50**	**3,421.50**
3030	**Replace furnace, gas, 200 MBH**	15	Q-9	Ea.							
	Remove furnace				4.000		188		188	237	296
	Replace furnace				8.000	2,800	375		3,175	3,550	4,100
	Total				12.000	2,800	563		3,363	**3,787**	**4,396**

D3053 320 Residential Furnace, Oil

	System Description	Freq. (Years)	Crew	Unit	Labor Hours	2012 Bare Costs				Total In-House	Total w/O&P
						Material	Labor	Equipment	Total		
1010	**Repair furnace, oil, 55 MBH**	10	Q-1	Ea.							
	Repair controls				.500		28		28	35	43.50
	Remove fan motor				.976		54.50		54.50	68	84.50
	Replace fan motor				1.951	193	101		294	335	395
	Remove auto vent damper				.473		22		22	28	35
	Replace auto vent damper				.945	146	44.50		190.50	217	253
	Remove burner				4.334		213		213	266	330
	Replace burner				8.667	289	425		714	850	1,025
	Total				17.846	628	888		1,516	**1,799**	**2,166**
1030	**Replace furnace, oil, 55 MBH**	15	Q-9	Ea.							
	Remove furnace				2.889		136		136	171	213
	Replace furnace, oil, 55 mbh				5.778	1,475	271		1,746	1,975	2,275
	Total				8.667	1,475	407		1,882	**2,146**	**2,488**

System Description	Freq. (Years)	Crew	Unit	Labor Hours	2012 Bare Costs				Total In-House	Total w/O&P
					Material	Labor	Equipment	Total		
2010 Repair furnace, oil, 100 MBH	10	Q-1	Ea.							
Repair controls				.500		28		28	35	43.50
Remove fan motor				.976		54.50		54.50	68	84.50
Replace fan motor				1.951	288	101		389	440	515
Remove auto vent damper				.495		23		23	29.50	36.50
Replace auto vent damper				.990	67.50	46.50		114	133	157
Remove burner				4.334		213		213	266	330
Replace burner				8.667	289	425		714	850	1,025
Total				17.914	644.50	891		1,535.50	1,821.50	2,191.50
2030 Replace furnace, oil, 100 MBH	15	Q-1	Ea.							
Remove furnace				3.059		144		144	181	226
Replace furnace, oil, 100 mbh				6.119	1,875	287		2,162	2,425	2,800
Total				9.177	1,875	431		2,306	2,606	3,026
3010 Repair furnace, oil, 200 MBH	10	Q-1	Ea.							
Repair controls				.500		28		28	35	43.50
Remove fan motor				.976		54.50		54.50	68	84.50
Replace fan motor				1.951	320	101		421	475	555
Remove auto vent damper				.520		24.50		24.50	31	38.50
Replace auto vent damper				1.040	87	49		136	157	186
Remove burner				4.334		213		213	266	330
Replace burner				8.667	289	425		714	850	1,025
Total				17.988	696	895		1,591	1,882	2,262.50
3030 Replace furnace, oil, 200 MBH	15	Q-1	Ea.							
Remove furnace				4.000		188		188	237	296
Replace furnace, oil, 200 mbh				8.000	2,450	375		2,825	3,175	3,650
Total				12.000	2,450	563		3,013	3,412	3,946

D3053 330 | **Residential Furnace, Electric**

	System Description	Freq. (Years)	Crew	Unit	Labor Hours	2012 Bare Costs Material	Labor	Equipment	Total	Total In-House	Total w/O&P
1010	**Repair furnace, electric, 25 MBH**	10	Q-20	Ea.							
	Repair controls				.500		28		28	35	43.50
	Remove fan motor				.976		54.50		54.50	68	84.50
	Replace fan motor				1.951	193	101		294	335	395
	Remove heat element				.867		41.50		41.50	52	65
	Replace heat element				1.733	1,225	83		1,308	1,450	1,650
	Total				6.027	1,418	308		1,726	1,940	2,238
1030	**Replace furnace, electric, 25 MBH**	15	Q-20	Ea.							
	Remove furnace				2.826		135		135	170	212
	Replace furnace, electric, 25 mbh				5.653	600	270		870	1,000	1,175
	Total				8.479	600	405		1,005	1,170	1,387
2010	**Repair furnace, electric, 50 MBH**	10	Q-20	Ea.							
	Repair controls				.500		28		28	35	43.50
	Remove fan motor				.976		54.50		54.50	68	84.50
	Replace fan motor				1.951	193	101		294	335	395
	Remove heat element				.929		44.50		44.50	56	69.50
	Replace heat element				1.857	1,275	89		1,364	1,525	1,725
	Total				6.212	1,468	317		1,785	2,019	2,317.50
2030	**Replace furnace , electric, 50 MBH**	15	Q-20	Ea.							
	Remove furnace				3.095		148		148	186	232
	Replace furnace, electric, 50 mbh				6.190	685	296		981	1,125	1,325
	Total				9.285	685	444		1,129	1,311	1,557
3010	**Repair furnace, electric, 85 MBH**	10	Q-20	Ea.							
	Repair controls				.500		28		28	35	43.50
	Remove fan motor				.976		54.50		54.50	68	84.50
	Replace fan motor				1.951	288	101		389	440	515
	Remove heat element				1.083		52		52	65	81.50
	Replace heat element				2.167	2,275	104		2,379	2,625	3,000
	Total				6.677	2,563	339.50		2,902.50	3,233	3,724.50
3030	**Replace furnace, electric, 85 MBH**	15	Q-20	Ea.							
	Remove furnace				4.000		188		188	237	296
	Replace furnace, electric, 85 mbh				6.842	745	325		1,070	1,225	1,450
	Total				10.842	745	513		1,258	1,462	1,746

D3053 410 Electric Baseboard Heating Units

System Description	Freq. (Years)	Crew	Unit	Labor Hours	2012 Bare Costs				Total In-House	Total w/O&P
					Material	Labor	Equipment	Total		
0010 Maintenance and repair										
Repair wiring connections	2	1 ELEC	Ea.	.615		31.50		31.50	39	49
Total				.615		31.50		31.50	**39**	**49**
0020 Maintenance and inspection										
Inspect and clean baseboard heater	0.50	1 ELEC	Ea.	1.143		59		59	72.50	91
Total				1.143		59		59	**72.50**	**91**
0030 Replace baseboard heater										
Remove baseboard heater	20	1 ELEC	Ea.	.667		34.50		34.50	42.50	53
Baseboard heater, 5' long				1.860	68	96		164	193	233
Total				2.527	68	130.50		198.50	**235.50**	**286**

D3053 420 Cast Iron Radiator, 10' section, 1 side

System Description	Freq. (Years)	Crew	Unit	Labor Hours	2012 Bare Costs				Total In-House	Total w/O&P
					Material	Labor	Equipment	Total		
0020 Refinish C.I. radiator, 1 side										
Prepare surface	5	1 PORD	Ea.	.296		11.40		11.40	14.60	18
Prime and paint 1 coat, brushwork				.471	3.80	18		21.80	27.50	33.50
Total				.767	3.80	29.40		33.20	**42.10**	**51.50**

D3053 710 Fireplaces, Firebrick

System Description	Freq. (Years)	Crew	Unit	Labor Hours	2012 Bare Costs				Total In-House	Total w/O&P
					Material	Labor	Equipment	Total		
0020 Replace firebrick										
Masonry demolition, fireplace, brick, 30" x 24"	75	2 BRIC	S.F.	1.155		40.63		40.63	54	66.50
Install new firebrick				.208	8.55	8.25		16.80	20	24
Total				1.363	8.55	48.88		57.43	**74**	**90.50**

D4013 110 | **Backflow Preventer**

System Description	Freq. (Years)	Crew	Unit	Labor Hours	2012 Bare Costs Material	2012 Bare Costs Labor	2012 Bare Costs Equipment	2012 Bare Costs Total	Total In-House	Total w/O&P
3010 **Rebuild 4" diam. reduced pressure backflow preventer**	10	1 PLUM	Ea.							
Notify proper authorities prior to closing valves				.250		13.65		13.65	17.05	21.50
Close valves at 4" diameter BFP and open by-pass				.167		9.10		9.10	11.35	14.20
Rebuild 4" diameter reduced pressure BFP				2.000	310	109		419	475	560
Test backflow preventer				.500		27.50		27.50	34	42.50
Total				2.917	310	159.25		469.25	537.40	638.20
3020 **Rebuild 6" diam. reduced pressure backflow preventer**	10	1 PLUM	Ea.							
Notify proper authorities prior to closing valves				.250		13.65		13.65	17.05	21.50
Close valves at 6" diameter BFP and open by-pass				.182		9.95		9.95	12.40	15.45
Rebuild 6" diameter reduced pressure BFP				3.008	330	164		494	570	670
Test backflow preventer				.500		27.50		27.50	34	42.50
Total				3.939	330	215.10		545.10	633.45	749.45
3030 **Rebuild 8" diam. reduced pressure backflow preventer**	10	1 PLUM	Ea.							
Notify proper authorities prior to closing valves				.250		13.65		13.65	17.05	21.50
Close valves at 8" diameter BFP and open by-pass				.200		10.90		10.90	13.65	17
Rebuild 8" diameter reduced pressure BFP				4.000	405	218		623	720	845
Test backflow preventer				.500		27.50		27.50	34	42.50
Total				4.950	405	270.05		675.05	784.70	926
3040 **Rebuild 10" diam. reduced pressure backflow preventer**	10	1 PLUM	Ea.							
Notify proper authorities prior to closing valves				.250		13.65		13.65	17.05	21.50
Close valves at 10" diameter BFP and open by-pass				.222		12.15		12.15	15.15	18.90
Rebuild 10" diameter reduced pressure BFP				5.000	475	273		748	865	1,025
Test backflow preventer				.500		27.50		27.50	34	42.50
Total				5.972	475	326.30		801.30	931.20	1,107.90

System Description	Freq. (Years)	Crew	Unit	Labor Hours	2012 Bare Costs				Total In-House	Total w/O&P
					Material	Labor	Equipment	Total		
1020 Inspect sprinkler system	1	1 PLUM	Ea.							
Inspect water pressure gauges				.044		2.40		2.40	3	3.80
Test fire alarm (wet or dry)				.030		1.60		1.60	2	2.50
Motor, exposed, inspect				.333		18.20		18.20	22.50	28.50
Inspect, visual				.060		3.30		3.30	4.10	5.10
Total				.467		25.50		25.50	**31.60**	**39.90**
1030 Replace sprinkler head	20	1 PLUM	Ea.							
Remove old sprinkler head				.325		17.55		17.55	22	27.50
Install new head				.650	10.25	35		45.25	55	68
Total				.975	10.25	52.55		62.80	**77**	**95.50**
1040 Rebuild double check 3″ backflow preventer	1	1 PLUM	Ea.							
Rebuild 3″ backflow preventer				3.910	365	213		578	670	790
Test system				1.300		71		71	88.50	111
Total				5.210	365	284		649	**758.50**	**901**
1050 Rebuild double check 4″ backflow preventer	1	1 PLUM	Ea.							
Rebuild 4″ backflow preventer				4.561	495	249		744	855	1,000
Test system				1.300		71		71	88.50	111
Total				5.861	495	320		815	**943.50**	**1,111**
1060 Rebuild double check 6″ backflow preventer	1	1 PLUM	Ea.							
Rebuild 6″ backflow preventer				5.202	585	284		869	1,000	1,175
Test system				1.300		71		71	88.50	111
Total				6.502	585	355		940	**1,088.50**	**1,286**
1070 Rebuild reduced pressure backflow preventer	1	1 PLUM	Ea.							
Rebuild 3″ backflow preventer				3.910	365	213		578	670	790
Test system				1.300		71		71	88.50	111
Total				5.210	365	284		649	**758.50**	**901**

	D40	FIRE PROTECTION		D4013		Sprinklers									
	D4013 410					**Fire Pump**									

							2012 Bare Costs					
	System Description	Freq. (Years)	Crew	Unit	Labor Hours	Material	Labor	Equipment	Total	Total In-House	Total w/O&P
1030	**Replace fire pump / electric motor assembly 100 H.P.**	25	Q-13	Ea.							
	Remove 100 H.P. electric-drive fire pump				31.373		1,625		1,625	2,025	2,525
	Install new electric-drive fire pump and controls, 100 H.P.				64.000	22,000	3,300		25,300	28,300	32,600
	Total				95.373	22,000	4,925		26,925	30,325	35,125

D5013 110 Primary Transformer, Liquid Filled

System Description	Freq. (Years)	Crew	Unit	Labor Hours	2012 Bare Costs				Total In-House	Total w/O&P
					Material	Labor	Equipment	Total		
0010 Repair 500 kVA transformer	10	1 ELEC	Ea.							
Remove transformer component				1.000		51.50		51.50	63.50	79.50
Transformer component				2.963	2,225	153		2,378	2,625	3,025
Total				3.963	2,225	204.50		2,429.50	**2,688.50**	**3,104.50**
0020 Maintenance and inspection	0.50	1 ELEC	Ea.							
Test energized transformer				.500		26		26	32	40
Total				.500		26		26	**32**	**40**
0030 Replace transformer	30	R-3	Ea.							
Remove transformer				13.793		705	91.50	796.50	965	1,200
Transformer 500 kVA, 5 KV primary, 277/480 V secondary				50.000	20,600	2,550	330	23,480	26,200	30,100
Total				63.793	20,600	3,255	421.50	24,276.50	**27,165**	**31,300**

D5013 120 Primary Transformer, Dry

System Description	Freq. (Years)	Crew	Unit	Labor Hours	2012 Bare Costs				Total In-House	Total w/O&P
					Material	Labor	Equipment	Total		
0010 Repair 15 KV primary transformer	15	1 ELEC	Ea.							
Repair transformer terminal				2.000	48.50	103		151.50	181	220
Total				2.000	48.50	103		151.50	**181**	**220**
0020 Maintenance and inspection	0.50	1 ELEC	Ea.							
Test energized transformer				.500		26		26	32	40
Total				.500		26		26	**32**	**40**
0030 Replace transformer	30	R-3	Ea.							
Remove transformer				13.793		705	91.50	796.50	965	1,200
Transformer 500 kVA, 15 KV primary, 277/480 V secondary				57.143	46,700	2,925	380	50,005	55,500	63,500
Total				70.936	46,700	3,630	471.50	50,801.50	**56,465**	**64,700**

D5013 210 Switchgear, Mainframe

System Description	Freq. (Years)	Crew	Unit	Labor Hours	2012 Bare Costs Material	Labor	Equipment	Total	Total In-House	Total w/O&P
0010 Repair switchgear 1200 A	5	1 ELEC	Ea.							
Remove relay				1.702		87.50		87.50	108	136
Relay				5.000	1,150	258		1,408	1,575	1,850
Total				6.702	1,150	345.50		1,495.50	1,683	**1,986**
0020 Maintenance and inspection	1	1 ELEC	Ea.							
Check & retighten switchgear connections				.800		41		41	51	63.50
Total				.800		41		41	**51**	**63.50**
0030 Replace switchgear 1200 A	20	3 ELEC	Ea.							
Remove switchgear 1200 A				6.000		310		310	380	480
Switchgear 1200 A				21.818	1,725	1,125		2,850	3,275	3,900
Test switchgear				2.000		103		103	127	159
Total				29.818	1,725	1,538		3,263	3,782	**4,539**

D5013 216 Fuses

System Description	Freq. (Years)	Crew	Unit	Labor Hours	2012 Bare Costs Material	Labor	Equipment	Total	Total In-House	Total w/O&P
0010 Replace fuse	25	1 ELEC	Ea.							
Remove fuse				.151		7.80		7.80	9.60	12
Fuse 600 A				.400	320	20.50		340.50	375	430
Total				.551	320	28.30		348.30	**384.60**	**442**

D5013 220 Switchgear, Indoor, Less Than 600 V

System Description	Freq. (Years)	Crew	Unit	Labor Hours	2012 Bare Costs Material	Labor	Equipment	Total	Total In-House	Total w/O&P
0010 Repair switchgear, - (5% of total C.B.)	10	1 ELEC	Ea.							
Remove circuit breaker				.400		20.50		20.50	25.50	32
Circuit breaker				1.143	222	59		281	315	370
Total				1.543	222	79.50		301.50	**340.50**	**402**
0020 Maintenance and inspection	3	1 ELEC	Ea.							
Inspect and clean panel				.500		26		26	32	40
Total				.500		26		26	**32**	**40**

D5013 220 Switchgear, Indoor, Less Than 600 V

System Description	Freq. (Years)	Crew	Unit	Labor Hours	2012 Bare Costs				Total In-House	Total w/O&P
					Material	Labor	Equipment	Total		
0030 Replace switchgear, 225 A	30	1 ELEC	Ea.							
Remove panelboard, 4 wire, 120/208 V, 225 A				4.000		206		206	255	320
Panelboard, 4 wire, 120/208 V, 225 A main circuit breaker				11.940	2,350	615		2,965	3,350	3,900
Test indoor switchgear				1.509		78		78	96	120
Total				17.450	2,350	899		3,249	3,701	4,340
0200 Replace switchgear, 400 A	30	2 ELEC	Ea.							
Turn power off, later turn on				.200		10.30		10.30	12.70	15.90
Remove panelboard, 4 wire, 120/208 V, 100 A				3.333		172		172	212	266
Remove panelboard, 4 wire, 120/208 V, 400 A				8.333		430		430	530	665
Panelboard, 4 wire, 120/208 V, 100 A main circuit breaker				17.021	1,150	875		2,025	2,350	2,800
Panelboard, 4 wire, 120/208 V, 400 A main circuit breaker				33.333	3,150	1,725		4,875	5,575	6,600
Test circuits				.145		7.50		7.50	9.25	11.60
Total				62.367	4,300	3,219.80		7,519.80	8,688.95	10,358.50
0240 Replace switchgear, 600 A	30	2 ELEC	Ea.							
Turn power off, later turn on				.300		15.45		15.45	19.05	24
Remove panelboard, 4 wire, 120/208 V, 200 A				6.667		345		345	425	530
Remove switchboard, incoming section, 600 A				4.848		250		250	310	385
Remove switchboard, distribution section, 600 A				4.000		206		206	255	320
Panelboard, 4 wire, 120/208 V, 225 A main circuit breaker				28.571	2,350	1,475		3,825	4,400	5,225
Switchboard, incoming section, 600 A				16.000	4,025	825		4,850	5,450	6,300
Switchboard, distribution section, 600 A				16.000	2,225	825		3,050	3,475	4,050
Test circuits				.218		11.25		11.25	13.90	17.40
Total				76.605	8,600	3,952.70		12,552.70	14,347.95	16,851.40
0280 Replace switchgear, 800 A	30	2 ELEC	Ea.							
Turn power off, later turn on				.400		20.60		20.60	25.50	32
Remove panelboard, 4 wire, 120/208 V, 200 A (2 panelboards)				13.333		690		690	850	1,050
Remove switchboard, incoming section, 800 A				5.517		284		284	350	440
Remove switchboard, distribution section, 800 A				4.444		229		229	283	355
Panelboard, 4 wire, 120/208 V, 225 A main lugs (2 panelboards)				47.059	2,750	2,450		5,200	6,000	7,200
Switchboard, incoming section, 800 A				18.182	4,025	935		4,960	5,575	6,475
Switchboard, distribution section, 800 A				18.182	2,925	935		3,860	4,375	5,100
Test circuits				.291		15		15	18.50	23
Total				107.408	9,700	5,558.60		15,258.60	17,477	20,675

D5013 220 Switchgear, Indoor, Less Than 600 V

System Description	Freq. (Years)	Crew	Unit	Labor Hours	2012 Bare Costs				Total In-House	Total w/O&P
					Material	Labor	Equipment	Total		
0320 Replace switchgear, 1200 A	30	3 ELEC	Ea.							
Turn power off, later turn on				.600		30.90		30.90	38	47.50
Remove panelboard, 4 wire, 120/208 V, 200 A (4 panelboards)				26.667		1,380		1,380	1,700	2,125
Remove switchboard, incoming section, 1200 A				6.667		345		345	425	530
Remove switchboard, distribution section, 1200 A				5.161		266		266	330	410
Panelboard, 4 wire, 120/208 V, 225 A main lugs (4 panelboards)				94.118	5,500	4,900		10,400	12,000	14,400
Switchboard, incoming section, 1200 A				22.222	4,850	1,150		6,000	6,750	7,850
Switchboard, distribution section, 1200 A				22.222	3,625	1,150		4,775	5,400	6,300
Test circuits				.436		22.50		22.50	28	35
Total				178.093	13,975	9,244.40		23,219.40	26,671	31,697.50
0360 Replace switchgear, 1600 A	30	3 ELEC	Ea.							
Turn power off, later turn on				.800		41.20		41.20	51	63.50
Remove panelboard, 4 wire, 120/208 V, 200 A (6 panelboards)				40.000		2,070		2,070	2,550	3,175
Remove switchboard, incoming section, 1600 A				7.273		375		375	465	580
Remove switchboard, distribution section, 1600 A				5.517		284		284	350	440
Panelboard, 4 wire, 120/208 V, 225 A main lugs (6 panelboards)				141.176	8,250	7,350		15,600	18,000	21,600
Switchboard, incoming section, 1600 A				24.242	4,850	1,250		6,100	6,875	8,000
Switchboard, distribution section, 1600 A				24.242	4,175	1,250		5,425	6,125	7,150
Test circuits				.582		30		30	37	46.50
Total				243.833	17,275	12,650.20		29,925.20	34,453	41,055
0400 Replace switchgear, 2000 A	30	3 ELEC	Ea.							
Turn power off, later turn on				1.000		51.50		51.50	63.50	79.50
Remove panelboard, 4 wire, 120/208 V, 200 A (8 panelboards)				53.333		2,760		2,760	3,400	4,250
Remove switchboard, incoming section, 2000 A				7.619		395		395	485	605
Remove switchboard, distribution section, 2000 A				5.926		305		305	375	470
Panelboard, 4 wire, 120/208 V, 225 A main lugs (8 panelboards)				188.235	11,000	9,800		20,800	24,000	28,800
Switchboard, incoming section, 2000 A				25.806	5,225	1,325		6,550	7,400	8,575
Switchboard, distribution section, 2000 A				25.806	4,875	1,325		6,200	7,000	8,150
Test circuits				.727		37.50		37.50	46.50	58
Total				308.454	21,100	15,999		37,099	42,770	50,987.50

311

D5013 224 Switchgear, Indoor, 600 V

	System Description	Freq. (Years)	Crew	Unit	Labor Hours	2012 Bare Costs				Total In-House	Total w/O&P
						Material	Labor	Equipment	Total		
0010	**Maintenance and repair, - (5% of total fuses)**	10	1 ELEC	Ea.							
	Remove fuse				.151		7.80		7.80	9.60	12
	Fuse				.400	320	20.50		340.50	375	430
	Total				.551	320	28.30		348.30	**384.60**	**442**
0020	**Maintenance and inspection**	3	1 ELEC	Ea.							
	Inspect and clean panel				.500		26		26	32	40
	Total				.500		26		26	**32**	**40**
0030	**Replace switchgear**	30	2 ELEC	Ea.							
	Remove indoor switchgear				4.000		206		206	255	320
	Switchgear				14.035	1,325	725		2,050	2,350	2,775
	Test indoor switchgear				2.000		103		103	127	159
	Total				20.035	1,325	1,034		2,359	**2,732**	**3,254**

D5013 230 Meters

	System Description	Freq. (Years)	Crew	Unit	Labor Hours	2012 Bare Costs				Total In-House	Total w/O&P
						Material	Labor	Equipment	Total		
0010	**Repair switchboard meter**	10	1 ELEC	Ea.							
	Repair meter				5.000	955	258		1,213	1,375	1,600
	Total				5.000	955	258		1,213	**1,375**	**1,600**
0020	**Replace switchboard meter**	20	1 ELEC	Ea.							
	Remove meter				.500		26		26	32	40
	Meter				1.600	4,775	82.50		4,857.50	5,350	6,100
	Total				2.100	4,775	108.50		4,883.50	**5,382**	**6,140**

D5013 240 Inverter

	System Description	Freq. (Years)	Crew	Unit	Labor Hours	2012 Bare Costs				Total In-House	Total w/O&P
						Material	Labor	Equipment	Total		
0010	**Maintenance and repair**	1	2 ELEC	Ea.							
	Repair inverter component				5.000	246	258		504	590	710
	Total				5.000	246	258		504	**590**	**710**

D5013 240 Inverter

System Description	Freq. (Years)	Crew	Unit	Labor Hours	2012 Bare Costs				Total In-House	Total w/O&P
					Material	Labor	Equipment	Total		
0020 **Maintenance and inspection**										
Check connections, controls & relays	0.25	1 ELEC	Ea.	1.600		82.50		82.50	102	127
Total				1.600		82.50		82.50	**102**	**127**
0030 **Replace 1 kVA inverter**										
Remove inverter	20	2 ELEC	Ea.	.500		26		26	32	40
Inverter				1.600	2,450	82.50		2,532.50	2,800	3,200
Total				2.100	2,450	108.50		2,558.50	**2,832**	**3,240**

D5013 250 Rectifier, Up To 600 V

System Description	Freq. (Years)	Crew	Unit	Labor Hours	2012 Bare Costs				Total In-House	Total w/O&P
					Material	Labor	Equipment	Total		
0010 **Maintenance and repair**										
Repair rectifier component	2	1 ELEC	Ea.	4.000	455	206		661	755	890
Total				4.000	455	206		661	**755**	**890**
0020 **Maintenance and inspection**										
Check connections, controls & relays	0.33	1 ELEC	Ea.	1.600		82.50		82.50	102	127
Total				1.600		82.50		82.50	**102**	**127**
0030 **Replace rectifier**										
Remove rectifier	20	2 ELEC	Ea.	.500		26		26	32	40
Rectifier				1.600	1,375	82.50		1,457.50	1,625	1,850
Total				2.100	1,375	108.50		1,483.50	**1,657**	**1,890**

D5013 264 Motor Starter, Up To 600 V

System Description	Freq. (Years)	Crew	Unit	Labor Hours	2012 Bare Costs				Total In-House	Total w/O&P
					Material	Labor	Equipment	Total		
0010 **Maintenance and repair**										
Remove motor starter coil	5	1 ELEC	Ea.	.500		26		26	32	40
Motor starter coil				1.600	52.50	82.50		135	160	193
Total				2.100	52.50	108.50		161	**192**	**233**

D5013 264 Motor Starter, Up To 600 V

System Description	Freq. (Years)	Crew	Unit	Labor Hours	2012 Bare Costs				Total In-House	Total w/O&P
					Material	Labor	Equipment	Total		
0020 Maintenance and inspection										
Inspect & clean motor starter	0.50	1 ELEC	Ea.	.667		34.50		34.50	42.50	53
Total				.667		34.50		34.50	**42.50**	**53**
0030 Replace starter										
Remove motor starter	18	1 ELEC	Ea.	.899		46.50		46.50	57	71.50
Magnetic motor starter 5 H.P., size 0				3.478	259	179		438	505	600
Cut, form, align & connect wires				.151		7.80		7.80	9.60	12
Check operation of motor starter				.018		.94		.94	1.17	1.46
Total				4.546	259	234.24		493.24	572.77	684.96

D5013 266 Motor Starter, 600 V

System Description	Freq. (Years)	Crew	Unit	Labor Hours	2012 Bare Costs				Total In-House	Total w/O&P
					Material	Labor	Equipment	Total		
0010 Maintenance and repair										
Remove motor starter coil	3	1 ELEC	Ea.	1.702		87.50		87.50	108	136
Motor starter coil				5.000	157	258		415	490	595
Total				6.702	157	345.50		502.50	**598**	**731**
0020 Maintenance and inspection										
Inspect & clean motor starter	0.25	1 ELEC	Ea.	.667		34.50		34.50	42.50	53
Total				.667		34.50		34.50	**42.50**	**53**
0030 Replace starter										
Remove motor starter	18	2 ELEC	Ea.	3.333		172		172	212	266
Motor starter FVNR 600 V, 3 P, 100 H.P. motor				13.333	3,200	685		3,885	4,375	5,050
Cut, form, align & connect wires				.170		8.75		8.75	10.85	13.55
Check operation of motor starter				.018		.94		.94	1.17	1.46
Total				16.855	3,200	866.69		4,066.69	4,599.02	5,331.01

D5013 272 Secondary Transformer, Liquid Filled

System Description	Freq. (Years)	Crew	Unit	Labor Hours	2012 Bare Costs				Total In-House	Total w/O&P
					Material	Labor	Equipment	Total		
0010 Maintenance and repair	25	1 ELEC	Ea.							
Remove transformer terminal				.348		17.95		17.95	22	27.50
Transformer terminal				1.000	63.50	51.50		115	134	159
Total				1.348	63.50	69.45		132.95	156	186.50
0020 Maintenance and inspection	0.50	1 ELEC	Ea.							
Check connections & fluid				.667		34.50		34.50	42.50	53
Total				.667		34.50		34.50	42.50	53

D5013 274 Secondary Transformer, Dry

System Description	Freq. (Years)	Crew	Unit	Labor Hours	2012 Bare Costs				Total In-House	Total w/O&P
					Material	Labor	Equipment	Total		
0010 Maintenance and repair	10	1 ELEC	Ea.							
Remove transformer terminal				.500		26		26	32	40
Transformer terminal				1.000	191	51.50		242.50	274	320
Total				1.500	191	77.50		268.50	306	360
0020 Maintenance and inspection	0.50	1 ELEC	Ea.							
Inspect connections & tighten				1.000		51.50		51.50	63.50	79.50
Total				1.000		51.50		51.50	63.50	79.50
0030 Replace 15 kVA transformer	30	2 ELEC	Ea.							
Remove transformer 15 kVA, incl. supp., wire & conduit terminations				3.810		196		196	242	305
Transformer 15 kVA, 240/480 V primary, 120/208 V secondary				14.545	1,275	750		2,025	2,325	2,750
Total				18.355	1,275	946		2,221	2,567	3,055
0040 Replace 112.5 kVA transformer	30	R-3	Ea.							
Remove transformer 112.5 kVA, incl. support, wire, conduit termination				6.897		350	45.50	395.50	480	595
Transformer 112.5 kVA, 240/480 V primary, 120/208 V secondary				22.222	3,100	1,125	147	4,372	4,975	5,775
Total				29.119	3,100	1,475	192.50	4,767.50	5,455	6,370
0050 Replace 500 kVA transformer	30	R-3	Ea.							
Remove transformer 500 kVA, incl. support,wire & conduit terminations				14.286		730	94.50	824.50	1,000	1,225
Transformer 500 kVA, 240/480 V primary, 120/208 V secondary				44.444	11,500	2,275	294	14,069	15,800	18,200
Total				58.730	11,500	3,005	388.50	14,893.50	16,800	19,425

D5013 280 Lighting Panel, Indoor

System Description	Freq. (Years)	Crew	Unit	Labor Hours	2012 Bare Costs				Total In-House	Total w/O&P
					Material	Labor	Equipment	Total		
0020										
Maintenance and inspection	3	1 ELEC	Ea.							
Inspect and clean panels				.500		26		26	32	40
Total				.500		26		26	**32**	**40**
0030										
Replace load center, 100 A	20	2 ELEC	Ea.							
Turn power off, later turn on				.100		5.15		5.15	6.35	7.95
Remove load center, 3 wire, 120/240 V				3.077		159		159	196	245
Load centers, 3 Wire, 120/240V, 100 A				6.667	370	345		715	830	995
Test circuits				.073		3.75		3.75	4.63	5.80
Total				9.916	370	512.90		882.90	**1,036.98**	**1,253.75**

D5023 110 Wireway

	System Description	Freq. (Years)	Crew	Unit	Labor Hours	2012 Bare Costs Material	Labor	Equipment	Total	Total In-House	Total w/O&P
0030	**Replace 8" x 8" wireway**	20	2 ELEC	L.F.							
	Remove and reinstall supply box				.050		2.60		2.60	3.20	4
	Remove wireway, fittings & support				.100		5.15		5.15	6.35	7.95
	Wireway 8" x 8", fittings & support				.400	33	20.50		53.50	62	73.50
	Total				.550	33	28.25		61.25	71.55	85.45

D5023 112 Conduit EMT

	System Description	Freq. (Years)	Crew	Unit	Labor Hours	2012 Bare Costs Material	Labor	Equipment	Total	Total In-House	Total w/O&P
0010	**Replace 1" EMT conduit**	50	2 ELEC	M.L.F.							
	Remove & reinstall cover plate				1.290		66.50		66.50	82	103
	Remove conduit w/ fittings & hangers				20.300		1,050		1,050	1,300	1,625
	Remove junction box				1.000		51.50		51.50	63.50	79.50
	1" EMT with couplings				38.650	1,480	1,990		3,470	4,100	4,925
	Outlet box square				4.000	29	205		234	285	355
	Box connector				.889	49.60	45.80		95.40	111	133
	Beam clamp				5.000	331	273		604	705	840
	Conduit hanger				5.926	615	305		920	1,050	1,250
	Total				77.055	2,504.60	3,986.80		6,491.40	7,696.50	9,310.50

D5023 120 Cable, Non-Metallic (NM) Sheathed

	System Description	Freq. (Years)	Crew	Unit	Labor Hours	2012 Bare Costs Material	Labor	Equipment	Total	Total In-House	Total w/O&P
0010	**Replace NM cable**	50	2 ELEC	M.L.F.							
	Shut off power, later turn on				.100		5.15		5.15	6.35	7.95
	Remove & reinstall cover plate				1.290		66.50		66.50	82	103
	Remove junction box				1.000		51.50		51.50	63.50	79.50
	Remove NM cable #12, 2 wire				12.720		660		660	810	1,000
	NM cable #12, 2 wire				32.000	450	1,650		2,100	2,525	3,125
	Staples, for Romex or BX cable				4.000	4	206		210	258	325
	NM #12-2 wire cable connectors				.602	12.90	31		43.90	52.50	64
	Outlet box square 4" for Romex or BX				4.000	123.50	205		328.50	390	475
	Total				55.712	590.40	2,875.15		3,465.55	4,187.35	5,179.45

D5023 122 Cable, Service

System Description	Freq. (Years)	Crew	Unit	Labor Hours	2012 Bare Costs				Total In-House	Total w/O&P
					Material	Labor	Equipment	Total		
0010										
Replace service cable	50	2 ELEC	M.L.F.							
Shut off power, later turn on				.100		5.15		5.15	6.35	7.95
Remove & reinstall cover plate				1.290		66.50		66.50	82	103
Remove junction box				1.000		51.50		51.50	63.50	79.50
Remove wire #6 XLPE				2.000		103		103	128	160
600 V, copper type XLPE-USE				12.308	1,150	635		1,785	2,050	2,425
Staples, for service cable				5.000	6	258		264	325	405
SER cable connectors				3.333	37.70	172		209.70	255	310
Outlet box square 4"				4.000	29	205		234	285	355
Total				29.031	1,222.70	1,496.15		2,718.85	3,194.85	3,845.45

D5023 124 Cable, Armored

System Description	Freq. (Years)	Crew	Unit	Labor Hours	2012 Bare Costs				Total In-House	Total w/O&P
					Material	Labor	Equipment	Total		
0010										
Replace armored cable	60	2 ELEC	M.L.F.							
Shut off power, later turn on				.100		5.15		5.15	6.35	7.95
Remove & reinstall cover plate				1.290		66.50		66.50	82	103
Remove junction box				1.000		51.50		51.50	63.50	79.50
Remove armored cable				13.220		680		680	840	1,050
BX #12, 2 wire				34.783	725	1,790		2,515	3,000	3,675
Staples, for Romex or BX cable				4.000	4	206		210	258	325
Cable connector				2.000	6.70	103		109.70	135	168
Outlet box square 4" for Romex or BX				4.000	123.50	205		328.50	390	475
Total				60.393	859.20	3,107.15		3,966.35	4,774.85	5,883.45

D5023 126 | Branch Wiring, With Junction Box

	Freq. (Years)	Crew	Unit	Labor Hours	2012 Bare Costs				Total In-House	Total w/O&P
System Description					Material	Labor	Equipment	Total		
0010 Replace branch wiring	50	2 ELEC	M.L.F.							
Shut off power, later turn on				.100		5.15		5.15	6.35	7.95
Remove & reinstall cover plate				1.290		66.50		66.50	82	103
Remove junction box				1.000		51.50		51.50	63.50	79.50
Remove #12 wire				1.455		75		75	92.50	116
Conductor THW-THHN, copper, stranded, #12				7.273	143.50	375		518.50	620	760
Outlet box square 4"				4.000	29	205		234	285	355
Wire connectors				1.000	3.30	51.60		54.90	67	83.50
Total				16.117	175.80	829.75		1,005.55	1,216.35	1,504.95

D5023 128 | Branch Wiring, 600 V

	Freq. (Years)	Crew	Unit	Labor Hours	2012 Bare Costs				Total In-House	Total w/O&P
System Description					Material	Labor	Equipment	Total		
0010 Replace branch wiring	50	2 ELEC	M.L.F.							
Shut off power, later turn on				.100		5.15		5.15	6.35	7.95
Remove #12 wire				1.455		75		75	92.50	116
Conductor THW-THHN, copper, stranded, #12				7.273	143.50	375		518.50	620	760
Cut, form and align 4 wires				.410		21		21	26	32.50
Splice, solder, insulate 2 wires				2.667		137		137	170	212
Total				11.904	143.50	613.15		756.65	914.85	1,128.45

D5023 130 | Circuit Breaker

	Freq. (Years)	Crew	Unit	Labor Hours	2012 Bare Costs				Total In-House	Total w/O&P
System Description					Material	Labor	Equipment	Total		
0010 Maintenance and repair breaker, molded case, 480 V, 1 pole	20	1 ELEC	Ea.							
Tighten connections				.889		46		46	56.50	71
Total				.889		46		46	56.50	71
0020 Maintenance and inspection C.B., molded case, 480 V, 1 pole	0.50	1 ELEC	Ea.							
Inspect, tighten C.B. wiring				.400		20.50		20.50	25.50	32
Total				.400		20.50		20.50	25.50	32

D5023 130   Circuit Breaker

System Description	Freq. (Years)	Crew	Unit	Labor Hours	Material	Labor	Equipment	Total	Total In-House	Total w/O&P
						2012 Bare Costs				
0030										
Replace C.B. molded case, 480 V, 1 pole	50	1 ELEC	Ea.							
Remove circuit breaker				.348		17.95		17.95	22	27.50
Circuit breaker molded case, 480 V, 70 to 100 A, 1 P				1.143	222	59		281	315	370
Cut, form, align & connect wires				.151		7.80		7.80	9.60	12
Check operation of breaker				.018		.94		.94	1.17	1.46
Total				1.660	222	85.69		307.69	347.77	410.96
1010										
Maintenance and repair breaker, molded case, 480 V, 2 pole	20	1 ELEC	Ea.							
Tighten connections				.889		46		46	56.50	71
Total				.889		46		46	**56.50**	**71**
1020										
Maintenance and inspection C.B., molded case, 480 V, 2 pole	0.50	1 ELEC	Ea.							
Inspect, tighten C.B. wiring				.400		20.50		20.50	25.50	32
Total				.400		20.50		20.50	**25.50**	**32**
1030										
Replace C.B. molded case, 480 V, 2 pole	50	1 ELEC	Ea.							
Remove circuit breaker				.500		26		26	32	40
Circuit breaker molded case, 480 V, 70 to 100 A, 2 P				1.600	560	82.50		642.50	720	825
Cut, form, align & connect wires				.151		7.80		7.80	9.60	12
Check operation of breaker				.018		.94		.94	1.17	1.46
Total				2.269	560	117.24		677.24	762.77	878.46
1040										
Maintenance and repair breaker, molded case, 480 V, 3 pole	20	1 ELEC	Ea.							
Tighten connections				.889		46		46	56.50	71
Total				.889		46		46	**56.50**	**71**
1050										
Maintenance and inspection C.B., molded case, 480 V, 3 pole	0.50	1 ELEC	Ea.							
Inspect & tighten C.B. wiring				.400		20.50		20.50	25.50	32
Total				.400		20.50		20.50	**25.50**	**32**
1060										
Replace C.B. molded case, 480 V, 3 pole	50	1 ELEC	Ea.							
Remove circuit breaker				.500		26		26	32	40
Circuit breaker molded case, 480 V, 70 to 100 A, 3 P				2.000	655	103		758	850	980
Cut, form, align & connect wires				.151		7.80		7.80	9.60	12
Check operation of breaker				.018		.94		.94	1.17	1.46
Total				2.669	655	137.74		792.74	892.77	1,033.46

D5023 130 | Circuit Breaker

System Description	Freq. (Years)	Crew	Unit	Labor Hours	2012 Bare Costs				Total In-House	Total w/O&P
					Material	Labor	Equipment	Total		
2010 Repair failed breaker, molded case, 600 V, 2 pole	10	1 ELEC	Ea.							
Remove trip switch				.500		26		26	32	40
Trip switch				1.600	206	82.50		288.50	330	385
Total				2.100	206	108.50		314.50	**362**	**425**
2020 Maintenance and inspection C.B., molded case, 600 V, 2 pole	0.33	1 ELEC	Ea.							
Inspect & tighten C.B. wiring				.400		20.50		20.50	25.50	32
Total				.400		20.50		20.50	**25.50**	**32**
2030 Replace C.B. molded case, 600 V, 2 pole	50	1 ELEC	Ea.							
Remove circuit breaker				.500		26		26	32	40
Circuit breaker molded case, 600 V, 70 to 100 A, 2 P				1.600	630	82.50		712.50	795	915
Cut, form, align & connect wires				.170		8.75		8.75	10.85	13.55
Check operation of breakers				.018		.94		.94	1.17	1.46
Total				2.289	630	118.19		748.19	**839.02**	**970.01**
3010 Repair failed breaker, molded case, 600 V, 3 pole	10	1 ELEC	Ea.							
Remove trip switch				.500		26		26	32	40
Trip switch				1.600	206	82.50		288.50	330	385
Total				2.100	206	108.50		314.50	**362**	**425**
3020 Maintenance and inspection C.B., molded case, 600 V, 3 pole	0.33	1 ELEC	Ea.							
Inspect & tighten C.B. wiring				.400		20.50		20.50	25.50	32
Total				.400		20.50		20.50	**25.50**	**32**
3030 Replace C.B. molded case, 600 V, 3 pole	50	1 ELEC	Ea.							
Remove circuit breaker				.889		46		46	56.50	71
Circuit breaker molded case, 600 V, 125 to 400 A, 3 P				3.478	2,650	179		2,829	3,125	3,600
Cut, form, align & connect wires				.170		8.75		8.75	10.85	13.55
Check operation of breakers				.018		.94		.94	1.17	1.46
Total				4.556	2,650	234.69		2,884.69	**3,193.52**	**3,686.01**
3040 Maintenance and repair breaker, enclosed, 240 V, 1 pole	25	1 ELEC	Ea.							
Tighten connections				.889		46		46	56.50	71
Total				.889		46		46	**56.50**	**71**

D5023 130 | **Circuit Breaker**

System Description	Freq. (Years)	Crew	Unit	Labor Hours	2012 Bare Costs				Total In-House	Total w/O&P
					Material	Labor	Equipment	Total		
3050										
Maintenance and inspection C.B., enclosed, 240 V, 1 pole										
Inspect & tighten C.B. wiring	1	1 ELEC	Ea.	.400		20.50		20.50	25.50	32
Total				.400		20.50		20.50	**25.50**	**32**
3060										
Replace C.B. enclosed, 240 V, 1 pole										
Remove circuit breaker	50	1 ELEC	Ea.	.500		26		26	32	40
Circuit breaker enclosed, 240 V, 15 to 60 A, 1 P				2.105	260	109		369	420	495
Cut, form, align & connect wires				.151		7.80		7.80	9.60	12
Check operation of breaker				.018		.94		.94	1.17	1.46
Total				2.775	260	143.74		403.74	462.77	548.46
4010										
Maintenance and repair breaker, enclosed, 240 V, 2 pole										
Tighten connections	25	1 ELEC	Ea.	.889		46		46	56.50	71
Total				.889		46		46	**56.50**	**71**
4020										
Maintenance and inspection C.B., enclosed, 240 V, 2 pole										
Inspect & tighten C.B. wiring	1	1 ELEC	Ea.	.400		20.50		20.50	25.50	32
Total				.400		20.50		20.50	**25.50**	**32**
4030										
Replace C.B. enclosed, 240 V, 2 pole										
Remove circuit breaker	50	1 ELEC	Ea.	.500		26		26	32	40
Circuit breaker enclosed, 240 V, 15 to 60 A, 2 P				2.286	375	118		493	560	650
Cut, form, align & connect wires				.151		7.80		7.80	9.60	12
Check operation of breaker				.018		.94		.94	1.17	1.46
Total				2.955	375	152.74		527.74	602.77	703.46
4040										
Maintenance and repair breaker, enclosed, 240 V, 3 pole										
Tighten connections	25	1 ELEC	Ea.	.889		46		46	56.50	71
Total				.889		46		46	**56.50**	**71**
4050										
Maintenance and inspection C.B., enclosed, 240 V, 3 pole										
Inspect & tighten C.B. wiring	1	1 ELEC	Ea.	.400		20.50		20.50	25.50	32
Total				.400		20.50		20.50	**25.50**	**32**

	System Description	Freq. (Years)	Crew	Unit	Labor Hours	2012 Bare Costs				Total In-House	Total w/O&P
						Material	Labor	Equipment	Total		
4060	**Replace C.B. enclosed, 240 V, 3 pole**	50	1 ELEC	Ea.							
	Remove circuit breaker				.500		26		26	32	40
	Circuit breaker enclosed, 240 V, 15 to 60 A, 3 P				2.500	490	129		619	700	810
	Cut, form, align & connect wires				.151		7.80		7.80	9.60	12
	Check operation of breaker				.018		.94		.94	1.17	1.46
	Total				3.169	490	163.74		653.74	**742.77**	**863.46**
5010	**Repair failed breaker, enclosed, 600 V, 2 pole**	4	1 ELEC	Ea.							
	Repair circuit breaker component				2.105	365	109		474	535	625
	Total				2.105	365	109		474	**535**	**625**
5020	**Maintenance and inspection C.B., enclosed, 600 V, 2 pole**	0.33	1 ELEC	Ea.							
	Inspect & tighten C.B. wiring				.400		20.50		20.50	25.50	32
	Total				.400		20.50		20.50	**25.50**	**32**
5030	**Replace C.B. enclosed, 600 V, 2 pole**	50	1 ELEC	Ea.							
	Remove circuit breaker				.800		41		41	51	63.50
	Circuit breaker enclosed, 600 V, 100 A, 2 P				3.200	630	165		795	895	1,050
	Cut, form, align & connect wires				.170		8.75		8.75	10.85	13.55
	Check operation of breaker				.018		.94		.94	1.17	1.46
	Total				4.189	630	215.69		845.69	**958.02**	**1,128.51**
6010	**Repair failed breaker, enclosed, 600 V, 3 pole**	4	1 ELEC	Ea.							
	Repair circuit breaker component				2.105	365	109		474	535	625
	Total				2.105	365	109		474	**535**	**625**
6020	**Maintenance and inspection C.B., enclosed, 600 V, 3 pole**	0.33	1 ELEC	Ea.							
	Inspect & tighten C.B. wiring				.400		20.50		20.50	25.50	32
	Total				.400		20.50		20.50	**25.50**	**32**
6030	**Replace C.B. enclosed, 600 V, 3 pole**	50	1 ELEC	Ea.							
	Remove circuit breaker				.889		46		46	56.50	71
	Circuit breaker enclosed, 600 V, 100 A, 3 P				3.478	685	179		864	975	1,125
	Cut, form, align & connect wires				.170		8.75		8.75	10.85	13.55
	Check operation of breaker				.018		.94		.94	1.17	1.46
	Total				4.556	685	234.69		919.69	**1,043.52**	**1,211.01**

D5023 130 | Circuit Breaker

System Description	Freq. (Years)	Crew	Unit	Labor Hours	2012 Bare Costs				Total In-House	Total w/O&P
					Material	Labor	Equipment	Total		
6830										
Replace C.B. enclosed, 600 V, 3 pole 800 A	50	2 ELEC	Ea.							
Remove circuit breaker				4.444		229		229	283	355
Circuit breaker enclosed, 600 V, 800 A, 3 P				17.021	5,100	875		5,975	6,700	7,725
Cut, form, align & connect wires				.340		17.50		17.50	21.50	27
Check operation of breaker				.037		1.88		1.88	2.34	2.92
Total				21.843	5,100	1,123.38		6,223.38	7,006.84	8,109.92
6930										
Replace C.B. enclosed, 600 V, 3 pole 1000 A	50	2 ELEC	Ea.							
Remove circuit breaker				5.161		266		266	330	410
Circuit breaker enclosed, 600 V, 1000 A, 3 P				19.048	6,425	980		7,405	8,275	9,550
Cut, form, align & connect wires				.516		26.52		26.52	33	41
Check operation of breaker				.055		2.85		2.85	3.55	4.42
Total				24.780	6,425	1,275.37		7,700.37	8,641.55	10,005.42
7130										
Replace C.B. enclosed, 600 V, 3 pole 1600 A	50	2 ELEC	Ea.							
Remove circuit breaker				5.714		295		295	365	455
Circuit breaker enclosed, 600 V, 1600 A, 3 P				22.222	15,100	1,150		16,250	18,000	20,700
Cut, form, align & connect wires				.681		35		35	43.50	54
Check operation of breaker				.073		3.76		3.76	4.68	5.85
Total				28.691	15,100	1,483.76		16,583.76	18,413.18	21,214.85
7230										
Replace C.B. enclosed, 600 V, 3 pole 2000 A	50	2 ELEC	Ea.							
Remove circuit breaker				6.400		330		330	405	510
Circuit breaker enclosed, 600 V, 2000 A, 3 P				25.000	16,300	1,300		17,600	19,500	22,400
Cut, form, align & connect wires				1.418		72.92		72.92	90.50	113
Check operation of breaker				.153		7.83		7.83	9.75	12.15
Total				32.971	16,300	1,710.75		18,010.75	20,005.25	23,035.15

D5023 132 | Safety Switch, Heavy Duty

System Description	Freq. (Years)	Crew	Unit	Labor Hours	2012 Bare Costs				Total In-House	Total w/O&P
					Material	Labor	Equipment	Total		
0010										
Maintenance and repair safety switch, H.D., 3 pole	8	1 ELEC	Ea.							
Resecure lugs				.500		26		26	32	40
Total				.500		26		26	32	40

D5023 132 | **Safety Switch, Heavy Duty**

	System Description	Freq. (Years)	Crew	Unit	Labor Hours	2012 Bare Costs				Total In-House	Total w/O&P
						Material	Labor	Equipment	Total		
0020	**Maintenance and inspection safety switch, 3 pole**	1	1 ELEC	Ea.							
	Inspect & clean safety switch				.500		26		26	32	40
	Total				.500		26		26	**32**	**40**
0030	**Replace safety switch, H.D. 30 A**	25	2 ELEC	Ea.							
	Remove safety switch				.650		33.50		33.50	41.50	52
	Fused safety switch, heavy duty, 600 V, 3 P, 30 A				2.500	325	129		454	515	605
	Fuses				.600	37.05	30.90		67.95	79.50	94
	Check operation of switch				.018		.94		.94	1.17	1.46
	Total				3.769	362.05	194.34		556.39	**637.17**	**752.46**
0130	**Replace safety switch, H.D. 100 A**	25	2 ELEC	Ea.							
	Remove safety switch				1.096		56.50		56.50	70	87.50
	Fused safety switch, heavy duty, 600 V, 3 P, 100 A				4.211	720	217		937	1,050	1,225
	Fuses				.667	132	34.35		166.35	188	218
	Check operation of switch				.018		.94		.94	1.17	1.46
	Total				5.991	852	308.79		1,160.79	**1,309.17**	**1,531.96**
0230	**Replace safety switch, H.D. 200 A**	25	2 ELEC	Ea.							
	Remove safety switch				1.600		82.50		82.50	102	127
	Fused safety switch, heavy duty, 600 V, 3 P, 200 A				6.154	1,050	315		1,365	1,550	1,800
	Fuses				.800	262.50	41.25		303.75	340	390
	Check operation of switch				.018		.94		.94	1.17	1.46
	Total				8.572	1,312.50	439.69		1,752.19	**1,993.17**	**2,318.46**
0430	**Replace safety switch, H.D. 400 A**	25	2 ELEC	Ea.							
	Remove safety switch				2.353		121		121	150	187
	Fused safety switch, heavy duty, 600 V, 3 P, 400 A				8.889	2,725	460		3,185	3,575	4,125
	Fuses				1.000	525	51.60		576.60	640	735
	Check operation of switch				.037		1.88		1.88	2.34	2.92
	Total				12.278	3,250	634.48		3,884.48	**4,367.34**	**5,049.92**
0630	**Replace safety switch, H.D. 600 A**	25	2 ELEC	Ea.							
	Remove safety switch				3.478		179		179	221	277
	Fused safety switch, heavy duty, 600 V, 3 P, 600 A				13.333	4,575	685		5,260	5,875	6,775
	Fuses				1.200	762	61.50		823.50	915	1,050
	Check operation of switch				.037		1.88		1.88	2.34	2.92
	Total				18.048	5,337	927.38		6,264.38	**7,013.34**	**8,104.92**

D5023 140 | Safety Switch, General Duty

System Description	Freq. (Years)	Crew	Unit	Labor Hours	2012 Bare Costs Material	Labor	Equipment	Total	Total In-House	Total w/O&P
2010 Maintenance and repair safety switch gen., 2 pole	8	1 ELEC	Ea.							
Resecure lugs				.500		26		26	32	40
Total				.500		26		26	**32**	**40**
2020 Maintenance and inspection safety switch, 2 pole	1	1 ELEC	Ea.							
Inspect & clean safety switch				.500		26		26	32	40
Total				.500		26		26	**32**	**40**
2030 Replace safety switch 240 V, 2 pole	25	2 ELEC	Ea.							
Remove safety switch				.650		33.50		33.50	41.50	52
Fused safety switch, general duty, 240 V, 2 P, 30 A				2.299	145	119		264	305	365
Fuse, dual element, time delay, 250 V, 30 A				.320	12.50	16.50		29	34	41
Cut, form, align & connect wires				.151		7.80		7.80	9.60	12
Check operation of switch				.018		.94		.94	1.17	1.46
Total				3.439	157.50	177.74		335.24	**391.27**	**471.46**
3010 Maintenance and repair safety switch gen., 3 pole	8	1 ELEC	Ea.							
Resecure lugs				.500		26		26	32	40
Total				.500		26		26	**32**	**40**
3020 Maintenance and inspection safety switch, 3 pole	1	1 ELEC	Ea.							
Inspect & clean safety switch				.500		26		26	32	40
Total				.500		26		26	**32**	**40**
3030 Replace safety switch 240 V, 3 pole	25	2 ELEC	Ea.							
Remove safety switch				.650		33.50		33.50	41.50	52
Fused safety switch, general duty, 240 V, 3 P, 30 A				2.500	192	129		321	370	440
Fuse, dual element, time delay, 250 V, 30 A				.480	18.75	24.75		43.50	51	61.50
Cut, form, align & connect wires				.151		7.80		7.80	9.60	12
Check operation of switch				.018		.94		.94	1.17	1.46
Total				3.800	210.75	195.99		406.74	**473.27**	**566.96**
4010 Replace low voltage cartridge	50	1 ELEC	Ea.							
Remove cartridge fuse cutouts				.100		5.15		5.15	6.35	7.95
Cartridge fuse cutouts 3 P				.296	13.50	15.25		28.75	33.50	40.50
Total				.396	13.50	20.40		33.90	**39.85**	**48.45**

RSMeans Professional Development Seminars

RSMeans Seminars are approved for Continuing Education Units (CEUs) by both the American Institute of Architects Continuing Education Systems (AIA/CES) and AACE International Certification Board.

Seminar Topics Include:

- Practical Project Management for Construction Professionals
- Scheduling with MSProject for Construction Professionals
- Assessing Scope of Work for Facilities Construction Estimating
- Site Work and Heavy Construction Estimating
- Facilities Construction Estimating
- Job Order Contracting
- Mechanical and Electrical Estimating
- Facilities Maintenance and Repair Estimating
- Unit Price Estimating
- RSMeans Product Training (MeansCostWorks.com and RSMeans CostWorks CD)

Ask us about on-site product training.
Call 1-800-334-3509, option 2.

For more information and a seminar schedule visit
www.reedconstructiondata.com/rsmeans/seminars.

RSMeans

D5023 140 Safety Switch, General Duty

	System Description	Freq. (Years)	Crew	Unit	Labor Hours	2012 Bare Costs				Total In-House	Total w/O&P
						Material	Labor	Equipment	Total		
5010	**Replace plug fuse**	25	1 ELEC	Ea.							
	Remove plug fuse				.080		4.12		4.12	5.10	6.35
	Fuse, plug, 120 V, 15 to 30 A				.160	7.90	8.25		16.15	18.85	22.50
	Total				.240	7.90	12.37		20.27	23.95	**28.85**

D5023 150 Receptacles And Plugs

	System Description	Freq. (Years)	Crew	Unit	Labor Hours	2012 Bare Costs				Total In-House	Total w/O&P
						Material	Labor	Equipment	Total		
0010	**Maintenance and repair**	20	1 ELEC	Ea.							
	Repair receptacle component (cover)				.500	2.50	26		28.50	34.50	43
	Total				.500	2.50	26		28.50	**34.50**	**43**
0020	**Replace receptacle/plug**	20	1 ELEC	Ea.							
	Turn power off, later turn on				.100		5.15		5.15	6.35	7.95
	Remove & install cover plates				.170		8.75		8.75	10.85	13.55
	Remove receptacle				.040		2.06		2.06	2.55	3.19
	Wiring devices, receptacle				.381	10.95	19.65		30.60	36.50	44
	Cut, form, align & connect wires				.026		1.34		1.34	1.65	2.07
	Test for operation				.015		.75		.75	.93	1.16
	Total				.732	10.95	37.70		48.65	**58.83**	**71.92**

D5023 154 4-Pin Receptacle

	System Description	Freq. (Years)	Crew	Unit	Labor Hours	2012 Bare Costs				Total In-House	Total w/O&P
						Material	Labor	Equipment	Total		
0010	**Repair 4-pin receptacle cover**	10	1 ELEC	Ea.							
	Repair receptacle(cover)				.615	8.85	31.50		40.35	49	60
	Total				.615	8.85	31.50		40.35	**49**	**60**
0020	**Replace 4 - pin receptacle**	20	1 ELEC	Ea.							
	Remove 4-pin receptacle				.200		10.30		10.30	12.75	15.95
	Receptacle locking, 4-pin				.615	83.50	31.50		115	131	153
	Total				.815	83.50	41.80		125.30	**143.75**	**168.95**

D5023 210   Contactors And Relays

System Description	Freq. (Years)	Crew	Unit	Labor Hours	2012 Bare Costs				Total In-House	Total w/O&P
					Material	Labor	Equipment	Total		
0010 Maintenance and repair	3	1 ELEC	Ea.							
Remove contactor coil				.602		31		31	38.50	48
Contactor coil				2.000	52	103		155	185	224
Total				2.602	52	134		186	223.50	272
0020 Maintenance and inspection	0.50	1 ELEC	Ea.							
Inspect and clean contacts				.250		12.90		12.90	15.90	19.90
Total				.250		12.90		12.90	15.90	19.90
0030 Replace contactor	18	1 ELEC	Ea.							
Remove magnetic contactor				.800		41		41	51	63.50
Magnetic contactor 600 V, 3 P, 25 H.P.				2.667	425	137		562	635	745
Cut, form, align & connect wires				.151		7.80		7.80	9.60	12
Check operation of contactor				.018		.94		.94	1.17	1.46
Total				3.636	425	186.74		611.74	696.77	821.96

D5023 220   Wiring Devices, Switches

System Description	Freq. (Years)	Crew	Unit	Labor Hours	2012 Bare Costs				Total In-House	Total w/O&P
					Material	Labor	Equipment	Total		
0010 Maintenance and repair	10	1 ELEC	Ea.							
Repair switch component (cover)				.500	2.50	26		28.50	34.50	43
Total				.500	2.50	26		28.50	34.50	43
0020 Replace switch	15	1 ELEC	Ea.							
Turn power off, later turn on				.100		5.15		5.15	6.35	7.95
Remove & install cover plates				.170		8.75		8.75	10.85	13.55
Remove switch				.040		2.06		2.06	2.55	3.19
Wiring devices, switch				.381	8.35	19.65		28	33.50	41
Cut, form, align & connect wires				.026		1.34		1.34	1.65	2.07
Test for operation				.015		.75		.75	.93	1.16
Total				.732	8.35	37.70		46.05	55.83	68.92

D5023 222 Switch, Pull Cord

System Description	Freq. (Years)	Crew	Unit	Labor Hours	2012 Bare Costs Material	Labor	Equipment	Total	Total In-House	Total w/O&P
0010 Maintenance and repair										
Repair switch component (cover)	5	1 ELEC	Ea.	.500	2.75	26		28.75	35	43.50
Total				.500	2.75	26		28.75	**35**	**43.50**
0020 Replace switch	15	1 ELEC	Ea.							
Turn power off, later turn on				.100		5.15		5.15	6.35	7.95
Remove & install cover plates				.170		8.75		8.75	10.85	13.55
Remove switch, pull cord				.040		2.06		2.06	2.55	3.19
Switch, pull cord				.381	12.10	19.65		31.75	37.50	45.50
Cut, form, align & connect wires				.026		1.34		1.34	1.65	2.07
Test for operation				.015		.75		.75	.93	1.16
Total				.732	12.10	37.70		49.80	**59.83**	**73.42**

D5023 230 Light Dimming Panel

System Description	Freq. (Years)	Crew	Unit	Labor Hours	2012 Bare Costs Material	Labor	Equipment	Total	Total In-House	Total w/O&P
0010 Minor repairs to light dimming panel	5	1 ELEC	Ea.							
Check and test components				.400		20.50		20.50	25.50	32
Remove dimming panel component				.222		11.45		11.45	14.15	17.70
Dimming panel component				.667	90	34.50		124.50	141	166
Total				1.289	90	66.45		156.45	**180.65**	**215.70**
0020 Maintenance and inspection	1	1 ELEC	Ea.							
Check light dimming panel				.533		27.50		27.50	34	42.50
Total				.533		27.50		27.50	**34**	**42.50**
0030 Replace light dimming panel	15	1 ELEC	Ea.							
Turn power off, later turn on				.100		5.15		5.15	6.35	7.95
Remove dimming panel				1.600		82.50		82.50	102	127
Dimming panel				8.000	620	410		1,030	1,200	1,400
Test circuits				.073		3.75		3.75	4.63	5.80
Total				9.773	620	501.40		1,121.40	**1,312.98**	**1,540.75**

D5023 240 | Incandescent Lighting Fixtures

System Description	Freq. (Years)	Crew	Unit	Labor Hours	2012 Bare Costs				Total In-House	Total w/O&P
					Material	Labor	Equipment	Total		
0010 **Maintenance and repair**										
Remove glass globe		1 ELEC	Ea.	.100		5.15		5.15	6.35	7.95
Glass globe	10			.296	26.50	15.25		41.75	48	56.50
Total				.396	26.50	20.40		46.90	54.35	64.45
0020 **Replace lamp**										
Remove incand. lighting fixture lamp		1 ELEC	Ea.	.022		1.13		1.13	1.40	1.75
Incand. lighting fixture lamp	5			.065	2.20	3.35		5.55	6.55	7.95
Total				.087	2.20	4.48		6.68	7.95	9.70
0030 **Replace lighting fixture**										
Turn circuit off and on for fixture		1 ELEC	Ea.	.018		.94		.94	1.17	1.46
Remove incand. lighting fixture				.258		13.30		13.30	16.45	20.50
Incand. lighting fixture, 75 W	20			.800	55	41		96	111	132
Total				1.076	55	55.24		110.24	128.62	153.96
0120 **Replace lamp, 200 W**										
Remove incand. lighting fixture lamp		1 ELEC	Ea.	.022		1.15		1.15	1.41	1.77
Incand. lighting fixture lamp, 200 W	5			.065	2.96	3.35		6.31	7.40	8.90
Total				.087	2.96	4.50		7.46	8.81	10.67
0220 **Replace lamp for explosion proof fixture**										
Remove incand. lighting fixture lamp		1 ELEC	Ea.	.044		2.30		2.30	2.82	3.54
Incand. lighting fixture lamp for explosion proof fixture	5			.130	5.92	6.70		12.62	14.80	17.80
Total				.175	5.92	9		14.92	17.62	21.34
0230 **Replace incan. lighting fixt., explosion proof, ceiling mtd., 200 W**										
Turn branch circuit off and on		1 ELEC	Ea.	.018		.94		.94	1.17	1.46
Remove incandescent lighting fixture, explosion proof				.920		47.50		47.50	58.50	73
Incan. lighting fixture, explosion proof, ceiling mtd, 200 W	20			2.000	1,050	103		1,153	1,275	1,475
Total				2.938	1,050	151.44		1,201.44	1,334.67	1,549.46
1230 **Replace incan. lighting fixt., high hat can type, ceiling mtd., 200 W**										
Turn branch circuit off and on		1 ELEC	Ea.	.018		.94		.94	1.17	1.46
Remove incandescent lighting fixture, can type				.258		13.30		13.30	16.45	20.50
Incan. lighting fixture, high hat can type, ceiling mtd, 200 W	20			1.194	95	61.50		156.50	181	214
Total				1.470	95	75.74		170.74	198.62	235.96

D5023 250 Quartz Fixture

	System Description	Freq. (Years)	Crew	Unit	Labor Hours	2012 Bare Costs Material	2012 Bare Costs Labor	2012 Bare Costs Equipment	2012 Bare Costs Total	Total In-House	Total w/O&P
0010	**Maintenance and repair**	10	1 ELEC	Ea.							
	Repair glass lens				.400		20.50		51.50	59.50	71
	Total				.400		20.50		51.50	**59.50**	**71**
0020	**Replace 1500 W quartz lamp**	10	1 ELEC	Ea.							
	Remove quartz lamp				.087		4.48		4.48	5.55	6.95
	Quartz lamp				.258	54.50	13.30		67.80	76.50	88.50
	Total				.345	54.50	17.78		72.28	**82.05**	**95.45**
0030	**Replace fixture**	20	1 ELEC	Ea.							
	Turn branch circuit off and on				.018		.94		.94	1.17	1.46
	Remove exterior fixt., quartz, 1500 W				.593		30.50		30.50	37.50	47
	Exterior fixt. quartz, 1500 W				1.905	118	98		216	251	300
	Total				2.516	118	129.44		247.44	**289.67**	**348.46**

D5023 260 Fluorescent Lighting Fixture

	System Description	Freq. (Years)	Crew	Unit	Labor Hours	2012 Bare Costs Material	2012 Bare Costs Labor	2012 Bare Costs Equipment	2012 Bare Costs Total	Total In-House	Total w/O&P
0010	**Replace fluor. ballast**	10	1 ELEC	Ea.							
	Remove indoor fluor. ballast				.333		17.20		17.20	21	26.50
	Fluorescent, electronic ballast				.667	36.50	34.50		71	82.50	98.50
	Test fixture				.018		.94		.94	1.17	1.46
	Total				1.018	36.50	52.64		89.14	**104.67**	**126.46**
0020	**Replace lamps (2 lamps), 4', 34 W energy saver**	10	1 ELEC	Ea.							
	Remove fluor. lamps in fixture				.078		4.02		4.02	4.96	6.20
	Fluor. lamp, 4' energy saver				.232	9.30	12		21.30	25	30
	Total				.310	9.30	16.02		25.32	**29.96**	**36.20**
0030	**Replace fixture, lay-in, recess mtd., 2' x 4', two 40 W**	20	1 ELEC	Ea.							
	Turn branch circuit off and on				.018		.94		.94	1.17	1.46
	Remove fluor. lighting fixture				.485		25		25	31	38.50
	Fluor. 2' x 4', recess mounted, two 40 W				1.509	58	78		136	160	193
	Total				2.013	58	103.94		161.94	**192.17**	**232.96**

D5023 260 Fluorescent Lighting Fixture

	System Description	Freq. (Years)	Crew	Unit	Labor Hours	2012 Bare Costs				Total In-House	Total w/O&P
						Material	Labor	Equipment	Total		
0040	**Replace fixture, lay-in, recess mtd., 2′ x 4′, four 32 W**	20	1 ELEC	Ea.							
	Turn branch circuit off and on				.018		.94		.94	1.17	1.46
	Remove fluor. lighting fixture				.533		27.50		27.50	34	42.50
	Fluor, lay-in, recess mtd., 2′ x 4′, four 32 W				1.702	78.50	87.50		166	195	234
	Total				2.254	78.50	115.94		194.44	230.17	277.96
0120	**Replace lamps (2 lamps), 8′, 60 W energy saver**	10	1 ELEC	Ea.							
	Remove fluor. lamps in fixture				.078		4.02		4.02	4.96	6.20
	Fluor. lamps, 8′ energy saver				.200	11.90	10.30		22.20	26	31
	Total				.278	11.90	14.32		26.22	30.96	37.20
0130	**Replace fixture, strip, surface mtd., 8′, two 75 W**	20	2 ELEC	Ea.							
	Turn branch circuit off and on				.018		.94		.94	1.17	1.46
	Remove fluor. lighting fixture				.400		20.50		20.50	25.50	32
	Fluor. strip, surface mounted, 8′, two 75 W				1.290	57	66.50		123.50	145	174
	Total				1.709	57	87.94		144.94	171.67	207.46
0140	**Replace fixture, strip, pendent mtd, 8′, two 75 W**	20	2 ELEC	Ea.							
	Turn branch circuit off and on				.018		.94		.94	1.17	1.46
	Remove fluor. lighting fixture				.593		30.50		30.50	37.50	47
	Fluor, strip, pendent mtd, 8′, two 75 W				1.818	96	93.50		189.50	221	265
	Total				2.429	96	124.94		220.94	259.67	313.46

D5023 270 Metal Halide Fixture

	System Description	Freq. (Years)	Crew	Unit	Labor Hours	2012 Bare Costs				Total In-House	Total w/O&P
						Material	Labor	Equipment	Total		
2010	**Replace M.H. ballast, 175 W**	10	1 ELEC	Ea.							
	Remove metal halide fixt. ballast				.333		17.20		17.20	21	26.50
	Metal halide fixt. 175 W, ballast				.667	136	34.50		170.50	192	223
	Test fixture				.018		.94		.94	1.17	1.46
	Total				1.018	136	52.64		188.64	214.17	250.96
2020	**Replace lamp, 175 W**	5	1 ELEC	Ea.							
	Remove metal halide fixt. lamp				.116		6		6	7.40	9.25
	Metal halide lamp, 175 W				.348	46	17.95		63.95	72.50	85
	Total				.464	46	23.95		69.95	79.90	94.25

	System Description	Freq. (Years)	Crew	Unit	Labor Hours	2012 Bare Costs				Total In-House	Total w/O&P
						Material	Labor	Equipment	Total		
2030	**Replace fixture, 175 W**	20	1 ELEC	Ea.							
	Turn branch circuit off and on				.018		.94		.94	1.17	1.46
	Remove metal halide fixt.				.800		41		41	51	63.50
	Metal halide, recessed, square 175 W				2.353	390	121		511	580	675
	Total				3.171	390	162.94		552.94	632.17	739.96
2210	**Replace M.H. ballast, 400 W**	10	1 ELEC	Ea.							
	Remove metal halide fixt. ballast				.333		17.20		17.20	21	26.50
	Metal halide fixt. 400 W, ballast				.762	219	39.50		258.50	289	335
	Test fixture				.018		.94		.94	1.17	1.46
	Total				1.114	219	57.64		276.64	311.17	362.96
2220	**Replace lamp, 400 W**	5	1 ELEC	Ea.							
	Remove metal halide fixt. lamp				.118		6.05		6.05	7.50	9.35
	Metal halide lamp, 400 W				.348	85.50	17.95		103.45	116	134
	Total				.465	85.50	24		109.50	123.50	143.35
2230	**Replace fixture, 400 W**	20	2 ELEC	Ea.							
	Turn branch circuit off and on				.018		.94		.94	1.17	1.46
	Remove metal halide fixt.				1.067		55		55	68	85
	Metal halide, surface mtd, high bay, 400 W				3.478	405	179		584	665	785
	Total				4.563	405	234.94		639.94	734.17	871.46
2310	**Replace M.H. ballast, 1000 W**	10	1 ELEC	Ea.							
	Remove metal halide fixt. ballast				.333		17.20		17.20	21	26.50
	Metal halide fixt. 1000 W, ballast				.889	375	46		421	470	540
	Test fixture				.018		.94		.94	1.17	1.46
	Total				1.241	375	64.14		439.14	492.17	567.96
2320	**Replace lamp, 1000 W**	5	1 ELEC	Ea.							
	Remove metal halide fixt. lamp				.118		6.05		6.05	7.50	9.35
	Metal halide lamp, 1000 W				.523	119	27		146	164	190
	Total				.641	119	33.05		152.05	171.50	199.35

333

D5023 270 Metal Halide Fixture

					2012 Bare Costs				Total In-House	Total w/O&P
System Description	Freq. (Years)	Crew	Unit	Labor Hours	Material	Labor	Equipment	Total		
2330										
Replace fixture, 1000 W	20	2 ELEC	Ea.							
Turn branch circuit off and on				.018		.94		.94	1.17	1.46
Remove metal halide fixt.				1.333		68.50		68.50	85	106
Metal halide, surface mtd, high bay, 1000 W				4.000	580	206		786	895	1,050
Total				5.352	580	275.44		855.44	981.17	1,157.46

D5023 280 H.P. Sodium Fixture, 250 W

					2012 Bare Costs				Total In-House	Total w/O&P
System Description	Freq. (Years)	Crew	Unit	Labor Hours	Material	Labor	Equipment	Total		
1010										
Replace H.P. sodium ballast	10	2 ELEC	Ea.							
Remove H.P. Sodium fixt. ballast				.333		17.20		17.20	21	26.50
H.P. Sodium fixt., 250 W, ballast				.667	370	34.50		404.50	450	515
Test fixture				.018		.94		.94	1.17	1.46
Total				1.018	370	52.64		422.64	472.17	542.96
1020										
Replace lamp	10	2 ELEC	Ea.							
Remove H.P. Sodium fixt. lamp				.116		6		6	7.40	9.25
H.P. Sodium fixt. lamp, 250 W				.348	63.50	17.95		81.45	92	107
Total				.464	63.50	23.95		87.45	99.40	116.25
1030										
Replace fixture	20	2 ELEC	Ea.							
Turn branch circuit off and on				.018		.94		.94	1.17	1.46
Remove H.P. Sodium fixt.				.889		46		46	56.50	71
H.P. Sodium fixt., recessed, square 250 W				2.667	645	137		782	880	1,025
Total				3.574	645	183.94		828.94	937.67	1,097.46

D5033 310 Telephone Cable

	System Description	Freq. (Years)	Crew	Unit	Labor Hours	2012 Bare Costs Material	Labor	Equipment	Total	Total In-House	Total w/O&P
0010	**Repair cable, 22 A.W.G., 4 pair**	8	1 ELEC	M.L.F.							
	Cut telephone cable				.080		4.12		4.12	5.10	6.35
	Splice and insulate telephone cable				.471	7.60	24.50		32.10	38.50	47
	Total				.551	7.60	28.62		36.22	**43.60**	**53.35**
0020	**Replace telephone cable , #22-4 conductor**	50	2 ELEC	M.L.F.							
	Turn power off, later turn on				.100		5.15		5.15	6.35	7.95
	Remove & reinstall cover plates				1.290		66.50		66.50	82	103
	Remove telephone cable				2.581		133		133	164	206
	Telephone twisted, #22-4 conductor				10.000	142	515		657	795	975
	Total				13.971	142	719.65		861.65	**1,047.35**	**1,291.95**
1020	**Replace telephone jack**	20	1 ELEC	Ea.							
	Remove telephone jack				.059		3.05		3.05	3.77	4.72
	Telephone jack				.250	4.80	12.90		17.70	21	26
	Total				.309	4.80	15.95		20.75	**24.77**	**30.72**

D5033 410 Master Clock Control

	System Description	Freq. (Years)	Crew	Unit	Labor Hours	2012 Bare Costs Material	Labor	Equipment	Total	Total In-House	Total w/O&P
0010	**Maintenance and repair**	10	1 ELEC	Ea.							
	Remove time control clock motor				.296		15.25		15.25	18.85	23.50
	Time control clock motor				1.000	55.50	51.50		107	125	149
	Total				1.296	55.50	66.75		122.25	**143.85**	**172.50**
0020	**Check operation**	1	1 ELEC	Ea.							
	Check time control clock operation				.533		27.50		27.50	34	42.50
	Total				.533		27.50		27.50	**34**	**42.50**
0030	**Replace time control clock**	15	1 ELEC	Ea.							
	Remove time control clock				.296		15.25		15.25	18.85	23.50
	Time control clock				1.333	139	68.50		207.50	238	280
	Total				1.630	139	83.75		222.75	**256.85**	**303.50**

D5033 410 Master Clock Control

System Description	Freq. (Years)	Crew	Unit	Labor Hours	2012 Bare Costs				Total In-House	Total w/O&P
					Material	Labor	Equipment	Total		
1120 Maintenance and inspection										
Check operation of program bell	1	2 ELEC	Ea.	.320		16.50		16.50	20.50	25.50
Total				.320		16.50		16.50	**20.50**	**25.50**
1130 Replace program bell										
Remove program bell	15	2 ELEC	Ea.	.667		34.50		34.50	42.50	53
Program bell				1.000	85	51.50		136.50	157	186
Total				1.667	85	86		171	**199.50**	**239**

D5033 510 TV Cable Outlet

System Description	Freq. (Years)	Crew	Unit	Labor Hours	2012 Bare Costs				Total In-House	Total w/O&P
					Material	Labor	Equipment	Total		
0010 Maintenance and repair										
Repair TV cable outlet (cover)	10	1 ELEC	Ea.	.615	2.75	31.50		34.25	42	52.50
Total				.615	2.75	31.50		34.25	**42**	**52.50**
0020 Replace TV cable outlet										
Remove TV cable outlet	20	1 ELEC	Ea.	.200		10.30		10.30	12.75	15.95
TV cable outlet				.615	15.30	31.50		46.80	56	68
Total				.815	15.30	41.80		57.10	**68.75**	**83.95**

D5033 610 Door Bell

System Description	Freq. (Years)	Crew	Unit	Labor Hours	2012 Bare Costs				Total In-House	Total w/O&P
					Material	Labor	Equipment	Total		
0010 Maintenance and repair										
Remove door bell transformer	10	1 ELEC	Ea.	.200		10.30		10.30	12.75	15.95
Door bell transformer				.667	24	34.50		58.50	69	83
Total				.867	24	44.80		68.80	**81.75**	**98.95**
0020 Maintenance and inspection										
Check operation of door bell	1	1 ELEC	Ea.	.320		16.50		16.50	20.50	25.50
Total				.320		16.50		16.50	**20.50**	**25.50**

D50 ELECTRICAL — D5033 — Communications and Security

D5033 610 | Door Bell

	System Description	Freq. (Years)	Crew	Unit	Labor Hours	2012 Bare Costs Material	2012 Bare Costs Labor	2012 Bare Costs Equipment	2012 Bare Costs Total	Total In-House	Total w/O&P
0030	**Replace door bell**	15	1 ELEC	Ea.							
	Remove door bell system				.667		34.50		34.50	42.50	53
	Door bell system				2.667	112	137		249	293	350
	Total				3.333	112	171.50		283.50	335.50	403

D5033 620 | Sound System Components

	System Description	Freq. (Years)	Crew	Unit	Labor Hours	2012 Bare Costs Material	2012 Bare Costs Labor	2012 Bare Costs Equipment	2012 Bare Costs Total	Total In-House	Total w/O&P
0030	**Replace speaker**	20	1 ELEC	Ea.							
	Turn power off, later turn on				.100		5.15		5.15	6.35	7.95
	Remove speaker				.333		17.20		17.20	21	26.50
	Speaker				1.000	115	51.50		166.50	190	223
	Test for operation				.015		.75		.75	.93	1.16
	Total				1.448	115	74.60		189.60	218.28	258.61
0120	**Inspect monitor panel**	0.50	1 ELEC	Ea.							
	Check monitor panel				.533		27.50		27.50	34	42.50
	Total				.533		27.50		27.50	34	42.50
0130	**Replace monitor panel**	15	1 ELEC	Ea.							
	Turn power off, later turn on				.100		5.15		5.15	6.35	7.95
	Remove monitor panel				1.667		86		86	105	133
	Monitor panel				2.000	380	103		483	545	635
	Test circuits				.073		3.75		3.75	4.63	5.80
	Total				3.839	380	197.90		577.90	660.98	781.75
0220	**Inspect volume control**	1	1 ELEC	Ea.							
	Check operation of volume control				.320		16.50		16.50	20.50	25.50
	Total				.320		16.50		16.50	20.50	25.50
0230	**Replace volume control**	15	2 ELEC	Ea.							
	Remove volume control				.333		17.20		17.20	21	26.50
	Volume control				1.000	86	51.50		137.50	158	187
	Total				1.333	86	68.70		154.70	179	213.50

D5033 620 Sound System Components

System Description	Freq. (Years)	Crew	Unit	Labor Hours	2012 Bare Costs				Total In-House	Total w/O&P
					Material	Labor	Equipment	Total		
0330 Replace amplifier	15	2 ELEC	Ea.							
Turn power off, later turn on				.100		5.15		5.15	6.35	7.95
Remove amplifier				1.667		86		86	105	133
Amplifier				8.000	1,225	410		1,635	1,850	2,175
Test for operation				.015		.75		.75	.93	1.16
Total				9.781	1,225	501.90		1,726.90	1,962.28	2,317.11

D5033 630 Intercom System Components

System Description	Freq. (Years)	Crew	Unit	Labor Hours	2012 Bare Costs				Total In-House	Total w/O&P
					Material	Labor	Equipment	Total		
0120 Inspect intercom master station	0.50	1 ELEC	Ea.							
Check intercom master station				2.133		110		110	136	170
Total				2.133		110		110	136	170
0130 Replace intercom master station	15	2 ELEC	Ea.							
Turn power off, later turn on				.100		5.15		5.15	6.35	7.95
Remove intercom master station				1.333		68.50		68.50	85	106
Intercom master station				8.000	2,250	410		2,660	2,975	3,450
Test circuits				.073		3.75		3.75	4.63	5.80
Total				9.506	2,250	487.40		2,737.40	3,070.98	3,569.75
0220 Inspect intercom remote station	1	1 ELEC	Ea.							
Check operation of intercom remote station				.320		16.50		16.50	20.50	25.50
Total				.320		16.50		16.50	20.50	25.50
0230 Replace intercom remote station	15	1 ELEC	Ea.							
Remove intercom remote station				.333		17.20		17.20	21	26.50
Intercom remote station				1.000	159	51.50		210.50	239	278
Total				1.333	159	68.70		227.70	260	304.50

D5033 640 Security System Components

	System Description	Freq. (Years)	Crew	Unit	Labor Hours	Material	Labor	Equipment	Total	Total In-House	Total w/O&P
							2012 Bare Costs				
0020	**Inspect camera and monitor**	0.50	1 ELEC	Ea.							
	Check camera and monitor				.808		41.67		41.67	51.50	64.50
	Total				.808		41.67		41.67	**51.50**	**64.50**
0030	**Replace camera and monitor**	12	2 ELEC	Ea.							
	Turn power off, later turn on				.100		5.15		5.15	6.35	7.95
	Remove closed circuit TV, one camera & one monitor				2.051		106		106	131	163
	Closed circuit TV, one camera & one monitor				6.154	1,300	315		1,615	1,825	2,125
	Test for operation				.015		.75		.75	.93	1.16
	Total				8.320	1,300	426.90		1,726.90	**1,963.28**	**2,297.11**
0120	**Inspect camera**	0.50	1 ELEC	Ea.							
	Check camera				.533		27.50		27.50	34	42.50
	Total				.533		27.50		27.50	**34**	**42.50**
0130	**Replace camera**	12	1 ELEC	Ea.							
	Turn power off, later turn on				.100		5.15		5.15	6.35	7.95
	Remove closed circuit TV, one camera				1.000		51.50		51.50	63.50	79.50
	Closed circuit TV, one camera				2.963	735	153		888	995	1,150
	Test for operation				.015		.75		.75	.93	1.16
	Total				4.078	735	210.40		945.40	**1,065.78**	**1,238.61**

D5033 710 Smoke Detector

	System Description	Freq. (Years)	Crew	Unit	Labor Hours	Material	Labor	Equipment	Total	Total In-House	Total w/O&P
							2012 Bare Costs				
0010	**Repair smoke detector**	10	1 ELEC	Ea.							
	Remove smoke detector lamp				.151		7.80		7.80	9.60	12
	Smoke detector lamp				.444	3.75	23		26.75	32.50	40
	Total				.595	3.75	30.80		34.55	**42.10**	**52**
0020	**Check operation**	1	1 ELEC	Ea.							
	Check smoke detector operation				.200		10.30		10.30	12.75	15.95
	Total				.200		10.30		10.30	**12.75**	**15.95**

D5033 710 Smoke Detector

System Description	Freq. (Years)	Crew	Unit	Labor Hours	2012 Bare Costs Material	Labor	Equipment	Total	Total In-House	Total w/O&P
0030 Replace smoke detector	15	1 ELEC	Ea.							
Turn power off, later turn on				.100		5.15		5.15	6.35	7.95
Remove smoke detector				.348		17.95		17.95	22	27.50
Smoke detector, ceiling type				1.290	127	66.50		193.50	222	262
Test for operation				.015		.75		.75	.93	1.16
Total				1.753	127	90.35		217.35	251.28	298.61

D5033 712 Heat Detector

System Description	Freq. (Years)	Crew	Unit	Labor Hours	2012 Bare Costs Material	Labor	Equipment	Total	Total In-House	Total w/O&P
0010 Repair heat detector	10	1 ELEC	Ea.							
Remove heat detector element				.151		7.80		7.80	9.60	12
Heat detector element				.444	8.40	23		31.40	37.50	46
Total				.595	8.40	30.80		39.20	47.10	58
0020 Check operation	1	1 ELEC	Ea.							
Check heat detector operation				.200		10.30		10.30	12.75	15.95
Total				.200		10.30		10.30	12.75	15.95
0030 Replace heat detector	15	1 ELEC	Ea.							
Turn power off, later turn on				.100		5.15		5.15	6.35	7.95
Remove heat detector				.348		17.95		17.95	22	27.50
Heat detector				1.000	49.50	51.50		101	118	141
Test for operation				.015		.75		.75	.93	1.16
Total				1.462	49.50	75.35		124.85	147.28	177.61

D5033 720 Manual Pull Station

System Description	Freq. (Years)	Crew	Unit	Labor Hours	2012 Bare Costs Material	Labor	Equipment	Total	Total In-House	Total w/O&P
0010 Check and repair manual pull station	10	1 ELEC	Ea.							
Remove pull station component				.200		10.30		10.30	12.75	15.95
Manual pull station component				.667	13.40	34.50		47.90	57	70
Total				.867	13.40	44.80		58.20	69.75	85.95

D5033 720 Manual Pull Station

System Description	Freq. (Years)	Crew	Unit	Labor Hours	2012 Bare Costs				Total In-House	Total w/O&P
					Material	Labor	Equipment	Total		
0020 Replace manual pull station	15	1 ELEC	Ea.							
Turn power off, later turn on				.100		5.15		5.15	6.35	7.95
Remove manual pull station				.348		17.95		17.95	22	27.50
Manual pull station				1.000	81	51.50		132.50	153	181
Test for operation				.015		.75		.75	.93	1.16
Total				1.462	81	75.35		156.35	182.28	217.61

D5033 760 Fire Alarm Control Panel

System Description	Freq. (Years)	Crew	Unit	Labor Hours	2012 Bare Costs				Total In-House	Total w/O&P
					Material	Labor	Equipment	Total		
0010 Minor repairs to fire alarm	5	1 ELEC	Ea.							
Check and test components				.400		20.50		20.50	25.50	32
Remove relay				.222		11.45		11.45	14.15	17.70
Relay				.667	41	34.50		75.50	87.50	104
Total				1.289	41	66.45		107.45	127.15	153.70
0020 Maintenance and inspection	0.50	1 ELEC	Ea.							
Check control panel				.533		27.50		27.50	34	42.50
Total				.533		27.50		27.50	34	42.50
0030 Replace fire alarm panel	15	1 ELEC	Ea.							
Turn power off, later turn on				.100		5.15		5.15	6.35	7.95
Remove fire alarm control panel				2.000		103		103	127	159
Fire alarm control panel				16.000	760	825		1,585	1,850	2,225
Test circuits				.073		3.75		3.75	4.63	5.80
Total				18.173	760	936.90		1,696.90	1,987.98	2,397.75

D5033 766 Annunciation Panel

System Description	Freq. (Years)	Crew	Unit	Labor Hours	2012 Bare Costs				Total In-House	Total w/O&P
					Material	Labor	Equipment	Total		
0010 Minor repairs to annunciation panel	5	1 ELEC	Ea.							
Check and test components				.400		20.50		20.50	25.50	32
Remove relay				.222		11.45		11.45	14.15	17.70
Relay				.667	41	34.50		75.50	87.50	104
Total				1.289	41	66.45		107.45	**127.15**	**153.70**
0020 Maintenance and inspection	0.50	1 ELEC	Ea.							
Check annunciator panel				.533		27.50		27.50	34	42.50
Total				.533		27.50		27.50	**34**	**42.50**
0030 Replace annunciation panel	15	1 ELEC	Ea.							
Turn power off, later turn on				.100		5.15		5.15	6.35	7.95
Remove annunciation panel				1.600		82.50		82.50	102	127
Annunciation panel				6.154	325	315		640	750	895
Test circuits				.073		3.75		3.75	4.63	5.80
Total				7.927	325	406.40		731.40	**862.98**	**1,035.75**

D5033 770 Fire Alarm Bell

System Description	Freq. (Years)	Crew	Unit	Labor Hours	2012 Bare Costs				Total In-House	Total w/O&P
					Material	Labor	Equipment	Total		
0010 Replace fire alarm bell, 6"	20	1 ELEC	Ea.							
Turn power off, later turn on				.100		5.15		5.15	6.35	7.95
Remove fire alarm bell				.348		17.95		17.95	22	27.50
Fire alarm bell				1.000	71	51.50		122.50	142	168
Test for operation				.015		.75		.75	.93	1.16
Total				1.462	71	75.35		146.35	**171.28**	**204.61**

D5093 110 Electrical Service Ground

	System Description	Freq. (Years)	Crew	Unit	Labor Hours	Material	Labor	Equipment	Total	Total In-House	Total w/O&P
						2012 Bare Costs					
0010	**Maintenance and repair**	25	1 ELEC	M.L.F.							
	Repair service ground (1 termination)				1.053	6.60	54.50		61.10	74.50	92.50
	Total				1.053	6.60	54.50		61.10	74.50	92.50
0020	**Replace electrical service ground**	50	1 ELEC	M.L.F.							
	Remove ground wire #6				2.000		103		103	128	160
	Excavate hole for ground rod				2.222		114.50		114.50	142	177
	Ground rod 5/8", 10'				17.391	230	895		1,125	1,350	1,675
	Ground clamp				2.500	66	129		195	230	282
	Backfill over top of ground rod				1.053		54.50		54.50	67	84
	Insulated copper wire #6				12.308	575	635		1,210	1,425	1,700
	Total				37.474	871	1,931		2,802	3,342	4,078

D5093 120 Building Structure Ground

	System Description	Freq. (Years)	Crew	Unit	Labor Hours	Material	Labor	Equipment	Total	Total In-House	Total w/O&P
						2012 Bare Costs					
0010	**Maintenance and repair**	7	1 ELEC	M.L.F.							
	Repair bldg structure ground (1 termination)				1.053	6.60	54.50		61.10	74.50	92.50
	Total				1.053	6.60	54.50		61.10	74.50	92.50
0020	**Replace building structure ground**	50	1 ELEC	M.L.F.							
	Remove ground wire #4				3.077		158.50		158.50	196	245
	Excavate hole for ground rod				2.222		114.50		114.50	142	177
	Ground rod 5/8", 10'				17.391	230	895		1,125	1,350	1,675
	Ground clamp				2.500	66	129		195	230	282
	Backfill over top of ground rod				1.053		54.50		54.50	67	84
	Insulated copper wire #4				15.094	900	780		1,680	1,950	2,325
	Total				41.337	1,196	2,131.50		3,327.50	3,935	4,788

D5093 130 Lightning Protection System

	System Description	Freq. (Years)	Crew	Unit	Labor Hours	2012 Bare Costs Material	2012 Bare Costs Labor	2012 Bare Costs Equipment	2012 Bare Costs Total	Total In-House	Total w/O&P
1010	**Maintenance and repair of general wiring**	1	1 ELEC	M.L.F.							
	Repair lightning protection (1 termination)				1.053	12.10	54.50		66.60	80.50	99
	Total				1.053	12.10	54.50		66.60	80.50	99
1020	**Replace lightning protection general wiring**	25	2 ELEC	M.L.F.							
	Remove lightning protection cable				4.000		206		206	255	320
	Excavate hole for ground rod				2.222		114.50		114.50	142	177
	Ground rod 5/8", 10'				17.391	230	895		1,125	1,350	1,675
	Ground clamp				2.500	66	129		195	230	282
	Backfill over top of ground rod				1.053		54.50		54.50	67	84
	Lightning protection cable				25.000	3,540	1,290		4,830	5,500	6,425
	Air terminals, copper 3/8" x 10"				10.000	290	515		805	955	1,150
	Total				62.166	4,126	3,204		7,330	8,499	10,113

D5093 140 Lightning Ground Rod

	System Description	Freq. (Years)	Crew	Unit	Labor Hours	2012 Bare Costs Material	2012 Bare Costs Labor	2012 Bare Costs Equipment	2012 Bare Costs Total	Total In-House	Total w/O&P
1010	**Maintenance and repair**	1	1 ELEC	Ea.							
	Repair ground rod connector				1.053	6.60	54.50		61.10	74.50	92.50
	Total				1.053	6.60	54.50		61.10	74.50	92.50
1020	**Replace lightning ground rod**	25	2 ELEC	Ea.							
	Excavate hole for ground rod				.333		17.20		17.20	21	26.50
	Ground rod 5/8", 10'				1.739	23	89.50		112.50	136	168
	Ground clamp				.250	6.60	12.90		19.50	23	28
	Backfill over top of ground rod				.157		8.10		8.10	10	12.50
	Total				2.479	29.60	127.70		157.30	190	235

D5093 150 Computer Ground System

	System Description	Freq. (Years)	Crew	Unit	Labor Hours	2012 Bare Costs Material	2012 Bare Costs Labor	2012 Bare Costs Equipment	2012 Bare Costs Total	Total In-House	Total w/O&P
0010	**Maintenance and repair**	4	1 ELEC	Ea.							
	Test bonding each connection				.267		13.75		13.75	16.95	21
	Total				.267		13.75		13.75	16.95	21

D5093 150 Computer Ground System

	System Description	Freq. (Years)	Crew	Unit	Labor Hours	2012 Bare Costs				Total In-House	Total w/O&P
						Material	Labor	Equipment	Total		
0020	**Replace computer ground system**	50	1 ELEC	M.L.F.							
	Remove ground wire #6				2.000		103		103	128	160
	Insulated ground wire #6				12.308	575	635		1,210	1,425	1,700
	Grounding connection				2.500	66	129		195	230	282
	Total				16.808	641	867		1,508	1,783	2,142

D5093 190 Special Ground System

	System Description	Freq. (Years)	Crew	Unit	Labor Hours	2012 Bare Costs				Total In-House	Total w/O&P
						Material	Labor	Equipment	Total		
0010	**Maintenance and repair**	4	1 ELEC	Ea.							
	Test bonding each connection				.267		13.75		13.75	16.95	21
	Total				.267		13.75		13.75	16.95	21
0020	**Replace special ground system**	50	2 ELEC	M.L.F.							
	Remove ground wire #6				2.000		103		103	128	160
	Insulated ground wire #6				12.308	575	635		1,210	1,425	1,700
	Grounding connection				2.500	66	129		195	230	282
	Total				16.808	641	867		1,508	1,783	2,142

D5093 210 Generator, Gasoline, 175 KW

	System Description	Freq. (Years)	Crew	Unit	Labor Hours	2012 Bare Costs				Total In-House	Total w/O&P
						Material	Labor	Equipment	Total		
0010	**Maintenance and inspection**	0.08	1 ELEC	Ea.							
	Run test gasoline generator				.800		41		41	51	63.50
	Total				.800		41		41	51	63.50
0020	**Replace generator component**	25	2 ELEC	Ea.							
	Remove gasoline generator				36.364		1,875		1,875	2,325	2,900
	Gasoline generator, 175 KW				106.000	83,000	5,500		88,500	98,000	112,500
	Total				142.364	83,000	7,375		90,375	100,325	115,400

D5093 220   Generator, Diesel, 750 KW

	System Description	Freq. (Years)	Crew	Unit	Labor Hours	2012 Bare Costs				Total In-House	Total w/O&P
						Material	Labor	Equipment	Total		
0010	**Maintenance and inspection**	0.08	1 ELEC	Ea.							
	Run test diesel generator				.800		41		41	51	63.50
	Total				.800		41		41	**51**	**63.50**
0020	**Replace diesel generator component**	25	4 ELEC	Ea.							
	Remove diesel generator				57.143		2,950		2,950	3,625	4,550
	Diesel generator, 750 KW				160.000	194,000	8,250		202,250	223,500	255,000
	Total				217.143	194,000	11,200		205,200	**227,125**	**259,550**

D5093 230   Transfer Switch

	System Description	Freq. (Years)	Crew	Unit	Labor Hours	2012 Bare Costs				Total In-House	Total w/O&P
						Material	Labor	Equipment	Total		
0010	**Maintenance and repair**	5	1 ELEC	Ea.							
	Remove transfer switch coil				.667		34.50		34.50	42.50	53
	Transfer switch coil				2.000	86.50	103		189.50	222	267
	Total				2.667	86.50	137.50		224	**264.50**	**320**
0020	**Maintenance and inspection**	0.50	1 ELEC	Ea.							
	Inspect and clean transfer switch				.500		26		26	32	40
	Total				.500		26		26	**32**	**40**
0030	**Replace transfer switch**	18	1 ELEC	Ea.							
	Remove transfer switch				.667		34.50		34.50	42.50	53
	Transfer switch, 480 V, 3 P, 30 A				3.478	2,575	179		2,754	3,050	3,500
	Cut, form, align & connect wires				.151		7.80		7.80	9.60	12
	Check operation of switch				.018		.94		.94	1.17	1.46
	Total				4.314	2,575	222.24		2,797.24	**3,103.27**	**3,566.46**

D5093 240   Emergency Lighting Fixture

	System Description	Freq. (Years)	Crew	Unit	Labor Hours	Material	Labor	Equipment	Total	Total In-House	Total w/O&P
						2012 Bare Costs					
0020	**Replace lamp**	2	1 ELEC	Ea.							
	Remove emergency remote lamp				.100		5.15		5.15	6.35	7.95
	Emergency remote lamp				.296	26	15.25		41.25	47.50	56
	Total				.396	26	20.40		46.40	53.85	63.95
0030	**Replace fixture**	20	1 ELEC	Ea.							
	Turn branch circuit off and on				.018		.94		.94	1.17	1.46
	Remove emergency light units				.667		34.50		34.50	42.50	53
	Emergency light units, battery operated				2.000	560	103		663	745	860
	Total				2.685	560	138.44		698.44	788.67	914.46

D5093 250   Exit Light

	System Description	Freq. (Years)	Crew	Unit	Labor Hours	Material	Labor	Equipment	Total	Total In-House	Total w/O&P
						2012 Bare Costs					
0010	**Maintenance and repair**	20	1 ELEC	Ea.							
	Remove exit light face plate				.100		5.15		5.15	6.35	7.95
	Exit light face plate				.296	17	15.25		32.25	37.50	45
	Total				.396	17	20.40		37.40	43.85	52.95
0020	**Replace lamp**	5	1 ELEC	Ea.							
	Remove exit light lamp				.022		1.13		1.13	1.40	1.75
	Exit light lamp				.065	8.75	3.35		12.10	13.75	16.15
	Total				.087	8.75	4.48		13.23	15.15	17.90
0030	**Replace lighting fixture**	20	1 ELEC	Ea.							
	Turn circuit off and on for fixture				.018		.94		.94	1.17	1.46
	Remove exit light				.333		17.20		17.20	21	26.50
	Exit light				1.000	38	51.50		89.50	105	127
	Total				1.352	38	69.64		107.64	127.17	154.96

D5093 255   Exit Light L.E.D.

System Description	Freq. (Years)	Crew	Unit	Labor Hours	2012 Bare Costs				Total In-House	Total w/O&P
					Material	Labor	Equipment	Total		
0020 Replace lamp with exit light L.E.D. retrofit kits	15	1 ELEC	Ea.							
Remove exit light lamp				.022		1.13		1.13	1.40	1.75
Exit light L.E.D. retrofit kits				.133	49.50	6.85		56.35	63	72.50
Total				.155	49.50	7.98		57.48	**64.40**	**74.25**
0030 Replace lighting fixture with exit light L.E.D. std.	20	1 ELEC	Ea.							
Turn circuit off and on for fixture				.018		.94		.94	1.17	1.46
Remove exit light				.333		17.20		17.20	21	26.50
Exit light, L.E.D. standard, double face				1.194	74.50	61.50		136	158	188
Total				1.546	74.50	79.64		154.14	**180.17**	**215.96**
0040 Replace lighting fixture with exit light L.E.D. w/battery unit	20	1 ELEC	Ea.							
Turn circuit off and on for fixture				.018		.94		.94	1.17	1.46
Remove exit light				.333		17.20		17.20	21	26.50
Exit light, L.E.D. with battery unit, double face				2.000	130	103		233	270	320
Total				2.352	130	121.14		251.14	**292.17**	**347.96**

D5093 260   Battery, Wet

System Description	Freq. (Years)	Crew	Unit	Labor Hours	2012 Bare Costs				Total In-House	Total w/O&P
					Material	Labor	Equipment	Total		
0010 Maintenance and inspection	0.02	1 ELEC	Ea.							
Clean & maintain wet cell battery				.500		26		26	32	40
Total				.500		26		26	**32**	**40**
0020 Replace battery	10	1 ELEC	Ea.							
Remove wet cell battery				.100		5.15		5.15	6.35	7.95
Wet cell battery				.296	355	15.25		370.25	410	465
Total				.396	355	20.40		375.40	**416.35**	**472.95**

D50 ELECTRICAL | D5093 | Other Electrical Systems

D5093 265 | Battery, Dry

	System Description	Freq. (Years)	Crew	Unit	Labor Hours	2012 Bare Costs				Total In-House	Total w/O&P
						Material	Labor	Equipment	Total		
0010	**Maintenance and inspection**	0.08	1 ELEC	Ea.							
	Clean & maintain dry cell battery				.500		26		26	32	40
	Total				.500		26		26	**32**	**40**
0020	**Replace battery**	5	1 ELEC	Ea.							
	Remove dry cell battery				.100		5.15		5.15	6.35	7.95
	Dry cell battery				.296	182	15.25		197.25	219	251
	Total				.396	182	20.40		202.40	**225.35**	**258.95**

D5093 270 | Battery Charger

	System Description	Freq. (Years)	Crew	Unit	Labor Hours	2012 Bare Costs				Total In-House	Total w/O&P
						Material	Labor	Equipment	Total		
0010	**Maintenance and repair**	2	1 ELEC	Ea.							
	Repair battery charger component				3.077	44.50	159		203.50	245	300
	Total				3.077	44.50	159		203.50	**245**	**300**
0020	**Maintenance and inspection**	0.25	1 ELEC	Ea.							
	Check battery charger				1.600		82.50		82.50	102	127
	Total				1.600		82.50		82.50	**102**	**127**
0030	**Replace charger**	20	1 ELEC	Ea.							
	Remove battery charger				.615		31.50		31.50	39	49
	Battery charger				1.600	850	82.50		932.50	1,025	1,200
	Total				2.215	850	114		964	**1,064**	**1,249**

D5093 280 | UPS Battery

	System Description	Freq. (Years)	Crew	Unit	Labor Hours	2012 Bare Costs				Total In-House	Total w/O&P
						Material	Labor	Equipment	Total		
0020	**Maintenance and inspection**	0.17	1 ELEC	Ea.							
	UPS battery electrical test				.800		41		41	51	63.50
	Total				.800		41		41	**51**	**63.50**

D5093 280 UPS Battery

	System Description	Freq. (Years)	Crew	Unit	Labor Hours	2012 Bare Costs				Total In-House	Total w/O&P
						Material	Labor	Equipment	Total		
0030	Replace motor generator UPS battery	15	1 ELEC	Ea.							
	Remove UPS battery				1.333		68.50		68.50	85	106
	UPS battery				4.000	269	206		475	550	655
	Total				5.333	269	274.50		543.50	635	761

D5093 920 Communications Components

	System Description	Freq. (Years)	Crew	Unit	Labor Hours	2012 Bare Costs				Total In-House	Total w/O&P
						Material	Labor	Equipment	Total		
0020	Maintenance and repair	10	1 ELEC	Ea.							
	Repair voice/data outlet				.615	2.75	31.50		34.25	42	52.50
	Total				.615	2.75	31.50		34.25	42	52.50
0030	Replace voice/data outlet	20	1 ELEC	Ea.							
	Remove voice/data outlet				.057		2.95		2.95	3.64	4.55
	Voice/data outlet, single opening, excludes voice/data device				.167	7.50	8.60		16.10	18.85	22.50
	Total				.224	7.50	11.55		19.05	22.49	27.05
0120	Maintenance and inspection	0.50	1 ELEC	Ea.							
	Check patch panel				1.067		55		55	68	85
	Total				1.067		55		55	68	85
0130	Replace patch panel	15	1 ELEC	Ea.							
	Remove patch panel				1.010		52.27		52.27	65	80.50
	Patch panel				4.000	370	206		576	660	785
	Test circuits				.996		51.37		51.37	63.50	79.50
	Total				6.006	370	309.64		679.64	788.50	945

E1023 710   Laboratory Equipment

	System Description	Freq. (Years)	Crew	Unit	Labor Hours	2012 Bare Costs				Total In-House	Total w/O&P
						Material	Labor	Equipment	Total		
0020	**Replace glove box gloves**	5	1 SKWK	Ea.							
	Laboratory equipment, remove bacteriological glove box gloves				.500		22.50		22.50	30	37
	Lab equipment, replace fiberglass, bacteriological glove box gloves				1.000	145	45.50		190.50	219	255
	Laboratory equipment, test replacement gloves				1.000		45.50		45.50	60	74
	Total				2.500	145	113.50		258.50	309	366
0080	**Replace fume hood sash**	20	2 SKWK	Ea.							
	Laboratory equipment, remove fume hood sash				1.000		45.50		45.50	60	74
	Laboratory equipment, replace fume hood sash				2.000	800	91		891	1,000	1,150
	Total				3.000	800	136.50		936.50	1,060	1,224

E1033 110 Automotive Equipment

	System Description	Freq. (Years)	Crew	Unit	Labor Hours	2012 Bare Costs				Total In-House	Total w/O&P
						Material	Labor	Equipment	Total		
0020	**Remove and replace vehicle lift hydraulic pump**	15	1 SKWK	Ea.							
	Automotive hoist, two posts, adj. frame, remove and replace pump				4.000	3,000	182		3,182	3,550	4,050
	Total				4.000	3,000	182		3,182	3,550	4,050
0100	**Remove and replace compressor, electric, 5 H.P.**	10	1 ELEC	Ea.							
	Automotive compressors, remove and replace 5 H.P. motor				2.000	720	103		823	920	1,050
	Total				2.000	720	103		823	920	1,050

E1093 310 Loading Dock Equipment

System Description	Freq. (Years)	Crew	Unit	Labor Hours	2012 Bare Costs				Total In-House	Total w/O&P
					Material	Labor	Equipment	Total		
0020 **Remove and replace hydraulic dock leveler lift cylinder**	15	2 SKWK	Ea.							
Loading dock, dock levelers, 10 ton cap., replace lift cylinder				4.000	5,750	182		5,932	6,575	7,475
Total				4.000	5,750	182		5,932	6,575	7,475
0040 **Remove and replace hydraulic dock leveler hydraulic pump**	20	1 SKWK	Ea.							
Loading dock, dock levelers, 10 ton cap., replace lift cylinder				3.077	1,325	140		1,465	1,650	1,875
Total				3.077	1,325	140		1,465	1,650	1,875

E1093 315 Dishwasher

System Description	Freq. (Years)	Crew	Unit	Labor Hours	2012 Bare Costs				Total In-House	Total w/O&P
					Material	Labor	Equipment	Total		
0020 **Replace commercial dishwasher, 10 to 12 racks per hour**	10	2 PLUM	Ea.							
Cleaning and disposal, dishwasher, commercial, rack type				12.000		645		645	800	1,000
Install new dishwasher				6.499	4,300	320		4,620	5,125	5,875
Total				18.499	4,300	965		5,265	5,925	6,875
0040 **Remove and replace dishwasher pump**	15	1 PLUM	Ea.							
Laboratory equip., glassware washer, remove and replace pump				1.778	710	97		807	900	1,050
Total				1.778	710	97		807	900	1,050
0080 **Replace commercial dishwasher, to 375 racks per hour**	20	L-4	Ea.							
Commercial dishwasher, to 275 racks per hour, selective demo				76.000		995		995	1,300	1,625
Dishwasher, automatic, 235 to 275 racks/hr.				24.000	31,900	3,225		35,125	39,100	44,900
				60.000						
Total				84.000	31,900	4,220		36,120	40,400	46,525

E1093 316 Waste Disposal, Residential

System Description	Freq. (Years)	Crew	Unit	Labor Hours	2012 Bare Costs				Total In-House	Total w/O&P
					Material	Labor	Equipment	Total		
0010 **Unstop disposal**	1	1 PLUM	Ea.							
Unstop clogged unit				.889		48.50		48.50	60.50	75.50
Total				.889		48.50		48.50	60.50	75.50

E1093 316 Waste Disposal, Residential

	System Description	Freq. (Years)	Crew	Unit	Labor Hours	2012 Bare Costs				Total In-House	Total w/O&P
						Material	Labor	Equipment	Total		
0020	Replace waste disposal unit, residential	8	1 PLUM	Ea.							
	Remove unit				1.040		55		55	68.50	85.50
	Install new disposal				2.080	197	110		307	355	415
	Total				3.120	197	165		362	423.50	500.50

E1093 320 Waste Handling Equipment

	System Description	Freq. (Years)	Crew	Unit	Labor Hours	2012 Bare Costs				Total In-House	Total w/O&P
						Material	Labor	Equipment	Total		
0020	Remove and replace waste compactor hydraulic cylinder	15	2 SKWK	Ea.							
	Replace ram, 5 C.Y. capacity				4.000	3,775	182		3,957	4,400	5,025
	Total				4.000	3,775	182		3,957	4,400	5,025
0040	Remove and replace waste compactor hydraulic pump	20	1 SKWK	Ea.							
	Replace hydraulic pump, 5 C.Y. capacity				3.200	755	145		900	1,025	1,175
	Total				3.200	755	145		900	1,025	1,175

E1093 510 Darkroom Dryer

	System Description	Freq. (Years)	Crew	Unit	Labor Hours	2012 Bare Costs				Total In-House	Total w/O&P
						Material	Labor	Equipment	Total		
0020	Remove and replace darkroom dryer fan	10	1 SKWK	Ea.							
	48″ x 25″ x 68″ high				1.600	166	72.50		238.50	278	325
	Total				1.600	166	72.50		238.50	278	325
0040	Remove and replace darkroom dryer heating element	15	1 SKWK	Ea.							
	Darkroom equip., dryers, dehumidifier, replace compressor				1.333	85	60.50		145.50	173	205
	Total				1.333	85	60.50		145.50	173	205

E1093 610 | Dust Collector

	System Description	Freq. (Years)	Crew	Unit	Labor Hours	2012 Bare Costs				Total In-House	Total w/O&P
						Material	Labor	Equipment	Total		
0100	Remove and replace 20" dia dust collector bag	5	1 SKWK	Ea.							
	Dust collector bag, 20" diameter				1.600	405	83.50		488.50	550	635
	Total				1.600	405	83.50		488.50	550	635

E1093 910 | Pump Systems

	System Description	Freq. (Years)	Crew	Unit	Labor Hours	2012 Bare Costs				Total In-House	Total w/O&P
						Material	Labor	Equipment	Total		
0500	Remove and replace 50 HP pump motor	25	2 ELEC	Ea.							
	Electrical dml, motors, 230/460 V, 60 Hz, 50 HP				1.667		86		86	106	133
	Install 50 HP motor, 230/460 V, totly encld, 1800 RPM				8.000	2,700	410		3,110	3,475	4,000
	Total				9.667	2,700	496		3,196	3,581	4,133

	System Description	Freq. (Years)	Crew	Unit	Labor Hours	2012 Bare Costs				Total In-House	Total w/O&P
						Material	Labor	Equipment	Total		
1010	**Remove 500 gal. underground storage tank(non-leaking)**	20	B-34P	Ea.							
	Saw cut asphalt				2.700	17	107	72.50	196.50	229	272
	Disconnect and remove piping				1.500		81.90		81.90	102	128
	Transfer liquids, 10% of volume				.250		13.50		13.50	17	21.50
	Insert solid carbon dioxide, 1.5 lbs./100 gal.				.150	7.05	5.25		12.30	14.70	17.45
	Cut accessway to inside of tank				1.501		52.50		52.50	70	86.50
	Remove sludge, wash and wipe tank				1.000		54.50		54.50	68	85
	Properly dispose of sludge/water					30			30	33	37.50
	Excavate, pull, & load tank, backfill hole				16.000		655	335	990	1,175	1,425
	Select structural backfill					172			172	188	215
	Haul tank to certified dump, 100 miles round trip				8.000		360	211	571	665	795
	Total				31.101	226.05	1,329.65	618.50	2,174.20	2,561.70	3,082.95
1020	**Remove 3000 gal. underground storage tank(non-leaking)**	20	B-34R	Ea.							
	Saw cut asphalt				5.400	34	214	145	393	455	545
	Disconnect and remove piping				2.500		136.50		136.50	171	213
	Transfer liquids, 10% of volume				1.500		81		81	102	129
	Insert solid carbon dioxide, 1.5 lbs./100 gal.				.900	42.30	31.50		73.80	88	105
	Cut accessway to inside of tank				1.501		52.50		52.50	70	86.50
	Remove sludge, wash and wipe tank				1.199		65.50		65.50	81.50	102
	Properly dispose of sludge/water					270			270	297	340
	Excavate, pull, & load tank, backfill hole				32.000		1,300	730	2,030	2,425	2,900
	Select structural backfill					645			645	705	805
	Haul tank to certified dump, 100 miles round trip				8.000		360	264	624	720	855
	Total				53.000	991.30	2,241	1,139	4,371.30	5,114.50	6,080.50
1030	**Remove 5000 gal. underground storage tank(non-leaking)**	20	B-34R	Ea.							
	Saw cut asphalt				5.940	37.40	235.40	159.50	432.30	505	600
	Disconnect and remove piping				2.500		136.50		136.50	171	213
	Transfer liquids, 10% of volume				2.500		135		135	170	215
	Insert solid carbon dioxide, 1.5 lbs./100 gal.				1.500	70.50	52.50		123	147	174
	Cut accessway to inside of tank				1.501		52.50		52.50	70	86.50
	Remove sludge, wash and wipe tank				1.301		71		71	88.50	111
	Properly dispose of sludge/water					450			450	495	565
	Excavate, pull, & load tank, backfill hole				32.000		1,300	730	2,030	2,425	2,900
	Select structural backfill					1,075			1,075	1,175	1,350
	Haul tank to certified dump, 100 miles round trip				8.000		360	264	624	720	855
	Total				55.242	1,632.90	2,342.90	1,153.50	5,129.30	5,966.50	7,069.50

	System Description	Freq. (Years)	Crew	Unit	Labor Hours	2012 Bare Costs				Total In-House	Total w/O&P
						Material	Labor	Equipment	Total		
1040	**Remove 8000 gal. underground storage tank(non-leaking)**	20	B-34R	Ea.							
	Saw cut asphalt				6.480	40.80	256.80	174	471.60	550	650
	Disconnect and remove piping				2.500		136.50		136.50	171	213
	Transfer liquids, 10% of volume				4.000		216		216	272	345
	Insert solid carbon cioxide, 1.5 lbs./100 gal.				2.400	112.80	84		196.80	235	279
	Cut accessway to inside of tank				1.501		52.50		52.50	70	86.50
	Remove sludge, wash and wipe tank				1.501		82		82	102	128
	Properly dispose of sludge/water					720			720	790	900
	Excavate, pull, & load tank, backfill hole				32.000		1,325	2,500	3,825	4,225	4,875
	Select structural backfill					1,505			1,505	1,650	1,875
	Haul tank to certified dump, 100 miles round trip				8.000		282	850	1,132	1,225	1,400
	Total				58.382	2,378.60	2,434.80	3,524	8,337.40	9,290	10,751.50
1050	**Remove 10000 gal. ugnd. storage tank(non-leaking)**	20	B-34S	Ea.							
	Saw cut asphalt				10.800	68	428	290	786	915	1,075
	Disconnect and remove piping				3.750		204.75		204.75	256	320
	Transfer liquids, 10% of volume				5.000		270		270	340	430
	Insert solid carbon dioxide, 1.5 lbs./100 gal.				3.000	141	105		246	294	350
	Cut accessway to inside of tank				1.501		52.50		52.50	70	86.50
	Remove sludge, wash and wipe tank				1.751		95.50		95.50	119	149
	Properly dispose of sludge/water					900			900	990	1,125
	Excavate, pull, & load tank, backfill hole				32.000		1,325	2,500	3,825	4,225	4,875
	Select structural backfill					1,935			1,935	2,125	2,425
	Haul tank to certified dump, 100 miles round trip				8.000		282	850	1,132	1,225	1,400
	Total				65.801	3,044	2,762.75	3,640	9,446.75	10,559	12,235.50
1060	**Remove 12000 gal. ugnd. storage tank(non-leaking)**	20	B-34S	Ea.							
	Saw cut asphalt				12.150	76.50	481.50	326.25	884.25	1,025	1,225
	Disconnect and remove piping				5.000		273		273	340	425
	Transfer liquids, 10% of volume				6.000		324		324	410	515
	Insert solid carbon dioxide, 1.5 lbs./100 gal.				3.600	169.20	126		295.20	355	420
	Cut accessway to inside of tank				1.501		52.50		52.50	70	86.50
	Remove sludge, wash and wipe tank				1.900		104		104	130	162
	Properly dispose cf sludge/water					1,080			1,080	1,200	1,350
	Excavate, pull, & load tank, backfill hole				32.000		1,325	2,500	3,825	4,225	4,875
	Select structural backfill					2,150			2,150	2,350	2,700
	Haul tank to certified dump, 100 miles round trip				8.000		282	850	1,132	1,225	1,400
	Total				70.151	3,475.70	2,968	3,676.25	10,119.95	11,330	13,158.50

G2023 210 Parking Lot Repairs

	System Description	Freq. (Years)	Crew	Unit	Labor Hours	2012 Bare Costs				Total In-House	Total w/O&P
						Material	Labor	Equipment	Total		
1010	**Parking lot repair and sealcoating**	5	B-1	M.S.F.							
	Thoroughly clean surface				.312		11.10	2.22	13.32	16.65	21
	Patch holes				.240	21.87	8.51	1.08	31.46	36.50	42.50
	Fill cracks				.715	52.50	25.50	9.50	87.50	101	117
	Install 2 coat petroleum resistant emulsion				3.330	142.08	118.77		260.85	315	375
	Restripe lot				.291	17.60	10.28	3.28	31.16	36	42.50
	Total				4.887	234.05	174.16	16.08	424.29	505.15	598
1020	**Parking lot repair and resurface**	10	B-25B	M.S.F.							
	Thoroughly clean surface				.312		11.10	2.22	13.32	16.65	21
	Patch holes				.240	21.87	8.51	1.08	31.46	36.50	42.50
	Fill cracks				.715	52.50	25.50	9.50	87.50	101	117
	Emulsion tack coat, .05 gal. per S.Y.				.710	41.07	28.86	36.63	106.56	120	138
	Install 1" thick asphaltic concrete wearing course				1.008	370.74	38.85	28.86	438.45	485	560
	Restripe lot				.291	17.60	10.28	3.28	31.16	36	42.50
	Total				3.276	503.78	123.10	81.57	708.45	795.15	921

G2023 310 General

	System Description	Freq. (Years)	Crew	Unit	Labor Hours	2012 Bare Costs				Total In-House	Total w/O&P
						Material	Labor	Equipment	Total		
1000	**Remove and replace steel guard rail**	7	B-80	L.F.							
	Remove old metal guide/guard rail and posts				.213		8.05	4.45	12.50	15	17.95
	Install metal guide/guard rail including posts 6'3"				.107	20	4.04	2.23	26.27	29.50	34
	Total				.320	20	12.09	6.68	38.77	44.50	51.95
1100	**Raise MH or catch basin frame and cover**	10	D-1	Ea.							
	Demolish pavement around frame				4.800		178	21	199	255	310
	Raise MH or catch basin frame with brick				1.332	7.16	52.95		60.11	77	94.50
	Total				6.132	7.16	230.95	21	259.11	332	404.50

G20 SITE IMPROVEMENTS | G2033 | Pedestrian Paving

G2033 130 | Asphalt Sidewalk & Curb

	System Description	Freq. (Years)	Crew	Unit	Labor Hours	2012 Bare Costs				Total In-House	Total w/O&P
						Material	Labor	Equipment	Total		
0100	**Remove & replace asphalt sidewalk, 4' wide**	15	B-37	L.F.							
	Remove existing asphalt pavement				.080		3	1.73	4.73	5.65	6.75
	Bank run gravel, 3" avg.				.002	.76	.09	.19	1.04	1.14	1.30
	Vibratory plate compaction				.003		.09	.01	.10	.13	.16
	Fine grade gravel base				.026		1.06	.99	2.05	2.37	2.80
	Place asphalt sidewalk, 2-1/2" thick				.027	2.32	.99	.08	3.39	3.93	4.60
	Total				.138	3.08	5.23	3	11.31	13.22	15.61
1000	**Remove and replace asphalt curb or berm**	10	B-37	L.F.							
	Demolish existing curb or berm				.096		3.56	.42	3.98	5.10	6.25
	Remove broken curb				.032		1.20	.69	1.89	2.26	2.70
	Asphalt curb, 8" wide, 6" high machine formed				.042	.04	1.48	.36	1.88	2.37	2.88
	Total				.170	.04	6.24	1.47	7.75	9.73	11.83

G2033 140 | Concrete Sidewalk & Curb

	System Description	Freq. (Years)	Crew	Unit	Labor Hours	2012 Bare Costs				Total In-House	Total w/O&P
						Material	Labor	Equipment	Total		
0100	**Remove and replace concrete sidewalk, 4' wide**	25	B-37	L.F.							
	Remove existing concrete pavement				.107		4.01	2.31	6.32	7.55	9.05
	Bank run gravel, 3" avg.				.002	.76	.09	.19	1.04	1.14	1.30
	Vibratory plate compaction				.003		.09	.01	.10	.13	.16
	Fine grade gravel				.026		1.06	.99	2.05	2.37	2.80
	Broom finished concrete sidewalk, 4" thick				.209	6.80	8.44	.99	15.24	18.50	22
	Total				.346	7.56	13.69	3.50	24.75	29.69	35.31
2000	**Remove and replace concrete curb or berm**	25	B-37	L.F.							
	Demolish existing curb or berm				.240		8.90	1.05	9.95	12.75	15.60
	Remove broken curb				.080		3	1.73	4.73	5.65	6.75
	Concrete curb, 6" x 18", steel forms				.091	3.56	3.89		7.45	9.10	10.80
	Total				.411	3.56	15.79	2.78	22.13	27.50	33.15

G2033 150 Patios

	System Description	Freq. (Years)	Crew	Unit	Labor Hours	2012 Bare Costs				Total In-House	Total w/O&P
						Material	Labor	Equipment	Total		
1030	**Refinish Concrete Patio**	3	1 PORD	S.F.							
	Prepare surface				.003		.12	.03	.15	.19	.22
	Paint 1 coat, roller & brush				.008	.07	.31		.38	.48	.59
	Total				.012	.07	.43	.03	.53	**.67**	**.81**
2030	**Refinish Masonry Patio**	3	1 PORD	S.F.							
	Prepare surface				.003		.12	.03	.15	.19	.22
	Apply 1 coat of sealer, roller & brush				.005	.24	.18		.42	.49	.59
	Total				.008	.24	.30	.03	.57	**.68**	**.81**
3030	**Refinish Stone Patio**	3	1 PORD	S.F.							
	Prepare surface				.003		.12	.03	.15	.19	.22
	Apply 1 coat of sealer, roller & brush				.005	.24	.18		.42	.49	.59
	Total				.008	.24	.30	.03	.57	**.68**	**.81**
4030	**Refinish Wood Patio**	3	1 PORD	S.F.							
	Prepare surface				.015		.57		.57	.73	.90
	Primer + 1 top coat, roller & brush				.022	.12	.85		.97	1.22	1.51
	Total				.037	.12	1.42		1.54	**1.95**	**2.41**

G2033 250 Handicap Ramp

	System Description	Freq. (Years)	Crew	Unit	Labor Hours	2012 Bare Costs				Total In-House	Total w/O&P
						Material	Labor	Equipment	Total		
1030	**Refinish Metal Handicap Ramp**	3	1 PORD	S.F.							
	Prepare surface				.015		.57		.57	.73	.90
	Prime & paint 1 coat, roller & brush				.015	.25	.56		.81	1	1.20
	Total				.029	.25	1.13		1.38	**1.73**	**2.10**
2030	**Refinish Wood Handicap Ramp**	3	1 PORD	S.F.							
	Prepare surface				.015		.57		.57	.73	.90
	Prime & paint 1 coat, roller & brush				.022	.12	.85		.97	1.22	1.51
	Total				.037	.12	1.42		1.54	**1.95**	**2.41**

G2043 105   Chain Link Fence and Gate Repairs

	System Description	Freq. (Years)	Crew	Unit	Labor Hours	2012 Bare Costs				Total In-House	Total w/O&P
						Material	Labor	Equipment	Total		
1010	**Minor chain link fence repairs (per 10 L.F.)**	1	2 CLAB	Ea.							
	Straighten bent 2" line post				.167		5.85		5.85	7.80	9.60
	Re-tie fence fabric				.167	1.66	5.85		7.51	9.60	11.65
	Refasten loose barbed wire arm				.083		2.92		2.92	3.89	4.80
	Refasten loose barbed wire, 3 strands				.083		2.92		2.92	3.89	4.80
	Total				.500	1.66	17.54		19.20	25.18	30.85
1110	**Replace bent 1-5/8" top rail (per 20 L.F.)**	2	2 CLAB	Ea.							
	Remove fabric ties, top rail & couplings				.333		11.70		11.70	15.55	19.20
	Install new top rail, couplings & fabric ties				.667	36.41	23.43		59.84	71.50	84
	Total				1.000	36.41	35.13		71.54	87.05	103.20
1120	**Replace broken barbed wire arm**	2	2 CLAB	Ea.							
	Remove fabric ties, top rail & couplings				.333		11.70		11.70	15.55	19.20
	Release barbed wires & remove old arm				.067		2.34		2.34	3.11	3.84
	Install new arm & refasten barbed wires				.167	.50	5.88		6.38	8.35	10.20
	Install old top rail, couplings & fabric ties				.667		23.40		23.40	31	38.50
	Total				1.234	.50	43.32		43.82	58.01	71.74
1130	**Replace barbed wire, 3 strands (per 100 L.F.)**	5	2 CLAB	Ea.							
	Remove old barbed wire				3.002		105		105	140	173
	Install new barbed wire				3.000	99.30	105.30		204.60	249	298
	Total				6.002	99.30	210.30		309.60	389	471
1140	**Replace fence fabric, 6' high, 9 ga. (per 10 L.F.)**	10	2 CLAB	Ea.							
	Remove ties from top rail, bottom tension wire & posts				.167		5.85		5.85	7.80	9.60
	Unstitch & remove section of fabric				.667		23.50		23.50	31	38.50
	Hang & stretch new fabric, stitch into existing fabric				1.333	66.20	46.80		113	136	160
	Re-tie fence fabric				.167	1.66	5.85		7.51	9.60	11.65
	Total				2.333	67.86	82		149.86	184.40	219.75
1150	**Replace double swing gates, 6' high, 20' opng.**	5	2 CLAB	Opng.							
	Remove 2 old gates (6'x10' ea.) & 4 hinges				1.111		39		39	52	64
	Supply 4 new gate hinges					23.08			23.08	25.50	29
	Install 2 new gates (6'x10' ea.), 4 hinges, adjust alignment				2.412	211.94	84.77		296.71	345	405
	Remove & replace gate latch				.914	5.68	32		37.68	49	60
	Remove & replace gate cane bolt				.883	5.68	30.80		36.48	47.50	58
	Total				5.320	246.38	186.57		432.95	519	616

G2043 105   Chain Link Fence and Gate Repairs

System Description	Freq. (Years)	Crew	Unit	Labor Hours	2012 Bare Costs				Total In-House	Total w/O&P
					Material	Labor	Equipment	Total		
1160 Replace 6'x18' cantilever slide gate	5	2 CLAB	Opng.							
Remove old gate & 4 rollers				.926		32.50		32.50	43	53.50
Supply 4 new cantilever gate rollers				.003	156.25	.03		156.28	173	195
Install new 6'x18' cantilever slide gate, 4 rollers, adjust				2.148	777.38	75.25		852.63	960	1,100
Remove & replace gate latch				.914	5.68	32		37.68	49	60
Total				3.991	939.31	139.78		1,079.09	1,225	1,408.50
1210 Replace 2" line post	5	B-55	Ea.							
Remove fabric ties, top rail & couplings				.333		11.70		11.70	15.55	19.20
Release barbed wires & remove old arm				.067		2.34		2.34	3.11	3.84
Unstitch & roll up section of fabric				1.000		35	41	76	87	102
Remove 2" post & concrete base from ground				.750		26	30.50	56.50	65.50	76.50
Install new 2" line post with concrete in old hole				1.500	57.93	52.33	61.43	171.69	194	226
Install old top rail, couplings & new fabric ties				.667		23.40		23.40	31	38.50
Unroll & stretch fabric, stitch into existing fabric				2.000		69.50	82	151.50	174	204
Re-tie fence fabric				.333	3.31	11.70		15.01	19.20	23.50
Total				6.650	61.24	231.97	214.93	508.14	589.36	693.54
1220 Replace 3" corner post	10	B-55	Ea.							
Remove fabric ties, retainer bars & ring fittings				.500		17.45	20.50	37.95	43.50	51
Roll back fabric				.250		8.70	10.25	18.95	22	25.50
Remove top rail & ring fittings				.500		17.45	20.50	37.95	43.50	51
Remove barbed wires & ring fittings				.750		26	30.50	56.50	65.50	76.50
Remove diagonal & horizontal braces, ring fittings				.500		17.45	20.50	37.95	43.50	51
Remove 3" post & concrete base from ground				1.000		35	41	76	87	102
Install new 3" post with concrete in old hole				2.000	84.50	69.50	82	236	267	310
Install old diagonal & horizontal braces, ring fittings				.500		17.45	20.50	37.95	43.50	51
Install old barbed wires & ring fittings				.750		26	30.50	56.50	65.50	76.50
Install old top rail & ring fittings				.500		17.45	20.50	37.95	43.50	51
Hang & stretch fabric, insert retainer bars & ring fittings				1.500		52.50	61.50	114	131	153
Re-tie fence fabric				.333	3.31	11.70		15.01	19.20	23.50
Total				9.083	87.81	316.65	358.25	762.71	874.70	1,022

G2043 105   Chain Link Fence and Gate Repairs

	System Description	Freq. (Years)	Crew	Unit	Labor Hours	2012 Bare Costs				Total In-House	Total w/O&P
						Material	Labor	Equipment	Total		
1230	**Replace 3″ gate post**	5	B-55	Ea.							
	Remove gate & hinges				.833		29	34	63	72.50	85
	Remove fabric ties, retainer bars & ring fittings				.500		17.45	20.50	37.95	43.50	51
	Roll back fabric				.250		8.70	10.25	18.95	22	25.50
	Remove top rail & ring fittings				.500		17.45	20.50	37.95	43.50	51
	Remove barbed wires & ring fittings				.750		26	30.50	56.50	65.50	76.50
	Remove diagonal & horizontal braces, ring fittings				.500		17.45	20.50	37.95	43.50	51
	Remove 3″ post & concrete base from ground				1.000		35	41	76	87	102
	Install new 3″ post with concrete in old hole				2.000	84.50	69.50	82	236	267	310
	Install old diagonal & horizontal braces, ring fittings				.500		17.45	20.50	37.95	43.50	51
	Install old barbed wires & ring fittings				.750		26	30.50	56.50	65.50	76.50
	Install old top rail & ring fittings				.500		17.45	20.50	37.95	43.50	51
	Hang & stretch fabric, insert retainer bars & ring fittings				1.500		52.50	61.50	114	131	153
	Re-tie fence fabric				.333	3.31	11.70		15.01	19.20	23.50
	Install old hinges & gate				1.807		63	74	137	157	185
	Total				11.724	87.81	408.65	466.25	962.71	1,104.20	1,292

G2043 110   Wood Fence

	System Description	Freq. (Years)	Crew	Unit	Labor Hours	2012 Bare Costs				Total In-House	Total w/O&P
						Material	Labor	Equipment	Total		
1020	**Refinish Wood Fence, 6′ High**	3	1 PORD	L.F.							
	Prepare surface				.089		3.42		3.42	4.38	5.40
	Prime & 1 top coat, roller & brush				.046	.42	1.74		2.16	2.76	3.35
	Total				.135	.42	5.16		5.58	7.14	8.75

G2043 710   Bleachers, Exterior

	System Description	Freq. (Years)	Crew	Unit	Labor Hours	2012 Bare Costs				Total In-House	Total w/O&P
						Material	Labor	Equipment	Total		
1020	**Refinish Wood Bleachers**	3	1 PORD	S.F.							
	Prepare surface				.015		.57		.57	.73	.90
	Prime & 1 top coat, roller & brush				.022	.12	.85		.97	1.22	1.51
	Total				.037	.12	1.42		1.54	1.95	2.41

G2043 750 Tennis Court Resurfacing

System Description	Freq. (Years)	Crew	Unit	Labor Hours	2012 Bare Costs				Total In-House	Total w/O&P
					Material	Labor	Equipment	Total		
1010 Resurface asphalt tennis court	7	2 SKWK	Ea.							
Remove/reinstall tennis net				1.000		35		35	46.50	57.50
Thoroughly clean surface				7.760		272		272	360	450
Install 3 coat acrylic emulsion sealcoat				16.000	4,640	560		5,200	5,850	6,725
Total				24.760	4,640	867		5,507	6,256.50	7,232.50
1020 Resurface cushioned asphalt tennis court	7	2 SKWK	Ea.							
Remove/reinstall tennis net				1.000		35		35	46.50	57.50
Thoroughly clean surface				7.760		272		272	360	450
Two cushion coats				16.000	2,100	560		2,660	3,050	3,550
Install 3 coat acrylic emulsion sealcoat				16.000	4,640	560		5,200	5,850	6,725
Total				40.760	6,740	1,427		8,167	9,306.50	10,782.50
2010 Clay tennis court preparation	1	2 SKWK	Ea.							
Remove/reinstall tennis net				1.000		35		35	46.50	57.50
Remove and reinstall tapes				6.015		211		211	281	345
Remove weeds and deteriorated surface material				2.000		70		70	93.50	115
Check court for level				1.000		35		35	46.50	57.50
Clay court top dressing, 1.5 tons				7.500	417	264		681	810	955
Clay court, roll after dressing				1.500		64	21.50	85.50	104	126
Total				19.015	417	679	21.50	1,117.50	1,381.50	1,656

G2043 810 Flag Pole

System Description	Freq. (Years)	Crew	Unit	Labor Hours	2012 Bare Costs				Total In-House	Total w/O&P
					Material	Labor	Equipment	Total		
1020 Refinish 25' Wood Flag Pole	5	1 PORD	Ea.							
Set up, secure and take down ladder				.258		9.85		9.85	12.70	15.75
Prepare surface				.370		14.25		14.25	18.25	22.50
Prime & 1 top coat, roller & brush				.556	3	21.25		24.25	30.50	38
Total				1.184	3	45.35		48.35	61.45	76.25

System Description	Freq. (Years)	Crew	Unit	Labor Hours	2012 Bare Costs Material	Labor	Equipment	Total	Total In-House	Total w/O&P
0100 **Prep & paint 100k gal. ground level water stor tank, 30' dia x 19' tall**	10	E-11	Ea.							
Scaffolding, outer ring				72.000		3,168		3,168	4,225	5,200
Scaffolding planks				35.666		1,572.90		1,572.90	2,100	2,575
Sandblast exterior, near white blast (SSPC-SP10), loose scale, fine rust				177.775	3,475	7,050	1,175	11,700	15,300	18,000
Epoxy primer, spray exterior				13.325	625	525		1,150	1,550	1,775
Epoxy topcoat, 2 coats, spray exterior				28.550	1,100	1,100		2,200	3,000	3,525
Clean up				10.000		375		375	550	675
Total				337.316	5,200	13,790.90	1,175	20,165.90	26,725	31,750
0200 **Prep & paint 250k gal. ground level water stor tank, 40' dia x 27' tall**	10	E-11	Ea.							
Scaffolding, outer ring				126.000		5,544		5,544	7,400	9,125
Scaffolding planks				63.333		2,793		2,793	3,725	4,550
Sandblast exterior, near white blast (SSPC-SP10), loose scale, fine rust				327.106	6,394	12,972	2,162	21,528	28,100	33,100
Epoxy primer, spray exterior				24.518	1,150	966		2,116	2,850	3,275
Epoxy topcoat, 2 coats, spray exterior				52.532	2,024	2,024		4,048	5,525	6,475
Clean up				18.400		690		690	1,000	1,250
Total				611.889	9,568	24,989	2,162	36,719	48,600	57,775
0300 **Prep & paint 500k gal. ground level water stor tank, 50' dia x 34' tall**	10	E-11	Ea.							
Scaffolding, outer ring				192.000		8,448		8,448	11,300	13,900
Scaffolding planks				96.666		4,263		4,263	5,675	6,950
Sandblast exterior, near white blast (SSPC-SP10), loose scale, fine rust				519.103	10,147	20,586	3,431	34,164	44,500	52,500
Epoxy primer, spray exterior				38.909	1,825	1,533		3,358	4,525	5,200
Epoxy topcoat, 2 coats, spray exterior				83.366	3,212	3,212		6,424	8,750	10,300
Clean up				29.200		1,095		1,095	1,600	1,975
Total				959.244	15,184	39,137	3,431	57,752	76,350	90,825
0400 **Prep & paint 750k gal. ground level water stor tank, 60' dia x 36' tall**	10	E-11	Ea.							
Scaffolding, outer ring				234.000		10,296		10,296	13,700	16,900
Scaffolding planks				117.332		5,174.40		5,174.40	6,875	8,450
Sandblast exterior, near white blast (SSPC-SP10), loose scale, fine rust				675.545	13,205	26,790	4,465	44,460	58,000	68,500
Epoxy primer, spray exterior				50.635	2,375	1,995		4,370	5,900	6,775
Epoxy topcoat, 2 coats, spray exterior				108.490	4,180	4,180		8,360	11,400	13,400
Clean up				38.000		1,425		1,425	2,100	2,575
Total				1224.002	19,760	49,860.40	4,465	74,085.40	97,975	116,600

G3013 400 Ground Level Water Storage Tank

System Description	Freq. (Years)	Crew	Unit	Labor Hours	2012 Bare Costs				Total In-House	Total w/O&P
					Material	Labor	Equipment	Total		
0500 Prep & paint 1M gal. ground level water stor tank, 70' dia x 35' tall	10	E-11	Ea.							
Scaffolding, outer ring				261.000		11,484		11,484	15,300	18,900
Scaffolding planks				131.332		5,791.80		5,791.80	7,700	9,450
Sandblast exterior, near white blast (SSPC-SP10), loose scale, fine rust				817.765	15,985	32,430	5,405	53,820	70,000	83,000
Epoxy primer, spray exterior				61.295	2,875	2,415		5,290	7,125	8,200
Epoxy topcoat, 2 coats, spray exterior				131.330	5,060	5,060		10,120	13,800	16,200
Clean up				46.000		1,725		1,725	2,525	3,100
Total				1448.722	23,920	58,905.80	5,405	88,230.80	116,450	138,850
0600 Prep & paint 2M gal. ground level water stor tank, 100' dia x 34' tall	10	E-11	Ea.							
Scaffolding, outer ring				354.000		15,576		15,576	20,800	25,600
Scaffolding planks				176.998		7,805.70		7,805.70	10,400	12,700
Sandblast exterior, near white blast (SSPC-SP10), loose scale, fine rust				1315.535	25,715	52,170	8,695	86,580	113,000	133,000
Epoxy primer, spray exterior				98.605	4,625	3,885		8,510	11,500	13,200
Epoxy topcoat, 2 coats, spray exterior				211.270	8,140	8,140		16,280	22,200	26,100
Clean up				74.000		2,775		2,775	4,075	5,000
Total				2230.408	38,480	90,351.70	8,695	137,526.70	181,975	215,600
0700 Prep & paint 4M gal. ground level water stor tank, 130' dia x 40' tall	10	E-11	Ea.							
Scaffolding, outer ring				531.000		23,364		23,364	31,200	38,400
Scaffolding planks				266.664		11,760		11,760	15,600	19,200
Sandblast exterior, near white blast (SSPC-SP10), loose scale, fine rust				2133.300	41,700	84,600	14,100	140,400	183,000	216,000
Epoxy primer, spray exterior				159.900	7,500	6,300		13,800	18,600	21,400
Epoxy topcoat, 2 coats, spray exterior				342.600	13,200	13,200		26,400	36,000	42,300
Clean up				120.000		4,500		4,500	6,600	8,100
Total				3553.464	62,400	143,724	14,100	220,224	291,000	345,400

G3013 405 Ground Level Water Storage Standpipe

System Description	Freq. (Years)	Crew	Unit	Labor Hours	2012 Bare Costs				Total In-House	Total w/O&P
					Material	Labor	Equipment	Total		
0100 Prep & paint 100k gal. grnd. level water standpipe, 24' dia x 30' tall	10	E-11	Ea.							
Scaffolding, outer ring				96.000		4,224		4,224	5,625	6,950
Scaffolding planks				47.666		2,102.10		2,102.10	2,800	3,425
Sandblast exterior, near white blast (SSPC-SP10), loose scale, fine rust				191.997	3,753	7,614	1,269	12,636	16,500	19,400
Epoxy primer, spray exterior				14.391	675	567		1,242	1,675	1,925
Epoxy topcoat, 2 coats, spray exterior				30.834	1,188	1,188		2,376	3,250	3,800
Clean up				10.800		405		405	595	730
Total				391.688	5,616	16,100.10	1,269	22,985.10	30,445	36,230
0200 Prep & paint 250k gal. grnd. level water standpipe, 32' dia x 42' tall	10	E-11	Ea.							
Scaffolding, outer ring				165.000		7,260		7,260	9,675	11,900
Scaffolding planks				82.666		3,645.60		3,645.60	4,850	5,950
Sandblast exterior, near white blast (SSPC-SP10), loose scale, fine rust				355.550	6,950	14,100	2,350	23,400	30,500	36,000
Epoxy primer, spray exterior				26.650	1,250	1,050		2,300	3,100	3,575
Epoxy topcoat, 2 coats, spray exterior				57.100	2,200	2,200		4,400	6,000	7,050
Clean up				20.000		750		750	1,100	1,350
Total				706.966	10,400	29,005.60	2,350	41,755.60	55,225	65,825
0300 Prep & paint 500k gal. grnd. level water standpipe, 40' dia x 53' tall	10	E-11	Ea.							
Scaffolding, outer ring				252.000		11,088		11,088	14,800	18,200
Scaffolding planks				125.665		5,541.90		5,541.90	7,375	9,050
Sandblast exterior, near white blast (SSPC-SP10), loose scale, fine rust				568.880	11,120	22,560	3,760	37,440	48,800	57,500
Epoxy primer, spray exterior				42.640	2,000	1,680		3,680	4,950	5,700
Epoxy topcoat, 2 coats, spray exterior				91.360	3,520	3,520		7,040	9,600	11,300
Clean up				32.000		1,200		1,200	1,750	2,150
Total				1112.545	16,640	45,589.90	3,760	65,989.90	87,275	103,900
0400 Prep & paint 750k gal. grnd. level water standpipe, 46' dia x 60' tall	10	E-11	Ea.							
Scaffolding, outer ring				318.000		13,992		13,992	18,700	23,000
Scaffolding planks				159.665		7,041.30		7,041.30	9,375	11,500
Sandblast exterior, near white blast (SSPC-SP10), loose scale, fine rust				739.544	14,456	29,328	4,888	48,672	63,500	75,000
Epoxy primer, spray exterior				55.432	2,600	2,184		4,784	6,450	7,400
Epoxy topcoat, 2 coats, spray exterior				118.768	4,576	4,576		9,152	12,500	14,700
Clean up				41.600		1,560		1,560	2,300	2,800
Total				1433.009	21,632	58,681.30	4,888	85,201.30	112,825	134,400

G3013 405 Ground Level Water Storage Standpipe

	System Description	Freq. (Years)	Crew	Unit	Labor Hours	2012 Bare Costs				Total In-House	Total w/O&P
						Material	Labor	Equipment	Total		
0500	**Prep & paint 1M gal. grnd. level water standpipe, 50' dia x 68' tall**	10	E-11	Ea.							
	Scaffolding, outer ring				384.000		16,896		16,896	22,500	27,800
	Scaffolding planks				192.998		8,511.30		8,511.30	11,300	13,900
	Sandblast exterior, near white blast (SSPC-SP10), loose scale, fine rust				903.097	17,653	35,814	5,969	59,436	77,500	91,500
	Epoxy primer, spray exterior				67.691	3,175	2,667		5,842	7,875	9,050
	Epoxy topcoat, 2 coats, spray exterior				145.034	5,588	5,588		11,176	15,200	17,900
	Clean up				50.800		1,905		1,905	2,800	3,425
	Total				1743.620	26,416	71,381.30	5,969	103,766.30	137,175	163,575
0600	**Prep & paint 2M gal. grnd. level water standpipe, 64' dia x 83' tall**	10	E-11	Ea.							
	Scaffolding, outer ring				579.000		25,476		25,476	34,000	41,900
	Scaffolding planks				290.664		12,818.40		12,818.40	17,000	20,900
	Sandblast exterior, near white blast (SSPC-SP10), loose scale, fine rust				1422.200	27,800	56,400	9,400	93,600	122,000	144,000
	Epoxy primer, spray exterior				106.600	5,000	4,200		9,200	12,400	14,300
	Epoxy topcoat, 2 coats, spray exterior				228.400	8,800	8,800		17,600	24,000	28,200
	Clean up				80.000		3,000		3,000	4,400	5,400
	Total				2706.864	41,600	110,694.40	9,400	161,694.40	213,800	254,700

G3013 410 Fire Hydrants

	System Description	Freq. (Years)	Crew	Unit	Labor Hours	2012 Bare Costs				Total In-House	Total w/O&P
						Material	Labor	Equipment	Total		
1010	**Remove and replace fire hydrant**	25	B-21	Ea.							
	Isolate hydrant from system				1.000		35		35	46.50	57.50
	Excavate to expose base and feeder pipe				.974		39.90	20.37	60.27	72	86
	Disconnect and remove hydrant and associated piping				4.000		140		140	187	230
	Install pipe to new hydrant				3.200	147.50	136.50		284	335	400
	Install hydrant, including lower barrel and shoe				4.000	1,650	162	18.90	1,830.90	2,050	2,350
	Install thrust blocks				1.200	49.80	50.70	.29	100.79	123	146
	Backfill excavation				5.091		178.50		178.50	238	294
	Fine grade, hand				8.000		280		280	375	460
	Total				27.465	1,847.30	1,022.60	39.56	2,909.46	3,426.50	4,023.50

G3013 470 Post Indicator Valve

	System Description	Freq. (Years)	Crew	Unit	Labor Hours	2012 Bare Costs				Total In-House	Total w/O&P
						Material	Labor	Equipment	Total		
1010	**Remove and replace post indicator valve**	35	B-21	Ea.							
	Isolate PIV from system				.126		6.90		6.90	8.60	10.70
	Excavate to expose base of valve				.139		5.70	2.91	8.61	10.25	12.30
	Disconnect and remove post indicator and valve				4.000		140		140	187	230
	Install new 4" diameter valve				4.000	1,375	153	55.50	1,583.50	1,775	2,025
	Install new post indicator				3.636	775	147	17.20	939.20	1,075	1,225
	Backfill excavation				.727		25.50		25.50	34	42
	Fine grade, hand				8.000		280		280	375	460
	Total				20.629	2,150	758.10	75.61	2,983.71	3,464.85	4,005

G3013 510 Elevated Water Storage Tank

	System Description	Freq. (Years)	Crew	Unit	Labor Hours	2012 Bare Costs				Total In-House	Total w/O&P
						Material	Labor	Equipment	Total		
0100	**Prep & paint 50K gal. stg tank, 30' dia x 10' tall, 50' above grnd.**	10	E-11	Ea.							
	Scaffolding, outer ring				225.000		9,900		9,900	13,200	16,300
	Scaffolding, center core under tank				80.000		3,520		3,520	4,675	5,775
	Scaffolding planks				58.333		2,572.50		2,572.50	3,425	4,200
	Sandblast exterior, near white blast (SSPC-SP10), loose scale, fine rust				167.464	3,273.45	6,641.10	1,106.85	11,021.40	14,400	17,000
	Epoxy primer, spray exterior				12.552	588.75	494.55		1,083.30	1,450	1,675
	Epoxy topcoat, 2 coats, spray exterior				26.894	1,036.20	1,036.20		2,072.40	2,825	3,325
	Clean up				9.420		353.25		353.25	520	635
	Total				579.663	4,898.40	24,517.60	1,106.85	30,522.85	40,495	48,910
0200	**Prep & paint 100K gal. stg tank, 30' dia x 20' tall, 50' above grnd.**	10	E-11	Ea.							
	Scaffolding, outer ring				261.000		11,484		11,484	15,300	18,900
	Scaffolding, center core under tank				80.000		3,520		3,520	4,675	5,775
	Scaffolding planks				153.332		6,762		6,762	9,000	11,000
	Sandblast exterior, near white blast (SSPC-SP10), loose scale, fine rust				227.552	4,448	9,024	1,504	14,976	19,500	23,000
	Epoxy primer, spray exterior				17.056	800	672		1,472	1,975	2,275
	Epoxy topcoat, 2 coats, spray exterior				36.544	1,408	1,408		2,816	3,850	4,500
	Clean up				12.800		480		480	705	865
	Total				788.284	6,656	33,350	1,504	41,510	55,005	66,315

G3013 510 Elevated Water Storage Tank

	System Description	Freq. (Years)	Crew	Unit	Labor Hours	2012 Bare Costs				Total In-House	Total w/O&P
						Material	Labor	Equipment	Total		
0300	**Prep & paint 250K gal. stg tank, 40' dia x 27' tall, 50' above grnd.**	10	E-11	Ea.							
	Scaffolding, outer ring				360.000		15,840		15,840	21,100	26,000
	Scaffolding, center core under tank				134.000		5,896		5,896	7,850	9,675
	Scaffolding planks				219.998		9,702		9,702	12,900	15,800
	Sandblast exterior, near white blast (SSPC-SP10), loose scale, fine rust				419.549	8,201	16,638	2,773	27,612	36,000	42,500
	Epoxy primer, spray exterior				31.447	1,475	1,239		2,714	3,650	4,200
	Epoxy topcoat, 2 coats, spray exterior				67.378	2,596	2,596		5,192	7,075	8,325
	Clean up				23.600		885		885	1,300	1,600
	Total				1255.972	12,272	52,796	2,773	67,841	89,875	108,100
0400	**Prep & paint 500K gal. stg tank, 50' dia x 34' tall, 50' above grnd.**	10	E-11	Ea.							
	Scaffolding, outer ring				480.000		21,120		21,120	28,200	34,700
	Scaffolding, center core under tank				202.000		8,888		8,888	11,800	14,600
	Scaffolding planks				296.664		13,083		13,083	17,400	21,400
	Sandblast exterior, near white blast (SSPC-SP10), loose scale, fine rust				661.323	12,927	26,226	4,371	43,524	56,500	67,000
	Epoxy primer, spray exterior				49.569	2,325	1,953		4,278	5,775	6,625
	Epoxy topcoat, 2 coats, spray exterior				106.206	4,092	4,092		8,184	11,200	13,100
	Clean up				37.200		1,395		1,395	2,050	2,500
	Total				1832.962	19,344	76,757	4,371	100,472	132,925	159,925
0500	**Prep & paint 750K gal. stg tank, 60' dia x 36' tall, 50' above grnd.**	10	E-11	Ea.							
	Scaffolding, outer ring				570.000		25,080		25,080	33,400	41,200
	Scaffolding, center core under tank				283.000		12,452		12,452	16,600	20,400
	Scaffolding planks				366.663		16,170		16,170	21,500	26,400
	Sandblast exterior, near white blast (SSPC-SP10), loose scale, fine rust				881.764	17,236	34,968	5,828	58,032	75,500	89,000
	Epoxy primer, spray exterior				66.092	3,100	2,604		5,704	7,700	8,825
	Epoxy topcoat, 2 coats, spray exterior				141.608	5,456	5,456		10,912	14,900	17,500
	Clean up				49.600		1,860		1,860	2,725	3,350
	Total				2358.727	25,792	98,590	5,828	130,210	172,325	206,675
0600	**Prep & paint 1M gal. stg tank, 65' dia x 40' tall, 50' above grnd.**	10	E-11	Ea.							
	Scaffolding, outer ring				645.000		28,380		28,380	37,800	46,700
	Scaffolding, center core under tank				329.000		14,476		14,476	19,200	23,800
	Scaffolding planks				413.329		18,228		18,228	24,200	29,800
	Sandblast exterior, near white blast (SSPC-SP10), loose scale, fine rust				1059.539	20,711	42,018	7,003	69,732	91,000	107,000
	Epoxy primer, spray exterior				79.417	3,725	3,129		6,854	9,250	10,600
	Epoxy topcoat, 2 coats, spray exterior				170.158	6,556	6,556		13,112	17,900	21,000
	Clean up				59.600		2,235		2,235	3,275	4,025
	Total				2756.043	30,992	115,022	7,003	153,017	202,625	242,925

G3063 410 Ground Level Fuel Storage Tank

	System Description	Freq. (Years)	Crew	Unit	Labor Hours	2012 Bare Costs				Total In-House	Total w/O&P
						Material	Labor	Equipment	Total		
0100	**Prep & paint 100k gal. ground level fuel storage tank, 24' dia x 30' tall**	25	E-11	Ea.							
	Scaffolding, outer ring				96.000		4,224		4,224	5,625	6,950
	Scaffolding planks				47.333		2,087.40		2,087.40	2,775	3,400
	Sandblast exterior, near white blast (SSPC-SP10), loose scale, fine rust				191.997	3,753	7,614	1,269	12,636	16,500	19,400
	Epoxy primer, spray exterior				14.391	675	567		1,242	1,675	1,925
	Epoxy topcoat, 2 coats, spray exterior				30.834	1,188	1,188		2,376	3,250	3,800
	Clean up				10.800		405		405	595	730
	Total				391.355	5,616	16,085.40	1,269	22,970.40	30,420	36,205

G4013 210 Overhead Service Cables

System Description	Freq. (Years)	Crew	Unit	Labor Hours	2012 Bare Costs				Total In-House	Total w/O&P
					Material	Labor	Equipment	Total		
0010 Repair cable splice										
Repair splice cable, polyethylene jacket	12	1 ELEC	M.L.F.	7.619	8.90	395		403.90	495	615
Total				7.619	8.90	395		403.90	**495**	**615**
0020 Cable inspection										
Check cables for damage	5	1 ELEC	M.L.F.	.667		34.50		34.50	42.50	53
Total				.667		34.50		34.50	**42.50**	**53**
0030 Replace service cable	30	2 ELEC	M.L.F.							
Remove overhead service cables				1.860		96		96	118	148
Overhead service 3 ACSR cable				16.000	3,350	825		4,175	4,700	5,475
Install 3 conductors at terminations				.941		48.50		48.50	60	75
Install conductors to insulators and clipping				2.500		129		129	159	199
Install and remove sag gauge				1.000		51.50		51.50	63.50	79.50
Make up & install conductor jumper				2.000		103		103	127	159
Total				24.302	3,350	1,253		4,603	**5,227.50**	**6,135.50**

G40 SITE ELEC. UTILITIES — G4023 — Site Lighting

G4023 210 — Outdoor Pole Lights

System Description	Freq. (Years)	Crew	Unit	Labor Hours	Material	Labor	Equipment	Total	Total In-House	Total w/O&P
1010 Replace 400W H.P.S. lamp, pole-mounted fixture	10	R-26	Ea.							
Position truck, raise and lower boom bucket				.289		14.90	5.20	20.10	23.50	29
Remove & install 400W H.P.S. lamp, pole-mounted fixture				.185	59	9.55	3.35	71.90	80	92
Total				.474	59	24.45	8.55	92	**103.50**	**121**
1020 Replace 400W H.P.S. ballast, pole-mounted fixture	10	R-26	Ea.							
Position truck, raise and lower boom bucket				.289		14.90	5.20	20.10	23.50	29
Remove & install 400W H.P.S. multi-tap ballast, pole-mounted fixt.				2.974	420	153	53.50	626.50	705	820
Test pole-mounted H.I.D. fixture				.074		3.82	1.34	5.16	6.05	7.35
Total				3.337	420	171.72	60.04	651.76	**734.55**	**856.35**
1030 Replace 400W H.P.S. pole-mounted fixt. w/ lamp & blst.	20	R-26	Ea.							
Turn branch cicuit off and on, pole light				.370		19.10	6.70	25.80	30.50	37
Turn branch cicuit off and on, pole light				.370		19.10	6.70	25.80	30.50	37
Position truck, raise and lower boom bucket				.289		14.90	5.20	20.10	23.50	29
Remove & install pole-mounted 400W H.P.S. fixture w/ lamp & blst.				9.456	365	485	171	1,021	1,175	1,400
Test pole-mounted H.I.D. fixture				.074		3.82	1.34	5.16	6.05	7.35
Total				10.560	365	541.92	190.94	1,097.86	**1,265.55**	**1,510.35**
1040 Replace light pole, 2 fixtures (conc. base not incl.)	10	R-3	Ea.							
Turn branch cicuit off and on, pole light				.370		19.10	6.70	25.80	30.50	37
Remove parking lot light pole with fixtures				2.500		128	16.55	144.55	175	216
Install 2 brackets arms onto aluminum light pole				2.602	490	134		624	700	820
Install two 400W H.P.S. fixtures w/ lamps & ballasts onto light pole				9.467	730	488		1,218	1,400	1,675
Install 30' aluminum light pole (incl. arms & fixtures) onto base				10.000	1,650	510	66	2,226	2,525	2,925
Pull new wires in existing underground conduits (3#10 500')				15.605	293.25	802.50		1,095.75	1,325	1,600
Test pole-mounted H.I.D. fixture				.074		3.82	1.34	5.16	6.05	7.35
Total				40.618	3,163.25	2,085.42	90.59	5,339.26	**6,161.55**	**7,280.35**

2012 Bare Costs span the Material, Labor, Equipment, and Total columns.

G4023 210 Outdoor Pole Lights

	System Description	Freq. (Years)	Crew	Unit	Labor Hours	2012 Bare Costs				Total In-House	Total w/O&P
						Material	Labor	Equipment	Total		
1050	**Replace concrete base for parking lot light pole**	20	B-18	Ea.							
	Sawcut asphalt paving				1.296	8.16	51.36	34.80	94.32	110	130
	Remove concrete light pole base				10.000		356	52.40	408.40	525	640
	Excavate by hand				12.987		455		455	605	745
	Install 1-1/4" PVC electrical conduit				.612	18.20	31.50		49.70	59	71.50
	Install 1-1/4" PVC electrical sweep				.433	35	22.50		57.50	66	78.50
	Install new concrete light pole base, 24" dia. x 8'				12.030	261	505		766	955	1,150
	Backfill excavation by hand				4.728		165		165	220	273
	Compact backfill				.578		20.30	2.35	22.65	29.50	36
	Install asphalt patch				.960	71.20	35.60	3	109.80	128	150
	Total				43.624	393.56	1,642.26	92.55	2,128.37	2,697.50	3,274

	System Description	Freq. (Years)	Crew	Unit	Labor Hours	2012 Bare Costs				Total In-House	Total w/O&P
						Material	Labor	Equipment	Total		
1010	**Daily use of crane, portal to portal, 12-ton**	1	A-3H	Day							
	12-ton truck-mounted hydraulic crane, daily use for small jobs				8.000		380	825	1,205	1,300	1,500
	Total				8.000		380	825	1,205	**1,300**	**1,500**
1020	**Daily use of crane, portal to portal, 25-ton**	1	A-3I	Day							
	25-ton truck-mounted hydraulic crane, daily use for small jobs				8.000		380	955	1,335	1,450	1,650
	Total				8.000		380	955	1,335	**1,450**	**1,650**
1030	**Daily use of crane, portal to portal, 40-ton**	1	A-3J	Day							
	40-ton truck-mounted hydraulic crane, daily use for small jobs				8.000		380	1,175	1,555	1,675	1,900
	Total				8.000		380	1,175	1,555	**1,675**	**1,900**
1040	**Daily use of crane, portal to portal, 55-ton**	1	A-3K	Day							
	55-ton truck-mounted hydraulic crane, daily use for small jobs				16.000		710	1,625	2,335	2,525	2,900
	Total				16.000		710	1,625	2,335	**2,525**	**2,900**
1050	**Daily use of crane, portal to portal, 80-ton**	1	A-3L	Day							
	80-ton truck-mounted hydraulic crane, daily use for small jobs				16.000		710	2,275	2,985	3,175	3,625
	Total				16.000		710	2,275	2,985	**3,175**	**3,625**
1060	**Daily use of crane, portal to portal, 100-ton**	1	A-3M	Day							
	100-ton truck-mounted hydraulic crane, daily use for small jobs				16.000		710	2,275	2,985	3,175	3,625
	Total				16.000		710	2,275	2,985	**3,175**	**3,625**

Preventive Maintenance

Table of Contents

Table of Contents (cont.)

How to Use the Preventive Maintenance Cost Tables

The following is a detailed explanation of a sample Preventive Maintenance Cost Table. The Preventive Maintenance Tables are separated into two parts: 1) the components and related labor-hours and frequencies of a typical system and 2) the costs for systems on an annual or annualized basis. Next to each bold number that follows is the described item with the appropriate component of the sample entry following in parentheses.

1 System/Line Numbers (D3025 130 4950)

Each Preventive Maintenance Cost Line has been assigned a unique identification number based on the UNIFORMAT II classification system.

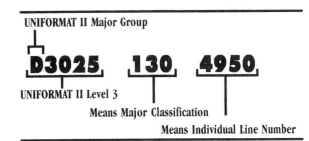

UNIFORMAT II Major Group

D3025   130   4950

UNIFORMAT II Level 3
Means Major Classification
Means Individual Line Number

D30 HVAC		D3025 130	Boiler, Hot Water, Oil/Gas/Comb.					
1 PM Components		**3** Labor-hrs.		W	M	Q	S	A
PM System D3025 130 4950					**4**			
Boiler, hot water; oil, gas or combination fired, over 1000 MBH								
1	Check combustion chamber for air or gas leaks.	.117						√
2	Inspect and clean oil burner gun and ignition assembly where applicable.	.987						√
3	Inspect fuel system for leaks and change fuel filter element, where applicable.	.147						√
4	Check fuel lines and connections for damage.	.035		√	√	√	√
5	Check for proper operational response of burner to thermostat controls.	.199			√	√	√
6	Check and lubricate burner and blower motors.	.120			√	√	√
7	Check main flame failure protection and main flame detection scanner on boiler equipped with spark ignition (oil burner).	.186		√	√	√	
8	Check electrical wiring to burner controls and blower.	.120					√
9	Clean firebox (sweep and vacuum).	.819					√
10	Check operation of mercury control switches (i.e., steam pressure, hot water temperature limit, atomizing or combustion air proving, etc.).	.215		√	√	√	√
11	Check operation and condition of safety pressure relief valve.	.046		√	√	√	√
12	Check operation of boiler low water cut off devices.	.085		√	√	√	√
13	Check hot water pressure gauges.	.109		√	√	√	√
14	Inspect and clean water column sight glass (or replace).	.191		√	√	√	√
15	Clean fire side of water jacket	.433					√
16	Check condition of flue pipe, damper and exhaust stack.	.221			√	√	
17	Check boiler operation through complete cycle, up to 30 minutes.	.887					√
18	Check fuel level with gauge pole, add as required.	.098		√	√	√	√
19	Clean area around boiler.	.182		√	√	√	√
20	Fill out maintenance checklist and report deficiencies.	.022		√	√	√	√
	5							
	Total labor-hours/period				1.169	1.709	1.709	5.219
	Total labor-hours/year				9.352	3.418	1.709	5.219

				Cost Each				
		7		2012 Bare Costs			Total	Total
	Description **6**	Labor-hrs.	Material	Labor **8**	Equip.	Total	In-House	w/O&P
4900	Boiler, hot water, O/G/C, over 1000 MBH, annually	5.219	113	291		404	485	595
4950	Annualized	19.698	118	1,100		1,218	1,500	1,850
							9	**10**

2 PM Components

The individual preventive maintenance operations required to be performed annually are listed separately to show what has been included in the development of the total system price. The cost table below the PM Components listing contains prices for the system on an annual or annualized basis.

3 Labor-hrs.

The "Labor-hrs." figure represents the number of labor-hours required to perform the individual operations one time.

4 Frequency

The columns marked with "W" for weekly, "M" for monthly, "Q" for quarterly, "S" for semi-annually, and "A" for annually indicate the recommended frequency for performing a task. For example, a check in the "M" column indicates the recommended frequency of the operation as monthly. Note that, as a result, checks also appear in the "Q," "S," and "A" columns, as they would be part of a monthly frequency.

5 Total Labor-hours

"Total Labor-hours" are provided on both a per-period and per-year basis. The per-period totals are derived by summing the hours for each operation recommended to be performed (indicated with a check mark) in a given period. In the example given here:

M	= .035 + .186 + .215 + .046 + .085		
	+ .109 + .191 + .098 + .182 + .022	= 1.169
Similarly		
Q	= .035 + .199 + .120 + ... + .098		
	+ .182 + .022	= 1.709
S	= .035 + .199 + .120 + ... + .098		
	+ .182 + .022	= 1.709
A	= .117 + .987 + .147 + .035 + ... + .887		
	+ .098 + .182 + .022	= 5.219

The per-year totals are derived by multiplying the per-period total by the net frequency for each time period. The net frequency per period is based on the following table using a 50-week work year:

Total Labor-hours		Labor-hours		
Annual	=	Annual	x	1
Semi-Annual	=	Semi-Annual	x	1
Quarterly	=	Quarterly	x	2
Monthly	=	Monthly	x	8
Weekly	=	Weekly	x	38
				50 wks.

Based on these values, the total labor-hours/year are calculated for the given example as follows:

M	=	(1.169)	x 8 = 9.352
Q	=	(1.709)	x 2 = 3.418
S	=	(1.709)	x 1 = 1.709
A	=	(5.219)	x 1 = 5.219
			= 19.698 hrs.

6 System Description (Boiler, Hot Water, O/G/C, etc.)

The "System Description" corresponds to that given at the beginning of the PM Components list. A description of the cost basis, annual or annualized, is given as well. Annual costs are based on performing each operation listed in the PM Components one time in a given year. Annualized costs are based on performing each operation at the recommended periodic frequencies in a given year.

7 Labor-hours: Annual/Annualized (5.219)/(19.698)

Annual labor-hours are based on performing each task once during a given year and are equal to the total labor-hours/period under the "A" column in the PM Components list. Annualized labor-hours are based on the recommended periodic frequencies and are equivalent to the sum of all the values in the total labor-hours/year row at the bottom of the PM Components list.

8 Bare Costs: Annualized

Material (118.00)

This figure for the system material cost is the "bare" material cost with no overhead and profit allowances included. *Costs shown reflect national average material prices for the current year and generally include delivery to the facility. Small purchases may require an additional delivery charge. No sales taxes are included.*

Labor (1100.00)

The labor costs are derived by multiplying bare labor-hour costs by labor-hour units. (The hourly labor costs are listed in the Crew Listings, or for a single trade, the wage rate is found on the inside back cover of the book.)

Equip. (Equipment) (0.00)

The unit equipment cost is derived by multiplying the bare equipment hourly cost by the labor-hour units. Equipment costs for each crew are listed in the description of each crew.

Total (1,218.00)

The total of the bare costs is the arithmetic total of the three previous columns: mat., labor, and equip.

Material	+	Labor	+	Equip.	=	Total
$118.00	+	$1100.00	+	$0.00	=	$1,218.00

9 Total In-House Costs Annualized (1,500)

"Total In-House Costs" include suggested markups to bare costs for the direct overhead requirements of in-house maintenance staff. The figure in this column is the sum of three components: the bare material cost plus 10% (for purchasing and handling small quantities); the bare labor cost plus workers' compensation and average fixed overhead (per the labor rate table on the inside back cover of the book or, if a crew is listed, from the Crew Listings); and the bare equipment cost.

10 Total Costs Including O & P Annualized (1,850)

"Total Costs Including O&P" include suggested markups to bare costs for an outside subcontractor's overhead and profit requirements. The figure in this column is the sum of three components: the bare material cost plus 25% for profit; the bare labor cost plus total overhead and profit (per the labor rate table on the inside back cover of the book or, if a crew is listed, from the Crew Listings); and the bare equipment cost plus 10% for profit.

PM Components	Labor-hrs.	W	M	Q	S	A
PM System B2035 110 1950						
Door, sliding, electric						
1 Check with operating or area personnel for deficiencies.	.035				√	√
2 Check for proper operation, binding or misalignment; adjust as necessary.	.062				√	√
3 Check and lubricate door guides, pulleys and hinges.	.142				√	√
4 Inspect and lubricate motor gearbox, drive chain (or belt), and motor; adjust as necessary.	.200				√	√
5 Check operation of limit switch; adjust as necessary.	.224				√	√
6 Check electrical operator, wiring, connections and contacts; adjust as necessary.	.473				√	√
7 Clean area around door.	.066				√	√
8 Fill out maintenance checklist and report deficiencies.	.022				√	√
Total labor-hours/period					1.224	1.224
Total labor-hours/year					1.224	1.224

		Cost Each					
		2012 Bare Costs				Total	Total
Description	Labor-hrs.	Material	Labor	Equip.	Total	In-House	w/O&P
1900 Door, sliding, electric, annually	1.224	26	54		80	100	121
1950 Annualized	2.448	32	108		140	179	217

PM Components	Labor-hrs.	W	M	Q	S	A
PM System B2035 110 2950						
Hanger doors, sliding						
1 Check with door operating personnel for deficiencies.	.027			√	√	√
2 Remove debris from door track.	.040			√	√	√
3 Operate door.	.050			√	√	√
4 Check alignment of hanger door, door guides and lubricate.	.650					√
5 Inspect and lubricate wheel drive chain.	.030			√	√	√
6 Adjust brake shoes and check for wear.	.150					√
7 Inspect and lubricate drive wheels, guides, stops and rollers.	.200			√	√	√
8 Fill out maintenance report.	.017			√	√	√
Total labor-hours/period				.364	.364	1.164
Total labor-hours/year				.728	.364	1.164

		Cost Each					
		2012 Bare Costs				Total	Total
Description	Labor-hrs.	Material	Labor	Equip.	Total	In-House	w/O&P
2900 Hanger doors, sliding, annually	1.164	25.50	57.50		83	117	139
2950 Annualized	2.256	46	111		157	223	265

383

PM Components	Labor-hrs.	W	M	Q	S	A
PM System B2035 225 1950						
Door, emergency egress, swinging						
1 Remove obstructions that restrict full movement/swing of door.	.013			√	√	√
2 Check swing of door; door must latch on normal closing.	.013			√	√	√
3 Test operation of panic hardware and local alarm battery.	.013			√	√	√
4 Lubricate hardware.	.013			√	√	√
5 Fill out maintenance checklist and report deficiencies.	.013			√	√	√
Total labor-hours/period				.065	.065	.065
Total labor-hours/year				.130	.065	.065

	Description	Labor-hrs.	Cost Each				Total In-House	Total w/O&P
			2012 Bare Costs					
			Material	Labor	Equip.	Total		
1900	Door, emergency egress, swinging, annually	.065	26	2.87		28.87	32.50	37
1950	Annualized	.260	31.50	11.45		42.95	50	58

PM Components	Labor-hrs.	W	M	Q	S	A
PM System B2035 300 1950						
Door, revolving, manual						
1 Check with operating or area personnel for deficiencies.	.043				√	√
2 Check for proper operation, binding or misalignment; adjust as necessary.	.043				√	√
3 Check for proper emergency breakaway operation of wings.	.043				√	√
4 Check top, bottom, edge and shaft weatherstripping.	.217				√	√
5 Check and lubricate pivots and bearings.	.217				√	√
6 Clean area around door.	.065				√	√
7 Fill out maintenance checklist and report deficiencies.	.022				√	√
Total labor-hours/period					.650	.650
Total labor-hours/year					.650	.650

			Cost Each				
			2012 Bare Costs			Total	Total
Description	Labor-hrs.	Material	Labor	Equip.	Total	In-House	w/O&P
1900 Door, revolving, manual, annually	.650	26	28.50		54.50	66.50	79.50
1950 Annualized	1.300	32	57.50		89.50	111	134

PM Components	Labor-hrs.	W	M	Q	S	A
PM System B2035 300 2950						
Door, revolving, electric						
1 Check with operating or area personnel for deficiencies.	.043				√	√
2 Check for proper operation, binding or misalignment; adjust as necessary.	.043				√	√
3 Check for proper emergency breakaway operation of wings.	.043				√	√
4 Check top, bottom, edge and shaft weatherstripping.	.217				√	√
5 Check elec. operator, safety devices and activators for proper operation.	.433				√	√
6 Check and lubricate pivots and bearings and operator gearbox.	.325				√	√
7 Clean area around door.	.065				√	√
8 Fill out maintenance checklist and report deficiencies.	.022				√	√
Total labor-hours/period					1.191	1.191
Total labor-hours/year					1.191	1.191

			Cost Each				
			2012 Bare Costs			Total	Total
Description	Labor-hrs.	Material	Labor	Equip.	Total	In-House	w/O&P
2900 Door, revolving, electric, annually	1.192	44.50	52.50		97	119	142
2950 Annualized	2.382	50.50	105		155.50	195	235

PM Components	Labor-hrs.	W	M	Q	S	A
PM System B2035 400 1950						
Door, overhead, manual, up to 24′ high x 25′ wide						
1 Check with operating or area personnel for deficiencies.	.035				✓	✓
2 Check for proper operation, binding or misalignment; adjust as necessary.	.135				✓	✓
3 Check and lubricate door guides, pulleys and hinges.	.880				✓	✓
4 Clean area around door.	.026				✓	✓
5 Fill out maintenance checklist and report deficiencies.	.022				✓	✓
Total labor-hours/period					1.098	1.098
Total labor-hours/year					1.098	1.098

			Cost Each				
			2012 Bare Costs			Total	Total
	Description	Labor-hrs.	Material	Labor	Equip.	Total	In-House	w/O&P
1900	Dr., overhead, manual, up to 24′H x 25′W, annually	1.098	26	48.50		74.50	93	112
1950	Annualized	2.196	32	97		129	164	199

PM Components	Labor-hrs.	W	M	Q	S	A
PM System B2035 410 1950						
Door, overhead, roll-up, electric, up to 24′ high x 25′ wide						
1 Check with operating or area personnel for deficiencies.	.035				✓	✓
2 Check for proper operation, binding or misalignment; adjust as necessary.	.135				✓	✓
3 Check and lubricate door guides, pulleys and hinges.	.880				✓	✓
4 Inspect and lubricate motor gearbox, drive chain (or belt), and motor; adjust as necessary.	.200				✓	✓
5 Check operation of limit switch; adjust as necessary.	.224				✓	✓
6 Check electrical operator, wiring, connections and contacts; adjust as necessary.	.473				✓	✓
7 Clean area around door.	.066				✓	✓
8 Fill out maintenance checklist and report deficiencies.	.022				✓	✓
Total labor-hours/period					2.035	2.035
Total labor-hours/year					2.035	2.035

			Cost Each				
			2012 Bare Costs			Total	Total
	Description	Labor-hrs.	Material	Labor	Equip.	Total	In-House	w/O&P
1900	Dr., overhead, electric, to 24′H x 25′W, annually	2.035	44.50	90		134.50	168	203
1950	Annualized	4.070	50.50	180		230.50	294	355

PM Components	Labor-hrs.	W	M	Q	S	A
PM System B2035 450 1950						
Shutter, roll-up, electric						
1 Check with operating or area personnel for deficiencies.	.035					√
2 Check for proper operation, binding or misalignment; adjust as necessary.	.135					√
3 Check and lubricate door guides, pulleys and hinges.	.880					√
4 Inspect and lubricate motor gearbox, drive chain (or belt), and motor; adjust as necessary.	.200					√
5 Check operation of limit switch; adjust as necessary.	.224					√
6 Check electrical operator, wiring, connections and contacts; adjust as necessary.	.473					√
7 Clean area around door.	.074					√
8 Fill out maintenance checklist and report deficiencies.	.022					√
Total labor-hours/period						2.043
Total labor-hours/year						2.043

				Cost Each				
			2012 Bare Costs				Total	Total
Description	Labor-hrs.	Material	Labor	Equip.	Total	In-House	w/O&P
1900	Shutter, roll up, electric, annually	2.043	26	90		116	148	181
1950	Annualized	2.043	32	90		122	155	188

PM Components	Labor-hrs.	W	M	Q	S	A
PM System C1025 110 1950						
Fire Door, Swinging						
1 Remove fusible link hold open devices.	.026			√	√	√
2 Remove obstructions that retard full movement/swing of door.	.013			√	√	√
3 Check swing of door. Door must latch on normal closing.	.013			√	√	√
4 Test operation of panic hardware.	.007			√	√	√
5 Check operation of special devices such as smoke detectors or magnetic door releases.	.013			√	√	√
6 Lubricate hardware.	.013			√	√	√
7 Fill out maintenance checklist and report deficiencies.	.013			√	√	√
Total labor-hours/period				.098	.098	.098
Total labor-hours/year				.196	.098	.098

			Cost Each				
			2012 Bare Costs			**Total**	**Total**
Description	**Labor-hrs.**	**Material**	**Labor**	**Equip.**	**Total**	**In-House**	**w/O&P**
1900 Fire doors, swinging, annually	.098	3.52	4.45		7.97	9.75	11.65
1950 Annualized	.392	7.05	17.80		24.85	31	38

PM Components	Labor-hrs.	W	M	Q	S	A
PM System C1025 110 2950						
Fire Door, Sliding						
1 Clean track.	.013			√	√	√
2 Lubricate pulleys.	.013			√	√	√
3 Inspect cable or chain for wear or damage and proper threading through pulleys.	.078			√	√	√
4 Replace fusible links or other heat activated devices that have been painted. Check operation of other heat activated devices.	.130			√	√	√
5 Permanently remove obstructions that prohibit movement of door.	.013			√	√	√
6 Check operation of door by disconnecting or lifting counterweight or other appropriate means.	.130			√	√	√
7 Check fit of door in binders and fit against stay roll.	.013			√	√	√
8 Check door for breaks in covering and examine for dry rot.	.013			√	√	√
9 Fill out maintenance checklist and report deficiencies.	.013			√	√	√
Total labor-hours/period				.416	.416	.416
Total labor-hours/year				.832	.416	.416

			Cost Each				
			2012 Bare Costs			**Total**	**Total**
Description	**Labor-hrs.**	**Material**	**Labor**	**Equip.**	**Total**	**In-House**	**w/O&P**
2900 Fire doors, sliding, annually	.416	4.33	18.90		23.23	29.50	36
2950 Annualized	1.664	8.65	75.50		84.15	109	134

PM Components	Labor-hrs.	W	M	Q	S	A
PM System C1025 110 3950						
Fire Door, Rollup						
1 Check with door operating personnel for deficiencies.	.027			√	√	√
2 Drop test heat activated or fusible link roll up fire door.	.070			√	√	√
3 Adjust rate of descent governor to desired closing speed.	.200					√
4 Inspect, clean and lubricate door gear assembly.	.200			√	√	√
5 Check alignment of overhead door guides, clean and lubricate.	.100			√	√	√
6 Check and adjust door counter balance assembly.	.250					√
7 Check electrical wiring and contacts for wear.	.200					√
8 Check and adjust limit switches.	.170					√
9 Inspect general condition of door for need of paint and repairs.	.005			√	√	√
10 Replace missing or tighten loose nuts and bolts.	.040			√	√	√
11 After maintenance clean around door and ensure access.	.050			√	√	√
12 Fill out maintenance report.	.017			√	√	√
Total labor-hours/period				.509	.509	1.329
Total labor-hours/year				1.018	.509	1.329

			Cost Each					
			2012 Bare Costs				Total	Total
Description	Labor-hrs.	Material	Labor	Equip.	Total	In-House	w/O&P
3900 Fire doors, roll-up, annually	1.329	4.60	65.50		70.10	107	128
3950 Annualized	2.856	18.40	141		159.40	238	285

PM Components	Labor-hrs.	W	M	Q	S	A
PM System D1015 100 1950						
Elevator, cable, electric, passenger/freight						
1 Ride car, check for any unusual noise or operation.	.411	√	√	√	√
2 Inspect machine room equipment.	.286	√	√	√	√
3 Motor room:						
A) visually inspect controllers and starters.	.012	√	√	√	√
B) visually inspect selector.	.012	√	√	√	√
C) lubricate and adjust tension of selector.	.113	√	√	√	√
D) inspect sleeve bearings of hoist motor.	.012	√	√	√	√
E) inspect brushes and commutator of hoist motor.	.012	√	√	√	√
F) inspect sleeve bearings of motor generator.	.012	√	√	√	√
G) inspect brushes and commutator of motor generator.	.014	√	√	√	√
H) inspect sleeve bearings of exciter.		√	√	√	√
I) inspect brushes and commutator of exciter.	.022	√	√	√	√
J) inspect sleeve bearings of regulator dampening motors and tach generators.	.022	√	√	√	√
K) inspect brushes and commutator of regulator dampening motors and tach generators.	.044	√	√	√	√
L) inspect and grease sleeve bearings of geared machines.	.047	√	√	√	√
M) inspect oil level in worm and gear of geared machines.	.044	√	√	√	√
N) visually inspect the brakes.	.022	√	√	√	√
O) inspect and grease, if necessary, sleeve bearings of drive deflectors and secondary sheaves.	.186	√	√	√	√
P) visually inspect and adjust contacts of controllers and starters.	.338		√	√	√
Q) inspect and adjust main operating contactor and switches of controllers and starters.	.338		√	√	√
R) inspect selector, adjusting contacts, brushes and cams if needed.	.103		√	√	√
S) inspect selsyn and advancer, motor brushes and commutators of selector.	.022		√	√	√
T) clean hoist motor brush rigging and commutator.	.068		√	√	√
U) clean motor generator and tighten brush rigging and clean commutator.	.068		√	√	√
V) clean exciter brush rigging and commutator.	.066			√	√	√
W) clean brush rigging and commutator of regulator dampening motors and tach generators.	.099			√	√	√
X) inspect machine worm and gear thrust and backlash and spider bolts; replace oil.	.047			√	√	√
Y) clean and lubricate brakes, pins and linkage.	.099			√	√	√
Z) inspect governors; lubricate sleeve bearings.	.099			√	√	√
Aa) inspect controllers and starters; adjust setting of overloads.	.169					√
Ab) tighten connections on controllers and starters; clean fuses and holders.	.169					√
Ac) set controllers and starter timers.	.169					√
Ad) clean controllers and starters.	.169					√
Ae) clean and inspect selector components.	.068					√
Af) inspect group operation controllers; clean and lubricate contacts, timers, steppers of operation controller.	.099					√
Ag) change oil and/or grease roller bearings of the hoist motor.	.094					√
Ah) vacuum and blowout the hoist motor.	.094					√
Ai) tighten all connections on the hoist motor.	.022					√

PM Components	Labor-hrs.	W	M	Q	S	A
Aj) change oil and/or grease generator's roller bearings.	.069					√
Ak) vacuum and blowout motor generator.	.094					√
Al) inspect all connections on the motor generator and tighten if necessary.	.022					√
Am) inspect roller bearings of the exciter and change oil and/or grease.	.069					√
An) vacuum and blowout exciter.	.094					√
Ao) change oil and/or grease roller bearings of regulator dampening motors and tach generators.	.094					√
Ap) vacuum/blowout regulator dampening motors and tach generators.	.044					√
Aq) inspect all regulator dampening motors and tach generator connections.	.047					√
Ar) change oil and/or grease roller bearings of the geared machines.	.094					√
As) clean and lubricate brake cores.	.099					√
At) inspect drive deflectors and secondary sheaves; change oil and grease roller bearings if necessary.	.170					√
Au) inspect drive deflectors and secondary sheaves' cable grooves for cracks.	.012					√
Av) inspect governors; change oil and grease roller bearings, if necessary.	.094					√
4 Hatch:						
A) lubricate rails of hoistway.	.733	√	√	√	√	
B) inspect car top and grease sleeve bearings if needed.	.151	√	√	√	√	
C) inspect counterweight and grease sleeve bearings if needed.	.068	√	√	√	√	
D) visually inspect cables, chains, hoist, compensating governor for wear and equalization.	.047	√	√	√	√	
E) lubricate cables, chain hoist and compensating governor if necessary.	.186	√	√	√	√	
F) inspect door operator; clean and lubricate chain and belt tension.	.177		√	√	√	
G) inspect door, clean and adjust safety edge, light ray and cables.	.052		√	√	√	
H) clean and adjust proximity devices on door.	.103		√	√	√	
I) inspect and lubricate governor tape and compensating sheave in pit.	.068		√	√	√	
J) clean and lubricate compensating tie down in pit.	.047		√	√	√	
K) inspect pit's run-by on counter weight.	.142		√	√	√	
L) inspect governor and compensating sheaves or chains for clearance to pit floor.	.022		√	√	√	
M) inspect/lubricate overhead hatch switches and cams.	.096					√
N) clean and lubricate rollers, cables, sight guards, chains, motors, closures, limit and zone switches.	.068					√
O) inspect door gibs and fastening.	.022					√
5 Inspect car top; change oil and grease roller bearings, if necessary.	.044					√
6 Check safety switches, indicators, leveling devices, selector tape, switches and hatches.	.044					√
7 Check and lubricate fan motor.	.072					√
8 Inspect counterweight; change oil and grease roller bearings, if necessary.	.094					√
9 Check safety linkage safety and cwt guides.	.098					√
10 Inspect compensation hatch.	.047					√
11 Inspect chains, hoist and compensating governor.	.094					√
12 Inspect traveling cables for tracking and wear.	.070					√

PM Components	Labor-hrs.	W	M	Q	S	A
13 Inspect door operator commutator and brushes.	.012					√
14 Inspect/clean/lubricate door operator clutch, retiring cam, door gib, rollers, tracks, upthrusts and relating cables.	.103					√
15 Under car:						
A) inspect/clean/lubricate safety devices, linkages, car guides, selector tape, switches and hitches.	.020					√
B) inspect cable hitch and loops; load weighing devices.	.027					√
16 Inspect/lubricate pit hatch switches, cams and pit oil buffer.	.083					√
17 In car:						
A) inspect and clean fixtures and signal in operating panel and car position and direction indicator.	.103		√	√	√	√
B) check operation of emergency lights and bells.	.228		√	√	√	√
C) check handrails, ceiling panels and hang on panels for tightness.	.027		√	√	√	√
D) check for tripping hazards.	.044		√	√	√	√
18 Hallway corridor:						
A) inspect hall buttons, signal lamps, lanterns and hall position indicator.	.046		√	√	√	√
B) inspect starter station, key operation and lamps.	.069		√	√	√	√
19 Clean equipment and surrounding area.	.066		√	√	√	√
20 Fill out maintenance checklist.	.022		√	√	√	√
Total labor-hours/period			3.061	5.019	5.019	8.068
Total labor-hours/year			24.488	10.038	5.019	8.068

			Cost Each					
			2012 Bare Costs				Total	Total
Description		Labor-hrs.	Material	Labor	Equip.	Total	In-House	w/O&P
1900	Elevator, cable, electric, passenger / freight, annually	8.068	1,175	570		1,745	2,000	2,350
1950	Annualized	47.613	2,100	3,375		5,475	6,475	7,850

PM Components	Labor-hrs.	W	M	Q	S	A
PM System D1015 110 1950						
Elevator, hydraulic, passenger/freight						
1 Ride car, checking for any unusual noise or operation.	.052		√	√	√	√
2 In car:						
A) inspect and clean fixtures and signal in operating panel and car position and direction indicator.	.103		√	√	√	√
B) check operation of emergency lights and bell.	.020		√	√	√	√
C) check handrails, ceiling panels and hang on panels for tightness.	.027		√	√	√	√
D) check for tripping hazards.	.012		√	√	√	√
3 Inspect and lubricate rails of hoistway.	.094		√	√	√	√
4 Hallway corridor:						
A) inspect hall buttons, signal lamps, lanterns and hall position indicator.	.046		√	√	√	√
B) inspect starter station, key operation and lamps.	.069		√	√	√	√
5 Motor room:						
A) inspect machine room equipment.	.077		√	√	√	√
B) lockout and log record.	.022		√	√	√	√
C) inspect tank oil level.	.012		√	√	√	√
D) inspect and adjust controller contacts; main operating contactors and switches.	.196			√	√	√
E) inspect pump and valve unit for leaks.	.051			√	√	√
F) inspect and adjust controller overloads; set timers.	.049					√
G) tighten connections and clean controller fuses and holders.	.020					√
H) inspect and lubricate pump motor bearings.	.099					√
6 Hatch:						
A) check hoistway car rails, brackets and fish plates.	.103					√
B) inspect/lubricate overhead hatch switches and cams.	.070					√
C) inspect/clean/lubricate hatch doors locks, rollers, tracks, upthrusts, relating cables, racks, sight guards and closers, motors, gear boxes, limit and zone switches.	.096					√
D) inspect door gibs and fastening.	.022					√
E) inspect/clean/lubricate cab top guides, steading devices, safety switches, inductors, leveling devices, selector tape, switches, hitches and fan motor.	.068					√
F) check traveling cables for wear.	.070					√
G) inspect/clean/lubricate door operator roller tracks, upthrusts, related cables, clutch, retiring cam and door gib.	.078					√
H) inspect door operator; clean and lubricate chain and belt tension.	.052			√	√	√
I) inspect door, clean and adjust safety edge, light ray and cables.	.103			√	√	√
J) clean and adjust proximity devices on door.	.068			√	√	√
7 Inspect pit gland packing.	.010			√	√	√
8 Inspect/clean/lubricate under car guides, selector tape, traveling cable, switches and platen plate assembly.	.068					√
9 Clean equipment and surrounding area.	.074		√	√	√	√
10 Fill out maintenance checklist.	.022		√	√	√	√
Total labor-hours/period			.630	1.110	1.110	1.853
Total labor-hours/year			5.040	2.220	1.110	1.853

			Cost Each					
			2012 Bare Costs				Total	Total
Description		Labor-hrs.	Material	Labor	Equip.	Total	In-House	w/O&P
1900	Elevator, hydraulic, passenger / freight, annually	1.853	1,075	131		1,206	1,350	1,550
1950	Annualized	10.223	1,250	725		1,975	2,275	2,700

PM Components	Labor-hrs.	W	M	Q	S	A
PM System D1015 310 1950						
Wheelchair Lift						
1 Check with operating personnel for any deficiencies.	.033				✓	✓
2 Check voltage and amperage under load.	.091				✓	✓
3 Check bolts securing drive cabinet and base, tighten accordingly.	.033				✓	✓
4 Check belt tension.	.033				✓	✓
5 Check lift nut assembly.	.026				✓	✓
6 Check cam rollers.	.026				✓	✓
7 Check wear pads for excessive wear.	.026				✓	✓
8 Inspect motor and shaft pulleys.	.039				✓	✓
9 Check Acme screw alignment.	.033				✓	✓
10 Inspect and lubricate upper and lower bearings.	.039				✓	✓
11 Check fastening of cable harness.	.026				✓	✓
12 Check alignment of platform and doors.	.033				✓	✓
13 Check door interlock switch for proper operation.	.039				✓	✓
14 Check operation of final limit switch and emergency stop/alarm.	.033				✓	✓
15 Check call/send controls at each station and on platform.	.039				✓	✓
16 Lube hinge of flip up ramp.	.033				✓	✓
17 Fill out maintenance checklist and report deficiencies.	.022				✓	✓
Total labor-hours/period					.604	.604
Total labor-hours/year					.604	.604

			Cost Each					
			2012 Bare Costs				**Total**	**Total**
Description		Labor-hrs.	Material	Labor	Equip.	Total	In-House	w/O&P
1900	Wheelchair lift, annually	.604		31		31	38.50	48
1950	Annualized	1.208		62.50		62.50	77	96

PM Components	Labor-hrs.	W	M	Q	S	A
PM System D1025 100 1950						
Escalator						
1 Ride escalator; check operation for smoothness, unusual vibration or noise, condition of handrails, etc.	.104	√	√	√	√	√
2 Deenergize, tag, and lockout the electrical circuit.	.017	√	√	√	√	√
3 Inspect comb plates at both ends of escalator for broken teeth and check for proper clearance between combs and step teeth and check for broken step treads.	.039	√	√	√	√	√
4 Check clearance between steps and skirt panel; look for loose trim, screws or bolts, that could snag or damage clothing or cause injury; check operation of handrail brushes.	.087	√	√	√	√	√
5 Clean escalator machine space.	.113	√	√	√	√	√
6 Lubricate step rollers, step chain, drive gears or chains, handrail drive chains, etc., according to manufacturers' instructions; observe gears and chains for signs of wear, misalignment, etc; adjust as required.	.267	√	√	√	√	√
7 Check motor for signs of overheating.	.004	√	√	√	√	√
8 Inspect controller for loose leads, burned contacts, etc.; repair as required.	.022	√	√	√	√	√
9 Clean handrails as required.	.217	√	√	√	√	√
10 Check escalator lighting; replace bulbs as required.	.099	√	√	√	√	√
11 Operate each emergency stop button and note that the escalator stops; if the escalator has the capabilities of running in both directions, stop buttons should function properly for each direction of travel; observe the stopping distance.	.013	√	√	√	√	√
12 Clean surrounding area.	.066	√	√	√	√	√
13 Fill out maintenance checklist and report deficiencies.	.022	√	√	√	√	√
Total labor-hours/period		1.070	1.070	1.070	1.070	1.070
Total labor-hours/year		40.660	8.560	2.140	1.070	1.070

	Description	Labor-hrs.	Cost Each						
			2012 Bare Costs				**Total In-House**	**Total w/O&P**	
			Material	Labor	Equip.	Total			
1900	Escalator, annually	1.070	1,625	76		1,701	1,900	2,150	
1950	Annualized	53.501	2,175	3,800		5,975	7,075	8,600	

PM Components	Labor-hrs.	W	M	Q	S	A
PM System D1095 100 1950						
Dumbwaiter, electric						
1 Check with operating or area personnel for any obvious deficiencies.	.086					√
2 Operate dumbwaiter through complete cycle and check operation for unusual noises or problems.	.052					√
3 Inspect and clean operating panel, starter station, key operation and lamps.	.072					√
4 Check operation of emergency lights and alarms.	.052					√
5 Inspect, clean and lubricate motor.	.072					√
6 Check operation of indicator lights and buttons.	.052					√
7 Inspect and lubricate rails of guides.	.148					√
8 Clean equipment and surrounding area.	.077					√
9 Fill out maintenance checklist and report deficiencies.	.022					√
Total labor-hours/period						.633
Total labor-hours/year						.633

			Cost Each					
			2012 Bare Costs				**Total**	**Total**
	Description	Labor-hrs.	Material	Labor	Equip.	Total	In-House	w/O&P
1900	Dumbwaiter, electric, annually	.633	47.50	45		92.50	109	129
1950	Annualized	.633	47.50	45		92.50	109	129

PM Components	Labor-hrs.	W	M	Q	S	A
PM System D1095 110 1950						
Dumbwaiter, hydraulic						
1 Check with operating or area personnel for any obvious deficiencies.	.086				√	√
2 Operate dumbwaiter through complete cycle and check operation for unusual noises or problems.	.052				√	√
3 Inspect and clean operating panel, starter station, key operation and lamps.	.072				√	√
4 Check operation of emergency lights and alarms.	.052				√	√
5 Inspect pump and valve unit for leaks.	.072				√	√
6 Inspect tank oil level; add as required.	.039				√	√
7 Inspect and lubricate rails of guides.	.148				√	√
8 Inspect jack seals.	.051				√	√
9 Clean equipment and surrounding area.	.077				√	√
10 Fill out maintenance checklist and report deficiencies.	.022				√	√
Total labor-hours/period					.671	.671
Total labor-hours/year					.671	.671

			Cost Each					
			2012 Bare Costs				**Total**	**Total**
	Description	Labor-hrs.	Material	Labor	Equip.	Total	In-House	w/O&P
1900	Dumbwaiter, hydraulic, annually	.671	47.50	47.50		95	112	133
1950	Annualized	1.342	95.50	95		190.50	223	266

PM Components	Labor-hrs.	W	M	Q	S	A
PM System D1095 200 1950						
Pneumatic Tube System						
1 Check with operating personnel for any deficiencies.	.039			√	√	√
2 Clean air intake screen.	.039			√	√	√
3 Check seal at doors.	.130			√	√	√
4 Inspect check valves	.026			√	√	√
5 Check blower motor and lubricate.	.065			√	√	√
6 Inspect carrier ends, latches and air washers	.026			√	√	√
7 Fill out maintenance checklist and report deficiencies.	.026			√	√	√
Total labor-hours/period				.351	.351	.351
Total labor-hours/year				.702	.351	.351

				Cost Each				
			2012 Bare Costs				**Total**	**Total**
Description	Labor-hrs.	Material	Labor	Equip.	Total	In-House	w/O&P
1900	Pneumatic Tube System, annually	.351		18.10		18.10	22.50	28
1950	Annualized	1.404		72.50		72.50	89.50	112

PM Components	Labor-hrs.	W	M	Q	S	A
PM System D2015 100 1950						
Urinals (Time is per fixture)						
1 Urinals - Flush and adjust water flow if required.	.020			√	√	√
2 Inspect for missing or damaged parts/caps and replace.	.020			√	√	√
3 Fill out maintenance checklist and report deficiencies.	.017			√	√	√
Total labor-hours/period				.057	.057	.057
Total labor-hours/year				.114	.057	.057

			Cost Each			
			2012 Bare Costs			Total	Total
Description	Labor-hrs.	Material	Labor	Equip.	Total	In-House	w/O&P
1900 Urinals, annually	.057		3.11		3.11	3.88	4.85
1950 Annualized	.228		12.45		12.45	15.55	19.40

PM Components	Labor-hrs.	W	M	Q	S	A
PM System D2015 100 2950						
Toilet, vacuum breaker type (Time is per fixture)						
1 Toilet (vacuum breaker type) - Flush and adjust water flow if required.	.020			√	√	√
2 Inspect for missing or damaged parts/caps, seat supports, and replace.	.020			√	√	√
3 Fill out maintenance checklist and report deficiencies.	.017			√	√	√
Total labor-hours/period				.057	.057	.057
Total labor-hours/year				.114	.057	.057

			Cost Each			
			2012 Bare Costs			Total	Total
Description	Labor-hrs.	Material	Labor	Equip.	Total	In-House	w/O&P
2900 Toilet (vacuum breaker type), annually	.057		3.11		3.11	3.88	4.85
2950 Annualized	.228		12.45		12.45	15.55	19.40

PM Components	Labor-hrs.	W	M	Q	S	A
PM System D2015 100 3950						
Toilet, tank type (Time is per fixture)						
1 Toilet - Clean flapper seat if leaking, adjust fill level if required.	.050			√	√	√
2 Inspect for missing or damaged parts/caps, seat supports, and replace.	.030			√	√	√
3 Fill out maintenance checklist and report deficiencies.	.017			√	√	√
Total labor-hours/period				.097	.097	.097
Total labor-hours/year				.194	.097	.097

			Cost Each			
			2012 Bare Costs			Total	Total
Description	Labor-hrs.	Material	Labor	Equip.	Total	In-House	w/O&P
3900 Toilet (tank type), annually	.097		5.30		5.30	6.60	8.25
3950 Annualized	.388		21		21	26.50	33

PM Components	Labor-hrs.	W	M	Q	S	A
PM System D2015 100 4950						
Lavatories (Time is per fixture)						
1 Lavatories - Operate faucets, replace washers/"O" Rings as necessary.	.040			√	√	√
2 Observe drain flow, clean trap if flow is obstructed.	.030			√	√	√
3 Fill out maintenance checklist and report deficiencies.	.017			√	√	√
Total labor-hours/period				.087	.087	.087
Total labor-hours/year				.174	.087	.087

		Cost Each					
		2012 Bare Costs				Total	Total
Description	Labor-hrs.	Material	Labor	Equip.	Total	In-House	w/O&P
4900 Lavatories, annually	.087	6.45	3.95		10.40	12.30	14.45
4950 Annualized	.348	6.45	15.80		22.25	28	33.50

PM Components	Labor-hrs.	W	M	Q	S	A
PM System D2015 100 5950						
Showers (Time is per fixture)						
1 Showers - Check for damaged, or missing shower heads/handles and replace if required.	.040			√	√	√
2 Fill out maintenance checklist and report deficiencies.	.017			√	√	√
Total labor-hours/period				.057	.057	.057
Total labor-hours/year				.114	.057	.057

		Cost Each					
		2012 Bare Costs				Total	Total
Description	Labor-hrs.	Material	Labor	Equip.	Total	In-House	w/O&P
5900 Showers, annually	.057	8.45	2.59		11.04	12.70	14.75
5950 Annualized	.228	8.45	10.35		18.80	23	27.50

PM Components	Labor-hrs.	W	M	Q	S	A
PM System D2015 800 1950						
Drinking fountain						
1 Check unit for proper operation, excessive noise or vibration.	.035					√
2 Clean condenser coils and fan as required.	.222					√
3 Check for water leaks in supply line and drain.	.077					√
4 Check water flow; adjust as necessary.	.039					√
5 Check drinking water temperature to ensure the unit is operating properly.	.039					√
6 Check electrical connections and cord; tighten and repair as necessary.	.120					√
7 Clean area around fountain.	.066					√
8 Fill out maintenance checklist and report deficiencies.	.022					√
Total labor-hours/period						.620
Total labor-hours/year						.620

		Cost Each					
		2012 Bare Costs				Total	Total
Description	Labor-hrs.	Material	Labor	Equip.	Total	In-House	w/O&P
1900 Drinking fountain, annually	.620	16.40	28		44.40	55	66.50
1950 Annualized	.620	16.40	28		44.40	55	66.50

PM Components	Labor-hrs.	W	M	Q	S	A
PM System D2025 120 1950						
Valve, butterfly, above 4″						
1 Lubricate valves that have grease fittings.	.022					√
2 Open and close valve using handle, wrench, or hand wheel to check operation.	.049					√
3 Check for leaks.	.007					√
4 Clean valve exterior and area around valve.	.066					√
5 Fill out maintenance report and report deficiencies.	.022					√
Total labor-hours/period						.166
Total labor-hours/year						.166

			Cost Each					
			2012 Bare Costs				**Total**	**Total**
Description	**Labor-hrs.**	**Material**	**Labor**	**Equip.**	**Total**		**In-House**	**w/O&P**
1900 Valve, butterfly, above 4″, annually	.166	7.50	7.55		15.05		18.15	21.50
1950 Annualized	.166	7.50	7.55		15.05		18.15	21.50

PM Components	Labor-hrs.	W	M	Q	S	A
PM System D2025 120 2950						
Valve, butterfly, auto, above 4″						
1 Lubricate valve actuator stem and valve stem, where possible.	.022					√
2 Check automatic valve for proper operation.	.062					√
3 Check packing gland for leaks; adjust as required.	.160					√
4 Check pneumatic operator and tubing for air leaks.	.047					√
5 Clean valve exterior and area around valve.	.034					√
6 Fill out maintenance report and report deficiencies.	.022					√
Total labor-hours/period						.347
Total labor-hours/year						.347

			Cost Each					
			2012 Bare Costs				**Total**	**Total**
Description	**Labor-hrs.**	**Material**	**Labor**	**Equip.**	**Total**		**In-House**	**w/O&P**
2900 Valve, butterfly, auto, above 4″, annually	.347	7.50	15.75		23.25		29.50	35
2950 Annualized	.347	7.50	15.75		23.25		29.50	35

PM Components	Labor-hrs.	W	M	Q	S	A
PM System D2025 125 1950						
Valve, check, above 4″						
1 Inspect valve for leaks; repair as necessary.	.009					√
2 Adjust system pressure/flow to verify that valve is opening and closing properly, if applicable.	.160					√
3 Clean valve and area around valve.	.066					√
4 Fill out maintenance report and report deficiencies.	.022					√
Total labor-hours/period						.257
Total labor-hours/year						.257

			Cost Each					
			2012 Bare Costs				**Total**	**Total**
Description	**Labor-hrs.**	**Material**	**Labor**	**Equip.**	**Total**		**In-House**	**w/O&P**
1900 Valve, check, above 4″, annually	.257	7.50	11.65		19.15		23.50	28.50
1950 Annualized	.257	7.50	11.65		19.15		23.50	28.50

D20 PLUMBING — D2025 130 Valve, Cock

PM Components	Labor-hrs.	W	M	Q	S	A
PM System D2025 130 1950						
Valve, ball, above 4″						
1 Lubricate valves that have grease fittings.	.022					√
2 Open and close valve using handle, wrench, or hand wheel to check operation.	.049					√
3 Check for leaks.	.007					√
4 Clean valve and area around valve.	.066					√
5 Fill out maintenance report and report deficiencies.	.022					√
Total labor-hours/period						.166
Total labor-hours/year						.166

			Cost Each					
			2012 Bare Costs				**Total**	**Total**
Description	**Labor-hrs.**	**Material**	**Labor**	**Equip.**	**Total**		**In-House**	**w/O&P**
1900 Valve, ball, above 4″, annually	.166	7.50	7.55		15.05		18.15	21.50
1950 Annualized	.166	7.50	7.55		15.05		18.15	21.50

D20 PLUMBING — D2025 135 Valve, Diaphragm

PM Components	Labor-hrs.	W	M	Q	S	A
PM System D2025 135 1950						
Valve, diaphragm, above 4″						
1 Lubricate valve stem, close and open valve to check operation.	.022					√
2 Check valve for proper operation and leaks; tighten packing and flange bolts as required.	.044					√
3 Clean valve exterior and area around valve.	.034					√
4 Fill out maintenance report and report deficiencies.	.022					√
Total labor-hours/period						.122
Total labor-hours/year						.122

			Cost Each					
			2012 Bare Costs				**Total**	**Total**
Description	**Labor-hrs.**	**Material**	**Labor**	**Equip.**	**Total**		**In-House**	**w/O&P**
1900 Valve, diaphragm, above 4″, annually	.122	7.50	5.55		13.05		15.55	18.40
1950 Annualized	.122	7.50	5.55		13.05		15.55	18.40

D20 PLUMBING — D2025 140 Valve, Gate

PM Components	Labor-hrs.	W	M	Q	S	A
PM System D2025 140 1950						
Valve, gate, above 4″						
1 Lubricate valve stem; close and open valve to check operation.	.049					√
2 Check packing gland for leaks; tighten packing and flange bolts as req.	.022					√
3 Clean valve exterior and area around valve.	.066					√
4 Fill out maintenance report and report deficiencies.	.022					√
Total labor-hours/period						.159
Total labor-hours/year						.159

			Cost Each					
			2012 Bare Costs				**Total**	**Total**
Description	**Labor-hrs.**	**Material**	**Labor**	**Equip.**	**Total**		**In-House**	**w/O&P**
1900 Valve, gate, above 4″, annually	.159	7.50	7.20		14.70		17.75	21
1950 Annualized	.159	7.50	7.20		14.70		17.75	21

PM Components	Labor-hrs.	W	M	Q	S	A
PM System D2025 145 1950						
Valve, globe, above 4″						
1 Lubricate stem, close and open valve to check operation.	.049					✓
2 Check packing gland for leaks; tighten packing and flange bolts as req.	.022					✓
3 Clean valve exterior.	.066					✓
4 Fill out maintenance report and report deficiencies.	.022					✓
Total labor-hours/period						.159
Total labor-hours/year						.159

			Cost Each					
			2012 Bare Costs				Total	Total
Description	Labor-hrs.	Material	Labor	Equip.	Total	In-House	w/O&P
1900 Valve, globe, above 4″, annually	.159	7.50	7.20		14.70	17.75	21
1950 Annualized	.159	7.50	7.20		14.70	17.75	21

PM Components	Labor-hrs.	W	M	Q	S	A
PM System D2025 145 2950						
Valve, globe, auto, above 4″						
1 Lubricate valve actuator stem and valve stem, where possible.	.022					✓
2 Check automatic valve for proper operation.	.062					✓
3 Check packing gland for leaks; adjust as required.	.160					✓
4 Check penumatic operator and tubing for air leaks.	.025					✓
5 Clean valve exterior and area around valve.	.034					✓
6 Fill out maintenance report and report deficiencies.	.022					✓
Total labor-hours/period						.325
Total labor-hours/year						.325

			Cost Each					
			2012 Bare Costs				Total	Total
Description	Labor-hrs.	Material	Labor	Equip.	Total	In-House	w/O&P
2900 Valve, globe, auto, above 4″, annually	.325	7.50	14.75		22.25	27.50	33.50
2950 Annualized	.325	7.50	14.75		22.25	27.50	33.50

PM Components	Labor-hrs.	W	M	Q	S	A
PM System D2025 150 1950						
Valve, motor operated, above 4″						
1 Lubricate valve actuator stem and valve stem, where possible.	.091					✓
2 Check motor and valve for proper operation, including limit switch; adjust as required.	.022				✓	✓
3 Check packing gland for leaks; adjust as required.	.113				✓	✓
4 Check electrical wiring, connections and contacts; repair as necessary.	.120				✓	✓
5 Inspect and lubricate motor gearbox as required.	.099				✓	✓
6 Clean valve exterior and area around valve.	.034				✓	✓
7 Fill out maintenance report and report deficiencies.	.022				✓	✓
Total labor-hours/period					.501	.501
Total labor-hours/year					.501	.501

			Cost Each					
			2012 Bare Costs				Total	Total
Description	Labor-hrs.	Material	Labor	Equip.	Total	In-House	w/O&P
1900 Valve, motor operated, above 4″, annually	.501	7.50	23		30.50	38.50	46.50
1950 Annualized	1.002	15.05	45.50		60.55	76.50	93

PM Components	Labor-hrs.	W	M	Q	S	A
PM System D2025 155 1950						
Valve, OS&Y, above 4″						
1 Lubricate stem; open and close valve to check operation.	.049					√
2 Check packing gland for leaks; tighten packing and flange bolts as required.	.022					√
3 Clean valve exterior and area around valve.	.066					√
4 Fill out maintenance report and report deficiencies.	.022					√
Total labor-hours/period						.159
Total labor-hours/year						.159

	Description	Labor-hrs.	Cost Each				Total In-House	Total w/O&P
			2012 Bare Costs					
			Material	Labor	Equip.	Total		
1900	Valve, OS&Y, above 4″, annually	.159	7.50	7.20		14.70	17.75	21
1950	Annualized	.159	7.50	7.20		14.70	17.75	21

PM Components	Labor-hrs.	W	M	Q	S	A
PM System D2025 190 1950						
Solar, closed loop hot water heating system, up to 6 panels						
1 Check with operating or area personnel for deficiencies.	.035				√	√
2 Inspect interior piping and connections for leaks and damaged insulation; tighten connections and repair damaged insulation as necessary.	.125				√	√
3 Check zone and circulating pump motors for excessive overheating; lubricate motor bearings.	.077				√	√
4 Check pressure and air relief valves for proper operation.	.030				√	√
5 Check control panel and differential thermostat for proper operation.	.094				√	√
6 Clean sight glasses, controls, pumps, and flow indicators on tanks.	.127				√	√
7 Check system pressure on closed loop for loss of fluid.	.046				√	√
8 Check fluid level on drain-back systems; add fluid as necessary.	.029				√	√
9 Test glycol strength in closed systems, as applicable; if required, drain system and replace with new fluid mixture.	.222					√
10 Check heat exchanger for exterior leaks.	.077				√	√
11 Clean strainers and traps.	.181					√
12 Check storage and expansion tanks; for leaks and deteriorated insulation.	.077					√
13 Inspect all collector piping for leaks and damaged insulation; tighten connections and repair as required.	.133				√	√
14 Inspect collector glazing for cracks and seals for tightness; tighten or replace seals as necessary.	.124				√	√
15 Wash/clean glazing on collector panels.	.585					√
16 Inspect ferrule around pipe flashing where solar piping runs through roof; repair as necessary.	.086				√	√
17 Check collector mounting brackets and bolts; tighten as required.	.094				√	√
18 Clean area.	.066				√	√
19 Fill out maintenance checklist and report deficiencies.	.022				√	√
Total labor-hours/period					1.165	2.230
Total labor-hours/year					1.165	2.230

			Cost Each					
			2012 Bare Costs				**Total**	**Total**
Description		**Labor-hrs.**	**Material**	**Labor**	**Equip.**	**Total**	**In-House**	**w/O&P**
1900	Wtr. htng. sys., solar clsd. lp., up to 6 panels, annually	2.230	225	124		349	405	475
1950	Annualized	3.395	227	189		416	485	580

PM Components	Labor-hrs.	W	M	Q	S	A
PM System D2025 260 1950						
Water heater, gas, to 120 gallon						
1 Check with operating or area personnel for deficiencies.	.035				√	√
2 Check for water leaks to tank and piping. check for fuel system leaks.	.077				√	√
3 Check gas burner and pilot for proper flame; adjust if required.	.118				√	√
4 Check operation and condition of pressure relief valve.	.010				√	√
5 Check automatic controls for proper operation (temperature regulators, thermostatic devices, automatic fuel shut off valve, etc.).	.094				√	√
6 Check draft diverter and clear openings, if clogged.	.027				√	√
7 Check electrical wiring for fraying and loose connections on oil burner.	.072				√	√
8 Check for proper water temperature setting; adjust as required.	.029				√	√
9 Check condition of flue pipe, and chimney.	.147				√	√
10 Drain sediment from tank.	.325					√
11 Clean up area around unit.	.066				√	√
12 Fill out maintenance checklist and report deficiencies.	.022				√	√
Total labor-hours/period					.697	1.022
Total labor-hours/year					.697	1.022

			Cost Each					
				2012 Bare Costs			Total	Total
Description		Labor-hrs.	Material	Labor	Equip.	Total	In-House	w/O&P
1900	Water heater, gas, to 120 gal., annually	1.022	60.50	57		117.50	138	164
1950	Annualized	1.719	60.50	96		156.50	186	225

PM Components	Labor-hrs.	W	M	Q	S	A
PM System D2025 260 2950						
Water heater, oil fired, to 100 gallon						
1 Check with operating or area personnel for deficiencies.	.035				√	√
2 Check for water leaks to tank and piping; check for fuel system leaks.	.077				√	√
3 Check burner flame and pilot on oil burner; adjust if required.	.073				√	√
4 Check operation and condition of pressure relief valve.	.010				√	√
5 Check automatic controls for proper operation (temperature regulators, thermostatic devices, automatic fuel shut off valve, etc.).	.094				√	√
6 Check fuel filter element on oil burner.	.068				√	√
7 Check fuel level in tank; check tank, fill pipe and fuel lines and connections for damage.	.022				√	√
8 Inspect, clean, and adjust electrodes and nozzles on oil burners; inspect fire box and flame detection scanner.	.254				√	√
9 Check electrical wiring for fraying and loose connections on oil burner.	.072				√	√
10 Check for proper water temperature setting; adjust as required.	.029				√	√
11 Clean fire box.	.577					√
12 Check for proper draft adjustment; adjust draft meter if necessary.	.005				√	√
13 Check condition of flue pipe, damper and chimney.	.147				√	√
14 Drain sediment from tank.	.325					√
15 Clean up area around unit.	.066				√	√
16 Fill out maintenance checklist and report deficiencies.	.022				√	√
Total labor-hours/period					.974	1.876
Total labor-hours/year					.974	1.876

			Cost Each					
				2012 Bare Costs			Total	Total
Description		Labor-hrs.	Material	Labor	Equip.	Total	In-House	w/O&P
2900	Water heater, oil fired, to 100 gal., annually	1.876	68	104		172	205	248
2950	Annualized	2.850	75.50	159		234.50	281	340

PM Components	Labor-hrs.	W	M	Q	S	A
PM System D2025 260 3950						
Water heater, steam coil, to 2500 gallon						
1 Check with operating or area personnel for deficiencies.	.035				√	√
2 Check for water leaks to tank and piping; check steam lines for leaks.	.077				√	√
3 Check operation and condition of pressure relief valve.	.010				√	√
4 Check steam modulating valve and steam condensate trap for proper operation.	.068				√	√
5 Check electrical wiring connections on controls and switches.	.094				√	√
6 Check for proper water temperature setting; adjust as required.	.029				√	√
7 Clean, test and inspect sight gauges, valves and drains.	.040				√	√
8 Check automatic controls for proper operation including temperature regulators and thermostatic devices.	.094				√	√
9 Check insulation on heater; repair as necessary.	.077				√	√
10 Drain sediment from tank.	.325					√
11 Clean up area around unit.	.066				√	√
12 Fill out maintenance checklist and report deficiencies.	.022				√	√
Total labor-hours/period					.612	.937
Total labor-hours/year					.612	.937

		Cost Each						
			2012 Bare Costs				Total	Total
Description		Labor-hrs.	Material	Labor	Equip.	Total	In-House	w/O&P
3900	Water heater, steam coil, to 2500 gal., annually	.937	30	52		82	98	119
3950	Annualized	1.549	30	86.50		116.50	141	172

D20 PLUMBING | D2025 262 | Valve, Pressure Relief

PM Components	Labor-hrs.	W	M	Q	S	A
PM System D2025 262 1950						
Valve, pressure relief, above 4″						
1 Inspect valve for leaks, tighten fittings as necessary.	.022					√
2 Manually operate to check operation.	.038					√
3 Clean valve and area around valve.	.066					√
4 Fill out maintenance report and report deficiencies.	.022					√
Total labor-hours/period						.148
Total labor-hours/year						.148

			Cost Each				
			2012 Bare Costs			Total	Total
Description	Labor-hrs.	Material	Labor	Equip.	Total	In-House	w/O&P
1900 Valve, pressure relief, above 4″, annually	.148		6.70		6.70	8.85	10.90
1950 Annualized	.148		6.70		6.70	8.85	10.90

D20 PLUMBING | D2025 265 | Valve, Pressure Regulator

PM Components	Labor-hrs.	W	M	Q	S	A
PM System D2025 265 1950						
Valve, pressure regulator, above 4″						
1 Inspect valve for leaks; repair as necessary.	.160					√
2 Manually operate to check operation; adjust as required.	.049					√
3 Check pressure mechanism for proper opening and closing action.	.062					√
4 Clean valve and area around regulator.	.066					√
5 Fill out maintenance report and report deficiencies.	.022					√
Total labor-hours/period						.359
Total labor-hours/year						.359

			Cost Each				
			2012 Bare Costs			Total	Total
Description	Labor-hrs.	Material	Labor	Equip.	Total	In-House	w/O&P
1900 Valve, pressure regular, above 4″, annually	.359		16.30		16.30	21.50	26.50
1950 Annualized	.359		16.30		16.30	21.50	26.50

D20 PLUMBING | D2025 270 | Valve, Sediment Strainer

PM Components	Labor-hrs.	W	M	Q	S	A
PM System D2025 270 1950						
Valve, sediment strainer, above 4″						
1 Inspect valve for leaks, tighten fittings as necessary.	.160					√
2 Open valve drain to remove collected sediment.	.065					√
3 Clean valve exterior and around strainer.	.066					√
4 Fill out maintenance checklist and report deficiencies.	.022					√
Total labor-hours/period						.313
Total labor-hours/year						.313

			Cost Each				
			2012 Bare Costs			Total	Total
Description	Labor-hrs.	Material	Labor	Equip.	Total	In-House	w/O&P
1900 Valve, sediment strainer, above 4″, annually	.313		14.20		14.20	18.70	23
1950 Annualized	.313		14.20		14.20	18.70	23

PM Components	Labor-hrs.	W	M	Q	S	A
PM System D2025 310 1950						
Valve, automatic, above 4″						
1 Lubricate valve actuator stem and valve stem, where possible.	.022					√
2 Check automatic valve for proper operation.	.062					√
3 Check packing gland for leaks; adjust as required.	.022					√
4 Check pneumatic operator and tubing for air leaks.	.025					√
5 Clean valve exterior and area around valve.	.034					√
6 Fill out maintenance report and report deficiencies.	.022					√
Total labor-hours/period						.187
Total labor-hours/year						.187

			Cost Each					
			2012 Bare Costs				Total	Total
Description		Labor-hrs.	Material	Labor	Equip.	Total	In-House	w/O&P
1900	Valve, automatic, above 4″, annually	.187	7.50	8.50		16	19.40	23
1950	Annualized	.187	7.50	8.50		16	19.40	23

PM Components	Labor-hrs.	W	M	Q	S	A
PM System D2025 310 2950						
Valve, auto diaphragm, above 4″						
1 Lubricate valve actuator mechanism and valve stem.	.022					√
2 Check valve for proper operation and leaks; tighten packing and flange bolts as required.	.044					√
3 Check pneumatic tubing and operator mechanism for proper alignment and damage; adjust as necessary and soap solution test for leaks after maintenance.	.053					√
4 Clean valve exterior and area around valve.	.034					√
5 Fill out maintenance report and report deficiencies.	.022					√
Total labor-hours/period						.175
Total labor-hours/year						.175

			Cost Each					
			2012 Bare Costs				Total	Total
Description		Labor-hrs.	Material	Labor	Equip.	Total	In-House	w/O&P
2900	Valve, auto diaphragm, above 4″, annually	.175	7.50	7.95		15.45	18.70	22.50
2950	Annualized	.175	7.50	7.95		15.45	18.70	22.50

PM Components	Labor-hrs.	W	M	Q	S	A
PM System D2095 905 1950						
Duplex sump pump						
1 Check electrical cords, plugs and connections.	.239				√	√
2 Activate float switches and check pumps for proper operation.	.078				√	√
3 Lubricate pumps as required.	.094				√	√
4 Inspect packing and tighten as required.	.062				√	√
5 Check pumps for misalignment and bearings for overheating.	.260				√	√
6 Clean out trash from sump bottom.	.072				√	√
7 Fill out maintenance checklist and report deficiencies.	.022				√	√
Total labor-hours/period					.827	.827
Total labor-hours/year					.827	.827

			Cost Each					
			2012 Bare Costs				Total	Total
Description	Labor-hrs.	Material	Labor	Equip.	Total	In-House	w/O&P
1900	Duplex sump pump, annually	.827	15.05	45		60.05	73	89.50
1950	Annualized	1.654	30	90.50		120.50	146	179

PM Components	Labor-hrs.	W	M	Q	S	A
PM System D2095 910 1950						
Submersible pump, 1 H.P. and over						
1 Check with operating personnel for any deficiencies.	.035				√	√
2 Remove pump from pit.	.585				√	√
3 Clean out trash from pump intake.	.338				√	√
4 Check electrical plug, cord and connection.	.120				√	√
5 Inspect pump body for corrosion; prime and paint as necessary.	.053				√	√
6 Check pump and motor operation for excessive vibration, noise and overheating.	.022				√	√
7 Lubricate pump and motor, where applicable.	.099				√	√
8 Return pump to pit; reset and check float switch for proper operation.	.585				√	√
9 Clean area.	.066				√	√
10 Fill out maintenance checklist and report deficiencies.	.022				√	√
Total labor-hours/period					1.925	1.925
Total labor-hours/year					1.925	1.925

			Cost Each					
			2012 Bare Costs				Total	Total
Description	Labor-hrs.	Material	Labor	Equip.	Total	In-House	w/O&P
1900	Submersible pump, 1 H.P. and over, annually	1.925	15.05	105		120.05	148	183
1950	Annualized	3.850	30	210		240	295	365

PM Components	Labor-hrs.	W	M	Q	S	A
PM System D2095 930 1950						
Oxygen monitor.						
1 Check alarm set points.	.167			√	√	√
2 Check alarm lights for replacement.	.167			√	√	√
3 Check audible annuciator for proper operation.	.167			√	√	√
4 Check battery backup for proper operation.	.167			√	√	√
5 Check and test oxygen sensor for proper operation.	.276			√	√	√
6 Replace oxygen sensor annually.	1.000					√
7 Clean area.	.034			√	√	√
8 Fill out maintenance checklist and report deficiencies.	.022			√	√	√
Total labor-hours/period				1.000	1.000	2.000
Total labor-hours/year				2.000	1.000	2.000

			Cost Each					
			2012 Bare Costs				**Total**	**Total**
Description		**Labor-hrs.**	**Material**	**Labor**	**Equip.**	**Total**	**In-House**	**w/O&P**
1900	Oxygen monitor annually	2.000	211	91		302	350	410
1950	Annualized	5.000	211	227		438	530	635

PM Components	Labor-hrs.	W	M	Q	S	A
PM System D3025 110 1950						
Boiler, electric, to 1500 gallon						
1 Check with operating or area personnel for deficiencies.	.035			√	√	√
2 Check hot water pressure gauges.	.073			√	√	√
3 Check operation and condition of pressure relief valve.	.030			√	√	√
4 Check for proper operation of primary controls for resistance-type or electrode-type heating elements; check and adjust thermostat.	.133			√	√	√
5 Check electrical wiring to heating elements, blower, motors, overcurrent protective devices, grounding system and other electrical components as required.	.238			√	√	√
6 Check over temperature and over-pressure limit controls for proper operation.	.143			√	√	√
7 Check furnace operation through complete cycle or up to 10 minutes.	.217			√	√	√
8 Clean area around boiler.	.066			√	√	√
9 Fill out maintenance checklist and report deficiencies.	.022			√	√	√
Total labor-hours/period				.957	.957	.957
Total labor-hours/year				1.914	.957	.957

			Cost Each					
			2012 Bare Costs				Total	Total
Description	Labor-hrs.	Material	Labor	Equip.	Total	In-House	w/O&P
1900	Boiler, electric, to 1500 gal., annually	.957	66	53.50		119.50	139	166
1950	Annualized	3.828	66	213		279	340	415

PM Components	Labor-hrs.	W	M	Q	S	A
PM System D3025 130 1950						
Boiler, hot water; oil, gas or combination fired, up to 120 MBH						
1 Check combustion chamber for air or gas leaks.	.077					√
2 Inspect and clean oil burner gun and ignition assembly, where applicable.	.658					√
3 Inspect fuel system for leaks and change fuel filter element, where applicable.	.098					√
4 Check fuel lines and connections for damage.	.023		√	√	√	√
5 Check for proper operational response of burner to thermostat controls.	.133			√	√	√
6 Check and lubricate burner and blower motors.	.079			√	√	√
7 Check main flame failure protection and main flame detection scanner on boiler equipped with spark ignition (oil burner).	.124		√	√	√	√
8 Check electrical wiring to burner controls and blower.	.079					√
9 Clean firebox (sweep and vacuum).	.577					√
10 Check operation of mercury control switches (i.e., steam pressure, hot water temperature limit, atomizing or combustion air proving, etc.).	.143		√	√	√	√
11 Check operation and condition of safety pressure relief valve.	.030		√	√	√	√
12 Check operation of boiler low water cut off devices.	.056		√	√	√	√
13 Check hot water pressure gauges.	.073		√	√	√	√
14 Inspect and clean water column sight glass (or replace).	.127		√	√	√	√
15 Clean fire side of water jacket boiler.	.433					√
16 Check condition of flue pipe, damper and exhaust stack.	.147			√	√	√
17 Check boiler operation through complete cycle, up to 30 minutes.	.650					√
18 Check fuel level with gauge pole, add as required.	.046		√	√	√	√
19 Clean area around boiler.	.066		√	√	√	√
20 Fill out maintenance checklist and report deficiencies.	.022		√	√	√	√
Total labor-hours/period			.710	1.069	1.069	3.641
Total labor-hours/year			5.680	2.138	1.069	3.641

			Cost Each					
			2012 Bare Costs				Total	Total
	Description	Labor-hrs.	Material	Labor	Equip.	Total	In-House	w/O&P
1900	Boiler, hot water, O/G/C, up to 120 MBH, annually	3.641	74	203		277	335	410
1950	Annualized	12.528	79	700		779	960	1,175

PM Components	Labor-hrs.	W	M	Q	S	A
PM System D3025 130 2950						
Boiler, hot water; oil, gas or combination fired, 120 to 500 MBH						
1 Check combustion chamber for air or gas leaks.	.077					√
2 Inspect and clean oil burner gun and ignition assembly where applicable.	.835					√
3 Inspect fuel system for leaks and change fuel filter element, where applicable.	.125					√
4 Check fuel lines and connections for damage.	.023		√	√	√	√
5 Check for proper operational response of burner to thermostat controls.	.169			√	√	√
6 Check and lubricate burner and blower motors.	.099			√	√	√
7 Check main flame failure protection and main flame detection scanner on boiler equipped with spark ignition (oil burner).	.155		√	√	√	√
8 Check electrical wiring to burner controls and blower.	.100					√
9 Clean firebox (sweep and vacuum).	.793					√
10 Check operation of mercury control switches (i.e., steam pressure, hot water temperature limit, atomizing or combustion air proving, etc.).	.185		√	√	√	√
11 Check operation and condition of safety pressure relief valve.	.038		√	√	√	√
12 Check operation of boiler low water cut off devices.	.070		√	√	√	√
13 Check hot water pressure gauges.	.073		√	√	√	√
14 Inspect and clean water column sight glass (or replace).	.160		√	√	√	√
15 Clean fire side of water jacket	.433					√
16 Check condition of flue pipe, damper and exhaust stack.	.183			√	√	√
17 Check boiler operation through complete cycle, up to 30 minutes.	.806					√
18 Check fuel level with gauge pole, add as required.	.046		√	√	√	√
19 Clean area around boiler.	.137		√	√	√	√
20 Fill out maintenance checklist and report deficiencies.	.022		√	√	√	√
Total labor-hours/period			.909	1.360	1.360	4.529
Total labor-hours/year			7.272	2.720	1.360	4.529

		Cost Each						
			2012 Bare Costs				Total	Total
Description	Labor-hrs.	Material	Labor	Equip.	Total	In-House	w/O&P
2900 Boiler, hot water, O/G/C, 120 to 500 MBH, annually	4.094	93.50	228		321.50	385	470
2950 Annualized	15.448	98.50	860		958.50	1,175	1,475

PM Components	Labor-hrs.	W	M	Q	S	A
PM System D3025 130 3950						
Boiler, hot water; oil, gas or combination fired, 500 to 1000 MBH						
1 Check combustion chamber for air or gas leaks.	.086					√
2 Inspect and clean oil burner gun and ignition assembly where applicable.	.910					√
3 Inspect fuel system for leaks and change fuel filter element, where applicable.	.140					√
4 Check fuel lines and connections for damage.	.026		√	√	√	√
5 Check for proper operational response of burner to thermostat controls.	.185			√	√	√
6 Check and lubricate burner and blower motors.	.109			√	√	√
7 Check main flame failure protection and main flame detection scanner on boiler equipped with spark ignition (oil burner).	.169		√	√	√	√
8 Check electrical wiring to burner controls and blower.	.111					√
9 Clean firebox (sweep and vacuum).	.875					√
10 Check operation of mercury control switches (i.e., steam pressure, hot water temperature limit, atomizing or combustion air proving, etc.).	.203		√	√	√	√
11 Check operation and condition of safety pressure relief valve.	.042		√	√	√	√
12 Check operation of boiler low water cut off devices.	.077		√	√	√	√
13 Check hot water pressure gauges.	.081		√	√	√	√
14 Inspect and clean water column sight glass (or replace).	.176		√	√	√	√
15 Clean fire side of water jacket	.433					√
16 Check condition of flue pipe, damper and exhaust stack.	.202			√	√	√
17 Check boiler operation through complete cycle, up to 30 minutes.	.887					√
18 Check fuel level with gauge pole, add as required.	.049		√	√	√	√
19 Clean area around boiler.	.151		√	√	√	√
20 Fill out maintenance checklist and report deficiencies.	.022		√	√	√	√
Total labor-hours/period			.996	1.492	1.492	4.934
Total labor-hours/year			7.968	2.984	1.492	4.934

			Cost Each					
				2012 Bare Costs			Total	Total
Description		Labor-hrs.	Material	Labor	Equip.	Total	In-House	w/O&P
3900	Boiler, hot water, O/G/C, 500 to 1000 MBH, annually	4.934	100	275		375	455	555
3950	Annualized	17.378	105	970		1,075	1,325	1,625

PM Components	Labor-hrs.	W	M	Q	S	A
PM System D3025 130 4950						
Boiler, hot water; oil, gas or combination fired, over 1000 MBH						
1 Check combustion chamber for air or gas leaks.	.117					✓
2 Inspect and clean oil burner gun and ignition assembly where applicable.	.987					✓
3 Inspect fuel system for leaks and change fuel filter element, where applicable.	.147					✓
4 Check fuel lines and connections for damage.	.035		✓	✓	✓	✓
5 Check for proper operational response of burner to thermostat controls.	.199			✓	✓	✓
6 Check and lubricate burner and blower motors.	.120			✓	✓	✓
7 Check main flame failure protection and main flame detection scanner on boiler equipped with spark ignition (oil burner).	.186		✓	✓	✓	✓
8 Check electrical wiring to burner controls and blower.	.120					✓
9 Clean firebox (sweep and vacuum).	.819					✓
10 Check operation of mercury control switches (i.e., steam pressure, hot water temperature limit, atomizing or combustion air proving, etc.).	.215		✓	✓	✓	✓
11 Check operation and condition of safety pressure relief valve.	.046		✓	✓	✓	✓
12 Check operation of boiler low water cut off devices.	.085		✓	✓	✓	✓
13 Check hot water pressure gauges.	.109		✓	✓	✓	✓
14 Inspect and clean water column sight glass (or replace).	.191		✓	✓	✓	✓
15 Clean fire side of water jacket	.433					✓
16 Check condition of flue pipe, damper and exhaust stack.	.221			✓	✓	✓
17 Check boiler operation through complete cycle, up to 30 minutes.	.887					✓
18 Check fuel level with gauge pole, add as required.	.098		✓	✓	✓	✓
19 Clean area around boiler.	.182		✓	✓	✓	✓
20 Fill out maintenance checklist and report deficiencies.	.022		✓	✓	✓	✓
Total labor-hours/period			1.169	1.709	1.709	5.219
Total labor-hours/year			9.352	3.418	1.709	5.219

			Cost Each					
			2012 Bare Costs				Total	Total
Description		Labor-hrs.	Material	Labor	Equip.	Total	In-House	w/O&P
4900	Boiler, hot water, O/G/C, over 1000 MBH, annually	5.219	113	291		404	485	595
4950	Annualized	19.698	118	1,100		1,218	1,500	1,850

PM Components	Labor-hrs.	W	M	Q	S	A
PM System D3025 140 1950						
Boiler, steam; oil, gas or combination fired, up to 120 MBH						
1 Inspect fuel system for leaks or damage.	.098		√	√	√	√
2 Change fuel filter element and clean strainers; repair leaks, where applicable.	.581					√
3 Check main flame failure protection, positive fuel shutoff and main flame detection scanner on boiler equipped with spark ignition (oil burner).	.124		√	√	√	√
4 Check for proper operational response of burner to thermostat controls.	.133			√	√	√
5 Inspect all gas, steam and water lines, valves, connections for leaks or damage; repair as necessary.	.195			√	√	√
6 Check feedwater system and feedwater makeup control and pump.	.056		√	√	√	√
7 Check and lubricate burner and blower motors as required.	.083			√	√	√
8 Check operation and condition of safety pressure relief valve.	.030		√	√	√	√
9 Check combustion controls, combustion blower and damper modulation control.	.133					√
10 Check all indicator lamps and water/steam pressure gauges.	.073		√	√	√	√
11 Check electrical panels and wiring to burner, blowers and other components.	.079			√	√	√
12 Clean blower air-intake dampers, if required.	.055			√	√	√
13 Check condition of flue pipe, damper and exhaust stack.	.147		√	√	√	√
14 Check boiler operation through complete cycle, up to 30 minutes.	.650		√	√	√	√
15 Check water column sight glass and water level system; clean or replace sight glass, if required.	.127		√	√	√	√
16 Clean firebox (sweep and vacuum).	.577					√
17 Check fuel level with gauge pole for oil burning boilers.	.046		√	√	√	√
18 Inspect and clean oil burner gun and ignition assembly where applicable.	.650					√
19 Clean area around boiler.	.066		√	√	√	√
20 Fill out maintenance checklist and report deficiencies.	.022		√	√	√	√
Total labor-hours/period			.789	1.984	1.984	3.925
Total labor-hours/year			6.312	3.968	1.984	3.925

			Cost Each					
			2012 Bare Costs				Total	Total
Description		Labor-hrs.	Material	Labor	Equip.	Total	In-House	w/O&P
1900	Boiler, steam, O/G/C, up to 120 MBH, annually	3.925	146	219		365	435	525
1950	Annualized	16.189	151	900		1,051	1,300	1,600

PM Components	Labor-hrs.	W	M	Q	S	A
PM System D3025 140 2950						
Boiler, steam; oil, gas or combination fired, 120 to 500 MBH						
1 Inspect fuel system for leaks or damage.	.098		√	√	√	√
2 Change fuel filter element and clean strainers; repair leaks, where applicable.	.835					√
3 Check main flame failure protection, positive fuel shutoff and main flame detection scanner on boiler equipped with spark ignition (oil burner).	.125		√	√	√	√
4 Check for proper operational response of burner to thermostat controls.	.169			√	√	√
5 Inspect all gas, steam and water lines, valves, connections for leaks or damage; repair as necessary.	.195			√	√	√
6 Check feedwater system and feedwater makeup control and pump.	.069		√	√	√	√
7 Check and lubricate burner, blowers and motors as required.	.099			√	√	√
8 Check operation and condition of safety pressure relief valve.	.039		√	√	√	√
9 Check combustion controls, combustion blower and damper modulation control.	.169					√
10 Check all indicator lamps and water/steam pressure gauges.	.073		√	√	√	√
11 Check electrical panels and wiring to burner, blowers and other components.	.104			√	√	√
12 Clean blower air-intake dampers, if required.	.069			√	√	√
13 Check condition of flue pipe, damper and exhaust stack.	.147		√	√	√	√
14 Check boiler operation through complete cycle, up to 30 minutes.	.806			√	√	√
15 Check water column sight glass and water level system; clean or replace sight glass, if required.	.127		√	√	√	√
16 Clean firebox (sweep and vacuum).	.793					√
17 Check fuel level with gauge pole for oil burning boilers.	.046		√	√	√	√
18 Inspect and clean oil burner gun and ignition assembly where applicable.	.819					√
19 Clean area around boiler.	.137		√	√	√	√
20 Fill out maintenance checklist and report deficiencies.	.022		√	√	√	√
Total labor-hours/period			.883	2.325	2.325	4.941
Total labor-hours/year			7.064	4.650	2.325	4.941

		Cost Each						
		2012 Bare Costs				Total	Total	
Description	Labor-hrs.	Material	Labor	Equip.	Total	In-House	w/O&P	
2900 Boiler, steam, O/G/C, 120 to 500 MBH, annually	4.941	181	275		456	545	655	
2950 Annualized	18.980	191	1,050		1,241	1,525	1,900	

PM Components	Labor-hrs.	W	M	Q	S	A
PM System D3025 140 3950						
Boiler, steam; oil, gas or combination fired, 500 to 1000 MBH						
1 Inspect fuel system for leaks or damage.	.098		√	√	√	√
2 Change fuel filter element and clean strainers; repair leaks, where applicable.	.910					√
3 Check main flame failure protection, positive fuel shutoff and main flame detection scanner on boiler equipped with spark ignition (oil burner).	.140		√	√	√	√
4 Check for proper operational response of burner to thermostat controls.	.185			√	√	√
5 Inspect all gas, steam and water lines, valves, connections for leaks or damage; repair as necessary.	.195			√	√	√
6 Check feedwater system and feedwater makeup control and pump.	.075		√	√	√	√
7 Check and lubricate burner, blowers and motors as required.	.109			√	√	√
8 Check operation and condition of safety pressure relief valve.	.052		√	√	√	√
9 Check combustion controls, combustion blower and damper modulation control.	.185					√
10 Check all indicator lamps and water/steam pressure gauges.	.091		√	√	√	√
11 Check electrical panels and wiring to burner, blowers and other components.	.117			√	√	√
12 Clean blower air-intake dampers, if required.	.069			√	√	√
13 Check condition of flue pipe, damper and exhaust stack.	.147		√	√	√	√
14 Check boiler operation through complete cycle, up to 30 minutes.	.884			√	√	√
15 Check water column sight glass and water level system; clean or replace sight glass, if required.	.127		√	√	√	√
16 Clean firebox (sweep and vacuum).	1.053					√
17 Check fuel level with gauge pole for oil burning boilers.	.046		√	√	√	√
18 Inspect and clean oil burner gun and ignition assembly where applicable.	.923					√
19 Clean area around boiler.	.151		√	√	√	√
20 Fill out maintenance checklist and report deficiencies.	.022		√	√	√	√
Total labor-hours/period			.949	2.508	2.508	5.579
Total labor-hours/year			7.592	5.016	2.508	5.579

		Cost Each					
		2012 Bare Costs				Total	Total
Description	Labor-hrs.	Material	Labor	Equip.	Total	In-House	w/O&P
3900 Boiler, steam, O/G/C, 500 to 1000 MBH, annually	5.579	194	310		504	600	730
3950 Annualized	20.695	204	1,150		1,354	1,675	2,050

PM Components	Labor-hrs.	W	M	Q	S	A
PM System D3025 140 4950						
Boiler, steam; oil, gas or combination fired, over 1000 MBH						
1 Inspect fuel system for leaks or damage.	.098		√	√	√	√
2 Change fuel filter element and clean strainers; repair leaks, where applicable.	1.027					√
3 Check main flame failure protection, positive fuel shutoff and main flame detection scanner on boiler equipped with spark ignition (oil burner).	.147		√	√	√	√
4 Check for proper operational response of burner to thermostat controls.	.199			√	√	√
5 Inspect all gas, steam and water lines, valves, connections for leaks abor damage; repair as necessary.	.195			√	√	√
6 Check feedwater system and feedwater makeup control and pump.	.091		√	√	√	√
7 Check and lubricate burner, blowers and motors as required.	.120			√	√	√
8 Check operation and condition of safety pressure relief valve.	.069		√	√	√	√
9 Check combustion controls, combustion blower and damper modulation control.	.199					√
10 Check all indicator lamps and water/steam pressure gauges.	.109		√	√	√	√
11 Check electrical panels and wiring to burner, blowers and other components.	.140			√	√	√
12 Clean blower air-intake dampers, if required.	.069			√	√	√
13 Check condition of flue pipe, damper and exhaust stack.	.147		√	√	√	√
14 Check boiler operation through complete cycle, up to 30 minutes.	.884			√	√	√
15 Check water column sight glass and water level system; clean or replace sight glass, if required.	.127		√	√	√	√
16 Clean firebox (sweep and vacuum).	1.144					√
17 Check fuel level with gauge pole for oil burning boilers.	.046		√	√	√	√
18 Inspect and clean oil burner gun and ignition assembly where applicable.	1.196					√
19 Clean area around boiler.	.182		√	√	√	√
20 Fill out maintenance checklist and report deficiencies.	.022		√	√	√	√
Total labor-hours/period			1.038	2.645	2.645	6.211
Total labor-hours/year			8.304	5.290	2.645	6.211

		Cost Each						
			2012 Bare Costs				Total	Total
Description	Labor-hrs.	Material	Labor	Equip.	Total	In-House	w/O&P
4900 Boiler, steam, O/G/C, over 1000 MBH, annually	6.211	214	345		559	665	810
4950 Annualized	22.450	224	1,250		1,474	1,800	2,225

PM Components	Labor-hrs.	W	M	Q	S	A
PM System D3025 210 1950						
Deaerator tank						
1 Check tank and associated piping for leaks.	.013				√	√
2 Bottom - blow deaerator tank.	.022				√	√
3 Perform sulfite test on deaerator water sample.	.013				√	√
4 Check low and high float levels for proper operation and respective water level alarms.	.337				√	√
5 Clean steam and feedwater strainers.	.143				√	√
6 Check steam pressure regulating valve operation.	.007				√	√
7 Check all indicator lights.	.066				√	√
8 Clean unit and surrounding area.	.022				√	√
9 Fill out maintenance checklist and report deficiencies.	.130				√	√
Total labor-hours/period					.753	.753
Total labor-hours/year					.753	.753

	Description	Labor-hrs.	Cost Each				Total In-House	Total w/O&P
			2012 Bare Costs					
			Material	Labor	Equip.	Total		
1900	Deaerator tank, annually	.753	39	42		81	95	114
1950	Annualized	1.506	39	84		123	148	180

PM Components	Labor-hrs.	W	M	Q	S	A
PM System D3025 310 1950						
Pump, boiler fuel oil						
1 Check with operating or area personnel for deficiencies.	.035				√	√
2 Check for leaks on discharge piping and seals, etc.	.077				√	√
3 Check pump and motor operation for vibration, noise, overheating, etc.	.022				√	√
4 Check alignment and clearances of shaft and coupler.	.290				√	√
5 Tighten or replace loose, missing, or damaged nuts, bolts, and screws.	.005				√	√
6 Lubricate pump and motor as required.	.099				√	√
7 Clean pump, motor and surrounding area.	.066				√	√
8 Fill out maintenance checklist and report deficiencies.	.022				√	√
Total labor-hours/period					.616	.616
Total labor-hours/year					.616	.616

			Cost Each					
			2012 Bare Costs				**Total**	**Total**
Description		**Labor-hrs.**	**Material**	**Labor**	**Equip.**	**Total**	**In-House**	**w/O&P**
1900	Pump, boiler fuel oil, annually	.616	50	34.50		84.50	98	116
1950	Annualized	1.232	51	68.50		119.50	142	171

PM Components	Labor-hrs.	W	M	Q	S	A
PM System D3025 310 2950						
Pump, condensate return, over 1 H.P.						
1 Check for proper operation of pump.	.022				√	√
2 Check for leaks on suction and discharge piping, seals, packing glands, etc.; make minor adjustments as required.	.077				√	√
3 Check pump and motor operation for vibration, noise, overheating, etc.	.022				√	√
4 Check alignment pump and motor; adjust as necessary.	.290				√	√
5 Lubricate pump and motor.	.099				√	√
6 Clean exterior of pump, motor and surrounding area.	.030				√	√
7 Fill out maintenance checklist and report deficiencies.	.022				√	√
Total labor-hours/period					.562	.562
Total labor-hours/year					.562	.562

			Cost Each					
			2012 Bare Costs				**Total**	**Total**
Description		**Labor-hrs.**	**Material**	**Labor**	**Equip.**	**Total**	**In-House**	**w/O&P**
2900	Pump, steam condensate return, over 1 H.P., annually	.562	50	31.50		81.50	94	112
2950	Annualized	1.124	51	62.50		113.50	134	161

PM Components	Labor-hrs.	W	M	Q	S	A
PM System D3025 310 3950						
Pump, steam condensate return, duplex						
1 Check with operating or area personnel for deficiencies.	.035				√	√
2 Check for proper operation.	.022				√	√
3 Check for leaks on suction and discharge piping, seals, packing glands, etc.; make minor adjustments as required.	.153				√	√
4 Check pumps and motors operation for excessive vibration, noise and overheating.	.044				√	√
5 Check pump controller for proper operation.	.130				√	√
6 Lubricate pumps and motors.	.099				√	√
7 Clean condensate return unit and surrounding area.	.066				√	√
8 Fill out maintenance checklist and report deficiencies.	.022				√	√
Total labor-hours/period					.571	.571
Total labor-hours/year					.571	.571

			Cost Each					
			2012 Bare Costs				Total	Total
Description		Labor-hrs.	Material	Labor	Equip.	Total	In-House	w/O&P
3900	Pump, steam condensate return, duplex, annually	.571	99.50	32		131.50	149	174
3950	Annualized	1.142	102	63.50		165.50	192	227

PM Components	Labor-hrs.	W	M	Q	S	A
PM System D3035 110 1950						
Water cooling tower, forced draft, up to 50 tons						
1 Check with operating or area personnel for deficiencies.	.035				√	√
2 Check operation of unit for water leaks, noise or vibration.	.077				√	√
3 Clean and inspect hot water basin.	.156				√	√
4 Remove access panel.	.048				√	√
5 Check electrical wiring and connections; make appropriate adjustments.	.120				√	√
6 Lubricate all motor and fan bearings.	.047				√	√
7 Check fan blades or blowers for imbalance and tip clearance.	.055				√	√
8 Check belt for wear, tension and alignment; adjust as required.	.029				√	√
9 Drain and flush cold water sump and clean strainer.	.382				√	√
10 Clean inside of water tower using water hose; scrape, brush and wipe as required; heavy deposits of scale should be removed with scale removing compound.	.598				√	
11 Refill with water, ck. make-up water asm. for leakage, adj. float if nec.	.211				√	√
12 Replace access panel.	.039				√	√
13 Remove, clean and reinstall conductivity and ph electrodes in chemical water treatment system.	.390				√	
14 Inspect and clean around cooling tower.	.066				√	√
15 Fill out maintenance checklist and report deficiencies.	.022				√	√
Total labor-hours/period					2.275	2.275
Total labor-hours/year					2.275	2.275

			Cost Each				
			2012 Bare Costs			Total	Total
Description	Labor-hrs.	Material	Labor	Equip.	Total	In-House	w/O&P
1900 Cooling tower, forced draft, up to 50 tons, annually	2.275	25.50	127		152.50	186	229
1950 Annualized	4.550	36	253		289	355	440

PM Components	Labor-hrs.	W	M	Q	S	A
PM System D3035 110 2950						
Water cooling tower, forced draft, 51 tons through 500 tons						
1 Check with operating or area personnel for deficiencies.	.074				√	√
2 Check operation of unit for water leaks, noise or vibration.	.163				√	√
3 Clean and inspect hot water basin.	.332				√	√
4 Remove access panel.	.103				√	√
5 Check electrical wiring and connections; make appropriate adjustments.	.255				√	√
6 Lubricate all motor and fan bearings.	.100				√	√
7 Check fan blades or blowers for imbalance and tip clearance.	.247				√	√
8 Check belt for wear, tension and alignment; adjust as required.	.096				√	√
9 Drain and flush cold water sump and clean strainer.	.819				√	√
10 Clean inside of water tower using water hose; scrape, brush and wipe as required; heavy deposits of scale should be removed with scale removing compound.	1.271				√	√
11 Refill with water, chk. make-up water aseb. for leakage, adj. float if nec.	.447				√	√
12 Replace access panel.	.078				√	√
13 Remove, clean and reinstall conductivity and ph electrodes in chemical water treatment system.	.832				√	√
14 Inspect and clean around cooling tower.	.117				√	√
15 Fill out maintenance checklist and report deficiencies.	.022				√	√
Total labor-hours/period					4.956	4.956
Total labor-hours/year					4.956	4.956

			Cost Each				
			2012 Bare Costs			Total	Total
Description	Labor-hrs.	Material	Labor	Equip.	Total	In-House	w/O&P
2900 Cooling tower, forced draft, 50 thru 500 tons, annually	4.956	47	276		323	395	490
2950 Annualized	9.912	65	550		615	760	940

PM Components	Labor-hrs.	W	M	Q	S	A
PM System D3035 110 3950						
Water cooling tower, forced draft, 500 tons through 1000 tons						
1 Check with operating or area personnel for deficiencies.	.109				√	√
2 Check operation of unit for water leaks, noise or vibration.	.239				√	√
3 Clean and inspect hot water basin.	.488				√	√
4 Remove access panel.	.151				√	√
5 Check electrical wiring and connections; make appropriate adjustments.	.374				√	√
6 Lubricate all motor and fan bearings.	.147				√	√
7 Check fan blades or blowers for imbalance and tip clearance.	.302				√	√
8 Check belt for wear, tension and alignment; adjust as required.	.220				√	√
9 Drain and flush cold water sump and clean strainer.	1.464				√	√
10 Clean inside of water tower using water hose; scrape, brush and wipe as required; heavy deposits of scale should be removed with scale removing compound.	2.259				√	√
11 Refill with water, check make-up water assembly for leakage, adjust float if necessary.	1.578				√	√
12 Replace access panel.	.117				√	√
13 Remove, clean and reinstall conductivity and ph electrodes in chemical water treatment system.	1.222				√	√
14 Inspect and clean around cooling tower.	.172				√	√
15 Fill out maintenance checklist and report deficiencies.	.022				√	√
Total labor-hours/period					8.864	8.864
Total labor-hours/year					8.864	8.864

			Cost Each				
			2012 Bare Costs			Total	Total
Description	Labor-hrs.	Material	Labor	Equip.	Total	In-House	w/O&P
3900 Cooling tower, forced draft, 500 to 1000 tons, annually	8.864	101	495		596	725	895
3950 Annualized	17.728	144	985		1,129	1,400	1,725

PM Components	Labor-hrs.	W	M	Q	S	A
PM System D3035 130 1950						
Chiller, reciprocating, air cooled, up to 25 tons						
1 Check unit for proper operation, excessive noise or vibration.	.033		√	√	√	√
2 Run system diagnostics test.	.325		√	√	√	√
3 Check oil level in sight glass of lead compressor only, add oil as necessary.	.042		√	√	√	√
4 Check superheat and subcooling temperatures.	.325					√
5 Check liquid line sight glass, oil and refrigerant pressures.	.036		√	√	√	√
6 Check contactors, sensors and mechanical safety limits.	.094					√
7 Check electrical wiring and connections; tighten loose connections.	.120					√
8 Clean intake side of condenser coils, fans and intake screens.	1.282					√
9 Inspect fan(s) or blower(s) for bent blades of imbalance.	.086					√
10 Lubricate shaft bearings and motor bearings as required.	.281					√
11 Inspect plumbing and valves for leaks, adjust as necessary.	.077		√	√	√	√
12 Check evaporator and condenser for corrosion.	.026		√	√	√	√
13 Clean chiller and surrounding area.	.066		√	√	√	√
14 Fill out maintenance checklist and report deficiencies.	.022		√	√	√	√
Total labor-hours/period			.627	.627	.627	2.815
Total labor-hours/year			5.016	1.254	.627	2.815

			Cost Each				
			2012 Bare Costs			Total	Total
Description	Labor-hrs.	Material	Labor	Equip.	Total	In-House	w/O&P
1900 Chiller, recip., air cooled, up to 25 tons, annually	2.815	50.50	157		207.50	251	305
1950 Annualized	9.712	50.50	540		590.50	730	910

PM Components	Labor-hrs.	W	M	Q	S	A
PM System D3035 130 2950						
Chiller, reciprocating, air cooled, over 25 tons						
1 Check unit for proper operation, excessive noise or vibration.	.033		√	√	√	√
2 Run system diagnostics test.	.455		√	√	√	√
3 Check oil level in sight glass of lead compressor only, add oil as necessary.	.042		√	√	√	√
4 Check superheat and subcooling temperatures.	.325					√
5 Check liquid line sight glass, oil and refrigerant pressures.	.036		√	√	√	√
6 Check contactors, sensors and mechanical safety limits.	.094					√
7 Check electrical wiring and connections; tighten loose connections.	.120					√
8 Clean intake side of condenser coils, fans and intake screens.	1.282					√
9 Inspect fan(s) or blower(s) for bent blades of imbalance.	.237					√
10 Lubricate shaft bearings and motor bearings as required.	.341					√
11 Inspect plumbing and valves for leaks, adjust as necessary.	.117		√	√	√	√
12 Check evaporator and condenser for corrosion.	.052		√	√	√	√
13 Clean chiller and surrounding area.	.117		√	√	√	√
14 Fill out maintenance checklist and report deficiencies.	.022		√	√	√	√
Total labor-hours/period			.874	.874	.874	3.273
Total labor-hours/year			6.992	1.748	.874	3.273

			Cost Each				
			2012 Bare Costs			Total	Total
Description	Labor-hrs.	Material	Labor	Equip.	Total	In-House	w/O&P
2900 Chiller, recip., air cooled, over 25 tons, annually	3.273	72	182		254	305	375
2950 Annualized	12.887	72	720		792	975	1,225

PM Components	Labor-hrs.	W	M	Q	S	A
PM System D3035 135 1950						
Chiller, reciprocating, water cooled, up to 50 tons						
1　Check unit for proper operation, excessive noise or vibration.	.033		√	√	√	√
2　Run system diagnostics test.	.325		√	√	√	√
3　Check oil level in sight glass of lead compressor only, add oil as necessary.	.042		√	√	√	√
4　Check superheat and subcooling temperatures.	.325					√
5　Check liquid line sight glass, oil and refrigerant pressures.	.036		√	√	√	√
6　Check contactors, sensors and mechanical limits, adjust as necessary.	.094					√
7　Inspect plumbing and valves for leaks, tighten connections as necessary.	.077		√	√	√	√
8　Check condenser and evaporator for corrosion.	.026		√	√	√	√
9　Clean chiller and surrounding area.	.066		√	√	√	√
10　Fill out maintenance checklist and report deficiencies.	.022		√	√	√	√
Total labor-hours/period			.627	.627	.627	1.046
Total labor-hours/year			5.016	1.254	.627	1.046

			Cost Each				
			2012 Bare Costs			Total	Total
Description	Labor-hrs.	Material	Labor	Equip.	Total	In-House	w/O&P
1900　Chiller, recip., water cooled, up to 50 tons, annually	1.046	50.50	58.50		109	128	154
1950　　Annualized	7.943	50.50	440		490.50	610	755

PM Components	Labor-hrs.	W	M	Q	S	A
PM System D3035 135 2950						
Chiller, reciprocating, water cooled, over 50 tons						
1　Check unit for proper operation, excessive noise or vibration.	.033		√	√	√	√
2　Run system diagnostics test.	.455		√	√	√	√
3　Check oil level in sight glass of lead compressor only, add oil as necessary.	.042		√	√	√	√
4　Check superheat and subcooling temperatures.	.325					√
5　Check liquid line sight glass, oil and refrigerant pressures.	.036		√	√	√	√
6　Check contactors, sensors and mechanical limits, adjust as necessary.	.094					√
7　Inspect plumbing and valves for leaks, tighten connections as necessary.	.117		√	√	√	√
8　Check condenser and evaporator for corrosion.	.052		√	√	√	√
9　Clean chiller and surrounding area.	.117		√	√	√	√
10　Fill out maintenance checklist and report deficiencies.	.022		√	√	√	√
Total labor-hours/period			.874	.874	.874	1.293
Total labor-hours/year			6.992	1.748	.874	1.293

			Cost Each				
			2012 Bare Costs			Total	Total
Description	Labor-hrs.	Material	Labor	Equip.	Total	In-House	w/O&P
2900　Chiller, recip., water cooled, over 50 tons, annually	1.293	58	72		130	154	185
2950　　Annualized	10.907	58	610		668	820	1,025

PM Components	Labor-hrs.	W	M	Q	S	A
PM System D3035 140 1950						
Chiller, centrifugal water cooled, up to 100 tons						
1 Check unit for proper operation.	.035	√	√	√	√	√
2 Check oil level; add oil as necessary.	.022	√	√	√	√	√
3 Check oil temperature.	.038	√	√	√	√	√
4 Check dehydrator or purge system; remove water if observed in sight glass.	.046	√	√	√	√	√
5 Run system control tests.	.325		√	√	√	√
6 Check refrigerant charge/level, add as necessary.	.272		√	√	√	√
7 Check compressor for excessive noise/vibration.	.025		√	√	√	√
8 Check sensor and mechanical safety limits; replace as necessary.	.094				√	√
9 Clean dehydrator float valve.	.195					√
10 Perform spectrochemical analysis of compressor oil; replace oil as necessary.	.039					√
11 Replace oil filters and add oil as necessary.	.081					√
12 Inspect cooler and condenser tubes for leaks; clean screens as necessary.	5.200					√
13 Inspect utility vessel vent piping and safety relief valve; replace as necessary.	.195					√
14 Inspect/clean the economizer (vane) gas line, damper valve and actuator arm.	.650					√
15 Run an insulation test on the centrifugal motor.	1.300					√
16 Clean area around equipment.	.066	√	√	√	√	√
17 Document all maintenance and cleaning procedures.	.022	√	√	√	√	√
Total labor-hours/period		.229	.851	.851	.945	8.605
Total labor-hours/year		8.702	6.808	1.702	.945	8.605

			Cost Each					
			2012 Bare Costs				**Total**	**Total**
Description		Labor-hrs.	**Material**	**Labor**	**Equip.**	**Total**	**In-House**	**w/O&P**
1900	Chiller, centrif., water cooled, up to 100 tons, annually	8.605	235	480		715	855	1,050
1950	Annualized	26.762	238	1,500		1,738	2,125	2,625

PM Components	Labor-hrs.	W	M	Q	S	A
PM System D3035 140 2950						
Chiller, centrifugal water cooled, over 100 tons						
1 Check unit for proper operation.	.035	√	√	√	√	√
2 Check oil level; add oil as necessary.	.022	√	√	√	√	√
3 Check oil temperature.	.038	√	√	√	√	√
4 Check dehydrator or purge system; remove water if observed in sight glass.	.046	√	√	√	√	√
5 Run system control tests.	.455		√	√	√	√
6 Check refrigerant charge/level, add as necessary.	.381		√	√	√	√
7 Check compressor for excessive noise/vibration.	.039		√	√	√	√
8 Check sensor and mechanical safety limits; replace as necessary.	.133				√	√
9 Clean dehydrator float valve.	.351					√
10 Perform spectrochemical analysis of compressor oil; replace oil as necessary.	.039					√
11 Replace oil filters and add oil as necessary.	.161					√
12 Inspect cooler and condenser tubes for leaks; clean screens as necessary.	5.200					√
13 Inspect utility vessel vent piping and safety relief valve; replace as necessary.	.247					√
14 Inspect/clean the economizer (vane), gas line damper valve and actuator arm.	.650					√
15 Run an insulation test on the centrifugal motor.	1.950					√
16 Clean area around equipment.	.117	√	√	√	√	√
17 Document all maintenance and cleaning procedures.	.022	√	√	√	√	√
Total labor-hours/period		.280	1.155	1.155	1.288	9.886
Total labor-hours/year		10.640	9.240	2.310	1.288	9.886

			Cost Each					
			2012 Bare Costs				**Total**	**Total**
Description		**Labor-hrs.**	**Material**	**Labor**	**Equip.**	**Total**	**In-House**	**w/O&P**
2900	Chiller, centrif., water cooled, over 100 tons, annually	9.886	264	550		814	975	1,200
2950	Annualized	33.364	267	1,850		2,117	2,600	3,225

PM Components	Labor-hrs.	W	M	Q	S	A
PM System D3035 150 1950						
Chiller, absorption unit, up to 500 tons						
1 Check with operating personnel for deficiencies; check operating log sheets for indications of increased temperature trends.	.035			√	√	√
2 Check unit for proper operation, excessive noise or vibration.	.026			√	√	√
3 Check and clean strainers in all lines as required.	1.300					√
4 Check pulley alignment and belts for condition, proper tension and misalignment on external purge pump system, if applicable; adjust for proper tension and or alignment.	.043			√	√	√
5 Check purge pump vacuum oil level, as required; add/change oil as necessary.	.650			√	√	√
6 Lubricate pump shaft bearings and motor bearings.	.281			√	√	√
7 Check and service system controls, wirings and connections; tighten loose connections.	.120					√
8 Inspect cooling and system water piping circuits for leakage.	.077			√	√	√
9 Clean area around equipment.	.066			√	√	√
10 Fill out maintenance checklist.	.022			√	√	√
Total labor-hours/period				1.200	1.200	2.620
Total labor-hours/year				2.400	1.200	2.620

			Cost Each				
			2012 Bare Costs			**Total**	**Total**
Description	**Labor-hrs.**	**Material**	**Labor**	**Equip.**	**Total**	**In-House**	**w/O&P**
1900 Chiller, absorption unit, up to 500 tons, annually	2.620	81	146		227	271	330
1950 Annualized	6.220	86.50	345		431.50	525	650

PM Components	Labor-hrs.	W	M	Q	S	A
PM System D3035 150 2950						
Chiller, absorption unit, 500 to 5000 tons						
1 Check with operating personnel for deficiencies; check operating log sheets for indications of increased temperature trends.	.035			√	√	√
2 Check unit for proper operation, excessive noise or vibration.	.026			√	√	√
3 Check and clean strainers in all lines as required.	2.340					√
4 Check pulley alignment and belts for condition, proper tension and misalignment on external purge pump system, if applicable; adjust for proper tension and or alignment.	.086			√	√	√
5 Check purge pump vacuum oil level, as required; add/change oil as necessary.	.975			√	√	√
6 Lubricate pump shaft bearings and motor bearings.	.320			√	√	√
7 Check and service system controls, wirings and connections; tighten loose connections.	.139					√
8 Inspect cooling and system water piping circuits for leakage.	.153			√	√	√
9 Clean area around equipment.	.117			√	√	√
10 Fill out maintenance checklist.	.022			√	√	√
Total labor-hours/period				1.734	1.734	4.213
Total labor-hours/year				3.468	1.734	4.213

			Cost Each				
			2012 Bare Costs			**Total**	**Total**
Description	**Labor-hrs.**	**Material**	**Labor**	**Equip.**	**Total**	**In-House**	**w/O&P**
2900 Chiller, absorption unit, 500 to 5000 tons, annually	4.213	164	235		399	475	570
2950 Annualized	9.415	224	525		749	900	1,100

PM Components	Labor-hrs.	W	M	Q	S	A
PM System D3035 160 1950						
Chiller, screw, water cooled, up to 100 tons						
1 Check unit for proper operation, excessive noise or vibration.	.033		√	√	√	√
2 Run system diagnostics test.	.325		√	√	√	√
3 Check oil level and oil temperature; add oil as necessary.	.022		√	√	√	√
4 Check refrigerant pressures; add as necessary.	.272		√	√	√	√
5 Replace oil filters and oil, if applicable.	.081				√	√
6 Check contactors, sensors and mechanical safety limits.	.094				√	√
7 Perform spectrochemical analysis of compressor oil.	.039				√	√
8 Check electrical wiring and connections; tighten loose connections.	.120				√	√
9 Inspect cooler and condenser tubes for leaks.	5.200					√
10 Check evaporator and condenser for corrosion.	.026					√
11 Clean chiller and surrounding area.	.066		√	√	√	√
12 Fill out maintenance checklist and report deficiencies.	.022		√	√	√	√
Total labor-hours/period			.740	.740	1.074	6.300
Total labor-hours/year			5.920	1.480	1.074	6.300

			Cost Each					
			2012 Bare Costs				Total	Total
Description		Labor-hrs.	Material	Labor	Equip.	Total	In-House	w/O&P
1900	Chiller, screw, water cooled, up to 100 tons, annually	6.300	235	350		585	695	840
1950	Annualized	14.774	238	825		1,063	1,300	1,575

PM Components	Labor-hrs.	W	M	Q	S	A
PM System D3035 160 2950						
Chiller, screw, water cooled, over 100 tons						
1 Check unit for proper operation, excessive noise or vibration.	.033		√	√	√	√
2 Run system diagnostics test.	.325		√	√	√	√
3 Check oil level and oil temperature; add oil as necessary.	.022		√	√	√	√
4 Check refrigerant pressures; add as necessary.	.381		√	√	√	√
5 Replace oil filters and oil, if applicable.	.081				√	√
6 Check contactors, sensors and mechanical safety limits.	.094				√	√
7 Perform spectrochemical analysis of compressor oil.	.039				√	√
8 Check electrical wiring and connections; tighten loose connections.	.120				√	√
9 Inspect cooler and condenser tubes for leaks.	5.200					√
10 Check evaporator and condenser for corrosion.	.052					√
11 Clean chiller and surrounding area.	.117		√	√	√	√
12 Fill out maintenance checklist and report deficiencies.	.022		√	√	√	√
Total labor-hours/period			.900	.900	1.234	6.486
Total labor-hours/year			7.200	1.800	1.234	6.486

			Cost Each					
			2012 Bare Costs				Total	Total
Description		Labor-hrs.	Material	Labor	Equip.	Total	In-House	w/O&P
2900	Chiller, screw, water cooled, over 100 tons, annually	6.486	264	360		624	740	895
2950	Annualized	16.720	267	930		1,197	1,450	1,775

D30 HVAC | D3035 170 | Evaporative Cooler

	PM Components	Labor-hrs.	W	M	Q	S	A
PM System D3035 170 1950							
Evaporative cooler							
1	Check with operating or area personnel for deficiencies.	.035					√
2	Check unit for proper operation, noise and vibration.	.016					√
3	Clean evaporation louver panels.	.083					√
4	Lubricate fan, bearings and motor.	.052					√
5	Check belt(s) for excessive wear and deterioration.	.095					√
6	Visually inspect wiring for damage or loose connections; tighten loose connections.	.120					√
7	Clean sump.	.039					√
8	Clean and adjust float.	.257					√
9	Check interior surfaces and check components for loose paint/lime deposits.	.016					√
10	Check/clean, adjust nozzles (6).	.039					√
11	Remove/clean and reinstall evaporative pads.	.352					√
12	Start unit and check for proper operation.	.055					√
13	Remove debris from surrounding area.	.066					√
14	Fill out maintenance checklist.	.022					√
	Total labor-hours/period						1.247
	Total labor-hours/year						1.247

				Cost Each				
				2012 Bare Costs			**Total**	**Total**
	Description	Labor-hrs.	Material	Labor	Equip.	Total	In-House	w/O&P
1900	Evaporative cooler, annually	1.247	29	69.50		98.50	119	144
1950	Annualized	1.247	29	69.50		98.50	119	144

D30 HVAC | D3035 180 | Evaporative Cooler, Rotating Drum

	PM Components	Labor-hrs.	W	M	Q	S	A
PM System D3035 180 1950							
Evaporative cooler, rotating drum							
1	Check with operating or area personnel for deficiencies.	.035					√
2	Check unit for proper operation, noise and vibration.	.016					√
3	Clean evaporation louver panels.	.083					√
4	Lubricate rotary and fan, bearings and motor.	.078					√
5	Check belt(s) for excessive wear and deterioration.	.095					√
6	Visually inspect wiring for damage or loose connections; tighten loose connections.	.120					√
7	Clean sump and pump intake.	.039					√
8	Clean and adjust float.	.257					√
9	Check interior surfaces and check components for loose paint/lime deposits.	.055					√
10	Check/clean, adjust nozzles.	.039					√
11	Remove/clean and reinstall evaporative pads.	.352					√
12	Start unit and check for proper operation.	.055					√
13	Remove debris from surrounding area.	.066					√
14	Fill out maintenance checklist.	.022					√
	Total labor-hours/period						1.312
	Total labor-hours/year						1.312

				Cost Each				
				2012 Bare Costs			**Total**	**Total**
	Description	Labor-hrs.	Material	Labor	Equip.	Total	In-House	w/O&P
1900	Evaporative cooler, rotating drum, annually	1.312	36	73		109	131	159
1950	Annualized	1.312	36	73		109	131	159

PM Components	Labor-hrs.	W	M	Q	S	A
PM System D3035 210 1950						
Condenser, air cooled, 3 tons to 25 tons						
1 Check with operating or area personnel for deficiencies.	.027			√	√	√
2 Check unit for proper operation, excessive noise or vibration.	.025			√	√	√
3 Pressure wash coils and fans with coil cleaning solution.	.470					√
4 Check electrical wiring and connections; tighten loose connections.	.092					√
5 Lubricate shaft bearings and motor bearings.	.036					√
6 Inspect fan(s) or blower(s) for bent blades or imbalance; adjust as necessary.	.024			√	√	√
7 Check belt(s) for condition, proper tension, and misalignment; adjust for proper tension and/or alignment, if applicable.	.060			√	√	√
8 Inspect piping and valves for leaks; tighten connections as necessary.	.059			√	√	√
9 Clean area around equipment.	.051			√	√	√
10 Fill out maintenance checklist and report deficiencies.	.017			√	√	√
Total labor-hours/period				.299	.299	.861
Total labor-hours/year				.598	.299	.861

			Cost Each				
			2012 Bare Costs			Total	Total
Description	Labor-hrs.	Material	Labor	Equip.	Total	In-House	w/O&P
1900 Condenser, air cooled, 3 tons to 25 tons, annually	.861	22.50	48		70.50	85	103
1950 Annualized	1.758	38	98		136	164	201

PM Components	Labor-hrs.	W	M	Q	S	A
PM System D3035 210 2950						
Condenser, air cooled, 26 tons through 100 tons						
1 Check with operating or area personnel for deficiencies.	.027			√	√	√
2 Check unit for proper operation, excessive noise or vibration.	.025			√	√	√
3 Pressure wash coils and fans with coil cleaning solution.	.570					√
4 Check electrical wiring and connections; tighten loose connections.	.092					√
5 Lubricate shaft bearings and motor bearings.	.042					√
6 Inspect fan(s) or blower(s) for bent blades or imbalance; adjust as necessary.	.030			√	√	√
7 Check belt(s) for condition, proper tension, and misalignment; adjust for proper tension and/or alignment, if applicable.	.080			√	√	√
8 Inspect piping and valves for leaks; tighten connections as necessary.	.059			√	√	√
9 Clean area around equipment.	.051			√	√	√
10 Fill out maintenance checklist and report deficiencies.	.017			√	√	√
Total labor-hours/period				.331	.331	.993
Total labor-hours/year				.662	.331	.993

			Cost Each				
			2012 Bare Costs			Total	Total
Description	Labor-hrs.	Material	Labor	Equip.	Total	In-House	w/O&P
2900 Condenser, air cooled, 26 tons to 100 tons, annually	.993	54	55.50		109.50	128	154
2950 Annualized	1.986	69.50	111		180.50	215	259

PM Components	Labor-hrs.	W	M	Q	S	A
PM System D3035 210 3950						
Condenser, air cooled, over 100 tons						
1 Check with operating or area personnel for deficiencies.	.027			√	√	√
2 Check unit for proper operation, excessive noise or vibration.	.031			√	√	√
3 Pressure wash coils and fans with coil cleaning solution.	.670					√
4 Check electrical wiring and connections; tighten loose connections.	.092					√
5 Lubricate shaft bearings and motor bearings.	.042			√	√	√
6 Inspect fan(s) or blower(s) for bent blades or imbalance; adjust as necessary.	.030			√	√	√
7 Check belt(s) for condition, proper tension, and misalignment; adjust for proper tension and/or alignment, if applicable.	.100			√	√	√
8 Inspect piping and valves for leaks; tighten connections as necessary.	.059			√	√	√
9 Clean area around equipment.	.051			√	√	√
10 Fill out maintenance checklist and report deficiencies.	.017			√	√	√
Total labor-hours/period				.357	.357	1.119
Total labor-hours/year				.714	.357	1.119

		Cost Each						
		2012 Bare Costs				Total	Total
Description	Labor-hrs.	Material	Labor	Equip.	Total	In-House	w/O&P
3900 Condenser, air cooled, over 100 tons, annually	1.119	84.50	62.50		147	171	203
3950 Annualized	2.190	100	122		222	262	315

PM Components	Labor-hrs.	W	M	Q	S	A
PM System D3035 220 1950						
Condensing unit, air cooled, 3 tons to 25 tons						
1 Check with operating or area personnel for deficiencies.	.035			√	√	√
2 Check unit for proper operation, excessive noise or vibration.	.033			√	√	√
3 Pressure wash coils and fans with coil cleaning solution.	.611					√
4 Check electrical wiring and connections; tighten loose connections.	.120					√
5 Lubricate shaft bearings and motor bearings.	.047			√	√	√
6 Inspect fan(s) or blower(s) for bent blades or imbalance; adjust as necessary.	.031			√	√	√
7 Check belt(s) for condition, proper tension, and misalignment; adjust for proper tension and/or alignment, if applicable.	.078			√	√	√
8 Inspect piping and valves for leaks; tighten connections as necessary.	.077			√	√	√
9 Check refrigerant pressure; add refrigerant, if necessary.	.272					√
10 Clean area around equipment.	.066			√	√	√
11 Fill out maintenance checklist and report deficiencies.	.022			√	√	√
Total labor-hours/period				.389	.389	1.392
Total labor-hours/year				.778	.389	1.392

			Cost Each				
			2012 Bare Costs			**Total**	**Total**
Description	**Labor-hrs.**	**Material**	**Labor**	**Equip.**	**Total**	**In-House**	**w/O&P**
1900 Condensing unit, air cooled, 3 to 25 tons, annually	1.392	81	77.50		158.50	186	222
1950 Annualized	2.559	86.50	143		229.50	273	330

PM Components	Labor-hrs.	W	M	Q	S	A
PM System D3035 220 2950						
Condensing unit, air cooled, 26 tons through 100 tons						
1 Check with operating or area personnel for deficiencies.	.035			√	√	√
2 Check unit for proper operation, excessive noise or vibration.	.033			√	√	√
3 Pressure wash coils and fans with coil cleaning solution.	.741					√
4 Check electrical wiring and connections; tighten loose connections.	.120					√
5 Lubricate shaft bearings and motor bearings.	.055			√	√	√
6 Inspect fan(s) or blower(s) for bent blades or imbalance; adjust as necessary.	.039			√	√	√
7 Check belt(s) for condition, proper tension, and misalignment; adjust for proper tension and/or alignment, if applicable.	.104			√	√	√
8 Inspect piping and valves for leaks; tighten connections as necessary.	.077			√	√	√
9 Check refrigerant pressure; add refrigerant, if necessary.	.390					√
10 Clean area around equipment.	.066			√	√	√
11 Fill out maintenance checklist and report deficiencies.	.022			√	√	√
Total labor-hours/period				.431	.431	1.682
Total labor-hours/year				.862	.431	1.682

			Cost Each				
			2012 Bare Costs			**Total**	**Total**
Description	**Labor-hrs.**	**Material**	**Labor**	**Equip.**	**Total**	**In-House**	**w/O&P**
2900 Condensing unit, air cooled, 26 to 100 tons, annually	1.682	110	93.50		203.50	238	284
2950 Annualized	2.975	116	166		282	335	405

PM Components	Labor-hrs.	W	M	Q	S	A
PM System D3035 220 3950						
Condensing unit, air cooled, over 100 tons						
1 Check with operating or area personnel for deficiencies.	.035			√	√	√
2 Pressure wash coils and fans with coil cleaning solution.	.871					√
3 Clean intake side of condenser coils, fans and intake screens.	.091			√	√	√
4 Check electrical wiring and connections; tighten loose connections.	.120					√
5 Lubricate shaft bearings and motor bearings.	.055			√	√	√
6 Inspect fan(s) or blower(s) for bent blades or imbalance; adjust as necessary.	.039			√	√	√
7 Check belt(s) for condition, proper tension, and misalignment; adjust for proper tension and/or alignment, if applicable.	.130			√	√	√
8 Inspect piping and valves for leaks; tighten connections as necessary.	.077			√	√	√
9 Check refrigerant pressure; add refrigerant, if necessary.	.455					√
10 Clean area around equipment.	.066			√	√	√
11 Fill out maintenance checklist and report deficiencies.	.022			√	√	√
Total labor-hours/period				.515	.515	1.961
Total labor-hours/year				1.030	.515	1.961

	Description	Labor-hrs.	2012 Bare Costs Material	2012 Bare Costs Labor	2012 Bare Costs Equip.	2012 Bare Costs Total	Total In-House	Total w/O&P
3900	Condensing unit, air cooled, over 100 tons, annually	1.961	139	109		248	289	345
3950	Annualized	3.506	144	195		339	400	485

PM Components	Labor-hrs.	W	M	Q	S	A
PM System D3035 240 1950						
Condensing unit, water cooled, 3 tons to 24 tons						
1 Check with operating or area personnel for deficiencies.	.035			√	√	√
2 Check unit for proper operation, excessive noise or vibration.	.033			√	√	√
3 Check electrical wiring and connections; tighten loose connections.	.120					√
4 Inspect piping and valves for leaks; tighten connections as necessary.	.077			√	√	√
5 Check refrigerant pressure; add refrigerant, if necessary.	.272					√
6 Clean area around equipment.	.066			√	√	√
7 Fill out maintenance checklist and report deficiencies.	.022			√	√	√
Total labor-hours/period				.233	.233	.625
Total labor-hours/year				.466	.233	.625

			Cost Each					
			2012 Bare Costs				Total	Total
Description	Labor-hrs.	Material	Labor	Equip.	Total	In-House	w/O&P
1900 Condensing unit, water cooled, 3 to 24 tons, annually	.625	29	35		64	75.50	91
1950 Annualized	1.324	29	74		103	124	151

PM Components	Labor-hrs.	W	M	Q	S	A
PM System D3035 240 2950						
Condensing unit, water cooled, 25 tons through 100 tons						
1 Check with operating or area personnel for deficiencies.	.035			√	√	√
2 Check unit for proper operation, excessive noise or vibration.	.033			√	√	√
3 Run system diagnostics test.	.216			√	√	√
4 Check electrical wiring and connections; tighten loose connections.	.120			√	√	√
5 Check oil level in sight glass of lead compressor only; add oil as necessary.	.029			√	√	√
6 Check contactors, sensors and mechanical limits, adjust as necessary.	.156					√
7 Check condenser for corrosion.	.026					√
8 Inspect piping and valves for leaks; tighten connections as necessary.	.077			√	√	√
9 Check refrigerant pressure; add refrigerant, if necessary.	.272					√
10 Clean area around equipment.	.066			√	√	√
11 Fill out maintenance checklist and report deficiencies.	.022			√	√	√
Total labor-hours/period				.598	.598	1.052
Total labor-hours/year				1.196	.598	1.052

			Cost Each					
			2012 Bare Costs				Total	Total
Description	Labor-hrs.	Material	Labor	Equip.	Total	In-House	w/O&P
2900 Condensing unit, WC, 25 to 100 tons, annually	1.052	72	58.50		130.50	152	182
2950 Annualized	2.846	72	159		231	277	335

PM Components	Labor-hrs.	W	M	Q	S	A
PM System D3035 240 3950						
Condensing unit, water cooled, over 100 tons						
1 Check with operating or area personnel for deficiencies.	.035			√	√	√
2 Check unit for proper operation, excessive noise or vibration.	.033			√	√	√
3 Run system diagnostics test.	.216			√	√	√
4 Check electrical wiring and connections; tighten loose connections.	.120			√	√	√
5 Check oil level in sight glass of lead compressor only; add oil as necessary.	.029			√	√	√
6 Check contactors, sensors and mechanical limits, adjust as necessary.	.156					√
7 Check condenser for corrosion.	.026					√
8 Inspect piping and valves for leaks; tighten connections as necessary.	.077			√	√	√
9 Check refrigerant pressure; add refrigerant, if necessary.	.272					√
10 Clean area around equipment.	.066			√	√	√
11 Fill out maintenance checklist and report deficiencies.	.022			√	√	√
Total labor-hours/period				.598	.598	1.052
Total labor-hours/year				1.196	.598	1.052

			Cost Each					
			2012 Bare Costs				**Total**	**Total**
Description		**Labor-hrs.**	**Material**	**Labor**	**Equip.**	**Total**	**In-House**	**w/O&P**
3900	Condensing unit, WC, over 100 tons, annually	1.052	116	58.50		174.50	202	237
3950	Annualized	2.846	116	159		275	325	390

PM Components	Labor-hrs.	W	M	Q	S	A
PM System D3035 260 1950						
Compressor, DX Refrigeration, to 25 tons	.070					
1 Remove/replace access panel/cover.	.070					
2 Check unit for proper operation, excessive noise or vibration.	.030			√	√	√
3 Run systems diagnostics test, if applicable.	.060			√	√	√
4 Check oil level in compressor, if possible, and add oil as required.	.030			√	√	√
5 Check refrigerant pressures; add refrigerant as necessary.	.200			√	√	√
6 Check contactors, sensors and mechanical limits, adjust as necessary.	.100			√	√	√
7 Inspect refrigerant piping and insulation.	.050			√	√	√
8 Clean compressor and surrounding area.	.050			√	√	√
9 Fill out maintenance checklist and report deficiencies.	.020			√	√	√
Total labor-hours/period				.610	.610	.610
Total labor-hours/year				1.220	.610	.610

			Cost Each			
			2012 Bare Costs			Total	Total
Description	**Labor-hrs.**	**Material**	**Labor**	**Equip.**	**Total**	**In-House**	**w/O&P**
1900 Compressor, DX refrigeration, to 25 tons, annually	.610	15.10	34		49.10	59	72
1950 Annualized	2.440	15.10	136		151.10	186	231

PM Components	Labor-hrs.	W	M	Q	S	A
PM System D3035 260 2950						
Compressor, DX refrigeration, 25 tons to 100 tons						
Check unit for proper operation, excessive noise or vibration.	.030					
2 Run system diagnostics test, if applicable.	.098			√	√	√
3 Check oil level in compressor; add oil as necessary.	.033			√	√	√
4 Check refrigerant pressures; add refrigerant as necessary.	.272			√	√	√
5 Check contactors, sensors and mechanical limits, adjust as necessary.	.216			√	√	√
6 Inspect refrigerant piping and insulation.	.077			√	√	√
7 Clean compressor and surrounding area.	.066			√	√	√
8 Fill out maintenance checklist and report deficiencies.	.022			√	√	√
Total labor-hours/period				.784	.784	.784
Total labor-hours/year				1.568	.784	.784

			Cost Each			
			2012 Bare Costs			Total	Total
Description	**Labor-hrs.**	**Material**	**Labor**	**Equip.**	**Total**	**In-House**	**w/O&P**
2900 Compressor, DX refrigeration, 25 to 100 tons, annually	.784	14.30	43.50		57.80	70.50	86
2950 Annualized	3.136	14.30	175		189.30	234	290

PM Components	Labor-hrs.	W	M	Q	S	A
PM System D3035 290 1950						
Fluid cooler, 2 fans (no compressor)						
1 Check with operating or area personnel for deficiencies.	.035					√
2 Check unit for proper operation, excessive noise or vibration.	.159					√
3 Clean intake side of condenser coils, fans and intake screens.	.473					√
4 Check electrical wiring and connections; tighten loose connections.	.120					√
5 Inspect fan(s) for bent blades or unbalance; adjust as necessary.	.040					√
6 Check belts for condition, proper tension and misalignment; adjust	.029					√
for proper tension and/or alignment, if required.						
7 Lubricate shaft bearings and motor bearings.	.047					√
8 Inspect piping and valves for leaks; tighten connections as necessary.	.077					√
9 Lubricate and check operation of dampers, if applicable.	.055					√
10 Clean area around fluid cooler.	.066					√
11 Fill out maintenance checklist and report deficiencies.	.022					√
Total labor-hours/period						1.123
Total labor-hours/year						1.123

			Cost Each					
			2012 Bare Costs				Total	Total
Description		Labor-hrs.	Material	Labor	Equip.	Total	In-House	w/O&P
1900	Fluid cooler, 2 fans (no compressor), annually	1.123	14.45	62.50		76.95	94	116
1950	Annualized	1.123	14.45	62.50		76.95	94	116

PM Components	Labor-hrs.	W	M	Q	S	A
PM System D3045 110 1950						
Air handling unit, 3 tons through 24 tons						
1 Check with operating or area personnel for deficiencies.	.035			√	√	√
2 Check controls and unit for proper operation.	.033			√	√	√
3 Check for unusual noise or vibration.	.033			√	√	√
4 Check tension, condition and alignment of belts, adjust as necessary.	.029			√	√	√
5 Clean coils, evaporator drain pan, blower, motor and drain piping, as required.	.380					√
6 Lubricate shaft and motor bearings.	.047			√	√	√
7 Replace air filters.	.078			√	√	√
8 Inspect exterior piping and valves for leaks; tighten connections as required.	.077			√	√	√
9 Clean area around equipment.	.066			√	√	√
10 Fill out maintenance checklist and report deficiencies.	.022			√	√	√
Total labor-hours/period				.420	.420	.800
Total labor-hours/year				.840	.420	.800

			Cost Each				
			2012 Bare Costs			**Total**	**Total**
Description	**Labor-hrs.**	**Material**	**Labor**	**Equip.**	**Total**	**In-House**	**w/O&P**
1900 Air handling unit, 3 thru 24 tons, annually	.800	44.50	44.50		89	105	125
1950 Annualized	2.060	96	115		211	249	299

PM Components	Labor-hrs.	W	M	Q	S	A
PM System D3045 110 2950						
Air handling unit, 25 tons through 50 tons						
1 Check with operating or area personnel for deficiencies.	.035			√	√	√
2 Check controls and unit for proper operation.	.033			√	√	√
3 Check for unusual noise or vibration.	.033			√	√	√
4 Clean coils, evaporator drain pan, blower, motor and condensate drain piping, as required.	.380					√
5 Lubricate shaft and motor bearings.	.047			√	√	√
6 Check belts for wear, proper tension, and alignment; adjust as necessary.	.029			√	√	√
7 Inspect exterior piping and valves for leaks; tighten connections as required.	.077			√	√	√
8 Check operation and clean dampers, louvers and shutters; lubricate all pivot points and linkages.	.078					√
9 Replace air filters.	.078			√	√	√
10 Clean area around equipment.	.066			√	√	√
11 Fill out maintenance checklist and report deficiencies.	.022			√	√	√
Total labor-hours/period				.420	.420	.878
Total labor-hours/year				.840	.420	.878

			Cost Each				
			2012 Bare Costs			**Total**	**Total**
Description	**Labor-hrs.**	**Material**	**Labor**	**Equip.**	**Total**	**In-House**	**w/O&P**
2900 Air handling unit, 25 thru 50 tons, annually	.878	139	49		188	214	250
2950 Annualized	2.138	375	119		494	565	655

PM Components	Labor-hrs.	W	M	Q	S	A
PM System D3045 110 3950						
Air handling unit, over 50 tons						
1 Check with operating or area personnel for deficiencies.	.035			√	√	√
2 Check controls and unit for proper operation.	.033			√	√	√
3 Check for unusual noise or vibration.	.033			√	√	√
4 Clean coils, evaporator drain pan, blower, motor and drain piping, as required.	.510					√
5 Lubricate shaft and motor bearings.	.047			√	√	√
6 Check belts for wear, proper tension, and alignment; adjust as necessary.	.055			√	√	√
7 Inspect exterior piping and valves for leaks; tighten connections as required.	.077			√	√	√
8 Check operation and clean dampers, louvers and shutters; lubricate all pivot points and linkages.	.078					√
9 Clean centrifugal fan.	.065					√
10 Replace air filters.	.286			√	√	√
11 Clean area around equipment.	.066			√	√	√
12 Fill out maintenance checklist and report deficiencies	.022			√	√	√
Total labor-hours/period				.654	.654	1.307
Total labor-hours/year				1.308	.654	1.307

		Cost Each					
		2012 Bare Costs				Total	Total
Description	Labor-hrs.	Material	Labor	Equip.	Total	In-House	w/O&P
3900 Air handling unit, over 50 tons, annually	1.307	199	73		272	310	360
3950 Annualized	3.269	485	182		667	760	890

PM Components	Labor-hrs.	W	M	Q	S	A
PM System D3045 112 1950						
Air handling unit, computer room						
1 Check with operating or area personnel for deficiencies.	.035			√	√	√
2 Run microprocessor check, if available, or check controls and unit for proper operation.	.216			√	√	√
3 Check for unusual noise or vibration.	.033			√	√	√
4 Clean coils, evaporator drain pan, blower, motor and drain piping, as required.	.380					√
5 Lubricate shaft and motor bearings.	.047			√	√	√
6 Check belts for wear, proper tension, and alignment; adjust as necessary.	.029			√	√	√
7 Check humidity lamp, replace if necessary.	.156			√	√	√
8 Inspect exterior piping and valves for leaks; tighten connections as required.	.077			√	√	√
9 Replace air filters.	.078			√	√	√
10 Clean area around equipment.	.066			√	√	√
11 Fill out maintenance checklist and report deficiencies.	.022			√	√	√
Total labor-hours/period				.759	.759	1.139
Total labor-hours/year				1.518	.759	1.139

		Cost Each					
		2012 Bare Costs				Total	Total
Description	Labor-hrs.	Material	Labor	Equip.	Total	In-House	w/O&P
1900 Air handling unit, computer room, annually	1.139	37	63.50		100.50	120	145
1950 Annualized	3.416	59	190		249	300	370

PM Components	Labor-hrs.	W	M	Q	S	A
PM System D3045 120 1950						
Fan coil unit						
1 Check with operating or area personnel for deficiencies.	.035			√	√	√
2 Check coil unit while operating.	.120				√	√
3 Remove access panel and vacuum inside of unit and coils.	.468				√	√
4 Check coils and piping for leaks, damage and corrosion; repair as necessary.	.077			√	√	√
5 Lubricate blower shaft and fan motor bearings.	.047				√	√
6 Clean coil, drip pan, and drain line with solvent.	.473				√	√
7 Replace filters as required.	.009			√	√	√
8 Replace access panel.	.023				√	√
9 Check operation after repairs.	.120				√	√
10 Clean area.	.066			√	√	√
11 Fill out maintenance checklist and report deficiencies.	.022			√	√	√
Total labor-hours/period				.209	1.460	1.460
Total labor-hours/year				.418	1.460	1.460

			Cost Each					
			2012 Bare Costs				Total	Total
Description	Labor-hrs.	Material	Labor	Equip.	Total		In-House	w/O&P
1900 Fan coil unit, annually	1.460	6.50	81.50		88		109	135
1950 Annualized	3.338	26	186		212		261	325

PM Components	Labor-hrs.	W	M	Q	S	A
PM System D3045 150 1950						
Filters, Electrostatic						
1 Review manufacturers instructions.	.091			√	√	√
2 Check indicators for defective tubes or broken ionizing wires.	.130			√	√	√
3 De-energize power supply,tag and lockout disconnect switch.	.130			√	√	√
4 Ground bus trips, top and bottom.	.065			√	√	√
5 Secure filter and fan unit.	.065			√	√	√
6 Wash each manifold until clean, approximately 4 minutes with hot water, 7 minutes with cold water.	.390			√	√	√
7 Clean or replace dry filters as necessary.	.260			√	√	√
8 Inspect for broken on hum supressors and wipe insulators with soft dry cloth.	.260			√	√	√
9 Disassemble unit as required, check it thoroughly, clean and adjust.	.650			√	√	√
10 Restore to service and check for shorts.	.130			√	√	√
11 Fill out maintenance checklist and report deficiencies.	.022			√	√	√
Total labor-hours/period				2.193	2.193	2.193
Total labor-hours/year				4.386	2.193	2.193

			Cost Each					
			2012 Bare Costs				Total	Total
Description	Labor-hrs.	Material	Labor	Equip.	Total		In-House	w/O&P
1900 Air filter, electrostatic, annually	2.193	11.80	99.50		111.30		144	177
1950 Annualized	8.772	23.50	400		423.50		550	675

D30 HVAC — D3045 160 — VAV Boxes

PM Components	Labor-hrs.	W	M	Q	S	A
PM System D3045 160 1950						
VAV Boxes						
1 Open/close VAV control box access.	.060				√	√
2 Check that pneumatic tubing/electrical connections are in place and tight.	.040				√	√
3 Tighten arm on motor output shaft.	.040				√	√
4 Cycle actuator while watching for proper operation.	.200				√	√
Verify that blades fully open and close.	.040				√	√
5 Lubricate actuator linkage and damper blade pivot points.	.070				√	√
6 Fill out maintenance checklist and report deficiencies.	.017				√	√
Total labor-hours/period					.467	.467
Total labor-hours/year					.467	.467

			Cost Each					
			2012 Bare Costs				Total	Total
Description	Labor-hrs.	Material	Labor	Equip.	Total	In-House	w/O&P
1900 VAV Boxes, annually	.467	7.50	26		33.50	41	50
1950 Annualized	.934	7.50	52		59.50	73.50	90.50

D30 HVAC — D3045 170 — Fire Dampers

PM Components	Labor-hrs.	W	M	Q	S	A
PM System D3045 170 1950						
Fire dampers						
1 Remove/replace access door.	.800					√
2 Clean out debris/dirt blown against damper.	.200					√
3 Remove fusible link and check that blades operate freely.	.070					√
4 Lubricate pivot points.	.050					√
5 Replace fusible link.	.020					√
6 Fill out maintenance checklist and report deficiencies.	.017					√
Total labor-hours/period						1.157
Total labor-hours/year						1.157

			Cost Each					
			2012 Bare Costs				Total	Total
Description	Labor-hrs.	Material	Labor	Equip.	Total	In-House	w/O&P
1900 Fire dampers, annually	1.157	5.75	64.50		70.25	87	107
1950 Annualized	1.157	5.75	64.50		70.25	87	107

PM Components	Labor-hrs.	W	M	Q	S	A
PM System D3045 210 1950						
Fan, axial, up to 5,000 CFM						
1 Start and stop fan with local switch.	.012				✓	✓
2 Check fan for noise and vibration.	.091				✓	✓
3 Check electrical wiring and connections; tighten loose connections.	.029				✓	✓
4 Check motor and fan shaft bearings for noise, vibration, overheating; lubricate as required.	.325				✓	✓
5 Clean area around fan.	.143				✓	✓
6 Fill out maintenance checklist and report deficiencies.	.022				✓	✓
Total labor-hours/period					.622	.622
Total labor-hours/year					.622	.622

		Cost Each					
		2012 Bare Costs				**Total**	**Total**
Description	**Labor-hrs.**	**Material**	**Labor**	**Equip.**	**Total**	**In-House**	**w/O&P**
1900 Fan, axial, up to 5,000 CFM, annually	.622	3.62	28		31.62	41	50.50
1950 Annualized	1.244	7.20	56.50		63.70	82.50	101

PM Components	Labor-hrs.	W	M	Q	S	A
PM System D3045 210 2950						
Fan, axial, 5,000 to 10,000 CFM						
1 Start and stop fan with local switch.	.012				✓	✓
2 Check motor and fan shaft bearings for noise, vibration, overheating; lubricate bearings.	.325				✓	✓
3 Check belts for wear, tension, and alignment, if applicable; adjust as required.	.057				✓	✓
4 Check fan pitch operator, lubricate; if applicable.	.029				✓	✓
5 Check electrical wiring and connections; tighten loose connections.	.057				✓	✓
6 Clean fan and surrounding fan.	.143				✓	✓
7 Fill out maintenance checklist and report deficiencies.	.022				✓	✓
Total labor-hours/period					.645	.645
Total labor-hours/year					.645	.645

		Cost Each					
		2012 Bare Costs				**Total**	**Total**
Description	**Labor-hrs.**	**Material**	**Labor**	**Equip.**	**Total**	**In-House**	**w/O&P**
2900 Fan, axial, 5,000 to 10,000 CFM, annually	.645	3.62	29.50		33.12	42.50	52
2950 Annualized	1.290	7.20	58.50		65.70	85	104

PM Components	Labor-hrs.	W	M	Q	S	A
PM System D3045 210 3950						
Fan, axial, 36″ to 48″ dia (over 10,000 CFM)						
1 Start and stop fan with local switch.	.012				√	√
2 Check motor and fan shaft bearings for noise, vibration, overheating; lubricate bearings.	.325				√	√
3 Check belts for wear, tension, and alignment, if applicable; adjust as required.	.086				√	√
4 Check fan pitch operator, lubricate; if applicable.	.029				√	√
5 Check electrical wiring and connections; tighten loose connections.	.078				√	√
6 Clean fan and surrounding area.	.143				√	√
7 Fill out maintenance checklist and report deficiencies.	.022				√	√
Total labor-hours/period					.695	.695
Total labor-hours/year					.695	.695

			Cost Each					
			2012 Bare Costs				Total	Total
Description		Labor-hrs.	Material	Labor	Equip.	Total	In-House	w/O&P
3900	Fan, axial, 36″ to 48″ dia (over 10,000 CFM), annually	.695	3.62	31.50		35.12	45.50	56
3950	Annualized	1.390	7.20	63		70.20	91	112

445

PM Components	Labor-hrs.	W	M	Q	S	A
PM System D3045 220 1950						
Fan, centrifugal, up to 5,000 CFM						
1 Start and stop fan with local switch.	.012				√	√
2 Check motor and fan shaft bearings for noise, vibration, overheating; lubricate bearings.	.325				√	√
3 Check belts for wear, tension, and alignment, if applicable; adjust as required.	.057				√	√
4 Check blower intake dampers, lubricate; if applicable.	.029				√	√
5 Check electrical wiring and connections; tighten loose connections.	.029				√	√
6 Clean fan and surrounding area.	.066				√	√
7 Fill out maintenance checklist and report deficiencies.	.022				√	√
Total labor-hours/period					.540	.540
Total labor-hours/year					.540	.540

			Cost Each					
			2012 Bare Costs				Total	Total
Description	**Labor-hrs.**	**Material**	**Labor**	**Equip.**	**Total**		**In-House**	**w/O&P**
1900 Fan, centrifugal, up to 5,000 CFM, annually	.540	3.62	24.50		28.12		36	44.50
1950 Annualized	1.080	7.20	49		56.20		72.50	88.50

PM Components	Labor-hrs.	W	M	Q	S	A
PM System D3045 220 2950						
Fan, centrifugal, 5,000 to 10,000 CFM						
1 Start and stop fan with local switch.	.012				√	√
2 Check motor and fan shaft bearings for noise, vibration, overheating; lubricate bearings.	.325				√	√
3 Check belts for wear, tension, and alignment, if applicable; adjust as required.	.057				√	√
4 Check blower intake dampers, lubricate; if applicable.	.029				√	√
5 Check electrical wiring and connections; tighten loose connections.	.057				√	√
6 Clean fan and surrounding area.	.066				√	√
7 Fill out maintenance checklist and report deficiencies.	.022				√	√
Total labor-hours/period					.568	.568
Total labor-hours/year					.568	.568

			Cost Each					
			2012 Bare Costs				Total	Total
Description	**Labor-hrs.**	**Material**	**Labor**	**Equip.**	**Total**		**In-House**	**w/O&P**
2900 Fan, centrifugal, 5,000 to 10,000 CFM, annually	.568	3.62	26		29.62		38	46.50
2950 Annualized	1.136	7.20	51.50		58.70		76	93

PM Components	Labor-hrs.	W	M	Q	S	A
PM System D3045 220 3950						
Fan, centrifugal, over 10,000 CFM						
1 Start and stop fan with local switch.	.007				√	√
2 Check motor and fan shaft bearings for noise, vibration, overheating; lubricate bearings.	.325				√	√
3 Check belts for wear, tension, and alignment, if applicable; adjust as required.	.086				√	√
4 Check blower intake dampers, lubricate; if applicable.	.029				√	√
5 Check electrical wiring and connections; tighten loose connections.	.057				√	√
6 Clean fan and surrounding area.	.066				√	√
7 Fill out maintenance checklist and report deficiencies.	.022				√	√
Total labor-hours/period					.592	.592
Total labor-hours/year					.592	.592

			Cost Each				
			2012 Bare Costs			Total	Total
Description	Labor-hrs.	Material	Labor	Equip.	Total	In-House	w/O&P
3900 Fan, centrifugal, over 10,000 CFM, annually	.592	3.62	27		30.62	39.50	48
3950 Annualized	1.184	7.20	54		61.20	78.50	96.50

PM Components	Labor-hrs.	W	M	Q	S	A
PM System D3045 250 1950						
Hood and blower						
1 Check with operating or area personnel for any deficiencies.	.044			√	√	√
2 Check unit for proper operation, including switches, controls and thermostat; calibrate thermostat and repair components as required.	.109			√	√	√
3 Check operation of spray nozzles for spray coverage and drainage, if applicable.	.022					√
4 Inspect soap and spray solution feeder lines.	.007			√	√	√
5 Check components for automatic cleaning system and automatic fire protection system - solenoid valve, line strainer, shut-off valve, detergent tank, etc.	.055			√	√	√
6 Clean spray nozzles.	1.104					√
7 Tighten or replace loose, missing or damaged nuts, bolts or screws.	.005			√	√	√
8 Check operation of exhaust blower on roof; lubricate bearings; adjust tension of fan belts and clean fan blades as required.	.056			√	√	√
9 Fill out maintenance checklist and report deficiencies.	.022			√	√	√
Total labor-hours/period				.298	.298	1.424
Total labor-hours/year				.596	.298	1.424

			Cost Each				
			2012 Bare Costs			Total	Total
Description	Labor-hrs.	Material	Labor	Equip.	Total	In-House	w/O&P
1900 Hood and blower, annually	1.424	57.50	64.50		122	149	177
1950 Annualized	2.318	82	105		187	229	274

PM Components	Labor-hrs.	W	M	Q	S	A
PM System D3045 410 1950						
Centrifugal pump over 1 H.P.						
1 Check for proper operation of pump.	.022				√	√
2 Check for leaks on suction and discharge piping, seals, packing glands, etc.; make minor adjustments as required.	.077				√	√
3 Check pump and motor operation for excessive vibration, noise and overheating.	.022				√	√
4 Check alignment of pump and motor; adjust as necessary.	.260				√	√
5 Lubricate pump and motor.	.099				√	√
6 Clean exterior of pump, motor and surrounding area.	.096				√	√
7 Fill out maintenance checklist and report deficiencies.	.022				√	√
Total labor-hours/period					.598	.598
Total labor-hours/year					.598	.598

			Cost Each				
			2012 Bare Costs			**Total**	**Total**
Description	**Labor-hrs.**	**Material**	**Labor**	**Equip.**	**Total**	**In-House**	**w/O&P**
1900 Centrifugal pump, over 1 H.P., annually	.598	7.50	32.50		40	49.50	60.50
1950 Annualized	1.196	15.05	65.50		80.55	98	121

PM Components	Labor-hrs.	W	M	Q	S	A
PM System D3045 410 2950						
Centrifugal pump w/reduction gear, over 1 H.P.						
1 Check with operating or area personnel for deficiencies.	.035				√	√
2 Clean pump exterior and check for corrosion on pump exterior and base plate.	.030				√	√
3 Check for leaks on suction and discharge piping, seals, packing glands, etc.	.077				√	√
4 Check pump, gear and motor operation for vibration, noise, overheating, etc.	.022				√	√
5 Check alignment and clearances of shaft reduction gear and coupler.	.260				√	√
6 Tighten or replace loose, missing, or damaged nuts, bolts and screws.	.005				√	√
7 Lubricate pump and motor as required.	.099				√	√
8 When available, check suction or discharge, pressure gauge readings and flow rate.	.022				√	√
9 Clean area around pump.	.066				√	√
10 Fill out maintenance checklist and report deficiencies.	.022				√	√
Total labor-hours/period					.638	.638
Total labor-hours/year					.638	.638

			Cost Each				
			2012 Bare Costs			**Total**	**Total**
Description	**Labor-hrs.**	**Material**	**Labor**	**Equip.**	**Total**	**In-House**	**w/O&P**
2900 Centrifugal pump, w/ red. gear, over 1H.P., annually	.638	7.50	35		42.50	52	64
2950 Annualized	1.276	15.05	69.50		84.55	104	128

PM Components	Labor-hrs.	W	M	Q	S	A
PM System D3045 420 1950						
Pump w/oil reservoir, over 1 H.P.						
1 Check for proper operation of pump.	.022				√	√
2 Check for leaks on suction and discharge piping, seals, packing glands, etc.; make minor adjustments as required.	.077				√	√
3 Check pump and motor operation for excessive vibration, noise and overheating.	.022				√	√
4 Check alignment of pump and motor; adjust as necessary.	.260				√	√
5 Lubricate motor; check oil level in pump reservoir.	.099				√	√
6 Clean exterior of pump and surrounding area.	.096				√	√
7 Fill out maintenance checklist and report deficiencies.	.022				√	√
Total labor-hours/period					.598	.598
Total labor-hours/year					.598	.598

			Cost Each					
			2012 Bare Costs				Total	Total
Description	Labor-hrs.	Material	Labor	Equip.	Total	In-House	w/O&P
1900 Pump w/ oil reservoir, electric, annually	.598	7.50	32.50		40	49.50	60.50
1950 Annualized	1.196	15.05	65.50		80.55	98	121

PM Components	Labor-hrs.	W	M	Q	S	A
PM System D3045 600 1950						
Heat exchanger, steam						
1　Check with operating or area personnel for deficiencies.	.035				√	√
2　Check temperature gauges for proper operating temperatures.	.091				√	√
3　Check steam modulating valve and steam condensate trap for proper operation.	.101				√	√
4　Inspect heat exchanger and adjacent piping for torn or deteriorated insulation.	.147				√	√
5　Clean heat exchanger and surrounding area.	.066				√	√
6　Fill out maintenance checklist and report deficiencies.	.022				√	√
Total labor-hours/period					.462	.462
Total labor-hours/year					.462	.462

			Cost Each					
			2012 Bare Costs				Total	Total
Description		Labor-hrs.	Material	Labor	Equip.	Total	In-House	w/O&P
1900	Heat exchanger, steam, annually	.462	25	25.50		50.50	59.50	71.50
1950	Annualized	.924	25	51.50		76.50	91.50	111

PM Components	Labor-hrs.	W	M	Q	S	A
PM System D3055 110 1950						
Unit heater, gas radiant						
1 Check with operating or area personnel for deficiencies.	.035					√
2 Inspect, clean and adjust control valves and thermo sensing bulbs on gas burners.	.254					√
3 Inspect fuel system for leaks.	.016					√
4 Check for proper operation of burner controls. check and adjust thermostat.	.133					√
5 Check fan and motor for vibration and noise. lubricate bearings.	.056					√
6 Check electrical wiring to blower motor.	.079					√
7 Check condition of flue pipe, damper and stack.	.147					√
8 Check unit heater operation through complete cycle or up to ten minutes.	.133					√
9 Clean area around unit heater.	.133					√
10 Fill out maintenance checklist and report deficiencies.	.022					√
Total labor-hours/period						1.008
Total labor-hours/year						1.008

			Cost Each				
			2012 Bare Costs			**Total**	**Total**
Description	Labor-hrs.	Material	Labor	Equip.	Total	**In-House**	**w/O&P**
1900 Unit heater, gas radiant, annually	1.008	3	56		59	73.50	91.50
1950 Annualized	1.008	3	56		59	73.50	91.50

PM Components	Labor-hrs.	W	M	Q	S	A
PM System D3055 110 2950						
Unit heater, gas infrared						
1 Check with operating or area personnel for deficiencies.	.035					√
2 Inspect fuel system for leaks around unit.	.016					√
3 Replace primary air intake filter.	.048					√
4 Blow out burner.	.130					√
5 Clean spark electrode and reset gap, replace if necessary.	.254					√
6 Clean pilot and thermo-sensor bulb, replace if necessary.	.133					√
7 Check alignment of thermo-sensor bulb.	.133					√
8 Check wiring and connections; tighten any loose connections.	.079					√
9 Check and clean pilot sight glass.	.091					√
10 Vacuum pump (fan):						
A) check motor bearings for overheating; adjust or repair as required.	.022					√
B) lubricate motor bearings.	.099					√
C) check motor mounting; adjust as required.	.030					√
D) check fan blade clearance; adjust as required.	.042					√
E) check wiring, connections, switches, etc.; tighten any loose connections.	.079					√
11 Operate unit to ensure that it is in proper working condition.	.225					√
12 Clean equipment and surrounding area.	.066					√
13 Fill out maintenance checklist and report deficiencies.	.022					√
Total labor-hours/period						1.504
Total labor-hours/year						1.504

			Cost Each				
			2012 Bare Costs			**Total**	**Total**
Description	Labor-hrs.	Material	Labor	Equip.	Total	**In-House**	**w/O&P**
2900 Unit heater, gas infrared, annually	1.504	30	84		114	138	169
2950 Annualized	1.504	30	84		114	138	169

PM Components	Labor-hrs.	W	M	Q	S	A
PM System D3055 110 3950						
Unit heater, steam						
1 Check with operating or area personnel for deficiencies.	.035					√
2 Inspect, clean and adjust control valves and thermostat.	.254					√
3 Inspect coils, connections, trap and steam piping for leaks; repair as necessary.	.195					√
4 Check fan and motor for vibration and noise; lubricate bearings.	.056					√
5 Check electrical wiring to motor.	.079					√
6 Check unit heater operation through complete cycle or up to ten minutes.	.133					√
7 Clean equipment and surrounding area.	.066					√
8 Fill out maintenance checklist and report deficiencies.	.022					√
Total labor-hours/period						.840
Total labor-hours/year						.840

			Cost Each					
			2012 Bare Costs				Total	Total
Description		Labor-hrs.	Material	Labor	Equip.	Total	In-House	w/O&P
3900	Unit heater, steam, annually	.840	30	47		77	91.50	111
3950	Annualized	.840	30	47		77	91.50	111

PM Components	Labor-hrs.	W	M	Q	S	A
PM System D3055 122 1950						
Forced air heater, oil or gas fired, up to 120 MBH						
1 Check with operating or area personnel for deficiencies.	.035			√	√	√
2 Inspect, clean and adjust electrodes and nozzles on oil burners or controls, valves and thermo-sensing bulbs on gas burners; lubricate oil burner motor bearings as applicable.	.254					√
3 Inspect fuel system for leaks.	.016			√	√	√
4 Change fuel filter element on oil burner, where applicable.						
5 Check for proper operation of burner primary controls. check and adjust thermostat.	.133			√	√	√
6 Replace air filters in air handler.	.009			√	√	√
7 Check blower and motor for vibration and noise. lubricate bearings.	.042			√	√	√
8 Check belts for wear and proper tension, tighten if required.	.029			√	√	√
9 Check electrical wiring to burner controls and blower.	.079					√
10 Inspect and clean firebox.	.577					√
11 Clean blower and air plenum.	.294					√
12 Check condition of flue pipe, damper and stack.	.147			√	√	√
13 Check furnace operation through complete cycle or up to 10 minutes.	.650			√	√	√
14 Clean area around furnace.	.066			√	√	√
15 Fill out maintenance checklist and report deficiencies.	.022			√	√	√
Total labor-hours/period				1.149	1.149	2.353
Total labor-hours/year				2.298	1.149	2.353

			Cost Each					
			2012 Bare Costs				**Total**	**Total**
Description	**Labor-hrs.**	**Material**	**Labor**	**Equip.**	**Total**		**In-House**	**w/O&P**
1900 Forced air heater, oil/gas, up to 120 MBH, annually	2.353	95	131		226		269	325
1950 Annualized	5.800	114	325		439		530	650

PM Components	Labor-hrs.	W	M	Q	S	A
PM System D3055 122 2950						
Forced air heater, oil or gas fired, over 120 MBH						
1 Check with operating or area personnel for deficiencies.	.035			√	√	√
2 Inspect, clean and adjust electrodes and nozzles on oil burners or controls valves and thermo-sensing bulbs on gas burners; lubricate oil burner motor bearings as applicable.	.358					√
3 Inspect fuel system for leaks.	.156			√	√	√
4 Change fuel filter element on oil burner, where applicable.	.120					√
5 Check for proper operation of burner primary controls. check and adjust thermostat.	.133			√	√	√
6 Replace air filters in air handler.	.182			√	√	√
7 Check blower and motor for vibration and noise. lubricate bearings.	.047			√	√	√
8 Check belts for wear and proper tension, tighten if required.	.057			√	√	√
9 Check electrical wiring to burner controls and blower.	.079					√
10 Inspect and clean firebox.	.577					√
11 Clean blower and air plenum.	.294					√
12 Check condition of flue pipe, damper and stack.	.147			√	√	√
13 Check furnace operation through complete cycle or up to 10 minutes.	.650			√	√	√
14 Clean area around furnace.	.066			√	√	√
15 Fill out maintenance checklist and report deficiencies.	.022			√	√	√
Total labor-hours/period				1.495	1.495	2.923
Total labor-hours/year				2.990	1.495	2.923

			Cost Each					
			2012 Bare Costs				**Total**	**Total**
Description	**Labor-hrs.**	**Material**	**Labor**	**Equip.**	**Total**		**In-House**	**w/O&P**
2900 Forced air heater, oil/gas, over 120 MBH, annually	2.923	123	163		286		340	410
2950 Annualized	7.408	152	415		567		680	835

PM Components	Labor-hrs.	W	M	Q	S	A
PM System D3055 210 1950						
Package unit, air cooled, 3 tons through 24 tons						
1 Check with operating or area personnel for deficiencies.	.035			√	√	√
2 Check tension, condition, and alignment of belts; adjust as necessary.	.029			√	√	√
3 Lubricate shaft and motor bearings.	.047			√	√	√
4 Replace air filters.	.055			√	√	√
5 Clean electrical wiring and connections; tighten loose connections.	.120					√
6 Clean coils, evaporator drain pan, blowers, fans, motors and drain piping as required.	.385					√
7 Perform operational check of unit; make adjustments on controls and other components as required.	.077			√	√	√
8 During operation of unit, check refrigerant pressure; add refrigerant as necessary.	.135			√	√	√
9 Check compressor oil level; add oil as required.	.033					√
10 Clean area around unit.	.066			√	√	√
11 Fill out maintenance checklist and report deficiencies.	.022			√	√	√
Total labor-hours/period				.466	.466	1.004
Total labor-hours/year				.932	.466	1.004

			Cost Each				
			2012 Bare Costs			**Total**	**Total**
Description	**Labor-hrs.**	**Material**	**Labor**	**Equip.**	**Total**	**In-House**	**w/O&P**
1900 Package unit, air cooled, 3 thru 24 ton, annually	1.004	45	56		101	119	143
1950 Annualized	2.402	72	134		206	246	298

PM Components	Labor-hrs.	W	M	Q	S	A
PM System D3055 210 2950						
Package unit, air cooled, 25 tons through 50 tons						
1 Check with operating or area personnel for deficiencies.	.035			√	√	√
2 Check tension, condition, and alignment of belts; adjust as necessary.	.029			√	√	√
3 Lubricate shaft and motor bearings.	.047			√	√	√
4 Replace air filters.	.078			√	√	√
5 Clean electrical wiring and connections; tighten loose connections.	.120					√
6 Clean coils, evaporator drain pan, blowers, fans, motors and drain piping as required.	.385					√
7 Perform operational check of unit; make adjustments on controls and other components as required.	.130			√	√	√
8 During operation of unit, check refrigerant pressure; add refrigerant as necessary.	.272			√	√	√
9 Check compressor oil level; add oil as required.	.033					√
10 Clean area around unit.	.066			√	√	√
11 Fill out maintenance checklist and report deficiencies.	.022			√	√	√
Total labor-hours/period				.679	.679	1.217
Total labor-hours/year				1.358	.679	1.217

			Cost Each				
			2012 Bare Costs			**Total**	**Total**
Description	**Labor-hrs.**	**Material**	**Labor**	**Equip.**	**Total**	**In-House**	**w/O&P**
2900 Package unit, air cooled, 25 thru 50 ton, annually	1.217	63	68		131	154	185
2950 Annualized	3.254	101	181		282	335	410

PM Components	Labor-hrs.	W	M	Q	S	A
PM System D3055 220 1950						
Package unit, water cooled, 3 tons through 24 tons						
1 Check with operating or area personnel for deficiencies.	.035			√	√	√
2 Check tension, condition, and alignment of belts; adjust as necessary.	.029			√	√	√
3 Lubricate shaft and motor bearings.	.047			√	√	√
4 Replace air filters.	.055			√	√	√
5 Clean electrical wiring and connections; tighten loose connections.	.120					√
6 Clean coils, evaporator drain pan, blowers, fans, motors and drain piping as required.	.385					√
7 Perform operational check of unit; make adjustments on controls and other components as required.	.077			√	√	√
8 During operation of unit, check refrigerant pressure; add refrigerant as necessary.	.135			√	√	√
9 Check compressor oil level; add oil as required.	.033					√
10 Clean area around unit.	.066			√	√	√
11 Fill out maintenance checklist and report deficiencies.	.022			√	√	√
Total labor-hours/period				.466	.466	1.004
Total labor-hours/year				.932	.466	1.004

		Cost Each						
			2012 Bare Costs				**Total**	**Total**
Description	**Labor-hrs.**	**Material**	**Labor**	**Equip.**	**Total**		**In-House**	**w/O&P**
1900 Package unit, water cooled, 3 thru 24 ton, annually	1.004	45	56		101		119	143
1950 Annualized	2.402	72	134		206		246	298

PM Components	Labor-hrs.	W	M	Q	S	A
PM System D3055 220 2950						
Package unit, water cooled, 25 tons through 50 tons						
1 Check with operating or area personnel for deficiencies.	.035			√	√	√
2 Check tension, condition, and alignment of belts; adjust as necessary.	.029			√	√	√
3 Lubricate shaft and motor bearings.	.047			√	√	√
4 Replace air filters.	.078			√	√	√
5 Clean electrical wiring and connections; tighten loose connections.	.120					√
6 Clean coils, evaporator drain pan, blowers, fans, motors and drain piping as required.	.385					√
7 Perform operational check of unit; make adjustments on controls and other components as required.	.130			√	√	√
8 During operation of unit, check refrigerant pressure; add refrigerant as necessary.	.272			√	√	√
9 Check compressor oil level; add oil as required.	.033					√
10 Clean area around unit.	.066			√	√	√
11 Fill out maintenance checklist and report deficiencies.	.022			√	√	√
Total labor-hours/period				.679	.679	1.217
Total labor-hours/year				1.358	.679	1.217

		Cost Each						
			2012 Bare Costs				**Total**	**Total**
Description	**Labor-hrs.**	**Material**	**Labor**	**Equip.**	**Total**		**In-House**	**w/O&P**
2900 Package unit, water cooled, 25 thru 50 ton, annually	1.217	63	68		131		154	185
2950 Annualized	3.254	101	181		282		335	410

PM Components	Labor-hrs.	W	M	Q	S	A
PM System D3055 230 1950						
Package unit, computer room						
1 Check with operating or area personnel for deficiencies.	.035			√	√	√
2 Run microprocessor check, if available, or check controls and unit for proper operation.	.216			√	√	√
3 Check for unusual noise or vibration.	.033			√	√	√
4 Clean coils, evaporator drain pan, humidifier pan, blower, motor and drain piping as required.	.380				√	√
5 Replace air filters.	.078			√	√	√
6 Lubricate shaft and motor bearings.	.047			√	√	√
7 Check belts for wear, proper tension, and alignment; adjust as necessary.	.029			√	√	√
8 Check humidity lamp, replace if necessary.	.156			√	√	√
9 During operation of unit, check refrigerant pressures; add refrigerant as necessary.	.270				√	√
10 Inspect exterior piping and valves for leaks; tighten connections as required.	.077			√	√	√
11 Clean area around unit.	.066			√	√	√
12 Fill out maintenance checklist and report deficiencies.	.022			√	√	√
Total labor-hours/period				.759	1.409	1.409
Total labor-hours/year				1.518	1.409	1.409

	Description	Labor-hrs.	Material	Labor	Equip.	Total	Total In-House	Total w/O&P
				Cost Each				
				2012 Bare Costs				
1900	Package unit, computer room, annually	1.409	52.50	78.50		131	157	188
1950	Annualized	4.336	58	242		300	365	450

PM Components	Labor-hrs.	W	M	Q	S	A
PM System D3055 240 1950						
Package unit, with duct gas heater						
1 Check with operating or area personnel for deficiencies.	.035			√	√	√
2 Check tension, condition and alignment of belts; adjust as necessary.	.029			√	√	√
3 Lubricate shaft and motor bearings.	.047			√	√	√
4 Replace air filters.	.078			√	√	√
5 Check electrical wiring and connections; tighten loose connections.	.120					√
6 Clean coils, evaporator drain pan, blowers, fans, motors and drain piping as required.	.385					√
7 Perform operational check of unit; make adjustments on controls and other components as required.	.077			√	√	√
8 During operation of unit, check refrigerant pressures; add refrigerant as necessary.	.272			√	√	√
9 Check compressor oil level; add oil as required.	.033					√
10 Inspect, clean and adjust control valves and thermo-sensing bulbs on gas burners.	.254					√
11 Inspect fuel system for leaks.	.016			√	√	√
12 Check for proper operation of burner primary controls. Check and adjust thermostat.	.133					√
13 Check electrical wiring to burner controls.	.079					√
14 Inspect and clean firebox.	.577					√
15 Check condition of flue pipe, damper and stack.	.147			√	√	√
16 Check heater operation through complete cycle or up to 10 minutes.	.225					√
17 Clean area around entire unit.	.066			√	√	√
18 Fill out maintenance checklist and report deficiencies.	.022			√	√	√
Total labor-hours/period				.789	.789	2.595
Total labor-hours/year				1.578	.789	2.595

			Cost Each					
			2012 Bare Costs				Total	Total
Description	Labor-hrs.	Material	Labor	Equip.	Total	In-House	w/O&P
1900	Package unit with duct gas heater, annually	2.595	43.50	145		188.50	228	279
1950	Annualized	4.962	65	276		341	415	510

PM Components	Labor-hrs.	W	M	Q	S	A
PM System D3055 250 1950						
Air conditioning split system, DX, air cooled, up to 10 tons						
1 Check with operating or area personnel for deficiencies.	.035			√	√	√
2 Clean intake side of condenser coils, fans and intake screens.	.055			√	√	√
3 Lubricate shaft and motor bearings.	.047			√	√	√
4 Pressure wash condenser coils with coil clean solution, as required.	.611					√
5 Replace air filters.	.078			√	√	√
6 Clean electrical wiring and connections; tighten loose connections.	.120					√
7 Clean evaporator coils, drain pan, blowers, fans, motors and drain piping as required.	.380					√
8 Perform operational check of unit; make adjustments on controls and other components as required.	.033			√	√	√
9 During operation of unit, check refrigerant pressure; add refrigerant as necessary.	.272			√	√	√
10 Clean area around equipment.	.066			√	√	√
11 Fill out maintenance checklist and report deficiencies.	.022			√	√	√
Total labor-hours/period				.608	.608	1.719
Total labor-hours/year				1.216	.608	1.719

			Cost Each				
			2012 Bare Costs			**Total**	**Total**
Description	Labor-hrs.	Material	Labor	Equip.	Total	In-House	w/O&P
1900	A/C, split sys., DX, air cooled, to 10 tons, annually	1.719	46	96		142	170	207
1950	Annualized	3.543	73.50	197		270.50	325	400

PM Components	Labor-hrs.	W	M	Q	S	A
PM System D3055 250 2950						
Air conditioning split system, DX, air cooled, over 10 tons						
1 Check with operating or area personnel for deficiencies.	.035			√	√	√
2 Check tension, condition, and alignment of belts; adjust as necessary.	.029			√	√	√
3 Lubricate shaft and motor bearings.	.047			√	√	√
4 Pressure wash condenser coils with coil clean solution, as required.	.611					√
5 Replace air filters.	.078			√	√	√
6 Clean electrical wiring and connections; tighten loose connections.	.120					√
7 Clean evaporator coils, drain pan, blowers, fans, motors and drain piping as required.	.380					√
8 Perform operational check of unit; make adjustments on controls and other components as required.	.033			√	√	√
9 During operation of unit, check refrigerant pressure; add refrigerant as necessary.	.272			√	√	√
10 Check compressor oil level; add oil as required.	.033			√	√	√
11 Clean area around equipment.	.066			√	√	√
12 Fill out maintenance checklist and report deficiencies.	.022			√	√	√
Total labor-hours/period				.615	.615	1.726
Total labor-hours/year				1.230	.615	1.726

			Cost Each				
			2012 Bare Costs			**Total**	**Total**
Description	Labor-hrs.	Material	Labor	Equip.	Total	In-House	w/O&P
2900	A/C, split sys., DX, air cooled, over 10 T, annually	1.726	64.50	96		160.50	191	231
2950	Annualized	3.571	103	199		302	360	440

PM Components	Labor-hrs.	W	M	Q	S	A
PM System D3055 310 1950						
Heat pump, air cooled, up to 5 tons						
1 Check with operating or area personnel for deficiencies.	.035			√	√	√
2 Check unit for proper operation, excessive noise or vibration.	.033			√	√	√
3 Clean intake side of condenser coils, fans and intake screens.	.055			√	√	
4 Check electrical wiring and connections; tighten loose connections.	.120					√
5 Inspect fan(s) for bent blades or unbalance; adjust and clean as necessary.	.027					√
6 Check belts for condition, proper tension and misalignment; adjust as required.	.029			√	√	√
7 Lubricate shaft bearings and motor bearings.	.047			√	√	√
8 Inspect piping and valves for leaks; tighten connections as necessary.	.077			√	√	√
9 Replace air filters.	.078			√	√	√
10 Check refrigerant pressure; add refrigerant as necessary.	.135			√	√	√
11 Clean evaporative drain pan, and drain piping as required.	.385					√
12 Cycle the reverse cycle valve to insure proper operation.	.091			√	√	√
13 Clean area around equipment.	.066			√	√	√
14 Fill out maintenance checklist and report deficiencies.	.022			√	√	√
Total labor-hours/period				.668	.668	1.200
Total labor-hours/year				1.336	.668	1.200

		Cost Each					
			2012 Bare Costs			**Total**	**Total**
Description	**Labor-hrs.**	**Material**	**Labor**	**Equip.**	**Total**	**In-House**	**w/O&P**
1900 Heat pump, air cooled, up to 5 ton, annually	1.200	27	67		94	113	138
1950 Annualized	3.204	43.50	178		221.50	271	330

PM Components	Labor-hrs.	W	M	Q	S	A
PM System D3055 310 2950						
Heat pump, air cooled, over 5 tons						
1 Check with operating or area personnel for deficiencies.	.035			√	√	√
2 Check unit for proper operation, excessive noise or vibration.	.033			√	√	√
3 Clean intake side of condenser coils, fans and intake screens.	.055			√	√	
4 Check electrical wiring and connections; tighten loose connections.	.120					√
5 Inspect fan(s) for bent blades or unbalance; adjust and clean as necessary.	.055					√
6 Check belts for condition, proper tension and misalignment; adjust as required.	.057			√	√	√
7 Lubricate shaft bearings and motor bearings.	.047			√	√	√
8 Inspect piping and valves for leaks; tighten connections as necessary.	.077					√
9 Replace air filters.	.156			√	√	√
10 Check refrigerant pressure; add refrigerant as necessary.	.135			√	√	√
11 Lubricate and check operation of dampers, if applicable.	.029					√
12 Check compressor oil level and add oil, if required.	.033			√	√	√
13 Cycle the reverse cycle valve to insure proper operation.	.091			√	√	√
14 Clean evaporative drain pan, and drain piping as required.	.385					√
15 Clean area around equipment.	.066			√	√	√
16 Fill out maintenance checklist and report deficiencies.	.022			√	√	√
Total labor-hours/period				.730	.730	1.396
Total labor-hours/year				1.460	.730	1.396

		Cost Each					
			2012 Bare Costs			**Total**	**Total**
Description	**Labor-hrs.**	**Material**	**Labor**	**Equip.**	**Total**	**In-House**	**w/O&P**
2900 Heat pump, air cooled, over 5 ton, annually	1.396	50.50	78		128.50	153	184
2950 Annualized	3.586	72	200		272	330	400

459

PM Components	Labor-hrs.	W	M	Q	S	A
PM System D3055 320 1950						
Heat pump, water cooled, up to 5 tons						
1 Check with operating or area personnel for deficiencies.	.035			√	√	√
2 Check unit for proper operation, excessive noise or vibration.	.033			√	√	√
3 Clean intake side of evaporator coil, fans and intake screens.	.055			√	√	√
4 Check electrical wiring and connections; tighten loose connections.	.120					√
5 Inspect fan(s) for bent blades or unbalance; adjust and clean as necessary.	.027					√
6 Check belts for condition, proper tension and misalignment; adjust as required.	.029			√	√	√
7 Lubricate shaft bearings and motor bearings.	.047			√	√	√
8 Inspect piping and valves for leaks; tighten connections as necessary.	.077			√	√	√
9 Replace air filters.	.078			√	√	√
10 Check refrigerant pressure; add refrigerant as necessary.	.135			√	√	√
11 Lubricate and check operation of dampers, if applicable.	.029					√
12 Clean evaporator drain pan and drain line with solvent.	.385					√
13 Cycle reverse cycle valve to insure proper operation.	.091			√	√	√
14 Backwash condenser coil to remove sediment.	.325					√
15 Clean area around equipment.	.066			√	√	√
16 Fill out maintenance checklist and report deficiencies.	.022			√	√	√
Total labor-hours/period				.668	.668	1.554
Total labor-hours/year				1.336	.668	1.554

		Cost Each					
		2012 Bare Costs				Total	Total
Description	Labor-hrs.	Material	Labor	Equip.	Total	In-House	w/O&P
1900 Heat pump, water cooled, up to 5 ton, annually	1.554	27	86.50		113.50	138	169
1950 Annualized	3.558	43.50	198		241.50	295	365

PM Components	Labor-hrs.	W	M	Q	S	A
PM System D3055 320 2950						
Heat pump, water cooled, over 5 tons						
1 Check with operating or area personnel for deficiencies.	.035			√	√	√
2 Check unit for proper operation, excessive noise or vibration.	.033			√	√	√
3 Clean intake side of condenser coils, fans and intake screens.	.055			√	√	√
4 Check electrical wiring and connections; tighten loose connections.	.120					√
5 Inspect fan(s) for bent blades or unbalance; adjust and clean as necessary.	.027					√
6 Check belts for condition, proper tension and misalignment; adjust as required.	.029			√	√	√
7 Lubricate shaft bearings and motor bearings.	.047			√	√	√
8 Inspect piping and valves for leaks; tighten connections as necessary.	.077			√	√	√
9 Replace air filters.	.078			√	√	√
10 Check refrigerant pressure; add refrigerant as necessary.	.135			√	√	√
11 Lubricate and check operation of dampers, if applicable.	.029					√
12 Clean evaporator drain pan and drain line with solvent.	.385					√
13 Cycle reverse cycle valve to insure proper operation.	.091			√	√	√
14 Clean area around equipment.	.066			√	√	√
15 Fill out maintenance checklist and report deficiencies.	.022			√	√	√
Total labor-hours/period				.668	.668	1.229
Total labor-hours/year				1.336	.668	1.229

		Cost Each					
		2012 Bare Costs				Total	Total
Description	Labor-hrs.	Material	Labor	Equip.	Total	In-House	w/O&P
2900 Heat pump, water cooled, over 5 ton, annually	1.229	50.50	68.50		119	141	170
2950 Annualized	3.233	72	180		252	305	370

PM Components	Labor-hrs.	W	M	Q	S	A
PM System D3065 100 1950						
Controls, central system, electro/pneumatic						
1 With panel disconnected from power source, clean patrol panel compartment with a vacuum.	.468					√
2 Inspect wiring/components for loose connections; tighten, as required.	.120					√
3 Check set point of controls temperature, humidity or pressure.	.033					√
4 Check unit over its range of control.	.033					√
5 Check for correct pressure differential on all two position controllers.	.195					√
6 Check source of the signal and its amplification on electronic controls.	.468					√
7 Check air systems for leaks; repair as necessary.	.156					√
8 Check relays, pilot valves and pressure regulators for proper operation; repair or replace as necessary.	.325					√
9 Replace air filters in sensors, controllers, and thermostats as necessary.	.029					√
10 Clean area around equipment.	.066					√
11 Fill out maintenance checklist and report deficiencies.	.022					√
Total labor-hours/period						1.915
Total labor-hours/year						1.915

			Cost Each					
			2012 Bare Costs				Total	Total
Description		Labor-hrs.	Material	Labor	Equip.	Total	In-House	w/O&P
1900	Controls, central system, electro/pneumatic, annually	1.915	43.50	107		150.50	181	220
1950	Annualized	1.915	43.50	107		150.50	181	220

PM Components	Labor-hrs.	W	M	Q	S	A
PM System D3095 110 1950						
Air compressor, gas engine						
1 Check with operating or area personnel for any obvious deficiencies.	.035		√	√	√	√
2 Check compressor oil level; add oil as required.	.022		√	√	√	√
3 Replace compressor oil.	.221				√	√
4 Clean air intake filter on air compressor(s); replace if necessary.	.177				√	√
5 Clean cylinder cooling fins and air cooler on compressor(s).	.156				√	√
6 Check tension, condition, and alignment of v-belts; adjust as necessary.	.030				√	√
7 Clean oil and water traps.	.178				√	√
8 Drain moisture from air storage tank and check discharge for indication of interior corrosion.	.046				√	√
9 Perform operation check of compressor; check the operation of low pressure cut-in and high pressure cut-out switches.	.221		√	√	√	√
10 Check operation of safety pressure relief valve.	.030				√	√
11 Check and tighten compressor foundation anchor bolts.	.022				√	√
12 Check radiator coolant; add if required.	.012		√	√	√	√
13 Check battery water; add if required.	.241		√	√	√	√
14 Check wiring, connections, switches, etc.; tighten loose connections.	.120				√	√
15 Check engine oil level; add if required.	.014		√	√	√	√
16 Change engine oil.	.224				√	√
17 Change engine oil filter.	.059				√	√
18 Check spark plug and reset cap.	.035				√	√
19 Check condition of engine air filter; replace if necessary.	.039				√	√
20 Test run engine for proper operation.	.413		√	√	√	√
21 Wipe dust and dirt from engine and compressor.	.109		√	√	√	√
22 Check muffler/exhaust system for corrosion.	.020				√	√
23 Clean area around equipment.	.066		√	√	√	√
24 Fill out maintenance checklist and report deficiencies.	.022		√	√	√	√
Total labor-hours/period			1.155	1.155	2.512	2.512
Total labor-hours/year			9.240	2.310	2.512	2.512

			Cost Each					
			2012 Bare Costs				Total	Total
Description		Labor-hrs.	Material	Labor	Equip.	Total	In-House	w/O&P
1900	Air compressor, gas engine powered, annually	2.512	100	140		240	285	345
1950	Annualized	16.574	243	925		1,168	1,425	1,750

PM Components	Labor-hrs.	W	M	Q	S	A
PM System D3095 114 1950						√
Air compressor, centrifugal, to 40 H.P.						
1 Check compressor oil level; add oil as necessary.	.022			√	√	√
2 Perform operational check of compressor system and adjust as required.	.221			√	√	√
3 Check motor for excessive vibration, noise and overheating; lubricate.	.039			√	√	√
4 Check operation of pressure relief valve.	.030			√	√	√
5 Clean cooling fans and air cooler.	.023			√	√	√
6 Check tension, condition, and alignment of V-belts; adjust as necessary.	.030			√	√	√
7 Drain moisture from air storage tank and check low pressure cut-in; while draining, check discharge for indication of interior corrosion.	.046			√	√	√
8 Replace air intake filter, as needed.	.177			√	√	√
9 Clean oil and water trap.	.177			√	√	√
10 Clean compressor and surrounding area.	.066			√	√	√
11 Fill out maintenance checklist and report deficiencies.	.022			√	√	√
Total labor-hours/period				.853	.853	.853
Total labor-hours/year				1.706	.853	.853

			Cost Each				
			2012 Bare Costs			Total	Total
Description	Labor-hrs.	Material	Labor	Equip.	Total	In-House	w/O&P
1900 Air compressor, centrifugal, to 40 H.P., annually	.853	43	47.50		90.50	107	128
1950 Annualized	3.412	64.50	190		254.50	310	375

PM Components	Labor-hrs.	W	M	Q	S	A
PM System D3095 114 2950						
Air compressor, centrifugal, over 40 H.P.						
1 Check with operating or area personnel for any obvious deficiencies.	.035		√	√	√	√
2 Perform control system check.	.325				√	√
3 Lubricate main driver coupling if necessary.	.047				√	√
4 Lubricate prelube pump motor and pump coupling, if necessary.	.047				√	√
5 Perform operation check of air compressor, adjust as required.	.221		√	√	√	√
6 Check main driver coupling alignment; realign if necessary.	.325				√	√
7 Check compressor and motor operation for excessive vibration, noise and overheating; lubricate motor.	.039		√	√	√	√
8 Check compressor scrolls, piping, and impeller housing for all leaks or cracks.	.325		√	√	√	√
9 Check intercoolers and aftercoolers for high cooling water temperatures or cooling water leakage.	.195		√	√	√	√
10 Check oil level in compressor oil reservoir; add oil as necessary.	.022		√	√	√	√
11 Replace compressor oil and oil filters.	.282					√
12 Record oil pressure and oil temperature.	.013		√	√	√	√
13 Check compressor for oil leaks.	.026		√	√	√	√
14 Visually inspect oil mist arrestor, clean housing, lines, and replace element if saturated, if applicable.	.177				√	√
15 Check operation of pressure relief valve.	.030		√	√	√	√
16 Visually inspect discharge check valve.	.009				√	√
17 Check oil and water trap.	.022		√	√	√	√
18 Check indicating lamps or gauges for proper operation if appropriate; replace burned out lamps or repair/replace gauges.	.020					√
19 Visually check all air intake filter elements; replace if necessary.	.022		√	√	√	√
20 Replace all air intake filter elements.	.177					√
21 Lubricate motor.	.047				√	√
22 Clean compressor, motor and surrounding area.	.066		√	√	√	√
23 Fill out maintenance check and report deficiencies.	.022		√	√	√	√
Total labor-hours/period			1.038	1.038	2.015	2.494
Total labor-hours/year			8.304	2.076	2.015	2.494

Description	Labor-hrs.	Material	Labor	Equip.	Total	Total In-House	Total w/O&P
		2012 Bare Costs					
2900 Air compressor, centrifugal, over 40 H.P., annually	2.494	86	139		225	268	325
2950 Annualized	14.889	200	830		1,030	1,250	1,550

PM Components	Labor-hrs.	W	M	Q	S	A
PM System D3095 118 1950						
Air compressor, reciprocating, less than 5 H.P.						
1 Replace compressor oil.	.341			√	√	√
2 Perform operation check of compressor system and adjust as required.	.221			√	√	√
3 Check motor operation for excessive vibration, noise and overheating.	.042			√	√	√
4 Lubricate motor.	.047			√	√	√
5 Check operation of pressure relief valve.	.030			√	√	√
6 Check tension, condition, and alignment of V-belts; adjust as necessary.	.030			√	√	√
7 Drain moisture from air storage tank and check low pressure cut-in; while draining, check discharge for indication of interior corrosion.	.046			√	√	√
8 Clean air intake filter on compressor.	.177			√	√	√
9 Clean oil and water trap.	.177			√	√	√
10 Clean exterior of compressor, motor and surrounding area.	.066			√	√	√
11 Fill out maintenance checklist and report deficiencies.	.022			√	√	√
Total labor-hours/period				1.199	1.199	1.199
Total labor-hours/year				2.398	1.199	1.199

		Cost Each					
		2012 Bare Costs				Total	Total
Description	Labor-hrs.	Material	Labor	Equip.	Total	In-House	w/O&P
1900 Air compressor, recip., less than 5 H.P., annually	1.199	21.50	67		88.50	107	131
1950 Annualized	4.796	86	267		353	430	525

PM Components	Labor-hrs.	W	M	Q	S	A
PM System D3095 118 2950						
Air compressor, reciprocating, 5 to 40 H.P.						
1 Replace compressor oil.	.341			√	√	√
2 Perform operation check of compressor system and adjust as required.	.221			√	√	√
3 Check motor operation for excessive vibration, noise and overheating; lubricate motor.	.042			√	√	√
4 Check operation of pressure relief valve.	.043			√	√	√
5 Clean cooling fans and air cooler on compressor.	.023			√	√	√
6 Check tension, condition, and alignment of V-belts; adjust as necessary.	.030			√	√	√
7 Drain moisture from air storage tank and check low pressure cut-in; while draining, check discharge for indication of interior corrosion.	.059			√	√	√
8 Clean air intake filter on compressor.	.177			√	√	√
9 Clean oil and water trap.	.190			√	√	√
10 Clean compressor and surrounding area.	.066			√	√	√
11 Fill out maintenance checklist and report deficiencies.	.022			√	√	√
Total labor-hours/period				1.214	1.214	1.214
Total labor-hours/year				2.428	1.214	1.214

		Cost Each					
		2012 Bare Costs				Total	Total
Description	Labor-hrs.	Material	Labor	Equip.	Total	In-House	w/O&P
2900 Air compressor, reciprocating, 5 to 40 H.P., annually	1.214	21.50	67.50		89	108	132
2950 Annualized	4.856	86	270		356	430	530

PM Components	Labor-hrs.	W	M	Q	S	A
PM System D3095 118 3950						
Air compressor, reciprocating, over 40 H.P.						
1 Check with operating or area personnel for deficiencies.	.035			√	√	√
2 Perform operation check of compressor system and adjust as required.	.221			√	√	√
3 Replace compressor oil.	.341			√	√	√
4 Check motor(s) operation for excessive vibration, noise and overheating; lubricate motor(s).	.042			√	√	√
5 Clean cylinder cooling fins and air cooler on compressor.	.023			√	√	√
6 Check tension, condition, and alignment of V-belts; adjust as necessary.	.056			√	√	√
7 Check operation of pressure relief valve.	.030			√	√	√
8 Check low pressure cut in and high pressure cut out switches.	.120			√	√	√
9 Drain moisture from air storage tank and check low pressure cut-in; while draining, check discharge for indication of interior corrosion.	.072			√	√	√
10 Clean air intake filter on air compressor(s); replace if necessary.	.177			√	√	√
11 Clean oil and water trap.	.204			√	√	√
12 Check indicating lamps or gauges for proper operation if appropriate; replace burned out lamps or repair/replace gauges.	.020			√	√	√
13 Clean area around equipment.	.066			√	√	√
14 Fill out maintenance checklist and report deficiencies.	.022			√	√	√
Total labor-hours/period				1.429	1.429	1.429
Total labor-hours/year				2.858	1.429	1.429

			Cost Each					
			2012 Bare Costs				Total	Total
Description		Labor-hrs.	Material	Labor	Equip.	Total	In-House	w/O&P
3900	Air compressor, reciprocating, over 40 H.P., annually	1.429	21.50	79.50		101	123	151
3950	Annualized	5.716	86	320		406	490	605

PM Components	Labor-hrs.	W	M	Q	S	A
PM System D3095 210 1950						
Steam Humidification System						
1 Operate humidistat through its throttling range to verify activation and deactivation.	.117				√	√
2 Inspect steam trap for proper operation.	.117				√	√
3 Turn off steam supply.	.065				√	√
4 Secure electrical service before servicing humidification unit.	.065				√	√
5 Clean strainer.	.195				√	√
6 Clean and/or replace water/steam nozzels as necessary.	.455				√	√
7 Inspect pneumatic controller for air leaks.	.039				√	√
8 Inspect steam lines for leaks and corrosion and repair leaks.	.195				√	√
9 Fill out maintenance checklist and report deficiencies	.022				√	√
Total labor-hours/period					1.270	1.270
Total labor-hours/year					1.270	1.270

			Cost Each					
				2012 Bare Costs			Total	Total
	Description	Labor-hrs.	Material	Labor	Equip.	Total	In-House	w/O&P
1900	Steam humidification system, annually	1.270	21.50	70.50		92	112	137
1950	Annualized	2.540	43.50	141		184.50	224	274

PM Components	Labor-hrs.	W	M	Q	S	A
PM System D3095 210 2950						
Evaporative Pan with Heating Coil Humidification System						
1 Operate humidistat through its throttling range to verify activation and deactivation.	.117				√	√
2 Inspect steam trap for proper operation.	.117				√	√
3 Turn off water and steam supply.	.065				√	√
4 Secure electrical service before servicing humidification unit.	.065				√	√
5 Drain and flush water pans, clean drains, etc.	.260				√	√
6 Check condition of heating element/steam coils and clean.	.065				√	√
7 Inspect pneumatic controller for air leaks.	.039				√	√
8 Inspect steam lines for leaks and corrosion and repair leaks.	.195				√	√
9 Fill out maintenance checklist and report deficiencies.	.022				√	√
Total labor-hours/period					.945	.945
Total labor-hours/year					.945	.945

			Cost Each					
				2012 Bare Costs			Total	Total
	Description	Labor-hrs.	Material	Labor	Equip.	Total	In-House	w/O&P
2900	Evap. pan with heating coil humidif. system, annually	.945	14.45	52.50		66.95	81.50	100
2950	Annualized	1.890	29	105		134	163	200

PM Components	Labor-hrs.	W	M	Q	S	A
PM System D3095 220 1950						
Dehumidifier, desiccant wheel						
1 Check with operating or area personnel for deficiencies.	.035		√	√	√	√
2 Check filters for any blockage or fouling, remove and clean as required.	.036		√	√	√	√
3 Check wheel seals for tears or punctures.	.055		√	√	√	√
4 Check the control valve, thermo sensor bulb and burner, if it has heaters; or check for scaling or leaking on steam heating coils, as applicable.	.094				√	√
5 Check that the outlet air temperature is within the proper heat range.	.105		√	√	√	√
6 Clean the desiccant wheel and check for softening of wheel faces.	.031				√	√
7 Check desiccant wheel and motor for vibration and noise, adjust as required.	.109				√	√
8 Check gear reducer oil level; add as required.	.035				√	√
9 Check wheel belt(s) for wear, proper tension and alignment; adjust as required.	.029				√	√
10 Check blower and motor for excessive vibration and noise; adjust as required.	.109				√	√
11 Check blower belt(s) for wear, proper tension and alignment; adjust as required.	.029				√	√
12 Lubricate wheel, blower and motor bearings.	.047				√	√
13 Check electrical wiring and connections; make appropriate adjustments.	.120				√	√
14 Check reactivation ductwork for condensation and air leaks.	.013				√	√
15 Clean the equipment and the surrounding area.	.066		√	√	√	√
16 Fill out maintenance checklist and report deficiencies.	.022		√	√	√	√
Total labor-hours/period			.319	.319	.935	.935
Total labor-hours/year			2.552	.638	.935	.935

	Description	Labor-hrs.	Cost Each				Total In-House	Total w/O&P
			2012 Bare Costs					
			Material	Labor	Equip.	Total	In-House	w/O&P
1900	Dehumidifier, desiccant wheel, annually	.935	30	52		82	98	119
1950	Annualized	5.060	94	282		376	455	560

PM Components	Labor-hrs.	W	M	Q	S	A
PM System D4015 100 1950						
Backflow prevention device, up to 4″						
NOTE: Test frequency may vary depending on local regulations and application.						
1 Test and calibrate check valve operation of backflow prevention device with test set.	.191					√
2 Bleed air from backflow preventer.	.047					√
3 Inspect for leaks under pressure.	.007					√
4 Clean backflow preventer and surrounding area.	.066					√
5 Fill out maintenance checklist and report deficiencies.	.022					√
Total labor-hours/period						.333
Total labor-hours/year						.333

	Description	Labor-hrs.	Material	Labor	Equip.	Total	Total In-House	Total w/O&P
			2012 Bare Costs					
1900	Backflow prevention device, up to 4″, annually	.333		18.20		18.20	22.50	28.50
1950	Annualized	.333		18.20		18.20	22.50	28.50

PM Components	Labor-hrs.	W	M	Q	S	A
PM System D4015 100 2950						
Backflow prevention device, over 4″						
NOTE: Test frequency may vary depending on local regulations and application.						
1 Test and calibrate check valve operation of backflow prevention device with test set.	.334					√
2 Bleed air from backflow preventer.	.065					√
3 Inspect for leaks under pressure.	.007					√
4 Clean backflow preventer and surrounding area.	.066					√
5 Fill out maintenance checklist and report deficiencies.	.022					√
Total labor-hours/period						.494
Total labor-hours/year						.494

	Description	Labor-hrs.	Material	Labor	Equip.	Total	Total In-House	Total w/O&P
			2012 Bare Costs					
2900	Backflow prevention device, over 4″, annually	.494		27		27	33.50	42
2950	Annualized	.494		27		27	33.50	42

PM Components	Labor-hrs.	W	M	Q	S	A
PM System D4015 150 1950						
Extinguishing system, wet pipe						
1 Notify proper authorities prior to testing any alarm systems.	.130		√	√	√	√
2 Open and close post indicator valve (PIV) to check operation; make minor adjustments such as lubricating valve stem, cleaning and/or replacing target windows as required.	.176					√
3 Open and close OS&Y (outside stem and yoke) cut-off valve to check operation; make minor repairs such as lubricating stems and tightening packing glands as required.	.176					√
4 Perform operational test of water flow detectors; make minor adjustments and restore system to proper operating condition.	.148					√
5 Check to ensure that alarm drain is open; clean drain line if necessary.	.081		√	√	√	√
6 Open water motor alarm test valve and ensure that outside alarm operates; lubricate alarm, make adjustments as required.	.176		√	√	√	√
7 Conduct main drain test by opening 2″ test valve; maintain a continuous record of drain tests; make minor adjustments if applicable; restore system to proper operating condition.	.333			√	√	√
8 Check general condition of sprinklers and sprinkler system; make minor adjustments as required.	.228					√
9 Check equipment gaskets, piping, packing glands, and valves for leaks; tighten flange bolts and loose connections to stop all leaks.	.013					√
10 Check condition of fire department connections; replace missing or broken covers as required.	.103					√
11 Trip test wet pipe system using test valve furthest from wet pipe valve (control valve); make minor adjustments as necessary and restore system to proper operating condition.	1.733					√
12 Inspect OS&Y and PIV cut-off valves for open position.	.066		√	√	√	√
13 Clean area around system components.	.433		√	√	√	√
14 Fill out maintenance checklist and report deficiencies.	.022		√	√	√	√
Total labor-hours/period			.475	1.241	1.241	3.818
Total labor-hours/year			3.800	2.482	1.241	3.818

		Cost Each					
		2012 Bare Costs				**Total**	**Total**
Description	**Labor-hrs.**	**Material**	**Labor**	**Equip.**	**Total**	**In-House**	**w/O&P**
1900 Extinguishing system, wet pipe, annually	3.818	79	206		285	345	420
1950 Annualized	11.341	158	615		773	940	1,150

PM Components	Labor-hrs.	W	M	Q	S	A
PM System D4015 180 1950						
Extinguishing system, deluge/preaction						
1 Notify proper authorites prior to testing any alarm systems.	.130		√	√	√	√
2 Open and close post indicator valve (PIV) to check operation; make minor repairs such as lubricating valve stem, cleaning and/or replacing target windows as required.	.176					√
3 Open and close outside stem and yoke (OS&Y) cut-off valve to check operation; make minor repairs such as lubricating stems, tightening packing glands as required.	.176					√
4 Perform operational test of supervisory initiating devices and water flow detectors; make minor adjustments and restore system to proper operating condition.	.148					√
5 Check to ensure that alarm drain is open; clean drain if necessary.	.081		√	√	√	√
6 Open water motor alarm test valve and ensure that outside alarm operates; lubricate alarm and adjust as required.	.176		√	√	√	√
7 Visually check water pressure to ensure adequate operating pressure is available; make adjustments as required.	.004		√	√	√	√
8 Conduct main drain test by opening 2″ test valve and observing drop in water pressure on gauge; pressure drop should not exceed 20 PSI; maintain a continuous record of drain tests; make minor adjustments; restore system to proper operating condition.	.333			√	√	√
9 Check general condition of sprinklers and sprinkler system; make minor adjustments as required.	.228					√
10 Check equipment gaskets, piping, packing glands, and valves for leaks; tighten flange bolts and loose connections to stop all leaks.	.013					√
11 Check condition of fire department connections; replace missing or broken covers as required.	.103					√
12 Check and inspect pneumatic system for physical damage and proper operation; make minor adjustments as required.	.320					√
13 Trip test deluge system (control valve closed); make minor adjustments as necessary and restore system to fully operational condition.	1.956					√
14 Inspect OS&Y and PIV cut-off valves for open position.	.066		√	√	√	√
15 Clean area around system components.	.066					√
16 Ensure that system is restored to proper operating condition.	.109		√	√	√	√
17 Fill out maintenance checklist and report deficiencies.	.022		√	√	√	√
Total labor-hours/period			.588	.921	.921	4.107
Total labor-hours/year			4.704	1.842	.921	4.107

	Description	Labor-hrs.	2012 Bare Costs				Total In-House	Total w/O&P
			Material	Labor	Equip.	Total		
1900	Extinguishing system, deluge / preaction, annually	4.107	79	222		301	365	445
1950	Annualized	11.574	158	625		783	955	1,175

PM Components	Labor-hrs.	W	M	Q	S	A
PM System D4015 210 1950						
Fire pump, electric motor driven						
1 Check control panel and wiring for loose connections; tighten connections as required.	.109			√	√	√
2 Ensure all valves relating to water system are in correct position.	.008	√	√	√	√	√
3 Open and close OS&Y(outside steam and yoke) cut-off valve to check operation; make minor repairs such as lubricating stems and tightening packing glands as required.	.176			√	√	√
4 Centrifugal pump:						
A) perform 10 minute pump test run; check for proper operation and adjust if required.	.217	√	√	√	√	√
B) check for leaks on suction and discharge piping, seals, packing glands, etc.	.077	√	√	√	√	√
C) check for excessive vibration, noise, overheating, etc.	.022	√	√	√	√	√
D) check alignment, clearances, and rotation of shaft and coupler (includes removing and reinstalling safety cover).	.160	√	√	√	√	√
E) tighten or replace loose, missing or damaged nuts, bolts, or screws.	.005	√	√	√	√	√
F) lubricate pump and motor as required.	.099			√	√	√
G) check suction or discharge pressure gauge readings and flow rate.	.078	√	√	√	√	√
H) check packing glands and tighten or repack as required; note that slight dripping is required for proper lubrication of shaft.	.113			√	√	√
5 Inspect and clean strainers after each use and flow test.	.260	√	√	√	√	√
6 Clean equipment and surrounding area.	.066	√	√	√	√	√
7 Fill out maintenance checklist and report deficiencies.	.022	√	√	√	√	√
Total labor-hours/period		.915	.915	1.412	1.412	1.412
Total labor-hours/year		34.770	7.320	2.824	1.412	1.412

		Cost Each					
		2012 Bare Costs				Total	Total
Description	Labor-hrs.	Material	Labor	Equip.	Total	In-House	w/O&P
1900 Fire pump, electric motor driven, annually	1.412	80.50	76.50		157	184	220
1950 Annualized	47.738	125	2,575		2,700	3,375	4,175

PM Components	Labor-hrs.	W	M	Q	S	A
PM System D4015 250 1950						
Fire pump, engine driven						
1 Ensure all valves relating to water system are in correct position.	.008	√	√	√	√	√
2 Open and close OS&Y (outside steam and yoke) cut-off valve to check operation; make minor repairs such as lubricating stems and tightening packing glands as required.	.176			√	√	√
3 Controller panel:						
A) check controller panel for proper operation in accordance with standard procedures for the type of panel installed, replace burned out bulbs and fuses; make other repairs as necessary.	.039			√	√	√
B) check wiring for loose connections and fraying; tighten or replace as required.	.109			√	√	√
4 Diesel engine:						
A) check oil level in crankcase with dipstick; add oil as necessary.	.014	√	√	√	√	√
B) drain and replace engine oil.	.511					√
C) replace engine oil filter.	.059					√
D) check radiator coolant level; add water if low.	.012	√	√	√	√	√
E) drain and replace radiator coolant.	.511					√
F) check battery water level; add water if low.	.012			√	√	√
G) check battery terminals for corrosion; clean if necessary.	.124			√	√	√
H) check belts for tension and wear; adjust or replace if required.	.012			√	√	√
I) check fuel level in tank; refill as required.	.046			√	√	√
J) check electrical wiring, connections, switches, etc.; adjust or tighten as necessary.	.120			√	√	√
K) perform 10 minute pump check for proper operation and adjust as required.	.217	√	√	√	√	√
5 Centrifugal pump:						
A) check for leaks on suction and discharge piping, seals, packing glands, etc.	.077	√	√	√	√	√
B) check pump operation; vibration, noise, overheating, etc.	.022	√	√	√	√	√
C) check alignment, clearances, and rotation of shaft and coupler (includes removing and reinstalling safety cover).	.160	√	√	√	√	√
D) tighten or replace loose, missing or damaged nuts, bolts, or screws.	.005	√	√	√	√	√
E) lubricate pump as required.	.099			√	√	√
F) check suction or discharge pressure gauge readings and flow rate.	.078	√	√	√	√	√
G) check packing glands and tighten or repack as required; note that slight dripping is required for proper lubrication of shaft.	.113			√	√	√
6 Inspect and clean strainers after each use and flow test.	.260	√	√	√	√	√
7 Clean equipment and surrounding area.	.433	√	√	√	√	√
8 Fill out maintenance checklist and report deficiencies.	.022	√	√	√	√	√
Total labor-hours/period		1.308	1.308	2.158	2.158	3.239
Total labor-hours/year		49.704	10.464	4.316	2.158	3.239

			Cost Each					
			2012 Bare Costs				Total	Total
Description		Labor-hrs.	Material	Labor	Equip.	Total	In-House	w/O&P
1900	Fire pump, motor/engine driven, annually	3.239	176	175		351	410	495
1950	Annualized	69.881	205	3,775		3,980	4,950	6,125

PM Components	Labor-hrs.	W	M	Q	S	A
PM System D4015 310 1950						
Extinguishing system, dry pipe						
1 Notify proper authorities prior to testing any alarm systems.	.130		√	√	√	√
2 Open and close post indicator valve to check operation; make minor repairs such as lubricating valve stem, cleaning and/or replacing target windows as required.	.176					√
3 Open and close OS&Y (outside stem and yoke) cut-off valve to check operation; make minor repairs such as lubricating stems and tightening packing glands as required.	.176					√
4 Perform operational test of water flow detectors; make minor adjustments and restore system to proper operating condition.	.148					√
5 Check to ensure that alarm drain is open; clean drain line if necessary.	.081		√	√	√	√
6 Open water motor alarm test valve and ensure that outside alarm operates; lubricate alarm, make adjustments as required.	.176		√	√	√	√
7 Visually check water pressure to ensure that adequate operating pressure is available; make adjustments as required.	.003		√	√	√	√
8 Conduct main drain test by opening 2″ test valve; maintain a continuous record of drain tests; make minor adjustments if applicable; restore system to proper operating condition.	.333			√	√	√
9 Check general condition of sprinklers and sprinkler system; make minor adjustments as required.	.228					√
10 Check equipment gaskets, piping, packing glands, and valves for leaks; tighten flange bolts and loose connections to stop all leaks.	.013					√
11 Check condition of fire department connections; replace missing or broken covers as required.	.103					√
12 Visually check system air pressure; pump up system and make minor adjustments as required.	.135		√	√	√	√
13 Trip test dry pipe system using test valve furthest from dry pipe valve (control valve partially open); make minor adjustments as necessary and restore system to fully operational condition.	1.733					√
14 Check operation of quick opening device.	.022					√
15 Inspect OS&Y and PIV cut-off valves for open position.	.066		√	√	√	√
16 Clean area around system components.	.433			√	√	√
17 Fill out maintenance checklist and report deficiencies.	.022		√	√	√	√
Total labor-hours/period			.613	1.379	1.379	3.978
Total labor-hours/year			4.904	2.758	1.379	3.978

			Cost Each				
			2012 Bare Costs			Total	Total
Description	Labor-hrs.	Material	Labor	Equip.	Total	In-House	w/O&P
1900 Extinguishing system, dry pipe, annually	3.978	122	215		337	405	490
1950 Annualized	13.019	201	705		906	1,100	1,350

PM Components	Labor-hrs.	W	M	Q	S	A
PM System D4095 100 1950						
Extinguishing system, CO$_2$						
1 Check that nozzles, heads and hand hose lines are clear from obstructions, have not been damaged and in proper position.	.098		√	√	√	√
2 Check to ensure that all operating controls are properly set.	.066		√	√	√	√
3 Clean nozzles as required.	.098		√	√	√	√
4 Visually inspect the control panel for obstructions or physical damage; clean dirt and dust from interior and exterior; make sure that all cards are plugged in tightly, tighten loose connections and make other minor adjustments as necessary.	.222		√	√	√	√
5 Check battery voltages where installed, recharge or replace as required.	.012		√	√	√	√
6 Weigh CO$_2$ cylinders; replace any that show a weight loss greater than 10%.	.650				√	√
7 Blow out entire system to make sure that the system is not plugged or restricted.	.325					√
8 Run out hose reels and check hoses.	.217					√
9 Conduct operational test of actuating devices, both automatic, manual and alarm system. Prior to conducting tests, close valves, disable CO$_2$ dumping control and manually override computer shutdown feature if applicable, all in accordance with the manufacturer's specifications.	.433					√
10 Check the operation and timing of the time delay control and check operation of the abort station.	.108					√
11 Restore system to proper operating condition and notify personnel upon completion of tests.	.079					√
12 Clean up around system.	.066		√	√	√	√
13 Fill out maintenance checklist and report deficiencies.	.022		√	√	√	√
Total labor-hours/period			.584	.584	1.234	2.396
Total labor-hours/year			4.672	1.168	1.234	2.396

			Cost Each					
				2012 Bare Costs			Total	Total
	Description	Labor-hrs.	Material	Labor	Equip.	Total	In-House	w/O&P
1900	Extinguishing system, CO$_2$, annually	2.396	64.50	130		194.50	233	283
1950	Annualized	9.470	201	510		711	860	1,050

PM Components	Labor-hrs.	W	M	Q	S	A
PM System D4095 200 1950						
Extinguishing system, foam bottle						
1　Check that all nozzles, heads and hand held lines are clear from obstructions, have not been damaged and are in proper position.	.195		√	√	√	√
2　Check to ensure that all operating controls are properly set.	.022		√	√	√	√
3　Observe pressure on system to ensure that proper pressure is being maintained.	.004		√	√	√	√
4　Clean area around system.	.066		√	√	√	√
5　Fill out maintenance checklist and report deficiencies.	.022		√	√	√	√
Total labor-hours/period			.309	.309	.309	.309
Total labor-hours/year			2.472	.618	.309	.309

				Cost Each				
				2012 Bare Costs			Total	Total
Description		Labor-hrs.	Material	Labor	Equip.	Total	In-House	w/O&P
1900	Extinguishing system, foam bottle, annually	.309		16.70		16.70	21	26
1950	Annualized	3.708		200		200	250	310

PM Components	Labor-hrs.	W	M	Q	S	A
PM System D4095 210 1950						
Extinguishing system, foam, electric pump, deluge system						
1 Check foam concentrate level in tank; add concentrate as required to maintain proper level.	.043		√	√	√	√
2 Ensure all valves relating to foam/water system are in correct position.	.008		√	√	√	√
3 Visually check proportioning devices, pumps, and foam nozzles; correct any observed deficiencies.	.386		√	√	√	√
4 Check water supply pressure; adjust as necessary.	.029		√	√	√	√
5 Open and close OS&Y (outside stem and yoke) cut-off valve to check operation; make minor repairs such as lubricating stems and tightening packing glands as required.	.059			√	√	√
6 Centrifugal pump:						
A) perform 10 minute pump test run, check for proper operation and adjust as required.	.217			√	√	√
B) test start pump without foam discharger.	.022		√	√	√	√
C) check for leaks on suction and discharge piping, seals, packing glands, etc.	.077			√	√	√
D) check for excessive vibration, noise, overheating, etc.	.022			√	√	√
E) check alignment, clearances, and rotation of shaft and coupler (includes removing and reinstalling safety cover).	.160			√	√	√
F) tighten or replace loose, missing or damaged nuts, bolts, or screws.	.005			√	√	√
G) lubricate pump and motor as required.	.099			√	√	√
H) check suction or discharge pressure gauge readings and flow rate.	.078			√	√	√
I) check packing glands and tighten or repack as required; note that slight dripping is required for proper lubrication of shaft.	.113			√	√	√
7 Inspect and clean strainers after each use and flow test.	.260		√	√	√	√
8 Clean equipment and surrounding area.	.433		√	√	√	√
9 Fill out maintenance checklist.	.022		√	√	√	√
Total labor-hours/period			1.203	2.033	2.033	2.033
Total labor-hours/year			9.624	4.066	2.033	2.033

			Cost Each					
			2012 Bare Costs				Total	Total
Description		Labor-hrs.	Material	Labor	Equip.	Total	In-House	w/O&P
1900	Extinguishing system, foam, electric pump, annually	2.033	117	110		227	266	315
1950	Annualized	17.756	161	960		1,121	1,375	1,700

PM Components	Labor-hrs.	W	M	Q	S	A
PM System D4095 220 1950						
Extinguishing system, foam, diesel pump, deluge system						
1 Check foam concentrate level in tank; add concentrate as required to maintain proper level.	.043		√	√	√	√
2 Ensure all valves relating to foam/water system are in correct position.	.008		√	√	√	√
3 Visually check proportioning devices, pumps, and foam nozzles; correct any observed deficiencies.	.386		√	√	√	√
4 Check water supply pressure; adjust as necessary.	.003	√	√	√	√	√
5 Open and close OS&Y (outside stem and yoke) cut-off valve to check operation; make minor repairs such as lubricating stems and tightening packing glands as required.	.059			√	√	√
6 Controller panel:						
A) check controller panel for proper operation in accordance with standard procedures for the type of panel installed, replace burned out bulbs and fuses; make other repairs as necessary.	.039			√	√	√
B) check wiring for loose connections and fraying; tighten or replace as required.	.109			√	√	√
7 Diesel engine:						
A) check oil level in crankcase with dipstick; add oil as necessary.	.014		√	√	√	√
B) drain and replace engine oil.	.511					√
C) replace engine oil filter.	.059					√
D) check radiator coolant level; add water if low.	.012		√	√	√	√
E) drain and replace radiator coolant.	.511					√
F) check battery water level; add water if low.	.012			√	√	√
G) check battery terminals for corrosion; clean if necessary.	.124			√	√	√
H) check belts for tension and wear; adjust or replace if required.	.012			√	√	√
I) check fuel level in tank; refill as required.	.046			√	√	√
J) check electrical wiring, connections, switches, etc.; adjust or tighten as necessary.	.120			√	√	√
K) perform 10 minute pump check for proper operation and adjust as required, start pump without foam discharger.	.217		√	√	√	√
8 Centrifugal pump:						
A) check for leaks on suction and discharge piping, seals, packing glands, etc.	.077			√	√	√
B) check pump operation; vibration, noise, overheating, etc.	.022			√	√	√
C) check alignment, clearances, and rotation of shaft and coupler (includes removing and reinstalling safety cover).	.160			√	√	√
D) tighten or replace loose, missing or damaged nuts, bolts, or screws.	.005			√	√	√
E) lubricate pump as required.	.099			√	√	√
F) check suction or discharge pressure gauge readings and flow rate.	.078			√	√	√
G) check packing glands and tighten or repack as as required; note that slight dripping is required for proper lubrication of shaft.	.113			√	√	√
9 Inspect and clean strainers after each use and flow test.	.260		√	√	√	√
10 Clean equipment and surrounding area.	.433		√	√	√	√
11 Fill out maintenance checklist.	.022		√	√	√	√
Total labor-hours/period			1.398	2.473	2.473	3.554
Total labor-hours/year			11.184	4.946	2.473	3.554

		Cost Each					
		2012 Bare Costs				Total	Total
Description	Labor-hrs.	Material	Labor	Equip.	Total	In-House	w/O&P
1900 Extinguishing system, foam, diesel pump, annually	3.554	213	192		405	475	565
1950 Annualized	22.157	242	1,200		1,442	1,750	2,175

PM Components	Labor-hrs.	W	M	Q	S	A
PM System D4095 400 1950						
Extinguishing system, dry chemical						
1 Check nozzles, heads, and fusible links or heat detectors to ensure that they are clean, have adequate clearance from obstructions and have not been damaged.	.098		√	√	√	√
2 Check hand hose lines, if applicable, to ensure that they are clear, in proper position and in good condition.	.098		√	√	√	√
3 Check to ensure that all operating controls are properly set.	.066		√	√	√	√
4 Observe pressure on system to ensure that proper pressure is maintained.	.004		√	√	√	√
5 Check expellant gas cylinders of gas cartridge systems for proper pressure or weight to ensure that sufficient gas is available.	.260				√	√
6 Test all actuating and operating devices; turn valve on dry chemical bottle or cylinder to off position in accordance with manufacturers specifications, and test operation of control head by removing fusible link, activating heat detectors or pulling test control. Restore system to normal operation and make minor adjustments as applicable.	.433					√
7 Open and check dry chemical in cylinder and stored pressure systems to ensure it is free flowing and without lumps.	.325					√
8 When an alarm system is reactivated, ensure that it functions in accordance with manufacturers specifications.	.079					√
9 Clean area around system.	.066		√	√	√	√
10 Fill out maintenance checklist and report deficiencies.	.022		√	√	√	√
Total labor-hours/period			.354	.354	.614	1.451
Total labor-hours/year			2.832	.708	.614	1.451

			Cost Each					
			2012 Bare Costs				Total	Total
Description		Labor-hrs.	Material	Labor	Equip.	Total	In-House	w/O&P
1900	Extinguishing system, dry chemical, annually	1.451	64.50	78.50		143	169	203
1950	Annualized	5.605	201	305		506	600	720

PM Components	Labor-hrs.	W	M	Q	S	A
PM System D4095 450 1950						
Extinguishing system, FM200						
1 Check that nozzles, heads and hand hose lines are clear from obstructions, have not been damaged and in proper position.	.098		√	√	√	√
2 Check to ensure that all operating controls are properly set.	.066		√	√	√	√
3 Clean nozzles as required.	.098		√	√	√	√
4 Visually inspect the control panel for obstructions or physical damage; clean dirt and dust from interior and exterior; make sure that all cards are plugged in tightly, tighten loose connections and make other minor adjustments as necessary.	.222		√	√	√	√
5 Check battery voltages where installed, recharge or replace as required.	.012		√	√	√	√
6 Weigh cylinders; replace any that show a weight loss greater than 5% or a pressure loss greater than 10%.	.650				√	√
7 Blow out entire system to make sure that the system is not plugged or restricted.	.333					√
8 Conduct operational test of actuating devices, both automatic, manual and alarm system; prior to conducting tests, close valves disable CO_2 dumping control and manually override computer shutdown feature if applicable, all in accordance with manufacturers specifications.	.436					√
9 Check the operation and timing of the time delay control and check operation of abort station.	.108					√
10 Restore system to proper operating condition and notify cognizant personnel upon completion of tests.	.079					√
11 Clean out around system.	.066		√	√	√	√
12 Fill out maintenance checklist and report deficiencies.	.022		√	√	√	√
Total labor-hours/period			.584	.584	1.234	2.190
Total labor-hours/year			4.672	1.168	1.234	2.190

			Cost Each					
				2012 Bare Costs			Total	Total
	Description	Labor-hrs.	Material	Labor	Equip.	Total	In-House	w/O&P
1900	Extinguishing system, FM200, annually	2.190	43	118		161	196	239
1950	Annualized	9.264	158	500		658	800	980

PM Components	Labor-hrs.	W	M	Q	S	A
PM System D5015 210 1950						
Switchboard, electrical						
1 Check with operating or area personnel for deficiencies.	.044					√
2 Check indicating lamps for proper operation, if appropriate; replace burned out lamps.	.018					√
3 Remove and reinstall cover.	.196					√
4 Check for discolorations, hot spots, odors and charred insulation.	.359					√
5 Clean switchboard exterior and surrounding area.	.066					√
6 Fill out maintenance checklist and report deficiencies.	.022					√
Total labor-hours/period						.705
Total labor-hours/year						.705

				Cost Each				
				2012 Bare Costs			Total	Total
Description		Labor-hrs.	Material	Labor	Equip.	Total	In-House	w/O&P
1900	Switchboard, electrical, annually	.705	7.15	36.50		43.65	53	65
1950	Annualized	.705	7.15	36.50		43.65	53	65

PM Components	Labor-hrs.	W	M	Q	S	A
PM System D5015 214 1950						
Switchboard w/air circuit breaker						
1 Check with operating or area personnel for deficiencies.	.035					√
2 Check indicating lamps for proper operation, if appropriate; replace burned out lamps.	.020					√
3 Remove switchboard from service, coordinate with appropriate authority.	.038					√
4 Remove and reinstall cover.	.051					√
5 Check for discolorations, hot spots, odors and charred insulation.	.016					√
6 Check the records on the circuit breaker for any full current rated trips which may indicate a potential problem.	.020					√
7 Examine the exterior of the switchboard for any damage or moisture.	.020					√
8 Check operation of circuit breaker tripping mechanism and relays.	.096					√
9 Check the operation of the circuit breaker charging motor.	.020					√
10 Check hardware for tightness.	.120					√
11 Check interlock for proper operation.	.013					√
12 Check that the charger is operating properly.	.022		√	√	√	√
13 Check for any signs of corrosion on the battery terminals or wires.	.020		√	√	√	√
14 Check the electrolyte level in the batteries; add if required.	.624		√	√	√	√
15 Check the specific gravity of the electrolyte in a 10% sample of the batteries.	.069		√	√	√	√
16 Check 25% of terminal-to-cell connection resistance; rehabilitate connections as required; add anti-corrosion grease to battery terminals and connections.	.113					√
17 Measure and record individual cell and string float voltages.	2.808					√
18 Place switchboard back in service, notify appropriate authority.	.057					√
19 Clean switchboard, charger and the surrounding area.	.066		√	√	√	√
20 Fill out maintenance checklist and report deficiencies.	.022		√	√	√	√
Total labor-hours/period			.823	.823	.823	4.250
Total labor-hours/year			6.584	1.646	.823	4.250

				Cost Each				
				2012 Bare Costs			Total	Total
Description		Labor-hrs.	Material	Labor	Equip.	Total	In-House	w/O&P
1900	Switchboard, with air circuit breaker, annually	4.250	7.15	219		226.15	278	350
1950	Annualized	13.303	30	685		715	880	1,100

PM Components	Labor-hrs.	W	M	Q	S	A
PM System D5015 217 1950						
Switchboard w/air circuit breaker and tie switch						
1 Check with operating or area personnel for deficiencies.	.035					√
2 Check indicating lamps for proper operation, if appropriate; replace burned out lamps.	.020					√
3 Remove switchboard from service, coordinate with appropriate authority.	.038					√
4 Remove and reinstall cover.	.051					√
5 Check for discolorations, hot spots, odors and charred insulation.	.016					√
6 Check the records on the circuit breaker for any full current rated trips which may indicate a potential problem.	.020					√
7 Examine the exterior of the switchboard for any damage or moisture.	.020					√
8 Check operation of circuit breaker tripping mechanism and relays.	.096					√
9 Check the operation of the circuit breaker charging motor.	.020					√
10 Check hardware for tightness.	.120					√
11 Check interlock for proper operation.	.013					√
12 Operate the switching handle and check the locking mechanism.	.052					√
13 Check that the charger is operating properly.	.022		√	√	√	√
14 Check for any signs of corrosion on the battery terminals or wires.	.020		√	√	√	√
15 Check the electrolyte level in the batteries; add if required.	.624		√	√	√	√
16 Check the specific gravity of the electrolyte in a 10% sample of the batteries.	.069		√	√	√	√
17 Check 25% of terminal-to-cell connection resistance; rehabilitate connections as required; add anti-corrosion grease to battery terminals and connections.	.113					√
18 Measure and record individual cell and string float voltages.	2.808					√
19 Place switchboard back in service, notify appropriate authority.	.057					√
20 Clean switchboard, charger and the surrounding area.	.066		√	√	√	√
21 Fill out maintenance checklist and report deficiencies.	.022		√	√	√	√
Total labor-hours/period			.823	.823	.823	4.302
Total labor-hours/year			6.584	1.646	.823	4.302

			Cost Each					
				2012 Bare Costs			**Total**	**Total**
Description		**Labor-hrs.**	**Material**	**Labor**	**Equip.**	**Total**	**In-House**	**w/O&P**
1900	Switchboard, with air C.B. and tie switch, annually	4.302	11	222		233	286	360
1950	Annualized	13.355	45	690		735	900	1,125

PM Components	Labor-hrs.	W	M	Q	S	A
PM System D5015 220 1950						
Circuit breaker, HV air						
1 Check the records on the circuit breaker for any full current rated trips which may indicate a potential problem.	.066					√
2 Examine the exterior of the circuit breaker for any damage or moisture.	.060					√
3 Remove the circuit breaker from service, coordinate with appropriate authority.	.038					√
4 Check operation of tripping mechanisms and relays.	.096					√
5 Check the operation of the charging motor, if applicable.	.038					√
6 Check hardware for tightness.	.005					√
7 Check interlock for proper operation.	.039					√
8 Clean area around switch.	.066					√
9 Place the circuit breaker back in service, coordinate with appropriate authority.	.040					√
10 Fill out maintenance checklist.	.022					√
Total labor-hours/period						.470
Total labor-hours/year						.470

					Cost Each			
				2012 Bare Costs			**Total**	**Total**
Description	Labor-hrs.	Material	Labor	Equip.	Total	In-House	w/O&P
1900 Circuit breaker, high voltage air, annually	.470		24		24	30	37.50
1950 Annualized	.470		24		24	30	37.50

PM Components	Labor-hrs.	W	M	Q	S	A
PM System D5015 222 1950						
Circuit breaker, HV oil						
1 Check the records on the circuit breaker for any full current rated trips which may indicate a potential problem.	.066					√
2 Examine the exterior of the circuit breaker for any damage, cracks, rust or leaks; check around the gaskets and the drain valves.	.074					√
3 Check the entrance bushings for cracks in the porcelain.	.321					√
4 Check the condition of the ground system.	.170					√
5 Draw oil sample from bottom of circuit breaker; have sample tested; replace removed oil to the proper level.	.042					√
6 Clean the exterior of the circuit breaker and operating mechanism.	.094					√
7 Clean the area around the circuit breaker.	.066					√
8 Fill out maintenance checklist.	.022					√
Total labor-hours/period						.855
Total labor-hours/year						.855

					Cost Each			
				2012 Bare Costs			**Total**	**Total**
Description	Labor-hrs.	Material	Labor	Equip.	Total	In-House	w/O&P
1900 Circuit breaker, high voltage oil, annually	.855	15	44		59	71	87
1950 Annualized	.855	15	44		59	71	87

| **D5015 230** | **Switch, Selector, HV Air**

PM Components	Labor-hrs.	W	M	Q	S	A
PM System D5015 230 1950						
Switch, selector, HV, air						
1 Examine the exterior of the selector switch for any damage.	.060					✓
2 Check that the switching handle is locked.	.044					✓
3 Check the condition of the ground system.	.170					✓
4 Clean the exterior of the selector switch and operating mechanism.	.046					✓
5 Clean the area around the selector switch.	.066					✓
6 Fill out maintenance checklist and report deficiencies.	.022					✓
Total labor-hours/period						.408
Total labor-hours/year						.408

				Cost Each				
				2012 Bare Costs			Total	Total
	Description	Labor-hrs.	Material	Labor	Equip.	Total	In-House	w/O&P
1900	Switch, selector, high voltage, air, annually	.408	14.25	21		35.25	41.50	50.50
1950	Annualized	.408	14.25	21		35.25	41.50	50.50

| **D5015 232** | **Switch, Selector, HV Oil**

PM Components	Labor-hrs.	W	M	Q	S	A
PM System D5015 232 1950						
Switch, selector, HV, oil						
1 Examine the exterior of the interrupt switch for any damage, cracks, rust or leaks; check around the gaskets and the drain valves.	.060					✓
2 Check that the switching handle is locked.	.044					✓
3 Check the condition of the ground system.	.170					✓
4 Draw oil sample from bottom of selector switch; have sample tested; replace removed oil to the proper level.	.042					✓
5 Clean the exterior of the selector switch and operating mechanism.	.046					✓
6 Clean the area around the selector switch.	.066					✓
7 Fill out maintenance checklist and report deficiencies.	.022					✓
Total labor-hours/period						.450
Total labor-hours/year						.450

				Cost Each				
				2012 Bare Costs			Total	Total
	Description	Labor-hrs.	Material	Labor	Equip.	Total	In-House	w/O&P
1900	Switch, selector, high voltage, oil, annually	.450	21.50	23		44.50	52.50	63
1950	Annualized	.450	21.50	23		44.50	52.50	63

PM Components	Labor-hrs.	W	M	Q	S	A
PM System D5015 234 1950						
Switch, automatic transfer						
1 Check with operating or area personnel for deficiencies.	.044		√	√	√	√
2 Inspect wiring, wiring connections, and fuse blocks for looseness,charring, evidence of short circuiting, overheating and tighten all connections.	.263		√	√	√	√
3 Inspect gen. cond. of transf. switch and clean exter. and surrounding area.	.114		√	√	√	√
4 Fill out maintenance checklist and report deficiencies.	.022		√	√	√	√
Total labor-hours/period			.443	.443	.443	.443
Total labor-hours/year			3.544	.886	.443	.443

			Cost Each					
			2012 Bare Costs				Total	Total
Description	Labor-hrs.	Material	Labor	Equip.	Total	In-House	w/O&P
1900 Switch, automatic transfer, annually	.443	14.25	23		37.25	44	53.50
1950 Annualized	5.316	14.25	274		288.25	355	445

PM Components	Labor-hrs.	W	M	Q	S	A
PM System D5015 236 1950						
Switch, interrupt, HV, fused air						
1 Examine the exterior of the interrupt switch for any damage.	.060					√
2 Check the condition of the ground system.	.170					√
3 Clean the exterior of the interrupt switch and operating mechanism.	.046					√
4 Clean the area around the interrupt switch.	.066					√
5 Fill out maintenance checklist and report deficiencies.	.022					√
Total labor-hours/period						.364
Total labor-hours/year						.364

			Cost Each					
			2012 Bare Costs				Total	Total
Description	Labor-hrs.	Material	Labor	Equip.	Total	In-House	w/O&P
1900 Switch, interrupt, high voltage, fused air, annually	.364	14.25	18.75		33	39	47
1950 Annualized	.364	14.25	18.75		33	39	47

PM Components	Labor-hrs.	W	M	Q	S	A
PM System D5015 238 1950						
Switch, interrupt, HV, w/auxiliary fuses, air						
1 Examine the exterior of the interrupt switch for any damage.	.060					√
2 Check the condition of the ground system.	.170					√
3 Clean the exterior of the interrupt switch and operating mechanism.	.046					√
4 Clean the area around the interrupt switch.	.066					√
5 Fill out maintenance checklist and report deficiencies.	.022					√
Total labor-hours/period						.364
Total labor-hours/year						.364

			Cost Each					
			2012 Bare Costs				Total	Total
Description	Labor-hrs.	Material	Labor	Equip.	Total	In-House	w/O&P
1900 Switch, interrupt, HV, w/ aux fuses, air, annually	.364	14.25	18.75		33	39	47
1950 Annualized	.364	14.25	18.75		33	39	47

PM Components	Labor-hrs.	W	M	Q	S	A
PM System D5015 240 1950						
Transformer, dry type 500 KVA and over						
1 Examine the exterior of the transformer for any damage.	.060					√
2 Remove the covers or open the doors.	.196					√
3 Check for signs of moisture or overheating.	.059					√
4 Check for voltage creeping over insulated surfaces, such as evidenced by tracking or carbonization.	.018					√
5 Check fans, motors and other auxiliary devices for proper operation; where applicable.	.049					√
6 Check the condition of the ground system.	.170					√
7 Replace the covers or close the doors.	.196					√
8 Fill out maintenance checklist and report deficiencies.	.022					√
Total labor-hours/period						.770
Total labor-hours/year						.770

	Description	Labor-hrs.	Cost Each				Total In-House	Total w/O&P
			2012 Bare Costs					
			Material	Labor	Equip.	Total		
1900	Transformer, dry type 500 KVA and over, annually	.770	14.25	39.50		53.75	64.50	79.50
1950	Annualized	.770	14.25	39.50		53.75	64.50	79.50

PM Components	Labor-hrs.	W	M	Q	S	A
PM System D5015 240 2950						
Transformer, oil, pad mounted						
1 Examine the exterior of the transformer for any damage, cracks, rust or leaks; check around bushings, gaskets and pressure relief device.	.014					√
2 Check the condition of the ground system.	.170					√
3 Check and record the oil level, pressure and temperature readings.	.263					√
4 Check fans, motors and other auxiliary devices for proper operation; where applicable.	.022					√
5 Draw oil sample from top of transformer and have sample tested for dielectric strength; replace removed oil.	.525					√
6 Clean transformer exterior and the surrounding area.	.066					√
7 Fill out maintenance checklist and report deficiencies.	.022					√
Total labor-hours/period						1.082
Total labor-hours/year						1.082

	Description	Labor-hrs.	Cost Each				Total In-House	Total w/O&P
			2012 Bare Costs					
			Material	Labor	Equip.	Total		
2900	Transformer, oil, pad mounted, annually	1.082	28.50	56		84.50	100	122
2950	Annualized	1.082	28.50	56		84.50	100	122

PM Components	Labor-hrs.	W	M	Q	S	A
PM System D5015 240 3950						
Transformer, oil, pad mounted, PCB						
1 Check with operating or area personnel for deficiencies.	.040			√	√	√
2 Examine the exterior of the transformer for any damage, cracks, rust or leaks; check around the gaskets, the pressure relief device and the cooling fins.	.014			√	√	√
3 Check and record the oil levels, pressure and temperature readings: level ____; pressure ____; temperature ____.	.263					√
4 Check fans, motors and other auxiliary devices for proper operation; where applicable.	.051					√
5 Check the exterior bushings for leaking oil.	.321			√	√	√
6 Check the condition of the ground system.	.170					√
7 Draw oil sample from top of transformer and have sample tested; replace removed oil.	.525					√
8 Clean transformer exterior and the surrounding area.	.066					√
9 Verify the PCB warning markings are intact and clearly visible.	.022					√
10 Fill out maintenance checklist and report deficiencies. Note: the EPA PCB regulations under 40 CFR 716.30 shall apply to all inspections, samples, disposal, cleanups, decontamination, reporting and record-keeping.	.022			√	√	√
Total labor-hours/period				.397	.397	1.494
Total labor-hours/year				.794	.397	1.494

			Cost Each					
			2012 Bare Costs				Total	Total
Description		Labor-hrs.	Material	Labor	Equip.	Total	In-House	w/O&P
3900	Transformer, oil, pad mounted, PCB, annually	1.494	42	77		119	141	172
3950	Annualized	2.655	42	137		179	215	264

D50 ELECTRICAL | D5015 260 | Panelboard, 225 Amps and Above

PM Components	Labor-hrs.	W	M	Q	S	A
PM System D5015 260 1950						
Panelboard, 225 amps and above						
1 Check with operating or area personnel for deficiencies.	.066					√
2 Check for excessive heat, odors, noise, and vibration.	.239					√
3 Clean and check general condition of panel.	.114					√
4 Fill out maintenance checklist and report deficiencies.	.022					√
Total labor-hours/period						.441
Total labor-hours/year						.441

			Cost Each					
			2012 Bare Costs				Total	Total
	Description	Labor-hrs.	Material	Labor	Equip.	Total	In-House	w/O&P
1900	Panelboard, 225 A and above, annually	.441	28.50	22.50		51	59.50	70.50
1950	Annualized	.441	28.50	22.50		51	59.50	70.50

D50 ELECTRICAL | D5015 280 | Motor Control Center

PM Components	Labor-hrs.	W	M	Q	S	A
PM System D5015 280 1950						
Motor control center, over 400 amps						
1 Check with operating or area personnel for deficiencies.	.044					√
2 Check starter lights, replace if required.	.018					√
3 Check for excessive heat, odors, noise, and vibration.	.239					√
4 Clean motor control center exterior and surrounding area.	.066					√
5 Fill out maintenance checklist and report deficiencies.	.022					√
Total labor-hours/period						.389
Total labor-hours/year						.389

			Cost Each					
			2012 Bare Costs				Total	Total
	Description	Labor-hrs.	Material	Labor	Equip.	Total	In-House	w/O&P
1900	Motor control center, over 400 A, annually	.389	28.50	20		48.50	56	66.50
1950	Annualized	.389	28.50	20		48.50	56	66.50

PM Components	Labor-hrs.	W	M	Q	S	A
PM System D5035 610 1950						
Clocks, Central System						
1 Clean dirt and dust from interior and exterior of cabinet.	.260				√	√
2 Adjust relays and check transmission of signal.	.117				√	√
3 Tighten contacts and terminal screws.	.065				√	√
4 Burnish contacts.	.195				√	√
5 Fill out maintenance checklist and report deficiencies.	.022				√	√
Total labor-hours/period					.659	.659
Total labor-hours/year					.659	.659

			Cost Each					
			2012 Bare Costs				Total	Total
Description		Labor-hrs.	Material	Labor	Equip.	Total	In-House	w/O&P
1900	Central clock systems, annually	.659	1.50	34		35.50	43.50	54.50
1950	Annualized	1.318	1.50	68		69.50	85.50	107

PM Components	Labor-hrs.	W	M	Q	S	A
PM System D5035 710 1950						
Fire alarm annunciator system						
1　Visually inspect all alarm equipment for obstructions or physical damage, clean dirt and dust from interior and exterior of panel/pull boxes, tighten loose connections.	.222		√	√	√	√
2　Notify cogniant personnel prior to testing.	.112		√	√	√	√
3　Conduct operational test of initiating and signal transmitting devices in populated buildings by building zone/area; for those circuits which do not operate properly, check detectors, control units, and annunciators for dust on defective components; make minor adjustments as required.	.112		√	√	√	√
4　Check battery voltages where installed; replace as required.	.012		√	√	√	√
5　Conduct operational test of 10% of total number of spot type heat detectors and all smoke detectors; for those circuits which do not operate properly, check to determine if problem relates to circuit, device, or control unit, make minor adjustments as required; if detector is defective but no replacement is immediately available, remove detector, re-establish Initiating circuit and tag location until a replacement detector is installed.	2.171				√	√
6　Restore system to proper operating condition and notify personnel upon completion of tests.	.079		√	√	√	√
7　Fill out maintenance checklist and report deficiencies.	.022		√	√	√	√
Total labor-hours/period			.559	.559	2.730	2.730
Total labor-hours/year			4.472	1.118	2.730	2.730

			Cost Each				
			2012 Bare Costs			**Total**	**Total**
Description	Labor-hrs.	Material	Labor	Equip.	Total	In-House	w/O&P
1900　Fire alarm annunciator system, annually	2.730	117	148		265	315	375
1950　　　Annualized	11.050	147	595		742	910	1,125

PM Components	Labor-hrs.	W	M	Q	S	A
PM System D5035 810 1950						
Security / intrusion alarm system						
1　Check in and out with area security officer, notify operating/facility personnel, obtain necessary alarm keys, alarm codes and escort when required.	.520			√	√	√
2　Inspect alarm control panel and conduct operational test of initiating and signal transmitting devices; make minor adjustments as required.	.241			√	√	√
3　Check indicating lamps for proper operation, replace if necessary.	.018			√	√	√
4　Check battery voltages where installed, replace as required.	.012			√	√	√
5　Restore system to proper operating condition and notify personnel upon completion of tests.	.079			√	√	√
6　Clean exterior of cabinet and surrounding area.	.066			√	√	√
7　Fill out maintenance checklist and report deficiencies.	.022			√	√	√
Total labor-hours/period				.958	.958	.958
Total labor-hours/year				1.916	.958	.958

			Cost Each				
			2012 Bare Costs			**Total**	**Total**
Description	Labor-hrs.	Material	Labor	Equip.	Total	In-House	w/O&P
1900　Security, intrusion alarm system, annually	.958	10.75	49.50		60.25	73	90
1950　　　Annualized	3.832	42	198		240	290	360

PM Components	Labor-hrs.	W	M	Q	S	A
PM System D5095 210 1950						
Emergency generator up to 15 KVA						
1 Check with the operating or area personnel for any obvious deficiencies.	.044		√	√	√	√
2 Check engine oil level; add as required.	.010		√	√	√	√
3 Change engine oil and oil filter.	.170					√
4 Check battery charge and electrolyte specific gravity, add water as required; check terminals for corrosion, clean as required.	.120		√	√	√	√
5 Check belt tension and wear; adjust as required, if applicable.	.012		√	√	√	√
6 Check engine air filter; change as required.	.042					√
7 Check spark plug or injector nozzle condition; service or replace as required.	.211					√
8 Check wiring, connections, switches, etc., adjust as required.	.036		√	√	√	√
9 Perform 30 minute generator test run; check for proper operation.	.650		√	√	√	√
10 Check fuel level; add as required.	.046		√	√	√	√
11 Wipe dust and dirt from engine and generator.	.056		√	√	√	√
12 Clean area around generator.	.066		√	√	√	√
13 Fill out maintenance checklist and report deficiencies.	.022		√	√	√	√
Total labor-hours/period			1.062	1.062	1.062	1.485
Total labor-hours/year			8.496	2.124	1.062	1.485

		Cost Each					
		2012 Bare Costs				Total	Total
Description	Labor-hrs.	Material	Labor	Equip.	Total	In-House	w/O&P
1900 Emergency diesel generator, up to 15 KVA, annually	1.485	32	76.50		108.50	130	158
1950 Annualized	13.167	126	680		806	975	1,200

PM Components	Labor-hrs.	W	M	Q	S	A
PM System D5095 210 2950						
Emergency diesel generator, over 15 KVA						
1 Check with the operating or area personnel for any obvious deficiencies.	.044		√	√	√	√
2 Check engine oil level; add as required.	.010		√	√	√	√
3 Change engine oil and oil filter.	.511					√
4 Check battery charge and electrolyte specific gravity, add water as required; check terminals for corrosion, clean as required.	.241		√	√	√	√
5 Check belts for wear and proper tension; adjust as necessary.	.012		√	√	√	√
6 Check that crank case heater is operating.	.038		√	√	√	√
7 Check engine air filter; change as required.	.042					√
8 Check wiring, connections, switches, etc.; adjust as required.	.036		√	√	√	√
9 Check spark plug or injector nozzle condition; service or replace as required.	.281					√
10 Perform 30 minute generator test run; check for proper operation.	.650		√	√	√	√
11 Check fuel level with gauge pole, add as required.	.046		√	√	√	√
12 Wipe dust and dirt from engine and generator.	.109		√	√	√	√
13 Clean area around generator.	.066		√	√	√	√
14 Fill out maintenance checklist and report deficiencies.	.025		√	√	√	√
Total labor-hours/period			1.277	1.277	1.277	2.111
Total labor-hours/year			10.216	2.554	1.277	2.111

		Cost Each					
		2012 Bare Costs				Total	Total
Description	Labor-hrs.	Material	Labor	Equip.	Total	In-House	w/O&P
2900 Emergency diesel generator, over 15 KVA, annually	2.111	36	109		145	174	213
2950 Annualized	16.158	139	835		974	1,175	1,450

PM Components	Labor-hrs.	W	M	Q	S	A
PM System D5095 210 3950						
Emergency diesel generator, turbine						
1 Check with the operating or area personnel for any obvious deficiencies.	.044		√	√	√	√
2 Check turbine oil level; add oil as required.	.036		√	√	√	√
3 Change turbine oil and oil filter; check transmission oil level.	.569					√
4 Check that the crankcase heater is operating properly.	.022		√	√	√	√
5 Replace turbine air filter.	.224					√
6 Check wiring, connections, switches, etc.; adjust as required.	.060					√
7 Check starter for proper operation; lubricate as necessary.	.047		√	√	√	√
8 Check fuel nozzles, fuel regulator and ignition device condition; service or replace as required.	.813					√
9 Perform 30 minute generator test run; check for proper operation.	.650		√	√	√	√
10 Check and record transmission oil pressure and temperature, and natural gas pressure: oil press:____ oil temp:____ gas press:____.	.021					√
11 Record running time: beginning ____ hours; ending ____ hours.	.010					√
12 Check that the charger is operating properly.	.127		√	√	√	√
13 Check for any signs of corrosion on battery terminals or wires.	.117		√	√	√	√
14 Check the electrolyte level in the batteries; add if required.	.049		√	√	√	√
15 Check the specific gravity of the electrolyte in a 10% sample of the batteries.	.069					√
16 Check 25% of terminal-to-cell connection resistance; rehabilitate connections as required; add anti-corrosion grease to battery terminals and connections.	.038					√
17 Measure and record individual cell and string float voltages.	.140					√
18 Clean area around generator.	.066		√	√	√	√
19 Fill out maintenance checklist and report deficiencies.	.022		√	√	√	√
Total labor-hours/period			1.180	1.180	1.180	3.124
Total labor-hours/year			9.440	2.360	1.180	3.124

			Cost Each					
			2012 Bare Costs				Total	Total
Description	Labor-hrs.		Material	Labor	Equip.	Total	In-House	w/O&P
3900 Emergency diesel generator, turbine, annually	3.124		58	161		219	263	320
3950 Annualized	16.104		237	830		1,067	1,275	1,575

PM Components	Labor-hrs.	W	M	Q	S	A
PM System D5095 220 1950						
Power stabilizer						
1 Remove the covers or open the doors.	.218					√
2 Check for signs of moisture or overheating.	.022					√
3 Check fans and other auxiliary devices for proper operation.	.027					√
4 Check for voltage creeping over transformer insulated surfaces, such as evidenced by tracking or carbonization.	.018					√
5 Check condition of the ground system.	.170					√
6 Check wiring, connections, relays, etc; tighten and adjust as necessary.	.060					√
7 Replace the covers or close the doors.	.022					√
8 Clean the surrounding area.	.066					√
9 Fill out maintenance checklist and report deficiencies.	.022					√
Total labor-hours/period						.625
Total labor-hours/year						.625

			Cost Each					
			2012 Bare Costs				Total	Total
Description		Labor-hrs.	Material	Labor	Equip.	Total	In-House	w/O&P
1900	Power stablizer, annually	.625		32		32	40	50
1950	Annualized	.625		32		32	40	50

PM Components	Labor-hrs.	W	M	Q	S	A
PM System D5095 230 1950						
Uninterruptible power system, up to 200 KVA						
1 Check with operating or area personnel for any obvious deficiencies.	.044		✓	✓	✓	✓
2 Check electrolyte level of batteries; add water as required; check terminals for corrosion, clean as required.	.878		✓	✓	✓	✓
3 Check 25% of the batteries for charge and electrolyte specific gravity.	.777			✓	✓	✓
4 Check batteries for cracks or leaks.	.059		✓	✓	✓	✓
5 Check 25% of the terminal-to-cell connection resistances; rehabilitate connections as required; add anti-corrosion grease to battery terminals and connections.	.143			✓	✓	✓
6 Measure and record individual cell and string float voltages.	.618			✓	✓	✓
7 Check integrity of battery rack.	.176		✓	✓	✓	✓
8 Check battery room temperature and ventilation systems.	.010		✓	✓	✓	✓
9 Replace air filters on UPS modules.	.036		✓	✓	✓	✓
10 Check output voltage and amperages, from control panel.	.007		✓	✓	✓	✓
11 Check UPS room temperature and ventilation system.	.062		✓	✓	✓	✓
12 Notify personnel and test UPS fault alarm system.	.112		✓	✓	✓	✓
13 Clean around batteries and UPS modules.	.066		✓	✓	✓	✓
14 Fill out maintenance checklist and report deficiencies.	.022		✓	✓	✓	✓
Total labor-hours/period			1.360	3.010	3.010	3.010
Total labor-hours/year			10.880	6.020	3.010	3.010

	Description	Labor-hrs.	Cost Each				Total	Total
			2012 Bare Costs				In-House	w/O&P
			Material	Labor	Equip.	Total		
1900	Uninter. power system, up to 200 KVA, annually	3.010	51.50	155		206.50	248	305
1950	Annualized	22.920	210	1,175		1,385	1,700	2,100

PM Components	Labor-hrs.	W	M	Q	S	A
PM System D5095 230 2950						
Uninterrupted power system, 200 KVA to 800 KVA						
1 Check with operating or area personnel for any obvious deficiencies.	.044		✓	✓	✓	✓
2 Check electrolyte level of batteries; add water as required; check terminals for corrosion, clean as required.	3.510		✓	✓	✓	✓
3 Check 25% of the batteries for charge and electrolyte specific gravity.	3.107			✓	✓	✓
4 Check batteries for cracks or leaks.	.585		✓	✓	✓	✓
5 Check 25% of the terminal-to-cell connection resistances; rehabilitate connections as required; add anti-corrosion grease to battery terminals and connections.	.234			✓	✓	✓
6 Measure and record individual cell and string float voltages.	.936			✓	✓	✓
7 Check integrity of battery rack.	.702		✓	✓	✓	✓
8 Check battery room temperature and ventilation systems.	.010		✓	✓	✓	✓
9 Replace air filters on UPS modules.	.036		✓	✓	✓	✓
10 Check output voltage and amperages, from control panel.	.007		✓	✓	✓	✓
11 Check UPS room temperature and ventilation system.	.062		✓	✓	✓	✓
12 Notify personnel and test UPS fault alarm system.	.112		✓	✓	✓	✓
13 Clean around batteries and UPS modules.	.066		✓	✓	✓	✓
14 Fill out maintenance checklist and report deficiencies.	.022		✓	✓	✓	✓
Total labor-hours/period			5.044	9.433	9.433	9.433
Total labor-hours/year			40.352	18.866	9.433	9.433

	Description	Labor-hrs.	Cost Each				Total	Total
			2012 Bare Costs				In-House	w/O&P
			Material	Labor	Equip.	Total		
2900	UPS, 200 KVA to 800 KVA, annually	9.433	70	485		555	675	840
2950	Annualized	78.087	285	4,025		4,310	5,275	6,575

PM Components	Labor-hrs.	W	M	Q	S	A
PM System D5095 240 1950						
Battery system and charger						
1 Check that the charger is operating properly.	.051		√	√	√	√
2 Check for any signs of corrosion on the battery terminals or wires.	.117		√	√	√	√
3 Check the electrolyte level in the batteries; add if required.	.062		√	√	√	√
4 Check the specific gravity of the electrolyte in a 10% sample of the batteries.	.069		√	√	√	√
5 Check 25% of terminal-to-cell connection resistance; rehabilitate connections as required; add anti-corrosion grease to battery terminals and connections.	.741			√	√	√
6 Measure and record individual cell and string float voltages.	.281			√	√	√
7 Clean area around batteries.	.066		√	√	√	√
8 Fill out maintenance checklist and report deficiencies.	.022		√	√	√	√
Total labor-hours/period			.387	1.409	1.409	1.409
Total labor-hours/year			3.096	2.818	1.409	1.409

	Description	Labor-hrs.	2012 Bare Costs				Total In-House	Total w/O&P
			Material	Labor	Equip.	Total		
1900	Battery system and charger, annually	1.409	7.05	72.50		79.55	97.50	121
1950	Annualized	8.732	28.50	450		478.50	585	730

PM Components	Labor-hrs.	W	M	Q	S	A
PM System D5095 250 1950						
Light, emergency, hardwired system						
1 Test for proper operation, replace lamps as required.	.013				✓	✓
2 Clean exterior of cabinet and light heads.	.025				✓	✓
3 Check wiring for obvious defects.	.026				✓	✓
4 Adjust lamp heads for maximum illumination of area.	.039				✓	✓
5 Fill out maintenance checklist and report deficiencies.	.022				✓	✓
Total labor-hours/period					.125	.125
Total labor-hours/year					.125	.125

			Cost Each				
			2012 Bare Costs			Total	Total
Description	Labor-hrs.	Material	Labor	Equip.	Total	In-House	w/O&P
1900 Light, emergency, hardwired system, annually	.125		6.45		6.45	7.95	9.95
1950 Annualized	.250		12.90		12.90	15.90	19.90

PM Components	Labor-hrs.	W	M	Q	S	A
PM System D5095 250 2950						
Light, emergency, dry cell						
1 Test for proper operation, replace lamps as required.	.013				✓	✓
2 Clean exterior of emergency light cabinet and lamp heads.	.025				✓	✓
3 Check condition of batteries and change as required.	.012				✓	✓
4 Clean interior of cabinet, top of battery, and battery terminal.	.009				✓	✓
5 Inspect cabinet, relay, relay contacts, pilot light, wiring, and gen. cond.	.065				✓	✓
6 Adjust lamp heads for maximum illumination of area.	.039				✓	✓
7 Fill out maintenance checklist and report deficiencies.	.022				✓	✓
Total labor-hours/period					.185	.185
Total labor-hours/year					.185	.185

			Cost Each				
			2012 Bare Costs			Total	Total
Description	Labor-hrs.	Material	Labor	Equip.	Total	In-House	w/O&P
2900 Light, emergency, dry cell, annually	.185	21	9.55		30.55	35	41
2950 Annualized	.370	42	19.05		61.05	70	82

PM Components	Labor-hrs.	W	M	Q	S	A
PM System D5095 250 3950						
Light, emergency, wet cell						
1 Test for proper operation; correct deficiencies as required.	.013				✓	✓
2 Clean exterior of emergency light cabinet and lamp heads.	.025				✓	✓
3 Clean interior of cabinet, top of battery, and battery terminal.	.009				✓	✓
4 Check battery charge and electrolyte specific gravity; add water if nec.	.012				✓	✓
5 Inspect cabinet, relay, relay contacts, pilot light, wiring, and gen. cond.	.065				✓	✓
6 Apply anti-corrosion coating to battery terminals.	.010				✓	✓
7 Adjust lamp heads for maximum illumination of area.	.039				✓	✓
8 Fill out maintenance checklist and report deficiencies.	.022				✓	✓
Total labor-hours/period					.195	.195
Total labor-hours/year					.195	.195

			Cost Each				
			2012 Bare Costs			Total	Total
Description	Labor-hrs.	Material	Labor	Equip.	Total	In-House	w/O&P
3900 Light, emergency, wet cell, annually	.195	32	10.05		42.05	47.50	55.50
3950 Annualized	.390	63	20		83	94	110

PM Components	Labor-hrs.	W	M	Q	S	A
PM System E1015 810 1950						
Personal Computers						
1 Check with operating personnel for any deficiencies.	.065				√	√
2 Check all cables for fraying, cracking, or exposed wires; ensure connections are secure.	.065				√	√
3 Remove metal casing and vacuum interior, power supply vents, keyboard, monitor, and surrounding work area.	.130				√	√
4 Check for secure connections of all interior wires and cables. Secure all peripheral cards.	.065				√	√
5 Replace PC cover and clean case, keyboard, monitor screen and housing with an anti-static spray cleaner. Apply cleaner to towel and not the components.	.130				√	√
6 Disassemble the mouse; clean the tracking ball, interior rollers and housing. Blow out the interior of the mouse with clean compressed air.	.065				√	√
7 Turn on PC and check for unusual noises.	.026				√	√
8 Clean floppy drive heads with cleaning diskette and solution.	.039				√	√
9 Defragment the hard drive using a defragmentation utility.	.234				√	√
10 Run diagnostics software to test all the PC's components.	.234				√	√
11 Fill out maintenance checklist and report deficiencies.	.029				√	√
Total labor-hours/period					1.082	1.082
Total labor-hours/year					1.082	1.082

		Cost Each					
		2012 Bare Costs				Total	Total
Description	Labor-hrs.	Material	Labor	Equip.	Total	In-House	w/O&P
1900 Personnel Computers, annually	1.082		56		56	69	86
1950 Annualized	2.164		112		112	138	172

PM Components	Labor-hrs.	W	M	Q	S	A
PM System E1035 100 1950						
Hydraulic lift						
1 Check for proper operation of pump.	.035				√	√
2 Check for leaks on suction and discharge piping, seals, packing glands, etc.; make minor adjustments as required.	.077				√	√
3 Check pump and motor operation for excessive vibration, noise and overheating.	.022				√	√
4 Check alignment of pump and motor; adjust as necessary.	.260				√	√
5 Lubricate pump and motor.	.099				√	√
6 Inspect hydraulic lift post(s) for wear or leaks.	.065				√	√
7 Inspect, clean and tighten valves.	.034				√	√
8 Inspect and clean motor contactors.	.026				√	√
9 Inspect and test control relays and check wiring terminals.	.034				√	√
10 Clean pump unit and surrounding area.	.099				√	√
11 Fill out maintenance checklist and report deficiencies.	.022				√	√
Total labor-hours/period					.773	.773
Total labor-hours/year					.773	.773

			Cost Each				
			2012 Bare Costs			**Total**	**Total**
Description	**Labor-hrs.**	**Material**	**Labor**	**Equip.**	**Total**	**In-House**	**w/O&P**
1900 Hydraulic lift, annually	.773	45	42		87	102	122
1950 Annualized	1.546	60	84.50		144.50	171	207

PM Components	Labor-hrs.	W	M	Q	S	A
PM System E1035 310 1950						
Hydraulic lift, loading dock						
1 Check for proper operation of pump.	.022				√	√
2 Check for leaks on suction and discharge piping, seals, packing glands, etc.; make minor adjustments as required.	.077				√	√
3 Check pump and motor operation for excessive vibration, noise and overheating.	.022				√	√
4 Check alignment of pump and motor; adjust as necessary.	.100				√	√
5 Lubricate pump and motor.	.099				√	√
6 Inspect hydraulic lift post(s) for wear or leaks.	.051				√	√
7 Inspect, clean and tighten valves.	.072				√	√
8 Inspect and clean motor contactors.	.148				√	√
9 Inspect and test control relays and check wiring terminals.	.137				√	√
10 Clean pump unit and surrounding area.	.066				√	√
11 Fill out maintenance checklist and report deficiencies.	.022				√	√
Total labor-hours/period					.816	.816
Total labor-hours/year					.816	.816

			Cost Each				
			2012 Bare Costs			**Total**	**Total**
Description	**Labor-hrs.**	**Material**	**Labor**	**Equip.**	**Total**	**In-House**	**w/O&P**
1900 Hydraulic lift, loading dock, annually	.816	8.15	37.50		45.65	56.50	69
1950 Annualized	1.632	16.30	75		91.30	113	138

	PM Components	Labor-hrs.	W	M	Q	S	A
	PM System E1095 122 1950						
	Crane, electric bridge, up to 5 ton						
1	Check with operating or area personnel for deficiencies.	.035					✓
2	Inspect crane for damaged structural members, alignment, worn pins, column fasteners, stops and capacity markings.	.235					✓
3	Inspect and lubricate power cable tension reel and inspect condition of cable.	.491					✓
4	Check hoist operation - travel function, up, down, speed stepping, upper and lower travel limit switches, etc.	.072					✓
5	Inspect, clean and lubricate trolley assembly and reduction gear bearings.	.112					✓
6	Inspect and clean hook assembly and chain or wire rope sheaves.	.452					✓
7	Inspect, clean and lubricate hoist motor.	.094					✓
8	Inspect hoist brake mechanism.	.445					✓
9	Lubricate rails.	.114					✓
10	Weight capacity test hoisting equipment at 125% of rated capacity in accordance with 29 CFR 1910.179.	.780					✓
11	Clean work area.	.066					✓
12	Fill out maintenance report and report deficiencies.	.022					✓
	Total labor-hours/period						2.918
	Total labor-hours/year						2.918

			Cost Each					
				2012 Bare Costs			Total	Total
	Description	Labor-hrs.	Material	Labor	Equip.	Total	In-House	w/O&P
1900	Crane, electric bridge, up to 5 ton, annually	2.918	31	134		165	204	250
1950	Annualized	2.918	31	134		165	204	250

	PM Components	Labor-hrs.	W	M	Q	S	A
	PM System E1095 122 2950						
	Crane, electric bridge 5 to 15 ton						
1	Check with operating or area personnel for deficiencies.	.035			✓	✓	✓
2	Inspect crane for damaged structural members, alignment, worn pins, column fasteners, stops and capacity markings.	.235			✓	✓	✓
3	Inspect and lubricate power cable tension reel and inspect condition of cable.	.491			✓	✓	✓
4	Check operation of upper and lower travel limit switches.	.072			✓	✓	✓
5	Inspect brake mechanism.	.250					✓
6	Inspect, clean and lubricate trolley assembly and reduction gear bearings.	.099			✓	✓	✓
7	Drain and replace reduction gear housing oil.	.170					✓
8	Inspect and clean hook assembly and chain or wire rope sheaves.	.099			✓	✓	✓
9	Inspect, clean and lubricate hoist motor.	.094			✓	✓	✓
10	Check pendent control for hoist operation - travel function, up, down, speed stepping, etc.	.088			✓	✓	✓
11	Lubricate rails.	.325			✓	✓	✓
12	Weight capacity test hoisting equipment at 125% of rated capacity in accordance with 29 CFR 1910.179.	1.040					✓
13	Clean work area.	.066			✓	✓	✓
14	Fill out maintenance report and report deficiencies.	.022			✓	✓	✓
	Total labor-hours/period				1.626	1.626	3.086
	Total labor-hours/year				3.252	1.626	3.086

			Cost Each					
				2012 Bare Costs			Total	Total
	Description	Labor-hrs.	Material	Labor	Equip.	Total	In-House	w/O&P
2900	Crane, electric bridge, 5 to 15 ton, annually	3.086	15.50	142		157.50	197	243
2950	Annualized	7.964	46.50	365		411.50	515	635

PM Components	Labor-hrs.	W	M	Q	S	A
PM System E1095 122 3950						
Crane, electric bridge, over 15 tons						
1 Check with operating or area personnel for deficiencies.	.035			√	√	√
2 Inspect crane for damaged structural members, alignment, worn pins, column fasteners, stops and capacity markings.	.235			√	√	√
3 Inspect and lubricate power cable tension reel and inspect condition of cable.	.491			√	√	√
4 Check operation of upper and lower travel limit switches.	.072			√	√	√
5 Inspect brake mechanism.	.250					√
6 Inspect, clean and lubricate trolley assembly and reduction gear bearings.	.099			√	√	√
7 Drain and replace reduction gear housing oil.	.170					√
8 Inspect and clean hook assembly and chain or wire rope sheaves.	.099			√	√	√
9 Inspect, clean and lubricate hoist motor.	.094			√	√	√
10 Check pendent control for hoist operation - travel function, up, down, speed stepping, etc.	.088			√	√	√
11 Lubricate rails.	.325			√	√	√
12 Inspect control cabinet.	.238					√
13 Weight capacity test hoisting equipment, at 125% of rated capacity in accordance with 29 CFR 1910.179.	1.170					√
14 Clean work area.	.066			√	√	√
15 Fill out maintenance report and report deficiencies.	.022			√	√	√
Total labor-hours/period				1.626	1.626	3.454
Total labor-hours/year				3.252	1.626	3.454

			Cost Each					
			2012 Bare Costs				Total	Total
	Description	Labor-hrs.	Material	Labor	Equip.	Total	In-House	w/O&P
3900	Crane, electric bridge, over 15 tons, annually	3.454	23.50	159		182.50	227	279
3950	Annualized	8.332	62	385		447	555	685

PM Components	Labor-hrs.	W	M	Q	S	A
PM System E1095 123 1950						
Crane, manual bridge, up to 5 tons						
1 Check with operating or area personnel for deficiencies.	.035					√
2 Operate crane and hoist, inspect underhung hoist monorail for damaged structural members, braces, stops and capacity markings.	.075					√
3 Inspect and lubricate trolley wheels and bearings.	.096					√
4 Inspect, clean and lubricate hooks and chain sheaves.	.099					√
5 Check operation of crane and hoist brakes.	.016					√
6 Make minor adjustments as required for operational integrity; tighten bolts, etc.	.135					√
7 Weight capacity test hoisting equipment at 125% of rated capacity in accordance with 29 CFR 1910.179.	.390					√
8 Clean work area.	.066					√
9 Fill out maintenance report and report deficiencies.	.022					√
Total labor-hours/period						.934
Total labor-hours/year						.934

		Cost Each						
			2012 Bare Costs				Total	Total
Description	Labor-hrs.	Material	Labor	Equip.	Total		In-House	w/O&P
1900 Crane, manual bridge, up to 5 ton, annually	.934	15.50	43		58.50		71.50	87
1950 Annualized	.934	15.50	43		58.50		71.50	87

PM Components	Labor-hrs.	W	M	Q	S	A
PM System E1095 123 2950						
Crane, manual bridge, 5 to 15 tons						
1 Check with operating or area personnel for deficiencies.	.035					√
2 Operate crane and hoist, inspect underhung hoist monorail for damaged structural members, braces, stops and capacity markings.	.130					√
3 Inspect and lubricate trolley wheels and bearings.	.096					√
4 Inspect, clean and lubricate hooks and chain sheaves.	.099					√
5 Check operation of crane and hoist brakes.	.016					√
6 Make minor adjustments as required for operational integrity; tighten bolts, etc.	.135					√
7 Weight capacity test hoisting equipment at 125% of rated capacity in accordance with 29 CFR 1910.179.	.772					√
8 Clean work area.	.066					√
9 Fill out maintenance report and report deficiencies.	.022					√
Total labor-hours/period						1.371
Total labor-hours/year						1.371

		Cost Each						
			2012 Bare Costs				Total	Total
Description	Labor-hrs.	Material	Labor	Equip.	Total		In-House	w/O&P
2900 Crane, manual bridge, 5 to 15 ton, annually	1.371	31	63		94		114	138
2950 Annualized	1.371	31	63		94		114	138

| |

PM Components	Labor-hrs.	W	M	Q	S	A
PM System E1095 123 3950						
Crane, manual bridge, over 15 tons						
1 Check with operating or area personnel for deficiencies.	.035					√
2 Operate crane and hoist, inspect for damaged structural members, alignment, worn pins, fasteners, stops and capacity markings.	.235					√
3 Inspect and lubricate trolley wheels and bearings.	.096					√
4 Inspect, clean and lubricate hooks and chain sheaves.	.099					√
5 Check operation of crane and hoist brakes.	.016					√
6 Make minor adjustments as required for operational integrity; tighten bolts, etc.	.135					√
7 Weight capacity test hoisting equipment at 125% of rated capacity in accordance with 29 CFR 1910.179.	1.162					√
8 Clean work area.	.066					√
9 Fill out maintenance report and report deficiencies.	.022					√
Total labor-hours/period						1.866
Total labor-hours/year						1.866

			Cost Each					
			2012 Bare Costs				Total	Total
Description	Labor-hrs.	Material	Labor	Equip.	Total	In-House	w/O&P
3900	Crane, manual bridge, over 15 tons, annually	1.866	46.50	86		132.50	160	193
3950	Annualized	1.866	46.50	86		132.50	160	193

| |

PM Components	Labor-hrs.	W	M	Q	S	A
PM System E1095 125 1950						
Hoist, pneumatic						
1 Check with operating or area personnel for deficiencies.	.035					√
2 Inspect for damaged structural members, alignment, worn pins, column fasteners, stops and capacity markings.	.235					√
3 Inspect and lubricate cable tension reel and inspect condition of cable.	.452					√
4 Check pendent control for hoist operation - travel function, up, down, speed stepping, upper and lower travel limit switches, etc.	.088					√
5 Inspect, clean and lubricate trolley assembly.	.099					√
6 Drain and replace reduction gear housing oil.	.170					√
7 Inspect brake mechanism.	.016					√
8 Inspect and clean hook assembly and chain or wire rope sheaves.	.099					√
9 Inspect, clean and lubricate hoist motor.	.029					√
10 Clean work area.	.066					√
11 Fill out maintenance report and report deficiencies.	.022					√
Total labor-hours/period						1.311
Total labor-hours/year						1.311

			Cost Each					
			2012 Bare Costs				Total	Total
Description	Labor-hrs.	Material	Labor	Equip.	Total	In-House	w/O&P
1900	Hoist, pneumatic, annually	1.311	54.50	60.50		115	136	163
1950	Annualized	1.311	54.50	60.50		115	136	163

E10 EQUIPMENT | E1095 126 | Hoist/Winch, Chain/Cable

PM Components	Labor-hrs.	W	M	Q	S	A
PM System E1095 126 1950						
Hoist/winch, chain fall/cable, electric						
1 Check with operating or area personnel for deficiencies.	.035					√
2 Inspect for damaged structural members, alignment, worn pins, column fasteners, stops and capacity markings.	.235					√
3 Inspect and lubricate power cable tension reel; inspect condition of cable.	.491					√
4 Check hoist operation - travel function, up, down, speed stepping, upper and lower travel limit switches, etc.	.088					√
5 Inspect, clean and lubricate trolley assembly and reduction gear bearings.	.099					√
6 Drain and replace reduction gear housing oil.	.170					√
7 Inspect brake mechanism.	.250					√
8 Inspect and clean hook assembly and chain or wire rope sheaves.	.099					√
9 Inspect, clean and lubricate hoist motor.	.094					√
10 Clean work area.	.066					√
11 Fill out maintenance report and report deficiencies.	.022					√
Total labor-hours/period						1.649
Total labor-hours/year						1.649

		Cost Each					
		2012 Bare Costs				Total	Total
Description	Labor-hrs.	Material	Labor	Equip.	Total	In-House	w/O&P
1900 Hoist / winch, chain / cable, electric, annually	1.649	19.45	76		95.45	117	143
1950 Annualized	1.649	19.45	76		95.45	117	143

E10 EQUIPMENT | E1095 302 | Beverage Dispensing Unit

PM Components	Labor-hrs.	W	M	Q	S	A
PM System E1095 302 1950						
Beverage dispensing unit						
1 Check with operating or area personnel for deficiencies.	.044			√	√	√
2 Remove access panels and clean coils, fans, fins, and other areas; vacuum, blow down with compressed air or CO_2, and/or wipe off.	.517			√	√	√
3 Lubricate motor bearings.	.008			√	√	√
4 Check electrical wiring and connections; tighten loose connections.	.120			√	√	√
5 Visually check for refrigerant, water, and other liquid leaks.	.153			√	√	√
6 Check door gaskets for proper sealing; adjust door catch as required.	.033			√	√	√
7 Inspect dispensing valves; adjust as necessary.	.108			√	√	√
8 Perform operational check of unit; make adjustments as necessary.	.040			√	√	√
9 Clean area around equipment.	.066			√	√	√
10 Fill out maintenance checklist and report deficiencies.	.022			√	√	√
Total labor-hours/period				1.111	1.111	1.111
Total labor-hours/year				2.222	1.111	1.111

		Cost Each					
		2012 Bare Costs				Total	Total
Description	Labor-hrs.	Material	Labor	Equip.	Total	In-House	w/O&P
1900 Beverage dispensing unit, annually	1.111	8.20	50.50		58.70	75.50	92.50
1950 Annualized	4.444	16.40	202		218.40	284	350

PM Components	Labor-hrs.	W	M	Q	S	A
PM System E1095 304 1950						
Braising pan, tilting, gas/electric						
1 Check with operating or area personnel for deficiencies.	.044			√	√	√
2 Check electric transformer, heating elements, insulators, connections and wiring; tighten connections and repair as required.	.239			√	√	√
3 Check surface temperature with meter for hot spots.	.073			√	√	√
4 Check piping and valves on gas operated units for leaks.	.077			√	√	√
5 Check pilot/igniter, burner and combustion chamber for proper operation; adjust as required.	.079			√	√	√
6 Check temperature control system for proper operation; adjust as required.	.458			√	√	√
7 Lubricate tilting gear mechanism and trunnion bearings.	.047			√	√	√
8 Check nuts, bolts and screws for tightness; tighten as required.	.007			√	√	√
9 Check complete operation of unit.	.055			√	√	√
10 Fill out maintenance checklist and report deficiencies.	.022			√	√	√
Total labor-hours/period				1.101	1.101	1.101
Total labor-hours/year				2.202	1.101	1.101

			Cost Each					
			2012 Bare Costs				Total	Total
	Description	Labor-hrs.	Material	Labor	Equip.	Total	In-House	w/O&P
1900	Braising pan, tilting, gas / electric, annually	1.101	154	50		204	235	274
1950	Annualized	4.404	181	200		381	460	550

PM Components	Labor-hrs.	W	M	Q	S	A
PM System E1095 306 1950						
Bread slicer, electric						
1 Check with operating or area personnel for deficiencies.	.044			√	√	√
2 Check electric motor, controls, wiring connections, insulation and contacts for damage and/or proper operation; adjust as required.	.338			√	√	√
3 Check V-belt for wear, tension and alignment; change/adjust belt as necessary.	.029			√	√	√
4 Lubricate bushings and check oil level in gear drive mechanism; add oil if required.	.065			√	√	√
5 Clean machine of dust, grease and food particles.	.074			√	√	√
6 Check motor and motor bearings for overheating.	.039			√	√	√
7 Check for loose, missing or damaged nuts, bolts, or screws; tighten or replace as necessary.	.005			√	√	√
8 Fill out maintenance checklist and report deficiencies.	.022			√	√	√
Total labor-hours/period				.616	.616	.616
Total labor-hours/year				1.232	.616	.616

			Cost Each					
			2012 Bare Costs				Total	Total
	Description	Labor-hrs.	Material	Labor	Equip.	Total	In-House	w/O&P
1900	Bread slicer, electric, annually	.616	63	28		91	106	124
1950	Annualized	2.464	90.50	112		202.50	247	295

PM Components	Labor-hrs.	W	M	Q	S	A
PM System E1095 310 1950						
Broiler, conveyor type, gas						
1 Check with operating or area personnel for deficiencies.	.044			√	√	√
2 Check broiler pilot/igniters and jets for uniform flame; adjust as required.	.166			√	√	√
3 Check air filter; change as required.	.059			√	√	√
4 Check operation of chains and counterweights.	.012			√	√	√
5 Check piping and valves for leaks.	.077			√	√	√
6 Check electrical connections and wiring for defects; tighten loose connections.	.120			√	√	√
7 Check thermocouple and thermostat; calibrate thermostat as required.	.646			√	√	√
8 Tighten and replace any loose nuts, bolts, or screws.	.005			√	√	√
9 Check operation of unit.	.055			√	√	√
10 Fill out maintenance checklist and report deficiencies.	.022			√	√	√
Total labor-hours/period				1.206	1.206	1.206
Total labor-hours/year				2.412	1.206	1.206

		Cost Each						
			2012 Bare Costs				Total	Total
Description	Labor-hrs.	Material	Labor	Equip.	Total		In-House	w/O&P
1900 Broiler, conveyor type, gas, annually	1.206	163	55		218		251	293
1950 Annualized	4.824	163	219		382		470	560

PM Components	Labor-hrs.	W	M	Q	S	A
PM System E1095 310 2950						
Broiler, hot dog, electric						
1 Check with operating or area personnel for deficiencies.	.044			√	√	√
2 Check electric motor, controls, contacts, wiring connections for damage and proper operation; adjust as required.	.152			√	√	√
3 Lubricate bushings.	.007			√	√	√
4 Inspect lines and unit for mechanical defects; adjust or repair as required.	.021			√	√	√
5 Clean machine of dust and grease.	.109			√	√	√
6 Check unit for proper operation.	.082			√	√	√
7 Fill out maintenance checklist and report deficiencies.	.022			√	√	√
Total labor-hours/period				.437	.437	.437
Total labor-hours/year				.874	.437	.437

		Cost Each						
			2012 Bare Costs				Total	Total
Description	Labor-hrs.	Material	Labor	Equip.	Total		In-House	w/O&P
2900 Broiler, hot dog type, electric, annually	.437	45	19.85		64.85		75.50	89
2950 Annualized	1.748	72.50	79.50		152		184	220

PM Components	Labor-hrs.	W	M	Q	S	A
PM System E1095 310 3950						
Broiler/oven (salamander), gas/electric						
1 Check with operating or area personnel for deficiencies.	.044			√	√	√
2 Check broiler pilot and oven for uniform flame; adjust as required.	.166			√	√	√
3 Check piping and valves for leaks.	.077			√	√	√
4 Check doors, shelves for warping, alignment, and seals; adjust as required.	.148			√	√	√
5 Check electrical connections and wiring for defects; tighten loose connections.	.241			√	√	√
6 Tighten and replace any loose nuts, bolts and/or screws.	.012			√	√	√
7 Check operation of broiler arm, adjust as required.	.007			√	√	√
8 Check thermocouple and thermostat; calibrate thermostat as required.	.569			√	√	√
9 Fill out maintenance checklist and report deficiencies.	.022			√	√	√
Total labor-hours/period				1.286	1.286	1.286
Total labor-hours/year				2.572	1.286	1.286

			Cost Each					
			2012 Bare Costs				Total	Total
Description	Labor-hrs.	Material	Labor	Equip.	Total	In-House	w/O&P
3900	Broiler / oven, (salamander), gas / electric, annually	1.286	145	58.50		203.50	237	276
3950	Annualized	5.144	145	234		379	465	560

PM Components	Labor-hrs.	W	M	Q	S	A
PM System E1095 312 1950						
Chopper, electric						
1 Check with operating or area personnel for deficiencies.	.044			√	√	√
2 Check cutting surfaces, clutch assembly and guards for damage and proper alignment; adjust as required.	.065			√	√	√
3 Check nuts, bolts, and screws for tightness; tighten or replace as required.	.005			√	√	√
4 Check switch and controls for proper operation; adjust as required.	.010			√	√	√
5 Clean machine of dust, grease and food particles.	.014			√	√	√
6 Check operation of motor and check motor bearings for overheating; lubricate as required.	.069			√	√	√
7 Check belt tension; replace belt and/or adjust if required.	.315			√	√	√
8 Fill out maintenance checklist and report deficiencies.	.022			√	√	√
Total labor-hours/period				.544	.544	.544
Total labor-hours/year				1.088	.544	.544

			Cost Each					
			2012 Bare Costs				Total	Total
Description	Labor-hrs.	Material	Labor	Equip.	Total	In-House	w/O&P
1900	Chopper, electric, annually	.544	77.50	24.50		102	119	137
1950	Annualized	2.176	95	99		194	236	280

506

PM Components	Labor-hrs.	W	M	Q	S	A
PM System E1095 314 1950						
Coffee maker/urn, gas/electric/steam						
1 Check thermostat, switch, and temperature gauge; calibrate if required.	.465			√	√	√
2 Check pilots and flame on gas operated units; adjust as required.	.038			√	√	√
3 Check working pressure on steam operated unit.	.005			√	√	√
4 Check electrical connections and wiring for defects; tighten connections.	.120			√	√	√
5 Check for clogged or defective steam trap.	.100			√	√	√
6 Inspect and clean steam strainer.	.207			√	√	√
7 Examine equipment, valves, and piping for leaks.	.077			√	√	√
8 Inspect for leaks at water gauge glasses and at valves; repack valves if necessary.	.046			√	√	√
9 Tighten or replace loose, missing, or damaged nuts, bolts, or screws.	.005			√	√	√
10 Lubricate water filter valve, check rings, tighten as required.	.033			√	√	√
11 Check operation of lights.	.027			√	√	√
12 Check timer mechanism and operation of unit.	.018			√	√	√
13 Fill out maintenance checklist and report deficiencies.	.022			√	√	√
Total labor-hours/period				1.163	1.163	1.163
Total labor-hours/year				2.326	1.163	1.163

				Cost Each				
			2012 Bare Costs				Total	Total
Description	Labor-hrs.	Material	Labor	Equip.	Total	In-House	w/O&P
1900	Coffee maker / urn, gas / electric / steam, annually	1.163	49.50	53		102.50	124	148
1950	Annualized	4.652	49.50	211		260.50	330	405

PM Components	Labor-hrs.	W	M	Q	S	A
PM System E1095 316 1950						
Cooker, gas						
1 Check with operating or area personnel for any deficiencies.	.044			√	√	√
2 Examine doors and door gaskets; make necessary adjustments.	.021			√	√	√
3 Visually inspect hinges and latches; lubricate hinges.	.091			√	√	√
4 Tighten or replace any loose nuts, bolts, screws; replace broken knobs.	.007			√	√	√
5 Check gas piping and valves for leaks.	.077			√	√	√
6 Check pilot and thermosensor bulb.	.079			√	√	√
7 Check gas burner for uniform flame.	.007			√	√	√
8 Check calibration of thermostats.	.458			√	√	√
9 Operate unit to ensure that it is in proper working condition.	.130			√	√	√
10 Fill out maintenance checklist and report deficiencies.	.022			√	√	√
Total labor-hours/period				.936	.936	.936
Total labor-hours/year				1.872	.936	.936

			Cost Each				
			2012 Bare Costs			Total	Total
Description	Labor-hrs.	Material	Labor	Equip.	Total	In-House	w/O&P
1900 Cooker, gas, annually	.936	115	42.50		157.50	183	213
1950 Annualized	3.744	115	170		285	350	420

PM Components	Labor-hrs.	W	M	Q	S	A
PM System E1095 316 2950						
Cooker, vegetable steamer						
1 Check with operating or area personnel for any deficiencies.	.044			√	√	√
2 Examine doors and door gaskets; make necessary adjustments.	.021			√	√	√
3 Visually inspect hinges and latches; lubricate hinges.	.091			√	√	√
4 Tighten or replace any loose nuts, bolts, screws; replace broken knobs.	.005			√	√	√
5 Check working pressure on steam gauge.	.005			√	√	√
6 Inspect piping and valves for leaks; tighten as necessary.	.077			√	√	√
7 Check operation of low water cut-off; adjust as required.	.030			√	√	√
8 Check water level sight glass; adjust as required.	.007			√	√	√
9 Fill out maintenance checklist and report deficiencies.	.022			√	√	√
Total labor-hours/period				.302	.302	.302
Total labor-hours/year				.604	.302	.302

			Cost Each				
			2012 Bare Costs			Total	Total
Description	Labor-hrs.	Material	Labor	Equip.	Total	In-House	w/O&P
2900 Cooker, vegetable steamer, annually	.302	39.50	13.70		53.20	61.50	72
2950 Annualized	1.208	39.50	55		94.50	116	138

PM Components	Labor-hrs.	W	M	Q	S	A
PM System E1095 316 3950						
Cooker, steam						
1 Check with operating or area personnel for any deficiencies.	.044			√	√	√
2 Examine doors and door gaskets; make necessary adjustments.	.021			√	√	√
3 Visually inspect hinges and latches; lubricate hinges.	.091			√	√	√
4 Tighten or replace any loose nuts, bolts, screws; replace broken knobs.	.005			√	√	√
5 Check for clogged or defective steam trap; clean trap.	.098			√	√	√
6 Inspect and clean steam strainer.	.207			√	√	√
7 Check working pressure on steam gauge.	.005			√	√	√
8 Turn unit on, allow pressure to build, inspect piping, valve and doors for leaks; adjust as required.	.077			√	√	√
9 Check operation of pressure relief valve; adjust as required.	.010			√	√	√
10 Check operation of low water cut-off; adjust as required.	.030			√	√	√
11 Check water level sight glass; adjust as required.	.007			√	√	√
12 Check timer mechanism and operation; adjust as required.	.018			√	√	√
13 Fill out maintenance checklist and report deficiencies.	.022			√	√	√
Total labor-hours/period				.635	.635	.635
Total labor-hours/year				1.270	.635	.635

	Description	Labor-hrs.	Cost Each						
			2012 Bare Costs				Total In-House	Total w/O&P	
			Material	Labor	Equip.	Total			
3900	Cooker, steam, annually	.635	79	29		108	125	146	
3950	Annualized	2.540	79	115		194	239	286	

PM Components	Labor-hrs.	W	M	Q	S	A
PM System E1095 318 1950						
Cookie maker, electric						
1 Check with operating or area personnel for any deficiencies.	.044			√	√	√
2 Check electrical panel switches, connections, timing device for loose, frayed wiring; tighten connections as required.	.120			√	√	√
3 Check operation of electric motor and bearings for overheating; lubricate motor bearings.	.086			√	√	√
4 Check belt; adjust tension or replace belt as required.	.369			√	√	√
5 Check conveyor and rollers by observing movement; lubricate rollers and adjust as required.	.127			√	√	√
6 Tighten or replace loose, missing or damaged nuts, bolts or screws.	.012			√	√	√
7 Wipe off and clean unit.	.096			√	√	√
8 Fill out maintenance checklist and report deficiencies.	.022			√	√	√
Total labor-hours/period				.876	.876	.876
Total labor-hours/year				1.752	.876	.876

	Description	Labor-hrs.	Cost Each						
			2012 Bare Costs				Total In-House	Total w/O&P	
			Material	Labor	Equip.	Total			
1900	Cookie maker, electric, annually	.876	57.50	40		97.50	117	136	
1950	Annualized	3.504	82	159		241	300	360	

PM Components	Labor-hrs.	W	M	Q	S	A
PM System E1095 320 1950						
Deep fat fryer, pressurized broaster, gas/electric						
1 Check with operating or area personnel for any deficiencies.	.044			√	√	√
2 Check piping and valves for leaks; tighten fittings as required.	.125			√	√	√
3 Check pilot and flame on gas operated unit; adjust as required.	.009			√	√	√
4 Check elements, switches, controls, contacts, and wiring on electrically heated units; repair or adjust as required.	.025			√	√	
5 Check thermostat; calibrate if necessary.	.439			√	√	√
6 Check basket/racks for bends, breaks or defects; straighten bends or repair as necessary.	.013			√	√	
7 Check cooking oil filter on circulating system; change as required.	.068			√	√	√
8 Check operation of unit.	.164			√	√	√
9 Check operation of motor for excessive noise and overheating.	.022			√	√	√
10 Check nuts, bolts, and screws for tightness; tighten or replace as necessary.	.005			√	√	√
11 Fill out maintenance checklist and report deficiencies.	.022			√	√	√
Total labor-hours/period				.936	.936	.936
Total labor-hours/year				1.872	.936	.936

			Cost Each			
			2012 Bare Costs		**Total**	**Total**
Description	**Labor-hrs.**	**Material**	**Labor**	**Equip.**	**Total**	**In-House**	**w/O&P**
1900 Fryer, pressurized broaster, gas / electric, annually	.936	115	42.50		157.50	183	213
1950 Annualized	3.744	164	170		334	405	480

PM Components	Labor-hrs.	W	M	Q	S	A
PM System E1095 320 2950						
Deep fat fryer, automatic conveyor belt type, gas/electric						
1 Check with operating or area personnel for any deficiencies.	.044			√	√	√
2 Check compartments, valves and piping for leaks; tighten as required.	.077			√	√	√
3 Check pilot and flame on gas operated fryers; adjust as required.	.168			√	√	√
4 Check elements, switches, controls, contacts and wiring on electrically heated units for defects; repair or adjust as necessary.	.051			√	√	√
5 Check thermostats; calibrate as necessary.	.439			√	√	√
6 Check cooking oil filter on circulating system; change as required.	.068			√	√	√
7 Check operation of motor for excessive noise and overheating; lubricate bearings.	.022			√	√	√
8 Check operation of belt hoist; lubricate and adjust as required.	.052			√	√	√
9 Check nuts, bolts and screws for tightness; replace or tighten as necessary.	.017			√	√	√
10 Clean machine of dust, grease and food particles.	.044			√	√	√
11 Clean area around unit.	.066			√	√	√
12 Fill out maintenance checklist and report deficiencies.	.022			√	√	√
Total labor-hours/period				1.070	1.070	1.070
Total labor-hours/year				2.140	1.070	1.070

			Cost Each			
			2012 Bare Costs		**Total**	**Total**
Description	**Labor-hrs.**	**Material**	**Labor**	**Equip.**	**Total**	**In-House**	**w/O&P**
2900 Fryer, conveyor belt type, gas / electric, annually	1.070	98.50	48.50		147	172	202
2950 Annualized	4.280	98.50	194		292.50	365	440

PM Components	Labor-hrs.	W	M	Q	S	A
PM System E1095 320 3950						
Deep fat fryer, conventional type, gas/electric						
1 Check with operating or area personnel for any deficiencies.	.044			√	√	√
2 Clean machine thoroughly of dust, grease, and food particles.	.014			√	√	√
3 Check compartments, valves, and piping for leaks; tighten as required.	.077			√	√	√
4 Check pilot and flame on gas operated deep fat fryer; adjust as required.	.005			√	√	√
5 Check thermostat; calibrate if necessary.	.439			√	√	√
6 On electrically heated units check elements, switches, controls, contacts, and wiring for defects; repair or adjust as necessary.	.025			√	√	√
7 Check basket or rack for bends, breaks or defects, straighten bends or repair as necessary.	.013			√	√	√
8 Check nuts, bolts and screws for tightness; tighten or replace as necessary.	.005			√	√	√
9 Fill out maintenance checklist and report deficiencies.	.022			√	√	√
Total labor-hours/period				.644	.644	.644
Total labor-hours/year				1.288	.644	.644

			Cost Each				
			2012 Bare Costs			Total	Total
Description	Labor-hrs.	Material	Labor	Equip.	Total	In-House	w/O&P
3900 Fryer, conventional type, gas / electric, annually	.644	82	29		111	129	150
3950 Annualized	2.576	82	117		199	244	293

PM Components	Labor-hrs.	W	M	Q	S	A
PM System E1095 322 1950						
Dishwasher, electric						
1 Check with operating or area personnel for any deficiencies.	.044			√	√	√
2 Check electric insulators, connections, and wiring (includes removing access panels).	.120			√	√	√
3 Check motor and bearings for excessive noise, vibration and overheating.	.039			√	√	√
4 Check dish conveyor by turning on switch and observing conveyor movement; adjust chain if necessary.	.070			√	√	√
5 Check operation of wash and rinse spray mechanism for spray coverage and drainage.	.022			√	√	√
6 Inspect soap and spray solution feeder lines; clean as necessary.	.013			√	√	√
7 Inspect water lines and fittings for leaks; tighten fittings as necessary.	.077			√	√	√
8 Lubricate conveyor drive bushings and chain drive.	.055			√	√	√
9 Check belt tension; adjust if required.	.100			√	√	√
10 Check doors for: operation of chains and counterweights, warping, alignment and water tightness; adjust if necessary.	.022			√	√	√
11 Check packing glands on wash, rinse, and drain valves; add or replace packing as required.	.147			√	√	√
12 Check lubricant in gear case; add oil if required.	.049			√	√	√
13 Inspect splash curtain for tears, clearance and water tightness; adjust if required.	.016			√	√	√
14 Check proper operation of solenoid valve and float in fill tank; adjust as required.	.096			√	√	√
15 Check pumps for leakage and obstructions; adjust as required.	.120			√	√	√
16 Check proper operation of micro-switch.	.010			√	√	√
17 Check water for proper temperature.	.004			√	√	√
18 Check operation of safety stop and clutch on conveyor belt motor; adjust cut-off switch mechanism as required.	.049			√	√	√
19 Check temperature regulator and adjust if necessary.	.017			√	√	√
20 Clean lime off thermostatic probe and heating elements.	.020			√	√	√
21 Clean area around equipment.	.066			√	√	√
22 Fill out maintenance checklist and report deficiencies.	.022			√	√	√
Total labor-hours/period				1.178	1.178	1.178
Total labor-hours/year				2.356	1.178	1.178

			Cost Each					
			2012 Bare Costs				**Total**	**Total**
Description		**Labor-hrs.**	**Material**	**Labor**	**Equip.**	**Total**	**In-House**	**w/O&P**
1900	Dishwasher, electric, annually	1.178	107	53.50		160.50	189	221
1950	Annualized	4.712	230	214		444	535	640

PM Components	Labor-hrs.	W	M	Q	S	A
PM System E1095 322 2950						
Dishwasher, steam						
1 Check with operating or area personnel for any deficiencies.	.044			√	√	√
2 Check electric insulators, connections, and wiring (includes removing access panels).	.120			√	√	√
3 Check motor and bearings for excessive noise, vibration and overheating.	.039			√	√	√
4 Check dish conveyor by turning on switch and observing conveyor movement; adjust chain if necessary.	.070			√	√	√
5 Check operation of wash and rinse spray mechanism for spray coverage and drainage.	.022			√	√	√
6 Inspect soap and spray solution feeder lines; clean as necessary.	.013			√	√	√
7 Inspect steam and water lines and fittings for leaks; tighten fittings as necessary.	.077			√	√	√
8 Lubricate conveyor drive bushings and chain drive.	.055			√	√	√
9 Check belt tension; adjust if required.	.100			√	√	√
10 Check doors for: operation of chains and counterweights, warping, alignment and water tightness; adjust if necessary.	.022			√	√	√
11 Tighten loose nuts, bolts and screws.	.005			√	√	√
12 Check packing glands on wash, rinse, and drain valves; add or replace packing as required.	.147			√	√	√
13 Check lubricant in gear case; add oil if required.	.049			√	√	√
14 Inspect splash curtain for tears, clearance and water tightness; adjust if required.	.016			√	√	√
15 Check proper operation of solenoid valve and float in fill tank; adjust as required.	.096			√	√	√
16 Check pumps for leakage and obstructions; adjust as required.	.120			√	√	√
17 Check proper operation of micro-switch.	.010			√	√	√
18 Check water for proper temperature readings.	.004			√	√	√
19 Check operation of safety stop and clutch on conveyor belt motor; adjust cut-off switch mechanism as required.	.049			√	√	√
20 Check temperature regulator and adjust if necessary.	.017			√	√	√
21 Clean lime off thermostatic probe.	.020			√	√	√
22 Clean area around equipment.	.066			√	√	√
23 Fill out maintenance checklist and report deficienceis.	.022			√	√	√
Total labor-hours/period				1.183	1.183	1.183
Total labor-hours/year				2.366	1.183	1.183

		Cost Each						
			2012 Bare Costs				Total	Total
Description	Labor-hrs.	Material	Labor	Equip.	Total	In-House	w/O&P
2900	Dishwasher, steam, annually	1.183	107	53.50		160.50	189	221
2950	Annualized	4.732	230	215		445	535	640

| | **Dispenser, Beverage**

PM Components	Labor-hrs.	W	M	Q	S	A
PM System E1095 328 1950						
Dispenser, carbonated beverage						
1 Check with operating or area personnel for any deficiencies.	.044			√	√	√
2 Check all lines, connections and valves for leaks.	.077			√	√	√
3 Check pressure gauges; adjust as required.	.018			√	√	√
4 Check water strainer screen on carbonator; clean as required.	.159			√	√	√
5 Check wiring, connectors and switches; repair as required.	.120			√	√	√
6 Check nuts, bolts and screws for tightness; replace or tighten as required.	.005			√	√	√
7 Wipe and clean unit.	.056			√	√	√
8 Fill out maintenance checklist and report deficiencies.	.022			√	√	√
Total labor-hours/period				.501	.501	.501
Total labor-hours/year				1.002	.501	.501

			Cost Each					
			2012 Bare Costs				Total	Total
Description		Labor-hrs.	Material	Labor	Equip.	Total	In-House	w/O&P
1900	Dispenser, carbonated beverage, annually	.501	65.50	23		88.50	102	119
1950	Annualized	2.004	65.50	91		156.50	192	230

| | **Disposal, Garbage**

PM Components	Labor-hrs.	W	M	Q	S	A
PM System E1095 332 1950						
Disposal, garbage, electric						
1 Check with operating or area personnel for any deficiencies.	.044			√	√	√
2 Check motor and drive shaft for excessive noise, vibration, overheating, etc.	.044			√	√	√
3 Inspect electrical wiring.	.014			√	√	√
4 Visually examine grinder; check for obstructions; adjust cutters if required.	.074			√	√	√
5 Check drive belt(s) for wear and tension; adjust if required.	.014			√	√	√
6 Check for leaks to supply and drain connections; tighten if required.	.103			√	√	√
7 Check electrical switch for proper operation.	.014			√	√	√
8 Lubricate grinder, drive, and motor.	.022			√	√	√
9 Check water sprayer operation.	.030			√	√	√
10 Fill out maintenance checklist and report deficiencies.	.022			√	√	√
Total labor-hours/period				.381	.381	.381
Total labor-hours/year				.762	.381	.381

			Cost Each					
			2012 Bare Costs				Total	Total
Description		Labor-hrs.	Material	Labor	Equip.	Total	In-House	w/O&P
1900	Disposal, garbage, electric, annually	.381	39.50	17.30		56.80	66	77.50
1950	Annualized	1.524	39.50	69		108.50	135	161

PM Components	Labor-hrs.	W	M	Q	S	A
PM System E1095 334 1950						
Dough divider						
1 Check with operating or area personnel for any deficiencies.	.044			√	√	√
2 Check motor and drive shaft for excessive noise, vibration, overheating, etc.	.039			√	√	√
3 Inspect electrical wiring.	.120			√	√	√
4 Visually examine plates; check for obstructions; adjust cutters if required.	.074			√	√	√
5 Check electrical switch for proper operation.	.014			√	√	√
6 Lubricate press, drive, and motor.	.218			√	√	√
7 Fill out maintenance checklist and report deficiencies.	.022			√	√	√
Total labor-hours/period				.531	.531	.531
Total labor-hours/year				1.062	.531	.531

				Cost Each				
			2012 Bare Costs				Total	Total
Description	Labor-hrs.	Material	Labor	Equip.	Total	In-House	w/O&P
1900 Dough divider, annually	.531	82	24		106	122	142
1950 Annualized	2.124	82	96.50		178.50	217	260

PM Components	Labor-hrs.	W	M	Q	S	A
PM System E1095 334 2950						
Dough roller						
1 Check with operating or area personnel for any deficiencies.	.044			√	√	√
2 Check electric motor, switches, controls, wiring, connections and insulation for defective materials; repair as necessary.	.241			√	√	√
3 Check belt tension; adjust or replace as required.	.446			√	√	√
4 Check operation of conveyor-roller clearance; adjust as necessary.	.109			√	√	√
5 Lubricate all moving parts, motors, pivot points and chain drives.	.017			√	√	√
6 Clean unit and treat for rust and/or corrosion.	.083			√	√	√
7 Tighten or replace loose, missing or damaged nuts, bolts and screws.	.005			√	√	√
8 Fill out maintenance checklist and report deficiencies.	.022			√	√	√
Total labor-hours/period				.967	.967	.967
Total labor-hours/year				1.934	.967	.967

				Cost Each				
			2012 Bare Costs				Total	Total
Description	Labor-hrs.	Material	Labor	Equip.	Total	In-House	w/O&P
2900 Dough roller, annually	.967	123	44		167	193	225
2950 Annualized	3.868	148	176		324	395	470

PM Components	Labor-hrs.	W	M	Q	S	A
PM System E1095 336 1950						
Drink cooler, with external condenser						
1 Check with operating or area personnel for deficiencies.	.035				✓	✓
2 Clean condenser coils, fans, and intake screens; lubricate motor.	.504				✓	✓
3 Inspect door gaskets for damage and proper fit; adjust as necessary.	.033				✓	✓
4 Check starter panels and controls for proper operation, burned or loose contacts, and loose connections.	.094				✓	✓
5 Clean coils, evaporator drain pan, blowers, fans, motors and drain piping as required; lubricate motor(s).	.473				✓	✓
6 During operation of unit, check refrigerant pressures and compressor oil level; add refrigerant and/or oil as necessary.	.066				✓	✓
7 Check operation of low pressure cut-out; adjust or replace as necessary.	.057				✓	✓
8 Inspect defrost systems for proper operation; adjust as required.	.027				✓	✓
9 Clean area around equipment.	.066				✓	✓
10 Fill out maintenance checklist and report deficiencies.	.022				✓	✓
Total labor-hours/period					1.377	1.377
Total labor-hours/year					1.377	1.377

		Cost Each					
		2012 Bare Costs				Total	Total
Description	Labor-hrs.	Material	Labor	Equip.	Total	In-House	w/O&P
1900 Drink cooler with external condenser, annually	1.377	16.40	62.50		78.90	100	123
1950 Annualized	2.754	33	125		158	202	244

PM Components	Labor-hrs.	W	M	Q	S	A
PM System E1095 338 1950						
Fluid cooler, air cooled condenser						
1 Check with operating or area personnel for deficiencies.	.035					✓
2 Check unit for proper operation, excessive noise or vibration.	.159					✓
3 Clean intake side of condenser coils, fans and intake screens.	.473					✓
4 Check electrical wiring and connections; tighten loose connections.	.120					✓
5 Inspect fan(s) for bent blades or unbalance; adjust as necessary.	.014					✓
6 Check belts for condition, proper tension and misalignment, if required.	.029					✓
7 Lubricate shaft bearings and motor bearings.	.047					✓
8 Inspect piping and valves for leaks; tighten connections as necessary.	.077					✓
9 Lubricate and check operation of dampers, if applicable.	.055					✓
10 Clean area around fluid cooler.	.066					✓
11 Fill out maintenance checklist and report deficiencies.	.022					✓
Total labor-hours/period						1.097
Total labor-hours/year						1.097

		Cost Each					
		2012 Bare Costs				Total	Total
Description	Labor-hrs.	Material	Labor	Equip.	Total	In-House	w/O&P
1900 Fluid cooler, annually	1.097	16.40	50		66.40	83.50	102
1950 Annualized	1.097	16.40	50		66.40	83.50	102

PM Components	Labor-hrs.	W	M	Q	S	A
PM System E1095 340 1950						
Food saw, electric						
1 Check with operating or area personnel for any deficiencies.	.044			√	√	√
2 Check operation of saw for excessive vibration, blade tension and proper adjustment of safety guards; repair or adjust as required.	.095			√	√	√
3 Check motor and bearings for overheating; lubricate motor bearings.	.039			√	√	√
4 Check switches, motor, controls and wiring for damage and proper operation; repair as required.	.120			√	√	√
5 Clean machine of dust and grease.	.044			√	√	√
6 Check nuts, bolts and screws for tightness; tighten as required.	.005			√	√	√
7 Check belt tension and alignment; adjust as required.	.029			√	√	√
8 Fill out maintenance checklist and report deficiencies.	.022			√	√	√
Total labor-hours/period				.398	.398	.398
Total labor-hours/year				.796	.398	.398

			Cost Each				
			2012 Bare Costs			**Total**	**Total**
Description	**Labor-hrs.**	**Material**	**Labor**	**Equip.**	**Total**	**In-House**	**w/O&P**
1900 Food saw, electric, annually	.398	57.50	18.05		75.55	87.50	101
1950 Annualized	1.592	82	72.50		154.50	185	221

PM Components	Labor-hrs.	W	M	Q	S	A
PM System E1095 340 2950						
Food slicer, electric						
1 Check with operating or area personnel for any deficiencies.	.044			√	√	√
2 Check nuts, bolts and screws for tightness; tighten or replace as required.	.005			√	√	√
3 Lubricate food slicer and add lubricant to gear case if required.	.085			√	√	√
4 Check condition of blade, blade guard, guides, and controls; adjust as required.	.047			√	√	√
5 Check operation of motor and check motor bearings for overheating; lubricate motor bearings.	.039			√	√	√
6 Check sharpening stones; install new stones as required.	.013			√	√	√
7 Clean machine of dust, grease, and food particles.	.014			√	√	√
8 Fill out maintenance checklist and report deficiencies.	.022			√	√	√
Total labor-hours/period				.269	.269	.269
Total labor-hours/year				.538	.269	.269

			Cost Each				
			2012 Bare Costs			**Total**	**Total**
Description	**Labor-hrs.**	**Material**	**Labor**	**Equip.**	**Total**	**In-House**	**w/O&P**
2900 Food slicer, electric, annually	.269	74	12.20		86.20	97.50	112
2950 Annualized	1.076	98.50	49		147.50	173	203

| **E1095 346** | **Grill, Gas/Electric**

PM Components	Labor-hrs.	W	M	Q	S	A
PM System E1095 346 1950						
Grill, gas/electric						
1 Check with operating or area personnel for any deficiencies.	.044			√	√	√
2 Check nuts, bolts and screws for tightness; tighten or replace as required.	.005			√	√	√
3 On gas operated units, check piping and valves for leaks.	.077			√	√	√
4 On gas operated units, check pilot and gas burners for uniform flame; adjust as required.	.079			√	√	√
5 On electrically operated units, check switches, connections, and wiring for proper operation; adjust as required.	.135			√	√	√
6 Check calibration of thermostats; adjust as required.	.458			√	√	√
7 Fill out maintenance checklist and report deficiencies.	.022			√	√	√
Total labor-hours/period				.820	.820	.820
Total labor-hours/year				1.640	.820	.820

			Cost Each				
			2012 Bare Costs			**Total**	**Total**
Description	Labor-hrs.	Material	Labor	Equip.	Total	In-House	w/O&P
1900 Grill, gas / electric, annually	.820	82	37		119	139	163
1950 Annualized	3.280	82	149		231	286	345

| **E1095 348** | **Ice Machine**

PM Components	Labor-hrs.	W	M	Q	S	A
PM System E1095 348 1950						
Ice machine, flake or cube						
1 Check with operating or area personnel for any deficiencies.	.044			√	√	√
2 Remove and install access panel.	.044			√	√	√
3 Lubricate all moving parts, pivot points and fan motor(s).	.023			√	√	√
4 Visually check for refrigerant, oil or water leaks.	.022			√	√	√
5 Open and close water valve.	.007			√	√	√
6 Replace in-line water filter.	.009			√	√	√
7 Check and clear ice machine draining system (drain vent and trap).	.198			√	√	√
8 Clean motor, compressor and condenser coil.	.403			√	√	√
9 Check and tighten any loose screw-type electrical connections.	.005			√	√	√
10 Inspect door(s) hinges, gaskets, handles; lubricate as required.	.053			√	√	√
11 Clean area around equipment.	.066			√	√	√
12 Fill out maintenance checklist and report deficiencies.	.022			√	√	√
Total labor-hours/period				.896	.896	.896
Total labor-hours/year				1.792	.896	.896

			Cost Each				
			2012 Bare Costs			**Total**	**Total**
Description	Labor-hrs.	Material	Labor	Equip.	Total	In-House	w/O&P
1900 Ice machine, flake or cube, annually	.896	24.50	40.50		65	80.50	96.50
1950 Annualized	3.584	98.50	163		261.50	325	390

PM Components	Labor-hrs.	W	M	Q	S	A
PM System E1095 350 1950						
Kettle, steam, fixed or tilt						
1 Check with operating or area personnel for any deficiencies.	.044			√	√	√
2 Check piping and fittings for leaks; tighten as required.	.085			√	√	√
3 Check operation of electric water valve.	.030			√	√	√
4 Inspect cover, hinges, and seals on units to equipped; lubricate hinge.	.053			√	√	√
5 Lubricate tilting gear mechanism and trunnion bearings, if applicable.	.047			√	√	√
6 Fill out maintenance checklist and report deficiencies.	.022			√	√	√
Total labor-hours/period				.281	.281	.281
Total labor-hours/year				.562	.281	.281

	Description	Labor-hrs.	Cost Each				Total In-House	Total w/O&P
			2012 Bare Costs					
			Material	Labor	Equip.	Total		
1900	Kettle, steam, fixed or tilt, annually	.281	41	12.75		53.75	62	72
1950	Annualized	1.124	41	51		92	112	134

519

PM Components	Labor-hrs.	W	M	Q	S	A
PM System E1095 354 1950						
Mixer, counter, electric						
1 Check with operating or area personnel for any deficiencies.	.044			√	√	√
2 Check operation of mixer at varying speeds for excessive noise and vibrations; align or adjust as required.	.033			√	√	√
3 Check belt for proper tension and alignment; adjust as required.	.068			√	√	√
4 Lubricate mixer gears.	.042			√	√	√
5 Clean machine thoroughly of dust, grease, and food particles.	.014			√	√	√
6 Check motor, switches, controls and motor bearings for overheating; lubricate motor bearings.	.039			√	√	√
7 Check anchor bolts for tightness; tighten as required.	.010			√	√	√
8 Fill out maintenance checklist and report deficiencies.	.022			√	√	√
Total labor-hours/period				.272	.272	.272
Total labor-hours/year				.544	.272	.272

			Cost Each				
			2012 Bare Costs			**Total**	**Total**
Description	**Labor-hrs.**	**Material**	**Labor**	**Equip.**	**Total**	**In-House**	**w/O&P**
1900 Mixer, counter, electric, annually	.272	41	12.35		53.35	61.50	71.50
1950 Annualized	1.088	65.50	49.50		115	137	162

PM Components	Labor-hrs.	W	M	Q	S	A
PM System E1095 354 2950						
Mixer, floor, electric						
1 Check with operating or area personnel for any deficiencies.	.044			√	√	√
2 Check operation of mixer at varying speeds for excessive noise and vibrations; align or adjust as required.	.120			√	√	√
3 Tighten loose bolts, nuts, and screws.	.005			√	√	√
4 Check oil level in transmission; add or replace oil if required.	.159			√	√	√
5 Lubricate mixer gears and bowl lift mechanism.	.042			√	√	√
6 Check switches and control for damage and proper operation; adjust as required.	.068			√	√	√
7 Check belt for proper tension and alignment; adjust as required.	.029			√	√	√
8 Clean machine of dust and grease.	.030			√	√	√
9 Check anchor bolts for tightness; tighten as required.	.010			√	√	√
10 Clean area around equipment.	.066			√	√	√
11 Fill out maintenance checklist and report deficiencies.	.022			√	√	√
Total labor-hours/period				.595	.595	.595
Total labor-hours/year				1.190	.595	.595

			Cost Each				
			2012 Bare Costs			**Total**	**Total**
Description	**Labor-hrs.**	**Material**	**Labor**	**Equip.**	**Total**	**In-House**	**w/O&P**
2900 Mixer, floor, electric, annually	.595	74	27		101	117	137
2950 Annualized	2.380	98.50	108		206.50	251	299

PM Components	Labor-hrs.	W	M	Q	S	A
PM System E1095 356 1950						
Oven, convection, gas/electric						
1 Check with operating or area personnel for any deficiencies.	.044		√	√	√	√
2 Check doors and seals for warping and misalignment; lubricate hinges and repair as necessary.	.027		√	√	√	√
3 Check piping and valves for leaks.	.077		√	√	√	√
4 Check nuts, bolts, and screws for tightness; replace or tighten as required.	.005		√	√	√	√
5 Check pilot and gas burner for uniform flame; adjust as required.	.083		√	√	√	√
6 Check element, switches, controls and wiring on electrically heated units for defects; repair as required.	.120		√	√	√	√
7 Check fan blades and fan motor for proper operation.	.120		√	√	√	√
8 Check operation of thermostat; calibrate as required.	.439		√	√	√	√
9 Fill out maintenance checklist and report deficiencies.	.022		√	√	√	√
Total labor-hours/period			.937	.937	.937	.937
Total labor-hours/year			7.496	1.874	.937	.937

			Cost Each				
			2012 Bare Costs			**Total**	**Total**
Description	**Labor-hrs.**	**Material**	**Labor**	**Equip.**	**Total**	**In-House**	**w/O&P**
1900 Oven, convection, gas / electric, annually	.937	82	42.50		124.50	146	172
1950 Annualized	11.244	82	510		592	760	935

PM Components	Labor-hrs.	W	M	Q	S	A
PM System E1095 356 2950						
Oven, rotary, electric						
1 Check with operating or area personnel for any deficiencies.	.044		√	√	√	√
2 Remove and reinstall access panel; lubricate main bearing bushings.	.064		√	√	√	√
3 Turn motor on and check operation of chain drive mechanism; lubricate chain.	.064		√	√	√	√
4 Inspect motor and wiring; sensory inspect motor and bearings for overheating; lubricate motor bearings.	.055		√	√	√	√
5 Check V-belt; adjust tension and/or pulley as required.	.029		√	√	√	√
6 Inspect shelves for defects and level if required.	.142		√	√	√	√
7 Tighten or replace any loose nuts, bolts, screws.	.005		√	√	√	√
8 Check thermostat with thermometer; adjust as required.	.439		√	√	√	√
9 Check operation of stop and reverse switch.	.008		√	√	√	√
10 Check timer mechanism and operation.	.018		√	√	√	√
11 Check lubricant in gear case; add as required.	.055		√	√	√	√
12 Check ventilator for proper operation.	.160		√	√	√	√
13 Clean area around equipment.	.066		√	√	√	√
14 Fill out maintenance checklist and report deficiencies.	.022		√	√	√	√
Total labor-hours/period			1.171	1.171	1.171	1.171
Total labor-hours/year			9.368	2.342	1.171	1.171

			Cost Each				
			2012 Bare Costs			**Total**	**Total**
Description	**Labor-hrs.**	**Material**	**Labor**	**Equip.**	**Total**	**In-House**	**w/O&P**
2900 Oven, rotary, electric, annually	1.171	271	53		324	370	425
2950 Annualized	14.052	360	640		1,000	1,225	1,475

PM Components	Labor-hrs.	W	M	Q	S	A
PM System E1095 356 3950						
Oven, rotary, gas						
1 Check with operating or area personnel for any deficiencies.	.044		√	√	√	√
2 Examine doors and door gaskets; make necessary adjustments.	.021		√	√	√	√
3 Visually inspect hinges and latches; lubricate hinges.	.091		√	√	√	√
4 Remove and reinstall access panel; lubricate main bearing bushings.	.025		√	√	√	√
5 Turn motor on and chk. operation of chain drive mechanism; lubricate chain.	.064		√	√	√	√
6 Inspect motor and wiring; sensory inspect motor and bearings for overheating; lubricate motor bearings.	.055		√	√	√	√
7 Check V-belt; adjust tension and/or pulley as required.	.029		√	√	√	√
8 Check pilot and thermosensor bulb.	.042		√	√	√	√
9 Check gas burner for uniform flame.	.042		√	√	√	√
10 Check piping and valves for leaks.	.077		√	√	√	√
11 Inspect shelves for defects and level if required.	.142		√	√	√	√
12 Tighten or replace any loose nuts, bolts, screws.	.005		√	√	√	√
13 Check thermostat with thermometer; calibrate if required.	.439		√	√	√	√
14 Check operation of stop and reverse switch.	.008		√	√	√	√
15 Check timer mechanism and operation.	.018		√	√	√	√
16 Check lubricant in gear case, add as required.	.055		√	√	√	√
17 Check ventilator for proper operation.	.160		√	√	√	√
18 Clean area around equipment.	.066		√	√	√	√
19 Fill out maintenance checklist and report deficiencies.	.022		√	√	√	√
Total labor-hours/period			1.405	1.405	1.405	1.405
Total labor-hours/year			11.240	2.810	1.405	1.405

			Cost Each				
			2012 Bare Costs			**Total**	**Total**
Description	Labor-hrs.	Material	Labor	Equip.	Total	In-House	w/O&P
3900 Oven, rotary, gas, annually	1.405	271	64		335	380	445
3950 Annualized	16.860	360	765		1,125	1,400	1,700

PM Components	Labor-hrs.	W	M	Q	S	A
PM System E1095 366 1950						
Peeler, vegetable, electric						
1 Check with operating or area personnel for any deficiencies.	.044			√	√	√
2 Check vegetable peeler for proper operation, including switches and controls; lubricate motor bearings.	.156			√	√	√
3 Lubricate vegetable peeler bushings, as required.	.062			√	√	√
4 Check door for loose hinges and latch fittings; adjust if required.	.007			√	√	√
5 Clean peeler of dust, grease, and food particles.	.014			√	√	√
6 Check piping and valves for leaks.	.077			√	√	√
7 Inspect abrasive disk.	.018			√	√	√
8 Tighten or replace loose, missing or damaged nuts, bolts, screws.	.005			√	√	√
9 Check belt for proper tension and alignment; adjust or replace as required.	.029			√	√	√
10 Fill out maintenance checklist and report deficiencies.	.022			√	√	√
Total labor-hours/period				.434	.434	.434
Total labor-hours/year				.868	.434	.434

			Cost Each				
			2012 Bare Costs			**Total**	**Total**
Description	Labor-hrs.	Material	Labor	Equip.	Total	In-House	w/O&P
1900 Peeler, vegetable, electric, annually	.434	41	19.70		60.70	71	83.50
1950 Annualized	1.736	65.50	79		144.50	176	210

PM Components	Labor-hrs.	W	M	Q	S	A
PM System E1095 368 1950						
Pie maker, electric						
1 Check with operating or area personnel for any deficiencies.	.044			√	√	√
2 Check electrical system for loose connections and frayed wiring; tighten connections as required.	.120			√	√	√
3 Check operation of motors and bearings for overheating; lubricate motor bearings.	.169			√	√	√
4 Check V-belt for alignment and proper tension; adjust or replace belt as required.	.345			√	√	√
5 Check drain drive and sprocket for excessive wear; lubricate if applicable.	.087			√	√	√
6 Tighten or replace loose, missing or damaged nuts, bolts or screws.	.005			√	√	√
7 Wipe clean the machine.	.096			√	√	√
8 Fill out maintenance checklist and report deficiencies.	.022			√	√	√
Total labor-hours/period				.888	.888	.888
Total labor-hours/year				1.776	.888	.888

	Description	Labor-hrs.	Material	Labor	Equip.	Total	Total In-House	Total w/O&P
			2012 Bare Costs					
1900	Pie maker, electric, annually	.888	90.50	40.50		131	153	179
1950	Annualized	3.552	115	161		276	340	405

PM Components	Labor-hrs.	W	M	Q	S	A
PM System E1095 370 1950						
Proofer, automatic, electric						
1 Check with operating or area personnel for any deficiencies.	.044			√	√	√
2 Check operation of electric motor, switches, controls and bearings; adjust, repair and lubricate as required.	.280			√	√	√
3 Check belt tension; adjust as required.	.029			√	√	√
4 Check chain drive operation for proper alignment and tension; repair as required.	.129			√	√	√
5 Check action of flour sifter mechanism, connecting linkage and conveyor; lubricate bushings as required.	.290			√	√	√
6 Check roller conveyor and connecting drive mechanism.	.113			√	√	√
7 Check door latch; adjust if needed.	.014			√	√	√
8 Check nuts, bolts and screws for tightness; replace or tighten as required.	.029			√	√	√
9 Fill out maintenance checklist and report deficiencies.	.022			√	√	√
Total labor-hours/period				.950	.950	.950
Total labor-hours/year				1.900	.950	.950

	Description	Labor-hrs.	Material	Labor	Equip.	Total	Total In-House	Total w/O&P
			2012 Bare Costs					
1900	Proofer, automatic, electric, annually	.950	131	43		174	201	234
1950	Annualized	3.800	156	173		329	400	475

PM Components	Labor-hrs.	W	M	Q	S	A
PM System E1095 380 1950						
Refrigerator, domestic						
1 Check with operating or area personnel for deficiencies.	.035					√
2 Clean coils, fans, fan motors, drip pan and other areas with vacuum, brush or wiping as necessary.	.066					√
3 Inspect door gaskets for damage and proper fit; adjust gaskets as required and lubricate hinges.	.022					√
4 Check door latch and adjust as necessary.	.023					√
5 Clean area around equipment.	.066					√
6 Fill out maintenance checklist and report deficiencies.	.022					√
Total labor-hours/period						.234
Total labor-hours/year						.234

Description	Labor-hrs.	2012 Bare Costs				Total In-House	Total w/O&P
		Material	Labor	Equip.	Total		
1900 Refrigerator, domestic, annually	.234	16.40	10.60		27	32	38
1950 Annualized	.234	16.40	10.60		27	32	38

PM Components	Labor-hrs.	W	M	Q	S	A
PM System E1095 380 2950						
Refrigerator, display case						
1 Check with operating or area personnel for deficiencies.	.035					√
2 Clean coils, fans, fan motors, drip pan and other areas with vacuum, brush or wiping as necessary.	.066					√
3 Inspect door gaskets for damage and proper fit; adjust gaskets as required and lubricate hinges.	.044					√
4 Check door latch and adjust as necessary.	.047					√
5 Clean area around equipment.	.066					√
6 Fill out maintenance checklist and report deficiencies.	.022					√
Total labor-hours/period						.280
Total labor-hours/year						.280

Description	Labor-hrs.	2012 Bare Costs				Total In-House	Total w/O&P
		Material	Labor	Equip.	Total		
2900 Refrigerator, display case, annually	.280	16.40	12.70		29.10	35	41
2950 Annualized	.280	16.40	12.70		29.10	35	41

PM Components	Labor-hrs.	W	M	Q	S	A
PM System E1095 380 3950						
Refrigerator/display, walk-in w/external condenser						
1 Check with operating or area personnel for deficiencies.	.035				√	√
2 Clean condenser coils, fans, and intake screens; lubricate motor.	.066				√	√
3 Inspect door gaskets for damage and proper fit; adjust gaskets as required and lubricate hinges.	.137				√	√
4 Check starter panels and controls for proper operation, burned or loose contacts, and loose connections.	.182				√	√
5 Clean coils, evaporator drain pan, blowers, fans, motors and drain piping as required; lubricate motor(s).	.473				√	√
6 During operation of unit, check refrigerant pressures and compressor oil level; add refrigerant and/or oil as necessary.	.066				√	√
7 Check operation of low pressure cut-out; adjust or replace as required.	.047				√	√
8 Inspect defrost systems for proper operation; adjust as required.	.094				√	√
9 Clean area around equipment.	.066				√	√
10 Fill out maintenance checklist and report deficiencies.	.022				√	√
Total labor-hours/period					1.188	1.188
Total labor-hours/year					1.188	1.188

			Cost Each					
			2012 Bare Costs				Total	Total
Description		Labor-hrs.	Material	Labor	Equip.	Total	In-House	w/O&P
3900	Refrig. display, walk-in w/ ext. condenser, annually	1.188	41	54		95	116	139
3950	Annualized	2.376	49.50	108		157.50	197	237

PM Components	Labor-hrs.	W	M	Q	S	A
PM System E1095 382 1950						
Refrigerator/freezer, walk-in box w/external condenser						
1 Check with operating or area personnel for deficiencies.	.035				✓	✓
2 Clean condenser coils, fans, and intake screens; lubricate motor.	.036				✓	✓
3 Inspect door gaskets for damage and proper fit; adjust gaskets as required and lubricate hinges.	.022				✓	✓
4 Check starter panels and controls for proper operation, burned or loose contacts, and loose connections.	.182				✓	✓
5 Clean coils, evaporator drain pan, blowers, fans, motors and drain piping as required; lubricate motor(s).	.114				✓	✓
6 During operation of unit, check refrigerant pressures and compressor oil level; add refrigerant and/or oil as necessary.	.083				✓	✓
7 Check operation of low pressure cut-out; adjust or replace as required.	.079				✓	✓
8 Inspect defrost systems for proper operation; adjust as required.	.094				✓	✓
9 Clean area around equipment.	.066				✓	✓
10 Fill out maintenance checklist and report deficiencies.	.022				✓	✓
Total labor-hours/period					.733	.733
Total labor-hours/year					.733	.733

			Cost Each				
			2012 Bare Costs			**Total**	**Total**
Description	Labor-hrs.	Material	Labor	Equip.	Total	In-House	w/O&P
1900 Refrig. freezer, walk-in box w/ext. condenser, annually	.733	41	33.50		74.50	89	105
1950 Annualized	1.466	49.50	66.50		116	142	170

PM Components	Labor-hrs.	W	M	Q	S	A
PM System E1095 382 2950						
Refrigerator unit/display case/freezer w/external condenser						
1 Check with operating or area personnel for deficiencies.	.035				✓	✓
2 Clean condenser coils, fans, and intake screens; lubricate motor.	.504				✓	✓
3 Inspect door gaskets for damage and proper fit; adjust gaskets as required and lubricate hinges.	.033				✓	✓
4 Check starter panels and controls for proper operation, burned or loose contacts, and loose connections.	.213				✓	✓
5 Clean coils, evaporator drain pan, blowers, fans, motors and drain piping as required; lubricate motor(s).	.473				✓	✓
6 During operation of unit, check refrigerant pressures and compressor oil level; add refrigerant and/or oil as necessary.	.066				✓	✓
7 Check operation of low pressure cut-out; adjust or replace as required.	.057				✓	✓
8 Inspect defrost systems for proper operation; adjust as required.	.027				✓	✓
9 Clean area around equipment.	.066				✓	✓
10 Fill out maintenance checklist and report deficiencies.	.022				✓	✓
Total labor-hours/period					1.496	1.496
Total labor-hours/year					1.496	1.496

			Cost Each				
			2012 Bare Costs			**Total**	**Total**
Description	Labor-hrs.	Material	Labor	Equip.	Total	In-House	w/O&P
2900 Refrig., display case, freezer w/ ext. cond., annually	1.496	16.40	68		84.40	107	131
2950 Annualized	2.992	33	136		169	216	262

PM Components	Labor-hrs.	W	M	Q	S	A
PM System E1095 386 1950						
Steam table						
1 Check with operating or area personnel for any deficiencies.	.044			√	√	√
2 Inspect water compartment, steam coil, valves, and piping for leaks.	.117			√	√	√
3 Check steam trap and strainer; clean as required.	.306			√	√	√
4 Check operation of pressure regulating valve and gauge.	.035			√	√	√
5 Check pilots and flame on gas burner units; adjust as required.	.085			√	√	√
6 Check insulators, connections, and wiring, if applicable; tighten connections.	.120			√	√	√
7 Check condition of covers and receptacles; adjust as required.	.025			√	√	√
8 Check thermostat and temperature gauge; calibrate thermostat if necessary.	.152			√	√	√
9 Fill out maintenance checklist and report deficiencies.	.022			√	√	√
Total labor-hours/period				.906	.906	.906
Total labor-hours/year				1.812	.906	.906

			Cost Each				
			2012 Bare Costs			Total	Total
Description	Labor-hrs.	Material	Labor	Equip.	Total	In-House	w/O&P
1900 Steam table, annually	.906	82	41		123	144	170
1950 Annualized	3.624	82	165		247	305	370

PM Components	Labor-hrs.	W	M	Q	S	A
PM System E1095 388 1950						
Steamer, vegetable, direct connected units						
1 Check with operating or area personnel for any deficiencies.	.044			√	√	√
2 Inspect doors, door hardware and gaskets; lubricate hinges.	.112			√	√	√
3 Tighten or replace loose, missing, or damaged nuts, bolts, screws.	.005			√	√	√
4 Check for clogged or defective steam and strainers; clean as required.	.304			√	√	√
5 Check working pressure on steam gauge and inspect piping, valves, and doors for leaks; make necessary repairs as required.	.082			√	√	√
6 Check operation of pressure relief valve, low water cut-off, timer operation and water level in sight glass.	.065			√	√	√
7 Fill out maintenance checklist and report deficiencies.	.022			√	√	√
Total labor-hours/period				.634	.634	.634
Total labor-hours/year				1.268	.634	.634

			Cost Each				
			2012 Bare Costs			Total	Total
Description	Labor-hrs.	Material	Labor	Equip.	Total	In-House	w/O&P
1900 Steamer, vegetable, annually	.634	82	29		111	128	150
1950 Annualized	2.536	82	115		197	242	290

PM Components	Labor-hrs.	W	M	Q	S	A
PM System E1095 390 1950						
Toaster, rotary, gas/electric						
1 Check with operating or area personnel for any deficiencies.	.044			√	√	√
2 Check operation of toaster by toasting sample slice of bread.	.034			√	√	√
3 Clean toaster.	.014			√	√	√
4 Check valves and piping for leaks on gas units.	.077			√	√	√
5 Check pilot light and burner flame on gas units; adjust when required.	.017			√	√	
6 Check insulators, heating elements, connections, and wiring on electric units; tighten connections and repair as necessary.	.134			√	√	√
7 Inspect alignment of baskets and conveyor chains; lubricate chains and align as necessary.	.044			√	√	√
8 Check motor and motor bearings for overheating; lubricate motor bearings.	.086			√	√	√
9 Tighten or replace loose, missing or damaged nuts, bolts, screws.	.005			√	√	√
10 Fill out maintenance checklist and report deficiencies.	.022			√	√	√
Total labor-hours/period				.477	.477	.477
Total labor-hours/year				.954	.477	.477

				Cost Each				
				2012 Bare Costs			Total	Total
	Description	Labor-hrs.	Material	Labor	Equip.	Total	In-House	w/O&P
1900	Toaster, rotary, gas / electric, annually	.477	41	21.50		62.50	73.50	86.50
1950	Annualized	1.908	65.50	86.50		152	186	223

PM Components	Labor-hrs.	W	M	Q	S	A
PM System E1095 930 1950						
Vacuum						
1 Check with operating or area personnel for deficiencies.	.035				√	√
2 Check for leaks on suction and discharge piping, seals, etc.	.077				√	√
3 Check pump and motor operation for excessive vibration, noise and overheating.	.022				√	√
4 Check alignment and clearances of shaft and coupler.	.260				√	√
5 Tighten or replace loose, missing, or damaged nuts, bolts and screws.	.005				√	√
6 Lubricate pump and motor as required.	.099				√	√
7 Clean pump, motor and surrounding area.	.096				√	√
8 Fill out maintenance checklist and report deficiencies.	.022				√	√
Total labor-hours/period					.616	.616
Total labor-hours/year					.616	.616

				Cost Each				
				2012 Bare Costs			Total	Total
	Description	Labor-hrs.	Material	Labor	Equip.	Total	In-House	w/O&P
1900	Vacuum, annually	.616	7.50	33.50		41	50.50	62
1950	Annualized	1.232	15.05	67.50		82.55	101	124

PM Components	Labor-hrs.	W	M	Q	S	A
PM System F1045 110 1950						
Swimming pool						
Quantities of chemicals used vary significantly by climate and pool usage, therefore the price of these materials are not provided.						
1 Clean strainer basket.	.050	√	√	√	√	√
2 Backwash pool water filter.	.120	√	√	√	√	√
3 Add soda ash to feeder.	.080	√	√	√	√	√
4 Clean/flush soda ash pump head.	.400		√	√	√	√
5 Check chlorine, change bottles and check for leaks.	.120	√	√	√	√	√
6 Clean chlorine pump, flush with acid, and check for signs of deterioration	.200		√	√	√	√
7 Check acid source, add acid, check for leaks.	.100	√	√	√	√	√
8 Clean acid pump head.	.400		√	√	√	√
9 Check circulating pump for leaks and unusual noises. Lubricate as required.	.050	√	√	√	√	√
10 Check diving board, tighten or replace missing hardware. Inspect for structural defects or deterioration.	.080	√	√	√	√	√
11 Wash exposed stainless steel ladders and scum gutters with tap water to remove oil and dirt.	.300	√	√	√	√	√
12 Fill out maintenance report.	.017	√	√	√	√	√
Total labor-hours/period		.917	1.917	1.917	1.917	1.917
Total labor-hours/year		34.846	15.336	3.834	1.917	1.917

			Cost Each					
			2012 Bare Costs				Total	Total
Description		Labor-hrs.	Material	Labor	Equip.	Total	In-House	w/O&P
1900	Swimming pool outdoor, annually	1.917		87		87	115	141
1950	Annualized	57.849		2,625		2,625	3,450	4,275

PM Components	Labor-hrs.	W	M	Q	S	A
PM System G2015 610 1950						
Traffic signal light						
1 Inspect and clean control cabinet.	.030					√
2 Check wiring for obvious defects and tighten control electrical connections.	.090					√
3 Check operation of cabinet exhaust fan and inspect vents.	.020					√
4 Inspect and tighten power line connections to control cabinet.	.034					√
5 Check operation of cabinet heater.	.037					√
6 Perform the following operational checks of traffic controller.	.082			√	√	√
A) Check controller phase timing with stop watch.						
B) Check controller pedestrian phase timing with stop watch.						
C) Check controller clocks for correct time and log settings.						
7 Walk a circuit of the intersection to ensure all lights are functioning, replace bulbs as required.	.070			√	√	√
8 Check operation of pedestrian push buttons, average two per intersection.	.084			√	√	√
9 Check operation of all informational signs.	.042			√	√	√
10 Check operation of phase detectors (loop amplifiers).	.144			√	√	√
11 Visually inspect road sensors.	.074			√	√	√
12 Check operation of flashers.	.018					√
13 Fill out maintenance checklist and report deficiencies.	.017			√	√	√
Total labor-hours/period				.513	.513	.742
Total labor-hours/year				1.026	.513	.742

	Description	Labor-hrs.	Cost Each				Total In-House	Total w/O&P
			2012 Bare Costs					
			Material	Labor	Equip.	Total		
1900	Traffic signal light, annually	.742		38.50		38.50	47	59
1950	Annualized	2.281		118		118	145	182

PM Components	Labor-hrs.	W	M	Q	S	A
PM System G2045 150 1950						
Manual swing gate						
1 Check gate and hinge alignment.	.325				√	√
2 Tighten diagonal brace turnbuckle.	.108				√	√
3 Check cane bolt alignment.	.108				√	√
4 Grease hinges.	.217				√	√
5 Oil latch.	.108				√	√
Total labor-hours/period					.866	.866
Total labor-hours/year					.866	.866

		Cost Each					
			2012 Bare Costs			Total	Total
Description	Labor-hrs.	Material	Labor	Equip.	Total	In-House	w/O&P
1900 Manual swing gate, annually	.866	7.50	30.50		38	49	59.50
1950 Annualized	1.732	7.50	61		68.50	89.50	109

PM Components	Labor-hrs.	W	M	Q	S	A
PM System G2045 150 2950						
Electric swing gate						
1 Check gate and hinge alignment.	.325				√	√
2 Tighten diagonal brace turnbuckle.	.108				√	√
3 Check cane bolt alignment.	.108				√	√
4 Grease hinges.	.217				√	√
5 Oil latch.	.108				√	√
6 Check electric motor and connections.	.325				√	√
7 Grease gearbox.	.217				√	√
Total labor-hours/period					1.408	1.408
Total labor-hours/year					1.408	1.408

		Cost Each					
			2012 Bare Costs			Total	Total
Description	Labor-hrs.	Material	Labor	Equip.	Total	In-House	w/O&P
2900 Electric swing gate, annually	1.408	7.50	49.50		57	74.50	90.50
2950 Annualized	2.816	7.50	99		106.50	140	171

PM Components	Labor-hrs.	W	M	Q	S	A
PM System G2045 150 3950						
Manual slide gate						
1 Check alignment of rollers and gate.	.325				√	√
2 Grease rollers.	.325				√	√
3 Oil latch.	.108				√	√
Total labor-hours/period					.758	.758
Total labor-hours/year					.758	.758

		Cost Each					
			2012 Bare Costs			Total	Total
Description	Labor-hrs.	Material	Labor	Equip.	Total	In-House	w/O&P
3900 Manual slide gate, annually	.758	7.50	26.50		34	44	53
3950 Annualized	1.516	7.50	53		60.50	79.50	97

PM Components	Labor-hrs.	W	M	Q	S	A
PM System G2045 150 4950						
Electric slide gate						
1　Check alignment of rollers and gate.	.325				√	√
2　Grease rollers.	.325				√	√
3　Oil latch.	.108				√	√
4　Check electric motor and connections.	.325				√	√
5　Clean and grease chain.	.650			√	√	√
Total labor-hours/period				.650	1.733	1.733
Total labor-hours/year				1.300	1.733	1.733

	Description	Labor-hrs.	Cost Each				Total In-House	Total w/O&P
			2012 Bare Costs					
			Material	Labor	Equip.	Total		
4900	Electric slide gate, annually	1.733	7.50	61		68.50	89.50	109
4950	Annualized	4.766	7.50	167		174.50	231	283

PM Components	Labor-hrs.	W	M	Q	S	A
PM System G3015 108 1950						
Storage tank, tower						
1 Inspect exterior of tank for leaks or damage, including tank base and base plates.	.151					√
2 Inspect condition of ladders, sway bracing hardware and structural forms.	.624					√
3 Tighten and lubricate altitude valve and inspect valve vault.	.039					√
4 Check operation of storage tank lighting.	.121					√
5 Check cathodic protection system.	.122					√
6 Operate elevated tank heat system, if installed, and inspect insulation and coils.	.107					√
7 Clean up around tank area.	.134					√
8 Fill out maintenance checklist and report deficiencies.	.022					√
Total labor-hours/period						1.320
Total labor-hours/year						1.320

		Cost Each						
			2012 Bare Costs				Total	Total
Description	Labor-hrs.	Material	Labor	Equip.	Total	In-House	w/O&P
1900	Storage tank, tower, annually	1.320	15.05	60		75.05	95.50	116
1950	Annualized	1.320	15.05	60		75.05	95.50	116

PM Components	Labor-hrs.	W	M	Q	S	A
PM System G3015 108 2950						
Storage tank, ground level						
1 Inspect exterior of tank for leaks or damage.	.053					√
2 Check condition of roof and roof hatches including locks; remove trash from roof.	.147					√
3 Inspect condition of ladders and tighten or replace missing hardware.	.088					√
4 Inspect valves, fittings, drains and controls for leakage or damage.	.039					√
5 Check for deterioration of tank foundation.	.077					√
6 Inspect ground drainage slope, and vent screens; where applicable.	.043					√
7 Inspect tank lighting system; replace bulbs as needed.	.121					√
8 Clean up around tank.	.134					√
9 Fill out maintenance checklist and report deficiencies.	.022					√
Total labor-hours/period						.724
Total labor-hours/year						.724

		Cost Each						
			2012 Bare Costs				Total	Total
Description	Labor-hrs.	Material	Labor	Equip.	Total	In-House	w/O&P
2900	Storage tank, ground level, annually	.724	15.05	33		48.05	60	72.50
2950	Annualized	.724	15.05	33		48.05	60	72.50

PM Components	Labor-hrs.	W	M	Q	S	A
PM System G3015 116 1950						
Water flow meter, turbine						
1 Inspect meter for leaks, corrosion or broken sight glass; replace broken glass as required.	.035				√	√
2 Check meter operation for unusual noise.	.034				√	√
3 Clean meter to remove mineral buildup.	.039				√	√
4 Clean out trash or sludge from bottom of pit.	.165				√	√
5 Fill out maintenance report and report deficiencies.	.022				√	√
Total labor-hours/period					.295	.295
Total labor-hours/year					.295	.295

			Cost Each					
			2012 Bare Costs				Total	Total
	Description	Labor-hrs.	Material	Labor	Equip.	Total	In-House	w/O&P
1900	Water flow meter, turbine, annually	.295	15.05	13.40		28.45	34	41
1950	Annualized	.590	15.05	27		42.05	52	62.50

PM Components	Labor-hrs.	W	M	Q	S	A
PM System G3015 118 1950						
Fresh water distribution reservoir controls						
1 Check with reservoir personnel for any known deficiencies.	.086			√	√	√
2 Visually inspect and clean interior and exterior of controls cabinet.	.061			√	√	√
3 Inspect electrical system for frayed wires or loose connections; repair as required.	.120			√	√	√
4 Inspect water level receiver at reservoir.	.192			√	√	√
5 Inspect and adjust chronoflo transmitter.	.467			√	√	√
6 Perform operational check of relays, safety switches and electrical contactors.	.542			√	√	√
7 Perform operational check of controls system.	.659			√	√	√
8 Clean up controls area and dispose of debris.	.066			√	√	√
9 Fill out maintenance checklist and report deficiencies.	.022			√	√	√
Total labor-hours/period				2.215	2.215	2.215
Total labor-hours/year				4.430	2.215	2.215

			Cost Each					
			2012 Bare Costs				Total	Total
	Description	Labor-hrs.	Material	Labor	Equip.	Total	In-House	w/O&P
1900	Reservoir controls, fresh water distribution, annually	2.215	30	101		131	165	201
1950	Annualized	8.860	30	400		430	560	695

PM Components	Labor-hrs.	W	M	Q	S	A
PM System G3015 126 0950						
Pump, air lift, well						
1 Check with pump operating personnel for any known deficiencies.	.035				√	√
2 Check operation of compressor and pump.	.033				√	√
3 Check water sample for air or oil contamination.	.009				√	√
4 Check compressor oil level; add oil as necessary and lubricate pump and compressor shaft bearings as applicable.	.121				√	√
5 Inspect electrical system for frayed wires or loose connections; repair as required.	.120				√	√
6 Check and cycle high and low shut off valves.	.130				√	√
7 Inspect and clean air intake filter.	.094				√	√
8 Clean pump body and tighten or replace loose hardware.	.086				√	√
9 Calibrate and adjust pressure gauge.	.191				√	√
10 Clean surrounding area.	.066				√	√
11 Fill out maintenance checklist and report deficiencies.	.022				√	√
Total labor-hours/period					.907	.907
Total labor-hours/year					.907	.907

		Cost Each					
		2012 Bare Costs				**Total**	**Total**
Description	Labor-hrs.	Material	Labor	Equip.	Total	In-House	w/O&P
0900 Pump, air lift, well, annually	.907	15.05	41		56.05	71	86
0950 Annualized	1.814	30	82.50		112.50	141	172

PM Components	Labor-hrs.	W	M	Q	S	A
PM System G3015 126 1950						
Pump, centrifugal ejector						
1 Check for proper operation of pump.	.022				√	√
2 Check for leaks on suction and discharge piping, seals, packing glands, etc.; make minor adjustments as required.	.077				√	√
3 Check pump and motor operation for excessive vibration, noise and overheating.	.022				√	√
4 Check alignment of pump and motor; adjust as necessary.	.260				√	√
5 Lubricate pump and motor.	.099				√	√
6 Clean exterior of pump, motor and surrounding area.	.096				√	√
7 Fill out maintenance checklist and report deficiencies.	.022				√	√
Total labor-hours/period					.598	.598
Total labor-hours/year					.598	.598

		Cost Each					
		2012 Bare Costs				**Total**	**Total**
Description	Labor-hrs.	Material	Labor	Equip.	Total	In-House	w/O&P
1900 Pump, centrifugal ejector, annually	.598	7.50	27		34.50	44.50	53.50
1950 Annualized	1.196	15.05	54.50		69.55	88	107

PM Components	Labor-hrs.	W	M	Q	S	A
PM System G3015 126 3950						
Pump, metering (slurry)						
1 Check with pump operating personnel for any obvious deficiencies.	.035				√	√
2 Obtain and put on safety equipment for working with fluoride: goggles, apron, gloves and respirator.	.014				√	√
3 Check oil level in pump with dipstick; add oil as necessary.	.009				√	√
4 Inspect belt condition and tension on pump; adjust as required.	.029				√	√
5 Flush slurry pump with fresh water.	.139				√	√
6 Pressure test pump.	.012				√	√
7 Inspect pump motor.	.039				√	√
8 Operate pump and check for leaks, excessive noise and vibration.	.099				√	√
9 Clean up area.	.066				√	√
10 Fill out maintenance checklist and report deficiencies.	.022				√	√
Total labor-hours/period					.464	.464
Total labor-hours/year					.464	.464

			Cost Each				
			2012 Bare Costs			Total	Total
Description	Labor-hrs.	Material	Labor	Equip.	Total	In-House	w/O&P
3900 Pump, metering (slurry), annually	.464	15.05	21		36.05	44.50	53
3950 Annualized	.928	30	42		72	88.50	106

PM Components	Labor-hrs.	W	M	Q	S	A
PM System G3015 126 4950						
Pump, mixed or axial flow velocity						
1 Check with pump operating personnel for any obvious deficiencies.	.035				√	√
2 Clean pump exterior.	.014				√	√
3 Check impeller and shaft for correct alignment and clearances.	.031				√	√
4 Check oil level; add oil as needed.	.009				√	√
5 Inspect packing for leaks and tighten as needed.	.031				√	√
6 Inspect bearings for wear, damage or overheating; lubricate as required.	.053				√	√
7 Inspect float operation and adjust as needed.	.098				√	√
8 Inspect V-belt tension and condition; adjust as required.	.029				√	√
9 Operate pump and check for leaks, excessive noise and vibration.	.099				√	√
10 Tighten loose nuts and bolts and replace missing hardware.	.005				√	√
11 Check electrical system for frayed wires and loose connections.	.120				√	√
12 Clean up area.	.066				√	√
13 Fill out maintenance checklist and report deficiencies.	.022				√	√
Total labor-hours/period					.612	.612
Total labor-hours/year					.612	.612

			Cost Each				
			2012 Bare Costs			Total	Total
Description	Labor-hrs.	Material	Labor	Equip.	Total	In-House	w/O&P
4900 Pump, mixed or axial flow, annually	.612	15.05	28		43.05	53	64
4950 Annualized	1.224	30	55.50		85.50	106	128

PM Components	Labor-hrs.	W	M	Q	S	A
PM System G3015 126 5950						
Pump, reciprocating positive displacement						
1 Check for proper operation of pump.	.022				√	√
2 Check for leaks on suction and discharge piping, seals, packing glands, etc.; make minor adjustments as required.	.077				√	√
3 Check pump and motor operation for excessive vibration, noise and overheating.	.022				√	√
4 Check operation of pressure controls.	.133				√	√
5 Check alignment of pump and motor; adjust as necessary.	.260				√	√
6 Lubricate pump and motor.	.099				√	√
7 Clean exterior of pump, motor and surrounding area.	.094				√	√
8 Fill out maintenance checklist and report deficiencies.	.022				√	√
Total labor-hours/period					.729	.729
Total labor-hours/year					.729	.729

		Cost Each					
			2012 Bare Costs			Total	Total
Description	Labor-hrs.	Material	Labor	Equip.	Total	In-House	w/O&P
5900 Pump, reciprocating displacement, annually	.729	7.50	33		40.50	52.50	63.50
5950 Annualized	1.458	15.05	66		81.05	104	127

PM Components	Labor-hrs.	W	M	Q	S	A
PM System G3015 126 6950						
Pump, rotary positive displacement						
1 Check with operating personnel for obvious defects.	.035				√	√
2 Clean surface of pump with solvent.	.014				√	√
3 Operate pump and check for leaks at pipes and connections and for excessive noise and vibration.	.099				√	√
4 Lubricate pump.	.047				√	√
5 Check shaft alignment and clearances and pump rotation.	.031				√	√
6 Inspect packing for leaks and tighten.	.031				√	√
7 Tighten loose bolts and nuts; replace loose and missing hardware as needed.	.009				√	√
8 Inspect electrical system for loose connections and frayed wires; repair as necessary.	.120				√	√
9 Operate pump upon completion of maintenance, read and record pressure gauge readings and check discharge pressure.	.221				√	√
10 Clean up area around pump after repairs.	.066				√	√
11 Fill out maintenance checklist and report deficiencies.	.022				√	√
Total labor-hours/period					.695	.695
Total labor-hours/year					.695	.695

		Cost Each					
			2012 Bare Costs			Total	Total
Description	Labor-hrs.	Material	Labor	Equip.	Total	In-House	w/O&P
6900 Pump, rotary displacement, annually	.695	7.50	31.50		39	50.50	61
6950 Annualized	1.390	15.05	63		78.05	99.50	122

PM Components	Labor-hrs.	W	M	Q	S	A
PM System G3015 126 7950						
Pump, sump, up to 1 H.P.						
1 Check electrical plug, cord and connections.	.120				√	√
2 Activate float switch and check pump for proper operation.	.039				√	√
3 Lubricate pump as required.	.047				√	√
4 Inspect packing and tighten as required.	.031				√	√
5 Check pump for misalignment and bearings for overheating.	.199				√	√
6 Clean out trash from sump.	.065				√	√
7 Fill out maintenance checklist and report deficiencies.	.022				√	√
Total labor-hours/period					.523	.523
Total labor-hours/year					.523	.523

			Cost Each				
			2012 Bare Costs			Total	Total
Description	Labor-hrs.	Material	Labor	Equip.	Total	In-House	w/O&P
7900 Pump, sump, up to 1 H.P., annually	.523	7.50	23.50		31	40	48
7950 Annualized	1.046	15.05	47.50		62.55	79	96

PM Components	Labor-hrs.	W	M	Q	S	A
PM System G3015 126 8950						
Pump, turbine, well						
1 Check with pump operating personnel for any known deficiencies.	.035				√	√
2 Remove turbine and pump from deep well.	.585				√	√
3 Inspect pump body, bowls, water passages and impeller for corrosion, wear or pitting; repair as necessary.	.057				√	√
4 Check packing for leaks; tighten or replace as necessary.	.325				√	√
5 Adjust impeller for optimum operation.	.228				√	√
6 Inspect wear ring clearances, thrust and pump bearings for wear; repair as necessary.	.142				√	√
7 Lubricate all pump parts as required.	.047				√	√
8 Clean suction strainer or replace if damaged.	.338				√	√
9 Inspect operation of discharge valve.	.026				√	√
10 Inspect electrical system for frayed wires or loose connections; repair as necessary.	.120				√	√
11 Check operation of pressure and thermal controls.	.052				√	√
12 Paint pump with underwater paint.	.259				√	√
13 Run pump and check for noise and vibration.	.022				√	√
14 Reinstall pump in deep well and test operation.	.585				√	√
15 Fill out maintenance checklist and report deficiencies.	.022				√	√
Total labor-hours/period					2.843	2.843
Total labor-hours/year					2.843	2.843

			Cost Each				
			2012 Bare Costs			Total	Total
Description	Labor-hrs.	Material	Labor	Equip.	Total	In-House	w/O&P
8900 Pump, turbine, well, annually	2.843	135	129		264	320	380
8950 Annualized	5.686	150	258		408	505	610

PM Components	Labor-hrs.	W	M	Q	S	A
PM System G3015 126 9950						
Pump, vacuum						
1 Check with pump operating personnel for any known deficiencies.	.035				√	√
2 Check for leaks on suction and discharge piping, seals, etc.	.077				√	√
3 Check pump and motor operation for vibration, noise, overheating, etc.	.022				√	√
4 Check alignment and clearances of shaft and coupler.	.260				√	√
5 Tighten or replace loose, missing, or damaged nuts, bolts, and screws.	.005				√	√
6 Lubricate pump and motor as required.	.099				√	√
7 Clean pump, motor and surrounding area.	.099				√	√
8 Fill out maintenance checklist and report deficiencies.	.022				√	√
Total labor-hours/period					.619	.619
Total labor-hours/year					.619	.619

			Cost Each					
			2012 Bare Costs				Total	Total
Description	Labor-hrs.	Material	Labor	Equip.	Total	In-House	w/O&P
9900 Pump, vacuum, annually	.619	7.50	28		35.50	45.50	55
9950 Annualized	1.238	15.05	56		71.05	90.50	110

PM Components	Labor-hrs.	W	M	Q	S	A
PM System G3015 310 1950						
Turbine well pump						
1 Check with operating personnel for any deficiencies.	.035				√	√
2 Remove turbine pump from deep well.	.585				√	√
3 Inspect pump body, bowls, water passages and impeller for corrosion, wear or pitting; repair as necessary.	.057				√	√
4 Check packing for leaks; tighten or repack as necessary.	.330				√	√
5 Adjust impeller for optimun operation.	.228				√	√
6 Inspect wear ring clearances, thrust and pump bearings for wear; repair as necessary.	.142				√	√
7 Lubricate all pump parts as required.	.047				√	√
8 Clean suction strainer or replace if damaged.	.338				√	√
9 Inspect operation of discharge valve.	.030				√	√
10 Inspect electrical system for frayed wires or loose connections; repair as necessary.	.120				√	√
11 Check operation of pressure and thermal controls.	.124				√	√
12 Paint pump with underwater paint.	.259				√	√
13 Run pump and check for noise and vibration.	.022				√	√
14 Reinstall pump in deep well and test operation.	.585				√	√
15 Fill out maintenance checklist and report deficiencies.	.022				√	√
Total labor-hours/period					2.924	2.924
Total labor-hours/year					2.924	2.924

	Description	Labor-hrs.	Cost Each						
			2012 Bare Costs				Total In-House	Total w/O&P	
			Material	Labor	Equip.	Total			
1900	Turbine well pump, annually	2.924	75	160		235	283	345	
1950	Annualized	5.848	150	320		470	565	685	

PM Components	Labor-hrs.	W	M	Q	S	A
PM System G3015 320 1950						
Vertical lift pump, over 1 H.P.						
1 Check for proper operation of pump.	.130				√	√
2 Check for leaks on suction and discharge piping, seals, packing glands, etc.; make minor adjustments as required.	.077				√	√
3 Check pump and motor operation for excessive vibration, noise and overheating.	.022				√	√
4 Check alignment of pump and motor; adjust as necessary.	.260				√	√
5 Lubricate pump and motor.	.099				√	√
6 When available, check and record suction or discharge gauge pressure and flow rate.	.022				√	√
7 Clean exterior of pump and surrounding area.	.096				√	√
8 Fill out maintenance checklist and report deficiencies.	.022				√	√
Total labor-hours/period					.728	.728
Total labor-hours/year					.728	.728

	Description	Labor-hrs.	Cost Each						
			2012 Bare Costs				Total In-House	Total w/O&P	
			Material	Labor	Equip.	Total			
1900	Vertical lift pump, over 1 H.P., annually	.728	30	40		70	82.50	99.50	
1950	Annualized	1.456	60	79.50		139.50	165	199	

G30 SITE MECH. UTILITIES | G3015 410 | Fire Hydrant

PM Components	Labor-hrs.	W	M	Q	S	A
PM System G3015 410 1950						
Fire hydrant						
1 Remove hydrant caps and check condition of gaskets; replace as required.	.241					√
2 Flush hydrant, lubricate cap threads and reinstall cap.	.374					√
3 Fill out maintenance checklist and report deficiencies.	.022					√
Total labor-hours/period						.637
Total labor-hours/year						.637

			Cost Each					
			2012 Bare Costs				Total	Total
Description		Labor-hrs.	Material	Labor	Equip.	Total	In-House	w/O&P
1900	Fire hydrant, annually	.637	7.35	34.50		41.85	51	62.50
1950	Annualized	.637	7.35	34.50		41.85	51	62.50

G30 SITE MECH. UTILITIES | G3015 420 | Valve, Post Indicator

PM Components	Labor-hrs.	W	M	Q	S	A
PM System G3015 420 1950						
Valve, post indicator						
1 Remove set screw, cap and wire seal.	.111				√	√
2 Apply lubricant to threads, open and close valve.	.293				√	√
3 Check operation of and sign and clean glass indicator windows.	.130				√	√
4 Install cap and tighten screw, install handle and wire seal with valve open.	.088				√	√
5 Clean valve exterior and area around valve.	.066				√	√
6 Fill out maintenance checklist and report deficiencies.	.022				√	√
Total labor-hours/period					.710	.710
Total labor-hours/year					.710	.710

			Cost Each					
			2012 Bare Costs				Total	Total
Description		Labor-hrs.	Material	Labor	Equip.	Total	In-House	w/O&P
1900	Valve, post indicator, annually	.710	7.35	38.50		45.85	56	69
1950	Annualized	1.420	7.35	77		84.35	104	129

PM Components	Labor-hrs.	W	M	Q	S	A
PM System G3015 612 1950						
Filter plant						
1 Check daily operating records for unusual occurances.	.035			√	√	√
2 Inspect plant sand or gravel filters.	.694			√	√	√
3 Inspect clear well for cleanliness.	.018			√	√	√
4 Inspect and lubricate flocculator chain and baffle mechanism and waste-line valves.	.163			√	√	√
5 Inspect and adjust rate-of-flow controller.	.036			√	√	√
6 Calibrate and adjust loss-of-head gauge.	.191			√	√	√
7 Inspect clear well vent screen and manhole.	.143			√	√	√
8 Inspect operation of pumps, water mixers, chemical feeders and flow measuring devices.	1.145			√	√	√
9 Check aerator nozzles for obstructions; clean as required.	.065			√	√	√
10 Drain, clean and inspect mixing chambers.	1.455					√
11 Drain sedimentation basins and clean with fire hose.	2.220					√
12 Drain, inspect and clean flocculator.	2.401					√
13 Clean up filter plant area.	.334			√	√	√
14 Fill out maintenance checklist and report deficiencies.	.022			√	√	√
Total labor-hours/period				2.846	2.846	8.922
Total labor-hours/year				5.692	2.846	8.922

			Cost Each					
			2012 Bare Costs				Total	Total
Description	Labor-hrs.	Material	Labor	Equip.	Total	In-House	w/O&P
1900 Filter plant, annually	8.922	7.50	485		492.50	615	770
1950 Annualized	17.460	30	955		985	1,225	1,525

PM Components	Labor-hrs.	W	M	Q	S	A
PM System G3015 630 1950						
Water de-ionization station						
1 Check with operating or area personnel for deficiencies.	.035				√	√
2 Check bulk storage tanks, pumps, valves and piping for damage, corrosion or leaks.	.130				√	√
3 Lubricate pumps.	.047				√	√
4 Check venting of bulk storage tanks.	.043				√	√
5 Check operation of sodium hydroxide tank and piping heating system.	.124				√	√
6 Check operation of resin vent, blower and motor; lubricate as required.	.033				√	√
7 Check calibration of meters.	.577				√	√
8 Clean and check probes of metering system.	.040				√	√
9 Check condition of carbon filter bed; replace annually.	.694					√
10 Check water softener system for proper operation.	.195				√	√
11 Clean equpment and surrounding area.	.066				√	√
12 Fill out maintenance checklist and report deficiencies.	.022				√	√
Total labor-hours/period					2.006	2.006
Total labor-hours/year					2.006	2.006

			Cost Each					
			2012 Bare Costs				Total	Total
Description	Labor-hrs.	Material	Labor	Equip.	Total	In-House	w/O&P
1900 Water de-ionization system, annually	2.006	293	110		403	460	535
1950 Annualized	4.012	300	219		519	605	715

PM Components	Labor-hrs.	W	M	Q	S	A
PM System G3015 632 1950						
Reverse osmosis system, 750 gallons/month						
1 Check with operating personnel for report of treatment effectiveness.	.046			√	√	√
2 Inspect unit, piping and connections for leaks.	.077			√	√	√
3 Check operation of pumps and motors; check shafts for alignment and lubricate as required.	.330			√	√	√
4 Inspect electrical system for frayed wires or loose connections; repair as required.	.120			√	√	√
5 Check filters; replace as required.	.036			√	√	√
6 Check water level controls; adjust as required.	.030			√	√	√
7 Check holding tank temperature control valve operation.	.030			√	√	√
8 Replace charcoal filters as indicated by water test.	.143			√	√	√
9 Check to ensure that chemical supply level is properly maintained in the chemical feed system.	.120			√	√	√
Total labor-hours/period				.932	.932	.932
Total labor-hours/year				1.864	.932	.932

			Cost Each					
			2012 Bare Costs				Total	Total
	Description	Labor-hrs.	Material	Labor	Equip.	Total	In-House	w/O&P
1900	Reverse osmosis system, annually	.932	52.50	42.50		95	114	135
1950	Annualized	3.728	165	169		334	405	480

PM Components	Labor-hrs.	W	M	Q	S	A
PM System G3015 634 1950						
Water ion exchange system						
1 Check with operating personnel for deficiencies.	.035			√	√	√
2 Clean unit and piping and check for leaks.	.077			√	√	√
3 Clean brine pump and check for proper operation.	.120			√	√	√
4 Clean and check strainers pilot valve, vents and orifices.	.595					√
5 Inspect electrical system including pump contactor and contacts; repair as required.	.120			√	√	√
6 Check regeneration cycle; make adjustments as required.	.325			√	√	√
7 Clean surrounding area.	.066			√	√	√
8 Fill out maintenance report and report deficiencies.	.022			√	√	√
Total labor-hours/period				.765	.765	1.360
Total labor-hours/year				1.530	.765	1.360

			Cost Each					
			2012 Bare Costs				Total	Total
	Description	Labor-hrs.	Material	Labor	Equip.	Total	In-House	w/O&P
1900	Water ion exchange system, annually	1.360		62		62	81.50	100
1950	Annualized	3.655		166		166	218	270

PM Components	Labor-hrs.	W	M	Q	S	A
PM System G3015 650 1950						
Water softener						
1 Check with building personnel for report of water softener effectiveness.	.086			√	√	√
2 Check pressure gauges for proper operation.	.191			√	√	√
3 Check density of brine solution in salt tank.	.124			√	√	√
4 Check operation of float control in brine.	.040			√	√	√
5 Inspect water softener piping, fittings and valves for leaks.	.077			√	√	√
6 Lubricate valves and motors.	.330			√	√	√
7 Make minor adjustments to water softener controls if required.	.014			√	√	√
8 Inspect softener base and brine tank for corrosion and repair as needed.	.259			√	√	√
9 Check operation of automatic fill valve in brine tank.	.030			√	√	√
10 Check softener electrical wiring and phasing.	.120			√	√	√
11 Clean up area around softener.	.066			√	√	√
12 Fill out maintenance report and report deficiencies.	.022			√	√	√
Total labor-hours/period				1.359	1.359	1.359
Total labor-hours/year				2.718	1.359	1.359

			Cost Each				
			2012 Bare Costs			Total	Total
Description	Labor-hrs.	Material	Labor	Equip.	Total	In-House	w/O&P
1900 Water softener, annually	1.359	15.05	61.50		76.55	98	119
1950 Annualized	5.436	15.05	247		262.05	340	420

PM Components	Labor-hrs.	W	M	Q	S	A
PM System G3015 660 1950						
Fluoride saturator						
1 Check with operating personnel for any obvious discrepancies.	.035		√	√	√	√
2 Obtain and put on safety equipment such as goggles, apron, gloves and respirator prior to working on the fluoride saturator.	.014		√	√	√	√
3 Check oil level in gearbox, agitator and injector pump; add oil as necessary.	.018		√	√	√	√
4 Check water level in fluoride mixing tank.	.007		√	√	√	√
5 Check operation of fluoride flow regulator, float switch and solenoid.	.127		√	√	√	√
6 Check saturator for leaks.	.077		√	√	√	√
7 Check operation of unit.	.098		√	√	√	√
8 Clean fluoride tank with brush and detergent.	.085		√	√	√	√
9 Clean surrounding area.	.066		√	√	√	√
10 Fill out maintenance checklist and report deficiencies.	.022		√	√	√	√
Total labor-hours/period			.549	.549	.549	.549
Total labor-hours/year			4.392	1.098	.549	.549

			Cost Each				
			2012 Bare Costs			Total	Total
Description	Labor-hrs.	Material	Labor	Equip.	Total	In-House	w/O&P
1900 Fluoride saturator, annually	.549	7.50	30		37.50	46	56
1950 Annualized	6.588	30	360		390	480	600

PM Components	Labor-hrs.	W	M	Q	S	A
PM System G3015 670 1950						
Chlorinator						
1 Check with operating or area personnel for deficiencies.	.035			√	√	√
2 Put on safety equipment prior to checking equipment.	.014			√	√	√
3 Clean chlorinator and check for leaks.	.057			√	√	√
4 Check water trap for proper level and bleed air.	.017			√	√	√
5 Check and clean water strainers.	.675			√	√	√
6 Grease fittings.	.023			√	√	√
7 Make minor adjustments to chlorinator as needed.	.094			√	√	√
8 Fill out maintenance checklist and report deficiencies.	.022			√	√	√
Total labor-hours/period				.937	.937	.937
Total labor-hours/year				1.874	.937	.937

		Cost Each						
			2012 Bare Costs				Total	Total
Description	Labor-hrs.	Material	Labor	Equip.	Total		In-House	w/O&P
1900 Chlorinator, annually	.937	7.50	51		58.50		72.50	89
1950 Annualized	3.748	15.05	205		220.05		272	340

PM Components	Labor-hrs.	W	M	Q	S	A
PM System G3015 670 2950						
Chlorine detector						
1 Put on safety equipment prior to checking equipment.	.014			√	√	√
2 Test alarm and inspect fan and sensor wiring.	.252			√	√	√
3 Test detector with chlorine test kit.	.044			√	√	√
4 Flush sensor unit with fresh water and drain and fill reservoir.	.068			√	√	√
5 Check drip rate and reservoir level in sight glass.	.013			√	√	√
6 Check "O" rings; replace as required.	.029			√	√	√
7 Inspect sensor mounting grommet, fan operation, detector mounting bolts and drain tube connection.	.147			√	√	√
8 Check charcoal filter cartridge; replace as needed.	.009			√	√	√
9 Check basket for cracked or worn areas.	.059			√	√	√
10 Check detector for leaks under pressure.	.077			√	√	√
11 Clean unit and surrounding area.	.066			√	√	√
12 Fill out maintenance checklist and report deficiencies.	.022			√	√	√
Total labor-hours/period				.800	.800	.800
Total labor-hours/year				1.600	.800	.800

		Cost Each						
			2012 Bare Costs				Total	Total
Description	Labor-hrs.	Material	Labor	Equip.	Total		In-House	w/O&P
2900 Chlorine detector, annually	.800	30	43.50		73.50		87.50	106
2950 Annualized	3.200	120	175		295		350	420

545

PM Components	Labor-hrs.	W	M	Q	S	A
PM System G3025 410 1950						
Ejector, pump, sewage						
1 Check for proper operation of pump.	.130				√	√
2 Check for leaks on suction and discharge piping, seals, packing glands, etc.; make minor adjustments as required.	.069				√	√
3 Check ejector and motor operation for excessive vibration, noise and overheating.	.022				√	√
4 Check float or pressure controls for proper operation.	.039				√	√
5 Lubricate ejector and motor.	.099				√	√
6 Clean pump unit and surrounding area.	.096				√	√
7 Fill out maintenance checklist and report deficiencies.	.022				√	√
Total labor-hours/period					.477	.477
Total labor-hours/year					.477	.477

	Description	Labor-hrs.	Material	Labor	Equip.	Total	Total In-House	Total w/O&P
1900	Ejector pump, sewage, annually	.477	7.50	26		33.50	41.50	50
1950	Annualized	.954	15.05	52		67.05	81.50	100

PM Components	Labor-hrs.	W	M	Q	S	A
PM System G3025 412 1950						
Ejector, pump						
1 Check for proper operation of pump.	.130				√	√
2 Check for leaks on suction and discharge piping, seals, packing glands, etc.; make minor adjustments as required.	.077				√	√
3 Check ejector and motor operation for excessive vibration, noise and overheating.	.022				√	√
4 Check float or pressure controls for proper operation.	.039				√	√
5 Lubricate ejector and motor.	.099				√	√
6 Clean pump unit and surrounding area.	.096				√	√
7 Fill out maintenance checklist and report deficiencies.	.022				√	√
Total labor-hours/period					.485	.485
Total labor-hours/year					.485	.485

		Cost Each						
			2012 Bare Costs				Total	Total
Description	Labor-hrs.	Material	Labor	Equip.	Total		In-House	w/O&P
1900 Ejector pump, annually	.485	8.50	22		30.50		38.50	46.50
1950 Annualized	.970	17	44		61		76.50	93

PM Components	Labor-hrs.	W	M	Q	S	A
PM System G3025 412 2950						
Ejector pump, sump type						
1 Operate float switch, if applicable, and check for proper operation of pump.	.130				√	√
2 Check for leaks on suction and discharge piping, seals, packing glands, etc.; make minor adjustments as required.	.077				√	√
3 Check pump and motor operation for excessive vibration, noise and overheating.	.022				√	√
4 Check alignment of pump and motor; adjust as necessary.	.260				√	√
5 Lubricate motor.	.099				√	√
6 Check electrical wiring and connections and repair as applicable.	.120				√	√
7 Clean exterior of pump and surrounding area.	.096				√	√
8 Fill out maintenance checklist and report deficiencies.	.022				√	√
Total labor-hours/period					.826	.826
Total labor-hours/year					.826	.826

		Cost Each						
			2012 Bare Costs				Total	Total
Description	Labor-hrs.	Material	Labor	Equip.	Total		In-House	w/O&P
2900 Ejector pump, sump type, annually	.826	8.50	37.50		46		58.50	71.50
2950 Annualized	1.652	17	75		92		117	143

PM Components	Labor-hrs.	W	M	Q	S	A
PM System G3025 420 1950						
Sewage lift pump, over 1 H.P.						
1 Check for proper operation of pump.	.130				√	√
2 Check for leaks on suction and discharge piping, seals, packing glands, etc.; make minor adjustments as required.	.077				√	√
3 Check pump and motor operation for excessive vibration, noise and overheating.	.022				√	√
4 Check alignment of pump and motor; adjust as necessary.	.260				√	√
5 Lubricate pump and motor.	.099				√	√
6 When available, check and record suction or discharge gauge pressure and flow rate.	.022				√	√
7 Clean exterior of pump, motor and surrounding area.	.096				√	√
8 . Fill out maintenance checklist and report deficiencies.	.022				√	√
Total labor-hours/period					.728	.728
Total labor-hours/year					.728	.728

			Cost Each					
			2012 Bare Costs				Total	Total
Description	Labor-hrs.	Material	Labor	Equip.	Total	In-House	w/O&P
1900	Sewage lift pump, over 1 H.P., annually	.728	7.50	40		47.50	58.50	71.50
1950	Annualized	1.456	15.05	79.50		94.55	116	143

PM Components	Labor-hrs.	W	M	Q	S	A
PM System G3025 530 1950						
Aerator, floating						
1 Check with operating or area personnel for deficiencies.	.035			√	√	√
2 Remove aerator from pond.	.390			√	√	√
3 Clean exterior of pump and motor.	.066			√	√	√
4 Check pump and motor operation for excessive vibration, noise and overheating.	.022			√	√	√
5 Check alignment of pump and motor; adjust as necessary.	.260			√	√	√
6 Lubricate pump and motor.	.099			√	√	√
7 Position aerator back in pond.	.390			√	√	√
8 Fill out maintenance checklist and report deficiencies.	.022			√	√	√
Total labor-hours/period				1.284	1.284	1.284
Total labor-hours/year				2.568	1.284	1.284

				Cost Each			
			2012 Bare Costs			Total	Total
Description	Labor-hrs.	Material	Labor	Equip.	Total	In-House	w/O&P
1900 Aerator, floating, annually	1.284	8.50	58.50		67	86	106
1950 Annualized	5.136	17	233		250	325	400

PM Components	Labor-hrs.	W	M	Q	S	A
PM System G3025 532 1950						
Barminutor						
1 Check with operating or area personnel for deficiencies.	.044		√	√	√	√
2 Check condition and clearance of cutting knives and inspect base seal.	.217		√	√	√	√
3 Check oil level in gearbox; add oil as necessary.	.035		√	√	√	√
4 Change oil in gearbox.	.681					√
5 Wire brush and lubricate directional flow valve stem.	.060		√	√	√	√
6 Check for rust and corrosion; scrape, wire brush and spot paint as necessary.	.105		√	√	√	√
7 Fill out maintenance checklist and report deficiencies.	.022		√	√	√	√
Total labor-hours/period			.483	.483	.483	1.164
Total labor-hours/year			3.864	.966	.483	1.164

				Cost Each			
			2012 Bare Costs			Total	Total
Description	Labor-hrs.	Material	Labor	Equip.	Total	In-House	w/O&P
1900 Barminutor, annually	1.164	30	53		83	103	124
1950 Annualized	6.477	68	294		362	460	565

PM Components	Labor-hrs.	W	M	Q	S	A
PM System G3025 534 1950						
Blower, aerator						
1 Check with operating or area personnel for deficiencies.	.035		√	√	√	√
2 Check blower oil level; add oil as necessary.	.046		√	√	√	√
3 Change blower oil.	.390				√	√
4 Check bolts and tighten as necessary: foundation, cylinder head, belt guard, etc.	.155		√	√	√	√
5 Check tension, condition, and alignment of V-belts on blower; adjust or replace as necessary.	.030		√	√	√	√
6 Check pump for excessive heat or vibration.	.042		√	√	√	√
7 Clean air intake filter on blower; replace as necessary.	.177		√	√	√	√
8 Perform operation check of air blower and adjust as required.	.221		√	√	√	√
9 Clean area around equipment.	.066		√	√	√	√
10 Fill out maintenance checklist and report deficiencies.	.022		√	√	√	√
Total labor-hours/period			.794	.794	1.184	1.184
Total labor-hours/year			6.352	1.588	1.184	1.184

			Cost Each					
			2012 Bare Costs				Total	Total
	Description	Labor-hrs.	Material	Labor	Equip.	Total	In-House	w/O&P
1900	Blower, aerator, annually	1.184	72.50	54		126.50	152	178
1950	Annualized	10.308	136	470		606	765	930

PM Components	Labor-hrs.	W	M	Q	S	A
PM System G3025 536 1950						
Clarifier						
1 Check with operating or area personnel for deficiencies.	.035		√	√	√	√
2 Check chain and sprocket for wear, where applicable.	.033		√	√	√	√
3 Grease drive gear fittings.	.150		√	√	√	√
4 Check gearbox oil level; add if necessary.	.046		√	√	√	
5 Drain and refill gearbox oil reservoir.	.681					√
6 Check unit for rust and corrosion; scrape, wire brush, and paint as required.	.105					√
7 Clean clarifier drive and surrounding area.	.098		√	√	√	√
8 Fill out maintenance checklist and report deficiencies.	.022		√	√	√	√
Total labor-hours/period			.384	.384	.384	1.170
Total labor-hours/year			3.072	.768	.384	1.170

			Cost Each					
			2012 Bare Costs				Total	Total
	Description	Labor-hrs.	Material	Labor	Equip.	Total	In-House	w/O&P
1900	Clarifier, annually	1.170	25.50	53		78.50	98	118
1950	Annualized	5.394	51	245		296	380	465

PM Components	Labor-hrs.	W	M	Q	S	A
PM System G3025 538 1950						
Comminutor						
1 Check with operating or area personnel for deficiencies.	.035			√	√	√
2 Change gearbox oil and lubricate fittings.	.681				√	√
3 Check comminutor and motor for excessive noise, vibration and overheating.	.022			√	√	√
4 Lubricate fittings and check oil in gearbox.	.150			√	√	√
5 Check operation.	.108			√	√	√
6 Fill out maintenance checklist and report deficiencies.	.022			√	√	√
Total labor-hours/period				.337	1.018	1.018
Total labor-hours/year				.674	1.018	1.018

			Cost Each					
			2012 Bare Costs				**Total**	**Total**
Description	Labor-hrs.	Material	Labor	Equip.	Total	In-House	w/O&P
1900 Comminutor, annually	1.018	25.50	46		71.50	89	107
1950 Annualized	2.710	68	123		191	237	285

PM Components	Labor-hrs.	W	M	Q	S	A
PM System G3025 540 1950						
Filter, trickling						
1 Lubricate fittings and check oil level in oil reservoir.	.035				√	√
2 Check distribution arms, support cables, clevis pins, and turnbuckles for deterioration.	.325				√	√
3 Check for leaks.	.077				√	√
4 Check operation.	.108				√	√
5 Fill out maintenance checklist and report deficiencies.	.022				√	√
Total labor-hours/period					.567	.567
Total labor-hours/year					.567	.567

			Cost Each					
			2012 Bare Costs				**Total**	**Total**
Description	Labor-hrs.	Material	Labor	Equip.	Total	In-House	w/O&P
1900 Filter, trickling, annually	.567	17	25.50		42.50	52.50	63.50
1950 Annualized	1.134	34	51.50		85.50	105	126

551

G30 SITE MECH. UTILITIES | G3025 542 | Grit Drive

PM Components	Labor-hrs.	W	M	Q	S	A
PM System G3025 542 1950						
Grit drive						
1 Check with operating personnel for obvious deficiencies.	.035				√	√
2 Lubricate fittings and check oil level in gearbox.	.047				√	√
3 Change oil in gearbox.	.681					√
4 Check chain linkage and operation.	.033				√	√
5 Clean area around drive mechanism.	.066				√	√
6 Fill out maintenance checklist and report deficiencies.	.022				√	√
Total labor-hours/period					.203	.884
Total labor-hours/year					.203	.884

			Cost Each					
				2012 Bare Costs			Total	Total
	Description	Labor-hrs.	Material	Labor	Equip.	Total	In-House	w/O&P
1900	Grit drive, annually	.884	25.50	40		65.50	81	97
1950	Annualized	1.087	34	49.50		83.50	102	123

G30 SITE MECH. UTILITIES | G3025 544 | Mixer, Sewage

PM Components	Labor-hrs.	W	M	Q	S	A
PM System G3025 544 1950						
Mixer, sewage						
1 Check with operating or area personnel for deficiencies.	.035			√	√	√
2 Clean drive motor exterior and check for corrosion on motor exterior and base plate.	.053			√	√	√
3 Check motor operation for vibration, noise, overheating; etc.	.022			√	√	√
4 Check alignment and clearances of shaft and coupler.	.031			√	√	√
5 Tighten or replace loose, missing, or damaged nuts, bolts and screws.	.005			√	√	√
6 Lubricate motor and shaft bearings as required.	.047			√	√	√
7 Clean area around motor.	.066			√	√	√
8 Fill out maintenance checklist and report deficiencies.	.022			√	√	√
Total labor-hours/period				.281	.281	.281
Total labor-hours/year				.562	.281	.281

			Cost Each					
				2012 Bare Costs			Total	Total
	Description	Labor-hrs.	Material	Labor	Equip.	Total	In-House	w/O&P
1900	Mixer, sewage, annually	.281	8.50	12.75		21.25	26	31
1950	Annualized	1.124	17	51		68	86	104

PM Components	Labor-hrs.	W	M	Q	S	A
PM System G3065 310 1950						
Fuel oil storage tank, above ground						
1 Inspect tank for corrosion.	.192					√
2 Inspect floating tank roof, lifter or cone and automatic float gauge, if applicable.	.233					√
3 Inspect fuel tank fire protection devices.	.022					√
4 Inspect berms around fuel storage tank for erosion.	.047					√
5 Inspect non-freeze draw valves.	.060					√
6 Inspect storage tank vacuum and pressure vents.	.179					√
7 Inspect vapor recovery line for deterioration.	.082					√
8 Run pump and check operation.	.159					√
9 Calibrate and adjust fuel oil pressure.	.382					√
10 Inspect fuel strainer and clean as needed.	.415					√
11 Inspect tank electrical grounds for breaks or loose fittings.	1.292					√
12 Inspect liquid level gauge for proper operation.	.191					√
13 Fill out maintenance checklist.	.022					√
Total labor-hours/period						3.276
Total labor-hours/year						3.276

			Cost Each					
			2012 Bare Costs				Total	Total
Description	Labor-hrs.	Material	Labor	Equip.	Total	In-House	w/O&P
1900	Fuel oil storage tank, above ground, annually	3.276	64	182		246	299	365
1950	Annualized	3.276	64	182		246	299	365

PM Components	Labor-hrs.	W	M	Q	S	A
PM System G4095 110 1950						
Cathodic protection system						
1 Inspect exterior of rectifier cabinet, all exposed connecting conduit, and fittings for corrosion, deteriorated paint, mechanical integrity and cleanliness, make minor repairs and clean/touch-up paint as required.	.060				√	√
2 Open and inspect interior of rectifier cabinet, inspect wiring for fraying, signs of overheating, deterioration mechanical damage, and loose connections; make adjustments as required.	.138				√	√
3 Check electrical contacts for overheating and pitting; make adjustments.	.075				√	√
4 Clean interior of rectifier cabinet.	.008				√	√
5 Check panel voltmeter and ampmeter with standard test instruments.	.075				√	√
6 Read and record panel meter voltage and current values.	.007				√	√
7 Measure and record rectifier voltage and current with portable instrument.	.059				√	√
8 Check potential at cathode locations; tighten loose connections.	.286				√	√
9 Fill out maintenance checklist and record deficiencies.	.022				√	√
Total labor-hours/period					.730	.730
Total labor-hours/year					.730	.730

			Cost Each					
			2012 Bare Costs				Total	Total
Description		Labor-hrs.	Material	Labor	Equip.	Total	In-House	w/O&P
1900	Cathodic protection system, annually	.730	7.05	37.50		44.55	54	67
1950	Annualized	1.460	14.15	75.50		89.65	109	134

General Maintenance

Table of Contents

How to Use the General Maintenance Pages

The following is a detailed explanation of a sample entry in the General Maintenance Section. Next to each bold number that follows is the described item with the appropriate component of the sample entry following in parentheses.

1 Division Number/Title
(01 93/Facility Maintenance)

Use the General Maintenance Section Table of Contents to locate specific items. This section is classified according to the CSI MasterFormat 2004 system.

2 Line Numbers
(01 93 04.40 0030)

Each General Maintenance unit price line item has been assigned a unique 12-digit code based on the CSI MasterFormat classification.

MasterFormat Division (01)
MasterFormat Level 2 (01 93 00)
MasterFormat Level 3

01 93 04.40   0030

MasterFormat Level 4
RSMeans 12-Digit Line Number

---

01 93 Facility Maintenance

01 93 04 – Landscaping Maintenance

01 93 04.15 Edging		Crew	Daily Output	Labor-Hours	Unit	Material	Labor	Equipment	Total	Total In-House	Total Incl O&P
							2012 Bare Costs				
0010	**EDGING**										
0020	Hand edging, at walks	1 Clam	16	.500	C.L.F.		13.20		13.20	16.40	20.50
0030	At planting, mulch or stone beds		7	1.143			30		30	37.50	46.50
0040	Power edging, at walks		88	.091			2.40		2.40	2.98	3.72
0050	At planting, mulch or stone beds		24	.333			8.80		8.80	10.90	13.65
0070	Weeding, mulched bed		20	.400			10.55		10.55	13.10	16.35
0080	Unmulched bed		8	1			26.50		26.50	33.00	41
0090	Trees, pruning from ground, 1-1/2" caliper		84	.095	Ea.		2.51		2.51	3.12	3.90

01 93 04.40 Lawn Renovation

		Crew	Daily Output	Labor-Hours	Unit	Material	Labor	Equipment	Total	Total In-House	Total Incl O&P
0010	**LAWN RENOVATION**										
0020	Lawn renovations, aerating, 18" walk behind cultivator	1 Clam	95	.084	M.S.F.		2.22		2.22	2.76	3.44
0030	48" tractor drawn cultivator	A-18	750	.011			.28	.41	.69	.76	.90
0040	72" tractor drawn cultivator	"	1100	.007			.19	.28	.47	.52	.61
0050	Fertilizing, dry granular, 4#/M.S.F., drop spreader	1 Clam	24	.333		2.59	8.80		11.39	13.75	16.90
0060	Rotary spreader	"	140	.057		2.59	1.51		4.10	4.72	5.60

556

3 Description (Lawn Renovations, etc.)

Each line item is described in detail. Sub-items and additional sizes are indented beneath the appropriate line items. The first line or two after the main item (in boldface) may contain descriptive information that pertains to all line items beneath this boldface listing.

4 Crew (A-18)

The "Crew" column designates the typical trade or crew used for the task. If the task can be accomplished by one trade and requires no power equipment, that trade and the number of workers are listed (for example, "2 Clam"). If the task requires a composite crew, a crew code designation is listed (for example, "A-18"). You'll find full details on all composite crews in the Crew Listings.

- For a complete list of all trades utilized in this book and their abbreviations, see the inside back cover of the book.

Crews										
Crew No.	Bare Costs		In-House Costs		Incl. Subs O&P				Cost Per Labor-Hour	
Crew A-18	Hr.	Daily	Hr.	Daily	Hr.	Daily	Bare Costs	In House	Incl. O&P
1 Maintenance Laborer	$26.35	$210.83	$32.75	$262.00	$40.90	$327.20	$26.35	$32.75	$40.90
1 Farm Tractor w/ Attachment		311.00		311.00		342.10	38.88	38.88	42.76
8 L.H., Daily Totals		$521.83		$573.00		$669.30	$65.22	$71.63	$83.66

5 Productivity: Daily Output (750)/ Labor-Hours (.011)

The "Daily Output" represents the typical number of units the designated crew will perform in a normal 8-hour day. To find out the number of days the given crew would require to complete your task, divide your quantity by the daily output. For example:

Quantity	÷	Daily Output	=	Duration
2000 M.S.F.	÷	750 M.S.F./ Crew Day	=	2.7 Crew Days

The "Labor-Hours" figure represents the number of labor-hours required to perform one unit of work. To find out the number of labor-hours required for your particular task, multiply the quantity of the item times the number of labor-hours shown. For example:

Quantity	x	Productivity Rate	=	Duration
2000 M.S.F.	x	.011 Labor-Hours/ LF	=	22 Labor-Hours

6 Unit (M.S.F.)

The abbreviated designation indicates the unit of measure upon which the price, production, and crew are based (M.S.F. = Thousand Square Feet). For a complete listing of abbreviations, refer to the Abbreviations Listing in the Reference Section of this book.

7 Bare Costs:

The unit material cost is the "bare" material cost with no overhead and profit included. *Costs shown reflect national average material prices for January of the current year and include delivery to the facility. Small purchases may require an additional delivery charge. No sales taxes are included.*

Labor (.28)

The unit labor cost is derived by multiplying bare labor-hour costs for Crew A-18 by labor-hour units. The bare labor-hour cost is found in the Crew Section under A-18. (If a trade is listed, the hourly labor cost—the wage rate—is found on the inside back cover of the book.)

Labor-Hour Cost Crew A-18	x	Labor-Hour Units	=	Labor
$23.70	x	.011	=	$0.28

Equip. (Equipment) (.41)

Equipment costs for each crew are listed in the description of each crew. Tools or equipment whose value justifies purchase or ownership by a contractor are considered overhead as shown on the inside back cover of the book. The unit equipment cost is derived by multiplying the bare equipment hourly cost by the labor-hour units.

Equipment Cost Crew A-18	x	Labor-Hour Units	=	Equip.
$37.10	x	.011	=	$0.41

Total (.69)

The total of the bare costs is the arithmetic total of the three previous columns: mat., labor, and equip.

Material	+	Labor	+	Equip.	=	Total
$0.00	+	$0.28	+	$0.41	=	$0.69

8 Total In-House Costs (.76)

"Total In-House Costs" include suggested markups to bare costs for the direct overhead requirements of in-house maintenance staff. The figure in this column is the sum of three components: the bare material cost plus 10% (for purchasing and handling small quantities); the bare labor cost plus workers' compensation and average fixed overhead (per the labor rate table on the inside back cover of the book or, if a crew is listed, from the Crew Listings); and the bare equipment cost.

Material is Bare Material Cost + 10% = $0.00 + $0.00	=	$0.00
Labor for Crew A-18 = Labor-Hour Cost ($31.65) x Labor-Hour Units (.011)	=	$0.34
Equip. is Bare Equip. Cost	=	$0.41
Total	=	$0.76

9 Total Costs Including O & P (.90)

"Total Costs Including O&P" include suggested markups to bare costs for an outside subcontractor's overhead and profit requirements. The figure in this column is the sum of three components: the bare material cost plus 25% for profit; the bare labor cost plus total overhead and profit (per the labor rate table on the inside back cover of the book or, if a crew is listed, from the Crew Listings); and the bare equipment cost plus 10% for profit.

Material is Bare Material Cost + 25% = $0.00 + $0.00	=	$ 0.00
Labor for Crew A-18 = Labor-Hour Cost ($39.65) x Labor-Hour Units (.011)	=	$ 0.42
Equip. is Bare Equip. Cost + 10% = $0.41 + $0.04	=	$ 0.45
Total	=	$0.90*

*Due to in-process computer rounding.

01 93 Facility Maintenance

01 93 04 – Landscaping Maintenance

01 93 04.15 Edging

	Crew	Daily Output	Labor-Hours	Unit	Material	2012 Bare Costs Labor	2012 Bare Costs Equipment	Total	Total In-House	Total Incl O&P
0010 **EDGING**										
0020 Hand edging, at walks	1 Clam	16	.500	C.L.F.		13.20		13.20	16.40	20.50
0030 At planting, mulch or stone beds		7	1.143			30		30	37.50	46.50
0040 Power edging, at walks		88	.091			2.40		2.40	2.98	3.72
0050 At planting, mulch or stone beds		24	.333			8.80		8.80	10.90	13.65

01 93 04.20 Flower, Shrub and Tree Care

	Crew	Daily Output	Labor-Hours	Unit	Material	2012 Bare Costs Labor	2012 Bare Costs Equipment	Total	Total In-House	Total Incl O&P
0010 **FLOWER, SHRUB & TREE CARE**										
0020 Flower or shrub beds, bark mulch, 3" deep hand spreader	1 Clam	100	.080	S.Y.	2.92	2.11		5.03	5.85	6.90
0030 Peat moss, 1" deep hand spreader		900	.009		2.80	.23		3.03	3.37	3.86
0040 Wood chips, 2" deep hand spreader		220	.036		1.75	.96		2.71	3.12	3.68
0050 Cleaning		1	8	M.S.F.		211		211	262.00	325
0060 Fertilizing, dry granular, 3 #/C.S.F.		85	.094		6	2.48		8.48	9.70	11.35
0070 Weeding, mulched bed		20	.400			10.55		10.55	13.10	16.35
0080 Unmulched bed		8	1			26.50		26.50	33.00	41
0090 Trees, pruning from ground, 1-1/2" caliper		84	.095	Ea.		2.51		2.51	3.12	3.90
0100 2" caliper		70	.114			3.01		3.01	3.74	4.67
0110 2-1/2" caliper		50	.160			4.22		4.22	5.25	6.55
0120 3" caliper		30	.267			7.05		7.05	8.75	10.90
0130 4" caliper	2 Clam	21	.762			20		20	25.00	31
0140 6" caliper		12	1.333			35		35	43.50	54.50
0150 9" caliper		7.50	2.133			56		56	70.00	87.50
0160 12" caliper		6.50	2.462			65		65	80.50	101
0170 Fertilize, slow release tablets	1 Clam	100	.080		.52	2.11		2.63	3.19	3.92
0180 Pest control, spray		24	.333		23.50	8.80		32.30	37.00	43
0190 Systemic		48	.167		24	4.39		28.39	32.00	37
0200 Watering, under 1-1/2" caliper		34	.235			6.20		6.20	7.70	9.60
0210 1-1/2" to 4" caliper		14.50	.552			14.55		14.55	18.05	22.50
0220 4" caliper and over		10	.800			21		21	26.00	32.50
0230 Shrubs, prune, entire bed		7	1.143	M.S.F.		30		30	37.50	46.50
0240 Per shrub, 3' height		190	.042	Ea.		1.11		1.11	1.38	1.72
0250 4' height		90	.089			2.34		2.34	2.91	3.64
0260 6' height		50	.160			4.22		4.22	5.25	6.55
0270 Fertilize, dry granular, 3#/M.S.F.		85	.094	M.S.F.	6	2.48		8.48	9.70	11.35
0280 Watering, entire bed		7	1.143	"		30		30	37.50	46.50
0290 Per shrub		32	.250	Ea.		6.60		6.60	8.20	10.25

01 93 04.35 Lawn Care

	Crew	Daily Output	Labor-Hours	Unit	Material	2012 Bare Costs Labor	2012 Bare Costs Equipment	Total	Total In-House	Total Incl O&P
0010 **LAWN CARE**										
0020 Mowing lawns, power mower, 18"-22"	1 Clam	80	.100	M.S.F.		2.64		2.64	3.28	4.09
0030 22"-30"		120	.067			1.76		1.76	2.18	2.73
0040 30"-32"		140	.057			1.51		1.51	1.87	2.34
0050 Self propelled or riding mower, 36"-44"	A-16	300	.027			.70	.23	.93	1.10	1.34
0060 48"-58"		480	.017			.44	.14	.58	.69	.84
0070 Tractor, 3 gang reel, 7' cut		930	.009			.23	.07	.30	.35	.43
0080 5 gang reel, 12' cut		1200	.007			.18	.06	.24	.28	.33
0090 Edge trimming with weed whacker	1 Clam	5760	.001	L.F.		.04		.04	.05	.06

01 93 04.40 Lawn Renovation

	Crew	Daily Output	Labor-Hours	Unit	Material	2012 Bare Costs Labor	2012 Bare Costs Equipment	Total	Total In-House	Total Incl O&P
0010 **LAWN RENOVATION**										
0020 Lawn renovations, aerating, 18" walk behind cultivator	1 Clam	95	.084	M.S.F.		2.22		2.22	2.76	3.44
0030 48" tractor drawn cultivator	A-18	750	.011			.28	.41	.69	.76	.90
0040 72" tractor drawn cultivator	"	1100	.007			.19	.28	.47	.52	.61
0050 Fertilizing, dry granular, 4#/M.S.F., drop spreader	1 Clam	24	.333		2.59	8.80		11.39	13.75	16.90
0060 Rotary spreader	"	140	.057		2.59	1.51		4.10	4.72	5.60

01 93 Facility Maintenance

01 93 04 – Landscaping Maintenance

01 93 04.40 Lawn Renovation

		Crew	Daily Output	Labor-Hours	Unit	Material	2012 Bare Costs Labor	Equipment	Total	Total In-House	Total Incl O&P
0070	Tractor drawn 8' spreader	A-18	500	.016	M.S.F.	2.59	.42	.62	3.63	3.99	4.57
0080	Tractor drawn 12' spreader	"	800	.010		2.59	.26	.39	3.24	3.57	4.08
0090	Overseeding, utility mix, 7#/M.S.F., drop spreader	1 Clam	10	.800		17	21		38	45.00	54
0100	Tractor drawn spreader	A-18	52	.154		17	4.05	6	27.05	29.50	34
0110	Watering, 1" of water, applied by hand	1 Clam	21	.381			10.05		10.05	12.50	15.60
0120	Soaker hoses	"	82	.098			2.57		2.57	3.20	3.99

01 93 04.65 Raking

		Crew	Daily Output	Labor-Hours	Unit	Material	2012 Bare Costs Labor	Equipment	Total	Total In-House	Total Incl O&P
0010	**RAKING**										
0020	Raking, leaves, by hand	1 Clam	7.50	1.067	M.S.F.		28		28	35.00	43.50
0030	Power blower		45	.178			4.68		4.68	5.80	7.25
0040	Grass clippings, by hand		7.50	1.067			28		28	35.00	43.50

01 93 04.85 Walkways and Parking Care

		Crew	Daily Output	Labor-Hours	Unit	Material	2012 Bare Costs Labor	Equipment	Total	Total In-House	Total Incl O&P
0010	**WALKWAYS AND PARKING CARE**										
0020	General cleaning, parking area and walks, sweeping by hand	1 Clam	15	.533	M.S.F.		14.05		14.05	17.45	22
0030	Power vacuum		100	.080			2.11		2.11	2.62	3.27
0040	Power blower		100	.080			2.11		2.11	2.62	3.27
0050	Hose down		30	.267			7.05		7.05	8.75	10.90

01 93 04.90 Yard Waste Disposal

		Crew	Daily Output	Labor-Hours	Unit	Material	2012 Bare Costs Labor	Equipment	Total	Total In-House	Total Incl O&P
0010	**YARD WASTE DISPOSAL**										
0030	On site dump or compost heap	2 Clam	24	.667	C.Y.		17.55		17.55	22.00	27.50
0040	Into 6 CY dump truck, 2 mile haul to compost heap	A-17	125	.064			1.69	1.69	3.38	3.79	4.48
0050	4 mile haul to compost heap, fees not included	"	85	.094			2.48	2.48	4.96	5.55	6.60

01 93 05 – Exterior General Maintenance

01 93 05.95 Window Washing

		Crew	Daily Output	Labor-Hours	Unit	Material	2012 Bare Costs Labor	Equipment	Total	Total In-House	Total Incl O&P
0010	**WINDOW WASHING**										
0030	Minimum productivity	1 Clam	1	8	M.S.F.	4.14	211		215.14	267.00	330
0040	Average productivity		2.50	3.200		4.14	84.50		88.64	109.00	136
0050	Maximum productivity		4	2		4.14	52.50		56.64	70.00	87

01 93 06 – Interior General Maintenance

01 93 06.20 Carpet Care

		Crew	Daily Output	Labor-Hours	Unit	Material	2012 Bare Costs Labor	Equipment	Total	Total In-House	Total Incl O&P
0010	**CARPET CARE**										
0100	Carpet cleaning, portable extractor with floor wand	1 Clam	20	.400	M.S.F.	6.50	10.55		17.05	20.50	24.50
0200	Deep carpet cleaning, self-contained extractor										
0210	24" path @ 100 feet per minute	1 Clam	64	.125	M.S.F.	8.15	3.29		11.44	13.05	15.30
0220	20" path		54	.148		8.15	3.90		12.05	13.80	16.25
0230	16" path		43	.186		8.15	4.90		13.05	15.05	17.80
0240	12" path		32	.250		8.15	6.60		14.75	17.15	20.50
0300	Carpet pile lifting, self-contained extractor										
0310	24" path at 90 feet per minute	1 Clam	60	.133	M.S.F.	8.95	3.51		12.46	14.20	16.65
0320	20" path		50	.160		8.95	4.22		13.17	15.10	17.75
0330	16" path		40	.200		8.95	5.25		14.20	16.40	19.40
0340	12" path		30	.267		8.95	7.05		16	18.60	22
0400	Carpet restoration cleaning, self-contained extractor										
0410	24" path at 50 feet per minute	1 Clam	32	.250	M.S.F.	9.80	6.60		16.40	18.95	22.50
0420	20" path		27	.296		9.80	7.80		17.60	20.50	24.50
0430	16" path		21	.381		9.80	10.05		19.85	23.50	28
0440	12" path		16	.500		9.80	13.20		23	27.00	33

01 93 06.25 Ceiling Care

		Crew	Daily Output	Labor-Hours	Unit	Material	2012 Bare Costs Labor	Equipment	Total	Total In-House	Total Incl O&P
0010	**CEILING CARE**										
0020	Washing hard ceiling from ladder, hand	1 Clam	2.05	3.902	M.S.F.	5.45	103		108.45	134.00	167

01 93 06 – Interior General Maintenance

01 93 06.25 Ceiling Care

		Crew	Daily Output	Labor-Hours	Unit	Material	2012 Bare Costs Labor	2012 Bare Costs Equipment	Total	Total In-House	Total Incl O&P
0030	Machine	1 Clam	2.52	3.175	M.S.F.	5.45	83.50		88.95	110.00	137
0035	Acoustic tile cleaning, chemical spray, including masking										
0040	Unobstructed floor	4 Clam	5400	.006	S.F.	.06	.16		.22	.26	.32
0045	Obstructed floor	"	4000	.008	"	.06	.21		.27	.33	.41
0048	Chemical spray cleaning and coating, including masking										
0050	Unobstructed floor	4 Clam	4800	.007	S.F.	.13	.18		.31	.36	.43
0055	Obstructed floor	"	3400	.009	"	.13	.25		.38	.45	.54

01 93 06.40 General Cleaning

		Crew	Daily Output	Labor-Hours	Unit	Material	2012 Bare Costs Labor	2012 Bare Costs Equipment	Total	Total In-House	Total Incl O&P
0010	**GENERAL CLEANING**										
0020	Sweep stairs & landings, damp wipe handrails	1 Clam	80	.100	Floor	.11	2.64		2.75	3.40	4.23
0030	Dust mop stairs & landings, damp wipe handrails		62.50	.128		.11	3.37		3.48	4.31	5.40
0040	Damp mop stairs & landings, damp wipe handrails		45	.178		.25	4.68		4.93	6.10	7.55
0050	Vacuum stairs & landings, damp wipe handrails, canister		41	.195		.11	5.15		5.26	6.50	8.15
0060	Vacuum stairs & landings, damp wipe handrails, backpack		58.22	.137		.11	3.62		3.73	4.62	5.75
0070	Vacuum stairs & landings, damp wipe handrails, upright		31.57	.253		.11	6.70		6.81	8.40	10.50
0080	Clean carpeted elevators		48	.167	Ea.	1.11	4.39		5.50	6.70	8.20
0090	Clean uncarpeted elevators		32	.250		.99	6.60		7.59	9.30	11.50
0100	Clean escalator		8	1		1.09	26.50		27.59	34.00	42.50
0110	Restrooms, fixture cleaning, toilets		180	.044		.09	1.17		1.26	1.56	1.93
0120	Urinals		192	.042		.07	1.10		1.17	1.44	1.79
0130	Sinks		206	.039		.02	1.02		1.04	1.29	1.62
0140	Utility sink		175	.046		.07	1.20		1.27	1.58	1.96
0150	Bathtub		85	.094		.19	2.48		2.67	3.29	4.09
0160	Shower		85	.094		.65	2.48		3.13	3.80	4.66
0170	Accessories cleaning, soap dispenser		1280	.006		.02	.16		.18	.22	.29
0180	Sanitary napkin dispenser		640	.013		.02	.33		.35	.43	.54
0190	Paper towel dispenser		1455	.006		.02	.14		.16	.20	.26
0200	Toilet tissue dispenser		1455	.006		.02	.14		.16	.20	.26
0210	Accessories, refilling/restocking, soap dispenser (1 bag)		640	.013		9.05	.33		9.38	10.35	11.80
0220	Sanitary napkin/tampon dispenser (25/50)		384	.021		17.45	.55		18	19.90	22.50
0230	Paper towel dispenser, folded (2 pkgs of 250)		545	.015		8.30	.39		8.69	9.60	11
0240	Paper towel dispenser, rolled (350' roll)		340	.024		6	.62		6.62	7.35	8.45
0250	Toilet tissue dispenser (500 2-ply sheet roll)		1440	.006		.77	.15		.92	1.03	1.19
0260	Sanitary seat covers (pkg of 250)		960	.008		4.74	.22		4.96	5.50	6.25
0270	Toilet partition cleaning		96	.083		.41	2.20		2.61	3.18	3.92
0280	Ceramic tile wall cleaning		2400	.003	S.F.	.01	.09		.10	.12	.15
0290	General cleaning, empty to larger portable container, wastebaskets		960	.008	Ea.		.22		.22	.27	.34
0300	Ash trays		2880	.003			.07		.07	.09	.11
0310	Cigarette stands		960	.008			.22		.22	.27	.34
0320	Sand urns		640	.013			.33		.33	.41	.51
0330	Pencil sharpeners		2880	.003			.07		.07	.09	.11
0340	Remove trash to central location		290	.028	Lb.		.73		.73	.90	1.13
0347	Bench		480	.017	Ea.	.07	.44		.51	.63	.77
0350	Chairs		960	.008		.03	.22		.25	.30	.38
0360	Chalkboard erasers		960	.008			.22		.22	.27	.34
0370	Chalkboards		16	.500	M.S.F.	5.45	13.20		18.65	22.50	27.50
0380	Desk tops		225	.036	Ea.	.08	.94		1.02	1.25	1.55
0390	Glass doors		168	.048	"	.17	1.25		1.42	1.75	2.16
0400	Hard surface audience type seating		40	.200	M.S.F.	6.80	5.25		12.05	14.05	16.70
0409	Locker, metal		320	.025	Ea.	.16	.66		.82	1.00	1.22
0410	Microwave ovens		240	.033		.03	.88		.91	1.12	1.40
0420	Office partitions, to 48 S.F.		160	.050		.26	1.32		1.58	1.93	2.38

01 93 06.40 General Cleaning

		Crew	Daily Output	Labor-Hours	Unit	Material	2012 Bare Costs Labor	Equipment	Total	Total In-House	Total Incl O&P
0430	Overhead air vents	1 Clam	175	.046	Ea.	.02	1.20		1.22	1.52	1.90
0440	Refrigerators		35	.229		.43	6		6.43	7.95	9.90
0450	Revolving doors		35	.229		1.04	6		7.04	8.65	10.65
0460	Tables		240	.033		.11	.88		.99	1.21	1.50
0470	Telephone		288	.028		.02	.73		.75	.93	1.17
0480	Telephone booth		190	.042		.54	1.11		1.65	1.97	2.40
0490	Water fountain		480	.017		.03	.44		.47	.58	.72
0500	Wastebaskets		260	.031		.03	.81		.84	1.04	1.30
0510	Dusting, beds		360	.022			.59		.59	.73	.91
0520	Bedside stand		960	.008			.22		.22	.27	.34
0530	Bookcase		960	.008			.22		.22	.27	.34
0540	Calculator		1920	.004			.11		.11	.14	.17
0550	Chair		1340	.006			.16		.16	.20	.24
0560	Coat rack		400	.020			.53		.53	.66	.82
0570	Couch		320	.025			.66		.66	.82	1.02
0580	Desk		550	.015			.38		.38	.48	.60
0590	Desk lamp		1200	.007			.18		.18	.22	.27
0600	Desk trays		1920	.004			.11		.11	.14	.17
0610	Dictaphone		1920	.004			.11		.11	.14	.17
0620	Dresser		480	.017			.44		.44	.55	.68
0630	File cabinets		960	.008			.22		.22	.27	.34
0640	Lockers		2400	.003			.09		.09	.11	.14
0650	Piano		425	.019			.50		.50	.62	.77
0660	Radio		960	.008			.22		.22	.27	.34
0665	Shelf, storage, 1' x 20'		480	.017			.44		.44	.55	.68
0670	Table		670	.012			.31		.31	.39	.49
0680	Table lamp		960	.008			.22		.22	.27	.34
0690	Telephones		960	.008			.22		.22	.27	.34
0700	Television		960	.008			.22		.22	.27	.34
0710	Typewriter		960	.008			.22		.22	.27	.34
0720	Vacuuming, armless chair		825	.010			.26		.26	.32	.40
0730	Armchair		480	.017			.44		.44	.55	.68
0740	Couch		320	.025			.66		.66	.82	1.02
0750	Entry mats		8	1	M.S.F.		26.50		26.50	33.00	41
0760	Overhead air vents		480	.017	Ea.		.44		.44	.55	.68
0770	Upholstered auditorium seating		5.27	1.518	M.S.F.		40		40	49.50	62

01 93 06.45 Hard Floor Care

		Crew	Daily Output	Labor-Hours	Unit	Material	2012 Bare Costs Labor	Equipment	Total	Total In-House	Total Incl O&P
0010	**HARD FLOOR CARE**										
0020	Damp mop w/bucket & wringer, 12 oz mop head, unobstructed	1 Clam	25	.320	M.S.F.	4.02	8.45		12.47	14.90	18.15
0030	Obstructed		17	.471		4.02	12.40		16.42	19.85	24.50
0040	20 oz. mop head, unobstructed		29	.276		4.02	7.25		11.27	13.45	16.35
0050	Obstructed		20	.400		4.02	10.55		14.57	17.50	21.50
0060	24 oz. mop head, unobstructed		35	.229		4.02	6		10.02	11.90	14.40
0070	Obstructed		23	.348		4.02	9.15		13.17	15.80	19.30
0080	32 oz. mop head, unobstructed		43	.186		4.02	4.90		8.92	10.50	12.65
0090	Obstructed		29	.276		4.02	7.25		11.27	13.45	16.35
0100	Dust mop, 12" mop, unobstructed		33	.242			6.40		6.40	7.95	9.90
0110	Obstructed		19	.421			11.10		11.10	13.80	17.20
0120	18" mop, unobstructed		49	.163			4.30		4.30	5.35	6.70
0130	Obstructed		28	.286			7.55		7.55	9.35	11.70
0140	24" mop, unobstructed		61	.131			3.46		3.46	4.30	5.35
0150	Obstructed		34	.235			6.20		6.20	7.70	9.60

01 93 06 – Interior General Maintenance

01 93 06.45 Hard Floor Care		Crew	Daily Output	Labor-Hours	Unit	Material	2012 Bare Costs Labor	2012 Bare Costs Equipment	Total	Total In-House	Total Incl O&P
0160	30" mop, unobstructed	1 Clam	74	.108	M.S.F.		2.85		2.85	3.54	4.42
0170	Obstructed		42	.190			5		5	6.25	7.80
0180	36" mop, unobstructed		92	.087			2.29		2.29	2.85	3.56
0190	Obstructed		52	.154			4.05		4.05	5.05	6.30
0200	42" mop, unobstructed		124	.065			1.70		1.70	2.11	2.64
0210	Obstructed		70	.114			3.01		3.01	3.74	4.67
0220	48" mop, unobstructed		185	.043			1.14		1.14	1.42	1.77
0230	Obstructed		104	.077			2.03		2.03	2.52	3.15
0240	60" mop, unobstructed		246	.033			.86		.86	1.07	1.33
0250	Obstructed		138	.058			1.53		1.53	1.90	2.37
0260	72" mop, unobstructed		369	.022			.57		.57	.71	.89
0270	Obstructed		208	.038			1.01		1.01	1.26	1.57
0280	Sweeping, 8" broom, light soil, unobstructed		19	.421			11.10		11.10	13.80	17.20
0290	Obstructed		14	.571			15.05		15.05	18.70	23.50
0300	Heavy soil, unobstructed		11	.727			19.15		19.15	24.00	30
0310	Obstructed		9	.889			23.50		23.50	29.00	36.50
0320	12" push broom, light soil, unobstructed		32	.250			6.60		6.60	8.20	10.25
0330	Obstructed		24	.333			8.80		8.80	10.90	13.65
0340	Heavy soil, unobstructed		19	.421			11.10		11.10	13.80	17.20
0350	Obstructed		14	.571			15.05		15.05	18.70	23.50
0360	16" push broom, light soil, unobstructed		40	.200			5.25		5.25	6.55	8.20
0370	Obstructed		30	.267			7.05		7.05	8.75	10.90
0380	Heavy soil, unobstructed		24	.333			8.80		8.80	10.90	13.65
0390	Obstructed		18	.444			11.70		11.70	14.55	18.20
0400	18" push broom, light soil, unobstructed		44	.182			4.79		4.79	5.95	7.45
0410	Obstructed		33	.242			6.40		6.40	7.95	9.90
0420	Heavy soil, unobstructed		36	.222			5.85		5.85	7.30	9.10
0430	Obstructed		20	.400			10.55		10.55	13.10	16.35
0440	24" push broom, light soil, unobstructed		57	.140			3.70		3.70	4.60	5.75
0450	Obstructed		43	.186			4.90		4.90	6.10	7.60
0460	Heavy soil, unobstructed		34	.235			6.20		6.20	7.70	9.60
0470	Obstructed		26	.308			8.10		8.10	10.10	12.60
0480	30" push broom, light soil, unobstructed		81	.099			2.60		2.60	3.23	4.04
0490	Obstructed		60	.133			3.51		3.51	4.37	5.45
0500	Heavy soil, unobstructed		48	.167			4.39		4.39	5.45	6.80
0510	Obstructed		36	.222			5.85		5.85	7.30	9.10
0520	36" push broom, light soil, unobstructed		100	.080			2.11		2.11	2.62	3.27
0530	Obstructed		75	.107			2.81		2.81	3.49	4.36
0540	Heavy soil, unobstructed		60	.133			3.51		3.51	4.37	5.45
0550	Obstructed		45	.178			4.68		4.68	5.80	7.25
0560	42" push broom, light soil, unobstructed		133	.060			1.59		1.59	1.97	2.46
0570	Obstructed		100	.080			2.11		2.11	2.62	3.27
0580	Heavy soil, unobstructed		80	.100			2.64		2.64	3.28	4.09
0590	Obstructed		60	.133			3.51		3.51	4.37	5.45
0600	48" push broom, light soil, unobstructed		200	.040			1.05		1.05	1.31	1.64
0610	Obstructed		150	.053			1.41		1.41	1.75	2.18
0620	Heavy soil, unobstructed		120	.067			1.76		1.76	2.18	2.73
0630	Obstructed		90	.089			2.34		2.34	2.91	3.64
0640	Wet mop/rinse w/bucket & wringer, 12 oz. mop, unobstructed		11	.727		5.45	19.15		24.60	30.00	37
0650	Obstructed		8	1		5.45	26.50		31.95	39.00	48
0660	20 oz. mop head, unobstructed		14	.571		5.45	15.05		20.50	24.50	30.50
0670	Obstructed		10	.800		5.45	21		26.45	32.00	39.50
0680	24 oz. mop head, unobstructed		20	.400		5.45	10.55		16	19.10	23

01 93 06.45 Hard Floor Care

		Crew	Daily Output	Labor-Hours	Unit	Material	2012 Bare Costs Labor	2012 Bare Costs Equipment	Total	Total In-House	Total Incl O&P
0690	Obstructed	1 Clam	15	.533	M.S.F.	5.45	14.05		19.50	23.50	29
0700	32 oz. mop head, unobstructed		27	.296		5.45	7.80		13.25	15.70	18.90
0710	Obstructed		20	.400		5.45	10.55		16	19.10	23
0720	Dry buffing or polishing, 175 RPM, 12" diameter machine		14.21	.563			14.85		14.85	18.45	23
0730	14" diameter machine		16.51	.485			12.75		12.75	15.85	19.80
0740	17" diameter machine		19.20	.417			11		11	13.65	17.05
0750	20" diameter machine		22.85	.350			9.25		9.25	11.45	14.30
0760	24" diameter machine		28.99	.276			7.25		7.25	9.05	11.30
0770	350 RPM, 17" diameter machine		30.76	.260			6.85		6.85	8.50	10.65
0780	20" diameter machine		40.60	.197			5.20		5.20	6.45	8.05
0790	24" diameter machine		47.06	.170			4.48		4.48	5.55	6.95
0800	1000 RPM, 17" diameter machine		62.09	.129			3.40		3.40	4.22	5.25
0810	20" diameter machine		67.68	.118			3.11		3.11	3.87	4.83
0820	24" diameter machine		88.79	.090			2.37		2.37	2.95	3.69
0830	27" diameter machine		99.34	.081			2.12		2.12	2.64	3.29
0840	Spray buffing, 175 RPM, 12" diameter		10.66	.750		.79	19.75		20.54	25.50	31.50
0850	14" diameter machine		11.95	.669		.79	17.65		18.44	23.00	28.50
0860	17" diameter machine		13.80	.580		.79	15.30		16.09	19.85	24.50
0870	20" diameter machine		16	.500		.79	13.20		13.99	17.25	21.50
0880	24" diameter machine		19.05	.420		.79	11.05		11.84	14.60	18.20
0890	350 RPM, 17" diameter machine		17.39	.460		.79	12.10		12.89	15.95	19.80
0900	20" diameter machine		22.13	.362		.79	9.55		10.34	12.70	15.80
0910	24" diameter machine		29.22	.274		.79	7.20		7.99	9.85	12.20
0920	1000 RPM, 17" diameter machine		41.02	.195		.79	5.15		5.94	7.25	9
0930	20" diameter machine		44.14	.181		.79	4.78		5.57	6.80	8.40
0940	24" diameter machine		52.21	.153		.79	4.04		4.83	5.90	7.25
0950	27" diameter machine		57.43	.139		.79	3.67		4.46	5.45	6.70
0960	Burnish, 1000 RPM, 17" diameter machine		60	.133			3.51		3.51	4.37	5.45
0970	2000 RPM, 17" diameter machine		72	.111			2.93		2.93	3.64	4.54
0980	Scrubbing, 12" brush by hand		2	4		4.02	105		109.02	135.00	169
0990	175 RPM, 12" diameter machine		10.05	.796		4.02	21		25.02	30.50	37.50
1000	14" diameter machine		11.62	.688		4.02	18.15		22.17	27.00	33
1010	17" diameter machine		14	.571		4.02	15.05		19.07	23.00	28.50
1020	20" diameter machine		17.61	.454		4.02	11.95		15.97	19.30	23.50
1030	24" diameter machine		23.58	.339		4.02	8.95		12.97	15.55	18.95
1040	350 RPM, 17" diameter machine		24.12	.332		4.02	8.75		12.77	15.30	18.60
1050	20" diameter machine		28.91	.277		4.02	7.30		11.32	13.50	16.35
1060	24" diameter machine		36.92	.217		4.02	5.70		9.72	11.50	13.90
1070	Automatic, 21" machine		60.75	.132		4.02	3.47		7.49	8.75	10.45
1080	24" machine		83.47	.096		4.02	2.53		6.55	7.55	8.95
1090	32" machine		128.68	.062		4.02	1.64		5.66	6.45	7.55
1100	Stripping, separate wet pick-up required, 175 RPM, 17" diameter		6.86	1.166		2.77	30.50		33.27	41.00	51
1110	20" diameter machine		7.68	1.042		2.77	27.50		30.27	37.00	46
1120	350 RPM, 17" diameter machine		8.80	.909		2.77	24		26.77	33.00	40.50
1130	20" diameter machine		10.50	.762		2.77	20		22.77	28.00	34.50
1140	Wet pick-up, 12" opening attachment		18	.444			11.70		11.70	14.55	18.20
1150	20" opening attachment		24.12	.332			8.75		8.75	10.85	13.55
1160	Finish application, mop		14	.571		9.60	15.05		24.65	29.50	35.50
1170	Gravity fed applicator		21	.381		9.60	10.05		19.65	23.00	27.50
1180	Lambswool applicator		17	.471		9.60	12.40		22	26.00	31.50
1190	Sealer application, mop		14	.571		14.50	15.05		29.55	34.50	41.50
1200	Gravity fed applicator		21	.381		14.50	10.05		24.55	28.50	33.50
1210	Lambswool applicator		17	.471		14.50	12.40		26.90	31.50	37.50

01 93 06 – Interior General Maintenance

01 93 06.80 Vacuuming	Crew	Daily Output	Labor-Hours	Unit	Material	2012 Bare Costs Labor	Equipment	Total	Total In-House	Total Incl O&P
0010 **VACUUMING**										
0020 Vacuum carpet, 12" upright, spot areas	1 Clam	73.68	.109	M.S.F.		2.86		2.86	3.56	4.44
0030 Traffic areas		44.21	.181			4.77		4.77	5.95	7.40
0040 All areas		21.05	.380			10		10	12.45	15.55
0050 14" upright , spot areas		79.98	.100			2.64		2.64	3.28	4.09
0060 Traffic areas		47.99	.167			4.39		4.39	5.45	6.80
0070 All areas		22.85	.350			9.25		9.25	11.45	14.30
0080 16" upright, spot areas		87.50	.091			2.41		2.41	2.99	3.74
0090 Traffic areas		52.50	.152			4.02		4.02	4.99	6.25
0100 All areas		25	.320			8.45		8.45	10.50	13.10
0110 18" upright, spot areas		96.53	.083			2.18		2.18	2.71	3.39
0120 Traffic areas		57.92	.138			3.64		3.64	4.52	5.65
0130 All areas		27.58	.290			7.65		7.65	9.50	11.85
0140 20" upright, spot areas		107.66	.074			1.96		1.96	2.43	3.04
0150 Traffic areas		64.60	.124			3.26		3.26	4.06	5.05
0160 All areas		30.76	.260			6.85		6.85	8.50	10.65
0170 22" upright, spot areas		121.73	.066			1.73		1.73	2.15	2.69
0180 Traffic areas		73.04	.110			2.89		2.89	3.59	4.48
0190 All areas		34.78	.230			6.05		6.05	7.55	9.40
0200 24" upright, spot areas		140	.057			1.51		1.51	1.87	2.34
0210 Traffic areas		84	.095			2.51		2.51	3.12	3.90
0220 All areas		40	.200			5.25		5.25	6.55	8.20
0230 14" twin motor upright, spot areas		98.81	.081			2.13		2.13	2.65	3.31
0240 Traffic areas		59.28	.135			3.56		3.56	4.42	5.50
0250 All areas		28.23	.283			7.45		7.45	9.30	11.60
0260 18" twin motor upright, spot areas		112	.071			1.88		1.88	2.34	2.92
0270 Traffic areas		67.20	.119			3.14		3.14	3.90	4.87
0280 All areas		32	.250			6.60		6.60	8.20	10.25
0290 Backpack, 12" opening carpet attachment, spot areas		77.77	.103			2.71		2.71	3.37	4.21
0300 Traffic areas		46.66	.171			4.52		4.52	5.60	7
0310 All areas		22.22	.360			9.50		9.50	11.80	14.75
0320 14" opening carpet attachment, spot areas		84.84	.094			2.48		2.48	3.09	3.86
0330 Traffic areas		50.90	.157			4.14		4.14	5.15	6.45
0340 All areas		24.24	.330			8.70		8.70	10.80	13.50
0350 16" opening carpet attachment, spot areas		93.35	.086			2.26		2.26	2.81	3.51
0360 Traffic areas		56.01	.143			3.76		3.76	4.68	5.85
0370 All areas		26.67	.300			7.90		7.90	9.80	12.25
0380 18" opening carpet attachment, spot areas		103.67	.077			2.03		2.03	2.53	3.16
0390 Traffic areas		62.20	.129			3.39		3.39	4.21	5.25
0400 All areas		29.62	.270			7.10		7.10	8.85	11.05
0410 20" opening carpet attachment, spot areas		116.66	.069			1.81		1.81	2.25	2.80
0420 Traffic areas		69.99	.114			3.01		3.01	3.74	4.67
0430 All areas		33.33	.240			6.30		6.30	7.85	9.80
0440 22" opening carpet attachment, spot areas		133.32	.060			1.58		1.58	1.97	2.45
0450 Traffic areas		79.99	.100			2.64		2.64	3.28	4.09
0460 All areas		38.09	.210			5.55		5.55	6.90	8.60
0470 24" opening carpet attachment, spot areas		155.54	.051			1.36		1.36	1.68	2.10
0480 Traffic areas		93.32	.086			2.26		2.26	2.81	3.51
0490 All areas		44.44	.180			4.74		4.74	5.90	7.35
0500 Tank / cannister, 12" opening carpet attachment, spot areas		70	.114			3.01		3.01	3.74	4.67
0510 Traffic areas		42	.190			5		5	6.25	7.80
0520 All areas		20	.400			10.55		10.55	13.10	16.35

01 93 Facility Maintenance

01 93 06 – Interior General Maintenance

01 93 06.80 Vacuuming

		Crew	Daily Output	Labor-Hours	Unit	Material	2012 Bare Costs Labor	2012 Bare Costs Equipment	Total	Total In-House	Total Incl O&P
0530	14" opening carpet attachment, spot areas	1 Clam	75.67	.106	M.S.F.		2.79		2.79	3.46	4.32
0540	Traffic areas		45.40	.176			4.64		4.64	5.75	7.20
0550	All areas		21.62	.370			9.75		9.75	12.10	15.15
0560	16" opening carpet attachment, spot areas		82.32	.097			2.56		2.56	3.18	3.97
0570	Traffic areas		49.39	.162			4.27		4.27	5.30	6.65
0580	All areas		23.52	.340			8.95		8.95	11.15	13.90
0590	18" opening carpet attachment, spot areas		90.30	.089			2.33		2.33	2.90	3.62
0600	Traffic areas		54.18	.148			3.89		3.89	4.84	6.05
0610	All areas		25.80	.310			8.15		8.15	10.15	12.70
0620	20" opening carpet attachment, spot areas		100	.080			2.11		2.11	2.62	3.27
0630	Traffic areas		60	.133			3.51		3.51	4.37	5.45
0640	All areas		28.57	.280			7.40		7.40	9.15	11.45
0650	22" opening carpet attachment, spot areas		112	.071			1.88		1.88	2.34	2.92
0660	Traffic areas		67.20	.119			3.14		3.14	3.90	4.87
0670	All areas		32	.250			6.60		6.60	8.20	10.25
0680	24" opening carpet attachment, spot areas		127.26	.063			1.66		1.66	2.06	2.57
0690	Traffic areas		76.36	.105			2.76		2.76	3.43	4.29
0700	All areas		36.36	.220			5.80		5.80	7.20	9
0710	Large area machine, no obstructions, 26" opening		44.44	.180			4.74		4.74	5.90	7.35
0720	28" opening		64	.125			3.29		3.29	4.09	5.10
0730	30" opening		80	.100			2.64		2.64	3.28	4.09
0740	32" opening		120	.067			1.76		1.76	2.18	2.73

01 93 06.90 Wall Care

		Crew	Daily Output	Labor-Hours	Unit	Material	2012 Bare Costs Labor	2012 Bare Costs Equipment	Total	Total In-House	Total Incl O&P
0010	**WALL CARE**										
0020	Dusting walls, hand duster	1 Clam	87	.092	M.S.F.		2.42		2.42	3.01	3.76
0030	Treated cloth		40	.200			5.25		5.25	6.55	8.20
0040	Hand held duster vacuum		53	.151			3.98		3.98	4.94	6.15
0050	Cannister vacuum		32	.250			6.60		6.60	8.20	10.25
0060	Backpack vacuum		45	.178			4.68		4.68	5.80	7.25
0070	Washing walls, hand, painted surfaces		2.50	3.200		5.45	84.50		89.95	111.00	138
0080	Vinyl surfaces		3.25	2.462		5.45	65		70.45	86.50	108
0090	Machine, painted surfaces		4.80	1.667		5.45	44		49.45	60.50	75
0100	Washing walls from ladder, hand, painted surfaces		1.65	4.848		5.45	128		133.45	165.00	205
0110	Vinyl surfaces		2.15	3.721		5.45	98		103.45	128.00	159
0120	Machine, painted surfaces		3.17	2.524		5.45	66.50		71.95	88.50	110

01 93 06.95 Window and Accessory Care

		Crew	Daily Output	Labor-Hours	Unit	Material	2012 Bare Costs Labor	2012 Bare Costs Equipment	Total	Total In-House	Total Incl O&P
0010	**WINDOW AND ACCESSORY CARE**										
0025	Wash windows, trigger sprayer & wipe cloth, 12 S.F.	1 Clam	4.50	1.778	M.S.F.	4.14	47		51.14	63.00	77.50
0030	Over 12 S.F.		12.75	.627		4.14	16.55		20.69	25.00	30.50
0040	With squeegee & bucket, 12 S.F. and under		5.50	1.455		4.14	38.50		42.64	52.00	64.50
0050	Over 12 S.F.		15.50	.516		4.14	13.60		17.74	21.50	26
0060	Dust window sill		8640	.001	L.F.		.02		.02	.03	.04
0070	Damp wipe, venetian blinds		160	.050	Ea.	.11	1.32		1.43	1.76	2.19
0080	Vacuum, venetian blinds, horizontal		87.27	.092			2.42		2.42	3.00	3.75
0090	Draperies, in place, to 64 S.F.		160	.050			1.32		1.32	1.64	2.05

01 93 08 – Facility Maintenance Equipment

01 93 08.50 Equipment

		Crew	Daily Output	Labor-Hours	Unit	Material	2012 Bare Costs Labor	2012 Bare Costs Equipment	Total	Total In-House	Total Incl O&P
0010	**EQUIPMENT**, Purchase										
0090	Carpet care equipment										
0110	Dual motor vac, 1 H.P., 16" brush				Ea.	980			980	1,075.00	1,225
0120	Upright vacuum, 12" brush					335			335	370.00	420
0130	14" brush					380			380	420.00	475

01 93 08 – Facility Maintenance Equipment

01 93 08.50 Equipment	Crew	Daily Output	Labor-Hours	Unit	Material	2012 Bare Costs Labor	Equipment	Total	Total In-House	Total Incl O&P
0140	Soil extractor, hot water 5' wand, 12" head				Ea.	2,075			2,075	2,275.00	2,600
0150	Dry foam, 13" brush					1,575			1,575	1,725.00	1,975
0160	24" brush					2,150			2,150	2,375.00	2,700
0240	Floor care equipment										
0260	Polishing, buffing, waxing machine, 175 RPM										
0270	.33 H.P., 11" dia. brush				Ea.	600			600	660.00	750
0280	1 H.P., 16" dia. brush					970			970	1,075.00	1,225
0290	18" dia. brush					1,125			1,125	1,250.00	1,400
0300	1.5 H.P., 20" dia. brush					1,275			1,275	1,400.00	1,600
0310	24" dia. brush					1,375			1,375	1,525.00	1,725
0330	Scrubber, automatic, 2 stage 1 H.P. vacuum motor										
0340	20" dia. brush				Ea.	9,350			9,350	10,300.00	11,700
0350	28" dia. brush				"	13,600			13,600	15,000.00	17,000
1200	Plumbing maintenance equipment										
1220	Kinetic water ram				Ea.	203			203	223.00	254
1240	Cable pipe snake, 104 ft., self feed, electric, .5 H.P.				"	2,250			2,250	2,475.00	2,825
1500	Specialty equipment										
1550	Litterbuggy, 9 H.P. gasoline				Ea.	5,075			5,075	5,575.00	6,350
1560	Propane					2,675			2,675	2,950.00	3,350
1570	Pressure cleaner, hot water, minimum					3,375			3,375	3,725.00	4,225
1580	Maximum					6,125			6,125	6,750.00	7,650
1590	Vacuum cleaners, steel canister										
1600	Dry only, two stage, 1 H.P.				Ea.	305			305	335.00	380
1610	Wet/dry, two stage, 2 H.P.					460			460	505.00	575
1620	4 H.P.					795			795	875.00	995
1630	Wet/dry, three stage, 1.5 H.P.					460			460	505.00	575
1670	Squeegee wet only, 2 stage, 1 H.P.					770			770	845.00	965
1680	2 H.P.					1,325			1,325	1,450.00	1,650
1690	Asbestos and hazardous waste dry vacs, 1 H.P.					1,900			1,900	2,100.00	2,375
1700	2 H.P.					1,925			1,925	2,125.00	2,400
1710	Three stage, 1 H.P.					2,300			2,300	2,525.00	2,875
1800	Upholstery soil extractor, dry-foam					3,450			3,450	3,800.00	4,325
1900	Snow removal equipment										
1920	Thrower, 3 H.P., 20", single stage, gas				Ea.	625			625	690.00	780
1930	Electric start					725			725	800.00	905
1940	5 H.P., 24", 2 stage, gas					1,200			1,200	1,325.00	1,500
1950	11 H.P., 36"					2,900			2,900	3,200.00	3,625
2000	Tube cleaning equip., for heat exchangers, condensers, evap.										
2010	Tubes/pipes 1/4"-1", 115 volt, .5 H.P. drive				Ea.	1,525			1,525	1,675.00	1,900
2020	Air powered					1,600			1,600	1,750.00	2,000
2040	1" and up, 115 volt, 1 H.P. drive					1,700			1,700	1,875.00	2,125

Facilities Audits

Table of Contents

Auditing the Facility

Introduction

Capital budget planning begins with compiling a complete inventory of the facility, including equipment, that identifies existing deficiencies. The Facilities Audit is a vehicle for producing such an inventory; it is a system for thoroughly assessing the existing physical condition and functional performance of buildings, grounds, utilities, and equipment. The results of this audit are used to address major and minor, urgent and long-term needs for corrective action, for short- and long-term financial planning. The basic principles presented here can be applied to any scale operation, from a single structure to a facility consisting of multiple building complexes in dispersed locations.

The first step is determining the scope of the audit. Next, the audit team is selected, and a set of forms is designed. A survey team then records field observations on the forms for individual building components. Finally, the information from these forms is summarized, prioritized, presented, and used to:

- compare a building's condition and functional performance to that of other buildings within a facility
- define regular maintenance requirements
- define capital repair and replacement projects in order to eliminate deferred maintenance
- develop cost estimates for capital repair and replacement projects
- restore functionally obsolete facilities to a usable condition
- eliminate conditions that are either potentially damaging to property or present life safety hazards
- identify energy conservation measures

The audit ultimately produces a database on the condition of a facility's buildings, identifying the physical adequacy of construction, material, and equipment, and assessing the functional adequacy of the facility to perform its designated purpose. This comprehensive inventory can be used to guide property management decisions and strategic planning of capital assets, such as determining those expenditures necessary to extend the life of a facility.

The audit procedures and forms included here are for the purpose of identifying the condition of buildings and assessing the cost and priority of their repair. While this is a comprehensive stand-alone process, it is for the limited purposes of assessing costs and establishing priorities for repairs. It represents only a portion of the requirements of a full facilities audit. For further information and guidance on conducting a full audit, contact the RSMeans Engineering staff.

The Rating Forms

The audit approach involves conducting a thorough inspection of a facility, then employing a systematic process of completing individual forms for each component, following the order in which building components are assembled. This is a self-evaluation process designed to fit all types of structures. The audit procedure described is a "generic" approach that can be used as a starting point; the facilities manager should incorporate the special characteristics of an organization and its facilities into an individualized facilities audit.

Audits are best performed by the in-house personnel familiar with the building being audited. However, outside consultants may be required when staff is not available or when special expertise is required to further examine suspected deficiencies.

Four types of forms that can be used to conduct the building audit are described here. A complete set of the blank forms ready for photocopying follows.

1. *Building Data Summary*
   This form can be used to summarize all buildings to be covered by the audit.

2. *Facilities Inventory Form*
   This form is designed to collect the basic data about a specific building's characteristics (name, identification number, location, area), including land data. One form is prepared for each building to be audited as summarized on the *Building Data Summary* form.

3. *Standard Inspection Form*
   The standard form for recording observed deficiencies, it provides a uniform way to comment on, prioritize, and estimate the cost to correct those deficiencies. The *Standard Inspection Form* is designed to make use of cost data from the Maintenance & Repair and Preventive Maintenance sections of this publication. Cost data from publications such as *RSMeans Facilities Construction Cost Data* may be utilized as well.

4. *System Checklists*
   For each major building system from foundations through site work, there is a checklist to guide the audit and record the review process. The checklists are intended as general guides and may not be totally comprehensive. Be sure to make any necessary modifications (additions or deletions) required for the specific building being audited. The forms prompt the user on what to check and provide a place to check off or indicate by "Yes" or "No" the presence of deficiencies requiring further detailed analysis on the *Standard Inspection Form.*

Completing the Inspection Forms

The standard inspection forms are designed to be used in conjunction with the system checklists. A system checklist of typical deficiencies for each building system is completed as part of the inspection process. Then for each building deficiency, a standard inspection report is generated listing the identifying information as required on the form. With the deficiency defined and described, the specific work items required to correct the deficiency can be entered, prioritized, and costed in Part 3 of the form. The priority rating is further described below.

Priority Ratings

Priority rating is the inspector's judgment of the priority of an observed deficiency. The rating provides guidance for facilities managers who must review overall deficiencies and develop maintenance schedules and capital budgets. The following priority rating terms, commonly used in maintenance management, are a suggested guideline for priority values. The scale may be expanded as required to fit specific needs.

1. *Emergency*: This designation indicates work that demands immediate attention to repair an essential operating system or building component, or because life safety or property is endangered. A response should occur within two hours of notification.

2. *Urgent*: Work demanding prompt attention to alleviate temporary emergency repairs or a condition requiring correction within one to five days to prevent a subsequent emergency is classified as urgent.

3. *Routine*: A specific completion date can be requested or required for routine work. This includes work that has no short range effect on life safety, security of personnel, or property. Routine work can be planned in detail and incorporated into a trade backlog for scheduling within twelve months.

4. *Deferred*: Projects that can be deferred into the following year's work planning are classified as deferred.

Cost Estimates for Maintenance

A major characteristic of the audit described here is the application of detailed cost estimates. To prepare cost estimates for work required to correct deficiencies, detailed information about the nature and extent of the facility's condition is required at the beginning of the audit. However, when cost estimates are incorporated, the audit process generates highly useful summaries outlining major maintenance costs and priorities. Including cost estimates allows for comparisons to be made in order to prioritize repair and replacement needs on a project-by-project and building-by-building basis.

Other Considerations

A problem which may have to be settled by the audit leader is what to do with mixed-use buildings, those that have recent additions to the original construction, or buildings that have, under emergency circumstances, been forced to house new activities for which they were not designed. Such problems will have to be dealt with individually by the audit team.

The data gathered in a facilities audit must be kept current, gathered consistently, and regularly updated. An annual cycle of inspections is recommended. Each organization initiating a comprehensive audit and continuing with annual cycles of inspections will benefit from organizing data in a systematic format. Conducting annual audits in a consistent format provides the basis for monitoring the backlog of deferred maintenance and preparing effective long-term plans and budgets for maintenance and repair operations.

The forms are designed for ease of field entry of data and manual preparation of summaries and reports. The forms can also be created using basic word processing and spreadsheet software or database programming. Although the self-evaluation process is readily adaptable to data processing programs, not every organization has the capabilities or resources available. For those without computer capabilities, a manual method of storing and updating must be developed and used.

Summarizing the Audit Data

Information collected on the audit forms is compiled and used to determine the condition of the facility's buildings and what should be done to maintain and/or improve them. Summaries of a building audit can serve several purposes, some of which are listed below.

- *Routine Maintenance Needs:* A current property owner may be interested in planning and estimating a program for the cost of routine operations and maintenance.

- *Major Maintenance:* A current or prospective property owner may want to evaluate major maintenance needs to plan and estimate the cost of a corrective program.
- *Deferred Maintenance:* A backlog of routine and major maintenance can be addressed using a survey of conditions to plan and budget a deferred maintenance program.
- *Renovations and/or Additions:* Prior to developing feasibility studies on alternatives to renovations and/or additions, a survey of existing conditions may be necessary.
- *Capital Budgeting and Planning:* A comprehensive audit of facilities conditions will incorporate major maintenance requirements into overall capital needs.

Conclusion

The information and forms for conducting an audit of the facility are included in *RSMeans Facilities Maintenance & Repair Cost Data* to provide a method for applying the cost data to the actual maintenance and repair needs of a specific facility. The Facility Audit presented here is a subset of a more comprehensive audit program. The more comprehensive approach includes assessment of the building's functional performance, as well as additional forms and procedures to incorporate the cost of maintenance and repair into a comprehensive multi-year facility management plan.

BUILDING DATA SUMMARY

Building Number	Building Name	Building Use*	Location / Address	Ownership** Own/Lea/O-L

*   Principal and Special Uses

** Own = Owned
     Lea = Leased
     O-L = Owned/Leased

FACILITIES INVENTORY FORM

Building Data

1. Organization Name _____

2. Approved by: Name _____ Title _____ Date _____

3. Building Number _____

4. Property Name _____

5. Property Address _____

6. Property Main Use/Special Use _____

7. Gross Area (Sq. Ft.) _____ 8. Net Area (Sq. Ft.) _____

9. Type of Ownership: Owned _____ Leased _____ Owned / Leased _____

10. Book Value $ _____ Year Appraised _____

11. Replacement Value $ _____

12. Year Built _____ Year Acquired _____

13. Year Major Additions _____

Land Data

14. Type of Ownership: Owned _____ Leased _____ Owned / Leased _____

15. Book Value $ _____ Year Appraised _____

16. Year Acquired _____

17. Size in Acres _____

18. Market Value $ _____

Notes _____
_____
_____

STANDARD INSPECTION FORM

1. Facility Inspection Data

Facility #: _____   Name: _____

Component #: _____   Name: _____

Inspector: _____   Date: _____

2. Component Description

_____

_____

_____

3. Component Repair Evaluation

Defi- ciency #	Component Description	Line Number	Pri- ority	Unit	Quant.	Unit Cost	Total In-House	Unit Cost	Total W/O&P

577

Deficiencies	Causes
_____ Settlement, alignment changes or cracks	_____ Soils - changes in load bearing capacity due to shrinkage, erosion, or compaction. Adjacent construction undermining foundations. Reduced soil cover resulting in frost exposure.
	_____ Design loads - building equipment loads exceeding design loads. Vibration from heavy equipment requiring isolated foundations.
	_____ Structural or occupancy changes - inadequate bearing capacities. Foundation settling.
	_____ Earthquake resistance non-functioning.
_____ Moisture penetration	_____ Water table changes - inadequate drainage.
	_____ Ineffective drains or sump pump/sump pits.
	_____ Roof drainage - storm sewer connections inadequate or defective. Installation of roof drain restrictors, gutters, and downspouts where required.
	_____ Surface drainage - exterior grades should slope away from building and structures.
	_____ Utilities - broken or improperly functioning utility service lines or drains.
	_____ Leakage - wall cracks, opening of construction joints, inadequate or defective waterproofing.
	_____ Condensation - inadequate ventilation, vapor barrier, and/or dehumidification.
_____ Temperature changes	_____ Insulation - improperly selected for insulating value, fire ratings, and vermin resistance.
_____ Surface material deterioration	_____ Concrete, masonry, or stucco - spalling, corrosion of reinforcing, moisture penetration, or chemical reaction between cement and soil.
	_____ Steel or other ferrous metals - corrosion due to moisture or contact with acid-bearing soils.
	_____ Wood - decay due to moisture or insect infestation.
_____ Openings deterioration	_____ Non-functioning of doors, windows, hatchways, and stairways.
	_____ Utilities penetration due to damage, weather, wear, or other cause.

Deficiencies	Causes
_____ Floors, concrete - cracking or arching	_____ Shrinkage, or settlement of subsoil.
	_____ Inadequate drainage.
	_____ Movement in exterior walls, or frost heave.
	_____ Improper compaction of base. Erosion of base.
	_____ Heaving from hydraulic pressure.
_____ Floors, wood - rotting or arching	_____ Excessive dampness or insect infestation.
	_____ Leak in building exterior.
	_____ Lack of ventilation.
_____ Wall deterioration	_____ Concrete or masonry (see *A10 Foundations*)
_____ Crawl space ventilation and maintenance	_____ Inadequate air circulation due to blockage of openings in foundation walls.
	_____ Moisture barrier ineffective.
	_____ Pest control, housekeeping, and proper drainage.

The primary materials encountered in the superstructure inspection are concrete, steel, and wood. Typical observations of deficiencies will be observed by: failures in the exterior closure systems of exterior walls, openings, and roofs; cracks; movement of materials; moisture penetration; and discoloration. The exterior visual survey will detect failures of surface materials or at openings that will require further inspection to determine whether the cause was the superstructure system.

Deficiencies	**Causes**

Concrete (columns, walls, and floor and roof slabs)

_____	Overall alignment	_____	Settlement due to design and construction techniques.
		_____	Under designed for loading conditions (see *A10 Foundations*).
_____	Deflection	_____	Expansion and/or contraction due to changes in design loads.
		_____	Original design deficient.
		_____	Original materials deficient.
_____	Surface Conditions		
_____	Cracks	_____	Inadequate design and/or construction due to changes in design loads.
		_____	Stress concentration.
		_____	Extreme temperature changes; secondary effects of freeze-thaw.
_____	Scaling, spalls, and pop-outs	_____	Extreme temperature changes.
		_____	Reinforcement corrosion.
		_____	Environmental conditions.
		_____	Mechanical damage.
		_____	Poor materials.
_____	Stains	_____	Chemical reaction of reinforcing.
		_____	Reaction of materials in concrete mixture.
		_____	Environmental conditions.
_____	Exposed reinforcing	_____	Corrosion of steel.
		_____	Insufficient cover.
		_____	Mechanical damage.

Deficiencies	Causes

Steel (structural members, stairs, and connections)

_____ Overall alignment	_____	Settlement due to design and construction techniques; improper fabrication.
_____ Deflection or cracking	_____	Expansion and/or contraction.
	_____	Changes in design loads.
	_____	Fatigue due to vibration or impact.
_____ Corrosion	_____	Electrochemical reaction.
	_____	Failure of protective coating.
	_____	Excessive moisture exposure.
_____ Surface deterioration	_____	Excessive wear.

Wood (structural members and connections)

_____ Overall alignment	_____	Settlement; design and construction techniques.
_____ Deflection or cracking	_____	Expansion and/or contraction.
	_____	Changes in design loads.
	_____	Fatigue due to vibration or impact.
	_____	Failure of compression members.
	_____	Poor construction techniques.
	_____	General material failure.
_____ Rot (Decay)	_____	Direct contact with moisture.
	_____	Condensation.
	_____	Omission or deterioration of vapor barrier.
	_____	Poor construction techniques.
	_____	Damage from rodents or insects.

General Inspection

- Overall appearance
- Displacement
- Paint conditions
- Caulking
- Window & door fit
- Flashing condition

- Material integrity
- Cracks
- Evidence of moisture
- Construction joints
- Hardware condition

Exterior Walls

_____ Wood (Shingles, weatherboard siding, plywood).
_____ Paint or surface treatment condition
_____ Rot or decay

_____ Moisture penetration
_____ Loose, cracked, warped, or broken boards and shingles.

_____ Concrete, Masonry, and Tile (Concrete, brick, concrete masonry units, structural tile, glazed tile, stucco, stone).
_____ Settlement
_____ Construction and expansion joints
_____ Surface deterioration
_____ Parapet movement

_____ Structural frame movement causing cracks
_____ Condition of caulking and mortar
_____ Efflorescence and staining
_____ Tightness of fasteners

_____ Metal (Corrugated iron or steel, aluminum, enamel coated steel, protected metals).
_____ Settlement
_____ Condition of bracing
_____ Tightness of fasteners
_____ Flashings

_____ Structural frame movement
_____ Surface damage due to impact
_____ Caulking
_____ Corrosion

_____ Finishes (Mineral products, fiberglass, polyester resins, and plastics).
_____ Settlement
_____ Surface damage due to impact
_____ Stains
_____ Adhesion to substrate
_____ Flashings
_____ Asbestos products

_____ Structural frame movement
_____ Cracks
_____ Fasteners
_____ Caulking
_____ Lead paint

_____ Insulation
_____ Insulation present

_____ Satisfactory condition

Windows and Doors

_____ Frame fitting
_____ Paint or surface finish
_____ Hardware and operating parts
_____ Cleanliness
_____ Rot or corrosion

_____ Frame and molding condition
_____ Putty and weatherstripping
_____ Security
_____ Material condition (glass, wood, & metal Panels)
_____ Screens and storm windows

Shading Devices

_____ Material conditions
_____ Cleanliness

_____ Operations

B30 ROOFING INSPECTION CHECKLIST

General Appearance

Good_____ Fair_____ Poor_____

_____ **Water tightness**

_____ Evidence of leaks on undersurface	_____ Surface weathering
_____ Faulty material	_____ Faulty design
_____ Faulty application	_____ Standing water
_____ Weather damage	_____ Mechanical damage
_____ Fastening failure	_____ Flashing failure

_____ **Roofing Surface**

_____ Built Up (Felt or bitumen surfacing)

_____ Adhesion	_____ Moisture meter readings
_____ Bare areas	_____ Blisters, wrinkles
_____ Cracks, holes, tears	_____ Fish mouths
_____ Alligatoring	_____ Ballast

_____ Single Ply (Thermosetting, thermoplastic, composites)

_____ Adhesion	_____ Moisture meter readings
_____ Bare areas	_____ Blisters, wrinkles
_____ Cracks	_____ Holes, tears
_____ Seam conditions	_____ Protective coating
_____ Ballast	

_____ Metal Roofing (Preformed, formed)

_____ Corrosion (%)	_____ Protective coating
_____ Seams	_____ Cracks or breaks
_____ Holes	_____ Expansion joints

_____ Shingles & Tiles (Metal, clay, mission, concrete, or others)

_____ Disintegration	_____ Broken or cracked (%)
_____ Missing (%)	_____ Fasteners
_____ Underlayment	

_____ Wood shingles

_____ Cracked	_____ Curled
_____ Missing (%)	

B30 ROOFING INSPECTION CHECKLIST

_____ **Insulation**

     _____ Full coverage (%)   _____ Full thickness (%)

     _____ Satisfactory condition

_____ **Roof Penetrations**

     _____ Weather tightness   _____ Operable

_____ **Flashing**

     _____ Deterioration   _____ Open joints

     _____ Holes or damage   _____ Anchoring

     _____ Protective coating

_____ **Drainage**

     _____ Alignment   _____ Free flowing

     _____ Clamping rings secure   _____ Screens

     _____ Corrosion

General Inspection

Overall Appearance

     Good _____   Fair _____   Poor _____

     _____ Evidence of moisture   _____ Settlement

     _____ Cracks   _____ Surface condition

     _____ Cleanliness   _____ Stains

     _____ Discoloration

_____ **Paint**

     _____ Repainting necessary   _____ Peeling, cracking, flaking

     _____ Reflectivity   _____ Maintainability

     _____ Lead paint

_____ **Coverings & Coatings**

     _____ Replacement necessary   _____ Peeling

     _____ Rips, tears   _____ Holes

     _____ Adhesion   _____ Seams

_____ **Interior glazing**

     _____ Cracks   _____ Seals

     _____ Frame condition   _____ Missing panes

     _____ Shading devices

General Inspection

- Strength & stability
- Acoustical quality
- Maintainability

- Physical condition
- Adaptability
- Code compliance

Deficiencies   **Causes**

Wall Material

	Deficiencies		Causes
_____	Cracks	_____	Settlement
_____	Holes	_____	Defective material
_____	Looseness	_____	Operational abuse or vibrations
_____	Missing segments	_____	Environmental attack
_____	Water stains	_____	Moisture
_____	Joints	_____	Structural expansion or contraction
_____	Surface appearance	_____	Wind pressure

Hardware

	Deficiencies		Causes
_____	Overall condition	_____	Appearance
_____	Keying system	_____	Operations
_____	Fit	_____	Locksets
_____	Cylinders	_____	Panic devices
_____	Maintainability	_____	Security operations

C30 WALLS & FINISHES INSPECTION CHECKLIST

General Inspection

Code compliance _____

Maintainability _____

Means of egress _____

Fire ratings _____

Audible & visual device condition _____

Extinguishing systems (see also *08 Mechanical/Plumbing*): _____

   Type _____

Lighting system (see also *09 Electrical Lighting/Power*): _____

   Type _____

Handicapped accessibility _____

Building user comments _____

_____

Exterior Lighting

Adequacy:

   Good _____   Fair _____   Poor _____

Condition _____

Controls (type & location) _____

Fire Alarm Systems

_____ Panel visible   _____ Operational

_____ Pull station condition   _____ Detector conditions

Stairs and Ramps

_____ Exits marked   _____ Hardware operational

_____ Tripping hazards   _____ Surface conditions

_____ Lighting adequate   _____ Handrails

General Inspection

Overall Appearance

Good_____   Fair_____   Poor_____

- Evidence of moisture
- Irregular surface
- Handicapped hazards

- Visible settlement
- Tripping hazards
- Replacement necessary

Carpet (Tufted, tile)

_____ Age
_____ Stains
_____ Holes, tears

_____ Excessive wear
_____ Discoloration
_____ Seam conditions

Resilient (Asphalt tile, cork tile, linoleum, rubber, vinyl)

_____ Broken tiles
_____ Shrinkage
_____ Fading
_____ Porosity

_____ Loose tiles
_____ Lifting, cupping
_____ Cuts, holes
_____ Asbestos present

Masonry (Stone, brick)

_____ Cracks
_____ Joints
_____ Porosity

_____ Deterioration
_____ Stains
_____ Sealing

Monolithic Topping (Concrete, granolithic, terrazzo, magnesite)

_____ Cracks
_____ Joints

_____ Porosity
_____ Sealing

Wood (Plank, strips, block, parquet)

_____ Shrinkage
_____ Excessive wear
_____ Decay

_____ Cupping, warpage
_____ Unevenness
_____ Sealing

General Inspection

Overall appearance

Good ____   Fair ____   Poor ____

- Settlement or sagging
- Attachment
- Stains, discoloration
- Suitability
- Code compliance

- Alignment
- Evidence of moisture
- Missing units
- Acoustic quality

Exposed Systems (Unpainted, painted, spray-on, decorative)

____   Cracks
____   Surface deterioration
____   Missing elements
____   Adhesion

Applied to Structure & Suspended

General Condition:

Good ____   Fair ____   Poor ____

____   Fasteners
____   Trim condition

Openings:

____   Panels   ____   Inserts
____   Lighting fixtures   ____   Air distribution
____   Fire protection   ____   Other

General Inspection (Passenger Conveying)

Overall appearance (interior)

       Good _____   Fair _____   Poor _____

Overall appearance (exterior)

       Good _____   Fair _____   Poor _____

_____ Maintenance history available

    _____ Regular inspection frequency

    _____ Door operations

    _____ Control systems

    _____ Noise

    _____ Code compliance

    _____ Handicapped access

    _____ Major repairs necessary

    _____ Replacement necessary

D20 MECHANICAL/PLUMBING INSPECTION CHECKLIST

General Inspection

    General appearance

        Good _____   Fair _____   Poor _____

    Leaks, dripping, running faucets and valves   _____

    Maintenance history   _____

    Supply adequacy   _____

    Sanitation hazards   _____

    Drain & waste connection   _____

    Backflow protection   _____

    Cross connections   _____

    Fixture quantity   _____

    Fixture types & conditions   _____

    Handicapped fixtures   _____

    Female facilities   _____

    Metal pipe & fittings corrosion   _____

    Pipe joints & sealing   _____

    Pipe insulation   _____

    Hanger supports & clamps   _____

    Filters   _____

    Building user comments   _____

_____ **Water System**

    _____ Water pressure adequate   _____ Odors, tastes
    _____ Main cutoff operable   _____ Water heating temperature setting
    _____ Pump condition   _____ Insulation condition

_____ **Sanitary & Storm System**

    _____ Flow adequate   _____ Cleanouts access
    _____ Floor drains   _____ Chemical resistance
    _____ Gradient   _____ On-site disposal system

_____ **Code Requirements**

    _____ EPA/local permits   _____ Other

_____ **Fire protection system**

    _____ Regular inspections   _____ Sprinkler heads operable
    _____ Complies with code   _____ Controls operable
    _____ Hose cabinets functional   _____ Water pressure sufficient

General Inspection

General appearance

Good _____   Fair _____   Poor _____

Lubrication: bearings and moving parts _____

Rust and corrosion _____

Motors, fans, drive assemblies, and pumps _____

Wiring and electrical controls _____

Thermostats and automatic temperature controls _____

Thermal insulation and protective coatings _____

Guards, casings, hangers, supports, platforms, and mounting bolts _____

Piping system identification _____

Solenoid valves _____

Burner assemblies _____

Combustion chambers, smokepipes, and breeching _____

Electrical heating units _____

Guards, casings, hangers, supports, platforms, and mounting bolts _____

Steam and hot water heating equipment _____

Accessible steam, water, and fuel piping _____

Traps _____

Humidifier assemblies and controls _____

Strainers _____

Water sprays, weirs, and similar devices _____

Shell-and tube-type condensers _____

Self-contained evaporative condensers _____

Air cooled condensers _____

Compressors _____

Liquid receivers _____

Refrigerant driers, strainers, valves, oil traps, and accessories _____

Building user comments _____

Cleaning, maintenance, repair, and replacement

_____ Registers   _____ Grills
_____ Dampers   _____ Draft diverters
_____ Plenum chambers   _____ Supply and return ducts
_____ Louvers   _____ Fire dampers

Air filters

_____ Correct type   _____ Replacement schedule

Heating System Evaluation

_____ Heating capacity   _____ Temperature control
_____ Heating:

      _____ Seasonal   _____ All year

_____ Noise level   _____ Energy consumption
_____ Air circulation & ventilation   _____ Filtration
_____ Humidity control

Cooling System Evaluation

_____ Cooling capacity   _____ Temperature and humidity control
_____ Cooling all season   _____ Noise level
_____ Energy consumption   _____ Air circulation & ventilation
_____ Filtration   _____ Reliability

Ventilation System Evaluation

_____ Air velocity   _____ Exhaust air systems
_____ Bag collection   _____ Wet collectors
_____ Steam and hot water coils   _____ Electrical heating units
_____ Fire hazards   _____ Fire protective devices

General Inspection

Safety conditions   _____

Service capacity, % used, and age   _____

Switchgear capacity, % used, and age   _____

Feeder capacity, % used, and age   _____

Panel capacity   _____

Thermo-scanning   _____

Maintenance records available   _____

Convenience outlets   _____

Building user comments   _____

Exterior Service

_____ Line drawing
_____ Feed source:
     _____ Utility/owned   _____ Above/below ground
_____ Transformer:
     _____ Transformer tested   _____ Transformer arcing or burning
     _____ Transformer PCB's   _____ Ownership (facility or utility)

Interior Distribution System

_____ Line drawing   _____ Incoming conduit marked
_____ Main circuit breaker marked   _____ Panel boards, junction boxes covered
_____ All wiring in conduit   _____ Conduit properly secured
_____ Panels marked   _____ Panel schedules
_____ Missing breakers

Emergency Circuits

Emergency generator(s):

_____ Condition and age   _____ Auto start and switchover
_____ Testing schedule   _____ Test records available
_____ Service schedule   _____ Service schedule records available
_____ Circuits appropriate   _____ Cooling & exhaust
_____ Fuel storage (capacity)

Emergency lighting/power systems:

_____ Battery operation   _____ Separate power feed
_____ Exit signs   _____ Stairways/corridors
_____ Elevators   _____ Interior areas
_____ HVAC   _____ Exterior

General Inspection

Overall appearance

Good _____   Fair _____   Poor _____

Maintainability _____

Repairs/replacements _____

Code compliance _____

Roads, Walks, and Parking Lots

Surface conditions _____

Subsurface conditions _____

Settling and uplift _____

Cracks, holes _____

Drainage and slope _____

Curbing

Alignment _____

Erosion _____

Repairs/replacements _____

Drainage and Erosion Controls

Surface drainage _____

Manholes, catch basins _____

Vegetation _____

Channels, dikes _____

Retention, detention _____

Drains _____

Parking Lot Controls

Location _____

Operation _____

Repairs/replacements _____

G20   SITE WORK INSPECTION CHECKLIST

General Inspection

Code compliance _____

Maintainability _____

Means of egress _____

Fire ratings _____

Audible & visual device condition _____

Extinguishing systems (see also *D20 Mechanical/Plumbing*): _____

      Type _____

Lighting system (see also *D50 Electrical Lighting/Power*): _____

      Type _____

Handicapped accessibility _____

Building user comments _____

_____

Exterior Lighting

Adequacy:

    Good _____   Fair _____   Poor_____

Condition _____

Controls (type & location) _____

Fire Alarm Systems

_____	Panel visible	_____	Operational
_____	Pull station condition	_____	Detector conditions

Stairs and Ramps

_____	Exits marked	_____	Hardware operational
_____	Tripping hazards	_____	Surface conditions
_____	Lighting adequate	_____	Handrails

H10 SAFETY INSPECTION CHECKLIST

General Inspection

Code compliance _____

Maintainability _____

Means of egress _____

Fire ratings _____

Audible & visual device condition _____

Extinguishing systems (see also *D20 Mechanical/Plumbing*): _____

    Type _____

Lighting system (see also *D50 Electrical Lighting/Power*): _____

    Type _____

Handicapped accessibility _____

Building user comments _____

_____

Exterior Lighting

Adequacy:

    Good _____   Fair _____   Poor_____

Condition _____

Controls (type & location) _____

Fire Alarm Systems

_____ Panel visible   _____ Operational

_____ Pull station condition   _____ Detector conditions

Stairs and Ramps

_____ Exits marked   _____ Hardware operational

_____ Tripping hazards   _____ Surface conditions

_____ Lighting adequate   _____ Handrails

H10 SAFETY INSPECTION CHECKLIST

Reference Section

All the reference information is in one section, making it easy to find what you need to know . . . and easy to use the book on a daily basis. This section is visually identified by a vertical gray bar on the page edges.

In this Reference Section we've included information on Equipment Rental Costs, Crew Listings, Travel Costs, Reference Tables, Life Cycle Costing, and a listing of Abbreviations.

Table of Contents

Estimating Tips

- This section contains the average costs to rent and operate hundreds of pieces of construction equipment. This is useful information when estimating the time and material requirements of any particular operation in order to establish a unit or total cost. Equipment costs include not only rental, but also operating costs for equipment under normal use.

Rental Costs

- Equipment rental rates are obtained from industry sources throughout North America–contractors, suppliers, dealers, manufacturers, and distributors.
- Rental rates vary throughout the country, with larger cities generally having lower rates. Lease plans for new equipment are available for periods in excess of six months, with a percentage of payments applying toward purchase.
- Monthly rental rates vary from 2% to 5% of the purchase price of the equipment depending on the anticipated life of the equipment and its wearing parts.
- Weekly rental rates are about 1/3 the monthly rates, and daily rental rates are about 1/3 the weekly rate.
- Rental rates can also be treated as reimbursement costs for contractor-owned equipment. Owned equipment costs include depreciation, loan payments, interest, taxes, insurance, storage, and major repairs.

Operating Costs

- The operating costs include parts and labor for routine servicing, such as repair and replacement of pumps, filters and worn lines. Normal operating expendables, such as fuel, lubricants, tires and electricity (where applicable), are also included.
- Extraordinary operating expendables with highly variable wear patterns, such as diamond bits and blades, are excluded. These costs can be found as material costs in the Unit Price section.
- The hourly operating costs listed do not include the operator's wages.

Equipment Cost/Day

- Any power equipment required by a crew is shown in the Crew Listings with a daily cost.
- The daily cost of equipment needed by a crew is based on dividing the weekly rental rate by 5 (number of working days in the week), and then adding the hourly operating cost times 8 (the number of hours in a day). This "Equipment Cost/Day" is shown in the far right column of the Equipment Rental pages.
- If equipment is needed for only one or two days, it is best to develop your own cost by including components for daily rent and hourly operating cost. This is important when the listed Crew for a task does not contain the equipment needed, such as a crane for lifting mechanical heating/cooling equipment up onto a roof.

- If the quantity of work is less than the crew's Daily Output shown for a Unit Price line item that includes a bare unit equipment cost, it is recommended to estimate one day's rental cost and operating cost for equipment shown in the Crew Listing for that line item.

Mobilization/ Demobilization

- The cost to move construction equipment from an equipment yard or rental company to the jobsite and back again is not included in equipment rental costs listed in the Reference section, nor in the bare equipment cost of any Unit Price line item, nor in any equipment costs shown in the Crew listings.
- Mobilization (to the site) and demobilization (from the site) costs can be found in the Unit Price section.
- If a piece of equipment is already at the jobsite, it is not appropriate to utilize mobil./demob. costs again in an estimate.

01 54 33 | Equipment Rental

		UNIT	HOURLY OPER. COST	RENT PER DAY	RENT PER WEEK	RENT PER MONTH	EQUIPMENT COST/DAY	
10	**0010**	**CONCRETE EQUIPMENT RENTAL** without operators R015433 -10						**10**
	0200	Bucket, concrete lightweight, 1/2 C.Y.	Ea.	.75	22	66	198	19.20
	0300	1 C.Y.		.80	26.50	80	240	22.40
	0400	1-1/2 C.Y.		1.05	36.50	110	330	30.40
	0500	2 C.Y.		1.15	43.50	130	390	35.20
	0580	8 C.Y.		5.80	255	765	2,300	199.40
	0600	Cart, concrete, self-propelled, operator walking, 10 C.F.		2.85	56.50	170	510	56.80
	0700	Operator riding, 18 C.F.		4.80	93.50	280	840	94.40
	0800	Conveyer for concrete, portable, gas, 16" wide, 26' long		11.00	122	365	1,100	161
	0900	46' long		11.40	147	440	1,325	179.20
	1000	56' long		11.50	157	470	1,400	186
	1100	Core drill, electric, 2-1/2 H.P., 1" to 8" bit diameter		1.40	59.50	179	535	47
	1150	11 H.P., 8" to 18" cores		5.40	112	335	1,000	110.20
	1200	Finisher, concrete floor, gas, riding trowel, 96" wide		10.90	145	435	1,300	174.20
	1300	Gas, walk-behind, 3 blade, 36" trowel		1.80	20	60	180	26.40
	1400	4 blade, 48" trowel		3.55	27	81	243	44.60
	1500	Float, hand-operated (Bull float) 48" wide		.08	13.65	41	123	8.85
	1570	Curb builder, 14 H.P., gas, single screw		13.10	245	735	2,200	251.80
	1590	Double screw		13.75	283	850	2,550	280
	1600	Floor grinder, concrete and terrazzo, electric, 22" path		1.84	117	350	1,050	84.70
	1700	Edger, concrete, electric, 7" path		.90	51.50	155	465	38.20
	1750	Vacuum pick-up system for floor grinders, wet/dry		1.35	81.50	245	735	59.80
	1800	Mixer, powered, mortar and concrete, gas, 6 C.F., 18 H.P.		7.60	117	350	1,050	130.80
	1900	10 C.F., 25 H.P.		9.45	142	425	1,275	160.60
	2000	16 C.F.		9.75	165	495	1,475	177
	2100	Concrete, stationary, tilt drum, 2 C.Y.		6.55	230	690	2,075	190.40
	2120	Pump, concrete, truck mounted 4" line 80' boom		23.95	875	2,620	7,850	715.60
	2140	5" line, 110' boom		31.05	1,150	3,465	10,400	941.40
	2160	Mud jack, 50 C.F. per hr.		6.55	125	375	1,125	127.40
	2180	225 C.F. per hr.		8.70	142	425	1,275	154.60
	2190	Shotcrete pump rig, 12 C.Y./hr.		13.75	220	660	1,975	242
	2200	35 C.Y./hr.		15.85	237	710	2,125	268.80
	2600	Saw, concrete, manual, gas, 18 H.P.		5.00	43.50	130	390	66
	2650	Self-propelled, gas, 30 H.P.		11.00	100	300	900	148
	2700	Vibrators, concrete, electric, 60 cycle, 2 H.P.		.30	8.65	26	78	7.60
	2800	3 H.P.		.43	11.65	35	105	10.45
	2900	Gas engine, 5 H.P.		1.70	16	48	144	23.20
	3000	8 H.P.		2.30	15	45	135	27.40
	3050	Vibrating screed, gas engine, 8 H.P.		2.81	71.50	215	645	65.50
	3120	Concrete transit mixer, 6 x 4, 250 H.P., 8 C.Y., rear discharge		52.20	570	1,705	5,125	758.60
	3200	Front discharge		61.30	695	2,090	6,275	908.40
	3300	6 x 6, 285 H.P., 12 C.Y., rear discharge		60.40	655	1,970	5,900	877.20
	3400	Front discharge	▼	63.10	705	2,115	6,350	927.80
20	**0010**	**EARTHWORK EQUIPMENT RENTAL** without operators R015433 -10						**20**
	0040	Aggregate spreader, push type 8' to 12' wide	Ea.	2.70	25.50	76	228	36.80
	0045	Tailgate type, 8' wide		2.55	33	99	297	40.20
	0055	Earth auger, truck-mounted, for fence & sign posts, utility poles		15.30	470	1,405	4,225	403.40
	0060	For borings and monitoring wells		41.30	645	1,940	5,825	718.40
	0070	Portable, trailer mounted		2.75	31.50	95	285	41
	0075	Truck-mounted, for caissons, water wells		89.05	2,875	8,645	25,900	2,441
	0080	Horizontal boring machine, 12" to 36" diameter, 45 H.P.		22.20	192	575	1,725	292.60
	0090	12" to 48" diameter, 65 H.P.		30.95	335	1,000	3,000	447.60
	0095	Auger, for fence posts, gas engine, hand held		.50	6	18	54	7.60
	0100	Excavator, diesel hydraulic, crawler mounted, 1/2 C.Y. capacity		18.80	370	1,105	3,325	371.40
	0120	5/8 C.Y. capacity		28.60	540	1,615	4,850	551.80
	0140	3/4 C.Y. capacity		34.90	615	1,840	5,525	647.20
	0150	1 C.Y. capacity	▼	42.70	680	2,035	6,100	748.60

01 54 33 | Equipment Rental

		UNIT	HOURLY OPER. COST	RENT PER DAY	RENT PER WEEK	RENT PER MONTH	EQUIPMENT COST/DAY	
0200	1-1/2 C.Y. capacity	Ea.	51.80	910	2,730	8,200	960.40	
0300	2 C.Y. capacity		68.70	1,175	3,515	10,500	1,253	
0320	2-1/2 C.Y. capacity		92.40	1,525	4,565	13,700	1,652	
0325	3-1/2 C.Y. capacity		124.00	2,025	6,095	18,300	2,211	
0330	4-1/2 C.Y. capacity		149.80	2,575	7,750	23,300	2,748	
0335	6 C.Y. capacity		188.25	2,875	8,615	25,800	3,229	
0340	7 C.Y. capacity		190.45	2,975	8,900	26,700	3,304	
0342	Excavator attachments, bucket thumbs		3.05	240	720	2,150	168.40	
0345	Grapples		2.75	208	625	1,875	147	
0347	Hydraulic hammer for boom mounting, 5000 ft lb.		13.70	425	1,275	3,825	364.60	
0349	11,000 ft lb.		22.35	755	2,260	6,775	630.80	
0350	Gradall type, truck mounted, 3 ton @ 15' radius, 5/8 C.Y.		39.75	875	2,630	7,900	844	
0370	1 C.Y. capacity		43.65	1,025	3,060	9,175	961.20	
0400	Backhoe-loader, 40 to 45 H.P., 5/8 C.Y. capacity		12.90	240	720	2,150	247.20	
0450	45 H.P. to 60 H.P., 3/4 C.Y. capacity		19.75	293	880	2,650	334	
0460	80 H.P., 1-1/4 C.Y. capacity		21.60	320	955	2,875	363.80	
0470	112 H.P., 1-1/2 C.Y. capacity		35.65	655	1,960	5,875	677.20	
0482	Backhoe-loader attachment, compactor, 20,000 lb.		5.50	142	425	1,275	129	
0485	Hydraulic hammer, 750 ft lb.		3.10	95	285	855	81.80	
0486	Hydraulic hammer, 1200 ft lb.		6.05	217	650	1,950	178.40	
0500	Brush chipper, gas engine, 6" cutter head, 35 H.P.		9.75	107	320	960	142	
0550	Diesel engine, 12" cutter head, 130 H.P.		18.60	225	675	2,025	283.80	
0600	15" cutter head, 165 H.P.		23.35	265	795	2,375	345.80	
0750	Bucket, clamshell, general purpose, 3/8 C.Y.		1.20	38.50	115	345	32.60	
0800	1/2 C.Y.		1.30	45	135	405	37.40	
0850	3/4 C.Y.		1.45	53.50	160	480	43.60	
0900	1 C.Y.		1.50	58.50	175	525	47	
0950	1-1/2 C.Y.		2.45	80	240	720	67.60	
1000	2 C.Y.		2.55	88.50	265	795	73.40	
1010	Bucket, dragline, medium duty, 1/2 C.Y.		.70	23.50	70	210	19.60	
1020	3/4 C.Y.		.70	24.50	74	222	20.40	
1030	1 C.Y.		.75	26.50	80	240	22	
1040	1-1/2 C.Y.		1.15	40	120	360	33.20	
1050	2 C.Y.		1.25	45	135	405	37	
1070	3 C.Y.		1.85	61.50	185	555	51.80	
1200	Compactor, manually guided 2-drum vibratory smooth roller, 7.5 H.P.		6.70	197	590	1,775	171.60	
1250	Rammer/tamper, gas, 8"		2.40	41.50	125	375	44.20	
1260	15"		2.60	48.50	145	435	49.80	
1300	Vibratory plate, gas, 18" plate, 3000 lb. blow		2.30	23	69	207	32.20	
1350	21" plate, 5000 lb. blow		2.85	30	90	270	40.80	
1370	Curb builder/extruder, 14 H.P., gas, single screw		13.10	245	735	2,200	251.80	
1390	Double screw		13.75	283	850	2,550	280	
1500	Disc harrow attachment, for tractor		.42	69.50	209	625	45.15	
1810	Feller buncher, shearing & accumulating trees, 100 H.P.		31.15	545	1,640	4,925	577.20	
1860	Grader, self-propelled, 25,000 lb.		27.85	525	1,580	4,750	538.80	
1910	30,000 lb.		31.10	605	1,810	5,425	610.80	
1920	40,000 lb.		48.75	1,025	3,105	9,325	1,011	
1930	55,000 lb.		64.25	1,500	4,530	13,600	1,420	
1950	Hammer, pavement breaker, self-propelled, diesel, 1000 to 1250 lb.		26.10	345	1,040	3,125	416.80	
2000	1300 to 1500 lb.		39.15	695	2,080	6,250	729.20	
2050	Pile driving hammer, steam or air, 4150 ft lb. @ 225 bpm		10.00	480	1,435	4,300	367	
2100	8750 ft lb. @ 145 bpm		12.00	665	2,000	6,000	496	
2150	15,000 ft lb. @ 60 bpm		13.55	805	2,415	7,250	591.40	
2200	24,450 ft lb. @ 111 bpm		14.60	895	2,680	8,050	652.80	
2250	Leads, 60' high for pile driving hammers up to 20,000 ft lb.		3.15	80.50	242	725	73.60	
2300	90' high for hammers over 20,000 ft lb.		4.75	143	430	1,300	124	
2350	Diesel type hammer, 22,400 ft lb.		27.60	620	1,860	5,575	592.80	
2400	41,300 ft lb.		35.35	675	2,020	6,050	686.80	

20

01 54 33 | Equipment Rental

		UNIT	HOURLY OPER. COST	RENT PER DAY	RENT PER WEEK	RENT PER MONTH	EQUIPMENT COST/DAY	
20	2450	141,000 ft lb.	Ea.	52.60	1,150	3,440	10,300	1,109	20
	2500	Vib. elec. hammer/extractor, 200 kW diesel generator, 34 H.P.		45.65	645	1,940	5,825	753.20	
	2550	80 H.P.		82.40	945	2,840	8,525	1,227	
	2600	150 H.P.		155.30	1,825	5,465	16,400	2,335	
	2800	Log chipper, up to 22" diameter, 600 H.P.		50.70	510	1,525	4,575	710.60	
	2850	Logger, for skidding & stacking logs, 150 H.P.		46.90	815	2,450	7,350	865.20	
	2860	Mulcher, diesel powered, trailer mounted		19.70	215	645	1,925	286.60	
	2900	Rake, spring tooth, with tractor		15.41	335	1,007	3,025	324.70	
	3000	Roller, vibratory, tandem, smooth drum, 20 H.P.		7.90	143	430	1,300	149.20	
	3050	35 H.P.		9.95	247	740	2,225	227.60	
	3100	Towed type vibratory compactor, smooth drum, 50 H.P.		23.60	335	1,000	3,000	388.80	
	3150	Sheepsfoot, 50 H.P.		24.90	370	1,105	3,325	420.20	
	3170	Landfill compactor, 220 H.P.		77.35	1,425	4,305	12,900	1,480	
	3200	Pneumatic tire roller, 80 H.P.		14.15	335	1,000	3,000	313.20	
	3250	120 H.P.		21.25	560	1,680	5,050	506	
	3300	Sheepsfoot vibratory roller, 240 H.P.		58.10	1,050	3,180	9,550	1,101	
	3320	340 H.P.		85.45	1,525	4,575	13,700	1,599	
	3350	Smooth drum vibratory roller, 75 H.P.		22.10	565	1,690	5,075	514.80	
	3400	125 H.P.		28.40	690	2,065	6,200	640.20	
	3410	Rotary mower, brush, 60", with tractor		19.80	310	925	2,775	343.40	
	3420	Rototiller, walk-behind, gas, 5 H.P.		2.23	67.50	203	610	58.45	
	3422	8 H.P.		3.47	103	310	930	89.75	
	3440	Scrapers, towed type, 7 C.Y. capacity		5.40	108	325	975	108.20	
	3450	10 C.Y. capacity		6.15	150	450	1,350	139.20	
	3500	15 C.Y. capacity		6.60	173	520	1,550	156.80	
	3525	Self-propelled, single engine, 14 C.Y. capacity		91.35	1,350	4,030	12,100	1,537	
	3550	Dual engine, 21 C.Y. capacity		131.60	1,525	4,605	13,800	1,974	
	3600	31 C.Y. capacity		181.80	2,350	7,070	21,200	2,868	
	3640	44 C.Y. capacity		230.40	3,200	9,625	28,900	3,768	
	3650	Elevating type, single engine, 11 C.Y. capacity		61.60	1,025	3,060	9,175	1,105	
	3700	22 C.Y. capacity		113.95	1,975	5,935	17,800	2,099	
	3710	Screening plant 110 H.P. w/5' x 10' screen		33.90	435	1,305	3,925	532.20	
	3720	5' x 16' screen		36.15	540	1,625	4,875	614.20	
	3850	Shovel, crawler-mounted, front-loading, 7 C.Y. capacity		200.60	2,750	8,270	24,800	3,259	
	3855	12 C.Y. capacity		268.10	3,500	10,520	31,600	4,249	
	3860	Shovel/backhoe bucket, 1/2 C.Y.		2.30	65	195	585	57.40	
	3870	3/4 C.Y.		2.40	71.50	215	645	62.20	
	3880	1 C.Y.		2.50	80	240	720	68	
	3890	1-1/2 C.Y.		2.60	93.50	280	840	76.80	
	3910	3 C.Y.		2.95	127	380	1,150	99.60	
	3950	Stump chipper, 18" deep, 30 H.P.		7.21	188	565	1,700	170.70	
	4110	Dozer, crawler, torque converter, diesel 80 H.P.		25.30	400	1,200	3,600	442.40	
	4150	105 H.P.		30.85	505	1,520	4,550	550.80	
	4200	140 H.P.		44.30	770	2,315	6,950	817.40	
	4260	200 H.P.		65.75	1,200	3,585	10,800	1,243	
	4310	300 H.P.		86.45	1,700	5,130	15,400	1,718	
	4360	410 H.P.		117.20	2,225	6,670	20,000	2,272	
	4370	500 H.P.		150.10	2,900	8,680	26,000	2,937	
	4380	700 H.P.		222.15	4,100	12,290	36,900	4,235	
	4400	Loader, crawler, torque conv., diesel, 1-1/2 C.Y., 80 H.P.		26.70	460	1,375	4,125	488.60	
	4450	1-1/2 to 1-3/4 C.Y., 95 H.P.		30.40	590	1,775	5,325	598.20	
	4510	1-3/4 to 2-1/4 C.Y., 130 H.P.		47.40	860	2,580	7,750	895.20	
	4530	2-1/2 to 3-1/4 C.Y., 190 H.P.		57.75	1,075	3,220	9,650	1,106	
	4560	3-1/2 to 5 C.Y., 275 H.P.		73.90	1,425	4,260	12,800	1,443	
	4610	Front end loader, 4WD, articulated frame, diesel, 1 to 1-1/4 C.Y., 70 H.P.		16.65	225	675	2,025	268.20	
	4620	1-1/2 to 1-3/4 C.Y., 95 H.P.		20.85	278	835	2,500	333.80	
	4650	1-3/4 to 2 C.Y., 130 H.P.		24.40	365	1,100	3,300	415.20	
	4710	2-1/2 to 3-1/2 C.Y., 145 H.P.		27.55	420	1,260	3,775	472.40	

01 54 33 | Equipment Rental

		UNIT	HOURLY OPER. COST	RENT PER DAY	RENT PER WEEK	RENT PER MONTH	EQUIPMENT COST/DAY	
20	4730	3 to 4-1/2 C.Y., 185 H.P.	Ea.	35.25	550	1,645	4,925	611	**20**
	4760	5-1/4 to 5-3/4 C.Y., 270 H.P.		56.50	845	2,540	7,625	960	
	4810	7 to 9 C.Y., 475 H.P.		98.35	1,775	5,345	16,000	1,856	
	4870	9 - 11 C.Y., 620 H.P.		132.15	2,500	7,495	22,500	2,556	
	4880	Skid steer loader, wheeled, 10 C.F., 30 H.P. gas		8.95	147	440	1,325	159.60	
	4890	1 C.Y., 78 H.P., diesel		16.90	243	730	2,200	281.20	
	4892	Skid-steer attachment, auger		.55	92	276	830	59.60	
	4893	Backhoe		.70	116	348	1,050	75.20	
	4894	Broom		.74	124	371	1,125	80.10	
	4895	Forks		.25	41	123	370	26.60	
	4896	Grapple		.57	94.50	283	850	61.15	
	4897	Concrete hammer		1.08	179	538	1,625	116.25	
	4898	Tree spade		.94	156	468	1,400	101.10	
	4899	Trencher		.76	126	378	1,125	81.70	
	4900	Trencher, chain, boom type, gas, operator walking, 12 H.P.		4.35	46.50	140	420	62.80	
	4910	Operator riding, 40 H.P.		17.10	293	880	2,650	312.80	
	5000	Wheel type, diesel, 4' deep, 12" wide		73.05	835	2,500	7,500	1,084	
	5100	6' deep, 20" wide		84.15	1,900	5,715	17,100	1,816	
	5150	Chain type, diesel, 5' deep, 8" wide		32.30	560	1,685	5,050	595.40	
	5200	Diesel, 8' deep, 16" wide		134.05	2,950	8,880	26,600	2,848	
	5202	Rock trencher, wheel type, 6" wide x 18" deep		19.05	320	960	2,875	344.40	
	5206	Chain type, 18" wide x 7' deep		103.05	2,825	8,465	25,400	2,517	
	5210	Tree spade, self-propelled		13.73	267	800	2,400	269.85	
	5250	Truck, dump, 2-axle, 12 ton, 8 C.Y. payload, 220 H.P.		27.80	225	675	2,025	357.40	
	5300	Three axle dump, 16 ton, 12 C.Y. payload, 400 H.P.		48.95	320	965	2,900	584.60	
	5310	Four axle dump, 25 ton, 18 C.Y. payload, 450 H.P.		58.00	470	1,405	4,225	745	
	5350	Dump trailer only, rear dump, 16-1/2 C.Y.		5.15	137	410	1,225	123.20	
	5400	20 C.Y.		5.60	155	465	1,400	137.80	
	5450	Flatbed, single axle, 1-1/2 ton rating		21.25	68.50	205	615	211	
	5500	3 ton rating		25.80	96.50	290	870	264.40	
	5550	Off highway rear dump, 25 ton capacity		67.70	1,225	3,645	10,900	1,271	
	5600	35 ton capacity		63.10	1,075	3,260	9,775	1,157	
	5610	50 ton capacity		85.40	1,475	4,425	13,300	1,568	
	5620	65 ton capacity		88.20	1,450	4,330	13,000	1,572	
	5630	100 ton capacity		113.50	1,950	5,815	17,400	2,071	
	6000	Vibratory plow, 25 H.P., walking		7.35	60	180	540	94.80	
40	0010	**GENERAL EQUIPMENT RENTAL** without operators							**40**
	0150	Aerial lift, scissor type, to 15' high, 1000 lb. capacity, electric	Ea.	3.00	53.50	160	480	56	
	0160	To 25' high, 2000 lb. capacity		3.40	68.50	205	615	68.20	
	0170	Telescoping boom to 40' high, 500 lb. capacity, gas		17.40	310	925	2,775	324.20	
	0180	To 45' high, 500 lb. capacity		18.50	355	1,070	3,200	362	
	0190	To 60' high, 600 lb. capacity		20.80	470	1,405	4,225	447.40	
	0195	Air compressor, portable, 6.5 CFM, electric		.31	12.65	38	114	10.10	
	0196	Gasoline		.77	19	57	171	17.55	
	0200	Towed type, gas engine, 60 CFM		11.55	46.50	140	420	120.40	
	0300	160 CFM		13.35	50	150	450	136.80	
	0400	Diesel engine, rotary screw, 250 CFM		14.00	108	325	975	177	
	0500	365 CFM		18.75	132	395	1,175	229	
	0550	450 CFM		23.70	165	495	1,475	288.60	
	0600	600 CFM		41.45	227	680	2,050	467.60	
	0700	750 CFM		41.60	237	710	2,125	474.80	
	0800	For silenced models, small sizes, add to rent		3%	5%	5%	5%		
	0900	Large sizes, add to rent		5%	7%	7%	7%		
	0930	Air tools, breaker, pavement, 60 lb.	Ea.	.50	9.65	29	87	9.80	
	0940	80 lb.		.50	10.35	31	93	10.20	
	0950	Drills, hand (jackhammer) 65 lb.		.60	16.65	50	150	14.80	
	0960	Track or wagon, swing boom, 4" drifter		55.90	815	2,450	7,350	937.20	
	0970	5" drifter		67.20	915	2,750	8,250	1,088	

R015433 -10

01 54 33 | Equipment Rental

		UNIT	HOURLY OPER. COST	RENT PER DAY	RENT PER WEEK	RENT PER MONTH	EQUIPMENT COST/DAY	
40	0975	Track mounted quarry drill, 6" diameter drill	Ea.	102.85	1,350	4,060	12,200	1,635	40
	0980	Dust control per drill		.63	22	66	198	18.25	
	0990	Hammer, chipping, 12 lb.		.55	25.50	77	231	19.80	
	1000	Hose, air with couplings, 50' long, 3/4" diameter		.03	4.67	14	42	3.05	
	1100	1" diameter		.04	6.35	19	57	4.10	
	1200	1-1/2" diameter		.06	9.65	29	87	6.30	
	1300	2" diameter		.07	12	36	108	7.75	
	1400	2-1/2" diameter		.11	19	57	171	12.30	
	1410	3" diameter		.14	23	69	207	14.90	
	1450	Drill, steel, 7/8" x 2'		.05	8.65	26	78	5.60	
	1460	7/8" x 6'		.05	9	27	81	5.80	
	1520	Moil points		.02	4	12	36	2.55	
	1525	Pneumatic nailer w/accessories		.48	31.50	95	285	22.85	
	1530	Sheeting driver for 60 lb. breaker		.04	6	18	54	3.90	
	1540	For 90 lb. breaker		.12	8	24	72	5.75	
	1550	Spade, 25 lb.		.45	6.65	20	60	7.60	
	1560	Tamper, single, 35 lb.		.55	36.50	109	325	26.20	
	1570	Triple, 140 lb.		.82	54.50	164	490	39.35	
	1580	Wrenches, impact, air powered, up to 3/4" bolt		.40	11.35	34	102	10	
	1590	Up to 1-1/4" bolt		.50	23.50	70	210	18	
	1600	Barricades, barrels, reflectorized, 1 to 99 barrels		.03	4.60	13.80	41.50	3	
	1610	100 to 200 barrels		.02	3.53	10.60	32	2.30	
	1620	Barrels with flashers, 1 to 99 barrels		.03	5.25	15.80	47.50	3.40	
	1630	100 to 200 barrels		.03	4.20	12.60	38	2.75	
	1640	Barrels with steady burn type C lights		.04	7	21	63	4.50	
	1650	Illuminated board, trailer mounted, with generator		3.25	133	400	1,200	106	
	1670	Portable barricade, stock, with flashers, 1 to 6 units		.03	5.25	15.80	47.50	3.40	
	1680	25 to 50 units		.03	4.90	14.70	44	3.20	
	1685	Butt fusion machine, wheeled, 1.5 HP electric, 2" - 8" diameter pipe		2.56	167	500	1,500	120.50	
	1690	Tracked, 20 HP diesel, 4"-12" diameter pipe		10.43	490	1,465	4,400	376.45	
	1695	83 HP diesel, 8" - 24" diameter pipe		27.52	975	2,930	8,800	806.15	
	1700	Carts, brick, hand powered, 1000 lb. capacity		.44	72.50	218	655	47.10	
	1800	Gas engine, 1500 lb., 7-1/2' lift		4.04	115	345	1,025	101.30	
	1822	Dehumidifier, medium, 6 lb./hr., 150 CFM		.93	60	180	540	43.45	
	1824	Large, 18 lb./hr., 600 CFM		1.89	122	366	1,100	88.30	
	1830	Distributor, asphalt, trailer mounted, 2000 gal., 38 H.P. diesel		9.80	330	990	2,975	276.40	
	1840	3000 gal., 38 H.P. diesel		11.25	360	1,080	3,250	306	
	1850	Drill, rotary hammer, electric		.82	26.50	80	240	22.55	
	1860	Carbide bit, 1-1/2" diameter, add to electric rotary hammer		.02	4.97	14.90	44.50	3.15	
	1865	Rotary, crawler, 250 H.P.		131.70	2,050	6,175	18,500	2,289	
	1870	Emulsion sprayer, 65 gal., 5 H.P. gas engine		2.85	97	291	875	81	
	1880	200 gal., 5 H.P. engine		7.25	162	485	1,450	155	
	1900	Floor auto-scrubbing machine, walk-behind, 28" path		3.76	247	740	2,225	178.10	
	1930	Floodlight, mercury vapor, or quartz, on tripod, 1000 watt		.30	16	48	144	12	
	1940	2000 watt		.55	30.50	91	273	22.60	
	1950	Floodlights, trailer mounted with generator, 1 - 300 watt light		3.35	71.50	215	645	69.80	
	1960	2 - 1000 watt lights		4.35	96.50	290	870	92.80	
	2000	4 - 300 watt lights		4.10	91.50	275	825	87.80	
	2005	Foam spray rig, incl. box trailer, compressor, generator, proportioner		27.23	475	1,430	4,300	503.85	
	2020	Forklift, straight mast, 12' lift, 5000 lb., 2 wheel drive, gas		22.00	198	595	1,775	295	
	2040	21' lift, 5000 lb., 4 wheel drive, diesel		17.90	243	730	2,200	289.20	
	2050	For rough terrain, 42' lift, 35' reach, 9000 lb., 110 H.P.		25.10	470	1,405	4,225	481.80	
	2060	For plant, 4 ton capacity, 80 H.P., 2 wheel drive, gas		13.40	98.50	295	885	166.20	
	2080	10 ton capacity, 120 H.P., 2 wheel drive, diesel		19.95	172	515	1,550	262.60	
	2100	Generator, electric, gas engine, 1.5 kW to 3 kW		3.10	11.35	34	102	31.60	
	2200	5 kW		4.00	15	45	135	41	
	2300	10 kW		7.50	36.50	110	330	82	
	2400	25 kW		8.80	85	255	765	121.40	

01 54 33 | Equipment Rental

		UNIT	HOURLY OPER. COST	RENT PER DAY	RENT PER WEEK	RENT PER MONTH	EQUIPMENT COST/DAY	
40	2500	Diesel engine, 20 kW	Ea.	10.10	71.50	215	645	123.80	40
	2600	50 kW		18.15	98.50	295	885	204.20	
	2700	100 kW		35.05	138	415	1,250	363.40	
	2800	250 kW		69.05	243	730	2,200	698.40	
	2850	Hammer, hydraulic, for mounting on boom, to 500 ft lb.		2.40	75	225	675	64.20	
	2860	1000 ft lb.		4.15	125	375	1,125	108.20	
	2900	Heaters, space, oil or electric, 50 MBH		1.84	8	24	72	19.50	
	3000	100 MBH		3.32	11.35	34	102	33.35	
	3100	300 MBH		10.62	36.50	110	330	106.95	
	3150	500 MBH		21.42	48.50	145	435	200.35	
	3200	Hose, water, suction with coupling, 20' long, 2" diameter		.02	3	9	27	1.95	
	3210	3" diameter		.03	4.33	13	39	2.85	
	3220	4" diameter		.03	5	15	45	3.25	
	3230	6" diameter		.11	17.65	53	159	11.50	
	3240	8" diameter		.20	33.50	100	300	21.60	
	3250	Discharge hose with coupling, 50' long, 2" diameter		.02	2.67	8	24	1.75	
	3260	3" diameter		.03	4.67	14	42	3.05	
	3270	4" diameter		.04	7.35	22	66	4.70	
	3280	6" diameter		.11	18.65	56	168	12.10	
	3290	8" diameter		.20	33.50	100	300	21.60	
	3295	Insulation blower		.67	6	18	54	8.95	
	3300	Ladders, extension type, 16' to 36' long		.14	24	72	216	15.50	
	3400	40' to 60' long		.20	32.50	98	294	21.20	
	3405	Lance for cutting concrete		2.17	104	313	940	79.95	
	3407	Lawn mower, rotary, 22", 5 H.P.		2.14	63.50	190	570	55.10	
	3408	48" self propelled		2.88	75	225	675	68.05	
	3410	Level, electronic, automatic, with tripod and leveling rod		1.64	109	328	985	78.70	
	3430	Laser type, for pipe and sewer line and grade		.69	46	138	415	33.10	
	3440	Rotating beam for interior control		1.15	76.50	230	690	55.20	
	3460	Builder's optical transit, with tripod and rod		.09	15.35	46	138	9.90	
	3500	Light towers, towable, with diesel generator, 2000 watt		4.10	91.50	275	825	87.80	
	3600	4000 watt		4.35	96.50	290	870	92.80	
	3700	Mixer, powered, plaster and mortar, 6 C.F., 7 H.P.		2.30	19.65	59	177	30.20	
	3800	10 C.F., 9 H.P.		2.45	30.50	92	276	38	
	3850	Nailer, pneumatic		.49	32.50	98	294	23.50	
	3900	Paint sprayers complete, 8 CFM		.73	48.50	145	435	34.85	
	4000	17 CFM		1.35	89.50	269	805	64.60	
	4020	Pavers, bituminous, rubber tires, 8' wide, 50 H.P., diesel		29.45	490	1,465	4,400	528.60	
	4030	10' wide, 150 H.P.		96.65	1,800	5,395	16,200	1,852	
	4050	Crawler, 8' wide, 100 H.P., diesel		83.45	1,800	5,410	16,200	1,750	
	4060	10' wide, 150 H.P.		103.55	2,225	6,645	19,900	2,157	
	4070	Concrete paver, 12' to 24' wide, 250 H.P.		88.70	1,550	4,660	14,000	1,642	
	4080	Placer-spreader-trimmer, 24' wide, 300 H.P.		127.05	2,525	7,575	22,700	2,531	
	4100	Pump, centrifugal gas pump, 1-1/2" diameter, 65 GPM		3.70	48.50	145	435	58.60	
	4200	2" diameter, 130 GPM		4.85	53.50	160	480	70.80	
	4300	3" diameter, 250 GPM		5.10	55	165	495	73.80	
	4400	6" diameter, 1500 GPM		25.55	173	520	1,550	308.40	
	4500	Submersible electric pump, 1-1/4" diameter, 55 GPM		.31	16.35	49	147	12.30	
	4600	1-1/2" diameter, 83 GPM		.35	18.65	56	168	14	
	4700	2" diameter, 120 GPM		1.35	23.50	70	210	24.80	
	4800	3" diameter, 300 GPM		2.25	41.50	125	375	43	
	4900	4" diameter, 560 GPM		9.65	158	475	1,425	172.20	
	5000	6" diameter, 1590 GPM		14.15	213	640	1,925	241.20	
	5100	Diaphragm pump, gas, single, 1-1/2" diameter		1.15	49.50	148	445	38.80	
	5200	2" diameter		3.95	61.50	185	555	68.60	
	5300	3" diameter		3.95	61.50	185	555	68.60	
	5400	Double, 4" diameter		5.90	107	320	960	111.20	
	5450	Pressure washer 5 GPM, 3000 psi		4.25	48.50	145	435	63	

01 54 33 | Equipment Rental

		UNIT	HOURLY OPER. COST	RENT PER DAY	RENT PER WEEK	RENT PER MONTH	EQUIPMENT COST/DAY	
40	5500	Trash pump, self-priming, gas, 2" diameter	Ea.	4.05	21	63	189	45	**40**
	5600	Diesel, 4" diameter		7.75	73.50	220	660	106	
	5650	Diesel, 6" diameter		20.50	140	420	1,250	248	
	5655	Grout Pump		21.80	177	530	1,600	280.40	
	5700	Salamanders, L.P. gas fired, 100,000 Btu		3.33	12.65	38	114	34.25	
	5705	50,000 Btu		2.50	10.35	31	93	26.20	
	5720	Sandblaster, portable, open top, 3 C.F. capacity		.55	26.50	80	240	20.40	
	5730	6 C.F. capacity		.90	40	120	360	31.20	
	5740	Accessories for above		.12	20.50	62	186	13.35	
	5750	Sander, floor		.59	19.65	59	177	16.50	
	5760	Edger		.54	21.50	64	192	17.10	
	5800	Saw, chain, gas engine, 18" long		1.95	19.65	59	177	27.40	
	5900	Hydraulic powered, 36" long		.70	63.50	190	570	43.60	
	5950	60" long		.70	65	195	585	44.60	
	6000	Masonry, table mounted, 14" diameter, 5 H.P.		1.25	56.50	170	510	44	
	6050	Portable cut-off, 8 H.P.		2.10	32.50	98	294	36.40	
	6100	Circular, hand held, electric, 7-1/4" diameter		.14	4.67	14	42	3.90	
	6200	12" diameter		.21	7.65	23	69	6.30	
	6250	Wall saw, w/hydraulic power, 10 H.P.		7.00	60	180	540	92	
	6275	Shot blaster, walk-behind, 20" wide		4.65	290	870	2,600	211.20	
	6280	Sidewalk broom, walk-behind		2.09	60.50	182	545	53.10	
	6300	Steam cleaner, 100 gallons per hour		3.35	66.50	200	600	66.80	
	6310	200 gallons per hour		4.65	81.50	245	735	86.20	
	6340	Tar Kettle/Pot, 400 gallons		5.50	78.50	235	705	91	
	6350	Torch, cutting, acetylene-oxygen, 150' hose, excludes gases		.30	14	42	126	10.80	
	6360	Hourly operating cost includes tips and gas		10.80				86.40	
	6410	Toilet, portable chemical		.12	20	60	180	12.95	
	6420	Recycle flush type		.14	24	72	216	15.50	
	6430	Toilet, fresh water flush, garden hose,		.17	28.50	85	255	18.35	
	6440	Hoisted, non-flush, for high rise		.14	23.50	71	213	15.30	
	6465	Tractor, farm with attachment		18.25	275	825	2,475	311	
	6500	Trailers, platform, flush deck, 2 axle, 25 ton capacity		5.20	112	335	1,000	108.60	
	6600	40 ton capacity		6.75	155	465	1,400	147	
	6700	3 axle, 50 ton capacity		7.25	172	515	1,550	161	
	6800	75 ton capacity		9.05	225	675	2,025	207.40	
	6810	Trailer mounted cable reel for high voltage line work		5.14	245	734	2,200	187.90	
	6820	Trailer mounted cable tensioning rig		10.22	485	1,460	4,375	373.75	
	6830	Cable pulling rig		68.64	2,725	8,180	24,500	2,185	
	6900	Water tank trailer, engine driven discharge, 5000 gallons		6.75	145	435	1,300	141	
	6925	10,000 gallons		9.20	202	605	1,825	194.60	
	6950	Water truck, off highway, 6000 gallons		75.60	800	2,400	7,200	1,085	
	7010	Tram car for high voltage line work, powered, 2 conductor		4.44	133	399	1,200	115.30	
	7020	Transit (builder's level) with tripod		.09	15.35	46	138	9.90	
	7030	Trench box, 3000 lb., 6' x 8'		.56	93	279	835	60.30	
	7040	7200 lb., 6' x 20'		1.05	175	525	1,575	113.40	
	7050	8000 lb., 8' x 16'		1.05	175	525	1,575	113.40	
	7060	9500 lb., 8' x 20'		1.19	199	597	1,800	128.90	
	7065	11,000 lb., 8' x 24'		1.25	209	627	1,875	135.40	
	7070	12,000 lb., 10' x 20'		1.36	227	680	2,050	146.90	
	7100	Truck, pickup, 3/4 ton, 2 wheel drive		11.50	58.50	175	525	127	
	7200	4 wheel drive		11.75	75	225	675	139	
	7250	Crew carrier, 9 passenger		16.30	86.50	260	780	182.40	
	7290	Flat bed truck, 20,000 lb. GVW		17.60	125	375	1,125	215.80	
	7300	Tractor, 4 x 2, 220 H.P.		24.60	197	590	1,775	314.80	
	7410	330 H.P.		36.35	270	810	2,425	452.80	
	7500	6 x 4, 380 H.P.		41.65	315	945	2,825	522.20	
	7600	450 H.P.		50.75	380	1,145	3,425	635	
	7610	Tractor, with A frame, boom and winch, 225 H.P.		27.40	272	815	2,450	382.20	

01 54 33 | Equipment Rental

		UNIT	HOURLY OPER. COST	RENT PER DAY	RENT PER WEEK	RENT PER MONTH	EQUIPMENT COST/DAY	
40	7620	Vacuum truck, hazardous material, 2500 gallons	Ea.	11.55	298	895	2,675	271.40	**40**
	7625	5,000 gallons		13.40	415	1,250	3,750	357.20	
	7650	Vacuum, HEPA, 16 gallon, wet/dry		.74	18	54	162	16.70	
	7655	55 gallon, wet/dry		.59	27	81	243	20.90	
	7660	Water tank, portable		.16	27	80.70	242	17.40	
	7690	Sewer/catch basin vacuum, 14 C.Y., 1500 gallons		17.81	625	1,880	5,650	518.50	
	7700	Welder, electric, 200 amp		2.14	16.35	49	147	26.90	
	7800	300 amp		3.11	20	60	180	36.90	
	7900	Gas engine, 200 amp		11.70	23.50	70	210	107.60	
	8000	300 amp		13.35	24.50	74	222	121.60	
	8100	Wheelbarrow, any size		.08	12.65	38	114	8.25	
	8200	Wrecking ball, 4000 lb.		2.25	70	210	630	60	
50	0010	**HIGHWAY EQUIPMENT RENTAL** without operators							**50**
	0050	Asphalt batch plant, portable drum mixer, 100 ton/hr.	Ea.	70.30	1,425	4,310	12,900	1,424	
	0060	200 ton/hr.		78.75	1,525	4,570	13,700	1,544	
	0070	300 ton/hr.		91.25	1,800	5,375	16,100	1,805	
	0100	Backhoe attachment, long stick, up to 185 H.P., 10.5' long		.34	22.50	67	201	16.10	
	0140	Up to 250 H.P., 12' long		.36	24	72	216	17.30	
	0180	Over 250 H.P., 15' long		.50	33	99	297	23.80	
	0200	Special dipper arm, up to 100 H.P., 32' long		1.02	67.50	203	610	48.75	
	0240	Over 100 H.P., 33' long		1.27	84.50	253	760	60.75	
	0280	Catch basin/sewer cleaning truck, 3 ton, 9 C.Y., 1000 gal.		37.35	395	1,185	3,550	535.80	
	0300	Concrete batch plant, portable, electric, 200 C.Y./hr.		27.69	510	1,530	4,600	527.50	
	0520	Grader/dozer attachment, ripper/scarifier, rear mounted, up to 135 H.P.		3.35	65	195	585	65.80	
	0540	Up to 180 H.P.		3.95	83.50	250	750	81.60	
	0580	Up to 250 H.P.		4.35	95	285	855	91.80	
	0700	Pavement removal bucket, for hydraulic excavator, up to 90 H.P.		1.80	51.50	155	465	45.40	
	0740	Up to 200 H.P.		2.00	71.50	215	645	59	
	0780	Over 200 H.P.		2.15	85	255	765	68.20	
	0900	Aggregate spreader, self-propelled, 187 H.P.		46.10	690	2,065	6,200	781.80	
	1000	Chemical spreader, 3 C.Y.		3.00	43.50	130	390	50	
	1900	Hammermill, traveling, 250 H.P.		68.15	1,950	5,880	17,600	1,721	
	2000	Horizontal borer, 3" diameter, 13 H.P. gas driven		5.65	53.50	160	480	77.20	
	2150	Horizontal directional drill, 20,000 lb. thrust, 78 H.P. diesel		28.00	665	1,990	5,975	622	
	2160	30,000 lb. thrust, 115 H.P.		34.65	1,025	3,045	9,125	886.20	
	2170	50,000 lb. thrust, 170 H.P.		49.60	1,300	3,895	11,700	1,176	
	2190	Mud trailer for HDD, 1500 gallons, 175 H.P., gas		27.15	153	460	1,375	309.20	
	2200	Hydromulcher, diesel, 3000 gallon, for truck mounting		19.10	252	755	2,275	303.80	
	2300	Gas, 600 gallon		7.55	100	300	900	120.40	
	2400	Joint & crack cleaner, walk behind, 25 H.P.		3.40	50	150	450	57.20	
	2500	Filler, trailer mounted, 400 gallons, 20 H.P.		8.55	213	640	1,925	196.40	
	3000	Paint striper, self-propelled, 40 gallon, 22 H.P.		6.70	158	475	1,425	148.60	
	3100	120 gallon, 120 H.P.		20.45	410	1,225	3,675	408.60	
	3200	Post drivers, 6" I-Beam frame, for truck mounting		15.15	405	1,210	3,625	363.20	
	3400	Road sweeper, self-propelled, 8' wide, 90 H.P.		35.10	565	1,700	5,100	620.80	
	3450	Road sweeper, vacuum assisted, 4 C.Y., 220 gallons		63.20	620	1,855	5,575	876.60	
	4000	Road mixer, self-propelled, 130 H.P.		43.95	770	2,305	6,925	812.60	
	4100	310 H.P.		76.25	2,125	6,360	19,100	1,882	
	4220	Cold mix paver, incl. pug mill and bitumen tank, 165 H.P.		90.00	2,150	6,460	19,400	2,012	
	4240	Pavement brush, towed		3.10	95	285	855	81.80	
	4250	Paver, asphalt, wheel or crawler, 130 H.P., diesel		89.70	2,125	6,390	19,200	1,996	
	4300	Paver, road widener, gas 1' to 6', 67 H.P.		44.75	875	2,620	7,850	882	
	4400	Diesel, 2' to 14', 88 H.P.		56.90	1,050	3,155	9,475	1,086	
	4600	Slipform pavers, curb and gutter, 2 track, 75 H.P.		40.75	725	2,175	6,525	761	
	4700	4 track, 165 H.P.		36.65	735	2,200	6,600	733.20	
	4800	Median barrier, 215 H.P.		41.40	755	2,260	6,775	783.20	
	4901	Trailer, low bed, 75 ton capacity		9.75	225	675	2,025	213	
	5000	Road planer, walk behind, 10" cutting width, 10 H.P.		3.20	32.50	98	294	45.20	

R015433 -10

01 54 33 | Equipment Rental

		UNIT	HOURLY OPER. COST	RENT PER DAY	RENT PER WEEK	RENT PER MONTH	EQUIPMENT COST/DAY	
50	5100	Self-propelled, 12" cutting width, 64 H.P.	Ea.	8.90	112	335	1,000	138.20	**50**
	5120	Traffic line remover, metal ball blaster, truck mounted, 115 H.P.		44.60	740	2,220	6,650	800.80	
	5140	Grinder, truck mounted, 115 H.P.		50.10	805	2,410	7,225	882.80	
	5160	Walk-behind, 11 H.P.		3.65	53.50	160	480	61.20	
	5200	Pavement profiler, 4' to 6' wide, 450 H.P.		227.55	3,350	10,035	30,100	3,827	
	5300	8' to 10' wide, 750 H.P.		353.65	4,375	13,150	39,500	5,459	
	5400	Roadway plate, steel, 1" x 8' x 20'		.07	12.35	37	111	7.95	
	5600	Stabilizer, self-propelled, 150 H.P.		43.25	610	1,825	5,475	711	
	5700	310 H.P.		84.85	1,500	4,530	13,600	1,585	
	5800	Striper, thermal, truck mounted, 120 gallon paint, 460 H.P.		54.85	495	1,485	4,450	735.80	
	5900	Thermal paint heating kettle, 115 gallons		3.64	25.50	77	231	44.50	
	6000	Tar kettle, 330 gallon, trailer mounted		5.15	60	180	540	77.20	
	7000	Tunnel locomotive, diesel, 8 to 12 ton		29.20	570	1,710	5,125	575.60	
	7005	Electric, 10 ton		25.40	650	1,955	5,875	594.20	
	7010	Muck cars, 1/2 C.Y. capacity		2.00	23.50	71	213	30.20	
	7020	1 C.Y. capacity		2.20	31.50	95	285	36.60	
	7030	2 C.Y. capacity		2.30	36.50	110	330	40.40	
	7040	Side dump, 2 C.Y. capacity		2.50	43.50	130	390	46	
	7050	3 C.Y. capacity		3.40	50	150	450	57.20	
	7060	5 C.Y. capacity		4.85	63.50	190	570	76.80	
	7100	Ventilating blower for tunnel, 7-1/2 H.P.		1.75	50	150	450	44	
	7110	10 H.P.		1.88	51.50	155	465	46.05	
	7120	20 H.P.		2.68	67.50	202	605	61.85	
	7140	40 H.P.		4.17	95	285	855	90.35	
	7160	60 H.P.		6.38	147	440	1,325	139.05	
	7175	75 H.P.		8.35	196	587	1,750	184.20	
	7180	200 H.P.		15.40	293	880	2,650	299.20	
	7800	Windrow loader, elevating		51.85	1,325	3,960	11,900	1,207	
60	0010	**LIFTING AND HOISTING EQUIPMENT RENTAL** without operators							**60**
	0120	Aerial lift truck, 2 person, to 80'	Ea.	26.70	705	2,120	6,350	637.60	
	0140	Boom work platform, 40' snorkel		15.80	270	810	2,425	288.40	
	0150	Crane, flatbed mounted, 3 ton capacity		14.55	193	580	1,750	232.40	
	0200	Crane, climbing, 106' jib, 6000 lb. capacity, 410 fpm		29.95	1,550	4,670	14,000	1,174	
	0300	101' jib, 10,250 lb. capacity, 270 fpm		36.20	1,975	5,920	17,800	1,474	
	0500	Tower, static, 130' high, 106' jib, 6200 lb. capacity at 400 fpm		33.60	1,800	5,400	16,200	1,349	
	0600	Crawler mounted, lattice boom, 1/2 C.Y., 15 tons at 12' radius		33.19	635	1,910	5,725	647.50	
	0700	3/4 C.Y., 20 tons at 12' radius		44.25	795	2,390	7,175	832	
	0800	1 C.Y., 25 tons at 12' radius		59.00	1,075	3,190	9,575	1,110	
	0900	1-1/2 C.Y., 40 tons at 12' radius		59.00	1,075	3,215	9,650	1,115	
	1000	2 C.Y., 50 tons at 12' radius		62.90	1,250	3,770	11,300	1,257	
	1100	3 C.Y., 75 tons at 12' radius		67.55	1,475	4,415	13,200	1,423	
	1200	100 ton capacity, 60' boom		76.50	1,700	5,080	15,200	1,628	
	1300	165 ton capacity, 60' boom		96.25	1,975	5,940	17,800	1,958	
	1400	200 ton capacity, 70' boom		118.45	2,475	7,440	22,300	2,436	
	1500	350 ton capacity, 80' boom		166.45	3,750	11,245	33,700	3,581	
	1600	Truck mounted, lattice boom, 6 x 4, 20 tons at 10' radius		35.08	1,125	3,350	10,100	950.65	
	1700	25 tons at 10' radius		37.95	1,225	3,650	11,000	1,034	
	1800	8 x 4, 30 tons at 10' radius		41.11	1,300	3,880	11,600	1,105	
	1900	40 tons at 12' radius		43.92	1,350	4,060	12,200	1,163	
	2000	60 tons at 15' radius		49.48	1,425	4,300	12,900	1,256	
	2050	82 tons at 15' radius		55.38	1,525	4,590	13,800	1,361	
	2100	90 tons at 15' radius		62.13	1,675	5,000	15,000	1,497	
	2200	115 tons at 15' radius		70.13	1,875	5,590	16,800	1,679	
	2300	150 tons at 18' radius		81.45	1,950	5,885	17,700	1,829	
	2350	165 tons at 18' radius		82.43	2,075	6,240	18,700	1,907	
	2400	Truck mounted, hydraulic, 12 ton capacity		36.75	530	1,590	4,775	612	
	2500	25 ton capacity		39.15	640	1,920	5,750	697.20	
	2550	33 ton capacity		39.70	655	1,970	5,900	711.60	

Reference boxes: R015433-10, R015433-15, R312316-45

01 54 33 | Equipment Rental

		UNIT	HOURLY OPER. COST	RENT PER DAY	RENT PER WEEK	RENT PER MONTH	EQUIPMENT COST/DAY	
60	2560	40 ton capacity	Ea.	51.70	770	2,305	6,925	874.60	**60**
	2600	55 ton capacity		67.65	930	2,795	8,375	1,100	
	2700	80 ton capacity		88.65	1,400	4,225	12,700	1,554	
	2720	100 ton capacity		84.25	1,450	4,365	13,100	1,547	
	2740	120 ton capacity		96.15	1,575	4,690	14,100	1,707	
	2760	150 ton capacity		114.30	2,075	6,190	18,600	2,152	
	2800	Self-propelled, 4 x 4, with telescoping boom, 5 ton		15.70	232	695	2,075	264.60	
	2900	12-1/2 ton capacity		28.15	370	1,115	3,350	448.20	
	3000	15 ton capacity		28.85	390	1,175	3,525	465.80	
	3050	20 ton capacity		31.05	450	1,355	4,075	519.40	
	3100	25 ton capacity		32.65	505	1,520	4,550	565.20	
	3150	40 ton capacity		40.25	570	1,710	5,125	664	
	3200	Derricks, guy, 20 ton capacity, 60' boom, 75' mast		23.51	380	1,144	3,425	416.90	
	3300	100' boom, 115' mast		37.04	655	1,970	5,900	690.30	
	3400	Stiffleg, 20 ton capacity, 70' boom, 37' mast		25.93	495	1,490	4,475	505.45	
	3500	100' boom, 47' mast		39.91	795	2,380	7,150	795.30	
	3550	Helicopter, small, lift to 1250 lb. maximum, w/pilot		97.18	3,075	9,240	27,700	2,625	
	3600	Hoists, chain type, overhead, manual, 3/4 ton		.10	.33	1	3	1	
	3900	10 ton		.70	6	18	54	9.20	
	4000	Hoist and tower, 5000 lb. capacity, portable electric, 40' high		3.96	220	659	1,975	163.50	
	4100	For each added 10' section, add		.10	17.35	52	156	11.20	
	4200	Hoist and single tubular tower, 5000 lb. electric, 100' high		5.43	305	920	2,750	227.45	
	4300	For each added 6'-6" section, add		.18	29.50	89	267	19.25	
	4400	Hoist and double tubular tower, 5000 lb., 100' high		5.89	340	1,013	3,050	249.70	
	4500	For each added 6'-6" section, add		.20	33	99	297	21.40	
	4550	Hoist and tower, mast type, 6000 lb., 100' high		6.25	350	1,051	3,150	260.20	
	4570	For each added 10' section, add		.12	20.50	62	186	13.35	
	4600	Hoist and tower, personnel, electric, 2000 lb., 100' @ 125 fpm		14.61	930	2,790	8,375	674.90	
	4700	3000 lb., 100' @ 200 fpm		16.68	1,050	3,170	9,500	767.45	
	4800	3000 lb., 150' @ 300 fpm		18.58	1,175	3,550	10,700	858.65	
	4900	4000 lb., 100' @ 300 fpm		19.09	1,200	3,620	10,900	876.70	
	5000	6000 lb., 100' @ 275 fpm		20.27	1,275	3,790	11,400	920.15	
	5100	For added heights up to 500', add	L.F.	.01	1.67	5	15	1.10	
	5200	Jacks, hydraulic, 20 ton	Ea.	.05	2	6	18	1.60	
	5500	100 ton		.40	11.65	35	105	10.20	
	6100	Jacks, hydraulic, climbing w/50' jackrods, control console, 30 ton capacity		1.89	126	378	1,125	90.70	
	6150	For each added 10' jackrod section, add		.05	3.33	10	30	2.40	
	6300	50 ton capacity		3.05	203	609	1,825	146.20	
	6350	For each added 10' jackrod section, add		.06	4	12	36	2.90	
	6500	125 ton capacity		8.00	535	1,600	4,800	384	
	6550	For each added 10' jackrod section, add		.55	36.50	109	325	26.20	
	6600	Cable jack, 10 ton capacity with 200' cable		1.59	106	317	950	76.10	
	6650	For each added 50' of cable, add		.19	12.35	37	111	8.90	
70	0010	**WELLPOINT EQUIPMENT RENTAL** without operators							**70**
	0020	Based on 2 months rental							
	0100	Combination jetting & wellpoint pump, 60 H.P. diesel	Ea.	15.87	315	938	2,825	314.55	
	0200	High pressure gas jet pump, 200 H.P., 300 psi	"	36.61	267	802	2,400	453.30	
	0300	Discharge pipe, 8" diameter	L.F.	.01	.51	1.53	4.59	.40	
	0350	12" diameter		.01	.75	2.24	6.70	.55	
	0400	Header pipe, flows up to 150 GPM, 4" diameter		.01	.46	1.38	4.14	.35	
	0500	400 GPM, 6" diameter		.01	.54	1.63	4.89	.40	
	0600	800 GPM, 8" diameter		.01	.75	2.24	6.70	.55	
	0700	1500 GPM, 10" diameter		.01	.79	2.36	7.10	.55	
	0800	2500 GPM, 12" diameter		.02	1.49	4.47	13.40	1.05	
	0900	4500 GPM, 16" diameter		.03	1.91	5.72	17.15	1.40	
	0950	For quick coupling aluminum and plastic pipe, add		.03	1.97	5.92	17.75	1.40	
	1100	Wellpoint, 25' long, with fittings & riser pipe, 1-1/2" or 2" diameter	Ea.	.06	3.94	11.81	35.50	2.85	

Note row 0010 contains reference box: R015433 -10

01 54 33 | Equipment Rental

			UNIT	HOURLY OPER. COST	RENT PER DAY	RENT PER WEEK	RENT PER MONTH	EQUIPMENT COST/DAY	
70	1200	Wellpoint pump, diesel powered, 4" suction, 20 H.P.	Ea.	6.89	180	541	1,625	163.30	70
	1300	6" suction, 30 H.P.		9.35	224	671	2,025	209	
	1400	8" suction, 40 H.P.		12.64	305	920	2,750	285.10	
	1500	10" suction, 75 H.P.		19.15	360	1,075	3,225	368.20	
	1600	12" suction, 100 H.P.		27.47	570	1,710	5,125	561.75	
	1700	12" suction, 175 H.P.		.36	630	1,890	5,675	700.90	
80	0010	**MARINE EQUIPMENT RENTAL** without operators							80
	0200	Barge, 400 Ton, 30' wide x 90' long R015433 -10	Ea.	16.65	1,075	3,230	9,700	779.20	
	0240	800 Ton, 45' wide x 90' long		20.15	1,300	3,915	11,700	944.20	
	2000	Tugboat, diesel, 100 H.P.		31.60	215	645	1,925	381.80	
	2040	250 H.P.		64.00	395	1,180	3,550	748	
	2080	380 H.P.		131.50	1,175	3,505	10,500	1,753	

Crews

Crew No.	Bare Costs		In-House Costs		Incl. Subs O&P		Cost Per Labor-Hour		
Crew A-3H	Hr.	Daily	Hr.	Daily	Hr.	Daily	Bare Costs	In House	Incl. O&P
1 Equip. Oper. (crane)	$47.80	$ 382.40	$60.65	$ 485.20	$75.50	$ 604.00	$ 47.80	$ 60.65	$ 75.50
1 Hyd. crane, 12 Ton (daily)		824.00		824.00		906.40	103.00	103.00	113.30
8 L.H., Daily Totals		$1206.40		$1309.20		$1510.40	$150.80	$163.65	$188.80
Crew A-3I	Hr.	Daily	Hr.	Daily	Hr.	Daily	Bare Costs	In House	Incl. O&P
1 Equip. Oper. (crane)	$47.80	$ 382.40	$60.65	$ 485.20	$75.50	$ 604.00	$ 47.80	$ 60.65	$ 75.50
1 Hyd. crane, 25 Ton (daily)		953.20		953.20		1048.52	119.15	119.15	131.07
8 L.H., Daily Totals		$1335.60		$1438.40		$1652.52	$166.95	$179.80	$206.57
Crew A-3J	Hr.	Daily	Hr.	Daily	Hr.	Daily	Bare Costs	In House	Incl. O&P
1 Equip. Oper. (crane)	$47.80	$ 382.40	$60.65	$ 485.20	$75.50	$ 604.00	$ 47.80	$ 60.65	$ 75.50
1 Hyd. crane, 40 Ton (daily)		1184.00		1184.00		1302.40	148.00	148.00	162.80
8 L.H., Daily Totals		$1566.40		$1669.20		$1906.40	$195.80	$208.65	$238.30
Crew A-3K	Hr.	Daily	Hr.	Daily	Hr.	Daily	Bare Costs	In House	Incl. O&P
1 Equip. Oper. (crane)	$47.80	$ 382.40	$60.65	$ 485.20	$75.50	$ 604.00	$ 44.52	$ 56.50	$ 70.33
1 Equip. Oper. Oiler	41.25	330.00	52.35	418.80	65.15	521.20			
1 Hyd. crane, 55 Ton (daily)		1471.00		1471.00		1618.10			
1 P/U Truck, 3/4 Ton (daily)		152.00		152.00		167.20	101.44	101.44	111.58
16 L.H., Daily Totals		$2335.40		$2527.00		$2910.50	$145.96	$157.94	$181.91
Crew A-3L	Hr.	Daily	Hr.	Daily	Hr.	Daily	Bare Costs	In House	Incl. O&P
1 Equip. Oper. (crane)	$47.80	$ 382.40	$60.65	$ 485.20	$75.50	$ 604.00	$ 44.52	$ 56.50	$ 70.33
1 Equip. Oper. Oiler	41.25	330.00	52.35	418.80	65.15	521.20			
1 Hyd. crane, 80 Ton (daily)		2119.00		2119.00		2330.90			
1 P/U Truck, 3/4 Ton (daily)		152.00		152.00		167.20	141.94	141.94	156.13
16 L.H., Daily Totals		$2983.40		$3175.00		$3623.30	$186.46	$198.44	$226.46
Crew A-3M	Hr.	Daily	Hr.	Daily	Hr.	Daily	Bare Costs	In House	Incl. O&P
1 Equip. Oper. (crane)	$47.80	$ 382.40	$60.65	$ 485.20	$75.50	$ 604.00	$ 44.52	$ 56.50	$ 70.33
1 Equip. Oper. Oiler	41.25	330.00	52.35	418.80	65.15	521.20			
1 Hyd. crane, 100 Ton (daily)		2129.00		2129.00		2341.90			
1 P/U Truck, 3/4 Ton (daily)		152.00		152.00		167.20	142.56	142.56	156.82
16 L.H., Daily Totals		$2993.40		$3185.00		$3634.30	$187.09	$199.06	$227.14
Crew A-16	Hr.	Daily	Hr.	Daily	Hr.	Daily	Bare Costs	In House	Incl. O&P
1 Maintenance Laborer	$26.35	$210.80	$32.75	$262.00	$40.90	$327.20	$26.35	$32.75	$40.90
1 Lawn Mower, Riding		68.05		68.05		74.86	8.51	8.51	9.36
8 L.H., Daily Totals		$278.85		$330.05		$402.06	$34.86	$41.26	$50.26
Crew A-17	Hr.	Daily	Hr.	Daily	Hr.	Daily	Bare Costs	In House	Incl. O&P
1 Maintenance Laborer	$26.35	$210.80	$32.75	$262.00	$40.90	$327.20	$26.35	$32.75	$40.90
1 Flatbed Truck, Gas, 1.5 Ton		211.00		211.00		232.10	26.38	26.38	29.01
8 L.H., Daily Totals		$421.80		$473.00		$559.30	$52.73	$59.13	$69.91
Crew A-18	Hr.	Daily	Hr.	Daily	Hr.	Daily	Bare Costs	In House	Incl. O&P
1 Maintenance Laborer	$26.35	$210.80	$32.75	$262.00	$40.90	$327.20	$26.35	$32.75	$40.90
1 Farm Tractor w/ Attachment		311.00		311.00		342.10	38.88	38.88	42.76
8 L.H., Daily Totals		$521.80		$573.00		$669.30	$65.22	$71.63	$83.66
Crew B-1	Hr.	Daily	Hr.	Daily	Hr.	Daily	Bare Costs	In House	Incl. O&P
1 Labor Foreman (outside)	$37.10	$296.80	$49.30	$ 394.40	$60.80	$ 486.40	$35.77	$47.53	$58.63
2 Laborers	35.10	561.60	46.65	746.40	57.55	920.80			
24 L.H., Daily Totals		$858.40		$1140.80		$1407.20	$35.77	$47.53	$58.63

Crew No.	Bare Costs Hr.	Bare Costs Daily	In-House Costs Hr.	In-House Costs Daily	Incl. Subs O&P Hr.	Incl. Subs O&P Daily	Cost Per Labor-Hour Bare Costs	Cost Per Labor-Hour In House	Cost Per Labor-Hour Incl. O&P
Crew B-17	Hr.	Daily	Hr.	Daily	Hr.	Daily	Bare Costs	In House	Incl. O&P
2 Laborers	$35.10	$ 561.60	$46.65	$ 746.40	$57.55	$ 920.80	$37.56	$49.06	$60.71
1 Equip. Oper. (light)	44.75	358.00	56.80	454.40	70.65	565.20			
1 Truck Driver (heavy)	35.30	282.40	46.15	369.20	57.10	456.80			
1 Backhoe Loader, 48 H.P.		334.00		334.00		367.40			
1 Dump Truck, 8 C.Y., 220 H.P.		357.40		357.40		393.14	21.61	21.61	23.77
32 L.H., Daily Totals		$1893.40		$2261.40		$2703.34	$59.17	$70.67	$84.48
Crew B-18	Hr.	Daily	Hr.	Daily	Hr.	Daily	Bare Costs	In House	Incl. O&P
1 Labor Foreman (outside)	$37.10	$296.80	$49.30	$ 394.40	$60.80	$ 486.40	$35.77	$47.53	$58.63
2 Laborers	35.10	561.60	46.65	746.40	57.55	920.80			
1 Vibratory Plate, gas, 21"		40.80		40.80		44.88	1.70	1.70	1.87
24 L.H., Daily Totals		$899.20		$1181.60		$1452.08	$37.47	$49.23	$60.50
Crew B-21	Hr.	Daily	Hr.	Daily	Hr.	Daily	Bare Costs	In House	Incl. O&P
1 Labor Foreman (outside)	$37.10	$ 296.80	$49.30	$ 394.40	$60.80	$ 486.40	$40.43	$53.15	$65.69
1 Skilled Worker	45.40	363.20	59.75	478.00	73.80	590.40			
1 Laborer	35.10	280.80	46.65	373.20	57.55	460.40			
.5 Equip. Oper. (crane)	47.80	191.20	60.65	242.60	75.50	302.00			
.5 S.P. Crane, 4x4, 5 Ton		132.30		132.30		145.53	4.72	4.72	5.20
28 L.H., Daily Totals		$1264.30		$1620.50		$1984.73	$45.15	$57.88	$70.88
Crew B-25B	Hr.	Daily	Hr.	Daily	Hr.	Daily	Bare Costs	In House	Incl. O&P
1 Labor Foreman (outside)	$37.10	$ 296.80	$49.30	$ 394.40	$60.80	$ 486.40	$39.08	$51.00	$63.14
7 Laborers	35.10	1965.60	46.65	2612.40	57.55	3222.80			
4 Equip. Oper. (med.)	46.55	1489.60	59.05	1889.60	73.50	2352.00			
1 Asphalt Paver, 130 H.P.		1996.00		1996.00		2195.60			
2 Tandem Rollers, 10 Ton		455.20		455.20		500.72			
1 Roller, Pneum. Whl, 12 Ton		313.20		313.20		344.52	28.80	28.80	31.68
96 L.H., Daily Totals		$6516.40		$7660.80		$9102.04	$67.88	$79.80	$94.81
Crew B-30	Hr.	Daily	Hr.	Daily	Hr.	Daily	Bare Costs	In House	Incl. O&P
1 Equip. Oper. (med.)	$46.55	$ 372.40	$59.05	$ 472.40	$73.50	$ 588.00	$ 39.05	$ 50.45	$ 62.57
2 Truck Drivers (heavy)	35.30	564.80	46.15	738.40	57.10	913.60			
1 Hyd. Excavator, 1.5 C.Y.		960.40		960.40		1056.44			
2 Dump Trucks, 12 C.Y., 400 H.P.		1169.20		1169.20		1286.12	88.73	88.73	97.61
24 L.H., Daily Totals		$3066.80		$3340.40		$3844.16	$127.78	$139.18	$160.17
Crew B-34P	Hr.	Daily	Hr.	Daily	Hr.	Daily	Bare Costs	In House	Incl. O&P
1 Pipe Fitter	$55.70	$ 445.60	$69.50	$ 556.00	$86.80	$ 694.40	$45.53	$57.82	$71.95
1 Truck Driver (light)	34.35	274.80	44.90	359.20	55.55	444.40			
1 Equip. Oper. (med.)	46.55	372.40	59.05	472.40	73.50	588.00			
1 Flatbed Truck, Gas, 3 Ton		264.40		264.40		290.84			
1 Backhoe Loader, 48 H.P.		334.00		334.00		367.40	24.93	24.93	27.43
24 L.H., Daily Totals		$1691.20		$1986.00		$2385.04	$70.47	$82.75	$99.38
Crew B-34Q	Hr.	Daily	Hr.	Daily	Hr.	Daily	Bare Costs	In House	Incl. O&P
1 Pipe Fitter	$55.70	$ 445.60	$69.50	$ 556.00	$86.80	$ 694.40	$45.95	$ 58.35	$ 72.62
1 Truck Driver (light)	34.35	274.80	44.90	359.20	55.55	444.40			
1 Eqip. Oper. (crane)	47.80	382.40	60.65	485.20	75.50	604.00			
1 Flatbed Trailer, 25 Ton		108.60		108.60		119.46			
1 Dump Truck, 8 C.Y., 220 H.P.		357.40		357.40		393.14			
1 Hyd. Crane, 25 Ton		697.20		697.20		766.92	48.47	48.47	53.31
24 L.H., Daily Totals		$2266.00		$2563.60		$3022.32	$94.42	$106.82	$125.93

Crews

Crew No.	Bare Costs		In-House Costs		Incl. Subs O&P		Cost Per Labor-Hour		
Crew B-34R	Hr.	Daily	Hr.	Daily	Hr.	Daily	Bare Costs	In House	Incl. O&P
1 Pipe Fitter	$55.70	$ 445.60	$69.50	$ 556.00	$86.80	$ 694.40	$ 45.95	$ 58.35	$ 72.62
1 Truck Driver (light)	34.35	274.80	44.90	359.20	55.55	444.40			
1 Eqip. Oper. (crane)	47.80	382.40	60.65	485.20	75.50	604.00			
1 Flatbed Trailer, 25 Ton		108.60		108.60		119.46			
1 Dump Truck, 8 C.Y., 220 H.P.		357.40		357.40		393.14			
1 Hyd. Crane, 25 Ton		697.20		697.20		766.92			
1 Hyd. Excavator, 1 C.Y.		748.60		748.60		823.46	79.66	79.66	87.62
24 L.H., Daily Totals		$3014.60		$3312.20		$3845.78	$125.61	$138.01	$160.24
Crew B-34S	Hr.	Daily	Hr.	Daily	Hr.	Daily	Bare Costs	In House	Incl. O&P
2 Pipe Fitters	$55.70	$ 891.20	$69.50	$1112.00	$86.80	$1388.80	$ 48.63	$ 61.45	$ 76.55
1 Truck Driver (heavy)	35.30	282.40	46.15	369.20	57.10	456.80			
1 Eqip. Oper. (crane)	47.80	382.40	60.65	485.20	75.50	604.00			
1 Flatbed Trailer, 40 Ton		147.00		147.00		161.70			
1 Truck Tractor, 6x4, 380 H.P.		522.20		522.20		574.42			
1 Hyd. Crane, 80 Ton		1554.00		1554.00		1709.40			
1 Hyd. Excavator, 2 C.Y.		1253.00		1253.00		1378.30	108.63	108.63	119.49
32 L.H., Daily Totals		$5032.20		$5442.60		$6273.42	$157.26	$170.08	$196.04
Crew B-34T	Hr.	Daily	Hr.	Daily	Hr.	Daily	Bare Costs	In House	Incl. O&P
2 Pipe Fitters	$55.70	$ 891.20	$69.50	$1112.00	$86.80	$1388.80	$ 48.63	$ 61.45	$ 76.55
1 Truck Driver (heavy)	35.30	282.40	46.15	369.20	57.10	456.80			
1 Eqip. Oper. (crane)	47.80	382.40	60.65	485.20	75.50	604.00			
1 Flatbed Trailer, 40 Ton		147.00		147.00		161.70			
1 Truck Tractor, 6x4, 380 H.P.		522.20		522.20		574.42			
1 Hyd. Crane, 80 Ton		1554.00		1554.00		1709.40	69.47	69.47	76.42
32 L.H., Daily Totals		$3779.20		$4189.60		$4895.12	$118.10	$130.93	$152.97
Crew B-35	Hr.	Daily	Hr.	Daily	Hr.	Daily	Bare Costs	In House	Incl. O&P
1 Labor Foreman (outside)	$37.10	$ 296.80	$49.30	$ 394.40	$60.80	$ 486.40	$43.54	$56.14	$69.64
1 Skilled Worker	45.40	363.20	59.75	478.00	73.80	590.40			
1 Welder (plumber)	54.60	436.80	68.15	545.20	85.05	680.40			
1 Laborer	35.10	280.80	46.65	373.20	57.55	460.40			
1 Equip. Oper. (crane)	47.80	382.40	60.65	485.20	75.50	604.00			
1 Equip. Oper. Oiler	41.25	330.00	52.35	418.80	65.15	521.20			
1 Welder, electric, 300 amp		36.90		36.90		40.59			
1 Hyd. Excavator, .75 C.Y.		647.20		647.20		711.92	14.25	14.25	15.68
48 L.H., Daily Totals		$2774.10		$3378.90		$4095.31	$57.79	$70.39	$85.32
Crew B-37	Hr.	Daily	Hr.	Daily	Hr.	Daily	Bare Costs	In House	Incl. O&P
1 Labor Foreman (outside)	$37.10	$ 296.80	$49.30	$ 394.40	$60.80	$ 486.40	$37.04	$48.78	$60.27
4 Laborers	35.10	1123.20	46.65	1492.80	57.55	1841.60			
1 Equip. Oper. (light)	44.75	358.00	56.80	454.40	70.65	565.20			
1 Tandem Roller, 5 Ton		149.20		149.20		164.12	3.11	3.11	3.42
48 L.H., Daily Totals		$1927.20		$2490.80		$3057.32	$40.15	$51.89	$63.69
Crew B-47H	Hr.	Daily	Hr.	Daily	Hr.	Daily	Bare Costs	In House	Incl. O&P
1 Skilled Worker Foreman (out)	$47.40	$ 379.20	$62.40	$ 499.20	$77.05	$ 616.40	$45.90	$60.41	$74.61
3 Skilled Workers	45.40	1089.60	59.75	1434.00	73.80	1771.20			
1 Flatbed Truck, Gas, 3 Ton		264.40		264.40		290.84	8.26	8.26	9.09
32 L.H., Daily Totals		$1733.20		$2197.60		$2678.44	$54.16	$68.67	$83.70
Crew B-55	Hr.	Daily	Hr.	Daily	Hr.	Daily	Bare Costs	In House	Incl. O&P
2 Laborers	$35.10	$ 561.60	$46.65	$ 746.40	$57.55	$ 920.80	$34.85	$46.07	$ 56.88
1 Truck Driver (light)	34.35	274.80	44.90	359.20	55.55	444.40			
1 Truck-mounted earth auger		718.40		718.40		790.24			
1 Flatbed Truck, Gas, 3 Ton		264.40		264.40		290.84	40.95	40.95	45.05
24 L.H., Daily Totals		$1819.20		$2088.40		$2446.28	$75.80	$87.02	$101.93

Crew No.	Bare Costs		In-House Costs		Incl. Subs O&P		Cost Per Labor-Hour		
Crew B-80	Hr.	Daily	Hr.	Daily	Hr.	Daily	Bare Costs	In House	Incl. O&P
1 Labor Foreman (outside)	$37.10	$ 296.80	$49.30	$ 394.40	$60.80	$ 486.40	$37.83	$49.41	$61.14
1 Laborer	35.10	280.80	46.65	373.20	57.55	460.40			
1 Truck Driver (light)	34.35	274.80	44.90	359.20	55.55	444.40			
1 Equip. Oper. (light)	44.75	358.00	56.80	454.40	70.65	565.20			
1 Flatbed Truck, Gas, 3 Ton		264.40		264.40		290.84			
1 Earth Auger, Truck-Mtd.		403.40		403.40		443.74	20.87	20.87	22.96
32 L.H., Daily Totals		$1878.20		$2249.00		$2690.98	$58.69	$70.28	$84.09
Crew B-80C	Hr.	Daily	Hr.	Daily	Hr.	Daily	Bare Costs	In House	Incl. O&P
2 Laborers	$35.10	$ 561.60	$46.65	$ 746.40	$57.55	$ 920.80	$34.85	$46.07	$56.88
1 Truck Driver (light)	34.35	274.80	44.90	359.20	55.55	444.40			
1 Flatbed Truck, Gas, 1.5 Ton		211.00		211.00		232.10			
1 Manual fence post auger, gas		7.60		7.60		8.36	9.11	9.11	10.02
24 L.H., Daily Totals		$1055.00		$1324.20		$1605.66	$43.96	$55.17	$66.90
Crew D-1	Hr.	Daily	Hr.	Daily	Hr.	Daily	Bare Costs	In House	Incl. O&P
1 Bricklayer	$44.10	$352.80	$57.35	$458.80	$71.00	$ 568.00	$39.85	$51.83	$64.15
1 Bricklayer Helper	35.60	284.80	46.30	370.40	57.30	458.40			
16 L.H., Daily Totals		$637.60		$829.20		$1026.40	$39.85	$51.83	$64.15
Crew D-7	Hr.	Daily	Hr.	Daily	Hr.	Daily	Bare Costs	In House	Incl. O&P
1 Tile Layer	$40.75	$326.00	$51.30	$410.40	$63.95	$511.60	$36.42	$45.85	$57.15
1 Tile Layer Helper	32.10	256.80	40.40	323.20	50.35	402.80			
16 L.H., Daily Totals		$582.80		$733.60		$914.40	$36.42	$45.85	$57.15
Crew D-8	Hr.	Daily	Hr.	Daily	Hr.	Daily	Bare Costs	In House	Incl. O&P
3 Bricklayers	$44.10	$1058.40	$57.35	$1376.40	$71.00	$1704.00	$40.70	$52.93	$65.52
2 Bricklayer Helpers	35.60	569.60	46.30	740.80	57.30	916.80			
40 L.H., Daily Totals		$1628.00		$2117.20		$2620.80	$40.70	$52.93	$65.52
Crew G-1	Hr.	Daily	Hr.	Daily	Hr.	Daily	Bare Costs	In House	Incl. O&P
1 Roofer Foreman (outside)	$39.40	$ 315.20	$57.80	$ 462.40	$70.00	$ 560.00	$34.96	$51.27	$62.11
4 Roofers, Composition	37.40	1196.80	54.85	1755.20	66.45	2126.40			
2 Roofer Helpers	27.85	445.60	40.85	653.60	49.50	792.00			
1 Application Equipment		179.20		179.20		197.12			
1 Tar Kettle/Pot		91.00		91.00		100.10			
1 Crew Truck		182.40		182.40		200.64	8.08	8.08	8.89
56 L.H., Daily Totals		$2410.20		$3323.80		$3976.26	$43.04	$59.35	$71.00
Crew G-5	Hr.	Daily	Hr.	Daily	Hr.	Daily	Bare Costs	In House	Incl. O&P
1 Roofer Foreman (outside)	$39.40	$ 315.20	$57.80	$ 462.40	$70.00	$ 560.00	$33.98	$49.84	$60.38
2 Roofers, Composition	37.40	598.40	54.85	877.60	66.45	1063.20			
2 Roofer Helpers	27.85	445.60	40.85	653.60	49.50	792.00			
1 Application Equipment		179.20		179.20		197.12	4.48	4.48	4.93
40 L.H., Daily Totals		$1538.40		$2172.80		$2612.32	$38.46	$54.32	$65.31
Crew G-8	Hr.	Daily	Hr.	Daily	Hr.	Daily	Bare Costs	In House	Incl. O&P
1 Roofer, Composition	$37.40	$299.20	$54.85	$ 438.80	$66.45	$ 531.60	$ 37.40	$ 54.85	$ 66.45
1 Aerial Lift Truck, 80'		637.60		637.60		701.36	79.70	79.70	87.67
8 L.H., Daily Totals		$936.80		$1076.40		$1232.96	$117.10	$134.55	$154.12
Crew L-2	Hr.	Daily	Hr.	Daily	Hr.	Daily	Bare Costs	In House	Incl. O&P
1 Carpenter	$44.10	$352.80	$58.60	$468.80	$72.30	$ 578.40	$38.70	$51.40	$63.42
1 Carpenter Helper	33.30	266.40	44.20	353.60	54.55	436.40			
16 L.H., Daily Totals		$619.20		$822.40		$1014.80	$38.70	$51.40	$63.42

Crew No.	Bare Costs		In-House Costs		Incl. Subs O&P		Cost Per Labor-Hour		
Crew Q-1	Hr.	Daily	Hr.	Daily	Hr.	Daily	Bare Costs	In House	Incl. O&P
1 Plumber	$54.60	$436.80	$68.15	$545.20	$85.05	$ 680.40	$49.15	$61.35	$76.58
1 Plumber Apprentice	43.70	349.60	54.55	436.40	68.10	544.80			
16 L.H., Daily Totals		$786.40		$981.60		$1225.20	$49.15	$61.35	$76.58
Crew Q-2	Hr.	Daily	Hr.	Daily	Hr.	Daily	Bare Costs	In House	Incl. O&P
2 Plumbers	$54.60	$ 873.60	$68.15	$1090.40	$85.05	$1360.80	$50.97	$63.62	$79.40
1 Plumber Apprentice	43.70	349.60	54.55	436.40	68.10	544.80	50.97	63.62	79.40
24 L.H., Daily Totals		$1223.20		$1526.80		$1905.60	$50.97	$63.62	$79.40
Crew Q-4	Hr.	Daily	Hr.	Daily	Hr.	Daily	Bare Costs	In House	Incl. O&P
1 Plumber Foreman (inside)	$55.10	$ 440.80	$68.75	$ 550.00	$85.85	$ 686.80	$52.00	$64.90	$81.01
1 Plumber	54.60	436.80	68.15	545.20	85.05	680.40			
1 Welder (plumber)	54.60	436.80	68.15	545.20	85.05	680.40			
1 Plumber Apprentice	43.70	349.60	54.55	436.40	68.10	544.80			
1 Welder, electric, 300 amp		36.90		36.90		40.59	1.15	1.15	1.27
32 L.H., Daily Totals		$1700.90		$2113.70		$2632.99	$53.15	$66.05	$82.28
Crew Q-5	Hr.	Daily	Hr.	Daily	Hr.	Daily	Bare Costs	In House	Incl. O&P
1 Steamfitter	$55.70	$445.60	$69.50	$ 556.00	$86.80	$ 694.40	$50.13	$62.55	$78.10
1 Steamfitter Apprentice	44.55	356.40	55.60	444.80	69.40	555.20			
16 L.H., Daily Totals		$802.00		$1000.80		$1249.60	$50.13	$62.55	$78.10
Crew Q-6	Hr.	Daily	Hr.	Daily	Hr.	Daily	Bare Costs	In House	Incl. O&P
2 Steamfitters	$55.70	$ 891.20	$69.50	$1112.00	$86.80	$1388.80	$51.98	$64.87	$81.00
1 Steamfitter Apprentice	44.55	356.40	55.60	444.80	69.40	555.20	51.98	64.87	81.00
24 L.H., Daily Totals		$1247.60		$1556.80		$1944.00	$51.98	$64.87	$81.00
Crew Q-7	Hr.	Daily	Hr.	Daily	Hr.	Daily	Bare Costs	In House	Incl. O&P
1 Steamfitter Foreman (inside)	$56.20	$ 449.60	$70.15	$ 561.20	$87.55	$ 700.40	$53.04	$66.19	$82.64
2 Steamfitters	55.70	891.20	69.50	1112.00	86.80	1388.80			
1 Steamfitter Apprentice	44.55	356.40	55.60	444.80	69.40	555.20			
32 L.H., Daily Totals		$1697.20		$2118.00		$2644.40	$53.04	$66.19	$82.64
Crew Q-8	Hr.	Daily	Hr.	Daily	Hr.	Daily	Bare Costs	In House	Incl. O&P
1 Steamfitter Foreman (inside)	$56.20	$ 449.60	$70.15	$ 561.20	$87.55	$ 700.40	$53.04	$66.19	$82.64
1 Steamfitter	55.70	445.60	69.50	556.00	86.80	694.40			
1 Welder (steamfitter)	55.70	445.60	69.50	556.00	86.80	694.40			
1 Steamfitter Apprentice	44.55	356.40	55.60	444.80	69.40	555.20			
1 Welder, electric, 300 amp		36.90		36.90		40.59	1.15	1.15	1.27
32 L.H., Daily Totals		$1734.10		$2154.90		$2684.99	$54.19	$67.34	$83.91
Crew Q-9	Hr.	Daily	Hr.	Daily	Hr.	Daily	Bare Costs	In House	Incl. O&P
1 Sheet Metal Worker	$52.15	$417.20	$65.90	$527.20	$82.10	$ 656.80	$46.92	$59.30	$73.88
1 Sheet Metal Apprentice	41.70	333.60	52.70	421.60	65.65	525.20			
16 L.H., Daily Totals		$750.80		$948.80		$1182.00	$46.92	$59.30	$73.88
Crew Q-10	Hr.	Daily	Hr.	Daily	Hr.	Daily	Bare Costs	In House	Incl. O&P
2 Sheet Metal Workers	$52.15	$ 834.40	$65.90	$1054.40	$82.10	$1313.60	$48.67	$61.50	$76.62
1 Sheet Metal Apprentice	41.70	333.60	52.70	421.60	65.65	525.20			
24 L.H., Daily Totals		$1168.00		$1476.00		$1838.80	$48.67	$61.50	$76.62
Crew Q-14	Hr.	Daily	Hr.	Daily	Hr.	Daily	Bare Costs	In House	Incl. O&P
1 Asbestos Worker	$48.85	$390.80	$63.40	$507.20	$78.55	$ 628.40	$43.98	$57.08	$70.70
1 Asbestos Apprentice	39.10	312.80	50.75	406.00	62.85	502.80			
16 L.H., Daily Totals		$703.60		$913.20		$1131.20	$43.98	$57.08	$70.70

Crews

Crew No.	Bare Costs Hr.	Daily	In-House Costs Hr.	Daily	Incl. Subs O&P Hr.	Daily	Cost Per Labor-Hour Bare Costs	In House	Incl. O&P
Crew Q-15	Hr.	Daily	Hr.	Daily	Hr.	Daily	Bare Costs	In House	Incl. O&P
1 Plumber	$54.60	$436.80	$68.15	$ 545.20	$85.05	$ 680.40	$49.15	$61.35	$76.58
1 Plumber Apprentice	43.70	349.60	54.55	436.40	68.10	544.80			
1 Welder, electric, 300 amp		36.90		36.90		40.59	2.31	2.31	2.54
16 L.H., Daily Totals		$823.30		$1018.50		$1265.79	$51.46	$63.66	$79.11
Crew Q-16	Hr.	Daily	Hr.	Daily	Hr.	Daily	Bare Costs	In House	Incl. O&P
2 Plumbers	$54.60	$ 873.60	$68.15	$1090.40	$85.05	$1360.80	$50.97	$63.62	$79.40
1 Plumber Apprentice	43.70	349.60	54.55	436.40	68.10	544.80			
1 Welder, electric, 300 amp		36.90		36.90		40.59	1.54	1.54	1.69
24 L.H., Daily Totals		$1260.10		$1563.70		$1946.19	$52.50	$65.15	$81.09
Crew Q-20	Hr.	Daily	Hr.	Daily	Hr.	Daily	Bare Costs	In House	Incl. O&P
1 Sheet Metal Worker	$52.15	$417.20	$65.90	$ 527.20	$82.10	$ 656.80	$47.85	$60.17	$75.03
1 Sheet Metal Apprentice	41.70	333.60	52.70	421.60	65.65	525.20			
.5 Electrician	51.55	206.20	63.65	254.60	79.65	318.60			
20 L.H., Daily Totals		$957.00		$1203.40		$1500.60	$47.85	$60.17	$75.03
Crew R-3	Hr.	Daily	Hr.	Daily	Hr.	Daily	Bare Costs	In House	Incl. O&P
1 Electrician Foreman	$52.05	$ 416.40	$64.30	$ 514.40	$80.40	$ 643.20	$51.00	$63.31	$79.12
1 Electrician	51.55	412.40	63.65	509.20	79.65	637.20			
.5 Equip. Oper. (crane)	47.80	191.20	60.65	242.60	75.50	302.00			
.5 S.P. Crane, 4x4, 5 Ton		132.30		132.30		145.53	6.62	6.62	7.28
20 L.H., Daily Totals		$1152.30		$1398.50		$1727.93	$57.62	$69.92	$86.40
Crew R-26	Hr.	Daily	Hr.	Daily	Hr.	Daily	Bare Costs	In House	Incl. O&P
2 Electricians	$51.55	$ 824.80	$63.65	$1018.40	$79.65	$1274.40	$51.55	$63.65	$79.65
1 Boom Work Pltfm, 40'		288.40		288.40		317.24	18.02	18.02	19.83
16 L.H., Daily Totals		$1113.20		$1306.80		$1591.64	$69.58	$81.67	$99.48

Travel Costs

The following table is used to estimate the cost of in-house staff or contractor's personnel to travel to and from the job site. The amount incurred must be added to the in-house total labor cost or contractor's billing application to calculate the total cost with travel.

In-House Staff–Travel Times versus Costs

Travel Time Versus Costs	Crew Abbr.	Skwk	Clab	Clam	Asbe	Bric	Carp	Elec	Pord	Plum	Rofc	Shee	Stpi
	Rate with Mark-ups	$59.75	$46.65	$32.75	$63.40	$57.35	$58.60	$63.65	$49.20	$68.15	$54.85	$65.90	$69.50
Round Trip Travel Time (hours)	Crew Size												
0.50	1	29.88	23.33	16.38	31.70	28.68	29.30	31.83	24.60	34.08	27.43	32.95	34.75
	2	59.75	46.65	32.75	63.40	57.35	58.60	63.65	49.20	68.15	54.85	65.90	69.50
	3	89.63	69.98	49.13	95.10	86.03	87.90	95.48	73.80	102.23	82.28	98.85	104.25
0.75	1	44.81	34.99	24.56	47.55	43.01	43.95	47.74	36.90	51.11	41.14	49.43	52.13
	2	89.63	69.98	49.13	95.10	86.03	87.90	95.48	73.80	102.23	82.28	98.85	104.25
	3	134.44	104.96	73.69	142.65	129.04	131.85	143.21	110.70	153.34	123.41	148.28	156.38
1.00	1	59.75	46.65	32.75	63.40	57.35	58.60	63.65	49.20	68.15	54.85	65.90	69.50
	2	119.50	93.30	65.50	126.80	114.70	117.20	127.30	98.40	136.30	109.70	131.80	139.00
	3	179.25	139.95	98.25	190.20	172.05	175.80	190.95	147.60	204.45	164.55	197.70	208.50
1.50	1	89.63	69.98	49.13	95.10	86.03	87.90	95.48	73.80	102.23	82.28	98.85	104.25
	2	179.25	139.95	98.25	190.20	172.05	175.80	190.95	147.60	204.45	164.55	197.70	208.50
	3	268.88	209.93	147.38	285.30	258.08	263.70	286.43	221.40	306.68	246.83	296.55	312.75
2.00	1	119.50	93.30	65.50	126.80	114.70	117.20	127.30	98.40	136.30	109.70	131.80	139.00
	2	239.00	186.60	131.00	253.60	229.40	234.40	254.60	196.80	272.60	219.40	263.60	278.00
	3	358.50	279.90	196.50	380.40	344.10	351.60	381.90	295.20	408.90	329.10	395.40	417.00

Installing Contractors–Travel Times versus Costs

Travel Time Versus Costs	Crew Abbr.	Skwk	Clab	Clam	Asbe	Bric	Carp	Elec	Pord	Plum	Rofc	Shee	Stpi
	Rate with O & P	$73.80	$57.55	$40.90	$78.55	$71.00	$72.30	$79.65	$61.05	$85.05	$66.45	$82.10	$86.80
Round Trip Travel Time (hours)	Crew Size												
0.50	1	36.90	28.78	20.45	39.28	35.50	36.15	39.83	30.53	42.53	33.23	41.05	43.40
	2	73.80	57.55	40.90	78.55	71.00	72.30	79.65	61.05	85.05	66.45	82.10	86.80
	3	110.70	86.33	61.35	117.83	106.50	108.45	119.48	91.58	127.58	99.68	123.15	130.20
0.75	1	55.35	43.16	30.68	58.91	53.25	54.23	59.74	45.79	63.79	49.84	61.58	65.10
	2	110.70	86.33	61.35	117.83	106.50	108.45	119.48	91.58	127.58	99.68	123.15	130.20
	3	166.05	129.49	92.03	176.74	159.75	162.68	179.21	137.36	191.36	149.51	184.73	195.30
1.00	1	73.80	57.55	40.90	78.55	71.00	72.30	79.65	61.05	85.05	66.45	82.10	86.80
	2	147.60	115.10	81.80	157.10	142.00	144.60	159.30	122.10	170.10	132.90	164.20	173.60
	3	221.40	172.65	122.70	235.65	213.00	216.90	238.95	183.15	255.15	199.35	246.30	260.40
1.50	1	110.70	86.33	61.35	117.83	106.50	108.45	119.48	91.58	127.58	99.68	123.15	130.20
	2	221.40	172.65	122.70	235.65	213.00	216.90	238.95	183.15	255.15	199.35	246.30	260.40
	3	332.10	258.98	184.05	353.48	319.50	325.35	358.43	274.73	382.73	299.03	369.45	390.60
2.00	1	147.60	115.10	81.80	157.10	142.00	144.60	159.30	122.10	170.10	132.90	164.20	173.60
	2	295.20	230.20	163.60	314.20	284.00	289.20	318.60	244.20	340.20	265.80	328.40	347.20
	3	442.80	345.30	245.40	471.30	426.00	433.80	477.90	366.30	510.30	398.70	492.60	520.80

617

Table H1010-101 General Contractor's Overhead

There are two distinct types of overhead on a construction project: Project Overhead and Main Office Overhead. Project Overhead includes those costs at a construction site not directly associated with the installation of construction materials. Examples of Project Overhead costs include the following:

1. Superintendent
2. Construction office and storage trailers
3. Temporary sanitary facilities
4. Temporary utilities
5. Security fencing
6. Photographs
7. Clean up
8. Performance and payment bonds

The above Project Overhead items are also referred to as General Requirements and therefore are estimated in Division 1. Division 1 is the first division listed in the CSI MasterFormat but it is usually the last division estimated. The sum of the costs in Divisions 1 through 49 is referred to as the sum of the direct costs.

All construction projects also include indirect costs. The primary components of indirect costs are the contractor's Main Office Overhead and profit. The amount of the Main Office Overhead expense varies depending on the the following:

1. Owner's compensation
2. Project managers and estimator's wages
3. Clerical support wages
4. Office rent and utilities
5. Corporate legal and accounting costs
6. Advertising
7. Automobile expenses
8. Association dues
9. Travel and entertainment expenses

These costs are usually calculated as a percentage of annual sales volume. This percentage can range from 35% for a small contractor doing less than $500,000 to 5% for a large contractor with sales in excess of $100 million.

Table H1010-102 Main Office Expense

A General Contractor's main office expense consists of many items not detailed in the front portion of the book. The percentage of main office expense declines with increased annual volume of the contractor. Typical main office expense ranges from 2% to 20% with the median about 7.2%

of total volume. This equals about 7.7% of direct costs. The following are approximate percentages of total overhead for different items usually included in a General Contractor's main office overhead. With different accounting procedures, these percentages may vary.

Item	Typical Range			Average
Managers', clerical and estimators' salaries	40 %	to	55 %	48%
Profit sharing, pension and bonus plans	2	to	20	12
Insurance	5	to	8	6
Estimating and project management (not including salaries)	5	to	9	7
Legal, accounting and data processing	0.5	to	5	3
Automobile and light truck expense	2	to	8	5
Depreciation of overhead capital expenditures	2	to	6	4
Maintenance of office equipment	0.1	to	1.5	1
Office rental	3	to	5	4
Utilities including phone and light	1	to	3	2
Miscellaneous	5	to	15	8
Total				100%

Table H1010-201   Architectural Fees

Tabulated below are typical percentage fees by project size, for good professional architectural service. Fees may vary from those listed depending upon degree of design difficulty and economic conditions in any particular area.

Rates can be interpolated horizontally and vertically. Various portions of the same project requiring different rates should be adjusted proportionately. For alterations, add 50% to the fee for the first $500,000 of project cost and add 25% to the fee for project cost over $500,000.

Architectural fees tabulated below include Structural, Mechanical and Electrical Engineering Fees. They do not include the fees for special consultants such as kitchen planning, security, acoustical, interior design, etc.

Building Types	Total Project Size in Thousands of Dollars						
	100	250	500	1,000	5,000	10,000	50,000
Factories, garages, warehouses, repetitive housing	9.0%	8.0%	7.0%	6.2%	5.3%	4.9%	4.5%
Apartments, banks, schools, libraries, offices, municipal buildings	12.2	12.3	9.2	8.0	7.0	6.6	6.2
Churches, hospitals, homes, laboratories, museums, research	15.0	13.6	12.7	11.9	9.5	8.8	8.0
Memorials, monumental work, decorative furnishings	—	16.0	14.5	13.1	10.0	9.0	8.3

Table H1010-202   Engineering Fees

Typical **Structural Engineering Fees** based on type of construction and total project size. These fees are included in Architectural Fees.

Type of Construction	Total Project Size (in thousands of dollars)			
	$500	$500-$1,000	$1,000-$5,000	Over $5000
Industrial buildings, factories & warehouses	Technical payroll times 2.0 to 2.5	1.60%	1.25%	1.00%
Hotels, apartments, offices, dormitories, hospitals, public buildings, food stores		2.00%	1.70%	1.20%
Museums, banks, churches and cathedrals		2.00%	1.75%	1.25%
Thin shells, prestressed concrete, earthquake resistive		2.00%	1.75%	1.50%
Parking ramps, auditoriums, stadiums, convention halls, hangars & boiler houses		2.50%	2.00%	1.75%
Special buildings, major alterations, underpinning & future expansion		Add to above 0.5%	Add to above 0.5%	Add to above 0.5%

For complex reinforced concrete or unusually complicated structures, add 20% to 50%.

Table H1010-203   Mechanical and Electrical Fees

Typical **Mechanical and Electrical Engineering Fees** based on the size of the subcontract. The fee structure for both are shown below. These fees are included in Architectural Fees.

Type of Construction	Subcontract Size							
	$25,000	$50,000	$100,000	$225,000	$350,000	$500,000	$750,000	$1,000,000
Simple structures	6.4%	5.7%	4.8%	4.5%	4.4%	4.3%	4.2%	4.1%
Intermediate structures	8.0	7.3	6.5	5.6	5.1	5.0	4.9	4.8
Complex structures	10.1	9.0	9.0	8.0	7.5	7.5	7.0	7.0

For renovations, add 15% to 25% to applicable fee.

Table H1010-301   Builder's Risk Insurance

Builder's Risk Insurance is insurance on a building during construction. Premiums are paid by the owner or the contractor. Blasting, collapse and underground insurance would raise total insurance costs above those listed. Floater policy for materials delivered to the job runs $.75 to $1.25 per $100 value. Contractor equipment insurance runs $.50 to $1.50 per $100 value. Insurance for miscellaneous tools to $1,500 value runs from $3.00 to $7.50 per $100 value.

Tabulated below are New England Builder's Risk insurance rates in dollars per $100 value for $1,000 deductible. For $25,000 deductible, rates can be reduced 13% to 34%. On contracts over $1,000,000, rates may be lower than those tabulated. Policies are written annually for the total completed value in place. For "all risk" insurance (excluding flood, earthquake and certain other perils) add $.025 to total rates below.

Coverage	Frame Construction (Class 1)			Brick Construction (Class 4)			Fire Resistive (Class 6)		
	Range		Average	Range		Average	Range		Average
Fire Insurance	$.350 to $.850		$.600	$.158 to $.189		$.174	$.052 to $.080		$.070
Extended Coverage	.115 to .200		.158	.080 to .105		.101	.081 to .105		.100
Vandalism	.012 to .016		.014	.008 to .011		.011	.008 to .011		.010
Total Annual Rate	$.477 to $1.066		$.772	$.246 to $.305		$.286	$.141 to $.196		$.180

Table H1010-302   Performance Bond

This table shows the cost of a Performance Bond for a construction job scheduled to be completed in 12 months. Add 1% of the premium cost per month for jobs requiring more than 12 months to complete. The rates are "standard" rates offered to contractors that the bonding company considers financially sound and capable of doing the work. Preferred rates are offered by some bonding companies based upon financial strength of the contractor. Actual rates vary from contractor to contractor and from bonding company to bonding company. Contractors should prequalify through a bonding agency before submitting a bid on a contract that requires a bond.

Contract Amount	Building Construction Class B Projects	Highways & Bridges	
		Class A New Construction	Class A-1 Highway Resurfacing
First $ 100,000 bid	$25.00 per M	$15.00 per M	$9.40 per M
Next 400,000 bid	$ 2,500 plus $15.00 per M	$ 1,500 plus $10.00 per M	$ 940 plus $7.20 per M
Next 2,000,000 bid	8,500 plus 10.00 per M	5,500 plus 7.00 per M	3,820 plus 5.00 per M
Next 2,500,000 bid	28,500 plus 7.50 per M	19,500 plus 5.50 per M	15,820 plus 4.50 per M
Next 2,500,000 bid	47,250 plus 7.00 per M	33,250 plus 5.00 per M	28,320 plus 4.50 per M
Over 7,500,000 bid	64,750 plus 6.00 per M	45,750 plus 4.50 per M	39,570 plus 4.00 per M

Table H1010-401   Workers' Compensation Insurance Rates by Trade

The table below tabulates the national averages for Workers' Compensation insurance rates by trade and type of building. The average "Insurance Rate" is multiplied by the "% of Building Cost" for each trade. This produces the "Workers' Compensation Cost" by % of total labor cost, to be added for each trade by building type to determine the weighted average Workers' Compensation rate for the building types analyzed.

Trade	Insurance Rate (% Labor Cost)		% of Building Cost			Workers' Compensation		
	Range	Average	Office Bldgs.	Schools & Apts.	Mfg.	Office Bldgs.	Schools & Apts.	Mfg.
Excavation, Grading, etc.	3.9 % to 18.1%	9.0%	4.8%	4.9%	4.5%	0.43%	0.44%	0.41%
Piles & Foundations	5.1 to 59.5	16.8	7.1	5.2	8.7	1.19	0.87	1.46
Concrete	4.9 to 29.7	12.7	5.0	14.8	3.7	0.64	1.88	0.47
Masonry	4.4 to 28.7	12.1	6.9	7.5	1.9	0.83	0.91	0.23
Structural Steel	5.1 to 124.1	36.9	10.7	3.9	17.6	3.95	1.44	6.49
Miscellaneous & Ornamental Metals	4.2 to 22.6	10.1	2.8	4.0	3.6	0.28	0.40	0.36
Carpentry & Millwork	5.1 to 37	15.0	3.7	4.0	0.5	0.56	0.60	0.08
Metal or Composition Siding	4.9 to 43.3	14.9	2.3	0.3	4.3	0.34	0.04	0.64
Roofing	5.1 to 75.2	28.8	2.3	2.6	3.1	0.66	0.75	0.89
Doors & Hardware	2.8 to 37	10.5	0.9	1.4	0.4	0.09	0.15	0.04
Sash & Glazing	4.9 to 33.1	12.6	3.5	4.0	1.0	0.44	0.50	0.13
Lath & Plaster	2.5 to 30.5	10.8	3.3	6.9	0.8	0.36	0.75	0.09
Tile, Marble & Floors	2.3 to 18.9	8.0	2.6	3.0	0.5	0.21	0.24	0.04
Acoustical Ceilings	3.2 to 30.3	7.8	2.4	0.2	0.3	0.19	0.02	0.02
Painting	4.3 to 28.9	10.7	1.5	1.6	1.6	0.16	0.17	0.17
Interior Partitions	5.1 to 37	15.0	3.9	4.3	4.4	0.59	0.65	0.66
Miscellaneous Items	2.5 to 90.6	14.6	5.2	3.7	9.7	0.76	0.54	1.42
Elevators	1.8 to 12.8	5.9	2.1	1.1	2.2	0.12	0.06	0.13
Sprinklers	1.9 to 17.2	7.0	0.5	—	2.0	0.04	—	0.14
Plumbing	2.7 to 17.1	6.9	4.9	7.2	5.2	0.34	0.50	0.36
Heat., Vent., Air Conditioning	3.8 to 19.3	8.5	13.5	11.0	12.9	1.15	0.94	1.10
Electrical	2.6 to 13.2	5.6	10.1	8.4	11.1	0.57	0.47	0.62
Total	1.8 % to 124.1%	—	100.0%	100.0%	100.0%	13.90%	12.32%	15.95%
	Overall Weighted Average 14.06%							

Workers' Compensation Insurance Rates by States

The table below lists the weighted average Workers' Compensation base rate for each state with a factor comparing this with the national average of 13.7%.

State	Weighted Average	Factor	State	Weighted Average	Factor	State	Weighted Average	Factor
Alabama	19.6%	143	Kentucky	17.0%	124	North Dakota	10.8%	79
Alaska	16.3	119	Louisiana	15.6	114	Ohio	8.7	64
Arizona	9.0	66	Maine	14.0	102	Oklahoma	14.7	107
Arkansas	10.2	74	Maryland	15.6	114	Oregon	12.0	88
California	27.9	204	Massachusetts	12.4	91	Pennsylvania	16.3	119
Colorado	7.1	52	Michigan	20.6	150	Rhode Island	11.9	87
Connecticut	23.1	169	Minnesota	24.1	176	South Carolina	20.1	147
Delaware	9.3	68	Mississippi	13.1	96	South Dakota	16.0	117
District of Columbia	11.2	82	Missouri	17.4	127	Tennessee	13.2	96
Florida	10.8	79	Montana	14.2	104	Texas	10.6	77
Georgia	27.8	203	Nebraska	18.1	132	Utah	7.8	57
Hawaii	9.0	66	Nevada	10.4	76	Vermont	14.6	107
Idaho	10.8	79	New Hampshire	21.1	154	Virginia	8.7	64
Illinois	22.6	165	New Jersey	13.4	98	Washington	11.1	81
Indiana	5.5	40	New Mexico	17.8	130	West Virginia	12.6	92
Iowa	10.8	79	New York	5.9	43	Wisconsin	14.9	109
Kansas	8.0	58	North Carolina	17.6	128	Wyoming	5.7	42
			Weighted Average for U.S. is 14.1% of payroll = 100%					

Rates in the following table are the base or manual costs per $100 of payroll for Workers' Compensation in each state. Rates are usually applied to straight time wages only and not to premium time wages and bonuses.

The weighted average skilled worker rate for 35 trades is 13.7%. For bidding purposes, apply the full value of Workers' Compensation directly to total labor costs, or if labor is 38%, materials 42% and overhead and profit 20% of total cost, carry 38/80 x 13.7% =6.5% of cost (before overhead and profit) into overhead. Rates vary not only from state to state but also with the experience rating of the contractor.

Rates are the most current available at the time of publication.

Table H1010-403   Workers' Compensation Insurance Rates by Trade and State

State	Carpentry — 3 stories or less 5651	Carpentry — interior cab. work 5437	Carpentry — general 5403	Concrete Work — NOC 5213	Concrete Work — flat (flr., sdwk.) 5221	Electrical Wiring — inside 5190	Excavation — earth NOC 6217	Excavation — rock 6217	Glaziers 5462	Insulation Work 5479	Lathing 5443	Masonry 5022	Painting & Decorating 5474	Pile Driving 6003	Plastering 5480	Plumbing 5183	Roofing 5551	Sheet Metal Work (HVAC) 5538	Steel Erection — door & sash 5102	Steel Erection — inter, ornam. 5102	Steel Erection — structure 5040	Steel Erection — NOC 5057	Tile Work — (interior ceramic) 5348	Waterproofing 9014	Wrecking 5701
AL	29.28	13.11	25.00	12.94	9.22	8.58	11.91	11.91	20.78	14.99	8.43	22.04	16.81	18.81	14.91	8.97	48.49	9.00	10.13	10.13	46.10	24.11	14.15	8.68	46.10
AK	12.44	9.33	13.86	11.33	10.80	6.86	9.06	9.06	32.79	17.54	8.30	16.08	11.68	33.22	13.00	7.53	25.29	7.47	7.41	7.41	25.75	41.66	5.15	5.48	25.75
AZ	11.78	5.44	15.76	6.99	4.24	4.37	4.81	4.81	6.09	10.18	3.64	7.06	7.21	8.53	5.15	4.56	18.34	6.49	9.20	9.20	21.81	10.32	2.89	3.58	21.81
AR	11.58	5.85	10.93	6.39	5.50	4.31	6.73	6.73	7.95	8.55	4.39	7.75	8.88	10.93	12.95	4.70	17.06	5.13	6.99	6.99	28.58	21.04	6.21	2.97	28.58
CA	36.98	36.98	36.98	19.36	19.34	13.20	18.05	18.05	27.35	17.74	16.02	27.71	21.08	23.37	30.46	17.05	64.15	19.29	22.60	22.60	41.64	23.39	2.30	21.08	23.39
CO	7.62	4.14	5.79	6.03	4.35	2.67	4.88	4.88	4.93	7.66	3.52	7.28	5.10	7.13	5.24	3.62	13.42	3.77	5.01	5.01	24.23	9.35	3.77	2.76	21.38
CT	19.80	17.42	27.18	22.71	13.56	7.85	14.62	14.62	19.83	24.28	12.69	27.26	21.51	23.20	18.28	10.85	48.23	13.52	15.52	15.52	64.75	22.28	13.05	6.77	65.75
DE	9.15	9.15	7.05	7.35	6.12	3.18	5.54	5.54	7.90	7.05	7.90	8.28	9.53	11.07	7.90	4.76	17.93	6.13	8.83	8.83	17.30	8.83	5.60	8.28	17.30
DC	8.25	8.16	7.71	12.10	7.65	4.34	9.06	9.06	13.00	6.41	6.70	10.21	5.60	15.02	8.73	7.96	16.80	7.20	15.77	15.77	19.23	10.98	9.00	4.18	19.23
FL	9.33	7.33	10.95	11.45	5.16	5.13	5.96	5.96	8.48	8.55	4.12	8.77	7.91	38.24	11.10	4.82	17.10	6.49	8.06	8.06	19.04	10.13	4.43	4.41	19.04
GA	43.26	19.77	27.19	20.25	15.13	10.28	16.31	16.31	18.41	19.10	12.62	28.72	28.86	23.32	21.44	12.2	75.23	17.15	19.64	19.64	73.28	34.09	12.76	10.18	73.28
HI	7.84	6.87	14.67	7.64	4.33	4.13	5.18	5.18	8.07	5.61	6.55	7.82	6.96	9.14	8.22	4.26	13.77	4.11	6.51	6.51	28.23	9.49	5.22	5.37	20.79
ID	12.77	6.43	10.55	11.76	5.76	3.47	7.06	7.06	9.63	7.67	6.29	7.80	8.43	9.30	13.57	4.27	22.62	7.21	8.55	8.55	32.97	8.02	6.84	4.80	27.50
IL	23.60	15.01	21.72	29.69	12.06	8.24	11.22	11.22	18.09	20.32	12.88	20.85	13.07	21.77	22.24	10.77	36.73	12.98	19.24	19.24	79.82	21.35	16.91	5.78	29.82
IN	8.38	4.15	6.38	4.95	3.41	2.68	4.15	4.15	5.28	6.02	3.24	4.43	4.34	5.34	3.28	2.65	10.05	4.13	4.21	4.21	11.63	5.11	2.89	2.59	11.63
IA	10.34	8.42	12.90	12.72	8.24	4.47	6.88	6.88	9.20	5.82	4.64	8.40	6.76	8.73	10.98	6.40	19.92	4.80	5.70	5.70	36.26	14.65	6.70	4.60	24.10
KS	12.27	5.30	8.09	6.46	5.62	3.67	4.59	4.59	8.35	8.35	3.41	6.73	6.60	7.80	5.04	4.43	13.94	4.61	4.75	4.75	18.81	13.14	5.31	3.99	13.14
KY	12.63	12.30	24.88	12.96	7.51	5.36	11.65	11.65	16.68	13.04	8.83	7.70	11.00	21.98	12.55	5.87	34.41	11.42	10.07	10.07	60.00	17.23	18.88	4.22	60.00
LA	18.20	12.54	20.92	11.92	9.35	6.46	12.02	12.02	14.16	10.50	6.61	13.71	15.78	15.66	10.45	6.08	32.48	12.91	12.19	12.19	44.77	9.67	7.08	6.58	44.77
ME	14.80	10.05	21.30	15.69	9.73	5.57	10.34	10.34	14.40	14.60	5.58	10.56	14.17	12.31	10.83	7.41	24.74	8.22	7.40	7.40	38.54	15.25	5.97	5.13	38.54
MD	17.56	13.32	14.28	19.37	5.51	7.07	7.60	7.60	12.50	14.18	5.58	10.00	7.28	21.24	10.47	7.02	30.67	7.73	10.49	10.49	59.74	22.48	6.69	5.43	22.48
MA	8.68	5.23	9.61	18.85	6.24	2.84	4.35	4.35	9.58	7.78	5.27	10.55	5.09	12.92	4.68	3.50	30.99	5.72	6.89	6.89	54.08	33.00	5.81	2.48	23.75
MI	21.01	11.98	21.01	17.15	10.48	6.35	14.00	14.00	15.12	13.11	13.59	18.32	13.30	59.47	10.34	7.71	42.64	12.58	12.03	12.03	59.47	16.23	11.70	6.95	59.47
MN	19.68	20.00	29.85	10.35	13.68	5.50	10.18	10.18	33.05	22.80	10.63	15.00	14.53	30.90	10.63	8.08	62.73	17.35	9.73	9.73	124.08	8.93	11.70	7.20	8.93
MS	17.32	9.93	13.14	9.84	5.57	4.62	9.84	9.84	11.42	9.11	4.97	12.50	9.60	17.78	10.10	8.54	33.19	6.45	13.01	13.01	30.00	8.32	7.92	4.45	30.00
MO	18.26	12.25	13.57	17.90	11.00	7.12	11.34	11.34	10.74	13.27	9.16	15.43	11.27	18.34	14.38	10.70	36.70	9.28	11.58	11.58	38.70	38.11	13.39	6.50	38.70
MT	13.20	10.71	20.41	12.22	10.37	5.23	12.92	12.92	10.67	19.74	7.41	9.78	8.66	15.08	10.75	7.27	39.34	8.38	9.64	9.64	24.14	9.36	8.36	7.78	9.36
NE	20.53	15.68	20.38	19.08	12.10	7.83	15.30	15.30	12.18	19.13	8.00	18.20	11.23	15.73	13.68	9.48	34.05	11.63	13.15	13.15	44.88	22.70	8.23	6.70	63.83
NV	10.76	7.25	11.35	10.52	7.16	4.80	8.48	8.48	6.75	8.06	3.45	6.62	6.07	8.88	6.41	6.22	17.81	8.84	7.73	7.73	25.26	15.85	13.93	5.16	15.85
NH	20.77	11.63	18.79	25.37	13.01	5.70	13.22	13.22	12.59	13.98	7.47	19.78	24.64	15.55	10.58	10.41	35.43	8.15	11.93	11.93	99.47	28.64	12.59	6.79	99.47
NJ	15.50	9.86	15.50	14.21	9.79	4.45	8.75	8.75	7.99	10.68	12.42	14.48	10.11	14.56	12.42	6.24	38.07	6.71	10.85	10.85	16.29	15.14	7.82	5.82	15.93
NM	19.58	8.17	18.99	13.33	10.11	8.08	8.28	8.28	18.17	11.75	6.68	15.36	11.43	18.20	14.39	8.14	37.47	9.92	12.79	12.79	54.49	40.63	7.66	6.66	54.49
NY	4.93	2.81	6.01	7.46	5.60	2.64	3.94	3.94	6.56	3.28	4.63	6.16	4.85	6.74	2.51	3.31	12.36	4.57	5.46	5.46	10.44	6.29	3.12	3.09	4.57
NC	15.50	11.55	18.63	17.12	8.14	9.96	13.11	13.11	11.87	12.57	9.34	11.05	11.85	16.82	13.63	8.92	33.88	11.87	11.97	11.97	70.40	20.61	8.12	5.41	70.40
ND	10.78	10.78	10.78	4.92	4.92	3.79	4.18	4.18	10.78	10.78	8.88	6.00	6.57	12.68	8.88	6.21	19.53	6.21	12.68	12.68	12.68	12.68	10.78	19.53	8.53
OH	6.82	4.77	6.03	4.98	4.96	3.17	4.83	4.83	9.26	9.83	30.29	7.62	7.64	7.67	7.20	3.94	15.01	4.87	6.17	6.17	12.91	6	6.11	4.90	6.00
OK	13.42	9.17	11.76	11.76	6.34	5.73	10.83	10.83	16.07	19.47	8.45	10.02	8.47	20.25	12.19	7.09	21.13	9.05	13.76	13.76	39.72	23.97	6.50	5.71	39.72
OR	19.79	8.26	13.53	10.34	8.96	5.18	9.03	9.03	10.65	10.89	6.79	11.80	10.85	12.18	9.08	5.38	26.12	6.49	6.82	6.82	20.28	15.61	6.68	5.72	20.28
PA	16.83	16.83	13.22	16.61	11.93	6.69	9.79	9.79	12.75	13.22	12.75	14.24	14.78	17.14	12.75	8.62	33.19	8.74	16.63	16.63	25.25	16.63	9.61	14.24	25.25
RI	9.69	10.13	12.42	13.18	10.51	4.12	8.56	8.56	10.26	13.56	4.93	8.95	9.48	20.95	8.02	5.77	19.37	6.38	6.06	6.06	28.84	20.64	4.60	4.61	28.84
SC	21.43	18.13	22.49	16.89	9.59	11.45	11.78	11.78	16.99	18.58	11.06	13.93	15.50	20.61	15.75	12.36	50.08	13.06	13.91	13.91	41.22	32.53	10.50	6.33	41.22
SD	18.86	13.19	18.65	20.78	8.58	4.84	9.13	9.13	14.61	14.35	6.47	11.88	10.04	15.98	10.23	9.60	31.05	9.72	11.92	11.92	45.18	23.68	6.07	6.02	45.18
TN	16.91	10.01	10.79	11.98	5.04	5.70	11.30	11.30	11.59	8.82	7.16	12.26	9.19	21.55	10.85	5.70	30.21	7.60	8.74	8.74	22.74	23.16	7.39	4.11	22.74
TX	9.68	7.76	9.68	8.61	6.25	5.65	7.33	7.33	7.82	10.32	4.91	8.32	8.04	12.94	8.04	5.47	17.96	13.94	7.16	7.16	29.32	11.95	5.11	5.97	8.11
UT	9.81	5.76	7.93	7.13	5.38	3.09	6.77	6.77	7.13	5.43	4.01	6.86	5.93	7.69	4.67	3.28	21.47	5.41	4.91	4.91	17.18	8.18	3.74	4.02	18.30
VT	13.01	12.79	15.72	11.55	8.77	4.46	10.51	10.51	13.83	14.05	6.01	13.93	9.03	12.33	8.89	8.77	26.46	7.73	10.42	10.42	45.01	23.47	7.90	7.15	45.01
VA	8.91	6.79	7.37	8.34	4.22	3.84	6.23	6.23	6.35	5.77	6.19	6.15	7.43	7.98	6.26	4.34	21.14	5.67	6.19	6.19	25.35	11.51	4.06	2.65	25.35
WA	8.93	8.93	8.93	8.93	8.93	3.27	5.79	5.79	13.83	8.00	8.93	11.74	14.05	20.72	10.68	4.12	19.61	4.58	8.62	8.62	8.62	8.62	7.66	19.61	8.62
WV	13.52	9.63	10.91	11.26	6.25	6.07	9.18	9.18	11.22	9.76	7.21	10.37	10.25	15.47	9.74	6.22	25.10	7.93	8.31	8.31	34.41	16.71	7.86	3.96	32.85
WI	13.04	10.81	16.27	12.16	8.90	5.66	7.72	7.72	12.52	12.83	4.69	15.44	12.07	26.59	10.07	5.82	31.84	8.36	11.02	11.02	21.68	30.03	16.47	5.33	21.68
WY	5.07	5.07	5.07	5.07	5.07	5.07	5.07	5.07	5.07	5.07	5.07	5.07	5.07	5.07	5.07	5.07	5.07	5.07	5.07	5.07	5.07	5.07	5.07	5.07	5.07
AVG.	14.90	10.53	14.96	12.70	8.24	5.58	9.01	9.01	12.57	11.85	7.82	12.10	10.70	16.76	10.78	6.91	28.83	8.47	10.07	10.07	36.86	17.78	8.01	6.41	30.43

Table H1010-404   Workers' Compensation (Canada in Canadian dollars)

Province		Alberta	British Columbia	Manitoba	Ontario	New Brunswick	Newfndld. & Labrador	Northwest Territories	Nova Scotia	Prince Edward Island	Quebec	Saskat-chewan	Yukon
Carpentry—3 stories or less	Rate	6.07	3.93	3.96	4.44	4.62	9.44	3.92	5.70	6.62	12.61	3.74	8.55
	Code	42143	721028	40102	723	238130	4226	4-41	4226	403	80110	B1226	202
Carpentry—interior cab. work	Rate	2.16	2.68	3.96	4.44	4.37	4.24	3.92	4.83	3.69	12.61	2.24	8.55
	Code	42133	721021	40102	723	238350	4279	4-41	4274	402	80110	B1127	202
CARPENTRY—general	Rate	6.07	3.93	3.93	4.44	4.62	4.24	3.92	5.70	6.62	12.61	3.74	8.55
	Code	42143	721028	40102	723	238130	4299	4-41	4226	403	80110	B1202	202
CONCRETE WORK—NOC	Rate	3.86	3.28	6.27	17.86	4.62	9.44	3.92	5.03	3.69	12.86	4.28	8.55
	Code	42104	721010	40110	748	238110	4224	4-41	4224	402	80100	B1314	203
CONCRETE WORK—flat (flr. sidewalk)	Rate	3.86	3.28	6.27	17.86	4.62	9.44	3.92	5.03	3.69	12.86	4.28	8.55
	Code	42104	721010	40110	748	238110	4224	4-41	4224	402	80100	B1314	203
ELECTRICAL Wiring—inside	Rate	1.72	1.71	1.74	3.60	2.09	2.57	2.67	2.68	3.69	4.55	2.24	4.96
	Code	42124	721019	40203	704	238210	4261	4-46	4261	402	80170	B1105	206
EXCAVATION—earth NOC	Rate	2.18	3.62	4.52	5.16	4.62	3.59	3.90	3.16	3.69	8.33	2.21	4.96
	Code	40604	721031	4	711	238190	4214	4-43	4214	402	80030	R1106	207
EXCAVATION—rock	Rate	2.18	3.62	4.19	5.16	4.62	3.59	3.90	3.16	3.69	8.33	2.21	4.96
	Code	40604	721031	40706	711	238190	4214	4-43	4214	402	80030	R1106	207
GLAZIERS	Rate	2.34	3.05	3.96	10.00	4.62	5.25	3.92	5.70	3.69	14.52	4.28	4.96
	Code	42121	715020	40109	751	238150	4233	4-41	4233	402	80150	B1304	212
INSULATION WORK	Rate	1.74	6.88	3.96	10.00	4.37	5.25	3.92	5.70	3.69	12.61	3.74	8.55
	Code	42184	721029	40102	751	238310	4234	4-41	4234	402	80110	B1207	202
LATHING	Rate	3.78	7.08	3.96	4.44	4.37	4.24	3.92	4.83	3.69	12.61	4.28	8.55
	Code	42135	721042	40102	723	238390	4279	4-41	4271	402	80110	B1316	202
MASONRY	Rate	3.84	3.02	3.96	12.39	4.62	5.25	3.92	5.70	3.69	12.86	4.28	8.55
	Code	42102	721037	40102	741	238140	4231	4-41	4231	402	80100	B1318	202
PAINTING & DECORATING	Rate	2.90	3.12	3.44	7.33	4.37	4.24	3.92	4.83	3.69	12.61	3.74	8.55
	Code	42111	721041	40105	719	238320	4275	4-41	4275	402	80110	B1201	202
PILE DRIVING	Rate	3.77	3.92	4.19	6.86	4.62	3.59	3.90	5.03	6.62	8.33	4.28	8.55
	Code	42159	722004	40706	732	238190	4129	4-43	4221	403	80030	B1310	202
PLASTERING	Rate	3.78	7.08	4.48	7.33	4.37	4.24	3.92	4.83	3.69	12.61	3.74	8.55
	Code	42135	721042	40108	719	238390	4271	4-41	4271	402	80110	B1221	202
PLUMBING	Rate	1.72	2.26	2.93	4.06	2.09	2.68	2.67	3.14	2.21	6.44	2.24	4.96
	Code	42122	721043	40204	707	238220	4241	4-46	4241	401	80160	B1101	214
ROOFING	Rate	5.85	6.52	6.74	14.44	4.62	9.44	3.92	7.76	3.69	19.78	4.28	8.55
	Code	42118	721036	40403	728	238160	4236	4-41	4236	402	80130	B1320	202
SHEET METAL WORK (HVAC)	Rate	1.72	2.26	6.74	4.06	2.09	2.68	2.67	3.14	2.21	6.44	2.24	4.96
	Code	42117	721043	40402	707	238220	4244	4-46	4244	401	80160	B1107	208
STEEL ERECTION—door & sash	Rate	1.74	12.03	8.24	17.86	4.62	9.44	3.92	5.70	3.69	20.90	4.28	8.55
	Code	42106	722005	40502	748	238120	4227	4-41	4227	402	80080	B1322	202
STEEL ERECTION—inter., ornam.	Rate	1.74	12.03	8.24	17.86	4.62	9.44	3.92	5.70	3.69	20.90	4.28	8.55
	Code	42106	722005	40502	748	238120	4227	4-41	4227	402	80080	B1322	202
STEEL ERECTION—structure	Rate	1.74	12.03	8.24	17.86	4.62	9.44	3.92	5.70	3.69	20.90	4.28	8.55
	Code	42106	722005	40502	748	238120	4227	4-41	4227	402	80080	B1322	202
STEEL ERECTION—NOC	Rate	1.74	12.03	8.24	17.86	4.62	9.44	3.92	5.70	3.69	20.90	4.28	8.55
	Code	42106	722005	40502	748	238120	4227	4-41	4227	402	80080	B1322	202
TILE WORK—inter. (ceramic)	Rate	2.80	3.34	1.90	7.33	4.37	4.24	3.92	4.83	3.69	12.61	4.28	8.55
	Code	42113	721054	40103	719	238340	4276	4-41	4276	402	80110	B1301	202
WATERPROOFING	Rate	2.90	3.10	3.96	4.44	4.62	4.24	3.92	5.70	3.69	17.81	3.74	8.55
	Code	42139	721016	40102	723	238190	4299	4-41	4239	402	80130	B1217	202
WRECKING	Rate	2.18	4.81	7.34	17.86	4.62	3.59	3.90	3.16	5.61	12.61	2.21	8.55
	Code	40604	721005	40106	748	238190	4211	4-43	4211	402	80110	R1125	202

Unemployment Taxes and Social Security Taxes

State Unemployment Tax rates vary not only from state to state, but also with the experience rating of the contractor. The Federal Unemployment Tax rate is 6.2% of the first $7,000 of wages. This is reduced by a credit of up to 5.4% for timely payment to the state. The minimum Federal Unemployment Tax is 0.8% after all credits.

Social Security (FICA) for 2012 is estimated at time of publication to be 7.65% of wages up to $110,100.

Overtime

One way to improve the completion date of a project or eliminate negative float from a schedule is to compress activity duration times. This can be achieved by increasing the crew size or working overtime with the proposed crew.

To determine the costs of working overtime to compress activity duration times, consider the following examples. Below is an overtime efficiency and cost chart based on a five, six, or seven day week with an eight through twelve hour day. Payroll percentage increases for time and one half and double time are shown for the various working days.

Days per Week	Hours per Day	Production Efficiency					Payroll Cost Factors	
		1 Week	2 Weeks	3 Weeks	4 Weeks	Average 4 Weeks	@ 1-1/2 Times	@ 2 Times
	8	100%	100%	100%	100%	100 %	100 %	100 %
	9	100	100	95	90	96.25	105.6	111.1
5	10	100	95	90	85	91.25	110.0	120.0
	11	95	90	75	65	81.25	113.6	127.3
	12	90	85	70	60	76.25	116.7	133.3
	8	100	100	95	90	96.25	108.3	116.7
	9	100	95	90	85	92.50	113.0	125.9
6	10	95	90	85	80	87.50	116.7	133.3
	11	95	85	70	65	78.75	119.7	139.4
	12	90	80	65	60	73.75	122.2	144.4
	8	100	95	85	75	88.75	114.3	128.6
	9	95	90	80	70	83.75	118.3	136.5
7	10	90	85	75	65	78.75	121.4	142.9
	11	85	80	65	60	72.50	124.0	148.1
	12	85	75	60	55	68.75	126.2	152.4

Sales Tax by State

State sales tax on materials is tabulated below (5 states have no sales tax). Many states allow local jurisdictions, such as a county or city, to levy additional sales tax.

Some projects may be sales tax exempt, particularly those constructed with public funds.

State	Tax (%)	State	Tax (%)	State	Tax (%)	State	Tax (%)
Alabama	4	Illinois	6.25	Montana	0	Rhode Island	7
Alaska	0	Indiana	7	Nebraska	5.5	South Carolina	6
Arizona	6.6	Iowa	6	Nevada	6.85	South Dakota	4
Arkansas	6	Kansas	5.3	New Hampshire	0	Tennessee	7
California	9.25	Kentucky	6	New Jersey	7	Texas	6.25
Colorado	2.9	Louisiana	4	New Mexico	5.13	Utah	4.75
Connecticut	6	Maine	5	New York	4	Vermont	6
Delaware	0	Maryland	6	North Carolina	5.75	Virginia	4
District of Columbia	6	Massachusetts	6.25	North Dakota	5	Washington	6.5
Florida	6	Michigan	6	Ohio	5.5	West Virginia	6
Georgia	4	Minnesota	6.875	Oklahoma	4.5	Wisconsin	5
Hawaii	4	Mississippi	7	Oregon	0	Wyoming	4
Idaho	6	Missouri	4.225	Pennsylvania	6	Average	5.07 %

Table H1040-101   Steel Tubular Scaffolding

On new construction, tubular scaffolding is efficient up to 60' high or five stories. Above this it is usually better to use a hung scaffolding if construction permits. Swing scaffolding operations may interfere with tenants. In this case, the tubular is more practical at all heights.

In repairing or cleaning the front of an existing building, the cost of tubular scaffolding per S.F. of building front increases as the height increases above the first tier. The first tier cost is relatively high due to leveling and alignment.

The minimum efficient crew for erection is three workers. For heights over 50', a crew of four is more efficient. Use two or more on top and two at the bottom for handing up or hoisting. Four workers can erect and dismantle about nine frames per hour up to five stories. From five to eight stories, they will average six frames per hour. With 7' horizontal spacing, this will run about 400 S.F. and 265 S.F. of wall surface, respectively. Time for placing

planks must be added to the above. On heights above 50', five planks can be placed per labor-hour.

The cost per 1,000 S.F. of building front in the table below was developed by pricing the materials required for a typical tubular scaffolding system eleven frames long and two frames high. Planks were figured five wide for standing plus two wide for materials.

Frames are 5' wide and usually spaced 7' O.C. horizontally. Sidewalk frames are 6' wide. Rental rates will be lower for jobs over three months' duration.

For jobs under twenty-five frames, add 50% to rental cost. These figures do not include accessories which are listed separately below. Large quantities for long periods can reduce rental rates by 20%.

Item	Unit	Monthly Rent	Per 1,000 S. F. of Building Front	
			No. of Pieces	Rental per Month
5' Wide Standard Frame, 6'-4" High	Ea.	$ 5.15	24	$123.60
Leveling Jack & Plate		2.00	24	48.00
Cross Brace		1.00	44	44.00
Side Arm Bracket, 21"		2.00	12	24.00
Guardrail Post		1.00	12	12.00
Guardrail, 7' section		1.00	22	22.00
Stairway Section		40.00	2	80.00
Walk-Thru Frame Guardrail	▼	2.50	2	5.00
			Total	$358.60
			Per C.S.F., 1 Use/Mo.	$ 35.86

Scaffolding is often used as falsework over 15' high during construction of cast-in-place concrete beams and slabs. Two-foot wide scaffolding is generally used for heavy beam construction. The span between frames depends upon the load to be carried, with a maximum span of 5'.

Heavy duty shoring frames with a capacity of 10,000#/leg can be spaced up to 10' O. C., depending upon form support design and loading.

Scaffolding used as horizontal shoring requires less than half the material required with conventional shoring.

On new construction, erection is done by carpenters.

Rolling towers supporting horizontal shores can reduce labor and speed the job. For maintenance work, catwalks with spans up to 70' can be supported by the rolling towers.

General: The following information on current city cost indexes is calculated for over 930 zip code locations in the United States and Canada. Index figures for both material and installation are based upon the 30 major city average of 100 and represent the cost relationship on July 1, 2011.

In addition to index adjustment, the user should consider:
1. productivity
2. management efficiency
3. competitive conditions
4. automation
5. restrictive union practices
6. unique local requirements
7. regional variations due to specific building codes

The weighted-average index is calculated from about 66 materials and equipment types and 21 building trades. The component contribution of these in a model building is tabulated in Table J1010-011 below.

If the systems component distribution of a building is unknown, the weighted-average index can be used to adjust the cost for any city.

Table J1010-011 Labor, Material, and Equipment Cost Distribution for Weighted Average Listed by System Division

Division No.	Building System	Percentage	Division No.	Building System	Percentage
A	Substructure	6.3%	D10	Services: Conveying	4.3%
B10	Shell: Superstructure	18.3	D20-40	Mechanical	23.0
B20	Exterior Closure	11.6	D50	Electrical	11.7
B30	Roofing	2.9	E	Equipment & Furnishings	2.3
C	Interior Construction	15.3	G	Site Work	4.3
				Total weighted average (Div. A-G)	100.0%

How to Use the Component Indexes: Table J1010-012 below shows how the average costs obtained from this book for each division should be adjusted for your particular building in your city. The example is a building adjusted for New York, NY. Indexes for other cities are tabulated in Division RJ1030. These indexes should also be used when compiling data on the form in Division K1010.

Table J1010-012 Adjustment of "Book" Costs to a Particular City

| Systems Division Number | System Description | New York, NY | | | | | | | |
		City Cost Index	Cost Factor	Book Cost	Adjusted Cost	City Cost Index	Cost Factor	Book Cost	Adjusted Cost
A	Substructure	142.4	1.424	$ 96,400	$ 137,300				
B10	Shell: Superstructure	134.0	1.340	266,300	356,800				
B20	Exterior Closure	139.2	1.392	180,500	251,300				
B30	Roofing	127.3	1.273	39,800	50,700				
C	Interior Construction	134.9	1.349	256,900	346,600				
D10	Services: Conveying	108.4	1.084	51,400	55,700				
D20-40	Mechanical	127.7	1.277	318,900	407,200				
D50	Electrical	140.3	1.403	178,400	250,300				
E	Equipment	104.5	1.045	27,000	28,200				
G	Site Work	124.4	1.244	75,800	94,300				
Total Cost, (Div. A-G)				$1,491,400	$1,978,400				

Alternate Method: Use the weighted-average index for your city rather than the component indexes. **For example:**

(Total weighted-average index A-G)/100 x (total cost)   =   Adjusted city cost
New York, NY 1.32 x $1,491,400   = $1,971,600

City to City: To convert known or estimated costs from one city to another, cost indexes can be used as follows:

$$\text{Unknown City Cost} = \text{Known Cost} \times \frac{\text{Unknown City Index}}{\text{Known City Index}}$$

For example: If the building cost in Boston, MA, is $2,000,000, how much would a duplicated building cost in Los Angeles, CA?

$$\text{L.A. Cost} = \$2,000,000 \times \frac{\text{(Los Angeles) } 106.9}{\text{(Boston) } 117.5} = \$1,819,500$$

The table below lists both the Means City Cost Index based on January 1, 1993 = 100 as well as the computed value of an index based on January 1, 2012 costs. Since the January 1, 2012 figure is estimated, space is left to write in the actual index figures as they become available through either the quarterly *Means Construction Cost Indexes* or as printed in the *Engineering News-Record*. To compute the actual index based on January 1, 2012 = 100, divide the Quarterly City Cost Index for a particular year by the actual January 1, 2012 Quarterly City Cost Index. Space has been left to advance the index figures as the year progresses.

Table J1020-011 Historical Cost Indexes

Year	Historical Cost Index Jan. 1, 1993 = 100		Current Index Based on Jan. 1, 2012 = 100		Year	Historical Cost Index Jan. 1, 1993 = 100	Current Index Based on Jan. 1, 2012 = 100		Year	Historical Cost Index Jan. 1, 1993 = 100	Current Index Based on Jan. 1, 2012 = 100	
	Est.	Actual	Est.	Actual		Actual	Est.	Actual		Actual	Est.	Actual
Oct 2012*					July 1997	112.8	58.5		July 1979	57.8	30.0	
July 2012*					1996	110.2	57.2		1978	53.5	27.7	
April 2012*					1995	107.6	55.8		1977	49.5	25.7	
Jan 2012*	192.8		100.0	100.0	1994	104.4	54.1		1976	46.9	24.3	
July 2011		185.7	96.3		1993	101.7	52.7		1975	44.8	23.2	
2010		183.5	95.2		1992	99.4	51.6		1974	41.4	21.5	
2009		180.1	93.4		1991	96.8	50.2		1973	37.7	19.6	
2008		180.4	93.6		1990	94.3	48.9		1972	34.8	18.0	
2007		169.4	87.9		1989	92.1	47.8		1971	32.1	16.6	
2006		162.0	84.0		1988	89.9	46.6		1970	28.7	14.9	
2005		151.6	78.6		1987	87.7	45.5		1969	26.9	14.0	
2004		143.7	74.5		1986	84.2	43.7		1968	24.9	12.9	
2003		132.0	68.5		1985	82.6	42.8		1967	23.5	12.2	
2002		128.7	66.8		1984	82.0	42.5		1966	22.7	11.8	
2001		125.1	64.9		1983	80.2	41.6		1965	21.7	11.3	
2000		120.9	62.7		1982	76.1	39.5		1964	21.2	11.0	
1999		117.6	61.0		1981	70.0	36.3		1963	20.7	10.7	
1998		115.1	59.7		1980	62.9	32.6		1962	20.2	10.5	

To find the **current cost** from a project built previously in either the same city or a different city, the following formula is used:

$$\text{Present Cost (City X)} = \frac{\text{Current HCI} \times \text{CCI (City X)}}{\text{Previous HCI} \times \text{CCI (City Y)}} \times \text{Former Cost (City Y)}$$

For example: Find the construction cost of a building to be built in San Francisco, CA, as of January 1, 2012 when the identical building cost $500,000 in Boston, MA, on July 1, 1968.

$$\text{Jan. 1, 2012 (San Francisco)} = \frac{\text{(San Francisco) } 192.8 \times 123.4}{\text{(Boston) } 24.9 \times 117.5} \times \$500,000 = \$4,066,000$$

Note: The City Cost Indexes for Canada can be used to convert U.S. national averages to local costs in Canadian dollars.

To Project Future Construction Costs: Using the results of the last five years average percentage increase as a basis, an average increase of 4.4% could be used.

The historical index figures above are compiled from the Means Construction Index Service.

How to Use the City Cost Indexes

What you should know before you begin

RSMeans City Cost Indexes (CCI) are an extremely useful tool to use when you want to compare costs from city to city and region to region.

This publication contains average construction cost indexes for 317 U.S. and Canadian cities covering over 660 three-digit zip code locations, as listed directly under each city.

Keep in mind that a City Cost Index number is a percentage ratio of a specific city's cost to the national average cost of the same item at a stated time period.

In other words, these index figures represent relative construction factors (or, if you prefer, multipliers) for Material and Installation costs, as well as the weighted average for Total In Place costs for each CSI MasterFormat division. Installation costs include both labor and equipment rental costs. When estimating equipment rental rates only, for a specific location, use 015433 CONTRACTOR EQUIPMENT index.

The 30 City Average Index is the average of 30 major U.S. cities and serves as a National Average.

Index figures for both material and installation are based on the 30 major city average of 100 and represent the cost relationship as of July 1, 2010. The index for each division is computed from representative material and labor quantities for that division. The weighted average for each city is a weighted total of the components listed above it, but does not include relative productivity between trades or cities.

As changes occur in local material prices, labor rates, and equipment rental rates, (including fuel costs) the impact of these changes should be accurately measured by the change in the City Cost Index for each particular city (as compared to the 30 City Average).

Therefore, if you know (or have estimated) building costs in one city today, you can easily convert those costs to expected building costs in another city.

In addition, by using the Historical Cost Index, you can easily convert National Average building costs at a particular time to the approximate building costs for some other time. The City Cost Indexes can then be applied to calculate the costs for a particular city.

Quick Calculations

Location Adjustment Using the City Cost Indexes:

$$\frac{\text{Index for City A}}{\text{Index for City B}} \times \text{Cost in City B} = \text{Cost in City A}$$

Time Adjustment for the National Average Using the Historical Cost Index:

$$\frac{\text{Index for Year A}}{\text{Index for Year B}} \times \text{Cost in Year B} = \text{Cost in Year A}$$

Adjustment from the National Average:

$$\frac{\text{Index for City A}}{100} \times \text{National Average Cost} = \text{Cost in City A}$$

Since each of the other RSMeans publications contains many different items, any *one* item multiplied by the particular city index may give incorrect results. However, the larger the number of items compiled, the closer the results should be to actual costs for that particular city.

The City Cost Indexes for Canadian cities are calculated using Canadian material and equipment prices and labor rates, in Canadian dollars. Therefore, indexes for Canadian cities can be used to convert U.S. National Average prices to local costs in Canadian dollars.

How to use this section

1. Compare costs from city to city.

In using the RSMeans Indexes, remember that an index number is not a fixed number but a ratio: It's a percentage ratio of a building component's cost at any stated time to the National Average cost of that same component at the same time period. Put in the form of an equation:

$$\frac{\text{Specific City Cost}}{\text{National Average Cost}} \times 100 = \text{City Index Number}$$

Therefore, when making cost comparisons between cities, do not subtract one city's index number from the index number of another city and read the result as a percentage difference. Instead, divide one city's index number by that of the other city. The resulting number may then be used as a multiplier to calculate cost differences from city to city.

The formula used to find cost differences between cities for the purpose of comparison is as follows:

$$\frac{\text{City A Index}}{\text{City B Index}} \times \text{City B Cost (Known)} = \text{City A Cost (Unknown)}$$

In addition, you can use RSMeans CCI to calculate and compare costs division by division between cities using the same basic formula. (Just be sure that you're comparing similar divisions.)

2. Compare a specific city's construction costs with the National Average.

When you're studying construction location feasibility, it's advisable to compare a prospective project's cost index with an index of the National Average cost.

For example, divide the weighted average index of construction costs of a specific city by that of the 30 City Average, which = 100.

$$\frac{\text{City Index}}{100} = \% \text{ of National Average}$$

As a result, you get a ratio that indicates the relative cost of construction in that city in comparison with the National Average.

3. Convert U.S. National Average to actual costs in Canadian City.

$$\frac{\text{Index for Canadian City}}{100} \times \text{National Average Cost} = \text{Cost in Canadian City in \$ CAN}$$

4. Adjust construction cost data based on a National Average.

When you use a source of construction cost data which is based on a National Average (such as RSMeans cost data publications), it is necessary to adjust those costs to a specific location.

$$\frac{\text{City Index}}{100} \quad \text{x} \quad \frac{\text{"Book" Cost Based on}}{\text{National Average Costs}} \quad = \quad \frac{\text{City Cost}}{\text{(Unknown)}}$$

5. When applying the City Cost Indexes to demolition projects, use the appropriate division installation index. For example, for removal of existing doors and windows, use Division 8 (Openings) index.

What you might like to know about how we developed the Indexes

The information presented in the CCI is organized according to the Construction Specifications Institute (CSI) MasterFormat 2010.

To create a reliable index, RSMeans researched the building type most often constructed in the United States and Canada. Because it was concluded that no one type of building completely represented the building construction industry, nine different types of buildings were combined to create a composite model.

The exact material, labor, and equipment quantities are based on detailed analysis of these nine building types, then each quantity is weighted in proportion to expected usage. These various material items, labor hours, and equipment rental rates are thus combined to form a composite building representing as closely as possible the actual usage of materials, labor and equipment used in the North American Building Construction Industry.

The following structures were chosen to make up that composite model:

1. Factory, 1 story
2. Office, 2–4 story
3. Store, Retail
4. Town Hall, 2–3 story
5. High School, 2–3 story
6. Hospital, 4–8 story
7. Garage, Parking
8. Apartment, 1–3 story
9. Hotel/Motel, 2–3 story

For the purposes of ensuring the timeliness of the data, the components of the index for the composite model have been streamlined. They currently consist of:

- specific quantities of 66 commonly used construction materials;
- specific labor-hours for 21 building construction trades; and
- specific days of equipment rental for 6 types of construction equipment (normally used to install the 66 material items by the 21 trades.) Fuel costs and routine maintenance costs are included in the equipment cost.

A sophisticated computer program handles the updating of all costs for each city on a quarterly basis. Material and equipment price quotations are gathered quarterly from 731 cities in the United States and Canada. These prices and the latest negotiated labor wage rates for 21 different building trades are used to compile the quarterly update of the City Cost Index.

The 30 major U.S. cities used to calculate the National Average are:

Atlanta, GA	Memphis, TN
Baltimore, MD	Milwaukee, WI
Boston, MA	Minneapolis, MN
Buffalo, NY	Nashville, TN
Chicago, IL	New Orleans, LA
Cincinnati, OH	New York, NY
Cleveland, OH	Philadelphia, PA
Columbus, OH	Phoenix, AZ
Dallas, TX	Pittsburgh, PA
Denver, CO	St. Louis, MO
Detroit, MI	San Antonio, TX
Houston, TX	San Diego, CA
Indianapolis, IN	San Francisco, CA
Kansas City, MO	Seattle, WA
Los Angeles, CA	Washington, DC

What the CCI does not indicate

The weighted average for each city is a total of the divisional components weighted to reflect typical usage, but it does not include the productivity variations between trades or cities.

In addition, the CCI does not take into consideration factors such as the following:

- managerial efficiency
- competitive conditions
- automation
- restrictive union practices
- unique local requirements
- regional variations due to specific building codes

Cost Indexes

ALABAMA

DIV. NO.	BUILDING SYSTEMS	BIRMINGHAM MAT.	INST.	TOTAL	HUNTSVILLE MAT.	INST.	TOTAL	MOBILE MAT.	INST.	TOTAL	MONTGOMERY MAT.	INST.	TOTAL	TUSCALOOSA MAT.	INST.	TOTAL
A	Substructure	95.4	77.6	84.8	89.3	73.0	79.5	95.4	71.4	81.0	96.1	61.9	75.7	91.6	64.9	75.6
B10	Shell: Superstructure	95.0	83.6	90.3	94.8	79.0	88.3	94.8	79.2	88.4	94.8	72.9	85.8	94.7	74.2	86.3
B20	Exterior Closure	94.1	79.6	87.2	94.0	61.7	78.6	94.4	58.4	77.3	93.5	46.2	71.0	93.5	53.5	74.4
B30	Roofing	95.0	82.3	90.3	92.7	76.4	86.6	92.7	75.4	86.2	92.2	68.0	83.1	92.8	71.4	84.8
C	Interior Construction	97.5	69.4	85.2	97.2	63.1	82.2	99.7	57.1	81.0	99.3	44.8	75.3	97.2	48.0	75.5
D10	Services: Conveying	100.0	91.2	97.6	100.0	87.8	96.7	100.0	85.0	96.0	100.0	85.0	95.9	100.0	86.9	96.5
D20 - 40	Mechanical	99.9	65.9	86.1	99.9	55.5	81.9	99.9	64.6	85.6	100.0	36.4	74.2	99.9	36.2	74.1
D50	Electrical	103.0	62.5	82.1	99.4	65.6	82.0	99.4	60.7	79.5	98.5	64.7	81.0	98.9	62.5	80.1
E	Equipment & Furnishings	100.0	70.5	98.5	100.0	64.7	98.2	100.0	55.9	97.7	100.0	45.4	97.2	100.0	47.6	97.3
G	Site Work	86.3	93.9	91.4	81.5	92.9	89.1	94.6	88.2	90.3	93.4	88.1	89.9	82.0	93.0	89.3
A-G	WEIGHTED AVERAGE	97.6	74.6	87.4	96.6	68.1	84.1	97.7	67.5	84.4	97.4	56.6	79.4	96.6	58.6	79.9

ALASKA / ARIZONA

DIV. NO.	BUILDING SYSTEMS	ANCHORAGE MAT.	INST.	TOTAL	FAIRBANKS MAT.	INST.	TOTAL	JUNEAU MAT.	INST.	TOTAL	FLAGSTAFF MAT.	INST.	TOTAL	MESA/TEMPE MAT.	INST.	TOTAL
A	Substructure	142.1	118.5	128.0	135.5	118.7	125.4	134.7	118.5	125.0	91.8	79.7	84.6	91.1	78.8	83.7
B10	Shell: Superstructure	125.3	107.9	118.2	121.9	108.1	116.2	121.3	107.9	115.8	94.3	75.0	86.4	91.2	74.4	84.3
B20	Exterior Closure	148.4	119.6	134.7	141.2	119.6	130.9	137.4	119.6	128.9	116.7	64.9	92.1	107.1	63.3	86.2
B30	Roofing	191.8	115.9	163.3	180.3	117.4	156.7	181.8	115.9	157.0	98.2	67.0	86.5	101.9	63.0	87.3
C	Interior Construction	134.6	118.2	127.4	129.2	119.0	124.7	127.2	118.2	123.2	102.8	63.4	85.5	97.1	64.5	82.3
D10	Services: Conveying	100.0	107.7	102.1	100.0	107.7	102.1	100.0	107.7	102.1	100.0	84.9	95.9	100.0	84.6	95.8
D20 - 40	Mechanical	100.3	104.5	102.0	100.3	108.2	103.5	100.3	104.0	101.8	100.2	83.0	93.2	100.2	76.9	90.8
D50	Electrical	133.3	116.7	124.7	143.5	116.7	129.6	129.3	116.7	122.8	100.4	62.3	80.7	93.6	62.3	77.4
E	Equipment & Furnishings	100.0	116.4	100.8	100.0	116.4	100.8	100.0	116.4	100.8	100.0	67.7	98.3	100.0	67.5	98.3
G	Site Work	127.6	130.2	129.4	119.9	130.3	126.8	127.3	130.2	129.3	81.5	98.5	92.8	87.1	100.5	96.0
A-G	WEIGHTED AVERAGE	124.5	114.0	119.9	122.4	115.0	119.1	120.3	113.9	117.5	100.3	73.9	88.7	97.4	72.4	86.3

ARIZONA / ARKANSAS

DIV. NO.	BUILDING SYSTEMS	PHOENIX MAT.	INST.	TOTAL	PRESCOTT MAT.	INST.	TOTAL	TUCSON MAT.	INST.	TOTAL	FORT SMITH MAT.	INST.	TOTAL	JONESBORO MAT.	INST.	TOTAL
A	Substructure	91.0	81.1	85.1	89.8	64.4	74.6	88.6	80.8	84.0	89.9	68.8	77.2	88.0	66.7	75.2
B10	Shell: Superstructure	92.3	76.5	85.8	94.1	61.4	80.7	91.3	75.7	84.9	98.1	67.2	85.4	92.3	68.8	82.7
B20	Exterior Closure	100.7	67.6	85.0	103.2	47.6	76.8	99.3	65.0	83.0	98.2	52.9	76.6	96.7	48.1	73.6
B30	Roofing	101.5	66.9	88.5	96.9	50.8	79.6	103.0	62.9	87.9	97.4	55.8	81.8	101.0	53.3	83.1
C	Interior Construction	98.9	67.7	85.2	101.4	44.6	76.4	94.2	65.2	81.5	94.2	59.7	79.0	92.0	51.8	74.4
D10	Services: Conveying	100.0	85.2	96.0	100.0	82.2	95.2	100.0	85.2	96.0	100.0	79.3	94.4	100.0	48.4	86.0
D20 - 40	Mechanical	100.2	83.1	93.2	100.2	71.2	88.4	100.2	73.5	89.4	100.3	51.6	80.5	100.5	54.5	81.9
D50	Electrical	100.7	70.9	85.3	100.1	62.2	80.5	95.6	59.9	77.2	95.7	68.6	81.7	103.4	63.4	82.8
E	Equipment & Furnishings	100.0	70.7	98.5	100.0	43.9	97.1	100.0	70.1	98.5	100.0	60.5	98.0	100.0	51.2	97.5
G	Site Work	87.6	101.0	96.5	70.2	96.6	87.7	82.9	100.7	94.7	77.8	85.7	83.0	96.6	99.1	98.3
A-G	WEIGHTED AVERAGE	97.9	76.6	88.5	98.2	62.1	82.2	96.1	72.1	85.5	97.1	62.5	81.8	96.8	60.7	80.9

ARKANSAS / CALIFORNIA

DIV. NO.	BUILDING SYSTEMS	LITTLE ROCK MAT.	INST.	TOTAL	PINE BLUFF MAT.	INST.	TOTAL	TEXARKANA MAT.	INST.	TOTAL	ANAHEIM MAT.	INST.	TOTAL	BAKERSFIELD MAT.	INST.	TOTAL
A	Substructure	90.8	69.7	78.2	84.1	64.4	75.4	91.3	56.8	70.6	94.2	117.7	108.3	98.1	116.6	109.2
B10	Shell: Superstructure	94.8	67.2	83.5	94.8	67.1	83.4	91.0	57.9	77.4	99.6	110.3	104.0	96.5	109.7	101.9
B20	Exterior Closure	96.7	53.3	76.1	110.3	53.3	83.2	95.4	38.3	68.2	95.4	116.7	105.5	101.2	114.7	107.6
B30	Roofing	96.5	56.5	81.5	96.3	56.5	81.4	97.0	47.6	78.5	101.7	124.0	110.0	100.5	113.3	105.3
C	Interior Construction	95.1	63.1	81.0	89.8	63.1	78.1	93.9	43.8	71.9	103.4	118.1	109.8	103.0	115.1	108.4
D10	Services: Conveying	100.0	79.3	94.4	100.0	79.3	94.4	100.0	34.0	82.2	100.0	109.1	102.5	100.0	105.9	101.6
D20 - 40	Mechanical	100.2	59.3	83.6	100.3	54.0	81.5	100.3	57.3	82.9	100.1	112.0	104.9	100.1	105.5	102.3
D50	Electrical	100.5	69.7	84.6	95.0	69.7	82.0	97.0	38.2	66.7	92.2	105.4	99.0	101.6	101.2	101.4
E	Equipment & Furnishings	100.0	66.0	98.3	100.0	66.0	98.3	100.0	43.6	97.1	100.0	120.6	101.1	100.0	120.1	101.0
G	Site Work	83.9	85.7	85.1	79.5	85.7	83.6	90.9	86.2	87.8	98.1	108.6	105.1	99.9	106.2	104.1
A-G	WEIGHTED AVERAGE	97.0	65.0	82.9	96.7	63.8	82.2	95.9	51.3	76.2	98.9	112.8	105.1	100.0	109.5	104.2

CALIFORNIA

DIV. NO.	BUILDING SYSTEMS	FRESNO MAT.	INST.	TOTAL	LOS ANGELES MAT.	INST.	TOTAL	OAKLAND MAT.	INST.	TOTAL	OXNARD MAT.	INST.	TOTAL	REDDING MAT.	INST.	TOTAL
A	Substructure	97.1	120.0	110.8	99.0	117.2	109.9	115.9	126.8	122.4	101.2	116.5	110.3	109.4	119.8	115.7
B10	Shell: Superstructure	100.0	112.9	105.3	98.5	111.1	103.7	103.3	117.2	109.0	97.2	110.0	102.4	102.4	112.9	106.7
B20	Exterior Closure	105.4	120.6	112.6	98.9	119.9	108.9	121.0	131.8	126.1	103.2	115.1	108.8	107.0	118.1	112.3
B30	Roofing	95.2	114.2	102.3	98.8	122.7	107.8	112.2	135.8	121.1	104.8	119.5	110.3	105.3	117.8	110.0
C	Interior Construction	106.3	133.0	118.1	102.3	118.1	109.3	105.9	144.7	123.0	103.4	117.5	109.6	105.6	129.4	116.0
D10	Services: Conveying	100.0	118.1	104.9	100.0	108.7	102.4	100.0	120.1	105.4	100.0	109.4	102.5	100.0	118.1	104.9
D20 - 40	Mechanical	100.2	113.2	105.5	100.2	111.9	104.9	100.2	147.5	119.4	100.1	112.0	104.9	100.1	108.9	103.6
D50	Electrical	91.7	100.4	96.2	101.7	122.2	112.3	105.8	143.6	125.3	96.2	107.5	102.0	99.3	103.8	101.6
E	Equipment & Furnishings	100.0	135.6	101.8	100.0	121.2	101.1	100.0	153.2	102.7	100.0	120.4	101.0	100.0	135.7	101.8
G	Site Work	102.6	105.7	104.6	99.3	107.7	104.9	128.5	105.4	113.2	102.8	104.2	103.8	106.2	105.1	105.5
A-G	WEIGHTED AVERAGE	100.5	115.7	107.2	100.1	115.5	106.9	106.3	133.9	118.5	100.2	112.3	105.5	102.8	114.4	107.9

CALIFORNIA

DIV. NO.	BUILDING SYSTEMS	RIVERSIDE MAT.	INST.	TOTAL	SACRAMENTO MAT.	INST.	TOTAL	SAN DIEGO MAT.	INST.	TOTAL	SAN FRANCISCO MAT.	INST.	TOTAL	SAN JOSE MAT.	INST.	TOTAL
A	Substructure	98.2	117.3	109.6	99.0	122.5	113.0	97.5	108.6	104.2	121.1	128.8	125.7	115.3	125.4	121.3
B10	Shell: Superstructure	100.8	110.3	104.7	96.8	110.8	102.5	98.5	100.5	101.5	109.4	122.9	114.9	99.2	120.7	108.0
B20	Exterior Closure	92.2	115.8	103.4	109.7	121.2	115.2	98.0	113.4	105.3	122.1	135.2	128.3	116.2	132.4	123.9
B30	Roofing	101.9	123.6	110.0	118.9	122.2	120.1	106.6	105.3	106.1	114.3	136.8	122.8	101.2	137.1	114.7
C	Interior Construction	103.3	118.1	109.8	111.1	132.6	120.6	100.4	109.7	104.5	109.3	145.7	125.3	98.3	144.5	118.6
D10	Services: Conveying	100.0	109.1	102.5	100.0	118.8	105.1	100.0	108.5	102.3	100.0	120.6	105.6	100.0	119.3	105.2
D20 - 40	Mechanical	100.1	112.0	104.9	100.1	116.8	106.9	100.1	110.4	104.3	100.2	169.6	128.3	100.1	146.7	118.9
D50	Electrical	92.4	104.4	98.6	101.1	113.3	107.4	96.0	101.0	98.6	105.9	155.0	131.2	102.1	152.2	128.0
E	Equipment & Furnishings	100.0	120.5	101.1	100.0	139.2	102.0	100.0	107.6	100.4	100.0	153.8	102.8	100.0	153.7	102.7
G	Site Work	96.7	106.6	103.3	103.6	111.0	108.5	101.0	103.0	102.4	130.1	111.0	117.4	133.8	100.0	111.4
A-G	WEIGHTED AVERAGE	98.9	112.4	104.9	102.9	118.6	109.9	99.3	107.8	103.0	108.5	142.3	123.4	103.2	135.1	117.3

CALIFORNIA / COLORADO

DIV. NO.	BUILDING SYSTEMS	SANTA BARBARA MAT.	INST.	TOTAL	STOCKTON MAT.	INST.	TOTAL	VALLEJO MAT.	INST.	TOTAL	COLORADO SPRINGS MAT.	INST.	TOTAL	DENVER MAT.	INST.	TOTAL
A	Substructure	101.1	116.8	110.5	101.0	120.0	112.4	105.3	126.7	118.1	102.3	86.0	92.5	99.0	88.0	92.4
B10	Shell: Superstructure	97.5	109.9	102.6	98.4	113.3	104.5	100.9	114.9	106.6	102.3	86.0	95.7	103.9	86.1	96.6
B20	Exterior Closure	101.9	115.6	108.4	103.1	121.6	111.9	95.3	132.4	113.0	101.1	77.9	90.1	99.0	77.9	89.0
B30	Roofing	101.5	118.4	107.8	105.0	119.5	110.8	114.4	132.8	121.3	105.9	83.4	97.4	104.2	76.4	93.8
C	Interior Construction	104.3	115.6	109.3	103.9	130.5	115.6	112.0	144.0	126.1	103.7	76.6	91.8	105.2	82.5	95.2
D10	Services: Conveying	100.0	109.4	102.5	100.0	118.1	104.9	100.0	118.6	105.0	100.0	92.0	97.8	100.0	91.6	97.7
D20 - 40	Mechanical	100.1	112.0	104.9	100.1	113.2	105.4	100.2	130.4	112.4	100.2	74.8	89.9	99.9	80.5	92.1
D50	Electrical	89.3	108.2	99.0	98.9	112.2	105.8	98.1	129.6	114.4	102.4	84.7	93.3	104.1	87.0	95.3
E	Equipment & Furnishings	100.0	120.4	101.0	100.0	136.2	101.9	100.0	152.4	102.7	100.0	81.9	99.1	100.0	82.1	99.1
G	Site Work	102.8	106.2	105.1	100.6	105.2	103.6	104.2	110.9	108.7	93.5	95.5	94.8	92.5	103.7	100.0
A-G	WEIGHTED AVERAGE	99.5	112.3	105.1	100.7	117.2	108.0	102.2	128.2	113.7	101.6	81.7	92.8	101.7	84.7	94.2

COLORADO / CONNECTICUT

DIV. NO.	BUILDING SYSTEMS	FORT COLLINS MAT.	INST.	TOTAL	GRAND JUNCTION MAT.	INST.	TOTAL	GREELEY MAT.	INST.	TOTAL	PUEBLO MAT.	INST.	TOTAL	BRIDGEPORT MAT.	INST.	TOTAL
A	Substructure	110.2	84.0	94.5	110.1	84.3	94.7	96.8	79.4	86.4	101.4	86.0	92.2	108.2	119.0	114.7
B10	Shell: Superstructure	102.9	80.7	93.8	99.9	81.4	92.3	99.9	78.4	91.1	99.0	86.6	94.0	100.6	124.4	110.3
B20	Exterior Closure	109.8	59.8	86.0	122.9	77.0	101.1	101.2	56.9	80.1	101.0	77.9	90.0	108.5	128.9	118.2
B30	Roofing	105.5	71.0	92.5	105.0	69.2	91.5	104.9	66.7	90.5	104.5	82.9	96.4	101.3	125.8	110.5
C	Interior Construction	102.3	73.7	89.7	106.9	76.3	93.4	101.6	76.0	90.3	102.3	79.1	92.1	102.3	124.8	112.2
D10	Services: Conveying	100.0	91.6	97.7	100.0	91.9	97.8	100.0	91.6	97.7	100.0	92.7	98.0	100.0	107.1	101.9
D20 - 40	Mechanical	100.0	80.1	91.9	100.0	88.6	95.4	100.0	80.0	91.9	100.0	74.8	89.8	100.0	114.7	106.0
D50	Electrical	98.9	86.8	92.6	94.8	57.2	75.4	98.9	86.8	92.6	95.7	75.1	85.1	102.2	109.9	106.2
E	Equipment & Furnishings	100.0	81.7	99.1	100.0	80.2	99.0	100.0	87.3	99.4	100.0	81.4	99.0	100.0	119.5	101.0
G	Site Work	104.3	96.9	99.4	123.7	98.3	106.8	91.2	96.3	94.6	115.1	94.3	101.3	109.2	103.5	105.4
A-G	WEIGHTED AVERAGE	102.6	79.1	92.2	104.2	79.6	93.4	100.0	78.2	90.4	100.4	80.8	91.8	102.2	118.7	109.5

CONNECTICUT

DIV. NO.	BUILDING SYSTEMS	BRISTOL MAT.	INST.	TOTAL	HARTFORD MAT.	INST.	TOTAL	NEW BRITAIN MAT.	INST.	TOTAL	NEW HAVEN MAT.	INST.	TOTAL	NORWALK MAT.	INST.	TOTAL
A	Substructure	103.9	119.0	112.9	106.2	119.0	113.8	104.9	119.0	113.3	106.0	119.1	113.9	107.0	119.6	114.6
B10	Shell: Superstructure	99.6	124.3	109.7	104.0	124.3	112.3	97.1	124.3	108.3	97.6	124.3	108.5	100.3	125.0	110.4
B20	Exterior Closure	105.0	128.9	116.4	105.4	128.9	116.6	105.7	128.9	116.7	120.2	128.9	124.3	104.9	130.2	117.0
B30	Roofing	101.4	122.4	109.3	102.7	122.4	110.1	101.4	122.4	109.3	101.5	122.2	109.3	101.4	126.1	110.7
C	Interior Construction	102.3	124.8	112.2	101.7	124.8	111.8	102.3	124.8	112.2	102.3	124.8	112.2	102.3	124.8	112.2
D10	Services: Conveying	100.0	107.1	101.9	100.0	107.1	101.9	100.0	107.1	101.9	100.0	107.1	101.9	100.0	107.1	101.9
D20 - 40	Mechanical	100.0	114.7	106.0	100.1	114.7	106.0	100.0	114.7	106.0	100.0	114.7	106.0	100.0	114.8	106.0
D50	Electrical	102.2	109.6	106.0	99.2	110.5	105.1	102.3	109.6	106.1	102.1	109.6	106.0	102.2	162.3	133.2
E	Equipment & Furnishings	100.0	119.5	101.0	100.0	119.6	101.0	100.0	119.5	101.0	100.0	119.5	101.0	100.0	122.1	101.1
G	Site Work	108.3	103.5	105.1	102.0	103.5	103.0	108.5	103.5	105.2	108.4	104.2	105.6	109.0	103.5	105.3
A-G	WEIGHTED AVERAGE	101.5	118.6	109.0	102.0	118.7	109.4	101.1	118.6	108.8	102.8	118.6	109.8	101.8	126.3	112.6

CONNECTICUT / D.C. / DELAWARE / FLORIDA

DIV. NO.	BUILDING SYSTEMS	STAMFORD MAT.	INST.	TOTAL	WATERBURY MAT.	INST.	TOTAL	WASHINGTON MAT.	INST.	TOTAL	WILMINGTON MAT.	INST.	TOTAL	DAYTONA BEACH MAT.	INST.	TOTAL
A	Substructure	108.2	119.6	115.0	108.1	119.0	114.6	118.7	87.7	100.1	93.4	104.7	100.1	97.3	77.7	85.5
B10	Shell: Superstructure	100.6	125.0	110.6	100.6	124.3	110.3	101.6	96.8	99.6	99.7	110.3	104.0	95.6	83.8	90.8
B20	Exterior Closure	105.3	130.2	117.1	105.3	128.9	116.5	102.2	84.5	93.8	103.8	101.2	102.6	95.3	70.5	83.5
B30	Roofing	101.4	126.1	110.7	101.4	122.2	109.2	100.2	85.1	94.5	98.3	114.9	104.5	94.9	78.1	88.6
C	Interior Construction	102.3	124.8	112.2	102.2	124.8	112.1	105.3	84.3	96.0	96.8	103.1	99.6	102.4	73.4	89.7
D10	Services: Conveying	100.0	107.1	101.9	100.0	107.1	101.9	100.0	101.9	100.5	100.0	92.5	98.0	100.0	79.0	94.3
D20 - 40	Mechanical	100.0	114.8	106.0	100.0	114.7	106.0	100.2	94.2	97.7	100.1	113.4	105.5	99.9	77.0	90.6
D50	Electrical	102.2	162.3	133.2	101.6	109.9	105.9	98.8	106.0	102.5	98.6	110.1	104.5	98.0	58.4	77.6
E	Equipment & Furnishings	100.0	122.1	101.1	100.0	119.5	101.0	100.0	80.6	99.0	100.0	112.5	100.1	100.0	72.5	98.6
G	Site Work	109.7	103.5	105.6	108.9	103.5	105.3	110.5	92.3	98.4	89.4	112.2	104.5	113.3	89.3	97.3
A-G	WEIGHTED AVERAGE	101.9	126.3	112.7	101.8	118.6	109.2	102.4	92.8	98.2	99.1	108.0	103.0	98.8	75.2	88.4

FLORIDA

DIV. NO.	BUILDING SYSTEMS	FORT LAUDERDALE MAT.	INST.	TOTAL	JACKSONVILLE MAT.	INST.	TOTAL	MELBOURNE MAT.	INST.	TOTAL	MIAMI MAT.	INST.	TOTAL	ORLANDO MAT.	INST.	TOTAL
A	Substructure	97.1	77.1	85.1	97.8	70.5	81.5	109.9	78.7	91.2	98.8	77.5	86.0	111.4	78.8	91.9
B10	Shell: Superstructure	96.0	85.2	91.6	94.6	76.4	87.2	104.4	84.5	96.2	100.3	84.8	93.9	103.2	84.6	95.6
B20	Exterior Closure	93.8	72.8	83.8	95.3	65.8	81.3	97.0	75.2	86.6	94.1	75.8	85.4	99.2	70.4	85.5
B30	Roofing	95.0	87.6	92.2	95.1	65.2	83.9	95.3	81.0	89.9	103.6	80.2	94.8	96.0	78.8	89.6
C	Interior Construction	100.4	72.1	87.9	102.4	59.0	83.4	101.2	76.0	90.1	101.2	73.0	88.8	103.3	77.0	91.7
D10	Services: Conveying	100.0	86.6	96.4	100.0	77.2	93.8	100.0	80.7	94.8	100.0	87.3	96.6	100.0	79.0	94.3
D20 - 40	Mechanical	99.9	70.6	88.1	99.9	68.6	87.3	99.9	79.2	91.5	99.9	71.3	88.3	99.9	60.6	84.0
D50	Electrical	98.0	74.3	85.8	97.7	66.1	81.4	99.4	68.0	83.2	99.9	76.9	88.0	100.1	62.8	80.8
E	Equipment & Furnishings	100.0	71.3	98.5	100.0	55.4	97.7	100.0	72.9	98.6	100.0	71.5	98.5	100.0	78.4	98.9
G	Site Work	98.7	77.5	84.6	113.3	88.6	96.9	121.7	88.6	99.7	100.7	77.2	85.1	114.2	88.5	97.1
A-G	WEIGHTED AVERAGE	98.1	75.9	88.3	98.7	69.4	85.7	101.5	78.2	91.2	99.6	76.7	89.6	101.8	73.0	89.1

FLORIDA

DIV. NO.	BUILDING SYSTEMS	PANAMA CITY MAT.	INST.	TOTAL	PENSACOLA MAT.	INST.	TOTAL	ST. PETERSBURG MAT.	INST.	TOTAL	TALLAHASSEE MAT.	INST.	TOTAL	TAMPA MAT.	INST.	TOTAL
A	Substructure	103.6	64.2	80.0	117.8	70.0	89.2	105.2	70.4	84.4	101.9	62.9	78.6	103.4	83.1	91.2
B10	Shell: Superstructure	96.4	73.6	87.1	100.6	78.0	91.4	99.6	79.7	91.4	91.9	71.5	83.6	98.6	92.2	95.9
B20	Exterior Closure	102.4	51.6	78.2	109.7	60.1	86.1	120.3	56.0	89.7	96.9	58.2	78.5	95.9	81.1	88.8
B30	Roofing	95.4	60.9	82.4	95.3	65.9	84.3	94.8	61.9	82.5	100.8	77.3	92.0	95.1	89.6	93.0
C	Interior Construction	101.4	48.2	78.0	100.4	58.0	81.8	100.8	56.0	81.1	103.3	50.6	80.1	102.5	76.5	91.1
D10	Services: Conveying	100.0	50.6	86.3	100.0	49.4	86.3	100.0	61.3	89.5	100.0	74.3	93.2	100.0	78.9	94.3
D20 - 40	Mechanical	99.9	55.8	82.1	99.9	56.2	82.2	99.9	60.1	83.8	99.9	41.8	76.4	99.9	86.7	94.6
D50	Electrical	96.7	60.1	77.8	100.7	57.2	78.3	98.3	65.4	81.3	103.8	60.1	81.3	98.0	65.4	81.2
E	Equipment & Furnishings	100.0	44.6	97.2	100.0	54.3	97.7	100.0	53.3	97.6	100.0	44.2	97.1	100.0	81.0	99.0
G	Site Work	127.5	87.5	101.0	127.4	88.0	101.2	114.5	88.1	97.0	110.1	87.7	95.2	114.6	88.7	97.4
A-G	WEIGHTED AVERAGE	100.1	60.5	82.7	102.6	64.1	85.6	102.5	65.8	86.3	99.4	59.3	81.7	99.8	82.1	92.0

GEORGIA

DIV. NO.	BUILDING SYSTEMS	ALBANY MAT.	ALBANY INST.	ALBANY TOTAL	ATLANTA MAT.	ATLANTA INST.	ATLANTA TOTAL	AUGUSTA MAT.	AUGUSTA INST.	AUGUSTA TOTAL	COLUMBUS MAT.	COLUMBUS INST.	COLUMBUS TOTAL	MACON MAT.	MACON INST.	MACON TOTAL
A	Substructure	98.2	59.7	75.1	107.8	80.0	91.2	103.5	69.4	83.1	98.0	66.1	78.9	97.8	66.8	79.2
B10	Shell: Superstructure	95.9	70.7	85.6	95.6	77.9	88.3	93.7	68.9	83.5	95.5	76.0	87.5	92.3	74.0	84.8
B20	Exterior Closure	94.8	46.8	71.9	93.0	69.0	81.6	90.6	44.8	68.8	94.7	59.6	78.0	98.8	43.5	72.5
B30	Roofing	92.6	65.4	82.4	94.3	74.4	86.9	94.1	61.4	81.8	92.6	66.9	82.9	91.1	67.2	82.2
C	Interior Construction	100.3	44.1	75.6	95.7	75.1	86.6	92.5	61.7	78.9	100.2	56.9	81.2	94.7	51.7	75.8
D10	Services: Conveying	100.0	85.9	96.2	100.0	86.4	96.3	100.0	51.3	86.8	100.0	85.9	96.2	100.0	83.8	95.6
D20 - 40	Mechanical	99.9	68.2	87.1	99.9	73.4	89.2	100.0	65.7	86.1	99.9	49.9	79.7	99.9	66.3	86.3
D50	Electrical	93.5	60.1	76.3	101.7	75.5	88.2	103.0	65.6	83.7	93.5	74.0	83.4	92.5	62.1	76.8
E	Equipment & Furnishings	100.0	41.1	97.0	100.0	77.2	98.8	100.0	71.3	98.5	100.0	55.8	97.7	100.0	54.2	97.7
G	Site Work	98.9	78.8	85.6	98.7	94.2	95.7	95.3	92.1	93.2	98.8	78.9	85.6	99.5	93.7	95.7
A-G	WEIGHTED AVERAGE	97.6	61.5	81.7	98.0	76.5	88.5	96.7	64.5	82.5	97.5	64.6	83.0	96.4	64.2	82.2

GEORGIA / HAWAII / IDAHO

DIV. NO.	BUILDING SYSTEMS	SAVANNAH MAT.	SAVANNAH INST.	SAVANNAH TOTAL	VALDOSTA MAT.	VALDOSTA INST.	VALDOSTA TOTAL	HONOLULU MAT.	HONOLULU INST.	HONOLULU TOTAL	STATES & POSS., GUAM MAT.	STATES & POSS., GUAM INST.	STATES & POSS., GUAM TOTAL	BOISE MAT.	BOISE INST.	BOISE TOTAL
A	Substructure	104.3	60.9	78.3	98.0	58.8	74.5	142.4	123.9	131.3	168.0	83.7	117.6	90.9	80.0	84.4
B10	Shell: Superstructure	94.2	70.3	84.4	94.4	68.1	83.6	131.5	118.3	126.1	143.9	76.5	116.3	98.2	74.7	88.6
B20	Exterior Closure	94.6	52.5	74.6	101.9	51.6	78.0	108.6	126.1	116.9	135.9	47.5	93.8	113.7	63.2	89.7
B30	Roofing	94.9	60.1	81.8	92.8	67.3	83.2	114.7	124.6	118.4	121.0	73.6	103.2	96.0	68.1	85.5
C	Interior Construction	102.2	50.3	79.4	96.6	44.9	73.9	116.9	136.0	125.3	148.3	61.6	110.2	97.3	71.0	85.5
D10	Services: Conveying	100.0	53.3	87.4	100.0	53.3	87.4	100.0	112.6	103.4	100.0	82.2	95.2	100.0	60.5	89.3
D20 - 40	Mechanical	99.9	61.6	84.4	99.9	68.1	87.0	100.1	109.7	104.0	102.1	40.0	76.9	100.0	67.6	86.9
D50	Electrical	95.0	57.4	75.6	91.6	59.8	75.2	105.9	127.2	116.9	154.1	43.8	97.2	96.4	73.0	84.3
E	Equipment & Furnishings	100.0	47.5	97.3	100.0	40.1	96.9	100.0	137.5	101.9	100.0	61.3	98.0	100.0	75.6	98.8
G	Site Work	100.0	79.7	86.5	108.5	78.8	88.8	127.1	107.6	114.1	161.3	103.7	123.1	79.2	98.2	91.8
A-G	WEIGHTED AVERAGE	98.1	60.5	81.5	97.6	60.8	81.4	113.3	121.2	116.8	131.1	60.8	100.1	99.3	72.4	87.4

IDAHO / ILLINOIS

DIV. NO.	BUILDING SYSTEMS	LEWISTON MAT.	LEWISTON INST.	LEWISTON TOTAL	POCATELLO MAT.	POCATELLO INST.	POCATELLO TOTAL	TWIN FALLS MAT.	TWIN FALLS INST.	TWIN FALLS TOTAL	CHICAGO MAT.	CHICAGO INST.	CHICAGO TOTAL	DECATUR MAT.	DECATUR INST.	DECATUR TOTAL
A	Substructure	100.9	80.1	88.5	93.2	79.9	85.3	95.9	55.0	71.4	106.3	139.3	126.0	97.4	109.9	104.9
B10	Shell: Superstructure	95.7	78.9	88.8	104.6	74.6	92.3	105.1	58.0	85.8	97.4	143.0	116.1	99.3	110.7	104.0
B20	Exterior Closure	123.1	79.6	102.4	110.9	63.0	88.1	118.7	35.1	78.9	96.1	152.0	122.7	84.9	114.3	98.9
B30	Roofing	148.7	72.7	120.1	96.0	61.5	83.1	96.8	38.6	74.9	99.7	144.0	116.4	98.7	108.2	102.2
C	Interior Construction	141.1	62.9	106.7	98.6	71.1	86.5	100.3	32.8	70.6	99.5	156.6	124.6	98.8	117.5	107.1
D10	Services: Conveying	100.0	66.8	91.0	100.0	60.5	89.3	100.0	36.5	82.8	100.0	121.1	105.7	100.0	102.6	100.7
D20 - 40	Mechanical	100.8	90.2	96.5	100.0	67.5	86.8	100.0	55.6	82.0	100.0	133.9	113.7	99.9	101.5	100.6
D50	Electrical	85.5	80.8	83.1	93.9	73.0	83.1	88.9	62.9	75.5	95.4	133.4	115.0	97.1	90.3	93.6
E	Equipment & Furnishings	100.0	52.3	97.6	100.0	75.6	98.8	100.0	29.1	96.4	100.0	155.4	102.8	100.0	117.3	100.9
G	Site Work	84.6	94.4	91.1	80.1	98.2	92.1	86.7	96.5	93.2	110.9	93.7	99.5	92.6	97.6	95.9
A-G	WEIGHTED AVERAGE	107.9	79.7	95.5	100.3	72.2	87.9	101.3	52.5	79.8	99.1	138.9	116.6	97.4	106.3	101.3

ILLINOIS

DIV. NO.	BUILDING SYSTEMS	EAST ST. LOUIS MAT.	EAST ST. LOUIS INST.	EAST ST. LOUIS TOTAL	JOLIET MAT.	JOLIET INST.	JOLIET TOTAL	PEORIA MAT.	PEORIA INST.	PEORIA TOTAL	ROCKFORD MAT.	ROCKFORD INST.	ROCKFORD TOTAL	SPRINGFIELD MAT.	SPRINGFIELD INST.	SPRINGFIELD TOTAL
A	Substructure	95.8	110.0	104.3	106.4	135.2	123.6	97.4	110.4	105.2	98.0	123.4	113.2	92.7	108.7	102.3
B10	Shell: Superstructure	96.3	116.6	104.6	95.8	136.6	112.5	98.9	112.6	104.5	99.1	129.9	111.7	99.6	110.2	103.9
B20	Exterior Closure	79.4	117.8	97.7	97.2	145.6	120.3	104.2	113.6	108.7	92.6	135.4	113.0	87.4	115.1	100.6
B30	Roofing	93.1	113.1	100.6	99.6	140.6	115.0	98.8	113.4	104.3	101.3	129.5	111.9	98.5	113.0	103.9
C	Interior Construction	92.9	112.6	101.6	98.2	153.0	122.3	99.0	116.5	106.7	99.0	130.6	112.9	99.4	116.2	106.8
D10	Services: Conveying	100.0	103.1	100.8	100.0	119.4	105.3	100.0	103.3	100.9	100.0	89.4	97.1	100.0	103.0	100.8
D20 - 40	Mechanical	99.9	97.1	98.8	100.1	133.2	113.5	99.9	105.7	102.3	100.0	115.6	106.3	99.8	104.8	101.8
D50	Electrical	94.0	105.4	99.8	94.7	137.9	117.0	96.2	97.2	96.7	96.6	131.8	114.8	97.5	92.4	94.9
E	Equipment & Furnishings	100.0	110.2	100.5	100.0	155.9	102.9	100.0	114.8	100.8	100.0	131.8	101.6	100.0	117.5	100.9
G	Site Work	106.7	98.3	101.1	110.7	92.6	98.7	100.4	96.6	97.9	99.6	97.9	98.5	98.8	97.6	98.0
A-G	WEIGHTED AVERAGE	95.1	108.3	100.9	98.6	136.4	115.3	99.5	108.3	103.4	98.4	124.3	109.8	97.8	107.1	101.9

INDIANA

DIV. NO.	BUILDING SYSTEMS	ANDERSON MAT.	ANDERSON INST.	ANDERSON TOTAL	BLOOMINGTON MAT.	BLOOMINGTON INST.	BLOOMINGTON TOTAL	EVANSVILLE MAT.	EVANSVILLE INST.	EVANSVILLE TOTAL	FORT WAYNE MAT.	FORT WAYNE INST.	FORT WAYNE TOTAL	GARY MAT.	GARY INST.	GARY TOTAL
A	Substructure	97.0	84.5	89.5	94.2	85.0	88.7	93.2	92.3	92.7	100.4	80.2	88.3	99.8	105.9	103.4
B10	Shell: Superstructure	95.0	85.7	91.2	95.2	80.2	89.0	89.7	83.4	87.1	95.9	81.6	90.0	95.6	106.3	100.9
B20	Exterior Closure	91.4	82.2	87.0	100.3	79.2	90.3	97.7	82.6	90.5	93.1	78.9	86.4	92.0	113.4	102.2
B30	Roofing	98.2	80.0	91.4	93.8	83.9	90.1	97.6	84.8	92.8	98.0	82.7	92.3	97.1	109.7	101.8
C	Interior Construction	96.7	80.7	89.7	101.8	82.0	93.1	96.6	81.1	89.8	96.6	75.5	87.3	96.3	112.5	103.4
D10	Services: Conveying	100.0	93.9	98.3	100.0	88.5	96.9	100.0	93.8	98.3	100.0	89.3	97.1	100.0	102.6	100.7
D20 - 40	Mechanical	100.0	77.4	90.8	99.8	80.8	92.1	99.9	81.1	92.3	100.0	74.5	89.7	100.0	105.7	102.3
D50	Electrical	88.2	86.3	87.2	99.7	85.7	92.5	95.8	85.6	90.6	89.0	74.1	81.3	100.4	114.3	107.6
E	Equipment & Furnishings	100.0	82.2	99.1	100.0	82.8	99.1	100.0	78.8	98.9	100.0	74.3	98.7	100.0	109.6	100.5
G	Site Work	95.9	94.7	95.1	80.5	95.5	90.5	85.5	125.0	111.7	97.1	94.4	95.3	96.5	98.1	97.6
A-G	WEIGHTED AVERAGE	96.1	83.4	90.5	98.4	82.9	91.6	96.0	86.5	91.8	96.7	78.7	88.8	97.6	108.5	102.4

INDIANA / IOWA

DIV. NO.	BUILDING SYSTEMS	INDIANAPOLIS MAT.	INDIANAPOLIS INST.	INDIANAPOLIS TOTAL	MUNCIE MAT.	MUNCIE INST.	MUNCIE TOTAL	SOUTH BEND MAT.	SOUTH BEND INST.	SOUTH BEND TOTAL	TERRE HAUTE MAT.	TERRE HAUTE INST.	TERRE HAUTE TOTAL	CEDAR RAPIDS MAT.	CEDAR RAPIDS INST.	CEDAR RAPIDS TOTAL
A	Substructure	95.1	88.2	90.9	98.4	84.7	90.2	96.2	83.1	88.3	91.4	93.6	92.7	108.9	85.3	94.8
B10	Shell: Superstructure	96.0	82.8	90.6	97.3	82.6	92.6	94.6	90.0	92.7	89.8	85.9	88.2	95.4	88.1	92.4
B20	Exterior Closure	98.7	82.6	91.0	96.8	82.2	89.8	87.0	81.0	84.1	105.3	82.3	94.3	100.7	80.6	91.2
B30	Roofing	96.2	85.1	92.1	96.4	80.3	90.4	92.8	84.3	89.6	97.6	82.8	92.1	107.9	80.9	97.8
C	Interior Construction	102.3	85.5	94.9	97.3	80.6	90.0	91.1	80.2	86.3	96.9	81.8	90.3	106.1	81.3	95.2
D10	Services: Conveying	100.0	94.9	98.6	100.0	93.4	98.2	100.0	70.1	91.9	100.0	96.7	99.1	100.0	89.4	97.1
D20 - 40	Mechanical	99.9	83.3	93.2	99.8	77.3	90.7	99.9	77.4	90.8	99.9	79.9	91.8	100.3	81.9	92.8
D50	Electrical	102.4	86.3	94.1	91.5	80.3	85.7	99.7	84.2	91.7	94.0	85.7	89.7	98.4	81.0	89.4
E	Equipment & Furnishings	100.0	85.7	99.3	100.0	81.9	99.1	100.0	79.0	98.9	100.0	79.1	98.9	100.0	80.5	99.0
G	Site Work	95.4	98.0	97.1	80.7	95.4	90.4	98.3	94.6	95.9	87.4	125.3	112.6	101.9	96.4	98.2
A-G	WEIGHTED AVERAGE	99.2	85.6	93.2	97.1	82.6	90.7	95.7	82.9	90.1	96.7	86.9	92.4	100.7	84.0	93.3

IOWA

DIV. NO.	BUILDING SYSTEMS	COUNCIL BLUFFS MAT.	INST.	TOTAL	DAVENPORT MAT.	INST.	TOTAL	DES MOINES MAT.	INST.	TOTAL	DUBUQUE MAT.	INST.	TOTAL	SIOUX CITY MAT.	INST.	TOTAL
A	Substructure	112.8	79.1	92.6	105.9	91.5	97.3	95.6	87.5	90.7	105.5	82.8	91.9	110.0	70.7	86.4
B10	Shell: Superstructure	99.3	82.8	92.5	94.8	95.7	95.2	92.9	88.5	91.1	93.1	85.9	90.1	95.3	73.7	86.5
B20	Exterior Closure	102.3	77.2	90.4	99.2	86.3	93.0	95.3	84.1	89.9	100.1	77.8	89.5	97.7	57.3	78.5
B30	Roofing	107.4	68.3	92.7	107.4	86.6	99.6	108.8	79.8	97.9	107.7	72.0	94.3	107.4	67.4	92.4
C	Interior Construction	100.7	73.8	88.9	103.8	88.5	97.1	102.0	79.5	92.1	103.0	71.8	89.3	104.9	64.2	87.0
D10	Services: Conveying	100.0	83.1	95.4	100.0	90.7	97.5	100.0	89.9	97.3	100.0	88.8	97.0	100.0	86.7	96.4
D20 - 40	Mechanical	100.3	74.6	89.9	100.3	89.6	96.0	100.2	81.3	92.5	100.3	76.4	90.6	100.3	69.3	87.7
D50	Electrical	103.6	82.0	92.5	95.3	86.7	90.8	107.5	82.5	94.6	102.2	79.1	90.3	98.4	74.4	86.0
E	Equipment & Furnishings	100.0	71.6	98.5	100.0	86.9	99.3	100.0	76.3	98.8	100.0	67.6	98.3	100.0	65.5	98.2
G	Site Work	107.9	92.7	97.8	99.7	99.4	99.5	89.8	100.1	96.6	100.0	93.6	95.7	110.7	96.0	101.0
A-G	WEIGHTED AVERAGE	101.7	78.8	91.6	99.6	90.4	95.5	99.1	84.7	92.7	99.9	79.7	91.0	100.5	70.7	87.3

IOWA / KANSAS

DIV. NO.	BUILDING SYSTEMS	WATERLOO MAT.	INST.	TOTAL	DODGE CITY MAT.	INST.	TOTAL	KANSAS CITY MAT.	INST.	TOTAL	SALINA MAT.	INST.	TOTAL	TOPEKA MAT.	INST.	TOTAL
A	Substructure	108.6	67.5	84.0	112.1	67.3	85.3	92.6	95.3	94.2	100.8	65.4	79.6	92.9	63.0	75.0
B10	Shell: Superstructure	95.5	75.6	87.3	99.6	69.3	87.2	100.1	97.7	99.1	97.0	70.4	86.1	99.6	76.1	90.0
B20	Exterior Closure	97.6	74.0	86.4	109.0	60.2	85.7	102.5	95.8	99.3	110.8	57.9	85.6	97.8	59.8	79.7
B30	Roofing	107.2	72.2	94.0	99.5	61.1	85.1	98.2	97.7	98.0	99.0	60.0	84.3	100.0	62.3	85.8
C	Interior Construction	102.1	55.9	81.8	98.6	56.1	79.9	96.5	94.0	95.4	97.8	56.5	79.7	98.0	49.7	76.8
D10	Services: Conveying	100.0	89.4	97.1	100.0	42.1	84.3	100.0	62.2	89.8	100.0	54.0	87.5	100.0	52.5	87.1
D20 - 40	Mechanical	100.3	81.2	92.6	99.9	67.4	86.8	99.9	99.0	99.5	99.9	67.5	86.8	99.9	57.4	82.7
D50	Electrical	98.4	59.1	78.1	96.7	73.7	84.8	102.3	95.9	99.0	96.4	73.7	84.7	102.0	73.6	87.4
E	Equipment & Furnishings	100.0	40.3	96.9	100.0	61.3	98.0	100.0	97.6	99.9	100.0	55.6	97.7	100.0	40.3	96.9
G	Site Work	100.2	96.5	97.7	115.0	93.2	100.5	96.3	91.7	93.2	104.9	93.6	97.4	96.7	90.4	92.5
A-G	WEIGHTED AVERAGE	99.7	72.2	87.6	101.2	66.8	86.0	99.5	95.4	97.7	100.0	66.9	85.4	99.2	64.5	83.9

KANSAS / KENTUCKY

DIV. NO.	BUILDING SYSTEMS	WICHITA MAT.	INST.	TOTAL	BOWLING GREEN MAT.	INST.	TOTAL	LEXINGTON MAT.	INST.	TOTAL	LOUISVILLE MAT.	INST.	TOTAL	OWENSBORO MAT.	INST.	TOTAL
A	Substructure	91.5	62.8	74.3	84.6	91.0	88.5	91.9	87.2	89.1	92.4	84.6	87.7	87.6	97.8	93.7
B10	Shell: Superstructure	99.4	69.5	87.1	91.0	86.8	89.3	94.2	85.6	90.7	99.6	84.8	93.5	85.7	88.7	86.9
B20	Exterior Closure	94.9	55.2	76.0	99.0	73.6	86.9	94.2	71.4	83.3	94.7	80.5	87.9	104.0	84.1	94.5
B30	Roofing	98.3	53.9	81.6	85.4	83.7	84.8	97.9	90.3	95.0	91.9	77.8	86.6	97.6	90.1	94.8
C	Interior Construction	97.8	50.4	77.0	95.5	80.8	89.1	97.9	76.1	88.3	96.7	81.1	89.8	94.3	84.7	90.1
D10	Services: Conveying	100.0	51.0	86.7	100.0	59.1	88.9	100.0	95.3	98.7	100.0	91.9	97.8	100.0	101.1	100.3
D20 - 40	Mechanical	99.7	63.6	85.1	99.9	83.9	93.5	99.9	76.7	90.5	100.0	82.3	92.8	99.9	77.2	90.7
D50	Electrical	99.9	73.7	86.4	94.8	83.7	89.1	95.3	83.7	89.3	102.7	80.8	91.4	94.3	83.9	88.9
E	Equipment & Furnishings	100.0	45.6	97.2	100.0	79.1	98.9	100.0	74.3	98.6	100.0	78.8	98.9	100.0	80.3	99.0
G	Site Work	96.7	92.3	93.8	72.5	99.0	90.1	81.1	101.7	94.8	70.4	98.8	89.3	85.8	125.5	112.1
A-G	WEIGHTED AVERAGE	98.4	64.1	83.3	95.0	83.5	90.0	96.5	81.8	90.0	97.8	83.5	91.5	95.2	87.9	92.0

LOUISIANA

DIV. NO.	BUILDING SYSTEMS	ALEXANDRIA MAT.	INST.	TOTAL	BATON ROUGE MAT.	INST.	TOTAL	LAKE CHARLES MAT.	INST.	TOTAL	MONROE MAT.	INST.	TOTAL	NEW ORLEANS MAT.	INST.	TOTAL
A	Substructure	94.9	51.9	69.2	96.8	66.1	78.4	102.0	66.7	80.8	94.6	56.3	71.7	102.0	72.8	84.5
B10	Shell: Superstructure	90.4	57.6	76.9	100.2	66.1	86.2	97.4	65.9	84.5	90.2	58.6	77.3	107.2	71.6	92.6
B20	Exterior Closure	107.6	49.9	80.1	101.2	52.0	77.8	100.5	56.9	79.8	105.4	48.0	78.0	100.9	63.3	83.0
B30	Roofing	97.5	49.1	79.3	95.4	57.2	81.0	96.9	56.9	81.9	97.4	49.1	79.3	97.4	71.6	87.7
C	Interior Construction	94.2	41.0	70.8	100.7	62.1	83.8	100.6	59.2	82.4	94.1	40.8	70.6	101.4	68.7	87.0
D10	Services: Conveying	100.0	53.1	87.3	100.0	81.3	94.9	100.0	81.4	95.0	100.0	48.3	86.0	100.0	85.4	96.0
D20 - 40	Mechanical	100.3	51.2	80.4	100.1	59.1	83.5	100.2	59.8	83.8	100.3	50.1	80.0	100.1	65.8	86.2
D50	Electrical	93.9	56.5	74.6	110.9	61.3	85.3	102.7	67.0	84.3	95.8	57.7	76.1	103.4	71.7	87.0
E	Equipment & Furnishings	100.0	35.4	96.7	100.0	66.3	98.3	100.0	60.2	98.0	100.0	35.8	96.7	100.0	69.9	98.5
G	Site Work	96.8	85.6	89.4	103.5	85.2	91.3	106.0	85.0	92.1	96.7	85.0	88.9	108.4	88.0	94.9
A-G	WEIGHTED AVERAGE	97.1	53.5	77.9	101.2	63.0	84.4	100.1	64.1	84.2	97.0	53.6	77.9	102.3	70.5	88.3

LOUISIANA / MAINE

DIV. NO.	BUILDING SYSTEMS	SHREVEPORT MAT.	INST.	TOTAL	AUGUSTA MAT.	INST.	TOTAL	BANGOR MAT.	INST.	TOTAL	LEWISTON MAT.	INST.	TOTAL	PORTLAND MAT.	INST.	TOTAL
A	Substructure	95.8	54.1	70.8	92.9	89.8	91.0	85.8	97.6	92.9	90.8	97.6	94.9	102.8	97.6	99.7
B10	Shell: Superstructure	88.5	57.7	75.9	88.2	87.5	87.9	85.9	88.5	87.0	89.6	88.5	89.2	93.6	88.5	91.5
B20	Exterior Closure	99.7	48.2	75.2	108.4	62.5	86.6	114.3	61.6	89.2	103.8	61.6	83.7	103.9	61.6	83.8
B30	Roofing	96.5	47.4	78.1	101.0	67.2	88.3	101.6	66.7	88.5	101.4	66.7	88.4	104.7	66.7	90.5
C	Interior Construction	94.9	42.7	72.0	98.6	90.4	95.0	98.3	83.8	91.9	101.2	83.8	93.5	100.5	83.8	93.2
D10	Services: Conveying	100.0	68.4	91.4	100.0	91.6	97.7	100.0	107.3	102.0	100.0	107.3	102.0	100.0	107.3	102.0
D20 - 40	Mechanical	100.2	55.1	81.9	99.9	65.4	85.9	100.0	61.4	84.4	100.0	61.4	84.4	99.9	61.4	84.3
D50	Electrical	100.0	66.6	82.8	98.5	80.1	89.0	100.1	80.1	89.8	102.3	80.1	90.9	103.9	80.1	91.6
E	Equipment & Furnishings	100.0	39.0	96.9	100.0	108.5	100.4	100.0	96.0	99.8	100.0	96.0	99.8	100.0	96.0	99.8
G	Site Work	98.9	84.8	89.6	87.7	100.3	96.0	89.9	98.0	95.2	86.1	98.0	94.0	84.6	98.0	93.5
A-G	WEIGHTED AVERAGE	96.7	56.3	78.9	97.6	79.8	89.8	97.7	78.9	89.4	98.1	78.9	89.7	99.5	78.9	90.4

MARYLAND / MASSACHUSETTS

DIV. NO.	BUILDING SYSTEMS	BALTIMORE MAT.	INST.	TOTAL	HAGERSTOWN MAT.	INST.	TOTAL	BOSTON MAT.	INST.	TOTAL	BROCKTON MAT.	INST.	TOTAL	FALL RIVER MAT.	INST.	TOTAL
A	Substructure	114.5	82.5	95.4	98.6	82.7	89.1	105.2	136.9	124.2	102.0	131.6	119.7	99.9	127.8	116.6
B10	Shell: Superstructure	100.5	87.5	95.2	94.1	85.9	90.7	102.2	136.5	116.3	99.1	131.9	112.5	98.6	123.8	108.9
B20	Exterior Closure	101.5	79.0	90.8	98.2	79.3	89.2	115.2	158.3	135.7	112.8	154.6	132.7	113.0	151.4	131.3
B30	Roofing	97.4	79.7	90.7	96.5	76.2	88.9	101.6	146.5	118.5	101.6	141.6	116.7	101.6	135.3	114.3
C	Interior Construction	95.9	76.7	87.5	92.9	77.8	86.3	98.6	149.4	120.9	97.2	136.9	114.7	97.2	135.6	114.1
D10	Services: Conveying	100.0	88.4	96.9	100.0	91.5	97.7	100.0	117.4	104.7	100.0	116.2	104.4	100.0	116.9	104.6
D20 - 40	Mechanical	99.9	83.8	93.4	99.9	84.4	93.6	100.1	128.6	111.6	100.0	111.9	104.8	100.0	111.7	104.7
D50	Electrical	99.4	93.8	96.5	96.9	82.0	89.2	101.5	132.0	117.2	100.6	98.8	99.7	100.5	98.8	99.7
E	Equipment & Furnishings	100.0	77.4	98.8	100.0	77.3	98.8	100.0	141.2	102.1	100.0	123.4	101.2	100.0	123.3	101.2
G	Site Work	101.6	94.0	96.6	90.9	90.7	90.7	95.0	107.5	103.3	92.1	104.1	100.1	91.1	104.2	99.8
A-G	WEIGHTED AVERAGE	100.2	84.7	93.3	96.8	82.9	90.7	102.2	136.8	117.5	100.8	124.7	111.4	100.6	122.2	110.1

MASSACHUSETTS

DIV. NO.	BUILDING SYSTEMS	HYANNIS MAT.	INST.	TOTAL	LAWRENCE MAT.	INST.	TOTAL	LOWELL MAT.	INST.	TOTAL	NEW BEDFORD MAT.	INST.	TOTAL	PITTSFIELD MAT.	INST.	TOTAL
A	Substructure	90.9	127.6	112.8	102.3	128.3	117.9	96.6	128.2	115.5	92.3	127.8	113.6	98.5	109.8	105.3
B10	Shell: Superstructure	93.7	123.5	105.9	97.2	127.3	109.5	95.7	125.7	108.0	96.9	123.8	107.9	96.0	106.4	100.3
B20	Exterior Closure	109.4	151.4	129.4	112.4	154.0	132.2	101.7	148.0	123.7	112.3	151.4	130.9	102.0	119.2	110.2
B30	Roofing	101.3	136.2	114.4	101.6	140.7	116.3	101.4	140.2	116.3	101.6	135.3	114.3	101.5	113.6	106.0
C	Interior Construction	93.5	135.4	111.9	97.1	136.2	114.3	100.9	136.2	116.4	97.2	135.6	114.1	100.9	111.9	105.7
D10	Services: Conveying	100.0	116.2	104.4	100.0	116.2	104.4	100.0	116.2	104.4	100.0	116.9	104.6	100.0	103.7	101.0
D20 - 40	Mechanical	100.0	111.6	104.7	100.0	119.0	107.7	100.0	124.5	109.9	100.0	111.7	104.7	100.0	97.6	99.1
D50	Electrical	98.1	98.8	98.5	101.8	128.4	115.5	102.3	124.2	113.6	101.4	98.8	100.1	102.3	93.0	97.5
E	Equipment & Furnishings	100.0	123.4	101.2	100.0	124.8	101.3	100.0	124.6	101.3	100.0	123.3	101.2	100.0	104.8	100.2
G	Site Work	89.4	104.1	99.1	92.9	104.1	100.3	91.7	104.1	99.9	89.4	104.2	99.2	92.9	102.3	99.1
A-G	**WEIGHTED AVERAGE**	98.0	122.1	108.6	100.5	129.0	113.1	99.4	128.5	112.3	99.9	122.2	109.7	99.6	105.3	102.1

MASSACHUSETTS / MICHIGAN

DIV. NO.	BUILDING SYSTEMS	SPRINGFIELD MAT.	INST.	TOTAL	WORCESTER MAT.	INST.	TOTAL	ANN ARBOR MAT.	INST.	TOTAL	DEARBORN MAT.	INST.	TOTAL	DETROIT MAT.	INST.	TOTAL
A	Substructure	99.0	113.5	107.7	98.7	128.8	116.7	85.5	109.7	100.0	84.3	110.9	100.2	91.4	111.0	103.1
B10	Shell: Superstructure	98.2	112.1	103.9	98.2	127.6	110.3	92.4	116.3	102.2	92.2	117.5	102.6	96.5	108.1	101.3
B20	Exterior Closure	101.9	123.5	112.1	101.6	148.3	123.9	97.7	108.9	103.0	97.6	111.9	104.4	97.4	110.7	103.7
B30	Roofing	101.4	115.8	106.8	101.4	134.0	113.7	101.3	110.2	104.7	100.0	115.1	105.6	98.3	115.1	104.6
C	Interior Construction	100.9	113.7	106.6	100.9	135.4	116.1	94.8	111.2	102.0	94.7	114.4	103.4	96.3	114.4	104.2
D10	Services: Conveying	100.0	105.4	101.5	100.0	108.6	102.3	100.0	106.4	101.7	100.0	106.7	101.8	100.0	106.7	101.8
D20 - 40	Mechanical	100.0	102.1	100.9	100.0	115.1	106.1	100.0	100.2	100.1	100.0	110.5	104.3	100.1	111.8	104.8
D50	Electrical	102.3	94.9	98.5	102.3	102.6	102.4	95.6	110.4	103.2	95.6	109.2	102.6	96.7	109.1	103.1
E	Equipment & Furnishings	100.0	105.2	100.3	100.0	123.3	101.2	100.0	110.3	100.5	100.0	114.6	100.7	100.0	114.6	100.7
G	Site Work	92.2	102.6	99.1	92.2	104.1	100.1	76.0	96.2	89.4	75.7	96.2	89.3	89.0	98.3	95.2
A-G	**WEIGHTED AVERAGE**	100.0	108.7	103.9	100.0	123.5	110.4	95.8	108.1	101.2	95.7	111.4	102.6	97.4	110.1	103.0

MICHIGAN

DIV. NO.	BUILDING SYSTEMS	FLINT MAT.	INST.	TOTAL	GRAND RAPIDS MAT.	INST.	TOTAL	KALAMAZOO MAT.	INST.	TOTAL	LANSING MAT.	INST.	TOTAL	MUSKEGON MAT.	INST.	TOTAL
A	Substructure	84.3	98.1	92.6	96.7	88.0	91.5	93.9	92.9	93.3	90.2	96.5	94.0	92.7	90.7	91.5
B10	Shell: Superstructure	92.8	107.7	98.9	95.1	86.4	91.5	93.5	90.0	92.1	92.3	106.4	98.1	91.5	88.2	90.2
B20	Exterior Closure	97.7	97.4	97.6	94.6	82.3	88.8	97.4	85.3	91.6	94.8	95.3	95.0	92.5	77.9	85.6
B30	Roofing	99.1	99.5	99.3	95.4	76.2	88.2	93.7	87.2	91.2	100.2	91.6	97.0	92.9	79.0	87.7
C	Interior Construction	94.4	90.3	92.6	96.7	78.6	88.8	95.0	86.3	91.2	96.6	87.6	92.7	92.9	83.6	88.8
D10	Services: Conveying	100.0	99.4	99.8	100.0	105.1	101.4	100.0	105.3	101.4	100.0	99.2	99.8	100.0	105.3	101.4
D20 - 40	Mechanical	100.0	94.1	97.6	99.9	83.2	93.1	99.9	83.0	93.1	99.9	92.2	96.8	99.8	85.2	93.9
D50	Electrical	95.6	95.0	95.3	99.1	75.1	86.7	94.7	86.9	90.7	98.7	93.0	95.8	95.2	80.1	87.4
E	Equipment & Furnishings	100.0	89.2	99.4	100.0	75.2	98.7	100.0	85.7	99.3	100.0	86.0	99.3	100.0	84.2	99.2
G	Site Work	66.8	95.5	85.8	87.2	88.5	88.1	86.1	88.6	87.8	83.6	95.4	91.4	83.5	88.6	86.9
A-G	**WEIGHTED AVERAGE**	95.5	97.1	96.2	97.2	83.0	90.9	96.3	87.4	92.4	96.4	95.1	95.9	94.9	84.9	90.5

MICHIGAN / MINNESOTA

DIV. NO.	BUILDING SYSTEMS	SAGINAW MAT.	INST.	TOTAL	DULUTH MAT.	INST.	TOTAL	MINNEAPOLIS MAT.	INST.	TOTAL	ROCHESTER MAT.	INST.	TOTAL	SAINT PAUL MAT.	INST.	TOTAL
A	Substructure	83.6	96.6	91.4	104.4	110.4	108.0	112.8	120.2	117.2	111.2	107.8	109.2	111.4	118.8	115.8
B10	Shell: Superstructure	92.4	106.4	98.1	100.7	119.8	108.5	104.9	128.6	114.6	102.3	120.8	109.9	101.8	128.3	112.6
B20	Exterior Closure	97.9	91.0	94.6	101.9	120.2	110.6	103.6	128.9	115.6	101.3	118.6	109.5	109.4	128.9	118.7
B30	Roofing	99.9	96.9	98.8	109.3	119.7	113.2	108.9	134.7	118.6	109.3	102.8	106.9	110.5	134.5	119.5
C	Interior Construction	93.4	87.9	90.9	95.6	119.9	106.3	98.3	131.4	112.9	96.2	115.4	104.6	93.7	130.9	110.0
D10	Services: Conveying	100.0	98.3	99.6	100.0	103.9	101.1	100.0	107.8	102.1	100.0	103.4	101.0	100.0	107.5	102.0
D20 - 40	Mechanical	100.0	87.5	95.0	100.1	101.0	100.5	100.0	121.6	108.8	100.0	99.4	99.8	100.0	117.1	106.9
D50	Electrical	92.7	91.3	92.0	99.5	108.9	104.3	101.6	113.1	107.6	100.6	89.1	94.7	98.7	113.1	106.1
E	Equipment & Furnishings	100.0	87.6	99.4	100.0	116.7	100.9	100.0	128.1	101.4	100.0	109.2	100.5	100.0	128.0	101.4
G	Site Work	69.5	95.3	86.6	98.8	102.2	101.0	101.5	107.6	105.5	100.5	102.0	101.5	101.6	102.8	102.4
A-G	**WEIGHTED AVERAGE**	95.0	93.5	94.4	100.1	112.0	105.4	102.1	123.0	111.3	100.9	107.6	103.8	101.1	121.5	110.1

MINNESOTA / MISSISSIPPI

DIV. NO.	BUILDING SYSTEMS	ST. CLOUD MAT.	INST.	TOTAL	BILOXI MAT.	INST.	TOTAL	GREENVILLE MAT.	INST.	TOTAL	JACKSON MAT.	INST.	TOTAL	MERIDIAN MAT.	INST.	TOTAL
A	Substructure	99.1	117.6	110.2	103.6	64.5	80.2	104.9	70.0	84.0	93.3	67.2	77.7	99.6	70.1	81.9
B10	Shell: Superstructure	95.3	125.9	107.8	94.9	71.7	85.4	93.1	76.3	86.2	92.4	73.1	84.5	92.1	75.1	85.1
B20	Exterior Closure	97.3	126.4	111.2	94.5	50.1	73.4	118.3	53.7	87.6	95.1	53.2	75.2	92.7	58.7	76.5
B30	Roofing	107.8	124.0	113.9	92.7	57.8	79.6	92.8	64.7	82.3	94.5	63.6	82.9	92.4	66.5	82.7
C	Interior Construction	91.4	127.9	107.4	100.6	56.1	81.1	98.1	67.4	84.6	100.3	61.6	83.3	97.5	67.1	84.1
D10	Services: Conveying	100.0	102.1	100.6	100.0	60.1	89.2	100.0	62.1	89.8	100.0	62.1	89.8	100.0	63.8	90.2
D20 - 40	Mechanical	99.7	121.3	108.4	99.9	50.4	79.9	99.9	51.1	80.1	99.9	56.5	82.3	99.9	58.7	83.2
D50	Electrical	102.1	113.1	107.8	98.8	59.0	78.3	98.1	66.6	81.9	99.5	66.6	82.5	97.8	59.2	77.9
E	Equipment & Furnishings	100.0	123.1	101.2	100.0	58.8	97.9	100.0	71.4	98.5	100.0	62.9	98.1	100.0	68.3	98.4
G	Site Work	92.2	105.4	101.0	101.2	88.6	92.8	105.0	88.6	94.1	96.3	88.6	91.2	96.9	88.9	91.6
A-G	**WEIGHTED AVERAGE**	97.6	120.8	107.9	98.3	60.2	81.5	100.3	65.1	84.7	97.4	64.4	82.9	96.7	66.1	83.2

MISSOURI

DIV. NO.	BUILDING SYSTEMS	CAPE GIRARDEAU MAT.	INST.	TOTAL	COLUMBIA MAT.	INST.	TOTAL	JOPLIN MAT.	INST.	TOTAL	KANSAS CITY MAT.	INST.	TOTAL	SPRINGFIELD MAT.	INST.	TOTAL
A	Substructure	94.5	82.9	87.6	92.9	89.4	90.8	100.6	77.4	86.7	93.8	106.8	101.6	97.2	84.0	89.3
B10	Shell: Superstructure	97.5	92.5	95.5	93.4	104.1	97.8	94.1	80.6	91.6	103.9	112.3	107.8	98.1	94.2	96.5
B20	Exterior Closure	109.0	78.4	94.4	106.4	90.0	98.6	94.0	83.5	89.0	96.1	109.9	103.1	92.9	84.5	88.9
B30	Roofing	100.9	81.7	93.7	93.2	85.2	90.2	97.3	69.7	87.0	96.9	109.3	101.6	97.6	78.8	90.5
C	Interior Construction	98.0	75.3	88.0	94.7	82.5	89.3	97.6	66.1	83.8	98.2	109.0	102.9	99.7	69.1	86.2
D10	Services: Conveying	100.0	92.7	98.0	100.0	97.7	99.4	100.0	60.5	89.3	100.0	100.7	100.2	100.0	96.2	99.0
D20 - 40	Mechanical	99.9	94.9	97.8	99.9	95.2	98.0	100.2	48.0	79.0	100.0	110.9	104.4	99.9	70.8	88.1
D50	Electrical	99.7	107.9	103.9	95.6	88.0	91.7	93.7	69.0	81.0	104.3	102.0	103.1	99.8	72.4	85.7
E	Equipment & Furnishings	100.0	73.7	98.7	100.0	77.3	98.8	100.0	73.7	98.7	100.0	107.4	100.4	100.0	72.8	98.6
G	Site Work	92.8	93.1	93.0	105.1	95.5	98.7	100.6	98.3	99.1	94.4	98.1	96.9	99.3	93.4	95.4
A-G	**WEIGHTED AVERAGE**	99.7	89.6	95.3	97.7	92.4	95.4	98.2	70.4	85.9	100.1	108.0	103.6	98.5	79.9	90.3

MISSOURI / MONTANA

DIV. NO.	BUILDING SYSTEMS	ST. JOSEPH MAT.	INST.	TOTAL	ST. LOUIS MAT.	INST.	TOTAL	BILLINGS MAT.	INST.	TOTAL	BUTTE MAT.	INST.	TOTAL	GREAT FALLS MAT.	INST.	TOTAL
A	Substructure	93.6	96.9	95.6	93.9	103.6	99.7	109.9	75.5	89.3	119.7	75.1	93.0	124.0	75.5	94.9
B10	Shell: Superstructure	100.8	103.8	102.0	101.5	112.0	105.8	110.1	80.0	97.8	106.0	79.8	95.3	110.3	80.0	97.9
B20	Exterior Closure	96.6	95.9	96.3	99.1	111.0	104.8	109.7	69.6	90.6	104.6	71.4	88.8	109.6	72.6	92.0
B30	Roofing	97.5	95.6	96.8	101.0	106.3	103.0	107.5	67.7	92.6	107.4	68.0	92.6	108.0	67.0	92.6
C	Interior Construction	97.9	89.5	94.2	100.1	102.6	101.2	100.5	66.8	85.7	99.7	65.9	84.9	103.5	67.9	87.8
D10	Services: Conveying	100.0	98.5	99.6	100.0	102.3	100.6	100.0	76.1	93.5	100.0	76.2	93.6	100.0	77.7	94.0
D20 - 40	Mechanical	100.2	87.3	94.9	99.9	101.7	100.6	100.2	71.4	88.5	100.3	68.4	87.4	100.3	73.5	89.4
D50	Electrical	102.7	76.5	89.2	102.2	108.3	105.3	97.3	76.7	86.7	104.9	72.6	88.2	97.5	73.5	85.1
E	Equipment & Furnishings	100.0	84.4	99.2	100.0	102.1	100.1	100.0	66.2	98.3	100.0	63.5	98.1	100.0	66.3	98.3
G	Site Work	96.0	93.9	94.6	92.4	97.2	95.5	98.6	96.9	97.5	108.0	96.2	100.2	111.7	97.0	101.9
A-G	WEIGHTED AVERAGE	99.3	91.8	96.0	100.0	105.7	102.5	103.5	74.7	90.8	103.5	73.5	90.3	105.0	75.3	91.9

MONTANA / NEBRASKA

DIV. NO.	BUILDING SYSTEMS	HELENA MAT.	INST.	TOTAL	MISSOULA MAT.	INST.	TOTAL	GRAND ISLAND MAT.	INST.	TOTAL	LINCOLN MAT.	INST.	TOTAL	NORTH PLATTE MAT.	INST.	TOTAL
A	Substructure	104.4	72.5	85.3	96.9	74.0	82.6	110.9	78.3	91.4	89.8	73.3	80.0	111.2	76.3	90.3
B10	Shell: Superstructure	105.4	74.0	92.5	98.9	78.2	90.4	98.1	80.8	91.0	97.5	76.3	88.8	98.3	79.9	90.8
B20	Exterior Closure	105.5	66.9	87.1	109.4	69.5	90.4	101.9	78.7	90.9	96.2	68.8	83.2	94.5	86.8	90.8
B30	Roofing	107.8	70.7	93.9	106.7	67.2	91.9	98.4	74.0	89.3	98.0	71.0	87.8	98.4	76.7	90.2
C	Interior Construction	101.9	64.3	85.4	99.4	64.5	84.0	95.1	80.0	88.4	98.0	65.2	83.6	94.7	77.7	87.2
D10	Services: Conveying	100.0	77.7	94.0	100.0	75.7	93.4	100.0	83.4	95.5	100.0	83.4	95.5	100.0	70.1	91.9
D20 - 40	Mechanical	100.2	69.9	87.9	100.3	67.6	87.0	99.9	78.2	91.1	99.8	78.2	91.1	99.9	73.7	89.3
D50	Electrical	101.9	73.5	87.3	102.7	71.9	86.8	91.0	67.3	78.8	99.8	67.3	83.0	93.0	81.9	87.3
E	Equipment & Furnishings	100.0	66.1	98.3	100.0	62.3	98.1	100.0	75.8	98.8	100.0	56.2	97.8	100.0	76.2	98.8
G	Site Work	100.9	96.2	97.7	88.7	96.1	93.6	104.1	91.8	96.0	91.7	91.8	91.8	105.1	91.1	95.8
A-G	WEIGHTED AVERAGE	102.6	72.0	89.1	100.8	72.2	88.2	98.7	78.4	89.8	98.0	73.6	87.2	98.1	79.4	89.9

NEBRASKA / NEVADA / NEW HAMPSHIRE

DIV. NO.	BUILDING SYSTEMS	OMAHA MAT.	INST.	TOTAL	CARSON CITY MAT.	INST.	TOTAL	LAS VEGAS MAT.	INST.	TOTAL	RENO MAT.	INST.	TOTAL	MANCHESTER MAT.	INST.	TOTAL
A	Substructure	93.9	79.3	85.2	94.6	98.4	96.9	94.9	112.4	105.4	100.4	99.3	99.7	106.9	96.4	100.6
B10	Shell: Superstructure	98.0	77.0	89.4	94.7	100.8	97.2	99.8	112.6	105.0	96.7	102.7	99.1	100.2	91.9	96.8
B20	Exterior Closure	98.4	79.5	89.4	109.5	83.4	97.1	107.4	109.2	108.3	110.2	81.5	96.6	104.5	79.2	92.5
B30	Roofing	92.9	79.8	88.0	99.6	89.5	95.8	115.2	102.2	110.3	101.0	89.5	96.7	100.8	88.2	96.0
C	Interior Construction	110.9	74.0	94.6	98.4	95.8	97.2	99.1	114.7	105.9	98.4	96.1	97.4	100.7	90.6	96.2
D10	Services: Conveying	100.0	82.1	95.2	100.0	96.7	99.1	100.0	90.3	97.4	100.0	96.7	99.1	100.0	58.6	88.8
D20 - 40	Mechanical	99.7	78.0	90.9	99.9	84.2	93.5	100.1	108.5	103.5	100.0	84.2	93.6	99.9	83.5	93.2
D50	Electrical	99.2	82.8	90.8	91.1	98.5	94.9	98.5	116.6	107.8	94.5	98.5	96.5	100.3	81.4	90.6
E	Equipment & Furnishings	100.0	72.9	98.6	100.0	100.0	100.0	100.0	115.4	100.8	100.0	100.0	100.0	100.0	89.0	99.4
G	Site Work	80.8	91.1	87.6	70.0	101.3	90.8	64.4	103.9	90.6	62.2	101.3	88.2	89.8	98.2	95.3
A-G	WEIGHTED AVERAGE	100.0	79.2	90.8	97.8	93.5	95.9	99.8	110.7	104.6	98.7	93.7	96.5	100.7	86.7	94.5

NEW HAMPSHIRE / NEW JERSEY

DIV. NO.	BUILDING SYSTEMS	NASHUA MAT.	INST.	TOTAL	PORTSMOUTH MAT.	INST.	TOTAL	CAMDEN MAT.	INST.	TOTAL	ELIZABETH MAT.	INST.	TOTAL	JERSEY CITY MAT.	INST.	TOTAL
A	Substructure	97.6	96.4	96.9	88.7	100.4	95.7	90.8	120.1	108.4	93.6	121.3	110.2	90.8	121.4	109.1
B10	Shell: Superstructure	97.8	91.9	95.4	92.9	95.4	93.9	95.9	114.1	103.3	93.8	118.5	103.9	96.0	117.2	104.7
B20	Exterior Closure	104.1	79.2	92.2	100.0	87.4	94.0	101.6	125.8	113.1	110.8	126.6	118.3	100.3	126.4	112.8
B30	Roofing	101.6	88.2	96.5	101.3	116.0	106.8	101.2	123.7	109.7	101.8	125.9	110.8	101.1	125.9	110.4
C	Interior Construction	101.2	90.6	96.6	99.3	93.0	96.5	101.5	124.8	111.8	103.6	129.9	115.2	101.5	129.9	114.0
D10	Services: Conveying	100.0	58.6	88.8	100.0	63.1	90.0	100.0	108.6	102.3	100.0	108.5	102.3	100.0	108.5	102.3
D20 - 40	Mechanical	100.0	83.5	93.3	100.0	89.6	95.8	100.0	124.9	110.1	100.0	125.6	110.4	100.0	125.7	110.4
D50	Electrical	102.1	81.4	91.5	100.0	81.5	90.5	102.6	136.9	120.3	99.3	137.0	118.8	103.8	136.9	120.9
E	Equipment & Furnishings	100.0	89.0	99.4	100.0	89.7	99.5	100.0	124.1	101.2	100.0	124.3	101.2	100.0	124.4	101.2
G	Site Work	94.0	98.2	96.7	88.4	99.7	95.9	97.5	103.8	101.7	113.9	104.3	107.5	97.5	104.8	102.3
A-G	WEIGHTED AVERAGE	100.2	86.7	94.3	97.8	91.2	94.9	99.4	122.6	109.6	100.6	124.5	111.2	99.4	124.4	110.4

NEW JERSEY / NEW MEXICO

DIV. NO.	BUILDING SYSTEMS	NEWARK MAT.	INST.	TOTAL	PATERSON MAT.	INST.	TOTAL	TRENTON MAT.	INST.	TOTAL	ALBUQUERQUE MAT.	INST.	TOTAL	FARMINGTON MAT.	INST.	TOTAL
A	Substructure	109.2	121.3	116.4	106.2	121.4	115.3	101.6	120.3	112.8	98.4	78.6	86.6	101.0	78.6	87.6
B10	Shell: Superstructure	99.8	118.5	107.4	95.5	118.5	104.9	94.8	115.4	103.2	100.3	79.5	91.8	99.2	79.5	91.1
B20	Exterior Closure	105.6	126.6	115.6	103.5	126.6	114.5	100.1	125.8	112.3	105.3	64.6	85.9	110.9	64.6	88.9
B30	Roofing	101.3	125.9	110.5	101.7	123.0	109.7	97.2	123.9	107.2	100.5	74.7	90.8	100.9	74.7	91.1
C	Interior Construction	104.8	129.9	115.8	105.4	129.9	116.2	101.1	129.3	113.5	98.2	65.8	83.9	99.1	65.8	84.4
D10	Services: Conveying	100.0	108.5	102.3	100.0	108.5	102.3	100.0	108.5	102.3	100.0	82.2	95.2	100.0	82.2	95.2
D20 - 40	Mechanical	100.1	126.1	110.6	100.0	125.7	110.4	100.2	124.7	110.1	100.1	68.2	87.2	100.0	68.2	87.1
D50	Electrical	105.5	136.9	121.7	103.8	137.0	120.9	105.1	137.6	121.9	89.5	71.1	80.0	87.8	71.1	79.2
E	Equipment & Furnishings	100.0	124.3	101.2	100.0	124.4	101.2	100.0	124.4	101.2	100.0	65.9	98.3	100.0	65.9	98.3
G	Site Work	113.2	104.3	107.3	111.2	104.8	106.9	95.1	104.7	101.4	79.6	106.8	97.6	86.5	106.8	100.0
A-G	WEIGHTED AVERAGE	102.7	124.6	112.4	101.4	124.5	111.6	99.6	123.6	110.2	98.7	73.6	87.7	99.4	73.6	88.0

NEW MEXICO / NEW YORK

DIV. NO.	BUILDING SYSTEMS	LAS CRUCES MAT.	INST.	TOTAL	ROSWELL MAT.	INST.	TOTAL	SANTA FE MAT.	INST.	TOTAL	ALBANY MAT.	INST.	TOTAL	BINGHAMTON MAT.	INST.	TOTAL
A	Substructure	92.5	70.9	79.6	96.5	78.6	85.8	101.7	78.6	87.9	82.2	99.6	92.6	98.0	90.6	93.6
B10	Shell: Superstructure	96.8	74.6	87.7	97.9	79.5	90.4	99.2	79.5	91.1	96.6	100.8	98.3	97.5	102.3	99.4
B20	Exterior Closure	89.1	64.0	77.1	114.6	64.6	90.8	105.5	64.6	86.1	100.3	99.2	99.8	99.1	90.0	94.8
B30	Roofing	87.1	69.3	80.4	101.1	74.7	91.2	100.2	74.7	90.6	88.5	92.8	90.1	103.6	82.0	95.5
C	Interior Construction	100.2	65.0	84.7	97.3	65.8	83.5	97.8	65.8	83.7	95.4	94.3	94.9	93.4	83.1	88.9
D10	Services: Conveying	100.0	79.1	94.3	100.0	82.2	95.2	100.0	82.2	95.2	100.0	93.6	98.3	100.0	96.1	99.0
D20 - 40	Mechanical	100.3	67.9	87.2	100.0	68.2	87.1	99.9	68.2	87.1	100.0	92.1	96.8	100.4	80.7	92.4
D50	Electrical	88.4	66.3	77.0	88.6	71.1	79.6	96.6	71.1	83.4	99.2	91.6	95.3	100.7	90.2	95.3
E	Equipment & Furnishings	100.0	65.0	98.2	100.0	65.9	98.3	100.0	65.9	98.3	100.0	94.0	99.7	100.0	80.8	99.0
G	Site Work	90.6	86.0	87.5	91.1	106.8	101.5	84.0	106.8	99.1	70.1	106.8	94.5	93.4	91.8	92.4
A-G	WEIGHTED AVERAGE	96.1	69.6	84.4	99.3	73.6	88.0	99.4	73.6	88.0	96.7	96.4	96.5	98.4	89.2	94.4

NEW YORK

DIV. NO.	BUILDING SYSTEMS	BUFFALO MAT.	INST.	TOTAL	HICKSVILLE MAT.	INST.	TOTAL	NEW YORK MAT.	INST.	TOTAL	RIVERHEAD MAT.	INST.	TOTAL	ROCHESTER MAT.	INST.	TOTAL
A	Substructure	102.0	110.0	106.8	94.9	147.4	126.3	103.8	168.2	142.4	96.4	147.7	127.1	96.2	96.6	96.5
B10	Shell: Superstructure	101.8	103.6	102.5	103.5	144.0	120.1	115.2	161.2	134.0	104.4	143.6	120.5	98.2	99.1	98.6
B20	Exterior Closure	106.3	113.0	109.5	110.1	159.5	133.6	106.5	175.3	139.2	111.9	161.2	135.4	114.1	95.7	105.3
B30	Roofing	101.0	107.7	103.5	105.1	146.0	120.5	104.0	165.9	127.3	105.7	147.1	121.3	96.6	93.0	95.2
C	Interior Construction	95.9	115.1	104.3	95.7	147.0	118.3	98.3	181.6	134.9	96.1	147.3	118.6	98.7	93.1	96.3
D10	Services: Conveying	100.0	105.2	101.4	100.0	119.9	105.4	100.0	131.2	108.4	100.0	120.8	105.6	100.0	94.5	98.5
D20 - 40	Mechanical	99.9	92.8	97.0	99.7	148.7	119.6	100.0	168.4	127.7	99.9	149.8	120.1	100.0	87.1	94.8
D50	Electrical	98.6	99.7	99.2	100.1	141.0	121.2	105.0	173.3	140.3	101.7	141.0	122.0	99.2	89.6	94.2
E	Equipment & Furnishings	100.0	115.7	100.8	100.0	146.3	102.4	100.0	187.8	104.5	100.0	146.4	102.4	100.0	91.2	99.5
G	Site Work	98.2	97.2	97.6	113.3	127.3	122.6	122.0	125.6	124.4	114.7	127.4	123.1	74.8	107.5	96.5
A-G	**WEIGHTED AVERAGE**	100.3	104.0	101.9	101.3	145.6	120.8	104.8	166.9	132.2	102.1	146.1	121.5	100.0	94.0	97.3

NEW YORK

DIV. NO.	BUILDING SYSTEMS	SCHENECTADY MAT.	INST.	TOTAL	SYRACUSE MAT.	INST.	TOTAL	UTICA MAT.	INST.	TOTAL	WATERTOWN MAT.	INST.	TOTAL	WHITE PLAINS MAT.	INST.	TOTAL
A	Substructure	90.8	99.3	95.9	93.7	95.7	94.9	86.8	89.2	88.2	95.3	96.2	95.8	92.9	133.2	117.1
B10	Shell: Superstructure	99.0	100.6	99.6	99.0	98.7	98.9	96.4	93.6	95.3	97.6	99.3	98.3	101.8	134.7	115.3
B20	Exterior Closure	100.1	98.4	99.3	102.8	98.7	100.9	99.5	88.2	94.1	106.9	99.8	103.5	99.3	131.5	114.6
B30	Roofing	89.1	92.3	90.3	99.5	94.9	97.8	88.9	88.0	88.6	89.2	94.7	91.2	104.7	137.0	116.9
C	Interior Construction	95.9	94.1	95.1	94.8	89.0	92.2	95.9	83.4	90.4	94.8	89.6	92.5	91.9	139.0	112.6
D10	Services: Conveying	100.0	93.2	98.1	100.0	97.1	99.2	100.0	87.9	96.7	100.0	96.6	99.1	100.0	115.1	104.1
D20 - 40	Mechanical	100.2	91.5	96.7	100.2	88.3	95.3	100.2	78.4	91.3	100.2	83.8	93.5	100.3	117.9	107.4
D50	Electrical	100.9	91.6	96.1	100.9	94.3	97.5	99.0	94.3	96.6	100.9	91.7	96.2	95.2	157.5	127.4
E	Equipment & Furnishings	100.0	94.0	99.7	100.0	85.8	99.3	100.0	81.8	99.1	100.0	89.2	99.4	100.0	132.9	101.7
G	Site Work	71.9	106.7	95.0	92.2	106.5	101.7	70.0	104.1	92.6	77.7	106.4	96.7	114.8	119.6	118.0
A-G	**WEIGHTED AVERAGE**	97.8	96.1	97.0	98.9	94.5	97.0	96.8	88.2	93.0	98.5	93.5	96.3	98.8	133.0	113.9

NEW YORK / NORTH CAROLINA

DIV. NO.	BUILDING SYSTEMS	YONKERS MAT.	INST.	TOTAL	ASHEVILLE MAT.	INST.	TOTAL	CHARLOTTE MAT.	INST.	TOTAL	DURHAM MAT.	INST.	TOTAL	FAYETTEVILLE MAT.	INST.	TOTAL
A	Substructure	102.3	133.2	120.8	110.1	49.6	73.9	114.7	50.4	76.2	111.8	52.7	76.4	114.1	53.8	78.0
B10	Shell: Superstructure	111.4	134.7	120.9	92.2	67.9	78.1	96.5	57.9	80.7	102.8	60.3	85.4	106.4	60.9	87.7
B20	Exterior Closure	106.2	131.5	118.3	94.2	40.0	68.4	97.3	43.3	71.6	96.9	37.6	68.7	94.9	41.5	69.5
B30	Roofing	105.0	137.0	117.1	99.8	41.4	77.8	97.1	42.3	76.5	100.6	44.0	79.3	99.7	41.7	77.9
C	Interior Construction	96.2	139.0	115.0	96.9	37.9	71.0	99.2	39.6	73.0	100.1	38.9	73.2	97.3	39.1	71.8
D10	Services: Conveying	100.0	118.8	105.1	100.0	68.4	91.4	100.0	66.8	91.5	100.0	77.0	93.8	100.0	77.9	94.0
D20 - 40	Mechanical	100.3	117.9	107.4	100.2	36.9	74.6	99.9	37.1	74.5	100.3	35.8	74.2	100.2	36.9	74.5
D50	Electrical	103.3	157.5	131.3	96.6	36.6	65.7	97.2	47.6	71.6	97.5	46.3	71.1	95.6	50.5	72.3
E	Equipment & Furnishings	100.0	132.8	101.7	100.0	35.9	96.7	100.0	38.4	96.8	100.0	37.5	96.8	100.0	37.8	96.8
G	Site Work	121.5	119.4	120.1	108.9	74.9	86.3	110.1	74.9	86.8	109.0	83.5	92.1	108.1	83.6	91.9
A-G	**WEIGHTED AVERAGE**	103.5	133.1	116.5	97.8	45.5	74.7	99.4	47.8	76.7	100.8	47.9	77.5	100.7	49.4	78.1

NORTH CAROLINA / NORTH DAKOTA

DIV. NO.	BUILDING SYSTEMS	GREENSBORO MAT.	INST.	TOTAL	RALEIGH MAT.	INST.	TOTAL	WILMINGTON MAT.	INST.	TOTAL	WINSTON-SALEM MAT.	INST.	TOTAL	BISMARCK MAT.	INST.	TOTAL
A	Substructure	111.0	54.4	77.1	116.3	55.0	79.6	110.0	53.5	76.2	112.9	51.0	75.8	103.4	63.4	79.4
B10	Shell: Superstructure	98.1	62.8	83.6	97.6	61.4	82.8	92.1	61.7	79.6	96.8	56.9	80.4	97.7	69.8	86.3
B20	Exterior Closure	96.0	38.4	68.6	95.9	42.1	70.3	89.5	42.5	67.1	96.1	38.5	68.7	99.9	60.0	80.9
B30	Roofing	100.3	41.7	78.3	99.3	42.0	77.8	99.8	47.2	80.0	100.3	40.9	78.0	107.6	50.7	86.2
C	Interior Construction	100.2	39.1	73.3	97.8	40.0	72.4	97.3	44.0	73.9	100.2	38.1	72.9	105.7	45.8	79.4
D10	Services: Conveying	100.0	68.4	91.5	100.0	78.2	94.1	100.0	78.9	94.3	100.0	68.1	91.4	100.0	87.0	96.5
D20 - 40	Mechanical	100.2	37.0	74.6	100.0	35.3	73.8	100.2	38.3	75.1	100.2	35.7	74.1	100.3	60.7	84.3
D50	Electrical	96.4	36.8	65.7	100.6	36.5	67.5	96.8	36.9	65.9	96.4	40.1	67.4	98.1	71.7	84.5
E	Equipment & Furnishings	100.0	37.1	96.8	100.0	37.8	96.8	100.0	42.7	97.1	100.0	36.7	96.8	100.0	38.5	96.8
G	Site Work	108.8	83.6	92.1	109.7	83.7	92.4	110.1	75.1	86.9	109.2	83.6	92.2	98.8	97.3	97.8
A-G	**WEIGHTED AVERAGE**	99.7	47.3	76.6	99.8	47.6	76.8	97.4	48.5	75.8	99.5	46.0	75.9	100.7	64.4	84.7

NORTH DAKOTA / OHIO

DIV. NO.	BUILDING SYSTEMS	FARGO MAT.	INST.	TOTAL	GRAND FORKS MAT.	INST.	TOTAL	MINOT MAT.	INST.	TOTAL	AKRON MAT.	INST.	TOTAL	CANTON MAT.	INST.	TOTAL
A	Substructure	101.3	64.1	79.1	111.0	59.5	80.2	111.0	69.6	86.2	94.7	96.7	95.9	95.3	90.5	92.4
B10	Shell: Superstructure	99.0	70.4	87.3	98.9	65.0	85.0	99.1	75.0	89.2	93.4	87.7	91.1	93.5	80.4	88.2
B20	Exterior Closure	110.3	60.0	86.4	106.8	62.7	85.8	104.8	64.6	85.6	95.5	94.8	95.2	95.1	84.9	90.2
B30	Roofing	105.9	51.9	85.6	108.7	45.9	85.1	108.4	53.9	87.9	107.3	97.1	103.5	108.3	93.7	102.8
C	Interior Construction	105.7	50.0	81.2	107.0	36.3	75.9	106.4	61.8	86.8	105.8	92.5	100.0	102.5	81.2	93.1
D10	Services: Conveying	100.0	87.0	96.5	100.0	35.2	82.5	100.0	87.0	96.5	100.0	94.4	98.5	100.0	93.0	98.1
D20 - 40	Mechanical	100.3	66.0	86.4	100.4	35.6	74.2	100.4	60.7	84.3	100.0	97.0	98.8	100.0	83.9	93.5
D50	Electrical	99.7	66.9	82.8	99.9	56.9	77.7	103.1	80.4	91.4	97.9	94.5	96.1	97.2	90.9	93.9
E	Equipment & Furnishings	100.0	38.7	96.9	100.0	34.3	96.6	100.0	61.8	98.0	100.0	91.1	99.5	100.0	80.9	99.0
G	Site Work	99.4	97.3	98.0	112.0	94.0	100.0	109.2	97.3	101.3	92.3	104.9	100.7	92.5	104.4	100.4
A-G	**WEIGHTED AVERAGE**	102.1	65.7	86.0	102.8	53.1	80.9	102.7	70.2	88.4	98.7	94.5	96.9	98.2	86.3	93.0

OHIO

DIV. NO.	BUILDING SYSTEMS	CINCINNATI MAT.	INST.	TOTAL	CLEVELAND MAT.	INST.	TOTAL	COLUMBUS MAT.	INST.	TOTAL	DAYTON MAT.	INST.	TOTAL	LORAIN MAT.	INST.	TOTAL
A	Substructure	91.5	89.1	90.1	93.7	100.9	98.0	92.7	91.7	92.1	87.3	88.8	88.2	91.8	96.4	94.6
B10	Shell: Superstructure	94.6	84.1	90.3	94.4	91.3	93.1	94.1	84.4	90.1	93.0	80.3	87.8	93.2	87.6	90.9
B20	Exterior Closure	89.3	86.6	88.0	96.1	101.4	98.7	95.1	92.5	93.9	89.1	83.3	86.3	93.2	96.4	94.7
B30	Roofing	99.3	91.8	96.5	105.9	109.0	107.1	100.8	95.4	98.7	104.2	89.9	98.9	108.3	101.2	105.6
C	Interior Construction	100.9	82.6	92.9	99.9	98.2	99.2	100.3	86.9	94.4	101.5	81.2	92.6	102.4	91.1	97.4
D10	Services: Conveying	100.0	94.0	98.4	100.0	98.8	99.7	100.0	95.9	98.9	100.0	93.4	98.2	100.0	96.5	99.1
D20 - 40	Mechanical	99.9	83.0	93.1	99.9	98.8	99.5	99.9	93.5	97.3	100.6	84.8	94.2	100.0	84.7	93.8
D50	Electrical	97.7	80.4	88.8	97.5	107.4	102.6	98.7	88.1	93.2	96.3	83.8	89.9	97.4	89.9	93.5
E	Equipment & Furnishings	100.0	80.2	99.0	100.0	95.5	99.8	100.0	85.3	99.2	100.0	80.5	99.0	100.0	84.9	99.2
G	Site Work	86.4	106.3	99.6	92.3	105.1	100.8	94.0	101.0	98.7	85.4	106.3	99.3	91.7	103.8	99.7
A-G	**WEIGHTED AVERAGE**	96.9	85.8	92.0	97.9	99.8	98.7	97.8	90.6	94.6	96.7	85.2	91.6	97.7	91.3	94.9

OHIO / OKLAHOMA

DIV. NO.	BUILDING SYSTEMS	SPRINGFIELD MAT.	INST.	TOTAL	TOLEDO MAT.	INST.	TOTAL	YOUNGSTOWN MAT.	INST.	TOTAL	ENID MAT.	INST.	TOTAL	LAWTON MAT.	INST.	TOTAL
A	Substructure	88.7	89.5	89.2	92.5	98.5	96.1	94.1	93.9	94.0	95.2	55.7	71.6	93.3	60.2	73.4
B10	Shell: Superstructure	93.3	81.0	88.3	93.9	91.9	93.1	93.3	84.5	89.7	93.1	57.7	78.6	95.6	60.9	81.4
B20	Exterior Closure	88.7	83.0	86.0	98.7	98.5	98.6	94.9	91.5	93.3	103.0	55.4	80.4	98.2	55.9	78.1
B30	Roofing	104.1	90.6	99.0	102.5	103.9	103.0	108.4	95.0	103.4	97.6	55.9	82.0	97.4	57.8	82.5
C	Interior Construction	100.5	84.0	93.2	98.9	96.3	97.7	102.4	86.5	95.4	93.2	36.8	68.4	95.1	46.5	73.7
D10	Services: Conveying	100.0	93.5	98.3	100.0	98.9	99.7	100.0	93.5	98.2	100.0	77.1	93.8	100.0	77.1	93.8
D20 - 40	Mechanical	100.6	85.0	94.3	100.0	99.2	99.7	100.0	92.1	96.8	100.3	61.3	84.5	100.3	61.3	84.5
D50	Electrical	96.3	84.0	89.9	98.7	104.1	101.5	97.4	86.1	91.5	95.5	68.6	81.6	97.1	68.6	82.4
E	Equipment & Furnishings	100.0	84.3	99.2	100.0	95.6	99.8	100.0	83.6	99.2	100.0	31.4	96.5	100.0	46.0	97.2
G	Site Work	85.7	105.0	98.5	93.3	101.9	99.0	92.2	105.3	100.9	102.5	89.3	93.7	98.0	90.7	93.2
A-G	WEIGHTED AVERAGE	96.6	85.8	91.8	97.9	98.3	98.1	98.1	90.1	94.6	97.3	58.7	80.3	97.5	61.4	81.6

OKLAHOMA / OREGON

DIV. NO.	BUILDING SYSTEMS	MUSKOGEE MAT.	INST.	TOTAL	OKLAHOMA CITY MAT.	INST.	TOTAL	TULSA MAT.	INST.	TOTAL	EUGENE MAT.	INST.	TOTAL	MEDFORD MAT.	INST.	TOTAL
A	Substructure	87.9	45.1	62.3	93.7	58.9	72.8	93.6	51.7	71.7	99.1	100.7	100.1	101.5	100.7	101.0
B10	Shell: Superstructure	91.9	45.3	72.8	97.1	59.5	81.7	95.5	64.9	83.0	90.2	98.2	93.5	89.9	98.2	93.3
B20	Exterior Closure	104.4	44.3	75.8	98.0	57.0	78.5	97.8	57.8	78.7	102.7	107.4	104.9	107.2	107.4	107.3
B30	Roofing	97.3	38.6	75.2	94.2	57.6	80.4	97.2	51.7	80.2	104.6	89.7	99.0	105.2	91.4	100.0
C	Interior Construction	94.1	31.6	66.6	95.1	41.3	71.5	94.8	41.3	71.3	100.9	94.0	97.8	103.4	93.3	99.0
D10	Services: Conveying	100.0	77.0	93.8	100.0	77.8	94.0	100.0	78.3	94.1	100.0	104.5	101.2	100.0	104.5	101.2
D20 - 40	Mechanical	100.3	23.4	69.1	100.2	62.1	84.7	100.3	47.3	78.8	100.1	97.6	99.1	100.1	97.6	99.1
D50	Electrical	95.1	28.0	60.5	98.7	68.6	83.2	97.1	36.5	65.9	99.1	93.9	96.4	102.6	83.4	92.7
E	Equipment & Furnishings	100.0	29.0	96.4	100.0	37.8	96.8	100.0	37.2	96.8	100.0	91.7	99.6	100.0	91.2	99.6
G	Site Work	89.7	84.9	86.5	96.6	91.3	93.1	95.5	86.3	89.4	101.8	103.9	103.2	109.9	103.9	105.9
A-G	WEIGHTED AVERAGE	96.7	39.3	71.4	97.8	60.6	81.4	97.4	53.5	78.0	98.6	98.5	98.6	100.1	97.0	98.7

OREGON / PENNSYLVANIA

DIV. NO.	BUILDING SYSTEMS	PORTLAND MAT.	INST.	TOTAL	SALEM MAT.	INST.	TOTAL	ALLENTOWN MAT.	INST.	TOTAL	ALTOONA MAT.	INST.	TOTAL	ERIE MAT.	INST.	TOTAL
A	Substructure	101.1	100.8	100.9	93.5	100.7	97.9	88.2	109.1	100.7	93.7	88.8	90.7	93.8	91.8	92.6
B10	Shell: Superstructure	91.3	98.4	94.2	89.2	98.3	92.9	98.0	117.8	106.1	93.6	98.1	95.4	94.5	100.0	96.8
B20	Exterior Closure	102.4	107.4	104.8	104.8	107.4	106.0	100.2	106.1	103.0	92.7	72.4	83.0	86.5	90.4	88.4
B30	Roofing	104.5	96.1	101.4	102.5	93.1	99.0	99.5	119.6	107.0	98.8	92.5	96.4	99.2	94.0	97.2
C	Interior Construction	99.6	94.0	97.2	100.3	94.0	97.5	93.7	109.0	100.4	89.8	84.7	87.5	90.8	89.3	90.1
D10	Services: Conveying	100.0	104.5	101.2	100.0	104.5	101.2	100.0	105.2	101.4	100.0	97.8	99.4	100.0	103.2	100.9
D20 - 40	Mechanical	100.1	100.9	100.4	100.1	97.6	99.1	100.2	112.2	105.0	99.7	83.7	93.2	99.7	93.0	97.0
D50	Electrical	99.4	100.2	99.8	103.5	93.9	98.6	99.9	97.7	98.7	89.8	107.8	99.1	91.7	87.4	89.5
E	Equipment & Furnishings	100.0	92.0	99.6	100.0	91.7	99.6	100.0	114.0	100.7	100.0	82.1	99.1	100.0	85.7	99.3
G	Site Work	104.9	103.9	104.2	97.3	103.9	101.7	91.1	105.7	100.8	93.9	105.3	101.5	90.6	106.0	100.8
A-G	WEIGHTED AVERAGE	98.8	100.3	99.5	98.6	98.6	98.6	97.9	109.2	102.9	94.8	90.6	93.0	94.6	93.6	94.1

PENNSYLVANIA

DIV. NO.	BUILDING SYSTEMS	HARRISBURG MAT.	INST.	TOTAL	PHILADELPHIA MAT.	INST.	TOTAL	PITTSBURGH MAT.	INST.	TOTAL	READING MAT.	INST.	TOTAL	SCRANTON MAT.	INST.	TOTAL
A	Substructure	88.8	97.3	93.9	99.6	125.8	115.3	102.4	101.2	101.7	82.5	97.1	91.2	90.5	96.6	94.2
B10	Shell: Superstructure	99.9	107.5	103.0	102.9	133.9	115.6	99.1	111.4	104.1	96.1	106.3	100.3	100.2	107.9	103.3
B20	Exterior Closure	98.4	94.5	96.5	98.5	131.0	114.0	97.3	105.3	101.1	99.0	97.2	98.1	100.4	98.3	99.4
B30	Roofing	105.2	110.6	107.2	98.3	133.5	111.5	104.9	101.5	103.6	97.8	110.3	102.5	99.4	97.3	98.6
C	Interior Construction	93.3	92.1	92.8	98.2	138.6	116.0	96.8	101.1	98.7	95.3	88.5	92.3	94.7	94.1	94.5
D10	Services: Conveying	100.0	99.4	99.8	100.0	116.7	104.5	100.0	104.3	101.2	100.0	101.8	100.5	100.0	98.5	99.6
D20 - 40	Mechanical	100.0	92.2	96.9	99.9	128.4	111.5	100.0	100.1	100.1	100.0	107.9	103.2	100.2	100.5	100.3
D50	Electrical	96.7	85.8	91.1	99.1	142.8	121.7	95.5	107.9	101.9	101.3	90.2	95.6	99.9	94.5	97.1
E	Equipment & Furnishings	100.0	89.3	99.5	100.0	135.9	101.8	100.0	96.2	99.8	100.0	82.8	99.1	100.0	86.9	99.3
G	Site Work	82.1	104.6	97.0	98.3	98.4	98.4	108.3	106.7	107.2	95.4	110.9	105.7	91.6	105.9	101.1
A-G	WEIGHTED AVERAGE	97.7	96.1	97.0	99.9	130.9	113.6	99.1	104.6	101.5	97.6	100.0	98.6	98.6	99.5	99.0

PENNSYLVANIA / PUERTO RICO / RHODE ISLAND / SOUTH CAROLINA

DIV. NO.	BUILDING SYSTEMS	YORK MAT.	INST.	TOTAL	SAN JUAN MAT.	INST.	TOTAL	PROVIDENCE MAT.	INST.	TOTAL	CHARLESTON MAT.	INST.	TOTAL	COLUMBIA MAT.	INST.	TOTAL
A	Substructure	84.1	96.1	91.3	124.7	37.7	72.6	101.5	113.1	108.4	105.8	56.4	76.2	107.3	56.2	76.7
B10	Shell: Superstructure	96.6	106.7	100.7	113.7	28.6	78.8	99.0	112.3	104.5	91.6	63.1	79.9	92.1	62.5	80.0
B20	Exterior Closure	101.9	93.5	97.9	100.5	17.0	60.8	111.4	120.4	115.7	99.8	41.9	72.2	97.1	40.1	70.0
B30	Roofing	98.4	109.7	102.6	129.1	22.4	89.0	99.1	112.6	104.2	99.9	42.7	78.4	98.7	41.7	77.3
C	Interior Construction	90.8	89.9	90.4	177.7	16.1	106.7	96.7	120.7	107.2	100.6	44.2	75.8	98.8	41.4	73.6
D10	Services: Conveying	100.0	98.9	99.7	100.0	17.2	77.6	100.0	101.3	100.4	100.0	74.2	93.0	100.0	74.2	93.0
D20 - 40	Mechanical	100.2	91.7	96.7	102.8	13.3	66.5	99.9	108.3	103.3	100.2	39.9	75.8	99.9	35.3	73.7
D50	Electrical	93.5	85.8	89.5	130.6	12.6	69.7	99.7	99.0	99.3	96.2	94.3	95.2	95.2	48.2	71.0
E	Equipment & Furnishings	100.0	86.2	99.3	100.0	15.5	95.7	100.0	116.2	100.8	100.0	41.8	97.0	100.0	39.2	96.9
G	Site Work	81.4	104.5	96.8	131.3	90.4	104.2	88.2	103.0	98.0	101.5	83.6	89.6	99.6	83.6	89.0
A-G	WEIGHTED AVERAGE	96.3	95.2	95.8	121.3	24.1	78.4	100.2	111.1	105.0	98.4	57.4	80.3	97.8	49.3	76.4

SOUTH CAROLINA / SOUTH DAKOTA

DIV. NO.	BUILDING SYSTEMS	FLORENCE MAT.	INST.	TOTAL	GREENVILLE MAT.	INST.	TOTAL	SPARTANBURG MAT.	INST.	TOTAL	ABERDEEN MAT.	INST.	TOTAL	PIERRE MAT.	INST.	TOTAL
A	Substructure	96.6	56.1	72.3	96.7	54.3	71.3	96.9	54.3	71.4	105.4	54.5	75.0	94.1	57.0	71.9
B10	Shell: Superstructure	87.7	62.6	77.4	88.4	59.4	76.5	88.6	59.4	76.6	103.3	54.8	83.5	100.7	60.8	84.3
B20	Exterior Closure	98.2	41.8	71.4	95.0	41.4	69.5	96.0	41.4	70.0	101.5	55.7	79.7	99.4	55.0	78.3
B30	Roofing	100.3	42.6	78.6	100.2	42.6	78.5	100.2	42.6	78.6	107.3	47.1	84.7	107.1	45.4	83.9
C	Interior Construction	97.1	41.8	72.8	98.0	43.1	73.9	98.3	43.1	74.1	101.4	40.6	74.7	101.3	40.6	74.6
D10	Services: Conveying	100.0	74.2	93.0	100.0	74.2	93.0	100.0	74.2	93.0	100.0	44.5	85.0	100.0	78.9	94.3
D20 - 40	Mechanical	100.2	35.3	73.9	100.2	33.9	73.3	100.2	33.9	73.3	100.2	42.7	76.9	100.1	42.4	76.7
D50	Electrical	94.2	45.9	69.3	96.2	49.6	72.2	96.2	49.6	72.2	100.3	54.4	76.6	100.1	52.1	75.3
E	Equipment & Furnishings	100.0	39.1	96.9	100.0	39.2	96.9	100.0	39.2	96.9	100.0	38.3	96.8	100.0	39.0	96.9
G	Site Work	111.8	83.6	93.1	106.5	83.2	91.1	106.3	83.2	91.0	98.5	94.8	96.0	93.7	94.8	94.4
A-G	WEIGHTED AVERAGE	96.6	49.3	75.8	96.6	49.0	75.6	96.8	49.0	75.7	101.6	52.2	79.8	100.1	53.8	79.7

DIV. NO.	BUILDING SYSTEMS	SOUTH DAKOTA RAPID CITY MAT.	INST.	TOTAL	SIOUX FALLS MAT.	INST.	TOTAL	TENNESSEE CHATTANOOGA MAT.	INST.	TOTAL	JACKSON MAT.	INST.	TOTAL	JOHNSON CITY MAT.	INST.	TOTAL
A	Substructure	102.2	56.5	74.8	96.5	58.5	73.8	96.6	69.3	80.3	99.1	62.7	77.3	84.9	60.9	70.5
B10	Shell: Superstructure	104.1	60.5	86.2	102.8	61.9	86.1	96.1	74.9	87.4	93.9	71.1	84.6	90.4	69.9	82.0
B20	Exterior Closure	100.6	55.8	79.3	97.5	56.7	78.1	99.4	53.5	77.6	107.7	52.7	81.5	121.6	49.6	87.3
B30	Roofing	107.7	47.1	84.9	109.6	48.3	86.5	95.5	60.3	82.3	92.5	50.4	76.7	91.0	55.7	77.7
C	Interior Construction	103.4	44.6	77.5	103.0	48.8	79.2	99.0	58.3	81.1	97.5	47.9	75.7	98.4	41.7	73.4
D10	Services: Conveying	100.0	79.2	94.4	100.0	78.9	94.3	100.0	42.5	84.4	100.0	46.3	85.5	100.0	47.6	85.8
D20-40	Mechanical	100.2	42.9	77.0	100.2	41.2	76.3	100.2	63.3	85.2	100.0	71.6	88.5	99.9	56.3	82.2
D50	Electrical	97.0	52.1	73.8	99.2	63.1	80.6	102.4	69.3	85.3	102.5	62.1	81.7	92.3	49.2	70.1
E	Equipment & Furnishings	100.0	35.7	96.7	100.0	42.1	97.0	100.0	58.7	97.9	100.0	48.0	97.3	100.0	39.0	96.9
G	Site Work	96.4	94.9	95.4	94.1	96.5	95.7	100.9	98.4	99.2	98.4	96.9	97.4	108.4	87.2	94.4
A-G	WEIGHTED AVERAGE	101.4	54.6	80.7	100.7	57.1	81.5	99.0	66.2	84.6	99.2	63.8	83.6	98.7	56.7	80.2

DIV. NO.	BUILDING SYSTEMS	TENNESSEE KNOXVILLE MAT.	INST.	TOTAL	MEMPHIS MAT.	INST.	TOTAL	NASHVILLE MAT.	INST.	TOTAL	TEXAS ABILENE MAT.	INST.	TOTAL	AMARILLO MAT.	INST.	TOTAL
A	Substructure	90.5	58.6	71.4	92.8	69.5	78.9	89.5	73.1	79.7	95.0	55.1	71.1	94.6	61.9	75.0
B10	Shell: Superstructure	95.6	68.8	84.6	96.7	77.0	88.6	95.8	77.9	88.5	98.4	57.8	81.8	98.3	62.2	83.5
B20	Exterior Closure	87.3	55.8	72.3	95.9	64.8	81.1	90.6	61.1	76.6	98.3	56.9	78.6	98.3	58.8	79.5
B30	Roofing	89.0	60.1	78.1	90.1	63.8	80.2	93.8	61.9	81.8	97.4	47.7	78.7	97.4	51.4	80.1
C	Interior Construction	93.0	46.4	72.5	98.8	56.8	80.3	98.9	65.3	84.1	93.5	46.4	72.8	93.7	57.4	77.7
D10	Services: Conveying	100.0	50.6	86.6	100.0	83.8	95.6	100.0	84.1	95.7	100.0	81.2	94.9	100.0	73.3	92.8
D20-40	Mechanical	99.9	66.7	86.5	100.0	70.2	87.9	100.0	77.3	90.8	100.3	45.2	78.0	100.2	51.2	80.3
D50	Electrical	97.9	58.1	77.3	103.7	65.9	84.2	95.6	61.9	78.2	97.3	50.5	73.1	99.5	67.1	82.8
E	Equipment & Furnishings	100.0	39.9	96.9	100.0	60.7	98.0	100.0	64.3	98.2	100.0	38.5	96.9	100.0	56.3	97.8
G	Site Work	87.5	87.7	87.7	89.9	93.1	92.0	96.2	99.3	98.3	96.0	86.0	89.3	96.0	87.1	90.1
A-G	WEIGHTED AVERAGE	95.4	61.4	80.4	98.2	69.6	85.6	96.8	72.2	86.0	97.9	54.2	78.6	98.1	61.0	81.7

DIV. NO.	BUILDING SYSTEMS	TEXAS AUSTIN MAT.	INST.	TOTAL	BEAUMONT MAT.	INST.	TOTAL	CORPUS CHRISTI MAT.	INST.	TOTAL	DALLAS MAT.	INST.	TOTAL	EL PASO MAT.	INST.	TOTAL
A	Substructure	91.2	59.7	72.4	87.6	58.7	70.3	104.8	52.6	73.5	98.9	66.2	79.3	90.6	54.2	68.8
B10	Shell: Superstructure	94.6	59.0	80.0	95.4	58.4	80.3	96.0	60.1	81.3	99.7	71.1	88.0	97.3	55.0	80.0
B20	Exterior Closure	93.3	49.8	72.6	103.3	57.8	81.7	92.8	49.8	72.3	100.6	59.0	80.8	97.3	48.0	73.8
B30	Roofing	86.6	50.3	72.9	103.6	54.8	85.3	95.3	43.7	75.9	92.5	64.3	81.9	93.5	52.6	78.2
C	Interior Construction	93.9	50.7	74.9	93.2	53.0	75.6	101.7	43.9	76.3	99.2	61.2	82.5	93.6	47.8	73.4
D10	Services: Conveying	100.0	80.9	94.8	100.0	84.3	95.5	100.0	82.2	95.2	100.0	84.1	95.7	100.0	82.0	95.1
D20-40	Mechanical	100.1	55.3	82.0	100.1	59.3	83.6	100.1	40.1	75.8	100.0	63.7	85.3	100.2	35.4	73.9
D50	Electrical	96.4	64.5	79.9	94.8	72.6	83.4	92.7	54.7	73.1	95.5	67.6	81.1	93.9	53.3	72.9
E	Equipment & Furnishings	100.0	56.4	97.8	100.0	50.8	97.5	100.0	37.8	96.8	100.0	66.4	98.3	100.0	46.8	97.3
G	Site Work	98.4	86.7	90.6	88.2	86.2	86.9	133.3	82.0	99.3	109.0	87.0	94.4	93.4	85.3	88.1
A-G	WEIGHTED AVERAGE	96.1	58.8	79.6	97.2	62.0	81.7	98.9	52.3	78.4	99.4	66.8	85.0	96.8	51.2	76.7

DIV. NO.	BUILDING SYSTEMS	TEXAS FORT WORTH MAT.	INST.	TOTAL	HOUSTON MAT.	INST.	TOTAL	LAREDO MAT.	INST.	TOTAL	LUBBOCK MAT.	INST.	TOTAL	ODESSA MAT.	INST.	TOTAL
A	Substructure	96.8	64.4	77.4	92.4	69.8	78.8	83.1	56.9	67.4	99.7	59.4	75.6	95.1	53.9	70.4
B10	Shell: Superstructure	96.3	64.3	83.2	98.5	77.1	89.7	93.4	55.7	77.9	101.2	67.6	87.4	97.9	56.4	80.9
B20	Exterior Closure	98.7	58.2	79.4	99.9	68.0	84.7	97.4	47.7	73.7	98.6	56.5	78.5	98.3	44.6	72.7
B30	Roofing	98.2	52.9	81.2	94.8	66.8	84.3	91.3	48.0	75.0	87.8	50.4	73.7	97.4	42.9	76.9
C	Interior Construction	93.4	59.8	78.7	100.9	60.7	83.3	94.0	43.5	71.8	99.4	51.1	78.2	93.5	41.9	70.8
D10	Services: Conveying	100.0	83.8	95.6	100.0	86.5	96.3	100.0	79.8	94.5	100.0	80.9	94.8	100.0	82.4	95.3
D20-40	Mechanical	100.2	59.1	83.5	100.0	66.6	86.5	100.0	38.8	75.2	99.9	44.3	77.3	100.3	44.4	77.6
D50	Electrical	93.4	62.4	77.4	96.5	67.5	81.5	94.3	62.2	77.7	95.9	51.5	73.0	97.4	41.8	68.8
E	Equipment & Furnishings	100.0	66.1	98.3	100.0	62.0	98.1	100.0	38.1	96.8	100.0	55.4	97.7	100.0	38.6	96.9
G	Site Work	97.7	86.4	90.2	104.6	85.0	91.6	97.7	86.4	90.2	118.2	83.9	95.4	96.0	86.3	89.5
A-G	WEIGHTED AVERAGE	97.2	63.2	82.2	99.1	69.8	86.2	95.8	52.7	76.8	99.6	56.8	80.7	97.8	50.2	76.8

DIV. NO.	BUILDING SYSTEMS	TEXAS SAN ANTONIO MAT.	INST.	TOTAL	WACO MAT.	INST.	TOTAL	WICHITA FALLS MAT.	INST.	TOTAL	UTAH LOGAN MAT.	INST.	TOTAL	OGDEN MAT.	INST.	TOTAL
A	Substructure	83.4	66.9	73.5	89.1	56.1	69.4	92.8	53.6	69.3	91.0	74.7	81.3	90.1	74.7	80.9
B10	Shell: Superstructure	94.0	63.9	81.7	97.0	56.9	80.6	97.9	56.8	81.0	97.8	71.9	87.1	98.3	71.9	87.5
B20	Exterior Closure	97.3	59.3	79.2	99.9	53.9	78.0	100.1	57.0	79.6	114.5	61.5	89.2	101.0	61.5	82.2
B30	Roofing	90.9	64.7	81.1	97.9	47.2	78.8	97.9	48.9	79.5	99.6	64.3	86.4	98.5	64.3	85.6
C	Interior Construction	95.2	56.5	78.2	93.0	39.7	69.6	93.2	44.9	72.0	95.1	58.4	79.0	94.1	58.4	78.4
D10	Services: Conveying	100.0	84.5	95.8	100.0	83.8	95.6	100.0	73.0	92.7	100.0	56.8	88.3	100.0	56.8	88.3
D20-40	Mechanical	99.9	66.1	86.2	100.3	51.3	80.4	100.3	46.6	78.5	100.0	71.3	88.4	100.0	71.3	88.4
D50	Electrical	94.7	62.3	78.0	97.5	67.6	82.0	99.2	57.9	77.9	94.5	73.7	83.8	94.8	73.7	83.9
E	Equipment & Furnishings	100.0	55.3	97.7	100.0	37.6	96.8	100.0	36.7	96.8	100.0	59.0	97.9	100.0	59.0	97.9
G	Site Work	97.4	91.3	93.3	94.7	86.4	89.2	95.5	86.0	89.2	90.2	98.3	95.6	79.1	98.3	91.9
A-G	WEIGHTED AVERAGE	96.2	65.0	82.4	97.4	56.4	79.4	98.0	54.8	79.0	99.2	70.0	86.3	97.3	70.0	85.3

DIV. NO.	BUILDING SYSTEMS	UTAH PROVO MAT.	INST.	TOTAL	SALT LAKE CITY MAT.	INST.	TOTAL	VERMONT BURLINGTON MAT.	INST.	TOTAL	RUTLAND MAT.	INST.	TOTAL	VIRGINIA ALEXANDRIA MAT.	INST.	TOTAL
A	Substructure	92.2	74.3	81.5	95.7	74.6	83.1	102.1	79.4	88.5	95.9	79.4	86.0	110.5	81.6	93.2
B10	Shell: Superstructure	96.8	71.8	86.6	103.3	71.8	90.4	100.5	75.0	90.0	97.8	75.0	88.5	99.0	87.1	94.1
B20	Exterior Closure	116.5	61.5	90.3	122.1	61.5	93.3	108.8	49.9	80.8	99.7	49.9	76.0	100.7	74.4	88.2
B30	Roofing	101.5	64.3	87.5	105.1	64.3	89.8	100.7	60.4	85.6	100.9	60.9	85.9	98.5	82.1	92.4
C	Interior Construction	97.6	57.4	79.9	95.4	57.4	78.7	99.6	51.0	78.2	99.8	51.0	78.3	100.7	76.8	90.2
D10	Services: Conveying	100.0	56.8	88.3	100.0	56.8	88.3	100.0	73.4	92.8	100.0	73.4	92.8	100.0	91.3	97.6
D20-40	Mechanical	100.0	71.3	88.4	100.1	71.3	88.4	99.9	62.1	84.5	100.0	62.1	84.6	100.2	88.8	95.6
D50	Electrical	95.4	63.5	78.9	97.8	63.5	80.1	99.4	64.9	81.6	102.0	64.9	82.9	96.3	102.5	99.5
E	Equipment & Furnishings	100.0	58.5	97.9	100.0	58.5	97.9	100.0	49.7	97.4	100.0	49.7	97.4	100.0	75.0	98.7
G	Site Work	87.1	96.6	93.4	78.9	98.3	91.7	84.5	96.5	92.5	85.0	96.5	92.6	120.7	88.0	99.0
A-G	WEIGHTED AVERAGE	99.7	68.3	85.8	101.6	68.4	86.9	100.6	65.4	85.1	99.2	65.4	84.3	100.6	86.0	94.2

Cost Indexes

DIV. NO.	BUILDING SYSTEMS	VIRGINIA ARLINGTON MAT.	INST.	TOTAL	NEWPORT NEWS MAT.	INST.	TOTAL	NORFOLK MAT.	INST.	TOTAL	PORTSMOUTH MAT.	INST.	TOTAL	RICHMOND MAT.	INST.	TOTAL
A	Substructure	112.3	77.3	91.4	112.1	70.7	87.3	118.8	71.0	90.2	110.5	65.9	83.8	108.9	66.8	83.7
B10	Shell: Superstructure	97.8	78.5	89.9	100.2	79.0	90.9	100.2	79.1	91.5	97.6	74.1	88.0	99.2	76.2	90.4
B20	Exterior Closure	111.1	68.2	90.7	100.2	56.7	79.5	103.0	56.7	81.0	102.8	55.9	80.4	99.2	58.1	79.6
B30	Roofing	100.5	67.9	88.3	99.9	55.6	83.3	97.3	55.6	81.6	100.0	52.9	82.3	98.5	55.0	82.2
C	Interior Construction	99.7	71.1	87.2	100.2	63.2	83.9	99.3	65.3	84.4	98.8	57.4	80.6	100.5	62.8	83.9
D10	Services: Conveying	100.0	69.7	91.8	100.0	79.7	94.5	100.0	79.7	94.5	100.0	79.7	94.5	100.0	75.0	93.2
D20-40	Mechanical	100.2	84.6	93.9	100.2	63.9	85.5	100.0	63.7	85.3	100.2	62.1	84.8	100.0	55.0	81.8
D50	Electrical	94.0	98.3	96.2	96.0	60.4	77.6	101.2	59.9	79.9	94.3	59.8	76.5	99.3	71.0	84.7
E	Equipment & Furnishings	100.0	74.5	98.7	100.0	67.8	98.4	100.0	67.8	98.4	100.0	53.1	97.6	100.0	60.7	98.0
G	Site Work	131.2	84.7	100.3	112.8	87.0	95.7	111.4	88.0	95.8	111.1	86.3	94.6	110.4	87.3	95.1
A-G	WEIGHTED AVERAGE	101.6	79.9	92.0	100.4	67.3	85.8	101.4	67.6	86.5	99.9	64.4	84.3	100.6	66.0	85.3

DIV. NO.	BUILDING SYSTEMS	VIRGINIA ROANOKE MAT.	INST.	TOTAL	WASHINGTON EVERETT MAT.	INST.	TOTAL	RICHLAND MAT.	INST.	TOTAL	SEATTLE MAT.	INST.	TOTAL	SPOKANE MAT.	INST.	TOTAL
A	Substructure	120.6	68.5	89.4	104.1	104.6	104.4	101.9	84.5	91.5	106.9	104.7	105.6	105.0	84.5	92.7
B10	Shell: Superstructure	101.2	76.1	90.9	102.1	96.9	100.0	91.3	82.4	87.6	103.6	98.4	101.5	94.0	82.3	89.2
B20	Exterior Closure	100.7	57.6	80.2	104.7	99.5	102.3	100.5	79.6	90.6	103.3	99.7	101.6	100.9	79.7	90.9
B30	Roofing	99.9	54.0	82.7	102.4	99.3	101.3	152.9	78.2	124.8	102.3	99.3	101.2	149.3	79.2	123.0
C	Interior Construction	100.1	60.0	82.5	104.9	96.2	101.1	113.5	78.2	98.0	105.1	98.4	102.2	113.5	79.1	98.4
D10	Services: Conveying	100.0	78.2	94.1	100.0	96.4	99.0	100.0	65.3	90.6	100.0	101.3	100.3	100.0	65.3	90.6
D20-40	Mechanical	100.2	47.5	78.9	100.0	90.9	96.3	100.4	100.1	100.3	100.0	122.1	109.0	100.3	89.0	95.7
D50	Electrical	96.0	40.4	67.3	103.8	82.3	92.7	97.1	93.1	95.1	103.6	107.9	105.8	95.1	79.1	86.8
E	Equipment & Furnishings	100.0	64.0	98.2	100.0	98.2	99.9	100.0	79.0	98.9	100.0	99.5	100.0	100.0	78.3	98.9
G	Site Work	110.9	84.4	93.3	93.2	113.2	106.5	101.5	91.2	94.7	96.9	111.4	106.5	100.7	91.2	94.4
A-G	WEIGHTED AVERAGE	101.2	59.8	82.9	102.2	95.6	99.3	102.1	86.8	95.4	102.5	106.3	104.2	102.5	82.7	93.7

DIV. NO.	BUILDING SYSTEMS	WASHINGTON TACOMA MAT.	INST.	TOTAL	VANCOUVER MAT.	INST.	TOTAL	YAKIMA MAT.	INST.	TOTAL	WEST VIRGINIA CHARLESTON MAT.	INST.	TOTAL	HUNTINGTON MAT.	INST.	TOTAL
A	Substructure	105.4	104.7	105.0	114.9	95.8	103.5	110.2	95.5	101.4	103.2	91.6	96.3	115.5	94.8	103.1
B10	Shell: Superstructure	103.3	97.0	100.7	103.2	93.1	99.1	103.0	89.2	97.3	97.7	94.2	96.2	100.2	97.0	98.9
B20	Exterior Closure	103.0	99.6	101.4	107.9	95.7	102.1	101.0	78.9	90.5	98.8	90.3	94.7	100.4	90.7	95.8
B30	Roofing	102.2	96.6	100.1	102.8	90.7	98.2	102.3	81.4	94.5	97.1	86.9	93.2	100.1	88.4	95.7
C	Interior Construction	104.4	97.1	101.2	101.0	87.4	95.0	103.8	87.2	96.5	99.8	91.0	95.9	99.6	91.8	96.2
D10	Services: Conveying	100.0	101.3	100.3	100.0	61.4	89.6	100.0	98.2	99.5	100.0	96.7	99.1	100.0	99.4	99.4
D20-40	Mechanical	100.1	90.9	96.4	100.2	93.0	97.3	100.1	100.2	100.1	100.0	82.2	92.8	100.2	84.4	93.8
D50	Electrical	103.6	97.0	100.2	108.5	98.0	103.1	106.6	93.1	99.6	97.2	90.9	93.9	96.0	93.9	94.9
E	Equipment & Furnishings	100.0	98.9	99.9	100.0	85.0	99.2	100.0	98.2	99.9	100.0	87.7	99.4	100.0	90.1	99.5
G	Site Work	96.2	113.2	107.5	106.6	100.2	102.3	99.1	112.7	108.1	103.1	88.1	93.1	109.8	89.0	96.0
A-G	WEIGHTED AVERAGE	102.2	97.9	100.3	103.5	93.0	98.8	102.5	92.6	98.1	99.2	89.5	94.9	100.6	91.4	96.6

DIV. NO.	BUILDING SYSTEMS	WEST VIRGINIA PARKERSBURG MAT.	INST.	TOTAL	WHEELING MAT.	INST.	TOTAL	WISCONSIN EAU CLAIRE MAT.	INST.	TOTAL	GREEN BAY MAT.	INST.	TOTAL	KENOSHA MAT.	INST.	TOTAL
A	Substructure	110.3	88.0	96.9	110.3	89.7	98.0	102.5	98.0	99.8	105.7	96.3	100.1	109.9	101.4	104.8
B10	Shell: Superstructure	97.3	91.6	95.6	97.5	92.8	95.6	97.2	99.9	98.3	99.9	96.3	98.4	99.7	101.6	100.6
B20	Exterior Closure	97.4	84.4	91.2	108.9	86.9	98.5	94.7	97.2	95.9	111.4	96.9	104.5	98.6	107.1	102.6
B30	Roofing	100.0	86.6	94.9	100.4	87.3	95.5	106.5	82.5	97.5	107.9	82.9	98.5	105.6	94.8	101.5
C	Interior Construction	99.2	86.7	93.7	99.8	86.9	94.1	100.8	99.3	100.2	100.6	97.4	99.2	100.4	105.0	102.4
D10	Services: Conveying	100.0	96.5	99.1	100.0	97.9	99.4	100.0	91.1	97.6	100.0	90.8	97.5	100.0	98.8	99.7
D20-40	Mechanical	100.2	87.8	95.1	100.2	87.7	95.2	100.2	84.8	93.9	100.4	82.9	93.3	100.1	94.8	97.9
D50	Electrical	96.4	90.3	93.3	93.7	91.5	92.6	103.7	90.2	96.7	98.4	82.8	90.3	101.7	99.4	100.5
E	Equipment & Furnishings	100.0	84.9	99.2	100.0	83.3	99.1	100.0	96.7	99.8	100.0	96.4	99.8	100.0	102.8	100.1
G	Site Work	114.3	88.0	96.9	115.1	87.2	96.6	98.3	103.4	101.6	101.4	99.5	100.1	103.6	103.7	103.7
A-G	WEIGHTED AVERAGE	99.6	88.4	94.7	100.7	89.2	95.7	99.7	94.3	97.3	101.8	91.6	97.3	100.8	101.0	100.9

DIV. NO.	BUILDING SYSTEMS	WISCONSIN LA CROSSE MAT.	INST.	TOTAL	MADISON MAT.	INST.	TOTAL	MILWAUKEE MAT.	INST.	TOTAL	RACINE MAT.	INST.	TOTAL	WYOMING CASPER MAT.	INST.	TOTAL
A	Substructure	94.2	95.9	95.2	96.7	98.6	97.8	101.6	110.2	106.7	101.7	102.2	102.0	97.5	67.0	79.2
B10	Shell: Superstructure	94.8	96.0	95.3	97.9	96.4	97.3	99.7	105.0	101.9	98.3	101.7	99.7	97.3	62.0	82.9
B20	Exterior Closure	91.5	95.3	93.3	98.7	101.6	100.1	100.1	119.7	109.4	99.8	107.0	103.3	102.7	38.2	72.0
B30	Roofing	106.0	82.0	97.0	102.5	88.7	97.3	103.9	114.4	107.9	106.0	94.3	101.6	97.8	50.1	79.9
C	Interior Construction	98.9	97.4	98.3	101.1	98.7	100.0	103.9	119.8	110.9	101.5	105.4	103.2	99.9	40.0	73.5
D10	Services: Conveying	100.0	91.9	97.8	100.0	91.6	97.7	100.0	102.1	100.6	100.0	98.8	99.7	100.0	79.0	94.3
D20-40	Mechanical	100.2	85.5	94.3	99.8	94.6	97.7	99.9	103.7	101.4	99.9	94.8	97.8	100.0	55.0	81.8
D50	Electrical	104.0	90.4	97.0	99.4	94.1	96.7	102.6	100.1	101.3	100.9	97.3	99.1	94.9	66.9	80.5
E	Equipment & Furnishings	100.0	96.8	99.8	100.0	97.1	99.8	100.0	120.0	101.0	100.0	102.6	100.1	100.0	39.2	96.9
G	Site Work	91.6	103.4	99.5	93.1	106.7	102.1	98.2	97.4	97.7	97.1	107.4	103.9	94.7	97.4	96.5
A-G	WEIGHTED AVERAGE	98.1	93.2	95.9	99.3	97.2	98.4	100.9	108.3	104.2	100.1	101.0	100.5	98.9	57.7	80.7

DIV. NO.	BUILDING SYSTEMS	WYOMING CHEYENNE MAT.	INST.	TOTAL	ROCK SPRINGS MAT.	INST.	TOTAL	CANADA CALGARY, ALBERTA MAT.	INST.	TOTAL	EDMONTON, ALBERTA MAT.	INST.	TOTAL	HALIFAX, NOVA SCOTIA MAT.	INST.	TOTAL
A	Substructure	94.3	72.3	81.1	94.5	61.7	74.8	175.9	98.0	129.2	185.5	98.0	133.1	153.3	81.3	110.2
B10	Shell: Superstructure	97.9	66.9	85.2	95.1	59.9	80.7	151.6	92.0	127.2	153.2	92.0	128.2	133.0	79.0	110.8
B20	Exterior Closure	102.0	50.3	77.4	127.6	45.8	88.7	158.9	88.9	125.5	153.2	88.9	122.6	136.8	80.0	110.2
B30	Roofing	99.4	53.1	82.0	100.9	45.8	80.2	123.6	95.7	113.1	125.1	95.7	114.0	107.0	76.4	95.5
C	Interior Construction	100.5	55.3	80.7	101.5	43.6	76.0	113.8	96.5	106.2	115.4	96.5	107.1	99.4	78.9	90.4
D10	Services: Conveying	100.0	79.0	94.3	100.0	58.9	88.9	140.0	102.2	129.8	140.0	102.2	129.8	140.0	70.9	121.3
D20-40	Mechanical	100.0	55.0	81.8	100.0	52.7	80.8	100.5	92.6	97.3	100.6	92.6	97.4	99.8	78.0	91.0
D50	Electrical	97.6	72.9	84.9	93.4	66.9	79.7	123.5	84.2	103.2	115.6	84.2	99.4	120.9	79.8	99.7
E	Equipment & Furnishings	100.0	57.7	97.8	100.0	44.9	97.2	141.3	95.4	139.0	141.3	95.4	139.0	141.3	76.3	138.0
G	Site Work	87.8	97.4	94.2	84.3	96.3	92.3	128.4	105.2	113.0	151.3	105.2	120.7	104.1	98.9	100.7
A-G	WEIGHTED AVERAGE	99.1	63.8	83.5	101.0	57.2	81.7	129.8	93.1	113.6	130.0	93.1	113.7	119.0	80.3	101.9

DIV. NO.	BUILDING SYSTEMS	CANADA														
		HAMILTON, ONTARIO			KITCHENER, ONTARIO			LAVAL, QUEBEC			LONDON, ONTARIO			MONTREAL, QUEBEC		
		MAT.	INST.	TOTAL	MAT.	INST.	TOTAL	MAT.	INST.	TOTAL	MAT.	INST.	TOTAL	MAT.	INST.	TOTAL
A	Substructure	148.1	97.9	118.0	127.3	90.6	105.4	132.1	95.5	110.2	150.6	93.3	116.3	162.1	95.0	121.9
B10	Shell: Superstructure	131.4	92.8	115.6	119.0	89.3	106.8	113.1	91.5	104.2	131.1	90.5	114.5	134.7	92.1	117.3
B20	Exterior Closure	141.1	99.5	121.3	123.1	92.3	108.4	131.9	87.5	110.7	144.0	96.6	121.4	135.1	87.7	112.5
B30	Roofing	122.4	94.8	112.1	110.6	89.7	102.8	105.6	94.6	101.5	123.2	92.4	111.7	119.3	93.9	109.8
C	Interior Construction	112.3	95.9	105.1	101.6	88.4	95.8	104.6	93.4	99.7	113.0	90.9	103.3	108.6	92.8	101.6
D10	Services: Conveying	140.0	105.4	130.7	140.0	103.1	130.0	140.0	90.6	126.6	140.0	104.7	130.5	140.0	90.8	126.7
D20 - 40	Mechanical	100.7	84.0	93.9	99.8	89.1	95.4	99.8	96.1	98.3	100.7	81.2	92.8	100.7	95.6	98.6
D50	Electrical	119.7	87.5	103.1	117.6	85.1	100.8	118.9	75.9	96.7	112.9	85.1	98.6	123.4	83.0	102.5
E	Equipment & Furnishings	141.3	93.3	138.8	141.3	84.8	138.4	141.3	91.3	138.7	141.3	86.5	138.5	141.3	89.3	138.6
G	Site Work	119.0	113.0	115.0	103.4	105.1	104.5	97.1	100.9	99.6	118.3	105.4	109.7	107.1	99.9	102.3
A-G	**WEIGHTED AVERAGE**	121.9	93.7	109.4	113.7	90.4	103.4	114.0	91.1	103.9	121.6	90.2	107.8	121.9	91.9	108.7

DIV. NO.	BUILDING SYSTEMS	CANADA														
		OSHAWA, ONTARIO			OTTAWA, ONTARIO			QUEBEC, QUEBEC			REGINA, SASKATCHEWAN			SASKATOON, SASKATCHEWAN		
		MAT.	INST.	TOTAL	MAT.	INST.	TOTAL	MAT.	INST.	TOTAL	MAT.	INST.	TOTAL	MAT.	INST.	TOTAL
A	Substructure	155.2	94.7	119.0	155.5	93.9	118.6	140.0	95.2	113.2	150.2	90.7	114.5	129.9	90.7	106.4
B10	Shell: Superstructure	118.9	93.9	108.2	136.3	91.0	117.8	129.5	92.4	114.3	119.8	85.8	105.9	110.8	85.8	100.5
B20	Exterior Closure	132.6	97.6	115.9	141.5	96.7	120.2	138.5	90.4	115.6	128.4	87.8	109.1	126.5	87.8	108.1
B30	Roofing	111.6	90.0	103.5	125.1	91.9	112.6	121.4	94.1	111.1	106.5	83.3	97.8	105.1	83.3	96.9
C	Interior Construction	105.9	95.9	101.5	115.2	91.9	105.0	110.6	92.8	102.8	105.8	84.7	96.5	102.7	84.7	94.8
D10	Services: Conveying	140.0	105.4	130.5	140.0	102.0	129.7	140.0	90.9	126.7	140.0	73.3	122.0	140.0	73.3	122.0
D20 - 40	Mechanical	99.8	106.3	102.4	100.7	81.7	93.0	100.6	95.7	98.6	99.9	82.3	92.8	99.8	82.3	92.7
D50	Electrical	118.7	94.5	106.2	112.3	85.9	98.7	116.5	83.0	99.2	119.9	87.3	103.1	121.9	87.3	104.1
E	Equipment & Furnishings	141.3	92.3	138.8	141.3	89.9	138.7	141.3	89.3	138.6	141.3	88.8	138.6	141.3	88.8	138.6
G	Site Work	116.1	104.9	108.7	115.9	105.2	108.8	104.3	100.0	101.4	119.0	98.4	105.3	109.1	98.4	102.0
A-G	**WEIGHTED AVERAGE**	117.1	98.2	108.7	122.9	90.7	108.7	119.8	92.3	107.7	116.7	86.2	103.2	113.2	86.2	101.3

DIV. NO.	BUILDING SYSTEMS	CANADA														
		ST CATHARINES, ONTARIO			ST JOHNS, NEWFOUNDLAND			THUNDER BAY, ONTARIO			TORONTO, ONTARIO			VANCOUVER, BRITISH COLUMBIA		
		MAT.	INST.	TOTAL	MAT.	INST.	TOTAL	MAT.	INST.	TOTAL	MAT.	INST.	TOTAL	MAT.	INST.	TOTAL
A	Substructure	123.2	95.2	106.5	157.1	81.5	111.8	130.6	93.9	108.6	152.7	103.4	123.2	153.8	95.1	118.6
B10	Shell: Superstructure	110.6	92.5	103.2	124.2	77.6	105.1	112.4	91.0	103.7	132.9	97.0	118.2	157.1	90.6	129.9
B20	Exterior Closure	122.8	99.0	111.4	149.1	75.9	114.2	126.3	98.0	112.8	146.5	104.0	126.3	146.9	93.4	121.4
B30	Roofing	110.6	95.6	105.0	110.1	75.5	97.1	110.9	92.3	103.9	123.4	100.0	114.6	133.8	88.4	116.8
C	Interior Construction	99.5	95.4	97.7	108.9	70.1	91.8	101.6	93.5	98.0	112.7	100.8	107.5	115.2	86.9	102.8
D10	Services: Conveying	140.0	77.0	123.0	140.0	72.4	121.7	140.0	77.2	123.0	140.0	106.7	131.0	140.0	101.5	129.6
D20 - 40	Mechanical	99.8	82.9	92.9	100.1	71.3	88.4	99.8	82.7	92.8	100.6	97.7	99.4	100.6	84.7	94.2
D50	Electrical	119.2	86.0	102.1	116.0	72.3	93.4	117.5	84.5	100.5	114.0	88.1	100.7	115.1	77.7	95.8
E	Equipment & Furnishings	141.3	93.2	138.8	141.3	71.0	137.7	141.3	90.2	138.7	141.3	97.9	139.1	141.3	84.7	138.4
G	Site Work	104.6	101.9	102.8	117.8	99.7	105.8	109.9	101.9	104.6	139.0	106.0	117.1	122.8	108.4	113.2
A-G	**WEIGHTED AVERAGE**	111.7	91.3	102.8	120.3	75.7	100.6	113.1	90.2	103.0	123.0	98.8	112.3	128.1	89.1	110.9

DIV. NO.	BUILDING SYSTEMS	CANADA														
		WINDSOR, ONTARIO			WINNIPEG, MANITOBA											
		MAT.	INST.	TOTAL	MAT.	INST.	TOTAL	MAT.	INST.	TOTAL	MAT.	INST.	TOTAL	MAT.	INST.	TOTAL
A	Substructure	125.4	93.4	106.2	169.2	77.5	114.3									
B10	Shell: Superstructure	111.4	91.0	103.0	158.8	73.0	123.6									
B20	Exterior Closure	122.6	97.2	110.5	147.4	69.8	110.5									
B30	Roofing	110.7	91.0	103.3	116.2	72.3	99.7									
C	Interior Construction	100.5	92.3	96.9	111.8	68.9	92.9									
D10	Services: Conveying	140.0	76.6	122.9	140.0	70.6	121.2									
D20 - 40	Mechanical	99.8	82.3	92.7	100.5	67.9	87.3									
D50	Electrical	122.0	86.0	103.4	117.9	68.3	92.3									
E	Equipment & Furnishings	141.3	88.8	138.6	141.3	69.8	137.6									
G	Site Work	99.1	101.8	100.9	125.1	101.5	109.4									
A-G	**WEIGHTED AVERAGE**	112.2	90.0	102.4	128.4	72.4	103.7									

Costs shown in RSMeans cost data publications are based on national averages for materials and installation. To adjust these costs to a specific location, simply multiply the base cost by the factor and divide by 100 for that city. The data is arranged alphabetically by state and postal zip code numbers. For a city not listed, use the factor for a nearby city with similar economic characteristics.

STATE/ZIP	CITY	MAT.	INST.	TOTAL
ALABAMA				
350-352	Birmingham	97.6	74.6	87.4
354	Tuscaloosa	96.6	58.6	79.9
355	Jasper	96.8	57.6	79.5
356	Decatur	96.5	60.1	80.5
357-358	Huntsville	96.6	68.1	84.1
359	Gadsden	96.6	57.6	79.4
360-361	Montgomery	97.4	56.6	79.4
362	Anniston	96.0	64.5	82.1
363	Dothan	96.6	52.0	76.9
364	Evergreen	96.2	53.4	77.3
365-366	Mobile	97.7	67.5	84.4
367	Selma	96.3	51.9	76.7
368	Phenix City	97.1	55.9	78.9
369	Butler	96.5	52.0	76.9
ALASKA				
995-996	Anchorage	124.5	114.0	119.9
997	Fairbanks	122.4	115.0	119.1
998	Juneau	120.3	113.9	117.5
999	Ketchikan	134.1	113.9	125.2
ARIZONA				
850,853	Phoenix	97.9	76.6	88.5
851,852	Mesa/Tempe	97.4	72.4	86.3
855	Globe	97.4	62.5	82.0
856-857	Tucson	96.1	72.1	85.5
859	Show Low	97.5	62.9	82.2
860	Flagstaff	100.3	73.9	88.7
863	Prescott	98.2	62.1	82.2
864	Kingman	96.4	73.4	86.3
865	Chambers	96.5	63.0	81.7
ARKANSAS				
716	Pine Bluff	96.7	63.8	82.2
717	Camden	94.1	50.1	74.7
718	Texarkana	95.9	51.3	76.2
719	Hot Springs	93.4	52.9	75.5
720-722	Little Rock	97.0	65.0	82.9
723	West Memphis	95.8	62.8	81.2
724	Jonesboro	96.8	60.7	80.9
725	Batesville	94.2	56.1	77.4
726	Harrison	95.5	52.3	76.5
727	Fayetteville	92.9	54.1	75.8
728	Russellville	94.1	55.4	77.0
729	Fort Smith	97.1	62.5	81.8
CALIFORNIA				
900-902	Los Angeles	100.1	115.5	106.9
903-905	Inglewood	95.3	113.1	103.2
906-908	Long Beach	96.9	113.2	104.1
910-912	Pasadena	95.2	113.6	103.3
913-916	Van Nuys	98.1	113.5	104.9
917-918	Alhambra	97.1	113.5	104.3
919-921	San Diego	99.3	107.8	103.0
922	Palm Springs	96.4	110.9	102.8
923-924	San Bernardino	94.3	110.5	101.4
925	Riverside	98.9	112.4	104.9
926-927	Santa Ana	96.1	110.8	102.6
928	Anaheim	98.9	112.8	105.1
930	Oxnard	100.2	112.3	105.5
931	Santa Barbara	99.5	112.3	105.1
932-933	Bakersfield	100.0	109.5	104.2
934	San Luis Obispo	99.7	109.4	104.0
935	Mojave	97.0	106.9	101.3
936-938	Fresno	100.5	115.7	107.2
939	Salinas	100.5	122.7	110.3
940-941	San Francisco	108.5	142.3	123.4
942,956-958	Sacramento	102.9	118.6	109.9
943	Palo Alto	101.3	129.9	113.9
944	San Mateo	103.8	131.3	115.9
945	Vallejo	102.2	128.2	113.7
946	Oakland	106.3	133.9	118.5
947	Berkeley	105.5	133.2	117.7
948	Richmond	104.7	129.7	115.7
949	San Rafael	106.0	129.5	116.4
950	Santa Cruz	105.0	122.8	112.9

STATE/ZIP	CITY	MAT.	INST.	TOTAL
CALIFORNIA (CONT'D)				
951	San Jose	103.2	135.1	117.3
952	Stockton	100.7	117.2	108.0
953	Modesto	100.7	116.9	107.9
954	Santa Rosa	100.3	135.0	115.6
955	Eureka	101.6	114.2	107.2
959	Marysville	100.9	114.4	106.8
960	Redding	102.8	114.4	107.9
961	Susanville	101.5	114.4	107.2
COLORADO				
800-802	Denver	101.7	84.7	94.2
803	Boulder	98.6	82.9	91.7
804	Golden	100.7	81.7	92.3
805	Fort Collins	102.6	79.1	92.2
806	Greeley	100.0	78.2	90.4
807	Fort Morgan	99.3	82.0	91.7
808-809	Colorado Springs	101.6	81.7	92.8
810	Pueblo	100.4	80.8	91.8
811	Alamosa	101.5	76.7	90.6
812	Salida	101.3	78.3	91.2
813	Durango	101.9	79.6	92.1
814	Montrose	100.8	79.3	91.3
815	Grand Junction	104.2	79.6	93.4
816	Glenwood Springs	101.6	82.2	93.1
CONNECTICUT				
060	New Britain	101.1	118.6	108.8
061	Hartford	102.0	118.7	109.4
062	Willimantic	101.7	118.4	109.1
063	New London	97.6	118.6	106.9
064	Meriden	99.7	118.6	108.0
065	New Haven	102.8	118.6	109.8
066	Bridgeport	102.2	118.7	109.5
067	Waterbury	101.8	118.6	109.2
068	Norwalk	101.8	126.3	112.6
069	Stamford	101.9	126.3	112.7
D.C.				
200-205	Washington	102.4	92.8	98.2
DELAWARE				
197	Newark	99.4	107.9	103.2
198	Wilmington	99.1	108.0	103.0
199	Dover	99.5	107.9	103.2
FLORIDA				
320,322	Jacksonville	98.7	69.4	85.7
321	Daytona Beach	98.8	75.2	88.4
323	Tallahassee	99.4	59.3	81.7
324	Panama City	100.1	60.5	82.7
325	Pensacola	102.6	64.1	85.6
326,344	Gainesville	100.4	69.7	86.9
327-328,347	Orlando	101.8	73.0	89.1
329	Melbourne	101.5	78.2	91.2
330-332,340	Miami	99.6	76.7	89.6
333	Fort Lauderdale	98.1	75.9	88.3
334,349	West Palm Beach	96.7	74.4	86.9
335-336,346	Tampa	99.8	82.1	92.0
337	St. Petersburg	102.5	65.8	86.3
338	Lakeland	99.0	82.0	91.5
339,341	Fort Myers	98.1	75.8	88.3
342	Sarasota	100.0	77.3	90.0
GEORGIA				
300-303,399	Atlanta	98.0	76.5	88.5
304	Statesboro	97.4	54.0	78.3
305	Gainesville	96.1	64.0	82.0
306	Athens	95.5	64.2	81.7
307	Dalton	97.6	60.1	81.1
308-309	Augusta	96.7	64.5	82.5
310-312	Macon	96.4	64.2	82.2
313-314	Savannah	98.1	60.5	81.5
315	Waycross	97.3	61.4	81.5
316	Valdosta	97.6	60.8	81.4
317,398	Albany	97.6	61.5	81.7
318-319	Columbus	97.5	64.6	83.0

STATE/ZIP	CITY	MAT.	INST.	TOTAL
HAWAII				
967	Hilo	110.3	121.2	115.1
968	Honolulu	113.3	121.2	116.8
STATES & POSS.				
969	Guam	131.1	60.8	100.1
IDAHO				
832	Pocatello	100.3	72.2	87.9
833	Twin Falls	101.3	52.5	79.8
834	Idaho Falls	98.9	58.7	81.2
835	Lewiston	107.9	79.7	95.5
836-837	Boise	99.3	72.4	87.4
838	Coeur d'Alene	107.2	76.3	93.6
ILLINOIS				
600-603	North Suburban	98.7	132.4	113.5
604	Joliet	98.6	136.4	115.3
605	South Suburban	98.7	132.4	113.5
606-608	Chicago	99.1	138.9	116.6
609	Kankakee	94.6	127.4	109.1
610-611	Rockford	98.4	124.3	109.8
612	Rock Island	95.9	98.9	97.2
613	La Salle	97.0	120.8	107.5
614	Galesburg	96.9	104.8	100.4
615-616	Peoria	99.5	108.3	103.4
617	Bloomington	96.3	109.3	102.0
618-619	Champaign	99.8	108.1	103.5
620-622	East St. Louis	95.1	108.3	100.9
623	Quincy	96.0	100.1	97.8
624	Effingham	95.3	103.9	99.1
625	Decatur	97.4	106.3	101.3
626-627	Springfield	97.8	107.1	101.9
628	Centralia	93.4	107.0	99.4
629	Carbondale	93.1	102.0	97.1
INDIANA				
460	Anderson	96.1	83.4	90.5
461-462	Indianapolis	99.2	85.6	93.2
463-464	Gary	97.6	108.5	102.4
465-466	South Bend	95.7	82.9	90.1
467-468	Fort Wayne	96.7	78.7	88.8
469	Kokomo	93.7	82.2	88.6
470	Lawrenceburg	92.5	79.6	86.8
471	New Albany	93.6	76.6	86.1
472	Columbus	96.0	81.5	89.6
473	Muncie	97.1	82.6	90.7
474	Bloomington	98.4	82.9	91.6
475	Washington	94.4	83.7	89.7
476-477	Evansville	96.0	86.5	91.8
478	Terre Haute	96.7	86.9	92.4
479	Lafayette	95.7	83.2	90.2
IOWA				
500-503,509	Des Moines	99.1	84.7	92.7
504	Mason City	97.6	67.8	84.5
505	Fort Dodge	97.9	59.7	81.0
506-507	Waterloo	99.7	72.2	87.6
508	Creston	98.1	78.8	89.6
510-511	Sioux City	100.5	70.7	87.3
512	Sibley	98.9	56.5	80.2
513	Spencer	100.6	56.5	81.2
514	Carroll	97.4	72.4	86.4
515	Council Bluffs	101.7	78.8	91.6
516	Shenandoah	98.2	72.3	86.8
520	Dubuque	99.9	79.7	91.0
521	Decorah	98.5	65.7	84.0
522-524	Cedar Rapids	100.7	84.0	93.3
525	Ottumwa	98.4	70.7	86.2
526	Burlington	97.6	77.3	88.6
527-528	Davenport	99.6	90.4	95.5
KANSAS				
660-662	Kansas City	99.5	95.4	97.7
664-666	Topeka	99.2	64.5	83.9
667	Fort Scott	97.7	73.9	87.2
668	Emporia	97.9	69.7	85.4
669	Belleville	99.6	65.5	84.6
670-672	Wichita	98.4	64.1	83.3
673	Independence	99.2	69.5	86.1
674	Salina	100.0	66.9	85.4
675	Hutchinson	94.8	65.4	81.8
676	Hays	98.8	65.8	84.3
677	Colby	99.5	65.8	84.6

STATE/ZIP	CITY	MAT.	INST.	TOTAL
KANSAS (CONT'D)				
678	Dodge City	101.2	66.8	86.0
679	Liberal	98.7	65.8	84.2
KENTUCKY				
400-402	Louisville	97.8	83.5	91.5
403-405	Lexington	96.5	81.8	90.0
406	Frankfort	97.2	83.5	91.2
407-409	Corbin	93.7	72.5	84.4
410	Covington	94.4	95.2	94.8
411-412	Ashland	93.3	98.5	95.6
413-414	Campton	94.5	81.2	88.6
415-416	Pikeville	95.6	91.7	93.9
417-418	Hazard	93.9	81.5	88.4
420	Paducah	92.6	85.7	89.6
421-422	Bowling Green	95.0	83.5	90.0
423	Owensboro	95.2	87.9	92.0
424	Henderson	92.4	87.9	90.4
425-426	Somerset	91.9	79.1	86.2
427	Elizabethtown	91.4	83.9	88.1
LOUISIANA				
700-701	New Orleans	102.3	70.5	88.3
703	Thibodaux	100.2	63.4	84.0
704	Hammond	97.5	56.1	79.3
705	Lafayette	99.9	61.5	83.0
706	Lake Charles	100.1	64.1	84.2
707-708	Baton Rouge	101.2	63.0	84.4
710-711	Shreveport	96.7	56.3	78.9
712	Monroe	97.0	53.6	77.9
713-714	Alexandria	97.1	53.5	77.9
MAINE				
039	Kittery	94.8	80.1	88.3
040-041	Portland	99.5	78.9	90.4
042	Lewiston	98.1	78.9	89.7
043	Augusta	97.6	79.8	89.8
044	Bangor	97.7	78.9	89.4
045	Bath	96.0	79.5	88.7
046	Machias	95.5	79.0	88.2
047	Houlton	95.7	78.9	88.3
048	Rockland	94.7	79.4	88.0
049	Waterville	96.1	79.8	88.9
MARYLAND				
206	Waldorf	98.5	82.4	91.4
207-208	College Park	98.5	84.2	92.2
209	Silver Spring	97.7	82.3	90.9
210-212	Baltimore	100.2	84.7	93.3
214	Annapolis	100.2	83.2	92.7
215	Cumberland	95.8	80.2	89.0
216	Easton	97.5	70.3	85.5
217	Hagerstown	96.8	82.9	90.7
218	Salisbury	97.9	65.3	83.5
219	Elkton	94.7	84.3	90.1
MASSACHUSETTS				
010-011	Springfield	100.0	108.7	103.9
012	Pittsfield	99.6	105.3	102.1
013	Greenfield	97.3	108.4	102.2
014	Fitchburg	96.1	123.3	108.1
015-016	Worcester	100.0	123.5	110.4
017	Framingham	95.5	129.9	110.7
018	Lowell	99.4	128.5	112.3
019	Lawrence	100.5	129.0	113.1
020-022, 024	Boston	102.2	136.8	117.5
023	Brockton	100.8	124.7	111.4
025	Buzzards Bay	94.9	122.1	106.9
026	Hyannis	98.0	122.1	108.6
027	New Bedford	99.9	122.2	109.7
MICHIGAN				
480,483	Royal Oak	93.4	106.2	99.1
481	Ann Arbor	95.8	108.1	101.2
482	Detroit	97.4	110.1	103.0
484-485	Flint	95.5	97.1	96.2
486	Saginaw	95.0	93.5	94.4
487	Bay City	95.2	93.6	94.5
488-489	Lansing	96.4	95.1	95.9
490	Battle Creek	96.0	89.2	93.0
491	Kalamazoo	96.3	87.4	92.4
492	Jackson	94.3	95.9	95.0
493,495	Grand Rapids	97.2	83.0	90.9
494	Muskegon	94.9	84.9	90.5

STATE/ZIP	CITY	MAT.	INST.	TOTAL
MICHIGAN (CONT'D)				
496	Traverse City	93.6	78.7	87.0
497	Gaylord	94.7	72.8	85.1
498-499	Iron mountain	96.7	87.8	92.8
MINNESOTA				
550-551	Saint Paul	101.1	121.5	110.1
553-555	Minneapolis	102.1	123.0	111.3
556-558	Duluth	100.1	112.0	105.4
559	Rochester	100.9	107.6	103.8
560	Mankato	97.7	104.6	100.7
561	Windom	96.4	93.8	95.2
562	Willmar	96.0	105.1	100.0
563	St. Cloud	97.6	120.8	107.9
564	Brainerd	97.6	105.3	101.0
565	Detroit Lakes	99.4	99.3	99.4
566	Bemidji	98.7	101.3	99.9
567	Thief River Falls	98.3	95.8	97.2
MISSISSIPPI				
386	Clarksdale	96.4	55.5	78.4
387	Greenville	100.3	65.1	84.7
388	Tupelo	98.0	57.9	80.4
389	Greenwood	97.6	55.1	78.8
390-392	Jackson	97.4	64.4	82.9
393	Meridian	96.7	66.1	83.2
394	Laurel	97.9	58.8	80.6
395	Biloxi	98.3	60.2	81.5
396	Mccomb	96.3	54.6	77.9
397	Columbus	97.8	56.9	79.8
MISSOURI				
630-631	St. Louis	100.0	105.7	102.5
633	Bowling Green	98.4	90.5	94.9
634	Hannibal	97.3	87.1	92.8
635	Kirksville	100.4	83.8	93.1
636	Flat River	99.4	92.9	96.5
637	Cape Girardeau	99.7	89.6	95.3
638	Sikeston	97.5	85.5	92.2
639	Poplar Bluff	97.0	86.8	92.5
640-641	Kansas City	100.1	108.0	103.6
644-645	St. Joseph	99.3	91.8	96.0
646	Chillicothe	96.1	70.0	84.6
647	Harrisonville	95.7	104.5	99.6
648	Joplin	98.2	70.4	85.9
650-651	Jefferson City	96.2	90.5	93.7
652	Columbia	97.7	92.4	95.4
653	Sedalia	96.6	92.8	94.9
654-655	Rolla	95.2	87.9	92.0
656-658	Springfield	98.5	79.9	90.3
MONTANA				
590-591	Billings	103.5	74.7	90.8
592	Wolf Point	103.1	67.5	87.4
593	Miles City	100.7	69.1	86.8
594	Great Falls	105.0	75.3	91.9
595	Havre	102.0	70.2	88.0
596	Helena	102.6	72.0	89.1
597	Butte	103.5	73.5	90.3
598	Missoula	100.8	72.2	88.2
599	Kalispell	99.6	70.1	86.6
NEBRASKA				
680-681	Omaha	100.0	79.2	90.8
683-685	Lincoln	98.0	73.6	87.2
686	Columbus	96.8	71.7	85.7
687	Norfolk	98.5	75.1	88.2
688	Grand Island	98.7	78.4	89.8
689	Hastings	97.8	79.3	89.6
690	Mccook	97.6	70.7	85.7
691	North Platte	98.1	79.4	89.9
692	Valentine	99.7	67.6	85.6
693	Alliance	99.7	65.8	84.8
NEVADA				
889-891	Las Vegas	99.8	110.7	104.6
893	Ely	98.5	98.1	98.3
894-895	Reno	98.7	93.7	96.5
897	Carson City	97.8	93.5	95.9
898	Elko	97.2	85.3	92.0
NEW HAMPSHIRE				
030	Nashua	100.2	86.7	94.3
031	Manchester	100.7	86.7	94.5

STATE/ZIP	CITY	MAT.	INST.	TOTAL
NEW HAMPSHIRE (CONT'D)				
032-033	Concord	98.6	82.4	91.5
034	Keene	96.9	49.4	76.0
035	Littleton	96.5	56.6	78.9
036	Charleston	96.3	47.1	74.6
037	Claremont	95.3	47.1	74.1
038	Portsmouth	97.8	91.2	94.9
NEW JERSEY				
070-071	Newark	102.7	124.6	112.4
072	Elizabeth	100.6	124.5	111.2
073	Jersey City	99.4	124.4	110.4
074-075	Paterson	101.4	124.5	111.6
076	Hackensack	99.4	124.5	110.5
077	Long Branch	99.0	123.3	109.7
078	Dover	99.7	124.6	110.7
079	Summit	99.6	124.7	110.7
080,083	Vineland	97.6	122.4	108.6
081	Camden	99.4	122.6	109.6
082,084	Atlantic City	98.1	122.1	108.7
085-086	Trenton	99.6	123.6	110.2
087	Point Pleasant	99.7	122.5	109.7
088-089	New Brunswick	100.1	124.3	110.8
NEW MEXICO				
870-872	Albuquerque	98.7	73.6	87.7
873	Gallup	98.8	73.6	87.7
874	Farmington	99.4	73.6	88.0
875	Santa Fe	99.4	73.6	88.0
877	Las Vegas	97.3	73.6	86.8
878	Socorro	96.8	73.6	86.6
879	Truth/Consequences	97.0	70.3	85.3
880	Las Cruces	96.1	69.6	84.4
881	Clovis	97.4	73.5	86.9
882	Roswell	99.3	73.6	88.0
883	Carrizozo	99.4	73.6	88.1
884	Tucumcari	98.1	73.5	87.3
NEW YORK				
100-102	New York	104.8	166.9	132.2
103	Staten Island	100.8	163.6	128.5
104	Bronx	98.9	163.6	127.4
105	Mount Vernon	98.6	133.0	113.8
106	White Plains	98.8	133.0	113.9
107	Yonkers	103.5	133.1	116.5
108	New Rochelle	99.0	133.0	114.0
109	Suffern	98.7	122.0	109.0
110	Queens	101.4	163.8	128.9
111	Long Island City	103.0	163.8	129.8
112	Brooklyn	103.4	163.8	130.0
113	Flushing	102.9	163.8	129.7
114	Jamaica	101.1	163.8	128.7
115,117,118	Hicksville	101.3	145.6	120.8
116	Far Rockaway	103.1	163.8	129.8
119	Riverhead	102.1	146.1	121.5
120-122	Albany	96.7	96.4	96.5
123	Schenectady	97.8	96.1	97.0
124	Kingston	100.9	117.4	108.2
125-126	Poughkeepsie	100.1	128.4	112.6
127	Monticello	99.4	118.0	107.6
128	Glens Falls	92.3	92.6	92.5
129	Plattsburgh	96.9	87.0	92.6
130-132	Syracuse	98.9	94.5	97.0
133-135	Utica	96.8	88.2	93.0
136	Watertown	98.5	93.5	96.3
137-139	Binghamton	98.4	89.2	94.4
140-142	Buffalo	100.3	104.0	101.9
143	Niagara Falls	97.9	106.1	101.5
144-146	Rochester	100.0	94.0	97.3
147	Jamestown	96.9	86.4	92.3
148-149	Elmira	96.7	91.0	94.2
NORTH CAROLINA				
270,272-274	Greensboro	99.7	47.3	76.6
271	Winston-Salem	99.5	46.0	75.9
275-276	Raleigh	99.8	47.6	76.8
277	Durham	100.8	47.9	77.5
278	Rocky Mount	96.8	42.5	72.9
279	Elizabeth City	97.8	40.6	72.6
280	Gastonia	98.6	45.4	75.1
281-282	Charlotte	99.4	47.8	76.7
283	Fayetteville	100.7	49.4	78.1
284	Wilmington	97.4	48.5	75.8
285	Kinston	95.2	43.8	72.6

STATE/ZIP	CITY	MAT.	INST.	TOTAL
NORTH CAROLINA (CONT'D)				
286	Hickory	95.5	42.3	72.1
287-288	Asheville	97.8	45.5	74.7
289	Murphy	96.4	33.2	68.5
NORTH DAKOTA				
580-581	Fargo	102.1	65.7	86.0
582	Grand Forks	102.8	53.1	80.9
583	Devils Lake	101.7	57.0	82.0
584	Jamestown	101.9	46.4	77.4
585	Bismarck	100.7	64.4	84.7
586	Dickinson	102.7	58.8	83.3
587	Minot	102.7	70.2	88.4
588	Williston	101.1	58.8	82.4
OHIO				
430-432	Columbus	97.8	90.6	94.6
433	Marion	93.9	85.4	90.2
434-436	Toledo	97.9	98.3	98.1
437-438	Zanesville	94.5	86.1	90.8
439	Steubenville	96.1	93.5	95.0
440	Lorain	97.7	91.3	94.9
441	Cleveland	97.9	99.8	98.7
442-443	Akron	98.7	94.5	96.9
444-445	Youngstown	98.1	90.1	94.6
446-447	Canton	98.2	86.3	93.0
448-449	Mansfield	95.2	87.4	91.7
450	Hamilton	96.6	85.6	91.7
451-452	Cincinnati	96.9	85.8	92.0
453-454	Dayton	96.7	85.2	91.6
455	Springfield	96.6	85.8	91.8
456	Chillicothe	95.2	93.4	94.4
457	Athens	98.0	83.1	91.4
458	Lima	98.4	86.1	93.0
OKLAHOMA				
730-731	Oklahoma City	97.8	60.6	81.4
734	Ardmore	95.0	60.1	79.6
735	Lawton	97.5	61.4	81.6
736	Clinton	96.5	58.8	79.8
737	Enid	97.3	58.7	80.3
738	Woodward	95.1	58.8	79.1
739	Guymon	96.2	31.0	67.5
740-741	Tulsa	97.4	53.5	78.0
743	Miami	93.8	67.9	82.3
744	Muskogee	96.7	39.3	71.4
745	Mcalester	93.6	50.6	74.6
746	Ponca City	94.1	58.7	78.5
747	Durant	94.1	57.7	78.1
748	Shawnee	95.7	56.5	78.4
749	Poteau	93.2	61.4	79.2
OREGON				
970-972	Portland	98.8	100.3	99.5
973	Salem	98.6	98.6	98.6
974	Eugene	98.6	98.5	98.6
975	Medford	100.1	97.0	98.7
976	Klamath Falls	99.8	97.0	98.6
977	Bend	98.8	98.6	98.7
978	Pendleton	94.1	100.0	96.7
979	Vale	91.9	90.5	91.3
PENNSYLVANIA				
150-152	Pittsburgh	99.1	104.6	101.5
153	Washington	95.9	102.1	98.6
154	Uniontown	96.4	100.8	98.3
155	Bedford	97.2	91.7	94.8
156	Greensburg	97.2	100.3	98.5
157	Indiana	96.0	99.1	97.4
158	Dubois	97.6	94.5	96.2
159	Johnstown	97.2	95.8	96.6
160	Butler	92.3	100.5	95.9
161	New Castle	92.4	97.5	94.6
162	Kittanning	92.8	102.4	97.0
163	Oil City	92.4	94.7	93.4
164-165	Erie	94.6	93.6	94.1
166	Altoona	94.8	90.6	93.0
167	Bradford	95.5	93.8	94.7
168	State College	95.0	91.8	93.6
169	Wellsboro	96.1	92.4	94.5
170-171	Harrisburg	97.7	96.1	97.0
172	Chambersburg	95.5	89.5	92.9
173-174	York	96.3	95.2	95.8
175-176	Lancaster	94.3	89.7	92.3

STATE/ZIP	CITY	MAT.	INST.	TOTAL
PENNSYLVANIA (CONT'D)				
177	Williamsport	93.0	79.6	87.1
178	Sunbury	95.1	95.1	95.1
179	Pottsville	94.2	96.8	95.4
180	Lehigh Valley	95.6	113.5	103.5
181	Allentown	97.9	109.2	102.9
182	Hazleton	95.1	97.2	96.0
183	Stroudsburg	94.9	103.0	98.5
184-185	Scranton	98.6	99.5	99.0
186-187	Wilkes-Barre	94.8	98.2	96.3
188	Montrose	94.5	97.0	95.6
189	Doylestown	94.7	120.1	105.9
190-191	Philadelphia	99.9	130.9	113.6
193	Westchester	96.1	122.8	107.9
194	Norristown	95.2	130.2	110.6
195-196	Reading	97.6	100.0	98.6
PUERTO RICO				
009	San Juan	121.3	24.1	78.4
RHODE ISLAND				
028	Newport	99.2	111.1	104.5
029	Providence	100.2	111.1	105.0
SOUTH CAROLINA				
290-292	Columbia	97.8	49.3	76.4
293	Spartanburg	96.8	49.0	75.7
294	Charleston	98.4	57.4	80.3
295	Florence	96.6	49.3	75.8
296	Greenville	96.6	49.0	75.6
297	Rock Hill	96.0	47.2	74.5
298	Aiken	96.8	72.8	86.2
299	Beaufort	97.5	42.5	73.3
SOUTH DAKOTA				
570-571	Sioux Falls	100.7	57.1	81.5
572	Watertown	99.8	51.6	78.5
573	Mitchell	98.6	51.0	77.6
574	Aberdeen	101.6	52.2	79.8
575	Pierre	100.1	53.8	79.7
576	Mobridge	99.3	51.4	78.2
577	Rapid City	101.4	54.6	80.7
TENNESSEE				
370-372	Nashville	96.8	72.2	86.0
373-374	Chattanooga	99.0	66.2	84.6
375,380-381	Memphis	98.2	69.6	85.6
376	Johnson City	98.7	56.7	80.2
377-379	Knoxville	95.4	61.4	80.4
382	Mckenzie	97.1	61.8	81.6
383	Jackson	99.2	63.8	83.6
384	Columbia	95.7	67.1	83.1
385	Cookeville	97.0	60.2	80.8
TEXAS				
750	Mckinney	98.5	50.2	77.2
751	Waxahackie	98.5	57.3	80.3
752-753	Dallas	99.4	66.8	85.0
754	Greenville	98.6	43.3	74.2
755	Texarkana	98.0	51.0	77.2
756	Longview	98.6	40.4	72.9
757	Tyler	99.0	54.4	79.4
758	Palestine	95.2	56.6	78.2
759	Lufkin	95.8	58.3	79.3
760-761	Fort Worth	97.2	63.2	82.2
762	Denton	97.1	47.8	75.4
763	Wichita Falls	98.0	54.8	79.0
764	Eastland	96.5	49.7	75.9
765	Temple	95.1	49.4	75.0
766-767	Waco	97.4	56.4	79.4
768	Brownwood	97.7	49.0	76.2
769	San Angelo	97.3	49.6	76.3
770-772	Houston	99.1	69.8	86.2
773	Huntsville	97.5	55.9	79.2
774	Wharton	98.5	54.0	78.9
775	Galveston	96.5	68.2	84.0
776-777	Beaumont	97.2	62.0	81.7
778	Bryan	94.3	61.7	79.9
779	Victoria	98.6	44.0	74.5
780	Laredo	95.8	52.7	76.8
781-782	San Antonio	96.2	65.0	82.4
783-784	Corpus Christi	98.9	52.3	78.4
785	Mc Allen	98.6	46.6	75.7
786-787	Austin	96.1	58.8	79.6

STATE/ZIP	CITY	MAT.	INST.	TOTAL
TEXAS (CONT'D)				
788	Del Rio	98.0	46.5	75.3
789	Giddings	95.1	56.2	77.9
790-791	Amarillo	98.1	61.0	81.7
792	Childress	97.3	57.2	79.6
793-794	Lubbock	99.6	56.8	80.7
795-796	Abilene	97.9	54.2	78.6
797	Midland	99.4	51.4	78.2
798-799,885	El Paso	96.8	51.2	76.7
UTAH				
840-841	Salt Lake City	101.6	68.4	86.9
842,844	Ogden	97.3	70.0	85.3
843	Logan	99.2	70.0	86.3
845	Price	99.5	65.9	84.7
846-847	Provo	99.7	68.3	85.8
VERMONT				
050	White River Jct.	98.0	54.4	78.8
051	Bellows Falls	96.5	72.7	86.0
052	Bennington	96.8	67.8	84.0
053	Brattleboro	97.2	72.9	86.5
054	Burlington	100.6	65.4	85.1
056	Montpelier	97.4	65.4	83.3
057	Rutland	99.2	65.4	84.3
058	St. Johnsbury	97.9	55.2	79.1
059	Guildhall	96.6	55.0	78.3
VIRGINIA				
220-221	Fairfax	100.1	82.0	92.1
222	Arlington	101.6	79.9	92.0
223	Alexandria	100.6	86.0	94.2
224-225	Fredericksburg	98.8	71.8	86.9
226	Winchester	99.4	62.2	83.0
227	Culpeper	99.3	67.0	85.1
228	Harrisonburg	99.6	63.0	83.4
229	Charlottesville	100.0	62.8	83.6
230-232	Richmond	100.6	66.0	85.3
233-235	Norfolk	101.4	67.6	86.5
236	Newport News	100.4	67.3	85.8
237	Portsmouth	99.9	64.4	84.3
238	Petersburg	99.9	66.0	85.0
239	Farmville	98.9	52.3	78.4
240-241	Roanoke	101.2	59.8	82.9
242	Bristol	98.6	54.3	79.1
243	Pulaski	98.3	50.3	77.1
244	Staunton	99.2	58.2	81.1
245	Lynchburg	99.3	63.6	83.5
246	Grundy	98.6	49.7	77.0
WASHINGTON				
980-981,987	Seattle	102.5	106.3	104.2
982	Everett	102.2	95.6	99.3
983-984	Tacoma	102.2	97.9	100.3
985	Olympia	99.4	97.9	98.7
986	Vancouver	103.5	93.0	98.8
988	Wenatchee	101.8	83.6	93.8
989	Yakima	102.5	92.6	98.1
990-992	Spokane	102.5	82.7	93.7
993	Richland	102.1	86.8	95.4
994	Clarkston	100.4	81.3	92.0
WEST VIRGINIA				
247-248	Bluefield	97.4	82.6	90.9
249	Lewisburg	99.1	82.7	91.9
250-253	Charleston	99.2	89.5	94.9
254	Martinsburg	98.9	79.1	90.2
255-257	Huntington	100.6	91.4	96.6
258-259	Beckley	97.3	86.6	92.6
260	Wheeling	100.7	89.2	95.7
261	Parkersburg	99.6	88.4	94.7
262	Buckhannon	98.8	89.0	94.5
263-264	Clarksburg	99.4	89.1	94.9
265	Morgantown	99.5	88.2	94.5
266	Gassaway	98.7	89.8	94.8
267	Romney	98.7	85.1	92.7
268	Petersburg	98.5	84.9	92.5
WISCONSIN				
530,532	Milwaukee	100.9	108.3	104.2
531	Kenosha	100.8	101.0	100.9
534	Racine	100.1	101.0	100.5
535	Beloit	100.0	96.0	98.3
537	Madison	99.3	97.2	98.4

STATE/ZIP	CITY	MAT.	INST.	TOTAL
WISCONSIN (CONT'D)				
538	Lancaster	97.6	91.5	94.9
539	Portage	96.1	94.5	95.4
540	New Richmond	97.3	94.4	96.0
541-543	Green Bay	101.8	91.6	97.3
544	Wausau	96.5	91.7	94.4
545	Rhinelander	99.8	90.5	95.7
546	La Crosse	98.1	93.2	95.9
547	Eau Claire	99.7	94.3	97.3
548	Superior	97.1	96.9	97.0
549	Oshkosh	97.2	82.6	90.8
WYOMING				
820	Cheyenne	99.1	63.8	83.5
821	Yellowstone Nat'l Park	96.4	59.3	80.1
822	Wheatland	97.5	58.2	80.2
823	Rawlins	99.0	57.0	80.5
824	Worland	97.1	57.0	79.4
825	Riverton	98.1	57.0	80.0
826	Casper	98.9	57.7	80.7
827	Newcastle	96.9	57.0	79.3
828	Sheridan	99.7	60.6	82.4
829-831	Rock Springs	101.0	57.2	81.7
CANADIAN FACTORS (reflect Canadian currency)				
ALBERTA				
	Calgary	129.8	93.1	113.6
	Edmonton	130.0	93.1	113.7
	Fort McMurray	126.5	95.8	113.0
	Lethbridge	120.8	95.3	109.5
	Lloydminster	116.0	91.8	105.4
	Medicine Hat	116.1	91.1	105.1
	Red Deer	116.6	91.1	105.3
BRITISH COLUMBIA				
	Kamloops	116.9	94.4	107.0
	Prince George	118.1	93.7	107.3
	Vancouver	128.1	89.1	110.9
	Victoria	118.1	87.2	104.5
MANITOBA				
	Brandon	116.2	79.0	99.8
	Portage la Prairie	116.0	77.2	98.9
	Winnipeg	128.4	72.4	103.7
NEW BRUNSWICK				
	Bathurst	114.1	70.1	94.7
	Dalhousie	114.1	70.3	94.8
	Fredericton	117.0	75.6	98.8
	Moncton	114.3	71.7	95.5
	Newcastle	114.1	70.8	95.0
	St. John	116.6	75.3	98.4
NEWFOUNDLAND				
	Corner Brook	119.5	70.5	97.9
	St Johns	120.3	75.7	100.6
NORTHWEST TERRITORIES				
	Yellowknife	123.5	88.9	108.3
NOVA SCOTIA				
	Bridgewater	115.6	77.8	98.9
	Dartmouth	117.2	77.8	99.8
	Halifax	119.0	80.3	101.9
	New Glasgow	115.3	77.8	98.8
	Sydney	112.8	77.8	97.4
	Truro	115.1	77.8	98.6
	Yarmouth	115.2	77.8	98.7
ONTARIO				
	Barrie	118.6	96.9	109.1
	Brantford	117.7	101.0	110.4
	Cornwall	117.7	97.2	108.7
	Hamilton	121.9	93.7	109.4
	Kingston	118.6	97.3	109.2
	Kitchener	113.7	90.4	103.4
	London	121.6	90.2	107.8
	North Bay	118.0	94.9	107.8
	Oshawa	117.1	98.2	108.7
	Ottawa	122.9	90.7	108.7
	Owen Sound	118.8	95.0	108.3
	Peterborough	117.7	97.0	108.6
	Sarnia	117.4	101.6	110.5
	Sault Ste Marie	112.6	94.5	104.6

STATE/ZIP	CITY	MAT.	INST.	TOTAL
ONTARIO (CONT'D)	St. Catharines	111.7	91.3	102.8
	Sudbury	112.3	90.4	102.7
	Thunder Bay	113.1	90.2	103.0
	Timmins	117.9	94.9	107.8
	Toronto	123.0	98.8	112.3
	Windsor	112.2	90.0	102.4
PRINCE EDWARD ISLAND				
	Charlottetown	118.2	65.4	95.0
	Summerside	117.0	65.5	94.3
QUEBEC				
	Cap-de-la-Madeleine	114.8	91.3	104.4
	Charlesbourg	114.8	91.3	104.4
	Chicoutimi	113.7	91.6	104.0
	Gatineau	114.4	91.1	104.2
	Granby	114.7	91.0	104.3
	Hull	114.5	91.1	104.2
	Joliette	114.9	91.3	104.5
	Laval	114.0	91.1	103.9
	Montreal	121.9	91.9	108.7
	Quebec	119.8	92.3	107.7
	Rimouski	114.2	91.6	104.2
	Rouyn-Noranda	114.4	91.1	104.1
	Saint Hyacinthe	113.6	91.1	103.7
	Sherbrooke	114.8	91.1	104.4
	Sorel	114.9	91.3	104.5
	St Jerome	114.4	91.1	104.1
	Trois Rivieres	115.1	91.3	104.6
SASKATCHEWAN				
	Moose Jaw	113.4	72.4	95.3
	Prince Albert	112.3	70.5	93.9
	Regina	116.7	86.2	103.2
	Saskatoon	113.2	86.2	101.3
YUKON				
	Whitehorse	116.5	71.3	96.6

L1010-101 Minimum Design Live Loads in Pounds per S.F. for Various Building Codes

Occupancy	Description	Minimum Live Loads, Pounds per S.F.
		IBC
Access Floors	Office use	50
	Computer use	100
Armories		150
Assembly	Fixed seats	60
	Movable seats	100
	Platforms or stage floors	125
Commercial & Industrial	Light manufacturing	125
	Heavy manufacturing	250
	Light storage	125
	Heavy storage	250
	Stores, retail, first floor	100
	Stores, retail, upper floors	75
	Stores, wholesale	125
Dance halls	Ballrooms	100
Dining rooms	Restaurants	100
Fire escapes	Other than below	100
	Single family residential	40
Garages	Passenger cars only	40
Gymnasiums	Main floors and balconies	100
Hospitals	Operating rooms, laboratories	60
	Private room	40
	Corridors, above first floor	80
Libraries	Reading rooms	60
	Stack rooms	150
	Corridors, above first floor	80
Marquees		75
Office Buildings	Offices	50
	Lobbies	100
	Corridors, above first floor	80
Residential	Multi family private apartments	40
	Multi family, public rooms	100
	Multi family, corridors	100
	Dwellings, first floor	40
	Dwellings, second floor & habitable attics	30
	Dwellings, uninhabitable attics	20
	Hotels, guest rooms	40
	Hotels, public rooms	100
	Hotels, corridors serving public rooms	100
	Hotels, corridors	100
Schools	Classrooms	40
	Corridors	100
Sidewalks	Driveways, etc. subject to trucking	250
Stairs	Exits	100
Theaters	Aisles, corridors and lobbies	See Assembly
	Orchestra floors	↓
	Balconies	
	Stage floors	125
Yards	Terrace, pedestrian	100

UBC = Uniform Building Code, International Conference of Building Officials, 2006 Edition

Table L1010-201   Design Weight Per S.F. for Walls and Partitions

Type	Wall Thickness	Description	Weight Per S.F.	Type	Wall Thickness	Description	Weight Per S.F.
Brick	4"	Clay brick, high absorption	34 lb.	Clay tile	2"	Split terra cotta furring	10 lb.
		Clay brick, medium absorption	39			Non load bearing clay tile	11
		Clay brick, low absorption	46		3"	Split terra cotta furring	12
		Sand-lime brick	38			Non load bearing clay tile	18
		Concrete brick, heavy aggregate	46		4"	Non load bearing clay tile	20
		Concrete brick, light aggregate	33			Load bearing clay tile	24
	8"	Clay brick, high absorption	69		6"	Non load bearing clay tile	30
		Clay brick, medium absorption	79			Load bearing clay tile	36
		Clay brick, low absorption	89		8"	Non load bearing clay tile	36
		Sand-lime brick	74			Load bearing clay tile	42
		Concrete brick, heavy aggregate	89		12"	Non load bearing clay tile	46
		Concrete brick, light aggregate	68			Load bearing clay tile	58
	12"	Common brick	120	Gypsum block	2"	Hollow gypsum block	9.5
		Pressed brick	130			Solid gypsum block	12
		Sand-lime brick	105		3"	Hollow gypsum block	10
		Concrete brick, heavy aggregate	130			Solid gypsum block	18
		Concrete brick, light aggregate	98		4"	Hollow gypsum block	15
	16"	Clay brick, high absorption	134			Solid gypsum block	24
		Clay brick, medium absorption	155		5"	Hollow gypsum block	18
		Clay brick, low absorption	173		6"	Hollow gypsum block	24
		Sand-lime brick	138	Structural facing tile	2"	Facing tile	15
		Concrete brick, heavy aggregate	174		4"	Facing tile	25
		Concrete brick, light aggregate	130		6"	Facing tile	38
Concrete block	4"	Solid conc. block, stone aggregate	45	Glass	4"	Glass block	18
		Solid conc. block, lightweight	34		1"	Structural glass	15
		Hollow conc. block, stone aggregate	30	Plaster	1"	Gypsum plaster (1 side)	5
		Hollow conc. block, lightweight	20			Cement plaster (1 side)	10
	6"	Solid conc. block, stone aggregate	50			Gypsum plaster on lath	8
		Solid conc. block, lightweight	37			Cement plaster on lath	13
		Hollow conc. block, stone aggregate	42	Plaster partition (2 finished faces)	2"	Solid gypsum on metal lath	18
		Hollow conc. block, lightweight	30			Solid cement on metal lath	25
	8"	Solid conc. block, stone aggregate	67			Solid gypsum on gypsum lath	18
		Solid conc. block, lightweight	48			Gypsum on lath & metal studs	18
		Hollow conc. block, stone aggregate	55		3"	Gypsum on lath & metal studs	19
		Hollow conc. block, lightweight	38		4"	Gypsum on lath & metal studs	20
	10"	Solid conc. block, stone aggregate	84		6"	Gypsum on lath & wood studs	18
		Solid conc. block, lightweight	62	Concrete	6"	Reinf concrete, stone aggregate	75
		Hollow conc. block, stone aggregate	55			Reinf. concrete, lightweight	36-60
		Hollow conc. block, lightweight	38		8"	Reinf. concrete, stone aggregate	100
	12"	Solid conc. block, stone aggregate	108			Reinf. concrete, lightweight	48-80
		Solid conc. block, lightweight	72		10"	Reinf. concrete, stone aggregate	125
		Hollow conc. block, stone aggregate	85			Reinf. concrete, lightweight	60-100
		Hollow conc. block, lightweight	55		12"	Reinf concrete stone aggregate	150
Drywall	6"	Drywall on wood studs	10			Reinf concrete, lightweight	72-120

Table L1010-202   Design Weight per S.F. for Roof Coverings

Type	Description		Weight lb. Per S.F.	Type	Wall Thickness	Description	Weight lb. Per S.F.
Sheathing	Gypsum	1" thick	4	Metal	Aluminum	Corr. & ribbed, .024" to .040"	.4-.8
	Wood	¾" thick	3		Copper	or tin	1.5-2.5
Insulation	per 1"	Loose	.5		Steel	Corrugated, 29 ga. to 12 ga.	.6-5.0
		Poured in place	2	Shingles	Asphalt	Strip shingles	1.7-2.8
		Rigid	1.5		Clay	Tile	8-16
Built-up	Tar & gravel	3 ply felt	5.5		Slate	¼" thick	9.5
		5 ply felt	6.5		Wood		2-3

Table L1010-203   Design Weight per Square Foot for Floor Fills and Finishes

Type		Description	Weight lb. per S.F.	Type		Description	Weight lb. per S.F.
Floor fill	per 1″	Cinder fill	5	Wood	Single 7/8″	On sleepers, light concrete fill	16
		Cinder concrete	9			On sleepers, stone concrete fill	25
		Lightweight concrete	3-9		Double 7/8″	On sleepers, light concrete fill	19
		Stone concrete	12			On sleepers, stone concrete fill	28
		Sand	8		3″	Wood block on mastic, no fill	15
		Gypsum	6			Wood block on ½″ mortar	16
Terrazzo	1″	Terrazzo, 2″ stone concrete	25		per 1″	Hardwood flooring (25/32″)	4
Marble	and mortar	on stone concrete fill	33			Underlayment (Plywood per 1″)	3
Resilient	1/16″-1/4″	Linoleum, asphalt, vinyl tile	2	Asphalt	1-1/2″	Mastic flooring	18
Tile	3/4″	Ceramic or quarry	10		2″	Block on ½″ mortar	30

Table L1010-204   Design Weight Per Cubic Foot for Miscellaneous Materials

Type		Description	Weight lb. per C.F.	Type		Description	Weight lb. per C.F.
Bituminous	Coal, piled	Anthracite	47-58	Masonry	Ashlar	Granite	165
		Bituminous	40-54			Limestone, crystalline	165
		Peat, turf, dry	47			Limestone, oolitic	135
		Coke	75			Marble	173
	Petroleum	Unrefined	54			Sandstone	144
		Refined	50		Rubble, in mortar	Granite	155
		Gasoline	42			Limestone, crystalline	147
	Pitch		69			Limestone, oolitic	138
	Tar	Bituminous	75			Marble	156
Concrete	Plain	Stone aggregate	144			Sandstone & Bluestone	130
		Slag aggregate	132		Brick	Pressed	140
		Expanded slag aggregate	100			Common	120
		Haydite (burned clay agg.)	90			Soft	100
		Vermiculite & perlite, load bearing	70-105		Cement	Portland, loose	90
		Vermiculite & perlite, non load bear	35-50			Portland set	183
	Reinforced	Stone aggregate	150		Lime	Gypsum, loose	53-64
		Slag aggregate	138		Mortar	Set	103
		Lightweight aggregates	30-120	Metals	Aluminum	Cast, hammered	165
Earth	Clay	Dry	63		Brass	Cast, rolled	534
		Damp, plastic	110		Bronze	7.9 to 14% Sn	509
		and gravel, dry	100		Copper	Cast, rolled	556
	Dry	Loose	76		Iron	Cast, pig	450
		Packed	95			Wrought	480
	Moist	Loose	78		Lead		710
		Packed	96		Monel		556
	Mud	Flowing	108		Steel	Rolled	490
		Packed	115		Tin	Cast, hammered	459
	Riprap	Limestone	80-85		Zinc	Cast rolled	440
		Sandstone	90	Timber	Cedar	White or red	24.2
		Shale	105		Fir	Douglas	23.7
	Sand & gravel	Dry, loose	90-105			Eastern	25
		Dry, packed	100-120		Maple	Hard	44.5
		Wet	118-120			White	33
Gases	Air	0C., 760 mm.	.0807		Oak	Red or Black	47.3
	Gas	Natural	.0385			White	47.3
Liquids	Alcohol	100%	49		Pine	White	26
	Water	4°C., maximum density	62.5			Yellow, long leaf	44
		Ice	56			Yellow, short leaf	38
		Snow, fresh fallen	8		Redwood	California	26
		Sea water	64		Spruce	White or black	27

Table L1010-225 Design Weight Per S.F. for Structural Floor and Roof Systems

Type Slab		Description	Weight in Pounds per S.F. Slab Depth in Inches												
Concrete Slab	Reinforced	Stone aggregate	1"	12.5	2"	25	3"	37.5	4"	50	5"	62.5	6"	75
		Lightweight sand aggregate		9.5		19		28.5		38		47.5		57
		All lightweight aggregate		9.0		18		27.0		36		45.0		54
	Plain, nonrein-forced	Stone aggregate		12.0		24		36.0		48		60.0		72
		Lightweight sand aggregate		9.0		18		27.0		36		45.0		54
		All lightweight aggregate		8.5		17		25.5		34		42.5		51
Concrete Waffle	19" x 19"	5" wide ribs @ 24" O.C.	6+3	77	8+3	92	10+3	100	12+3	118				
			6+4½	96	8+4½	110	10+4½	119	12+4½	136				
	30" x 30"	6" wide ribs @ 36" O.C.	8+3	83	10+3	95	12+3	109	14+3	118	16+3	130	20+3	155
			8+4½	101	10+4½	113	12+4½	126	14+4½	137	16+4½	149	20+4½	173
Concrete Joist	20" wide form	5" wide rib	8+3	60	10+3	67	12+3	74	14+3	81				
		6" wide rib		63		70		78		86	16+3	94	20+3	111
		7" wide rib										99		118
		5" wide rib	8+4½	79	10+4½	85	12+4½	92	14+4½	99				
		6" wide rib		82		89		97		104	16+4½	113	20+4½	130
		7" wide rib										118		136
	30" wide form	5" wide rib	8+3	54	10+3	58	12+3	63	14+3	68				
		6" wide rib		56		61		67		72	16+3	78	20+3	91
		7" wide rib										83		96
		5" wide rib	8+4½	72	10+4½	77	12+4½	82	14+4½	87				
		6" wide rib		75		80		85		91	16+4½	97	20+4½	109
		7" wide rib										101		115
Wood Joists	Incl. Subfloor	12" O.C.	2x6	6	2x8	6	2x10	7	2x12	8	3x8	8	3x12	11
		16" O.C.		5		6		6		7		7		9

Table L1010-226 Superimposed Dead Load Ranges

Component	Load Range (PSF)
Ceiling	5-10
Partitions	20-30
Mechanical	4-8

Table L1010-301 Design Loads for Structures for Wind Load

Wind Loads: Structures are designed to resist the wind force from any direction. Usually 2/3 is assumed to act on the windward side, 1/3 on the leeward side.

For more than 1/3 openings, add 10 psf for internal wind pressure or 5 psf for suction, whichever is critical.

For buildings and structures, use psf values from Table L1010-301.

For glass over 4 S.F. use values in Table L1010-302 after determining 30' wind velocity from Table L1010-303.

Type Structure	Height Above Grade	Horizontal Load in Lb. per S.F.
Buildings	Up to 50 ft.	15
	50 to 100 ft.	20
	Over 100 ft.	20 + .025 per ft.
Ground signs & towers	Up to 50 ft.	15
	Over 50 ft.	20
Roof structures		30
Glass	See Table below	

Table L1010-302 Design Wind Load in PSF for Glass at Various Elevations (BOCA Code)

Height From Grade	Velocity in Miles per Hour and Design Load in Pounds per S.F.																			
	Vel.	PSF	Vel.	PSF	Vel.	PSF	Vel.	PSF	Vel.	PSF	Vel.	PSF	Vel.	PSF	Vel.	PSF	Vel.	PSF	Vel.	PSF
To 10 ft.	42	6	46	7	49	8	52	9	55	10	59	11	62	12	66	14	69	15	76	19	83	22
10-20	52	9	58	11	61	11	65	14	70	16	74	18	79	20	83	22	87	24	96	30	105	35
20-30*	60	12	67	14	70	16	75	18	80	20	85	23	90	26	95	29	100	32	110	39	120	46
30-60	66	14	74	18	77	19	83	22	88	25	94	28	99	31	104	35	110	39	121	47	132	56
60-120	73	17	82	21	85	12	92	27	98	31	104	35	110	39	116	43	122	48	134	57	146	68
120-140	81	21	91	26	95	29	101	33	108	37	115	42	122	48	128	52	135	48	149	71	162	84
240-480	90	26	100	32	104	35	112	40	119	45	127	51	134	57	142	65	149	71	164	86	179	102
480-960	98	31	110	39	115	42	123	49	131	55	139	62	148	70	156	78	164	86	180	104	197	124
Over 960	98	31	110	39	115	42	123	49	131	55	139	62	148	70	156	78	164	86	180	104	197	124

*Determine appropriate wind at 30' elevation Fig. L1010-303 below.

Table L1010-303 Design Wind Velocity at 30 Ft. Above Ground

SPEEDS ARE FOR NORMAL EXPOSURE WHERE SURFACE FRICTION IS RELATIVELY UNIFORM FOR A FETCH OF ABOUT 25 MILES. IF THE EXPOSURE IS ELEVATED, SUBJECT TO CHANNELING, OR OTHER SPECIAL CONDITIONS AFFECTING THE EXTREME WIND SPEEDS, ADJUSTMENTS MUST BE MADE TO THE MAP VALUES.

Table L1010-401   Snow Load in Pounds Per Square Foot on the Ground

Based on 50 year storm for INDUSTRIAL BUSINESS, MERCANTILE, & RESIDENTIAL

Table L1010-402   Snow Load in Pounds Per Square Foot on the Ground

Based on 100 year storm for ASSEMBLY INSTITUTIONAL, HIGH HAZARD MOTELS

Table L1010-403   Snow Loads

To convert the ground snow loads on the previous page to roof snow loads, the ground snow loads should be multiplied by the following factors depending upon the roof characteristics.

Note, in all cases $\frac{\alpha - 30}{50}$ is valid only for > 30 degrees.

Description	Sketch	Formula	Angle	Conversion Factor = C_f	
				Sheltered	Exposed
Simple flat and shed roofs	Load Diagram	For $\alpha > 30°$ $C_f = 0.8 - \frac{\alpha - 30}{50}$	0° to 30°	0.8	0.6
			40°	0.6	0.45
			50°	0.4	0.3
			60°	0.2	0.15
			70° to 90°	0	0
				Case I	Case II
Simple gable and hip roofs	Case I Load Diagram — Case II Load Diagram	$C_f = 0.8 - \frac{\alpha - 30}{50}$ $C_f = 1.25 \left(0.8 - \left(\frac{\alpha - 30}{50}\right)\right)$	10°	0.8	—
			20°	0.8	—
			30°	0.8	1.0
			40°	0.6	0.75
			50°	0.4	0.5
			60°	0.2	0.25
Valley areas of Two span roofs	Case I — Case II	$\beta = \frac{\alpha_1 + \alpha_2}{2}$ $C_f = 0.8 - \frac{\alpha - 30}{50}$	$\beta \le 10°$ use Case I only $\beta > 10°$ $\beta < 20°$ use Case I & II $\beta \ge 20°$ use Case I, II & III		
Lower level of multi level roofs (or on an adjacent building not more then 15 ft. away)	W = 2h	$C_f = 15 \frac{h}{g}$ h = difference in roof height in feet g = ground snow load in psf w = width of drift For h < 5, w = 10 h > 15, w = 30	When $15 \frac{h}{g} < .8$, use 0.8 When $15 \frac{h}{g} > 3.0$, use 3.0		

Summary of above:

1. For flat roofs or roofs up to 30°, use 0.8 x ground snow load for the roof snow load.
2. For roof pitches in excess of 30°, conversion factor becomes lower than 0.8.
3. For exposed roofs there is a further 25% reduction of conversion factor.
4. For steep roofs a more highly loaded half span must be considered.
5. For shallow roof valleys conversion factor is 0.8.
6. For moderate roof valleys, conversion factor is 1.0 for half the span.
7. For steep roof valleys, conversion factor is 1.5 for one quarter of the span.
8. For roofs adjoining vertical surfaces the conversion factor is up to 3.0 for part of the span.
9. If snow load is less than 30 psf, use water load on roof for clogged drain condition.

Table L1020-101 Floor Area Ratios

Table below lists commonly used gross to net area and net to gross area ratios expressed in % for various building types.

Building Type	Gross to Net Ratio	Net to Gross Ratio	Building Type	Gross to Net Ratio	Net to Gross Ratio
Apartment	156	64	School Buildings (campus type)		
Bank	140	72	Administrative	150	67
Church	142	70	Auditorium	142	70
Courthouse	162	61	Biology	161	62
Department Store	123	81	Chemistry	170	59
Garage	118	85	Classroom	152	66
Hospital	183	55	Dining Hall	138	72
Hotel	158	63	Dormitory	154	65
Laboratory	171	58	Engineering	164	61
Library	132	76	Fraternity	160	63
Office	135	75	Gymnasium	142	70
Restaurant	141	70	Science	167	60
Warehouse	108	93	Service	120	83
			Student Union	172	59

The gross area of a building is the total floor area based on outside dimensions.

The net area of a building is the usable floor area for the function intended and excludes such items as stairways, corridors, and mechanical rooms.

In the case of a commercial building, it might be considered as the "leasable area."

Table L1020-201 Partition/Door Density

Building Type		Stories	Partition/Density	Doors	Description of Partition
Apartments		1 story	9 SF/LF	90 SF/door	Plaster, wood doors & trim
		2 story	8 SF/LF	80 SF/door	Drywall, wood studs, wood doors & trim
		3 story	9 SF/LF	90 SF/door	Plaster, wood studs, wood doors & trim
		5 story	9 SF/LF	90 SF/door	Plaster, metal studs, wood doors & trim
		6-15 story	8 SF/LF	80 SF/door	Drywall, metal studs, wood doors & trim
Bakery		1 story	50 SF/LF	500 SF/door	Conc. block, paint, door & drywall, wood studs
		2 story	50 SF/LF	500 SF/door	Conc. block, paint, door & drywall, wood studs
Bank		1 story	20 SF/LF	200 SF/door	Plaster, wood studs, wood doors & trim
		2-4 story	15 SF/LF	150 SF/door	Plaster, metal studs, wood doors & trim
Bottling Plant		1 story	50 SF/LF	500 SF/door	Conc. block, drywall, metal studs, wood trim
Bowling Alley		1 story	50 SF/LF	500 SF/door	Conc. block, wood & metal doors, wood trim
Bus Terminal		1 story	15 SF/LF	150 SF/door	Conc. block, ceramic tile, wood trim
Cannery		1 story	100 SF/LF	1000 SF/door	Drywall on metal studs
Car Wash		1 story	18 SF/LF	180 SF/door	Concrete block, painted & hollow metal door
Dairy Plant		1 story	30 SF/LF	300 SF/door	Concrete block, glazed tile, insulated cooler doors
Department Store		1 story	60 SF/LF	600 SF/door	Drywall, metal studs, wood doors & trim
		2-5 story	60 SF/LF	600 SF/door	30% concrete block, 70% drywall, wood studs
Dormitory		2 story	9 SF/LF	90 SF/door	Plaster, concrete block, wood doors & trim
		3-5 story	9 SF/LF	90 SF/door	Plaster, concrete block, wood doors & trim
		6-15 story	9 SF/LF	90 SF/door	Plaster, concrete block, wood doors & trim
Funeral Home		1 story	15 SF/LF	150 SF/door	Plaster on concrete block & wood studs, paneling
		2 story	14 SF/LF	140 SF/door	Plaster, wood studs, paneling & wood doors
Garage Sales & Service		1 story	30 SF/LF	300 SF/door	50% conc. block, 50% drywall, wood studs
Hotel		3-8 story	9 SF/LF	90 SF/door	Plaster, conc. block, wood doors & trim
		9-15 story	9 SF/LF	90 SF/door	Plaster, conc. block, wood doors & trim
Laundromat		1 story	25 SF/LF	250 SF/door	Drywall, wood studs, wood doors & trim
Medical Clinic		1 story	6 SF/LF	60 SF/door	Drywall, wood studs, wood doors & trim
		2-4 story	6 SF/LF	60 SF/door	Drywall, metal studs, wood doors & trim
Motel		1 story	7 SF/LF	70 SF/door	Drywall, wood studs, wood doors & trim
		2-3 story	7 SF/LF	70 SF/door	Concrete block, drywall on metal studs, wood paneling
Movie Theater	200-600 seats	1 story	18 SF/LF	180 SF/door	Concrete block, wood, metal, vinyl trim
	601-1400 seats		20 SF/LF	200 SF/door	Concrete block, wood, metal, vinyl trim
	1401-22000 seats		25 SF/LF	250 SF/door	Concrete block, wood, metal, vinyl trim
Nursing Home		1 story	8 SF/LF	80 SF/door	Drywall, metal studs, wood doors & trim
		2-4 story	8 SF/LF	80 SF/door	Drywall, metal studs, wood doors & trim
Office		1 story	20 SF/LF	200-500 SF/door	30% concrete block, 70% drywall on wood studs
		2 story	20 SF/LF	200-500 SF/door	30% concrete block, 70% drywall on metal studs
		3-5 story	20 SF/LF	200-500 SF/door	30% concrete block, 70% movable partitions
		6-10 story	20 SF/LF	200-500 SF/door	30% concrete block, 70% movable partitions
		11-20 story	20 SF/LF	200-500 SF/door	30% concrete block, 70% movable partitions
Parking Ramp (Open)		2-8 story	60 SF/LF	600 SF/door	Stair and elevator enclosures only
Parking garage		2-8 story	60 SF/LF	600 SF/door	Stair and elevator enclosures only
Pre-Engineered	Steel	1 story	0		
	Store	1 story	60 SF/LF	600 SF/door	Drywall on metal studs, wood doors & trim
	Office	1 story	15 SF/LF	150 SF/door	Concrete block, movable wood partitions
	Shop	1 story	15 SF/LF	150 SF/door	Movable wood partitions
	Warehouse	1 story	0		
Radio & TV Broadcasting		1 story	25 SF/LF	250 SF/door	Concrete block, metal and wood doors
& TV Transmitter		1 story	40 SF/LF	400 SF/door	Concrete block, metal and wood doors
Self Service Restaurant		1 story	15 SF/LF	150 SF/door	Concrete block, wood and aluminum trim
Cafe & Drive-in Restaurant		1 story	18 SF/LF	180 SF/door	Drywall, metal studs, ceramic & plastic trim
Restaurant with seating		1 story	25 SF/LF	250 SF/door	Concrete block, paneling, wood studs & trim
Supper Club		1 story	25 SF/LF	250 SF/door	Concrete block, paneling, wood studs & trim
Bar or Lounge		1 story	24 SF/LF	240 SF/door	Plaster or gypsum lath, wooded studs
Retail Store or Shop		1 story	60 SF/LF	600 SF/door	Drywall metal studs, wood doors & trim
Service Station	Masonry	1 story	15 SF/LF	150 SF/door	Concrete block, paint, door & drywall, wood studs
	Metal panel	1 story	15 SF/LF	150 SF/door	Concrete block, paint, door & drywall, wood studs
	Frame	1 story	15 SF/LF	150 SF/door	Drywall, wood studs, wood doors & trim
Shopping Center	(strip)	1 story	30 SF/LF	300 SF/door	Drywall, metal studs, wood doors & trim
	(group)	1 story	40 SF/LF	400 SF/door	50% concrete block, 50% drywall, wood studs
		2 story	40 SF/LF	400 SF/door	50% concrete block, 50% drywall, wood studs
Small Food Store		1 story	30 SF/LF	300 SF/door	Concrete block drywall, wood studs, wood trim
Store/Apt. above	Masonry	2 story	10 SF/LF	100 SF/door	Plaster, metal studs, wood doors & trim
	Frame	2 story	10 SF/LF	100 SF/door	Plaster, metal studs, wood doors & trim
	Frame	3 story	10 SF/LF	100 SF/door	Plaster, metal studs, wood doors & trim
Supermarkets		1 story	40 SF/LF	400 SF/door	Concrete block, paint, drywall & porcelain panel
Truck Terminal		1 story	0		
Warehouse		1 story	0		

Table L1020-301 Occupancy Determinations

Description		S.F. Required per Person IBC
Assembly Areas	Fixed seats**	# fixed seats
	Without fixed seats	
	Concentrated (chairs only)	7 net
	Standing Space	5 net
	Unconcentrated (tables and chairs)	15 net
	Gaming floors (Keno, slots, etc.)	11 gross
Educational	Classroom area	20 net
	Shops and other vocational room areas	50 net
Institutional	Inpatient treatment areas	240 gross
	Outpatient areas	100 gross
	Sleeping Areas	120 gross
Mercantile	Areas on other floors	60 gross
	Basement and grade floor areas	30 gross
	Storage, stock, shipping areas	300 gross
Business Areas		100 gross

IBC = *International Building Code,* 2006 Edition

** The occupancy load for assembly area with fixed seats shall be determined by the number of fixed seats installed.

Table L1020-302 Length of Exitway Access Travel (ft.)

Use Group	Without Fire Suppression System	With Fire Suppression System
Assembly	200	250
Business	200	300
Factory and industrial	300	400
High hazard	—	75
Institutional	200	250
Mercantile	200	250
Residential	200	250
Storage, low hazard	300	400
Storage, moderate hazard	200	250

Note: The maximum length of exitway access travel in unlimited area buildings shall be 400′.

Table L1020-303 Capacity Per Unit Egress Width*

Use Group	Without Fire Suppression System (Inches per Person)*		With Fire Suppression System (Inches per Person)*	
	Stairways	Doors, Ramps and Corridors	Stairways	Doors, Ramps and Corridors
Assembly, Business, Educational, Factory Industrial, Mercantile, Residential, Storage	0.3	0.2	0.2	0.15
Institutional—1	0.3	0.2	0.2	0.15
Institutional—2	—	0.7	0.3	0.2
Institutional—3	0.3	0.2	0.2	0.15
High Hazard	0.7	0.4	0.3	0.2

* 1″ = 25.4 mm

Table L1030-401   Resistances ("R") of Building and Insulating Materials

Material	Wt./Lbs. per C.F.	R per Inch	R Listed Size
Air Spaces and Surfaces			
Enclosed non-reflective spaces, E=0.82			
50° F mean temp., 30°/10° F diff.			
.5"			.90/.91
.75"			.94/1.01
1.50"			.90/1.02
3.50"			.91/1.01
Inside vert. surface (still air)			0.68
Outside vert. surface (15 mph wind)			0.17
Building Boards			
Asbestos cement, 0.25" thick	120		0.06
Gypsum or plaster, 0.5" thick	50		0.45
Hardboard regular	50	1.37	
Tempered	63	1.00	
Laminated paper	30	2.00	
Particle board	37	1.85	
	50	1.06	
	63	0.85	
Plywood (Douglas Fir), 0.5" thick	34		0.62
Shingle backer, .375" thick	18		0.94
Sound deadening board, 0.5" thick	15		1.35
Tile and lay-in panels, plain or			
acoustical, 0.5" thick	18		1.25
Vegetable fiber, 0.5" thick	18		1.32
	25		1.14
Wood, hardwoods	48	0.91	
Softwoods	32	1.25	
Flooring Carpet with fibrous pad			2.08
With rubber pad			1.23
Cork tile, 1/8" thick			0.28
Terrazzo			0.08
Tile, resilient			0.05
Wood, hardwood, 0.75" thick			0.68
Subfloor, 0.75" thick			0.94
Glass			
Insulation, 0.50" air space			2.04
Single glass			0.91
Insulation Blanket or Batt, mineral, glass			
or rock fiber, approximate thickness			
3.0" to 3.5" thick			11
3.5" to 4.0" thick			13
6.0" to 6.5" thick			19
6.5" to 7.0" thick			22
8.5" to 9.0" thick			30
Boards			
Cellular glass	8.5	2.63	
Fiberboard, wet felted			
Acoustical tile	21	2.70	
Roof insulation	17	2.94	
Fiberboard, wet molded			
Acoustical tile	23	2.38	
Mineral fiber with resin binder	15	3.45	
Polystyrene, extruded,			
cut cell surface	1.8	4.00	
smooth skin surface	2.2	5.00	
	3.5	5.26	
Bead boards	1.0	3.57	
Polyurethane	1.5	6.25	
Wood or cane fiberboard, 0.5" thick			1.25

Material	Wt./Lbs. per C.F.	R per Inch	R Listed Size
Insulation Loose Fill			
Cellulose	2.3	3.13	
	3.2	3.70	
Mineral fiber, 3.75" to 5" thick	2-5		11
6.5" to 8.75" thick			19
7.5" to 10" thick			22
10.25" to 13.75" thick			30
Perlite	5-8	2.70	
Vermiculite	4-6	2.27	
Wood fiber	2-3.5	3.33	
Masonry Brick, Common	120	0.20	
Face	130	0.11	
Cement mortar	116	0.20	
Clay tile, hollow			
1 cell wide, 3" width			0.80
4" width			1.11
2 cells wide, 6" width			1.52
8" width			1.85
10" width			2.22
3 cells wide, 12" width			2.50
Concrete, gypsum fiber	51	0.60	
Lightweight	120	0.19	
	80	0.40	
	40	0.86	
Perlite	40	1.08	
Sand and gravel or stone	140	0.08	
Concrete block, lightweight			
3 cell units, 4"-15 lbs. ea.			1.68
6"-23 lbs. ea.			1.83
8"-28 lbs. ea.			2.12
12"-40 lbs. ea.			2.62
Sand and gravel aggregates,			
4"-20 lbs. ea.			1.17
6"-33 lbs. ea.			1.29
8"-38 lbs. ea.			1.46
12"-56 lbs. ea.			1.81
Plastering Cement Plaster,			
Sand aggregate	116	0.20	
Gypsum plaster, Perlite aggregate	45	0.67	
Sand aggregate	105	0.18	
Vermiculite aggregate	45	0.59	
Roofing			
Asphalt, felt, 15 lb.			0.06
Rolled roofing	70		0.15
Shingles	70		0.44
Built-up roofing .375" thick	70		0.33
Cement shingles	120		0.21
Vapor-permeable felt			0.06
Vapor seal, 2 layers of			
mopped 15 lb. felt			0.12
Wood, shingles 16"-7.5" exposure			0.87
Siding			
Aluminum or steel (hollow backed)			
oversheathing			0.61
With .375" insulating backer board			1.82
Foil backed			2.96
Wood siding, beveled, ½" x 8"			0.81

Table L1030-502 Maximum Depth of Frost Penetration in Inches

THIS MAP IS REASONABLY ACCURATE FOR MOST PARTS
OF THE UNITED STATES BUT IS NECESSARILY HIGHLY
GENERALIZED, AND CONSEQUENTLY NOT TOO ACCURATE IN
MOUNTAINOUS REGIONS, PARTICULARLY IN THE ROCKIES.

Table L1040-101 Fire-Resisting Ratings of Structural Elements (in hours)

Description of the Structural Element	No. 1 Fireproof		No. 2 Non Combustible			No. 3 Exterior Masonry Wall			No. 4 Frame	
			Protected		Unprotected	Heavy Timber	Ordinary		Protected	Unprotected
							Protected	Unprotected		
	1A	1B	2A	2B	2C	3A	3B	3C	4A	4B
Exterior, Bearing Walls	4	3	2	1½	1	2	2	2	1	1
Nonbearing Walls	2	2	1½	1	1	2	2	2	1	1
Interior Bearing Walls and Partitions	4	3	2	1	0	2	1	0	1	0
Fire Walls and Party Walls	4	3	2	2	2	2	2	2	2	2
Fire Enclosure of Exitways, Exit Hallways and Stairways	2	2	2	2	2	2	2	2	1	1
Shafts other than Exitways, Hallways and Stairways	2	2	2	2	2	2	2	2	1	1
Exitway access corridors and Vertical separation of tenant space	1	1	1	1	0	1	1	0	1	0
Columns, girders, trusses (other than roof trusses) and framing: Supporting more than one floor	4	3	2	1	0	—	1	0	1	0
Supporting one floor only	3	2	1½	1	0	—	1	0	1	0
Structural members supporting wall	3	2	1½	1	0	1	1	0	1	0
Floor construction including beams	3	2	1½	1	0	—	1	0	1	0
Roof construction including beams, trusses and framing arches and roof deck 15' or less in height to lowest member	2	1½	1	1	0	—	1	0	1	0

Note: a. Codes include special requirements and exceptions that are not included in the table above.

b. Each type of construction has been divided into sub-types which vary according to the degree of fire resistance required. Sub-types (A) requirements are more severe than those for sub-types (B).

c. Protected construction means all structural members are chemically treated, covered or protected so that the unit has the required fire resistance.

Type No. 1, Fireproof Construction — Buildings and structures of fireproof construction are those in which the walls, partitions, structural elements, floors, ceilings, and roofs, and the exitways are protected with approved noncombustible materials to afford the fire-resistance rating specified in Table L1040-101; except as otherwise specifically regulated. Fire-resistant treated wood may be used as specified.

Type No. 2, Noncombustible Construction — Buildings and structures of noncombustible construction are those in which the walls, partitions, structural elements, floors, ceilings, roofs and the exitways are approved noncombustible materials meeting the fire-resistance rating requirements specified in Table L1040-101; except as modified by the fire limit restrictions. Fire-retardant treated wood may be used as specified.

Type No. 3, Exterior Masonry Wall Construction — Buildings and structures of exterior masonry wall construction are those in which the exterior, fire and party walls are masonry or other approved noncombustible materials of the required fire-resistance rating and structural properties. The floors, roofs, and interior framing are wholly or partly wood or metal or other approved construction. The fire and party walls are ground-supported; except that girders and their supports, carrying walls of masonry shall be protected to afford the same degree of fire-resistance rating of the supported walls. All structural elements have the required fire-resistance rating specified in Table L1040-101.

Type No. 4, Frame Construction — Buildings and structures of frame construction are those in which the exterior walls, bearing walls, partitions, floor and roof construction are wholly or partly of wood stud and joist assemblies with a minimum nominal dimension of two inches or of other approved combustible materials. Fire stops are required at all vertical and horizontal draft openings in which the structural elements have required fire-resistance ratings specified in Table L1040-101.

Table L1040-201 Fire Grading of Building in Hours for Fire Walls and Fire Separation Walls

Fire Hazard for Fire Walls

The degree of fire hazard of buildings relating to their intended use is defined by ''Fire Grading'' the buildings. Such a grading system is listed in the Table L1040-201 below. This type of grading determines the requirements for fire walls and fire separation walls (exterior fire exposure). For mixed use occupancy, use the higher Fire Grading requirement of the components.

Building Type	Hours	Building Type	Hours
Businesses	2	Recreation Centers	2
Churches	1½	Residential Hotels	2
Factories	3	Residential, Multi-family Dwellings	1½
High Hazard*	4	Residential, One & Two Family Dwellings	¾
Industrial	3	Restaurants	2
Institutional, Incapacitated Occupants	2	Schools	1½
Institutional, Restrained Occupants	3	Storage, Low Hazard*	2
Lecture Halls	2	Storage, Moderate Hazard*	3
Mercantile	3	Terminals	2
Night Club	3	Theatres	3

Note: *The difference in "Fire Hazards" is determined by their occupancy and use.

High Hazard: Industrial and storage buildings in which the combustible contents might cause fires to be unusually intense or where explosives, combustible gases or flammable liquids are manufactured or stored.

Moderate Hazard: Mercantile buildings, industrial and storage buildings in which combustible contents might cause fires of moderate intensity.

Low Hazard: Business buildings that ordinarily do not burn rapidly.

Table L1040-202 Interior Finish Classification

Flame Spread for Interior Finishes

The flame spreadability of a material is the burning characteristic of the material relative to the fuel contributed by its combustion and the density of smoke developed. The flame spread classification of a material is based on a ten minute test on a scale of 0 to 100. Cement asbestos board is assigned a rating of 0 and select red oak flooring a rating of 100. The four classes are listed in Table L1040-202.

The flame spread ratings for interior finish walls and ceilings shall not be greater than the Class listed in the Table L1040-203 below.

Class of Material	Surface Burning Characteristics
I	0 to 25
II	26 to 75
III	76 to 200
IV	201 to 5000

Table L1040-203 Interior Finish Requirements by Class

Building Type	Vertical Exitways & Passageways	Corridors Providing Exitways	Rooms or Enclosed Spaces	Building Type	Vertical Exitways & Passageways	Corridors Providing Exitways	Rooms or Enclosed Space
Assembly Halls	I	I	II	Mercantile Walls	I	II	III
Businesses	I	II	III	Night Clubs	I	I	II
Churches	I	I	II	Residential Hotels	I	II	III
Factory	I	II	III	Residential, Multi-family	I	II	III
High Hazard	I	II	II	Residential, 1 & 2 Family	IV	IV	IV
Industrial	I	II	III	Restaurants	I	I	II
Institutional, Incapacitated	I	II	I	Storage, Low Hazard	I	II	III
Institutional, Restrained	I	I	I	Storage, Moderate Hazard	I	II	III
Mercantile Ceilings	I	II	II	Terminals	I	I	II

Description: This table is primarily for converting customary U.S. units in the left hand column to Sl metric units in the right hand column.

In addition, conversion factors for some commonly encountered Canadian and non-Sl metric units are included.

Table L1090-101   Metric Conversion Factors

If You Know		Multiply By		To Find
Length	Inches	x	25.4[a]	=	Millimeters
	Feet	x	0.3048[a]	=	Meters
	Yards	x	0.9144[a]	=	Meters
	Miles (statute)	x	1.609	=	Kilometers
Area	Square inches	x	645.2	=	Square millimeters
	Square feet	x	0.0929	=	Square meters
	Square yards	x	0.8361	=	Square meters
Volume (Capacity)	Cubic inches	x	16,387	=	Cubic millimeters
	Cubic feet	x	0.02832	=	Cubic meters
	Cubic yards	x	0.7646	=	Cubic meters
	Gallons (U.S. liquids)[b]	x	0.003785	=	Cubic meters[c]
	Gallons (Canadian liquid)[b]	x	0.004546	=	Cubic meters[c]
	Ounces (U.S. liquid)[b]	x	29.57	=	Milliliters[c, d]
	Quarts (U.S. liquid)[b]	x	0.9464	=	Liters[c, d]
	Gallons (U.S. liquid)[b]	x	3.785	=	Liters[c, d]
Force	Kilograms force[d]	x	9.807	=	Newtons
	Pounds force	x	4.448	=	Newtons
	Pounds force	x	0.4536	=	Kilograms force[d]
	Kips	x	4448	=	Newtons
	Kips	x	453.6	=	Kilograms force[d]
Pressure, Stress, Strength (Force per unit area)	Kilograms force per square centimeter[d]	x	0.09807	=	Megapascals
	Pounds force per square inch (psi)	x	0.006895	=	Megapascals
	Kips per square inch	x	6.895	=	Megapascals
	Pounds force per square inch (psi)	x	0.07031	=	Kilograms force per square centimeter[d]
	Pounds force per square foot	x	47.88	=	Pascals
	Pounds force per square foot	x	4.882	=	Kilograms force per square meter[d]
Bending Moment Or Torque	Inch-pounds force	x	0.01152	=	Meter-kilograms force[d]
	Inch-pounds force	x	0.1130	=	Newton-meters
	Foot-pounds force	x	0.1383	=	Meter-kilograms force[d]
	Foot-pounds force	x	1.356	=	Newton-meters
	Meter-kilograms force[d]	x	9.807	=	Newton-meters
Mass	Ounces (avoirdupois)	x	28.35	=	Grams
	Pounds (avoirdupois)	x	0.4536	=	Kilograms
	Tons (metric)	x	1000	=	Kilograms
	Tons, short (2000 pounds)	x	907.2	=	Kilograms
	Tons, short (2000 pounds)	x	0.9072	=	Megagrams[e]
Mass per Unit Volume	Pounds mass per cubic foot	x	16.02	=	Kilograms per cubic meter
	Pounds mass per cubic yard	x	0.5933	=	Kilograms per cubic meter
	Pounds mass per gallon (U.S. liquid)[b]	x	119.8	=	Kilograms per cubic meter
	Pounds mass per gallon (Canadian liquid)[b]	x	99.78	=	Kilograms per cubic meter
Temperature	Degrees Fahrenheit	(F-32)/1.8		=	Degrees Celsius
	Degrees Fahrenheit	(F+459.67)/1.8		=	Degrees Kelvin
	Degrees Celsius	C+273.15		=	Degrees Kelvin

[a]The factor given is exact
[b]One U.S. gallon = 0.8327 Canadian gallon
[c]1 liter = 1000 milliliters = 1000 cubic centimeters
   1 cubic decimeter = 0.001 cubic meter

[d]Metric but not SI unit
[e]Called "tonne" in England and
   "metric ton" in other metric countries

Life Cycle Costing (LCC)
for Evaluating Economic Performance of Building Investments

Introduction

A complete analysis of maintenance costs requires consideration of life cycle costs, or LCC, as it is often called. Under current conditions, facilities managers have to wisely spend their limited operating and maintenance budgets. When deciding how to allocate limited budgets, maintenance professionals are constantly faced with the economic decision of when to stop maintaining and start replacing. Once the decision to replace has been made, LCC analysis can enhance the choice of alternatives as well.

The American Society of Testing and Materials (ASTM) Subcommittee E06.81 on Building Economics has developed a series of standards for evaluating the economic performance of building investments. These standards, which have been endorsed by the American Association of Cost Engineers (AACE), are intended to provide uniformity in both the terminology and calculation methods utilized for Life Cycle Costing. Without these standards as a basis for calculations, life cycle cost comparisons could be misleading or incomplete. This chapter is based on the current ASTM standards which are listed in the references at the end of this section.

Definition of Life Cycle Costing
(ASTM Standard Terminology of Building Economics E833-89)

A technique of economic evaluation that sums over a given study period the cost of initial investment less resale value, replacements, operations, energy use, and maintenance and repair of an investment decision. The costs are expressed in either lump sum present value terms or in equivalent uniform annual values.

This technique for life cycle costing is important to the facilities manager, as it is a valuable tool for evaluating investment alternatives and supports his or her decision-making.

To understand Life Cycle Costing, one should be familiar with the notions of compounding, discounting, present value, and equivalent uniform annual value.

Compounding
Definition of Compounding *(Webster's New Collegiate Dictionary)*

The process of computing the value of an original principal sum based on interest calculated on the sum of the original principal and accrued interest.

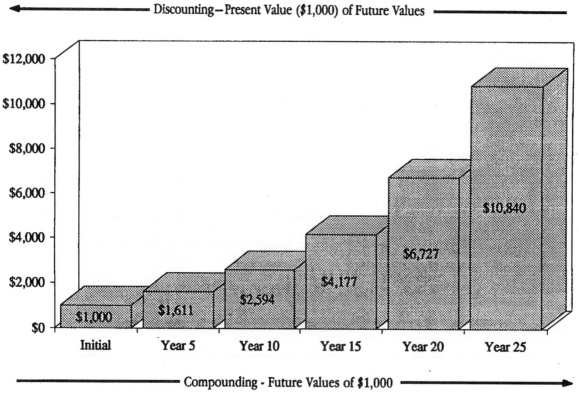

◄ — Discounting—Present Value ($1,000) of Future Values —

$12,000

$10,000

$8,000

$6,000

$4,000

$2,000

$0

| Initial | Year 5 | Year 10 | Year 15 | Year 20 | Year 25 |

$1,000 $1,611 $2,594 $4,177 $6,727 $10,840

— Compounding - Future Values of $1,000 ►

Figure 1: Compounding and Discounting at 10% Per Annum

Figure 1 illustrates compounding. As shown, a principal sum of $1,000 at a compound interest rate of 10% per annum increases to $1,611 in 5 years, $2,594 in 10 years, $4,177 in 15 years, $6,727 in 20 years, and $10,840 in 25 years; this process (compounding) is usually well understood in that it represents the amount accumulated in a bank account for a specific amount at a given interest rate and calculated on the sum of the original principal and accrued interest.

Discounting

ASTM Definition of Discounting

A technique for converting cash flows that occur over time to equivalent amounts at a common time (base time).

It is also evident from Figure 1 that if one had to pay out or meet an obligation of either $1,611 in 5 years, $2,594 in 10 years, $4,177 in 15 years, $6,727 in 20 years, or $10,840 in 25 years, the amount to be invested initially at 10% interest would be $1,000. This amount is referred to as the present value (PV) of a future amount and it is calculated by "discounting" a future value (F) in a specific year at a given rate of interest.

Present Value

ASTM Definition of Present Value

The value of a benefit or cost found by discounting future cash flows to the base time. (Syn. present worth)

The basic mathematics for calculating present values are relatively simple:

Given:

P	=	Present sum of money
F	=	Future sum of money
i	=	Interest or discount rate (expressed as a decimal and not a percentage)
n	=	Number of years

The future value (F) of a present sum of money (P) may be computed as shown in Table 1, a relatively simple process.

Year	Future Value (F)
1	$P (1 + i)$
2	$P (1 + i) (1 + i) = P (1 + i)^2$
3	$P (1 + i)^2 (1 + i) = P (1 + i)^3$
n	$P (1 + i)^n$

Table 1: The Future Value of a Present Sum of Money

Since $\qquad F = P (1 + i)^n$

Therefore $\qquad P = \dfrac{F}{(1 + 1)^n} \quad = \quad F \times \dfrac{1}{(1 + i)^n}$

Example

What is the present value (P) of an anticipated maintenance expense of $300 in year 3 (F) if the interest rate is 10%?

$$P = F \times \frac{1}{(1 + i)^n} = 300 \times \frac{1}{(1 + 0.10)^n} = 300 \times \frac{1}{1.33}$$

$$= 300 \times 0.75$$

$$= \$225$$

From an interest standpoint, this tells us that $225 is the amount that would have to be deposited today into an account paying 10% interest per annum in order to provide $300 at the end of year 3 to meet the anticipated expense. From the economist's point of view, discounting using the investor's minimum acceptable rate of return (10% in this case) makes the economic outlook the same, whether it is the future amount of $300 or a present value of $225.

Note that $(1 + i)^n$ is commonly referred to as the *Single Compound Amount (SCA)* factor, and $1/(1 + i)^n$ as the *Single Present Value Factor (SPV)*. Both factors may be readily found in standard discount factor tables for a wide range of interest rates and time periods, thus simplifying calculations. The use of these factors in calculating life cycle costs by the formula method is discussed later in this section.

A life cycle cost analysis can be performed in *constant dollars* (dollars of constant purchasing power, net of general inflation) or *current dollars* (actual prices inclusive of general inflation). If you use constant dollars, you must use a "real" discount rate (i.e., a rate which reflects the time value of money, net of general inflation) and differential escalation rates (also net of general inflation) for future cost items. Constant dollars are generally tied to a specific year. If you use current dollars, the discount rates and escalation rate must include general inflation (i.e., they must be "nominal" or "market" rates). In this chapter, all costs are expressed in current dollars and rates in nominal terms. When taxes are included in the analysis, the current dollar approach is generally preferred.

The Cash Flow Method for Calculating Life Cycle Costs

There are basically two approaches to calculating life cycle costs—the *cash flow* method and the *formula* method which, when applicable, is somewhat more simple.

To illustrate the cash flow method, a relatively simple example follows.

Example

A facility manager is considering the purchase of maintenance equipment required for a four-year period for which initial costs, energy costs and maintenance costs of alternative proposals vary.

The financial criteria on which the economic evaluation will be based are the following:

Interest/Discount Rate	– 10%
Energy Escalation Rate	– 8% per annum
Labor and Material Escalation Rate	– 4% per annum
Period of Study	– 4 years

The following data is provided in one of the alternative proposals to be analyzed:

- Initial Capital Cost – $1,000
- Maintenance Costs – A fixed annual cost of $100 per year quoted by the supplier (no escalation to be considered)
- Annual Energy Costs – Initially $100 per year and subject to 8% annual escalation – i.e., $108 for year one.
- Salvage Value – At the end of the four-year period, the equipment has no further useful life and the supplier agrees to purchase it as scrap for $50.

What is the present value of this alternative proposal?

The steps to resolve this problem are the following:

Step 1 – Prepare a Cash Flow Diagram.

Step 2 – Establish a Time Schedule of Costs.

Step 3 – Calculate Annual Net Cash Flows.

Step 4 – Calculate Present Value Factors.

Step 5 – Calculate Present Values of Annual Cash Flows and Life Cycle Costs.

Step 1: Prepare a Cash Flow Diagram

To better understand the problem, cash flow diagrams are often prepared. Revenues are noted as vertical lines above a horizontal time axis, and disbursements are noted as vertical lines below it.

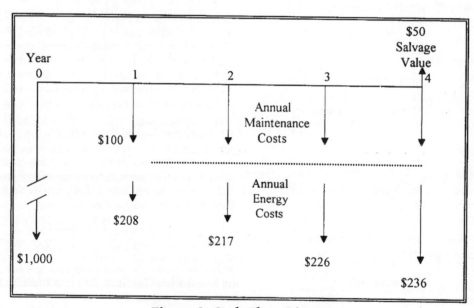

Figure 2: Cash Flow Diagram

Step 2: Establish a Time Schedule of Costs

Table 2 below presents revenues and disbursements for each year of the study:

A Year	B Capital Costs	C Maintenance Costs	D Energy Cost (8% escalation)
0	1,000	–	–
1	–	100	108
2	–	100	117
3	–	100	126
4	(50)	100	136

Table 2

Note that the disbursements in this example are considered positive, and revenues for the salvage value are negative.

Step 3: Calculate Annual Net Cash Flows

Table 3 below provides the net cash flow (NCF) for each year, which could be a disbursement or a revenue.

A Year	B Capital Costs	C Maintenance Costs	D Energy Cost (8% escalation)	E NCF (B + C + D)
0	1,000	–	–	1,000
1	–	100	108	208
2	–	100	117	217
3	–	100	126	226
4	(50)	100	136	186

Table 3

Step 4: Calculate Present Value Factors

As in a previous example, present value factors based on 10% interest will be calculated for each year to convert the annual net cash flows to present values.

Year n	PV Factor	$\dfrac{1}{(1+i)^n}$
0		1
1		$\dfrac{1}{(1+0.1)^1}$ = 0.91
2		$\dfrac{1}{(1+0.1)^2}$ = 0.83
3		$\dfrac{1}{(1+0.1)^3}$ = 0.75
4		$\dfrac{1}{(1+0.1)^4}$ = 0.68

Table 4

Step 5: Calculate Present Values of Annual Cash Flows and Life Cycle Costs

Annual net cash flows are converted to present values of the base year. Their sum (Total Present Value) will represent the life cycle costs of the alternative.

Year n	NCF	PV Factor	PV $
0	1,000	1	1,000
1	208	0.91	189
2	217	0.83	180
3	226	0.75	170
4	186	0.68	126
PV Life Cycle Cost	–	–	1,665

Table 5

The total life cycle cost of this alternative in terms of today's dollar (if this year is the base year) is $1,665. This means that if a present sum of $1,665 were deposited today at an interest rate of 10%, all expenses could be paid over a four-year period, at which time the bank balance would be zero.

Once the costs of the other proposals have been calculated in present value dollars, the facilities manager will be in a position to quantify the differences in life cycle costs and decide which proposal represents the lowest cost of ownership in the long run.

The approach outlined is a practical one when considering the purchase of equipment such as elevators, controls, etc.; quotations should not only include capital costs, but also the costs of long-term maintenance contracts which could make a higher initial cost proposal lower over the life cycle of the equipment.

The Formula Method for Calculating Life Cycle Costs

It is also possible to solve the previous problem utilizing the formula method if the problem is adaptable to this technique. Business calculators or discount factor tables such as those published by ASTM can be employed to generate the present value factors, and results may be obtained more quickly.

In some cases, the complexity of the calculations (such as when taxes on net revenues are considered) will necessitate the "cash flow" method, with calculations done manually or using a spreadsheet program.

With the formula method approach, the calculations for the life cycle cost of the maintenance equipment alternative analyzed would be as follows:

1. PV of Initial Investment $1,000
2. PV of Maintenance Costs
   Annual Cost (A) x UPV factor
   100 x 3.17 $ 317
3. PV of Energy Costs
   Base Year Cost (A) x UPV* $ 382
   100 x 3.82
4. Salvage (Scrap) Value
   Future Value (F) x SPV
   (50) x 0.68   (34)
5. Life Cycle Cost / Total Present Value $1,665

Note: The above factors can be found in Discount Factor Tables.

  UPV–Uniform Present Value
  SPV–Single Present Value
  UPV*–Uniform Present Value Modified (*)

The calculated life cycle cost of $1,665 is identical to that obtained with the cash flow method, but is arrived at with less effort.

Equivalent Uniform Annual Value
ASTM Definition of Equivalent Uniform Annual Value
A uniform annual amount equivalent to the project costs or benefits, taking into account the time value of money throughout the study period. (Syn. annual value)

As noted previously in the definition of Life Cycle Costs, these may be expressed as a lump sum present value with a base time reference, or in equivalent uniform annual values (EUAV) over the study period; decision-makers may prefer one or the other, or require both for the analysis of investment alternatives.

To express life cycle costs in annual values, it is necessary to first determine the lump sum present value of an alternative and multiply it by the Uniform Capital Recovery (UCR) factor given the interest rate and time period. This process is identical to calculating annual payments for a mortgage.

Example
The present value life cycle cost for one of the maintenance equipment alternatives analyzed amounted to $1,665; what is the equivalent uniform annual value "A"?

Given: P   (a principal sum
      or present value
      life cycle cost)   = $1,665
      i   = 10%
      n   = 4 years
      UCR Factor   = 0.32 (from standard factor
            tables for i)
            = 10%, n = 4 years
      A   = equivalent uniform annual
            value – to be determined

Solution: A   = P x UCR
           = $1,665 x 0.32
           = $530

The life cycle cost of the alternative may be expressed as a lump sum, $1,665, or an annual value of $530 based on a four-year time period.

Other Methods of Evaluating Economic Performance

While calculating life cycle costs is a helpful tool for the facilities manager evaluating alternatives, there are other approaches for evaluating economic performance of building investments. Among these other methods are *payback, net benefits,* and *internal rate of return;* these are described in detail in an ASTM compilation of *Building Economics Standards* which are endorsed by the American Association of Cost Engineers (AACE). These standards, as well as adjuncts available such as discount factor tables and a life cycle cost analysis computer program, are included in the References at the end of this section.

ASTM has also developed a Standard Classification of Building Elements and Related Site Work entitled UNIFORMAT II (Designation E-1557-93). One of the many applications for this classification for facilities managers is its use to structure operating and maintenance cost data by building elements or systems, thus facilitating life cycle costing studies. This classification can also be the basis of life cycle cost plans for new facilities that should be developed during the design period with the assistance of the facility manager.

References (Annual Book of ASTM Standards Vol. 04.07)
ASTM Standards

E 833   Terminology of Building Economics

E 917   Practice for Measuring Life Cycle Costs of Buildings and Building Systems

E 964   Practice for Measuring Benefit-to-Cost and Savings-to-Investment Ratios for Buildings and Building Systems

E 1057   Practice for Measuring Internal Rates of Return and Adjusted Internal Rates of Return for Investments in Buildings and Building Systems

E 1074   Practice for Measuring Net Benefits for Investments in Buildings and Building Systems

E 1121   Practice for Measuring Payback for Investments in Buildings and Building Systems

E 1185   Guide for Selecting Economic Methods for Evaluating Investments in Buildings and Building Systems

E 1369   Guide for Selecting Techniques for Treating Uncertainty and Risk in the Economic Evaluation of Buildings and Building Systems

E 1557   Standard Classification for Building Elements and Related Site Work–UNIFORMAT II

ASTM Adjuncts

Discount Factor Tables, Adjunct to Practices E 917, E 964, E 1057, and E 1074.

Computer Program and User's Guide to Building Maintenance, Repair, and Replacement Database for Life Cycle Cost Analysis, Adjunct to Practices E 917, E 964, E 1057, and E 1121.

     Note: The Standards noted above, other than E 1557, are available in one publication entitled *ASTM Standards on Building Economics, Second Edition.*

Abbreviations

A	Area Square Feet; Ampere	BTUH	BTU per Hour	Cwt.	100 Pounds
ABS	Acrylonitrile Butadiene Stryrene; Asbestos Bonded Steel	B.U.R.	Built-up Roofing	C.W.X.	Cool White Deluxe
A.C.	Alternating Current; Air-Conditioning; Asbestos Cement; Plywood Grade A & C	BX	Interlocked Armored Cable	C.Y.	Cubic Yard (27 cubic feet)
		°C	degree centegrade	C.Y./Hr.	Cubic Yard per Hour
		c	Conductivity, Copper Sweat	Cyl.	Cylinder
		C	Hundred; Centigrade	d	Penny (nail size)
A.C.I.	American Concrete Institute	C/C	Center to Center, Cedar on Cedar	D	Deep; Depth; Discharge
AD	Plywood, Grade A & D	C-C	Center to Center	Dis., Disch.	Discharge
Addit.	Additional	Cab.	Cabinet	Db.	Decibel
Adj.	Adjustable	Cair.	Air Tool Laborer	Dbl.	Double
af	Audio-frequency	Calc	Calculated	DC	Direct Current
A.G.A.	American Gas Association	Cap.	Capacity	DDC	Direct Digital Control
Agg.	Aggregate	Carp.	Carpenter	Demob.	Demobilization
A.H.	Ampere Hours	C.B.	Circuit Breaker	d.f.u.	Drainage Fixture Units
A hr.	Ampere-hour	C.C.A.	Chromate Copper Arsenate	D.H.	Double Hung
A.H.U.	Air Handling Unit	C.C.F.	Hundred Cubic Feet	DHW	Domestic Hot Water
A.I.A.	American Institute of Architects	cd	Candela	DI	Ductile Iron
AIC	Ampere Interrupting Capacity	cd/sf	Candela per Square Foot	Diag.	Diagonal
Allow.	Allowance	CD	Grade of Plywood Face & Back	Diam., Dia	Diameter
alt.	Altitude	CDX	Plywood, Grade C & D, exterior glue	Distrib.	Distribution
Alum.	Aluminum			Div.	Division
a.m.	Ante Meridiem	Cefi.	Cement Finisher	Dk.	Deck
Amp.	Ampere	Cem.	Cement	D.L.	Dead Load; Diesel
Anod.	Anodized	CF	Hundred Feet	DLH	Deep Long Span Bar Joist
Approx.	Approximate	C.F.	Cubic Feet	Do.	Ditto
Apt.	Apartment	CFM	Cubic Feet per Minute	Dp.	Depth
Asb.	Asbestos	c.g.	Center of Gravity	D.P.S.T.	Double Pole, Single Throw
A.S.B.C.	American Standard Building Code	CHW	Chilled Water; Commercial Hot Water	Dr.	Drive
Asbe.	Asbestos Worker			Drink.	Drinking
ASCE	American Society of Civil Engineers	C.I.	Cast Iron	D.S.	Double Strength
A.S.H.R.A.E.	American Society of Heating, Refrig. & AC Engineers	C.I.P.	Cast in Place	D.S.A.	Double Strength A Grade
		Circ.	Circuit	D.S.B.	Double Strength B Grade
A.S.M.E.	American Society of Mechanical Engineers	C.L.	Carload Lot	Dty.	Duty
		Clab.	Common Laborer	DWV	Drain Waste Vent
A.S.T.M.	American Society for Testing and Materials	Clam	Common maintenance laborer	DX	Deluxe White, Direct Expansion
		C.L.F.	Hundred Linear Feet	dyn	Dyne
Attchmt.	Attachment	CLF	Current Limiting Fuse	e	Eccentricity
Avg., Ave.	Average	CLP	Cross Linked Polyethylene	E	Equipment Only; East
A.W.G.	American Wire Gauge	cm	Centimeter	Ea.	Each
AWWA	American Water Works Assoc.	CMP	Corr. Metal Pipe	E.B.	Encased Burial
Bbl.	Barrel	C.M.U.	Concrete Masonry Unit	Econ.	Economy
B&B	Grade B and Better; Balled & Burlapped	CN	Change Notice	E.C.Y	Embankment Cubic Yards
		Col.	Column	EDP	Electronic Data Processing
B.&S.	Bell and Spigot	CO₂	Carbon Dioxide	EIFS	Exterior Insulation Finish System
B.&W.	Black and White	Comb.	Combination	E.D.R.	Equiv. Direct Radiation
b.c.c.	Body-centered Cubic	Compr.	Compressor	Eq.	Equation
B.C.Y.	Bank Cubic Yards	Conc.	Concrete	EL	elevation
BE	Bevel End	Cont.	Continuous; Continued, Container	Elec.	Electrician; Electrical
B.F.	Board Feet	Corr.	Corrugated	Elev.	Elevator; Elevating
Bg. cem.	Bag of Cement	Cos	Cosine	EMT	Electrical Metallic Conduit; Thin Wall Conduit
BHP	Boiler Horsepower; Brake Horsepower	Cot	Cotangent		
		Cov.	Cover	Eng.	Engine, Engineered
B.I.	Black Iron	C/P	Cedar on Paneling	EPDM	Ethylene Propylene Diene Monomer
Bit., Bitum.	Bituminous	CPA	Control Point Adjustment		
Bit., Conc.	Bituminous Concrete	Cplg.	Coupling	EPS	Expanded Polystyrene
Bk.	Backed	C.P.M.	Critical Path Method	Eqhv.	Equip. Oper., Heavy
Bkrs.	Breakers	CPVC	Chlorinated Polyvinyl Chloride	Eqlt.	Equip. Oper., Light
Bldg.	Building	C.Pr.	Hundred Pair	Eqmd.	Equip. Oper., Medium
Blk.	Block	CRC	Cold Rolled Channel	Eqmm.	Equip. Oper., Master Mechanic
Bm.	Beam	Creos.	Creosote	Eqol.	Equip. Oper., Oilers
Boil.	Boilermaker	Crpt.	Carpet & Linoleum Layer	Equip.	Equipment
B.P.M.	Blows per Minute	CRT	Cathode-ray Tube	ERW	Electric Resistance Welded
BR	Bedroom	CS	Carbon Steel, Constant Shear Bar Joist	E.S.	Energy Saver
Brg.	Bearing			Est.	Estimated
Brhe.	Bricklayer Helper	Csc	Cosecant	esu	Electrostatic Units
Bric.	Bricklayer	C.S.F.	Hundred Square Feet	E.W.	Each Way
Brk.	Brick	CSI	Construction Specifications Institute	EWT	Entering Water Temperature
Brng.	Bearing			Excav.	Excavation
Brs.	Brass	C.T.	Current Transformer	Exp.	Expansion, Exposure
Brz.	Bronze	CTS	Copper Tube Size	Ext.	Exterior
Bsn.	Basin	Cu	Copper, Cubic	Extru.	Extrusion
Btr.	Better	Cu. Ft.	Cubic Foot	f.	Fiber stress
Btu	British Thermal Unit	cw	Continuous Wave	F	Fahrenheit; Female; Fill
		C.W.	Cool White; Cold Water	Fab.	Fabricated

FBGS	Fiberglass	H.P.	Horsepower; High Pressure	LE	Lead Equivalent
F.C.	Footcandles	H.P.F.	High Power Factor	LED	Light Emitting Diode
f.c.c.	Face-centered Cubic	Hr.	Hour	L.F.	Linear Foot
f'c.	Compressive Stress in Concrete;	Hrs./Day	Hours per Day	L.F. Nose	Linear Foot of Stair Nosing
	Extreme Compressive Stress	HSC	High Short Circuit	L.F. Rsr	Linear Foot of Stair Riser
F.E.	Front End	Ht.	Height	Lg.	Long; Length; Large
FEP	Fluorinated Ethylene Propylene	Htg.	Heating	L & H	Light and Heat
	(Teflon)	Htrs.	Heaters	LH	Long Span Bar Joist
F.G.	Flat Grain	HVAC	Heating, Ventilation & Air-	L.H.	Labor Hours
F.H.A.	Federal Housing Administration		Conditioning	L.L.	Live Load
Fig.	Figure	Hvy.	Heavy	L.L.D.	Lamp Lumen Depreciation
Fin.	Finished	HW	Hot Water	lm	Lumen
Fixt.	Fixture	Hyd.;Hydr.	Hydraulic	lm/sf	Lumen per Square Foot
Fl. Oz.	Fluid Ounces	Hz.	Hertz (cycles)	lm/W	Lumen per Watt
Flr.	Floor	I.	Moment of Inertia	L.O.A.	Length Over All
F.M.	Frequency Modulation;	IBC	International Building Code	log	Logarithm
	Factory Mutual	I.C.	Interrupting Capacity	L-O-L	Lateralolet
Fmg.	Framing	ID	Inside Diameter	long.	longitude
Fdn.	Foundation	I.D.	Inside Dimension; Identification	L.P.	Liquefied Petroleum; Low Pressure
Fori.	Foreman, Inside	I.F.	Inside Frosted	L.P.F.	Low Power Factor
Foro.	Foreman, Outside	I.M.C.	Intermediate Metal Conduit	LR	Long Radius
Fount.	Fountain	In.	Inch	L.S.	Lump Sum
fpm	Feet per Minute	Incan.	Incandescent	Lt.	Light
FPT	Female Pipe Thread	Incl.	Included; Including	Lt. Ga.	Light Gauge
Fr.	Frame	Int.	Interior	L.T.L.	Less than Truckload Lot
F.R.	Fire Rating	Inst.	Installation	Lt. Wt.	Lightweight
FRK	Foil Reinforced Kraft	Insul.	Insulation/Insulated	L.V.	Low Voltage
FRP	Fiberglass Reinforced Plastic	I.P.	Iron Pipe	M	Thousand; Material; Male;
FS	Forged Steel	I.P.S.	Iron Pipe Size		Light Wall Copper Tubing
FSC	Cast Body; Cast Switch Box	I.P.T.	Iron Pipe Threaded	M²CA	Meters Squared Contact Area
Ft.	Foot; Feet	I.W.	Indirect Waste	m/hr.; M.H.	Man-hour
Ftng.	Fitting	J	Joule	mA	Milliampere
Ftg.	Footing	J.I.C.	Joint Industrial Council	Mach.	Machine
Ft lb.	Foot Pound	K	Thousand; Thousand Pounds;	Mag. Str.	Magnetic Starter
Furn.	Furniture		Heavy Wall Copper Tubing, Kelvin	Maint.	Maintenance
FVNR	Full Voltage Non-Reversing	K.A.H.	Thousand Amp. Hours	Marb.	Marble Setter
FXM	Female by Male	KCMIL	Thousand Circular Mils	Mat; Mat'l.	Material
Fy.	Minimum Yield Stress of Steel	KD	Knock Down	Max.	Maximum
g	Gram	K.D.A.T.	Kiln Dried After Treatment	MBF	Thousand Board Feet
G	Gauss	kg	Kilogram	MBH	Thousand BTU's per hr.
Ga.	Gauge	kG	Kilogauss	MC	Metal Clad Cable
Gal., gal.	Gallon	kgf	Kilogram Force	M.C.F.	Thousand Cubic Feet
gpm, GPM	Gallon per Minute	kHz	Kilohertz	M.C.F.M.	Thousand Cubic Feet per Minute
Galv.	Galvanized	Kip.	1000 Pounds	M.C.M.	Thousand Circular Mils
Gen.	General	KJ	Kiljoule	M.C.P.	Motor Circuit Protector
G.F.I.	Ground Fault Interrupter	K.L.	Effective Length Factor	MD	Medium Duty
Glaz.	Glazier	K.L.F.	Kips per Linear Foot	M.D.O.	Medium Density Overlaid
GPD	Gallons per Day	Km	Kilometer	Med.	Medium
GPH	Gallons per Hour	K.S.F.	Kips per Square Foot	MF	Thousand Feet
GPM	Gallons per Minute	K.S.I.	Kips per Square Inch	M.F.B.M.	Thousand Feet Board Measure
GR	Grade	kV	Kilovolt	Mfg.	Manufacturing
Gran.	Granular	kVA	Kilovolt Ampere	Mfrs.	Manufacturers
Grnd.	Ground	K.V.A.R.	Kilovar (Reactance)	mg	Milligram
H	High Henry	KW	Kilowatt	MGD	Million Gallons per Day
H.C.	High Capacity	KWh	Kilowatt-hour	MGPH	Thousand Gallons per Hour
H.D.	Heavy Duty; High Density	L	Labor Only; Length; Long;	MH, M.H.	Manhole; Metal Halide; Man-Hour
H.D.O.	High Density Overlaid		Medium Wall Copper Tubing	MHz	Megahertz
H.D.P.E.	high density polyethelene	Lab.	Labor	Mi.	Mile
Hdr.	Header	lat	Latitude	MI	Malleable Iron; Mineral Insulated
Hdwe.	Hardware	Lath.	Lather	m	Meter
Help.	Helper Average	Lav.	Lavatory	mm	Millimeter
HEPA	High Efficiency Particulate Air	lb.; #	Pound	Mill.	Millwright
	Filter	L.B.	Load Bearing; L Conduit Body	Min., min.	Minimum, minute
Hg	Mercury	L. & E.	Labor & Equipment	Misc.	Miscellaneous
HIC	High Interrupting Capacity	lb./hr.	Pounds per Hour	ml	Milliliter, Mainline
HM	Hollow Metal	lb./L.F.	Pounds per Linear Foot	M.L.F.	Thousand Linear Feet
HMWPE	high molecular weight	lbf/sq.in.	Pound-force per Square Inch	Mo.	Month
	polyethylene	L.C.L.	Less than Carload Lot	Mobil.	Mobilization
H.O.	High Output	L.C.Y.	Loose Cubic Yard	Mog.	Mogul Base
Horiz.	Horizontal	Ld.	Load	MPH	Miles per Hour
				MPT	Male Pipe Thread

MRT	Mile Round Trip
ms	Millisecond
M.S.F.	Thousand Square Feet
Mstz.	Mosaic & Terrazzo Worker
M.S.Y.	Thousand Square Yards
Mtd., mtd.	Mounted
Mthe.	Mosaic & Terrazzo Helper
Mtng.	Mounting
Mult.	Multi; Multiply
M.V.A.	Million Volt Amperes
M.V.A.R.	Million Volt Amperes Reactance
MV	Megavolt
MW	Megawatt
MXM	Male by Male
MYD	Thousand Yards
N	Natural; North
nA	Nanoampere
NA	Not Available; Not Applicable
N.B.C.	National Building Code
NC	Normally Closed
N.E.M.A.	National Electrical Manufacturers Assoc.
NEHB	Bolted Circuit Breaker to 600V.
N.L.B.	Non-Load-Bearing
NM	Non-Metallic Cable
nm	Nanometer
No.	Number
NO	Normally Open
N.O.C.	Not Otherwise Classified
Nose.	Nosing
N.P.T.	National Pipe Thread
NQOD	Combination Plug-on/Bolt on Circuit Breaker to 240V.
N.R.C.	Noise Reduction Coefficient/ Nuclear Regulator Commission
N.R.S.	Non Rising Stem
ns	Nanosecond
nW	Nanowatt
OB	Opposing Blade
OC	On Center
OD	Outside Diameter
O.D.	Outside Dimension
ODS	Overhead Distribution System
O.G.	Ogee
O.H.	Overhead
O&P	Overhead and Profit
Oper.	Operator
Opng.	Opening
Orna.	Ornamental
OSB	Oriented Strand Board
O.S.&Y.	Outside Screw and Yoke
Ovhd.	Overhead
OWG	Oil, Water or Gas
Oz.	Ounce
P.	Pole; Applied Load; Projection
p.	Page
Pape.	Paperhanger
P.A.P.R.	Powered Air Purifying Respirator
PAR	Parabolic Reflector
Pc., Pcs.	Piece, Pieces
P.C.	Portland Cement; Power Connector
P.C.F.	Pounds per Cubic Foot
P.C.M.	Phase Contrast Microscopy
P.E.	Professional Engineer; Porcelain Enamel; Polyethylene; Plain End
Perf.	Perforated
PEX	Cross linked polyethylene
Ph.	Phase
P.I.	Pressure Injected
Pile.	Pile Driver
Pkg.	Package

Pl.	Plate
Plah.	Plasterer Helper
Plas.	Plasterer
Pluh.	Plumbers Helper
Plum.	Plumber
Ply.	Plywood
p.m.	Post Meridiem
Pntd.	Painted
Pord.	Painter, Ordinary
pp	Pages
PP, PPL	Polypropylene
P.P.M.	Parts per Million
Pr.	Pair
P.E.S.B.	Pre-engineered Steel Building
Prefab.	Prefabricated
Prefin.	Prefinished
Prop.	Propelled
PSF, psf	Pounds per Square Foot
PSI, psi	Pounds per Square Inch
PSIG	Pounds per Square Inch Gauge
PSP	Plastic Sewer Pipe
Pspr.	Painter, Spray
Psst.	Painter, Structural Steel
P.T.	Potential Transformer
P. & T.	Pressure & Temperature
Ptd.	Painted
Ptns.	Partitions
Pu	Ultimate Load
PVC	Polyvinyl Chloride
Pvmt.	Pavement
Pwr.	Power
Q	Quantity Heat Flow
Qt.	Quart
Quan., Qty.	Quantity
Q.C.	Quick Coupling
r	Radius of Gyration
R	Resistance
R.C.P.	Reinforced Concrete Pipe
Rect.	Rectangle
Reg.	Regular
Reinf.	Reinforced
Req'd.	Required
Res.	Resistant
Resi.	Residential
Rgh.	Rough
RGS	Rigid Galvanized Steel
R.H.W.	Rubber, Heat & Water Resistant; Residential Hot Water
rms	Root Mean Square
Rnd.	Round
Rodm.	Rodman
Rofc.	Roofer, Composition
Rofp.	Roofer, Precast
Rohe.	Roofer Helpers (Composition)
Rots.	Roofer, Tile & Slate
R.O.W.	Right of Way
RPM	Revolutions per Minute
R.S.	Rapid Start
Rsr	Riser
RT	Round Trip
S.	Suction; Single Entrance; South
SC	Screw Cover
SCFM	Standard Cubic Feet per Minute
Scaf.	Scaffold
Sch., Sched.	Schedule
S.C.R.	Modular Brick
S.D.	Sound Deadening
S.D.R.	Standard Dimension Ratio
S.E.	Surfaced Edge
Sel.	Select
S.E.R., S.E.U.	Service Entrance Cable
S.F.	Square Foot

S.F.C.A.	Square Foot Contact Area
S.F. Flr.	Square Foot of Floor
S.F.G.	Square Foot of Ground
S.F. Hor.	Square Foot Horizontal
S.F.R.	Square Feet of Radiation
S.F. Shlf.	Square Foot of Shelf
S4S	Surface 4 Sides
Shee.	Sheet Metal Worker
Sin.	Sine
Skwk.	Skilled Worker
SL	Saran Lined
S.L.	Slimline
Sldr.	Solder
SLH	Super Long Span Bar Joist
S.N.	Solid Neutral
S-O-L	Socketolet
sp	Standpipe
S.P.	Static Pressure; Single Pole; Self-Propelled
Spri.	Sprinkler Installer
spwg	Static Pressure Water Gauge
S.P.D.T.	Single Pole, Double Throw
SPF	Spruce Pine Fir
S.P.S.T.	Single Pole, Single Throw
SPT	Standard Pipe Thread
Sq.	Square; 100 Square Feet
Sq. Hd.	Square Head
Sq. In.	Square Inch
S.S.	Single Strength; Stainless Steel
S.S.B.	Single Strength B Grade
sst, ss	Stainless Steel
Sswk.	Structural Steel Worker
Sswl.	Structural Steel Welder
St.; Stl.	Steel
S.T.C.	Sound Transmission Coefficient
Std.	Standard
Stg.	Staging
STK	Select Tight Knot
STP	Standard Temperature & Pressure
Stpi.	Steamfitter, Pipefitter
Str.	Strength; Starter; Straight
Strd.	Stranded
Struct.	Structural
Sty.	Story
Subj.	Subject
Subs.	Subcontractors
Surf.	Surface
Sw.	Switch
Swbd.	Switchboard
S.Y.	Square Yard
Syn.	Synthetic
S.Y.P.	Southern Yellow Pine
Sys.	System
t.	Thickness
T	Temperature; Ton
Tan	Tangent
T.C.	Terra Cotta
T & C	Threaded and Coupled
T.D.	Temperature Difference
Tdd	Telecommunications Device for the Deaf
T.E.M.	Transmission Electron Microscopy
TFE	Tetrafluoroethylene (Teflon)
T. & G.	Tongue & Groove; Tar & Gravel
Th., Thk.	Thick
Thn.	Thin
Thrded	Threaded
Tilf.	Tile Layer, Floor
Tilh.	Tile Layer, Helper
THHN	Nylon Jacketed Wire
THW.	Insulated Strand Wire

Abbreviations

THWN	Nylon Jacketed Wire	USP	United States Primed	Wrck.	Wrecker
T.L.	Truckload	UTP	Unshielded Twisted Pair	W.S.P.	Water, Steam, Petroleum
T.M.	Track Mounted	V	Volt	WT., Wt.	Weight
Tot.	Total	V.A.	Volt Amperes	WWF	Welded Wire Fabric
T-O-L	Threadolet	V.C.T.	Vinyl Composition Tile	XFER	Transfer
T.S.	Trigger Start	VAV	Variable Air Volume	XFMR	Transformer
Tr.	Trade	VC	Veneer Core	XHD	Extra Heavy Duty
Transf.	Transformer	Vent.	Ventilation	XHHW,	Cross-Linked Polyethylene Wire
Trhv.	Truck Driver, Heavy	Vert.	Vertical	XLPE	Insulation
Trlr	Trailer	V.F.	Vinyl Faced	XLP	Cross-linked Polyethylene
Trlt.	Truck Driver, Light	V.G.	Vertical Grain	Y	Wye
TTY	Teletypewriter	V.H.F.	Very High Frequency	yd	Yard
TV	Television	VHO	Very High Output	yr	Year
T.W.	Thermoplastic Water Resistant	Vib.	Vibrating	Δ	Delta
	Wire	V.L.F.	Vertical Linear Foot	%	Percent
UCI	Uniform Construction Index	Vol.	Volume	~	Approximately
UF	Underground Feeder	VRP	Vinyl Reinforced Polyester	Ø	Phase; diameter
UGND	Underground Feeder	W	Wire; Watt; Wide; West	@	At
U.H.F.	Ultra High Frequency	w/	With	#	Pound; Number
U.I.	United Inch	W.C.	Water Column; Water Closet	<	Less Than
U.L.	Underwriters Laboratory	W.F.	Wide Flange	>	Greater Than
Uld.	unloading	W.G.	Water Gauge	Z	zone
Unfin.	Unfinished	Wldg.	Welding		
URD	Underground Residential	W. Mile	Wire Mile		
	Distribution	W-O-L	Weldolet		
US	United States	W.R.	Water Resistant		

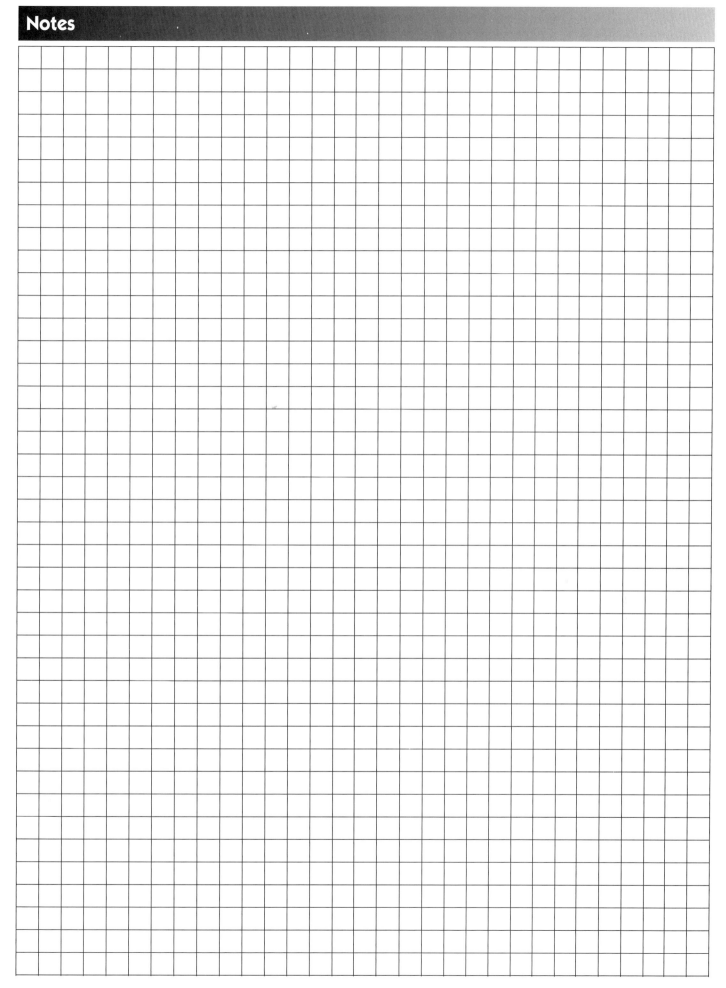

..

For more information visit the RSMeans website at **www.rsmeans.com**

Unit prices according to the latest MasterFormat!

Book Selection Guide The following table provides definitive information on the content of each cost data publication. The number of lines of data provided in each unit price or assemblies division, as well as the number of reference tables and crews, is listed for each book. The presence of other elements such as equipment rental costs, historical cost indexes, city cost indexes, square foot models, or cross-referenced indexes is also indicated. You can use the table to help select the RSMeans book that has the quantity and type of information you most need in your work.

Unit Cost Divisions	Building Construction	Mechanical	Electrical	Commercial Renovation	Square Foot	Site Work Landsc.	Green Building	Interior	Concrete Masonry	Open Shop	Heavy Construction	Light Commercial	Facilities Construction	Plumbing	Residential
1	571	392	407	495		515	124	319	461	570	505	231	1001	408	174
2	745	264	83	684		965	180	363	219	742	704	439	1174	288	240
3	1539	222	212	906		1342	874	313	1847	1539	1481	386	1567	189	366
4	902	24	0	698		701	183	573	1137	878	593	490	1149	0	405
5	1912	263	168	1022		871	1799	1021	834	1903	1118	893	1905	339	724
6	1986	67	69	1573		401	534	1294	300	1965	380	1667	1602	22	2179
7	1456	208	125	1484		555	778	543	505	1453	26	1161	1516	217	915
8	2081	61	10	2277		296	1155	1765	658	2036	0	1661	2495	0	1412
9	1875	72	26	1670		306	444	1966	386	1817	15	1589	2111	54	1400
10	988	17	10	612		215	27	808	159	988	29	494	1074	231	221
11	1029	208	166	493		126	54	885	28	1014	0	235	1049	169	110
12	562	0	2	318		248	150	1707	12	551	19	364	1757	23	317
13	732	117	111	247		347	128	249	69	731	261	80	760	72	79
14	280	36	0	229		28	0	259	0	279	0	12	299	21	6
21	78	0	16	30		0	0	249	0	78	0	60	430	436	224
22	1144	7289	155	1108		1536	1100	609	20	1106	1660	834	7150	9008	662
23	1201	7048	605	784		157	900	691	38	1121	110	688	5126	1870	411
26	1249	496	9967	1010		763	572	1085	55	1237	539	1095	9903	441	559
27	67	0	261	34		9	0	59	0	67	35	48	263	0	4
28	96	58	124	71		0	21	78	0	99	0	40	139	44	25
31	1477	735	608	798		3186	290	7	1208	1421	3257	600	1540	660	606
32	767	54	0	838		4324	343	359	274	738	1797	380	1645	166	428
33	506	1008	465	205		1964	41	0	228	505	1887	117	1549	1197	115
34	109	0	20	4		144	0	0	31	64	122	0	129	0	0
35	18	0	0	0		166	0	0	0	18	281	0	83	0	0
41	52	0	0	24		7	0	22	0	52	30	0	59	14	0
44	75	83	0	0		0	0	0	0	0	0	0	75	75	0
46	23	16	0	0		162	149	0	0	23	152	0	33	33	0
48	0	0	0	0		0	19	0	0	0	0	0	0	0	0
Totals	23520	18738	13610	17614		19334	9865	15224	8469	22995	15001	13564	47583	15977	11582

Assem Div	Building Construction	Mechanical	Electrical	Commercial Renovation	Square Foot	Site Work Landscape	Assemblies	Green Building	Interior	Concrete Masonry	Heavy Construction	Light Commercial	Facilities Construction	Plumbing	Asm Div	Residential
A		15	0	188	150	577	598	0	0	536	571	154	24	0	1	368
B		0	0	825	2472	0	5572	56	330	1914	368	2032	143	0	2	211
C		0	0	647	864	0	1233	0	1558	146	0	763	245	0	3	588
D		1067	812	712	1798	72	2425	281	769	0	0	1272	1027	1083	4	859
E		0	0	86	259	0	297	0	5	0	0	256	5	0	5	392
F		0	0	0	122	0	122	0	0	0	0	122	3	0	6	357
G		527	294	317	202	3006	668	0	0	535	1372	200	293	685	7	300
															8	760
															9	80
															10	0
															11	0
															12	0
Totals		1609	1106	2775	5867	3655	10915	337	2662	3131	2311	4799	1740	1768		3915

Reference Section	Building Construction Costs	Mechanical	Electrical	Commercial Renovation	Square Foot	Site Work Landscape	Assem.	Green Building	Interior	Concrete Masonry	Open Shop	Heavy Construction	Light Commercial	Facilities Construction	Plumbing	Resi.
Reference Tables	yes	yes	yes	yes	no	yes	yes	yes	yes	yes	yes	yes	yes	yes	yes	yes
Models					107								46			28
Crews	527	527	527	505		527		527	527	527	503	527	503	505	527	503
Equipment Rental Costs	yes	yes	yes	yes		yes		yes	yes	yes	yes	yes	yes	yes	yes	yes
Historical Cost Indexes	yes	yes	yes	yes	yes	yes	yes	yes	yes	yes	yes	yes	yes	yes	yes	no
City Cost Indexes	yes	yes	yes	yes	yes	yes	yes	yes	yes	yes	yes	yes	yes	yes	yes	yes

RSMeans Building Construction Cost Data 2012

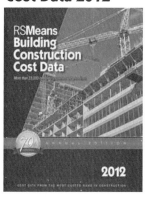

Offers you unchallenged unit price reliability in an easy-to-use format. Whether used for verifying complete, finished estimates or for periodic checks, it supplies more cost facts better and faster than any comparable source. Over 23,000 unit prices have been updated for 2012. The City Cost Indexes and Location Factors cover over 930 areas, for indexing to any project location in North America. Order and get *RSMeans Quarterly Update Service* FREE. You'll have year-long access to the RSMeans Estimating **HOTLINE** FREE with your subscription. Expert assistance when using RSMeans data is just a phone call away.

$177.95 per copy | Available Sept. 2011 | Catalog no. 60012

RSMeans Mechanical Cost Data 2012

Total unit and systems price guidance for mechanical construction. . . materials, parts, fittings, and complete labor cost information. Includes prices for piping, heating, air conditioning, ventilation, and all related construction.

Plus new 2012 unit costs for:

- Thousands of installed HVAC/controls assemblies components
- "On-site" Location Factors for over 930 cities and towns in the U.S. and Canada
- Crews, labor, and equipment

$174.95 per copy | Available Oct. 2011 | Catalog no. 60022

RSMeans Square Foot Costs 2012

Accurate and Easy To Use

- **Updated price information** based on nationwide figures from suppliers, estimators, labor experts, and contractors
- "How-to-Use" sections, with **clear examples** of commercial, residential, industrial, and institutional structures
- Realistic graphics, offering true-to-life illustrations of building projects
- Extensive information on using square foot cost data, including sample estimates and alternate pricing methods

$187.95 per copy | Available Oct. 2011 | Catalog no. 60052

RSMeans Green Building Cost Data 2012

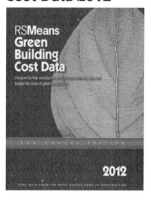

Estimate, plan, and budget the costs of green building for both new commercial construction and renovation work with this first edition of RSMeans Green Building Cost Data. More than 9,000 unit costs for a wide array of green building products plus assemblies costs. Easily identified cross references to LEED and Green Globes building rating systems criteria.

$147.95 per copy | Available Nov. 2011 | Catalog no. 60552

RSMeans Facilities Construction Cost Data 2012

For the maintenance and construction of commercial, industrial, municipal, and institutional properties. Costs are shown for new and remodeling construction and are broken down into materials, labor, equipment, and overhead and profit. Special emphasis is given to sections on mechanical, electrical, furnishings, site work, building maintenance, finish work, and demolition.

More than 47,000 unit costs, plus assemblies costs and a comprehensive Reference Section are included.

$453.95 per copy | Available Nov. 2011 | Catalog no. 60202

RSMeans Commercial Renovation Cost Data 2012

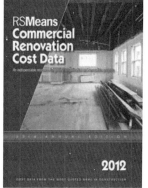

Commercial/Multifamily Residential

Use this valuable tool to estimate commercial and multifamily residential renovation and remodeling.

Includes: New costs for hundreds of unique methods, materials, and conditions that only come up in repair and remodeling, PLUS:

- Unit costs for more than 17,000 construction components
- Installed costs for more than 2,000 assemblies
- More than 930 "on-site" localization factors for the U.S. and Canada

$144.95 per copy | Available Oct. 2011 | Catalog no. 60042

RSMeans Electrical Cost Data 2012

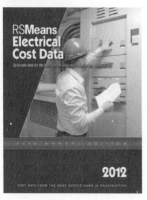

Pricing information for every part of electrical cost planning. More than 13,000 unit and systems costs with design tables; clear specifications and drawings; engineering guides; illustrated estimating procedures; complete labor-hour and materials costs for better scheduling and procurement; and the latest electrical products and construction methods.

- A variety of special electrical systems including cathodic protection
- Costs for maintenance, demolition, HVAC/mechanical, specialties, equipment, and more

$179.95 per copy | Available Oct. 2011 | Catalog no. 60032

RSMeans Electrical Change Order Cost Data 2012

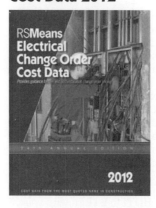

RSMeans Electrical Change Order Cost Data provides you with electrical unit prices exclusively for pricing change orders—based on the recent, direct experience of contractors and suppliers. Analyze and check your own change order estimates against the experience others have had doing the same work. It also covers productivity analysis and change order cost justifications. With useful information for calculating the effects of change orders and dealing with their administration.

$174.95 per copy | Available Dec. 2011 | Catalog no. 60232

RSMeans Assemblies Cost Data 2012

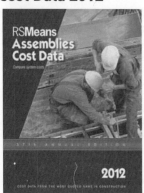

RSMeans Assemblies Cost Data takes the guesswork out of preliminary or conceptual estimates. Now you don't have to try to calculate the assembled cost by working up individual component costs. We've done all the work for you.

Presents detailed illustrations, descriptions, specifications, and costs for every conceivable building assembly—over 350 types in all—arranged in the easy-to-use UNIFORMAT II system. Each illustrated "assembled" cost includes a complete grouping of materials and associated installation costs, including the installing contractor's overhead and profit.

$290.95 per copy | Available Sept. 2011 | Catalog no. 60062

RSMeans Open Shop Building Construction Cost Data 2012

The latest costs for accurate budgeting and estimating of new commercial and residential construction. . . renovation work. . . change orders. . . cost engineering.

RSMeans Open Shop "BCCD" will assist you to:

- Develop benchmark prices for change orders
- Plug gaps in preliminary estimates and budgets
- Estimate complex projects
- Substantiate invoices on contracts
- Price ADA-related renovations

$152.95 per copy | Available Dec. 2011 | Catalog no. 60152

RSMeans Residential Cost Data 2012

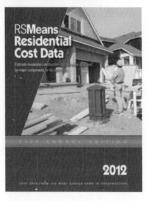

Contains square foot costs for 28 basic home models with the look of today, plus hundreds of custom additions and modifications you can quote right off the page. Includes costs for more than 700 residential systems. Complete with blank estimating forms, sample estimates, and step-by-step instructions.

Now contains line items for cultured stone and brick, PVC trim lumber, and TPO roofing.

$127.95 per copy | Available Oct. 2011 | Catalog no. 60172

RSMeans Site Work & Landscape Cost Data 2012

Includes unit and assemblies costs for earthwork, sewerage, piped utilities, site improvements, drainage, paving, trees and shrubs, street openings/repairs, underground tanks, and more. Contains 78 types of assemblies costs for accurate conceptual estimates.

Includes:

- Estimating for infrastructure improvements
- Environmentally-oriented construction
- ADA-mandated handicapped access
- Hazardous waste line items

$172.95 per copy | Available Dec. 2011 | Catalog no. 60282

RSMeans Facilities Maintenance & Repair Cost Data 2012

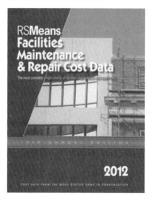

RSMeans Facilities Maintenance & Repair Cost Data gives you a complete system to manage and plan your facility repair and maintenance costs and budget efficiently. Guidelines for auditing a facility and developing an annual maintenance plan. Budgeting is included, along with reference tables on cost and management, and information on frequency and productivity of maintenance operations.

The only nationally recognized source of maintenance and repair costs. Developed in cooperation with the Civil Engineering Research Laboratory (CERL) of the Army Corps of Engineers.

$399.95 per copy | Available Nov. 2011 | Catalog no. 60302

RSMeans Concrete & Masonry Cost Data 2012

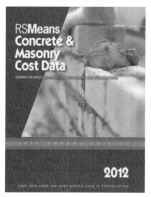

Provides you with cost facts for virtually all concrete/masonry estimating needs, from complicated formwork to various sizes and face finishes of brick and block—all in great detail. The comprehensive Unit Price Section contains more than 8,000 selected entries. Also contains an Assemblies [Cost] Section, and a detailed Reference Section that supplements the cost data.

$162.95 per copy | Available Dec. 2011 | Catalog no. 60112

RSMeans Construction Cost Indexes 2012

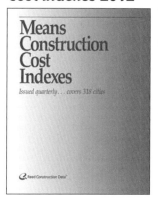

What materials and labor costs will change unexpectedly this year? By how much?

- Breakdowns for 318 major cities
- National averages for 30 key cities
- Expanded five major city indexes
- Historical construction cost indexes

$362.00 per year (subscription) | Catalog no. 50142
$90.50 individual quarters | Catalog no. 60142 A,B,C,D

RSMeans Light Commercial Cost Data 2012

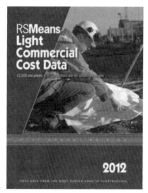

Specifically addresses the light commercial market, which is a specialized niche in the construction industry. Aids you, the owner/designer/contractor, in preparing all types of estimates—from budgets to detailed bids. Includes new advances in methods and materials.

Assemblies Section allows you to evaluate alternatives in the early stages of design/planning.

Over 13,000 unit costs ensure that you have the prices you need. . . when you need them.

$132.95 per copy | Available Nov. 2011 | Catalog no. 60182

RSMeans Labor Rates for the Construction Industry 2012

Complete information for estimating labor costs, making comparisons, and negotiating wage rates by trade for more than 300 U.S. and Canadian cities. With 46 construction trades listed by local union number in each city, and historical wage rates included for comparison. Each city chart lists the county and is alphabetically arranged with handy visual flip tabs for quick reference.

$395.95 per copy | Available Dec. 2011 | Catalog no. 60122

RSMeans Interior Cost Data 2012

Provides you with prices and guidance needed to make accurate interior work estimates. Contains costs on materials, equipment, hardware, custom installations, furnishings, and labor costs. . . for new and remodel commercial and industrial interior construction, including updated information on office furnishings, and reference information.

$182.95 per copy | Available Nov. 2011 | Catalog no. 60092

Annual Cost Guides

Cost Guides also available online
at meanscostworks.com

For more information visit the RSMeans website at **www.rsmeans.com**

Unit prices according to the latest MasterFormat!

RSMeans Heavy Construction Cost Data 2012

A comprehensive guide to heavy construction costs. Includes costs for highly specialized projects such as tunnels, dams, highways, airports, and waterways. Information on labor rates, equipment, and materials costs is included. Features unit price costs, systems costs, and numerous reference tables for costs and design.

$177.95 per copy | Available Dec. 2011 | Catalog no. 60162

RSMeans Plumbing Cost Data 2012

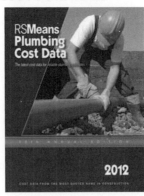

Comprehensive unit prices and assemblies for plumbing, irrigation systems, commercial and residential fire protection, point-of-use water heaters, and the latest approved materials. This publication and its companion, *RSMeans Mechanical Cost Data*, provide full-range cost estimating coverage for all the mechanical trades.

Now contains updated costs for potable water and radiant heat systems and high efficiency fixtures.

$179.95 per copy | Available Oct. 2011 | Catalog no. 60212

2012 RSMeans Seminar Schedule

Note: call for exact dates and details.

Location	Dates
Las Vegas, NV	March
Washington, DC	April
San Francisco, CA	June
Washington, DC	September
Dallas, TX	September

Location	Dates
Las Vegas, NV	October
Orlando, FL	November
San Diego, CA	December

1-800-334-3509, ext. 925115

2012 Regional Seminar Schedule

Note: call for exact dates and details.

Location	Dates
Seattle, WA	January and August
Dallas/Ft. Worth, TX	January
Austin, TX	February
Oklahoma City, OK	February
Anchorage, AK	March and September
Phoenix, AZ	March
San Bernardino, CA	April
Aiea, HI	April
Kansas City, MO	April
Toronto	May
Denver, CO	May
Bethesda, MD	June

Location	Dates
Columbus, GA	June
El Segundo, CA	August
Jacksonville FL	September
Birmingham, AL	October
St. Louis, MO	October
Houston, TX	October
Portland, OR	November
Baltimore, MD	November
San Antonio, TX	December
Raleigh, NC	December

1-800-334-3509, ext. 925115

Registration Information

Register early... Save up to $100! Register 30 days before the start date of a seminar and save $100 off your total fee. *Note: This discount can be applied only once per order. It cannot be applied to team discount registrations or any other special offer.*

How to register Register by phone today! The RSMeans toll-free number for making reservations is **1-800-334-3509, ext. 925115.**

Individual seminar registration fee - $935. *Means CostWorks®* **training registration fee - $375.** To register by mail, complete the registration form and return, with your full fee, to: RSMeans Seminars, 700 Longwater Drive, Norwell, MA 02061.

Government pricing All federal government employees save off the regular seminar price. Other promotional discounts cannot be combined with the government discount.

Team discount program for two to four seminar registrations. Call for pricing: 1-800-334-3509, ext. 925115

Multiple course discounts When signing up for two or more courses, call for pricing.

Refund policy Cancellations will be accepted up to ten business days prior to the seminar start. There are no refunds for cancellations received later than ten working days prior to the first day of the seminar. A $150 processing fee will be applied for all cancellations. Written notice of cancellation is required. Substitutions can be made at any time before the session starts. **No-shows are subject to the full seminar fee.**

AACE approved courses Many seminars described and offered here have been approved for 14 hours (1.4 recertification credits) of credit by the AACE International Certification Board toward meeting the continuing education requirements for recertification as a Certified Cost Engineer/Certified Cost Consultant.

AIA Continuing Education We are registered with the AIA Continuing Education System (AIA/CES) and are committed to developing quality learning activities in accordance with the CES criteria. Many seminars meet the AIA/CES criteria for Quality Level 2. AIA members may receive (14) learning units (LUs) for each two-day RSMeans course.

Daily course schedule The first day of each seminar session begins at 8:30 a.m. and ends at 4:30 p.m. The second day begins at 8:00 a.m. and ends at 4:00 p.m. Participants are urged to bring a hand-held calculator, since many actual problems will be worked out in each session.

Continental breakfast Your registration includes the cost of a continental breakfast, and a morning and afternoon refreshment break. These informal segments allow you to discuss topics of mutual interest with other seminar attendees. (You are free to make your own lunch and dinner arrangements.)

Hotel/transportation arrangements RSMeans arranges to hold a block of rooms at most host hotels. To take advantage of special group rates when making your reservation, be sure to mention that you are attending the RSMeans seminar. You are, of course, free to stay at the lodging place of your choice. **(Hotel reservations and transportation arrangements should be made directly by seminar attendees.)**

Important Class sizes are limited, so please register as soon as possible.

Note: Pricing subject to change.

Registration Form   ADDS-1000

Call 1-800-334-3509, ext. 925115 to register or FAX this form 1-800-632-6732. Visit our website: www.rsmeans.com

Please register the following people for the RSMeans construction seminars as shown here. We understand that we must make our own hotel reservations if overnight stays are necessary.

☐ Full payment of $_____enclosed.

☐ Bill me.

Please print name of registrant(s).

(To appear on certificate of completion)

_____

_____

_____

P.O. #: _____
    GOVERNMENT AGENCIES MUST SUPPLY PURCHASE ORDER NUMBER OR
    TRAINING FORM.

Firm name_____

Address_____

City/State/Zip_____

Telephone no._____ Fax no._____

E-mail address_____

Charge registration(s) to: ☐ MasterCard ☐ VISA ☐ American Express

Account no._____Exp. date_____

Cardholder's signature_____

Seminar name_____

Seminar City _____

Please mail check to: RSMeans Seminars, 700 Longwater Drive, Norwell, MA 02061 USA

Professional Development

For more information visit the RSMeans website at **www.rsmeans.com**

Means CostWorks.com Training

Construction estimating is vital to the decision-making process at each state of every project. Means CostWorks.com works the way you do. It's systematic, flexible and intuitive. In this one day class you will see how you can estimate any phase of any project faster and better.

Some of what you'll learn:
- Customizing Means CostWorks.com
- Making the most of RSMeans "Circle Reference" numbers
- How to integrate your cost data
- Generate reports, exporting estimates to MS Excel, sharing, collaborating and more

Who should attend: architects & engineers, facility managers, contractors, construction estimators, and anyone using this powerful web-based tool.

Facilities Construction Estimating

In this *two-day* course, professionals working in facilities management can get help with their daily challenges to establish budgets for all phases of a project.

Some of what you'll learn:
- Determining the full scope of a project
- Identifying the scope of risks and opportunities
- Creative solutions to estimating issues
- Organizing estimates for presentation and discussion
- Special techniques for repair/remodel and maintenance projects
- Negotiating project change orders

Who should attend: facility managers, engineers, contractors, facility tradespeople, planners, and project managers.

Scheduling with Microsoft Project

Two days of hands-on training gives you a look at the basics to putting it all together with MS Project to create a complete project schedule. Learn to work better and faster, manage changes and updates, enhance tracking, generate actionable reports, and boost control of your time and budget.

Some of what you'll learn:
- Defining task/activity relationships: link tasks, establish predecessor/successor relationships and create logs
- Baseline scheduling: the essential what/when
- Using MS Project to determine the critical path
- Integrate RSMeans data with MS Project
- The dollar-loaded schedule: enhance the reliability of this "must-know" technique for scheduling public projects.

Who should attend: Contractors' project-management teams, architects and engineers, project owners and their representatives, and those interested in improving their project planning and scheduling and management skills.

Site Work & Heavy Construction Estimating

This *two-day* course teaches attendees how to estimate earthwork, site utilities, foundations, and site improvements, using the assemblies and the unit price methods.

Some of what you'll learn:
- Basic site work and heavy construction estimating skills
- Estimating foundations, utilities, earthwork, and site improvements
- Correct equipment usage, quality control, and site investigation for estimating purposes

Who should attend: project managers, design engineers, estimators, and contractors doing site work and heavy construction.

Practical Project Management for Construction Professionals

In this *two-day* course, acquire the essential knowledge and develop the skills to effectively and efficiently execute the day-to-day responsibilities of the construction project manager.

Covers:
- General conditions of the construction contract
- Contract modifications: change orders and construction change directives
- Negotiations with subcontractors and vendors
- Effective writing: notification and communications
- Dispute resolution: claims and liens

Who should attend: architects, engineers, owner's representatives, project managers.

Mechanical & Electrical Estimating

This *two-day* course teaches attendees how to prepare more accurate and complete mechanical/electrical estimates, avoiding the pitfalls of omission and double-counting, while understanding the composition and rationale within the RSMeans mechanical/electrical database.

Some of what you'll learn:
- The unique way mechanical and electrical systems are interrelated
- M&E estimates—conceptual, planning, budgeting, and bidding stages
- Order of magnitude, square foot, assemblies, and unit price estimating
- Comparative cost analysis of equipment and design alternatives

Who should attend: architects, engineers, facilities managers, mechanical and electrical contractors, and others who need a highly reliable method for developing, understanding, and evaluating mechanical and electrical contracts.

Professional Development

For more information visit the RSMeans website at **www.rsmeans.com**

Unit Price Estimating

This interactive *two-day* seminar teaches attendees how to interpret project information and process it into final, detailed estimates with the greatest accuracy level.

The most important credential an estimator can take to the job is the ability to visualize construction and estimate accurately.

Some of what you'll learn:
- Interpreting the design in terms of cost
- The most detailed, time-tested methodology for accurate pricing
- Key cost drivers—material, labor, equipment, staging, and subcontracts
- Understanding direct and indirect costs for accurate job cost accounting and change order management

Who should attend: Corporate and government estimators and purchasers, architects, engineers, and others who need to produce accurate project estimates.

RSMeans CostWorks® CD Training

This one-day course helps users become more familiar with the functionality of *RSMeans CostWork*s program. Each menu, icon, screen, and function found in the program is explained in depth. Time is devoted to hands-on estimating exercises.

Some of what you'll learn:
- Searching the database using all navigation methods
- Exporting RSMeans data to your preferred spreadsheet format
- Viewing crews, assembly components, and much more
- Automatically regionalizing the database

You are required to bring your own laptop computer for this course.

When you register for this course you will receive an outline for your laptop requirements.

Also offering web training for CostWorks CD!

Facilities Maintenance & Repair Estimating

This *two-day* course teaches attendees how to plan, budget, and estimate the cost of ongoing and preventive maintenance and repair for existing buildings and grounds.

Some of what you'll learn:
- The most financially favorable maintenance, repair, and replacement scheduling and estimating
- Auditing and value engineering facilities
- Preventive planning and facilities upgrading
- Determining both in-house and contract-out service costs
- Annual, asset-protecting M&R plan

Who should attend: Facility managers, maintenance supervisors, buildings and grounds superintendents, plant managers, planners, estimators, and others involved in facilities planning and budgeting.

Square Foot Estimating using Means CostWorks

This *two day* class uses the leading industry data and a powerful software package to develop highly accurate conceptual estimates for your construction projects. All attendees must bring a laptop computer loaded with the current year *Square Foot Model Costs* and the *Assemblies Cost Data* CostWorks titles.

Some of what you'll learn:
- Introduction to conceptual estimating
- Types of conceptual estimates
- Helpful hints
- Order of magnitude estimating
- Square foot estimating
- Assemblies estimating

Who should attend: architects, engineers, contractors, construction estimators, owner's representatives, and anyone looking for an electronic method for performing square foot estimating.

Assessing Scope of Work for Facility Construction Estimating

This *two-day* practical training program addresses the vital importance of understanding the SCOPE of projects in order to produce accurate cost estimates for facility repair and remodeling.

Some of what you'll learn:
- Discussions of site visits, plans/specs, record drawings of facilities, and site-specific lists
- Review of CSI divisions, including means, methods, materials, and the challenges of scoping each topic
- Exercises in SCOPE identification and SCOPE writing for accurate estimating of projects
- Hands-on exercises that require SCOPE, take-off, and pricing

Who should attend: corporate and government estimators, planners, facility managers, and others who need to produce accurate project estimates.

685

Reference Books

For more information visit the RSMeans website at **www.rsmeans.com**

Value Engineering: Practical Applications

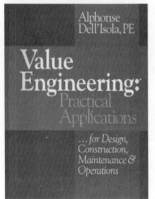

For Design, Construction, Maintenance & Operations
by Alphonse Dell'Isola, PE

A tool for immediate application—for engineers, architects, facility managers, owners, and contractors. Includes making the case for VE—the management briefing; integrating VE into planning, budgeting, and design; conducting life cycle costing; using VE methodology in design review and consultant selection; case studies; VE workbook; and a life cycle costing program on disk.

$79.95 per copy | Over 450 pages, illustrated, softcover | Catalog no. 67319A

The Building Professional's Guide to Contract Documents

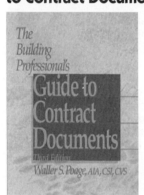

3rd Edition
by Waller S. Poage, AIA, CSI, CVS

A comprehensive reference for owners, design professionals, contractors, and students

- Structure your documents for maximum efficiency.
- Effectively communicate construction requirements.
- Understand the roles and responsibilities of construction professionals.
- Improve methods of project delivery.

$64.95 per copy | 400 pages Diagrams and construction forms, hardcover
Catalog no. 67261A

Cost Planning & Estimating for Facilities Maintenance

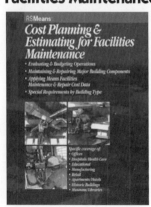

In this unique book, a team of facilities management authorities shares their expertise on:

- Evaluating and budgeting maintenance operations
- Maintaining and repairing key building components
- Applying *RSMeans Facilities Maintenance & Repair Cost Data* to your estimating

Covers special maintenance requirements of the ten major building types

$89.95 per copy | Over 475 pages, hardcover | Catalog no. 67314

Facilities Operations & Engineering Reference

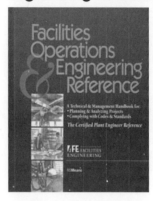

by the Association for Facilities Engineering and RSMeans

An all-in-one technical reference for planning and managing facility projects and solving day-to-day operations problems. Selected as the official certified plant engineer reference, this handbook covers financial analysis, maintenance, HVAC and energy efficiency, and more.

$109.95 per copy | Over 700 pages, illustrated, hardcover | Catalog no. 67318

Complete Book of Framing

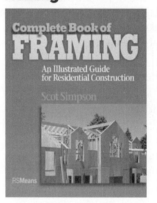

by Scot Simpson

This straightforward, easy-to-learn method will help framers, carpenters, and handy homeowners build their skills in rough carpentry and framing. Shows how to frame all the parts of a house: floors, walls, roofs, door & window openings, and stairs—with hundreds of color photographs and drawings that show every detail.

The book gives beginners all the basics they need to go from zero framing knowledge to a journeyman level.

$29.95 per copy | 336 pages, softcover | Catalog no. 67353

Life Cycle Costing for Facilities

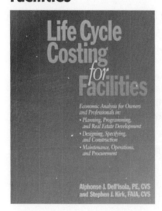

by Alphonse Dell'Isola and Dr. Steven Kirk

Guidance for achieving higher quality design and construction projects at lower costs! Cost-cutting efforts often sacrifice quality to yield the cheapest product. Life cycle costing enables building designers and owners to achieve both. The authors of this book show how LCC can work for a variety of projects — from roads to HVAC upgrades to different types of buildings.

$99.95 per copy | 396 pages, hardcover | Catalog no. 67341

Reference Books

For more information visit the RSMeans website at **www.rsmeans.com**

Interior Home Improvement Costs

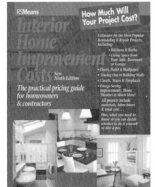

9th Edition

Updated estimates for the most popular remodeling and repair projects—from small, do-it-yourself jobs to major renovations and new construction. Includes: kitchens & baths; new living space from your attic, basement, or garage; new floors, paint, and wallpaper; tearing out or building new walls; closets, stairs, and fireplaces; new energy-saving improvements, home theaters, and more!

$24.95 per copy | 250 pages, illustrated, softcover | Catalog no. 67308E

Exterior Home Improvement Costs

9th Edition

Updated estimates for the most popular remodeling and repair projects—from small, do-it-yourself jobs, to major renovations and new construction. Includes: curb appeal projects—landscaping, patios, porches, driveways, and walkways; new windows and doors; decks, greenhouses, and sunrooms; room additions and garages; roofing, siding, and painting; "green" improvements to save energy & water.

$24.95 per copy | Over 275 pages, illustrated, softcover | Catalog no. 67309E

Builder's Essentials: Plan Reading & Material Takeoff

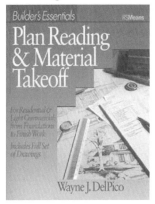

For Residential and Light Commercial Construction
by Wayne J. DelPico

A valuable tool for understanding plans and specs, and accurately calculating material quantities. Step-by-step instructions and takeoff procedures based on a full set of working drawings.

$35.95 per copy | Over 420 pages, softcover | Catalog no. 67307

Means Unit Price Estimating Methods

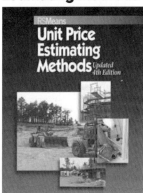

New 4th Edition

This new edition includes up-to-date cost data and estimating examples, updated to reflect changes to the CSI numbering system and new features of RSMeans cost data. It describes the most productive, universally accepted ways to estimate, and uses checklists and forms to illustrate shortcuts and timesavers. A model estimate demonstrates procedures. A new chapter explores computer estimating alternatives.

$59.95 per copy | Over 350 pages, illustrated, softcover | Catalog no. 67303B

Concrete Repair and Maintenance Illustrated

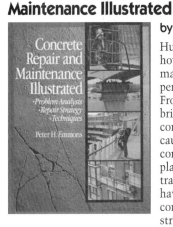

by Peter Emmons

Hundreds of illustrations show users how to analyze, repair, clean, and maintain concrete structures for optimal performance and cost effectiveness. From parking garages to roads and bridges to structural concrete, this comprehensive book describes the causes, effects, and remedies for concrete wear and failure. Invaluable for planning jobs, selecting materials, and training employees, this book is a must-have for concrete specialists, general contractors, facility managers, civil and structural engineers, and architects.

$69.95 per copy | 300 pages, illustrated, softcover | Catalog no. 67146

Total Productive Facilities Management

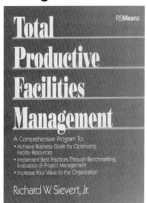

by Richard W. Sievert, Jr.

Today, facilities are viewed as strategic resources. . . elevating the facility manager to the role of asset manager supporting the organization's overall business goals. Now, Richard Sievert Jr., in this well-articulated guidebook, sets forth a new operational standard for the facility manager's emerging role. . . a comprehensive program for managing facilities as a true profit center.

$79.95 per copy | 275 pages, softcover | Catalog no. 67321

Reference Books

For more information visit the RSMeans website at **www.rsmeans.com**

Means Illustrated Construction Dictionary

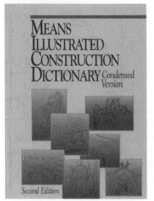

Condensed, 2nd Edition

The best portable dictionary for office or field use—an essential tool for contractors, architects, insurance and real estate personnel, facility managers, homeowners, and anyone who needs quick, clear definitions for construction terms. The second edition has been further enhanced with updates and hundreds of new terms and illustrations . . . in keeping with the most recent developments in the construction industry.

Now with a quick-reference Spanish section. Includes tools and equipment, materials, tasks, and more!

$59.95 per copy | Over 500 pages, softcover | Catalog no. 67282A

Facilities Planning & Relocation

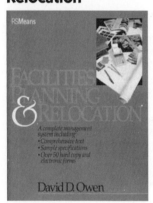

by David D. Owen

A complete system for planning space needs and managing relocations. Includes step-by-step manual, over 50 forms, and extensive reference section on materials and furnishings.

New lower price and user-friendly format.

$89.95 per copy | Over 450 pages, softcover | Catalog no. 67301

Electrical Estimating Methods

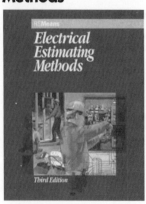

3rd Edition

Expanded edition includes sample estimates and cost information in keeping with the latest version of the CSI MasterFormat and UNIFORMAT II. Complete coverage of fiber optic and uninterruptible power supply electrical systems, broken down by components, and explained in detail. Includes a new chapter on computerized estimating methods. A practical companion to *RSMeans Electrical Cost Data.*

$64.95 per copy | Over 325 pages, hardcover | Catalog no. 67230B

Square Foot & UNIFORMAT Assemblies Estimating Methods

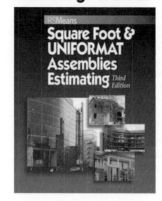

3rd Edition

Develop realistic square foot and assemblies costs for budgeting and construction funding. The new edition features updated guidance on square foot and assemblies estimating using UNIFORMAT II. An essential reference for anyone who performs conceptual estimates.

$69.95 per copy | Over 300 pages, illustrated, softcover | Catalog no. 67145B

Mechanical Estimating Methods

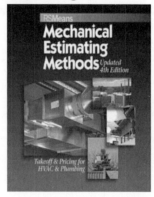

4th Edition

Completely updated, this guide assists you in making a review of plans, specs, and bid packages, with suggestions for takeoff procedures, listings, substitutions, and pre-bid scheduling for all components of HVAC. Includes suggestions for budgeting labor and equipment usage. Compares materials and construction methods to allow you to select the best option.

$64.95 per copy | Over 350 pages, illustrated, softcover | Catalog no. 67294B

Residential & Light Commercial Construction Standards

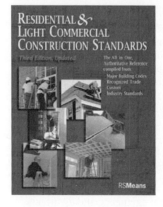

3rd Edition, Updated by RSMeans and contributing authors

This book provides authoritative requirements and recommendations compiled from leading professional associations, industry publications, and building code organizations. This all-in-one reference helps establish a standard for workmanship, quickly resolve disputes, and avoid defect claims. Updated third edition includes new coverage of green building, seismic, hurricane, and mold-resistant construction.

$59.95 | Over 550 pages, illustrated, softcover | Catalog no. 67322B

Reference Books

For more information visit the RSMeans website at **www.rsmeans.com**

Construction Business Management

by Nick Ganaway

Only 43% of construction firms stay in business after four years. Make sure your company thrives with valuable guidance from a pro with 25 years of success as a commercial contractor. Find out what it takes to build all aspects of a business that is profitable, enjoyable, and enduring. With a bonus chapter on retail construction.

$49.95 per copy | 200 pages, softcover | Catalog no. 67352

The Practice of Cost Segregation Analysis

by Bruce A. Desrosiers and Wayne J. DelPico

This expert guide walks you through the practice of cost segregation analysis, which enables property owners to defer taxes and benefit from "accelerated cost recovery" through depreciation deductions on assets that are properly identified and classified.

With a glossary of terms, sample cost segregation estimates for various building types, key information resources, and updates via a dedicated website, this book is a critical resource for anyone involved in cost segregation analysis.

$99.95 per copy | Over 225 pages | Catalog no. 67345

How to Estimate with Means Data & CostWorks

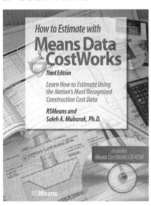

New 3rd Edition
by RSMeans and Saleh A. Mubarak, Ph.D.

New 3rd Edition—fully updated with new chapters, plus new CD with updated *CostWorks* cost data and MasterFormat organization. Includes all major construction items—with more than 300 exercises and two sets of plans that show how to estimate for a broad range of construction items and systems—including general conditions and equipment costs.

$59.95 per copy | 272 pages, softcover | Includes CostWorks CD
Catalog no. 67324B

Project Scheduling & Management for Construction

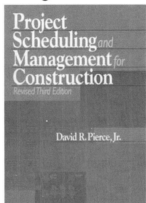

3rd Edition
by David R. Pierce, Jr.

A comprehensive yet easy-to-follow guide to construction project scheduling and control—from vital project management principles through the latest scheduling, tracking, and controlling techniques. The author is a leading authority on scheduling, with years of field and teaching experience at leading academic institutions. Spend a few hours with this book and come away with a solid understanding of this essential management topic.

$64.95 per copy | Over 300 pages, illustrated, hardcover | Catalog no. 67247B

Preventive Maintenance for Multi-Family Housing

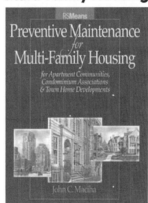

by John C. Maciha

Prepared by one of the nation's leading experts on multi-family housing.

This complete PM system for apartment and condominium communities features expert guidance, checklists for buildings and grounds maintenance tasks and their frequencies, a reusable wall chart to track maintenance, and a dedicated website featuring customizable electronic forms. A must-have for anyone involved with multi-family housing maintenance and upkeep.

$89.95 per copy | 225 pages | Catalog no. 67346

Job Order Contracting Expediting Construction Project Delivery

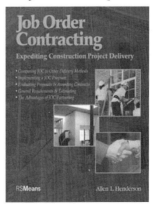

by Allen Henderson

Expert guidance to help you implement JOC—fast becoming the preferred project delivery method for repair and renovation, minor new construction, and maintenance projects in the public sector and in many states and municipalities. The author, a leading JOC expert and practitioner, shows how to:

- Establish a JOC program
- Evaluate proposals and award contracts
- Handle general requirements and estimating
- Partner for maximum benefits

$89.95 per copy | 192 pages, illustrated, hardcover | Catalog no. 67348

Reference Books

For more information visit the RSMeans website at **www.rsmeans.com**

Estimating Building Costs

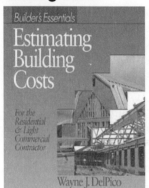

For the Residential & Light Commercial Contractor
by Wayne J. DelPico

Step-by-step estimating methods for residential and light commercial contractors. Includes a detailed look at every construction specialty—explaining all the components, takeoff units, and labor needed for well-organized, complete estimates. Covers correctly interpreting plans and specifications, and developing accurate and complete labor and material costs.

$29.95 per copy | Over 400 pages, illustrated, softcover | Catalog no. 67343

The Homeowner's Guide to Mold

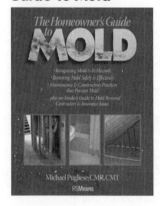

By Michael Pugliese

Expert guidance to protect your health and your home.

Mold, whether caused by leaks, humidity or flooding, is a real health and financial issue—for homeowners and contractors.

This full-color book explains:

- Construction and maintenance practices to prevent mold
- How to inspect for and remove mold
- Mold remediation procedures and costs
- What to do after a flood
- How to deal with insurance companies

$21.95 per copy | 144 pages, softcover | Catalog no. 67344

Landscape Estimating Methods

5th Edition

Answers questions about preparing competitive landscape construction estimates, with up-to-date cost estimates and the new MasterFormat classification system. Expanded and revised to address the latest materials and methods, including new coverage on approaches to green building. Includes:

- Step-by-step explanation of the estimating process
- Sample forms and worksheets that save time and prevent errors

$64.95 per copy | Over 350 pages, softcover | Catalog no. 67295C

Building & Renovating Schools

This all-inclusive guide covers every step of the school construction process—from initial planning, needs assessment, and design, right through moving into the new facility. A must-have resource for anyone concerned with new school construction or renovation. With square foot cost models for elementary, middle, and high school facilities, and real-life case studies of recently completed school projects.

The contributors to this book—architects, construction project managers, contractors, and estimators who specialize in school construction—provide start-to-finish, expert guidance on the process.

$99.95 per copy | Over 425 pages, hardcover | Catalog no. 67342

Universal Design Ideas for Style, Comfort & Safety

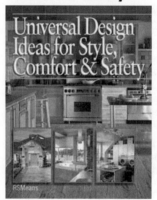

by RSMeans and Lexicon Consulting, Inc.

Incorporating universal design when building or remodeling helps people of any age and physical ability more fully and safely enjoy their living spaces. This book shows how universal design can be artfully blended into the most attractive homes. It discusses specialized products like adjustable countertops and chair lifts, as well as simple ways to enhance a home's safety and comfort. With color photos and expert guidance, every area of the home is covered. Includes budget estimates that give an idea how much projects will cost.

$21.95 | 160 pages, illustrated, softcover | Catalog no. 67354

Plumbing Estimating Methods

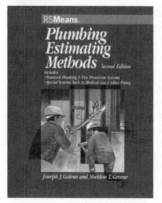

3rd Edition
by Joseph Galeno and Sheldon Greene

Updated and revised! This practical guide walks you through a plumbing estimate, from basic materials and installation methods through change order analysis. *Plumbing Estimating Methods* covers residential, commercial, industrial, and medical systems, and features sample takeoff and estimate forms and detailed illustrations of systems and components.

$59.95 per copy | 330+ pages, softcover | Catalog no. 67283B

Reference Books

For more information visit the RSMeans website at **www.rsmeans.com**

Understanding & Negotiating Construction Contracts

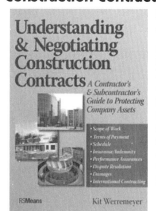

by Kit Werremeyer

Take advantage of the author's 30 years' experience in small-to-large (including international) construction projects. Learn how to identify, understand, and evaluate high risk terms and conditions typically found in all construction contracts—then negotiate to lower or eliminate the risk, improve terms of payment, and reduce exposure to claims and disputes. The author avoids "legalese" and gives real-life examples from actual projects.

$69.95 per copy | 300 pages, softcover | Catalog no. 67350

How Your House Works

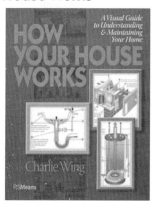

by Charlie Wing

A must-have reference for every homeowner, handyman, and contractor—for repair, remodeling, and new construction. This book uncovers the mysteries behind just about every major appliance and building element in your house—from electrical, heating and AC, to plumbing, framing, foundations and appliances. Clear, "exploded" drawings show exactly how things should be put together and how they function—what to check if they don't work, and what you can do that might save you having to call in a professional.

$21.95 per copy | 160 pages, softcover | Catalog no. 67351

RSMeans Estimating Handbook

3rd Edition

Widely used in the industry for tasks ranging from routine estimates to special cost analysis projects, this handbook has been completely updated and reorganized with new and expanded technical information.

RSMeans Estimating Handbook will help construction professionals:

- Evaluate architectural plans and specifications
- Prepare accurate quantity takeoffs
- Compare design alternatives and costs
- Perform value engineering
- Double-check estimates and quotes
- Estimate change orders

$99.95 per copy | Over 900 pages, hardcover | Catalog No. 67276B

Spanish/English Construction Dictionary

2nd Edition
by RSMeans and the International Code Council

This expanded edition features thousands of the most common words and useful phrases in the construction industry with easy-to-follow pronunciations in both Spanish and English. Over 800 new terms, phrases, and illustrations have been added. It also features a new stand-alone "Safety & Emergencies" section, with colored pages for quick access.

Unique to this dictionary are the systems illustrations showing the relationship of components in the most common building systems for all major trades.

$23.95 per copy | Over 400 pages | Catalog no. 67327A

The Gypsum Construction Handbook

by USG

An invaluable reference of construction procedures for gypsum drywall, cement board, veneer plaster, and conventional plaster. This new edition includes the newest product developments, installation methods, fire- and sound-rated construction information, illustrated framing-to-finish application instructions, estimating and planning information, and more. Great for architects and engineers; contractors, builders, and dealers; apprentices and training programs; building inspectors and code officials; and anyone interested in gypsum construction. Features information on tools and safety practices, a glossary of construction terms, and a list of important agencies and associations. Also available in Spanish.

$29.95 | Over 575 pages, illustrated, softcover | Catalog no. 67357A

Means Illustrated Construction Dictionary

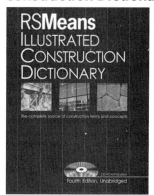

Unabridged 4th Edition, with CD-ROM

Long regarded as the industry's finest, *Means Illustrated Construction Dictionary* is now even better. With nearly 20,000 terms and more than 1,400 illustrations and photos, it is the clear choice for the most comprehensive and current information. The companion CD-ROM that comes with this new edition adds extra features such as: larger graphics and expanded definitions.

$99.95 per copy | Over 790 pages, illust., hardcover | Catalog no. 67292B

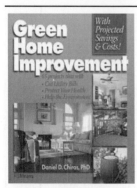

Green
Home Improvement

by Daniel D. Chiras, PhD

With energy costs rising and environmental awareness increasing, people are looking to make their homes greener. This book, with 65 projects and actual costs and projected savings help homeowners prioritize their green improvements.

Projects range from simple water savers that cost only a few dollars, to bigger-ticket items such as HVAC systems. With color photos and cost estimates, each project compares options and describes the work involved, the benefits, and the savings.

$24.95 | 320 pages, illustrated, softcover | Catalog no. 67355

New Titles

Construction
Supervision

This brand new title inspires supervisory excellence with proven tactics and techniques applied by thousands of construction supervisors over the past decade. Recognizing the unique and critical role the supervisor plays in project success, the book's leadership guidelines carve out a practical blueprint for motivating work performance and increasing productivity through effective communication.

Features:

• A unique focus on field supervision and crew management

• Coverage of supervision from the foreman to the superintendent level

• An overview of technical skills whose mastery will build confidence and success for the supervisor

• A detailed view of "soft" management and communication skills

$90.00 per copy | Over 450 pages, softcover | Catalog no. 67358

Risk Management
for Design and Construction

This book introduces risk as a central pillar of project management and shows how a project manager can be prepared for dealing with uncertainty. Written by experts in the field, *Risk Management for Design and Construction* uses clear, straightforward terminology to demystify the concepts of project uncertainty and risk.

Highlights include:

• Integrated cost and schedule risk analysis

• An introduction to a ready-to-use system of analyzing a project's risks and tools to proactively manage risks

• A methodology that was developed and used by the Washington State Department of Transportation

• Case studies and examples on the proper application of principles

• Information about combining value analysis with risk analysis

$125.00 per copy | Over 250 pages, softcover | Catalog no. 67359

Green Building: Project
Planning & Cost Estimating

3rd Edition

Since the widely read first edition of this book, green building has gone from a growing trend to a major force in design and construction.

This new edition has been updated with the latest in green building technologies, design concepts, standards, and costs. Full-color with all new case studies—plus a new chapter on commercial real estate.

$99.95 per copy | Over 450 pages, softcover | Catalog no. 67338B

For more information visit the RSMeans website at **www.rsmeans.com**

Qty.	Book no.	COST ESTIMATING BOOKS	Unit Price	Total
	60062	Assemblies Cost Data 2012	$290.95	
	60012	Building Construction Cost Data 2012	177.95	
	60112	Concrete & Masonry Cost Data 2012	162.95	
	50142	Construction Cost Indexes 2012 (subscription)	362.00	
	60142A	Construction Cost Index–January 2012	90.50	
	60142B	Construction Cost Index–April 2012	90.50	
	60142C	Construction Cost Index–July 2012	90.50	
	60142D	Construction Cost Index–October 2012	90.50	
	60342	Contr. Pricing Guide: Resid. R & R Costs 2012	39.95	
	60232	Electrical Change Order Cost Data 2012	174.95	
	60032	Electrical Cost Data 2012	179.95	
	60202	Facilities Construction Cost Data 2012	453.95	
	60302	Facilities Maintenance & Repair Cost Data 2012	399.95	
	60552	Green Building Cost Data 2012	147.95	
	60162	Heavy Construction Cost Data 2012	177.95	
	60092	Interior Cost Data 2012	182.95	
	60122	Labor Rates for the Const. Industry 2012	395.95	
	60182	Light Commercial Cost Data 2012	132.95	
	60022	Mechanical Cost Data 2012	174.95	
	60152	Open Shop Building Const. Cost Data 2012	152.95	
	60212	Plumbing Cost Data 2012	179.95	
	60042	Commercial Renovation Cost Data 2012	144.95	
	60172	Residential Cost Data 2012	127.95	
	60282	Site Work & Landscape Cost Data 2012	172.95	
	60052	Square Foot Costs 2012	187.95	
	62011	Yardsticks for Costing (2011)	174.95	
	62012	Yardsticks for Costing (2012)	176.95	
		REFERENCE BOOKS		
	67329	Bldrs Essentials: Best Bus. Practices for Bldrs	29.95	
	67298A	Bldrs Essentials: Framing/Carpentry 2nd Ed.	24.95	
	67298AS	Bldrs Essentials: Framing/Carpentry Spanish	24.95	
	67307	Bldrs Essentials: Plan Reading & Takeoff	35.95	
	67342	Building & Renovating Schools	99.95	
	67339	Building Security: Strategies & Costs	89.95	
	67353	Complete Book of Framing	29.95	
	67146	Concrete Repair & Maintenance Illustrated	69.95	
	67352	Construction Business Management	49.95	
	67358	Construction Supervision	90.00	
	67314	Cost Planning & Est. for Facil. Maint.	89.95	
	67328A	Designing & Building with the IBC, 2nd Ed.	99.95	
	67230B	Electrical Estimating Methods, 3rd Ed.	64.95	
	67343	Estimating Bldg. Costs for Resi. & Lt. Comm.	29.95	
	67276B	Estimating Handbook, 3rd Ed.	99.95	
	67318	Facilities Operations & Engineering Reference	109.95	
	67301	Facilities Planning & Relocation	89.95	
	67338B	Green Building: Proj. Planning & Cost Est., 3rd Ed.	99.95	
	67355	Green Home Improvement	24.95	
	67357A	The Gypsum Construction Handbook	29.95	
	67357S	The Gypsum Construction Handbook (Spanish)	29.95	
	67148	Heavy Construction Handbook	99.95	
	67323	Historic Preservation: Proj. Planning & Est.	99.95	

Qty.	Book no.	REFERENCE BOOKS (Cont.)	Unit Price	Total
	67308E	Home Improvement Costs–Int. Projects, 9th Ed.	24.95	
	67309E	Home Improvement Costs–Ext. Projects, 9th Ed.	24.95	
	67344	Homeowner's Guide to Mold	21.95	
	67324B	How to Est.w/Means Data & CostWorks, 3rd Ed.	59.95	
	67351	How Your House Works	21.95	
	67282A	Illustrated Const. Dictionary, Condensed, 2nd Ed.	59.95	
	67292B	Illustrated Const. Dictionary, w/CD-ROM, 4th Ed.	99.95	
	67348	Job Order Contracting	89.95	
	67295C	Landscape Estimating Methods, 5th Ed.	64.95	
	67341	Life Cycle Costing for Facilities	99.95	
	67294B	Mechanical Estimating Methods, 4th Ed.	64.95	
	67283B	Plumbing Estimating Methods, 3rd Ed.	59.95	
	67345	Practice of Cost Segregation Analysis	99.95	
	67346	Preventive Maint. for Multi-Family Housing	89.95	
	67326	Preventive Maint. Guidelines for School Facil.	149.95	
	67247B	Project Scheduling & Manag. for Constr. 3rd Ed.	64.95	
	67322B	Resi. & Light Commercial Const. Stds., 3rd Ed.	59.95	
	67359	Risk Management for Design & Construction	125.00	
	67327A	Spanish/English Construction Dictionary, 2nd Ed.	23.95	
	67145B	Sq. Ft. & Assem. Estimating Methods, 3rd Ed.	69.95	
	67321	Total Productive Facilities Management	79.95	
	67350	Understanding and Negotiating Const. Contracts	69.95	
	67303B	Unit Price Estimating Methods, 4th Ed.	59.95	
	67354	Universal Design	21.95	
	67319A	Value Engineering: Practical Applications	79.95	

MA residents add 6.25% state sales tax	
Shipping & Handling**	
Total (U.S. Funds)*	

Prices are subject to change and are for U.S. delivery only. *Canadian customers may call for current prices. **Shipping & handling charges: Add 7% of total order for check and credit card payments. Add 9% of total order for invoiced orders.

Send order to: ADDV-1000

Name (please print) _____

Company _____

☐ Company

☐ Home Address _____

_____

City/State/Zip _____

Phone # _____ P.O. # _____

(Must accompany all orders being billed)

Mail to: RSMeans, 700 Longwater Drive, Norwell, MA 02061

RSMeans Project Cost Report

By filling out this report, your project data will contribute to the database that supports the RSMeans Project Cost Square Foot Data. When you fill out this form, RSMeans will provide a $30 discount off one of the RSMeans products advertised in the preceding pages. Please complete the form including all items where you have cost data, and all the items marked (☑).

$30.00 Discount per product for each report you submit

Project Description (no remodeling projects, please)

☑ Building Use (Office School...)_____

☑ Address (City, State)_____

_____

☑ Total Building Area (SF) _____

☑ Ground Floor (SF) _____

☑ Frame (Wood, Steel...) _____

☑ Exterior Wall (Brick, Tilt-up...) _____

☑ Basement: (checkone)   ☐ Full   ☐ Partial   ☐ None

☑ Number of Stories _____

☑ Floor-to-Floor Height_____

☑ Volume (C.F.)_____

% Air Conditioned _____ Tons_____

Total Project Cost $ _____

Owner _____

Architect_____

General Contractor _____

☑ Bid Date _____

☑ Typical Bay Size _____

☑ Capacity _____

☑ Labor Force: _____ % Union _____ % Non-Union

☑ Project Description (Circle one number in each line.)

1. Economy   2. Average   3. Custom   4. Luxury

1. Square   2. Rectangular   3. Irregular   4. Very Irregular

Comments _____

_____

A	☑	General Conditions	$
B	☑	Site Work	$
C	☑	Concrete	$
D	☑	Masonry	$
E	☑	Metals	$
F	☑	Wood & Plastics	$
G	☑	Thermal &Moisture Protection	$
GR		Roofing & Flashing	$
H	☑	Doors and Windows	$
J	☑	Finishes	$
JP		Painting & Wall Covering	$

K	☑	Specialties	$
L	☑	Equipment	$
M	☑	Furnishings	$
N	☑	SpecialConstruction	$
P	☑	ConveyingSystems	$
Q	☑	Mechanical	$
QP		Plumbing	$
QB		HVAC	$
R	☑	Electrical	$
S	☑	Mech./Elec. Combined	$

Please specify the RSMeans product you wish to receive. Complete the address information.

Product Name _____

Product Number _____

Your Name _____

Title _____

Company_____
   ☐ Company
   ☐ Home   Street Address_____

City, State, Zip _____

Return by mail or fax 888-492-6770.

Method of Payment:

Credit Card # _____

Expiration Date _____

Check_____

Purchase Order _____

Phone Number _____
(for those not comfortable mailing in credit card information)

RSMeans
a division of Reed Construction Data
Square Foot Costs Department
700 Longwater Drive
Norwell, MA 02061